ISBN 978-1-5284-3520-8
PIBN 10917164

1 MONTH OF
FREE
READING

at

www.ForgottenBooks.com

By purchasing this book you are eligible for one month membership to ForgottenBooks.com, giving you unlimited access to our entire collection of over 1,000,000 titles via our web site and mobile apps.

To claim your free month visit:

www.forgottenbooks.com/free917164

English
Français
Deutsche
Italiano
Español
Português

www.forgottenbooks.com

Mythology Photography **Fiction**
Fishing Christianity **Art** Cooking
Essays Buddhism Freemasonry
Medicine **Biology** Music **Ancient
Egypt** Evolution Carpentry Physics
Dance Geology **Mathematics** Fitness
Shakespeare **Folklore** Yoga Marketing
Confidence Immortality Biographies
Poetry **Psychology** Witchcraft
Electronics Chemistry History **Law**
Accounting **Philosophy** Anthropology
Alchemy Drama Quantum Mechanics
Atheism Sexual Health **Ancient History**
Entrepreneurship Languages Sport
Paleontology Needlework Islam
Metaphysics Investment Archaeology
Parenting Statistics Criminology
Motivational

ANNUAL REPORT

OF THE

BOARD OF REGENTS

OF THE

SMITHSONIAN INSTITUTION,

SHOWING

THE OPERATIONS, EXPENDITURES, AND CONDITION
OF THE INSTITUTION

TO

JULY, 1888.

———••◆••———

WASHINGTON:
GOVERNMENT PRINTING OFFICE.
1890.

Concurrent resolution adopted by the House of Representatives May 27, 1890, and by the Senate, June 17, 1890.

Resolved by the House of Representatives (the Senate concurring), That there be printed of the Report of the Smithsonian Institution and National Museum for the years ending June 30, 1888, and June 30, 1889, in two octavo volumes for each year, 16,000 copies; of which 3,000 copies shall be for the use of the Senate, 6,000 for the use of the House of Representatives, and 7,000 for the use of the Smithsonian Institution.

II

LETTER

FROM THE

SECRETARY OF THE SMITHSONIAN INSTITUTION,

ACCOMPANYING

The annual report of the Board of Regents of that Institution to the end of June, 1888.

SMITHSONIAN INSTITUTION,
Washington, D. C., July 1, 1888.

To the Congress of the United States:

In accordance with section 5593 of the Revised Statutes of the United States, I have the honor, in behalf of the Board of Regents, to submit to Congress the annual report of the operations, expenditures, and condition of the Smithsonian Institution for the year ending June 30, 1888.

I have the honor to be, very respectfully, your obedient servant,

S. P. LANGLEY,
Secretary of Smithsonian Institution.

Hon. JOHN. J. INGALLS,
President of the Senate, pro tem.
Hon. JOHN G. CARLISLE,
Speaker of the House of Representatives.

ANNUAL REPORT OF THE SMITHSONIAN INSTITUTION TO THE END OF JUNE, 1888.

SUBJECTS.

1. Proceedings of the Board of Regents for the sessions of January and March, 1888.

2. Report of the Executive Committee, exhibiting the financial affairs of the Institution, including a statement of the Smithson fund, and receipts and expenditures for the year 1887–'88.

3. Annual report of the Secretary, giving an account of the operations and condition of the Institution for the year 1887–'88, with statistics of exchanges, etc.

4. General appendix, comprising a selection of miscellaneous memoirs of interest to collaborators and correspondents of the Institution, teachers, and others engaged in the promotion of knowledge.

The report of the National Museum for the year 1887–'88 will be published in a separate volume.

CONTENTS.

REPORT OF THE SECRETARY.

GENERAL APPENDIX.

LIST OF ILLUSTRATIONS.

Article on Meteorology.

Article on the name America.

THE SMITHSONIAN INSTITUTION.

MEMBERS EX OFFICIO OF THE "ESTABLISHMENT."

(January, 1888.)

REGENTS OF THE INSTITUTION.

(List given on the following page.)

OFFICERS OF THE INSTITUTION.

REGENTS OF THE SMITHSONIAN INSTITUTION.

By the organizing act approved August 10, 1846 (Revised Statutes, Title LXXIII, section 5580), "The business of the Institution shall be conducted at the city of Washington by a Board of Regents, named the Regents of the Smithsonian Institution, to be composed of the Vice-President, the Chief Justice of the United States [and the Governor of the District of Columbia], three members of the Senate, and three members of the House of Representatives, together with six other persons, other than members of Congress, two of whom shall be resident in the city of Washington, and the other four shall be inhabitants of some State, but no two of the same State."

REGENTS FOR THE YEAR 1888.

The Vice-President of the United States:
  JOHN J. INGALLS (elected President of the Senate February 26, 1887).

The Chief-Justice of the United States:
  MORRISON R. WAITE...died March 23, 1888.
  SAMUEL F. MILLER, Acting Chief-Justice, elected Chancellor and President of the Board *pro tempore* March 27, 1888.

United States Senators: Term expires.
  JUSTIN S. MORRILL (appointed February 21, 1883)............ Mar. 3, 1891.
  SHELBY M. CULLOM (appointed March 23, 1885) ....' Mar. 3, 1889.
  RANDALL L. GIBSON (appointed December 19, 1887) .... Mar. 3, 1889.

Members of the House of Representatives:
  SAMUEL S. COX (appointed January 5, 1888).................. Dec. 26, 1889.
  JOSEPH WHEELER (appointed January 5, 1888) .... Dec. 26, 1889.
  WILLIAM W. PHELPS (appointed January 5, 1888) .... Dec. 26, 1889.

Citizens of a State:
  ASA GRAY, of Massachusetts (first appointed in 1874).......died Jan , 30, 1888.
  HENRY COPPÉE, of Pennsylvania (first appointed in 1874)..... Dec. 26, 1891.
  NOAH PORTER, of Connecticut (first appointed in 1878)....... Mar. 3, 1890.
  JAMES B. ANGELL, of Michigan (appointed January 19, 1887) . Jan. 19, 1893.
  ANDREW D. WHITE, of New York (appointed February 15, 1888, to succeed Asa Gray, deceased)..................................... Feb. 15, 1894.

Citizens of Washington:
  JAMES C. WELLING (appointed May 13, 1884) .... May 13, 1890.
  MONTGOMERY C. MEIGS (appointed December 26, 1885)....... Dec. 26, 1891.

Executive Committee of the Board of Regents.

JAMES C. WELLING.   HENRY COPPÉE   MONTGOMERY C. MEIGS.

JOURNAL OF PROCEEDINGS OF THE BOARD OF REGENTS OF THE SMITHSONIAN INSTITUTION.

WASHINGTON, *January* 11, 1888.

The stated annual meeting of the Board of Regents of the Smithsonian Institution was held this day at 10:30 o'clock A. M.

Present: Chief-Justice M. R. WAITE, Chancellor of the Institution, Hon. S. S. COX, Hon. W. W. PHELPS, Hon. JOSEPH WHEELER, Dr. HENRY COPPÉE, Dr. J. B. ANGELL, Dr. J. C. WELLING, General M. C. MEIGS, and the Secretary, Professor LANGLEY.

Excuses for non-attendance were read from Dr. NOAH PORTER and Senator J. S. MORRILL. The Secretary made a statement that the absence of Dr. ASA GRAY was caused by his severe illness.

The journal of the proceedings of the Board at the meetings on January 12 and November 18, 1887, was read and approved.

The Secretary stated that in accordance with the instructions of the Board at the last meeting, he had again consulted with the widow of the late Professor BAIRD, and ascertained that while she desired to defer to the wishes of the Regents, her own preference would be that the interment of the remains of her husband should be strictly private. It was necessary therefore to depart from the arrangements which had been contemplated at the last meeting of the Board, and by the advice of the Executive Committee, a meeting of the Board of Regents was not called as had been anticipated in December, and the stated annual meeting is therefore now held at the regular time, as provided by the regulations of the Board of Regents.

The Chancellor announced the appointment by the President of the Senate, on December 19, 1887, of Hon. Randall L. Gibson, of Louisiana, as a regent of the Smithsonian Institution, *vice* Senator Maxey, whose term had expired.

The Chancellor also announced the appointment by the Speaker of the House of Representatives, on January 5, 1888, of Hon. S. S. Cox, of New York, as regent, *vice* Hon. O. R. Singleton, who had not been re-elected to Congress; and on the 10th of January, of Hon. Joseph Wheeler, of Alabama, *vice* Hon. W. L. Wilson, and the re-appointment of Hon. W. W. Phelps, of New Jersey.

Dr. Welling, chairman of the Executive Committee, presented its annual report for the year ending June 30, 1887.

Dr. Welling, in presenting the report, called attention to a paragraph on the third page, relative to the appropriation for "ethnological researches," and he wished it understood—not as a matter of criticism, but in explanation—that the Executive Committee made no examination or inspection of the accounts of the Bureau of Ethnology. These were exclusively under the control—according to the acts of Congress making the appropriations—" of the *Secretary* of the Smithsonian Institution." In this respect a difference existed between the duty of the committee in regard to these accounts and those of the Museum or of other trusts committed to the Institution, of which careful examination was made of every voucher.

The Secretary stated that he would be very willing to be relieved of this weighty responsibility and would be gratified if it could be assumed by the Regents. He had no desire to assume a personal responsibility in regard to the appropriation referred to, and he hoped that in the future it might be found possible to make the appropriations to the " *Smithsonian Institution* " instead of to the " *Secretary.*"

Dr. Welling remarked that the Executive Committee does not care to share this responsibility.

Dr. Coppée said he thought it the *duty* of the Regents to share in this; and that if the language of the act was doubtful, and if in relation to one trust it was the duty of the Secretary to confer with the Executive Committee, he thought that in others, although the Regents or the Institution were not specially mentioned, he ought to come under the same arrangement.

General Meigs said that *Congress* made the distinction referred to by Dr. Welling, and it was not for the Board to advise or dictate to Congress.

[This view was assented to by various members of the Board.]

The Secretary having stated that the accounts of the Museum were settled by the Interior Department, and that the estimates for preservation, etc., of the collections were sent by him through the Secretary of the Interior to the Secretary of the Treasury, the Chancellor remarked that he thought that all the accounts of the Institution in regard to any operations committed to it, should be settled directly with the Treasury Department, and not through an intermediate department.

The Secretary said that the Chancellor had anticipated what he was about to say. As the Executive Committee had observed, the relations of the Museum with the Department of the Interior on the one hand and with the Regents on the other, are undoubtedly ambiguous, since the late Secretary of the Interior himself wrote to say that he did not understand them. At present the Secretary of the Institution transmits the estimates for the Bureau of Ethnology to the Secretary of the Treasury, but does not transmit those of the Museum, which are sent through the Secretary of the Interior. It would seem desirable that some arrangement should be made by which in the future all the estimates should be submitted to the Secretary of the Treasury, and all appropriations for the Museum, as well as for the Bureau of Ethnology, made to the Smithsonian Institution, and that the sundry civil bill should be changed in the items relating to the Museum and the Bureau of Ethnology.

The Chancellor expressed the opinion that all the appropriations ought to be disbursed and controlled by the Institution.

After remarks by several of the Regents, on motion of Dr. Welling, the following resolution was adopted:

Resolved, That the Regents recommend to Congress that the form of the sundry civil appropriation bill be so changed in the items relating to the Museum and the Bureau of Ethnology as to provide,

First, That these moneys shall be disbursed under the direction of the Smithsonian Institution.

Second, That the estimates for the appropriations of the Museum in future shall be sent direct to the Secretary of the Treasury by the Smithsonian Institution through its Secretary.

On motion, it was resolved that the report of the Executive Committee be accepted.

The Secretary presented the annual report for the year ending June 30, 1887, which had been printed; but he regretted to say that he had not been able to procure copies from the Public Printer in December, in accordance with the resolutions of the Board.

The Chancellor suggested that some action ought to be taken by Congress to avoid delay in printing the annual reports of the Institution. He thought provision might be made by law for the printing of the Smithsonian Institution outside of the Government Printing Office, as is done in the case of the printing for the Supreme Court. The attention of the Congressional Regents was especially called to this subject.

The Secretary stated that a large amount of indispensable printing was now done through the Department of the Interior, and some provision ought to be made for this if the connection of the Museum with the Department should cease. He hoped that the Congressional Regents would take some action in this matter.

On motion of Mr. Cox, it was resolved that the report of the Secretary for the year ending June 30, 1887, be accepted, and that the Secretary transmit the same to Congress.

The Chancellor announced that on December 2, 1887, in accordance with the statute, he had appointed Mr. G. Brown Goode to act as Acting Secretary in case of the absence or disability of the Secretary.

The Secretary called the attention of the Board to a bill introduced in the Senate by Senator Edmunds on the 12th of December, as follows:

A BILL to provide for paying the widow of the late Spencer F. Baird for the services rendered by him as Commissioner of Fish and Fisheries.

Be it enacted by the Senate and House of Representatives of the United States of America in Congress assembled, That the Secretary of the Treasury be, and he is hereby, directed to pay Mrs. Mary C. Baird, widow of the late Spencer F. Baird, the sum of fifty thousand dollars, out of any money in the Treasury not otherwise appropriated, in full compensation for the services and expenses of the said Spencer F. Baird during his administration of the office of Commissioner of Fish and Fisheries, from February twenty-fifth, eighteen hundred and seventy-one, to the time of his death in August, eighteen hundred and eighty-seven.

The Secretary also called attention to the fact that Senator Morrill had introduced a bill in the Senate on the 12th of December, 1887, as follows :

A BILL for the erection of a bronze statue of Spencer F. Baird, late Secretary of the Smithsonian Institution.

Be it enacted by the Senate and House of Representatives of the United States of America in Congress assembled, That the Regents of the Smithsonian Institution be, and are hereby, authorized to contract for a statue in bronze of Spencer F. Baird, late Secretary of the Smithsonian Institution, to be erected upon the grounds in front of the National Museum; and for this purpose, and for the entire expense of the foundation and pedestal of the monument, the sum of fifteen thousand dollars, or so much of said sum as may be needed, is hereby appropriated, out of any moneys in the Treasury not otherwise appropriated.

On motion of Mr. Phelps it was resolved that the Executive Committee and the Secretary be authorized to act for the Board of Regents in case of the passage of any act of Congress relative to the erection of a statue of Professor Baird. .

The Secretary stated that he had but one more matter to which to call the attention of the Board ; it was brief, but of considerable importance.

It may be remembered that several years ago the Secretary of the Institution, Professor Baird, called the attention of the Regents to a bill introduced in the House of Representatives as follows, viz :

"For the erection of a fire-proof building on the south portion of the Smithsonian Reservation for the accommodation of the U. S. Geological Survey, and for other purposes.

" *Be it enacted by the Senate and House of Representatives of the United States of America in Congress assembled,* That the sum of two hundred thousand dollars be, and hereby is, appropriated out of any money in the Treasury not otherwise appropriated, for the erection of a fire-proof building on the south portion of the Smithsonian Reservation for the accommodation of the U. S. Geological Survey, and for other purposes: *Provided,* That the consent of the Regents of the Smithsonian Institution be first obtained thereto, and that the building be under their direction when completed : *And provided further,* That the building be erected by the Architect of the Capitol in accordance with plans approved by the Director of the United States Geological Survey, the Secretary of the Smithsonian Institution, and the Architect of the Capitol, acting as a board therefor.

"After a very full expression by the Regents in favor of immediate action, on motion of General Sherman, it was

"*Resolved,* That the Board of Regents of the Smithsonian Institution recommend to Congress to enlarge the National Museum, so as properly to exhibit the mineral, geological, and other collections already on hand and increasing each year, by the erection of a fire-proof building on the southwest corner of the Smithsonian Reservation, similar in style to the present National Museum, and they request an appropriation of $300,000 therefor, to be expended under the direction of the Regents of the Institution." *

The Secretary remarked that the placing of the offices of the Geological Survey upon land heretofore reserved exclusively for Smithsonian purposes might be perhaps considered as committing the Institution toward the policy of a union with other scientific bureaus of the Government. It was in view of the questions of general policy thus involved, that it seemed proper that he should ask instruction from the Regents. He could only infer their opinion on the former bill from the language of the resolution, which apparently implied,

First. That increased provision was desirable for the Museum collections.

Second. From its silence as to the Geological Survey, that the building proposed in the bill was not to be appropriated to that use.

The Secretary had lately been informally advised that it was the desire of the Geological Survey to obtain his opinion with reference to this, in anticipation of a bill to be brought before the present Congress, and he desired to be favored with the judgment of the Regents.

The Chancellor stated that it was desirable that new Museum buildings should be erected in any case, but that since by act of Congress a certain part of the public grounds had been set apart and appropriated absolutely and exclusively to the Smithsonian Institution, he for one did not want to see anything else placed on these grounds. He further said : "If the Smithsonian Institution is to grow it will need them all, and whatever is put upon them should be under our exclusive control."

After remarks by a number of Regents, expressing concurrence in the views of the Chancellor, it was suggested by Mr. Phelps that the unanimous opinion of the Board ought to be embodied in a resolution.

The Chancellor did not think this was necessary. He supposed all the Secretary wanted was the moral support of the Board in a policy which would forbid the placing of any building on the Smithsonian grounds except for the exclusive use of the Smithsonian Institution.

The Secretary alluded to another bill, which proposed to occupy part of the public grounds, including the Smithsonian reservation, with buildings for the Columbian celebration in 1892. It was here remarked by a Regent that there was no danger of this being done immediately, to which the Chancellor said, " With my consent, never."

On motion of Dr. Angell, it was resolved that the income of the Institution for the fiscal year beginning July 1, 1888, and ending June 30, 1889, be appropriated for the service of the Institution, to be expended by the Secretary, with the advice of the Executive Committee, upon the

---

* Proceedings of the Board, January 17, 1883. Smithsonian Report for 1882, pp. xii, xiii.

basis of the operations described in the last annual report of said committee, with full discretion on the part of the Secretary as to items of expenditures properly falling under each of the heads embraced in the established conduct of the Institution.

The Chancellor informed the Board that he had the melancholy duty to perform of announcing the death, yesterday, of Dr. PETER PARKER, who had been for many years a Regent of the Institution and chairman of its Executive Committee.

On motion of Dr. Angell, it was resolved that the Executive Committee prepare resolutions relative to the death of Dr. Parker.

Dr. Welling, of the Executive Committee, presented the following resolutions, which were adopted:

Whereas the Board has received the afflictive intelligence that the venerable Dr. PETER PARKER, who, for sixteen years, was a member of the Board of Regents, and who for this whole period served with fidelity on its Executive Committee, has departed this life after a long career filled with useful labors in the service of God and of man: Therefore, be it

Resolved, That in the retrospect of such a life-career, protracted as it was beyond the limits usually allotted to men, and yet at each stage of its progress, dedicated to beneficent works in the cause of religion, philanthropy, and science, we desire to testify our respect for the exalted worth and scrupulous conscientiousness which Dr. Parker brought to the discharge of every duty, and which, during his connection with the government of this Institution, were nobly exemplified by the zeal and diligence with which he ever watched and worked for its prosperity and usefulness, even during the later period of his honorable service, when the burden of years was added to the burden of his official cares, and when with a less conscientious sense of public duty he might have claimed an exemption from the tasks of life.

Resolved, That since the retirement of our departed colleague from the membership of this Board we have continued to follow him with the grateful recollections inspired by the association of this council chamber, as well as with a reverent respect for the Christian patience with which he bore the infirmities of advancing age and the unfaltering Christian hope with which he awaited "the inevitable hour" in full assurance of immortality.

Resolved, That these resolutions be spread upon the minutes of the Board, and that the Secretary of the Institution is hereby requested to transmit a copy of them to the family of our late colleague.

On motion, the Board then adjourned *sine die.*

SPECIAL MEETING OF THE REGENTS.

A special meeting of the Board of Regents was held this day at 11 o'clock A. M.

Present, Hon. J. J. INGALLS (President of the United States Senate *pro tem.*); Hon. SAMUEL F. MILLER (acting Chief Justice of the United States); Hon. J. S. MORRILL, Hon. S. M. CULLOM, Hon. S. S. COX, Hon. JOSEPH WHEELER, Hon. WILLIAM W. PHELPS, Dr. JAMES C. WELLING, General M. C. MEIGS, and the Secretary, Prof. S. P. LANGLEY.

The Secretary called the Board to order.

On motion of Senator Morrill, Hon. J. J. Ingalls was elected Chairman.

Excuses for non-attendance were read from Dr. PORTER, Dr. COPPÉE, Dr. ANGELL, and Dr. WHITE.

The Secretary stated that this special meeting had been called at the request of three of the Regents as provided in the organic act. There were two subjects requiring consideration: First, the recent death of the Chancellor of the Institution, Chief Justice Waite; second, the election of a Chancellor.

Professor Langley remarked that it would be for others who had known the late Chancellor longer than he had to speak of his worth and public services. He could only say that Judge Waite was not only a tower of strength to the Institution; he was much more; he had the regard, the respect, and the reverence of all those who were brought into relation with him. He could only speak of him with the real affection he felt, and say that the loss the Institution had experienced was to him that of a dear and revered personal friend.

On the second point, the Secretary stated that the joint signatures of the Chancellor and Secretary were required on requisitions for money from the United States Treasury for carrying on the operations of the Institution, and that on the 1st of next July the semi annual interest would be due, and some one who could act as Chancellor, within the provisions of the law, must sign the requisition in connection with the Secretary, at that time.

On motion of Dr. Welling, a committee was appointed to express the sense of the Board in relation to the death of the Chancellor.

The Chair appointed Dr. Welling, Senator Morrill, and Professor Langley.

The committee retired and on its return reported through the chairman, Dr. Welling, the following preamble and resolutions, which were
unanimously adopted:

Whereas the Board of Regents of the Smithsonian Institution has
been called to meet in extraordinary session by the afflicting intelligence that MORRISON REMICK WAITE, late Chief-Justice of the
Supreme Court of the United States, and late Chancellor of the Smithsonian Institution, has been removed by the hand of death from the
scene of his high activities and distinguished usefulness; therefore be it

Resolved, That sitting as we do at this time and place, in the very
center of that dark shadow which has fallen upon the whole land in the
lamented death of the late Chief-Justice Waite, and appalled as we
are by the suddenness as well as by the magnitude of the great affliction which in coming to the nation at large has come to us individually,
with an added pathos of sorrow because of the nearer view we have
had, for so many years, of the talents, virtues, and graces which found
their familiar home in the person of our honored friend, we could with
much good reason crave for ourselves, in this hour of bereavement, the
humble permission of mourning apart, that we might silently gauge
the depth and the dimensions of a calamity which brings to us its
message of personal grief and which has also torn away from our highest seat of justice its venerated and beloved chief; from the legal profession of the country its foremost official representative and therefore
its crowning exponent; from the walks of social life in this national
capital a commanding presence no less remarkable for his genial and
open-hearted sincerity than for his affable and gracious benignity; and
from the Christian communion a true and faithful disciple who witnessed a good confession as much by the simplicity and humility with
which he walked before God as by the unswerving consistency with
which he wore the ornament of a pure heart and of a meek and quiet
spirit before the scrutiny of his fellow-men.

Resolved, That while an obvious sense of propriety must dictate that
we should leave to others in that great forum which was the chosen
arena of his life's career the sad privilege of depicting, with minute
and detailed analysis, the remarkable combination of strong and lovely
traits which met in the person of the late Chief-Justice and gave to the
symmetrical character of our beloved friend its blended sweetness and
light, we can not omit, even in this hour of our special sorrow, to bear
our cheerful testimony to the pleasing amenity with which he presided
over the deliberations of this council chamber as the Chancellor of the
Smithsonian Institution, and sharing, as we all do, in a profound admiration for the intelligence he brought to our discussions, while ever
moderating them by the guidance of his clear thought and mild wisdom,
we can but render our reverent homage to the engaging personal qualities which endeared him to us as a man, while at the same time gratefully confessing our obligations to him for the provident care and deep
interest which he always brought to the discharge of his official duties
in this place, where, through all the years of his honorable and useful
service at the head of this Board, the Secretary of the Institution in
common with ourselves has leaned on him as the wise and true counsellor who could be trusted as well for the rectitude of his moral intuitions as for the clear perceptions of his calm and judicious intellect.

Resolved, That we will attend the funeral of our departed Chancellor
in a body, and that the Secretary of the Institution, together with a
deputation from the members of the Board, be requested to accompany

the other friends and associates of the late Chief-Justice who will bear his remains to their last resting place in Ohio.

Resolved, That these resolutions be entered on the minutes of the Board. and that the Secretary be requested to send a copy of them to the family of our departed friend in token of our sincere condolence with them in their great affliction.

On motion of Senator Cullom it was resolved, that Acting Chief-Justice SAMUEL F. MILLER be elected Chancellor *pro tem.*

On taking the chair, Justice Miller remarked that in this hour of grief it was a consolation to be honored with the appointment which had just been conferred upon him, especially as it was not a necessity of law that he as Acting Chief-Justice should have been selected to fill this important position.   While it would not be expected of him on the present occasion to deliver a eulogy on the late Chancellor, it was only proper for him to say that, sitting beside Judge Waite as he had done for four hours a day for about fourteen years, he felt as well qualified to appreciate his character as any man living.   He was an able judge, an upright man, honest in every fiber of his nature.   No sophistry could induce him to act in violation of his conscience.   He never was led to believe only what he desired to believe, or to decide against his convictions of *right.*   He was a sound jurist, and above all an able manager of our complicated legal administrative affairs.   We can not do too much to honor his memory.

He thanked the gentlemen of the Board for the honor they had conferred in electing him Chancellor.

On motion of Mr. Phelps, it was resolved, that all or any of the members of the Board, and the Secretary, who wish to attend the funeral services of the late Chancellor at Toledo, be appointed to represent the Board of Regents.

On motion, the Board then adjourned *sine die.*

REPORT OF THE EXECUTIVE COMMITTEE OF THE BOARD OF REGENTS OF THE SMITHSONIAN INSTITUTION.

(For the year ending 30th of June, 1888.)

To the Board of Regents of the Smithsonian Institution:

The Executive Committee of the Board of Regents of the Smithsonian Institution respectfully submits the following report in relation to the funds of the Institution, the appropriations by Congress for the National Museum and other purposes, and the receipts and expenditures for the Institution and the Museum for the year ending June 30, 1888.

Condition of the fund July 1, 1888.

The amount of the bequest of James Smithson deposited in the Treasury of the United States, according to the act of Congress of August 10, 1846, was $515,169. To this was added, by authority of Congress, act of February 8, 1867, the residuary legacy of Smithson, and savings from annual income and other sources, $134,831. To this $1,000 was added by a bequest of James Hamilton, $500 by a bequest of Simeon Habel, and $51,500 as the proceeds of the sale of Virginia bonds owned by the Institution, making in all, as the permanent Smithson fund in the United States Treasury, $703,000.

Statement of the Receipts and Expenditures of the Smithsonian Institution July 1, 1887, to June 30, 1888.

RECEIPTS.

Cash on hand July 1, 1887		$1,423.14
Interest on the fund, July 1, 1887 ⎱		42,180.00
Interest on the fund, January 1, 1888 ⎰		
Cash from sales of publications	$481.75	
Cash from repayments of freight, etc	271.11	
		752.86
Total receipts		$44,356.00

EXPENDITURES.

Building:		
Repairs, care, and improvements	$2,682.37	
Furniture and fixtures	1,088.64	
		$3,771.01
Expenditures (carried over)	3,771.01	

General expenses:

Meetings	$576.00	
Postage and telegraph	313.50	
Stationery	953.11	
General printing	359.71	
Incidentals (fuel, gas, ice, stable, etc.)	1,625.92	
Library (books, periodicals, binding, etc.)	2,828.00	
Salaries	18,430.08	
		$25,086.32

Publications and researches:

Smithsonian Contributions	342.00	
Miscellaneous Collections	3,835.00	
Reports	2,413.61	
Explorations	545.22	
		7,135.83
Literary and scientific exchanges		3,113.46
Portraits of the late Chancellor, and of the Secretary		440.15
Total expenditure		$39,546.77
Balance unexpended June 30, 1888		4,809.23

The cash received from sales of publications, repayments for freight, etc., is to be credited on the items of expenditure above as follows:

Postage	$3.80
Incidentals	61.56
Smithsonian Contributions	124.40
Miscellaneous Collections	337.67
Reports	19.68
Exchanges	205.75
	$752.86

The net expenditure of the Institution for the year was therefore $38,793.91, or $752.86 less than the total expenditure, $39,546.77, above given.

In addition to the aggregate of salaries, above stated at $18,430.08, the sum of $4,289.98 was paid as salaries for services rendered in connection with the subjects of building ($1,240), exchanges ($1,050), library ($1,200), and reports ($799.98), and makes a part of the charges reported under those heads.

All the moneys received by the Smithsonian Institution from interest, sales, refunding of moneys temporarily advanced, or otherwise, are deposited with the Treasurer of the United States to the credit of the Secretary of the Institution, and all payments are made by his checks on the Treasurer of the United States.

INTERNATIONAL EXCHANGES.

Appropriated by Congress for the fiscal year ending June 30, 1888, "for expenses of the system of international exchanges between the United States and foreign countries under the direction of the Smithsonian Institution, including salaries or compensation of all necessary employés," (sundry civil act, approved March 3, 1887) $12,000.00

Expenditures during 1887–'88.

Salaries or compensation:

1 curator (part of year), at $175 per month	$598. 39
1 clerk, twelve months, at $150 per month	1,800. 00
1 clerk, twelve months, at $100 per month	1,200. 00
1 clerk, eight months, at $75 per month	600. 00
1 clerk, six months, at $75 per month	450. 00
1 clerk, eight months, at $65 per month	520. 00
1 clerk, twelve months, at $60 per month	720. 00
1 clerk, six months, at $60 per month	360. 00
1 clerk, eight months, at $60 per month	480. 00
1 clerk, four months, at $60 per month	240. 00
1 clerk, four months, at $55 per month	220. 00
1 copyist, four months, at $40 per month	160. 00
1 copyist, special	40. 65
1 packer, nine months, at $75 per month	675. 00
1 packer, five months, at $50 per month	250. 00
1 messenger, nine months, at $20 per month	180. 00
1 laborer, two months, at $40 per month	80. 00
1 agent (Germany), one year	1,000. 00
1 agent (England), one year	500. 00

Total salaries and compensation		$10,074. 04
Freight		924. 54
Packing-boxes		527. 00
Printing		230. 50
Postage		100. 00
Binding records		88. 00
Date stamps		5. 75
Total expenditure		$11,949. 83
Balance unexpended July 1, 1888		50. 17

NORTH AMERICAN ETHNOLOGY.

An appropriation of $40,000 was made by Congress for the fiscal year ending June 30, 1888, for the prosecution of ethnological researches under the direction of the Secretary of the Smithsonian Institution. The actual conduct of these investigations has been placed by the Secretary in the hands of Maj. J. W. Powell, Director of the Geological Survey. The abstracts of expenditures and balance sheets for this appropriation have been exhibited to us; the vouchers for the expenditures, after approval by the Secretary, are paid by the disbursing clerk of the Bureau of Ethnology and transmitted to the accounting officers of the Treasury Department for settlement.

The balance available to meet outstanding liabilities on the 1st of July, 1888, as reported by the official disbursing agent, is $7,847.08.

The following is a classified statement of all expenditures made during the last fiscal year from this appropriation:

Classification of expenditures (A).

Salaries and compensation per year, viz:

1 ethnologist ($3,000)	$3,000.00
2 ethnologists ($2,400)	4,800.00
2 ethnologists ($1,800)	3,600.00
3 assistant ethnologists ($1,500)	4,500.00
4 assistant ethnologists ($1,200)	4,800.00
1 assistant ethnologist ($1,000)	1,000.00
1 assistant ethnologist ($720)	720.00
1 modeler ($720)	720.00
1 copyist ($720)	720.00
2 ethnologic assistants ($600)	1,200.00
3 copyists ($600)	1,800.00
1 messenger ($600)	600.00
1 translator ($480)	480.00
1 copyist ($300)	300.00
	28,240.00
Unclassified and paid by day	598.33
Total salaries and compensation	$28,838.33
Traveling expenses	3,637.66
Transportation of property	444.91
Field subsistence	242.06
Field supplies and expenses	2,431.04
Field material	351.06
Instruments	32.50
Laboratory material	42.67
Photographic material	116.17
Books and maps	181.00
Stationery and drawing materials	9.10
Illustrations for reports	926.30
Goods for distribution to Indians	511.30
Office furniture	85.00
Office supplies and repairs	18.62
Correspondence	6.49
Specimens	844.95
	38,719.16
Bonded railroad accounts settled by Treasury Department	.74
Total expenditure	$38,719.90

Classification of expenditures (B).

Illustrations for report...	$926.30
Contingent expenses	298.99
Collections and specimens.......................	844.95
	38,719.16
Bonded railroad accounts settled by Treasury Department	.74
Total expenditure..	$38,719.90

SUMMARY.

July 1, 1887:

Balance on hand of appropriation for 1886-'87......................	6,553.08
Amount credited to appropriation by disallowance by Comptroller .	13.90
Appropriation by Congress "for the purpose of continuing ethnological researches among the American Indians, under the direction of the Secretary of the Smithsonian Institution, including salaries or compensation of all necessary employés" (sundry civil act of March 3, 1887)..	40,000.00
Total available for the year ending June 30, 1888................	46,566.98
Expended during the year ending June 30, 1888..................	38,719.90

July 1, 1888:

Balance to meet outstanding liabilities................................	$7,847.08

SMITHSONIAN BUILDING REPAIRS.

Appropriation by Congress "for urgent and necessary repairs to central and western portions of the Smithsonian Institution Building" (sundry civil act of March 3, 1887)		15,000.00
Expenditures:		
Cut-stone, brick, metal, carpenters', and miscellaneous work	$9,800.00	
Iron-work	1,848.00	
Steam-fitters', laborers', and day work	466.30	
Steam, water, and gas pipes...............................	147.58	
Clerk-hire	275.00	
Nails and lumber	61.32	
Advertising and printing....................................	49.10	
Hardware	72.66	
		12,719.96
Balance July 1, 1888		$2,280.04

(Of this appropriation $131.80 was expended in 1887, leaving $14,868.20 available during the year ending June 30, 1888.)

NATIONAL MUSEUM.

PRESERVATION OF COLLECTIONS, JULY 1, 1887, TO JUNE 30, 1888

Appropriation by Congress for fiscal year ending June 30, 1888, "for the preservation, exhibition, and increase of the collections from the surveying and exploring expeditions of the Government and from other sources, including salaries or compensation of all necessary employés"	$116,000.00
Classification of expenditures:	
Salaries and compensation	$96,511.43
Supplies	2,608.38
Stationery...	1,792.20

Classification of expenditures—Continued.

Specimens	$2,038.65	
Books	500.36	
Travel	822.85	
Freight	1,381.08	
Total expenditure		$105,654.95

Balance July 1, 1888, to meet outstanding liabilities $10,345.05

Salaries and compensation paid from the appropriation for preservation of collections,
                 1887–1888.

(All of these persons were employed by the month or by the day, and many for part of the year only.)

Direction.

Assistant Secretary Smithsonian Institution, in charge U. S. National Museum (per month)	$300.00	$3,600.00

Scientific staff :

5 curators (per month), at	175.00	
1 curator (per month), at	166.00	
1 acting curator (per month), at	90.00	
1 assistant curator (per month), at	150.00	
2 assistant curators (per month), at	125.00	
1 assistant curator (per month), at	90.00	
1 assistant (per month), at	125.00	
1 assistant (per month), at	100.00	
1 collector (per month), at	100.00	
2 aids (per month), at	75.00	
1 aid (per month), at	65.00	
3 aids (per month), at	60.00	
3 aids (per month), at	50.00	
5 aids (per month), at	40.00	
		25,726.39

Clerical staff :

1 chief clerk (per month), at	166.66	
1 executive clerk (per month), at	150.00	
1 registrar (per month), at	158.83	
1 agent (per month), at	100.00	
1 draughtsman (per month), at	75.00	
1 assistant draughtsman (per month), at	30.00	
1 clerk (per month), at	115.00	
1 clerk (per month), at	110.00	
2 clerks (per month), at	100.00	
1 clerk (per month), at	90.00	
1 clerk (per month), at	75.00	
1 clerk (per month), at	70.00	
1 clerk (per month), at	60.00	
3 clerks (per month), at	50.00	
1 typewriter (per month), at	45.00	
1 copyist (per month), at	55.00	
7 copyists (per month), at	50.00	
1 copyist (per month), at	45.00	
7 copyists (per month), at	40.00	
1 copyist (per month), at	35.00	
2 copyists (per month), at	30.00	
1 copyist (per month), at	25.00	
		25,123.45

Preparators :

1 artist (per month), at	$110. 00	
1 photographer (per month), at	150. 00	
1 taxidermist (per month), at	150. 00	
1 taxidermist (per month), at	80. 00	
1 taxidermist (per month), at	70. 00	
1 assistant taxidermist (per month), at	60. 00	
1 modeler (per month), at	125. 00	
1 modeler (per diem),	4. 00	
2 preparators (per month), at	100. 00	
1 preparator (per month), at	75. 00	
1 preparator (per month), at	65. 00	
1 preparator (per month), at	60. 00	
1 preparator (per month), at	50. 00	
		$13, 675. 07

Buildings and labor :

1 superintendent of buildings (per month), at	135. 00	
1 assistant superintendent (per month), at	100. 00	
1 assistant superintendent (per month), at	75. 00	
13 watchmen (per month), at	50. 00	
4 skilled laborers (per month), at	50. 00	
2 skilled laborers (per diem), at	2. 00	
1 laborer (per month), at	46. 00	
2 laborers (per month), at	45. 00	
8 laborers (per month), at	40. 00	
12 laborers (per diem), at	1. 50	
1 attendant (per month), at	40. 00	
2 attendants (per month), at	35. 00	
3 cleaners (per month), at	30. 00	
1 cleaner (per month), at	20. 00	
2 cleaners (per diem), at	1. 00	
1 messenger (per month) at	75. 00	
1 messenger (per month) at	65. 00	
1 messenger (per month) at	45. 00	
1 messenger (per month) at	37. 00	
1 messenger (per month) at	20. 00	
		22, 336. 52

Total salaries and compensation ... $96, 511. 53

NATIONAL MUSEUM —FURNITURE AND FIXTURES.

Appropriation for fiscal year ending June 30, 1888 : For cases, furniture, fixtures, and appliances required for the exhibition and safe-keeping of the collections of the National Museum, including salary or compensation of all necessary employés $40, 000. 00

Classification of expenditures.

Salaries and compensation :

Engineer of property, work inspector, clerks, and copyists	$3, 970. 00	
Carpenters	7, 807. 75	
Painters	2, 020. 00	
Laborers	4, 926. 04	
Cleaners	480. 00	
		$19, 203. 79

Materials, etc:

Exhibition case frames	$7,383.44
Designs and drawings for cases	305.00
Glass	2,790.11
Drawers, trays, boxes, etc	595.14
Hardware and interior fittings for cases	874.91
Iron brackets	126.30
Cloth, cotton, felt (lining for cases)	420.24
Glass jars and containers for specimens	223.29
Chemicals and apparatus	378.33
Lumber	2,140.98
Tools	191.68
Paints and oils	749.99
Office furniture and other fixtures	1,784.75
Plumbing, tin, lead, etc	889.54
Slate, tiles, etc	29.50
Brushes, brooms, pitchers, etc	111.47
Paper	49.50
Traveling expenses	35.08

$19,079.25

Total expenditure $38,283.04

Balance July 1, 1888, to meet outstanding liabilities.................. $1,716.96

Salaries and compensation paid from the appropriation for furniture and fixtures, 1887–'88.

(Many of these persons were employed only part of the year)

1 engineer of property (per month) at	$150.00
1 work inspector (for one month only) at	100.00
1 clerk (per month) at	110.00
1 clerk (per month) at	90.00
1 clerk (per month) at	80.00
1 clerk (per month) at	50.00
1 copyist (per month) at	60.00
3 copyists (per month) at	50.00
2 copyists (per month) at	40.00
1 copyist (per month) at	30.00
1 carpenter (per diem) at	3.50
11 carpenters (per diem) at	3.00
2 carpenters (per diem) at	2.00
1 painter (per month) at	50.00
1 painter (per diem) at	2.50
1 painter (per diem) at	2.00
2 laborers (per month) at	50.00
4 laborers (per month) at	40.00
18 laborers (per diem) at	1.50
2 cleaners (per month) at	30.00

Total salaries and compensation.................................... $19,203.79

NATIONAL MUSEUM.—HEATING AND LIGHTING.

Appropriation for fiscal year ending June 30, 1888: For expense of heating, lighting, and electrical and telephonic service for the National Museum 12,000.00

Classification of expenditures.

Salaries and compensation:

Engineer	$1,440.00
Telegraph and telephone clerks	1,140.00
Firemen and machinists	3,473.36

Total salaries and compensation ... $6,053.36

Coal and wood	3,014.08
Gas	795,09
Telephones	588.65
Electric work	293.20
Rental of call boxes	110.00
Heating repairs	389.73

5,190.75

Total expenditures ... $11,244.11

Balance July 1, 1888, to meet outstanding liabilities ... $755.89

Salaries and compensation paid from the appropriation for heating and lighting, 1887–1888.

1 engineer (per month), at	$120.00
1 telegraph clerk (per month), at	40.00
1 telephone clerk (per month), at	55.00
1 fireman and machinist (per month), at	65.00
1 fireman (per month), at	50.00
8 firemen (temporary) (per month), at	50.00

Total salaries and compensation ... $6,053.36

NATIONAL MUSEUM.—OTHER APPROPRIATIONS.

Preservation of collections, 1886:

Balance of appropriation July 1, 1887	1.96

This balance remains July 1, 1888.

Preservation of collections, 1887:

Balance of appropriation July 1, 1887	5,991.17
Expended during year ending June 30, 1888	5,991.15

Balance unexpended July 1, 1888 ... .02

Furniture and fixtures, 1886:

Balance of appropriation July 1, 1887	45.05

This balance remains July 1, 1888.

Furniture and fixtures, 1887:

Balance of appropriation July 1, 1887	2,809.80
Expended during year ending June 30, 1888	2,734.83

Balance unexpended July 1, 1888 ... 74.97

Preservation of collections, armory, 1886:

Balance of appropriation July 1, 1887	46.14
Expended during year ending June 30, 1888	38.50

Balance unexpended July 1, 1888 ... 7.64

Heating and lighting, 1887 :

Balance of appropriation July 1, 1887..........................	$391.73	
Expended during year ending June 30, 1888................	373.19	
Balance unexpended July 1, 1888......................................		$18.54
Balances reported last year on July 1, 1887, viz :		
Preservation of collections 1885...............................	2.00	
Expended during 1887–'88................................	1.50	
Balance July 1, 1888..		.50
Preservation of collections 1885–'86.......		1.48
Armory, 1885...		8.25
Furniture and fixtures, 1885..		.16

The above sums have, under the action of Revised Statutes, section 3090, been carried by the Treasury Department to the credit of the surplus fund July 1, 1888.

RECAPITULATION.

The total amount of the funds administered by the Institution during the year ending 30th of June, 1888, appears, from the foregoing statements and the account books, to have been as follows:

Smithsonian Institution:			
From balance of last year....................................		$1,423.14	
From interest on the Smithsonian fund.....................		42,180.00	
From sales of publications.........................	$481.75		
From repayments for freight, etc.................	271.11		
		752.86	
			$14,356.00
Appropriations committed by Congress to the care of the Institution, for the year 1888, and balances of appropriations unexpended in previous years :			
International exchanges		12,000.00	
Ethnological researches....................................		46,556.98	
Smithsonian building repairs............................		14,868.20	
Preservation of collections:			
1886		1.96	
1887		5,991.17	
1888		116,000.00	
		121,993.13	
Preservation, armory....................................		46.14	
Furniture and fixtures...................................		42,854.85	
Heating, lighting, etc...................................		12,391.73	
		250,711.03	
Total..			$295,067.03

The committee has examined the vouchers for payments made from the Smithsonian income during the year ending June 30, 1888, all of which bear the approval of the Secretary of the Institution, and a certificate that the materials and services charged were applied to the purposes of the Institution.

The committee has also examined the accounts of the National Museum, and find that the balances above given correspond with the certificates of the disbursing officers of the Interior and Treasury Departments.

The quarterly accounts current, the vouchers, and journals have been examined and found correct.

Statement of regular income from the Smithsonian fund, to be available for use in the year ending June 30, 1889.

Balance on hand June 30, 1888... $4,809.23
Interest due and receivable July 1, 1888 .... 21,090.00
Interest due and receivable January 1, 1889.............................. 21,090,00

Total available for year ending June 30, 1889 .... $46,989.23

Respectfully submitted.

JAMES C. WELLING,
M. C. MEIGS,
of Executive Committee.

WASHINGTON, *December* 6, 1888.

ACTS AND RESOLUTIONS OF CONGRESS RELATIVE TO THE SMITHSONIAN INSTITUTION, NATIONAL MUSEUM, ETC.

(In continuation from previous reports.)

[Forty-ninth Congress, first session, 1885-'86.]

SMITHSONIAN INSTITUTION.

JOINT RESOLUTION (No. 2) filling existing vacancies in the Board of Regents of the Smithsonian Institution.

Resolved by the Senate and House of Representatives of the United States of America in Congress assembled, That the existing vacancies in the Board of Regents of the Smithsonian Institution of the class "other than Members of Congress," shall be filled by the re-appointment of John Maclean, of New Jersey; Asa Gray, of Massachusetts; Henry Coppée, of Pennsylvania, and the appointment of Montgomery C. Meigs, of the city of Washington, vice William T. Sherman, whose term has expired and who is no longer a citizen of Washington.

(Approved, December 26, 1885. Forty-ninth Congress, first session. Statutes, 1885-'86.)

INTERNATIONAL EXCHANGES.

NAVAL OBSERVATORY: For payment to Smithsonian Institution for freight on observatory publications sent to foreign countries, one hundred and thirty-six dollars.

(Legislative, executive, and judicial appropriation act. Approved July 31, 1886, chapter 827.)

WAR DEPARTMENT.—For the transportation of reports and maps to foreign countries, through the Smithsonian Institution, one hundred dollars.

(Sundry civil appropriation act. Approved August 4, 1886, chapter 902.)

INTERNATIONAL EXCHANGES, SMITHSONIAN INSTITUTION: For expenses of the system of international exchanges between the United States and foreign countries, under the direction of the Smithsonian Institution, including salaries or compensation of all necessary employés, ten thousand dollars.

(Sundry civil appropriation act. Approved August 4, 1886, chapter 902.)

NORTH AMERICAN ETHNOLOGY.

NORTH AMERICAN ETHNOLOGY, SMITHSONIAN INSTITUTION: For the purpose of continuing ethnological researches among the American

Indians, under the direction of the Secretary of the Smithsonian Institution, including salaries or compensation of all necessary employés, forty thousand dollars.

(Sundry civil appropriation act. Approved August 4, 1886, chapter 902.)

NATIONAL MUSEUM.

HEATING AND LIGHTING THE NATIONAL MUSEUM.—For expense of heating, lighting, and electrical and telephonic service for the National Museum, eleven thousand dollars.

PRESERVATION OF COLLECTIONS OF THE NATIONAL MUSEUM.— For the preservation, exhibition, and increase of the collections received from the surveying and exploring expeditions of the Government, and from other sources, including salaries or compensation of all necessary employés, one hundred and six thousand five hundred dollars.

FURNITURE AND FIXTURES OF THE NATIONAL MUSEUM.—For cases, furniture, and fixtures required for the exhibition and safe-keeping of the collections of the National Museum, including salaries or compensation of all necessary employés, forty thousand dollars.

(Sundry civil appropriation act. Approved August 4, 1886, chapter 902.)

NATIONAL MUSEUM: For expense of heating, lighting, and electrical and telephonic service, six hundred and thirty-one dollars and sixty-seven cents.

Preservation of collections, eighteen hundred and eighty-three and prior years, one hundred and forty-nine dollars and sixteen cents.

(Act to supply deficiencies. Approved August 4, 1886, chapter 903.)

JOINT RESOLUTION (No. 35), accepting from Julia Dent Grant and William H. Vanderbilt objects of value and art presented by various foreign Governments to the late General Ulysses S. Grant.

Whereas Julia Dent Grant and William H. Vanderbilt, by deed of trust executed on the tenth day of January, eighteen hundred and eighty-five, presented to the United States certain swords, medals, paintings, bronzes, portraits, commissions, and addresses, and objects of value and art presented by various Governments in the world to General Ulysses S. Grant as tokens of their high appreciation of his illustrious character as a soldier and a statesman : Therefore,

Resolved by the Senate and House of Representatives of the United States of America in Congress assembled, That the United States accept, with grateful acknowledgments, the said property and articles, more fully described in the schedule attached to said deed of trust, to be held by the United States and preserved and protected in the city of Washington for the use and inspection of the people of the United States.

SEC. 2. That the said property and articles be placed under the custody of the Director of the National Museum ; and he is hereby directed to receive the same for safe-keeping therein.

(Approved August 5, 1886. Forty-ninth Congress, first session. Statutes, 1885–'86.)

[Forty-ninth Congress, second session, 1886-1887.]

SMITHSONIAN INSTITUTION.

JOINT RESOLUTION (No. 5) appointing James B. Angell a member of the Board of Regents of the Smithsonian Institution.

Resolved by the Senate and House of Representatives of the United States of America in Congress assembled, That the existing vacancy in the Board of Regents of the Smithsonian Institution of the class " other than members of Congress," shall be filled by the appointment of James B. Angell, of the State of Michigan, in place of John Maclean, deceased.

(Approved January 19, 1887. Forty-ninth Congress, second session, Statutes, 1886-'87.)

SMITHSONIAN INSTITUTION : For urgent and necessary repairs to central and western portions of the Smithsonian Institution building, fifteen thousand dollars.

(Sundry civil appropriation act. Approved March 3, 1887, chapter 362.)

INTERNATIONAL EXCHANGES.

INTERNATIONAL EXCHANGES, SMITHSONIAN INSTITUTION : For expenses of the system of international exchanges between the United States and foreign countries, under the direction of the Smithsonian Institution, including salaries or compensation of all necessary employés, twelve thousand dollars.

NAVAL OBSERVATORY : For payment to Smithsonian Institution for freight on Observatory publications sent to foreign countries, one hundred and thirty-six dollars.

(Legislative, executive, and judicial appropriation act. Approved March 3, 1887, chapter 392.)

NORTH AMERICAN ETHNOLOGY.

NORTH AMERICAN ETHNOLOGY, SMITHSONIAN INSTITUTION : For the purpose of continuing ethnological researches among the American Indians, under the direction of the Secretary of the Smithsonian Institution, including salaries or compensation of all necessary employés, forty thousand dollars.

(Sundry civil appropriation act. Approved March 3, 1887, chapter 362.)

NATIONAL MUSEUM.

HEATING AND LIGHTING THE NATIONAL MUSEUM : For expense of heating, lighting, and electrical and telephonic service for the National Museum, twelve thousand dollars.

PRESERVATION OF COLLECTIONS OF THE NATIONAL MUSEUM : For the preservation, exhibition, and increase of the collections from the surveying and exploring expeditions of the Government, and from other sources, including salaries or compensation of all necessary employees, one hundred and sixteen thousand dollars.

FURNITURE AND FIXTURES OF THE NATIONAL MUSEUM : For cases, furniture, fixtures, and appliances required for the exhibition and safe-keeping of the collections of the National Museum, including salaries or compensation of all necessary employees, forty thousand dollars.

(Sundry civil appropriation act. Approved March 3, 1887, chapter 362.)

HISTORICAL MANUSCRIPTS.

COMMISSION TO REPORT ON HISTORICAL VALUE OF MANUSCRIPTS, ETC. : That the Secretary of State, the Librarian of Congress, and the Secretary of the Smithsonian Institution, and their successors in office, are hereby constituted a commission whose duty it shall be to report to Congress the character and value of the historical and other manuscripts belonging to the Government of the United States, and what method and policy should be pursued in regard to editing and publishing the same, or any of them.
(Sundry civil appropriation act. Approved March 3, 1887, chapter 362.)

MINNEAPOLIS EXPOSITION.

JOINT RESOLUTION (No.19.) authorizing the several Executive Departments of the Government to loan to the Minneapolis Industrial Exposition certain articles for exhibit.

Resolved by the Senate and House of Representatives of the United States of America in Congress assembled, That it is desirable, in any way consistent with existing laws and without risk to Government property or expense to the National Treasury, to encourage the effort being made for the opening and holding of a grand industrial and educational exposition of the Northwest, at the city of Minneapolis, in the State of Minnesota, and the interests of the whole northwestern section of our country demand it be made an unqualified success; and it be, and is hereby, approved that the heads of the several Executive Departments shall, in whatever respects they may in their judgment see convenient and proper, loan any articles or material suitable to such purpose: *Provided,* That such loan be made entirely on the responsibility of said Minneapolis Industrial Exposition, and shall not be of material needed for use in either Department, and shall not in any way interrupt the daily routine of duty or order in any branch of the Government, and shall be returned to the proper Department, in good order, within one month after the close of the exposition: *And provided further,* That before any such loan shall be made the proper head of the Department shall require and receive a good and sufficient bond, by or in behalf of such exposition, for the safe return thereof as aforesaid, and to indemnify and save harmless the Government of the United States, or any Department thereof, from any liability or expense on account thereof, or on account of this resolution.

Approved, March 3, 1887.

[Fiftieth Congress, first session, 1887–'88.]

SMITHSONIAN INSTITUTION.

JOINT RESOLUTION (No. 4.) appointing Andrew D. White a member of the Board of Regents of the Smithsonian Institution.

Resolved by the Senate and House of Representatives of the United States of America in Congress assembled, That the existing vacancy in the Board of Regents of the Smithsonian Institution of the class "other than members of Congress," shall be filled by the appointment of Andrew D. White, of the State of New York, in place of Asa Gray, deceased.
(Approved, February 15, 1888.)

NORTH AMERICAN ETHNOLOGY.

For North American Ethnology, Smithsonian Institution, forty-nine dollars and nine cents.

(Urgent deficiency act. Approved March 30, 1888, chapter 47.)

NATIONAL MUSEUM.

CHAP. 124.—AN ACT to purchase of the widow and children of the late General James Shields certain swords.

Whereas the State of Illinois and the State of South Carolina, after the war with Mexico, each presented to the late General James Shields a sword, in consideration of gallant and meritorious services rendered by him in said war; and

Whereas he has left surviving him a widow and three minor children, with but limited means of support, and said swords, though costly and valuable, can not be divided and apportioned between said children, and their value is needed for the education and support of said children : Therefore,

Be it enacted by the Senate and House of Representatives of the United States of America in Congress assembled, That the Secretary of War be, and he is hereby, authorized and directed to purchase of said widow and children said swords, at their actual cost, not to exceed the sum of ten thousand dollars, to be paid for out of any money in the Treasury not otherwise appropriated, and when so purchased the same to be deposited with the other military archives of the nation, in some public place at the National Museum.

(Approved, April 19, 1888, chapter 124.)

CINCINNATI EXPOSITION.

AN ACT making an appropriation to enable the several Executive Departments of the Government and the Bureau of Agriculture and the Smithsonian Institution, including the National Museum and Commission of Fish and Fisheries to participate in the Centennial Exposition of the Ohio Valley and Central States, to be held at Cincinnati, Ohio, from July fourth to October twenty-seventh, eighteen hundred and eighty-eight.

Whereas the States which comprise the Northwest Territory and the adjacent States will hold at Cincinnati, Ohio, from July fourth to October twenty-seventh, eighteen hundred and eighty-eight, a centennial exposition commemorative of the organization of the Northwest Territory, under the ordinance of seventeen hundred and eighty-seven, in which exposition all the States and Territories of the United States and the General Government have been invited to participate, the object being in said exposition to present a panorama of the nation's resources and present state of progressive development by an exhibition of the products of agriculture, of the various industries and fine arts; also the results of advancement made in the sciences ; the whole illustrating the opportunities secured to and the possibilities which wait upon the citizens of this Republic ; and

Whereas the citizens of the Ohio Valley and the several States adjacent thereto have made suitable and adequate preparation and arrangements for holding said exposition, and are desirous—and it being fit and proper—that the several Executive Departments of the Government, the Department of Agriculture, the Smithsonian Institution, including the National Museum and Commission of Fish and Fisheries, should participate in said exhibition : Therefore,

Be it enacted ,by the Senate and House of Representatives of the United States of America in Congress assembled, That the head of each of the several Executive Departments of the Government, the Commissioner of Agriculture, and the Smithsonian Institution, including the National Museum and Commission of Fish and Fisheries, under the direction of the President of the United States, be, and they are hereby authorized and directed to prepare and make suitable exhibits at the said Centennial Exposition of the Ohio Valley and Central States, to be held at Cincinnati, beginning on the fourth of July and closing October twenty-seventh, eighteen hundred and eighty-eight.

That there shall be appointed a committee of Congress composed of ten members, five to be appointed by the President of the Senate and five by the Speaker of the House of Representatives. Said committee is authorized and directed to visit said exposition and make such report to Congress in that behalf as they may deem needful and proper: *Provided*, That the President may in the exercise of his discretion allow such documents, and exhibits as relate to early settlement at Marietta, Ohio, and the establishment of civil government in the territory northwest of the Ohio River, to be taken to Marietta, and exhibited during the time from July fifteenth to nineteenth, eighteen hundred and eighty-eight, inclusive, under such restrictions and custody as he may direct.

That to enable the several Executive Departments of the Government, the Department of Agriculture and the Smithsonian Institution, including the National Museum and the Commission of Fish and Fisheries, to participate in said exposition, to be held as aforesaid, there is hereby appropriated, out of any money in the Treasury not otherwise appropriated, one hundred and forty-seven thousand seven hundred and fifty dollars, apportioned as follows :

For the War Department, seven thousand one hundred and fifty dollars.

For the Navy Department, fifteen thousand dollars.

For the State Department, two thousand five hundred dollars.

For the Treasury Department, seven thousand five hundred dollars.

For the Interior Department, thirty-six thousand one hundred dollars.

For the Department of Agriculture, twenty thousand dollars.

For the Post-Office Department, five thousand dollars.

For the Department of Justice, two thousand dollars.

For the Smithsonian Institution, including the Commission of Fish and Fisheries, fifty thousand dollars.

For expenses of the committee of Congress, two thousand five hundred dollars.

That the President may, if in his judgment it shall be deemed necessary and expedient in order to secure the best results with greatest economy, transfer a part of the fund hereby apportioned to one Department or Bureau to another Department or Bureau. The term Bureau wherever used herein shall be construed to include the Agricultural Department, the Smithsonian Institution, and Commission of Fish and Fisheries.

That the President of the United States is hereby authorized to detail an officer of the pay department of the Army or Navy to disburse the fund appropriated by this act.

The payments on account of expenses incurred in carrying out and into effect the provisions hereof shall be made on itemized vouchers approved by the representative of the Department incurring the liability, and a person to be designated by the President to make final audit of said accounts: *Provided*, That payment of the expenses incurred by the committee of Congress shall be made on vouchers approved by the chairman of said committee.

That the head of each of said Executive Departments and of the Department of Agriculture, Smithsonian Institution, and Commission of Fish and Fisheries shall, from among the officers or employees thereof, appoint a suitable person to act as representative of such Department or Bureau, and said representative shall, under the direction and control of the head of the Department or Bureau, supervise the preparation and conduct of the exhibits herein provided for.

That no officer or employee appointed as aforesaid shall be paid extra or additional compensation by reason of services rendered in virtue of such employment; but nothing herein shall be so construed as to prevent the payment of the just and reasonable expenses of any committee, officer, or employee appointed or employed under and by virtue of the provisions of this act.

That all articles imported from the Republic of Mexico or the Dominion of Canada for the purpose of being exhibited at said exposition shall be admitted free of duty, subject, however, to such conditions and regulations as the Secretary of the Treasury may impose and prescribe.

Approved, May, 28, 1888.

JOINT RESOLUTION (No. 30) declaring the true intent and meaning of the act approved May twenty-eighth, eighteen hundred and eighty-eight.

Resolved by the Senate and House of Representatives of the United States of America in Congress assembled, That it is the true intent and meaning of the act of Congress approved May twenty eighth, eighteen hundred and eighty-eight, by the President of the United States, entitled " An act making appropriation to enable the several Executive Departments of the Government, and the Bureau of Agriculture, and the Smithsonian Institution, including the National Museum and the Commission of Fish and Fisheries, to participate in the Centennial Exposition of the Ohio Valley and Central States, to be held at Cincinnati, Ohio, from July fourth to October seventh, eighteen hundred and eighty-eight," that the President of the United States may, in his discretion make an order directing that any documents, papers, maps not original, books or other exhibits which properly and pertinently relate to the establishment of civil government in the territory northwest of the Ohio River, may be sent upon an executive order from any of the several Departments in said act named, or from the exhibits now at Cincinnati, and that the appropriation of money in said act to defray the expenses of such exhibits, may be made applicable, in so far as the President of the United States may direct, to the payment of the expenses of the care, transportation to and return of such exhibits from Marietta. And the same shall be paid from such fund heretofore set apart for each Department as the President may order. Nor shall anything in said act be so construed as to prevent the purchase of suitable materials, and the employment of proper persons, to complete or modify series of objects, and classes of specimens, when in the judgment of the head of any Department such purchase or employment, or both is necessary in the proper preparation and conduct of an exhibit. Nor to authorize the removal from their places of deposit in Washington of any original paper or document or laws or ordinances whatever.

Approved, July 16, 1888.

JOINT RESOLUTION (No. 57), authorizing the exhibits made by the Government at the Centennial Exposition of the Ohio Valley and Central States, at Cincinnati, Ohio, to remain at said exposition until and including the fifteenth day of November, eighteen hundred and eighty-eight.

Resolved by the Senate and House of Representatives of the United States of America in Congress assembled, That authority is hereby granted to continue until and including November fifteenth, eighteen hundred and eighty-eight, the exhibits made by the Government at the Centennial Exposition of the Ohio Valley and Central States, at Cincinnati, Ohio, under authority of the act approved May twenty-eighth, eighteen hundred and eighty-eight.

(Approved October 20, 1888)

INTERNATIONAL EXCHANGES.

NAVAL OBSERVATORY.—For payment to Smithsonian Institution for freight on Observatory publications sent to foreign countries, one hundred and thirty-six dollars.

(Legislative, executive, and judicial appropriation act. Approved July 11, 1888, chapter 615.)

UNITED STATES GEOLOGICAL SURVEY.—For the purchase of necessary books for the library, and the payment for the transmission of public documents through the Smithsonian exchange, five thousand dollars.

(Sundry civil appropriation act. Approved October 2, 1888, chapter 1069.)

INTERNATIONAL EXCHANGES, SMITHSONIAN INSTITUTION: For expenses of the system of international exchanges between the United States and foreign countries, under the direction of the Smithsonian Institution, including salaries or compensation of all necessary employees, fifteen thousand dollars.

WAR DEPARTMENT.—Transportation of reports and maps to foreign countries: For the transportation of reports and maps to foreign countries through the Smithsonian Institution, one hundred dollars.

(Sundry civil appropriation act, approved October 2, 1888, chapter 1069.)

NORTH AMERICAN ETHNOLOGY.

NORTH AMERICAN ETHNOLOGY: For the purpose of continuing ethnological researches among the American Indians, under the direction of the Secretary of the Smithsonian Institution, including salaries or compensation of all necessary employees, forty thousand dollars.

NATIONAL MUSEUM.

Under the Secretary of the Smithsonian Institution as Director of the National Museum.

NATIONAL MUSEUM, HEATING AND LIGHTING: For expense of heating, lighting, and electrical and telephonic service for the National Museum, twelve thousand dollars.

PRESERVATION OF COLLECTIONS OF THE NATIONAL MUSEUM: For the preservation, exhibition, and increase of the collections from the surveying and exploring expeditions of the Government, and from other sources, including salaries or compensation of all necessary employees, one hundred and twenty-five thousand dollars.

FURNITURE AND FIXTURES OF THE NATIONAL MUSEUM : For cases, furniture, fixtures, and appliances required for the exhibition and safe-keeping of the collections of the National Museum, including salaries or compensation of all necessary employees, forty thousand dollars.

That the Secretary of the Smithsonian Institution shall submit to Congress at its next session a detailed statement of the expenditures of the fiscal year eighteen hundred and eighty-eight under appropriations for "International Exchanges," "North American Ethnology," and the "National Museum," and annually thereafter a detailed state-ment of expenditures under said appropriations shall be submitted to Congress at the beginning of each regular session thereof.

(Sundry civil appropriation act. Approved October 2, 1888, chapter 1069.)

For the National Museum, for printing labels and blanks and for the "Bulletins" and annual volumes of the "Proceedings" of the Museum, ten thousand dollars.

(Sundry civil appropriation act, approved October 2, 1888, chapter 1069.)

For preservation of collections, National Museum, eighteen hundred and eighty-five and prior years. to pay the claim numbered fifty-two thousand one hundred and eighty-two, in said Executive Document, number three hundred and seventy-seven, sixty dollars.

(Deficiency appropriation act, approved, October 19, 1888, chapter 1210.)

AN ACT for the relief of Semon Bache and Company.

Be it enacted by the Senate and House of Representatives of the United States of America in Congress assembled, That the Secretary of the Treas-ury be, and he is hereby, authorized to pay to Semon Bache and Com-pany, of New York, the sum of three thousand five hundred and sixty-two dollars and fifty-six cents, out of any money in the Treasury not otherwise appropriated, for the purpose of refunding the duty paid by said firm upon glass from imported stock furnished to the National Museum and the New Orleans, Louisville, and Cincinnati Expositions or exhibition cases.

(Approved September 26, 1888. Private laws, chapter 1043.)

REPORT OF SAMUEL P. LANGLEY,

SECRETARY OF THE SMITHSONIAN INSTITUTION, FOR 1887-'88.

To the Board of Regents of the Smithsonian Institution:

GENTLEMEN: I have the honor to present with this the customary report for the year ending June 30, 1888.

This year is memorable for the loss to the Institution, not only of its Chancellor and of others to be mentioned later, but of its late Secretary, Spencer F. Baird.

I have endeavored elsewhere to characterize his character and services, while yet feeling that one who has been so recently called to fill his place is hardly the fittest person to adequately describe them; but that may surely be repeated here which is no secret to any one, that a most honored and useful life, which might have been prolonged for many years, came to an end which can not but be called premature, largely through a too self-sacrificing devotion to the public service.

I shall also have to speak later of the loss to the Institution of its Chancellor, the late Chief-Justice of the United States—a man whom those honored with his acquaintance grew, in proportion to their knowledge of him, to look up to and trust; and of one of its Regents, Prof. Asa Gray, pre-eminent in science, but in whom, as in the Chief-Justice, the qualities of the intellect were supplemented by others, such that both inspired even in their official relations, a feeling not only of respect, but of affection, which the formal intercourse of public life rarely brings.

The past has, indeed, been a fatal year to the Institution; but these great losses have been spoken of at length in its necrology, and I will now ask to be allowed to preface this and the rest of my report by a few personal words.

Although long acquainted with both Professor Henry and Professor Baird I had no official relationship with either until two years ago, when the latter, in view of the end which he must have felt to be approaching, asked me if I was disposed to assume a connection with the Institution while continuing the scientific researches to which my life had been chiefly devoted.

The position then tendered me, and later at your hands, that of Secretary, was accepted, from the knowledge that in your view such researches for the increase of knowledge, no less than administrative la-

bors, formed the essential duties of the place to which I was honored
by your invitation, though it has happened that this, the first year of
these duties, has been passed all but exclusively in purely administrative work, of which there is alone occasion at present to speak.

The year was begun with the feeling that it was best to closely follow
the methods of my predecessors till a longer experience should have
brought material for independent judgment; but at its close I desire to
be allowed to say that every experience has enhanced my confidence in
their policy as a permanent guide; and if it be true, as has sometimes been
said, that men eminent in science are apt to be devoid of capacity in the
management of daily affairs, we must conclude that Professor Henry
was a singular exception to such a rule; for the practical wisdom of the
general lines of conduct laid down by him, and adopted by my honored
predecessor, so commend themselves to me in the light of daily service
that more trust in them is felt with every new trial.

From them there may, it seems to me, be deduced some general considerations with reference to the Smithsonian Institution and its associate interests, of which the following brief summary represents those
general principles of official action by which I have sought to be guided.

If the position of the Smithsonian is that of a ward of the Government, having property of its own, for which that Government acts the
part of a trustee, while leaving its administration wholly with the Regents, it follows that the Institution enjoys a measure of independence,
and in it a power of initiative for good which ought to be deemed its
most privileged possession ; so that any action which is taken by one
having its interests at heart, ought to be with this consideration of its
independence always in mind.

The Institution is for "the increase and diffusion of knowledge among
men." It is not primarily for the promotion of utilitarian interests,
which can be advanced through other channels, but for knowledge
in the highest and widest sense, including not only all pure science,
but even, in the words of Henry, "the true, the beautiful, as well as the
immediately practical;" and these interests it is to guard from all entangling alliances.

In dealing with the circumstances of to-day, the Institution should
still be guided by these principles; but in bringing them to the test of
present needs, we are daily reminded that these same principles are now
to be often applied to quite new conditions.

The Smithsonian has under its charge besides the Museum, the Bureau
of Ethnology, which will be referred to later, and some minor interests,
which are, however, insignificant in comparison.

It has from time to time been proposed by friends outside of this
Institution that it should take on much wider cares than these, and
that it should be the center around which all the scientific establishments of the Government might cluster. In the writer's opinion it

would not be perhaps impossible, but it would certainly be difficult, to make such a permanent arrangement consistently with the independence of the Smithsonian, and its continued devotion to the original objects of its being; but since the project is from time to time renewed, it may not be superfluous to observe that in any case the Museum would stand on an entirely different footing from any other governmental bureau of applied science, if only because it has been created in a very considerable degree out of the endowment income of the Institution; while other scientific bureaus have grown up wholly independent of the Smithsonian, which has neither legal nor moral title to their property.

It must be admitted, however, that the line of demarcation, even in the Museum, between the property to which the Smithsonian has an undoubted legal title; that to which this claim is only presumptive; and that to which it has no claim, is not in all cases at present clearly drawn, and we are endeavoring to remedy this uncertainty. As regards the care of this property, a great gain has been made in the past year by carrying out (with the concurrence of the Secretary of the Interior) the wishes which the Regents expressed in regard to the Museum at their last meeting; so that it is no longer uncertain how far this care falls upon the Institution, and how far upon the Interior Department.

Reference has just been made to the question of the general policy to be followed by the Smithsonian with regard to its accepting the charge of other Government departments of science, and this question is so far from being an idle one that the Secretary has been called upon during the past year to consider whether it was his duty to advise that the Fish Commission, which until lately had such intimate though unofficial relations with the Institution, should be united with it by a legal bond, or not. While feeling that it would be in many respects most desirable to connect with the Smithsonian the purely scientific portions of the Fish Commission and its apparatus of research, he could not but recognize that these were almost indissolubly mingled with certain great utilitarian interests, which were not equally proper subjects of the Smithsonian's care; and after consultation with those Regents whose advice he could separately obtain, he felt unable to urge such a union with any confidence that it would meet the approbation of the Board.

The President saw fit to appoint as Commissioner, Dr. G. Brown Goode, the Assistant Secretary of the Smithsonian Institution, who, while still, with my full consent, retaining that place, accepted the office provisionally, from a sense of duty to the interests of the Fish Commission, concerning which he had obtained an intimate acquaintance under the late Professor Baird.

Having placed these interests on a proper footing; after a brief period of laborious but wholly gratuitous service, he declined the higher salary and permanent appointment of Commissioner which was pressed upon him, and resumed the duties here to which his scientific life has been chiefly devoted.

On the 2d of December, 1887, the chancellor, Chief-Justice Waite, under the provision of the law, designated Dr. G. Brown Goode as Acting Secretary of the Smithsonian Institution during the absence of the Secretary.

If only from the ordinary need of a periodical revision, nearly every department of the Institution has been the subject of examination, and in some cases of considerable modification during the past year, and I now proceed to speak of these in some detail, prefacing each with a brief statement of such considerations as seem to me deserving of the particular attention of the Regents.

BOARD OF REGENTS.

Meetings of the Board.—A special meeting of the Board was held November 18, 1887, to take action in regard to the death of the Secretary, Spencer Fullerton Baird, and at this meeting Samuel Pierpont Langley was elected his successor.

The stated annual meeting of the Board was held on the 11th January, 1888.

A special meeting of the Board was also held on the 27th March, 1888, to take action in regard to the death of the chancellor of the Institution, Chief-Justice Waite.

The journal of proceedings of the Board is given in full, as usual, in the introduction of the Regents' report.

Changes in the Board of Regents.—Other vacancies than those already mentioned have occurred in the membership of the Board during the year by the expiration of the legal terms of service.

Senator Maxey's term ended March 3, 1887, and with the close of the Forty-ninth Congress the terms of the Hon. O. R. Singleton, of the Hon. W. L. Wilson, and of the Hon. W. W. Phelps, members of the House of Representatives, also expired; and on the 19th of December, 1887, the President of the Senate appointed the Hon. Randall Lee Gibson, Senator from Louisiana, a Regent for the term of six years, to fill the vacancy occasioned by Senator Maxey's retirement. On the 5th of January, 1888, the Speaker of the House of Representatives appointed the Hon. Samuel S. Cox, of New York, a Regent in the place of the Hon. Otho R. Singleton; and on the 10th of January, 1888, he appointed the Hon. Joseph Wheeler, of Alabama, a Regent in the place of the Hon. William L. Wilson, and re-appointed the Hon. William Walter Phelps, of New Jersey, to continue his service as Regent. Lastly, by joint resolution of Congress, approved by President Cleveland, February 15, 1888, Dr. Andrew D. White, of New York, was elected a Regent for the term of six years, to fill the place of Dr. Asa Gray, deceased.

At the special meeting of the Board of Regents, held March 27, 1888, Mr. Justice Samuel F. Miller, senior Associate and acting Chief Justice of the United States Supreme Court, was elected to act as chancellor of the Institution *pro tempore.*

FINANCES.

While with this is presented the report of the Executive Committee and other statements, showing that the funds are in the usual sense in a satisfactory condition, this seems to be a proper occasion to say something about the larger questions of finance, for, as time passes, the purchasing power of money imperceptibly but surely alters, until finally the consideration is forced upon us that these slow changes, though almost inappreciable from year to year, have, in the half century already elapsed since Congress accepted Smithson's bequest, essentially diminished the actual value of the fund, while its nominal value remains unchanged.

I do not now refer merely to the fact that we measure all things by another scale in 1888 from what we did in 1836; or that, owing to the immense increase of public wealth, the capital of the original bequest, which then was greater than any but a few private fortunes, has become relatively so inconsiderable to-day. More than this is meant. It is meant that the actual purchasing power of each dollar is, for our purposes, notably less; that it is being forced upon us that we can not print as many books, or pay as many employés, or make as many researches as when the scheme of expenditure was first fixed, and that, consequently, a scheme which was wise then, because not only desirable but feasible, is not necessarily so now.

I know that this consideration is not presented to the Regents for the first time, and that a committee of their number, as long ago as 1877, observed—

"That the income of the Smithsonian fund, while nominally fixed, is growing actually less year by year, with the rapidly-changing value of money, and of less and less importance in the work that it accomplishes with reference to the immense extension of the country since the Government accepted the trust."

In a time, short with reference to the probable life of the Institution, the income of the Smithsonian fund proper will necessarily become entirely inadequate to carry on the object of Henry's care on the scale which he inaugurated. Even when this is the case, it seems to me that this income of the Smithsonian bequest will still have a value wholly beyond its nominal one, for it will at least maintain the Institution in that position of independence and disinterestedness which are its most potent means of influencing others to aid in carrying out the intention of its founder.

It is, nevertheless, most evidently desirable that the fund should be enlarged both by Governmental recontribution and by private bequest, so as to constantly represent at least the original position of its finances relatively to those of the country and contemporary institutions of learning; a position which we can estimate from the observation that there are several such institutions, which were at first scarcely on a par with it financially, but whose funds, having been invested so as to share in the growth of the country, and aided by private benefaction, now surpass ours from ten to twenty fold.

We can never regret the generous spirit which has dictated the direction of the expenditure of the Smithsonian income in the past, but it is true that if a less absolutely unselfish policy had been followed—if, for instance, though keeping up all proper expenditures for the increase and diffusion of knowledge, those funds whose expenditure has practically inured chiefly to the benefit of the General Government had been allowed to accumulate—the Institution would have been comparatively wealthy to-day.

I will instance, in explanation of my meaning, the remark of Professor Henry in 1872, to the effect that the Government, in equity, should *then* have paid the Institution $300,000 for the use of the present building. This building, erected wholly out of Smithsonian funds at the cost of over half a million dollars, has, with the exception of a small portion, been ever since that time used rent-free by the Government; and if the observation had force then, it has double force to-day.

Again, the Institution has left in perpetual charge of the nation, in the Museum alone, property acquired out of its private fund (and to which it has apparently the same title), which is probably now more than equal in value to the whole amount of the Smithsonian bequest.

While it is gratefully recognized that Congress has never dealt in any ungenerous spirit with the Institution, I can not think it superfluous to keep such facts as those just cited in mind at a time when it becomes necessary to review the whole scheme of expenditure, in view of an income practically diminishing, and which would, if not for these facts, be more than double its actual amount.

The will of James Smithson, of England, "to found at Washington, under the name of the Smithsonian Institution, an establishment for the increase and diffusion of knowledge among men," was made October 23, 1826.

•The existence of the bequest was communicated to Congress by a message from the President of the United States December 17, 1835, and by an act of Congress approved July 1, 1836, the bequest was accepted, and the President was authorized and enabled to assert and prosecute with effect the claim of the United States to the property thereby bequeathed and then held in trust by the English court of chancery.

Under this authority the sum of $508,318.46 was received in gold by the United States and placed in the Treasury.

The "Smithsonian Institution" provided for in the will of Smithson was not established, however, by Congress until August 10, 1846, when a definite plan of organization was adopted and operations commenced.

By act of Congress February 8, 1867, the Secretary of the Treasury was authorized to receive a residuary legacy of Smithson, which had been received by the Institution in 1863, amounting to $26,210.63, on the same terms as the original bequest. By the same act the Regents were authorized to add to the Smithsonian fund such other sum as they might see fit to deposit, not exceeding, with the original bequest, the sum of $1,000,000.

The original bequest and the sums since added are therefore as follows:

Bequest of Smithson, 1846	$515, 169. 00
Residuary legacy of Smithson, 1867	26, 210. 63
Deposits from savings of income, etc., 1867	108, 620. 37
Bequest of James Hamilton, 1874	1, 000. 00
Bequest of Simeon Habel, 1880	500. 00
Deposit from proceeds of sale of bonds, 1881	51, 500. 00

Total permanent Smithsonian fund in the Treasury of the United States, bearing interest at 6 per cent. per annum............ 703, 000. 00

At the beginning of the fiscal year the balance on hand of the income from the fund was $1,423.14. The interest paid semi-annually July 1, 1887, and January 1, 1888, was $42,180.

To this was added from sales of publications and miscellaneous sources $752.86, making a total available amount for carrying on the operations of the Institution of $44,356; total expenditures for the year, $39,546.77; leaving a balance July 1, 1888, of $4,809.23.

It is proper in this connection to state that the Institution is charged by Congress with the care and disbursement of sundry appropriations, those for the past year being as follows:

For international exchanges	$12,000
For ethnological researches	40,000
For preservation of Government and other collections in natural history, ethnology, etc., in the National Museum	116,000
For furniture and fixtures for the National Museum	40,000
For heating, lighting, and electrical service for the Museum	12,000

The vouchers for all the expenditures from these appropriations as well as those from the Smithsonian income are carefully examined and passed upon by the Executive Committee of the Board of Regents, with one exception—those for ethnological researches.

The disbursement of this appropriation from its commencement has been made under the direction of Maj. J. W. Powell, who has been in charge of the Bureau of Ethnology.

The necessity of greatly increased appropriations for the proper conduct of the interests committed by Congress to the care of the Institution is daily more manifest, and has been made known in the strongest terms to the National Legislature.

The estimates prepared to be submitted for the fiscal year ending June 30, 1889, are as follows:

International exchanges	$27,500
Ethnological researches	50,000
Preservation of collections	150,000
Furniture and fixtures	40,000
Heating, lighting, etc	12,000
	279,500

In accordance with the instructions of the Board of Regents at its last annual meeting, I requested the Committee on Appropriations of the House of Representatives to make certain changes in the assignment of appropriations and the method of their disbursement.

The following is the correspondence on the subject with the Secretary of the Interior and with the chairman of the Committee on Appropriations.

SMITHSONIAN INSTITUTION,
February 29, 1888.

SIR: I have the honor to make the following requests in regard to the assignment of the appropriations for the maintenance of the U. S. National Museum for the coming fiscal year:

(1) That the items for "preservation of collections," "heating and lighting," "furniture and fixtures" be transferred from their present position in the schedule of "Estimates of Appropriations, 1888–'89" (p. 237), under the Department of the Interior, to a place under the general head of "under the Smithsonian Institution," and along with and in proximity to the other items to be expended under the direction of the Smithsonian Institution or its Secretary.

(2) That each of these items be placed directly under the subhead "Under the direction of the Secretary of the Smithsonian Institution as director of the National Museum."

(3) That a special item be inserted under the caption "Public printing and binding," providing the sum of $10,000 for printing labels and blanks for the use of the National Museum and for the "Bulletins" and annual volumes of the "Proceedings" of the Museum.

In explanation of these requests, I submit the following statements:

The act of Congress establishing the Smithsonian Institution, approved August 10, 1846 (Revised Statutes, Title LXXIII, sections 5579, 5594), provided that all objects of art and of foreign and curious research, and all objects of natural history, plants, and geological and mineralogical specimens belonging or hereafter to belong to the United States, which may be in the city of Washington, shall be delivered to the Regents of the Smithsonian Institution, and, together with new specimens obtained by exchange, donation, or otherwise, shall be so arranged and classified as best to facilitate their examination and study.

The National Museum, as it is now called, was thus placed under the sole control and direction of the Smithsonian Institution, and has ever since remained under its control; Congress having, since 1858, made annual appropriations for its maintenance. Until 1880, however, the sums thus appropriated were inadequate, and the yearly deficiences were paid from the income of the Institution.

In accordance with a practice of nearly thirty years the estimates for the annual appropriations have been each year, at the request of the Secretary of this Institution, forwarded by the Secretary of the Interior to the Secretary of the Treasury for transmission to Congress, and the disbursement of the appropriation has been made by the disbursing agent of the Interior Department.

This arrangement is somewhat inconvenient and cumbersome, and at the last meeting of the Board of Regents of the Smithsonian Institution the following resolution was adopted:

"*Resolved*, That the Regents recommend to Congress that the form of the sundry civil appropriation bill be so changed in the terms relating to the Museum and the Bureau of Ethnology as to provide—

"(1) That these moneys shall be disbursed under the direction of the Smithsonian Institution.

"(2) That the estimates for the appropriations of the Museum in the future shall be sent direct to the Secretary of the Treasury by the Smithsonian Institution through its Secretary."

In obedience to the wishes of the Board of Regents thus expressed, the matter was brought to the attention of the Secretary of the Interior, in a recent interview, by Chief-Justice Waite (the Chancellor of the Smithsonian Institution) and myself. As a result of this meeting a letter has been received from the Secretary of the Interior, in which he expresses the opinion that changes may be made with great propriety both in the manner of voting the appropriation and in the method of its disbursement. A copy of this letter is herewith inclosed, together with a copy of a second letter received in response to an inquiry as to the manner in which this change may best be effected.

In further explanation of the third request, I wish to say that this does not involve a new appropriation, since the estimate for this amount is included, as I understand it, in the sum of $375,525 estimated by the Secretary of the Treasury for the printing of the Interior Department and its Bureaus (see page 129 of the "Estimates of Appropriations, 1888–'89"). I may say in further explanation of this item that an appropriation has thus been made for the printing of the National Museum for at least twelve years past, and I am informed that the amount allotted during recent years has usually been $10,000.

I believe these changes will be in the interest of the public service, and respectfully ask that they be made.

I am, sir, your obedient servant,

S. P. LANGLEY,
Secretary.

Hon. SAMUEL J. RANDALL,
Chairman of Committee on Appropriations,
House of Representatives.

DEPARTMENT OF THE INTERIOR,
Washington, February 14, 1888.

SIR: I have considered the topic of the conference which I had the honor to have yesterday with the Chancellor of the Smithsonian Institution and yourself, being the relation of the Interior Department to the expenditure of the appropriation for the increase and care of the National Museum, which is a part of the Smithsonian Institution, and whether there be objection to the recommendation of an independency in the disbursement of the funds provided for its support as well as in its management.

The first collection of scientific curiosities which appears to have been a special object of care on the part of Congress was that made by the Wilkes Exploring Expedition, provided for by the act of May 14, 1836 (5 Stats., 29). This collection was first placed in the care of the National Institution for the Promotion of Science, and afterwards was transferred to the hall in the second story of the Patent Office. In 1846, when the act for the establishment of the Smithsonian Institution was passed, it was provided that, "as suitable arrangements could be made for their reception, all objects of art, and of foreign and curious research, and all objects of natural history, plants, geological and mineralogical specimens, belonging or hereafter to belong to the United

States, which may be in the city of Washington, in whosesover custody the same may be, shall be delivered to such persons as may be authorized by the Board of Regents to receive them, and shall be arranged in such order and so classed as best to facilitate the examination and study of them in the building so as aforesaid to be erected for the Institution;" provision having been made in the act for a suitable building, etc. It was provided by Congress that the Smithsonian Institution might be constructed adjacent to the Patent Office Building, but the project was not accepted, and an independent building, where now located, was arranged, this being completed in the year 1853.

It is said that the Secretary of the Interior and the Commissioner of Patents were desirous of removing the collections of the exploring expedition and of the National Institution out of the Patent Office Building, and requested the Regents of the Smithsonian Institution to receive them. This appears to have been acceded to by the Regents on the condition imposed that the Secretary of the Interior should provide for the payment of the expenses of the keeping and care of the collections.

An appropriation of $15,000 was made by Congress in the act of March 3, 1857, for the construction of cases, and of $2,000 for the removal of the articles. It was then held by the Attorney-General, in response to a request of the Secretary of the Interior for his opinion, that the provision in the eighth section of the act of the 4th of August, 1854 (10 Stats., 572), placing the collections under the control of the Commissioner of Patents, and authorizing the employment by him of keepers therefor, was designed to be temporary only, and that the act establishing the Smithsonian Institution, as well as that making the appropriation in 1857, were to be regarded as indicating the purpose of Congress respecting permanent provision for these collections.

In 1858, by the act of the 2d of June (11 Stats., 301), an appropriation of $4,000 " for the preservation of the collection of the exploring and surveying expeditions of the Government" was made as a contingent expense in the office of the Secretary of the Interior. This appears to have been the product of the condition acceded to by the Secretary of the Interior upon the occasion of the removal of the collections from the Patent Office to the Smithsonian; and, pursuing the same practice in October, 1858, Professor Henry, your illustrious predecessor, requested of the Secretary of the Interior the renewal of the same appropriation. Since that time this course appears to have been pursued without any other reason for its support than this summary narration indicates.

By the seventh section of the act for the establishment of the Smithsonian Institution (9 Stats., 105) the Secretary is directed to discuarge the duties of " keeper of the Museum," and authorized, with the consent of the board, to employ assistants. No power of appointment of any of the officers who expend the money provided by these annual appropriations is supposed to exist, or, since the transfer to the Smithsonian, has ever been exercised by any officer of this Department.

The manner of the appropriation has operated to impose upon the disbursing officer of this Department the duties of an auditor and a treasurer for this fund, as an officer for whom the Secretary is responsible. But no authority over the expenditures appears to rest with the Secretary of the Interior or at least ever to have been exercised, so that any scrutiny supposable has been that only of an auditor. Practically the disbursement of this appropriation has been made by the officers of the Smithsonian Institution, subject to two audits, one by this Department and the other by the Treasury, while the disbursing officer of the In-

REPORT OF THE SECRETARY.

terior Department acts as the disbursing officer for the Smithsonian, and a clerk has been assigned, as I am informed, by the Smithsonian to duty in the Interior Department to assist the disbursing officer.

Obviously there is nothing in the relations between the Smithsonian and the Interior Department to require the continuance of this state of things. The National Museum enjoys now an annual appropriation of a large amount in the various items, not usually less than $150,000. In the last act the appropriation was of $12,000 for heating, lighting, electrical, and telephonic service; of $116,000 for the preservation, exhibition, and increase of the collections; and of $40,000 for cases, furniture, fixtures, and appliances; both of the latter items embracing salaries. These items indicate not only the considerable proportions which the Museum has attained, but that their disbursement should be in the hands of those who have the government of the Museum and a direct responsibility exacted.

So far, then, from there appearing to be objection, the facts suggest to my mind the wisdom and desirability of providing for the National Museum directly, and imposing responsibility for the disbursement of the appropriation immediately upon the officers of that Institution, and with accountability to the Treasury, as in other cases.

The act of July 7, 1884 (23 Stats., 214), was a step in the direction of this independency of requiring the director of the National Museum to report annually to Congress the progress of the Museum during the year and its present condition.

The papers you kindly loaned me are herewith returned.

I have the honor to be, very respectfully,

WM. F. VILAS,
Secretary.

Prof. S. P. LANGLEY,
Secretary of the Smithsonian Institution.

DEPARTMENT OF THE INTERIOR,
Washington, February 20, 1888.

SIR: Replying to your favor of the 16th instant, I beg to say that it seems to me that so long as Congress has made the appropriation for the current year "under the Interior Department" in terms, it is necessary that it should be expended according to the practice hitherto prevailing; and that, if the same terms of appropriation should be continued, it would be with the expectation that the fixed practice of disbursement would continue also. It is therefore probably necessary that the language of the appropriation should be changed in order to effect the object desired. It may be presumed the accounting officers of the Treasury would require it.

The same observations may be applied to the appropriation for printing. I think it desirable that that should be separately made, so that the Smithsonian Institution should be independent, in its use of the provisions made by Congress, of this Department, and this Department freed of care in respect to it.

Yours, respectfully,

WM. F. VILAS,
Secretary.

Prof. S. P. LANGLEY,
Secretary of the Smithsonian Institution.

It was anticipated that when the wishes of the Regents were communicated to the Appropriations Committee of the House, the objection might be raised that the Secretary of the Smithsonian Institution, as such, was not an officer of the Government in the sense that the head of an executive department is, and that this might be an obstacle to the proposed transfer.

Such objection was, in fact, made in the committee, and for this reason the bill as reported from the House committee places the Museum appropriation "under the Secretary of the Smithsonian Institution as director of the National Museum;" while at the same time this, with the other appropriations, is subordinated to the general title "under the Smithsonian Institution."

In regard to the Bureau of Ethnology, the Secretary had already represented to the Regents his desire to see such a modification of the wording as might relieve him from the personal responsibility imposed by the language of former bills. The change actually introduced by the committee consists in making the former words "under the direction of the Secretary of the Smithsonian Institution" subordinate to the same general title "under the Smithsonian Institution."

Should the bill as reported pass both houses the disbursements for the National Museum will hereafter be made by an officer designated by the Secretary of the Smithsonian Institution, duly qualified and bonded to the acceptance of the Secretary of the Treasury, whose office will be in the Smithsonian building, instead of by the disbursing officer of the Department of the Interior, as heretofore.

The appropriations for " international exchanges " will also be disbursed by the same clerk at the Institution, instead of the disbursing clerk of the Treasury Department.

This new arrangement, while adding greatly to the responsibilities and cares of the officers of the Institution, will, it is believed, secure good results.

International exchanges.—The regular estimate submitted to Congress was as follows:

For expenses of the system of international exchanges between the United States and foreign countries, under the direction of the Smithsonian Institution, including salaries or compensation of all necessary employés, $15,000.

A *revised* estimate was submitted to Congress through the Secretary of the Treasury, on May 31, 1888, asking for $27,050 for the exchanges.

The House committee declined to recommend the proposed increase. It was then laid before the Senate Committee on Appropriations and an argument presented in favor of the increase, which induced the committee to report an amendment to the sundry civil bill increasing the appropriation from $15,000 to $20,000.*

---

* See Congressional Record, July 29, 1888, page 7666.

This amendment was adopted by the Senate, rejected by the House, and finally lost in conference committee of the two houses, so that the increase of appropriation for exchanges is only $3,000 for the next fiscal year.

Preservation of collections.—The appropriation asked for this service was $150,000. The House committee reported $120,000; the Senate committee, $125,000, and this latter amount was finally agreed to.

Furniture and fixtures.—An estimate of $40,000 was submitted, accepted by both committees, and passed by Congress.

Heating and lighting.—The original estimate " for expense of heating, lighting, and electrical and telephonic service for the National Museum," was $12,000. This sum was reported by the House Committee on Appropriations and adopted by Congress without change.

Armory building.—For several years this building has been occupied jointly by the National Museum and the U. S. Fish Commission, the latter paying the expenses of its care and repairs since July 1, 1885.

The House Committee on Appropriations in reporting the item of $120,000, for "preservation of the collection of the National Museum" inserted the following clause : " *And for the care and custody of the so-called Armory building,*" thus transferring the whole of the building and its maintenance to the Museum.

The Senate Committee on Appropriations, after hearing a statement from the U. S. Fish Commissioner,* struck out this clause, and inserted the following under the items for the Fish Commission :†

Provided, That the building known as the Armory building, Washington, District of Columbia, is hereby transferred to the charge of the United States Commission of Fish and Fisheries for use as a hatching and distributing station and for offices.

These diverse views were finally reconciled by the conference committees, who reported the following, which became a law : " *Under the U. S. Commission of Fish and Fisheries.*"

Provided, That the building known as the Armory building, Washington, District of Columbia, shall be occupied as at present, jointly by the United States Commission of Fish and Fisheries and the National Museum.

North American Ethnology.—The regular estimate for "continuing ethnological researches among the American Indians, under the direction of the Secretary of the Smithsonian Institution, including salaries or compensation of all necessary employés," was $50,000.

The House Committee on Appropriations, however, only reported $40,000, the sum which has been appropriated annually since 1884. This sum was accepted by both the House and the Senate, and is the amount appropriated. The appropriation is placed in the language of former years "under the direction of the Secretary," but at his request this with other departments is placed under the general caption "under the Smithsonian Institution."

---

* Senate Report No. 1814, p. 26.   † Act No. 1877, p. 47.

Report of the expenditures to be made to Congress.—The House Committee on Appropriations proposed a clause in the sundry civil bill for the next fiscal year which was agreed to by Congress and forms part of the act (No. 307), which is as follows:

That the Secretary of the Smithsonian Institution shall submit to Congress at its next session a detailed statement of the expenditures of the fiscal year 1888, under appropriations for "International Exchanges," "North American Ethnology," and the "National Museum," and annually thereafter a detailed statement of expenditures under said appropriations shall be submitted to Congress at the beginning of each regular session thereof.

BUILDINGS.

Among other matters discussed at the last meeting of the Regents was the erection of a new Museum building. On this occasion the Regents tacitly re-affirmed their resolution of 1882, recommending to Congress the enlargement of the National Museum by the erection of a fire-proof building on the southwest corner of the Smithsonian reservation, similar in style to the present National Museum; but on viewing the sketch plans, which had been prepared subsequently to the resolution, so as to include offices for the Geological Survey, they added an expression of their opinion that the new building should be planned exclusively for Museum purposes.

It was not at first intended to take action in this matter during the present year, but the overcrowded condition of the building, on account of which not only the current work but the proper development of the collections is greatly impeded, seemed to render immediate action necessary. A still more urgent need appeared to be the unsatisfactory sanitary condition of the new Museum building. A committee, consisting of Dr. J. H. Kidder, chairman, Dr. James M. Flint, U. S. Navy, and Mr. J. E. Watkins, was appointed on April 14 to make a careful study of the water supply, ventilation, and drainage, and in May submitted a preliminary report, from which it appeared that an alarming amount of sickness and mortality has been manifest among the employés since 1881—a mortality which can not be attributed to the location of the building, which has sometimes been pronounced unsanitary, since there has been no corresponding percentage of ill health in the old Smithsonian building adjoining. The number of days lost by employés on account of sickness in 1886 was 796; in 1887, 875; and in 1888, up to May 10, 213, by far the largest part of this loss of time being attributed on the books of the Museum to miasmatic diseases. The committee states that there is no reasonable doubt that some, if not all, of the ten deaths since 1881 were hastened or induced by the unwholesome condition of this building. The committee suggested repairs and modifications of considerable extent, including the construction of continuous cellars under each of the four sides of the building, which, in addition to the other necessary expenses, would cost in the neighborhood of $40,000.

This state of affairs seemed to demand decided action, and it being absolutely impossible to make any changes in the present building without entirely vacating a portion of it for a considerable period of time, the exigency for more accommodation seemed a great deal more urgent than had been at first supposed.

While it became evident, on study of the question, that for the ultimate needs of the Museum, a building of but one story occupying the same area as the present Museum would be insufficient, the question of immediate action was unexpectedly brought up in May by one of the senior Regents, a member of the Senate, who, when visiting the Museum with some friends, noticed its crowded and unsatisfactory condition. Having learned from me of the mortality and sickness of the employés, he inquired as to the feasibility of erecting a new building, and offered to use his influence to procure an appropriation, if I could obtain for him a set of sketch plans within a week, time being, as he stated, a very essential condition. After consulting with the chairman of your Executive Committee, I had no hesitation in accepting such an offer, but a difficulty arose from the fact that the sketch plans which had been laid before the Regents in 1882 were in part for purposes which the Regents had at their last meeting disapproved, and that hence they could not be used. By great diligence, however, plans for a building to be devoted exclusively to Museum purposes were prepared within the time mentioned. These were based upon an extensive accumulation of notes and drawings, embodying the record of the best recent work of museum construction in this country and in Europe, and they were for a building, as far as was consistent with these improvements, like the existing Museum. The report submitted by Senator Morrill, to accompany Senate bill 3134, contains the correspondence on which action was taken, and I have discussed the acts therein presented elsewhere under the proper heads.*

The following bill was introduced by Senator Morrill on June 12, was passed by the Senate on June 20, and at the end of the fiscal year was in the hands of the House Committee on Public Buildings and Grounds:

A BILL for the erection of an additional fire-proof building for the use of the National Museum.

Be it enacted by the Senate and House of Representatives of the United States of America in Congress assembled, That the sum of five hundred thousand dollars is hereby appropriated, out of any money in the Treasury not otherwise appropriated, or so much thereof as may be necessary, for the erection of a fire-proof building for the use of the National Museum, to cover three hundred feet square, and to consist of two stories and basement, to be erected under the direction of the Regents of the Smithsonian Institution, in accordance with the plans now on file with the Committee on Public Buildings and Grounds, on the southwestern portion of the grounds of the Smithsonian Institution. Said building to be placed west of the Smithsonian Institution, leaving a

---

* See museum, etc.

roadway between it and the latter of not less than forty feet, with the north front on a line with the south face of the building of the Agricultural Department and of the Smithsonian Institution; and all expenditures for the purpose herein mentioned shall be audited by the proper officers of the Treasury Department.

The building, as proposed, covers the same area as the present Museum, and is of the same general style, so far as is consistent with the introduction of a second story, thus affording nearly three times as much accommodation under the same area of roof as the building now in use. The arrangement of the interior of the proposed new structure is, however, considerably modified, as the result of the experience of seven years' occupation of the present building. The eighteen exhibition halls, on the two main floors are completely isolated from each other, and are capable of subdivision into smaller halls. The lighting will be equally as good as in the present building, the ventilation will be much better, and in other important respects the sanitary arrangements will be far more satisfactory.

A basement story is absolutely necessary, not only with a view to promoting the comfort and health of visitors and employés, as well as for securing greater dryness and better preservation of the specimens, but also for the purpose of providing large apartments for store-rooms and workshops. These proposed improvements in arrangement will not, however, interfere with the possibility of constructing a building which shall conform in the essential points of exterior proportion with the main features of the present building.

The present building contains about 80,000 square feet of floor space available for exhibition and storage. The building proposed will contain about 220,000 square feet. The amount of room for offices and laboratories would be about the same in each. The net area in the new building available for exhibition, storage, and office rooms, as estimated, would be between 5 and 6 acres.

For the construction of the present Museum Building an appropriation of $250,000 was made. This sum was supplemented by the following special appropriations: $25,000 for steam-heating apparatus, $26,000 for marble floors, $12,500 for water and gas fixtures and electrical apparatus, and $1,900 for special sewer connections. The total amount expended on this building was therefore $315,400, and it is generally admitted that the cost of its construction was considerably less than that of any other similar building in existence; in fact, perhaps too cheap to secure the truest economy.

The proposed structure can be erected at a proportionately smaller cost. I have obtained from responsible bidders, who are willing to give bonds for the completion of the work in accordance with the bids which they have submitted, estimates for the erection of the building complete, with steam-heating apparatus and all other essential appliances, excepting the electrical equipment, amounting in the aggregate to $473,000. These bids, upon which the estimates of cost have been made, were not competitive, and it is possible that something may be saved through competition. It is, however, necessary to provide also for the architect's superintendence, and for the removal and reconstruction of the Smithsonian stable, which now occupies the site. I therefore think it advisable to make request for the sum of $500,000, in order that these additional items and other contingencies may be covered.

The plans, though drawn in the limited time imposed, represent the results of an exhaustive study—which has extended over several years—of plans of the best modern museum buildings in Europe and America, nearly all of which have been personally inspected by officers of the Smithsonian Institution.

It will be remembered by the Regents that neither the central portion of the Smithsonian Building nor the so-called " chapel," at its western extremity, has ever been made fire-proof. The first contains valuable collections, which are in somewhat menacing neighborhood to the paint shop outside and to alcoholic stores within. These ought to be provided for separately, but the representations made of the necessity have not yet obtained attention from Congress. A special occasion having arisen which made it desirable, at any rate, to complete the fire-proofing of the " chapel," on the 21st May, at the request of the Secretary, Hon. J. S. Morrill reported from the Committee on Public Buildings the following bill :

A BILL to provide for making the west end of the Smithsonian Building fire-proof, and for other purposes.

Be it enacted by the Senate and House of Representatives of the United States of America in Congress assembled, That for the purpose of making the roof of the Gothic chapel at the west end of the Smithsonian Building fire-proof, and for other purposes, under the direction of the Regents of the Smithsonian Institution, the sum of seventeen thousand five hundred dollars, or so much thereof as may be necessary, is hereby appropriated out of any money in the Treasury not otherwise appropriated.

This bill was adopted without a dissenting vote by the United States Senate.

It was referred in the House May 22, 1888, to the Committee on Public Buildings, but no report was made by the committee. The same bill was offered in the Senate on the 28th of June by Senator Morrill as an amendment reported by the Senate Committee on Public Buildings and Grounds to the sundry civil bill. This was referred to the Senate Committee on Appropriations, but was not reported back.

Fire-proofing west range of Smithsonian building.—In 1887 Congress made an appropriation of $15,000 " for urgent and necessary repairs to central and western portions of the Smithsonian Institution."[*]

This was expended in removing the combustible material in the west range, as this was the most urgent work required. The contents of

---

[*] Sundry civil act, No. 148, March 3, 1887

this part of the building, consisting of the alcoholic collections, were very inflammable and dangerous. The fire-proofing was intrusted to Messrs. Cluss and Schulze, architects, from whose report the following account of the work is taken :

"The reconstruction extended over the curtain between the main building and the west wing, a building of 60 feet in length and 54 feet in width, with an adjoining turret containing stairs. It contains a basement where alcoholic specimens are kept.

"The main story is mostly occupied by an exhibition hall, extending up into the roof, with a clere-story. Along the north front was originally an open cloister, which had been, for many years, temporarily fitted up, by frame-work, for offices.

"Permanent provision was made for these purposes, and a mezzanine story formed by the insertion of a fire proof upper floor.

"Besides the old, rotten, combustible floors and roofs, a complicated system of decorative hollow columns and vaults, framed of wooden scantlings, boards, and lathed plastering, had to be carefully removed, so as not to injure the outside walls, consisting of a thin cut-stone facing, backed by ordinary rubble-work.

"In the reconstruction the Romanesque general character of the building was preserved with the greatest simplicity compatible with the surroundings, and also made a necessity by the limited appropriation, in conjunction with the increased cost of decorations in fire proof materials.

"The first advertisement for bids for the work was confined to what was required for making the reconstructed building ready for occupancy; and to leave desirable but not absolutely necessary improvements and internal finishings to any balance left from the appropriation.

"Under date of June 27, 1887, an advertisement was issued for the wrought and cast iron work, and the award made to C. A. Schneider's Sons, of this city, at $1,848, the lowest bid received.

"On July 6, 1887, another advertisement was issued for cut-stone work, brick-work, fire-proofing, metal-roofing, lighter iron-work, corrugated-iron lathing, carpenter's work, plastering, and miscellaneous work. There was no bid below that of D. T. Cissel, of Washington, which amounted to $9,850, and was within the estimates.

"Miscellaneous minor operations, such as cleaning and clearing the building, steam fitting, and electric work, were done by day's work and settled for on pay-rolls.

"The hardware was obtained in open market, by competition among the principal dealers of the city, on specifications.

"The contractors have satisfactorily and for the sums agreed upon completed their work.

"The cost of the work to June 30, 1888, has been—

Pay-rolls of laborers, carpenters, and steam-fitters	$466.30
Advertising, printing, and type-writing	49.10
Brick repairs, nails, and lumber	61.32
Contract for iron-work by C. A. Schneider's Sons	1,848.00
Contract for miscellaneous work by D. T. Cissel	9,800.00
Hardware	72.66
Steam and water pipes	147.58
Clerk-hire	275.00
	12,719.96

"leaving a balance of $2,280.04 for frescoing and decoration and completion of the work."

The east room, used for the meeting of the Regents, has had such improvements made in its ventilation as the defective construction of the building in this respect admitted, and I have taken occasion to draw on the different departments of the Smithsonian for its furniture, so that this may recall in some measure the various interests under the Regents' care.

RESEARCHES.

From the foundation of the Institution the promotion of original research has been regarded as one of its important functions under the general provision of Smithson's bequest, and by encouraging and facilitating the discovery of new truths it is obvious that the primary purpose of the founder—the increase of knowledge—can be most efficiently attained.

Natural science falls into two great divisions, the biological and the physical, and since it has been the case that of late years the first of these has been almost exclusively encouraged by the Smithsonian, it was the desire of the late Secretary, Professor Baird, to do something to restore the balance, and with this end in view he had made preparations to secure an astro-physical observatory and laboratory, and though these preparations were interrupted by his death it is understood that through his action some friends of the Institution have already offered to give the means for the erection of the modest structure needed for the accommodation of such a special observatory. The site would necessarily be suburban, on account of the especial need of seclusion and the absence of tremor in the soil, such as is felt in the neighborhood of the streets of a city.

No steps have yet been taken to secure a site, but in view of the promise of means for the building, and the fact that the construction of the necessary apparatus will occupy a long time, I have ordered such of the essential pieces as are not likely to be ready, even under these conditions, till the building is prepared to receive it. With the exception of this preparation there has been nothing done for the increase of knowledge in the physical branches of science in the past year, but it may be remarked that the Institution is in possession of a certain amount of philosophical apparatus. This is formed of the débris of its first collection (nearly destroyed by the fire) and of a certain few pieces purchased by Professor Henry in the later years of his life.

There are also a number of historical relics, as the philosophical instruments used by Dr. Joseph Priestly and others. These were on exhibition in the new Museum Building, but the room they occupied being wanted for other purposes the collection was transferred to the Smithsonian Building where they were placed in an apartment adjoining the laboratory. Arrangements are now being made for a more suitable depository and for the exhibition to the public of such articles of this class as may be of general interest.

The Institution has continued to give an important impulse to the prosecution of the biological sciences, but most largely so, indirectly through the Museum and Bureau of Ethnology.

The chief research has been under an arrangement made by the late Secretary. Prof. E. D. Cope has been engaged during the entire year in completing and preparing for publication the results of an investigation upon the reptiles and batrachians of North America, which has been in progress under the direction of the Institution for more than twenty years. The first part, consisting of a Monograph on the Batrachians, has been handed in and sent to the Public Printer, and the work of printing it as one of the bulletins of the National Museum has been already begun.

The expense entailed in the publication has been much greater than the late Secretary anticipated, but I have felt it proper to continue it, not only to carry out a purpose which had engaged the interest of Professor Baird, but on account of the great intrinsic importance and value of the work itself. No complete memoir on the Batrachians of North America has ever been published; while the projected work enters fully into questions of anatomy and geographical distribution, in addition to the customary discussion of classification and synonymy, and will supply a long-felt need of biologists not alone in America but throughout the world.

The second part, relating to the Reptiles, is in progress, and its completion is promised during the coming year.

Important investigations are in progress at the hands of the curators and their assistants in every department of the Museum, for which reference may be made to that portion of my report.

EXPLORATIONS.

Our function in promoting the increase of knowledge has always been regarded as including in its scope and object explorations at distant or less familiar localities. Though no special explorations independent of those already undertaken in connection with the Fish Commission have been made during the past year, I am in hearty accord with the policy of giving such encouragement to the lines of investigation heretofore prosecuted in this respect as may be practicable from the portion of our income which can be thus appropriated.

The activity in exploration this year is not less than heretofore, but it has chiefly been carried on by the appropriation for ethnological researches. This has been placed by law under your Secretary, who has continued the arrangement, in some sense inherited from his predecessors, under which the direction of the expenditure has been left almost wholly within the discretion of Maj. J. W. Powell, from the confidence felt equally in his scientific acquirements as an ethnologist and his known capacity as an administrator. The usual report of the Bureau of Ethnology is given elsewhere.

There has also been a limited amount of exploration carried on in connection with the Museum.

Mr. Romyn Hitchcock, one of the curators of the Museum, has been for two years on leave of absence, while performing the duty of professor of English at the University Osaka, Japan, and has been assisted as far as has been practicable in his explorations in the west and north of the Japanese Archipelago.

Two of the geological curators have explored numerous mineral localities in connection with the work of completing the sets of minerals for distribution. Their work is referred to in the report of the Museum.

Two employés of the Museum accompanied the Fish Commission schooner *Grampus* on her trip to the Gulf of St. Lawrence, for the purpose of taking advantage of the opportunity, should any offer, of exploring the natural history of the islands of that region, and particularly to make search for the remains of the Great Auk. They were successful in their efforts, obtaining important collections and material for a report which will be presented in connection with the work of the Museum.

At the beginning of the fiscal year Mr. Charles H. Townsend, of the U. S. Fish Commission, was engaged in the joint service of the Commission and the Museum in natural history exploration in Central America. He returned in October, 1887.

Ensign A. P. Niblack, U. S. Navy, (for three years attached to the scientific staff of the Museum,) during a cruise upon the coast of Alaska made extensive collections and obtained material for a report on the ethnology of that region.

PUBLICATIONS.

Classes of publications.—Of the Smithsonian publications, the first class—both in priority of introduction and in scientific importance—is the quarto series of *Contributions to Knowledge.* This series, numbering twenty-five volumes, was inaugurated forty years ago.

An early hope had been entertained that the Institution might be enabled to issue one volume of the quarto series each year, but it was soon discovered that original memoirs of merit, embodying new acquisitions to our knowledge, could not be procured at any such rate. Partly by reason of the rapid growth of scientific institutions in our country, and partly by reason of the largely increased endowments of some of them, other channels of scientific publication have been opened, and there has been a steady reduction both in the number of memoirs presented to this Institution for publication and in the numbers of these judged deserving of a place in the ranks of the "Contributions." This diminution of fertility is perhaps best exhibited by the following table of volumes issued during each successive period of ten years:

During first decade (from 1848 to 1857), nine volumes.

During second decade (ending 1867), six volumes.

During third decade (ending 1877), six volumes. .

During fourth decade (ending 1887), four volumes.

It may be stated that the last volume of this series (Volume XXV) was issued in 1885, and that one memoir of 196 pages, with five chromo-lithographic plates, "Researches upon the Venoms of Poisonous Serpents" (by Dr. S. Weir Mitchell and Dr. Edward T. Reichert) has since been published (1886) as an installment for Volume XXVI:

The second class of Smithsonian publications is the octavo series of *Miscellaneous Collections*, which was not organized until nearly a quarter of a century later than the "Contributions," the first volume having been published in 1862.

As estimated by the number of volumes published during the period of its existence, now amounting to thirty-three, this series (as was to have been expected) has grown about twice as rapidly as the former.

In addition to these two classes of works, published at the expense of the Smithsonian fund, three other series of works are issued under the direction of the Institution, the publication of which is provided for by Congressional appropriations.

Of these, first in order may be mentioned the *Annual Reports* to Congress of the Board of Regents of the Institution, in accordance with the provisions of Revised Statutes, section 5593, enacting that the Board shall submit to Congress at each session thereof a report of the operations, expenditures, and condition of the Institution. These are in octavo form, and have gradually increased in bulk from a few hundred pages to two thick volumes per annum. Although printed by the General Government, these reports have been a constant and increasing charge upon the funds of the Institution, required by the preparation of suitable material for the usual appendix, in illustration of particular investigations, or of the principal advances made in science. For a number of years past the expenditure for this purpose has amounted to several thousand dollars for each year, and it has become a serious question whether we can longer afford to bear the burden. If Congress can be induced to make a small appropriation for the collection and preparation of information relative to the annual progress in the United States of scientific discovery, and of its technological applications, to be appended to the Smithsonian Report, such a record would not only be in keeping with the great objects of this Institution, but would maintain for its report its high popular and educational character as well as promote the industrial interests of our country, and the trifling expenditure would seem to be well justified by the precedents of similar appropriations for obtaining and diffusing valuable information through the medium of the Agricultural and other official reports.

In the original "programme of organization," approved by the Regents December 8, 1847, was specified among the details of the plan for diffusing knowledge "the publication of a series of reports giving an account of the new discoveries in science, and of the changes made from year to year in all branches of knowledge not strictly professional." And it was added, "The reports are to be prepared by collaborators eminent in the different branches of knowledge."

In the Smithsonian Report for 1854 appeared for the first time an "appendix," containing an account of American explorations for the years 1853 and 1854, by Prof. S. F. Baird; a full report of lectures delivered before the Institution by Marsh, Brainard, Loomis, Channing, Reed, and Russell; extracts from the scientific correspondence of the Institution; and miscellaneous papers relating to American archæology, geology, etc. This general appendix to the Annual Report of the Regents has been regularly continued to the present time (for more than the third of a century), and has served to bring the Smithsonian Report into great popular demand.

In the Report for 1880 (after the abandonment by the publishing house—the Harpers, of New York—of an "Annual Record of Science and Industry"), a systematic "Record of Scientific Progress," compiled by various specialists, was made the principal feature of the general appendix by my predecessor. This annual scientific summary, however acceptable and however conformable to the plans originally laid down, has labored under two very serious difficulties: First, that from the vexatious delay of publication the record of recent science lost much of its interest and value; and, secondly, that the expense of its preparation (averaging $2,500 per annum) has become more and more a tax upon the Smithsonian income that could be but illy afforded. To this may be added a practical difficulty in getting all the different summaries completed at the time of making up the general appendix, so that an omission of one or more branches occurred in every report. Under these circumstances, it has become a serious question as to the manner in which this appendix to the Report is to be maintained, if maintained at all.

An additional complication of the question may be referred to, arising out of the construction given to an act of Congress approved August 4, 1886, and since continued from year to year, which prescribes that heads of departments "before transmitting their annual reports to Congress, the printing of which is chargeable to this appropriation, shall cause the same to be carefully examined, and shall exclude therefrom all matter including engravings, maps, drawings, and illustrations, except such as they shall certify in their letters transmitting such reports to be necessary, and to relate entirely to the transaction of public business." (Statutes, Forty-ninth Congress, first session; chapter 902, page 255.)

This restriction has been held by the Public Printer to apply equally to the reports of the Regents to Congress, which are printed under the provisions of this appropriation. This consideration seems to furnish an additional reason for having the supplementary matter of the report placed under a special clause of authorization, for the avoidance of all question as to the "necessity and entire relation to the public business" of such general scientific information.

The second series to be mentioned under this head consists of the publications of the U. S. National Museum, comprising its "Bulletins" and its "Proceedings." The Bulletins of the National Museum were instituted for the purpose of furnishing a prompt publication of original descriptions of specimens received, and of thus illustrating the mineral, botanical, zoological, and ethnological collections belonging to the Museum. They consist of monographs on biological subjects, check-lists, taxonomic systems, etc., and are prepared mainly by the curators and other attachés of the establishment. This series was commenced in 1875, and now numbers thirty-two Bulletins. These memoirs, from their variety of subject, are naturally of very unequal extent, ranging from fifty to over one thousand pages. Collected, they form nine large-sized octavo volumes.

The Proceedings of the National Museum consist of shorter and less elaborate papers, designed to give early accounts of its recent acces-sions, or of freshly acquired facts relating to natural history, etc., and are promptly issued in single " signatures," as soon as matter sufficient to fill sixteen pages has been prepared, the date of issue being given on each signature. These " Proceedings" thus partake of the character of an irregular periodical, the numbers of which—continuously paged—form an annual volume.

This series was commenced in 1878, and now extends to nine annual volumes, averaging about 650 pages, and illustrated with numerous wood-cut plates. Both these series of publications of the National Museum have hitherto been printed at the expense of a fund under the authority of the Interior Department; but it is proposed to ask for legislation which will permit them to be printed at the Government Printing Office on the requisition of your secretary.

The third and last series to be mentioned comprises the annual re-ports of the Bureau of Ethnology, which are large sized volumes of royal octavo form, well printed and well illustrated with cuts and lithographic plates. These volumes (of which four only have thus far been issued, but of which the material for four more awaits the printer) present matter of great interest to the anthropologist, and in their production reflect credit upon the scientific staff of the Bureau of Ethnology.

Distribution of publications.—Since the diffusion of knowledge, next to efforts for its increase, is one of the principal functions and duties of the Institution, it would doubtless be desirable if we could offer a copy of its works to every intelligent inquirer specially interested in any subject of which some of these volumes might treat. Since, however, the Institution can not afford to print, in ordinary cases, more than from 1,250 to 1,500 copies of one work, three-fourths of which are required to be supplied to our regular list of " correspondents," for the mainte-nance of our exchange series, it has been found necessary to restrict the gratuitous distribution to these, and to hold the small reserve, more strictly than in earlier times, for sale to those sufficiently interested to purchase them.

The remarks made on this subject by the first secretary so long ago as 1850, are no less pertinent to-day: "It must be evident that from the small portion of the income which can be devoted to this object the distribution must be circumscribed. Fifteen hundred copies of each memoir have been printed; but this number, though all that the income could furnish, has not been found sufficient to meet a tenth part of the demand. It should be recollected that though these memoirs consist of the results of new investigations of the highest importance to the well-being of man in extending the bounds of his knowledge of the universe of mind and matter of which he forms a part, yet they are not in all cases of such a character as to be immediately appreciated by the popular mind, and indeed they are better adapted to instruct the teacher than to interest the general reader. They should therefore be distributed in such a way as most readily to meet the eye of those who will make the best use of them in diffusing a knowledge of their contents."

That our present circulation, however, is placed on a liberal basis, is sufficiently shown by the published conditions on which we are enabled still to offer them gratuitously. This distribution is made, first, to those learned societies of the first class which give to the Institution in return complete sets of their own publications. Secondly, to colleges of the first class furnishing catalogues of their libraries and students, and publications relative to their organization and history. Thirdly, to public libraries in this country having twenty-five thousand volumes. Fourthly, they are presented in some cases to still smaller libraries, especially if no other copies of the Smithsonian publications are given in the same place and a large district would be otherwise unsupplied. Lastly, to institutions devoted exclusively to the promotion of particular branches of knowledge, such of its publications are given as relate to their special objects.

These rules apply chiefly to distribution in the United States. The number sent to foreign countries, under somewhat different conditions, is about the same as that distributed in this country.

Economy of publication demanded.—In view of the natural expansion of the Smithsonian operations with advancing years, with its resources fixed to a rigidly measured income which, as I have already observed, is itself undergoing a slow depreciation in intrinsic value or actual purchasing power, it would seem that some curtailment will be necessary in the appropriations for preparing and printing the works that may be offered. In looking to see in what direction this economy may be most advantageously exercised it has seemed to me that a more critical supervision over the series of "Miscellaneous Collections" might be adopted so as to limit it to works of a more general interest or of a higher scientific value. This series already extending (as above stated) to thirty-three volumes, has included a number of the Museum Bulletins and Proceedings as well as the proceedings of several scientific societies established in this city. In the infancy of the Philosoph-ical, the Anthropological, and the Biological Societies of Washington this form of patronage appeared to be a very proper method of pro-moting the increase and diffusion of knowledge. But now that these societies are well established on a permanent basis, with a large mem-bership for each, such a support appears to be less required. In like manner the publications of the National Museum being provided for by a Congressional appropriation, this Institution may well relinquish the expense of any re-issue of them, while still employing its exchange service for the gratuitous transmission of such copies of the "Bulle-tins" and "Proceedings" as may be intrusted to its care. Thus far eight volumes of the Miscellaneous Collections have been occupied with these issues, to wit: Volumes XIII, XIX, XXII, XXIII, and XXIV, with the publications of the National Museum; and Volumes XX, XXV, and XXXIII, with those of the societies named. I propose to discard these from the series in the future and to make such other restrictions as may seem judicious under present conditions. In con-nection with this I have had in mind the renewal of an experiment made by your first secretary of placing (in certain exceptional cases) the excess of copies beyond those regularly distributed, in the hands of a publisher.

With regard to the quarto series of Smithsonian Contributions to Knowledge there will probably be no occasion to suggest any change, at least for the present.

THE SMITHSONIAN EXCHANGE SYSTEM.

The "diffusion of knowledge among men," which, next to its "in-crease," is the reason for the existence of this Institution, has been, ever since its foundation, largely carried out by means of the exchange sys-tem, under which all knowledge, but especially new knowledge, as em-bodied in scientific and other literature, is disseminated by the gratu-itous efforts of the Smithsonian.

The system of exchanges, even in its present condition, involved in 1886–'87, the shipping of about ten thousand domestic and over forty thousand foreign packages of books, and this has been increased to over twelve thousand domestic and sixty-two thousand foreign packages by the operations of the past year.

Before the writer's connection with the Smithsonian Institution he had abundant opportunity to know that the regard and confidence in which it is held by all scientific men did not prevent a then general rec-ognition of the fact that its exchange system did not work the benefits contemplated, in that it took a time which ordinarily seemed excessive to send a package to Europe or to get one in return.

The writer having been assigned to the charge of exchanges on his first connection with the Institution as Assistant Secretary, gave early attention to this subject. The result of his investigation appears to show that the reproach for delay was then well founded, but that the blame did not lie at the door of the Institution, which did not, and does not, possess the means to efficiently fulfill the tasks now imposed upon it. He hopes some improvement has already been effected ; but much doubtless remains to be done.

In the early period of the history of the exchanges nearly all transportation was slow, but if it took the Smithsonian two or three months to send a package to Europe and as much to bring it back, it took the private individual the same time. The early steam-ship lines, then or a little later, generously aided the Smithsonian plan by giving the exchanges free transportation, a privilege which the Institution has often used, but now that rapid transportation is general, does not wish to abuse by making a request that such companies should continue to transport the whole of its greatly increased freight without charge.

There is another reason why they should not be requested to do so in the fact that the character of the freight the exchange department sends has changed, as the greater part of it is now the property of the nation, and if the General Government desires this to go by rapid transit, it is certainly able to pay for it. As Congress does not pay for rapid transit, it is a reasonable conclusion that it does not desire it, but it may be doubted whether either the extent of the actual use of the Smithsonian exchanges by the Government or the degree of delay of governmental business is understood.

To bring the facts in the case to mind let me recall, first, that the original exchange system commenced in 1846, and, second, that after twenty years of useful work exclusively in the interests of knowledge, an entirely new duty was imposed upon it by the act of March, 1867, which established the International Exchange of Government Publications and made the Smithsonian Institution the agency for this exchange, giving it for distribution 50 copies of all documents printed by order of either house of Congress, 50 additional copies of all documents printed in excess of the usual number, together with 50 of each publication issued by any Department or Bureau of the Government; while the resolution of July 25, 1868, makes it obligatory upon the Departments to furnish 50 copies of each publication issued by them, wherever printed.

Accordingly, of late years, there has been added to the primitive Smithsonian exchange system and merged with it the additional feature of carrying the Government's exchanges.

The Institution possessed unequaled experience and facilities for such work, and though the new class of books brought to its exchange department was partly foreign to its original object, the propriety of its assuming such a service, if the Government's interests could be promoted by this experience, is evident. It certainly, however, was not to have been anticipated that the Institution should conduct a purely administrative work for the General Government out of its private funds, as it appears to have done for thirteen years from 1868 to 1881, when the first appropriation of $3,000 was made by Congress.* If we look back to the commencement of the Government system we find that up to 1880, inclusive, the Smithsonian had paid $92,386.29 for exchanges, of which it is estimated that more than two-thirds were on Government account, for which the Government paid nothing whatever. Subsequently to 1880, as the foot-note more exactly shows, the service has cost $96,065.85, for which the Government has paid $57,500, leaving nearly $30,000 of the cost to be borne by the Smithsonian Institution, and this exclusive of the rent of the rooms, which represents about $3,000 a year more.

All exchanges are now conducted by Government, but here "Governmental" signifies all publications received from or for any bureau or office of this or any Government, and "Miscellaneous" all others.†

It would appear that there is no doubt that in the intent of Congress, as expressed in the act of 1881, these appropriations should now be applied indifferently to all exchanges, whether to those which it undertakes for the Congressional publications, for those of governmental bureaus, or for other literary and scientific objects; but the amount as-

---

Proportion of the amount and cost of foreign exchanges for the years 1881 to 1887-'88.

Year.	Governmental		Miscellaneous.		Total		Paid by Government.
	Packages.	Cost.	Packages	Cost.	Packages	Cost	
1881	25, 747	$7, 219. 72	11, 915	$3, 248. 12	37, 662	$10, 467. 84	$3, 000
1882	42, 731	7, 347. 46	15, 316	2, 633. 73	58, 047	9, 981. 19	5, 000
1883	50, 634	10, 834. 83	13. 260	2, 857. 51	63, 894	13, 692. 34	7, 500
1884	51, 813	9, 955. 77	13, 294	2, 554. 94	65, 107	12, 510. 71	10, 000
1885 (6 months).	37, 618	7, 335. 51	5, 982	972 08	43, 600	8, 307. 59	....
1885-'86	71, 446	9, 101. 75	22, 647	2, 904. 05	94, 093	12, 005. 80	10, 000
1886-'87	27, 530	7, 788. 04	24, 688	6, 198. 59	52, 218	13, 986. 63	10, 000
1887-'88	50, 691	10, 200.02	24, 416	4, 913. 73	75, 107	15, 113. 75	12, 000
Total.....	358, 210	69, 783 10	131, 518	26, 282 75	489, 728	96, 065. 85	57, 500

† Under the classification which has prevailed heretofore the publications passing through the exchange office have been divided into "official" and "literary and scientific," meaning by the former designation only the publications furnished by the Public Printer for distribution among the national libraries of the Governments participating in the international exchanges, and including in the latter all of the publications sent or received by the bureaus of this Government in direct exchange with the bureaus of others, and for the benefit of the bureau libraries. The classification appears to be misleading, since this latter subdivision of the exchanges is quite as strictly official, or for the service of the Government, as the former. I have therefore directed that hereafter all publications issued or received by the Government, whether by legislative, judicial, or Executive authority, shall be designated as "Governmental," and all others as "Miscellaneous."

signed is inadequate for the proper conduct even of the former, as has just been shown.*

Having been assigned to the charge of the international exchanges when Assistant Secretary, the writer has always taken particular interest in this part of the work of the Institution; but so far as its success depends upon the provision by Congress of the indispensable means to meet the expenses which it has just been shown that the Government connection has made needful, his labors have been but partially successful. The department of exchanges, however, has continued to be the object of more than usual attention, first under the immediate care of the writer, and later under that of Dr. J. H. Kidder, appointed curator of laboratory and exchanges on the 19th of March, 1888.

· It has been remarked that the present system is unsatisfactory because of the delay involved, while it will shortly be shown that the expenses of shipment by a prompt and efficiently conducted system would be substantially the same per ton of freight as by the present inefficient and slow one, which is largely carried on by what might be called the charity of the transportation lines. Unsatisfactory as is the service, however, and necessarily conducted as it is (under the present appropriations) in a manner prejudicial to every interest concerned with it, these appropriations do not, as we have seen, meet all the inevitable expenditures, and the deficiency still continues to be met from the proper funds of the Institution.

The expense for the service for this fiscal year has been $15,113.75, of which sum $12,000 were voted by Congress and $205.75 were refunded by the Patent Office, Signal Office, and a correspondent in South America, leaving a net deficit of $2,908, paid by the Smithsonian fund. In the coming fiscal year, at the present rate of expenditure, the cost will be $16,050, making no allowance for the usual annual increase in the quantity of business or for increased salaries of employés. The domestic exchanges, it will be understood, form no part of this estimate. Finally, it should be stated that nearly every department of the Government has some small appropriation to partially cover services which should be gratuitously rendered.

Recurring now to one of the effects of this insufficient appropriation, the writer repeats that there are too many and too great delays in the transit of packages sent by the international exchanges. These delays do not occur in the office at Washington, nor in those of the agents of the Institution at London and Leipzig. They are due, broadly speaking, to the fact just stated that the Institution has not the means to

---

* The act approved in 1882 reads, "For expenses of the international exchanges between the United States and foreign countries, in accordance with the Paris convention of 1877;" and this wording is repeated in 1883. Although the phrase referring to the Paris convention was afterwards dropped from the law, there seems to be no doubt that it has fixed its meaning, since the point has been raised more than once by the accounting officers of the Treasury, and so decided.

pay for rapid transit on land or sea, and that for what it obtains on the latter it is dependent upon the courtesy of several ocean steam-ship companies, with the natural result that the free freight is often delayed to make room for that which is paid for.* A subordinate cause, however, lies in the apathy or indifference, or possible insufficient clerical force, of most of the foreign-exchange bureaus.

In a recent test case parcels shipped on the same day to London, Leipzig, and Paris, with letters requesting immediate notification of receipt, were acknowledged by the agents of the Institution at London on the fourteenth day, at Leipzig on the fifteenth, and by the Bureau des Échanges at Paris on the fortieth day.

In the hope of insuring a regular and certain ocean-steamer service, I requested, on the 30th of May last, through the honorable Secretary of the Treasury, an increase in the appropriation for the fiscal year 1888–'89 to $27,050, based upon a careful consideration of the cost of "fast freight" at the ordinary commercial rates and upon the quantity of material which past experience has made probable.

The following brief statement wil give the essential facts on which the application was based.

It should be premised that only about one-third of the Government's publications are actually received from the office of the Public Printer and elsewhere, for transmission abroad, and that while special application on our part might call out the remainder, we can not undertake to do this while only partly paid the actual outlay for the portion we carry already, while a sufficient appropriation to justify the employment of a special exchange agent in Europe, as has been frequently and earnestly recommended by the Librarian of Congress, would bring back in return probably about eight times what we now receive. Accordingly, in the subjoined estimate of what should be done, if Congress paid the actual cost of efficient service (the services of the officers of this Institution being given without charge), more packages appear under the new plan than under the old.

---

* A shipment sent from Rome in December, 1887, for example, lay at Naples until the latter part of March, 1888, before the steam-ship company forwarded it.

Statement of exchanges during the fiscal year ended June 30, 1887, *together with estimates for proposed new departure.*

	Old plan, 1886–'87.	Estimate, new plan.
I. Amount of exchanges sent Abroad.	*Packages.*	*Packages.*
Congressional	21,600	40,000
Departmental	16,901	30,000
Society and private	13,145	15,000
Total sendings	51,646	85,000
Weight in tons	52	87
Average number of packages to box		30
Average weight of box ....pounds		175
II. Time.	*Days.*	*Days.*
Average time in transit to western Europe * ......days	36	15

	Delayed.	Prompt.
III. Expenses.		
Freight to New York	$684	$2,280
Freight across the ocean	Free.	5,000
Freight from port of debarcation to destination	750	1,750
Total sendings	1,434	9,038

	Conveyance.	
*Average time in transit to Western Europe:	Delayed	Prompt.
	Days.	*Days.*
To seaboard	2	¼
Interval between steamers :		
For England	14	3½
For Germany	14	3½
For France	7	7
Ocean transport :		
To England	15	8
To Germany	15	9
To France	12	9
Discharging cargo	4	2
Continental freight :		
England	4	2
Germany	7	3
France	4	2
Giving average time as above	36	15

All this refers to sendings abroad.

	Actual.	Estimated.
The receipts are:		
Congressional packages	$1,348	$10,784
Departmental packages..............................	7,211	14,000
Society and private packages.........................	2,926	3,000
Total	11,485	27,784

The average time for receipts will be probably reduced to less than one-half that at present.

	1886–'87.	Estimated.
Expenses of the service:		
Service, including salaries *	$11,630.36	$16,500
Transportation	2,064.91	9,000
Boxes	575.77	950
Incidentals, paper, printing, etc	412.41	600
Total..	14,683.11	27,050

This estimate does not include any charge for office rent.

Summary at present, 85 tons annually in thirty-six days at a total cost of... $14,683

By proposed plan, 150 tons annually in fifteen days at a total cost of........ 27,050

The following memorandum appears in the Congressional Record of July 29, 1888, page 7666, and contains the leading facts in a succinct form:

"*International Exchanges.*—Present system established by resolution of Congress approved March 2, 1867, and by subsequent legislation. Fifty copies of all Government publications put at disposal of Committee on Library for international exchange.

Uniform system agreed upon at international geographical conference, Paris, 1875, and modified by conferences for this particular purpose at Brussels in 1880, 1883, and 1886. Treaty now before Senate is the result of these conferences. There is now no completed treaty obligation. England, Germany, and France have declined to ratify the treaty, and were not represented at the last conference.

The Smithsonian is not concerned with the system otherwise than as the agent of the Government, but has paid a material part of the cost annually from its private fund.

As the office is now organized the annual expenditure is at the following rates:

Pay-rolls, $965 per month $11,580
Foreign agents 1,500
Boxes, freight, etc., estimated................................. 3,000

    16,080

---

* It is not superfluous to repeat that these services are those of persons engaged in addition to the proper personnel of this institution, the services of whose officers are given without charge.

This means 'slow' freight, and for the most part gratuitous, on the ocean. The average time for transmission of a parcel to western Europe is now thirty-six days. By ordinary fast freight it could be reduced to sixteen days. Extraordinary delays occur frequently because of the fact that the freight is carried gratuitously. Boxes shipped from Rome, for example, in December last were held in Naples three months by the steam ship line because its steamer's space was all filled by paying freight. The same thing has occurred frequently on this side of the ocean. As at present organized, the Smithsonian sends out about one-third of the United States Government publications, and receives from foreign governments less than one-tenth of their official publications. Very much is thus lost which is of great interest and value to our Government offices.

Many of the Executive Departments which wish to use the exchange system are obliged to adopt other measures at considerably increased cost. Some of them have special appropriations to defray part of the cost of special transmissions by the Smithsonian.

The sum estimated for ($27,050), is the result of careful calculation, based upon a comparison of the details of the business for several years back. It is the Secretary's opinion that it will far more than repay itself by an increased efficiency in the service and by the number of valuable works which it will bring to Congress and the Executive Departments of the Government."

I am aware that it hardly lies within the power of the Regents as a body to correct the evils I have referred to, but I present this summary and imperfect statement of them, in the hope that those of the Regents who are legislators will perhaps be able and willing, in their individual capacity, to do something to remedy the state of things which I have just shown to be actually existing.

I have represented a wearisome and trying matter very briefly. For a statement more at large of the actual condition of the exchanges, I beg to refer to the valuable report made to the Secretary by the·curator of exchanges, which will be found in the appendix.

Preparation of new exchange lists.—In March, 1887, the writer, then Assistant Secretary, acting under the general instructions of the Secretary, Professor Baird, with a view to perfecting the collections of the Smithsonian Library so that they might include scientific periodicals published throughout the world, where these were obtainable by exchange, undertook to ascertain as far as possible the names of all useful (particularly of all modern) publications which were not on the old Smithsonian lists.

To do this it was necessary to get information not existing in print, and as the search for the names of desired publications was necessarily on an extended scale, it seemed proper to enlist as many expert coadjutors as possible. To this end the principal branches of human knowledge to the number of thirty were indexed on as many separate lists. Several copies were made of each list, and then it was sought, by sending a copy of each to an eminent specialist in the branch in question, to enlist his services as a coadjutor by obtaining from him a list of the publications not actually on our records which would be most desirable in his own department.

Medicine was omitted, but Belles Lettres, History, Law, Fine Arts, and, in fact, Theology are evidently to be considered even in a purely scientific list, at least so far as they illustrate anthropology.

Periodicals devoted to science in its more restricted interpretation generally fall under one of two great divisions:

First, those connected with the biological, and second, those connected with the physical, sciences.

As the former are represented by many distinguished specialists connected with the Smithsonian Institution as curators in the Museum there was at first prepared a circular letter (Appendix IV) to these biological curators, requesting them to furnish—

(1) "A list of those periodicals, whether transactions of societies or otherwise, which were deemed most nearly indispensable to their respective departments;" and

(2) "A list of recent serials, whether transactions or otherwise, of interest in connection with the special investigations of the curators, even if not exclusively devoted to them."

Pending the replies, which related almost altogether to biology, the writer himself prepared a list of the main divisions and subdivisions of physical science meant, with the preceding exceptions, to represent every department of knowledge outside of the biological sciences.

This list was submitted in April to Professors F. A. P. Barnard, Samuel H. Scudder, and H. Carrington Bolton, with the requests—

First. "To examine the list and see whether these headings themselves are judiciously chosen;" and

Next. "To indicate the names of the two most fitting persons, under each head, to give advice as to the periodicals belonging to their respective departments." The list was also submitted to the Hon. A. R. Spofford, Librarian of Congress, and Mr. William J. Rhees, the Chief Clerk of the Smithsonian Institution.

A full list of the names of eminent specialists who could advise in each branch having been thus obtained, and the classification of subjects having been determined in the manner above indicated, circular letters (in three forms) were forwarded on the 9th of May, 1887. A third or supplementary circular (in two forms) was mailed on the 15th of June, 1887. One of these, which will indicate the general character of all, is given in Appendix IV.

The circular letter of March 19, sent to twenty-six curators of the National Museum, was responded to by twenty-two curators, among whom Prof. L. F. Ward was pre-eminent for the extent and character of the lists of periodicals specified (352 titles).

Of the circulars of May 9 and June 15, 1887, 274 copies were sent out and 152 replies received, among which those of the following deserve special mention for completeness of lists furnished :

	Titles.
Prof. Richard Ely	805
E. J. Farquhar, assistant librarian Patent Office	701
W. H. Wahl, secretary Franklin Institute	542
Prof. William Libbey, jr	183
Mr. Justin Winsor	157
Maj. J. W. Powell	147
Hon. A. R. Spofford	113

The result of the inquiry was to bring in 5,730 names, of which, after deducting those found on more than one list, 3,594 independent titles remain; but of these, as will appear, a considerable portion was on our list already. It may be interesting, however, to notice how these titles are distributed throughout the world, the little tables in the foot-note* giving incidentally an interesting exposition of the activities of different peoples as well as of different professions in this direction.

*Geographical arrangement of the numbers of titles and references received in reply to the "Circular for the increase of the Smithsonian Library."

Country.	Titles	References.	Country.	Titles.	References.
AFRICA			**AUSTRALASIA—cont'd.**		
Algeria	3	4	Victoria	5	6
Cape Colony	1	1	New Zealand	7	12
Egypt	2	4	**EUROPE.**		
AMERICA.			Austria-Hungary	124	168
British	44	61	Belgium	66	105
United States	866	1,445	Denmark	14	20
Mexico	8	10	France	439	695
Argentine Republic	11	16	Germany	669	993
Brazil	9	11	Great Britain and Ireland	439	809
Chili	4	4	Greece	4	9
Colombia	1	1	Iceland	1	2
Costa Rica	2	2	Italy	154	217
Ecuador	1	1	Netherlands	37	49
Venezuela	1	1	Norway	19	31
ASIA.			Portugal	12	20
			Roumania	2	2
China	3	4	Russia	52	74
India	23	31	Servia	1	1
Japan	9	13	Spain	35	38
Java	5	8	Sweden	26	44
AUSTRALASIA.			Switzerland	51	66
New South Wales	7	13	Turkey	1	1
Queensland	1	1	Unclassified	433	734
South Australia	1	1	Total	3,594	5,730
Tasmania	1	2			

Of which number 433 are titles of and 734 references to books, the remainder relating to pamphlets or periodicals.

The second list* subjoined is a subject index, and is also not without interest.

It is a striking testimony to the complexity of modern science that when a number of its representatives are asked to indicate the independent periodicals, desirable in their opinion for its study, these periodicals (each representing monthly contributions of numerous original

* *Subject arrangement of the references received in reply to the circular for the increase of the Library.*

Agriculture	72	Mechanical engineering	18
Animal products and fisheries	51	Mechanics and machinery	5
Archæology	6	Medicine and surgery	7
Archæology and art	90	Metallurgy	24
Architecture	10	Marine engineering	10
Architecture and engineering	7	Metaphysics and psychology	13
Art	46	Microscopy	19
Assyriology	26	Military engineering	17
Astronomy	30	Military science	36
Botany	380	Mineralogy	50
Brewing and distillation	2	Mineralogy, chemistry, and physics	39
Bridge engineering	12	Mining	101
Chemistry	105	Mining and metallurgy	3
Chemistry and physics	14	Music	8
Civil engineering	54	Naval architecture	28
Classical philology	1	Naval arts	113
Comparative anatomy	35	Naval engineering	12
Costumes	3	Naval machinery	11
Education	192	Numismatics	13
Education of deaf and dumb	2	Ordnance	15
Electricity	60	Ornithology	49
Electrical engineering	35	Paper and printing	4
Electrotyping	6	Patents	11
Engineering	59	Pedagogy	33
Engineering and industries	528	Philology	16
Ethics	3	Photography	13
Ethnology	160	Physics	14
Fencing	7	Political economy	3
Gas	2	Political science	41
General science	9	Prime motors	7
Geography	340	Psychology	28
Graphic arts	16	Railroads	7
Historical sciences	82	Reptiles	10
History	27	Sanitary engineering	8
Industries	12	Social science	24
Insects	86	Sport	5
Instruments of precision	2	Statistics	80
International law	6	Telegraphy	1
Invertebrate palæontology	119	Textile fabrics and dyeing	3
Librarians' art and bibliography	150	Theology	170
Literature, ancient and classical	72	Trades	17
Lithology	68	Wind engines	4
Logic	7	Johns Hopkins exchange list	805
Machine construction	16	List of books, Patent Office	700
Mammals	58		5,756
Marine invertebrates	50	Less duplication	26
Mathematics	16		
Mathematics and algebra	27	Total	5,730

articles) are found to reach the enormous number of 3,594; and yet these by no means comprise, as it will be seen, all that the Smithsonian lists contain.

Five thousand seven hundred and thirty names were in fact received, but many of these were duplicates, after striking out which, 3,594 titles remain, and a careful investigation by Mr. Boehmer, then in charge of exchanges, shows that of these, 2,328 were foreign, and 1,266 were domestic; and that of the foreign titles but 792 were on our old lists. As regards these latter, then, the final result of the inquiry is the nearly trebling of our foreign lists by adding to them 1,536 new titles (consisting largely of periodicals begun in the past twelve or fifteen years), and this list will be used by the library in obtaining, so far as possible, the periodicals themselves.

LIBRARY.

Chiefly through its exchange system, the Smithsonian had in 1865 accumulated about forty thousand volumes, largely publications of learned societies, containing the record of the actual progress of the world in all that pertains to the mental and physical development of the human family, and affording the means of tracing the history of at least every branch of positive science since the days of revival of letters until the present time.*

These books, in many cases presents from old European libraries, and not to be obtained by purchase, formed even then one of the best collections of the kind in the world.

The danger incurred from the fire of that year, and the fact that the greater portion of these volumes, being unbound and crowded into insufficient space, could not be readily consulted, while the expense to be incurred for this binding, enlarged room, and other purposes connected with their use threatened to grow beyond the means of the Institution, appear to have been the moving causes which determined the Regents to accept an arrangement by which Congress was to place the Smithsonian Library with its own in the Capitol, subject to the right of the Regents to withdraw the books on paying the charges of binding, etc. Owing to the same causes (which have affected the Library of Congress itself) these principal conditions, except as regards their custody in a fire proof building, have never been fulfilled.

The books are still deposited chiefly in the Capitol, but though they have now accumulated from 40,000 to fully 250,000 volumes and parts of volumes, and form without doubt the most valuable collection of the kind in existence, they not only remain unbound, but in a far more crowded and inaccessible condition than they were before the transfer. It is hardly necessary to add that these facts are deplored by no one more than by the present efficient Librarian of Congress, who would, I am confident, gladly give, as far as it lies in his power, effect to any ex-

*See Smithsonian Report of 1867.

pression of the wish of the Regents that in the new building a hall or
halls worthy of this really magnificent collection of a quarter of a million titles should be exclusively devoted to it, under the name of the
" Smithsonian Halls", or in any such other method as may point it out
as an acquisition of national importance due to the Institution under
the Regents' care.

It will be remembered that a small portion of these volumes, representing in number something like one-twentieth of the whole, is ordinarily retained for consultation in the National Museum.

A certain limited number of books, chiefly of works of reference,
obtained by purchase from the Smithsonian fund, is kept in the Smithsonian building, under the titles of "The Secretary's Library" and
" Editor's Library."

With these exceptions, it will be understood that a large part of the
Smithsonian exchange system, and a considerable portion of the best
rooms in the main building of the Smithsonian, continue to be given to
this portion of the Library of Congress without any return.

On April 1, 1887, upon the resignation of Miss J. A. Turner, who had
for many years performed the duties of librarian with the greatest diligence and faithfulness, the provisions for the care of the books supplied
to the Congressional Library were reorganized under the regulations
which I had prepared upon my appointment as assistant secretary.*
Mr. John Murdoch, formerly assistant librarian in the National Museum, was appointed librarian in Miss Turner's place, and was also
given the charge of the collection of books kept in the Museum as a
working library for the use of the curators and other officers.

A force of three clerks was detailed to report to the librarian, in
order to enable him to carry out the new regulations, which require
greater promptness in disposing of accessions than it was possible to
effect when one person alone was employed on this work. All accessions received during any week must now be completely recorded and
ready for a final disposition to be made of them on the Saturday of the
same week. All accessions, as heretofore, except the comparatively
few retained for use at the Institution, and certain medical publications
which are specially loaned to the library of the Surgeon-General's Office,
U. S. Army, are sent to the Library of Congress.

Publications retained for the use of the Institution must, under the
regulations, be entered and ready for use within twenty-four hours
from the time they are received.

A "full entry" of any publication, according to the regulations, is
" to consist of both a day-book and a ledger account entry."

The day-book is simply a continuation of the old Smithsonian record
of accessions, in which the running numbers reached on June 30, 1888,
182,059. The ledger account is supplementary to the manuscript catalogue in thirteen large bound volumes, called " Publications of Learned

---

* These regulations are given in Appendix V.

Societies, Periodicals, etc., in the Library of the Smithsonian Institution," which was complete up to April 1, 1887. The new record is kept on large cards, one for each institution or individual from whom the Institution has received any publication, and on each card is entered the title of everything received from the person or institution whose name appears at the head of the card, each marked with its accession or "day book" number, by means of which reference can be made to the "day-book" for further particulars. These cards are now arranged alphabetically by the name of the donor's residence.

These regulations have been carried out without failure since the reorganization of the library, though there have been weeks when, owing to the arrival of large invoices through the department of foreign exchanges, the librarian and his clerks have been hard pressed to complete the work in the time specified. Upwards of five hundred accessions have been recorded in a single week.

The books destined for the Library of Congress are sent regularly on Monday of each week, and it is impossible for publications to be delayed at the Institution for the length of time which was frequently unavoidable under the former arrangements. It is, however, to be regretted that the Librarian of Congress is unable to take advantage of the increased promptness of the Smithsonian library administration. Owing, as I am informed, to the pressure of copyright work and the overcrowded condition of the present quarters of the Library, the chests sent up from the Institution frequently lie for months unopened, so that their contents are inaccessible to readers.

This is the more to be regretted as, on account of the limited space at the disposal of the Institution for keeping books and periodicals, only the most important publications can be retained for use here.

The books thus retained for use at the Institution form part of the National Museum library (the rest of which consists of such publications as are donated directly to the Museum or purchased from the Museum appropriation for the use of its curators), and are loaned under certain necessary conditions to the officers of the Smithsonian Institution, the Smithsonian editor, the scientific staff of the Museum, and such persons as are authorized to borrow books by special written permission from one of the officers of the Smithsonian Institution.

How important these contributions from the Smithsonian accessions are to the Museum library may be seen from the fact that out of the 6,063 accessions to the Museum library (including parts of regular serials) during the fiscal year, 3,045, or a trifle more than 50 per cent., were from this source.

From lack of space in the Museum library it had been practically impossible to provide for the proper display of new accessions to the library, and especially of the current numbers of periodicals. At my direction, therefore, the librarian prepared plans for a reading-room in the Smithsonian Building. This room was opened to readers in the latter part of April, 1887, and has remained in active use since then It now contains the current numbers of two hundred and sixty-five serials, embracing most of the chief scientific and technical publications, and including also a few of the more important literary periodicals. It is much used by the employés of the Smithsonian Institution and the Museum, and to a less degree by other persons in Washington who wish to consult the scientific periodicals. Such a scientific reading-room has long been needed at the Institution, and the one now in operation appears to fill the want satisfactorily.

The policy that has been pursued in regard to the library has been, in general, to obtain as large and as valuable a return as possible for the works published by the Institution, and to make the best possible use of these returns when they are received. With this end in view, the librarian has been instructed to watch for all opportunities of obtaining new publications by exchange and to bring to my knowledge every occasion of this kind. The results of this increased activity in seeking new exchanges are to be seen in the fact that for the fiscal year 1887–'88 the total number of accessions amounted to 18,948, an increase of 2,401 over the total number for the preceding fiscal year (1886–'87), which was 16,547.

As has been previously stated, 3,045 of these accessions have been transferred to the Museum library, and, in addition to these, 675 medical dissertations have been loaned to the library of the Surgeon-General's Office, U. S. Army. The remainder, 15,228 in number, have been transferred to the Library of Congress. It is impossible, as it seems to me, not to consider this as an ample return for whatever expense the Library of Congress is put to in paying for the recording of these accessions.

The following is a statement of the books, maps, and charts received by the Smithsonian Institution from July 1, 1887, to June 30, 1888:

```
Volumes :
    Octavo or smaller ............................. 1,010
    Quarto or larger ..............................  575
                                                         ——— 1,585
Parts of volumes :
    Octavo or smaller............................. 6,188
    Quarto or larger ............................. 6,420
                                                         ——— 12,608
Pamphlets :
    Octavo or smaller............................. 3,607
    Quarto or larger.............................   681
                                                         ——— 4,288
Maps......................................................  467
                                                         ———
    Total ............................................ 18,948
```

Were I to attempt to mention the titles of the publications received, it would expand this report beyond all reasonable dimensions.

I may, however, specify the following publications as among the most important additions to our list of serials :

L'Aérostat.	Ethnologische Mittheilungen aus Ungarn.
American Anthropologist.	
American Geologist.	Fernschau.
American Journal of Psychology.	Geografisk Tidskrift.
American Yachtsman.	Globus.
Anales del Museo Michoacano.	Honduras-Progress (the first English
Astronomische Nachrichten.	newspaper published in Honduras).
Boletin mensual del Observatorio Meteorologico del collegio pio·de Villa Colon.	Indian Annals and Magazine of Natural Sciences.
Boletin mensual del Observatorio Meteorologico-magnetico, Mexico.	"Notes from the Leyden Museum." Notes and Queries (Manchester, N. H.).
Boletin de Sanidad, Madrid.	Record of American and Foreign Shipping.
Centralblatt für Bacteriologie und Parasitenkunde.	
	Scottish Geographical Magazine.
Entomologist.	Societas Entomologica.
Entomologists' Monthly Magazine.	Zeitschrift für Luftschifffahrt.

The following universities have sent complete sets of all their academic publications for the year, including the inaugural dissertations delivered by the students on graduation : Bern, Bonn, Dorpat, Erlangen, Freiburg-im-Breisgau, Giessen, Göttingen, Greifswald, Halle-an-der-Saale, Heidelberg, Helsingfors, Jena, Kiel, Königsberg, Leipzig, Liège, Lund, Marburg, Strassburg, Tübingen, Utrecht, Würzburg, and Zürich.

Among other important accessions during the year, I may mention the following : "Les premiers âges du métal dans le Sud-est de l'Espagne," from the authors, MM. Henri and Louis Siret, Antwerp, a magnificent illustrated work; a full set of the publications of the Physicalische Anstalt im-Bernoullianum, Basel ; vol. 4 (the first issued) of the reports of the German commission for the observation of the transit of Venus ; a full set of parliamentary publications from the German Reichstags-Bibliothek; two volumes of the magnificent "Corpus Inscriptionum Latinorum," published by the Berlin Academy; a full set of the publications of the Birmingham Natural History and Microscopical Society, since 1872 ; "Voyages en Moscovie et Tartarie," by Adam Olearius, and Mandelslo's "Voyages de Perse aux Indes Orientales," both published in 1727, from Hon. William T. Rice, United States consul at Horgen, Switzerland; the first 2 volumes of Houzeau and Lancaster's great "Bibliographie Générale de l'Astronomie," from Prof. A. Lancaster, of Brussels ; twenty-eight ichthyological publications from the author, Dr. Francis Day, Cheltenham, England ; volumes 17 and 18 of the report of the Norwegian North Atlantic Expedition ; a full set of government publications from Saxony ; the great "Catalogus Librorum Bibliothecæ Collegii S. S. Trinitatis," in 8 folio volumes, from Trinity College, Dublin; a valuable set of 16 volumes on forestry, from the author, Dr. John Croumbie Brown, Haddington, England ; Haeckel's "Kalkschwämme," in 3 volumes, and his "Allgemeine Naturgeschichte der Radiolarien," volume 2, from the author; a full set of their publications for the year from the British Admiralty; volumes 20, 21, and 22 of the *Challenger* Report (Zoology) from the British Government; a full set of Indian Government publications from the India office; volume 1 of Lieutenant-General Pitt-Rivers's great work, " Excavations in Cramborne Chase," from the author; a full set of catalogues and handbooks published during the year from the science and art department, South Kensington; Seebohm's magnificent " Geographical Distribution of the Family Charadridæ ", from the author; 110 volumes and pamphlets of " Columbiana " from Columbia College, New York; a full set of parliamentary papers, etc., for the year, from the library of Parliament, Ottawa, Canada; volumes 2, 3, 4, and 6 of the " Mission Scientifique du Cap Horn " and other important Government publications from the Bureau Français des Échanges Internationaux; a full set of all the results that have yet been published of the scientific cruises of his yacht *L'Hirondelle*, from Prince Albert of Monaco; a full set of Government publications for the year from the Italian Government; the memorial edition of the "Botanical Works of George Engelmann," from Henry Shaw, esq., Saint Louis; a set of the " Jahresberichte des Comités für ornithologische Beobachtungs-Stationen in Oesterreich " from Victor Ritter Tschusi zu Schmidhoffen, Salzburg, Austria; the concluding volumes (volumes 4 and 5) of " Vega-Expeditionens Vetenskapliga Iakttagelser " from Baron Nordenskiöld, Stockholm; a large series of government publications from the Government of New Zealand.

ZOOLOGICAL PARK.

Collections of living Animals.—It has been customary, ever since the Institution commenced to form collections, that skeletons and skins of wild animals should be sent here for preparation, so that a certain regular supply of such material now comes in without solicitation every year, together with occasional live animals, which have been usually sent to the Zoological Gardens in Philadelphia. It seemed to me worth while to try the experiment of having all animals sent on alive when this could be done without enhanced cost; and thus has been formed the nucleus of a collection of living animals, which, though still small, has attracted the popular interest in a very marked degree.

It is understood that this interest, and the consideration that the buffalo, the mountain sheep and goat, the elk, and other vanishing races of the continent deserve protection at the hands of the Government, was the cause of a bill which was introduced by Senator Beck to create a Zoological Garden on Rock Creek, such that these animals might not only form the subject of study, but be expected to increase as they do not do in ordinary captivity.

I present herewith the amendment to the sundry civil appropriation bill reported by Senator Morrill, of the Committee on Public Buildings and Grounds, June 4, 1888. This is identical with the bill proposed by Senator Beck April 23, 1888 (S. 2752), which was read twice and referred to the Committee on Public Buildings and Grounds with the additions of the paragraphs inclosed in brackets.

This establishment it is proposed, when completed, to place under the care of the Regents, with a proper provision for its maintenance. The bill has not yet become a law, but in the event of its doing so, the trust created, being in the interest of knowledge, and incidentally offering a most obvious means for its popular diffusion, seems to be one which falls entirely within the proper function of the Smithsonian Institution, and I hope I may be able to state that the trust is one of a nature which the Regents, if called upon, are likely to favor.

[A BILL for the establishment of a zoological park in the District of Columbia.]

That, in order to establish a Zoological Park in the District of Columbia, for the advancement of science and the instruction and recreation of the people, a commission shall be constituted, composed of three persons, namely: the Secretary of the Interior, the president of the board of Commissioners of the District of Columbia, and the Secretary of the Smithsonian Institution, which shall be known and designated as the commission for the establishment of a zoological park.

That the said commission is hereby authorized and directed to make an inspection of the country along Rock Creek, beginning at the point on that creek where the Woodley road crosses said creek, and extending upward along its course to where said creek is crossed by the Klingle road, and to select from that district of country such a tract of land, of not more than one hundred acres, which shall include a section of the creek, as said commission shall deem to be suitable and appropriate for a zoological park.

That the said commission shall cause to be made a careful map of said zoological park, showing the location, quantity, and character of each parcel of private property to be taken for such purpose, with the names of the respective owners inscribed thereon, and the said map shall be filed and recorded in the public records of the District of Columbia; and from and after that date the several tracts and parcels of land embraced in such zoological park shall be held as condemned for public uses, subject to the payment of just compensation, to be determined by the said commission and approved by the President of the United States, provided that such compensation be accepted by the owner or owners of the several parcels of land.

That if the said commission shall be unable to purchase any portion of the land so selected and condemned within thirty days after such condemnation, by agreement with the respective owners, at the price approved by the President of the United States, it shall, at the expiration of such period of thirty days, make application to the Supreme Court of the District of Columbia, by petition, at a general or special term, for an assessment of the value of such land, and said petition shall contain a particular description of the property selected and condemned, with the name of the owner or owners thereof, and his, her, or their residences, as far as the same can be ascertained, together with a copy of the recorded map of the park; and the said Court is hereby authorized and required, upon such application, without delay, to notify the owners and occupants of the land and to ascertain and assess the value of the land so selected and condemned by appointing three commissioners to appraise the value or values thereof, and to return the appraisement to the Court, and when the values of such land are thus ascertained, said values shall be paid to the owner or owners, and the United States shall be deemed to have a valid title to said lands.

That when the said commission shall have obtained the land for a zoological park, as herein provided, it shall have power to lay out the same as a park and to erect such building or buildings thereon as may be necessary for the scientific purposes to which the park is dedicated and proper, for the custody, care, and exhibition of a collection of animals.

That when the said commission shall have established a zoological park in the District of Columbia under the provisions of this act, by acquiring the necessary lands and by laying out the same as a park and by the erection of the necessary buildings, thereupon it shall be the duty of said commission to turn over the said zoological park, with all its buildings and appurtenances, to the custody and care of the Regents of the Smithsonian Institution ; and when such transfer of the custody and care of the zoological park shall be made, the duties of said commission shall cease and its existence terminate.

That when the said commission shall tender to the Regents of the Smithsonian Institution the care and custody of the zoological park provided for in this act, the Regents of the Smithsonian Institution are hereby authorized to assume the care and custody of the same; and the said Regents of the Smithsonian Institution are hereby authorized to make such rules and regulations for the management of the park, and of the property, appurtenances, and collections of the park, as they may deem necessary and wise to secure the use of the same for the advancement of science and the instruction and recreation of the people.

[That the said commission is hereby authorized to call upon the Director of the Geological Survey to make such surveys as may be necessary to carry into effect the provisions of this act; and the Director of the Geological Survey is hereby authorized and required to make such surveys under the direction of said commission.]

I will take this occasion to observe that we have found great liberality in the donors of specimens. Among those to whom we are especially indebted is the Hon. Eugene G. Blackford, commissioner of fisheries for the State of New York, and an old and valued supporter of the work of the Institution, who has presented us with two buffaloes, an animal now become so rare as to have a high money value.

The proposition for the establishment of a National Zoological Park has met with a very surprising amount of support from all parts of the United States.*

---

* The following extract from " Public Opinion " will serve to give somewhat of an idea of the character and extent of this support:

[Public Opinion, New York.]

The National Zoological Park.—Of all the bills that have been introduced in Congress this session, no other has been more universally approved by the press than Senator Beck's bill for the establishment of a National Zoological Park at Washington, on a grand and liberal scale, " for the advancement of science and the instruction and recreation of the people." With all our great game animals being swept out of existence by modern breech-loaders, a magnificent site within 2 miles of the Executive Mansion, a huge surplus in the Treasury, gifts of live animals pouring into

ART AND MISCELLANEOUS SUBJECTS.

Art collections.—The words of your first secretary, that the Institution exists for knowledge in the highest sense, including not only science commonly so called, but "the true, the beautiful, as well as the immediately practical," remind us that one of the lines on which the Institution was to develop according to the views of Congress, that of its connection with art, has been allowed almost entirely to lapse. It is now, however, understood that a very valuable collection of art objects, representing, perhaps, over $1,000,000 in value, has been left to the Smithsonian Institution; and it is not an abstract question when we ask what these relations are to be. It seems to me that here again the fact of the independence of the Smithsonian is of inestimable value in its possible future usefulness. No possessor of a great private gallery like either of the two or three in this country which are rising now to almost national importance—no possessor of such a gallery, knowing on the one hand what art is and on the other hand what the relations of the Government to art have been in the past, is likely to bequeath it to the nation without some guaranty, not only for its care and maintenance, but for its judicious use in the cause of national art itself.

the Smithsonian, the public clamoring for a National " Zoo," and a competent naturalist ready and anxious to build it up, what reason is there why the bill should not be passed and work begun at once? If it is neglected much longer some of our grandest game species will have become so nearly extinct it will be almost, if not quite, impossible to procure living representatives of them at any price. At the rate mountain goats are now being killed off for their pelts five years hence it will be impossible to procure a living specimen. A live buffalo is now worth from $500 to $1,000, according to sex and size, whereas three or four years ago they were worth only one-fifth as much. As an index to public sentiment in regard to the proposed zoological park at Washington, we may quote a few editorial expressions from our exchanges. It is interesting to note the unanimity of the opinions that come to us in journals of all kinds and parties, from Boston to San Francisco. The Boston Globe exclaims: " Give us a National *Zoo.* Senator Beck has introduced a bill of great interest to the people of the United States, concerning which there can be no partisan difference of opinion, and which ought to be passed. This is the only great nation in the world which does not possess such an institution, and it is the one of all others which needs it most. A national museum of living animals would be one of the leading attractions of Washington, and would show the citizen and foreign visitor at a glance the animals of this country as they could never be seen otherwise. By all means let this country have a National ' Zoo.' Senator Beck's bill ought to pass." The Pittsburgh Dispatch declares that the bill " should meet with the hearty indorsement it deserves. That a nation so far in advance in the march of progress as the United States should be entirely without some such institution under Government protection seems almost incredible." The New York Forest and Stream asserts that " the importance of preserving living North American mammals can hardly be overestimated. The buffalo is practically extinct, and the range of the elk has become so contracted in the last few years that it is apparent the same fate awaits that noble species. There are others that will survive longer, but the people at large know nothing, and never can know, about them, unless they shall be brought close to their homes. All these animals should be secured before it is too late." The Chicago Inter-Ocean, in a lengthy and very earnest editorial on this sub-

The Smithsonian stands here in the position of a disinterested and independent party, absolutely responsible, having a permanency such as no individual or private corporation can represent, and it might very well, it seems to me, in pursuit of its proper objects accept a trust of this kind on the condition either of seeing itself that the Government accepted it and provided for it in a proper way or handing it back to the heirs of the conditional donor. It is perhaps not too much to say that an important function of the Smithsonian which has lain long in abeyance may yet be developed in this direction.

Assignment of rooms for scientific work.—During the past year the use of rooms in the Smithsonian building has been granted to the Director of the Geological Survey for draughtsmen; to the Coast and Geodetic Survey for pendulum experiments under the direction of Assistant C. S. Peirce; to the Fish Commission, during the commissionership of Dr. Goode for the sessions of a committee for revising the work and organization of the Commission, and for the storage of the stereotype plates of its publications.

Rooms and facilities for work have also been granted to Dr. J. F. Bransford, surgeon, U. S. Navy, for the preparation of a report on the

---

ject, dwells with special emphasis on the fact that "if the Government purchases and fits up a park or extensive gardens there will not be the slightest difficulty in obtaining suitable inhabitants. No better illustration need be cited than the menagerie at the Smithsonian. Nearly all the really valuable animals there have been presented to it. The *zoo* in London, the gardens in Paris, the parks in the cities of the United States, not the least of which are those of Chicago, set forth, with pointed object-lessons, the value and interest these zoological exhibitions possess. A great garden at the national capital could, on the plan proposed, be made one of the most interesting and instructive of public resorts." The Minneapolis Journal says with confidence that "inasmuch as the expense would be comparatively trifling under the management of that object of national pride, the Smithsonian, there is every reason to expect that the project will meet the approval of Congress." The San Francisco Call earnestly advocates the measure as one of interest to the entire American people. It says: "That such a park would be of advantage 'for the advancement of science and the instruction and the recreation of the people' needs no demonstration. It would be a national benefit, as similar gardens have proved themselves to be in other countries. But there are peculiar reasons for establishing an American *zoo*. The original wild animals of this country are being rapidly exterminated. The American bison, better known as the buffalo, is almost extinct. There are a few in a remote corner of Texas, and a few still survive in the Yellowstone Park. But if nothing is done to preserve them, in a few years they will have disappeared as completely as the pterodactyl. A few moose can still be found in northern New York and Maine; there are still a few specimens of the mountain sheep and goat in the mountains of Colorado; an occasional caribou is still shot in the Adirondacks; a herd of antelope is still seen, once in the way, on the prairies; a few grizzlies survive in the Rocky Mountains, but hunters know to their sorrow that these creatures, once so plentiful, are growing scarcer every year, and will soon have vanished altogether. The traveler on the eastern slopes of the Rockies finds plenty of beaver dams, but few beavers, and the mountain lion is almost a thing of the past. To find a complete collection of the wild beasts which once roamed in freedom over the mountain slopes and the prairies one must now go to the northern section of the Dominion of Canada.

antiquities of Central America; and to Paymaster William J. Thomson, U. S. Navy, for the preparation of a report on the antiquities of Easter Island, Pacific Ocean.

Toner Lecture Fund.—The Secretary of the Institution is *ex-officio* chairman of the board of trustees. No lectures have been delivered for several years. The fund remains as originally invested, increased annually by the unexpended income. It consists partly in real estate in Washington, and partly in Government bonds, the estimated value of which is about $3,000.

American Historical Association.—A bill was introduced in the Senate by Hon. G. F. Hoar on the 21st of May, 1888, and in the House on the 4th of June by Hon. James Phelan, to incorporate the "American Historical Association," and as the bill proposes an intimate connection between the association and the Smithsonian Institution it is here given in full:

[A BILL to incorporate the American Historical Association.]

Be it enacted by the Senate and House of Representatives of the United States of America in Congress assembled, That Andrew D. White, of Ithaca, in the State of New York; George Bancroft, of Washington, in the District of Columbia; Justin Winsor, of Cambridge, in the State of Massachusetts; William F. Poole, of Chicago, in the State of Illinois; Herbert B. Adams, of Baltimore, in the State of Maryland; Clarence W. Bowen, of Brooklyn, in the State of New York, their associates and successors, are hereby created a body corporate and politic, by the name of the American Historical Association, for the promotion of historical studies, the collection and preservation of historical manuscripts, and for kindred purposes in the interest of American history and of history in America. Said association is authorized to hold real and personal estate to an amount not exceeding five hundred thousand dollars, to adopt a constitution, and to make by-laws. Said association shall have its headquarters at Washington, in the District of Columbia, and shall hold its annual meetings in such places as the said incorporators shall determine. Said association shall report annually to the Secretary of the Smithsonian Institution concerning its proceedings and the condition of historical study in America. Said Secretary shall communicate to Congress the whole of such reports, or such portion thereof as he shall see fit. The Regents of the Smithsonian Institution are authorized to permit said association to deposit its collections, manuscripts, books, pamphlets, and other material for history in the Smithsonian Institution or in the National Museum, at their discretion, upon such conditions and under such rules as they shall prescribe.

Eighth centenary of the University of Bologna.—In accordance with the request of Prof. J. Capellini, rector of the University of Bologna, the Smithsonian Institution appointed two representatives to be present at the eighth centenary of the university, which occurred on the 12th of June, 1888. Dr. S. Weir Mitchell, of Philadelphia, and Dr. C. Gardini,

United States consul at Bologna, were appointed.   A letter from Doctor Mitchell is herewith appended:

To the REGENTS OF THE SMITHSONIAN INSTITUTION:

GENTLEMEN : As representing the Institution over which you preside
I went to Bologna, and was present at the eight hundredth anniversary
of its famous university.   The ceremonies consisted in addresses and a
poem by Professor Carducci, with presentations to the King and Queen,
and with the conferring of degrees in law, letters, science, and medicine.   Mr. James Russell Lowell was thus honored in letters, Mr. David
Dudley Field in law, Alexander Agassiz in science, and myself in medicine.   The "Laureati" were not given LL.D.'s but were made doctors
in their respective branches; a more sensible plan.   I shall send a medal
and the volumes presented to me, that of these you may make such disposal as seem best.

    And I have the honor to be, very respectfully,   •
                                             WEIR MITCHELL.

Grants and subscriptions.—In accordance with a precedent established
by the first Secretary to encourage meritorious scientific enterprises
undertaken wholly for the advance of knowledge and not for pecuniary
gain, a subscription of twenty copies was made for the Astronomical
Journal of Dr. B. A. Gould, published at Boston.

Privilege of floor of the House of Representatives.—A resolution having
been introduced in the House of Representatives on the 6th of February,
1888, to admit to the privileges of the floor certain officials of the Government, Hon. Mr. Cox, of New York, one of the Regents, introduced a
resolution, which was referred to the Committee on Rules, to confer the
privilege on the Secretary of the Smithsonian Institution.

It is proper to state that for many years this privilege has been extended to the Secretary by the Senate of the United States.

Reception.—It was the habit of the first Secretary, when he resided in
the Smithsonian building, to give receptions there from time to time,
which many still pleasantly remember.   It is, perhaps, proper for the
writer to mention that though these rooms are now devoted to official purposes he, desiring that the traditions of this kindly hospitality should
not entirely lapse, used them on the 17th of April of the present year
on an occasion, which, so far as he was able to make it so, was not dis-
similar in kind to the former ones in the same place, and which he has
reason to hope will be pleasantly associated with them in the recollections of old friends of the Institution.

Employés of the Institution.—Few changes have occurred in the clerical force.   Owing to the independence of the Smithsonian Institution of
those alterations which take place with changes of administration in
Government Departments, the tenure of office of all its employés is
justly regarded as more secure than in other public establishments;
and acceptable persons are commonly found willing to take employment

under the Regents on lower terms than the same nominal service is elsewhere paid for by the Government. At the same time with this fixity of tenure and permanence of position, closer and perhaps kindlier relations are found to arise than exist else where in the midst of frequent change; and the writer is happy to believe that the best and most valuable part of this service is often an unbought and voluntary one, and that this is recognized by both employer and employed.

U. S. NATIONAL MUSEUM.

The relations of the Museum to the Smithsonian Institution have so frequently been discussed, that it is unnecessary to dwell upon them at the present time. The connection of the Museum with the present establishment has not only always been very much more intimate than that of many of the other undertakings which were projected at the time of the foundation of the Institution, but as has already been observed, it rests on a radically distinct footing from any other, since the Smithsonian Institution has actual property in the Museum, equalling probably its whole original fund. Through the agency of the Museum the Institution is able to direct the work of a goodly number of investigators, who, in addition to their regular administrative work, are doing each year important service in the increase and diffusion of knowledge. In fact so much is done in the name of the Institution by the officers of the Museum and the Bureau of Ethnology in all the fields of biological, anthropological, and geological work, that the Institution can devote a larger proportion of its own funds to the encouragement of investigation in physical sciences than it could were not the biological sciences thus well provided for.

The statement of the work of the year in the Museum some years since became so great in extent that it was found necessary to add a second volume to the Smithsonian Report to contain it. Referring then to the report of Dr. G. Brown Goode, the assistant secretary in charge of the Museum, for a history of the work as performed in its various departments, I need here refer only to some of the most important general considerations.

Prominent among these are the financial relations of the Museum to the Smithsonian and to the General Government, and the changes obtained by legislation in the past year, with regard to placing the appropriations more immediately under the care of the Regents, but these I have already spoken of under the head of "Finance."

During the past year a committee appointed by me to investigate the sanitary condition of the present Museum structure, has reported in urgent terms on the need in the interest of health, of very great changes such as can not be undertaken till another building exists to receive the present personnel, the collections, and the public during the changes,

Through the agency of one of your body this is likely to be provided. The particulars have already been stated under the subject of "Building."

I may add in this connection that the present Museum building is not more than large enough for the ethnological and technological material already available. The proposed new building will afford accommodation for the natural history collections which are at present very inadequately housed. For instance, the amount of space assigned to the collection of mammals is about 6,500 feet. At least double that amount of space will be needed to accommodate the material now on hand, as soon as the taxidermists of the Museum shall have been able to prepare it for exhibition, it being our desire to have mounted groups, similar to the buffalo family recently finished, in order to preserve for future generations representations of the large quadrupeds native to this continent, which are on the verge of extinction.

At the close of the last fiscal year (June 30, 1887), a very careful estimate showed that the collections were about fifteen times as great in number of specimens as in the year 1882. I desire to call your attention especially to the inclosed statement bearing upon this point.

The Museum is growing, as it is fitting that the National Museum of a great country should grow; and it is not only necessary to care for what is already here, but to provide for the reception and display of what is certain to be placed in our hands within the next few years.

Since the erection of the present Museum building there have been more than 12,000 groups or lots of specimens added to the collection, chiefly by gifts. From the year 1859 to 1880 the accessions numbered 8,475. It is thus evident that within the last eight years the number of accessions has been half as large again as during the previous twenty-one.

Many of the more recent accessions are of very great extent, as for instance the bequest of the late Isaac Lea, of Philadelphia, which contains 20,000 specimens of shells, besides minerals and other objects; the Jeffreys collection of fossil and recent shells of Europe, including 40,000 specimens; the Stearns collections of mollusks, numbering 100,000 specimens; the Riley collection of insects, containing 150,000 specimens; the Catlin collection of Indian paintings, about 500 in number; the collection of the American Institute of Mining Engineers, for the transportation of which to Washington several freight-cars were required.

There are also the extensive collections obtained at the Fisheries Exhibition at Berlin and London and at the close of the New Orleans Cotton Centennial; the Shepard collection of meteorites; the Wilson collection of archæological objects (more than 12,0.0 specimens); the Lorrillard collection of Central American antiquities, and very many others nearly as extensive. In addition to these are the annual accretions from the work of the U. S. Fish Commission, the U. S. Geological Survey, and the Bureau of Ethnology, as well as the contributions from several expeditions of the Government, from Army and Navy officers, and from other Government officials. These are very extensive, and are yearly increasing in bulk and value.

In the Armory building are stored many hundreds of boxes of valuable material which we have not room to unpack, and the great vaults under the Smithsonian building and many of the attic and tower rooms are similarly occupied.

For several important departments of the Museum no exhibition space whatever is available, and no portion of the collection can be publicly displayed. Indeed, the growth of many of the departments is in large measure prevented by the fact that we have no room for additional exhibition cases, or even for storage. Many valuable collections elsewhere than in Washington are at the service of the Museum, but we have no space for their reception.

The collection of birds, which, so far as North America is concerned, is the finest in the world, is very inadequately shown, and requires double the case room now available.

The collection of mollusks, which is one of the most complete in the world and contains more than 450,000 specimens, is at present almost entirely unprovided for.

The collection of insects, which, though smaller, is, so far as North America is concerned, equally perfect, is also practically without any exhibition space. And so I might continue.

It should be borne in mind that under the roofs of the Smithsonian and new Museum buildings are grouped together collections which in London, Paris, or any other of the European capitals, are provided for in a group of museums, for the accommodation of which a much larger number of equally commodious buildings is found needful.

One of the most striking features in connection with the affairs of the Museum is the remarkable increase in the extent of its collections, which each year becomes greater. This increase is in a large degree spontaneous, only a very small sum of money being available for the purchase of new material. As might be supposed, a considerable proportion of the objects given duplicate material already on hand, and although these contributions can, with the utmost advantage, be used for distribution to other museums and schools, they do not increase as much as is desired the value of the collections for study by specialists, and for general educational purposes. The need of a larger fund for the purchase of specimens is yearly more manifest. Exceedingly important material is constantly offered to us at prices very much below what it would cost to obtain it by collecting, and in many instances, when refused, it is eagerly taken by the museums and institutions of Europe. The extent and character of the recent additions to the collections may, perhaps, be better shown by the appended table than in any other way. This table shows comparatively the results of a census of the collections, taken for the past six years, and from it appears that the number of specimens or of lots of specimens on hand at the close of the year is more than 2,800,000. These figures are in many instances estimated, and are always subject to revision.

Name of department.	1882.	1883.	1884.	¹1885.	1885–'86.	1886–'87.	1887–'88.
Arts and industries:							
Materia medica...............	....	4,000	4,442	......	4,850	5,516	5,763
Foods...	....	²1,244	1,580	......	³822	⁴877	⁵877
Textiles.....................	....	... .	2,000	......	3,064	3,144	⁵3,144
Fisheries	....	....	5,000	......	³9,870	10,078	⁵10,078
Animal products..............	....	....	1,000	......	2,792	2,822	⁵2,822
Naval architecture...........	... .	....	600	......	....	....	....
Historical relics.............	....	....	....	......	1,002		
Coins, medals, paper money, etc......					1,055	13,634	14,640
Musical instruments.........	....	....	....	.....	400	417	427
Modern pottery, porcelain, and bronzes	....	....	....	.....	2,278	2,238	3,011
Paints and dyes	....	....	....	.....	³77	100	⁵100
" The Catlin Gallery "......	....	....	....	.....	500	500	⁵500
Physical apparatus..........	....	.. ..	....	.....	250	251	⁵251
Oils and gums.............	....	....	....	.....	³197	198	⁵198
Chemical products	....	....	....	.....	³659	661	⁵661
Ethnology....................	....	....	200,000	.....	⁶500,000	503,764	505,464
American aboriginal pottery....	....	....	12,000	.....	25,000	⁶26,022	⁶27,122
Prehistoric anthropology........	35,512	40,491	45,252	.....	65,314	101,659	108,631
Mammals (skins and alcoholics)..	4,660	4,920	5,694	.....	7,451	7,811	8,058
Birds-.......................	44,354	47,246	50,350	.....	55,945	54,987	56,484
Oology......................	....	....	40,072	.....	44,163	⁷48,173	50,055
Reptiles and batrachians........	....	....	23,495	.....	25,344	27,542	27,664
Fishes........................	50,000	65,000	68,000	.....	75,000	100,000	101,350
Mollusks.....................	⁸33,375	....	400,000	.....	⁹460,000	425,000	455,000
Insects......................	1,000	....	¹⁰151,000	.....	⁶500,000	⁶585,000	595,000
Marine invertebrates...........	⁸11,781	⁸14,825	⁶200,000	.....	⁶350,000	⁶450,000	515,000
Comparative anatomy:							
Osteology....................	3,535	3,640	4,214		10,210	⁶11,022	11,558
Anatomy.....................	70	103	3,000				
Palæozoic fossils..............	....	20,000	73,000	......	80,482	84,491	84,649
Mesozoic fossils.......	... .	....	100,000	......	69,742	70,775	70,925
Cenozoic fossils..................	(Included with mollusks)			......			
Fossil plants	....	4,624	¹¹7,291		¹²7,429	8,462	10,000
Recent plants	....	....	....		30,000	⁶32,000	⁶38,000
Minerals......	....	14,550	16,610	......	18,401	18,601	21,896
Lithology and physical geology..	¹³9,075	12,500	18,000	.....	20,647	⁶21,500	22,500
Metallurgy and economic geology	.. ..	30,000	40,000	......	48,000	⁶49,000	51,412
Living animals..................	....	....	....		....	....	220
Total.....	193,362	263,143	1,472,600	......	2,420,944	2,666,335	2,803,459

¹ No census of collection taken.
² Including paints, pigments, and oils.
³ Duplicates not included.
⁴ Foods only.
⁵ No entries of material received during the year have been made on the catalogue.
⁶ Estimated.
⁷ 2,335 are nests.
⁸ Catalogue entries.
⁹ Including Cenozoic fossils.
¹⁰ Professor Riley's collection numbers 15,000 specimens.
¹¹ Fossil and recent
¹² Exclusive of Professor Ward's collection.
¹³ In reserve series.

The number of entries made in the Department catalogues during the year, as far as can now be ascertained, is 25,415. This number may be increased before the publication of the Museum report for the year, in which a complete tabulated statement will be given.

The registrar states that 12,400 boxes and packages were received during the year and entered upon the transportation records of the Smithsonian Institution. In this number are included 1,482 "accession lots" for the Museum.

Many valuable contributions have been made, as in past years, through the friendly co-operation of the Departments and Bureaus of the Government and of officers of the Army and Navy. For this assistance the sincere thanks of the Museum are tendered. The geographical index to the "list of accessions," which will be published in the report of the assistant secretary in charge of the Museum, will show the sources of the material received during the year. Among the most important accessions are the following: A collection of old coins, chiefly Roman, deposited by Mr. Thomas Wilson; a collection of archæological and ethnographical specimens bequeathed to the Museum by Dr. Charles Rau; the Lea collection of shells and minerals presented during Professor Baird's life-time, but not received until this year; ethnological objects from Egypt, presented by Dr. James Grant Bey, and from the Congo region, by Lieut. E. H. Taunt, U. S. Navy; a collection of birds from Central America and islands in the Caribbean Sea, collected by Mr. Charles H. Townsend; a pair of living buffaloes presented by Mr. E. G. Blackford; a skin of an unusually large moose, purchased from Mr. A. B. Douglas; the first cast made in the mold taken from the living face of Abraham Lincoln, by Leonard Volk, in 1860; also the first casts made in the molds from Lincoln's hands, and the first bronze cast of the face mold, and bronze casts of the hands presented to the Government of the United States, for deposit in the Museum, by thirty-three subscribers, through a committee composed of Thomas B. Clarke, Augustus St. Gaudens, Richard Watson Gilder, and Erwin Davis; Indian pottery from the pueblos of the Jemez Valley, in New Mexico, collected by Col. James Stevenson, of the Bureau of Ethnology; a collection of bird eggs from Lieut. H. C. Benson, U. S. Army, and from Dr. J. C. Merrill, U. S. Army; a collection of reptiles and batrachians from Dr. R. Ellsworth Call; extensive collections of fishes and marine invertebrates, collected by the U. S. Fish Commission; a large collection of Syrphidæ from Dr. S. W. Williston, forming the types of Bulletin 31 of the National Museum; a valuable series of paleozoic fossils from the New York State Museum of Natural History; a series of fossil plants, several of them new to science, from the coal-measures of Alabama, presented by Prof. I. C. Russell, of the U. S. Geological Survey; a large collection of eruptive, metamorphic, and sedimentary rocks from Colorado, collected by Dr. S. F. Emmons, of the U. S. Geological Survey; an extensive series of rocks, collected by Mr. G. P. Merrill in New Jersey, Rhode Island, Massachusetts, and Maine; a very interesting series of aluminum bronzes and other rare alloys, made by Bierman, of Hanover, d presented by the "Iron Age," of New York City. Some objects of lue have also been added to other sections and departments of the useum, especially to those of Transportation and Graphic Arts. These ll be enumerated in the "list of accessions" already referred to.

A collection intended to illustrate the application of photography to ientific purposes is now being prepared by Mr. T. W. Smillie for exhibition at the Cincinnati Exposition. This collection includes interestg contributions from Prof. E. C. Pickering, of Harvard University; . S. Magnetic Station, U. S. Coast Survey, Army Medical Museum, U. Light-House Board, U. S. Signal Office, the proving ground at Anpolis, Commander C. F. Goodrich, U. S. Navy; Mr. J. W. Osborne, and r. Thomas Taylor, of the Department of Agriculture.

The increasing popularity of the Museum seems to be proved by the ct that during the year the number of visitors to the Museum Building was 249,025, or 32,463 more than last year, and the number of visits to the Smithsonian Building was 103,442, or 4,891 more than last ar.

Following the usual policy, free access to the collections has been anted to students in the various branches of natural history, and in any instances specimens have been lent to specialists for comparison d study. Instruction in taxidermy and photography have been given several applicants. This has in some instances been done at the rest of an executive department; otherwise, the students have been pected to render voluntary service as an equivalent. Permission has en granted by the Superintendent of Police, upon the indorsement of e Smithsonian Institution, to several young men to shoot birds in the strict of Columbia for scientific purposes. This privilege is provided by law in section 14, chapter 213, vol. I of the "Supplement to the Reed Statutes of the United States." The use of the lecture hall in the seum has been granted for lectures and meetings of scientific societies, as follows: A course of Saturday lectures, twelve in number, comncing on February 18; four lectures given under the auspices of the ateur Botanical Club of Washington, on December 10, 21, January 21; the annual meeting of the National Academy of Sciences, April -21. The Biological Society of Washington and the Botanical Secn of this society also held some of their meetings in the Museum. e usual courtesies have been extended to other public institutions the gift and loan of photographs and working drawings of Museum ses, drawings and photographs of specimens, and copies of Museum els.

Two hundred and sixty-four lots of specimens have been distributed museums, colleges, and individuals. Applications for duplicate spec. ens are each year increasing in number. During this year fifty-three ve been received. It has always been the policy of the Smithsonian stitution to distribute in this way the duplicate material which accumulates in the departments of the Museum, and the importance of this policy has been repeatedly commented upon in previous reports. It has not yet, however, been found practicable to comply with these applications as fast as received, because the curators have not yet had time to arrange the duplicate material into sets for distribution. It is to be hoped that in future it may be possible to relieve the curators of some of the routine work which they are now obliged to attend to personally, in order that among other things they may devote more of their time to the classification of duplicate material.

The importance of museum collections for purposes of education in schools is becoming of late years much more fully appreciated, and it seems desirable to make some changes in the manner of distributing specimens; especially to make the collections sent out so complete—within such limits as it may be possible to develop them by methods of arrangement and labels—that they may be ready for immediate use in instruction. In order to do this it is often necessary to supplement duplicate material on hand by other material specially collected. With this in view the curators of mineralogy and physical geology have been requested to obtain during the year in large quantities, for the special purpose of distribution, specimens of minerals from certain rich localities. By this means material for a considerable number of series of minerals and rocks have been obtained, while at the same time valuable additions have been made to the Museum collections. Mr. Merrill, curator of physical geology, visited during the summer, points in North Carolina, Pennsylvania, Massachusetts, Maine, New Hampshire, Vermont, and New York. Mr. Yeates, assistant curator of minerals, visited the States of New York, New Jersey, Pennsylvania, and North Carolina. Special attention has been thus given to obtaining geological and mineralogical material for distribution, owing to the fact that there is on file a very large number of applications for specimens of this kind, which it has been impossible so far to meet. Collections of this character are, furthermore, much better suited for school museums, especially those which have not much money to spend in the preparation and installation of specimens, than are the more fragile and perishable zoölogical collections. It is hoped that during the coming year it will also be practical to make up a considerable number of sets of bird-skins, illustrating the classification of birds into families.

The report on the operations of the National Museum for the first half of 1885, and forming Part II of the Report of the Smithsonian Institution, has been received from the Public Printer. This report includes Mr. Thomas Donaldson's paper on "The George Catlin Indian Gallery." The bound volumes of volume 9 of the "Proceedings of the U. S. National Museum" were received from the Public Printer in August. Two hundred copies of this volume had been distributed, signature by signature, to the collaborators of the Museum and other scientists throughout the world. This volume consists of 720 pages, and is illustrated by twenty-five plates and six figures. It includes fifty-five papers by Messrs. Ridgway, Rathbun, Stejneger, Dall, True, and other officers of the Museum, and by Messrs. Jordan, Eigenmann, Evermann, Lawrence, and other collaborators. Six new genera and fifty-one new species of animals are described for the first time in this volume. Signatures 7–31 of volume 10 of the "Proceedings of the U. S. National Museum," were printed and distributed. These include 400 pages, and embrace thirty-three papers by Messrs. Bean, Bollman, Cope, Eigenmann, C. H. Gilbert, Lilljeborg, Linton, Lucas, McNeill, Rathbun, Ridgway, R. W. Shufeldt, J. B. Smith, Stejneger, Townsend, and Vasey. In these signatures are contained descriptions of fifty-one new genera and species of birds, mammals, reptiles, fishes, and insects. Bulletin 32, "Catalogue of Batrachians and Reptiles of Central America and Mexico," by E. D. Cope, has been issued. Considerable progress has been made in the printing of Bulletin 33, "Catalogue of Minerals," by Thomas Egleston, and of Bulletin 34, "Batrachia of North America," by E. D. Cope.

The Museum report for 1887–'88 is now being prepared, and will include literary contributions from Dr. H. C. Yarrow, Prof. Otis T. Mason, Mr. F. A. Lucas, and others.

Circular 36, "Concerning the Department of Antiquities," was printed and widely distributed by the curator of that department. A large correspondence has resulted, and valuable facts have been collated therefrom. These will be published in the report of the curator.

Nearly 250 papers have been published by the officers of Museum and about 50 by collaborators. In the latter case the papers are based upon material in the Museum. Of the entire number, 79 relate to insects, 70 to birds, 12 to reptiles, 11 to fossil invertebrates, 9 to minerals, and 8 to plants.

The number of labels printed for the Museum during the year is 2,600. In addition, copy for more than 2,000 labels was sent to the Government Printing Office, but the labels had not been printed at the end of the fiscal year. It is hoped that next year it may be possible to secure quicker returns of labels from the Printing Office, since upon them depends in great part the instructive value of the objects exhibited.

The number of publications added to the Library during the year is 6,063, of which 1,316 are volumes of more than a hundred pages. The most important accession was the bequest of Dr. Charles Rau's library, consisting of 715 volumes and 1,722 pamphlets and other documents.

Through the co-operation of the U. S. Fish Commission the Smithsonian Institution has been enabled to secure from Funk Island, for the National Museum, a collection of bones of the Great Auk, and incidentally important collections of mammals, birds, bird eggs, fishes, plants, ores, rocks, stone implements, and fossils were obtained from

Newfoundland, Magdalen Islands, and adjacent islands. An account of this expedition will be given in a paper by Mr. F. A. Lucas in Part II of the Report of the Smithsonian Institution for 1888.

The collection of the department of Ethnology has been enriched by the receipt of a most valuable and interesting contribution of specimens brought from Easter Island, and also of a series of photographs taken on the island by Paymaster William J. Thomson, U. S. Navy.

Mr. W. T. Hornaday, curator of living animals, made a collecting trip to the Northwest in November and secured a large number of living animals.

Under the joint auspices of the Fish Commission and Smithsonian Institution Mr. Charles H. Townsend made a collecting tour on Swan Island and in Central America. As a result large collections of mammals and birds were obtained for the Museum.

During the summer Mr. F. H. Knowiton made a collection of the plants, rocks, and ores of Vermont.

During the year important changes have taken place in connection with some of the scientific departments of the Museum. Dr. Charles Rau, Curator of the Department of Prehistoric Anthropology, died on June 26, 1887.* His successor is Mr. Thomas Wilson, who received his appointment as Honorary Curator on December 1. In November Dr. H. G. Beyer, U. S. Navy, Honorary Curator of the Section of Materia Medica, was ordered to other duties, and Dr. J. M. Flint, U. S. Navy, the first Curator of this collection, has again taken charge. The Museum has commenced the formation of a collection of casts of Assyrian and Babylonian antiquities, in association with the Johns Hopkins University. Dr. Paul Haupt, Professor of Semitic Languages in the Johns Hopkins University, was in February appointed Honorary Curator, Dr. Cyrus Adler, of the same university, consenting to act as Honorary Assistant Curator. The Section of Transportation, under the care of Mr. J. E. Watkins, has now reached that point in its history where it may take rank with the other sections of the Department of Arts and Industries. The Section of Graphic Arts, under the curatorship of Mr. S. R. Koehler, has made excellent progress toward the illustration of the resources of the art of engraving in all its branches. On May 9 the Department of Living Animals was organized, with Mr. W. T. Hornaday, Chief Taxidermist, as curator.

As in years past, we have been called upon to contribute to local exhibitions, and numerous applications have been made for material, which has always been refused on the ground that nothing could be done without an order from Congress. Numerous bills of this kind have been before Congress for consideration. One of these, passed during the fiscal year of 1887, applied to the present year. This was the bill authorizing

---

* See Necrology, in a subsequent section.

the sending of collections to Minneapolis. The joint resolution, which was approved March 3, 1887, is here quoted:

[Public resolution No. 18.]

JOINT RESOLUTION authorizing the several Executive Departments of the Government to loan to the Minneapolis Industrial Exposition certain articles for exhibit.

Resolved by the Senate and House of Representatives of the United States of America in Congress assembled, That it is desirable, in any way consistent with existing laws, and without risk to Government property or expense to the National Treasury, to encourage the effort being made for the opening and holding of a grand industrial and educational exposition of the Northwest, at the city of Minneapolis, in the State of Minnesota, and the interests of the whole northwestern section of our country demand it be made an unqualified success; and it be, and is hereby, approved that the heads of the several Executive Departments shall, in whatever respects they may in their judgment see convenient and proper, loan any articles or material suitable to such purpose: *Provided,* That such loan be made entirely on the responsibility of said Minneapolis Industrial Exposition, and shall not be of material needed for use in either Department, and shall not in any way interrupt the daily routine of duty or order in any branch of the Government, and shall be returned to the proper Department, in good order, within one month after the close of the exposition: *And provided further,* That before any such loan shall be made, the proper head of the Department shall require and receive a good and sufficient bond, by or in behalf of such exposition, for the safe return thereof as aforesaid, and to indemnify and save harmless the Government of the United States, or any Department thereof, from any liability or expense on account thereof, or on account of this resolution.

Approved, March 3, 1887.

The exhibit of the Smithsonian Institution was prepared under the direction of Mr. W. V. Cox, Chief Clerk of the National Museum, who was appointed representative of the Institution on this occasion. The exhibit may be classified under the following heads: Ethnology, Textiles and Fabrics, Metallurgy, Deer Antlers and Horns, Casts of Fishes of North America, Photographs of Government Buildings, including the Smithsonian Institution and National Museum, collection of specimens illustrating the composition of the human body. The total weight of this exhibit was 21,507 pounds. The entire Government exhibit attracted much attention, and repeated requests were made by the managers of the exposition for the privilege of keeping the articles for another exhibition.

A much more extensive enterprise was the Ohio Valley and Central States Exposition at Cincinnati, opening July 4, 1888, which, together with an exhibition at Marietta on July 15 to July 19, was made the subject of a bill which, having passed both Houses, was approved May 28, 1888. A copy of the act approved May 28, and of the explanatory act approved July 16, is here given.

AN ACT making an appropriation to enable the several Executive Departments of the Government and the Bureau of Agriculture and the Smithsonian Institution, including the National Museum and Commission of Fish and Fisheries, to participate in the Centennial Exposition of the Ohio Valley and Central States, to be held at Cincinnati, Ohio, from July fourth to October twenty-seventh, eighteen hundred and eighty-eight.

Whereas the States which comprise the Northwest Territory and the adjacent States will hold at Cincinnati, Ohio, from July fourth to October twenty-seventh, eighteen hundred and eighty-eight, a centennial exposition commemorative of the organization of the Northwest Territory, under the ordinance of seventeen hundred and eighty-seven, in which exposition all the States and Territories of the United States and the General Government have been invited to participate, the object being in said exposition to present a panorama of the nation's resources and present state of progressive development by an exhibition of the products of agriculture, of the various industries and fine arts; also the results of advancement made in the sciences; the whole illustrating the opportunities secured to and the possibilities which wait upon the citizens of this Republic; and

Whereas the citizens of the Ohio Valley and the several States adjacent thereto have made suitable and adequate preparation and arrangements for holding said exposition, and are desirous—and it being fit and proper—that the several Executive Departments of the Government, the Department of Agriculture, the Smithsonian Institution, including the National Museum and Commission of Fish and Fisheries, should participate in said exhibition: Therefore,

Be it enacted by the Senate and House of Representatives of the United States of America in Congress assembled, That the head of each of the several Executive Departments of the Government, the Commissioner of Agriculture, and the Smithsonian Institution, including the National Museum and Commission of Fish and Fisheries, under the direction of the President of the United States, be, and they are hereby, authorized and directed to prepare and make suitable exhibits at the said Centennial Exposition of the Ohio Valley and Central States, to be held at Cincinnati, beginning on the fourth of July and closing October twenty-seventh, eighteen hundred and eighty-eight.

That there shall be appointed a committee of Congress composed of ten members, five to be appointed by the President of the Senate and five by the Speaker of the House of Representatives. Said committee is authorized and directed to visit said exposition and make such report to Congress in that behalf as they may deem needful and proper: *Provided,* That the President may in the exercise of his discretion allow such documents, and exhibits as relate to early settlement at Marietta, Ohio, and the establishment of civil government in the territory northwest of the Ohio River, to be taken to Marietta, and exhibited during the time from July fifteenth to nineteenth, eighteen hundred and eighty-eight, inclusive, under such restrictions and custody as he may direct.

That to enable the several Executive Departments of the Government, the Department of Agriculture and the Smithsonian Institution, including the National Museum and the Commission of Fish and Fisheries, to participate in said exposition, to be held as aforesaid, there is hereby appropriated, out of any money in the Treasury not otherwise appropriated, one hundred and forty-seven thousand seven hundred and fifty dollars, apportioned as follows:

For the War Department, seven thousand one hundred and fifty dollars.

For the Navy Department, fifteen thousand dollars.

For the State Department, two thousand five hundred dollars.

For the Treasury Department, seven thousand five hundred dollars.

For the Interior Department, thirty-six thousand one hundred dollars.

For the Department of Agriculture, twenty thousand dollars.

For the Post-Office Department, five thousand dollars.

For the Department of Justice, two thousand dollars.

For the Smithsonian Institution, including the Commission of Fish and Fisheries, fifty thousand dollars.

For expenses of the committee of Congress, two thousand five hundred dollars.

That the President may, if in his judgment it shall be deemed necessary and expedient in order to secure the best results with greatest economy, transfer a part of the fund hereby apportioned to one Department or Bureau to another Department or Bureau. The term Bureau wherever used herein shall be construed to include the Agricultural Department, the Smithsonian Institution, and Commission of Fish and Fisheries.

That the President of the United States is hereby authorized to detail an officer of the pay department of the Army or Navy to disburse the fund appropriated by this act.

The payments on account of expenses incurred in carrying out and into effect the provisions hereof shall be made on itemized vouchers approved by the representative of the Department incurring the liability, and a person to be designated by the President to make final audit of said accounts : *Provided*, That payment of the expenses incurred by the committee of Congress shall be made on vouchers approved by the chairman of said committee.

That the head of each of said Executive Departments and of the Department of Agriculture, Smithsonian Institution, and Commission of Fish and Fisheries shall, from among the officers or employees thereof, appoint a suitable person to act as representative of such Department or Bureau, and said representative shall, under the direction and control of the head of the Department or Bureau, supervise the preparation and conduct of the exhibits herein provided for.

That no officer or employee appointed as aforesaid shall be paid extra or additional compensation by reason of services rendered in virtue of such employment; but nothing herein shall be so construed as to prevent the payment of the just and reasonable expenses of any committee, officer, or employee appointed or employed under and by virtue of the provisions of this act.

That all articles imported from the Republic of Mexico or the Dominion of Canada for the purpose of being exhibited at said exposition shall be admitted free of duty, subject, however, to such conditions and regulations as the Secretary of the Treasury may impose and prescribe.

Approved, May 28, 1888.

JOINT RESOLUTION declaring the true intent and meaning of the act approved May twenty-eighth, eighteen hundred and eighty-eight.

Resolved by the Senate and House of Representatives of the United States of America in Congress assembled, That it is the true intent and meaning of the act of Congress approved May twenty-eighth, eighteen hundred and eighty-eight, by the President of the United States, entitled "An act making appropriation to enable the several Executive Departments of the Government, and the Bureau of Agriculture, and the Smithsonian

Institution, including the National Museum and the Commission of Fish and Fisheries, to participate in the Centennial Exposition of the Ohio Valley and Central States, to be held at Cincinnati, Ohio, from July fourth to October seventh, eighteen hundred and eighty-eight," that the President of the United States may, in his discretion make an order directing that any documents, papers, maps not original, books or other exhibits which properly and pertinently relate to the establishment of civil government in the territory northwest of the Ohio River, may be sent upon an executive order from any of the several Departments in said act named, or from the exhibits now at Cincinnati, and that the appropriation of money in said act to defray the expenses of such exhibits, may be made applicable, in so far as the President of the United States may direct, to the payment of the expenses of the care, transportation to and return of such exhibits from Marietta. And the same shall be paid from such fund heretofore set apart for each Department as the President may order. Nor shall anything in said act be so construed as to prevent the purchase of suitable materials, and the employment of proper persons, to complete or modify series of objects, and classes of specimens, when in the judgment of the head of any Department such purchase or employment, or both is necessary in the proper preparation and conduct of an exhibit. Nor to authorize the removal from their places of deposit in Washington of any original paper or document or laws or ordinances whatever.

Approved, July 16, 1888.

The Assistant Secretary, Dr. Goode, was appointed representative of the Smithsonian Institution in the preparation of this display, in accordance with the provisions of the act. Preparations for these exhibitions were nearly completed at the close of the fiscal year, and some fourteen car-loads of material have been sent by this Institution to Cincinnati. The sum of $50,000 was appropriated for the use of the Smithsonian Institution (including the National Museum and Fish Commission), and $10,000 of this sum was transferred to the Commissioner of Fisheries.

In this connection it may be well to say that, although sympathizing with the effort to extend the educational work of the Institution and of the National Museum throughout the country, the growing tendency to withdraw for a considerable portion of each year some of the most interesting and valuable parts of the collections, is liable to many objections,—objections which are much stronger now, since the Museum is approaching a final arrangement in classification than some years ago, when the collections were unsettled and unformed. Not only is the work of the entire Museum seriously impaired, but the collections sent out are invariably damaged, some irreparably, some to such a degree that it requires much time and expense to restore them. Furthermore, the standard of local exhibitions is yearly becoming higher, and the local managers are no longer satisfied to accept from us the specimens which, in the judgment of the Museum officials, can be spared, but are disposed to insist upon having the most valuable and costly objects, which if destroyed would be irreplaceable, and if sent at all are especially liable to damage. In addition to this should be taken into account the fact that temporary exposition buildings are never fire-proof, and that the time is sure to come, if the present practice prevails, when some exhibition building containing Government collections, to the value of hundreds of thousands of dollars, will be destroyed. The experience of the Mexican Government in its participation at the New Orleans Exposition and of the Government of New South Wales in 1883 may be taken as warnings. If, however, in future years Congress is disposed to order such participation in exhibitions, I would urge as a necessity that legislation should be provided at least six months in advance of the date of the exhibition; otherwise, the participation can not but be unsatisfactory and expensive. I am also disposed to lay stress upon the necessity of liberal appropriations, which should be made with the understanding that new material may be obtained, which shall not only replace that which has been lost in past exhibitions, but shall enrich the Museum collections for home use and for use in future exhibition work. If this necessity is not recognized, the result will be that in a few years the Museum will be greatly impoverished, not only by the destruction of material, but also by the dissipation of the energy of its staff, which being applied to temporary purposes in this way is taken away from its legitimate work. It would indeed seem only fair that a distraction of this kind, which affects in large degree every officer and employé, should be compensated for by the opportunity to purchase new material which will remain permanently the property of the Government and increase the usefulness of the Governmental Museum work.

BUREAU OF ETHNOLOGY.

The prosecution of ethnologic researches among the North American Indians, under the Secretary of the Smithsonian Institution, and in compliance with acts of Congress, was continued during the year 1887–'88 in charge of Maj. J. W. Powell, as director, who has furnished the following account of operations.

The work of the year is most conveniently reported upon under two general heads of field work and office work.

FIELD WORK.

The field work of the year is divided into (1) mound explorations and (2) general field studies, which during the year were chiefly directed to archæology, linguistics, and pictography.

Mound explorations.—The work of exploring the mounds of the eastern United States was, in former years, under the superintendence of Prof. Cyrus Thomas.

Much of his attention and that of his assistants was directed to the preparation for the publication of his reports on the work of the mound division during the previous years of its labors.

As the work of writing up the report from the field-notes, examining the collections, and preparing the plats and illustrations proceeded, it was found that here and there were omissions in the original examinations which left the details of certain sections incomplete. It therefore became necessary to close these gaps as far as possible. The most important hiatus was filled by an examination of the lake border of the United States from Detroit westward to the head of Lake Superior, to ascertain whether the historic Indian localities along that line were marked by mounds or other ancient works.

Another undertaking which had been begun during the last month of the preceding year was a survey of certain inclosures and other ancient remains of Ohio, to test the reliability and accuracy of the surveys made by Squier and Davis and others. This was continued during a portion of the past year.

A third item consisted in completing, as far as possible, the list of mound localities to be used in preparing the maps.

During the year the assistants were Messrs. James D. Middleton, Gerard Fowke, and Henry L. Reynolds.

On July 15 Messrs. Middleton and Fowke went to Ohio, where they were engaged about one month in surveying the ancient works of that region. During the same time Mr. Reynolds was employed in the same State collecting data for the archæologic maps. From Ohio Mr. Fowke went to Michigan, making the tour of the lake border of the United States from Detroit westward to Duluth at the head of Lake Superior. He made careful examinations for ancient works and aboriginal remains, especially at the following-named points: Detroit; Port Huron; Saginaw; Ogeman County; about Traverse Bay; Beaver Island; Mackinac Island and the main land on both sides; Sault Ste. Marie; Marquette; Munissing; the copper region; Ontonagon; Ashland; Bayfield; La Pointe (the Old Chaquamagon), and Duluth. Returning by way of Prairie du Chien, Wis., and Davenport, Iowa, he stopped at Carbondale, Ill., the point selected as headquarters for the season. After writing out a preliminary report of his trip he went to Kentucky to examine certain works in the northern part of that State, and thence to Washington. During May and June, 1888, he was engaged in exploring mounds in Pike County, Ohio.

From Ohio Mr. Middleton went to Wisconsin to survey certain groups of works in the southern and southwestern part of that State, which occupied him until autumn. He then went to Carbondale where he was engaged most of the winter in working up the plats and other results of his surveys. Before the close of the winter he made a survey of certain groups in southeastern Missouri and of the Seltzertown group in Mississippi. During April, May, and June he was engaged in surveying and examining groups in southern Ohio and northern Kentucky.

Mr. Reynolds, after leaving Ohio, was engaged during the remainder of the summer, and until he went to Carbondale in autumn, collecting

material for maps, in Michigan and Wisconsin. He remained at Carbondale until the last of December.

General field studies.—While engaged in making a geological reconnaissance of the Tewan Mountains, the Director was enabled to study
on the ground a large field of archæology. This is an extensive district
of country drained by the Chama and Jemez, and other tributaries of
the Rio Grande del Norte. In prehistoric and early historic times the
region was mainly occupied by tribes of the Tewan stock. The people
lived in villages or pueblos, many of which were built of the rude stone
that abounds in convenient forms for such structures. The cliffs of the
cañons carved by the many streams that drain the mountain area are
often composed of volcanic tufa so soft that it can be easily worked with
rude stone tools, and many of the people had learned to hew it into
convenient shapes for architectural purposes.

Some of the tribes at different periods in their history left their stone
pueblos and constructed homes for themselves by excavating chambers
in the tufa cliffs. These cavate dwellings, now abandoned and in ruins,
and the ruins of many other ancient dwellings, are scattered throughout this entire country.

On the northern flank of the Tewan Mountains, near the river Chama
and about 3 miles below Abiquiu, an extensive ruin was visited, the
walls of which were constructed of clay built up in a mass. By what
mechanical devices they were built was not discovered, but it is evident
that the clay was not made into adobes. During the study of all these
ruins interesting archæologic collections were made, especially of articles
in stone and clay.

Mr. James Stevenson, who had accompanied the Director in the above-
mentioned explorations, proceeded, at the beginning of October, 1887,
to the pueblo of Silla, about 8 miles south of Jemez, and spent six weeks
engaged, with remarkable success, in making a collection and studying
the customs, sociology, and mythology of the people.

The Silla retain their ancient religion in great purity in spite of the
efforts of Christian priests which have been continued for centuries.
Their ceremonial chambers contained brightly-colored altars of wood,
before which many idols and other sacred objects were placed, while the
walls were hung with various mythologic emblems of great delicacy and
beauty. Mr. Stevenson was invited to inspect all these freely. The
fact was disclosed that the people had a finer variety of idols than even
the Zuñi. Their stone idols in human form presented a special feature,
the carving being of a higher type than any before seen in the region.

From one of the large ceremonial chambers he was passed through a
concealed opening into a much smaller room literally filled with masks
made in imitation of their idols, all of which he was permitted to examine
at leisure, a most unusual privilege, as these people have a superstitious
dread of their masks being seen when off the person. This collection of
masks is not only large but interesting in variety. Sketches were made
of many of them.

The Silla, like the other pueblos, have shrines scattered around the village near and far, which Mr. Stevenson was invited to visit and inspect, finding some of them guarded by colossal stone animals crudely formed. Having unexpectedly discovered, while studying their mythology, that these people, like the Moki, held ceremonials with living snakes, including the rattlesnake, he asked to be shown the exact place where the snake ceremonies were held. This proved to be 5 or 6 miles distant from the pueblo, in a desolate spot among arid hills, where there was a small square log structure in which the snake order held ceremonies previous to the dance, the snakes being contained in two large pottery vases. The cave when found was closed and completely concealed by a stone slab, upon the removal of which two splendid specimens of ancient vases were disclosed, decorated with pictures of the rattlesnake, mountain lion, and bear, and one of these vases now occupies a position in the National Museum as a part of the collection of the past season.

This collection, consisting of 864 specimens, is in many respects the most valuable ever secured by Mr. Stevenson, as it not only includes a great variety of form and decoration in pottery (some of the pieces being very old), but it embraces the largest and most interesting collection of idols and fetiches yet made. Many of the stone images are in human form and different from anything possessed by the Zuñi or Moki Indians; those of the latter being, with few exceptions, carved in wood, while the Silla possessed a large number of well-carved stone idols in human form. The stone animal idols are also superior to and larger than any heretofore collected. One of the features of the collection is the beautiful variety of plumed and other fetiches.

Mr. Stevenson made copious notes on the mythology and sociology of the Silla, and obtained the most complete cosmogony ever secured by him from any people.

He closed his field season with the Zuñi priest-doctors, obtaining from them additional detailed accounts of their secret medicine order.

During the months of August and September Mr. W. H. Holmes was engaged in studying the antiquities of Jemez Valley, New Mexico. This valley is tributary to the Rio Grande on the west, and its middle portion is about 50 miles west of Santa Fé.

Fifteen important ruined pueblos and village sites were examined. They correspond closely in type to those of the north, and bear evidence in most cases of pre-Spanish occupation. Besides the larger ruins there are a multitude of minor ruins, small houses and lodges of stone, scattered through the forests. Mr. Holmes carried his investigations of the ruins of Colorado and New Mexico as far south as Abiquiu, which village lies at the northern end of the group of mountains in which the Rio Jemez takes its rise. His work of the year has therefore enabled him to connect his studies of the northern localities with those of the south in which the numerous modern pueblos are located. The chain of observations thus secured is of value in a study of the art products of the vast region formerly occupied by town-building tribes.

Particular attention was given to an examination of the ceramic remains. These constitute one of the means of developing the history of the pre-Columbian inhabitants. A large series of specimens was forwarded to the Museum.

Mr. Victor Mindeleff, with Mr. Cosmos Mindeleff as his assistant, left Washington for the field, September 1, 1887, and returned March 18, 1888. A group of cave lodges, excavated in the top and sides of a cinder cone at the base of San Francisco Mountain, and situated about 18 miles northeast of Flagstaff, Ariz., was visited and sketches and diagrams were made. The cliff dwellings of Walnut Cañon, about 12 miles southeast of Flagstaff, were also examined.

Later the work of the field party was among the ruined pueblos near Keams Cañon, which connect traditionally with the present Moki villages. These ruins, six in number, are distributed on the north border of the Jeditoh Valley, and are scattered along for a distance of 12 miles.

The party afterwards camped for some time in the vicinity of Oraibe, the largest of the present villages of Tusayan. Here a study was made of the primitive constructional devices still in use. Two interesting ruins were discovered in this neighborhood and their ground plans secured. In the northern ruin a cave or underground apartment was found containing vestiges of stone walls and supporting timbers. The small village of Moen-Kopi was surveyed. This is an outlying farming pueblo, occupied mainly during the planting and harvesting seasons. A very extensive system of irrigation is in operation in this vicinity.

Subsequently the party spent six weeks at the Chaco ruins in New Mexico. An accurate architectural survey of the more important ruins was made, and the plans secured reveal many points of interest. The degree of mechanical knowledge displayed by the builders of these pueblos has been greatly exaggerated by earlier explorers, as also the quality of the masonry. Close examination reveals on the part of the builders ignorance of some of the simplest principles of construction. Several ruins, not previously known, were surveyed and others were visited. Late in the season the party platted the pueblo of Jemez, situated upon a river of the same name, a tributary of the Rio Grande.

At various times during the progress of the field-work studies were made of the more primitive Navajo architecture, and many sketches and diagrams were prepared illustrating the Navajo system of framing these "hogans," or conical wood and earth houses. Several photographs of typical examples were taken.

Mr. Cosmos Mindeleff left Washington for the field September 1 and returned February 23. In addition to general assistance to the party under charge of Mr. Victor Mindeleff, he was in immediate charge of the surveying. Ground plans of thirteen important ruins, in addition to sketch plans of a number of others of less importance, and of two inhabited pueblos, were added to those already in the possession of the Bureau. The methods of surveying followed in previous years were continued in this. The plans, as a rule, are drawn to a scale of 20 feet to 1 inch, and the drawing is finished in the field. The topography is in all cases indicated by contour lines of 5-foot intervals, sketched upon a basis of a number of points determined with a level. The ground plan was usually drawn over a number of points and lines, which were located with an instrument, and the direction of all the walls was determined by a compass, in order to detect any irregularities. It was found that the regularity and symmetry of plan which characterizes many published ground plans of ruins in the southwest—notably those of the Chaco ruins—are not justified by the facts exhibited by the ruins themselves, though upon cursory examination, and even upon preliminary survey, the ground plans of many of these ruins are apparently symmetric. The plans obtained will be published in articles now being prepared.

Mr. A. M. Stephen was engaged during half of the fiscal year in collecting traditions and other matter from the Tusayan villages and among the Navajos. He has transmitted a number of valuable short papers on these topics and also on the house-lore of the Moki Indians, and has furnished descriptions and drawings of the "Kisis" or rude temporary shelters of the Moki, comparing these with the primitive structures of the Navajos.

The publications of Henry R. Schoolcraft, issued in 1853, upon the pictographs of the Ojibwa, give the impression that they were nearly as far advanced in hieroglyphic writing as were the Egyptians immediately before their pictorial representations had become syllabic. Doubts had been entertained of the accuracy of this account which it was considered to be the duty of the Bureau of Ethnology to resolve; therefore at the beginning of the fiscal year Col. Garrick Mallery and Dr. W. J. Hoffman were directed to proceed to Indian reservations in Minnesota and Wisconsin and learn whatever remained accessible on the subject.

Dr. Hoffman proceeded to the White Earth and Red Lake Reservations, Minnesota, and remained for three months, making the required researches among the Ojibwa. He found that the most important birchbark records are those relating to the Ojibwa cosmogony, the institution of the Midewin or Grand Medicine Society (in which is preserved all that pertains to the supposed sacred mission of the Shaman), and the songs used in connection with the ritual and the initiation of candidates into that society.

The pictographic charts are, as a rule, in the possession of the Midé or Grand Medicine Man, though records relating to hunting and personal exploits, as well as directions for killing game, gathering fruits, and making journeys, and even personal letters, are made by other members of the tribe who possess more than ordinary intelligence.

The great mass of charts consist of mnemonic songs, pertaining to incantations, exorcism, and other ceremonies, and a considerable number of these records were obtained, together with their interpretations. Sketches of tattooed Indians were also made, but it was learned that this custom is almost extinct, the only modern markings being those applied to various portions of the face for the exorcism of evil spirits causing neuralgia, headache, and other pains. Hasty sketches were obtained also of an old Grand Medicine chart at Red Lake, a protracted examination of it not being permitted by the keeper of the record.

In addition to the pictographic material, a quantity of mythologic matter was collected, all or nearly all of which was intimately connected with the rites of the secret society of the Midewin, or Grand Medicine.

Colonel Mallery directed his attention chiefly to the examination of the Ojibwa on the La Pointe and Red Cliff Reservations in Wisconsin, and although it is a less favorable field for ethnologic research than those mentioned in Minnesota, owing to the larger and closer influence of civilization, he obtained evidence complementing the observations and conclusions of Dr. Hoffman. As a general result it is found that there still exists among the Ojibwa a remarkable degree of pictographic skill and it is employed in ordinary affairs of life as well as in the service of religion and ceremonial rites. The statements of Schoolcraft, however, are shown to be exaggerated, or at least erroneous, especially in their attribution of mystic symbolism to devices purely ideographic or mnemonic. The apparently significant coloration of his figures is deceptive, as colors are not now and probably never have been used in the genuine records.

In August, Colonel Mallery proceeded alone to Cape Breton and Prince Edward Islands, Nova Scotia, and Maine, to investigate the bark records and petroglyphs of Micmacs and the Abnaki. Special study was made as to the probability of an aboriginal source for many of the characters supposed to have been first used by French missionaries in 1652, and afterward printed at Vienna, Austria, in 1862, with additions and changes, under the direction of Rev. Charles Kauder, and now generally styled the "Micmac Hieroglyphs."

A most interesting and unique body of rock etchings was discovered at and near Kejimkoojic Lake, Nova Scotia, and accurate copies of many of them were secured. On account of their number, their intrinsic interest and the evidences of their antiquity, these etchings form a highly important addition to the collections before made, especially as they are in a region from which no representation of that nature had been reported. A petroglyph of interest near Machias, Me., not before known, was also copied. A valuable collection was for the first time obtained of birch-bark pictographs still made or formerly used by the Passamaquoddy and Penobscot tribes of the Abnaki in Maine, showing a similarity in the use of picture-writing between the members of the extensive Algonkian stock in the regions west of the Great Lakes and those on the northeastern sea-board. The correlation of the pictographic practice in manner and extent was before inferentially asserted, but no satisfactory evidence of it had been presented until the researches of the present year brought into direct comparison the pictography of the Ojibwa with that of the Micmacs and Abnaki. Colonel Mallery returned to Washington in October.

Mr. James Mooney spent the earlier months of the fiscal year in the examination of the northern division of Cherokees with reference to the dialectic difference of vocabulary between them and the main body of the same tribe in the Indian Territory from which they have long been separated, and also, in studying for the same comparison their religious practices, traditions, social customs, and arts. The northern Cherokees are found to have been less affected by civilization than those of the south, and they can therefore be studied with manifest advantage. Mr. Mooney procured a large amount of valuable material from them.

OFFICE WORK.

Director Powell was frequently occupied during the year in the examination of undetermined problems pertaining to his work upon the classification of the Indian linguistic stocks, the scope of which has been explained in his former reports. It was found necessary to defer decision respecting some of the stocks until after obtaining the result of additional field-work planned for the ensuing year.

Colonel Mallery, after his return from the field-work, was engaged in study of important and novel points developed thereby, and in continued research and correspondence on sign language and pictography.

Dr. Hoffman, while assisting in the same work, prepared an atlas and topograhic chart showing all the petroglyphs within the limits of the United States and adjacent countries so far recorded in the archives of the Bureau, and all particulars of manipulation, coloration, position, and other characteristics of interest, with descriptions and references to authorities.

Mr. H. W. Henshaw was chiefly employed in a solution of problems relating to the geographic distribution of the linguistic families of North American Indians in the territory north of Mexico. When not engaged in this work or with executive duties he continued the preparation of a dictionary in the nature of a synonomy of tribal names of the North American Indians, now well advanced toward completion, the general character and object of which have been set forth in a former report.

While in general charge of that division of the office work he specially attended to the Sahaptinian, Salishan, Chemakuman, Chinookan, and several other linguistic stocks of the Pacific slope.

During the first live months of the year Mr. A. S. Gatschet was engaged in digesting the results of his recent trip to Louisiana, Texas, and

Mexico, and utilizing them in the compilation of the Indian tribal synonomy now in course of preparation by the Bureau.

His designated share in that work comprised the families of the southern Indians from the Rio Grande to the Atlantic sea-board of Florida, namely, the stocks of the Natchez, Atákapa, Shetimasha, Tonkawè, Pakawá (otherwise known under the vague designation of "Coahuilteco o Tejano"), Tonica, Yuchi. and Timmucua, and the most important stock of them all, the Maskóki family. His work of correlating the information of these tribes for the synonomy can now be considered as completed, though some important tribes can not be classified linguistically, *e. g.*, the Kóroas and Pascagoulas, on account of the absence of all information in the documents of early chroniclers relating to these extinct tribes. The Adai, classed by Gallatin as a distinct family, is believed by Mr. Gatschet to be affiliated with the Caddoan stock as a dialect distantly related to Yátassi and Caddo proper.

After concluding his labors on the tribal synonomy, Mr. Gatschet resumed his work on the grammar of the Klamath language of southwestern Oregon. He combined all the results of his recent studies of both dialects, the northern and the southern, with the facts previously acquired by him and composed a treatise on the morphology of the language. This has now been rewritten three times by him in order to secure completeness and accuracy. The "phonetics" are already cast in plates as are the chapters on radicals and on prefixion.

From July to December, 1887, Rev. J. Owen Dorsey was engaged in translating the Teton texts of Mr. George Bushotter, a Dakotan, who was working under his direction. Mr. Bushotter's collection consists of myths, legends, historical papers, an autobiography, accounts of games, folk-lore and epistles, amounting to two hundred and fifty eight textual manuscripts. This work was continued until the following December when Bushotter resigned, leaving one hundred and twenty-nine texts to be translated. Mr. Dorsey then continued the work alone until April 18, 1888, when another Dakotan, Mr. John Bruyier, of Cheyenne .River Agency, began to revise and interpret the Teton texts, making many corrections in the originals, and supplying important parts omitted by Bushotter.

Mr. Bruyier also furnished Mr. Dorsey with many examples of the Teton, as spoken at the Cheyenne River Reservation, which showed that it differed considerably from that spoken at the Lower Brulé and Pine Ridge Reservations. He also wrote new versions of several myths, continuing his work until June 30, 1888.

During the autumn of 1887, Mr. Dorsey completed his work on the Siouan, Caddoan, Athapascan, Takilman, Kusan, and Yakonan cards for the Indian synonomy referred to in a former report of the Director. He also prepared nearly four hundred type-written foolscap pages of Çegiha epistles, legends, and other texts, which constitute an important addition to those published in the Contributions to North American

Ethnology, vol. VI, part 1. He also transliterated on slips in alphabetic order his Winnebago material, obtained in 1878-'79, collating it with the additional material obtained in 1886. This contains fully four thousand entries.

He gave much attention to the Catawba language, collating parts of a recent vocabulary (that procured by Mr. Gatschet) with all others which were accessible.

Mr. Jeremiah Curtin contributed to the Indian synonomy with reference to several tribes in Oregon and California, and devoted much study to the large number of myths obtained by him from the same tribes, also to those of the Iroquois.

Mr. James C. Pilling has continued throughout the year to give a portion of his time to the preparation of bibliographies of the more important stocks of North American languages. As stated in the last report, the manuscript for the Siouan bibliography, the second of the series, was sent to the printer late in the fiscal year 1886-'87. The proof was read during the summer months and the work received from the Public Printer November 12. Work was then begun on the Iroquoian stock of languages, and the close of the fiscal year found it ready for the printer. Some preliminary work was also done on the Muskokian bibliography. Late in December Mr. Pilling made a visit to the library of the Historical Society of Pennsylvania, at Philadelphia, for the purpose of inspecting and taking descriptions of several important manuscripts in Indian languages, written by Moravian missionaries, manuscripts then temporarily in that city and permanently preserved in the Moravian archives at Bethlehem, Pa., and Fairfield, Canada.

Mr. James Mooney, when not in the field, continued to be charged with the synonomy relating to the Iroquoian and Algonkin linguistic stocks, and also worked upon the vocabularies, myths, and notes of information procured by him from the northern Cherokees.

During the entire year, except at short intervals when he visited the field to make personal observations, Professor Thomas has been busily engaged upon his report. The manuscript for the first volume with the illustrations was presented for publication about a month before the close of the fiscal year. The manuscript, illustrations, and maps for the second volume are well under way and will soon be ready for publication. Mr. Henry L. Reynolds, from December until the close of the fiscal year, was at Washington occupied in the preparation of maps, plates, and diagrams for the report.

During the winter and until the 1st of May, 1888, Mr. Gerard Fowke was engaged in preparing a paper for a report on the articles of stone in the Bureau collections.

Mr. W. H. Holmes has charge of the illustrations intended for the Bureau publications as in previous years, and has as far as possible continued his studies in aboriginal art and archæology.

The collections acquired during the summer, although not lacking interest and value, are not so extensive as those of previous years. Acquisitions are made in three distinct ways: first, through members of the Bureau and the Geological Survey who act as collectors; second, by means of exchange for publications or duplicate specimens from previous collections; and third, by donation. Professor Thomas and his assistants, working in the Mississippi Valley and on the Atlantic slope, report but few accessions during the year. Mr. James Stevenson secured important collections from the Pueblo country, especially from the villages of Jemez and Silla, in the Jemez Valley, New Mexico. These collections include about five hundred specimens of pottery and nearly four hundred of stone, wood, and other substances. A large percentage of these specimens are ancient. A considerable number of ancient relics of pottery and stone were obtained from ancient ruin sites in the Jemez and Rio Grande Valleys, New Mexico, by the Director and Mr. Holmes. Mr. A. P. Davis collected a number of fragments of ancient pottery from the ruin of Pueblo Alto, New Mexico. A very interesting series of objects, illustrating the present condition of the arts among the Cherokee and Catawba Indians, was procured by Mr. James Mooney of the Bureau. Mr. DeLancey W. Gill, of the Geological Survey, has added to the collection many specimens of rude stone implements from the vicinity of Washington. Donations have been received from the following persons: Mr. C. C. Jones, fragments of ancient pottery from Stallings Island, near Augusta, Ga.; Dr. Taylor, fragments of ancient pottery from Baldwin County, Ala.; General G. P. Thruston, fragment of an enormous earthen vase from a suburb of Nashville, Tenn.; Mr. W. W. Adams, articles of stone from Union Springs, N. Y.; Mr. C. L. R. Wheeler, cast of a unique stone knife from Westchester County, N. Y.; and Mr. James Tilton, fragments of pottery from Plum Island, Massachusetts.

By exchange for books and duplicates from the National Museum the following acquisitions have been made:

From Mr. H. P. Hamilton, fragments of ancient pottery from Two Rivers, Wis., and from Mr. H. W. Hakes, fragments of pottery from Broome County, N. Y.

By purchase or part purchase the Bureau has obtained from Mr. J. A. McNiel one hundred and seventy pieces of ancient pottery from Chiriqui, Panama, besides some very interesting objects of stone. From Mr. Ward Bachelor it has acquired a fine collection of earthen and stone objects from Mexico. From Dr. E. Boban a few fine samples of Mexican pottery were obtained. All these have been catalogued and turned over to the National Museum.

Mr. L. B. Case, of Richmond, Ind., has presented to the Bureau the records of the State Archæologic Association of Indiana, which fell into his hands as secretary at the discontinuance of the society several years ago.

Valuable photographs of archæologic subjects have been received irom Prof. Anastasio Alfaro, secretary of the National Museum of Costa Rica; also from Mr. C. F. Low, of Cincinnati; from Mr. A. F. Sears, of Portland, Oregon; and Mr. D. S. Sears, of Cuba, Ill.

During the first two months of the fiscal year Mr. Victor Mindeleff was engaged upon a report on the architecture of the Cibola and Tusayan groups of pueblos, in New Mexico and Arizona. Subsequent to his return from the field on March 18 that report was resumed, but it was not completed at the end of the fiscal year. The additional data secured from the Tusayan district during the field season is being prepared for incorporation into the same report.

During the early part of the year Mr. Cosmos Mindeleff was occupied upon that portion of the report on pueblo architecture which had been assigned to him. On his return from the field on February 23 he resumed work upon that report, but it was suspended in order to take up the preparation of an exhibit to be made by the Bureau at the Cincinnati Centennial Exposition. An exhibit to cover nearly 2,000 square feet of floor space was prepared, but as the space was limited only the field work of the Bureau in one especial region, viz, the Pueblo country, was illustrated, though a small amount of other material was added for purposes of comparison. This work was not completed at the close of the fiscal year.

The work of the modeling room was continued throughout the year in his charge. No new work was taken up, all available labor being used in preparing a series of duplicates of models previously deposited in the National Museum. This work was continued from last year. The series is not yet completed, but the accumulations on hand at the end of the fiscal year were sufficient to enable the Bureau to make a creditable display at the Cincinnati Centennial Exposition without withdrawing, to any large extent, the models deposited in the National Museum. During the year eight models were added to the duplicate series, and three other models commenced.

Dr. Washington Matthews, surgeon U. S. Army, continued work upon a grammar and dictionary of the Navajo language.

Mr. E. W. Nelson was still engaged in the completion of his paper mentioned in the last report upon the Eskimo of northern Alaska, comprising a dictionary with notes upon the grammar of the language and also upon the myths and customs of the people.

Mr. J. N. B. Hewitt has continued the study of the Iroquoian languages and the preparation of a Tuscarora-English dictionary. He also worked upon the comparison of words, radicals, and terms in the Iriquoian languages with those in the Cherokee, and in determining the prehistoric habitat of the Iroquois.

The work of Mr. Charles C. Royce, before reported upon, presenting the former title of Indian tribes to lands within the present boundaries of the United States, and the methods of securing their relinquishment, was substantially prepared for publication, the charts having all been finished.

For several years past it has been part of the work of the Bureau to take advantage of the frequent presence in Washington of parties styled "delegations," of the several Indian tribes visiting the capital, for the purpose of photographing all the individuals composing them. These are generally the prominent men of the tribes represented by them and their photographs have biographic and historic interest as well as anthropologic importance. Mr. J. K. Hillers has been in charge of this branch of the work, and during the past year has secured ninety-nine photographs of prominent Indians in both full face and profile, in order to exhibit to better advantage all their facial characteristics. The subjects were from the following tribes, viz:

White Mountain Apache, 15 persons; Chiracahua Apaches, 20; Jicarilla Apaches, 8; Sac and Fox, 7; Utes, 4; Shawnee, 9; Omaha, 20; Dakota, 11; Oto and Missouri, 5.

In connection with the name of each Indian photographed it has been the practice to note his age, status in the tribe, and such biographic information as could be obtained.

LIST OF PUBLICATIONS OF THE BUREAU OF ETHNOLOGY.

ANNUAL REPORTS.

First Annual Report of the Bureau of Ethnology, 1879–'80. 1881. xxxv, + 603 pp. 8vo.

Second Annual Report of the Bureau of Ethnology, 1880–'81. 1883. xxxvii, + 477 pp. 8vo.

Third Annual Report of the Bureau of Ethnology, 1881–'82. 1884. lxxiv, + 606 pp. 8vo.

Fourth Annual Report of the Bureau of Ethnology, 1882–'83. 1886. lxxiii, + 532 pp. 8vo.

Fifth Annual Report of the Bureau of Ethnology, 1883–'84. 1887. liii, + 564 pp. 8vo.

CONTRIBUTIONS.

Contributions to North American Ethnology, Vol. I. 1877. xiv. + 361 pp. 4to.

Contributions to North American Ethnology, Vol. III. 1877. 3. 635 pp. 4to.

Contributions to North American Ethnology, Vol. IV. 1881. xiv, + 231 pp. 4to.

Contributions to North American Ethnology, Vol. V. 1882. 112. 32. xxxvii, + 237 pp. 4to.

INTRODUCTIONS.

Powell, J. W. Introduction to the Study of Indian Languages. 1877. 104 pp. 4to.

Powell, J. W. Introduction to the Study of Indian Languages. 2nd ed. 1880. xi, + 228 pp. 4to.

Mallery, Garrick. Introduction to the Study of Indian Languages. 1880. iv, + 72 pp. 4to.

Yarrow, H. C. Introduction to the Study of Mortuary Customs. 1880. ix, + 114 pp. 4to.

Mallery, Garrick. Collection of Gesture Signs and Signals. 1880. 329 pp. 4to.

Pilling, J. C. Proof-sheets of Bibliography of North American Indian Languages. 1885. xl, + 1135 pp. 4to.

Pilling, J. C. Bibliography of the Eskimo Language. 1887. v, + 116 pp. 8vo.
Henshaw, H. W. Perforated Stones from California. 1887. 34 pp. 8vo.
Holmes, W. H. The Use of Gold and other Metals among the Ancient Inhabitants of Chiriqui, Isthmus of Darien. 1887. 27 pp. 8vo.
Thomas, C. Work in Mound Exploration of the Bureau of Ethnology. 1887. 15 pp. 8vo.
Pilling, J. C. Bibliography of the Siouan Languages. 1887. v, + 87 pp. 8vo.

NECROLOGY.

MORRISON R. WAITE, CHANCELLOR.

In the order of official precedence, I am called on to first mention the loss sustained by the Institution during the year, of its Chancellor, the late eminent Chief-Justice of the United States Supreme Court, Morrison R. Waite, who died in this city on the 23d of March last (1888).

His biography belongs to the whole country; but though I have only to speak of his relations to this Institution, yet one who knew him even in this limited part of his important duties can not but feel that his was a character of a singular sincerity, in the proper meaning of the word; so that it has been well said of him that he possessed not only a moral but an intellectual integrity. Of the affection, as well as respect, he inspired, I have already spoken. Remarkable for this admirable simplicity of character as for his kindness of heart, in his unwavering conscientiousness of purpose in the discharge of every duty, he made himself, perhaps, the most influential and efficient Chancellor among the very able ones the Institution has been so fortunate as to possess. Taking pains to acquaint himself accurately with the character and requirements of the Institution, evincing an earnest sympathy in its objects and in its adopted policy, he was a faithful attendant on the meetings of the Board during the fourteen years of his presidency.

It seems proper to here record, as a part of the official history of this bereavement, that a special meeting of the Board of Regents was called on the 27th of March, 1888, to take appropriate action on the occasion, and that the following resolutions, expressive of the general sentiment, were unanimously adopted and placed upon the journal of the Board:

Whereas the Board of Regents of the Smithsonian Institution has been called to meet in extraordinary session by the afflicting intelligence that Morrison Remick Waite, late Chief-Justice of the Supreme Court of the United States and late Chancellor of the Smithsonian Institution, has been removed by the hand of death from the scenes of his high activities and distinguished usefulness: Therefore be it

Resolved, That sitting as we do at this time and place, in the very center of that dark shadow which has fallen upon the whole land in the lamented death of the late Chief-Justice Waite, and appalled as we are by the suddenness as well as by the magnitude of the great affliction

which in coming to the nation at large has come to us individually with
an added pathos of sorrow, because of the nearer view we have had for
so many years of the talents, virtues, and graces which found their familiar home in the person of our honored friend, we could with much
good reason crave for ourselves, in this hour of bereavement, the humble
permission of mourning apart, that we might silently gauge the depth and
the dimensions of a calamity which brings to us its message of personal
grief and which has also torn away from our highest seat of justice its
venerated and beloved chief; from the legal profession of the country
its foremost official representative and therefore its crowning exponent;
from the walks of social life in this National Capital a commanding
presence, no less remarkable for his genial and open-hearted sincerity
than for his affable and gracious benignity; and from the Christian
communion a true and faithful disciple who witnessed a good confession
as much by the simplicity and humility with which he walked before
God as by the unswerving consistency with which he wore the ornament
of a pure heart and of a meek and quiet spirit before the scrutiny of his
fellow men.

Resolved, That while an obvious sense of propriety must dictate that
we should leave to others in that great forum which was the chosen
arena of his life's career, the sad privilege of depicting, with minute and
detailed analysis, the remarkable combination of strong and lovely
traits which met in the person of the late Chief-Justice and gave to the
symmetrical character of our beloved friend its blended sweetness and
light, we can not omit, even in this hour of our special sorrow, to bear
cheerful testimony to the pleasing amenity with which he presided over
the deliberations of this council chamber as the Chancellor of the Smithsonian Institution, and sharing as we all do in a profound admiration
for the intelligence he brought to our discussions, while ever moderating them by the guidance of his clear thought and mild wisdom, we can
but render our reverent homage to the engaging personal qualities which
endeared him to us as a man; while at the same time gratefully confessing our obligations to him for the provident care and deep interest
which he always brought to the discharge of his official duties in this
place, where through all the years of his honorable and useful service
at the head of this Board, the Secretary of the Institution, in common
with ourselves, has leaned on him as the wise and true counsellor who
could be trusted as well for the rectitude of his moral intuitions as for
the clear perceptions of his calm and judicious intellect.

Resolved, That we will attend the funeral of our departed Chancellor
in a body, and that the Secretary of the Institution, together with a
deputation from the members of the Board, be requested to accompany
the other friends and associates of the late Chief-Justice, who will bear
his remains to their last resting-place in Ohio.

Resolved, That these resolutions be entered on the minutes of the
Board, and that the Secretary be requested to send a copy of them to
the family of our departed friend, in token of our sincere condolence
with them in their great affliction.

It only remains for your Secretary to add that, in accordance with
your request, he proceeded to Toledo, where he was joined by one of
your body, Dr. J. B. Angell, and in his company paid the final tribute
of respect, by representing your honorable body at the obsequies of
this eminent and good man.

PROFESSOR BAIRD.

I have referred, at the beginning of this report, to the death of the late Secretary. Both the greatness of the loss to science and to this Institution make me feel the need of speaking again and more particularly both of him and of his work.

When, in January, 1887, the Secretary asked of your honorable body authority to appoint two assistant secretaries to relieve him from the growing burden of his official occupations, it was doubtless with the consciousness that his failing strength no longer permitted the continuous attention to his varied duties which he had previously, with ready zeal, bestowed. When, under the imperative orders of his physician, he withdrew himself (as much as his active mental interest permitted) from the executive operations of his position, the comparative relaxation of effort and responsibility seemed to have been accepted too late to give him its expected relief and recuperation; and his exhausted powers continued to decline until he quietly breathed his last, on the afternoon of the 19th of August, 1887, at the headquarters of the U. S. Commission of Fisheries, at Wood's Holl.

In recognition of his distinguished services, a bill was introduced in the Senate of the United States, and passed by that body February 10, 1888, making an appropriation for the erection of a bronze statue to commemorate his merits.

A bill was also introduced in the Senate for the benefit of his widow.

At a special meeting of the Board of Regents, held November 18, 1887, the following resolutions were passed:

Whereas, in the dispensation of Divine Providence, the mortal life of Spencer Fullerton Baird was ended on the 19th of August last, the Regents of the Smithsonian Institution, now at the earliest practicable moment assembled, desire to express and to record their profound sense of the great loss which this Institution has thereby sustained, and which they personally have sustained. And they accordingly *resolve:*

1. That, in the lamented death of Professor Baird, the Institution is bereaved of its honored and efficient Secretary, who has faithfully and unremittingly devoted to its service his rare administrative abilities for thirty-seven years—that is, almost from the actual foundation of the establishment—for the last nine years as its chief executive officer, under whose sagacious management it has greatly prospered and widely extended its usefulness and its renown.

2. That the National Museum, of which this Institution is the administrator, and the Fish Commission, which is practically affiliated to it, both organized and in a just sense created by our late Secretary, are by this bereavement deprived of the invaluable and unpaid services of their indefatigable official head.

3. That the cultivators of science, both in this country and abroad, have to deplore the loss of a veteran and distinguished naturalist, who was from early years a sedulous and successful investigator; whose native gifts and whose experience in systematic biological work served in no small degree to adapt him to the administrative duties which filled the later years of his life, but whose knowledge and whose interest in science widened and deepened as the opportunities for special

investigation lessened, and who accordingly used his best endeavors to promote the researches of his fellow naturalists in every part of the world.

4. That his kindly disposition, equable temper, singleness of aim, and unsullied purity of motive, along with his facile mastery of affairs, greatly endeared him to his subordinates, secured to him the confidence and trust of those whose influence he sought for the advancement of the interests he had at heart, and won the high regard and warm affection of those who, like the members of this Board, were officially and intimately associated with him.

5. That, without intruding into the domain of private sorrow, the Regents of the Institution would respectfully offer to the family of their late Secretary the assurance of their profound sympathy.

6. That the Regents invite the near associate of the late Secretary, Professor Goode, to prepare a memorial of the life and services of Professor Baird for publication in the ensuing annual report of the Institution.

The address made by Maj. J. W. Powell, an old and personal friend of the late Secretary, at the memorial meeting held by the scientific societies of Washington January 11, 1888, contained so just and eloquent a tribute to Professor Baird's memory, that I feel inclined to quote from it a few words which, it seems to me, will characterize the large purpose and attainment of his life, and its relation to others, better than any of my own:

"Baird was one of the learned men of the world. He knew the birds of the air; he knew the beasts of the forests and the prairies, and the reptiles that crawl through desert sands or slimy marshes; he knew the fishes that scale mountain torrents, that bask in quiet lakes, or that journey from zone to zone through the deep waters of the sea. The treasures of the land did not satisfy the desires of Baird; he must also have the treasures of the sea, and so he organized a fish commission, with its great laboratories and vessels of research.

"The Fish Commission was an agency of research; but it was more; he made it an agency by which science is applied to the relief of the wants of mankind—by which a cheap, nutritious, healthful, and luxurious food is to be given to the millions of men.

"In the research thus organized the materials for the work of other scientific men were gathered. He incited the men personally to undertake and continuously prosecute their investigations. He enlisted the men himself; he trained them himself; he himself furnished them with the materials and instruments of research, and, best of all, was their guide and great exemplar. Thus it was that the three institutions over which he presided—the Smithsonian Institution, the National Museum, and the Fish Commission—were woven into one great organization, a university of instruction in the methods of scientific research, including in its scope the entire field of biology and anthropology.

"In his work with his assistants, he scrupulously provided that every one should receive the meed of honor due for successful research, and treated all with generosity. Many an investigation begun by himself, was turned over to assistants when he found that valuable conclusions could be reached; and these assistants, who were his warm friends, his younger brothers, reaped the reward; and he had more joy over every young man's success than over the triumphs and honors heaped upon himself from every quarter of the globe. He was the sympathetic counselor of many men; into his ears were poured the sorrows and joys of others, and he mourned with the mourning, and rejoiced with the rejoicing. His life at home was pure and sweet and full of joys, for he gave and received love and trust and tender care. But the history of his home life is sacred.

"For many long months he contemplated the day of parting. Labor that knew no rest, responsibility that was never lifted from his shoulders, too soon brought his life to an end. In the summer of the past year he returned to his work by the sea-side, that he might die in its midst. There at Wood's Holl he had created the greatest biologic laboratory of the world ; and in that laboratory, with the best results of his life-work all about him, he calmly and philosophically waited for the time of times."

The memorial which is being prepared, in obedience to the desire of the Regents, by the Assistant Secretary of the Institution, is partly written, but the pressure of official work has prevented its completion in time for publication in the present report.

It seems essential, however, that this report should not be published without at least a brief biographical sketch of my predecessor from one of his scientific family, and the following notice, which anticipates the coming fuller memorial by Dr. Goode, has accordingly been prepared by him at my request.

" Spencer Fullerton Baird was born February 3, 1823, in Reading, a town in southeastern Pennsylvania about 60 miles from Philadelphia, where his ancestors, people of education and prominent in the community, had lived for several generations. About 1834 his mother, then a widow, removed to Carlisle. Carlisle was the seat of Dickinson College, where he was graduated in 1840, at the age of seventeen. His tastes for scientific investigation had already developed in such a remarkable manner that his mother felt that she was justified in allowing him, after graduation, to devote himself for a time to his favorite pursuits, and his time for several years was devoted to studies in general natural history, to long pedestrian excursions for the purpose of observing animals and plants, and collecting specimens, and to the organization of a private cabinet of natural history, which a few years later became the nucleus of the museum of the Smithsonian Institution. During this period he published a number of original papers on natural history. There were at that time no schools for young naturalists, and his education was in large degree self-directed ; during this time, however, he partially completed a course in medicine at the College of Physicians and Surgeons in New York,* and drew inspiration and instruction from such men as Audubon and others of the older naturalists whom at this period he visited, forming the foundation of lifelong friendships. His home studies continued for six years, and were scarcely interrupted by his election in 1841 to the chair of natural his-

---

* He read medicine with Dr. Middleton Goldsmith, and attended a winter course of lectures at the College of Physicians and Surgeons in New York, in 1842. His medical course was never formally completed, although in 1848 he received the degree of M. D., *honoris causa*, from the Philadelphia Medical College.

tory and chemistry in his own college, where he remained until 1850, having married, meantime, Miss Mary H. Churchill, the daughter of General Sylvester Churchill, U. S. Army, for many years Inspector-General.

"The inheritance of a love of nature and a taste for scientific classification, together with the companionship of a brother similarly gifted, tended to the development of the young naturalist. In 1841, at the age of eighteen, we find him making an ornithological excursion through the mountains of Pennsylvania, walking 400 miles in twenty-one days, the last day 60 miles between daylight and rest. The following year he walked more than 2,200 miles. His fine physique and consequent capacity for work are doubtless due in part to his outdoor life during these years.

"The coming of Agassiz to the United States in 1846, was an inspiration to him, and one of the first great works projected by the Swiss savant was a joint memoir upon the fishes of North America, which was enthusiastically begun by the young Dickinson professor, but never brought to the point of publication.

"Agassiz did not become established in Cambridge until 1848, and it is to Baird rather than to him that should belong the credit of having introduced into American schools the system of laboratory practice and field explorations in connection with natural history instruction. Moncure D. Conway, who was one of his pupils, has often told me how fascinating were Professor Baird's explanations of natural phenomena, and how the contagion of his enthusiasm spread among his pupils, who frequently followed him through the fields and woods 20 or 30 miles a day.

"His mentor at this period was the Hon. George P. Marsh, of Vermont, already prominent in public affairs, and his warm friend and admirer.* To him Professor Baird felt that he owed his real start in life, for Mr. Marsh, feeling that his *protége* was disposed to bury himself too deeply in the technicalities of a specialty, proposed that he should undertake the translation and editorship of an edition of the ' Iconographic Encyclopædia,' a version of Heck's *Bilder-Atlas*, published in connection with the famous *Conversations-Lexikon* of Brockhaus. This task, though exceedingly laborious and confining to a young man of twenty-six, entirely untrained in literary methods, was efficiently and rapidly performed, and resulted in a great extension of his tastes and sympathies, while the training which he acquired was an excellent preparation for the tremendous literary tasks which he undertook without hesitation in later years. It was also to the interest of Mr. Marsh, who was one of the earliest Regents of the Smithsonian Institution, that he owed his nomination to the position of Assistant Secretary of that Institution, then recently organized, which he accepted July 5, 1850, and October 3, at the age of twenty-seven years, entered upon his life-work in con-

---

* In Mrs. Caroline Marsh's lately published biography of her husband many interesting letters from Mr. Marsh to Professor Baird are quoted.

nection with that foundation, "the increase and diffusion of knowledge among men." His appointment, if we may judge from a statement in Professor Henry's fifth report, was due quite as much to his training in editorial methods as to his professional acquirements. His appointment, it is stated, was made at this time more particularly in order that his services might be secured to take charge of the publications, and that the Institution might take advantage of the ample experience which he had gained in this kind of work.

"It was, of course, impossible that the Regents of the Smithsonian Institution could have appreciated the fact that he had invented, in connection with his work upon his own private collections, a system of museum administration which was to be of the utmost value in the development of the great National Museum which he afterward was instrumental in founding. All the elaborate and efficient methods of administration which are now in use in the National Museum were present, in germ at least, in the little private museum which grew up under his control at home, and which he brought with him in a single freight car to form the nucleus of the great Smithsonian collections.* Among the treasures of this collection, which are still cherished by the Institution, were a number of the choicest bird skins collected by Audubon, who had always felt for him a sincere friendship from the time when he proposed to the boy of seventeen that he should accompany him on a voyage to the headwaters of the Missouri, and become his partner in the preparation of a great work on the quadrupeds of North America, which afterward he brought out in conjunction with Bachman, of South Carolina.

"The first grant made by the Institution for scientific exploration

---

* The only specimens in possession of the Institution at the time of his arrival were a few boxes of minerals and plants. The collections of the Wilkes Exploring Expedition, which constitute the legal foundation of the National Museum of the United States, were at that time under the charge of the National Institute; and although by the act of incorporation the Smithsonian Institution was the legal custodian of the national cabinet of curiosities, it was not until 1857 that the Regents finally accepted the trust, and the National Museum was definitely placed under the control of the Smithsonian Institution and transferred to its building. Until this time Congress had granted no funds for the support of the Smithsonian cabinets, and the collections had been acquired and cared for at the expense of the endowment fund. They had, however, become so large and important in 1857 that the so-called "National Collection" at that time acquired was small in comparison.

The National Museum thus had a double origin. Its actual although not its legal nucleus was the collection gathered in the Smithsonian building prior to 1857. Its methods of administration, which were in fact the very same that had been developed by Professor Baird in Carlisle as early as 1845, are those which are still in use, and which have stood the test of thirty years without any necessity for their modification becoming apparent. In the Fifth Annual Report of the Smithsonian Institution, now exceedingly rare, is a report by the assistant secretary in charge of the natural history department, for the year 1850, which enumerates the specimens belonging to the Museum on January 1, 1851, including a full account of his own deposit.

and field research was in 1848 to Spencer F. Baird, of Carlisle, for the exploration of the bone caves and the local natural history of southeastern Pennsylvania.

"From the start the department of explorations was under his charge, and in his reports to the Secretary, published year by year in the annual report of the Institution, may be found the only systematic record of Government explorations which has ever been prepared.

"The decade beginning with 1850 was a period of great activity in exploration. Our frontier was being rapidly extended toward the West, but in the territory between the Mississippi and the Pacific coast were immense stretches of country practically unknown. Numerous Government expeditions were sent forth, and immense collections in every department of natural history were gathered and sent to Washington to be studied and reported upon. The Smithsonian Institution had been designated by law the custodian of these collections, and within the walls of its buildings assembled the naturalists by whose exertions these collections had been brought together. Professor Baird was surrounded by conditions most congenial and stimulating, for he found full scope for his administrative skill in the work of arranging the scientific outfits for these expeditions, preparing instructions for the explorers, and above all in inspiring them with enthusiasm for the work. To him also fell in large part the task of receiving the collections, arranging for the necessary investigations, and the collation and publication of their results. The natural history portions of the reports of the Mexican boundary survey, the Pacific Railroad surveys, the expeditions of Ives, Emory, Stansbury, and others, were under his supervision, as well as, in considerable degree, the natural history collections of the Wilkes exploring expedition, which were still under investigation.

"The period of the civil war was one of comparative quiet, but much was accomplished by Baird and his pupils, and two of his most important memoirs, viz, Review of North American Birds and The Distribution and Migrations of North American Birds, were published. During this decade, too, continued the summer expeditions usually extending over three months, which were becoming yearly more and more exclusively devoted to the investigation of marine life, and which ultimately led to the organization of the Fish Commission in 1871. During the latter part of this decade the early impressions of his work in connection with the Iconographic Encyclopædia began to revive, and a new interest was shown by Professor Baird in the popularization of scientific subjects. At the solicitation of Mr. George W. Childs, in 1867 he began to devote a column to scientific intelligence in the Philadelphia Public Ledger, and about 1870 he became the scientific editor of the periodicals published by the Harper Brothers, of New York. His connection with this firm continued until 1878, and in addition to the weekly and monthly issues there resulted eight annual volumes of the Annual

Record of Science and Industry, the successor of the Annual of Scientific Discovery, established by David A. Wells, in 1850. When Professor Baird became Secretary of the Smithsonian Institution his editorial labors were abandoned, but the idea of his Annual Record of Science and Industry was continued in the yearly appendices to the Smithsonian report under the title of Record of Progress, and the scientific work of the world for as many consecutive years is passed in review in the thirty-eight volumes which combine the three series just referred to.

"In the memoir which the writer is preparing it is his intention to discuss in detail the great labors of Professor Baird in scientific administration and investigation, but his life was so full that it is only by careful condensation that even an outline of its eventful features can be brought within the brief limits of this notice.

"There may be noted in the career of Professor Baird several distinct phases of activity, namely : (1) A period of twenty-six years (1843-1869) occupation in laborious investigation and voluminous publication upon the vertebrate fauna of North America; (2) forty years (1840-1880) of continuous contribution to scientific editorship; (3) five years (1845-1850) devoted to educational work; (4) forty-four years (1843-1887) devoted to the encouragement and promotion of scientific enterprises and the development of new workers among the young men with whom he was brought in contact; (5) thirty-seven years (1850-1887) devoted to administrative work as an officer of the Smithsonian Institution and in charge of the scientific collections of the Government, twenty-eight (1850-1878) as principal executive officer, and nine (1878-1887) as Secretary and responsible head; (6) sixteen years (1871-1887) as head of the Fish Commission, a philanthropic labor for the increase of the food supply of the world, and, incidentally, in promoting the interests of biological and physical investigation of the waters.

"The extent of his contributions to science and scientific literature may be at least partially comprehended by an examination of the bibliography of his publications issued by the Institution in 1883.* The list of his writings is complete to the end of the year 1882, and contains 1,063 titles. Of this number, 775 are brief notices and critical reviews contributed to the Annual Record of Science and Industry, while under his editorial charge; 31 are reports relating to the work of the Smithsonian Institution; 7 are reports upon the American fisheries ; 25 are schedules and circulars officially issued, and 25 are volumes or papers edited. Out of the remaining 200 the majority are formal contributions to scientific literature, among them the two classical works upon the Mammals of North America and the Birds of North America (Volumes VIII and IX of the Pacific Railroad Reports). These were the only extended systematic treatises upon those groups which had at that time been prepared, of scope sufficient to embrace the fauna of the entire continent. They are still standard works of reference, and every spec-

---

* Bulletin XX, U. S. National Museum.

ialist who uses them bears testimony to their extreme accuracy and merit.

"Of the total number of papers enumerated in the list, 73 relate to mammals, 80 to birds, 43 to reptiles, 431 to fishes, 61 to invertebrates (these being chiefly reviews), 16 to plants, 88 to geographical distribution, 46 to geology, mineralogy, and palæontology; 45 to anthropology, 31 to industry and art, and 109 to exploration and travel.

"While the number of new species described does not necessarily afford any clew to the value of the work accomplished, it may not be uninteresting to refer to it as an indication of the pioneer work which it was necessary to do even in so prominent a group as the vertebrates. I note among mammals 49, birds 70, reptiles 186, fishes 56. Forty-nine of 220, or nearly one-fourth, of the mammals discussed in the Mammals of North America were there described for the first time. In the catalogue of serpents not more than 60 per cent. had been named, and in preparation for studying the specimens each was carefully ticketed with its locality, and then the 2,000 or more individuals were thrown indiscriminately into one great pile, and the work of sorting them out by resemblances was begun. Not the least valuable have been the numerous accurate figures of North American vertebrates, prepared under Professor Baird's supervision. These include representatives of 170 species of mammals and 160 species of reptiles, besides many hundreds of birds.

"On the 9th of February, 1874, Congress passed a joint resolution which authorized the appointment of a Commissioner of Fish and Fisheries. The duties of the Commissioner were thus defined: 'To prosecute investigations on the subject (of the diminution of valuable fishes) with the view of ascertaining whether any and what diminution in the number of the food-fishes of the coast and the lakes of the United States has taken place, and, if so, to what causes the same is due; and also whether any and what protective, prohibitory, or precautionary measures should be adopted in the premises, and to report upon the same to Congress.'

"The resolution establishing the office of Commissioner of Fisheries required that the person to be appointed should be a civil officer of the Government, of proved scientific and practical acquaintance with the fishes of the coast, to serve without additional salary. The choice was thus practically limited to a single man. Professor Baird, at that time Assistant Secretary of the Smithsonian Institution, was appointed, and, at once entering upon his duties, soon developed a systematic scheme of investigation.

"The Fish Commission now fills a place tenfold more extensive and useful than at first. Its work is naturally divided into three sections:

"(1) The systematic investigation of the waters of the United States and the biological and physical problems which they present. The scientific studies of the Commission are based upon a liberal and philosophical interpretation of the law. In making his original plans the Commissioner insisted that to study only food-fishes would be of little importance, and that useful conclusions must needs rest upon a broad foundation of investigations purely scientific in character. The life history of species of economic value should be understood from beginning to end, but no less requisite is it to know the histories of the animals and plants upon which they feed or upon which their food is nourished; the histories of their enemies and friends, and the friends and foes of their enemies and friends, as well as the currents, temperatures, and other physical phenomena of the waters in relation to migration, reproduction, and growth. A necessary accomplishment to this division is the amassing of material for research to be stored in the National and other museums for future use.

"(2) The investigation of the methods of fisheries, past and present, and the statistics of production and commerce of fishery products. Man being one of the chief destroyers of fish, his influence upon their abundance must be studied. Fishery methods and apparatus must be examined and compared with those of other lands, that the use of those which threaten the destruction of useful fishes may be discouraged, and that those which are inefficient may be replaced by others more serviceable. Statistics of industry and trade must be secured for the use of Congress in making treaties or imposing tariffs, to show to producers the best markets, and to consumers where and with what their needs may be supplied.

"(3) The introduction and multiplication of useful food fishes throughout the country, especially in waters under the jurisdiction of the General Government, or those common to several States, none of which might feel willing to make expenditures for the benefit of the others. This work, which was not contemplated when the Commission was established, was first undertaken at the instance of the American Fish Cultural Association, whose representatives induced Congress to make a special appropriation for the purpose.

"His relation to the organizations with which he was so closely identified, the Smithsonian Institution, its ward, the National Museum, and the Fish Commission, can in this place only be incidentally mentioned, and the numerous biographical notices which have appeared since his death have not failed to review critically the significance of his connection with them and his influence upon them. To his friends who knew him best and miss him most it seems pleasanter to dwell upon the recognition which his labors received than upon the labors themselves, his devotion to which shortened his life so many years.

"Almost every civilized country in the world has paid him honor. In 1875 he received the decoration of Knight of the Royal Norwegian order of St. Olaf from the King of Norway and Sweden. In 1878 he was awarded the silver medal of the Acclimatization Society of Melbourne, and in 1879 the gold medal of the Société d'Acclimation of France. In 1856 he received the degree of doctor of physical science from Dickinson College, and in 1875 that of doctor of laws from Columbian University. A few months before his death, on the occasion of the two hundred and fiftieth anniversary of Harvard University, the same degree, *ad eundem*, was conferred on him as an eminent promoter of science. This was one of the few occasions upon which he was induced to ascend the platform in a public place. He was one of the early members of the National Academy of Sciences, and ever since the organization was a member of its council. In 1850 and 1851 he served as permanent secretary of the American Association for the Advancement of Science, and since 1878 was one of the trustees of the Corcoran Gallery of Art, Washington. He was a president of the Cosmos Club, and for many years a trustee of Columbian University. Among his honorary relations to numerous scientific societies of the United States and other countries are included those of foreign membership in the Linnæan Society of London and the Zoological Society of London, honorary membership in the Linnæan Society of New South Wales, and corresponding membership in the K. K. Zoologisch-botanische Gesellschaft, Vienna; the Sociedad de Geographia, Lisbon; the New Zealand Insti. tute; the Koninklijke Natuurkundige Vereeniging in Nederlandsch Indië, Batavia; the Magyar Tudományos Akademia, Buda-Pesth; the Société Nationale des Sciences Naturelles, Cherbourg; the Academia Germanica Naturæ Curiosorum, Jena; the Naturforschende Gesellschaft, Halle; the Naturhistorische Gesellschaft, Nuremberg; the Geographical Society, of Quebec; the Historical Society of New York; the Deutsche Fischerei-Verein, Berlin.

"The nomenclature of zoology contains many memorials of his connection with its history. A partial enumeration shows that over twenty-five species and one genus of fishes bears his name, and that not less than forty species have been named in his honor. These will for all time be monuments to his memory as undying as the institutions which he founded.

"A post-office in Shasta County, Cal., located near the McCloud River Salmon Hatching Station of the U. S. Fish Commission, was named Baird by the Postmaster-General in 1877.

"Even Japan was not unmindful of Professor Baird's services to science, for from distant Yezo, the most northern island of the Japanese Archipelago, came, soon after his death, a little volume beautifully printed upon silk, containing his portrait and the story of his character.

"The importance of his services to fish-culture was perhaps more fully recognized in Germany than in any other country, not excluding the United States. In 1880, on the occasion of the first great International Fishery Exhibition held in Berlin, his name was found to be widely known among the scientific men there present. The magnificent silver trophy which was the chief prize was awarded to him by the Emperor William. This now stands in the fishery hall of the National Museum. While Professor Baird's portrait hung over the entrance to the American section at Berlin, the Kammerherr von Behr, the president of the German Fishery Union, the most powerful and influential fishery organization in the world, never passed under it without taking off his hat in honor of the 'first fish-culturist of the world,' as he delighted to call him. He also insisted that any who might be in his company should pay the same respect to Professor Baird. Indeed, I am not sure that the late Emperor Frederick, at that time Crown Prince and protector of the German fisheries, did not do homage in this way to the American philanthropist. After Professor Baird's death a circular was issued by the German Fishery Union which contained a most appreciative eulogy.

"His ever ready assistance to his fellow-workers in Europe won for him their deep regard. Mr. R. Bowdler Sharpe, of the British Museum, writes as follows to *Nature*: 'As chief of the Smithsonian Institution Professor Baird possessed a power of conferring benefits to the world of science exercised by few directors of public museums, and the manner in which he has utilized these powers has resulted not only in the wonderful success of the United States National Museum under his direction, but in the enrichment of many other museums. We know by experience that the British Museum is indebted to Professor Baird beyond measure. We had only to express our wants, and immediately every effort was made to supply all the desiderata in our ornithological collection.'

"Professor Baird was the most modest of men. He seemed never to care for public recognition. In speaking of any honors which he had received he appeared to deprecate what had been done, as if ashamed of the attentions, feeling himself unworthy to receive them.

"He once remarked to me, some years before his death, that he was satisfied that no man's life was of such importance to the people among whom he lived that he could not shortly be replaced by another who would fully fill his place. As I looked at the man before me, a giant in body and in mind, a treasury of untransferable experience and wisdom, I thought to myself that if this judgment was a true one (which I did not believe, nor, at his heart, I suppose, did he), in him at least there was an exception. I speak not now of his official usefulness alone, but of the broader and more essential relationships which he held to science and to humanity.

"Such a man has a thousand sides, each most familiar to a few, and perhaps entirely strange to the greater part of those who know him.

"Future historians of American science will be better able than are we to estimate justly the value of the contributions to scientific literature which are enumerated in his bibliography; but no one not living in the present can form an accurate idea of the personal influence of a leader upon his associates and upon the progress of thought in his special department, nor can such an influence as this well be set down in words. This influence is apparently due not only to extraordinary skill in organization, to great power of application and concentration of thought constantly applied, and to a philosophical and comprehensive mind, but to an entire and self-sacrificing devotion to the interests of his work and that of others.

"His extreme diffidence and lack of self-seeking were among his conspicuous characteristics. He was always averse to addressing audiences, and this is all the more remarkable to his friends, who remember how winning and persuasive his eloquence was when he talked in the presence of a few. His ability as a talker and organizer was never better seen than when, as already observed, in the presence of Congressional committees, before whom he was summoned from year to year to give reasons for his requests for money to be used in expanding the work of the Fish Commission or the National Museum. He was always received by the members with the heartiest welcome; and it seemed that always these pushing, brusque men of business, who ordinarily rushed with the greatest haste through the routine of committee work, forgot their usual hurry when Professor Baird was before them. They listened attentively as long as he could be induced to talk about his plans for the development of the organizations whose success he had at heart. Not unfrequently they would wander from the business before them as they asked him questions upon subjects which his suggestive remarks impressed upon their attention.

"No man was more easily approached than Professor Baird. He seemed especially fond of meeting young persons, whom he immediately set at their ease by his geniality and frankness of manner. A writer in the *Nation* has said: 'It seemed as if in his mind he had an epitome of all the characteristics of mind and habit of each and every man. No thought of self seemed to enter into his calculations. Those who felt themselves the object of his personal regard sometimes halted for a moment in a comical dismay, perceiving themselves frankly moved, like chessmen, in directions which they would not themselves have selected, but an overwhelming sense of Baird's entire devotion to the promotion of science, his perfect unselfishness, and his incomparable good judgment, always carried the day.'

"From his early youth until his failing strength forbade, he kept a journal of his daily pursuits, and this, together with the immense piles of copy-books and files of letters received, will afford a boundless treasure to his biographer; and when his biography is written, if it be properly done in accordance with the modern theory of biography-making, it will form essentially a history of the natural sciences in America for the past half century.

"For many months before his death he knew that his life was drawing to a close. In the summer of 1887, a few weeks before he died, he went to Wood's Holl, as usual, to direct the operations of the Fish Commission. Of all the tributes to his character none were more eloquent or touching than one at the funeral service at Wood's Holl. The simple burial service was read, and then the clergyman recited these sentences from the Sermon on the Mount: 'Blessed are the merciful, for they shall obtain mercy. Blessed are the pure in heart, for they shall see God. Blessed are the peace-makers, for they shall be called the children of God.' So appropriate were these words that scarcely one of those present could refrain from tears, realizing how great, how benevolent, how simple-hearted had been the friend whom they had lost."

A memorial meeting was held January 11, 1888, in the lecture-room of the Columbian University of Washington, under the joint auspices of the Philosophical, Anthropological, and Biological Societies of this city, at which addresses were made by members of the several societies commemorating the life and scientific work of Professor Baird.

An oil portrait of Professor Baird, of life-size, painted by Mr. Henry Ulke, of this city, was purchased by the Regents for the Institution.

PROFESSOR ASA GRAY, REGENT.

In addition to the loss of our honored Chancellor and Secretary, the Institution has further been called upon to mourn the decease of one of the oldest and most distinguished members of the Board of Regents, Dr. Asa Gray, whose death took place on the 30th day of January last (1888), and brought the mournful loss not only of a great man of science, intimately and long connected with the Institution, but of one personally endeared to all who knew him.

Professor Gray may be said to have been identified with the Institution from its very beginning as a chosen and trusted counselor of its first Secretary, and an active member of the Board from January, 1874.

Born in the town of Paris, Oneida County, N. Y., on the 18th of November, 1810, Professor Gray was at the time of his death, therefore, over seventy-seven years of age, though few would have so supposed, judging from his continued activity and vigor. He was graduated at the Fairfield College of Physicians and Surgeons, Herkimer County, N. Y., in 1831, as doctor of medicine. Relinquishing, however, his profession, he devoted himself to the study of botany under Professor Torrey; and he prosecuted for years this branch of natural history with such zeal and energy as ultimately to even surpass the fame of his distinguished preceptor, and to become the acknowledged chief of American naturalists in his chosen field.

In 1842 he was elected the Fisher professor of natural history at Harvard College, a position he retained for more than thirty years. From this college he received, in 1844, the degree of A. M., and from Hamilton College, in 1860, the degree of LL. D. He published various botanical manuals and systematic treatises, several of which became universally-accepted popular text-books. He was one of the original members of the National Academy of Sciences, incorporated by act of Congress March 3, 1863. From 1863 to 1873 he was president of the

American Academy of Arts and Sciences, and was president of the American Association for the Advancement of Science for the year 1872.

More than forty years ago, in the very infancy of this Institution, Dr. Gray, at the instance of its Secretary, undertook to prepare for publication, under its auspices, a comprehensive illustrated work on American Forest Trees. In the Secretary's third report (for 1849) it is recorded, with reference to contemplated "Reports on the Progress of Knowledge," that " the most important report now in progress is that on the Forest Trees of North America, by Dr. Gray, professor of botany in Harvard University. It is intended in this work to give figures from original drawings of the flowers, leaves, fruit, etc., of each principal species in the United States proper, for the most part of the size of nature, and so executed as to furnish colored or uncolored copies; the first being intended to give an adequate idea of the species, and the second for greater cheapness and more general diffusion. This work will be completed in three parts, in octavo, with an atlas of quarto plates, the first to be published next spring. - - - As the work will be adapted to general comprehension, it will be of interest to the popular as well as the scientific reader."

This very interesting and important enterprise, delayed by Dr. Gray's visit to Europe the following year, and afterward from time to time postponed by various hindrances, was never completed. Simultaneously with his engagement upon this great work, other interests and investigations were pressing upon his attention. A botanical expedition—assisted by the Institution—made by Mr. Charles Wright, through Texas and New Mexico in the summer and autumn of 1849, was rewarded by an extensive and valuable collection of the plants of these regions, which were placed in the hands of Dr. Gray; and in 1851 it was announced that his report on this new material was ready for publication. This memoir was issued in two parts, quarto size. Part I, comprising 146 pages of text, illustrated by ten engraved plates, was included in Vol. III of the Smithsonian Contributions to Knowledge, and Part II, comprising 119 pages, illustrated by 4 plates, was included in Vol. V of Contributions to Knowledge.

In the winter of 1854–'55 Dr. Gray delivered, in the lecture-room of this Institution, a course of nine lectures " On Vegetation."

In 1884, Dr. Gray presented to Harvard College his herbarium, containing more than 200,000 specimens, and his botanical library of more than 2,500 works; for the reception of which a fire-proof building was provided. In 1873, he resigned his professorship in the college, retaining, however, the charge of its herbarium. In 1874, he was selected by joint resolution of Congress a Regent of this Institution, taking the place made vacant by the death of Professor Agassiz, who had been a Regent for the preceding ten years.

DR. PETER PARKER, EX-REGENT.

While recounting the inroads made by death on the earlier portion of the membership of the Institution and its Board of Regents, it seems proper to notice also the demise of Dr. Peter Parker, who had been a Regent from 1868 to 1884, when he was induced to resign his position on the Board in consequence of infirmity and failing health. His death occurred at his residence in this city on the 10th day of January last (1888).

The stated annual meeting of the Board occurring on the following day (January 11, 1888), expression was given to the regret occasioned thereby, in the following preamble and resolution:

Whereas the Board has received the afflictive intelligence that the venerable Dr. Peter Parker, who for sixteen years was a member of the Board of Regents, and who for this whole period served with fidelity on its executive committee, has departed this life after a long career filled with useful labors in the service of God and of man: Therefore,

Be it resolved, That in the retrospect of such a life-career, protracted as it was beyond the limit usually allotted to men, and yet at each stage of its progress dedicated to beneficent works in the cause of religion, philanthropy, and science, we desire to testify our respect for the exalted worth and scrupulous conscientiousness which Dr. Parker brought to the discharge of every duty, and which during his connection with the government of this Institution were nobly exemplified by the zeal and diligence with which he ever watched and worked for its prosperity and usefulness, even during the later period of his honorable service, when the burden of years was added to the burden of official cares, and when with a less conscientious sense of public duty he might have claimed an exemption from the tasks of life.

DR. CHARLES RAU, CURATOR OF ANTIQUITIES.

Dr. Charles Rau, for many years in charge of the department of antiquities in the National Museum, was born in Belgium in 1826. He lived for a time in Germany and as a political exile came to America thirty years ago, landing at New Orleans December 23, 1848; lived for a time in Saint Louis; engaged in teaching at Belleville, Ill., and later went to New York City, still occupied as a teacher of languages. He had always been a deeply interested student of aboriginal remains, and had written many articles on the prehistoric condition of man. In 1875 he had charge of an exhibition of North American archæology for the display of the Institution in the Centennial Exhibition at Philadelphia.

He was in 1881 appointed curator of the department of antiquities in the National Museum. His health gave way in 1886, and in July, 1887, he went to the hospital of the University of Pennsylvania, where he died on the 25th of July. His body was brought to Washington and was buried in Oak Hill Cemetery, where a modest grave-stone bearing a suitable inscription has been erected to his memory.

Ile bequeathed to the National Museum his library, consisting of 715 bound volumes, and 1,722 volumes unbound; his archæological collec- tion comprising 1,920 specimens (ethnologic) and his collection of minerals and fossils.

These objects have been transferred to the Museum by his adminis- trator, Mr. Thomas Wilson. The books comprising the library are being arranged and catalogued, and will form the nucleus of a departmental library. The archæological specimens will be kept together and dis- played under the name of their donor. Almost the entire life of Dr. Rau was spent in archæologic studies. He was faithful, zealous, and devoted to science. He had the courage of his convictions and was ready to defend them before any person or tribunal, however august. He did what he could for the alleviation of human suffering and regret- ted he could not do more. The fruits of his scientific labors will be de- scribed in the Bibliographical Appendix to the Report of the National Museum in Part II of this Report.

In addition to the above, mention should be made of the deaths of the following employés of the Institution:

On June 8, 1888, Charles Wickliffe Beckham, formerly an assistant in the Department of Birds, died at his home near Bardstown, Ky. He had made several valuable contributions to American ornithological literature.

Mrs. L. S. Weaver, clerk and translator, died November 26, 1887. She had been employed in the Institution since 1876, having been ap- pointed upon the death of her first husband, L. Stoerzer, at that time chief taxidermist; and she rendered always willing and efficient service.

Capt. C. W. C. Dunnington, a respected citizen of Washington, for several years a watchman in the Museum, Frederick R. Parker, a clerk in the Institution, and Isaac Diggs, for twenty years a laborer and at- tendant, have also died during the year.

The following notice of Dr. Emil Bessels has been supplied by Dr. Dall:

Dr. Emil Bessels was born in Heidelberg, June 2, 1847. Educated at the University, and securing the degree of doctor in medicine, he was more disposed toward science and belles-lettres than to the practice of his profession. Being in easy circumstances he was enabled to follow his natural bent, and for a time was a student in zoology under Van Bene- den, and an assistant of Krauss at the Naturalien Cabinet, or Royal Museum of Würtemberg in Stuttgart. He became interested in Arctic discovery, and his first essay in this direction, under the encouragement of Petermann, of Gotha, was the well-known voyage of 1869 into the sea between Spitzbergen and Nova Zembla. By his observations on this journey he traced the influence of the Gulf Stream water east of Spitzbergen and added much to the scanty knowledge of this region then available. In 1870 he was called to the field as military surgeon, rendering services in the hospitals, which brought him a public commendation from the Grand Duke of Baden. In 1871 he came to America at Petermann's suggestion to join Hall's Polar Expedition as naturalist and surgeon. Most of the scientific results of this voyage were the fruit of his personal efforts. After the rescue of the survivors he returned to America, where for some years he was busy at the Smithsonian Institution in preparing for publication the scientific results of the voyage, one of the most striking of which was the proof first brought out by him of the insularity of Greenland, which he deduced from the tidal observations secured on the expedition. In 1876 his work was printed in quarto, under the title of "Report on the Scientific Results of the Polaris Expedition." Three years later he published through Englemann, at Leipzig, a German narrative of the expedition, illustrated largely from his own very artistic sketches. He projected a work on the Eskimo, to which he devoted much labor. An ethnological voyage undertaken on the United States steamer *Saranac* to the northwest coast of America was prematurely terminated by the wreck of that vessel in Seymour Narrows, British Columbia. He returned to Washington, where he prepared several contributions to Arctic and zoological literature. Through an unfortunate fire at his residence he lost his library, manuscripts, and collections in 1885, and subsequently returned to Germany, where he settled at Stuttgart. Here he was engaged in literary pursuits, the study of art, and in geographical instruction. He died after a short illness, March 30, 1888, and his remains were interred in the Cemetery, at Heidelberg.

Respectfully submitted.

S. P. LANGLEY,
Secretary of Smithsonian Institution.

APPENDIX TO SECRETARY'S REPORT.

APPENDIX I.

PROGRAMME OF ORGANIZATION OF THE SMITHSONIAN INSTITUTION.

[Presented in the First Annual Report of the Secretary, and adopted by the Board of Regents, December 13, 1847]

INTRODUCTION.—General considerations which should serve as a guide in adopting a plan of organization.

1. Will of Smithson. The property is bequeathed to the United States of America " to found at Washington, under the name of the Smithsonian Institution, an establishment for the increase and diffusion of knowledge among men."

2. The bequest is for the benefit of mankind. The Government of the United States is merely a trustee to carry out the design of the testator.

3. The Institution is not a national establishment, as is frequently supposed, but the establishment of an individual, and is to bear and perpetuate his name.

4. The objects of the Institution are (1) to increase, and (2) to diffuse knowledge among men.

5. These two objects should not be confounded with one another. The first is to enlarge the existing stock of knowledge by the addition of new truths; and the second, to disseminate knowledge, thus increased, among men.

6. The will makes no restriction in favor of any particular kind of knowledge; hence all branches are entitled to a share of attention.

7. Knowledge can be increased by different methods of facilitating and promoting the discovery of new truths; and can be most extensively diffused among men by means of the press.

8. To effect the greatest amount of good, the organization should be such as to enable the Institution to produce results, in the way of increasing and diffusing knowledge, which can not be produced either at all or so efficiently by the existing institutions in our country.

9. The organization should also be such as can be adopted provisionally, can be easily reduced to practice, receive modifications, or be abandoned, in whole or in part, without a sacrifice of the funds.

10. In order to compensate, in some measure, for the loss of time occasioned by the delay of eight years in establishing the Institution, a considerable portion of the interest which has accrued should be added to the principal.

11. In proportion to the wide field of knowledge to be cultivated, the funds are small. Economy should therefore be consulted in the construction of the building; and not only the first cost of the edifice should be considered, but also the continual expense of keeping it in repair, and of the support of the establishment necessarily connected with it. There should also be but few individuals permanently supported by the Institution.

12. The plan and dimensions of the building should be determined by the plan of the organization, and not the converse.

13 It should be recollected that mankind in general are to be benefited by the bequest, and that, therefore, all unnecessary expenditure on local objects would be a perversion of the trust.

14. Besides the foregoing considerations, deduced immediately from the will of Smithson, regard must be had to certain requirements of the act of Congress establishing the Institution. These are, a library, a museum, and a gallery of art, with a building on a liberal scale to contain them.

SECTION I

Plan of organization of the Institution in accordance with the foregoing deductions from the will of Smithson.

To increase knowledge: It proposed (1) to stimulate men of talent to make original researches, by offering suitable rewards for memoirs containing new truths; and (2) to appropriate annually a portion of the income for particular researches, under the direction of suitable persons.

To diffuse knowledge: It is proposed (1) to publish a series of periodical reports on the progress of the different branches of knowledge; and (2) to publish occasionally separate treatises on subjects of general interest.

DETAILS OF THE PLAN TO INCREASE KNOWLEDGE.

I. *By stimulating researches.*—1. Facilities afforded for the production of original memoirs on all branches of knowledge. 2 The memoirs thus obtained to be published in a series of volumes, in a quarto form, and entitled Smithsonian Contributions to Knowledge. 3. No memoir, on subjects of physical science, to be accepted for publication, which does not furnish a positive addition to human knowledge, resting on original research; and all unverified speculations to be rejected. 4. Each memoir presented to the Institution to be submitted for examination to a commission of persons of reputation for learning in the branch to which the memoir pertains; and to be accepted for publication only in case the report of this commission is favorable. 5. The commission to be chosen by the officers of the Institution, and the name of the author, as far as practicable, concealed, unless a favorable decision be made. 6. The volumes of the memoirs to be exchanged for the transactions of literary and scientific societies, and copies to be given to all the colleges and principal libraries in this country. One part of the remaining copies may be offered for sale; and the other carefully preserved, to form complete sets of the work, to supply the demand from new institutions. 7. An abstract, or popular account, of the contents of these memoirs to be given to the public through the annual report of the Regents to Congress.

II. *By appropriating a part of the income, annually, to special objects of research, under the direction of suitable persons.*—1. The objects and the amount appropriated to be recommended by counselors of the Institution. 2. Appropriations in different years to different objects, so that in course of time each branch of knowledge may receive a share. 3. The results obtained from these appropriations to be published, with the memoirs before mentioned, in the volumes of the Smithsonian Contributions to Knowledge. 4. Examples of objects for which appropriations may be made. (*a*) System of extended meteorological observations for solving the problem of American storms. (*b*) Explorations in descriptive natural history and geological, magnetical, and topographical surveys, to collect materials for the formation of a physical atlas of the United States (*c*) Solution of experimental problems, such as a new determination of the weight of the earth, of the velocity of electricity, and of light; chemical analyses of soils and plants; collection and publication of scientific facts accumulated in the offices of Government. (*d*) Institution of statistical inquiries with reference to physical, moral, and political subjects. (*e*) Historical researches and accurate surveys of places celebrated in American history. (*f*) Ethnological researches, particularly with reference to the different races of men in North America; also, explorations and accurate surveys of the mounds and other remains of the ancient people of our country.

I. *By the publication of a series of reports giving an account of the new discoveries in science, and of the changes made from year to year in all branches of knowledge not strictly professional.*—1. These reports will diffuse a kind of knowledge generally interesting, but which, at present, is inaccessible to the public. Some of the reports may be published annually, others at longer intervals, as the income of the Institution or the changes in the branches of knowledge may indicate. 2. The reports are to be prepared by collaborators eminent in the different branches of knowledge. 3. Each collaborator to be furnished with the journals and publications, domestic and foreign, necessary to the compilation of his report; to be paid a certain sum for his labors, and to be named on the title-page of the report. 4. The reports to be published in separate parts, so that persons interested in a particular branch can procure the parts relating to it without purchasing the whole. 5. These reports may be presented to Congress for partial distribution, the remaining copies to be given to literary and scientific institutions and sold to individuals for a moderate price.*

II. *By the publication of separate treatises on subjects of general interest.*—1. These treatises may occasionally consist of valuable memoirs translated from foreign languages, or of articles prepared under the direction of the Institution, or procured by offering premiums for the best exposition of a given subject. 2. The treatises should, in all cases, be submitted to a commission of competent judges previous to their publication. 3. As examples of these treatises, expositions may be obtained of the present state of the several branches of knowledge mentioned in the table of reports.

Section II.

Plan of organization, in accordance with the terms of the resolutions of the Board of Regents, providing for the two modes of increasing and diffusing knowledge.

1. The act of Congress establishing the Institution contemplated the formation of a library and a museum, and the Board of Regents, including these objects in the plan of organization, resolved to divide the income into two equal parts.

2. One part to be appropriated to increase and diffuse knowledge by means of publications and researches, agreeably to the scheme before given. The other part to be appropriated to the formation of a library and a collection of objects of nature and of art.

3. These two plans are not incompatible with one another.

4. To carry out the plan before described, a library will be required, consisting, first, of a complete collection of the transactions and proceedings of all the learned societies in the world; second, of the more important current periodical publications and other works necessary in preparing the periodical reports.

5. The Institution should make special collections, particularly of objects to illustrate and verify its own publications.

6. Also, a collection of instruments of research in all branches of experimental science.

---

* The following are some of the subjects which may be embraced in the reports:

I. *Physical Class.*—(1) Physics, including astronomy, natural philosophy, chemistry, and meteorology. (2) Natural history, including botany, zoology, geology, etc. (3) Agriculture. (4) Application of science to arts.

II. *Moral and Political Class.*—(5) Ethnology, including particular history, comparative philology, antiquities, etc. (6) Statistics and political economy. (7) Mental and moral philosophy. (8) A survey of the political events of the world, penal reform, etc.

III. *Literature and the Fine Arts.*—(9) Modern literature. (10) The fine arts, and their application to the useful arts. (11) Bibliography. (12) Obituary notices of distinguished individuals.

7. With reference to the collection of books, other than those mentioned above, catalogues of all the different libraries in the United States should be procured, in order that the valuable books first purchased may be such as are not to be found in the United States.

8. Also, catalogues of memoirs, and of books and other materials, should be collected for rendering the Institution a center of bibliographical knowledge, whence the student may be directed to any work which he may require.

9. It is believed that the collections in natural history will increase by donation as rapidly as the income of the Institution can make provision for their reception, and therefore it will seldom be necessary to purchase articles of this kind.

10. Attempts should be made to procure for the gallery of art casts of the most celebrated articles of ancient and modern sculpture.

11. The arts may be encouraged by providing a room, free of expense, for the exhibition of the objects of the Art Union and other similar societies.

12. A small appropriation should annually be made for models of antiquities, such as those of the remains of ancient temples, etc.

13. For the present, or until the building is fully completed, besides the Secretary, no permanent assistant will be required, except one to act as librarian.

14. The Secretary, by the law of Congress, is alone responsible to the Regents. He shall take charge of the building and property, keep a record of proceedings, discharge the duties of librarian and keeper of the museum, and may, with the consent of the Regents, *employ assistants.*

15. The Secretary and his assistants, during the session of Congress, will be required to illustrate new discoveries in science, and to exhibit new objects of art; distinguished individuals should also be invited to give lectures on subjects of general interest.

This programme, which was at first adopted provisionally, has become the settled policy of the Institution. The only material change is that expressed by the following resolutions, adopted January 15, 1855, viz:

Resolved, That the seventh resolution passed by the Board of Regents on the 26th of January, 1847, requiring an equal division of the income between the active operations and the museum and library, when the buildings are completed, be, and it is hereby, repealed.

Resolved, That hereafter the annual appropriations shall be apportioned specifically among the different objects and operations of the Institution in such manner as may, in the judgment of the Regents, be necessary and proper for each, according to its intrinsic importance, and a compliance in good faith with the law.

[Resolution of Board of Regents, adopted January 17, 1880, and at each successive annual meeting]

Resolved, That the income for the year be appropriated for the service of the Institution upon the basis of the report [of the Executive Committee], to be expended by the Secretary, with full discretion as to the items, subject to the approval of the Executive Committee.

APPENDIX II.

PUBLICATIONS OF THE YEAR.

SMITHSONIAN CONTRIBUTIONS TO KNOWLEDGE.

Of this series, no work has been published during the past year. A memoir on the archæology of North America has been for several years in course of preparation by Dr. Charles Rau, the late curator of the department of Pre-historic Antiquities, and several thousand dollars have been expended in the production of drawings by Mr. C. F. Trill and others, under Dr. Rau's direction, for the purpose of properly illustrating the work. Dr. Rau's illness at the beginning of the past fiscal year, and his death in July, 1887, have arrested the progress of this undertaking. The unfinished work will, however, be taken up by his successor, Mr. Thomas Wilson, and prosecuted to an early completion, and it is not improbable that this work may be published in the above series.

SMITHSONIAN MISCELLANEOUS COLLECTIONS.

Of this series three volumes have been published during the year, besides several independent treatises. Taking these in the order in which they appear in the printed lists, they are as follows:

591. "Synoptical Flora of North America: The Gamopetalæ; being a second edition of Vol. I, Part II, and Vol. II, Part I, collected," by Asa Gray, LL. D. Of these two portions, the earlier—the last part of the proposed first volume—comprises 480 pages, and the latter—being the commencing part of the proposed second volume—comprises 494 pages; forming in the aggregate, with introductory matter, an octavo volume of 986 pages. As long as forty years ago, Dr. Gray, in co operation with Dr. Torrey, undertook a comprehensive classification of the North American flora, which, however, never was completed, stopping with a synopsis of the polypetalous, and about half the gamopetalous divisions of the Dicotyledons, or to the close of the order of *Compositæ*. Ambitious of reconstructing and completing the long contemplated work, Dr. Gray, postponing the first part of Vol. I (the *Polypetalæ*), has taken up, for the second part of the volume, the *Gamopetalæ* as far as the completion of the *Compositæ*, and has continued the remaining orders of the Gamopetalæ as the first part of the succeeding volume. The lamented death of the author has left his great work still unfinished; the third division of the Dicotyledons (the *Apetalæ*), and the Monoctyledons having been designed to form the second part of Vol. II. The present two detached portions of successive volumes, however, have a unity in being occupied entirely with the *Gamopetalæ*, and they constitute a full and systematic descriptive catalogue or synopsis of this great division.

Several thousand dollars have been expended by the Institution in furthering this important botanical work, which probably cost the author nearly as much more. In consideration of this, Dr. Gray was allowed to issue for his own benefit a first edition of the work of 500 copies before the Institution attempted to publish its own edition, which has thus only lately appeared.

"Miscellaneous Collections, Vol. xxxi." This volume is occupied with the two parts of the "Flora of North America," by Dr. Asa Gray, just described; a separate edition of 500 copies of the work having been issued as "No. 591," for special distribution, according to the long-established policy of the Institution, and an edition of 1,000 copies being issued as a numbered volume of the "Collections," for deposit with the principal libraries and scientific societies of the world.

658. "Index to the Literature of the Spectroscope," by Alfred Tuckerman. This bibliography is designed to give a list of all the books and smaller treatises, especially contributions to scientific periodicals, on the spectroscope and spectrum analysis from the beginning of our knowledge upon the subject until July, 1887. The work is arranged as an alphabetical index to topics as well as of substances which have been spectroscopically examined, followed by an alphabetical list of the authors. It comprises 3,829 titles and the names of 799 authors, and forms an octavo volume of 433 pages, including introductory matter and supplement.

659. "A Table of Specific Gravity for Solids and Liquids (new edition, revised and enlarged)," by Frank Wigglesworth Clark. This work is a revised edition, entirely re-written, of specific gravity tables, by the same author, published by this Institution December, 1873, and a supplement to the same, published April, 1876. The melting and boiling temperature appended to many of the substances in these earlier tables have been omitted in the present. A general idea of the expansion given to this important series of density determinations may be suggested by the statement that the original work gave a list of 2,263 different substances, to which the supplement added nearly 700 more, while the present work presents a list of 5,227 distinct substances. And as many of the substances have had their specific gravities independently investigated by several eminent chemists, with slight variations in their results, it may be well to add that the tables actually include 14,465 separate determinations of these constants, averaging about two and three-fourths independent examinations to every substance catalogued. The large mass of material thus exhibited furnishes a creditable record, both of the rapid extension of minute chemical investigation in the last dozen years and of the diligence of the present compiler, Mr. Clark, who has himself, moreover, done very meritorious work in the direction of specific gravity determinations.

The work forms an octavo volume of 417 pages in all, and it is under consideration whether it may not be well, in view of the interest of chemists in the table and the demand for them, to put the sale copies in the hand of a publisher.

660. "Miscellaneous Collections," Vol. XXXII. This volume is made up of the two works last mentioned, in the order, first, Clark's Table of Specific Gravity; second, Tuckerman's Bibliography of Spectroscopic Analysis. It forms an octavo volume of 855 pages.

661. "Bulletin of the Philosophical Society of Washington," Vols. IX, X. Containing the minutes of the society and of the mathematical section for the years 1886, 1887, together with the proceedings of the Baird memorial meeting, held January 11, 1888. The bulletin for these two years forms an octavo volume of 376 pages, embellished with a phototype likeness of Professor Baird.

662. "Miscellaneous Collections," Vol. XXXIII. This volume consists entirely of the bulletins of the Philosophical Society of Washington, and is made up of No. 543. Bulletin, Vol. VI, for the year 1883; No. 592, Bulletin, Vol. VII, for the year 1884; No. 636, Bulletin, Vol. VIII, for the year 1885, and No. 661, just previously described, Bulletin, Vol. IX, for 1886, and Vol. X, for 1887. The following note is appended to the general table of contents on page 5: "With this volume (containing the last five volumes of the bulletins of the Philosophical Society of Washington) is terminated the re-issue of these proceedings in the series of Miscellaneous Collections. It may be stated that volumes 1, 2, and 3 of these bulletins formed Vol. XX of the Miscellaneous Collections; volumes 4 and 5 were included in Vol. XXV of the Miscellaneous Collections; and, lastly, volumes 6, 7, 8, 9, and 10, together with the Memorial Proceedings in honor of Professor Baird, and a full index of the whole ten volumes, constitute the present Vol. XXXIII of the Miscellaneous Collections." This last forms in all an octavo volume of 910 pages, with several wood-cuts and one plate portrait.

654. "Annual Report of the Board of Regents of the Smithsonian Institution," 1885, Part II. This second part, being the report of the United States National Museum to July, 1885, has at last been received from the Government Printing Office, more than a year later than the first part of the report for the same period, which related to the operations of the Smithsonian Institution proper. This long-delayed Part II consists of five sections: The first being the "Report upon the Condition and Progress of the U. S. National Museum during the half year ending June 30, 1885," by G. Brown Goode, assistant director, and occupying the first 54 pages of the work. The second, "Reports of the Curators and Acting Curators of the Museum upon the Progress of their Work" during the period, occupying pages 55 to 146. The third, a "Bibliography of the Museum" during the period, including the publications of the Museum and those of its officers and others relative to the museum material, and occupying pages 149 to 173. The fourth, a "List of Accessions to the Museum" during the period, together with descriptive notes and indices, occupying pages 175 to 243. The fifth, an appendix, consisting of a very full description of the "George Catlin Indian Gallery in the Museum, with memoir and statistics," by Thomas Donaldson, occupying 939 pages, illustrated by 142 plates and maps. This historical sketch (forming the greater portion of the volume) has proved to be in great popular demand, the applications made for it through Members of Congress having been unusually numerous, so that our stock of 7,000 copies is already nearly exhausted. The whole number of pages of this Part II of the report, including introductory matter and indices, is 1,220. If to this be added the illustrations, the aggregate would be equal to 1,500 octavo pages.

657. "Report of Prof. Spencer F. Baird, Secretary of the Smithsonian Institution, for the year 1886-'87." This last report of my lamented predecessor forms an octavo pamphlet of 27 pages. The volume to contain the above report, with its accompanying papers and general appendix, has not yet been set up at the Government Printing Office.

655. "Proceedings of the United States National Museum, Vol. IX, 1886." As already stated, this series, though primarily published at the expense of the Government by the authority of the Interior Department, has heretofore been re-issued by the Smithsonian Institution. The present volume, completed and collected during the past year, consists of descriptive papers by James E. Benedict, T. W. Blackiston, George H. Boehmer, Charles H. Bollman, E. D. Cope, W. H. Dall, George E. Doering, Charles L. Edwards, Carl H. Eigenmann, Barton W. Evermann, Fernando Ferari-Perez, Morton W. Fordyce, Elizabeth G. Hughes, David S. Jordan, George N. Lawrence, John Belknap Marcou, William G. Masyk, George P. Merrill, Richard Rathbun, Robert Ridgway, John A. Rider, John B. Smith, Rosa Smith, Leonard Steineger, Frederick W. True, and John Grant Wells. The collection forms an octavo volume of 720 pages, including introduction and index, and is illustrated by 25 plates, of which one is a chromo-lithograph.

565. "Bulletin of the United States National Museum, No. 32." This work is a Catalogue of Batrachians and Reptiles of Central America and Mexico, by E. D. Cope. The systematic catalogue is very largely based on the specimens contained in the National Museum. To each species is added a list of the localities at which it has been discovered, together with the name of the discoverer, or, in the absence of that, with the name of the author who is responsible for the correctness of the locality. The total number of genera included in the catalogue is 197, and of species 705, of which 135 are Batrachians and 570 Reptilians. The Bulletin forms a pamphlet of 98 octavo pages.

For many years the greater portion of the stereotype plates of Smithsonian publications has been stored in Philadelphia, in the fire-proof vaults of the Academy of

Natural Sciences, generously offered for that purpose. There having been no safe depository here for them, and much of the printing having been done in Philadelphia, the plates have been allowed to remain there undisturbed.

As the institution now has suitable store-rooms entirely fire-proof, and it is found that new editions of works can be printed to better advantage in this city, thereby avoiding the cost of transportation of the whole editions of publications, it is proposed to bring all these plates together in one depository—the basement of the Smithsonian Building.

It is to be regretted that the early volumes of "Smithsonian Contributions to Knowledge" were not stereotyped, and thus that it is impossible at the present time to reproduce full sets.

The plates of the annual reports from 1862 to 1886 (twenty-five years) are in possession of the Institution; and if supplies should be wanted for libraries or individuals, an edition might at any time be ordered by Congress, at the mere cost of paper and press-work.

Appendix III.

REPORT UPON INTERNATIONAL EXCHANGES, UNDER THE DIRECTION OF THE SMITHSONIAN INSTITUTION, FOR THE YEAR ENDING JUNE 30, 1888.

By J. H. KIDDER, Curator.

The business of the exchange office has increased during the year, as shown by the following table:

	1886–'87.	1887–'88.	Increase.
Packages received	52,218	75,107	22,889
Packages shipped, domestic	10,294	12,301	2,007
Packages shipped, foreign	41,424	62,306	20,882

or over 40 per cent. more packages were handled than during the previous year. This large increase is partly offset by the fact that an unusually large number of the packages received during the year just passed were single publications and of small size. The business of the office is set forth in detail by Exhibit A, hereto appended.

EXPENSE.

The expense of the service for the fiscal year has been $15,113.75, of which sum $12,000 were voted by Congress for the support of the "international exchanges with foreign countries," and $205.75 were refunded by the Patent Office, Signal Office, and a correspondent in South America, leaving a net deficit of $2,908, which has been paid from the Smithsonian fund.

The expenditure for the fiscal year 1888–'89 at the present rate, making no allowance for increase in the business of the office or in the pay of its employés, will be $16,050. If the amount estimated for last October, $15,000, shall be voted by Congress, there will be a deficit at the end of the year of at least $1,050, to be paid by the Smithsonian fund. Considering the probability that the business of the office will continue to increase during the next fiscal year, I think it reasonable to expect that the deficit will amount to as much as $2,000 by the 30th of June, 1889.

RE-IMBURSEMENT OF EXPENSES.

In former years a part of the deficit in the expense of transportation has been re-paid to the Smithsonian Institution by the different departments and bureaus of the Government, to which occasional appropriations have been granted by Congress for the purpose. During the past year such payments have been made by the Signal Office and Patent Office, but only of a part of their indebtedness, the usual appropriations to other bureaus having been omitted. The Institution has, therefore, desisted from sending bills during the year to offices of the National Government, bal-

103

ances against which now stand on its books to the following amounts, on the 30th of June, 1888 :.

Naval Observatory	$94.70
Office of Engineers, U. S. Army	16.80
Signal Office, U. S. Army	115.97
Geological Survey	1,922.25
Patent Office	112.25
Total	2,261.97

By the terms of the pending sundry civil bill for the year ending June 30, 1889, the Geological Survey will have an appropriation of $5,000 " for the purchase of necessary books for the library, and the payment for the transmission of public documents through the Smithsonian exchange." Other appropriations of a similar purport are to the Signal Office " for expenses * * * of prepaying, printing, *distributing*, and displaying weather maps, etc., $15,000," and to the War Department " for the transportation of charts and maps to foreign countries through the Smithsonian Institution, $100." By the legislative and executive bill it is proposed to appropriate to the Naval Observatory " for payment to the Smithsonian Institution for freight on Observatory publications sent to foreign countries, $136," and to the Library of Congress " for expenses of exchanging public documents for the publications of foreign governments, $1,500." By the same act an indefinite part of an appropriation of $3,000 to the Patent Office is " for the purchase of books and expenses of transporting publications of patents issued by the Patent Office to foreign governments," and a similar appropriation of $2,000 to the Bureau of Education is " for the distribution and exchange of educational documents," among other purposes.

It appears then to have been the intention of Congress that its specific appropriation for the exchange business shall be supplemented by special appropriations to some of the bureaus and departments of the Government, so that the charge of 5 cents per pound weight, imposed by the Regents of the Smithsonian Institution in 1878, may be met by them.

It is my opinion, and I therefore respectfully recommend, that this procedure, which had become necessary at the time of its original adoption by reason of the heavy annual expense of the exchanges to the Smithsonian fund, is no longer advantageous or economical and may wisely be discontinued. The average annual amount collected in this way between the years 1878 and 1887 was about $1,650. Allowing for the increased business of later years $2,000 should be added to the annual appropriation for Exchanges. The expense to the Government would be no greater than it now is, while the entire cost of the Exchanges would appear in a single appropriation. By the present system the cost of the service is actually larger than appears in the specific appropriation for Exchanges, and as the special appropriations to the different departments of the Government vary from year to year, and are often omitted altogether, an uncertain burden, which can not be accurately foreseen, is imposed upon the Smithsonian fund.

CORRESPONDENTS.

The number of correspondents has been increased during the year by 1,721 new names. There have been 100 losses by deaths of individuals or discontinuance of organizations.

The additions are classified as follows :

	Foreign.	Domestic.
Societies and institutions	240	96
Libraries	28	38
Individuals	953	366
Total	1,221	500

The total number of correspondents is now 10,973, classified as follows:

Foreign societies 4,194
Domestic societies 1,070
Foreign individuals 4,153
Domestic individuals 1,556

Total 10,973

GRAND DUCHY OF BADEN.

The Grand Duchy of Baden was one of the governments which were the first to accede to the proposition for international exchanges conveyed by Professor Henry's circular letter dated May 16, 1867, and two cases were shipped to Karlsruhe through the Smithsonian agent at Leipzig, on the 13th of June, 1873. After that time exchanges with Baden were discontinued until the visit of Mr. George H. Boehmer, special agent of the Exchange Office and of the National Library, to Europe in 1884. Mr. Boehmer succeeded in procuring from the Government of the Grand Duchy a set of the statutes (Official Gazette) from 1803 to 1885, and the proceedings of the Diet since 1849. Continuations of these series were shipped by the Government of Baden in August, 1887, and in February, 1888, Baden was again added to the list of governments receiving official international exchanges. Twenty-four boxes were sent thither on the 29th of February, 1888, and three shipments have been made since that time.

The number of Governments now taking part with the United States in these official exchanges is 41, as follows:

Argentine Republic,	England,	Prussia,
Austria,	Greece,	Queensland,
Baden,	Hayti,	Russia,
Bavaria,	Holland,	Saxony,
Belgium,	Hungary,	South Australia,
Buenos Ayres,	India,	Spain,
Brazil,	Italy,	Sweden,
Canada (Ottawa),	Japan,	Switzerland,
Canada (Toronto),	Mexico,	Tasmania,
Chili,	New South Wales,	Turkey,
Colombia, United States of,	New Zealand,	Venezuela,
Denmark,	Norway,	Victoria,
France,	Peru,	Wurtemberg.
North German Empire,	Portugal,	

It will be observed that several of these Governments are provincial or subordinate members of an empire, kingdom, or republic.

Of this number only seven, to wit, Belgium, Brazil, Italy, Portugal, Servia, Spain, and Switzerland, have acceded to the first of the two conventions, based upon a conference of representatives of different Governments at Brussels in 1886, and now pending before the Senate of the United States. *

The first of the two conventions relates to the "International Exchange of official documents and scientific publications;" the second, to the "immediate exchange of the daily official journals" of legislative assemblies.

To this second convention only six nations besides the United States have acceded, Switzerland withdrawing.

These conventions have been brought about mainly through the active interest of the Government of Belgium in the success and extension of the international exchange system. The history of the present agreements is of some interest in this connection, and has been set forth at length by Mr. George H. Boehmer in previous reports (see

---

* These conventions have been ratified by the President since the end of the fiscal year, but final ratifications have not yet been exchanged by the representatives of the contracting powers

especially Secretary's Reports for 1881, 1883, and 1887). It may be briefly summarized, as follows:

The delegates to the International Geographic Congress, which met at Paris in 1875, who were for the most part the diplomatic representatives of the Governments participating, passed a unanimous resolution, on the 12th of August, pledging themselves to request their Governments each to establish a bureau of International Exchanges; and on the 29th of January, 1876, those delegates who remained in Paris prepared and signed a set of rules for the management of the exchange business. At this time the "Bureau des Échanges" was established in Paris, under the direction of the Baron de Vatteville, and the rules agreed upon by the delegates and issued by this bureau were generally accepted by the Governments concerned, but no ratifications or other formal and international agreements were exchanged. England and Germany refused from the first to participate in either conferences or conventions relating to international exchanges.

With the hope of bringing about a more formal agreement, which should have the force and obligation of a treaty, the Government of Belgium called another conference, which met at Brussels in 1880, but at which the United States was not represented. This conference prepared an amended agreement for future consideration.

In the year 1883 (April 10) there was another, more formal, conference at Brussels, at which this country was represented by Mr. Nicholas Fish, the United States minister resident. By this conference the articles prepared by the meeting of 1880 were revised and further amended. At the instance of France the exchange bureaus were relieved from the duty of collecting official publications from the several departmental offices for transmission. The articles, as amended, were agreed to by the representative of the United States. A second special agreement was also drawn up, providing for the immediate transmission of parliamentary journals, annals, and public documents, which the representative of the United States refused to sign. A protocol, signed by all the powers represented, stated the purpose of the proposed conventions to be (1) the collection into a national library of each country of all official publications of every other; and (2) as many literary, scientific, and art publications as the bureaus could procure.

The articles agreed upon in 1883 were signed at a third Brussels conference in 1886, and on this occasion the representative of the United States, Mr. Lambert Tree, the minister resident, signed the additional convention providing for the immediate transmission of parliamentary daily journals, etc., which his predecessor had rejected in 1883. At this time France declined to participate further in the conferences, England and Germany still persisting in their refusal. As already stated, only seven Governments besides the United States have acceded to the general convention for international exchanges, and only six to the special agreement for the immediate exchange of the daily journals of legislative assemblies. With the thirty-four other Governments which take part in the international official exchanges this friendly commerce will probably continue in the future as it has in the past, upon the basis of mutual agreements between the parties concerned, but without the sanction or compulsion of treaty obligations.

The principal advantage accruing from these several conferences and conventions has been the establishment of a certain uniformity of procedure in the transactions of the exchange business by the agents of the countries interested.

The conventions themselves do not promise any definite improvement in the present system, from the point of view held by the Smithsonian Institution, the main stipulations for which it has contended not having been retained in the agreements now under consideration. These are, as stated by Professor Henry (circular letter dated May 16, 1867), and by Professor Baird (letter to Baron de Vatteville, dated February 8, 1879), that each exchange agency shall, (1) furnish an annual list of all the official publications of its Government, and (2) shall charge itself with the collection and forwarding of such publications. These provisions appeared in the agreement of

1875, the authorship of which is attributed principally to the representatives of France; were stricken out of the amended articles considered in 1883 at the instance of France; and in 1886 that Government declined to take further part in the conference.

It is, in fact, scarcely possible for the exchange offices of most foreign countries to procure all of the official publications of their Governments for exchange purposes, the publishing arrangements of the governmental departments being for the most part quite separate and distinct from one another, and there being no law, except in the United States and Belgium, requiring them to furnish copies for this purpose. It is indeed extremely difficult even for the exchange agent of a Government to ascertain what the official publications of the different departments and bureaus are.

The text of the two conventions as finally agreed to by the conference of 1886 is presented herewith as Exhibit B.

During the past year some unusual pains have been taken in the efforts to increase the number of official publications received from foreign countries, it appearing that the United States Government now sends out about twenty times as many packages to other Governments as it receives from them, and that this disproportion has been annually on the increase for several years past. (See Exhibit C.) With some difficulty and at the cost of much correspondence a list, still not complete, of French official publications has been compiled, containing four hundred and twenty-one titles. Of these the library of the Smithsonian Institution received during the calendar year 1887 thirty-nine titles and the National Library forty-one titles.

During the fiscal year 1887–'88 three shipments were received from the French Bureau des Échanges, on the 6th of June and the 8th of December, 1887, and the 12th of April, 1888, containing nine official packages for the Library of Congress. The number of titles contained in these nine packages can not now be precisely stated, but was probably not greater than that received during the calendar year.

On the other hand, there were four shipments of official publications to France from this country during the fiscal year, containing seven hundred and sixty-three packages of official publications.

What has just been said relates only to the international exchange of official publications, intended for the national libraries of the Governments participating. By far the larger part of all of the business of this office is actually governmental business, a considerable proportion of the so-called "literary and scientific" exchanges being really an exchange of official publications between the bureaus or official subdivisions of the different Governments, for the benefit of the bureau libraries, and not for that of central or national libraries already referred to (Exhibit B). *

Most of the foreign Government bureaus, and of our own as well, desire to enrich their individual libraries, and do not regard the deposit of one set of the publications

---

* These publications are as strictly a part of the "official or governmental" exchanges as are those provided for by the resolution of Congress granting fifty copies for foreign national libraries. While, therefore, long usage has sanctioned the designations "literary and scientific" and "official," in the sense explained above, I think that in the interest of convenience and intelligibility, hereafter it will be better to express simply the distinction which really exists, namely, that between the official and unofficial exchanges, by the adjections "governmental" and "miscellaneous;" meaning by the former all publications sent or received by the Government or its bureaus, and by the latter all others. The publications of the Smithsonian Institution, which are partly "governmental" and partly "miscellaneous," although divided so far as the exchange records and statistics are concerned, are accounted for as a whole by the office routine of the Institution. I am not aware of any other office or organization whose publications would not fall wholly within one or the other of these classes.

of other countries in the national library as an equivalent for some forty copies of their own publications.

If the clauses proposed by the Paris conference of 1875, and always urged by the Smithsonian Institution, requiring the preparation and exchange of annual lists of *all* official publications, and that all of those named in the lists should be furnished to each of the contracting parties, had been retained in the convention of 1886, and if the convention could be faithfully executed, an effective remedy for the shortcomings already indicated might have been found. The opposition of some of the Governments participating in the conferences however (notably France and Switzerland), and the final withdrawal of France and continued indifference of England and Germany, have made this remedy impossible. Something has been done during the past year, by persevering correspondence, and more may doubtless be effected hereafter in the same way, but the most promising plan yet tried has been the employment of a special agent to visit the European (as the most important) Government offices, and excite there an interest in the subject by personal explanation and argument. Mr. George H. Boehmer, of this office, was employed in this way in 1884, as has been already stated, with the result of much larger receipts than have been shown by any one year before or since. After Mr. Boehmer's return, however, the temporary interest which his mission had excited rapidly weakened. Many sets of publications which had been freely promised him (notably a complete set of the publications of the British Government) have not been sent, mainly because of indifference, and of the considerable labor and time required for preparing the sets for shipment.

It is not only foreign Governments, however, which show shortcomings in this matter. According to Hickox' monthly catalogue of Government publications, there were issued by the National Government and its bureaus, during the first six months of the year 1888, about eleven hundred separate titles, not considering single laws or articles forming parts of reports as distinct publications. While it is not possible until the volumes of Executive Documents, Miscellaneous Documents, and Reports have been finally collected and bound, to state precisely the number of separate volumes as finally distributed, it is safe to say that the total number for the six months was greatly in excess of the number of titles furnished for official exchanges. Of all the Executive Departments, for example, only the Light-House Board and the Signal Office furnished a part of their publications for this purpose.

The total number of separate titles furnished by the Public Printer during the six months for which this comparison is drawn was two hundred and ninety-five, including a considerable number of Army orders, reports of contested-election cases, and other matter not of a kind most valuable to foreign libraries. Such a comparison as this can, however, only be regarded as illustrative, since the publications furnished by the Public Printer are always at least a year old at the time of distribution.

The resolution of Congress, passed July 25, 1868, directing that fifty copies of every Government publication and every publication issued under the direction of the Government, shall be placed at the disposal of the joint committee of Congress on the Library for the purpose of the international exchanges, is sufficiently mandatory in its provisions, but, as above stated, has never been fully carried out. Efforts have been made from time to time by the Secretary of the Smithsonian Institution and the Librarian of Congress, with the assistance and support of the State Department and of members of both branches of Congress, which have been set forth at length in the reports on exchanges attached to the Secretary's reports for 1886 and 1887. I am pleased to be able to report that the receipts from the Public Printer during the last six months of the year, far as they fall short of the full and complete distribution contemplated by the law, show a decided increase over the number of titles received and shipped in previous months and years. The resolution is recited in Exhibit D, hereto appended.

As I have already said, it is not easy to get data for complete lists of the official publications of foreign countries, since they have not, to my knowledge, been brought together in a single catalogue by any government. Such lists are now in course of preparation by this office, and in April last a special card catalogue was begun of the titles of all foreign official publications which passed through the exchange office, so that by the end of another year it will be possible to state with some certainty which official publications each government gives to the international exchanges and which it withholds.

EFFICIENCY OF THE SERVICE.

Upon assuming general control of the office (March 19, 1888), I found that complaints and criticisms of the efficiency of the exchange system by individuals, societies, and Government bureaus were not infrequent. In some instances packages from abroad, notification of the shipment of which had been long ago received, had not been delivered; in others, packages sent hence had failed to reach their destination or had been unreasonably delayed. Every such complaint has been promptly and diligently followed up by correspondence, with the result, in all but three instances thus far, of tracing the missing package and explaining the delay. It has happened, rather surprisingly often, that the receipt of the complaining correspondent for the package he writes of is on file in this office, having been signed by some assistant in his absence, or by himself and forgotten. In the three cases not yet settled no reply has yet been received from the distributing agencies to which inquiries have been addressed.

The fact remains, however, that there have been and are still too many and too great delays in the transmission of exchange matter from its place of shipment to its destination, and for this state of things there are several reasons.

In the first place, delays occur in this office in forwarding packages addressed to countries which receive and send but few publications (such as Hawaii, Hayti, and many of the Central American republics), until a sufficient number has accumulated to fill one of the ordinary boxes. If these packages should be forwarded as soon as they are received the expense would be greater than the resources of the exchange service could bear. But the most serious delays occur in the exchange bureaus of other countries. For example, in a recent experimental shipment to London, Leipzig, and Paris, the boxes having been shipped on the same day and accompanied by letters asking for immediate acknowledgments, the agents of the Smithsonian Institution at London and Leipzig reported receipt in fourteen and fifteen days, respectively, and the Bureau des Échanges at Paris in forty days. Consignments frequently remain in the hands of foreign agencies for several months before being forwarded, while their consignees, having received prompt notice of their shipment from the consignor, very naturally regard such delays as unreasonable and unnecessary. Delays of this sort are, of course, quite beyond the control of the Smithsonian Institution, which can do nothing to remedy them otherwise than by correspondence and persuasion. Every such case is followed up as soon as brought to the notice of the office, and I fancy that I can already perceive some improvement in the promptness of shipment and some increased interest in the subject on the part of foreign correspondents.

Another occasional cause of delay arises from the fact that the Smithsonian Institution continues to be indebted to the generosity and public spirit of most of the ocean steam-ship lines for free transportation of its exchange boxes, as it has been for many years past. The list of transportation companies and business firms which continue to extend this valuable privilege has undergone no change since its publication in the report for 1886-'87, and is reproduced as Exhibit E, hereto annexed. It naturally and necessarily follows from this relation between the exchange service and the transportation companies that boxes bearing the Smithsonian mark are shipped, for the most part, by slow freight, and are subject to delays at times when paid freight is offered in excess of the capacity of the steamers. Under special circumstances the delay may become considerable, as, for instance, in the case of steamers from Naples, which have been hard pressed for space on account of the use of some of them as transports in the military operations of the Italian Government in Africa last year, when boxes shipped by the exchange office at Rome on December 1, 1887, were received in Washington on the 9th of April, 1888, having been detained meanwhile at Naples in the warehouses of the steam-ship company. At this writing boxes the shipment of which from Rome was announced more than four months ago have not yet been received. Delays of this sort are also beyond the control of the Smithsonian Institution, and will be likely to recur so long as the Institution continues to be unable to pay for its freight in the same way as other shippers.

With a view to doing away with this last-named cause of delay and to establishing the transportation service of the international exchanges upon an assured business basis an estimate of the probable annual cost of the service was drawn up last May, based upon the usual ocean steam-ship charges and the average amount of freight which may be expected to be forwarded yearly to each country. The sum estimated was $27,050, which you presented to Congress as an amended estimate, through the honorable Secretary of the Treasury, on the 31st of May last, but which has not yet been acted upon.

So far as my own observations extend, and, as I have every reason to believe, for a considerable time previous to my appointment, no avoidable delay has occurred either in the Smithsonian exchange bureau or in the offices of its paid agents at London and Leipzig. The quantity and frequency of shipments to and receipts from the different countries concerned in the international exchanges are set forth as Exhibit F, presented herewith.

But few changes in the routine have been made during the year. Since last March a printed card has been placed in each outgoing package, stating the date of its shipment from the Smithsonian Institution, and requesting that any unusual delay in its receipt be promptly reported. On the 1st of June the shipping office was separated from the receiving office with the result of a considerable economy of time and labor. Two circulars have been issued during the year; one on March 2, requesting the bureaus of the National Government to correct and complete their list of publications prepared in response to a circular issued in the previous year, and described in the annual report upon international exchanges for the year ending June 30, 1887; the other on May 31, requesting an expression of opinion from all the bureaus and offices of the National Government, as to the advantage to their business of increased speed in transmitting their publications. Both circulars were very generally answered and have been the means of procuring valuable information for use in the future.

I take pleasure in being able to bear witness to the faithfulness and efficiency of the employés in the exchange office. Although the greater part of them receive a less compensation than employés in other offices of the Government, and the duties which they perform are both laborious and responsible, the business of the office has not at any time been in arrears, nor has any employé incurred censure for misconduct or neglect. The foreign agencies of the exchange service, conducted by Messrs. William Wesley & Son at London and by Dr. Felix Flügel at Leipzig, are also in every way satisfactory as regards promptness and efficiency.

, Exhibit A.

Transactions of the exchange office of the Smithsonian Institution during the fiscal year 1887-'88.

	July.	August.	September.	October.	November.	December.	January.	February.	March.	April.	May.	June.	Total.
Number of packages received	17,974	3,985	1,056	10,641	1,875	2,045	4,415	9,686	2,845	3,120	11,184	6,281	75,107
Weight of packages received	21,506	13,060	3,190	13,958	9,126	8,089	11,197	15,920	6,385	6,215	18,415	22,567	149,630
Entries made:													
Foreign	4,412	5,702	1,178	1,536	1,794	2,366	4,086	2,850	2,858	2,050	2,074	9,242	40,148
Domestic	4,484	1,834	604	2,358	698	1,690	3,586	1,404	2,766	1,400	2,474	812	23,510
Ledger accounts:													
Foreign societies	4,159												4,194
Domestic societies	970												1,070
Foreign individuals	3,237												4,153
Domestic individuals	1,195												1,556
Domestic packages sent	2,242	917	302	1,179	559	845	1,793	702	1,383	700	1,237	442	12,301
Invoices written		1,864	840	744	847	555	925	1,159	605	725	1,365	3,896	13,525
Cases shipped abroad	43	63	38	63	28	19	32	81	43	20	86	147	663
Acknowledgments recorded:													
Foreign	731	849	383	1,171	769	1,061	612	607	341	443	584	419	7,970
Domestic	818	418	495	207	428	405	206	378	400	670	570	313	4,808
Letters recorded	81	83	77	91	92	85	103	91	72	80	69	138	1,062
Letters written	129	93	130	169	130	92	89	137	266	92	247	230	1,804

Exhibit B.

CONVENTION CONCERNING THE INTERNATIONAL EXCHANGES FOR OFFICIAL DOCUMENTS AND SCIENTIFIC AND LITERARY PUBLICATIONS.

[Translation from the French.]

The President of the United States of America, His Majesty the King of the Belgians, His Majesty the Emperor of Brazil, Her Majesty the Queen Regent of Spain, His Majesty the King of Italy, His Majesty the King of Portugal and of the Algarves, His Majesty the King of Servia, the Federal Council of the Swiss Confederation, desiring to establish, on the basis adopted by the conference which met at Brussels from the 10th to the 14th April, 1883, a system of international exchanges of the official documents and of the scientific and literary publications of their respective States, have appointed for their plenipotentiaries, to wit:

The President of the United States of America, Mr. Lambert Tree, minister resident of the United States of America at Brussels, His Majesty the King of the Belgians, the Prince de Caraman, his minister of foreign affairs and the Chevalier de Moreau, his minister of agriculture, industry, and public works,

His Majesty the Emperor of Brazil, the Count de Villeneuve, his envoy extraordinary and minister plenipotentiary near His Majesty the King of the Belgians,

Her Majesty the Queen Regent of Spain, Mr. de Tavira, chargé d'affaires ad interim of Spain at Brussels,

His Majesty, the King of Italy, the Marquis Maffei, his envoy extraordinary and minister plenipotentiary near His Majesty the King of the Belgians,

His Majesty the King of Portugal and of the Algarves, the Baron de Sant'Anna, envoy extraordinary and minister plenipotentiary of His Very Faithful Majesty,

His Majesty the King of Servia, Mr. Marinovitch, his envoy extraordinary and minister plenipotentiary near His Majesty the King of the Belgians,

The Federal Council of the Swiss Confederation, Mr. Rivier, its special plenipotentiary,

Who, after having communicated between themselves their full powers, which are found in good and due form, have agreed upon the following articles:

ARTICLE I. There shall be established in each of the contracting states, a bureau charged with the duty of the exchanges.

ART. II. The publications which the contracting states agree to exchange are the following:

1st. The official documents, parliamentary and administrative, which are published in the country of their origin.

2nd. The works executed by order and at the expense of the Government.

ART. III. Each bureau shall cause to be printed a list of the publications that it is able to place at the disposal of the contracting states.

This list shall be corrected and completed each year and regularly addressed to all the bureaus of exchange.

ART. IV. The bureaus of exchange will arrange between themselves the number of copies which they may be able eventually to demand and furnish.

ART. V. The transmission shall be made directly from bureau to bureau. Uniform models and formulas will be adopted for the memoranda of the contents of the cases, as well as for all the administrative correspondence, requests, acknowledgments of reception, etc.

ART. VI. For exterior transmissions, each state assumes the expense of packing and transportation to the place of destination. Nevertheless when the transmissions shall be made by sea, special arrangements will regulate the share of each state in the expense of transportation.

ART. VII. The bureaus of exchange will serve, in an official capacity, as intermediaries between the learned bodies and literary and scientific societies, etc., * * * of the contracting states for the reception and transmission of their publications.

It remains, however, well understood that, in such case, the duty of the bureaus of exchange will be confined to the free transmission of the works exchanged, and that these bureaus will not in any manner take the initiative to bring about the establishment of such relations.

ART. VIII. These provisions apply only to the documents and works published after the date of the present convention.

ART. IX. The states which have not taken part in the present convention are admitted to adhere to it on their request.

This adhesion will be notified diplomatically to the Belgian Government, and by that Government to all the other signatory states.

ART. X. The present convention will be ratified and the ratifications will be exchanged at Brussels as soon as practicable. It is concluded for ten years from the day of the exchange of ratifications, and it will remain in force beyond that time, so long as one of the Governments shall not have declared six months in advance that it renounces it.

In witness whereof the respective plenipotentiaries have signed it, and have thereunto affixed their seals.

Done at Brussels in eight copies the 15th of March, 1886.

LAMBERT TREE.	[SEAL.]	JOSÉ MA. DE TAVIRA.	[SEAL.]
PR. DE CARAMAN.	[SEAL.]	MAFFEI.	[SEAL.]
CHEVALIER DE MOREAU.	[SEAL.]	BARON DE SANT'ANNA,	[SEAL.]
COMTE DE VILLENEUVE.	[SEAL.]	I. MARINOVITCH.	[SEAL.]
		ALPHONSE RIVIER,	[SEAL.]

CONVENTION FOR ASSURING THE IMMEDIATE EXCHANGE OF THE OFFICIAL JOURNAL, AS WELL AS OF THE PARLIAMENTARY ANNALS AND DOCUMENTS.

[Translation from the French]

¯ The President of the United States of America, His Majesty the King of the Belgians, His Majesty the Emperor of Brazil, Her Majesty the Queen Regent of Spain, His Majesty the King of Italy, His Majesty the King of Portugal and of the Algarves, His Majesty the King of Servia, desiring to assure the immediate exchange of the Official Journal, as well as of the parliamentary annals and documents of their respective states, have named as their plenipotentiaries, to wit:

The President of the United States of America, Mr. Lambert Tree, minister resident of the United States of America at Brussels,

His Majesty the King of the Belgians, the Prince de Caraman, his minister of foreign affairs, and the Chevalier de Moreau, his minister of agriculture, industry, and public works,

His Majesty the Emperor of Brazil, the Count de Villeneuve, his envoy extraordinary and minister plenipotentiary near His Majesty the King of the Belgians,

Her Majesty the Queen Regent of Spain, Mr. de Tavira, chargé d'affaires ad interim of Spain, at Brussels,

His Majesty the King of Italy, the Marquis Maffei, his envoy extraordinary and minister plenipotentiary near His Majesty the King of the Belgians,

His Majesty the King of Portugal and of the Algarves, the Baron de Sant'Anna, envoy extraordinary and minister plenipotentiary of His Very Faithful Majesty,

His Majesty the King of Servia, Mr. Marinovitch, his envoy extraordinary and minister plenipotentiary near His Majesty the King of the Belgians,

Who, after having communicated between themselves their full powers, found in good and due form, have agreed upon the following articles:

ARTICLE I. Independently of the obligations which result from article 2 of the General Convention of this day, relative to the exchange of official documents and of scientific and literary publications, the respective Governments undertake to have transmitted to the legislative chambers of each contracting State, as fast as their publication, a copy of the official journal, as well as of the parliamentary annals and documents which are given publicity.

ART. II. The States which have not taken part in the present Convention are admitted to adhere thereto on their request.

This adhesion will be notified diplomatically to the Belgian Government, and by that Government to all the other signatory States.

ART. III. The present Convention will be ratified, and the ratifications will be exchanged at Brussels as soon as practicable. It is concluded for ten years from the day of the exchange of the ratifications, and it will remain in force beyond that time, so long as one of the Governments shall not have declared six months in advance that it renounces it.

In witness whereof, the respective Plenipotentiaries have signed it, and have thereunto affixed their seals.

Done at Brussels, in seven copies, the 15th of March, 1886.

LAMBERT TREE.	[SEAL.]	JOSÉ MA. DE TAVIRA.	[SEAL.]
PRINCE DE CARAMAN.	[SEAL.]	MAFFEI.	[SEAL.]
CHEVALIER DE MOREAU.	[SEAL.]	BARON DE SANT'ANNA.	[SEAL.]
COMTE DE VILLENEUVE.	[SEAL.]	I. MARINOVITCH.	[SEAL.]

— — —

EXHIBIT C.

OFFICIAL GOVERNMENT EXCHANGES.

During the year ending June 30, 1888, the number of packages sent abroad to those Governments participating in the Government exchanges was 36,445.

The number of packages received during the same time (besides 13 boxes of book purchased by the Library of Congress in England) was 1,530, as follows:

From Austria	219	From Italy	164
From France	9	From Norway	2
From Great Britain	2	From Sweden	30
From Germany	1,104		
			1,530

EXHIBIT D.

A RESOLUTION TO CARRY INTO EFFECT THE RESOLUTION APPROVED MARCH 2, 1867, PROVIDING FOR THE EXCHANGE OF CERTAIN PUBLIC DOCUMENTS. (No. 72.)

Resolved by the Senate and House of Representatives of the United States in Congress assembled, That the Congressional Printer, whenever he shall be so directed by the Joint Committee on the Library, be, and he hereby is, directed to print fifty copies, in addition to the regular number, of all documents hereafter printed by order of either house of Congress, or by order of any Department or Bureau of the Government; and whenever he shall be so directed by the Joint Committee on the Library one hundred copies additional of all documents ordered to be printed, in excess of the usual number, said fifty or one hundred copies to be delivered to the Librarian of Congress, to be exchanged, under the direction of the Joint Committee on the Library, as provided by the joint resolution approved March 2, 1867.

SEC. 2. *And be it further resolved,* That fifty copies of each publication printed under the direction of any Department or Bureau of the Government, whether at the Congressional Printing Office or elsewhere, shall be placed at the disposal of the Joint Committee on the Library, to carry out the provision of said resolution.

Passed July 25, 1868.

EXHIBIT E.

LIST OF STEAM-SHIP COMPANIES AND OTHERS GRANTING TO THE SMITHSONIAN INSTITUTION FREE TRANSPORTATION FOR ITS BOXES AND PACKAGES, DURING THE YEAR ENDING JUNE 30, 1888.

Allan Steam-ship Company (A. Schumacher & Co., agents), Baltimore.
Anchor Steam-ship Line (Henderson & Brother, agents), New York.
Atlas Steam-ship Company (Pim, Forwood & Co., agents), New York.
Bailey, H. B., & Co., New York.
Bixby, Thomas E., & Co., Boston, Mass.
Borland, B. R., New York.
Boulton, Bliss & Dallett, New York.
Cameron, R. W.. & Co., New York.
Compagnie Générale Transatlantique (L. de Bébian, agent), New York.
Cunard Royal Mail Steam-ship Line (Vernon H. Brown & Co., agents), New York.
Dennison, Thomas, New York.
Florio Rubattino Line, New York.
Hamburg American Packet Company (Kunhardt & Co., agents), New York.
Inman Steam-ship Company, New York.
Merchants' Line of Steamers, New York.
Muñoz y Espriella, New York.
Murray, Ferris & Co., New York.
Netherlands American Steam Navigation Company (H. Cazaux, agent), New York.
New York and Brazil Steam-ship Company, New York.
New York and Mexico Steam-ship Company, New York.

North German Lloyd (agents, Oelrichs & Co., New York; A. Schumacher & Co., Baltimore).

Pacific Mail Steam-ship Company, New York.

Panama Railroad Company, New York.

Red Star Line (Peter Wright & Sons, agents), Philadelphia and New York.

White Cross Line of Antwerp (Funch, Edye & Co., agents), New York.

Wilson & Asmus, New York.

Exhibit F.

SHIPMENTS AND RECEIPTS BY INTERNATIONAL EXCHANGE DURING THE YEAR ENDING JUNE 30, 1888.

Country.	Shipments		Receipts	
	No. of cases.	No. of shipments.	No. of cases.	No. of shipments.
Algeria*	1	1		
Argentine Republic	11	8		
Austria-Hungary†	36	21		
Baden†	26	3		
Bavaria†	4	4		
Belgium	19	12	8	3
Brazil	11	8	2	1
British Guiana	1	1		
Buenos Ayres	4	4		
Canada	15	11	7	1
Cape of Good Hope	1	1		
Chili	8	8		
China	2	2		
Colombia (United States of)	5	5		
Costa Rica	1	1		
Cuba	2	2		
Denmark	10	8	2	2
Dutch Guiana	1	1		
Ecuador	1	1		
Egypt	2	2		
France	59	21	7	2
Germany	76	22	55	17
Great Britain and Ireland (including the colonies not mentioned separately)	96	28	51	32
Greece	5	5		
Guatemala	1	1		
Hayti	4	4		
India‡	11	8		
Italy	33	13	13	5
Jamaica	1	1		
Japan	18	9		
Liberia	2	2		
Mexico	13	8	3	3
Netherlands	14	9	3	2
New South Wales‡	10	7		
New Zealand§	10	7		
Norway	11	8	1	1
Peru	6	6		

SHIPMENTS AND RECEIPTS BY INTERNATIONAL EXCHANGE DURING THE YEAR ENDING
JUNE 30, 1888—Continued.

Country.	Shipments.		Receipts.	
	No. of cases.	No. of shipments.	No. of cases.	No. of shipments.
Polynesia........	1	1	....	....
Portugal.............	8	6	....	....
Prussia†	4	4	....	....
Queensland§..............................	8	7	....	....
Russia.......	26	12	8	4
Saxony†	4	4	....	... .
South Australia§	7	7	....	....
Spain...	8	7	....	....
Sweden§	15	9	....	....
Switzerland†	19	9	....	....
Tasmania§.....................................	5	5	....	....
Trinidad	1	1	....	....
Turkey	5	5	....	....
Uruguay	2	2	....	....
Venezuela	6	6	....	....
Victoria§	9	7	....	....
Würtemberg†	4	4	....	....
	603	359	160	73

* Returns made through French Exchange Bureau.
† Returns included under Germany.
‡ Returns included under Great Britain and a portion received directly by mail.
§ Returns received directly by mail (a small number of parcels).

APPENDIX IV.

CIRCULARS RESPECTING PERIODICALS.

CIRCULAR TO THE CURATORS OF THE U. S. NATIONAL MUSEUM.

MARCH 19, 1887.

DEAR SIR: It is my desire to obtain from you (1) a list of those periodicals, whether transactions of societies or otherwise, which you deem most nearly indispensable to your own department. This inquiry is irrespective of the fact that the Museum does already possess them or not, and the list should be confined to the most essentially necessary titles; if possible, not over twenty in number.

I may add, to make my meaning plainer, that standard transactions of well-known societies concerned in all branches of science, such as the Royal Society of London, the Comptes Rendus de l'Institut of Paris, etc., and well known periodicals admitting the discussion of all scientific topics; such as Science, the American Journal of Science, Nature, etc., are excluded from such a list, which is meant to cover only those technical periodicals of most special use to your own department.

In addition to this list, and quite distinct from it, I should be pleased to have you give a list (2) of recent serials, whether transactions or otherwise, of interest in connection with your special investigations, even if not exclusively devoted to them. To be more definite, let us say anything of real importance or even considerable promise commenced within the past twelve years. There need be no limit to the number of titles in *this* list, but the more important one should have a distinctive check; and I should be very glad if it might suit your convenience to let me have it in this week or next.

While the above two lists are especially important and are desired at your earliest convenience, I should be pleased to have you supply me in addition with a list of every serial publication which a worker in your field may expect to have not wholly infrequent occasion to consult; and here again I should be glad to have you indicate those of most value.

S. P. LANGLEY,
Assistant Secretary.

GENERAL CIRCULAR.

JUNE 15, 1887.

DEAR SIR: The Smithsonian Institution, in pursuit of the object of its foundation, the "increase and diffusion of knowledge among men," has always aimed to keep a complete list of all transactions and proceedings of learned societies and of all journals devoted to science and the useful arts throughout the world. This, at least, is the aim; but it must often fall short of the fulfillment of so large a purpose and from time to time find its lists need revising, and this in two different particulars. First, in adding to its lists new societies or new periodicals which have arisen since the last revisal; second, in repairing lacunæ in its sets of long established society transactions or technical journals, and for this end it needs to know which still maintains a prominent place, so that gaps in the more important ones shall receive first attention.

It has been suggested to me that you are able, and may perhaps be willing, to assist us by supplying under these two heads the names of those special transactions

117

or journals which you would like to see made accessible to every student of the subject of ———— ————, with which your own name is here associated.

The subject of ———— ———— is, of course, divisible into others, such as ————
————, and we address ourselves to you in the hope that you can oblige us with the
names of any meritorious publications, whether foreign or domestic, devoted either
to ———— ———— in general, or to any such of its subdivisions.

To make our wants entirely clear, let me explain that the Institution does not ordinarily need to be informed of the names of societies or journals dealing with all
departments of knowledge, but only of such transactions of societies and the names
of such journals as are concerned chiefly, if not wholly, with the subject in question, or which, at any rate, are frequently consulted by its special students.

It is chiefly for such technical publications that we desire lists under the two
heads already named. To repeat: First, of those transactions of societies or periodicals devoted to the principal subject in question, or to some of its branches which
have been established within the past twelve or fifteen years and which you know
to be frequently consulted; second, of those which, being long established, are of
now most generally recognized importance.

I venture to address to you this outlined plan without having any claim upon
your kindness other than this, that the single purpose of this request is to make the
Smithsonian Library more immediately useful to every student in your own department, and that nothing can contribute more directly to this end than your furnishing the desired list, with which, if you can oblige me, I beg we may be favored
within the coming month.

In case you do not feel that your time will allow you to make it complete, I beg
you will not, on this account, refuse your help altogether, but rather that you will
put down, if only imperfectly, the transactions or journals best known to you and
which seem most desirable in connection with the general subject or with any of its
divisions as indicated.

I have the honor to be, very respectfully, your obedient servant,

S. P. LANGLEY,
Acting Secretary.

Blank form accompanying the circular.

List of desirable journals or transactions commenced within the past fifteen years,
specially devoted to ———— ———— or to any of its departments or subdivisions, as

APPENDIX V.

ORGANIZATION OF LIBRARY.

1. By act of Congress of April 5, 1866, the Library of the Smithsonian Institution is to be kept with the Library of Congress, but with the provision that the Institution shall continue to enjoy its customary use of it. The following regulations refer only to those books which, under the above proviso, are retained at the Smithsonian Institution proper, or in its Museum Library.

2. By order of the Secretary, after April 1, 1887, these are under the general direction of the Assistant Secretary, in charge of the library placed in the immediate charge of a librarian, whose title shall be Librarian of the Smithsonian Institution, and whose duty it shall be to decide what books shall be retained from the Library of Congress in a central library under his charge. The following regulations are intended for the better execution of the aforesaid order.

SECTIONAL LIBRARIES.

3. Sectional libraries may be formed by the officers of the Smithsonian Institution, namely, the assistant secretaries and the chief clerk, and also by the curators and acting curators and the editor. Curators and acting curators are permitted, subject to the approval of the assistant secretary in charge of the Museum, to form sectional libraries to be kept in their respective offices, but this shall only be done by withdrawing from the general collection such books as relate exclusively to the objects under their care. Dictionaries, cyclopædias, journals, or any works other than such as relate exclusively to the special department can not form a part of such a sectional library, except upon the recommendation of the librarian, approved by one of the assistant secretaries.

4. The official in charge of each sectional library shall be responsible for its safe keeping, and shall on no account lend the books.

5. Books in the sectional library must be returned to the central library before they can be issued for use outside of the office or room to which they are accredited.

6. The books of each sectional library shall be kept separate from all other books in the rooms of the official or curator, in distinct cases, the locks of which shall be controlled by a master key in the hands of the librarian, who may, at stated times, examine them, and call the attention of the curators to any deficiencies.

7. No person who is not a member of the scientific staff of the Museum shall withdraw books or other matter without special written permission from one of the officers of the Smithsonian Institution. Persons taking books from the central library shall be responsible for the safe keeping of the same, and shall make good any losses. They shall not be allowed to withdraw other books until those which are lost have been restored.

8. The librarian shall have authority to decide what books are suitable for any curator's sectional library, and to recall any book not in a sectional library within two weeks. Permanent recalls of books from sectional libraries may be made, as well as temporary calls. In case of certain rare or costly or encyclopedic works, or in other special instances, the librarian shall be authorized to designate books which shall in no case be taken from the library. This regulation shall not apply to

119

any books now actually in the office of the editor. All books and other matter not in the sectional library shall be at all times subject to recall by the librarian.

9. The librarian will be expected to exercise his discretion as to the books to be withdrawn from the Congressional Library, but will (in the absence of special cause to the contrary) recall any book upon receiving a written request for the same.

10. The librarian shall annually, or oftener, report to the Assistant Secretary, in charge of the library, any defective series, any missing books, or any new serials, or books which are specially desirable.

REGULATIONS CONCERNING ENTRY AND ACKNOWLEDGMENT OF BOOKS.

11. All books, pamphlets, periodicals, maps, and other publications acquired by the Smithsonian Institution through exchange or donation or purchase shall be separately entered by the librarian, who shall prepare a reference list, with the aid of which he shall immediately upon their receipt from the chief clerk divide them into two classes, one of which is to be fully entered within a day of its receipt; the other to be fully entered in any case at some time within the current week.

12. It shall be an invariable rule that such a full entry, to consist of both a day-book and a ledger-account entry, shall be made within the above-specified time for every separate book, or pamphlet or map, without exception ; but it is understood that this ledger account may be in the form of a card catalogue.

13. Against every title there shall be entered in the day-book the letter " C " (Smithsonian Library, deposited in Library of Congress), or "G" (Smithsonian Library, deposited with Surgeon General), or " I " (Smithsonian Library, deposited at the Institution) ; and it shall be the duty of the librarian to see that all books of the first class are prepared for delivery to the Librarian of Congress within the current week.

14. The librarian shall notify the exchange department within the current week of any new correspondent on his books, and shall also acknowledge receipt to the senders or donors of every article at stated times, at intervals of not more than a year, and shall make a record of such entry, with the date of acknowledgment opposite to the entry of the work in question.

15. It shall be the duty of the librarian at all times to hold these books open to the inspection of the Librarian of Congress, and to report to him the place and condition of any work under his charge in answer to any specific inquiry.

16. In addition to the books which are included in the Smithsonian deposit in the Library of Congress, and so stamped, there are certain books procured by the Smithsonian Institution for use in the National Museum. These shall be distinctively marked ; and it is understood that while they form no part of the above-described books of the Smithsonian deposit in the Library of Congress, they are in other respects to be treated in accordance with the above regulations. No book or chart belonging to the Smithsonian Institution is exempt from them unless procured for the specific use of an officer of the Smithsonian, as above designated, and distinctively stamped as belonging to his office.

The above rules will take effect on and after this date.

S. P. LANGLEY,
Assistant Secretary, in charge of Library.

NOTE (added December 3, 1887).—Under the last clause come books purchased especially for the office of the Secretary, Assistant Secretary, or chief clerk, forming "office libraries," and for these it is understood that the librarian's responsibility ceases when he has distinctively stamped each, entered it distinctively on the card catalogue, and also in a separate list catalogue. Indispensable books of reference in exchange department, etc., form part of chief clerk's office library.

S. P. LANGLEY,
Secretary.

NOTE (added February 13, 1888).—This last clause above cited is to be understood as including the books purchased at the expense of the Museum appropriation, but not necessarily books obtained by exchange for Museum publications, as it would be difficult, if not impossible, always to discriminate these under our present system. This point is reserved for future consideration, but provisionally it is understood that the librarian is to send books to the Library of Congress if not evidently meant for the Museum.

S. P. LANGLEY,
Secretary.

GENERAL APPENDIX

TO THE

SMITHSONIAN REPORT FOR 1888.

ADVERTISEMENT.

The object of the GENERAL APPENDIX to the Annual Report of the Smithsonian Institution is to furnish summaries of scientific discovery in particular directions; occasional reports of the investigations made by collaborators of the Institution; memoirs of a general character or on special topics, whether original and prepared expressly for the purpose, or selected from foreign journals and proceedings; and briefly to present (as fully as space will permit) such papers not published in the "Smithsonian Contributions" or in the "Miscellaneous Collections" as may be supposed to be of interest or value to the numerous correspondents of the Institution.

124

RECORD OF SCIENCE FOR 1887 AND 1888.

ASTRONOMY FOR 1887, 1888.

By WILLIAM C. WINLOCK.

The following record of the progress of Astronomy during the years 1887 and 1888 is presented in essentially the form adopted by Professor Holden in 1879. It is thought that this form is most suitable for an annual record, as it furnishes a series of reference notes for those especially interested in the study of astronomy, and at the same time a condensed review for the general reader.

The writer has made free use of reviews and abstracts which have appeared in the Bulletin Astronomique, the Observatory, Nature, the Athenæum, and other periodicals.

COSMOGONY.

Dr. Carl Braun, S. J., formerly director of the Kalocsa Observatory, has collected in a book of 167 pages a series of essays, first published in the Catholic periodical Natur und Offenbarung in 1885–'86, in which he enters into a scientific discussion of the evolution of the universe, more particularly the formation of the sun and planets. His theory demands a structureless, motionless, tenuous nebula, its particles endowed with gravity and atomic repulsion. Such a nebula, if perfectly homogeneous, should give birth to one portentous solitary sun. But, in point of fact, it would possess innumerable, almost imperceptible, local irregularities, which, forming so many centers of attraction, would eventually lead to the breaking up of the nebula into a vast multitude of separate fragments. On one of these, the destined progenitor of the solar system, we are asked to concentrate our attention. The manner of its development is, however, a widely different one from that traced by Laplace, who assumed the needful rotation and left the rest to work itself out spontaneously. Dr. Braun, on the other hand, assumes less to begin with, but invokes adventitious aid in emergencies. He ascribes the rotation of the original solar nebula to the impact of masses drawn in from the depths of space, comet-like projectiles, endowed with energy external to the system. These masses would affect the outer shell con-

stituting the nebula more than they would the inner, and the result is
a central condensation surrounded by an ellipsoidal atmosphere revolving with increasing velocity as we proceed outwards from the center.
Instead of supposing that the planets are formed from rings detached
from this nebula by over-spinning, Braun assumes that their formation
is determined simply by centers of condensation which existed in the
nebula itself. These formations have commenced at distances from the
central nucleus much greater than the present distances of the planets,
and the immediate result is an approach to the sun within a distance
at which its attraction is balanced by the outward gaseous pressure and
the centrifugal force. The incipient planet, animated with the greater
angular velocity of the stratum to which it originally belonged, revolves
now at a rate slightly superior to that of the new medium in which it
finds itself. Hence the possibility of its sweeping up and annexing
fresh matter as it proceeds along the coils of its narrowing orbit, until
a point is reached when the planet, or even sun, has drawn in all the
matter which stood in its way, and gravity alone exactly balances centrifugal force. The planet then revolves in an orbit sensibly the same
as at present.

As the planet in approaching the sun has encountered strata of increasing density, so that the tangential resistance on the side towards
the sun has always been greater than on the opposite side, it is easy to
see that a planetary or "direct" rotation must be set up in the direction
of revolution. In order to explain the rotation of Neptune, which is
probably, like its satellite, retrograde, it is necessary to suppose that
the birth of the planet was preceded by the formation of a ring, while
Uranus is regarded as a "limiting instance" between the annular and
the nuclear methods of generation.

Ingenious explanations are derived for the rapid motion of Phobos,
the inner satellite of Mars, for the swifter rotation of the larger planets,
and for the increase in their density and decrease in their mass as we
approach the sun. Mars is an exception; but there are reasons for
thinking it of later formation, so that when it came into existence the
space allotted for its growth was already greatly exhausted, owing
chiefly to the powerful attraction of Jupiter.

While many of Father Braun's conclusions will not be accepted by
cosmogonists, his work forms an able contribution to the subject. Its
appearance may be said to mark the definite abandonment by sound
thinkers of the annular method of planet and satellite formation, and
gradually it is becoming clear that "while the various members of the
solar family owned unquestionably a common origin, they can scarcely
be said to have had a common history."

Janssen delivered an interesting discourse bearing upon the same subject at Paris, October 25, 1887—"The age of the stars," in which he
reviewed the steps leading us to the belief that each star must have a
beginning, a period of activity, a decline, and an end; and he points

out that upon the hypothesis that stars of higher temperature will last longer than stars of lower, we must conclude, from the testimony of the spectroscope, that Sirius, Vega, and the greater number of the stars visible to the naked eye are in their youth, while Aldebaran, Arcturus, and our own sun have long since passed their period of greatest activity.

NEBULÆ AND STAR-CLUSTERS.

Dr. Dreyer's new general catalogue of nebulæ and clusters of stars is essentially a new edition of Sir John Herschel's catalogue, revised, corrected, and brought down to December, 1887. It therefore forms a complete list of all known nebulæ, and is of the greatest value to observers. Herschel's General Catalogue was published in 1864 and contained 5,079 objects. D'Arrest's work, published three years later, gave the means of correcting many of the errors in the earlier observations, and in 1876 Dr. Dreyer compiled a supplement from the material at that time available. Recent discoveries have given rise to a demand for a second supplement which has been wisely met by recasting the whole work. The present catalogue contains 7,840 objects, the positions being given in right ascension to seconds of time and in declination to tenths of a minute of arc. The epoch of the first general catalogue and of D'Arrest's final positions—1860—has been retained ; precessions are given for 1880. There is an index to published figures of nebulæ and clusters, and an appendix giving the places of new nebulæ published too late to be incorporated in the catalogue itself. Further additions in numbers or in accuracy of positions might, perhaps, now be made from the recently published lists of Bigourdan, von Engelhardt, Ginzel, Stone, and Swift.

The largest refractor devoted almost exclusively to the observation of nebulæ is the 26-inch equatorial of the Leander McCormick Observatory. Professor Stone's object is to obtain as accurate positions as possible and thus to establish the means of detecting the proper motion of these objects if any exists. His working list embraces all nebulæ north of —30° which are as bright as the fourteenth magnitude.

Dr. Dreyer has submitted to a rigid examination all reported cases of variability or proper motion in nebulæ, and concludes that in not one case can either be considered as well established. It seems that the only well-authenticated changes are changes of brightness only, while we so far do not possess any clear evidence of change of form or change of place.

Detection of new nebulæ by photography.—Professor Pickering in order to test the efficacy of photography in the discovery of new nebulæ has compared the number of nebulæ shown in a series of photographs of the regions about the great nebulæ in Orion with the number in the same region given by Dreyer's catalogue. The instrument employed was the Bache telescope, which has a photographic doublet with an aperture of 8 inches and focal length of 44 inches. Each plate covered a region 10 degrees square, the great nebulæ being about the center ;

the definition was good in a central circular area about 7 degrees in diameter. Fourteen of the objects photographed are contained in Dreyer's catalogue; four in the catalogue are not photographed; twelve that are photographed are not in the catalogue. Professor Pickering concludes that in carrying out the same proportion we might expect to discover four or five thousand such objects by photographing the whole sky; but, he adds, "there is one consideration that may seriously modify this conclusion. The successive improvements in photography have continually increased the limits of the nebula in Orion. These plates show that it not only includes the sword-handle, c, ι, and θ, but a long nebulosity extends south from ζ, others surround this star, while others, both north and south, indicate that perhaps the next increase in sensitiveness of our plates will join them all in a vast nebula many degrees in length."

Herr von Gothard has obtained extraordinary results with a 10-inch reflector. His photographs, though small, show a great richness of detail; several of them are reproduced in an article by Dr. Vogel, in No. 2854 of the Nachrichten. The photographs of clusters Dr. Vogel was able to enlarge without great difficulty, but for the nebulæ it was necessary to resort to drawings; among the latter the reproduction of a photograph of the spiral nebula in Canes Venatici is particularly interesting.

The Ring Nebula in Lyra.—Professor Holden reports that nearly all the nebulæ examined with the 36 inch Lick telescope show a multitude of new details of structure. In the Ring Nebula in Lyra, for example, Lassell's 4-foot reflector and the Washington 26-inch refractor show thirteen stars in an oval outside the ring, and only one star within it, while the Lick glass shows twelve stars within the ring or projected on it, and renders it obvious that the nebula consists of a series of ovals or ellipses—first the ring of stars, then the outer and inner edges of the nebulosity; next a ring of faint stars round the edges of the inner ring, and last a number of stars situated on the various parts of the nebulosity and outer oval.

Mr. Roberts' photographs of the Ring Nebula in Lyra, the Great Nebula in Andromeda, and others, also require special mention.

The Great Nebula in Orion.—In the spectrum of this nebula, Dr. Copeland has observed a new line apparently identical with D_3, wave-length 587.4. The occurrence of this line in the spectrum of a nebula is of great interest as affording another connecting link between gaseous nebulæ and the sun and stars with bright-line spectra, especially with that remarkable class of stars, of which the first examples were detected by Wolf and Rayet in the constellation Cygnus.

The Pleiades.—The initial volume of publications of the Yale Observatory is a valuable memoir by Dr. W. L. Elkin on the positions of the principal stars in the Pleiades as determined with the new Yale heliometer, and it is, we believe, the first heliometer work done in this country. Dr. Elkin has taken in all the stars in the Durchmusterung down to 9.2 magnitude, which may reasonably be said to fall within the group, and in so doing he has rejected one of the stars used by Bessel in his celebrated work with the Königsberg heliometer as too faint for accurate measurement, but he has added seventeen stars to Bessel's list of fifty-three, so that he has taken sixty-nine stars in all. Two practically independent methods of measurement were adopted. The first plan was to measure the distance of each star of the group from each one of four reference stars situated so as to form a quadrilateral symmetrically placed about the group; the position of each star thus depended on measures of distance alone. The second plan was to measure the position-angle and distance of each star from η Tauri or Alcyone, the central star of the group. The work on the quadrilateral plan was commenced in March, 1884, and lasted to December—the measures from η Tauri occupied the first three and last four months of 1885, the mean epoch of the second triangulation falling about a year later than that of the first. Dr. Elkin gives a brief description of the instrument with his method of using it, and this is followed by a determination of the instrumental constants and by the observations in detail. The definitive results are then critically compared with Bessel's heliometer work and with the filar micrometer measures of Wolf at Paris and Pritchard at Oxford. The comparison with the Königsberg observations shows that for the six largest stars there is a striking community of motion, both in direction and in amount, and it is remarkable that this general direction of drift is very similar to the reversed absolute motion of Alcyone as given by Newcomb. Dr. Elkin thinks the coincidence is sufficiently close for two of the stars at least, and possibly for the other four, to warrant the conclusion that they are only optically members of the group. Of the remaining twenty-six of the thirty-two stars showing some displacement since 1840, the epoch of Bessel's catalogue, the distribution of the direction of motion is by no means equable, six stars only having an easterly motion, while twenty move towards the west, and here too there seems to be a tendency to community of drift in certain groups in the same part of the cluster.

"The general character of the internal motions of the group appears to be thus extremely minute. If for the six stars mentioned as with more or less probability not belonging to the group this proves to be the case, there are but five stars for which the displacement amounts to over one second in forty-five years. The bright stars especially seem to form an almost rigid system, as for only one is there really much evidence of motion, and in this case (star b) the total amount is barely one second per century. The hopes of obtaining any clew to the internal mechanism of this cluster seem therefore not likely to be realized in an immediate future."

Professor Hall has measured with the 26 inch Washington refractor the positions of sixty-three small stars in the group relatively to the brighter stars determined by Bessel and Elkin, thus furnishing further data for testing in the future any movement that may be going on in the system.

Since the discovery of the nebula in the Pleiades around the star Maia, the Henrys have been at work perfecting their apparatus, and upon repeating their ·examination of the Pleiades with an exposure of four hours, and very sensitive plates, they have defined with considerable detail a great mass of cosmic matter covering a large part of the group. The most interesting detail is a straight nebulous filament 35' to 40' long and only 3'' to 4'' wide projecting from the main mass in an east and west direction. This filament passes over seven stars, which it seems to connect like beads on a string; a slight change in direction takes place where it meets the largest star. The plate contains nearly twice as many stars as the first plate—about 2,000 down to the eighteenth magnitude.

Excellent photographs of the Pleiades have also been taken by Mr. Roberts near Liverpool with an 18-inch silvered-glass reflector.

ASTRONOMICAL CONSTANTS.

Constant of precession.—Dr. Ludwig Struve has deduced a new value of the constant of precession and the motion of the solar system in space from an elaborate comparison of recent Pulkowa catalogues with Bradley's observations as reduced by Auwers, thus obtaining an interval of a century—1755.0 to 1855.0—for the determination of proper motions. These proper motions, computed with O. Struve's precession constant (of 1841), were affected by the apparent displacement due to the motion of the solar system in space and by the error of the assumed precession constant.

They thus furnished a means of determining these two quantities. After rejecting seven stars which seem to be exceptionally near us, the remaining 2,509 are divided into 120 groups, forming 240 equations of condition to be solved by least squares for the determination of the five unknowns, the co-ordinates X, Y, Z of the sun's "goal" (or point in space towards which the sun is traveling, to adopt the term introduced by Professor Newton) and the corrections $\triangle m$ and $\triangle n$ to Bessel's constants. The following table shows the resulting value of the luni-solar precession compared with that of previous calculators:

Bessel	50.''3635	Bolte	50.''3584
O. Struve	50. 3798	Bolte	50. 3570
Nyrén	50. 3269	Bolte	50. 3621
Dreyer	50. 3820	L. Struve	50. 3514

At the end of the paper the author treats of the planetary precession and the secular variation, and gives a list of stars whose proper motions as found by him differ from those deduced by Auwers from Greenwich and Berlin observations. The results obtained for the motion of the solar system are quoted elsewhere in this report.

Constant of aberration.—Herr Küstner of the Berlin Observatory has made a determination of the constant of aberration with a 4½ inch broken-back, universal instrument, employing what is commonly known in this country as Talcott's method. His result is a correction of $-0''.132$ to Struve's constant of aberration with the small probable error of $\pm 0''.011$. A further exhaustive discussion of the observations has led the author to conclude that the latitude of his instrument in the spring of 1884 was $0''.204 \pm 0''.021$ greater than in the spring of 1885—important evidence upon the mooted question of the variability of terrestrial latitudes.

Professor Hall has recently reduced a series of observations of α Lyræ made with the prime vertical instrument at the U. S. Naval Observatory between the years 1862 and 1867. These observations had been designed to give corrections to the assumed values of the constants of nutation and aberration, and an absolute determination of the parallax of the star. The series was not continued for a sufficient period for the first purpose, and a preliminary examination having shown that a negative parallax would result, the work has been set aside till the present time. The mean resulting parallax from the 436 observations is $\pi = -0''.079 \pm 0''.0134$, and the constant of aberration $= 20''.4506 \pm 0''.0142$.

On account of the uncertainty in the parallax, Professor Hall has introduced a parallax of $+0''.15$, about the mean value indicated by numerous observations of this star, and he then obtains a constant of aberration $= 20''.4542 \pm 0''.0144$. To this result he gives the preference and deduces for the solar parallax $8''.810 \pm 0''.0062$, adopting Hansen's value of the mean anomaly of the earth and eccentricity, Clarke's value for the equatorial radius of the earth, and Michelson and Newcomb's determination of the velocity of light, 186,325 miles per second.

Herr Nyrén has found in a discussion of the Pulkowa observations of the difference of right ascension between Polaris and its companion, evidence to confirm the hypothesis, upon which determinations of the aberration constant rest, that the velocity of light is independent of the state whether of motion or rest of the luminous body.

On the other hand the experiments of Michelson and Morley seem to throw some doubt upon Fresnel's hypotheses that the ether is at rest except in transparent media, and that there it participates in the motion of translation in the ratio $\frac{n^2 - 1}{n^2}$, n being the index of refraction.

Loewy's method of determining the constant of aberration from differential measurements of the changes in the distances of suitably-chosen pairs of stars is to be tested at the Paris Observatory with an equatorial condé, and by Professor Comstock at the Washburn Observatory with suitable apparatus fitted to the 6-inch equatorial. The method is essentially to bring the two stars, which may be, say, 90 degrees apart in the sky, into the field of an equatorial by reflection from the surfaces of a double mirror at the objective: any change in the distance between the two stars can then be measured with extreme nicety. It should perhaps be mentioned that Houzeau claimed to have suggested this principle in 1871.

Diurnal nutation.—M. Niesten, in applying Folie's formulæ for diurnal nutation to the Greenwich observations of γ Draconis, has found a positive parallax where Main and Downing obtained a negative value, and a constant of aberration more closely agreeing with that generally adopted. Introducing similar corrections in Hall's discussion of the prime vertical observations of α Lyræ has, however, had no appreciable effect.

STAR-CATALOGUES AND CHARTS.

Paris Catalogue.—The first two volumes of the great work undertaken by Leverrier a third of a century ago, the re observation of the stars of Lalande's catalogue, have recently been published. The first volume is the first installment of the catalogue proper, viz, stars from 0^h to 6^h of right ascension, observed during the years 1837 to 1881; the second volume gives the separate observations. Each series when complete will extend to four volumes. The observations were made with the five meridian instruments of the Paris Observatory, and include some 20,000 or 30,000 observations made between 1837 and 1854; they have therefore been divided into three periods, 1837–'53, 1854–'67, and 1868–'81, and severally reduced to the mean epochs 1845, 1860, or 1875. Observations subsequent to 1881, about one-fourth of the entire number, will be published separately. The present section of the catalogue contains 7,245 stars, and represents about 80,000 observations in both elements. It gives for each of the three periods the number of observations, the mean date, the right ascension and north polar distance reduced to the mean epoch, and a comparison with Lalande. The precessions for 1875 are also added. The introduction, by M. Gaillot, who has superintended the reduction, contains a discussion of the probable errors of the observations, and is followed by a comparison of the present catalogue with Auwers' Bradley, and an important investigation by M. Bossert of the proper motions of a large number of stars, followed by a table of errors in Lalande's catalogue which the present and other catalogues have brought to light.

Cincinnati Zone Catalogue.—Professor Porter has published the results of observations made with a 3-inch transit instrument, at the Cincinnati Observatory, upon 4,050 stars between the declinations —18° 50′ and —22° 20′, during the years 1885 to 1887. The faintest stars were of about 8.5 magnitude, and nearly all the stars were observed three times. The observations were made in zones, the telescope being clamped. The transits which were recorded by the chronograph were generally taken over five wires, and two bisections were made in declination whenever time allowed. The probable errors of a single observation are $\pm 0^s.123$ and $\pm 1.''84$. An appendix gives the proper motion of seventy-five stars deduced from a comparison with other catalogues.

Dunsink Catalogue.—The sixth part of the Dunsink observations is devoted to a catalogue of 1,012 stars, between —2° and —23° declination, observed with the meridian circle from 1881 to 1885. The standard stars employed are those of the Berlin Jahrbuch, and the observations are reduced to Auwers' system. The mean right ascensions and declinations, with the annual precessions for the epoch 1885.0, the mean epoch, and the number of observations are given.

Pulkowa.—Volume XII contains a catalogue for 1865.0 of the principal stars, to the fourth magnitude—381 in number—as far as 15 degrees south declination deduced from observations in the years 1861–1872. The formation of a catalogue of these stars for the epoch 1845.0 was the first piece of work completed by this observatory, and the present work is thus enhanced in value by being an almost exact repetition of that undertaken twenty years before.

Auwers' new reduction of Bradley.—The third volume of Auwers' new reduction of Bradley, which has been five years in going through the press, was finally published in 1888. This volume contains, in addition to the catalogue proper, tables giving the quantities in the reduction to the apparent place that depend upon the star's position, and a comparison of Bradley's positions, reduced to 1865, with Berlin and Greenwich observations of about the same date. The catalogue contains 3,268 stars, and gives for each star the magnitude, right ascension, and declination for 1775.0, corrections to the *Fundamenta* of Bessels, number of observations, epoch, precessions for 1755, 1810, and 1865, proper motions, references to Greenwich catalogues, and to double-star catalogues, where the star was double, and a column of notes.

An important list of 480 stars to be used as fundamental stars for zone observations between —20° and —80° declination, is published by Dr. Auwers in the Monthly Notices for June, 1887.

Dr. C. H. F. Peters has contributed two valuable papers to the third volume of the Memoirs of the National Academy of Sciences; the first is a critical examination of all data bearing on Flamsteed's twenty-two "missing" stars, for each of which a plausible explanation is found; and the second paper is a list of corrigenda in the catalogues, O. Arg. S., Bonn VI, Weisse (1 and 2), Rümker, Schjellerup, Baily's Lalande zones, Yarnall, Glasgow, Santiago, and Geneva.

A very useful index to stars in Airy's six Greenwich catalogues not found in Flamsteed—the work of Miss Lamb—will be found in the fifth volume of publications of the Washburn Observatory.

Astronomische Gesellschaft Zones.—The following notes condensed from the reports presented at the meeting of the Gesellschaft in August, 1887, show the progress of the work at that time:

Kasan, 80°–75°.—The second volume of observations has been printed, and the reductions to 1875.0 and the formation of the catalogue have been begun.

Dorpat, 75°–70°.—Partly printed.

Christiania, 70°–65°.—Greater part printed.

Helsingfors-Gotha, 65°-55°.—Catalogue finished to the precessions; 0ʰ ready for press.

Cambridge (Harvard), 55°-50°.—Reductions nearly completed.

Bonn, 50°-40°.—Reductions well advanced.

Lund, 40°-35°.—Two-thirds reduced to 1875.0.

Leiden, 35°-30°.—Zones printed, and precessions for catalogue partly finished.

Cambridge (England), 30°-25°.—Observations nearly complete; reductions proceeding rapidly.

Berlin, 25°-20°.—Reductions nearly finished.

Berlin, 20°-15°.—Reductions under way.

Leipzig, 15°-5°.—Observations practically finished.

Albany, 5°-1°.—In press.

Nicolaief, +1° . . . −2°.—Observations finished; reductions progressing.

Observations of zero stars for the zones −2° to −23° 10′ are in progress at Leiden, Strassburg and Karlsruhe. Two of these zones have been undertaken in the United States—9° 50′ to −14° 20′ at Cambridge and −13° 50′ to −18° 10′ at Washington.

Star-charts.—Sections III and IV of the Southern Durchmusterung charts (sheets 48, 53–63) have been published, bringing to a close that most valuable work. Professor Schönfel● has issued with these last numbers a short list of errata detected, which is reprinted in No. 2834 of the Nachrichten.

A series of charts embracing all the stars visible to the naked eye— that is, down to about the sixth and one-half magnitude—has been published by Mr. Cottam, and has been very highly complimented. There are in all thirty-six sheets, the scale being one-third of an inch to one degree of a great circle. Another useful book of the same kind is Klein's New Star-Atlas, which has appeared in both English and German editions. There are eighteen maps, containing about the same number of stars as Mr. Cottam's, and giving also all the nebulæ and clusters visible in telescopes of moderate power—a great help to comet hunters.

STELLAR PARALLAX.

Parallax of α Tauri.—Prof. Asaph Hall has published in No. 156 of the Astronomical Journal, a determination of the parallax of α Tauri from a series of observations with the 26-inch Washington equatorial, extending from October 2, 1886, to March 15, 1887. The comparison-star was an eleventh magnitude companion distant about 116″, in position angle 34°.5. The resulting values of the relative parallax are: From measures of position angle, $\pi = +0''.163 \pm 0''.0409$; and from measures of distance, $\pi = +0''.035 \pm 0''.0431$. The mean value of the parallax of α Tauri from these observations is, therefore, $\pi = 0''.102 \pm 0''.0296$.

Prof. O. Struve, using the same comparison-star, recently obtained a value nearly five times as great, namely, $\pi = 0''.516 \pm 0''.057$.

Parallax of Σ 1516.—Dr. L. de Ball, of the observatory of the University of Liège, has determined in a similar manner the parallax of the brighter component (which has a sensible proper motion) of this optically double star. From measures of position angle he finds $\pi = +0''.091$ $\pm 0''.013$; and from measures of distance, $\pi = +0''.112 \pm 0''.010$. The mean result is $\pi = +0''.104 \pm 0''.008$.

Parallax of $\Sigma 2398$.—A new investigation of the parallax of the double star Σ 2398 has been made by Dr. Lamp, based upon observations between May 20, 1885, and March 15, 1887. In this he not only obtains a very satisfactory confirmation of his previous value of the parallax $(0''.34)$ of the larger star, but he is able to show that the two stars are at practically the same distance. For the principal star he finds the annual parallax equal to $0''.3520 \pm 0''.0140$; for the smaller, $0''.3548$ $\pm 0''.0131$; or for the mean, $0''.353 \pm 0''.014$. The magnitudes are 8.7 and 8.2, respectively, and the common proper motion about $-0^s.17$ in right ascension, and $+1''.90$ in declination annually.

Parallax of first-magnitude stars in the northern hemisphere.—Dr. Elkin has completed his heliometer measures for the determination of the parallax of the ten stars of the first magnitude in the northern hemisphere, and summarizes his results in the following table:

Star.	Parallax.	Probable error.	No. of comparative stars.	No. of observations.	Proper motion.
	"	*"*			*"*
α Tauri	+0.116	±0.029	6	64	0.202
α Aurigæ	+0.107	.047	2	16	0.442
α Orionis	−0.009	.049	2	16	0.022
α Canis minoris	+0.266	.047	2	16	1.257
β Geminorum	+0.068	.047	2	16	0.628
α Leonis	+0.093	.048	4	15	0.255
α Bootis	+0.018	.022	10	89	2.287
α Lyræ	+0.034	.045	2	30	0.344
α Aquilæ	+0.199	.047	4	16	0.647
α Cygni	−0.042	.047	4	16	0.010

The mean of the ten parallaxes gives for the mean parallax of a first-magnitude star, $+0''.039 \pm 0''.015$, a result according well with the values deduced by Gyldén $(0''.084)$ and Peters $(0''.102)$.

The probable errors include an estimation of the probable systematic error of the measures. They are therefore considerably larger than those generally assigned to such results, which, as a rule, only take into account the mere *casual* error of observation.

It will be seen on inspection of the table that of the ten stars six may be said to give indications of a measurable parallax, but in only two cases, α Canis Minoris and α Aquilæ, are the values in any degree remarkable, and these confirm closely results of former investigators; Auwers and Wagner having obtained $+0''.240 \pm 0''.029$ and $+0''.299$ $\pm 0''.038$ respectively for Procyon, and W. Struve $+0''.181 \pm 0''.094$ for Altair. On the other hand, the next two largest results, those for

α Bootis and α Aurigæ, do not confirm the large values found by O. Struve, $+0''.516$ and $+0''.305$; but in the case of the former star there is a close agreement with Hall, who got $+0''.102 \pm 0''.030$, and there seems to be but little doubt that the Pulkowa value is largely in error.

Of the four stars where the parallactic displacement has been inappreciable, Arcturus, with its large proper motion of over $2''$, second only to that of α Centauri in all of the 200 brightest stars down to the fourth magnitude, is especially note-worthy. The minuteness of the parallax is beyond doubt, depending, as it does, on five pairs of comparison stars, all in reasonable agreement, and it can not be considered as seriously at variance with the results previously obtained by Peters and Johnson, $+0''.127 \pm 0''.073$ and $+0''.138 \pm 0''.052$ respectively, when their liability to systematic error is taken into account. The Yale result for α Lyræ does not fall in well with those hitherto deduced for this star. If we commence at the epoch of W. Struve and neglect the earlier attempts to find the absolute parallax, we have the following list of values:

	Parallax.	Probable error.
	$''$	$''$
W. Struve, at Dorpat, 1837–'40	$+0.261$	± 0.025
Peters, at Pulkowa, 1842............	$.103$	$.053$
O. Struve, at Pulkowa, 1851–'53	$.147$	$.009$
Johnson, at Oxford, 1854–'55	$.154$	$.046$
Brünnow, at Dublin, 1868–'69	$.212$	$.010$
Brünnow, at Dublin, 1870......	$.188$	$.033$
Hall, at Washington, 1880–'81	$.134$	$.0055$

from which a parallax of about $+0''.17$ would seem well assured. The pair of comparison stars used by Elkin are very symmetrical, and so large a value would seem incompatible with the heliometer measures.

Photographic determination of stellar parallax.—Professor Pritchard, of the Oxford University Observatory, pursuing his experimental work upon the determination of stellar parallax by the help of photography, has published the following interesting results. The last three are provisional, having been determined from only six months' observations:

	Parallax.	Probable error.
	$''$	$''$
61¹ Cygni	$+0.4289$	± 0.0180
61² Cygni	$.4353$	$.0152$
μ Cassiopeæ	$.0356$	$.0250$
Polaris	$.052$	$.0314$
α Cassiopeæ	$.072$	$.042$
β Cassiopeæ	$.187$	$.039$
γ Cassiopeæ	$< .050$	$.047$

For comparison we may cite the following results obtained by other astronomers working with equatorials and heliometers in the usual way:

61 Cygni	Bessel, 1840................	+0″.348
	Auwers, 1863	+0 .564
	Ball, 1878...................	+0 .468
	Hall, 1880.................	+0 .261
μ Cassiopeæ	Bessel	−0 .12
	Struve	+0 .342
Polaris	Lindenau................ ...	+0 .144
	Struve and Peters............	+0 .172
	C. A. F. Peters.........	+0 .067

Professor Pritchard lays stress upon the fact that each photographic plate must be considered as carrying its own scale; and, due regard being paid to the unavoidable, though slight, variations of scale in the different plates, he is of opinion that in this delicate class of work photography will give as accurate results as any other known method.

For 61 Cygni the value given rests upon the measurement of three hundred and thirty plates, taken upon eighty-nine nights; each component was referred to four comparison stars. On each of fifty-three nights four photographic plates were taken of μ Cassiopeæ, the exposures varying from five to ten minutes. Experiments seemed to indicate, however, that sufficiently approximate results, with a great saving of labor, would be obtained by confining the observations to about five nights in each of four periods of the year indicated by the position of the parallactic ellipse. Professor Pritchard proposes to apply this method systematically to all those stars between magnitudes one and one-half and two and one-half which attain at Oxford a suitable altitude; and he hopes to obtain good results for all of these stars that have a parallax not less than the thirtieth of a second of arc.

DOUBLE AND MULTIPLE STARS.

Extension of the law of gravitation to stellar systems.—Professor Hall, in a discussion of this question in the Astronomical Journal, after a review of the various speculations upon the subject, says: "The weakness of the proof that the Newtonian law governs the motions of double stars arises from two sources. In the first place, the errors of observation have a large ratio to the quantities measured. This condition makes it difficult to compute the orbits with much accuracy, or we may satisfy the observations with very different elements. - - - The insufficiency in the data can only be removed by further observation. Since there is no theoretical difficulty in the way, the continuation of the observations of double stars and the improvement of methods of observation will, in time, give the means for the accurate determination of their apparent orbits. The theoretical difficulty in proving the law of Newton for double stars can not be overcome. But we can increase the probability of the existence of this law by determining more orbits

and those that are very differently situated. If the law prove satisfactory in all cases, we shall have a probability of its universality increasing with the progress of astronomy." But, although this probability may be very great, it can not constitute a proof offering the character of experimental certainty which clothes the law of Newton itself
in our planetary system.

A serious difficulty is encountered in the enormous velocities with
which quite a number of stars appear to be moving through space, "run-
away" Groombridge—1830, μ Cassiopeæ, β Hydri, α Bootis, and others.
Some of these velocities are comparable to that of a comet in close proximity to the sun, but in most cases there is no visible object near the
one in motion to which we can ascribe an attractive force, acting according to the Newtonian law, which would produce the velocity observed,
unless we assume enormous masses.

An interesting article upon this subject is contributed by M. Tisserand to the Bulletin Astronomique for January, 1887.

Milan Double star observations.—Professor Schiaparelli has published,
in the Milan volume 33, his first series of double star observations made
at that observatory with the 8-inch refractor from 1874 to 1885. There
are four hundred and sixty-five stars in his list, and in most of them
the components are less than 5″ apart. In an appendix are given the
mean results for a number of the closest pairs as measured with .the
18 inch refractor. With this instrument he discovered that the principal star of ε Hydræ is itself a very close double, the magnitudes of the
two components being 4 and 5.5, and distance 0″.2 or 0″.25. The first
part of the volume contains a detailed description of the optical performance of the 8-inch refractor, a discussion of the errors of the micrometer and of the accidental errors of observation, and a very full
comparison with Dembowski's measures. The differences in the determination of position angle due to the varying inclination of the line
joining the two stars to the line of the observer's eyes are also investigated, but the reversion prism was not used. Professor Schiaparelli
finds that his measures of distance are free from systematic errors, due
to personality, but his position angles have a tendency to be small as
compared with those of other observers.

Professor Hough has published a catalogue of two hundred and nine
new double stars discovered and measured by himself with the 18½-inch
refractor of the Dearborn Observatory. Short lists of new doubles
discovered with the McCormick 26-inch, and the Lick 36-inch, have also
been published. Burnham's list of his discoveries with the 36-inch refractor in three months is very interesting, containing as it does new
companions to γ Cassiopeæ, 11 mag., 2″.2 distant; and α Tauri, 12 mag.,
2″.3 distant.

The following table contains the results of recent computations of
the orbits of binary stars. The star δ Equulei is of especial interest,
as the period of eleven and a half years assigned to it is the shortest of

any known pair. The elements, however, are only to be regarded as provisional.

For 85 Pegasi, Mr. Schaeberle has deduced proper motions of $+0^{s}.833$ in right ascension, and $-1''.005$ in declination.

Elements of binary stars.

Star.	Time of periastron T	Position of node Ω	Position of periastron λ	Inclination ι	Eccentricity ε	Semiaxis major a	Mean motion ν	Period in years P	Computer
		°	°	°		''	°		
δ Equulei... ...	1892 03	24. 05	26. 61	81. 75	0. 2011	0. 406	....	11. 478	Wrublewsky.
β Delphini	1868. 850	10. 938	220. 952	61. 582	0. 09622	0. 46000	......	16. 955	Celoria.
85 Pegasi	1834. 00	306. 1	70. 3	68. 6	0. 35	0. 96	......	22 3	Schaeberle.
Σ 3121..............	1878. 5198	21. 847	129. 454	75. 436	0. 30863	0. 67254	.. ....	34. 6188	Celoria.
O : 2"8	1882 857	2. 130	21. 899	65. 847	0. 58360	0. 88349	.. ....	f6 653	Celoria.
70 (p) Ophiuchi ..	1807. 65	120. 1	171. 8	58. 5	0. 4912	4. 50	−4. 098	87. 84	Gore.
14 (i) Orionis... .	1959. 05	99. 6	302. 7	45. 0	0. 2465	1. 22	−1. 89	190. 48	Gore.
Σ 1757	1791. 98	87. 6	185. 4	40. 9	0. 4498	2. 05	+1. 30	276. 92	Gore.
p Eridani	1823. 55	135. 0	240. 0	38. 5	0. 674	6. 96	−1. 19	302 37	Gore.
λ O hinchi	1787. 9	105. 5	152. 5	38. 1	0. 4424	1. 53	+0. 9638	373. 5	Glasenapp.
Σ 948..............	1710. 0	166. 5	93. 6	46. 0	0. 229	1. 64	−0. 741	485. 8	Gore.

The multiple star ζ Cancri.—Professor Seeliger's recent investigations have confirmed the results of his earlier work, and those obtained by Struve in 1874. "The three stars A, B, and C have the magnitudes respectively, 5.0, 5.7, and 5.3. The proper motion of the system amounts in a century to $+10^{s}.6$ in right ascension, and to $-11''$ in declination. The close pair, A and B, have a motion round each other in about sixty years; their apparent distance varying from about $0''.6$ to $1''.1$; whilst C, the more distant companion, has moved through about 55° of position angle round the other two since Herschel's observations in 1781, its distance never very greatly varying from $5\frac{1}{2}''$. The motion of A and B round their common center of gravity does not appear to be disturbed to any appreciable extent by the influence of C, which is so placed as not to affect their apparent relative motions, even though a very considerable mass be assigned to it, and as a fact Professor Seeliger finds, for the most probable value of the mass of C, $\frac{m'}{1+m}=2.386$, where $1, m$, and m' are the masses of A, B, and C respectively. But there is a periodical retrogression of C itself which is most easily accounted for by supposing the presence of a close companion, one hitherto undetected, and therefore either entirely dark or but faintly luminous. The distance of this companion is probably only a few tenths of a second, the distance of C from the point, s_2, round which it appears to revolve, and which may reasonably be assumed to be the center of gravity of itself and of D, the as yet undiscovered fourth member of the family, being only about one-fifth of a second. The entire group may then be considered as a double double.

VARIABLE AND COLORED STARS.

Chandler's catalogue of variable stars.—The most important work upon variable stars since Schoenfeld's " Zweiter Catalog," now thirteen years old, is a new catalogue published by Mr. S. C. Chandler as Nos. 179 and 180 of the Astronomical Journal. In the absence of any later catalogue from Schoenfeld this immediately takes its place as the standard, though the author states that it is preliminary to a more complete catalogue which will embody a series of observations and definitive investigations now in hand.

An analysis of the catalogue shows that of the 225 stars comprised in it 160 are distinctly variable; in 12 the periodic character is rather uncertainly defined; 14 are distinctly irregular; 12 belong to the so-called *novæ*, or have been seen at only one appearance; and the 27 remaining have been too little observed for the character of the variation to be properly known. Of the 160 periodical variables, epochs of both maximum and minimum are assigned for 63; maximum epochs alone for 82; minimum epochs alone for 14, 9 of these being of the Algol type, while in one the period alone is given. The elements of 124 stars are the results of Mr. Chandler's own investigations; 22 are taken from Schoenfeld; and 14 from other computers after Mr. Chandler had carefully confirmed them. The systematic perturbations shown by many of the periods have received attention, and the further study of this subject promises important additions to our knowledge of the causes of stellar variation.

A useful novelty introduced in numbering the stars calls for unqualified approval. Instead of giving them consecutive numbers each is distinguished by a number equal to one-tenth of the right ascension expressed in time-seconds for the equinox 1900.0. In this way the numeration need not be disturbed by fresh discoveries.

The catalogue gives in successive columns a serial number assigned in the way just described; Schoenfeld's number; the right ascension and declination for 1855, and the annual variations; the discoverer; date of discovery; redness on an arbitrary scale; magnitude at maximum and at minimum; Greenwich mean time of maximum and minimum; period; remarks; and approximate place for 1900.

A very ingenious method of estimating the colors was employed by Mr. Chandler; it consists in estimating the relative change in brightness effected in two stars by the interposition, first, of a blue and then of a red shade glass. If a red and a white star appear of the same brightness, when viewed directly, the red star will seem the fainter when the blue glass is interposed, but the brighter with the red glass; and these differences of brightness can be very precisely estimated by Argelander's method, and they thus afford definite measures of the differences in color of the two stars on an arbitrary scale depending upon the glasses employed. Mr. Chandler finds that the effect of brightness upon the scale-estimates is imperceptible, at least between the second and ninth magnitudes. An important result of his observations is the intimate connection shown between the length of period and the depth of color of the star; the very short-period variables are nearly white; those of longer period somewhat redder, the tint growing deeper, the longer the period.

Several new variable stars have been detected by Chandler, Sawyer, Espin, and others, and among them are two of more than ordinary interest, as they apparently belong to the well-known "Algol-type." The first was discovered by Mr. Chandler in the constellation Cygnus (Y Cygni), right ascension $=20^h$ $47^m.5$; declination $=+34°$ $14'$ (DM. + 34°, 4181). Its light varies from 7.1 magnitude to about 7.9 magnitude, and the period is probably 1^d 11^h 56^m 48^s. The second star referred to, was discovered by Mr. Sawyer in March, 1887, in the constellation Canis Major, and as it is the first undoubted variable found in that constellation, it will probably be known as R Canis Majoris. Its position for 1887 is right ascension $=7^h$ $14^m.4$; declination $=-16°$ $11'$. The minimum observed by Mr. Sawyer was 6.7 magnitude, and the period is 1^d 3^h 15^m 55^s. Mr. Chandler has collected the observations of U Ophiuchi, of all variables the one with shortest period and the most rapid fluctuations of light, and he finds a curious but well-marked retardation in the increase of brilliancy some half-hour or so after minimum is passed. A similar irregularity has been noticed in the light-curve of S Cancri and occasionally in that of Algol.

Mr. Chandler strongly urges the possessors of large refractors to devote a portion of their time to the observation of the minima of variables that become too faint for ordinary telescopes, our knowledge of such variables being extremely deficient. Argelander's method of observation is recommended.

Professor Pickering has in preparation an index to observations of variable stars which will give for each star the number of observations each year since the discovery of variability. This index will be published in volume 18 of the Annals of the Harvard Observatory.

In an interesting article published in the Observatory (April, 1888), Miss Clerke has collected a series of notes upon variable double stars. These stars show for the most part a spectrum analogous to that of Sirius, that is of Class I, although single stars of that class hardly ever show any fluctuations in brightness. Algol-variables, if the eclipse theory of their changes be admitted, make no exceptions to this rule; Gore's catalogue contains three examples: δ Orionis, S Monocerotis, and Y Virginis, and among the well-known doubles are γ Virginis, ζ Bootis, π Bootis, 3S Geminorum, α Piscium, θ Serpentis, and β Scorpii, and perhaps δ Cygni. With few and doubtful exceptions, revolving double stars vary in concert, if they vary at all. The changes of γ Virginis illustrate the mode of procedure in this respect of couples intrinsically equal. They alternate in each component, and can thus be detected only by close attention. Each may be described as nor-

mally of the third magnitude; and each in turn declines by about half
a magnitude and recovers within a few days, yet so that the general
preponderance, during a cycle of several years, remains to the same
star. Miss Clerke suggests that simultaneous variation in the color of
neighboring stars may lead to the discovery of their physical dependence.

Mr. G. F. Chambers has prepared a catalogue (still in manuscript) of
seven hundred and eleven red stars, brighter than the eight and one-
half magnitude, the result of observations made from 1870 to 1886;
less than twelve stars, according to Mr. Chambers, can properly be
termed carmine or ruby.

STELLAR PHOTOMETRY.

The magnitudes of the standard stars of the British, French, German,
Spanish, and American nautical almanacs have been rediscussed by
Professor Pickering, and his results will probably be adopted in future
issues of the French, Spanish, and American works. The plan proposed was, that the magnitude adopted for each star should be the
mean of those derived from the Harvard Photometry, the photometric
observations of Wolff, the Uranometria Oxoniensis, and the Uranometria Argentina. The list published embraces 800 stars, and of these
the magnitudes of all but 64 depend upon at least two and generally
upon three authorities; 132 stars being common to all four of the
adopted standard catalogues of brightness.

A "wedge-photometer," constructed under the direction of Professor
Pritchard for the Harvard Observatory, has been submitted to a careful
examination by Professors Langley, Young, and Pickering, and it appears from Professor Langley's investigation of the wedge, by means
of his bolometer, that there is a selective absorption of light throughout
the wedge; feeble in the more luminous portion of the spectrum, but
of such a character that, broadly speaking, the transmissibility always
increases from the violet toward the red, increasing very greatly in the
infra-red. These results have been confirmed by Professor Pickering's
experiments, and they emphasize the danger, already recognized by
Professor Pritchard, of employing an instrument of this kind in the
observation of deeply-colored stars.

From a comparison of the star-magnitudes of the Oxford Uranometry
with those of Wolff's second catalogue, and with those of the Harvard
Photometry, Professor Pickering has found that the Oxford magnitudes
are, on the average, less than the Harvard magnitudes for stars down
to the third magnitude, but greater for the fourth and fifth, and less
again for stars below the sixth. The Harvard catalogue differs less
from those of Wolff and Pritchard than the two latter do from each
other.

STELLAR SPECTRA.

Photographic study of stellar spectra. Henry Draper memorial.—Professor Pickering, in his annual report for 1888, presents the progress made in the various investigations of stellar spectra as follows: A catalogue has been prepared of the spectra of 10,875 stars, covering the entire sky north of −25°. The 8-inch Bache telescope has been used for this work. Six hundred and thirty-three plates have been taken, and 27,953 spectra have been examined. The type of spectrum is given in each case, and in about six thousand cases additional lines are visible and have accordingly been described. The photographic intensities of the spectra have also been measured, giving a photometric measure of the stars by which those of different colors may be compared. The first draft of a spectroscopic catalogue has been prepared, including the place of each star for 1900, its designation and magnitude in various catalogues, its photographic brightness, and the description of each spectrum. The photographs required for the second investigation on the spectra of the fainter stars are nearly completed. The instruments employed in both of these investigations were prepared for shipment to Peru, where the work will be continued among the southern constellations. The detailed study of the brighter stars with the 11-inch Draper telescope has been extended by the use of plates stained with erythrosin. The sodium line D in these spectra has thus been photographed as a double line. A catalogue has been formed of the lines in some of the brighter stars. In Sirius the lines, except those due to hydrogen, are very faint. But nearly four hundred of them have been measured in different photographs of this star; fifteen are recorded between the lines H and K. A beginning has also been made of the study of the spectra of the variable stars.

Dr. von Konkoly and his assistant, Dr. Kövesligethy, have carried the spectroscopic survey of the heavens begun by Vogel and Dunér to 15 degrees south declination, and have published their work in volume 8, part 2, of the O'Gyalla observations. The instrument used was a Zöllner spectroscope. Vogel's arrangement of types was followed. The catalogue contains in all 2,022 stars, down to 7.5 magnitude. But one bright line spectrum was suspected, a star of 6.5 magnitude 50′ north of ζ Orionis, and this star, as well as β, δ, and ε Orionis, is found to have a variable spectrum.

Among the peculiarities detected in stellar spectra may be noted the discovery by Espin on August 13, 1888, of a bright line in the spectrum of the variable star R Cygni; and as Dunér found it in 1879–'82 of a weak III type, an extraordinary change seems to have taken place. Espin's bright line was apparently of a temporary character, and faded rapidly.

Motion of stars in the line of sight.—The spectroscopic observations for the determination of the motions of stars in the line of sight have been continued at Greenwich and at the Temple Observatory, Rugby, the only two observatories that have thus far given systematic attention to this important line of work. The most interesting results are in the case of Sirius, which, when first observed at Greenwich in the winter of 1875-'76, seemed to be receding from us at the rate of 24 miles per second. This recession gradually changed to an *approach* of 5 miles per second in 1882-'83, increasing to 24 miles in 1885-'86, and then dropping to 1 mile in 1886-'87, and now becoming a recession again, in 1887, of 6 miles per second. As the Astronomer Royal remarks, these results are to be accepted with caution; the F line for which the measures were made would seem to have changed somewhat its characteristics, and the observation is moreover one of extreme difficulty, the discordances obtained on different nights being almost as great as the whole range of displacement noted.

Dr. Vogel, of Potsdam, has successfully applied photography to the determination of the displacement of lines in stellar spectra due to a motion of the star in the line of sight. Two Rutherford prisms were used, the observations being made on the third line of hydrogen, Hγ. Dr. Scheiner, who has been carrying out these experiments, has examined the spectra of Sirius, Procyon, Castor, Arcturus, Aldebaran, Pollux, and Rigel. Of these, Sirius showed a slight displacement toward the red, thus indicating a motion away from us; Procyon a decided displacement, and Rigel a very large one in the same direction, while Arcturus showed a considerable displacement towards the violet. A systematic examination of all stars of the first and second magnitudes is to be undertaken with improved apparatus.

ASTRONOMICAL PHOTOGRAPHY.

The Paris International Astrophotographic Congress.—The general interest in the application of photography to astronomical observations has resulted in a meeting called by the French Academy of Sciences, at the instance of Admiral Mouchez, for the purpose of uniting upon a plan for preparing by international co-operation a photographic chart of the heavens more extensive than any hitherto attempted by the usual methods. The Congress was opened at the Paris Observatory on April 16, 1887, by M. Flourens, minister of foreign affairs of the French Government, and addresses were made by M. Bertrand, the eminent mathematician, by Admiral Mouchez, director of the Paris Observatory, and by Professor Struve, director of the Pulkowa Observatory. Fifty-six members were present, including thirty-seven foreign astronomers, representing sixteen nations. Admiral Mouchez was chosen honorary president; Struve, president; Auwers, Christie, and Faye, vice-presidents; Bakhuyzen and Tisserand, secretaries, and Dunér and Trépied, assistant secretaries. At the first meeting a committee of nineteen was appointed to consider and report upon the size and construction of the instruments to be employed, and upon the limit of star-magnitudes to be included in the photographs. This committee reported on April 19, and after some discussion it was decided to divide the Congress into two sections—one to deal with purely astronomical questions, and the other with questions pertaining to the photographic side of the problem. Each section drew up a series of resolutions which were further discussed and amended by the Congress in full session, the result being an agreement to adopt refracting telescopes of 13 inches aperture and 11¼ feet focal length, and to undertake two series of photographs of the entire sky, one taking in stars as faint as the fourteenth magnitude, the other stopping at the eleventh. The ultimate aim is to convert the positions of the stars upon these last plates into the usual co-ordinates of right ascension and declination, and to publish them in the form of a star catalogue, and to prepare from the series embracing the fainter stars a set of glass positives for each of the co-operating observatories or nations.

Following are the resolutions in detail as finally adopted:

(1) The progress made in astronomical photography demands that astronomers of the present day should unite in undertaking a description of the heavens by photorahpic means.

(2) This work shall be carried out at selected stations, and the instruments shall be identical in their essential parts.

(3) The principal objects shall be: *a.* To prepare a general photographic chart of the heavens for the present epoch, and to obtain data which shall enable us to determine the positions and magnitudes of all stars down to a certain magnitude, with the greatest possible accuracy (magnitudes being understood in a photographic sense to be defined later). *b.* To be able to utilize in the best way, both in the present and in the future, the data obtained by photographic means.

(4) The instruments employed shall be exclusively refractors.

(5) The stars shall be photographed as far as the fourteenth magnitude, inclusive; this magnitude being indicated provisionally by the scale actually in use in France, and with the reservation that its photographic value shall be definitely fixed afterward.

(6) The aperture of the object-glasses shall be 0.33 meter (13. inches), and the focal length about 3.43 meters (11¼ feet), so that a minute of arc shall be represented approximately by 0.001 meter.

(7) The directors of observatories shall be at liberty to have the object-glasses made where they desire, provided they fulfill the general conditions laid down by the Congress.

(8) The aplanatism and achromatism of the objectives shall be calculated for radiations near the Fraunhofer ray G.

(9) All the plates shall be prepared according to the same formula; this formula to be subsequently agreed upon.

(10) A permanent control of these plates from the point of view of their relative sensibility to the different radiations shall be instituted.

(11) Questions in regard to the preservation and reproduction of the negatives can not at present be settled, and shall be referred to a special committee.

(12) The same conclusions are adopted in regard to the photographic magnitudes of the stars.

(13) Resolution 8 above, in regard to the aplanatism and achromatism of the object-glasses, shall be understood in the sense that the minimum focal distance shall be that of a ray near G, so as to attain the maximum sensibility of the photographic plates.

(14) The object-glasses shall be constructed in such a manner that the field to be measured.shall extend at least 1 degree from the center.

(15) In order to eliminate fictitious stars and to avoid inconvenience from minute specks which may exist upon the plates, two series of negatives shall be made for the whole sky.

(16) The two series of negatives shall be so made that the image of a star situated in the corner of a plate of the first series shall be found as nearly as possible in the center of a plate of the second series.

(17) Besides the two negatives giving the stars down to the four-teenth magnitude another series shall be made with shorter exposures, to assure a greater precision in the micrometrical measurement of the fundamental stars, and render possible the construction of a catalogue.

(18) The supplementary negatives, destined for the construction of the catalogue, shall contain all the stars down to the eleventh magnitude approximately. The executive committee shall determine the steps to be taken to insure the fulfillment of this condition.

(19) Each photographic plate to be used in the formation of the cata-logue shall be accompanied by all the data necessary to obtain the orientation and the value of its scale; and, as far as possible, these data shall be written on the plate itself. Each plate of this kind shall show a well-centered copy of a system of cross-wires for the purpose of elimi-nating errors which may be produced by a subsequent deformation of the photographic film. Further details of this nature shall be deter-mined by the executive committee.

(20) In the negatives intended for the map the number of cross-wires to be used in their control and reduction shall be reduced to a mini-mum.

(21) The tubes of the photographic instruments shall be constructed of the metal most likely to give an invariable focal plane and shall carry a graduation for the determination and regulation of the position of the plate.

(22) The executive committee shall choose the reference stars to be used.

(23) The question of the methods of measurement and the conversion of the numbers obtained into right ascensions and declinations for the equinox of 1900 is left to the executive committee. That committee shall first occupy itself with the study and methods of use of measuring-instruments, giving either rectangular or polar co-ordinates, and based upon the simultaneous use of scales for the larger distances, and mi-crometer screws for scale subdivisions.

(24) The connection of the plates will be effected in conformity with resolution No. 16.

At the last general session, April 25, the Congress delegated its pow-ers to a permanent committee, consisting of the directors of the observa-tories actually taking part in the work, and the following eleven mem-bers chosen by ballot, viz.: Christie, Dunér, Gill, Prosper Henry, Janssen, Loewy, Pickering, Struve, Tacchini, Vogel, and Weiss. The observa-tories of Algiers, Bordeaux, Cape of Good Hope, Greenwich, La Plata, Melbourne, Oxford, Paris, Potsdam, Rio de Janeiro, Santiago, San Fer-nando, Sydney, Tacubaya, Toulouse, have been pledged to co-operate, and the instruments for several of them are well advanced. No observa-tory in the United States has thus far signified definitely its intention of co-operating, though the Government has been appealed to to appropriate the necessary funds for the Washington Observatory. The business of the permanent committee is transacted through an executive bureau, consisting of Admiral Mouchez, president; Christie, Dunér, Janssen, Struve, and Tacchini, members, and Gill, Loewy, and Vogel, secretaries. It is expected that meetings of the permanent committee will be held every three years, though they may be called more frequently if found desirable. Before adjourning, the Congress elected also a special committee, to occupy itself with the application of photography to astronomy other than the construction of a map, acting in concert with the permanent committee. Messrs. Common and Janssen were requested to take charge of this matter. They have communicated by circular with all who are likely to be interested in this work, and propose to call a meeting at Paris, and form a committee for the consideration of the best means of carrying out the plan suggested by the Congress.

As many preliminary experiments are necessary in arranging details, special subjects of investigation have been referred to different astronomers. For instance, the study of the proper form of reticule, to Vogel; photographic magnitudes, to Struve and Pickering; optical deformation of images, to Struve; study of three or four stars nearly in a straight line, embracing an angular distance of about 1 degree, and photographed necessarily at the center and corner of a plate, to the observatories of Algiers, Leyden, Paris, Pulkowa; distortion of the sensitive film, to Algiers, Meudon, Potsdam; curved plates, Christie; orientation of the plates, the Cape, Paris; measuring apparatus, to a special committee; formula for the preparation of the plates, Abney, Eder; the effect of colors of the stars upon the photographic magnitude, Dunér.

The permanent committee has published, through the Paris Academy, three reports: the first, a full account of the Congress held in April, 1887; the other two, "bulletins," containing correspondence and results of the preliminary investigations. These papers are of great importance in the proposed photographic work, but they can hardly be reviewed satisfactorily here. The most extensive are: "Note sur l'application de la photographie aux mesures micrométriques des étoiles, T.-N. Thiele; De l'influence des durées de la pose sur l'exactitude des photographies stellaires, J. Scheiner; Travaux préparatoires effectués à l'observatoire de Potsdam, Vogel; Exposé de la méthode parallactique de mesure,—réduction des clichés, J. C. Kapteyn; Recherches faites à l'observatoire de Harvard College sur les résultats photométriques, E. C. Pickering; Étendue du champ des clichés photographiques de l'observatoire de Paris, MM. Henry."

It is strongly recommended that the plates be measured at a central bureau established in the neighborhood of Paris.

Professor Pritchard having undertaken, for the photographic committee of the Royal Society, an examination of two silver-on-glass mirrors of the same aperture but of very different focal lengths, with a view of ascertaining the practical effects of focal length on the photographic

field, has concluded that mirrors are unsuitable for any extensive charting, particularly mirrors of short focal length; at the same time there
is no doubt as to their capacity for the singularly accurate delineation
of small portions of the heavens, and for such operations as those connected with stellar parallax or the charting of the moon.

Mr. Roberts has described in the Monthly Notices (49 : 5–13) an instrument which he calls the "stellar pantograver," intended to surmount
the difficulties of reproducing the negatives after they have been obtained. It is essentially an instrument for engraving upon copper plates
points of the same size and in the same relative positions as those depicted by the photographs.

In the long exposures of two hours and upwards that some of the
photographs have required there is considerable danger of displacements of the images upon the plates due to variations in the refraction.
Dr. Dreyer has found that in latitude $+50°$ such displacements are not
likely to exceed $0''.5$ (and will therefore not affect sensibly the symmetry
of the images) in the case of an equatorial star moving from 27^m east
to 27^m west of the meridian or in the case of a star of $+25°$ declination
moving from 39^m east to 39^m west.

The photographic work of Professor Pickering upon stellar spectra,
and of Gothard, Vogel and Roberts upon nebulæ, has been mentioned
under these headings. Rapid progress has been made by Dr. Gill with
his southern photographic Durchmusterung.

COMETS.

Comet Encke (1888 II).—Encke's well-known periodic comet was
picked up by Mr. Tebbutt, of Windsor, New South Wales, with the
help of the ephemeris of Backlund and Seraphimoff, on July 8, 1888,
ten days after it had passed perihelion. In a $4\frac{1}{2}$-inch telescope it appeared as a small, bright, well-condensed nebula, about $1'$ in diameter, without a nucleus. It was observed at Windsor till August 1,
when it was "of the last degree of faintness," and at the Cape to
August 9, but it was unfavorably situated for observation in the
northern hemisphere.

Berberich has discussed the brightness of Encke's comet as seen at
different returns from 1786 to 1885, and calls attention to the rather
remarkable circumstance that the comet has been most conspicuous
when seen near a time of maximum of solar spots, and least when returning near a minimum.

Comet Faye (1888 IV).—Found by Perrotin, at Nice, August 9, 1888,
by the help of a sweeping ephemeris prepared by Kreutz. It was described as a very faint, circular nebulosity about one minute in extent,
with a slight central condensation. Although it remained visible as
late as February, 1889, on account of its extreme faintness but few
observations seemed to have been secured. Maximum brightness was
reached about the beginning of December. The correction to the

ephemeris computed directly from the elements was −4ᵐ.4; + 4′, corre·
sponding to a retardation of the perihelion time of about two days.

Comet Olbers, originally discovered by the celebrated Dr. Olbers on
March 6, 1815, was picked up by Brooks on August 24, 1887, inde-
dependently of Ginzel's ephemeris. Bessel, who made a discussion of
the earlier observations, predicted a return to perihelion on February
9, 1887, and Dr. Ginzel, rediscussing the orbit in a very elaborate
manner, found the most probable date of perihelion to be December 17, 1886, with an uncertainty of 1.6 years. Perihelion actually
occurred on October 8, 1887. Especial interest attaches to this comet
as the third member of the group of comets having a period of about
seventy-five years (Halley's, Pons', and Olbers'), which has returned
to perihelion in conformity with prediction. Kammermann, at Geneva,
described it on August 29, 1887, as a bright 7.8 magnitude, with a faint
tail. There seems to be no reason for supposing that it has lost any·
thing of its light-giving power since its previous appearance in 1815.
The last observation at this return was made at the Lick Observatory
on July 5, 1888, when the theoretical brightness was less than one-
tenth that at the time of discovery.

Comet Tempel.—The comet discovered by Tempel on July 3, 1873, and
found to have a period of five and one quarter years, was observed at its
return in 1878, but escaped observation in 1883 when it was due at perihelion on November 20. The conditions of visibility seem to be even
worse for the return of 1889, the comet remaining too near the sun,
while the circumstances of the return in 1894 are but little different
from those of 1883.

Comet Winnecke.—Von Haerdtl has rediscussed the motion of Winnecke's comet, making use of observations at a later return than Oppolzer could employ in 1880. The object was to detect, if possible, any
increase in the mean motion similar to that exhibited by Encke's comet,
though not sensible in Faye's comet, possibly owing to its great perihelion distance. He finds no acceleration whatever of the mean motion,
the actual figures indicating rather a slight retardation, but far too
small to justify any conclusion other than absence of change in the
mean motion and length of period.

Comet 1886 VIII:
=Comet c 1887.
Discovered by Barnard on January 23, 1887; last
observed on May 22, 1887; perihelion November 28,
1886.

Comet 1887 I:
=Comet a 1887.
=The great southern comet.
A cable dispatch from Dr. Thome, the director of the Cordoba Observatory in South
America, announced his discovery on Jan-
uary 18, 1887, of a large comet, or rather the tail of a large comet, faint
and illusory in the twilight and mist of the horizon. From later information it appeared that the comet was seen at Blauwberg, near Cape
Town, on the same evening, by a farmer and a fisherman, and a day or
two later it was seen at several places in Australia. Dr. Thome was

not able to confirm his discovery till January 20. From the 22d to the 25th the comet was a beautiful object to the naked eye—a narrow, straight, sharply defined, graceful tail, over 40 degrees long, shining with a soft starry light against the dark sky, beginning, apparently, without a head, and gradually widening and fading as it extended up. wards. At the Cape of Good Hope it was observed from January 22 to 28, the long, straight tail recalling the comet of February, 1880. The Revista do observatorio for February, published by Dr. Cruls at Rio Janeiro, gives a sketch of the comet made on January 24. The nucleus was then somewhere beyond the bright star α Gruis, invisible in the haze of the horizon, and the tail stretched up beyond β Hydrae, a narrow ribbon 52 degrees in length and about half a degree in width. As far as we have been able to learn the comet was not seen at all in the northern hemisphere, and was not followed in the southern hemisphere beyond the end of January.

Unfortunately, also, no well-defined nucleus, or even the slightest condensation as a point of observation could be made out at any of the observatories at which the comet was visible, and from the rough observations which were obtained it is impossible to determine the orbit with any degree of precision. The earlier dispatches suggested the identity of the new comet with the great comet of 1880, apparently on the ground of a general similarity of the circumstances of the apparition, and on the fact that the line of sight nearly intersected the orbit of the comet of 1880; but Mr. Chandler, who has made a critical discussion of all the observations obtained, has been unable to reconcile them with an orbit similar to that of the group of great comets of 1843, 1880, and 1882; the orbit that he obtains bears a closer resemblance, in fact, to those of the comets of 1680 and 1689. The unavoidable uncertainty in the observations must, however, leave the question of identity unsettled. The extremely small perihelion distance is worthy of notice, and may, perhaps, account for the lack of nucleus. Indeed, if we accept the orbit computed by Dr. Oppenheim (q=0.0047), the comet must have ploughed through the surface of the sun itself.

Comet 1887 II :
= Comet b 1887.
Discovered by W. R. Brooks, at Phelps, New York, on the evening of January 22, 1887, in the constellation Draco. In the early part of February it reached its greatest northern declination, 80°, then went south again, and was last observed by Plummer at Orwell Park, on April 23. From the time of discovery it increased gradually in brightness till about the middle of February, when it was described as a bright telescopic object about 3' in diameter with well marked central condensation of the tenth magnitude. According to the yet unfinished investigation of Dr. Stechert the orbit shows a well-marked ellipticity.

Comet 1887 III :
= Comet d 1887.
Discovered by Barnard at Nashville on the night of February 16, 1887, in 8ʰ right ascension, and 15° south declination, a very faint nebulous object with rapid motion to-

wards the north and west; last observed on April 10, at Orwell Park. The ordinary formula for brightness, which assumes that the comet shines by reflected sunlight only, seems to have failed in this case, as in many others; in the middle of March, when its theoretical brightness was 0.12 that at the time of discovery, it was apparently as well seen as during the first days of its appearance.

Comet 1887 IV: | Barnard's third comet of 1887 was discovered at
=Comet e 1887. | 11 o'clock on the evening of May 12, in right ascension 15^h, declination—31°. On May 13 it was described by Boss as having a star like nucleus of the 11.5 magnitude. It increased somewhat in brightness till about the middle of June, developing a tail which attained a length of 5'. It moved rapidly north, and on account of its brightness and favorable situation was well observed, till August 11. Mr. Muller has already completed a definitive orbit, and finds that the observations are represented by an ellipse somewhat better than by a parabola.

Comet 1887 V: | Found by W. R. Brooks, of Phelps, New
—Comet f 1887. | York, on August 24, 1887. (See comet Olbers.)
=Comet 1815.
=Olbers' comet.
=Olbers-Brooks comet.

Comet 1888 I: | Discovered by Sawerthal, at the Cape of Good
=Comet a 1888. | Hope, on February 18, 1888, or the early morning of February 19, civil reckoning, the comet being readily seen with the naked eye, with sharply defined nucleus of the seventh magnitude in right ascension 19^h, declination —56°; a tail 2° in length was visible with an opera glass. The rapid northerly motion brought it, by the 12th of March, into view in the northern hemisphere, where it was followed until September, being reported visible to the naked eye until the first part of May. Thome, at Cordoba, described it as a fine nakedeye object, with a tail, at its maximum, 5° in length and a nucleus of three and one-half magnitude. Remarkable fluctuations occurred in the brightness of the head, during the months of March and May, resembling the phenomena noted in the great September comet of 1882 and the Pons-Brooks comet of 1884.

On the 19th of March the main eighth magnitude nucleus was seen to have an eleventh magnitude companion, and on the 27th of the month a third faint nucleus was detected; the triple nucleus was last seen on the 4th of June. Between the 19th and 21st of May it became five or six times brighter than during the days immediately preceding, and from the nucleus two bright streamers were shot out, curving backward on either side of the nucleus into the tail. This sudden outburst is all the more difficult to account for as it occurred two months after perihelion; it is to be regretted that no spectroscopic observations were obtained at this critical period. The spectroscopic observations made in March and April showed a faint, broad, continuous spectrum, in addition to the three characteristic hydrogen bands. The orbit, according to Berberich, is undoubtedly elliptic, the period, from his preliminary computation, being 2,370 years.

Comet 1888 II:
 =Comet b 1888.
 =Encke's comet.

First observed at this return by Tebbutt, at Windsor, New South Wales, on July 8. (See comet Encke.)

Comet 1888 III:
 =Comet c 1888.

Discovered by W. R. Brooks, at the new Smith Observatory, Geneva, New York, about 8:45 P. M., August 7, 1888—right ascension 10ʰ 5ᵐ, declination +44°.30′. The head was round, one-half minute in diameter; the nucleus was of the ninth to tenth magnitude, and there was a little tail 5′ long in position angle 270°. Perihelion had been passed on July 31; the last observation reported was on October 10.

Comet 1888 IV:
 =Comet d 1888.
 =Faye's comet.

Found by Perrotin, at Nice, August 9, 1888. (See Comet Faye.)

Comet 1888 V:
 =Comet f 1888.

Discovered by Mr. E. E. Barnard, at the Lick Observatory, on October 30; a faint suspicious object, the head well developed, with ill-defined nucleus, and a short tail. Perihelion had taken place some forty-eight days before discovery, but the increasing distance from the sun was largely compensated for by the approach to the earth, so that the comet was observed for several months in 1889.

Comet 1889 I:
 =Comet e 1888.

This comet was discovered by Barnard at the Lick Observatory, with a 4-inch comet-seeker, on September 2, 1888, or the morning of September 3, and also independently by Brooks, at Geneva, on the following morning. It was a round nebulous mass 1′, in diameter, with a central condensation of 11–12 magnitude and no tail. At the end of November it reached its maximum brightness, twelve times as bright as at discovery, and appeared to the naked eye like a nebulous star of the sixth magnitude. It will not pass perihelion till January 31, 1889.

The spectrum, according to Dr. Copeland, on November 14, instead of being composed of the usual feeble separate bands, was continuous, rather long, extending from wave-lengths 575 to 450 of Angström's scale, brighter in the middle and fading gradually at both ends; it resembled the spectrum of a close globular star-cluster or of a non-gaseous nebula, rather than that of a self-luminous gas. Faint patches of light were made out in the positions usually occupied by the second and third cometary bands. Similar observations were made later, and on December 8, all three bands were distinctly visible, but on each occasion the continuous spectrum formed the ground on which the brighter spectrum was superposed. "It seems probable that the comet shines mainly by reflected light, - - - to which the action of the sun on the cometary material is slowly adding the usual bright bands."

Approximate elements of the comets of 1887 and 1888.

Designation.	Perihelion = T Greenwich mean time.	☊	ω	i	q	e	Discoverer.	Date of discovery.	Synonym.	
		° ′	° ′	° ′						
1886 VIII ●	1886. Nov. 28.38	258 12	31 53	65 35	1.480	.....	Barnard	1887. Jan. 23	1887 e	Great Southern Comet.
1887 I	1887. Jan. 11.23	337 43	63 36	137 ...	0.005	.....	Thome	Jan. 18	1887 a	
II	Mar. 17.03	279 51	159 11	104 17	1.633	.....	Brooks	Jan. 22	1887 b	
III	Mar. 28.40	135 27	36 29	139 49	1.007	.....	Barnard	Feb. 16	1887 d	
IV	June 16.66	245 13	15 8	17 33	1.394	0.996	...do	May 12	1887 c	Olbers's.
V	Oct. 8.46	84 29	65 19	44 34	1.199	0.931	Brooks	Aug. 24	1887 f	
1888 I	1888. Mar. 17.00	359 55	245 23	42 15	0.699	0.995	Sawerthal	1888. Feb. 18	1888 a	Encke's.
II	June 27.99	334 89	183 57	12 53	0.343	0.846	Tebbutt	July 8	1888 b	
III	July 31.15	101 30	59 14	74 12	0.902	.....	Brooks	Aug. 7	1888 c	
IV	Aug. 19.54	209 42	201 14	11 20	1.738	0.549	At Nice	Aug. 9	1888 d	Faye's.
V	Sept. 13.00	137 35	291 4	56 27	1.522	.....	Barnard	Oct. 30	1888 f	Elliptic?

Prof. Daniel Kirkwood has suggested that certain comets of short period may have originated within the solar system. Wolf's comet (1884 III), for example, before its last near approach to Jupiter, had an eccentricity of 0.28, which is exceeded by twelve known asteroids, and the elements of Tempel's comet (1867 II) do not differ greatly from those of an eccentric asteroid. Out of twenty short-period comets, seven have disappeared either by dissolution, like Biela's comet, or by the transformation of the orbit by Jupiter as in the case of Lexell's comet. Five, or, including Encke's and Biela's, seven, have periods commensurable with that of Jupiter; all have direct motion; all but one have a smaller inclination than Pallas, and there is a tendency of the perihelia to concentrate in the 180° (from 290° to 110°), as in the asteroids.

One of the most able of recent contributions to cometary astronomy is a monograph by Dr. Kreutz upon the orbit of the great September comet of 1882. In connection with investigations being carried on by Professor Weiss this will form a complete discussion of the system of comets with remarkably small perihelion distance, 1843 I, 1880 I, and 1882 II.

Dr. Galle is compiling a catalogue of recent comets embracing the various supplements to the list given in 1847 in Encke's edition of "Olbers' Methode."

METEORITES.

Researches on meteorites.—Mr. Lockyer presented at the meeting of the Royal Society on November 17, 1887, a paper giving the results of his "Researches on Meteorites," which has attracted much attention. He has examined meteoric spectra under various conditions, particularly that of feeble temperature, and has found it possible to obtain from meteorites spectra that show the most peculiar features of solar, stellar, nebular, or cometary spectra. "In the spectra of nebulæ, for instance, seven lines have been detected, of which three were traced to hydrogen, three to low-temperature magnesium, and the seventh, which has not yet been traced to its originating element, has been given by the glow from the Dhurmsala meteorite. The most characteristic nebular line was identified with the low-temperature fluting of magnesium, and the unusual spectrum obtained from the comets of 1866 and 1867 was ascribed to the same cause. The changes observed in the spectrum of the great comet of 1882 were such as would correspond to the changes induced by the change of temperature in the spectrum of a meteorite; and the changes in the spectrum of Nova Cygni, and the bright lines in such a star as R Geminorum received a similar explanation; while a very full, in parts almost perfect, reproduction of a considerable portion of the solar spectrum has been obtained by taking a composite photograph of the arc spectrum of several stony meteorites, taken at random between iron meteoric poles. These and similar observations have led Mr. Lockyer to regard all self-luminous bodies in the celestial spaces as composed of meteorites, or masses of meteoritic vapor produced by heat brought about by condensation of meteor-swarms due to gravity, so that the existing distinction between stars, comets, and nebulæ rests on no physical basis. All alike are meteoritic in origin, the differences between them depending upon differences in temperature, and upon the closeness of the compouent meteorites to one another. *Novæ* (new stars that blaze forth suddenly) are explained as produced by the clash of meteor-streams, and most variable stars are regarded as uncondensed meteor-streams. Stars with spectra like that of Alpha Orionis (Rigel) are considered not as true suns, but as mere clouds of incandescent stones; probably the first stage of meteoritic condensation. Stars with spectra of the first and second type represent the condensed swarm in its hottest stages, while spectra of Secchi's fourth type indicate an advanced state of cooling."

The general conclusions arrived at by Mr. Lockyer may be thus summarized: All self-luminous bodies in space are composed of meteorites variously aggregated, and at various stages of temperatuie depending upon the frequency and violence of their mutual collisions. Comets, nebulæ, bright-line stars, stars showing banded spectra of the third type, including most long-period variables, are to be regarded as veritable meteor-swarms; they are made up, that is to say, of an indefinite multitude of separate and (in a sense) independent solid bodies, bathed in evolved gases, and glowing with the heat due to their arrested motions. "The existing distinction," we are told, "between stars, comets, and nebulæ rests on no physical basis." Stars, on the other hand, of the Sirian and solar types (constituting the only true "suns") are vaporized meteor-swarms; their high temperatures represent the surrendered velocities of myriads of jostling particles, drawn together by the victorious power of gravity.

"Collisions" are not however exclusively relied upon for the cosmical production of light and heat. It is admitted that the luminosity of comets and nebulæ must be largely due to electrical excitement; nor is any reason apparent why its influence should be restricted to these two classes of bodies. Destruction of movement by impacts can scarcely be made to supply its place. Occasional illuminative effects may be derived from it, but none that are uniform and permanent.

The small bodies which, more or less plentifully distributed, appear to pervade space, are in this theory treated as the fundamental atoms of the universe. But it is evident that we can not begin there. They have a history, marked perhaps by strange vicissitudes. They may be agents of regeneration, but they are almost certainly products of destruction. Possibly they are seed as well as dust, and serve as the material link between the creation and decay of successive generations of suns.

The orbits of meteorites.—Prof. H. A. Newton, of Yale College, has carefully studied the evidence available for determining the "former orbits of those meteorites that are in our collections and that were seen to fall." Of these stone-falls there are three classes: (*a*) 116 falls for which we have statements as to the direction of the path through the air; (*b*) 94 falls of which we know the time of day; (*c*) 50 or more falls of which the history is too scanty to give the time of day. He is led to the following three propositions:

1. The meteorites which we have in our cabinets, and which were seen to fall, were originally (as a class and with a very small number of exceptions) moving about the sun in orbits that had inclinations less than 90°; that is, their motions were direct, not retrograde.

2. The reason why we have only this class of stones in our collections is not one wholly or even mainly dependent upon the habits of men; nor on the times when men are out of doors; nor on the places where men live; nor on any other principle of selection acting at or after the arrival of the stones at the ground. Either the stones, which are moving in the solar system across the earth's orbit, move in general in direct orbits, or else for some reason the stones which move in retrograde orbits do not in general come through the air in solid form.

3. The perihelion-distances of nearly all the orbits in which these stones moved were not less than 0.5 nor more than 1.0, the earth's radius-vector being unity. (*Observatory* 11: 331.)

At the meeting of the Royal Society, November 15, 1888, Prof. G. H. Darwin read an important paper dealing with the mechanical conditions of a swarm of meteorites from a mathematical stand-point.

SOLAR SYSTEM.

Motion of the solar system in space.—Dr. Ludwig Struve has made a careful comparison of the Pulkowa catalogues for 1855 with Auwer's re-reduction of Bradley (epoch 1755), and, as one of his results, has obtained a value of the motion of our system to which a good deal of interest attaches. As it was necessary to assume some connection between the magnitude of a star and its distance, he adopted the following relative scale, regarding a star of the sixth magnitude as at the distance unity:

Mag.	Dist.	Mag.	Dist.
1	0.13	5	0.70
2	0.23	6	1.00
3	0.36	7	1.49
4	0.51	8	2.25

The result he obtains—4.″36—is then the angular motion of the sun in one hundred years, as seen from the average sixth magnitude star. The actual velocity corresponding to this is about 13 miles per second. The point in the sky towards which the sun is moving is in the constel-

lation Hercules. By combining his results with those of other astronomers, Struve adopts for the mean a displacement of about 5″, corresponding to a velocity of 15 miles per second. The point toward which
the system is moving is still in Hercules, right ascension 266°.7, declination +31°.0.

The following table shows how the various determinations of these co-
ordinates agree:

	A.	D.	Epoch.	No. of stars.
	°	°		
W. Herschel	260.6	+26.3	....	....
Do	245.9	+40.4	....	....
Gauss	259.2	+30.8	....	....
Argelander	259.9	+32.5	1792.5	390
Lundahl	252.5	+14.4	1792.5	147
O. Struve	261.5	+37.6	1790	392
Galloway	260.1	+34.4	1790	78
Mädler	261.6	+39.9	1800	2,163
Airy	261.5	+24.7	1800	113
Dunkin	263.7	+25.0	1800	1,167
Gyldén	273.9	....	1800 ?	(?)
Do	260.5	....	1800	(?)
L. de Ball	269.0	+23.2	1860	67
Raucken	284.6	+31.9	1855 ?	106
Bischof	285.2	+48.5	1855	480
Ubaghs	262.4	+26.6	1810 ?	464
L. Struve	273.3	+27.3	1805	2,509
Plummer	270.1	+20.3	....	274
Do	276.1	+26.5	....	274

For the magnitude of the motion in a century we have—

$$\begin{aligned}
\text{O. Struve} & \dots\dots\dots\dots\dots\dots\dots\dots\dots\dots\dots\dots\dots\dots & 4.″31 \\
\text{Dunkin} & \dots\dots\dots\dots\dots\dots\dots\dots\dots\dots\dots\dots\dots\dots & 5.\ 22 \\
\text{L. Struve} & \dots\dots\dots\dots\dots\dots\dots\dots\dots\dots\dots\dots\dots\dots & 4.\ 36 \\
\text{Gyldén} & \dots\dots\dots\dots\dots\dots\dots\dots\dots\dots\dots\dots\dots\dots & 6.\ 80 \\
\text{Do} & \dots\dots\dots\dots\dots\dots\dots\dots\dots\dots\dots\dots\dots\dots & 5.\ 89
\end{aligned}$$

as seen from a star of the sixth magnitude.

SUN.

Rotation time of the sun.—Mr. Crew, of Johns Hopkins University,
has made a new determination of the time of revolution of the sun on
its axis by comparing the wave-lengths of certain lines in the spectrum
when measured in light coming from two opposite limbs of the sun. By
Doppler's principle the wave-length of the line in light from the approaching limb ought to be shorter than in the light from the receding
limb. The results obtained give a velocity of the photosphere at the
sun's equator of 2.437 miles per second; from this the rotation time is
determined to be 25.88 days. Mr. Crew's observations indicate an increase in the angular velocity of the surface with increase in the helio-
graphic latitude. This result is opposed to that obtained by Carrington
and Spoerer from observations of sunspots.

Dr. Wilsing has found the rotation period from observations of faculae to be 25.23, and has detected no variation in velocity depending upon the latitude. The difficulty of identifying faculae on their reappearance, and of measuring their positions with exactness, makes the result some· what doubtful.

Diameter of the sun.—Dr. Auwers has made a very exhaustive dis· cussion of the sun's horizontal and vertical diameters from the meridian observations of Greenwich, Washington, Oxford and Neuchâtel with special reference to the alleged variations in the mean annual diameters following the period of the sunspot cycle. He concludes that there is no valid reason for supposing the sun's diameter to vary, and that the apparent changes arise from insufficiently determined personal equa· tions. He also points out that meridian observations are quite unsuited for the determination of any possible ellipticity in the sun's disk, and that there is no reason to conclude from these results that such ellip· ticity exists. The several mean values of the sun's (assumed circular) diameter are:

Greenwich............32′ 2″.36.	Oxford............32′ 3″.19.
Washington..........32′ 2″.51.	Neuchâtel.........32′ 3″.27.

The discordances are ascribed to instrumental or uneliminated per· sonal peculiarities.

In a second paper Dr. Auwers discusses the apparent changes of both the horizontal and vertical diameter during the course of a year, de· duced from meridian observations, and he concludes that the periodic variations in the monthly value of the diameters result not from physical changes in the sun, but from the effect of temperature on the instruments and from difference in the quality of the telescopic images at opposite seasons of the year.

Another discussion of the horizontal diameter of the sun has been made by Professor di Legge from meridian transits of the sun observed at Campidoglio from 1874 to 1883. The mean horizontal diameter at mean distance deduced from 5796 transits by four observers on 2213 days is 32′ 2″.38.

Solar activity in 1887, 1888.—The decrease in spots, faculae and promi· nences which was so marked during 1886, and particularly during the latter part of that year, continued in 1887, and although there was no spotless period as long as that of November, 1886, the mean spotted area for the year was much below that of the year preceding. The days of greatest spotted area were July 6, 7, and 8. The agreement in the general form of the curves for spot numbers and magnetic variation was not so close as in some previous years. The fluctuations in the num· bers and dimensions of the prominences were less than for the spots, but they also showed a maximum in July. Faculae accorded well with the prominences, neither faculae nor prominences following the spots in the marked depression of November.

During 1888 spots were few, small and in low latitudes, and there were frequent intervals in which no spots at all were seen, longer intervals in fact than any since the minimum of 1879. The most prolific month as to entire spotted area, though not as to number of spots, was November, following immediately a long period of quiescence. There was a rough tendency of spots to certain solar longitudes and in latitude, they continued to be more numerous in the southern than in the northern hemisphere. Faculæ did not vary simultaneously with spots, but their diminution as compared with 1886 and 1887, was slight. They showed a very noticeable development during the secondary maximum of September, while the prominences fell off considerably both in September and November, but attained their greatest development in March and April.

Solar spectrum.—Experiments made by Professor Trowbridge and Mr. C. C. Hutchins at the Jefferson Physical Laboratory in Cambridge, have overthrown the proof brought forward in 1879 by Dr. Henry Draper of the existence of oxygen in the sun. They show that when sufficiently powerful apparatus is used to bring out minute details of the spectrum of oxygen and of the sun, the bright regions of the solar spectrum disappear, and hence also the apparent coincidences between them and the spectrum of oxygen upon which Dr. Draper based his proof. The bright bands obtained by Dr. Draper are in fact occupied by numerous dark lines of variable intensity.

Continuing their experiments however they have been led to conclude that there is unmistakable evidence of the existence of carbon in the sun.

In a valuable paper by Mr. C. C. Hutchins and Mr. E. L. Holden, evidence is brought forward to show the probable existence in the sun of bismuth, silver, and platinum, while tin potassium, and lithium are more doubtful. For cadmium two perfect coincidences were found, while there was no good evidence in favor of the presence of lead cerium, molybdenum, uranium or vanadium.

Prof. S. P. Langley has published in the American Journal of Science an abstract of a memoir on the invisible solar and lunar spectrum, in which he summarizes the result of investigations carried on at the Allegheny Observatory in continuation of his previous researches on the infra-red of the solar spectrum to the extent of about three microns. By means of the improved apparatus described, the extreme infra-red solar spectrum has now been searched from three to over eighteen microns; and it is shown that in this region the ratios between solar and lunar heat are completely changed from what they are in the visible spectrum. While the solar light in the latter is about five hundred thousand times that of moonlight, the solar heat received in the invisible part of the spectrum is probably less than five hundred times the lunar. These studies also promise important results for meteorology, by opening to observation the hitherto unknown region of the spectrum, in which are to be found the nocturnal and diurnal radiations, not only from the moon towards the earth, but from the soil of the earth towards space. (*Nature.*)

Total eclipse of the sun, August 19, 1887.—Unusual preparations were made throughout Europe for observing this eclipse, and great popular interest was manifested in the event, but, unfortunately, very few observations of value were obtained on account of the generally cloudy weather that prevailed over the whole region west of the Ural mountains. The central line of the eclipse first struck the earth at a point 53 miles west-northwest of Leipsic, where the sun was just rising. The line of totality, which was about 135 miles wide, then crossed Germany, Russia, Siberia, China and Japan, and left the earth at a point in the Pacific Ocean in latitude 24° 27' north, longitude 173° 30' east.

Eclipse of the moon, January 28, 1888.—The total eclipse of the moon on January 28, 1888, presented an unusually favorable opportunity for observing the occultations of a large number of faint stars, and, in order to secure as many observations of these phenomena as possible, Dr. Döllen, of Pulkowa, prepared and sent out to the principal observatories in Europe and America, a list of the stars to be occulted at each. He reports that he has received three hundred and ninety-six observations of disappearances and three hundred and eighty-seven of re-appearances, the places of observation being so favorably situated, that he considers that there is ample material for determining the position, the diameter, and possibly the ellipticity and parallax of the moon.

SOLAR PARALLAX AND THE TRANSITS OF VENUS.

Professor Harkness, at the meeting of the American Association in Cleveland on August 20, 1888, gave a description of the instruments and reduction processes employed by the United States Transit of Venus Commission in determining the solar parallax from the measurement of photographs taken at the ten American stations in December, 1882; Washington, Cedar Keys, San Antonio, Cerro Roblero, Princeton, and the Lick Observatory, in the United States; Santa Cruz and Santiago, South America; Wellington, South Africa, and Auckland, New Zealand. The preliminary value of the parallax deduced from the measured distances of the centres of the sun and of Venus on 1,475 photographs is $\pi = 8''.847 \pm 0''.012$. The American photographs in 1874 gave $\pi = 8''.883 \pm 0''.034$, and the French $\pi = 8''.80$. The distance of the sun corresponding to the value now obtained—8''.847—is 92,385,000 miles, with a probable error of only 125,000 miles. These numbers are doubtless close approximations to the results which will be obtained from the complete discussion of all the photographs, but they cannot be regarded as final for several reasons, chief among which is the fact that the reduction of the position angles of Venus relatively to the sun's center is still unfinished.

The report of the committee appointed to superintend the arrangements for the expeditions sent out by the British Government to observe the transit of Venus in 1882 has been published. It consists almost entirely of a discussion by Mr. Stone of the observations of contact Expeditions were sent from England to Jamaica, Barbadoes, Bermuda, Cape of Good Hope, Madagascar, New Zealand, and Brisbane, Queensland, and the observers at all these stations were successful, except at Brisbane, where the weather was cloudy. It will be remembered that the English committee did not feel satisfied with the photographic work in 1874, and for various reasons they determined in the second transit to put their reliance entirely upon contact observations. From the observations of external contact at ingress Mr. Stone obtains a parallax of $8.''700 \pm 0''.122$; from those of internal contact at ingress, $8''.823 \pm 0''.023$; from those of internal contact at egress, $8''.855 \pm 0''.036$, and from external contact at egress $8''.953 \pm 0''.048$. The most probable combined result he considers to be $8''.832 \pm 0''.024$, which corresponds to a mean distance of $92,500,000 \pm$ miles between the earth and sun, with an uncertainty of 250,000 miles.

The fourth volume of the report of the German Transit of Venus Commission was published in 1887, under the editorship of Dr. Auwers. It contains the observations in detail made with the heliometer by various observers, both before and after the transits of 1874 and 1882, for the purpose of determining the instrumental constants.

The report of the Brazilian expeditions has been printed in a quarto volume of 700 pages. Three stations were occupied: St. Thomas, in the Antilles; Olinda, Brazil; and Punta Arenas, in the Straits of Magellan. The transit was observed by projecting the sun's image formed by an equatorial refractor of 6.3 inches aperture upon a screen and noting the times of contact. The result given for the value of the parallax from the internal contacts is $8''.808$.

Professor Hall, using a value of the constant of aberration $20''.4542$, deduced from a series of observations of α Lyrae, made at the U. S. Naval Observatory during the years 1862 to 1867, and introducing Michelson and Newcomb's determination of the velocity of light, has found for the solar parallax $8''.810 \pm 0''.0062$.

PLANETS.

MARS.—The observations of Perrotin, Terby, and Denning have confirmed the presence of most of the so-called "canals," or narrow, dark lines, that were discovered by Schiaparelli in 1877, and at subsequent oppositions, and in some cases the gemination or doubling of the canals has been detected.

Considerable interest has been aroused in regard to Mars on account of the recent changes reported in the markings upon its surface by Perrotin and others. The chief change reported was the apparent inundation or disappearance of the "triangular continent," to which the name of Libya has been assigned, but the report has not been confirmed by the observations of Schiaparelli, Terby, Niesten, and Holden. The observations of Professor Holden and his assistants with the 36 inch refractor began on July 16, 1888, and were continued to August 10; the planet was therefore very unfavorably situated, its diameter being less than 9″. Several of the most important canals were seen, but they were not double, appearing rather "as broad bands covering the spaces on M. Schiaparelli's map which are occupied by pairs of canals and by the spaces separating the members of each pair." Professor Hall, with the Washington 26 inch refractor, has never been able to see these markings so sharply drawn by European observers. The only remarkable change he noticed was the diminution in the size of the white spot at the south pole of the planet.

Numerous sketches of Mars showing the canals or other markings have been published by Holden, Perrotin, Terby, and Niesten. No adequate explanation of the canals, or of the changes observed, has yet been offered.

JUPITER'S SATELLITES.—Astronomers have always been puzzled by the discordant appearances of the satellites during transit, but more especially by the fact that the phenomena do not apply equally to all the satellites, or even in some instances to the same satellite in two successive revolutions. The fourth, for instance, as it approaches the disk of Jupiter becomes rapidly fainter till it arrives at contact. When once on the limb it shines with a moderate brilliancy for about ten or fifteen minutes, then becomes suddenly lost to view for a similar period, and lastly reappears, but as a dark spot, which grows darker and darker until it equals the blackness of its own shadow on the planet. The appearance of the second satellite, however, is entirely different, for it seems never to have been seen otherwise than pure white during transit; whereas the first and third differ yet again from the preceding two. The former is sometimes a steel-gray, and at others a little darker, whereas the latter has been seen perfectly white and yet so black as to be mistaken for the fourth. Mr. E. J. Spitta has made a careful investigation of these interesting phenomena, communicating his results in a paper of some length, read at the meeting of the Royal Astronomical Society, in November, 1887. His experiments consisted essentially of numerous observations upon suitably prepared models representing the planet and satellites, and he concludes (see Nature 37:468, March 15, 1888) that the probable reason the fourth satellite is uniformly black during transit, when it has passed its period of disappearance, is, that its albedo is so low as to grant the difference between it and the background necessary for a body to appear black when superimposed on another. Its preliminary whiteness and disappearance are also shown to be a question of relative albedo, for they are due to the fact that a sphere at its limb loses so much in reflective power that up to that moment the satellite possesses sufficient albedo (as compared with the background in that situation) to maintain its whiteness. So, too, with the second satellite. Its albedo proves to be so high that it is capable of preserving its brilliancy throughout the entire transit.

The third and first satellites evidently possess sides of different albedo, one high enough to maintain a brighter aspect than the other, or even, as in the case of the third, to make it appear white when one side is presented to the earth and dark when the other. Finally, to quote from the original paper, " it is not unreasonable to conclude that these anomalous phenomena are due to functional idiosyncrasies in the eye itself, rather than to physical peculiarities of the Jovian system."

Mr. Denning has obtained from observations of the red spot made between February 12 and August 22, 1888, a rotation of $9^h 55^m 40^s.21$, nearly one second less than the spot gave in 1885–'86, though six seconds greater than in 1879.

The value obtained for the mass of Jupiter by von Haerdtl in his discussion of Winnecke's comet is 1 : 1047.152 $\pm$ 0.0136.

SATURN.—The first number of a new series of publications called Supplements to the Pulkowa Observations contains an interesting memoir by Dr. Hermann Struve on the outer satellites of Saturn. He discusses his own observations made with the 15-inch refractor in the years 1884–1886 on Iapetus, Titan, Rhea, and Dione, with a view to correcting the elements of these satellites, and also the values of the mass and ellipticity of Saturn. The mass of Saturn was found by Bessel to be 1 : 3501.6 $\pm$ 0.77, or with a slight correction indicated in the present paper, 1 : 3502.5. Prof. Asaph Hall, on the other hand, obtained the value 1 : 3481.3 $\pm$ 0.54. Struve considers the rather large discordance between these values due to systematic error in measuring the distance of a satellite from a limb, and his own observations consist entirely of comparisons of one satellite with another, either by differences of right ascension and north polar distance or of distance and position angle. His resulting value of the mass of Saturn agrees closely with Bessel's, being 1 : 3498. The correction of the elements has been carefully and laboriously carried out by the method of least squares. (*The Observatory*, 11 : 303, July, 1888.)

Mr. G. W. Hill, in his paper on the motion of Hyperion and the mass of Titan, has obtained for the latter 1 : 4714, Saturn's mass being unity. Newcomb's corrected value, and Ormond Stone's value, accord well with this.

URANUS.—Dr. Valentiner, of the Karlsruhe Observatory, and his assistant, Dr. von Rebeur-Paschwitz, were able to detect in April, 1887, a slight ellipticity in the disk of the planet Uranus, but their instrument, a 6-inch equatorial, was not of sufficient power to make satisfactory measures.

NEPTUNE.—Tisserand has shown that the progressive changes in the node and inclination of the orbit of the satellite of Neptune can be explained by supposing a slight flattening of the surface of the planet; but the flattening would probably be too slight to be measured. Further observations may enable the amount of the inclination to be more exactly determined, and at the same time will show whether the changes in question are due to this cause alone.

THE MINOR PLANETS.—Seventeen of these small bodies were added to the group during the years 1887 and 1888, making the total number now known 281.

The new discoveries, with approximate elements, are given in the following table. All except number 270 were below the eleventh magnitude, and some slight confusion at first occurred in the numbering, owing to the difficulty of distinguishing a new asteroid from one already known in the absence of a very carefully computed ephemeris. For instance, numbers 268 and 279 were at first thought to be identical with 149, Medusa; 277 with 228, Agathe; 280 with 255, Oppavia; while an asteroid detected by Luther on April 11, 1887, and independently by Coggia on April 16, proved to be 69, Hesperia, which had been looked for in vain in 1882 and 1885; and one found by Borelly on May 12, 1888, to which the number 278 was assigned, though it was suspected to be identical with 156, Xanthippe, eventually proved to be 116, Sirona.

List of minor planets discovered in 1887 and 1888.

Number and name.	Discoverer.	Date of discovery.	Longitude of perihelion.	Longitude of node.	Inclination.	Eccentricity.	Mean daily motion.	Mean distance from sun.	Period in years.
		1887.	°	°	°		''		
265 Anna	Palisa, at Vienna	Feb. 25	226.0	335.4	25.8	0.26	942	2.42	3.77
266 Aline	...do	May 17	23.8	236.3	13.3	.16	754	2.81	4.70
267 Tirza	Charlois, at Nice	May 27	264.3	74.0	6.0	.10	768	2.77	4.62
268 Adorea	Borrelly, at Marseilles	June 9	184.8	121.8	7.3	.13	655	3.08	5.42
269 Justina	Palisa, at Vienna	Sept. 21	274.6	157.3	5.4	.20	838	2.62	4.23
270 Anahita	Peters, at Clinton	Oct. 8	333.1	254.5	2.4	.15	1090	2.20	3.26
271 Penthesilea.	Knorre, at Berlin	Oct. 13	24.8	337.5	3.6	.10	681	3.01	5.21
		1888.							
272 Antonia	Charlois, at Nice	Feb. 4	21.4	37.0	4.6	.03	770	2.77	4.61
273 Atropos	Palisa, at Vienna	Mar. 8	285.0	158.8	20.8	.14	974	2.37	3.64
274 Philagoria	....do	Apr. 3	212.8	93.6	3.7	.12	668	3.04	5.31
275 Sapientia	.. do	Apr. 15	162.9	134.9	4.8	.17	769	2.77	4.61
276 Adelheid	....do	Apr. 17	120.6	211.6	21.7	.06	644	3.12	5.51
277 Elvira	Charlois, at Nice	May 3	......	233.5	1.1	.09	......	2.87	......
278 Paulina	Palisa, at Vienna	May 16	224.8	62.4	7.5	.11	786	2.73	4.52
279 Thule	.. do	Oct. 25	298.8	75.2	2.4	.11	405	4.25	8.75
280 Philia	.. do	Oct. 29	96.9	10.9	7.4	.14	692	2.97	5.12
281 Lucretia	...do	Oct. 31	45.9	31.0	5.3	.13	1096	2.19	3 24

Number 265 is remarkable on account of the very considerable inclination of the plane of its orbit to that of the ecliptic, and also on account of its near approach to the earth, its least distance from us being 0.96, in terms of the earth's mean distance from the sun; it would therefore seem to offer an additional means of determining the value of the solar parallax. Number 270 also approaches quite near the earth, $\triangle = 0.81$. It will be noticed that 279, with its mean distance from the sun of 4.25, considerably greater than that of any other asteroid, lies upon the extreme outer limit of the group, and will at certain times, therefore, be brought quite close to Jupiter, and by the perturbations thus experienced may furnish further knowledge of the mass of that planet. Number 281, with its small mean distance of 2.19 lies, on the other hand, near the inner border of the group; it is the sixty-eighth asteroid discovered by Dr. J. Palisa.

Prof. Tietjen discontinues with the year 1888, the regular issue of the Circulars and Correspondence of the Berlin Jahrbuch, relating to asteroids. Special attention will be given hereafter to the orbits of newly discovered planets presenting interesting peculiarities.

The Annals of the Harvard Observatory, volume 18, No. 3, contains a discussion of a series of photometric observations of the asteroids by Mr. H. M. Parkhurst, extending from April to December, 1887. The method of observation was to note the time that the asteroid took to disappear after passing a transit wire, the telescope being stationary, and the light of the asteroid or comparison star suffering diminution either by a wedge or more frequently by a deflector—a piece of glass with nearly parallel sides placed in the telescope tube, about one seventh of the way from the focus to the object glass, and covering half the field. The conclusions reached by the author are as follows:

(1) The phase correction can not be neglected, and is peculiar to each asteroid.

(2) There may be, for certain asteroids, large errors from rotation.

(3) In most cases, after the phase correction has been determined, the remaining unknown errors are less than the average variation of the fixed stars.

REPORTS OF OBSERVATORIES.

In collecting the following notes upon observatories the latest avail-able information has been utilized, but it has been found impossible to b.ing the report in each case down to the end of 1888. The Viertel-jahrsschrift, for instance, from which the data for many European ob servatories are drawn, contains reports no later than 1887, and compar atively few observatories publish independent annual reports. The writer's thanks are due to Sr. Felipe Valle for notes on the observatories of Mexico.

Ann Arbor.—Prof. W. W. Campbell has been appointed assistant to fill the vacancy made by the removal of Mr. Schaeberle to the Lick Ob-servatory.

Armagh.—Dr. Dreyer has devoted a large part of his time to the pre-paration and passing through the press of a new general catalogue of nebulæ.

Bamberg.—An interesting description of the new observatory is given in the Vierteljahrsschrift for 1887, p. 333, by the director, Dr. E. Hart-wig. The sum of $45,000 was available for buildings, $17,500 for in-struments, the interest on $20,000 for salaries, and on $12,500 for main-tenance, with a reserve fund of about $20,000. The observatory con-sists of two buildings, the observing-rooms being in one and the offices and dwelling in the other. In the first there are two towers surmounted by domes and connecting them is the transit room. A long covered way from the dwelling gives easy access to the instruments. The latter are a 7-inch Repsold-Merz heliometer similar to the one at the Cape, a 10 inch refractor, a Repsold-Merz transit with zenith-telescope attach-ment, 6-inch Merz comet-seeker, clocks, chronometers, and subsidiary apparatus.

Basel (1886).—The astronomical observatory and meteorological sta-tion are under the direction of Dr. E. Hagenbach-Bischoff, assisted by Dr. Riggenbach. The instruments are used principally for the deter-mination of time and for the instruction of students.

Beloit.—The equipment of the Smith Observatory, Beloit College, which was built in 1883 and ready for work in 1884, consists of an equatorial refractor of $9\frac{1}{2}$ inches aperture, objective by Clark, mount-ing by Warner and Swasey; a combined transit and zenith telescope of 2.6 inches aperture, made by Prof. C. S. Lyman (*see* Amer. Jour. Sc., XXX, p. 52); clocks, sidereal chronometer, chronograph and minor ap-paratus, and meteorological and photographic outfit. Directors: John Tatlock, jr., 1884-'85; O. A. Bacon, 1885. A local time service is main-tained, and meteorological observations are published daily.

Berkeley, California.—The "Students'" observatory of the University of California, established in 1887, is designed to furnish to under grad-uates instruction in geodesy and the more practical parts of astronomy generally; as rating clocks and chronometers, determining geographical latitudes and longitudes, etc. It is also designed to encourage study, on the part of the more advanced under-graduates, of astronomical phenomena, as far as they may be within the reach of young amateurs.

. A neat and sufficiently commodious observatory building, 50 feet long by 20 feet wide, on the average, has been built on a knoll in the university grounds 320 feet above mean sea-level. In the dome-room, at the east end of the observatory, is an equatorial refractor of 6½ inches clear aperture, objective (achromatic), by J. Byrn, of New York, the mounting, driving-clock, pier, etc., being by Fauth & Co., of Washington. With this telescope are six negative and as many more positive eyepieces, and a fine position filar micrometer made by the same firm. A spectroscope, capable of attachment to the equatorial or of being used on a stand, is furnished with a flint prism, and also with one of Rowland's diffraction gratings, having 14,334 lines to the inch.

In the room next west are two of J. Green's standard barometers, and in a specially prepared shed upon the north side, a wet bulb, a dry bulb, a maximum, and also a minimum thermometer, by H. J. Green, of New York. In this shed is also placed one of Draper's self-registering "thermographs."

On the northwest tower of the College of Letters are mounted a Robinson anemometer and a wind-vane. These instruments are connected by telegraph wires with an anemograph in the observatory, where the velocity and direction of the wind are automatically recorded. Meteorological observations and records are made at 7 A. M., 2 P. M., and 9 P. M. (standard or mean time of the 120th meridian of longitude). Monthly printed reports are made to the U. S. Signal Service office in San Francisco.

In the next room west is mounted a fine, large, portable " transit and zenith telescope," of the type used by the U. S. Coast and Geodetic Survey, but having an objective 3 inches in diameter.

Two diagonal and two direct eye-pieces belong to this instrument. In the same room is a Howard Standard mean time clock, with gravity escapement, mercurial compensating pendulum, and electric circuit connections. The clock is fastened to a solid granite pier 18 inches square and 6 feet long, which is inclosed in a brick pier reaching to solid rock 5 feet below the surface of the ground. The transit and equatorial are similarly founded. All the piers are disconnected from the floors of the observatory. A sidereal chronometer, made by Negus Bros., New York, is mounted upon one side of the transit pier.

On a shelf at one side of the transit-room is an electro chronograph, by Fauth & Co., of Washington, and on another the switch-board made by the San Francisco Electric Company. An electric circuit runs through the clock, chronometer, chronograph, sounder, and relay, and also into the equatorial-room, from which time may be marked on the chronograph by means of a break-circuit key. The switch-board is connected with the Western Union telegraph line by a shortline to Dwight Way-Station, Berkeley.

The two rooms further west are used respectively as a repair shop and a sleeping-room for the assistant.

In a small house at the rear of the observatory, upon a brick pier specially made for the purpose, are mounted three seismographs, the Duplex, the Ewing rotating, and the Gray.

The latitude of the mercury basin in the center of the transit pier of the observatory has been found from the first series of observations (preliminary to a continued series) to be $+ 37° 52' 21''.7$. Longitude west of Greenwich $8^h 9^m 2^s.52$.

The observatory is in charge of Prof. Frank Soulé, professor of civil engineering and astronomy, University of California.

Berlin.—The principal work of the meridian circle has been upon the Pulkowa list of stars and Argelander's stars, with considerable proper motion; a few comparison stars were observed, and preliminary experiments made to determine the influence of brightness of stars upon the observed time of transit. The 9-inch equatorial has been employed upon comets, asteroids, and comparison stars, and the declinograph attached to this instrument in observing zones in the thicker parts of the milky-way. With the smaller meridian instrument a series of observations of comparison stars has been begun, and with the heliometer measures of double stars and the Pleiades. In the annual reports of this observatory, given by Professor Foerster in the Vierteljahrsschrift, will be found interesting notes upon the performance of the clocks and time service.

The Recheninstitut, under Professor Tietjen, has published, as usual, the Jahrbuch, and circulars relating to the minor planets.

Bonn.—Dr. Schoenfeld reports satisfactory progress of the observations and reductions of zone $+40°$ to $+50°$. The remaining charts of the Southern Durchmusterung have been completed and distributed, and an investigation of errors in star catalogues covered by these charts is approaching completion. A few observations of variables have been made. Dr. Mönnichmeyer succeeded Dr. Scheiner as assistant on January 1, 1887, the latter having accepted a position at Potsdam.

Bordeaux.—The second volume of Annales, published in 1887, contains a memoir by Flamme upon elliptic motion of the planets, a determination of the latitude by Rayet, and a series of observations made with the meridian circle for a revision of Oeltzen's catalogue of Argelander's southern stars; also magnetic and meteorological observations.

Breslau.—Observations mainly meteorological and magnetic, and for the time service.

Brighton (Massachusetts).—Mr. E. F. Sawyer, of Cambridgeport, has removed to Brighton, upon the outskirts of Boston, and continues his observations of variables.

Brooklyn (New York).—Mr. H. M. Parkhurst's private observatory was originally built in 1862 and provided with a 6-inch telescope. It was rebuilt in 1877 and a 9-inch refractor was mounted. A series of photometric observations made by Mr. Parkhust has been published in the Harvard Observatory Annals, vol. 18, No. 3. Approximate position, latitude, $+40^\circ$ 41' 2''; longitude, 4^h 55^m $50^s.1$ west of Greenwich.

Brussels.—A catalogue of 10,792 stars upon which work was begun more than thirty years ago by Quetelet has at length been finished. M. Stuyvaert is engaged upon the formation of a catalogue of comparison-stars, which have appeared in volumes 107 and 108 of the Astronomische Nachrichten. Double stars, comets, and occultations by the moon have been observed with the equatorials of 38 and 15 centimeters, and numerous physical observations of the moon and planets have also been made. M. l'abbé Spée is especially occupied with a study of solar spots and protuberances, and M. Fievez with the study of the solar spectrum. The new observatory at Uccle is practically finished.

Cambridge (England).—Considerable progress has been made with the zone $+25^\circ$ to $+30^\circ$.

Camden (New Jersey).—Mr. E. E. Reed has erected a small private observatory, with 6-inch equatorial.

Cape of Good Hope—With the transit-circle regular observations have been continued of the Sun, Mercury, Venus, stars on the list of the Cape ten-year catalogue for 1890, comet comparison stars, stars occulted by the Moon, stars employed in the latitude and longitude determinations of the Geodetic Survey, and stars employed in zones for determining the scale value of the heliometer. The large theodolite has been used for observations of circumpolars and latitude stars, the zenith telescope for latitude, and the equatorial for observations of comets. The photographic "Durchmusterung" is proceeding rapidly, the instrument being kept at work by two observers from evening twilight till dawn. The reduction of the plates from declination -90° to $-77\frac{1}{2}^\circ$ has been completed by Professor Kapteyn, and plates for measurement to -57° have been sent to him. It is expected that the photographs will be completed by the end of 1889; their reduction will probably require two years longer. The new heliometer was received from Repsold, and mounted in the latter part of 1887; it is pronounced by Dr. Gill the most powerful and convenient instrument for refined micrometric research at present in existence. A complete working programme has been prepared, including the determination of the parallax of all the southern stars brighter than magnitude 2.0 and all the stars most remarkable for proper motion. Some progress has been made in the determination of the constants of the instrument. The meridian observations for 1882, 1883, and 1884, occultations observed from 1835 to 1880, forming vol. 1, part 4 of the Annals, and a discussion of the variations of the instrumental adjustments of the transit circle have been published.

Carleton College.—An illustrated description of the building and instruments is given in the Sidereal Messenger for October, 1888. The length of the building east and west is 80 feet, north and south 100 feet. The clock-room is on the first floor of the main building, and is 27 feet in diameter. The large circular pier for the 16-inch equatorial (to be constructed by Brashear) is in the middle of this room, suitably cased to a height of $7\frac{1}{2}$ feet, and provided with shelving. The meantime and sidereal clocks, both by Howard, are mounted in recesses in the east and west faces of this pier. In the west wing, upon the same floor, is the library with about 1,400 bound volumes, a small study or class-room, and a janitor's room; to the north is the prime vertical of 3-inch aperture (Fauth), and beyond this a class and lecture room. A small dome over the north wing covers the $8\frac{1}{4}$ inch Clark refractor. In the east wing is mounted a fine Repsold meridian circle of 4.8 inches aperture, which is under the charge of Dr. H. C. Wilson. The chronograph, chronometer, and time-distributing apparatus are in the clock-room. A time-service over more than 12,000 miles of railway is under the immediate care of Miss C. R. Willard.

The co-ordinates of the observatory provisionally adopted are (Astron. Nachr. 120: 85): latitude $+44^\circ$ 27′ 41″; longitude 6^h 12^m $36^s.0$ west of Greenwich.

Cincinnati.—A zone catalogue of 4,050 stars observed with the 3-inch transit was published in 1887. In September, 1888, a new meridian circle, by Fauth & Co., was mounted, one of the first large instruments of this class made in the United States. The clear aperture of the object-glass is $5\frac{1}{8}$ inches, and the focal length 70 inches; object-glass and micrometer are inter-changeable. The piers are of masonry to the floor-level, and from there up an iron frame work bricked inside to within a foot of the top. The pivots are of steel, glass hard. There are two solid circles, 24 inches in diameter; one is divided very coarsely to half degrees only: the other has two sets of graduation upon a silver band, both of them to 5′. The inner one is somewhat heavier than the other, and does not pretend to great accuracy, being used merely for setting. The outer graduation alone is visible in the reading miscroscopes; as far as Professor Porter has carried his investigation the errors of this graduation are very small. Electric illumination has been used throughout and has been found practically perfect. A detailed description of the instrument will be found in the Sidereal Messenger for January, 1889.

Cointe (Liège).—Observations of Titan and Iapetus have furnished a determination of the mass of Saturn. The meridian circle has been used for zone observations.

Copenhagen.—Mr. Nielsen has recently erected a private observatory with a $6\frac{1}{2}$ inch refractor by Reinfelder & Hertel, intended principally for selenographical work.

Cordoba.—Volumes 6 and 9, containing the zone observations made in 1875 and 1876, have been published.

Dearborn.—The report for 1885 and 1886, which has not previously been noticed, contains a list of nebulæ discovered by Professor Safford in 1866-'68; papers on the motion of the lunar apsides and on the companion of Sirius by Professor Colbert; and an illustrated paper on the physical aspect of Jupiter, a catalogue of 209 new double stars, and a description of a printing chronograph by Professor Hough. In the course of the two years referred to 130 new double stars were discovered and measured.

In consequence of the dissolution of the University of Chicago the Chicago Astronomical Society dismounted their instruments in the early part of 1888, and transferred the care of the observatory to the Northwestern University, at Evanston, Illinois, 12 miles from the business center of Chicago, about 16 miles north and 3 miles west of the old site, and some 300 feet from the shore of Lake Michigan. The corner stone of a new building, the gift of James B. Hobbs, was laid June 24, 1888. The plan includes a tower and dome for the $18\frac{1}{2}$-inch equatorial, meridian circle room, library, and about eight rooms for other purposes; the whole to be erected at a cost of $25,000. The approximate position is given: Latitude, $+42°$ 3'; longitude, $5^h 50^m 42^s$ west of Greenwich.

Denver.—A new observatory, the gift of Mr. H. B. Chamberlin to the University of Denver, is being built, about 7 miles from the city of Denver, at an altitude of 5,000 feet above sea-level. The principal instrument is to be a 20-inch Clark refractor. Director, Prof. H. A. Howe.

Dresden.—Baron von Engelhardt's older observatory was built in 1877 (latitude, $+51°$ 2' 31''; longitude, $0^h 54^m 53^s.3$ east of Greenwich), and contained an 8-inch Grubb equatorial, a 2-inch Cooke transit, and a sidereal clock by Knoblich. The present observatory was built in 1879 somewhat nearer the outskirts of Dresden (latitude, $+51°$ 2' 19''; longitude, $0^h 54^m 54^s.7$ east of Greenwich). It consists of a three-story tower, the upper story being surmounted by a cylindrical " dome " covering a 12-inch Grubb equatorial. The second floor connects with the transit-room, in which is a " broken-back " transit, by Bamberg, of 2.7 inches aperture. There is also a very complete equipment of subsidiary apparatus, clocks, chronometers, chronograph, etc. Upon the adjoining roof of the baron's residence is a little comet observatory arranged for two instruments, one of 6.4 inches aperture and the other of 3.7 inches. The larger instrument, which is similar to the Strassburg comet-seeker, is of somewhat novel construction. The telescope is fastened by two long arms to the back of a chair so that the eye-end comes at a convenient position for the observer; the arms are pivoted to the chair-back, permitting a motion in altitude, while the chair may be rotated in azimuth, so that the astronomer can examine the whole sky rapidly and without fatigue.

The numerous and valuable observations of occultations, phenomena of Jupiter's satellites, comets, planets, new stars, nebulæ, and clusters were collected and published in the latter part of 1886, together with an illustrated description of the observatory and instruments. Similar observations have been continued during the past two years, and considerable progress has also been made with a series of micrometric measures of all stars in Bradley and Argelander, which have an annual proper motion of at least $0''.1$, with companions not below the tenth magnitude, and distance not greater than $3'$.

Dresden (K. math. Salon).—Meteorological observations and a local time-service.

Dunecht.—Spectroscopic work has consisted of measures upon stars and nebulæ and a study of the low-sun atmospheric lines, as seen from an observing station established upon a neighboring hill. Circulars of astronomical information, the weekly firing of the time-gun, and the daily meteorological observations have been continued as in former years. A catalogue of the library is in press.

Dunsink.—The meridian circle has been devoted to observations of a list of about 1,000 stars suspected of large proper motion. Part VI of "Observations" was issued in 1888, containing the observations from 1881 to 1885 made with the meridian circle on 1,012 stars of the southern Durchmusterung requiring re-observation.

Düsseldorf.—Observations of comets and asteroids and ephemerides of the latter.

Ealing.—Mr. Common has completed his 5-foot reflector.

Edinburgh.—Prof. C. Piazzi Smyth resigned in August, 1888, the appointments (which he has held since 1846) of regius professor of practical astronomy in the University of Edinburgh and astronomer royal for Ireland, and he has given a very discouraging account of the financial condition of the institution. Dr. Ralph Copeland, of the Dun Echt Observatory, has been appointed as his successor.

Geneva.—In addition to the regular work of rating chronometers and watches, observations have been made of comets, of nebulæ, and of the rings of Saturn. A series of observations made by Plantamour and von Oppolzer, in 1881, for the purpose of determining the difference of longitude between Geneva and Vienna, have been discussed, giving a mean value of the difference of longitude of $40^m 44^s.64$ (Geneva west of Vienna).

Geneva (New York).—Mr. William Smith built in 1888 a small private observatory, which he has placed in charge of Mr. W. R. Brooks, well known for his discoveries of comets. The instrumental equipment is as follows: equatorial refractor, objective, by Clacey, of $10\frac{1}{4}$ inches aperture and 9 feet 9 inches focal length, with a photographic corrector of the same aperture. The mounting is by Warner & Swasey, and embodies numerous convenient devices. There is a large Gundlach periscopic comet eye-piece of 3 inches equivalent focus, with a silvered flat diagonal of $3\frac{1}{4}$ inches, a position micrometer, polarizing eye piece, universal Brashear spectroscope fitted with grating and prisms, and suited for stellar, solar, or laboratory work. The meridian circle is by Warner

& Swasey, 4-inch aperture and 40-inch focus, with 16-inch circles: one circle is coarsely divided, the other is divided to 5′ and is read by two microscopes to 1″. The sidereal clock was made by the Self-winding Clock Company, of Brooklyn, New York; it has Gerry's patent gravity escapement, and is automatically wound by a small electric motor. The chronograph was designed and constructed by the director. Outside the observatory proper, but ready for occasional use, are the 9-inch, 5-inch, and 3-inch reflectors, also built by Mr. Brooks, and used by him at Phelps, New York, in searching for comets.

Georgetown (*District of Columbia*).—The observatory of Georgetown College (built in 1845) was placed under the charge of Father J. G. Hagen, S. J., in the winter of 1888. The buildings and instruments, which have been but little used for nearly forty years, have been thoroughly renovated at considerable expense. Father Hagen has not as yet laid out any plan for the future work of the institution.

Glasgow (*Scotland*).—Observations with the transit circle of a list of stars in the earlier volume of Weisse's Bessel.

Glasgow (*United States*).—See Morrison Observatory.

Gohlis.—The private observatory of Herr Winkler was transferred in 1887 from Gohlis, near Leipzig, to the neighborhood of Jena—latitude, +50° 55′ 35″.6; longitude, 0ʰ 46ᵐ 20ˢ.8 east of ʻGreenwich.

Gotha.—Considerable progress has been made in the reduction of the zone observations (25°—20°). With the meridian circle observations of moon culminations and of stars of Mayer's catalogue have been made, and with the equatorial, observations of comets, of asteroids, and of Gore's variable near χ^1 Orionis.

Dr. Becker has, at the request of Professor Newcomb, collected in a convenient form Hansen's formulæ for the general perturbations by Jupiter and has applied them to the planet Eurynome. It will be remembered that Prof. J. C. Watson made provision in his will for the computation of tables of the asteroids discovered by him, which will readily give the places of the planets at future oppositions. Dr. Becker's work is for the purpose of facilitating these computations.

Dr. Paul Harzer succeeded Dr. Becker as director on December 1, 1887.

Göttingen (1886).—Dr. Schur assumed charge of the observatory on April 1, 1886, and immediately set to work to have much needed and very extensive repairs made in the buildings and instruments. As most of the instruments have been dismounted, the principal work done has been upon a new reduction of the zone observations made by Klinkerfues from 1858 to 1863. A 6-inch Repsold heliometer has been ordered. The personnel of the observatory consists (with the director) of observator, Dr. Battermann; assistant, Herr Clemens, and computer, Heidorn.

Greenwich.—The regular meridian observations of the sun, moon, and major and minor planets have been kept up as before, and satisfactory progress has been made with the reductions for a new ten-year catalogue (1877–′86). Observations of the moon have been made with the

altazimuth, and of comets with the equatorial. The spectroscopic observations for determining the motions of stars in the line of sight, the
photoheliographic record of the sun's surface, the magnetic and meteorological observations, the chronometer and time service are also continued as heretofore. A crown disk for the 28-inch objective, has, after
several failures, been obtained by Grubb from Chance & Co., and the
Treasury has granted the necessary funds for a 13 inch photographic
telescope to enable the observatory to take its share in the scheme for
forming a photographic map of the heavens. Numerous experiments
have been made in stellar photography in preparation for this work.
An 18-foot dome for a photographic equatorial was built in 1888, and
at the same time an addition was made to the space available for computing rooms. The annual volume for 1886 has been printed and distributed. We learn that provision has been made for a redetermina-
tion of the difference of longitude between Greenwich and Paris. The
astronomer royal in his last report draws attention to the recently
averted danger from a proposed railway tunnel within 840 yards of the
observatory. He also points out the inadequacy of the present staff to
handle properly the ever increasing amount of work demanded from a
national observatory, as new fields of research are opened up for investigation.

Grignon.—Sketches of the planets, observations of meteors, meteorological observations, and microscopical studies of cosmical dust. Director, Fr. Mayeul Lamey.

Grinnell.—Iowa College has a small observatory, for instruction, with
an 8-inch Clark refractor, mounted in April, 1888.

Guadalajara (Mexico).—Private observatory of Ingeneiro Carlos F. de
Landero; latitude, $+ 20° 40' 31''.9$; longitude, $6^h 53^m 23^s.66$ west of
Greenwich.

Haiphong (Tonkin).—The longitude of the small observatory as telegraphically determined by connection with Hong Kong April 5, 6, 7,
1887, is $7^h 6^m 44^s.04$ east of Greenwich.

Harrow.—The work of determining the places of comparision stars
and other selected small stars has been continued with the meridian
circle. Observations of comets have been made with the equatorial.

Harvard.—Professor Pickering describes the progress of his work
under three principal heads: The older instruments of the observatory,
the Draper memorial, and the Boyden fund. The 15-inch equatorial has
been used upon comets, eclipses of Jupiter satellites, and photometric
observations of asteroids. The meridian circle zone catalogue is passing through the press, and some progress has been made in observing
the new zone, $—9° 50'$ to $—14° 10'$. The work upon which the meridian
photometer has been employed since 1882 was finished September 29,
1888. The most laborious part of this work was the determination of
the brightness of stars of the ninth magnitude in zones 20 minutes in
width at intervals of 5 degrees from the north pole to the declination

—20°. This instrument has been dismounted and sent to Peru, where the work will be continued to the south pole, and in order to extend the investigation from stars of the ninth to stars of the fourteenth magnitude, an instrument of somewhat similar form but with an objective of 12 inches aperture (described under Instruments) has been mounted at Cambridge.

The first extensive research undertaken with the Henry Draper memorial funds, a catalogue of the spectra of 10,875 stars, covering the entire sky north of —25°, is nearly completed. This work has been done with the 8-inch Bache telescope. A second series of photographs made with longer exposures, and so taking in fainter stars, will soon be finished, and this instrument will likewise be sent to Peru, where the observations will be extended to the south pole. The detailed study of the brighter stars with the 11-inch Draper telescope has been continued, and the 15-inch and 28-inch reflectors constructed by Dr. Draper have been mounted and are employed in studying the spectra of variables.

The Boyden fund has been devoted to collecting necessary information in regard to the meteorological conditions at high altitudes, and in furtherance of this object several stations in Colorado were occupied during the summer of 1887 by a party from the observatory provided with special photographic apparatus. In December, 1888, a fully equipped expedition went out to California to observe the total solar eclipse on January 1, 1889, and having successfully completed that task, they proceeded to the southern hemisphere to occupy for several years an elevated station in Peru, and to carry out the photographic and photometric work mentioned above.

The compilation of observations of variable stars, the telegraphic announcement of astronomical discoveries, and the time service have been continued as in previous years. Volume 18 of the Annals is issued in parts in order to provide prompt publication for special investigations. These, as well as the Draper-memorial Reports, have received notice elsewhere. The Bulletin of the New England Meteorological Society and a good deal of other meteorological work will also appear in the Annals. The observatory buildings have been increased by the addition of two neighboring houses, and also by the erection of small detached and inexpensive buildings to cover the different telescopes that have been added to the equipment.

Haverford.—Founded in 1852, enlarged in 1883. Instruments: 10-inch refractor, by Clark; 8¼-inch refractor, re-ground, by Clark; 8¼ inch silver-on-glass reflector; 1¾-inch zenith telescope. Directors: Joseph G. Harlan, 1853; Samuel J. Gummere, ——; Samuel Alsop, jr., 1875; Isaac Sharpless, 1882; Francis P. Leavenworth, 1887. Professor Leavenworth has published a number of observations of comets.

Helsingfors.—The 7-inch refractor has been used for observations of comets, both determinations of position and careful examination of physical characteristics. The transit instrument has been re-modelled by the Repsolds and provided with a circle 48 centimeters in diameter, divided to 2′ and read by four microscopes.

Halifax —Observations of the phenomena of Jupiter's and Saturn's satellites, occultations, and transits of stars for time.

Herény.—The chief work has been on celestial photography. Photo. graphs of numerous star-clusters, of the moon, planets, comets, and of stellar spectra have been obtained.

Hurstside, West Molesey, England.—Sir Henry Thompson has built a private observatory with a 12-inch Cooke equatorial, to which is fitted a photographic objective and large prismatic objective for photograph. ing stellar spectra.

Kalocsa.—A careful series of observations of solar phenomena is carried on by the director, Father Julius Fényi.

Kew.—Magnetic, meteorological, and solar observations, verification of instruments, and the rating of watches and chronometers have been continued.

Kiel.—The zone catalogue, +55° to +65°, containing 14,680 stars, was finished and prepared for press in 1887. The Kiel observatory is the central station for the telegraphic distribution of astronomical information upon the continent, and in connection with this service considerable work has been done upon the new comets and asteroids by members of its staff.

Königsberg.—Observations of the sun and major planets, of time stars and comparison stars, have been made with the Repsold circle; observations of double stars, comets, and measures for stellar parallax with the heliometer. The director, Dr. E. Luther, died October 17, 1887, and was succeeded April 1, 1888, by Dr. C. F. W. Peters.

Kremsmünster.—The meridian circle has been repaired and remounted in a new building 4″.023 north and 0ˢ.22 west of its old position. Comet observations have been made with the refractor.

La Plata.—Observations of comets by M. Beuf and his assistants have been published. The position of the observatory is given as, latitude, −34° 54′ 30″.3; longitude, 4ʰ 0ᵐ 58ˢ.0 west of Paris. (Compt. Rend., 106:1590.) The construction is progressing rapidly, and when completed this will be one of the best equipped observatories in the southern hemisphere.

Leipzig (University Observatory).—The zone observations +5° to +15° are practically finished. A new Repsold heliometer of 162 millimeters aperture was mounted in 1886, and is described, together with its new dome, at some length in Dr. Bruns' report for 1887; an important addition to the working force is Herr " Mechaniker" Lohm.

Leipzig.—Dr. Engellman devoted most of his time to measures of double stars.

Lick.—An important event of the year 1888 was the transfer, on June 1, of the Lick Observatory to the regents of the University of California. The equipment of the Lick Observatory has been previously described in these reports and elsewhere, but it may not perhaps be superfluous to recapitulate briefly here, referring for details to Vol. 1 of the observatory publications, or to an article by Professor Holden in the Sidereal Messenger for February, 1888. The mounting of the 36-inch equatorial is referred to at some length in the present report under the heading " INSTRUMENTS."

The main observatory building is 287 feet long, including the 75 foot dome at its southern end, and contains a hall 12 feet wide running the whole length, offices and computing-rooms, the library, clock-room, visitors' room, etc., and at the northwest corner stands the 25-foot dome for the 12-inch equatorial. The other buildings on the mountain summit are the meridian-circle house, transit-house, photoheliograph, laboratory, several temporary workshops, and the dwelling for the astronomers. The instrumental equipment consists of the 36-inch, 12-inch, and 6½-inch equatorials, 4-inch comet-seeker, 6 inch meridian-circle, 4-inch transit and zenith telescope, 2-inch universal instrument, photoheliograph, declinograph, five clocks, several chronometers, four chronographs, and minor apparatus. The cost of the instruments with their mountings and transportation, aggregated about $200,000; buildings and other expenses amounted to about $375,000; leaving in the neighborhood of $125,000 for a permanent endowment fund. In addition to what may be derived from the investment of this sum, the observatory is to be allowed for its maintenance as a department of the University of California the sum of $19,188 a year. The astronomical staff consists of E. S. Holden, director and astronomer; S. W. Burnham, J. M. Schaeberle, J. E. Keeler, E. E. Barnard, astronomers; C. B. Hill, assistant astronomer, secretary, and librarian. The first volume of "Publications" appeared before the real work of the observatory had begun, and it is, therefore, mainly historical and descriptive. It contains Mr. Lick's deeds of trust, Professor Newcomb's report on glass for objectives, Mr. Burnham's reports upon the site in 1879 and 1881, descriptions of the buildings and instruments, an account of the engineering and building at Mount Hamilton in the years 1880–1885, observations of the transit of Mercury in 1881 and of Venus in 1882, geological reports, meteorological observations, 1880–1885, and an extensive series of reduction tables for the latitude of the observatory. There have been published in scientific journals and in the daily press interesting notes upon nebulæ and planetary markings as shown by the 36-inch refractor, and the discoveries of new comets and double stars. Professor Holden attributes the steady-seeing at Mount Hamilton to the coast fogs, which roll in from the sea every afternoon in the summer, rising 1,500 to 2,000 feet, covering the hot valley and preventing radiation from it. The nights of summer and autumn—April to October or November—are found to be excellent both as to clearness and steadiness; the daylight hours are less satisfactory, and in winter the seeing is not much better than at lower altitudes.

Liège (Ougrée).—See Cointe.

Litchfield.—Dr. Peters is still at work upon his ecliptic charts; he expects to issue shortly a second installment of twenty.

Liverpool.—The time-gun has been fired with regularity, chronometers tested, and meteorological observations conducted as heretofore.

Lund.—Dr. Dunér has continued his observations of variable stars and spectra of red stars, and with a large solar spectroscope, provided with one of Rowland's gratings, he has made an important investigation of the period of rotation of the sun. Photographs of the solar spectrum were made as a check upon the micrometer measures.

Lyme Regis.—See Rousdon.

McCormick.—The 26 inch equatorial is still devoted chiefly to the study of nebulæ. Mr. Leavenworth resigned as assistant in September, 1887, to take charge of the Haverford College observatory. Professor Stone expresses continued satisfaction with the electric illumination of the equatorial.

Madras.—Mr. Norman R. Pogson has published in two volumes the results of a series of observations of star places made with the 5½-inch meridian circle, the first volume giving, after a brief history and description of the observatory, the "separate results" and annual catalogues for 1862, 1863, and 1864, and the second volume "separate results" and annual catalogues for 1865, 1866, and 1867.

Mauritius.—Principal activity is in the observation of meteorological and magnetic phenomena, and in the photographic record of the state of the solar surface by means of the photoheliograph.

Mazatlan (Sinaloa).—Founded in 1879 and intended principally for the time service, and is supported by the department of public works. Its directors have been: Ingo. Fiacro Quijano, 1879-'84; L. Gutierrez, 1884; F. Weidner, 1884; C. Camiña, 1885-'87; L. Acosta, 1887. Instruments: Meridian instrument, by Fauth & Co., aperture $0^m.076$ (3 inches), focal length $0^m.787$ (31 inches); equatorial, by. W. Gregg, New York, $0^m.15$ (6 inches), aperture; Troughton & Simms altazimuth, and Negus chronometer. Latitude, $+23° 11' 22''.81$; longitude, $7^h 5^m 35^s.67$ west of Greenwich.

Melbourne.—The mirrors of the 4 foot Cassegrainian reflector have become so tarnished as to interfere materially with the observation of the fainter nebulæ. The sum of $5,000 has been appropriated to enable the observatory to take part in the stellar photographic scheme of the Paris conference.

Mexico.—The Central Astronomical Observatory in the city of Mexico was founded in 1878. It is intended for purposes of instruction, and especially for co-operating in geodetic work and for maintaining the time-service of the capital. The principal instruments are a meridian telescope, by Troughton & Simms, of $0^m.069$ aperture and $1^m.16$ focus; a zenith telescope, by the same makers, of $0^m.076$ aperture $1^m.22$ focus; an altazimuth, by the same, with $0^m.305$ (12-inch) circles; a small Buron refractor, Fauth chronograph, sidereal clock by Vasquez, two Bliss break-circuit chronometers, several mean-time chronometers, and a fillet chronograph. The director has also under his charge the geodetic, topographic, and astronomical instruments of the department of public works. Position of the observatory: Latitude, +19° 26′ 1″.3; longitude, 6ʰ 36ᵐ 31ˢ.5; altitude, 2,285ᵐ.4 (7,500 feet). Directors: Sr. Ingeneiro Geografo Don Francisco Jiminez from 1878 till his death, November 4, 1881, when he was succeeded by Sr. Don Leandro Fernandez.

Milan.—A new 18-inch refractor, objective by Merz, mounting by Repsold, was put in place in 1886, and has been devoted principally to the measurement of double stars. The smaller (8 inch) equatorial has been used for observations of comets and of double stars in rapid orbital motion. The markings on Mars were examined with both instruments.

Morrison observatory was established in 1875 through the efforts of the present director, Prof. C. W. Pritchett, aided by the liberality of Miss Berenice Morrison, whose name the institution bears. The principal instruments are a 12¼-inch Clark equatorial and an excellent 6-inch Troughton & Simms meridian circle, similar in plan to the meridian circle of the Harvard Observatory. The first number of the publications is a well printed volume of 111 pages, giving an account of the founding of the observatory, a full description of the building and instruments, and the observations in detail. The latter consist mainly of measures of double stars, observations of planets, comets, occultations by the moon, etc. A full discussion is given of the geographical co-ordinates of the meridian pier, the longitude being determined by an exchange of signals with Washington in 1880. There are several drawings of the observatory, and sketches of Saturn and of comets. The work is now much restricted owing to the inadequacy of funds.

Munich.—The zone observations with the meridian circle are continued, and a new Munich catalogue is going through the press. The 10½ inch refractor has been used for observations of comets, measures of stars in the cluster *h* Persei, and observations for stellar parallax. Some photometric observations have also been made.

Natal.—Recent work has been largely in meteorology. The observatory has been seriously crippled by the lack of funds.

Nice.—The first volume of the annals is to contain a description of the observatory and instruments, and is expected shortly; the second volume has already been published, and the third volume, also in preparation, will contain Thollon's study of the solar spectrum. Vol. 2 is devoted mainly to the determination of the co ordinates of the observatory and to measures of double stars. There are also observations of comets and planets, and notes on solar spectroscopy and the red-glows. The position of the observatory at present adopted is: Latitude, + 43° 43′ 16″.9; longitude, 0ʰ 19ᵐ 51ˢ.22 east of Paris.

North Carolina University.—Professor Love, of the University of North Carolina, Chapel Hill, has called attention to an early attempt to establish an astronomical observatory in the United States which seems to have remained unnoticed by astronomers. Professor Caldwell, the president of the university, went to Europe in 1824 to purchase books and apparatus, and spent the greater part of $3,361.35 for astronomical instruments; this was four years before the purchase of a telescope by Yale. The foundations of the observatory were laid in 1831, and the building was finished in 1832, six years before the Hopkins Observatory at Williams. There was but one room, 15 feet by 25 feet and about 25 feet high. A Simms transit of 3-inch aperture and 44-inch focus was mounted upon a masonry pier in this room, and a Simms altitude and azimuth instrument upon a pier projecting through the roof and covered by a small house moving on rails. The observatory possessed also a 2½-inch (52-inch focus) Dolland refractor, an astronomical clock by Molyneaux, reflecting circle, sextant, and quadrant. The instruments were removed from the observatory owing to a leaky roof, soon after Dr. Caldwell's death, in 1835, and in 1838 the building was partly destroyed by fire, and astronomical activity was never renewed. All records of observations have been lost.

Oakland.—The private observatory of Mr. F. G. Blinn, in East Oakland, contains a 5-inch Clark equatorial and 1¾-inch Latimer-Clark transit, with mean-time and sidereal clocks.

Oakland.—The observatory of Mr. Burckhalter, at West Oakland, California, contains a 10½-inch reflector by Brashear, and 1⅔-inch transit. The mechanical work of the building and equatorial mounting was done by the owner.

O'Gyalla.—Observations of sun spots, spectroscopic and photometric observations of planets, new stars, comets, and stars with variable spectra. The observations for a "spectroscopic Durchmusterung" from 0° to –15° declination have been finished and the catalogue printed. Dr. von Kövesligethy, Dr. von Konkoly's assistant, accepted a position in the meteorological office in Budapest, April 1, 1887. Considerable spectroscopic and photographic apparatus has been added to the equipment.

Omaha, Nebraska.—A new observatory at Creighton College was completed in 1887. The instruments are a 5 inch Steward equatorial, 3-inch Fauth transit, clocks, chronograph, etc. Director, J. Rigge, S. J. Latitude, +41° 16′ 6″; longitude, 6ʰ 23ᵐ 47ˢ west of Greenwich.

Orwell Park.—An extensive and valuable series of observations of recent comets has been published.

Oxford University.—Great attention has been paid to photography, and particularly to its application to the determination of stellar parallax (*q. v.*), with very gratifying results. The large equatorial is to be re-modelled as a photographic telescope of 13 inches aperture in conformity with the plans adopted by the Paris congress, the necessary funds having been provided by Dr. De La Rue.

Palermo.—Observations of comets, planets, sun spots, and meteors.

Paris.—The approaching completion of the observations for the Lalande catalogue has modified the plan of operations carried on with the meridian instruments for some years past. The large transit circle has been used for observations of the sun, moon, minor planets, and such stars of Lalande's list still requiring re-observation; the Gambey transit, for observations of the absolute right ascensions of fundamental stars; the Gambey circle and the "cercle du jardin," for a re investigation of the latitude, and the latter also for fundamental declinations. Comets, asteroids, nebulæ, and occultations of stars by the moon have been observed with the equatorials. The most important addition to the instrumental equipment is the apparatus adapted to the equatorial *coudé* for determining the constants of refraction and aberration by Loewy's method. Work in astronomical photography is continued by the Henrys. A fine engraving of the Pleiades, compiled from three of their photographs, accompanies Admiral Mouchez's report for 1887. The time service, which of late has not been entirely satisfactory, is undergoing renovation.

Paris (École militaire).—M. Bigourdan gives in the Bulletin Astronomique (4 : 497 ; 5 : 30) an interesting historical account of the observatories of the École militaire, famous for the labors of Lalande and d'Agelet.

Pekin.—An interesting historical account of this observatory (established in 1279) is given in abstract, in Nature for November 8, 1888.

Phelps (New York).—The Red House Observatory was abandoned in 1888, Mr. Brooks having become director of the Smith Observatory at Geneva.

Poona.—An observatory has been established at the College of Science with a 16½ inch silver-on-glass Newtonian reflector by Grubb, 6-inch refractor by Cooke, with photographic, photometric, and spectroscopic accessories. It is intended at present to restrict the work of the observatory to certain branches of spectroscopic research, with occasional observations of comets, etc. The curator is Mr. K. D. Naegamvala.

Potsdam.—Dr. Vogel has applied photography to the determination of the motions of stars in the line of sight, and has obtained most satisfactory results. He proposes to observe regularly all stars (about sixty) that are as bright as 2.5 magnitude. The observations of solar phenomena, sketches, and photometric observations of comets and planets have been continued with little interruption. Progress is reported upon the " photometric Durchmusterung," which is to take in all stars in the northern hemisphere down to the 7.5 magnitude. The instruments required to enable the observatory to take part in the photographic work planned by the Paris congress have been ordered, and numerous preliminary experiments have been carried out for the permanent committee of that body.

Prague.—Professor Safarik has continued his observations of variable stars. In 1887 he changed his residence, and made considerable improvements in his observatory. The instruments are a 6-inch refractor, which is to be replaced by one more powerful, and a small transit and clock. The provisional co-ordinates of the meridian room are : latitude, +50° 4' 21''; longitude, 0ʰ 57ᵐ 48ˢ east of Greenwich.

Puebla (Mexico).—Observatory of the College of the Sacred Heart. Director, P. Capelleli, S. J.

Pulkowa.—The great routine work of the observatory, the determinations of star positions with the transit, meridian circle, and vertical circle has proceeded on the same lines as before. Romberg is credited with having made no less than 9,000 observations with the meridian circle in a single year. The 30 inch refractor has been used on close double stars and satellites, the 15-inch on similar work, and also for experiments in stellar photography. The astro-physical laboratory is reported in working order. Volume 12, a catalogue of the principal stars to the fourth magnitude, as far as —15° declination, has been published, and several other volumes, though interrupted by the death of Wagner, are well advanced. The first number of a new series of publications— " Supplements to the Pulkowa Observations"—is an interesting memoir by Dr. Hermann Struve on the outer satellites of Saturn.

Radcliffe.—The transit circle has been used for observing the sun, moon, and a list of stars down to the seventh magnitude between the equator and —25°; the Barclay equatorial for the measurement of double stars and observations of comets. The volume for 1885 has been published, and all reductions are remarkably well advanced.

Rousdon.—Systematic observation of some twenty long-period variables has been taken up; time signals are furnished for the neighboring district.

Scholl Observatory.—At Lancaster City, Pennsylvania, a new observatory, named the Daniel Scholl Observatory, has been erected on the grounds of Franklin and Marshall College. The equipment as described by Mr. J. E. Kershner in Science for May 13, 1887, consists of an 11-inch Clark-Repsold equatorial, a 3-inch transit, a Seth Thomas clock, a chronometer, chronograph, and meteorological apparatus. The equatorial has a set of positive and negative eye pieces, with reversion prisms for three of the micrometer eye-pieces, a Mertz solar eye-piece, and a comet eye-piece, together with a micrometer and complete illuminating apparatus for bright and dark field, as worked out by the Repsolds.

Smith College (Northampton).—An exchange of longitude signals with the Harvard Observatory was made in the summer of 1888.

Stockholm.—Dr. Gyldén has devoted himself to investigations in celestial mechanics.

Stonyhurst College.—The solar observations consist of (1) a drawing of the sun's disk, 10½ inches in diameter, including the careful delineation of all spots and faculæ visible; (2) a spectroscopic measurement with a radial slit of the height of the chromosphere and of all the gaseous prominences; (3) a study of the general surface of the sun whenever ·the definition has been unusually good; (4) a sketch of the chromospheric flames, with a wide tangential slit; (5) the spectrum of the solar spots between the lines B and D. Observations of lunar occultations, of comets, and of the phenomena of Jupiter's satellites have been made as before. The sky-glows have also been watched with care. A 5½-inch Clark equatorial, formerly the property of Rev. T. W. Webb, was purchased for the observation of the total solar eclipse of August 29, 1886.

Strassburg.—Dr. E. Becker was appointed director December 1, 1887, relieving Dr. Kobold, the "observator," temporarily in charge. Observations of nebulæ, comets, and satellites have been made with the refractor; observations of the sun, moon, and planets and of zero stars for the southern zones with the meridian circle, and measures of the sun's diameter and sunspots with the heliometer. The transit instrument has been used by Dr. Wislicenus for investigations with a personal equation apparatus of his own design. All reductions are well advanced. The library has been thoroughly overhauled and recatalogued.

Syracuse (New York).—The new observatory of the University of Syracuse, a memorial to Charles Demarest Holden, of the class of 1877, was dedicated November 18, 1887, with an appropriate address by Professor Newcomb. The instruments are an 8 inch Clark equatorial, 3-inch Troughton and Simms transit, clock chronograph, and chronometer. Director, Prof. J. R. French.

Syracuse (New York.).—Private observatory of H. P. Stark; 5-5/16-inch Spencer equatorial refractor; 12-foot dome.

Tacubaya.—The National Mexican observatory, which is in the department of the secretary of public works, was founded May 5, 1878. The instruments were at first mounted at Chapultepec, but in 1883 they were transferred to the present building, erected at a cost of $200,000. The instruments are as follows: A refractor of $0^m.381$ (15 inches) aperture and $5^m.40$ (17 feet 8 inches) focal length, by Grubb, provided with a fine micrometer and an 11-prism spectroscope; a meridian circle of $0^m.203$ (8 inches) aperture and $2^m.743$ (9 feet) focal length, by Troughton & Simms, with circles $0^m.914$ (36 inches) in diameter, divided to 5′ and read by four microscopes, and with collimators of $0^m.152$ (6 inches) aperture and $2^m.15$ (7 feet) focus; a Dallmeyer photoheliograph of $0^m.102$ (4 inches) aperture and $1^m.53$ (5 feet) focus, with parallactic mounting and an enlarging apparatus; an alt-azimuth, also by Troughton & Simms, of $0^m.083$ (3¼ inches) aperture and $0^m.85$ (2 feet 9 inches) focal length, with circles $0^m.60$ (2 feet) in diameter, divided to 5′. In addition to these there are, not yet mounted, a Grubb equatorial of $0^m.152$ (6 inches) aperture and $2^m.54$ focal length, an Ertel meridian instrument of $0^m.152$ aperture and $2^m.20$ focal length, and a Troughton & Simms zenith telescope, $0^m.076$ aperture and $1^m.15$ focal length. Of

subsidiary apparatus there is a cylindrical chronograph, Barraud &
Lund; a fillet chronograph, made in 1867 by direction of Commodore
Maury; a sidereal clock, by F. Vazquez, Mexico; sidereal and mean-time
clocks, by Barraud & Lund; two sidereal chronometers, by Negretti &
Zambra; seven mean time chronometers, by various makers, and magnetic and meteorological instruments. A photographic refractor of
$0^m.33$ (13 inches) aperture and $3^m.43$ (11 feet) focal length has been ordered from Grubb, to enable the observatory to co-operate in the international plan of charting the sky by photography. The personnel consists of Sr. Ingeneiro Angel Anguiano, director; Sr. Ingeneiro Felipe
Valle, Sr. Lieut. Col. Teodoro Quintana, Sr. Ingeneiro Francisco Rodriguez Rey, Sr. Apolonio Romo, Sr. M. Moreno; two more astronomers
will be added during 1889. The work of the meridian circle has been
upon comparison stars, comets, and asteroids; the 15-inch equatorial
has been used upon comets, and asteroids, and these bodies, as well as
a list of southern nebulæ, will be carefully observed in future. The
photoheliograph has been used almost daily, and with the alt-azimuth
observations for time and latitude have been made, and observations of
lunar culminations and of comets. Considerable time has been devoted
to co-operating with longitude parties. The position of the observatory
is: Latitude, $+19° 24' 17''.5$; longitude, $6^h 36^m 46^s.53$ west of Greenwich (determined telegraphically from St. Louis); altitude $2,322^m$ (7,618
feet). An "annuario" is published regularly.

Tacubaya.—Private observatory of M. G. Prieto: Bardou equatorial,
$0^m.11$ (4¼ inches) aperture, $1^m.60$ (5 feet 3 inches) focal length; spectroscope, and clock.

Taschkent.—The refractor has been used for observations of sun-spots,
comets, and occultations by the moon; the meridian circle, principally
for determining the positions of comet comparison stars. The observatory has co-operated in determining the geographical positions of a number of places in central Asia. Several chronometers have been tested,
and the noon signal has been given by the discharge of a cannon, as in
previous years. The director, M. Pomerantzeff, is assisted by MM.
Zalessky and Schwarz. A new determination of the latitude in 1887
gave: $\varphi = +41° 19' 31''.35 \pm 0''.05$.

Temple observatory (Rugby).—Spectroscopic observations of the motion
of stars in the line of sight, and measures of double stars.

Tokio.—An observatory was founded in 1888 at Tokio, Japan, by
combining the astronomical department of the old Marine observatory,
the observatory of the Ministry of the Interior, and that of the Imperial University. The new observatory occupies the buildings of the
Marine observatory, its position as provisionally determined being latitude, $+35° 39' 17''.5$; longitude, $9^h 18^m 58^s.0$ east of Greenwich. The
principal instruments are a 5¼-inch Repsold transit, a 5 inch Merz and
Repsold meridian circle, and equatorials of 6½ and 8 inches aperture.
The director is H. Terao.

Turin.—Observations of comets, meteorological observations, and a determination of the latitude of a station at Termoli have been published.

United States Naval Observatory.—The work of 1887-'88 was similar to that of previous years. With the 26-inch equatorial observations were made of double stars, satellites, and of Saturn and Mars, and observations for stellar parallax; with the 9.6-inch, observations of comets and asteroids. The observations with the transit-circle for a catalogue of miscellaneous stars were completed in 1888, and preparations have been made for observing with this instrument the zone —14° to —18°. The time service has been considerably extended. The contract for the erection of the nine buildings comprising the new observatory was awarded in 18·8, and some progress has been made with the necessary excavations.

Upsala.—Dr. Hermann Schultz describes at some length in the Vierteljahrsschrift (23: 144) the recent additions to his instrumental outfit: a transit and a vertical circle, both by Repsold, with objectives of 96^{mm} (4 inches) aperture; a transit, by Steinheil, of 54^{mm} (2 inches) aperture, mounted in the prime vertical; a 4-inch refractor, parallactic mounting, by Simms; clock Hohwü 34, three chronometers, two chronographs, and minor apparatus. The principal instrument of the observatory is a 9-inch refractor.

Vassar College.—Miss Mary W. Whitney has been appointed to fill the vacancy caused by the resignation of Miss Maria Mitchell.

Vienna (Wien-Ottakring).—The private observatory of Herr von Kuffner, which was begun in 1884, was completed in 1887. The building is in the shape of a cross, 82 feet from east to west and 61 feet from north to south. The instruments are: A meridian circle, by Repsold, of 4.8 inches aperture and 5 feet focal length, with circle 21.6 inches in diameter, divided to 2' and read by four microscopes; and a refractor, also by Repsold, of 10.6 inches aperture and 12½ feet focal length, with filar, double image, and ring micrometers. The position of the observatory, as provisionally determined by Dr. Herz, is: Latitude, +48° 12' 47''.2; longitude, 1^h 5^m 11^s.1 east of Greenwich.

Warner (Rochester, New York).—Search for new nebulæ.

Washburn.—The fifth volume of publications contains the observations made with the meridian circle by Miss Lamb and Mr. Updegraff from the latter part of 1886 to April 1, 1887, observations made with the 15½-inch equatorial, and a summary of meteorological observations made by various observers at Madison from 1853 to 1886. Miss Lamb contributes a very useful index to stars in Airy's six Greenwich catalogues not found in Flamsteed, and Mr. Updegraff a discussion of the latitude of the observatory. Professor Davies was succeeded by Prof. G. C. Comstock as director, and Prof. Asaph Hall as consulting director. Mr. Updegraff and Miss Lamb (now Mrs. Updegraff) have removed to the Cordoba observatory. The assistants now at the observatory are

Mr. Π. V. Egbert, formerly of the Albany observatory, and Prof. S. J. Brown. The free use of the Washburn observatory was tendered to the Navy Department during the contemplated removal of the naval observatory to its new site.

West Point.—A new observatory was built in 1883, the old site having been rendered worthless as an astronomical station by a railroad tunnel cut immediately beneath it. The instruments are a 12-inch Clark equatorial, mounted in 1884, and an 8-inch Repsold meridian circle, mounted in 1885. Geographical position: Latitude, +41° 23′ 22″.1; longitude, 4ʰ 55ᵐ 50ˢ.6 west of Greenwich. Height above sea level, 480 feet.

Williams College.—On the 28th of June 1888, the fiftieth anniversary of the dedication of the Hopkins Observatory of Williams College was celebrated with suitable ceremony and a discourse upon "The Development of Astronomy in the United States," by Prof T. H. Safford. The Hopkins Observatory seems entitled to the honor of being the first permanent American observatory, having been projected about 1834, chiefly built in 1837, and dedicated June 12, 1838. The University of North Carolina had built an observatory in 1831 and provided an excellent instrumental equipment, but in 1838 the building was partially destroyed by fire, and little or no astronomical work was ever done with the instruments. Professor Safford published in 1888 a catalogue of the right ascensions of some 201 circumpolar stars, the results of several years' labor with the Repsold meridian circle.

Wilmington, Delaware.—The private observatory of Francis G. du Pont is at his residence about 4 miles to the north of Wilmington, Del. It was designed by the owner, and consists of two polygonal buildings, covered by domes of peculiar construction, and connected by a third building, which forms the transit room. The instruments are: A good 12-inch reflector by Brashear, well mounted, with driving-clock, etc.; a 4½-inch equatorial refractor, objective by Clark and mounting by Brashear; a small transit by Horne & Thornethwaite, London; sidereal and mean time clocks, and Morse register for recording transits. The whole building is lighted by the electric light, and the electric light is also used for instrumental illumination. The 12-inch reflector has been used for astronomical photography. The approximate latitude is +39° 16′.

Windsor, New South Wales.—Mr. Tebbutt published in pamphlet form in 1887 an interesting history and description of his observatory. It is situated, with the owner's residence, at the eastern extremity of the town of Windsor, upon a hill 50 feet above mean tide. Occasional astronomical observations were made here with a sextant and 1⅜-inch telescope from 1854 to 1864. To these instruments were added a 3¼-inch refractor by Jones in 1861, and a Frodsham chronometer in 1864. At the close of 1863 a small building, comprising transit and prime vertical rooms and a dome, was erected on the west of the dwelling, and a small transit and the 3¼-inch refractor already referred to were mounted. This refractor gave place to one of 4½ inches aperture in 1872, and in 1874 a further addition was made to the buildings. In 1879 a substantial observatory of brick was erected a few yards southwest of the old building. It consists of an equatorial room (under which is an office) and meridian and prime vertical rooms, the meridian room containing a Cooke transit, mounted in 1879. In 1882 an 8-inch Grubb equatorial supplanted the 4½-inch. Mr. Tebbutt has published many valuable observations of comets, asteroids, double and variable stars, occultations of stars by the moon, etc., during the more than twenty-five years' existence of his observatory.

Wolsingham.—Rev. T. E. Espin has continued his sweeps for red stars and stars with remarkable spectra, and has announced the discovery of several new variables. A 4.8-inch Troughton & Simms eqatorial has been added to the equipment, and a new edition of Birmingham's red star catalogue has been published. In the latter part of 1888 the observatory was removed to a new site at Towlaw, Darlington, 3 miles northeast of its old position and 1,000 feet above sea-level.

Yale.—The initial volume of " Transactions of the Astronomical Observatory of Yale University," a valuable memoir by Dr. W. L. Elkin upon the relative positions of the principal stars in the Pleiades, as determined with the new heliometer, was published in 1887, the expense of printing having been borne by Professor Loomis. Upon the completion of this work Dr. Elkin took up the investigation of the parallaxes of the ten first-magnitude stars in the northern hemisphere, and the results obtained we have already referred to under stellar parallax. The heliometer has also been used for measures of various double stars and of the diameters of the sun and Mars, and more recently in a triangulation of twenty-four stars within 100′ of the north pole, and in observations of Iris for the determination of the solar parallax. Mr. Hall has nearly completed the reduction of his work upon Titan, the expense of which is defrayed by the Bache fund, and he has taken up the investigation of the parallaxes 6 B Cygni and Lalande 18115, 22. Mr. O. T. Sherman, who had charge of the thermometric bureau, resigned in November, 1886, and his work has since been carried on by Mr. Peck. The testing of time-pieces has been discontinued, but the time-service is still maintained. The subscription of $1,000 annually for the support of the work with the heliometer has been renewed for three years, beginning with 1887.

Zacatecas (Mexico).—Latitude +22° 46′ 34.″9, longitude 6ʰ 50ᵐ 17.ˢ5 west of Greenwich ; altitude 2,475ᵐ (?). Instruments : Equatorial of 6 French inches aperture with astronomical and photographic objectives, a small transit, altazimuth, clock, chronometer, spectroscope, and meteorological apparatus. Director, Ingeneiro José A. y Bonilla.

Zürich (1886).—Dr. Rudolf Wolf has continued his observations of sun-spots.

ASTRONOMICAL INSTRUMENTS.

The 36-inch Lick telescope.—The great equatorial was mounted in 1887. The visual objective has a clear aperture of 36 inches and focal length of 56 feet 6 inches. The flint disk for this objective was obtained by Clark from Feil & Co., of Paris, in 1882, the crown in 1885, and the objective was completed and delivered by Clark in 1886. These two disks are separated in their cell by a space of 6.5 inches. In 1887 a third (crown) lens of 33 inches aperture and 46 feet focus was procured as a "photographic corrector." The mounting was made by Warner & Swasey, of Cleveland, Ohio, and put in place in the autumn of 1887. The pier is a hollow cast-iron column of rectangular section, and for convenience in transit is built up of five sections, bolted together by internal flanges. At the top the column measures 4 feet by 8 feet, increasing to 5 feet by 9 feet at the floor line, and then spreading out rapidly to a base 10 feet by 16 feet bearing on a masonry foundation. At this point the weight is distributed over a series of large steel screws, which afford the means of adjusting the position of the polar axis. At the top of the column is the head carrying the bearings for the polar axis, and around the head is a balcony reached by a spiral staircase. The intersection of polar and declination axes is 37 feet above the base. Column and head weigh together 21 tons, and the total weight of the telescope is 40 tons. The tube consists of a central section of cast-iron, strongly ribbed, to which two sections of sheet-steel are attached. The diameter of the tube is 4 feet at the center, 38 inches at the object-glass end, and 36 inches at the eye end, while the sheet-steel portions vary from one-eighth of an inch thick at the center to one-twelfth of an inch thick at the ends. When the telescope is in a horizontal position the flexure of the tube with the object glass and permanent counterbalance is one-eighth of an inch only, while with a load of 1 ton added at each end the flexure is increased to one-quarter of an inch.

The polar axis is of steel, 10 feet long, 12 inches in diameter at its upper and 10 inches at its lower end, with a 6-inch hole through its entire length; the bearings are of Babbitt metal, relieved by anti-friction rolls. The declination axis is also of steel, 10 feet 6 inches long, 10 inches tapering to $9\frac{1}{2}$ inches diameter, with a 4-inch hole running through it; Babbitt-metal bearings, with anti-friction rolls, upon hard steel balls are used, as in the polar axis. To facilitate counterpoising the telescope is arranged for carrying always its maximum load, so that when the photographic corrector, the spectroscope, or any physical apparatus is attached an equivalent weight is taken off at the same place. There are three regular finders of 6, 4, and 3 inches aperture; in addition to these the 12-inch equatorial can be quickly attached as a pointer for photographic work if necessary. The hour circle on the polar axis is 3 feet in diameter, and has coarse graduations to 5 minutes, and large figures on its outer edge, while on the northern face it is graduated to 20 seconds. Attached to the head, at the upper end, is a fixed hour

THE LICK TELESCOPE

Length, 57 feet   Diameter of Object-glass, 36 inches,   Total weight, 40 tons
Warner & Swasey, designers and builders   Object glass by Alvan Clark & Sons.

circle graduated to 20 seconds and read through a series of prisms, at the eye end to 4 seconds. On the declination sleeve near the tube is a fine declination circle 3 feet in diameter graduated to 5 minutes of arc, and read from the eye end to 12 seconds, while on the outer end of the axis is a coarse declination circle 6 feet in diameter graduated to degrees. The driving clock is regulated by a frictional governor of the cross-armed type and by an electric control from the standard clock. One of the shafts carries a chronograph drum. For photographic work an opening is cut in the side of the tube about 10 feet from the eye end, and a plate 20 inches square can here be inserted and suitably adjusted. The eye end is so arranged that the micrometer can be quickly re-moved and two steel bars inserted in bearings. These bearings are part of a jacket revolving 360° in position angle, and to them can be attached spectroscopes, photometers, enlarging cameras, etc. The eye end is also surrounded by a large ring, which supports the various handles for actuating the clamps and slow motions, and carries the read-ing microscopes and finders as well as a small sidereal chronometer. The clamps and slow motions are operated as follows:

An observer at the eye end can—

    (1) Clamp in declination.
    (2) Give slow motion in declination. ·
    (3) Read the declination circle (two verniers).
    (4) Clamp in right ascension.
    (5) Stop the clock.
    (6) Give slow motion in right ascension.
    (7) Read right ascension circle (one microscope).

An assistant on either side of the balcony below the axes can—

    (8) Clamp in declination.
    (9) Give rapid motion in declination.
    (10) Give slow motion in declination.
    (11) Give quick motion in right ascension.
    (12) Give slow motion in right ascension.
    (13) Clamp in right ascension.
    (14) Stop or start the driving clock.
    (15) Read the right ascension circle (two microscopes).
    (16) Read a dial showing the nearest quarter degree of declina-
        tion.

Detailed drawings of the mounting are given in Engineering, volume 46, London, 1888.

The almucantar.—In volume 17 of the Annals of Harvard College Observatory, Mr. S. C. Chandler, jr., has given a complete description and investigation of his "almucantar," and a discussion of a series of observations made with it in 1884 and 1885. The almucantar, as its name implies, is an equal altitude instrument, and was devised by Mr. Chandler in 1879. It consists, essentially, of a telescope attached to a frame-work which is floated on a small quantity of mercury contained in a shallow trough. The trough is supported on an upright pillar, and can be turned about a vertical axis, and set with the telescope it carries to any azimuth. If the telescope is clamped at a given altitude, the sight line will mark accurately in the heavens a parallel of altitude, or "almucantar," and the observation of the time of transits of stars as they rise or fall over this circle in different azimuths will furnish the means of determining instrumental and clock corrections, the latitude, or right ascensions and declinations. The particular parallel of altitude which has been found most convenient, as it materially simplifies the formulæ of reduction, is the parallel passing through the pole, to which the name "co-latitude circle" is given. Mr. Chandler gives the mathematical theory of the new instrument, and illustrates the various formulæ for reducing observations by numerous examples. He then proceeds to examine critically the results of his observations (which are given in detail in the last chapter), and to describe a number of experiments on the stability of the instrument. He also suggests several modifications of construction, which he hopes in time to incorporate in a more complete form of the apparatus.

The almucantar as a field instrument seems to possess many advantages over the transit and zenith telescope for the determination of time and of terrestrial latitudes and longitudes, and Mr. Chandler states that it can be constructed at a much less cost than these instruments; but for the determination of accurate positions of the fixed stars—a class of work for which meridian instruments have hitherto been exclusively employed—it offers a new and independent method, free from many of the systematic errors inherent in the older system. The remarkable results that Mr. Chandler has already obtained with his instrument of only about 4 inches aperture certainly justify great confidence in the "almucantar system."

Horizontal telescope.—Professor Pickering has had made for the Harvard Observatory a horizontal telescope of 12 inches aperture and 17 feet focal length, possessing some of the conveniences of the equatorial coudé. The tube is placed east and west, the object-glass at the western end. Before the object-glass is a plane mirror 18 inches in diameter, so mounted that the light of a celestial object not more than one hour on either side of the meridian can be thrown by its means into the field of the telescope. A small building covering the eye-piece at the eastern end protects the observer, and may be heated in winter so that he can work in comfort. The instrument may be used for almost any class of observations, but is intended primarily as a photometer, and with this end in view an auxiliary telescope of 5 inches aperture is employed to bring into the field an image of the Pole-star, which is reduced by polarizing apparatus to equality with the image of a star observed in the principal telescope. The angular apertures of the two telescopes are such that the emergent pencils are coincident.

A device adopted at Greenwich in the observations of occultations during the eclipse of the moon on January 28, 1888, seems worthy of record. The eye-piece of the telescope was mounted eccentrically from the axis at the distance of the moon's radius, so that, without disturbing the position of the telescope, any point of the limb could be brought into the center of the field. For setting the position-circles rapidly in the dark, card-board circles, with notches cut at important points which could be felt with the fingers, were used; and in another case luminous paint was found to work admirably for indicating the figures.

In the report of the Melbourne Observatory Mr. Ellery describes a form of micrometer used successfully on the great reflector for making sketches of nebulæ. It consists of a number of silver threads crossing at right angles, and rendered visible at will by means of an electric current.

M. Périgaud has found that the essential condition in the artificial horizon aevised by Gautier for the meridian work of the Paris Observatory is that the mercury should form an extremely thin covering upon the bottom of the containing vessel. For the inner basin used in Gautier's apparatus he has substituted a plate of such diameter as to leave a space of 5 millimeters between its edge and the side of the outer vessel, and the plate being carefully levelled, it is possible to flow over it a mere film of mercury, which will give sharp images under most adverse circumstances.

It may not be out of place here to call attention to the suggestion made by Brashear and others in regard to standard dimensions in astronomical and physical instruments. The great convenience which would result from having the fittings of telescopes, eye pieces, draw tubes, etc., interchangeable can hardly be over-estimated.

MISCELLANEOUS.

The Lalande prize of the Paris Academy in 1887 was awarded to Dr. Dunér, of the Lund Observatory, Sweden, for his double-star work and his researches on stellar spectra; the Valz prize to Périgaud for his valuable investigations of the meridian instruments of the Paris Observatory and other important astronomical work. The Janssen prize for progress in astronomical physics, awarded this year for the first time, was decreed to the late Dr. Kirchhoff; the Arago medal, also awarded for the first time, to Bischoffsheim the founder of the Nice Observatory; and the La Caze physical prize to Paul and Prosper Henry for their work in astronomical photography. The Rumford medal of the Royal Society was presented to Professor Tacchini, for his investigations on the physics of the sun, November 30, 1888.

In 1888 the Lalande prize was awarded to Bossert for his extensive and valuable astronomical computations; the Valz prize, to Prof. E. C. Pickering for photometric work ; the Janssen prize, to Dr. Huggins for his researches in spectrum analysis. The Damoiseau prize was not awarded.

The gold medal of the Royal Astronomical Society was awarded on February 10, 1888, to Dr. Auwers, for his re-reduction of Bradley's observations. The Draper medal of the National Academy of Sciences was awarded in April to Professor Pickering, and the Lawrence Smith medal, to Professor Newton for his original work on the subject of meteorites.

Prizes amounting in value to about $1,000 were distributed at the December, 1887, meeting of the French Astronomical Society for the best schemes submitted for reforming the calendar. The chief prize was secured by M. Gaston Armelin, of Paris.

Telegraphic transmission of astronomical data.—Early in 1888 a new code book, "The Science Observer Code," for the convenient and accurate transmission of astronomical data by telegraph, was published by Messrs. Chandler and Ritchie as "Occasional Publications No. 1" of the Boston Scientific Society. The new code book supersedes the dictionary formerly in use, and as the words are conveniently numbered it is used with great facility. The number code of 200 quarto pages is followed by a phrase code with numerous examples, covering 17 pages, and by tables for reducing decimals of a day to hours, minutes, and seconds, and *vice versa*.

The number words have been selected from the dictionaries of several languages, it being the intention that the literal arrangement of any word should differ from that of every other by at least two letters; all words of more than ten letters are excluded. The words are arranged in 400 sections, numbered from 0 to 399, each section comprising 100 words, numbered from 0 to 99; any integral number up to 39,999 can therefore be represented by a single letter. The phrase code is arranged for the transmission of information in regard to comets, planets, variable stars, the state of the weather, and for reference, also, to stars in the Durchmusterung and Gould's zone catalogue. Checks are provided for correcting errors which have been introduced in the transmission. After the lapse of suffic.ent time for all astronomers so desiring to provide themselves with a copy of the code, it finally went into effect on October 1, 1888. The observatory of Harvard College is the central station for the distribution of astronomical information in this country, and Dr. Krueger, at Kiel, serves in a like capacity for Europe.

A paper in No. 2791 of the Astronomische Nachrichten, on the meteorological conditions favorable for establishing a large telescope, should command the attention of any one upon whom may rest the responsibility of locating a new observatory. It is manifestly important that a careful examination of the meteorological conditions of any proposed site for a large telescope should be made, particularly with reference to

II, Mis, 142——13

the quality of the images of the stars. This can be done with a scin-tilloscope or more accurately with the scintillometer, for it is this scin-tillation or superposition of an infinite number of movable images that causes the unsatisfactory seeing so often encountered. Herr Exner, in studying the scintillation at Vienna, has not found a single night on which this disagreeable phenomenon was not present.

"The Observatory" on completing its tenth volume with the number for December, 1887, passed from the hands of Messrs. Maunder, Down-ing and Lewis to Messrs. Turner and Common. The editors' address remains Hyde House, Westcombe Park, Blackheath, S. E., England.

The twelfth meeting of the International Astronomische Gesellschaft was held at Kiel from the 29th to the 31st of August, 1887, under the presidency of Dr. Auwers. The next meeting will be at Brussels in 1889.

A new society for encouraging the study of nature, the "Gesellschaft Urania," has been established at Berlin under the presidency of Pro-fessor Förster, of the Berlin observatory. Popular lectures are given on scientific subjects, and a very well-written popular journal, "Him-mel und Erde," is published, especial attention being paid to astron-omy.

Another new society, the "Société Astronomique de France," founded January 28, 1887, at Paris, by M. Flammarion, has met with remark-able success. Reports are published in the "Observatory," and in "L'Astronomie," and the proceedings appear in an annual bulletin.

Among recent works of general interest to astronomers are Professor Langley's "New Astronomy," Young's "Text-book on Astronomy," Proctor's "Old and New Astronomy," which is being published in parts, and volume I, part 1, of Houzeau and Lancaster's admirable "Bibliographie générale de l'astronomie."

ASTRONOMICAL BIBLIOGRAPHY FOR 1888.

The following list contains the titles of the most important books and journal articles published during the year 1888, with a few papers of earlier date, that have come under the writer's notice. A number of titles have also been taken from reviews or catalogues where the pub-lications themselves have not been accessible. A more complete bibliog-raphy for the year 1887 has already been published in the Smithsonian Miscellaneous Collections, No. 664, and it has not seemed advisable to extend the present list by including references to observations of comets and asteroids, or the titles of journals or other annual publications. The prices quoted are generally from Friedländer's Naturæ Novitates, in German "marks" (1 mark=100 pfennige=1 franc 25 centimes=25 cents, nearly).

In the references to periodicals the volume and page are simply sep-arated by a colon; thus: "Astron. Nachr., 118 : 369," indicates volume

118, page (or column) 369. Among imprint and other abbreviations there occur:

Abstr.= Abstract.	Lfg.= Lieferung.	p.= page.
Am.= American.	M.= marks.	pl.= plates.
Bd.= Band.	n. d.= no date.	portr.= portrait.
d.= die, der, del, etc.	n. p.= no place of publica-	pt.= part.
ed.= edition.	tion.	r.= reale.
Hft.= Heft.	n. F.= neue Folge.	Rev.= review.
hrsg.= herausgegeben.	n. s.= new series.	s.= series.
il.= illustrated.	Not.= notices.	sc.= science, scientific.
j., jour.= journal.	obsrvs.= observations.	sup.= supplement.
k. k.= kaiserlich könliigch.	Obsry.= Observatory.	v., vol.= volume.

Aberration.

BATTERMANN (H.) Einige Berichtungen aus dem Gebiete der Aberration und Fortpflanzungsgeschwindigkeit des Lichts. Astron. Nachr., 118: 369.

NYRÉN (M.) Aberration der Fixsterne. Mél. math. astron. Acad. imp. de St.-Pétersb., 6: 653-667.

Aberration (Constant of).

BATTERMANN (H.) Erwiderung auf das Schreiben von Herrn Folie. Astron. Nachr., 119: 297.

COMSTOCK (G. C.) Examination of some errors possibly affecting measures of distance made with the prism apparatus of M. Loewy. Astron. Jour., 8: 17-21.

FOLIE (F.) Schreiben . . . betr. die Aberrationsconstante. Astron. Nachr., 119: 185.

HALL (A.) [Value of the constant of aberration deduced from Washington prime vertical observations, 1862-'67.] Astron. Jour., 8: 1-5, 9-13.

KÜSTNER (F.) Neue Methode zur Bestimmung der Aberrationsconstante, nebst Untersuchungen über die Veränderlichkeit der Polhöhe. 59 p. 4to. Berlin, 1888 ....(M. 3)
> Beob.-Ergeb d k. Struwrt zu Berl, Heft 3.

Altazimuth.

SCHUR (W.) Untersuchungen und Beobachtungen am Altazimuth der Strassburger Sternwarte. Astron. Nachr., 120: 1-30.

American Astronomical Society.

PAPERS . . . No. 3. 85 p. 8vo. Brooklyn, 1888.

Asteroid 11.

LUTHER (R.) Berechnung des Planeten 11, Parthenope. Astron. Nachr., 118: 301-304.

Asteroid 111.

HOLETSCHEK (J.) Ueber die Bahn des Planeten 111, Ate. Theil 3. 31 p. 8vo. Wien, 1888.

Asteroid 114.

ANTON (F.) Specielle Störungen und Ephemeriden . . . 38 p. 8vo. Wien, 1888 ....(M. 0.60)

Asteroid 139.

COMSTOCK (G. C.) Historical note relative to the name of the planet Juewa. Sid. Mess., 7: 214.

Asteroid 154.

ANTON (F.) Specielle Störungen und Ephemeriden . . . 38 p. 8vo. Wien, 1888 ....(M. 0.60)

Asteroid 183.

DONNER (A.) Bahn des Planeten 183, Istria. Astron. Nachr., 119: 37–40.

LUTHER (W.) Bahnbestimmung des Planeten 183, Istría. Astron. Nachr., 118: 365.

Asteroids.

BERBERICH (A.) Versuch die Gesammtmasse und Anzahl der Planetoiden zwischen Mars und Jupiter zu ermitteln. Astron. Nachr., 118: 289–296.

MONCK (W. H. S.) Companion asteroids. Sid. Mess., 7: 334.

PARKHURST (H. M.) Photometric observations of asteroids. Ann. Harv. Coll. Obsry., 18: 29–72 (v. 18, pt. 3). *Also*, Reprint.

PARMENTIER (*Gen.*) Distribution des petites planètes dans l'espace. il. L'Astron., 7: 226–231.

Asteroids of 1887.

LEHMANN (P.) Zusammenstellung der Planeten-Entdeckungen im Jahre 1887. Vrtljschr. d. astron. Gesellsch., 23: 8–12.

Astronomy.

NEWCOMB (S.) Place of astronomy among the sciences. Sid. Mess., 7: 14–20, 65–73. *Also, transl.:* Ciel et Terre, 9: 145–157. *Also, transl.:* Rev. d. obsrio., 3: 105, 120.

Astronomy (Bibliography of).

WINLOCK (W. C.) Bibliography of astronomy for the year 1887. 63 p. 8vo. Washington, 1888.
Smithson. Miscel. Coll., 664.

Astronomy (Descriptive).

BERNEIKE (M. L.) Astronomy note book. 36 p. 8vo. New York, 1888..(M. 2 50)

EMMERICH (A.) Unser nächtlicher Sternenhimmel. 12 + 74 p. il. 8vo. Bamberg, 1888 .... (M. 2)

GORE (J. E.) Planetary and stellar studies. 264 p. il. 12mo. London, 1888.

JEANS (H. W.) Hand-book for the stars; containing rules for finding the names and positions of all the stars of the first and second magnitudes. 4. ed., revised by W. R. Martin. 4to. 3 maps. London, 1888. .... (M. 5.30)

PROCTOR (R. A.) Old and new Astronomy. Pts. 1—7. 448 p. 4to. London, 1888.
In twelve parts. Each part 2s. 6d.

QUEKETT CLUB MAN (*pseud.*) My telescope and some objects which it shows me. 84 p. 12mo. London, 1888 .... (M. 2.70)

SERVISS (G. P.) Astronomy with an opera glass ... New York, 1888..(M. 7.80)

Astronomy (History of). *See, also,* ASTRONOMY (Progress of).

CLERKE (A. M.) Geschichte der Astronomie während des neunzehnten Jahrhunderts gemeinfasslich dargestellt. Autorisierte deutsche Ausgabe von H. Maser. 15 + 540 p. 8vo. Berlin, 1889 [1888] .... (M. 10)

DETAILLE (C.) L'astronomie des anciens Égyptiens. il. L'Astron., 7: 339–347.

Astronomy (Progress of).

FLAMMARION (C.) Les progrès de l'astronomie pendant l'année 1887. L'Astron., 7: 161–173.

[HARKNESS (W.)] Astronomical progress and phenomena [1887]. Appleton's Ann. Cycl., 27 (n. s., 12): 35–45.

KLEIN (H. J.) Fortschritte der Astronomie. Nr. 13, 1887. 139 p. 12mo. Leipzig, 1888 .... (M. 2)
Repr. from: Rev d. Naturwissensch., Nr 76.

SAFFORD (T. H.) Development of astronomy in the United States: a discourse read June 25, 1888, to commemorate the fiftieth anniversary of the Hopkins Observatory of Williams College. 32 p. 8vo. Williamstown, 1888. *Also:* Sid. Mess., 7: 430.

Astronomy (Spherical and Practical).

CASPARI (E.) Cours d'astronomie pratique . . . Partie 1. 12 + 287 p. il. 8vo. Paris, 1888 ....(M. 7.80)

WEISS (E.) Anweisung zur Beobachtung allgemeiner Phänomene am Himmel mit freiem Auge oder mittelst solcher Instrumente wie sie dem Reisenden zur Verfügung stehen. *In:* Anleitung zu wissensch. Beob. auf Reisen . . . von G. Neumayer, 1: 359–402.

Berlin Observatory.

MARCUSE (A.) Untersuchung der grossen Schraube am Bamberg'schen Mikrometerapparat . . . Astron. Nachr., 119: 247.

Calendar.

ARMELIN (G.) [Projet de la] réforme du calendrier. L'Astron., 7: 347.

——. La réforme du calendrier. Ciel et Terre, 9: 318–328.

RAAB (D. L.) Universalkalender für die julianische, gregorianische, jüdische, jüdisch-julianische und jüdisch-gregorianische Zeitrechnung. 8 + 649 p. 4to. Budapest, 1887.

Carleton College Observatory.

[DESCRIPTION of the building and instruments.] Sid. Mess., 7: 321–325.

Christiania Observatory.

GEELMUYDEN (H.) Christiania Observatoriums Polhöide bestemt ved Observationer i förste Vertical. 50 p. 8vo. Christiania, 1888 ....(M. 1.30)

Chronology.

MAHLER (E.) Chronologische Vergleichungstabellen, nebst einer Anleitung zu den Grundzügen der Chronologie. 1. Heft. Wien, 1888.

Chronometers.

HILFIKER (J.) Einfluss des Luftdruckes auf den Gang von Marinechronometern. Astron. Nachr., 120: 109.

Clocks.

CORNU (A.) Sur une objection faite à l'emploi d'amortisseurs électro-magnétiques dans les appareils de synchronisation. Co.pt. Rend., 106: 26–31.

——. Réglage du courant électrique donnant à l'oscillation synchronisée une amplitude déterminée. il. Compt. Rend., 106: 96–100.

——. Réglage de l'amortissement et de la phase d'une oscillation synchronisée réduisant au minimum l'influence des actions perturbatrices. Compt. Rend., 106: 1206–1213.

DEFFORGES (—.) Sur un point de l'histoire du pendule. Compt. Rend., 106: 1657–1660.

DOBERCK (W.) Rate of the Hong-Kong standard clock. Astron. Nachr., 120: 183.

FORSTER (W.) Untersuchungen über Pendel-Uhren. *In his:* Studien zur Astrometrie, 115–150.

GERLAND (E.) Die Erfindung der Penduluhr. Ztschr. f. Instrmknd., 8: 77–83.

KEELER (J. E) Experiments with electrical contact apparatus for astronomical clocks. Sid. Mess., 7: 9–14.

WOLF (C.) Remarques sur la dernière note de M. Cornu relative à la synchronisation des pendules. Compt. Rend., 106: 31, 93.

ZWINK (M.) Pendeluhren im luftdicht verschlossenen Raume mit besonderer Anwendung auf die bezüglichen Einrichtungen der Berliner Sternwarte. 32 p. 4to. Kiel, 1888 ....(M. 1.80)

Code (Astronomical).

ANNOUNCEMENT as to the new Science Observer code. Astron. Jour., 8: 102.

[CHANDLER (S. C.), jr., and RITCHIE (J.), jr.] Science observer code. [400] + 17 + p. 4to. Boston, 1888 ....($5.00)

Boston Scientific Soc Occasional publns, No 1

Code (Astronomical)—Continued.

KRÜGER (A.) Angelegenheiten der Centralstelle für astronomische Telegramme.
Astron. Nachr., 119: 17–22.

—— [Number of subscribers to astronomical telegrams.] Month. Not., 48: 352.

RITCHIE (J.) Announcement with reference to the astronomical code. Astron.
Jour., 7: 189.

Cointe Observatory.

UBAGHS (P.) Notice sur l'observatoire de Cointe. 14 p. 8vo. Liège,
1888 ....(M. 0.80)
    Repr. from : Mém. Soc. d. sc , Liège.

Collimators.   .

CORNU (A.) Sur l'emploi du collimateur à réflexion de Fizeau comme mire loin-
taine. Compt. Rend., 107 : 708–713.

Colored stars.

FRANCS (W. S.) Introduction to a catalogue of the mean colors of 758 stars;
with appendix containing the colors of 26 southern stars. Month. Not., 48:
265–267.

SCHRÖDER (H. C.) Chambers' neues Verzeichniss von roten Sternen. Sirius,
20 : 223, 256, 279 ; 21 : 7, 63, 78, 106, 127.

Comet Encke.

BERBERICH (A.) Helligkeit des Encke'schen Cometen. Astron. Nachr., 119.
49–66. *Also :* Sirius, 21: 151.

SHERMAN (O. T.) A study in the elements of Encke's comet. Astron. Jour.,
8: 99.

Comet Tempel.

GAUTIER (R.) Étude consacrée spécialement aux apparitions de 1873 et de 1879.
4 + 110 p. 4to. Genève, 1888 ....(M. 4.50)

Comet Winnecke.

VON HAERDTL (E.) Bahn des periodischen Cometen Winnecke in den Jahren
1858–1886, nebst einer neuen Bestimmung der Jupitermasse. Anzeig. Wien.
Akad., 1888, Nr. 18..(M. 4.80)

Comet 1666.

LYNN (W. T.) [Account of the comet in February, 1666, by Robert Knox.]
Obsry., 11 : 375.

Comet 1680.

LYNN (W. T.) First discovery of the great comet of 1680. Obsry., 11: 437.

Comet 1833.

SCHULHOF (L.) Orbites des deux comètes de 1833 et 1883. Bull. astron., 5:
248, 480, 532.

Comet 1862 II.

CERULLI (V.) Sull' orbita della cometa del Luglio 1862. Astron. Nachr., 118:
193–204.

Comet 1863 III.

ERICSSON (G.) Definitive Bahnelemente des Cometen 1863 III. Astron. Nachr.,
118 : 353–360 ....(M. 1.30)

Comet 1873 II.

SCHULHOF (L.) Éléments et éphémdride de la comète 1873 II (Tempel). Bull.
astron., 5 : 425. *Also :* Astron. Nachr., 120 : 173.

Comet 1879 IV.

MILLOSEVICH (E.) Orbita della comèta 1879 IV. Mem. Soc. spettrscp. ital.,
17 : 55.

Comet 1882 II.

KREUTZ (H.) Untersuchungen über das Cometensystem 1843 I, 1880 I und 1882 II. I. Theil. Der grosse September comet 1882 II. 110 p. 4to. Kiel, 1888. Publ d Strnwrt. in Ciel.

Comet 1885 III

CAMPBELL (W. W.) Definitive determination of the orbit of comet 1885 III. Astron. Nachr., 120: 49-58.

Comet 1887 IV.

MULLER (F.) Definitive determination of the orbit of comet 1887 IV. Astron. Jour., 8: 44-56, 71.

Comet seeker.

HILL (G. A.) [Altazimuth mounting of 6½-inch reflector.] il. Sid. Mess., 7: 241.

Comets.

BACCHOUSE (T. W.) Naked-eye comets. Obsry., 11: 343.

BERBERICH (A.) [Method and desirability of photometric observations of comets.] Astron. Nachr., 119: 66.

FAYE (H.) Hypothèse de Lagrange sur l'origine des comète set des aérolithes. Compt. Rend., 106: 1703-1708. Also: Ciel et Terre, 9. 237-243.

HALL (A.) Problem of alignment. Astron. Jour., 8: 143.

HOLETSCHEK (J.) Richtungen der grossen Axen der Cometenbahnen. Abstr.: Astron. Nachr., 120: 137.

KIAER (H. J.) Équations servant à déterminer les formes des queues cométaires. Astron. Nachr, 119: 369-378; 120: 107.

MONCK (W. H. S.) Cometary statistics. Obsry., 11: 432.

—— Dissipation of comets. Sid. Mess, 7: 239.

TEBBUTT (J.) Comet nomenclature. Obsry., 11: 436.

Comets and meteors.

KIRCWOOD (D.) Relation of short-period comets to the zone of asteroids. Sid. Mess., 7: 177-181.

Comets of 1887.

KREUTZ (H.) Zusammenstellung der Cometen-Erscheinungen des Jahres 1887. Vrtljschr d. astron. Gesellsch., 23: 13-20.

WILSON (H C.) [Account of the comets of 1887, with elements and references to observations.] Sid. Mess., 7: 153-160. Also, Reprint.

Comets (Orbits of)

LOHNSTEIN (T.) Ermittelung der geocentrischen Distanzen eines Cometen. Astron. Nachr., 119: 99-106.

Constellations.

PLOIX (C.) [Légendes de] la grande ourse. Ciel et Terre, 9: 25-37.

Corona (Solar).

NEUE Hypothese über die Natur der Sonnen-Korona. Sirius, 21: 1.

WESLEY (W. H.) Corona of 1886. il. Obsry., 11: 357-360.

Cosmogony. See, also, NEBULÆ; NEBULAR HYPOTHESIS; METEORITES.

JANSSEN (J.) L'âge des étoiles. Ciel et Terre, 9: 449, 465. Also: L'Astron., 7: 19, 59. Also, transl.: Sirius, 21: 49-57.

Dearborn Observatory.

HOUGH (G. W.) [Removal to new site.] Astron. Nachr., 119: 207.

JOHNSON (H. A.) [Address at the laying of the corner-stone of the new building, June 24, 1888.] Sid. Mess., 7: 381-385.

TENNANT (J. F.) [Position and constants for the new observatory.] Month. Not., 49: 95.

Domes.

CROSSLEY (E.) Description of a new observatory for a 3-foot reflector. 1 pl. Month. Not., 48: 356–359.

Double stars.

BURNHAM (S. W.) New double stars discovered at the Lick Observatory. Astron. Jour., 8: 141.

CLER(E (A. M.) Historical and descriptive list of some double stars suspected to vary in light. Nature, 39: 55–58.

—— Variable double stars. Obsry., 11: 188.

FLAMMARION (C.) Nouveaux systèmes stellaires. L'Astron., 7: 66.

MONC((W. H. S.) Brightness and density of binary stars. Obsry., 11: 341.

—— Distances of double stars. Sid. Mess., 7: 290

SCHIAPARELLI (G. V.) Osservazioni sulle stelle doppie Serie 1 .. 1875–1885, 85+144 p. 4to. Milano, 1888................................. ....(M. 7)

Earth.

BISCHOFF (J.) Neue Beziehungen auf dem Geoid. Astron. Nachr., 119: 177–184.

BONNEY (T. G.) Foundation-stones of the earth's crust. Nature, 39: 89–94.

CALLANDREAU (O.) Remarques sur la théorie de la figure de la terre. Bull. Astron., 5: 473–480.

HAYWOOD (J.) The earth and its chief motions, and the tangent index. 28 p. 12mo. Dayton, 1888...(M. 0.80)

HELMERT (F. R.) Mittheilung über eine beabsichtigte Cooperation mehrerer deutscher Sternwarten in Bezug auf die Untersuchung kleiner Bewegungen der Erdaxe. Astron. Nachr., 120: 225–230.

HILL (G. W.) Interior constitution of the earth as respects density. Ann. Math. 4: 19–29. *Also*, Reprint.

LÉVY (M.) Théorie de la figure de la terre. Compt. Rend., 106: 1270–1276, 1314–1320, 1375–1381.

POINCARÉ (H.) Sur la figure de la terre. Compt. Rend., 107: 67–71.

RICCÒ (A.) Immagine del sole riflessa nel mare prova della rotondità della terra. il. Mem. Soc. spettrscp. ital., 17: 203–220.

Eclipse of Thales.

PETERS (C. F. W.) Sonnenfinsterniss des Thales. Astron. Nachr., 120: 231.

Eclipse of the Moon, 1888, Jan. 28.

BODDICKER (O.) Veränderungen der Wärmestrahlung des Mondes während der totalen Mondfinsterniss 1888, Jan. 28. 1 pl. Astron. Nachr., 118: 310. *See, also :* Nature, 37: 318.

Eclipse of the Sun, 1886, Aug. 28-29.

TURNER (H. H.) Report of the observations . . . made at Grenville, in the Island of Grenada. 2 pl. Mem. Soc. spettrscp. ital., 17: 46.

Eclipse of the Sun, 1887, Aug. 18.

HAR(NESS (W.) [Résumé of observations.] Sid. Mess., 7: 1–8.

NIESTEN (L.) L'éclipse totale de soleil du 19 août 1887, observée à Jurjewetz, Russie. 21 p. 12mo. Bruxelles, 1888.
Repr. from Ann. de l'obs. roy. de Bruxelles, 1889

TODD (D. P.) Preliminary report . . . 16 p. 8vo. Amherst, 1888.

UPTON (W.) and ROTCH (A. L.) Meteorological observations . . . 25 p. 8vo. Ann Arbor, 1888.
Repr from : Am. Meteorol. J., 1888

VOGEL (H. C.) [Instructions for observing the eclipse.] Vrtljschr. d. astron. Gesellsch., 23: 130–135.

Eclipse of the Sun, 1889, Jan. 1..

HOLDEN (E. S.) Suggestions for observing the total eclipse of the Sun on Jan. 1, 1889. 21 p., 1 map. 8vo. Sacramento, 1888.

Eclipse of the Sun, 1889, Jan 1—Continued.

—— [Probable meteorological conditions at that time.] Month. Not., 48: 302-307.

TODD (D. P) Instructions for observing the total eclipse of the Sun, 1889, Jan. 1. il. 16 p. 8vo. Amherst, 1888 ....(M. 1.20)

Eclipses.

FLAMMARION (C.) Éclipses [de soleil] du 19e siècle visibles en France on aux environs. L'Astron., 7 : 306-311.

GINZEL (F. K.) Finsterniss Canon für das Untersuchungsgebiet der römischen Chronologie. 36 p. 8vo. Berlin Akad., 1887......................(M. 1.50)

LYNN (W. T.) Earliest recorded eclipse. Obsry., 11 : 197.

MAHLER (E.) Astronomische Untersuchungen über die angebliche Finsterniss unter Thakelath II. von Aegypten. 14 p. 4to. Wien, 1888.........(M. 0.80)

Eclipses of the moon.

BRUNS (H.) Heliometermessungen bei Mondfinsternissen. Astron. Nachr., 118: 363.

JOHNSON (S. J.) Earliest recorded lunar eclipse. Obsry., 11 : 340.

LYNN (W T.) Earliest recorded lunar eclipse. Obsry., 11 : 376.

Edinburgh Observatory.

SMYTH (C. Piazzi). Report on the Royal Observatory, Edinburgh, for 30 June, 1888, and the Edinburgh equatorial in 1887. 16 p. 4to. [n. p., 1888.]

Electric light.

BRUNS (H.) [Electric illumination of the Leipzig heliometer.] Vitljschr. d. astron. Gesellsch., 23: 109.

SPITTA (E. J.) Simple electric light for the telescope. il. Obsry., 11 : 368.

Engelmann (Friedrich Wilhelm Rudolf). [1841-1888.]

BRUNS (H.) Todes-Anzeige. Astron. Nachr., 119: 47.

PETER (B.) Nekrolog. Vrtljschr. d. astron. Gesellsch., 23 : 153-157.

Equatorial coudé.

LOEWY (M.) and PUISEUX (P.) Théorie nouvelle de l'equatorial coudé et des équatoriaux en général. (Exposé de l'ensemble des méthodes permettant de rectifier et d'orienter ces instruments.) Compt. Rend., 106 : 704-711, 793-800, 891-898, 970-976, 1199-1206, 1320-1326, 1483-1489.

Equatorials. *See, also,* TELESCOPES.

FÖRSTER (W.) Untersuchungen über das Fraunhofer'sche Aequatorial. *In his :* Studien zur Astrometrie, 160-206

GRUBB (H.) New arrangement of electrical control for driving clocks of equatorials. Month. Not., 48: 352-356.

RANYARD (A. C.) Simple method of applying electrical control to the driving clock of an equatorial. il. Month. Not., 48 : 336.

Eudoxus.

LYNN (W. T.) Narrien and the observations of Eudoxus of Cnidus. Obsry., 11 : 300.

Flexure.

BAUSCHINGER (J.) Biegung von Meridianfernröhren. 18 p., 1 pl. 4to Munchen, 1888 ....(M. 2)

STREHL (K.) Beugung im Fernrohr. Sirius, 21 : 132-138.

Galileo.

LYNN (W. T.) Galileo Galilei and his condemnation. Obsry., 11 ; 314-317.

Geographical positions.

STADTHAGEN (H.) Beiträge zur Untersuchung des Genauigkeitsgrades astronomischer Berechnungen mit Anwendung auf eine in der geographischen Ortsbestimmung häufig vorkommende Aufgabe. 84 p. 8°. Berlin, 1888 .....(M. 2.)

TIETJEN (F.) Geographische Ortsbestimmung. *In :* Anleitung zu wissensch Beob. auf. Reisen ... von G Neumayer, 1 : 1-40.

Gravitation.

CALLANDREAU (O.) Énergie potentielle de la gravitation d'une planète. Compt. Rend., 107 : 555.

HALL (A.) The extension of the law of gravitation to stellar systems. Astron. Jour., 8: 65–68.

Greenwich Observatory.

ASTRONOMICAL and magnetical and meteorological observations . . . 1886 [1027+] p. 4 to. London, 1888.

Harvard College Observatory.

ANNALS . . . vol. 13, pt. 2. Zone observations made with the transit wedge photometer . . . 149 p. 4to. Cambridge, 1888.

ANNALS . . . vol. 18, pt. 3. Photometric observations of asteroids. 44 p. 4to. Cambridge, 1888.

DRAPER (Henry) memorial. Second annual report of the photographic study of stellar spectra . . . [by] E. C. Pickering. 8 p. 2 pl. 4to. Cambridge, Mass., 1888.

REPORT (43d annual) of the director . . . E. C. Pickering . . . Dec. 15, 1888. 11 p. 8vo. Cambridge, 1888.

Houzeau (Jean Charles). [1820–1888.]

L[ANCASTER] (A.) Notes biographiques. Ciel et Terre, 9, 313, 361, 385, 409, 457, 481.

See, also, Ibid. 249-270. Also Obsry., 11. 318-320

Instruments (Astronomical). *See, also,* ALTAZIMUTH ; EQUATORIALS ; LEVELS, etc.

BRASHEAR (J. A.) Standard dimensions in astronomical and physical instruments. Proc. Am. Assn. Adv. Sc., 36: 61. *Also,* Sid. Mess., 7 : 77.

Jena Observatory.

WINKLER (W.) Verlegung seiner Privatsternwarte nach Jena . . . Astron. Nachr., 118 : 205.

Journals (Astronomical).

HIMMEL und Erde. Illustrirte naturwissenschaftliche Monatschrift. Hrsg. von der Gesellschaft Urania. Redacteur ; M. Wilhelm Meyer.

1. Jahrgang, Heft 1 October, 1888. Preis vierteljährlich, M 3 60 ; einzelne Hefte..(M.2)

Jupiter.

DENNING (W. F.) Rotation of Jupiter. Obsry., 11 : 88.

——. Motion of the red spot on Jupiter. Obsry., 11 : 406.

LYNN (W. T.) Rotation of Jupiter. Obsry., 11 : 125.

SCHULTZ-STEINHEIL (C. A.) [Werth für den Halbmesser des Planeten.] Astron. Nachr., 119 : 129-138.

Jupiter (Satellites of).

ANDRÉ (C.) Ligament lumineux des passages et occultations des satellites. Compt. Rend., 107 : 216.

——. Ligament lumineux des passages et occultations des satellites de Jupiter. Moyen de l'éviter. Compt. Rend., 107 : 615.

Kepler's problem.

SEYDLER (A.) Zur Lösung des Kepler'schen Problems. Astron. Nachr., 118: 261-271.

Kew Observatory.

REPORT of the Kew committee for the year ending October 31, 1888. 28 p. 8vo. London, 1888.

Levels.

MYLIUS (F.) Störungen der Libellen. Ztschr. f. Instrmknd., 8 : 267-283, 428.

Lick Observatory.

[DESCRIPTION of buildings and instruments.] il. Engineering, 46: 1, 81, 149, 151, 396.

[HISTOIRE de] l'observatoire Lick. il. Ciel et Terre, 9: 105–112.

HOLDEN (E. S.) [Description of] the Lick Observatory. il. Sid. Mess., 7: 49–65.

——. [First astronomical observations, etc.] Nature, 38: 355.

——. [Formal transfer to the University of California.] Astron. Jour., 8: 43.

——. Hand-book of the Lick Observatory of the University of California. 135 p. 16°. il. San Francisco, 1888.

NEUES Spektroskop des Lick-Observatoriums und die photographische Beobachtung der Sternenspektren. Sirius, 21: 230.

Light.

BELL (L.) Absolute wave-length of light. Am. J. Sc., 135: 265–282, 348–368.

Longitude. *See, also,* GEOGRAPHICAL POSITIONS.

CASPARI (—.) Formule pour le calcul des longitudes par les chronomètres. Compt. Rend., 107: 78.

Lunar theory.

ADAMS (J. C.) Remarks on Airy's numerical lunar theory. Month. Not., 48: 319–322.

AIRY (G. B.) The numerical lunar theory. Month. Not., 48: 253; 49: 2.

FRANZ (J.) Neue Berechnung von Hartwig's Beobachtungen der physischen Libration des Mondes. 8 p. 4to. Berlin, 1887 .... (M. 0.30)

HARZER (P.) Apsidenbewegung der Mondbahn. Astron. Nachr., 118: 273–280.

OPPOLZER (T.) and SCHRAM (R.) Entwurf einer Mondtheorie gehörende Entwicklung der Differentialquotienten ... 188 p. 4to. Wien. 1888 .... (M. 10)

Repr from· Denkschr d k. Akad d. Wissensch. Math. naturw. Cl. Wien 54 59–244.

TISSERAND (F.) Sur un point de la théorie de la lune. Compt. Rend., 106: 788–793.

Lyons Observatory.

ANDRÉ (C.) Travaux de l'observatoire de Lyon. Partie 1. Influence de l'altitude sur la marche diurne du baromètre. 153 p., 5 pl. 4to. Lyon, 1888.

McCormick Observatory.

REPORT ... for the year ending June 1, 1888. 3 p. 8vo. [n. p., n. d.]

Madras Observatory.

RESULTS of observations of the fixed stars made with the meridian circle at ... Madras in the years 1862, 1863, and 1864, under the direction of N. R. Pogson. 47+314 p. 4to. Madras, 1887.

——. Same. 1865, 1866, 1867. 22+362 p. 4 to. Madras, 1888.

Mars.

ERKLÄRUNG der Kanäle. Sirius, 21: 227–230.

FAYE (H.) [Les canaux et la région Libya.] Comp. Rend., 106: 1718.

FIZEAU (H. L.) Les canaux ... Compt. Rend., 106: 1759–1762.

F[LAMMARION] (C.) Inondations de la planète Mars: variations observées dans les canaux, les lacs et les mers. il. L'Astron, 7: 241–253.

——. Nouvelles observations sur la planète Mars: ses neiges, ses eaux et ses climats. il. L'Astron. 7: 281–291.

——. Un dernier mot sur la planète Mars. il. L'Astron., 7: 412–422.

——. Fleuves de la planète Mars. il. L'Astron., 7: 457–462.

——. Les neiges, les glaces et les eaux de la planète Mars. Compt. Rend., 107: 19–22.

HALL (A.) Appearance of Mars, June, 1888. Astron. Jour., 8: 79.

HOLDEN (E. S.) Physical observations of Mars during the opposition of 1888, at the Lick Observatory. Astron. Jour., 8: 97.

MAUNDER (E. W.) Canals on Mars. Obsry., 11: 345–348.

Mars—Continued.

NIESTEN (L.) Sur l'aspect physique de la planète Mars, pendant l'opposition de 1888. 12 p. 1 pl. 8vo. Bruxelles, 1888.
  Bull. de l'Acad. roy. de Belg., 3 s., vol. 16, No. 7.

PERROTIN (J.) Canaux de Mars. Nouveaux changements observés sur cette planète. il. L'Astron., 7: 213.

——. Nouvelles observations sur la planète Mars. il. L'Astron., 7: 366-370.

——. Observation des canaux de Mars. Compt. Rend., 106: 1393.

——. [Croquis de Mars.] Compt. Rend., 107: 161, 496.

PICKERING (W. H.) Physical aspect of the planet Mars. Science, 12: 82.

PROCTOR (R. A.) Note on [the canals of] Mars. Month. Not., 48: 307.

TERBY (F.) [Dessins de] la planète Mars. il. L'Astron., 7: 324.

——. Les canaux de Mars, leur gémination et les observations de 1888. il. Ciel et Terre, 9: 271-286, 289-302.

——. Premières observations de Mars et de Saturne faites à l'observatoire Lick ... en 1888, et réponses à quelques objections. Ciel et Terre, 9: 370-380.

——. Étude de la planète Mars. Compt. Rend, 106: 1470.

——. [Vérification des cartes de Schiaparelli.] Obsry., 11: 298.

WISLICENUS (W. F.) Anwendung von Mikrometermessungen bei physischen Beobachtungen des Mars. il. Astron. Nachr., 120: 241-250.

Mars (Satellites of).

DUBOIS (E.) [Peut-être petites planètes devenues les satellites.] Compt. Rend., 107: 439.

POINCARÉ (H.) [L'hypothèse qu'ils sont de petites planètes.] Compt. Rend., 107: 890.

Maury (Matthew Fontaine) [1806-73].

CORBIN (Diana F. M.) Life of Matthew Fontaine Maury. 306 p. portr. 8vo. London, 1888.

Mechanics (Celestial).

DZIOBEK (O.) Mathematische Theorien der Planetenbewegungen. 8+305 p. 8vo. Leipzig, 1888 ....(M. 9)

Mercury.

SHERMAN (O. T.) A study of the residual discordances for Mercury. Astron. Jour., 8: 34-36.

Meteorites. See, also, METEORS.

BORNITZ (H.) Zusammenstellung der Meteoritenfälle nach Monat, Tag u. Stunde. Sirius, 21: 157-161.

DARWIN (G. H.) Mechanical conditions of a swarm of meteorites. Abstr.: Nature, 39: 81, 105.

DERBY (O. A.) Notas sobre meteoritos Brasilieros. Rev. d. obstio.. 3: 3, 17, 33.

HUNTINGTON (O. W.) Catalogue of all recorded meteorites . . . Proc. Am· Acad. Arts & Sc., 23: 37-110. 1887. Also, Reprint

LOCKYER (J. N.) Notes on meteorites. il. Nature, 38: 424, 456, 530, 556, 602; 39: 139.

LOCKYER's Untersuchungen über die Spektra der Meteoriten. Sirius, 21: 111-115.

NEWTON (H. A.) Orbits of aerolites. Astron. Jour, 8: 41.

——. Relation which the former orbits of those meteorites that are in our collections, and that were seen to fall, had to the earth's orbit. Am. J. Sc., 136: 1-14.

Meteors. See, also, COMETS AND METEORS.

BOOTH (D.) Radiant of the August Perseids. Obsry, 11: 379.

BREDICHIN (T.) Quelques remarques sur l'origine des météores. Astron. Nachr., 120: 249. Also: Bull. astron., 5: 521-523.

DENNING (W. F.) History of the August meteors. Nature, 38: 393.

——. The chief meteor showers. Month. Not., 48: 110.

Meteors—Continued.

DENNING (W. F.) Heights of fire-balls and shooting stars. Month. Not., 48 : 112.

KLEIBER (J.) Vertheilung der Meteore in Meteorschwärmen. Astron. Nachr., 118 : 345.

MEUNIER (S.) Rapports mutuels des météorites et des étoiles filantes. Compt. Rend., 107 : 834.

DE TILLO (A.) Recherches sur la répartition des points radiants d'après les mois de l'année et d'après les coordonnées célestes. Bull. Astron., 5 : 237-248, 283-91.

Meteors (Observations of). *See, also,* METEORS.

DENNING (W. F.) Height of a Perseid fire-ball. il. Month. Not., 49 : 19-21.

—— Height of a Leonid fire-ball. il. Month. Not., 49 : 66.

—— Leonid meteor-shower, 1888. Nature, 39 : 84.

Micrometers.

COMSTOCK (G. C.) Value of one revolution of a micrometer screw. Sid. Mess., 7 : 343-409.

KEMPF (P.) Ueber Lamellen-mikrometer. Astron. Nachr., 119 : 33-38.

OUDEMANS (J. A. C.) Condition that in a double-image micrometer the value of a revolution of the micrometer screw may be independent of the accommodation of the eye. Month. Not., 48 : 334.

TUPMAN (G. L.) On the cross reticule. il. Month. Not., 48 : 96-103.

—— Description of a cross-bar micrometer. Obsry., 11 : 58-61.

Mirrors.

COMMON (A. A.) Testing polished flat surfaces. Month. Not., 48 : 105.

MADSEN (H. F.) Notes on the process of polishing and figuring 18-inch glass specula by hand, and experiments with flat surfaces. Jour. and Proc. Roy. Soc. N. S. Wales, 20 : 79-91, 1886.

Rev. by COMMON (A. A). Nature, 37 382.

Mitchel (Ormsby Mcknight) [1809-'62].

MITCHEL (F. A.) Ormsby Macknight Mitchel, astronomer and general: a biographical narrative. 8 + 392 p. portr. 12mo. Boston, 1887.

Moon. *See, also,* LUNAR THEORY.

ELGER (T. G.) Sir William Herschel's observations of volcanoes in the moon. Obsry., 11 : 377.

GRENSTED (F. F.) Theory to account for the airless and waterless condition of the moon . . . 8vo. Liverpool, 1888.

HOLDEN (E. S.) Sir William Herschel's observations of volcanoes in the moon. Obsry., 11 : 334.

HUNT (G.) Sir William Herschel's observations of volcanoes in the moon. Obsry , 11 : 403.

THUREIN (—) Elementare Darstellung der Mondbahn. 4to. Berlin, 1888.. (M. 1)

WILLIAMS (A. S.) Sir William Herschel's observations of volcanoes in the moon. Obsry , 11 : 378.

WOLF (M.) Aufnahme von Mondphotographien. il. Sirius, 21 : 97-100.

Moscow Observatory.

Annales de l'observatorie de Moscou . . . 2 s., v. 1. 2. livraison. 128 p. 6 pl. 4to. Moscow, 1888... (M. 6)

Nadir.

PÉRIGAUD (E.-L.-A.) Nouveau bain de mercure pour l'observation du nadir. Compt. Rend., 106 : 919-921.

—— Observations d'étoiles par réflexion et la mesure de la flexion du cercle de Gambey. Compt. Rend., 107 . 613.

Natal Observatory.

REPORT of the superintendent . . . 1887. 26 p. 4to. [n. p., n. d.]

Nebulæ.   *See. also,* PLEIADES.

COMMON (A. A.) Photographs of nebulæ. Obsry., 11 : 390–394.

DREYER (J. L. E.) New general catalogue of nebulæ and clusters of stars, being the catalogue of the late Sir John F. W. Herschel, revised, corrected, and enlarged. 237 p. 4to. London, 1888..(M. 21.)

    Mem. Roy. Astron. Soc., v. 49, pt 1. *Review.*—Nature, 37 : 353, Astron. Nachr., 118 : 367.

GINZEL (F. K.) Beobachtungen von Nebelflecken [vom Dec. 1884 bis Apr. 1886]. Astron. Nachr., 118 : 321–344.

LOCKYER (J. N). Suggestions on the classification of the various species of heavenly bodies. il. Proc. Roy. Soc. 46: 1–93. *Also*, Reprint. *Also:* Nature, 37 : 585, 606; 38 : 8, 31, 56, 79...(M. 3. 70)

PICKERING (E. C.) Detection of new nebulæ by photography. Ann. Harv. Coll. Obsry., 18 : 113–117 (v. 18, no. 6). *Also*, Reprint.

ROBERTS (I.) Photographs of the nebulæ M, 31, *h* 44 and *h* 51 Andromedæ and M. 27 Vulpeculæ. Month. Not., 49 : 65.

SWIFT (L.) Catalogue No. 7 of nebulæ discovered at the Warner Observatory. Astron. Nachr., 120 : 33–38.

VOGEL (H. C.) Bedeutung der Photographie zur Beobachtung von Nebelflecken. il. Astron. Nachr., 119 : 337–342.

Nebular hypothesis.

COAKLEY (G. W.) On the nebular hypothesis of La Place. 85 p. 8vo. Brooklyn, 1888.

    Papers Am. Astron. Soc., No 3.

KERZ (F.) Beitrag zur Nebular hypothese. Sirius, 20: 265; 21: 10, 34.

——. Weitere Ausbildung der Laplace'schen Nebular-hypothese. Nachtrag. 8+ 127 p., 3 pl. 8vo. Leipzig, 1888...(M. 3)

Neptune (Satellite of).

HALL (A.) [Orbit of] the satellite of Neptune. Astron. Jour., 8: 78.

NEWCOMB (S.) Note on the [orbit of the] satellite of Neptune. Astron. Jour., 8 : 143.

TISSERAND (F.) [Orbite du satellite.] Compt. Rend., 107: 804–810.

Nice Observatory.

Grand équatorial de l'observatoire de Nice. il. L'Astron., 7 : 447–451.

Nieuport Observatory.

DELPORTE (A.) L'observatoire astronomique temporaire de Nieuport. Ciel et Terre, 9: 423–429.

North Carolina University Observatory.

LOVE (J. L.) First college observatory in the United States. Sid. Mess., 7 : 417–420; Nation, 47 : 131.

Nutation.

FÖRSTER (W.) Ueber die bisherigen Annahmen in den Transformations-Elementen der astronomischen Ortsangaben. *In his ;* Studien zur Astrometrie, 1–49.

NIESTEN (L.) Influence de la nutation diurne dans la discussion des observations de γ Draconis faites à l'observatoire de Greenwich. 22 p. 8vo. [Bruxelles, 1887.]

    Repr. from Mém. cour. publ. par l'Acad. roy. de Belg , 1887.

——. Influence de la nutation diurne dans la discussion des observations de α Lyræ faites à l'observatoire de Washington. 6 p. 12mo. Bruxelles, 1888.

    Repr. from: Ann. de l'Obs. roy. de Brux., 1889.

Objectives.

CZAPSKI (S.) Bemerkungen zu der Abhandlung von E. v. Hoegh, "Die sphärische Abweichung ..." Ztschr. f. Instrmknd., 8 : 203–206.

GRUBB (H.) [Objectives adapted to either photographic or other work.] Nature, 37 : 439.

Objectives—Continued.

HASSELBERG (B.) Méthode à déterminer avec grande exactitude les distances focales d'un système optique pour une raie quelconque du spectre. Mem. Soc. spettrsep. ital., 17 : 182–188.

VON HOEGH (E.) Die sphärische Abweichung und deren Correction speciell bei Fernrohrobjectiven. Ztschr. f. Instrmknd., 8 : 117.

KRÜSS (H.) Die Farben-Correction der Fernrohr-Objective von Gauss und von Fraunhofer. Ztschr. für Instrmknd., 8 : 7, 53, 83.

PICKERING (E. C.) New photographic objective. Nature, 37 : 558.

SCHUR (W.) Untersuchungen und Rechnungen über das Objectiv des grossen Refractors der Strassburger Sternwarte. Astron. Nachr., 119 : 249–254.

VOGEL (H. C.) Ueber die Methoden zur Bestimmung der chromatischen Abweichung von Fernrohrobjectiven. Astron. Nachr., 119 : 293.

WOLF (M.) Bestimmung der Farbenabweichung grosser Objective. Astron. Nachr., 120 : 73.

——. Trennung der Objectivlinsen für photographische Zwecke. il. Astron. Nachr., 119 : 161.

Observatories.

HOLDEN (E. S.) Principal observatories of the world. il. *In his :* Handbook Lick Obsry., 104–125.

JAHRESBERICHTE der Sternwarten für 1887. Vrtljschr. d. astron. Gesellsch. 23 : 73–151.

LOVE (J. J.) [First observatory founded in the United States, at the University of North Carolina in 1831.] Nation, 47 : 131.

[REPORTS of observatories, 1887.] Month. Not., 48 : 175–198.

TENNANT (J. F.) Table of the positions of observatories with constants useful in correcting extra-meridian observations for parallax. Month. Not., 49 : 22–32, 95.

O'Gyalla Observatory.

Beobachtungen angestellt am astrophysikalischen Observatorium in O'Gyalla, hrsg. von Dr. von Konkoly. 9. Bd., enthaltend Beobachtungen vom Jahre 1886. 106 p. 4to. Halle, 1888.

Orbits. *See, also,* COMETS (Orbits of) ; THREE BODIES (Problem of).

BRUNS (H.) Der Lambert'sche Satz. Astron. Nachr., 118 : 241–250.

ISRAEL-HOLTZWART (K.) Beiträge zur Anwendung unendlicher Reihen im Gebiete der Bahnberechnung der Planeten und Kometen. 82 p. 8vo. Wiesbaden, 1888 .... (M. 2.40)

RADAU (R.) Formules pour la variation des éléments d'une orbite. Bull. astron., 5 : 5–12.

SEARLE (G. M.) An improvement in the computation of an orbit. Astron. Jour., 8 : 125.

Parallax (Solar).

HARKNESS (W.) Value of the solar parallax deducible from the American photographs of the last transit of Venus. Astron. Jour., 8 : 108.

Parallax (Stellar).

FOLIE (F.) Détermination de la vitesse systématique et de la parallaxe des étoiles. Astron. Nachr., 119 : 343.

PRITCHARD (C.) Results of recent investigations of stellar parallax made at the University Observatory, Oxford. Month. Not., 49 : 2–4.

Paris Observatory.

FAYE (H.) Latitude du cercle de Gambey. Compt. Rend., 107 : 810.

MOUCHEZ (E.-A.-B.) Difficulté d'obtenir la latitude de l'observatoire de Paris. Compt. Rend , 107 : 848.

· PÉRIGAUD (E.-L.-A.) Triple détermination de la latitude du cercle de Gambey. Compt. Rend., 107 : 722.

Paris Observatory—Continued.

RAPPORT annual sur l'état de l'Observatoire de Paris présenté au conseil . . . 21 janvier 1888. 26 p. 1 pl. 4vo. Paris, 1888.

Pekin Observatory.

RUSSELL (S. M.) History and description of the Pekin Observatory. Nature, 39: 46. *See, also: Ibid.*, 55.

Personal equation.

BIGOURDAN (G.) Variations de l'équation personnelle dans les mesures d'étoiles doubles. Compt. Rend., 106: 1645.

HILFIKER (J.) Sur l'équation personnelle dans les observations de passage. 7 p 12mo. Neuchâtel, 1888.
    Repr. from Bull. Soc. sc. nat. de Neuchâtel, vol. 16.

RENZ (F.) Versuch einer Bestimmung der persönlichen Gleichung bei der Beobachtung von Sternbedeckungen. Astron. Nachr., 119: 145–150.

SANFORD (E. C.) Personal equation. Am. J. Psychol., 2: 1–38, 271–298, 403–430.

WISLICENUS (W. F.) Untersuchungen über den absoluten persönlichen Fehler bei Durchgangsbeobachtungen. 50 p. 1 pl. 4vo. Leipzig, 1888 . . . . . . (M. 3)

Perturbations.

GAILLOT (A.) Théorie analytique du mouvement des planètes. Expression générale des perturbations qui sont du troisième ordre par rapport aux masses. Bull. astron., 5: 329, 377. *Also*, Reprint.

GYLDÉN (H.) Convergenz einer in der Störungstheorie vorkommenden Reihe. Astron. Nachr., 119: 321–330.

HARZER (P.) Differentialgleichung der Störungstheorie. Astron. Nachr., 119: 273–294.

LÁSKA (W.) Zur Theorie der planetarischen Störungen. 5 p. 8vo. Wien, 1888 . . . . (M. 0.20)

WEILER (A.) Störungen werden als Functionen zweier Anomalien dargestellt. Astron. Nachr., 120: 97–108.

Photographic Congress, Paris, 1887.

BULLETIN du comité international permanent pour l'exécution photographique de la carte du ciel. 1. et 2. fascicules, 80 p. 4to. Paris, 1888 . . . . (M. 8)
    Institut de France. Académie des Sciences.

Photography.

VON KONKOLY (N.) Das Hydroxylamin als Entwickler photographischer Platten. Sitzungsb. d. k. Akad. d. Wissensch. in Wien, math.-nat. Kl., 97. *Also*: Sirius, 21: 128–132.   .

Photography (Astronomical). *See, also*, MOON ; NEBULÆ.

GILL (D.) Note on some investigations of the accuracy of the Paris photographs. Obsry., 11: 292–296.

VON GOTHARD (E.) Universalcamera für Himmelsphotographie. 11. Ztschr. f. Instrmknd., 8: 41–46.

——. Erfahrungen auf dem Gebiete der Himmels- und Spektral-Photographie. Sirius, 21: 100–104.

JESSE (O.) Bestimmung von Sternschnuppenhöhen durch photographische Aufnahmen. Astron. Nachr., 119: 153.

[REVIEW of astronomical photography. | Edinb. Rev. 145: 23–46 *Also :* Sid. Mess., 7: 138, 181.

Photography (Stellar).

GILL (D.) [Progress of the southern photographic Durchmusterung.] Astron. Nachr., 119: 257.

HOLDEN (E. S.) Stellar photography. 4 p. 8vo [n. p., 1888].
    Repr. from Overland month.

VON KOVESLIGETHY (R.) Invisible stars of perceptible actinic power. Month. Not., 48: 114–116.

Photography (Stellar)—Continued.

[REPORT of photographic committee Royal Astronomical Society.] Month. Not., 48 : 351.

ROBERTS (I.) An instrument for measuring the positions and magnitudes of stars on photographs and for engraving them upon metal plates . . . il. Month. Not., 49 : 5-13.

TENNANT (J. F.) Note on the definition of reflecting telescopes and on the images of bright stars on photographic plates. Month. Not., 48: 104.

VOGEL (H. C.) Mittheilungen über die von dem astrophysikalischen Observatorium zu Potsdam übernommenen Voruntersuchungen zur Herstellung der photographischen Himmelskarte. Astron. Nachr., 119 : 1-6

Photometer.

CERASKI (W.) Photomètre de Zöllner à deux oculaires. Astron. Nachr., 120: 218.

PARKHURST (H. M.) Obliteration from illumination. Sid. Mess., 7 : 337-343.

Photometry. *See, also,* ASTEROIDS.

DORST (—.) Reduction der von Zöllner photometrisch bestimmten Sterne. Astron. Nachr., 118: 209-226.

MONCK (W. H. S.) [Comparison of the] Harvard and Oxford photometry. Sid. Mess., 7 : 92.

PICKERING (E. C.) Zone observations made with the transit wedge photometer attached to the equatorial of 15 inches aperture . . . 1882-'86. Ann. Harv. Coll. Obsry. 13: 211-359 (v. 13, pt. 2).

Planets. *See, also,* SOLAR SYSTEM.

[NEWCOMB (S.)]. New tables of the planets. Rept. Supt. Am. Naut. Almanac, 1887 : 4.

ROGER (—.) Distances moyennes des planètes au soleil. Compt. Rend., 106: 249.

ZENGER (C. V.) Periods of the planets. Obsry., 11: 87.

Planets (Orbits of).

LOHNSTEIN (T.) Ueber die Gleichungen v. Oppolzer's zur Bestimmung der helio-centrischen Distanzen eines Planeten. Astron. Nachr., 119 : 243.

Pleiades.

MOUCHEZ (E.) Nouvelles nébuleuses découvertes à l'aide de la photographie dans les Pléiades. Compt. Rend., 106: 912.

Prague Observatory.

WEINEK (L.) Neuer Zeitbestimmungsraum der Sternwarte in Prag. Sirius, 21: 174, 205.

Precession.

See STAR-PLACES (Reduction of).

Proctor (Richard Anthony). [1837-'88.]

NOBLE (W.) [Obituary notice.] Obsry., 11: 366-368. Knowledge, 11: 265. [Portrait.]

Prominences (Solar). *See, also,* SUN ; SUN (Statistics, etc.).

RICCÒ (A.) Grandes protubérances solaires observées à Palermo de 1881 à 1887. . . . il. L'Astron., 7: 215, 254.

Pulkowa Observatory.

OBSERVATIONS de Poulkova . . . v. 14. Déduction des déclinaisons moyennes du catalogue des étoiles principales pour 1865.0. Mémoire de M. Nyrén. Observations faites au cercle vertical 1871-1875. 228 p. 4to. St. Pétersbourg, 1888..(M. 26.40)

SUPPLEMENT 1 aux observations de Poulkova. Beobachtungen der Saturnstrabanten. 1 Abtheilung. 132 p. 4to. St. Pétersbourg, 1888......(M. 10.60)

H. Mis. 142——14

Refraction.

GRUEY (L.-J.) Sur une forme géométrique des effets de la réfraction dans le mouvement diurne. Bull. astron., 5: 91, 193.

SCHAEBERLE (J. M.) Note on a short method for computing the true refractions. Astron. Nachr., 118: 381.

TUTTLE (H. P.) Bessel's "log B" for great elevations. Sid. Mess., 7: 406.

Royal Astronomical Society.

MEMOIRS . . . vol. 49, pt. 1. 237 p. 4°. London, 1888 . . . . (M. 21)
New general catalogue of nebulæ and clusters of stars. By J. L E. Dreyer.

Saturn.

ELGER (T. G) Physical observations of Saturn in 1883. il. Month. Not., 48: 362-370.

——. [Observations of rings and belts.] Obsry., 11: 153.

KEELER (J. E.) First observations of Saturn with the 36-inch equatorial of the Lick Observatory. il. Sid. Mess., 7: 79-83.

PERROTIN (J.) Anneaux de Saturne. Compt. Rend., 106: 1716.

TERBY (F.) [Dessins des anneaux et des bandes.] il. Obsry., 11: 195.

——. Premières observations de Mars et de Saturne faites à l'observatoire Lick. . . en 1888, et réponses à quelques objections. Ciel et Terre, 9: 370-380.

TROUVELOT (E.-L.) Nouvelles observations sur la variabilité des anneaux de Saturne. Compt. Rend., 106: 464-467. *Also*, Reprint.

Saturn (Satellites of).

HALL (A) Motion of Hyperion. Astron. Jour., 7: 164.

HILL (G. W.) Motion of Hyperion and the mass of Titan. Astron. Jour., 8: 57-62.

LYNN (W. T.) Discovery of Titan. Obsry., 11: 338.

NEWCOMB (Simon). Mutual action of the satellites of Saturn. Astron. Jour., 8: 105.

OUDEMANS (J. A. C.) Retrogradation of the plane of Saturn's ring and of those of his satellites whose orbits coincide with that plane. Month. Not., 49: 54-64.

STRUVE (H.) Beobachtungen der Saturus-trabanten. Abtheilung I. Beobachtungen am 15-zölligen Refractor. 132 p. 4to. St. Petersburg, 1888 . . . (M. 10.60)
Supplement 1 aux observations de Poulkova

Scintillation.

COLEMAN (W.) Jumping stars. Obsry., 11: 434.

INFLUENCE des bourrasques sur la scintillation des étoiles. Ciel et Terre, 9: 489-494.

MAW (W. H.) Jumping stars. Obsry., 11: 404.

MONTIGNY (C.) De l'intensité de la scintillation des étoiles dans les différentes parties du ciel. Bruxelles, 188².
Repr from · Bull. Acad. roy. de Belg, 3 s , 16
Abstr Astron. Nachr , 120: 223 *Also, abstr* Ciel et Terre, 9: 393-400.

SEARLE (A.) Apparent instability of stars near the horizon. Astron. Nachr., 120: 109.

TENNANT (J. F.) Jumping stars. Obsry., 11: 433.

WEYER (G. D. E.) Sternschwanken. Astron. Nachr., 119: 143.

Sextant.

COMSTOCK (G. C.) Adjustment of a sextant. Sid. Mess., 7: 129-132.

GRUEY (L.-J.) Application de l'oculaire nadiral à la détermination des constantes de l'horizon gyroscopique. Compt. Rend., 106: 727-729.

SCHAEBERLE (J. M.) Adjustment of the sextant. Sid. Mes., 7: 223.

——. Eccentricity of the sextant. Astron. Nachr., 118: 383.

Sirius.

MANN (N. M.) System of Sirius. Sid. Mess., 7: 25, 94,

Société astronomique de France.

BULLETIN de la société astronomique de France. Première année: 1887. 128 p. 8vo. Paris, 1888.

FLAMMARION (C.) Discours prononcé à la séance générale annuelle du 4 avril 1888. 15 p. 8vo. Paris, 1888.

Solar system.

FLAMMARION (C.) Les centres de gravité. il. L'Astron., 7: 361–365.

STONE (O.) Motions of the solar system. Proc. Am. Ass. Adv. Sc., 37: 47–59. *Also,* Reprint. *Also:* Science, 12: 89. *Also:* Obsry., 11: 363–366. *Also, abstr.:* Nature, 39: 162.

Spectra (Stellar).

CLERKE (A. M.) Southern star spectra. Obsry., 11: 429–432.

DUNÉR on stars with spectra of Class III. Nature, 37: 234, 260.

ESPIN (T. E.) Stars with remarkable spectra. Astron. Nachr., 118: 257; 119: 309.

——. [Remarkable change in the spectrum of R Cygni.] Astron. Nachr., 119: 365. *See, also: Ibid* , 120: 41. *Also:* Astron. Jour., 8: 96. *Also:* Month. Not., 49: 18.

VOGEL (H. C.) Zwei Stern Spectraltafeln. [Mit Text.] 100 × 70 cm. Wien, 1888 ....(M. 10)

Spectroscope.

KRÜSS (H.) Automatisches Spektroskop mit festem Beobachtungsfernrohr. il. Ztschr. f. Instrnknd., 8: 388–392.

Spectrum.

JANSSEN (J.) Spectres de l'oxygène. Mem. soc. spettrscp. ital., 17: 31.

——. Spectre tellurique dans les hautes stations. L'Astron., 7: 443–446.

Spectrum analysis.

KURLBAUM (F.) Bestimmung der Wellenlänge einiger Fraunhofer'scher. Linien. 96 p., 1 pl. 8vo. Berlin, 1887.

LANGLEY (S. P.) Energy and vision. Am. J. Sc., 136: 359–379.

Spectrum (Solar).

DÉTAILLE (C.) Photographie du spectre solaire à l'aide de petits instruments. il. L'Astron., 7: 26.

LANGLEY (S. P.) The invisible solar and lunar spectrum. il. Am. J. Sc., 136: 397–410.

MENGARINI (G.) Massimo d' intensità luminosa dello spettro solare. Mem. Soc. spettrscp. ital., 17: 117–129.

Star-catalogues.

AUWERS (A.) Neue Reduction der Bradley'schen Beobachtungen aus den Jahren 1750 bis 1762. 3. Band den Sterncatalog für 1755, und seine Verglei- chung mit neuen Bestimmungen enthaltend. 5+352 p. 4to. St. Petersburg, 1888 ....(M. 9.20)

BACKLUND (O.) Ueber die Herleitung der im 8. Bande der Observations de Poulkova enthaltenen Stern-Cataloge, nebst einigen Untersuchungen über den Pulkowaer Meridiankreis. 100 p. 4to. St. Petersburg, 1888 ....(M. 2 80)

BECKER (E.) Resultate aus Beobachtungen von 521 Bradley'schen Sternen am grossen Berliner Meridiankreise. 8vo. Berlin, 1888.

DOWNING (A. M. W.) Positions for 1750.0 and proper motions of 154 stars south of —29° declination, deduced from a revision of Powalky's reduction of the star places of Lacaille's Astronomiæ fundamenta. Month. Not , 48: 322–333.

FRANZ (J.) Zur Bonner Durchmusterung bei 23ʰ, +8°. Astron. Nachr., 120: 75.

Star-catalogues—Continued.

MARCUSE (A.) Ableitung der Sterne des Fundamental-Cataloges der astronomischen Gesellschaft aus den von H. Romberg in den Jahren 1869–1873, am
grösseren Meridian-Instrumente der Berliner Sternwarte angestellten Beobachtungen. 84 p. 4to. Berlin, 1888.
   Beob.-Ergeb. d. k. Sternw. zu Berlin, Heft 4.

OERTEL (K.) Vergleichung der iu den "Greenwich Observations" von 1877 bis
1884 enthaltenen Sternverzeichnisse mit den beiden Catalogen der astronomischen Gesellschaft. Astron. Nachr., 118: 177–188.

——— Untersuchungen über die aus Beobachtungen an den Pariser Meridianinstru-
menten abgeleiteten Sternpositionen. Astron. Nachr., 119: 194.

STRUVE (O.) [Declinationen in dem Catalogue von 3542 Sternen.] Astron. Nachr.,
119: 81.

Star-charts.

KLEIN (H. J.) Stern-Atlas enthaltend sämmtliche Sterne der 1–6.5 Grösse
zwischen dem Nordpol und 34 Grad südlicher Declination. 8+71 p. 18 maps.
4to. Leipzig, 1888 ....(M. 16)

——— Star atlas, containing maps of all the stars from 1 to 6.5 magnitude between
the north pole and 34° south declination, and of all nebulæ and star clusters in
the same region which are visible in telescopes of moderate powers. With explanatory text ... Translated ... by E. McClure. 72 p., 18 pl. 4to. London
and Leipsic, 1888.

MESSER (J.) Stern-Atlas für Himmelsbeobachtung. 11 + 175 p. il. Map. St.
Petersburg, 1888..(M. 10)

SCHÖNFELD (E.) Fehlerverzeichniss zur zweiten Serie der Bonner Sternkarten.
Astron. Nachr., 119: 31.

Star-clusters.

CLERKE (A. M.) Globular star-clusters. Nature, 38: 365.

——— Irregular star-clusters. Nature, 39: 13. See also, Ibid., 61.

Star-places (Reduction of).

BOQUET (F.) Note sur la détermination géométrique des positions apparentes
des étoiles circumpolaires. Bull. Astron., 5: 137.

——— Application de la méthode de Gaillot. Ibid., 5: 233-237.

FABRITIUS (W.) Sur le calcul des lieux apparents des étoiles. Ibid., 5: 187-193.

FOLIE (F.) Sur l'incorrection des formules proposées par Fabritius pour la
réduction des circumpolaires. Ibid., 5: 47-50.

——— Sur les formules de M. Fabritius. Réplique aux notes de MM. Gonnessiat et
Herz. Ibid., 5: 185, 384.

——— Traité des réductions stellaires. Fascicule 1. Bruxelles, 1888 ..... (M. 22)
   Repr from Bull Acad Roy. d Belg, 1888.

GONNESSIAT (F) Calcul des positions apparentes des étoiles circumpolaires:
Méthode de M. Fabritius. Bull. Astron., 5: 135-145.

HERZ (N.) Sur la réduction des circumpolaires d'après les formules de Fabritius.
Ibid., 5: 145-147.

SAFFORD (T. H.) Reduction of star-places by Bohnenberger's method. Astron.
Nachr., 119: 21-28.

——— Note concerning Fabritius's method of reducing from one equinox to another.
Ibid., 119: 83.

SCHULHOF (L.) Sur les formules de M. Fabritius. Bull. Astron., 5: 281-283.

Stars (Distribution of).

MONCK (W. H. S.) Note on the distribution of the stars. Sid. Mess., 7: 20-25,
73-77, 105, 236.

Stars (Motion of) in the line of sight.

SPECTROSCOPIC results for the motions of stars in the line of sight, obtained at
... Greenwich ... 1887. Month. Not., 48: 116-122.

Stars (Motion of) in the line of sight—Continued.

VOGEL (H. C.) Bestimmung der Bewegung von Sternen im Visionsradius. Astron. Nachr., 119: 97.

—— Bestimmung der Bewegung von Sternen im Visionsradius durch spectrographische Beobachtung. Mem. Soc. spettrscp. ital, 17: 33.

Sun. See, also, CORONA; PROMINENCES; SPECTRUM; SUN (Diameter of), etc.

FLAMMARION (C.) Les grandes manifestations de l'activité solaire. il. L'Astron., 7: 121-133.

—— Une année de l'histoire du soleil. il. L'Astron., 7: 201-213.

FRITZ (H.) Beiträge zur Beziehung irdischer Erscheinungen zur Sonnenthätigkeit. Sirius, 21: 206-210, 217-222, 245-246.

SCHULZ (J. F. H.) Zur Sonnenphysik. II. 1 pl. Astron. Nachr., 119: 225-242.

SEARLE (A.) Atmospheric economy of solar radiation. Proc. Am. Acad. Arts and Sc., 26-29. Also, Reprint.

Sun (Diameter of).

WELLMAN (V.) Einfluss der Blendgläser bei Beobachtungen des Sonnendurchmessers. Astron. Nachr., 119: 241.

Sun (Rotation of).

CREW (H.) Period of the rotation of the sun as determined by the spectroscope. Am. J. Sc., 135: 151-159.

WILSING (J.) Ableitung der Rotationsbewegung der Sonne aus Positionsbestimmungen von Fackeln. Astron. Nachr., 119: 311-316.

Sun (Statistics of faculæ, prominences, and spots).

FLAMMARION (C.) Fluctuations de l'activité solaire depuis le dernier maximum de 1883-'84 jusqu'au delà du dernier minimum. Taches facules, éruptions et magnétisme terrestre. il. L'Astron., 7: 41-53.

SPOERER (A.) Verschiedenheit der Häufigkeit der Sonnenflecken auf der nördlichen und südlichen Halbkugel in den Jahren 1886 und 1887. Astron. Nachr., 118: 307.

TETENS (O.) Sonnenflecke im Jahre 1887 nach den Beobachtungen zu O'Gyalla. Astron. Nachr, 119: 267.

WOLF (R.) Sonnen-Statistik des Jahres 1887. Astron. Nachr., 118: 307.

Sun-spots.

BOSSI (B.) Le macchie solari; cause ed effetti. Sui terremoti avvenuti e futuri come da predizioni dell' autore. 3. ed., enl. 116 p. 16mo. Genova, 1888. (M. 1.50)

FAYE (H.) Remarques sur une objection de M. Khandrikoff à la théorie des taches et des protubérances solaires. Compt. Rend., 106: 399-403.

—— Taches et protubérances solaires. L'Astron., 7: 89-93.

Tables (Logarithmic).

NELL (A. M.) Fünfstellige Logarithmen . . . 6. ed. 19+104 p. 8vo. Darmstadt, 1888..(M. 1.80)

Taschkent Observatory.

POMERANTZEFF (H.) Latitude de l'observatoire de Tachkent. Astron. Nachr., 119: 317.

[MEMOIRS of the Taschkent astronomical and physical observatory. Publication II.] 104 p 4to Москва, 1888

Telegrams (Astronomical). See CODE (Astronomical).

Telescopes. See, also, EQUATORIALS: MIRRORS; OBJECTIVES.

CROSSLEY (E.) Improved centering tube for reflecting telescopes. Month. Not., 48: 280.

GRUBB (H.) Good astronomical telescopes. Sid. Mess., 7: 106, 259.

HARKNESS (W.) Visibility of objects as conditioned by their magnitude and brightness with applications to the theory of telescopes. Abstr.: Proc. Am. Assn. Adv. Sc., 36: 64.

Telescopes—Continued.

SMITH (H. L.) Telescopes of short focal length. Sid. Mess., 7: 293-296, 360.

TENNANT (J. F.) Note on the definition of reflecting telescopes, and on the images of bright stars on photographic plates. Month. Not., 48: 104.

TODD (D. P.) American telescopes. 4 p. 4to. [Philadelphia? 1888.] *Repr. from:* Encyc. Brit Amer. Reprint. Vol. 23, Appendix, p. 932-936.

Temple Observatory.

SEABROKE (G. M.) Report . . . 1888. 3 p. 8vo. [n. p., n. d.]

Three bodies (Problem of).

CHARLIER (C. V. L.) Ueber eine mit dem Problem der drei Körper verwandte Aufgabe. 18 p. 4to. St. Petersburg, 1888 ....(M. 0.80.

HARZER (P.) Argumento des Problems der *n* Körper. Astron. Nachr., 120: 193-218.

Time (Determination of).

BIGELOW (F. H.) Computation of clock corrections. Sid. Mess., 7: 97-100.

Time (Standard).

BOUQUET DE LA GRYE (J.-J.-A.) Note sur l'adoption d'une heure légale en France. Compt. Rend., 107 : 429.

FOREL (F.-A.) L'unification de l'heure: l'heure nationale. L'Astron., 7 : 327-333.

LAUSSEDAT (A.) L'heure nationale. L'Astron., 7 : 454-457.

Transit instrument.

BIGELOW (F. H.) An automatic transit instrument. il. Sid. Mess., 7 : 205-209.

BIGOURDAN (G.) Disposition qui permettrait l'emploi de puissants objectifs dans les observations méridiennes. Compt. Rend., 106 : 998.

DEVAUX (—.) Recherches sur la forme des tourillons d'une lunette méridienne. Bull. astron., 5 : 523-532.

FÖRSTER (W.) Theorie des Durchgangs-Instrumentes. *In his:* Studien zur Astrometrie, 50-114.

GEELMUYDEN (H.) Collimation des lunettes brisées. Astron. Nachr., 119: 151, 183.

GRUEY (L.-J.) Nouvel oculaire pour les observations méridiennes. Compt. Rend., 106: 585-587.

REPSOLD (J.) Durchgangs-Instrument mit Uhrbewegung. Astron. Nachr., 118: 305.

Transit observations.

GONESSIAT (F.) Quelques erreurs affectant les observations de passages. Compt. Rend., 107 : 647-650.

RAYET (G.) Recherches sur les erreurs accidentelles des observations de passages dans la méthode de l'œil et de l'oreille. Compt. Rend., 106 : 1713-1716.

United States Naval Observatory.

CIRCULAR relating to the construction of a new naval observatory. 44 p. 12mo. Washington, 1888.

ESTIMATE for the purchase of photographic telescope and pointers, and construction of buildings for same, for the proposed international project of charting the sky. 4 p. 8vo. [Washington, 1888.] 50th Congr., 2d sess., House of Rep., Ex. Doc. 46.

REPORT of the Superintendent . . . June 30, 1888. 24 p. 8vo. Washington, 1888.

Urania.

URANIA—Volksakademie der Naturwissenschaften in Berlin. Sirius, 21: 84-88.

Variable stars.

CHANDLER (S. C.) Period of Algol. Astron. Jour., 7: 165, 177.

——. On the observation of the variables of the Algol type. *Ibid.*, 7: 187.

——. New variable of long period. *Ibid.*, 8: 24.

Variable stars—Continued.

——. Ephemeris of variables of the Algol type. *Ibid.*, 8: 40.

——. Catalogue of variable stars. 14 p. 4to Lynn, 1888. *Repr. from:* Astron. Jour., 8: 81–96 (Nos. 179–180).

——. Observation of the fainter minima of the telescopic variables. Astron. Jour., 8: 114–117.

——. Some remarkable anomalies in the period of Y Cygni. *Ibid.*, 8: 130.

——. Colors of the variable stars. *Ibid.*, 8: 137–140.

CLERCE (A. M.) Variable double-stars. Obsry., 11: 188.

ESPIN (T. E.) [Discovery of variability of DM. $+40°$, 2694, 13^h 42^m 4.^{s}; $+40°$ 15′.9 (1855) 1888, Apr. 6.] Astron. Nachr., 119: 39.

——. [New star in Cygnus.] *Ibid.*, 119: 127.

——. Variable star near 26 Cygni. *Ibid.*, 119: 307.

LOCKYER (J. N.) Maximum of Mira Ceti [and its spectrum]. Nature, 38: 621. *See. also:* Compt. Rend., 107: 832.

OUDEMANS (J. A. C.) Request to observers of variable stars. Month. Not., 48: 85.

PLASSMANN (J.) Beobachtungen veränderlicher Sterne angestellt in den Jahren 1881–1888. Mit Erläuterungen und Notizen über die Helligkeit der Planeten Venus und Uranus und anderer Sterne. 44 p. 8vo. Münster, 1888...... (M. 2)
Beilage. zum Jahresb d. math -phys -chem Sect. d. westfäl. Provinzialver f. Wissensch und Kunst, Munster, 1888

SAFARIK (A.) Zwei neue veränderliche Sterne in den Sternbildern Cetus und Sagittarius. Astron. Nachr., 119: 109.

——. Lichtwechsel einer Anzahl von Sternen aus der Bonner Durchmusterung und aus den Katalogen rother Sterne von Schjellerup und Birmingham. 16 p. 8vo. Prag, 1887.. ...(M. 1.20)

SAWYER (E. F.) [Observations and period of U Ceti.] Astron. Journ , 7: 185.

——. [Observations and period of T Vulpeculæ]. *Ibid.*, 8: 5.

——. Definitive discussion of observations of U Ophiuchi. *Ibid.*, 8: 70.

——. Observations of some suspected variable stars. *Ibid.*, 8: 121–125.

Venus.

ELGER (T. G.) Visibility of the unilluminated part of Venus. Obsry., 11: 198.

LYNN (W. T.) Visibility of the unilluminated part of Venus. *Ibid.*, 11: 155.

Venus (Transit of).

HARKNESS (W.) Value of the solar parallax deducible from the American photographs of the last transit of Venus. Astron. Jour., 8: 108.

Vienna Observatory.

Annalen . . . 6. Bd. Jahrg., 1886. 3+160 p. 4°, Wien, 1888.

Watson (James Craig.) [1838–'80.]

COMSTOCK (G. C.) Biographical memoir of James Craig Watson. [Portr.] Sid. Mess., 7: 273–286.

Williams College Observatory.

SAFFORD (T. H.) Commemoration of the 50th anniversary of the dedication of the Hopkins Observatory. 32 p. 8vo. Williamstown, 1888. *Also:* Sid. Mess., 7: 430.

Wolsingham Observatory.

ESPIN (T. E.) [Site of new observatory]. Astron. Nachr., 120: 191.

Yale College Observatory.

REPORT for the year 1887–'88 . . . 16 p. 8vo. [New Haven, 1888.]

Zodiacal light.

BARNARD (E. E.) Observations of the zodiacal counterglow. [1883–'87.] Astron. Jour., 7: 186.

SHERMAN (O. T.) [Connection between the zodiacal light and sun-spots.] Nature, 38: 595: 39: 128. *See, also·* Science, 12· 180.

NECROLOGY OF ASTRONOMERS FOR 1887-'88.

BAXENDELL (JOSEPH), b. at Manchester, 1815; d. at Birkdale, Southport, October 7, 1887, æt. 72.

CAPRON (JOHN RAND); b. at London, February 19, 1829; d. at Guildown, Guildford, November 12, 1888, æt. 59.

CLARK (ALVAN); b. at Ashfield, Massachusetts, March 8, 1804; d. at Cambridgeport, August 22, 1887, æt. 83.

ENGELMANN (FRIEDRICH WILHELM RUDOLF); b. at Leipzig, June 1, 1841; d. at Leipzig, March 28, 1888, æt. 47.

FEDORENKO (IWAN); b. at Charkow, February 6, 1827; d. at Charkow, December 26, 1888, æt. 62.

FELLOCKER (SIEGMUND); b. 1816; d. September 5, 1887, æt. 71.

GRUBER (LUDWIG); b. at Fünfkirchen, May 12, 1851; d. at Budapest, January 25, 1888, æt. 37.

HOUZEAU DE LEHAIE (JEAN-CHARLES); b. at Mons (Hainaut), October 7, 1820; d. at Bruxelles, July 12, 1888, æt. 68.

JEDRZEJEWICZ (J. J.); b. in Warschau, 1835; d. at Plonsk, December 31, 1887, æt. 52.

KIRCHHOFF (GUSTAV ROBERT); b. at Königsberg. March 12, 1824; d. at Berlin, October 17, 1887, æt. 63.

LUTHER (EDWARD); b. at Hamburg, February 24, 1816; d. at Königsberg, October 17, 1887, æt. 71.

PROCTOR (RICHARD ANTHONY); b. at Chelsea, March 23, 1837; d. at New York, September 12, 1888, æt. 51.

SCHJELLERUP (HANS CARL FREDERIK CHRISTIAN); b. at Odense, February 8, 1827; d. at Copenhagen, November 13, 1887, æt. 60.

TEMPEL (GUGLIELMO ERNESTO); b. at Nieder-Cunersdorf, December 4, 1821; d. at Florence, March 16, 1888, æt. 66.

THOLLON (L.); b. 1827; d. at Nice, April 8, 1887, æt. 50.

GEOLOGY FOR 1887 AND 1888.

By W J McGee, Geologist, U. S. Geological Survey.

INTRODUCTORY NOTE.

At its birth each branch of science is fostered and promoted by individual effort, and its early history is an account of individuals; in the youth of a vigorous branch of science it is cultivated and developed not only by individual effort, but by groups of men and definitely organized scientific and educational institutions, and its history is an account of individuals, of institutions, and of its own first fruits; when a branch of science approaches maturity it is further promoted and applied, and its influence generally diffused, chiefly by groups of individuals organized as institutions of learning and research, and its history is an account of institutions rather than individuals and of its results in the promotion of human welfare; and there is a final stage in the history of the development of a branch of science in which the previously technical knowledge becomes generally diffused among and applied by certain classes or all classes of men, in which it gradually passes from the domain of pure science into that of the arts, and in which its history is an account of the people and of the material progress of a country or of the civilized world. Such has been the course of development in different branches of science; and such is the course pursued through one or more stages in those branches of science not yet completely developed.

Geology is one of the younger and at the same time one of the more vigorous branches of the tree of knowledge; and so rapidly has it developed, that within the memory of men yet living, it has passed from the infantile stage represented by individual effort to the adolescent stage represented by combination of effort among definitely organized institutions. Its problems are of such magnitude and such profound importance to the people at large that the states, as well as the learned institutions of the civilized world, have joined in the effort to solve them and render their results available. Geologic surveys are carried on in the states of this and some other countries; the general governments in this and other countries maintain bureaus of geologic information; many scientific societies have geologic sections and departments, and some such institutions are entirely devoted to the promotion of geol-

ogy; and many of the educational institutions have departments in
which the science of geology is taught not only from text-books, but
through original investigation, whereby the science is extended and its
field enlarged. So, while the results of individual effort are of inesti-
mable value to the growing science of geology, and while any account
of the science must deal primarily with the contributions of individuals,
it would seem desirable to preface even a short chapter in the history
of progress by some notice of the institutions to which, in conjunction
with the individual workers, that progress is due ; and accordingly the
following descriptive list of the principal American institutions now
promoting geologic science is prefixed to the account of actual progress
during recent years, and particularly the biennial period 1887, 1888.
The sources of information concerning these institutions are diverse,
widely scattered, and not easily accessible, and accordingly the list may
not be exhaustive.

All necessity for incorporating in this record lists of the individuals
by which geology has been promoted during the biennial period and of
the publications containing the contributions is obviated by a contemporaneous publication. Mr. N. H. Darton is now preparing a bibliography
of American geology for the same period, which will shortly be published by the U. S. Geological Survey.

INSTITUTIONS PROMOTING GEOLOGY.

GEOLOGIC SURVEYS.

The Federal Government.—The U. S. Geological Survey was organized
several years ago to prepare a geologic map of the United States, and
by implication to prosecute such investigations as are essential to the
accomplishment of that task. It is indicative of the recognized importance of geology that during recent years geographic exploration and
study have, in this country at least, been carried on largely as a means
to geologic investigation. The western States and Territories were in
great part explored by geographers and engineers for geologic purposes; in many of the States it was found necessary to make geographic
and topographic surveys before the geologic investigations could be
completed and their results made available to citizens ; and the dearth
of maps of the country at large is such, that a large part of the energies
of the national geologic institution are expended in preliminary geographic surveys. So the scientific corps of the U. S. Geological Survey,
which includes about forty geologists and assistants, about fifteen paleontologists and assistants, and seven chemists and physicists with
their assistants, comprises also about eighty geographers and topog-
raphers with their assistants ; and there is in addition an executive and
office force of about seventy-five persons. Hon. J. W. Powell is the
Director. During the biennial period just closed the institution has
published two royal octavo annual reports, three quarto monographs

(two accompanied by folio atlases), fifteen or sixteen octavo bulletins (or monographs upon minor subjects), and two octavo volumes relating to the mineral resources of the country.

The U. S. Coast and Geodetic Survey was organized many years since, for the purpose of accurately surveying the coast line and harbors of the country and ascertaining and recording their changes, and for the purpose also of connecting the coasts by transcontinental systems of triangulation, and so determining the elements of the geoid relating to our domain. The surveys and maps of this institution are immediately available as a basis for geologic investigations over the areas which they cover; and, moreover, the topographic and hydrographic configuration of the coasts and harbors represents a condition in the geologic evolution of the American continent, and so the investigations of the institution are in another way available to the geologist. Important contributions to geology annually result from the work of the Coast and Geodetic Survey.

The U. S. Signal Office is maintained for meteorologic observation and prognostication, and observations are regularly made and recorded over nearly all parts of the country. Now, climate (including the fall of rain and the action of resulting rivers upon the surface of the earth) is the most potent agency in geology; and so the results of the Signal Office are immediately available to the geologist, and some of the notable contributions made to geological science during the biennial period just closed have resulted indirectly from the operations of this bureau.

The Corps of Engineers of the U. S. Army is engaged in different lines of investigation, some of which bear upon the action of rivers, the relative position of land and sea, and other geologic agencies and conditions; and this Federal institution must accordingly be enumerated among those whose operations annually result in geologic progress.

Canada.—Second only to the U. S. Geological Survey in the magnitude and geographic extent of its operations is the Geological Survey of Canada, which, under the directorship of Dr. A. R. C. Selwyn, has been energetically prosecuted in various parts of the British dominion on the American continent during the past two years. The Canadian survey to-day occupies very much the position occupied by the several geologic and geographic surveys of the Federal Government during the last generation, when an important function of the geologist was geographic exploration : to-day the Canadian geologist is (except when employed in the relatively small portion of the Dominion now thickly populated) pre-eminently an explorer; his journeys carry him over unknown or little known tracts in the broad Saskatchewan plains, the extended Hudson Bay region, and the inhospitable foot-hills and river valleys of the northern Rocky Mountains; before he can satisfactorily represent the results of his studies or even complete his field-work it is necessary for him to map the tracts surveyed; and even in the more populous portions of the Dominion maps have to be compiled or constructed from original surveys in order that the results of the work may be properly set forth. In Canada as in America the needs of thé geologist stimulates geographic research; and in Canada as in America, too, geography is practically reduced to a subordinate part of the broad science of geology, and the derived signification of the terms is the true one. The corps of the geological survey of Canada includes, in addition to the director, ten geologists and about the same number of assistants (who are employed chiefly in topographic work); two paleontologists and a paleontologic artist; three chemists and lithologists; a topographer with two assistants; a librarian; and an accounting and office force. The principal publications of the survey appear in the form of annual reports, sometimes accompanied by portfolios or atlases of maps. During the biennial period just closed two annual reports have appeared.

Alabama.—Geologic surveys have been maintained for some years in this State; and Dr. Eugene A. Smith, the State geologist, has, with one or more assistants, been employed during the period 1887–88 in both scientific and economic investigations in geology. One octavo report of 571 pages has been published during the period, and a more voluminous publication is in press.

Arkansas.—Early in 1887 a geologic survey was instituted in this State, with Prof. John C. Branner as State geologist; provision being made for two or more assistants. The work of the survey has been pushed forward rapidly, with the co-operation of the U. S. Geological Survey in certain lines of study; and preliminary reports and one volume of the more elaborate annual report have been published. The latter is of special interest, since it settles definitely certain questions concerning a region reported to be rich in precious metals which had long agitated the citizens of the State, and indeed led to the establishment of the survey.

California.—Although this State does not now maintain a geologic survey under that name, there are two State institutions engaged in work which is partly geologic. The first is the State mining bureau, now in charge of William Irelan, jr., State mineralogist, which issues annual reports (that for 1887 containing 315 and that for 1888 948 pages octavo); and the second is the State engineering department, in charge of Wm. Ham. Hall, with a corps of assistants. The work of the department relates largely to irrigation and to the regimen and control of rivers, and so directly and indirectly to geology. Two octavo reports have been issued during the biennial period.

Colorado.—There is in this State a mining bureau, in charge of a nominal State geologist (the present incumbent is Fred. Bulkley), by which specific information is conveyed to citizens and others; but no reports have appeared during the years 1887 and 1888.

Florida.—In 1887 Dr. J. Kost was commissioned State geologist, and proceeded at once upon a geologic survey of the State; and a small report upon the progress of the work during the year was published. No provision was made, however, for continuing the work.

Georgia.—A State geologist is commonly employed under the auspices of the department of agriculture. During the greater part of the biennial period the incumbent was Augustus R. McCutchen; but after his death, early in 1888, the position remained vacant for several months, when it was filled by the appointment of Dr. J. W. Spencer, professor of geology in the State University at Athens. A law of 1874 provides in addition for the appointment of a State geologist by the governor; and Dr. Spencer has received this appointment also. No publications have appeared during the biennial period.

Illinois.—While no geologic surveys are in progress in this State, there is maintained at Springfield a State cabinet of geology and natural history, which is virtually a geologic bureau, and the curator of which is virtually State geologist. This position was held by Prof. A. H. Worthen until his decease, and is now occupied by Joshua Lindahl. No official publications have emanated from the bureau during the last two years.

Indiana.—A State geologic survey is in progress here, under the direction of Maurice Thompson, State geologist, with two or three assistants; and reports are issued annually.

Kentucky —Prof. John R. Proctor has charge of the State geologic survey, and, with three or four assistants, has carried forward important researches in structural and economic geology during the biennial period; and an octavo monograph and several minor papers have been published.

Michigan.—In this State there is a geologic survey, the personnel of which has been changed during the biennial period by the death of State Geologist C. E. Wright early in 1888, and the subsequent appointment of Prof. M. E. Wadsworth, president of the State mining school at Houghton. The survey in this State now partakes of the character of a mining bureau, designed to convey specific information upon definite subjects to citizens of the State, and no important publications have been made during the biennial period.

Minnesota.—A geologic survey has been under way for some years, under the direction of State Geologist N. H. Winchell, with a corps of assistants. Annual reports are published in octavo; and during the biennial period the second volume of the final report, in large quarto, has appeared.

New York.—A State geologic survey is in progress here under the direction of the board of regents of the University of the State of New York, the veteran paleontologist Prof. James Hall being State geologist. Two volumes of the elaborate series of quarto paleontologic monographs, and two annual reports in octavo, have been issued by the survey during 1887–'88.

North Carolina.—By the death of State Geologist W. C. Kerr, in 1834, a large amount of geologic material was left among the State archives in crude condition; and in order that this material might be rendered available to the State, Prof. Joseph A. Holmes, of the State University, at Chapel Hill, was appointed to collate, digest, and publish it. This report, which represents the work of the State survey during the biennial period, is now in press.

Ohio.—The activity of the State geologic survey of Ohio declined with the publication of the elaborate series of final reports by Dr. J. S. Newberry during the period 1873–1878; but the economic results to which the scientific investigations reported upon in these volumes were preliminary were subsequently elaborated and expanded by Dr. Newberry's successor, Prof. Edward Orton, of the State University. During the biennial period there was renewed activity in economic investigation under the stimulus of the discovery of rock gas and petroleum in large quantities within the State; and two editions of a preliminary report upon these substances, together with an elaborate final report upon the various mineral resources of the State, have been published since the beginning of 1887.

Pennsylvania—The most elaborate geologic survey ever conducted under the auspices of a single American State was recently made in Pennsylvania. As the local studies in various counties approached completion the results were published in seventy or eighty octavo volumes; the activity of the survey then diminished somewhat, and the energies of the director, Dr. J. P. Lesley, and his chief assistant, C. A. Ashburner, were directed toward the digestion of the material thus collected and the preparation of final reports. Annual reports have however been regularly issued; and during the biennial period advance sheets of a dictionary of fossils, which although primarily paleontologic is designed for the use of geologists, have also been issued.

Texas.—The second State geologic survey created within the biennial period is that of Texas, instituted and endowed liberally in 1888, with E. T. Dumble as State geologist, and provision for two or more assistants. No publications have thus far appeared.

Wyoming.—A Territorial geologist (Louis D. Ricketts) has been employed in investigating the geologic structure and mineral resources of this Territory during the biennial period, and an annual report covering the operations during 1887 has been published.

EDUCATIONAL INSTITUTIONS.

There are a number of universities and colleges in America which promote geologic science by providing (sometimes indirectly) for original investigations on the part of officers and pupils, and by publishing the results of these investigations.

Colorado State School of Mines.—In this institution researches in geology, mineralogy, mining, etc., are prosecuted by the president, Dr.

Regis Chauvenet, and by Prof. Arthur Lakes and Prof. Magnus C. Ihlseng. These officers are sometimes accompanied by advanced pupils, but rather for their instruction than for any assistance they may be able to give. The results of these field researches are generally published annually by the school in suitably illustrated octavo volumes.

Columbia College.—No specific provision is made here for original researches in geology in connection with the regular course of instruction; but the professor of geology in the School of Mines forming a part of the institution, Dr. J. S. Newberry, devotes his vacations and leisure to geologic work in field and office; and in this work he sometimes receives the assistance of, and his example is sometimes imitated by, advanced pupils. Part of the results of these researches appear in the School of Mines Quarterly, which is regularly published by the College Alumni Association. It should be understood that in this as in some other cases (and indeed in some measure in all cases) the credit for the original work belongs rather to individuals than to the institution.

Dakota School of Mines.—This institution is located at the same time in the only notable mining region in the State and in one of the most interesting geologic provinces on the face of the globe; and while, as in Colorado, the course of instruction relates rather to technology than pure science, field-work is carried on not only in connection with the teaching but during vacations, chiefly by the dean, Prof. Franklin R. Carpenter. A preliminary report upon this work was published in 1888 in an illustrated octavo volume of 171 pages.

Denison University.—Original investigations in field and office are carried on in this institution in connection with the regular course of instruction by C. L. Herrick, professor of geology and natural history, and some of his associates and pupils; and the results of these researches are published in excellent style in the Bulletin and Transactions of the scientific laboratories of the University.

State University of Iowa.—Special provision for original investigation is not made in this institution; but the energetic incumbent of the chair of geology and zoology, Prof. Samuel Calvin, carries forward, in connection with his university duties and during vacations, original researches in geology and paleontology; and in 1888 the publication was commenced of a "Bulletin from the Laboratories of Natural History," in which the results of the work of Professor Calvin and some of his associates and pupils are printed.

Johns Hopkins University.—There is in this university a fellowship assigned to geology which is worth $500 per year; and during the fiscal year there has been allotted in addition a small sum for the payment of field expenses incurred by the fellow of geology. Moreover, field-work is recognized as an important aid in class instruction, and the professor of geology, Dr. George H. Williams, introduces his pupils to practical work in the field upon the crystalline rocks of eastern Mary-

(and. The outcome of this work by Dr. Williams, that of some of his pupils, and that of the fellow in geology, Dr. William B. Clark, is published in condensed form in the University circulars. Both Dr. Williams and Dr. Clark, however, spend their vacations in field and office work for the U. S. Geological Survey.

Massachusetts Institute of Technology.—Geologic investigations are conducted by the incumbent of the chair of geology in this institution, Prof. W. O. Crosby, chiefly during vacations; classes are sometimes taken into the field; and the results of the various studies are sometimes printed in the Technological Quarterly published by the Institute.

University of Nebraska.—The professor of geology (Lewis E. Hicks, in this institution is *ex officio* State geologist, and divides his energies between class instruction and field investigation within the State; the classes are sometimes introduced to practical field-work in the vicinity of the University, and the advanced pupils sometimes aid the professor in his work in more distant parts of the State; and the results are published in a bulletin of the University.

Princeton (College of New Jersey.)—Field-work in geology and paleontology is carried on in connection with class instruction in this institution, and several expeditions have been fitted out in this department for exploration and surveys in the western Territories under the direction of Prof. Henry F. Osborn. The more important results of the original work so performed are published in the Bulletin and Memoirs of the E. M. Museum of Geology and Archæology of the College of New Jersey. The activity in original investigation has apparently declined somewhat during recent years.

University of Texas.—In the summer of 1888 a chair of geology was established in this institution; and it is the policy of its incumbent, Prof. Robert T. Hill, and of the president of the university, Dr. Leslie Waggener, to carry on field studies in connection with class work. It is proposed to publish the more important results of original work in circulars or bulletins.

Vassar College.—Although specific provision is not made in this college for field studies in connection with class work, the professor of geology, William B. Dwight, frequently carries his classes into the field and thus enlivens the prosaic courses of the text books. A part of the results of Professor Dwight's studies in field and office find a place in the Proceedings of the Vassar Brothers' Institute, which is connected with the college.

Washburn College.—No provision is made for original investigation in connection with class work in this institution, but Prof. F. W. Cragin, of the natural history department, devotes his vacations and leisure to geologic investigations in which he is sometimes assisted by associates and pupils. The preliminary and some of the final results of this work are printed in the Bulletin of the Washburn College Laboratory—a periodical maintained chiefly by personal enterprise.

Wisconsin State University.—Nine fellowships have recently been established in this university through the influence of President T. C. Chamberlin, and one or more of these is assigned to geology from time to time, as the bent of thought of fellows may indicate to be wise. A chair of agricultural physics is also maintained; and the incumbent, Prof. F. H. King, devotes a large part of his time to original work more or less closely connected with geology. A part of President Chamberlin's own time is devoted to researches in geology, the results of which are published by the U. S. Geological Survey.

There are several American universities and colleges which make no specific provision for original investigation in geology, but nevertheless promote the science through officers who are connected with State surveys, who divide their energies between research and didactic work, and who publish the results of their researches in State documents.

University of Alabama.—Dr. Eugene A. Smith is at the same time professor of geology in the university and State geologist, and frequently receives the assistance of pupils in the prosecution of his State work.

University of Georgia.—During 1888, Dr. J. W. Spencer was called to the chair of geology and natural history in this university, and about the end of that year was appointed State geologist. The plans for the co-ordination of research and instruction here are not yet matured, and thus far no publications have emanated either from the university or the survey.

University of Minnesota.—The professor of geology in this institution, N. H. Winchell, is also State geologist. Although but little field instruction is introduced in class work, advanced pupils are sometimes inducted into practical geology by assisting Professor Winchell in the State survey.

University of North Carolina.—No provision is made in this institution for original investigation, but the professor of geology and natural history, Joseph A. Holmes, has adopted the policy of combining class instruction with field study; and in his capacity as acting State geologist he avails himself of the assistance of advanced pupils in the paleontologic and chemic work carried forward by the State.

State University of Ohio.—Prof. Edward Orton, State geologist and professor of geology in the university, divides his time between survey work (in which he is sometimes assisted by advanced pupils) and class instruction; and field studies are occasionally undertaken in connection with the courses of the text-books.

Rutgers College.—The professor of geology in this institution, Dr. George H. Cook, is also State geologist, and the greater part of his energies (and sometimes the assistance of advanced pupils) are devoted to State work.

There are in addition several educational institutions in which no provision is made for publication of the results of original investigation, and in which there is no connection with State surveys or other institutions organized for original work, but in which geologic science is indirectly promoted—either by the combination of class instruction with original investigation or through partly independent work on the part of the professors of geology or other officers, etc.

Amherst College.—Prof. B. K. Emerson, of this institution, regularly carries his classes into the field; and the field work of instructor and pupils is in part directed toward certain specific problems upon which Professor Emerson is now at work. In addition that geologist spends his vacations in field work, the results of which are designed to be published *in extenso* by the U. S. Geological Survey.

Cornell University.—Prof. H. S. Williams, of this university, regularly combines his course of instruction in geology and paleontology with field investigations in southern New York, and sometimes secures the assistance of advanced pupils in work upon the special problems which engage his attention from time to time.

Dartmouth College.—In this institution field work is combined in some measure with the regular class instruction, and the vacations and leisure of the professor of geology, C. H. Hitchcock, are occupied in original investigation.

Harvard University.—There is in this university a summer school of geology, maintained by special fees, and the advanced pupils are given practical instruction in field work each year by the instructor in geology, William M. Davis. Moreover, Profs. N. S. Shaler and J. D. Whitney, as well as Prof. Davis, devote a large share of their energies to original investigations in geology, and important contributions to the science are thereby made each year.

McGill College.—Special provision is not made in this institution either for carrying on or publishing results of original investigation; but Sir William Dawson devotes a large share of his time to researches in geology and paleontology, and McGill College has, in consequence, come to be known as one of the principal centers of geologic work on the American continent. It was almost within the period covered in this report that this geologist received the distinguished honor of knighthood, in recognition of his abilities as an original investigator in geology.

Middlebury College.—President Ezra Brainerd and Prof. G. H. Seelye, of this institution, combine class instruction and field investigation in some measure, and, moreover, carry on original researches during vacations.

University of the City of New York.—Prof. John J. Stevenson, of this institution, has, during recent years, devoted his annual vacations to original investigations in the Appalachian Mountains, chiefly in the Virginias.

University of Virginia.—Prof. William M. Fontaine, of the chair of geology and natural history, devotes a part of his time to original work in paleo-botany and geology, in which he is sometimes assisted by advanced pupils.

Wesleyan University.—In this institution, like the last, some field instruction is given in connection with the regular class work, and, in addition, Prof. William North Rice devotes his leisure, in part, to original investigation.

University of West Virginia.—Prof. I. C. White, of this institution, divides his labors between educational work and original investigation, conducted under the auspices of the U. S. Geological Survey.

Yale University.—Although there is no specific appropriation for maintaining field investigations in connection with class instruction, the venerable James D. Dana, professor of geology, occupies his vacations and his leisure in field work, and occasionally carries advanced classes into the field in the vicinity of New Haven. The professor of mineralogy, Edward S. Dana, also carries on original investigations in his department. Moreover, the eminent professor of paleontology, O. C. Marsh, is largely occupied in original work, at his own cost in part, and in part under the auspices of the U. S. Geological Survey.

SCIENTIFIC INSTITUTIONS.

There are in this country a number of learned societies and other institutions of scientific character which either have funds available for original investigation in geology or employ officers whose work is in part original, and which publish the results of such investigations.

Academy of Natural Sciences of Philadelphia.—There are in this institution professorships in geology and paleontology, and the beneficiaries (particularly Prof. Angelo Heilprin and Dr. Joseph Leidy) are occupied in original work, the results of which generally find place among the regular publications to the academy.

American Museum of Natural History.—Provision is made in the organization of this institution for a curator of the collections in geology and paleontology, whose energies are largely devoted to original research. The position is held by Prof. R. P. Whitfield; and though his original work relates mainly to paleontology, much of it has geologic bearing. The results of his work and of certain other original investigations in geology are published mainly in the Bulletin of the museum.

New York State Cabinet of Natural History.—This institution is maintained by the State, and its curator (John C. Smock) not only has charge of the collections, but carries on original investigations in general and economic geology. Annual reports, and of late bulletins, are issued.

Peabody Museum of Comparative Zoology.—Provision is made in this institution for original investigation, and the results thereof (part of which are geologic) are printed in the regular series of publications of the museum.

Peabody Museum of Yale University.—In this museum, too, specialists are employed in original investigation, as well as in caring for the collections; and the publications, which are primarily paleontologic and only incidentally contain geologic matter, appear in the memoirs of the museum.

Smithsonian Institution.—In carrying out the purpose of its founder to increase and diffuse knowledge among men, the Smithsonian Institution has at various periods in its existence undertaken geologic investigations, some of which were of great importance and extent, and the results of these were generally published in part or in entirety. Moreover, the results of geologic work carried on under other auspices have been published from time to time. Since the organization of the U. S. Geological vey, however, the necessity for geologic work on the part of the Institution has diminished, and its activity has declined.

U. S. National Museum.—There is provision in this institution for the employment of a number of specialists as curators; and many of these officers are employed in original investigation. A part of the work relates to geology directly, and also indirectly through paleontology. The results are made public in the Proceedings and Bulletins of the National Museum.

Wagner Free Institute of Science.—There are connected with this institution four professors, who have charge of the museum and library, give free public lectures, and teach the method of—and also make—research. The most important original work thus far undertaken was an exploration of the west coast of Florida and part of the Okeechobee wilderness, with special reference to the geology and zoology of the Floridian peninsula, the results of which form an elaborate memoir, prepared by Prof. Angelo Heilprin and published by the Institute in 1887.

There are in America a large number of scientific societies which publish the results of geologic investigation, and thus indirectly promote geologic science, although no original work is directly carried on. Most of those not noted above are included in the following list:

Albany Institute,
American Academy of Arts and Sciences.
American Association for the Advancement of Science.
American Geographic Society.
American Institute of Mining Engineers.
American Philosophical Society.
American Society of Civil Engineers.
Anthropological Society of Washington.
Appalachian Mountain Club.
Biological Society of Washington.
Boston Society of Natural History.
Brookville (Indiana) Society of Natural History.
Buffalo Society of Natural Science.
California Academy of Science.
Canadian Institute.
Central Ohio Scientific Association.

Chicago Academy of Science. ·
Cincinnati Society of Natural History.
Colorado Scientific Society.
Connecticut Academy of Arts and Sciences.
Davenport Academy of Sciences.
Elliott Society of Natural History.
Elisha Mitchell Natural History Society.
Essex Institute.
Franklin Institute.
Hamilton Association.
Kansas Academy of Science.
Lackawanna Institute of History and Science.
Manitoba Historical and Scientific Society.
Meriden Scientific Association.
Minnesota Academy of Science.
National Academy of Science.
National Geographic Society.
New Brunswick Natural History Society.
Newport Natural History Society.
New York Academy of Science.
Nova Scotian Institute of Natural Science.
Ohio Mechanics' Institute.
Pacific Coast Technical Society.
Peoria Scientific Association.
Philosophical Society of Washington.
Portland Society of Natural History.
Quebec Literary and Historical Society.
Royal Society of Canada.
San Diego Lyceum of Science.
Santa Barbara Natural History Society.
Sedalia Natural History Society.
State Historical Society of Iowa.
Staten Island Natural Science Association.
St. Louis Academy of Science.
Texas Geological and Scientific Association.
Trenton Natural History Society.
Wisconsin Academy of Arts, Sciences, and Letters.
Worcester Natural History Society.
Wyoming Historical and Geological Society.

MISCELLANEOUS.

The most noteworthy event of the biennial period in American geology was the birth of the Geological Society of America. The project of organizing such a society has been under consideration by the leading geologists of the country for a decade; and a call issued by some of its promoters during the summer of 1888, inviting those interested to meet at Cleveland on the day before the opening of the session of the American Association for the Advancement of Science (August 14), received hearty response; and temporary organization was there effected. A meeting for completing the organization was held at Ithaca on December 27, and the society was there formally created with an original fellowship of one hundred and two. The veteran geologist and paleontologist. Prof. James Hall, was made president; and the following additional officers were elected: First vice-president, James D. Dana; second vice-president, Alex. Winchell; secretary, John J. Stevenson; Treasurer, Henry S. Williams; members at large of the council, John S. Newberry, J. W. Powell, and Charles H. Hitchcock.

Another event of moment was the session of the Congrés Géologique International at London on August 28 to September 3. The session was made notable to American geology by the attendance of a considerable number of our countrymen, and more particularly by the decision of the Congrés to hold its next session at Philadelphia in September, 1891. The American committee of the Congrés Géologique International has during the biennial period been actively engaged in formulating schemes for the classification and cartography of geologic phenomena, and has published several reports by which the literature of American systematic geology was materially augmented.

Still another noteworthy event was the establishment of a strictly geologic journal, The American Geologist, in 1888. The establishment of this journal is largely due to western enterprise, and it has been maintained largely by western talent. The editors and proprietors are: Prof. Samuel Calvin, Prof. Edward W. Claypole, Dr. Persifor Frazer, Prof. L. E. Hicks, Mr. E. O. Ulrich, Dr. Alexander Winchell, and Prof. N. H. Winchell.

LEADING EVENTS IN THE PROGRESS OF THE BIENNIAL PERIOD.

Although there is a stage in the development of every science in which progress may be best measured by the work of institutions, and another in which the advance is best shown by its own fruits, there is no stage in which the progress is not primarily due either directly or indirectly to individual effort: at first a branch of science is promoted directly by the individual often at great personal sacrifice; as its field widens and its problems deepen the energies of others are enlisted, and many individuals combine their labors; thus the institution is formed, and knowledge is promoted by the united efforts of many workers; but whether he is isolated or one of a hundred, whether he is unaided or has a score of associates, it is always the individual whose eyes perceive new facts and whose mind conceives new ideas. So, however progress is measured, it is impossible to state that progress except in the conceptions originating in individual minds.

Every advance in science is made through conceptions which spring like buds from the growing tree of knowledge, sometimes from the main trunk when each marks an epoch in intellectual development, more frequently from a main branch, and still more frequently from a minor branch, when the advance in knowledge is less striking; and sometimes the shooting buds meet and by their union bring forth new conceptions of the highest value,—for the conceptions resulting from the convergence of many lines of thought are always of higher grade than those resulting from divergent lines. While the conceptions constituting progress originate with individuals, the devices for facilitating interchange of thought in modern times are so numerous and complete that many conceptions are disseminated with their growth, students keep pace with the progress of their fellows in distant lands, and so contributions to a general conception may be made by many individuals. The rapid advance of human knowledge within recent years must be attributed not less to the facilities for free interchange of thought now existing than to that ever-increasing liberality of modern students which leads them to share even the first fruits of their work with the entire world.

Geologic science has been enriched by many notable conceptions during the biennial period 1887–'88; some of these are the product of individual minds, while some represent the work of many students upon related or identical problems; but only a few of the more prominent can be noted.

GEOLOGIC PHILOSOPHY.

Philosophic doctrine is the outcome of thought upon different lines; when comprehensive it is little affected by the movements upon any one line; and it is thus so nearly stable that little advance can be perceived within a year or even a decade. But the time has now come for noting an important step in the development of geologic philosophy; for although the movement began some years since among advanced thinkers, and although it has not yet extended to the text-books or even to the rank and file of workers, its influence is seen in geologic literature and is rapidly extending.

The primary geologic classification was based directly upon the objective phenomena of geology; and early geologic literature was pervaded, and the science shaped, by this fundamental idea. As time went on this classification was found too narrow to represent intelligibly the facts and their relations, and the desire for a more comprehensive taxonomy was indicated by the semi arbitrary division of the science into various departments in which the minor classes were variously defined and grouped: Physical geology; Structural geology; Stratigraphic geology; Historical geology; etc. Although all such divisions were partly arbitrary, they contained the germ of a more philosophic classification in which the agencies and conditions of geology are recognized. Progress in this direction culminated in 1884 in a classification devised by Powell to serve as a basis for a bibliography of North American geology. The following divisions are recognized in this classification:

I. Volcanic geology.	VIII. Lithic geology.
II. Diastrophic geology.	IX. Petromorphic geology.
III. Hydric geology.	X. Geochronic geology.
IV. Glacic geology.	XI. Choric geology.
V. Eolic geology.	XII. Geomorphic geology.
VI. Biotic geology.	XIII. Economic geology.
VII. Anthropic geology.	XIV. Geologic technology.*

---

* 5th Ann. Rep. U. S. Geol. Survey, 1885, p. xxxiii.

Examination of this system of classification shows that it has a triple basis — the agencies and conditions of geology form one of the elements, the generalized objective phenomena of geology form another, and the applications of geologic science form a third ; and the classes are neither co-ordinate nor definitely seriate, while the minor divisions of each must be made on unlike bases. The classification is intermediate between the purely objective systems which went before and the predominantly genetic systems which were evolved from it.

In the autumn of 1884 a more elaborate scheme of classification of geology was developed by Gilbert, and discussed at the meeting of the British Association for the Advancement of Science, at Montreal, under the title of a " Plan for a Subject-Bibliography of North American Geology."* It is as follows:

CLASSIFICATION OF GEOLOGY.

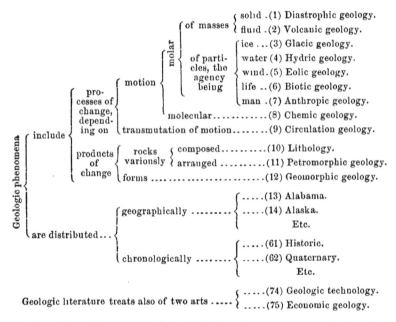

While the subject-matter is thus divided into processes and products, and their distribution in time and space are also elements in this scheme, the category of processes is given a leading place in the classification.

During 1887 and 1888 some minor contributions were made to the subject by different authors, and the influence of gradual modification in fundamental conceptions as to the relative importance of agencies and conditions in classification on the one hand and objective phenom-

---

* Rep. British Assn., 1884, p. 732. The plan was also set forth in a printed leaflet of four pages.

ena on the other have become apparent, and a purely genetic taxonomy of geology, designed also to include geography, has been published by McGee.* Although this classification can only be regarded as provisional, it may be introduced in brief. It is as follows:

Classification of geologic processes.

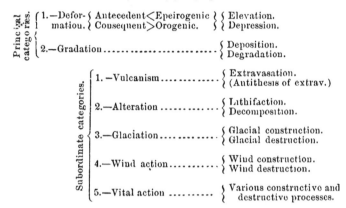

(The matter of this record is arranged in accordance with the last classification.)

DEFORMATION.

The initial geologic movements (so far as may be inferred from the present condition of the rocks of the earth) were distortion or displacement of the solid or solidifying crust in such manner as to produce irregularities in the surface of the globe. These are the movements involved in mountain growth and in the elevation of continents; they have been in operation from the earliest eons recognized by the geologist to the present time; and the advances in knowledge concerning them include not only current observations upon the movements now in progress, but observations upon crumpled and otherwise deformed strata, and also legitimate inferences concerning the causes of the movements whose effects are recorded in these strata.

It has long been known that the waters of the Atlantic are advancing upon the New Jersey coast, in consequence not only of wave-cutting, but also of sinking of the land. So rapid indeed is the sinking of the land, particularly towards Sandy Hook, that notable geographic changes have occurred within the last hundred years, and the mining of timber, which grew upon dry land, but is now lodged among its stumps many feet beneath tide level and buried beneath the oceanic and fluvial deposits, has become an industry of some importance. The

---

* Nat. Geog. Mag., vol. I, 1888, pp. 27–36; Geol. Mag., Decade III, vol. v, 1888, pp. 489–495.

rate of sinking has been estimated by Cook at 2 feet per century;* and the observations of the last two years corroborate this estimate.

This land movement is not confined to the coast of New Jersey, nor to historical time. It has recently been shown (1) that the entire coastal plain of the Middle Atlantic slope is now undergoing depression so rapid that sedimentation in the numerous estuaries by which it is dissected lags behind the sinking, so that sub-aerial alluvium is practically absent from the region; (2) that the Piedmont plain overlooking the coastal lowlands is rising so rapidly that the rivers are unable to cut down their gorges to tide level; and (3) that the differential movement culminates in a line of displacement, which every river crosses in a cascade or rapid, and along which the principal cities of the eastern United States have been located.† It would appear that this displacement began in early Pleistocene time, that it is yet in progress at a rate probably about as high as quiet orogenic movement ever acquires, and that the amount of displacement increases northward from perhaps 100 feet at Washington to 400 or 500 feet at New York.

It is improbable that the great earth-movement of the Middle Atlantic slope extends into New England; for although this part of the country is now suffering deformation as recently shown by Shaler, the tilting is southward rather than northward as in New Jersey. The modern deformation of New England is best shown in the behavior of streams. Throughout Massachusetts, Connecticut, and southern New Hampshire and Vermont, the greater part of the streams flow from north to south or with slight deviations from this direction. Except at the headwaters of these streams, where their volume is too slight to clean their beds of the glacial waste which encumbers them, their valleys are without swamps, and the streams flow upon beds of hard rock flanked by terraces of glacial material which record the stages of valley-excavation—*i. e.*, all of these south-flowing streams have high declivity and are energetically corrading their beds. A much smaller number of New England streams flow to the northward; and these, unlike their south-flowing neighbors, all flow sluggishly in débris-clogged valleys and are bordered by swamps instead of terraces—*i. e.*, all of these streams have low declivity and are employed in sedimentation rather than corrasion. The behavior of both classes of streams suggests southward tilting of the land and can not be satisfactorily explained in any other way;‡ and this inference is in line with the conclusions of Dana, the elder Hitchcock, and many others who have shown that the southward inclination of the terraces of the Connecticut River and its tributaries indicates a rise of the land to the northward since the recession of the last ice-sheet of the Pleistocene. It is in line, too, with the work of Gilbert, Spencer, and others in the region of the

---

* Geology of New Jersey, 1868, pp. 3623–64.
† McGee, 7th Ann. Rep. U. S. Geol. Surv., 1888, pp. 616, *et seq.*
‡ Shaler, Am. Jour. Sci., 1887, vol. XXXIII, pp. 210–221.

Great Lakes, where, as shown by the first-named geologist in particular, there has been so decided tilting of the land since the retreat of the latest ice-sheet that some of the terraces and shore lines carved out
• by Lake Ontario when its northern confine was the receding ice-sheet, now incline southward as much as 5 feet per mile in western New York. Southward tilting in the western part of the Great Lake region is also indicated by the backing of water in the southern affluents of Lake Michigan and the consequent conversion of their mouths into swamps and lakes as shown by Wooldridge.*

The inferences of Shaler in New England and Gilbert in New York as to the southward tilting of the land are in line with a notable investigation of the ancient terraces and beaches of the extinct Lake Agassiz by Upham. As the last ice-sheet of the Pleistocene withdrew beyond the divide between the Mississippi drainage and that of Hudson's Bay, the waters formed by its melting were dammed by the divide and so accumulated in swamps, ponds, and lakes along its front. The largest of the lakes occupied the valley now drained by the Red River of the North. It was a veritable mediterranean sea, albeit of fresh water, and confined on the north by walls of ice alone; for at the period of its maximum size it was fully 600 miles long and 200 miles in maximum breadth. Pending the final melting of the northern mer de glace this lake found outlet over the portage between Lakes Traverse and Big Stone, and thence through the Minnesota and Mississippi Rivers to the Gulf; and, although it has now utterly disappeared from the face of the earth, it has left an unmistakable record of its existence and its extent in the terraces and beach lines already traced by Upham over many hundreds of miles, and in the vast beds of lacustral sediments which make the valley of the Red River the paradise of the wheat grower.† Now the old shore lines of this extinct lake (named in honor of the illustrious Swiss naturalist by Upham) are no longer horizontal as when fashioned by the wind-swept waters, but incline southward about 6 inches per mile on an average. This departure from horizontality in the beach lines has indeed been ascribed (in part at least) by Upham to deformation of the surface of the lake by the gravitational attraction of the contiguous ice sheet; but since it has been shown by Woodward that this cause is alone incompetent under probable assumptions as to volume of the ice sheet,‡ most geologists who concern themselves with such questions have settled down to the conviction that there is here another example of that southward tilting of the area of Pleistocene glaciation already noted in New England by Dana and others, in New York by Gilbert and his contemporaries, and about Lake Michigan by Chamberlain, and more recently by Woolbridge. Leading students of the general subject of terrestrial deformation are indeed dis-

---

* Am. Geologist, 1888, vol. I, pp. 143–146.

† Final Report of the Geology of Minnesota, 1888, vol. II, pp. 517, 527 ; Bull. U. S. Geol. Surv. No. 39, 1887.

‡ Bull. U. S. Geol. Surv. No. 48, 1888, p. 67.

posed to look upon the tilting of the glaciated region as but an exemplification of one of the fundamental laws of earth movement: Babbage, Hall, Hunt, and Dana long ago, and Dutton, Fisher, Reade, Alexander Winchell, and others within the last lustrum, have shown that the exterior portions of the earth behave as if in a state of hydrostatic equilibrium, ready to rise with the removal and sink with the addition of the matter transferred by the processes of gradation. Now it is evident that an ice sheet must depress the surface upon which it rests, just as does a mass of oceanic sediments, directly by its weight, and also indirectly by chilling and so condensing the underlying rocks; and since, as all students of the primary agencies and conditions of geology are agreed, the viscous mass of the earth responds slowly to stresses tending to produce deformation, it is equally evident that the resumption of original attitude by any part of the surface after the recession of an ice sheet must be gradual and perhaps exceedingly slow. So the southward tilting indicated by the shore lines of Lake Agassiz, by the half drowned estuaries of Lake Michigan, by the beaches of the ancient Lake Ontario, and by the terraces of the Connecticut River, all seem attributable to the effort of the resilient terrestrial crust to return to its original form on relief from the pressure of the Pleistocene ice sheet; and the diversity in behavior of the north-flowing and south-flowing streams of New England would indicate that the restoration is even yet barely complete.

The ideas current among the leading geologists of the country concerning the behavior of the earth as an isostatic body when compressed beneath a great continental glacier have been summarized by Alexander Winchell within a few months.*

But there are certain comparatively recent changes in level which can not be attributed to movements due to the weighting of the land beneath the Pleistocene ice sheet. One of the more important contributions of the biennial period to the general subject of deformation is that by Le Conte, on the recent changes of physical geography in California indicated by the flora of the coast islands.† Sometime during the Pleistocene there was a depression of the Pacific coast by which the westernmost of the two ranges belonging to the trans-Sierra mountain system was nearly submerged, only the commanding summits rising above tide-level to form the islands of Santa Rosa and her companions; and this drowned mountain range displays no disposition to return to its former altitude. The period of this submergence is indicated, in so far as plants may be regarded as chronometers of geologic time, by the distinctive Pliocene flora of the islands, which has, according to Le Conte, been preserved by reason of its isolation, while the flora of the mainland has undergone modification in the struggle against competitors, enemies, and climatic conditions proper to a great continent.

---

*Am. Geologist, 1888, vol. I, pp. 139–143.
† Bull. of Cal. Acad. Sci., 1889, vol. II, p. 575.

The most notable North American advances of recent years in the observation and interpretation of the results of diastatic movement relate to faulting. Two genetic classes of faults have long been recognized—*i. e.*, normal faults, in which the hade (or inclination of the plane of fracture) is toward the thrown side, and reversed or overthrust faults, in which the hade is toward the heaved side; and in general the normal faults have been attributed to stresses not accompanied by horizontal compression, and the overthrust faults primarily to horizontal compression.

A few years ago Archibald Geikie and his collaborators upon the Geological Survey of Great Britain concluded that the peculiar structure of the Scottish Highlands is determined by overthrust faulting upon a grand scale—older strata being pushed over newer, sometimes for distances amounting to miles. This conclusion was so novel and striking, and so widely at variance from prevailing opinion, that despite the ability of the geologists by whom it was enunciated and the apparent conclusiveness of the evidence upon which it was based, many conservative students in this country hesitated to accept it; yet within the last two years there have been brought to light on this side of the Atlantic almost as striking examples of overthrust faulting as those of the Scottish Highlands.

During 1886 McConnell made an extended exploration of the Rocky Mountains among the passes followed by the Canadian Pacific Railroad, under the direction and auspices of the Geological Survey of Canada. In the course of this exploration he determined the limits of a remarkable faulted region, now about 25 miles wide, though a rough estimate places its original width at over 50 miles (the difference indicating the amount of compression suffered), in which the faults are generally of the overthrust type. The whole region is broken by a number of parallel, or nearly parallel, longitudinal fractures into a series of oblong blocks, and these are tilted and shoved one over the other until they have taken the form of a westerly dipping compound monocline, rising into a succession of ridges. A section through almost any of these ridges, starting from the west, shows, first, Cretaceous shales folded under older formations, ranging from upper Carboniferous downward through the Devonian and Silurian, and even to the Cambrian. The overthrusts on the south fork of Ghost River reach 3 or 4 miles; and in these, as in some other cases, the rocks thus faulted have been subsequently corrugated, and the original fault surface has been flexed into anticlinals and synclinals, parallel to those of the planes of deposition.*

Recent studies in the Appalachian region by Willis and other officers of the U. S. Geological Survey have brought to light examples of overthrust faulting, differing only in degree from those of the Scottish Highlands and the Canadian Rocky Mountains; and these observa-

---

* Rpt. D, of Annl. Rpt. Geol. and Natl. Hist. Canada for 1886-'87,

tions have corrected certain early inferences as to the mechanism of such faulting; inferences originating partly in Europe and partly in the Appalachians, and current for many years on both sides of the Atlantic. Heim noticed that in the Alps the inverted limb of an anticlinal is stretched or even crushed out between the anticlinal and synclinal curves of an overturn and the flexure thus converted into a fracture, and inferred that overthrust faults are always formed in this manner; but Willis points out that this explanation fails to account for many of the faults of the Appalachians because the essential fact of squeezed beds has not been found in that region. He shows also that the Appalachian sedimentary series, from the Cambrian upward, is composed of strata differing greatly in their capacity for resistance to horizontal thrusts, and that these variations in rigidity occur from place to place in the same strata as well as in the different strata superimposed one on the other, and that the rigid strata may not fold at the place where a vertically adjacent flexible stratum does fold, but that the rigid stratum may ride forward on its bedding plane until it reaches an axis (anticlinal or synclinal) in which both beds have suffered flexure, and that the forward movement may then sheer across the beds on the opposite dip, producing a fault.* Under this view it would appear that the yielding of rocks to horizontal pressure may take place, (1) as corrugation; (2) as overthrusts, perhaps originating in incipient corrugations; (3) as various combinations of corrugation and overthrust faulting, the difference in effect depending upon difference in structure, difference in the pressure beneath superincumbent beds, and other differences in conditions.

Willis's inferences from Appalachian structure have been checked by experimentation. During the past year he has subjected masses of wax consisting of alternating layers of varying rigidity, built up in imitation of the rocky strata of the earth's crust, to horizontal compression, the waxen strata being variously loaded in different experiments; and he finds that the deformation of the miniature strata in his models imitates the deformation displayed on a grander scale in the Appalachian Mountains.

Another order of faults, also resulting from horizontal compression, has recently been developed by Davis. There are in the Connecticut Valley extensive deposits of sandstone and shale of Triassic age, of unknown thickness, generally dipping eastward at a considerable angle; and there are in New Jersey, Pennsylvania, and northern Virginia similar deposits of Triassic sandstone, also of unknown thickness, dipping westward at high angles. In both of these areas the existence of faults has long been suspected, and in a few cases minor faults have actually been discovered; so the feeling has gained ground that despite the persistent and high dips over broad areas, the deposits are only of limited thickness. Now Davis has shown† that in the Connecticut area there are

---

* Bull. Phil. Soc. Wash., 1889, vol. XI (in press).
† 7th Ann. Rpt. U. S. Geol. Survey, 1888, pp. 461–490

intercalated within the sandstones certain sheets of trap, mainly intrusive; and using these distinctive beds as data planes in the otherwise homogeneous deposits, he finds that the same beds re appear many times, and that in some cases several successive trap ridges are formed by outcropping edges of a single sheet, the mass having been thrown into a series of parallel blocks and subsequently so degraded as to leave the harder trap projecting in the form of strongly accented surface features. His explanation of the faulting in this region is unique. He supposes that the Triassic sandstones were originally deposited in horizontal beds upon an eroded surface of highly inclined (but not vertical) schists, gneises, etc.; that after the completion of Triassic deposition, horizontal compression occurred; that the inclined crystalline strata slipped upon each other, as does a row of fallen books when pushed to upright position, and thus became more nearly vertical; and that as the successive blocks (defined perhaps by intercalations of softer matter) approached verticality the veneer of Triassic sediments above was broken through by a succession of approximately vertical faults coinciding with the planes of slipping among the crystalline strata. Davis's hypothesis is certainly suggestive, and, if valid, constitutes a notable advance in the branch of geology dealing with the deformation of the earth.

The *terra incognita* of American geographers for many years has been, singularly enough, not the comparatively inaccessible mountains and deserts of the West, but a tract in southwestern Missouri, northwestern Arkansas, and eastern Indian Territory. Somewhere here was supposed to belong that will-o'-the-wisp of geographers and geologists alike, the Ozark Mountain system—a half-ideal mountanic tract commonly named in geographic treatises and sometimes vaguely located in small-scale maps, though no geographer knew their exact position and no geologist knew their structure. Now during the last year or two a part of this tract has been surveyed topographically by officers of the U. S. Geological Survey and its general configuration ascertained; and moreover the work of the geological survey of Arkansas has extended along its southern flanks and the predominant structural characteristics ascertained. According to Branner and Comstock, the region suffered post-Paleozoic deformation now expressed by corrugation approaching the Appalachian type, the strata lying in a series of folds of nearly east-west direction;[*] and as pointed out by the former in a communication before the American Association for the Advancement of Science at Cleveland, the crystalline rocks found along the southern flanks of the corrugated tract are not eruptive, as they have hitherto been regarded, but Archæan, so that the region would appear to be homologous with and probably a continuation of the Appalachian region of eastern United States.

---

[*]Ark. Geol. Survey, Ann. Rpt. 1888, vol. i, maps, and p. xxx.

During the biennial period there have been some valuable foreign contributions to our knowledge of the causes and conditions of mountain-making, notably the development of the conception of the "level-of-no-strain;" for as shown upon physical grounds, by Reade, Fisher, G. H. Darwin, and Davison, there is at limited depth within the terrestrial crust a horizon or *couche* in which tangential stress disappears. This conception has modified American as well as foreign thought, but thus far no important contributions to the subject have been made on this side of the Atlantic.

Apropos to the conclusions of geologists and physicists concerning the isostatic condition (or condition of hydrostatic equilibrium) of the exterior crust of the earth, and of the bearing of these conclusions upon the general problem of mountain-making, reference may be made to a practically new conception as to certain relations between sedimentation and depression which bears upon the theory of mountain-making recently advocated by Reade. It may be thus stated : Lines of sedimentation are the margins of continents, and the sediments are laid down not upon horizontal surfaces, but upon seawardly sloping bottoms; so the sediments do not form horizontal beds, but take a variable seaward slope, determined by marine currents, wave action, etc. Thus the mass of sediments is collectively in the condition of a mass of snow upon a roof or upon a mountain side; *i. e.*, in a condition of potential instability or *inequipotentiality*. If the mass is stable in either case, it is because the friction among the particles exceeds the attraction of gravitation upon the particles; it is obvious that if particle friction were reduced by augmentation of temperature or by alteration of constitution, or if the efficiency of gravitation were increased by addition to the mass, the point of stability might be passed, when the mass would move in the direction of the slope; and it is equally obvious that if an inequipotential mass expand, the resulting movement will not take place equally in all directions, but mainly or wholly in the direction of least resistance, which is that of the slope. Since the sediments fringing continents are in a condition of inequipotentiality, any movement due to the rise of isogeotherms or other cause must take place in a single direction ; and it might not be limited to that due to expansion, for other factors co-operate. Supplemented by this additional conception, the hypothesis of mountain growth so ably advocated by Herschel[*] (who alone recognized vaguely the conception), Babbage, Hall, Dana, Le Conte, Reade, and a score of others, appears to gain much in acceptability.[†] The great displacement of the Middle Atlantic slope has been attributed to downward and seaward settling of the inequipotential mass of Mesozoic and Cenozoic sediments constituting the coastal plain.[‡]

[*] L. E. & D. Phil. Mag., 1856, 4th ser., XII, pp. 197–198.
[†] McGee, Geol. Mag., Decade III, 1888, vol. V, pp. 494, 495.
[‡] 7th Ann. Report U. S. Geol. Survey, 1888, p. 634.

Since diastatic movements are predominantly vertical and measured from sea-level as a datum plane, the determination of the mean sea-level (commonly called the "figure of the earth," or, more properly, the *geoid*) is important to geologists. The "figure of the earth" is also important to geologists in another way: It has long been known that despite the gravitational attraction of mountains and continental masses a plumb-line suspended at the sea-shore is generally deflected seaward, and that in some cases a plumb-line suspended at the base of a mountain range is deflected toward the plain rather than the mountains; and accordingly it has been supposed by many physicists, astronomers, and geologists that the rocks constituting the ocean bottom are heavier than those of the land, and that the rocks underlying plains are often heavier than those forming mountain masses. Suess and some others have indeed maintained that such mountain systems as the Andes must attract and materially elevate the surface of contiguous ocean waters; but Pratt and several other careful students have, on the contrary, advocated the simple inference from observation; and Faye has attributed the great inequalities of the earth's surface to the more rapid refrigeration and consequent condensation of sea bottoms than of land surfaces. Now, the determination of the differences in density indicated by the anomalous deflection of the plumb-line in certain cases, and so the solution of some of the most profound problems with which geologists have ever grappled, depends, first, upon the determination of the general form of the geoid, and second, upon the development of a formula by which the gravitational attractions of adventitious rock masses, and of rock masses varying in density, can be computed. The importance of these inquiries has been recognized by some of the ablest mathematicians, physicists, and geologists, including Thomson, Clarke, Pratt, Fisher, Stokes, Helmert, G. H. Darwin, Fischer, and others. For some years past Woodward has been engaged upon these problems; and during 1888 he published an elaborate discussion of the whole subject, including analyses of the results reached by former investigators, and formulæ applicable in evaluating the deformation of water surfaces by the gravitational attraction of ice masses, continents, and mountains, the changes in level of inconstant lakes, etc.* While the immediate result of Woodward's researches can scarcely be regarded as a contribution to knowledge of the general phenomena of deformation, his contribution is worthy of note as a sound basis for further investigation.

DEGRADATION.

All portions of the earth standing above the level of the sea are subject to degradation. Different processes effect degradation, but incomparably the most potent is the action of rain and rivers. Now the whole subject of hydro-dynamic action has received more attention from Amer-

---

*Bull. of the U. S. Geol. Survey, No. 48.

ican geologists than from those of any other country, and the greater part of our knowledge of the subject must be credited to American investigators. Thus, it was American geologists employed in the cañon-cut plateaus and mountains of the western Territories who discovered that the water of a river is not so much the agent of corrasion (which is one of the principal modes of degradation) as the vehicle by which the agent is rendered operative, and that the real agent of corrasion is the sand or other material with which the water of rivers is loaded. Pure water is practically impotent as a corrading agent; but when furnished with tools in the form of sand grains it rapidly cuts away the hardest rocks. And this is only one of many American contributions to the subject.

Until recently it has been commonly believed that while the sand grains and other matter held in suspension in river water directly increases corrasion, there is an indirect diminution in corrading capacity going with the addition of such matter, due to the absorption of a portion of the energy of the stream in transporting the solid matter. According to one of the highest authorities on the subject, "where a stream has all the load of a given degree of comminution which it is capable of carrying, the entire energy of the descending water and load is consumed in the translation of the water and load, and there is none applied to corrasion. - - - The work of transportation may thus monopolize a stream to the exclusion of corrasion, or the two works may be carried forward at the same time."* The same geologist has assumed the practical equality of the two elements, and thus that corrasion is little affected by load. Such has been the state of opinion on this subject for a decade.

Within a few months another American contribution of the first importance has been made to this subject: In a paper read before the National Academy of Sciences in November, 1888, Powell pointed out that there is a distinction between the sediment rolled or pushed along the bottom of a stream, and that which is of such degree of comminution as to float in the running water; and that to the extent that materials are rolled along the bottom by impact the energy of the water is indeed utilized in transportation, as held by Gilbert and others, but that to the extent that transportation is accomplished by flotation, the gravity of the particles themselves is the entire force of transportation; so that whatever is driven is transported by the energy of the water, while whatever floats is transported by its own inherent gravity. Thus within certain wide limits, and under certain conditions of comminution of the load, the energy of a stream would appear not to be diminished but on the contrary greatly increased by the addition of load. If the law thus formulated be valid (and its validity has not thus far been questioned) its discovery will become of great and wide-reaching practical value to

---

* Gilbert, Geology of the Henry Mountains, 1877, p. 111.

students of engineering problems, as well as to geologists concerned with the various and increasingly important problems of degradation.

Unquestionably the most noteworthy contribution to objective geology during the biennial period is the recognition by several students of the intimate relation between topographic configuration and geologic history. Although fully matured only within a few months, the conception found birth during the days of active geologic investigation in western Territories, originating, as have so many other wide-reaching inductions, in the fertile brain of Powell, but receiving notable impetus through the early work of Dutton. The former geologist pointed out that one of the leading determinants of degradation is found in the declivity of streams, and that there is a certain minimum declivity beyond which there is neither corrasion nor transportation. It is of course evident that no stream can sink its channel below the level of the sea; and as Powell pointed out, it is equally evident that at a distance from the sea a stream can not sink its channel below a certain altitude above tide which will give a slope just sufficient to permit flowage; and also that no tributary can corrade its channel below the level of its primary. This lowest limit of corrasion and transportation may be called the *base level of erosion*.[*] The importance of this conception was realized by several of the leading geologists of the world, but circumstances prevented further development of the subject, and the conception lay dormant for years.

Recently, different geologists at work in eastern United States have noticed certain intermontane plains and ancient terraces which can be explained only upon the hypothesis that during some past period the land stood lower than now, and remained stationary until not only the rivers and their tributaries, but the minor streamlets—and even the rain-born rills and so the entire surface, were reduced to a level below which degradation was impossible; and the term base level was extended not only to rivers and their tributaries, but to whole continents, so that to-day the term is applied to a bi-dimensional surface rather than a series of uni-dimensional lines. Moreover, it was found that the intermontane plains are in many cases bounded by steep slopes and intersected by sharp-cut gorges and ravines which could only be explained on the assumption that at the close of the base-level period the land was lifted so high that degradation was greatly accelerated, but for a period too short to permit the general reduction of the area to a new base level; and the geologists concluded that the plains tell of alterations in level of the land as well as of long standing at a single level. The conception expanded still further as study progressed until it came to be perceived that every hill and valley is a record of geologic activity depending upon the relation between land and sea, and thus indicating the geographic configuration of past periods. So a new geologic

---

[*] Exploration of the Colorado River, 1875, p. 203.

alphabet was devised, and now geologists read geologic history from the hills as well as from the strata and their contained fossils.

This line of investigation has .been successfully pursued by Davis,[*] who has acquired such skill in the interpretation of geologic history from topographic forms as to be able to read the principal events in the geologic development of New Jersey and Pennsylvania from topographic maps; it has been pursued by McGee with such success that " probably for the first time important practical conclusions, involving the consideration of hypogeal structure and orogenic movement, have been based on the interpretation of topography and on inferences from the present behavior of the streams by which the topography has been determined;"[†] and it has also been pursued with success by Willis in the central Appalachian region. So complete has been the development of this method of investigation that nearly as much information concerning the geologic history of the Atlantic slope has been obtained from the topographic configuration of the region within two years as was gathered from the sediments of the costal plain and their contained fossils in two generations.

The interpretation of geologic history from topographic configuration may well be called the *New Geology*. It opens a new field for the science so extensive as to nearly double its domain; and this field has been fully entered by American geologists alone and within the last two years.

DEPOSITION.

The clastic rocks—the products of deposition—have been more extensively studied than any other class of geologic phenomena; out of their study has grown the greater part of geologic literature; surveys and commissions have been endowed chiefly for the purpose of investigating them; national and international conventions have been established to discuss them; and their relations to science in general, to the arts, and to the welfare of the race have been elaborated by a host of students.

During the biennial period special attention has been given to this branch of geology under the stimulus afforded by the organization and active work of the Congrès Géologique International abroad and the American committee of the Congrès in this country. The American committee operated mainly through subcommittees, consisting of a few specialists (one of whom was the reporter of the subcommittee) and sometimes associates. Each subcommittee sought to develop a taxonomy applicable to a particular part of the geologic column, and the various subclassifications are designed to be thrown together into a general taxonomic system similar to but more refined than those current in objective geology for a generation. The reporters were, on the Archean Persifer Frazer; on the Lower Paleozoic, N. H. Winchell; on the

---

* Nat. Geog. Mag., vol. I, pp. 11-26.
†7th Ann. Rep. U. S. Geol. Survey, 1888, pp. 547-548.

Upper Paleozoic, H. S. Williams (Devonian), and J. J. Stevenson (Carboniferous); on the Mesozoic, G. H. Cook; on the Cenozoic, E. A. Smith (marine Cenozoic), and E. D. Cope (interior Cenozoic); and on the Quaternary and recent, C. H. Hitchcock. The several reports were edited and prefaced with a history of the committee by Frazer, printed in an octavo volume of about 250 pages, and distributed at the London session of the Congrès Géologique International. It should be observed that these reports, and the general system into which they are designed to be thrown, generally represent the primitive analytic classification or classification by products, and not the synthetic classification or classification by genesis, mentioned in an earlier paragraph.

The formal reports of the American committee represent however but a part of the activity in current thought awakened through the organization of the Congrés. In his vice-presidential address before the American Association at New York in 1887, Gilbert developed certain fundamental considerations in geologic taxonomy, nomenclature, and cartography. The address brought out clearly the distinction between classifications based upon structural units, and upon time units respectively—classifications which may be perfectly distinct, though both may traverse the same ground and which are both valuable for different purposes; e. g., the mining geologist may only be interested in the structural classification, while the paleontologist or student of geochrony may be interested only in the time classification. It is just to say that this address elicited adverse criticism, notably by Frazer.* A year later Vice-President Cook addressed his section of the American Association at Cleveland on a similar subject. A statement of the methods of cartography in use by the U. S. Geological Survey in 1885 was presented before the Congrès Géologique International at Berlin in that year by McGee, and was published in 1888 in the compte rendu of the session; and other contributions to the taxonomy of the clastic rocks have appeared.

It is to be noted that the interest awakened by these discussions resulted not only in much writing on geologic taxonomy based upon information already in hand, but also in much valuable work in the field; and the outcome of this work comprises several of the most important contributions to geologic progress made during the last two years.

Foremost among these must be placed the recognition by Irving and his associates (Chamberlin and Van Hise) of a vast mass of sediments, nearly 6 miles in vertical thickness, below the base of the previously known fossiliferous rocks of the terrestrial crust and above the original crystalline nucleus which everywhere forms the foundation upon which the clastic strata are built. This newly-recognized series of rocks is best developed in the Lake Superior region, where it was studied by Irving and his associates; but apparent equivalents have been found in

---

*Am. Naturalist, vol. XXI, pp. 841, 847, and elsewhere.

New England by Pumpelly, in the Grand Cañon region by Walcott and Powell, in Central Texas by Walcott, and in some other parts of the country. Irving was disposed to separate the series into two groups, each co-ordinate with the Devonian, Silurian, Cambrian, etc.—viz, the Keweenawan and Huronian,—and to class the entire series as a great system co-ordinate with the Paleozoic, for which he proposed the term Agnotozoic.* The present disposition among leading American geologists is, however, to reduce the series to the taxonomic rank of the groups (Devonian, Silurian, etc.), and to combine its divisions under the name Algonkian.

Second in importance to the recognition of the Algonkian must be placed the discovery in Texas during 1887 of a series of Cretaceous deposits underlying the Dakota formation (the supposed base of the cretaceous in this country), which is paleontologically equivalent to the lower half of the European cretaceous. The bridging of this break in the history recorded in American sediments is due to the labors of Hill† and C. A. White.‡ The evidence upon which the conclusions of these investigators rest is largely paleontologic, and their discovery is of interest to paleontologists as well as geologists.

Another noteworthy event, also of interest to the paleontologist, while at the same time important in statigraphy, is the elucidation of the structure of the Taconic Mountains in western New England, largely by Walcott, during 1887 and 1888. There is in eastern New York and western New England a region of faulted and metamorphosed crystalline or subcrystalline rocks, generally deeply mantled by drift, which has been the intellectual battle-ground of nearly all American geologists given to controversy for over half a century. In the early forties some of these rocks were erroneously grouped, and efforts were made to give this fictitious group a place in systematic geology under the name "Taconic system" and the "Taconic question" has been before the geologic world from that day almost to this. Late in 1886, and again in 1887, Walcott visited the region, and after much labor discovered the defective arrangement, ascertained the true relations of the strata, and made public his conclusions. In this work he was greatly aided, by the results of careful field studies extending over many years, by the eminent geologist of Yale, James D. Dana. The careful work in the field by Dana and Walcott has however been criticised. The contributors to the subject during the biennial period include Hunt, Marcou, Miller, Newberry, Vogdes, A. Winchell, N. H. Winchell, and others. But to the geologist interested in substantial progress rather than polemics, and to the layman interested in the practical results of geologic investigation, the most satisfactory contribution ever made to the "Taconic

---

*7th Ann. Rep. U. S. Geol. Survey, 1888, p. 453.
† Am. Jour. Sci., vol. xxxiv, p. 288, and elsewhere.
‡ Proc. Nat. Acad. Sci. Phil., 1887, pp. 39–47.

question" was that of the venerable Dana in December, 1888, and it may easily be quoted at length:

"1841-1888."*

An event of some importance to students of the multifarious products of deposition is the definition of the Columbia formation. There is a break in geologic history, as commonly interpreted, between the Neocene and the Pleistocene,—a hiatus partly natural and partly taxonomic, and exceedingly difficult to close by reason of diverse methods of classification as well as by reason of the dearth of common phenomena. But the formation under consideration is a superficial deposit of known genesis, intimately connected with the other Pleistocene deposits of the country; it is at the same time a fossiliferous sedimentary deposit as intimately connected with the Neocene and Eocene formations of the middle Atlantic slope as these are connected among themselves; and thus the formation not only covers the natural discontinuity between the Neocene and Pleistocene, but, since it is susceptible of classification with either, closes the taxonomic hiatus as well.†

There has long been grave uncertainty as to the relations among certain members of that Silurian or Cambrian rock series of the upper Mississippi Valley known in part as the Lower Magnesian Limestone of Owen; and it is a source of gratification to geologists to note that, in the second volume of his final report, N. H. Winchell has clearly set forth the relations of the various members of this series, particularly in Minnesota and Wisconsin. The series, beginning at the base of the well characterized St. Peter Sandstone, is as follows: (1) Shakopee Limestone; (2) New Richmond Sandstone; (3) main body of limestone, ("Lower Magnesian" in part); (4) Jordan Sandstone; (5) St. Lawrence Limestone; (6) a bed of shales; (7) Dresbach Sandstone (the last four representing the St. Croix); (8) a bed of shales; and (9) Hinckley Sandstone (the last six constituting the Potsdam of Wisconsin); the whole resting upon the red shales and sandstones which pass into the copper-bearing series.‡

One of the most puzzling problems which the geologists employed in the western Territories have been called upon to solve is the absence of formations elsewhere of great volume, without marked unconformity between the older and newer deposits. This condition is especially conspicuous in the Rocky Mountains, where the Silurian is sometimes reduced to a few feet of shales or limestones, and is sometimes almost unrecognizable. It is also conspicuous in the Black Hills, where, according to Newton, the Cambrian includes but 250 feet of sandstones and quartzites, while the Silurian proper and the Devonian are absent,§ although there are no marked unconformities. Newton's observations were verified and the anomalous relation of the Black Hills rocks dis-

---

*Am. Jour. Sci., 3rd series, vol. XXXVI, p. 427.

† McGee, Am. Journ. Sci., 3d series, vol. XXXV, p. 466.

‡ *Op. cit.* 1888, page xxii.

§ Rep. on Geology and Resources of the Black Hills, 1880, pp. 40, 41.

cussed during the past year by Crosby;* and it was shown that during
Silurian and Devonian time the region now upheaved as an isolated
mountain tract in the midst of a great continent must have been the bottom of an ocean so broad and deep that sediments were not transported
to it in sufficient quantity to form deposits of any considerable volume—
that during a large part of the Paleozoic the region must have been
in much the same condition as are to-day the abyssmal depths of the
south Atlantic and Pacific, in which dredges gather modern shells, Tertiary shark teeth, and Cretaceous otoliths at a single sweep.

The same author has recently discussed also the origin of the quartzites, cherty concretions, and other siliceous aggregations found in deep-
sea deposits, and shown that they must result in large part from solution of the organic silica contained in sponge spicules, diatom shells,
etc., and subsequent deposition of the silica in the mineral form ; the
mineral silica thus disseminated among the mechanical sediments sometimes segregating therefrom in solid nodules or the hollow bodies called
geodes.[1]

VULCANISM.

The recently renewed volcanic activity on the Hawaiian Islands led
to an interesting incident—i. e., a second visit to the islands by the
venerable Dana, for the purpose of re-examining in the light of modern
knowledge the phenomena studied by him half a century before.   Certain results of the new observations were summarized in a general
discussion of volcanic action, in which the principal movements are
classified as follows: (1) the ascending movement of the liquid rock
in the subterrranean conduit of the volcano from the deep-seated
crustal or sub-crustal region of fusion ; (2) the projection of the lava
aerially upward from the surface of the liquid lava in the vent, which is
accompanied by outflow whenever the height reached by the lavas is such
that they find an outlet either over or through fissures in the walls of
the crater.   Each of these operations (upflow and outflow) involves an
expulsion of material from subterranean regions ; and a usual consequence is (3) a subsidence or down plunge of the overlying rock or of
portions of the cone.   These movements of upthrow, ejection, and subsidence are the most universal and strongly marked of the entire series
of volcanic phenomena.   Connected with them, there are in addition
however (4) the escape of vapors from the crater, and (5) displacements
and the opening of fissures.[2]   The last movements are frequently accompanied by earth tremors, and sometimes by destructive earthquakes.
These observations upon the behavior of living volcanoes throw light
upon the history of the extinct volcanoes whose craters, lava sheets, or
even "necks" alone remain for examination by the geologist.

* Proc. Bost. Soc. Nat. Hist., vol. xxiii, pp. 501–6.

†Technology Quarterly, 1888, pp. 397–407; Scientific American Supplement, 1888,
vol. xxvi, pp. 10466–'68.

‡ Am. Jour., Sci., 1887, 3d series, vol. xxxiii, p. 103.

Next to active volcanoes in significance to systematic geologists, and in interest and instructiveness to laymen, come those recently extinct; and during the past two years such a volcano has been investigated by Diller. This volcano is perhaps the most recent within the United States. Its crater, overlooking Snag Lake 10 miles northeast of Lassen Peak in northern California, is indeed cold, but the lapilli and scoria of which it is composed have been scarcely affected by the action of the elements, and its slopes are as high as such material will maintain; the lava sheet which flowed from it, and which by damming a small creek formed Snag Lake, is scarcely discolored by weathering; the volcanic ashes which it vomited yet lie as they fell, little touched by the winter rains or the summer thunder showers; the stumps of trees smothered by the ashes and charred by the lava have not yet decayed; and all the phenomena indicate that this debris-swathed volcano was in active operation but a few scores or at most a few hundreds of years ago.*

This, although probably the youngest of the series, is only one of those volcanoes which, beginning in early Tertiary time and culminating in activity about the Pliocene or early Pleistocene, flooded hundreds of thousands of square miles of the Pacific slope with lava sheets the most extensive of the globe. Most of the orifices from which these lavas welled have been obliterated or buried by geologic changes; but one of them remains, and is of such vast dimensions that the water with which it is partly filled forms the deepest lake on the continent. This "Crater Lake," which lies in the heart of the Cascade range in southern Oregon, is 2,000 feet deep, and the bounding walls rise 900 to 2,000 feet above its level. It was explored by Dutton in 1886.†

Kilauea represents active vulcanism; Snag Lake represents the effects of vulcanism yet untouched by time; Crater Lake is a mighty volcano long dead and already mouldering into dust; the older lava sheets and degraded craters of Oregon and northern California contain a record of vulcanism partly effaced by the ever operative agencies of degradation; but there is a still later stage in the obliteration of the volcanic record which has been brought to light within two years: About Mount Taylor in northern New Mexico there is an extensive area now occupied chiefly by sedimentary rocks of Mesozoic age, which have evidently suffered great degradation during Cenozoic time; and through the strata project cylindrical masses of basalt, sometimes large enough to be dignified by the name of mountains, which evidently represent the contents of the pipes or ducts through which lava was extruded during past ages, probably in sufficient volume to sheet vast areas with lava, as southern Oregon was sheeted during the later epoch; but these lava sheets have been completely denuded over hundreds of square miles,

*Am. Journ. Sci., 1888, 3d series, vol. XXXIII, pp. 45-50.
†Science, vol. VII, p. 179.

and nothing remains to indicate their existence save the indurated contents of the pipes by which they were supplied. These remnants of
lava columns, or "volcanic necks" as they are called by Dutton (by
whom they were discovered and interpreted), are among the most interesting records of vulcanism extant, since by means of them the geologist
descends far into the crust of the earth toward the ultimate seat of volcanic action.

In the early days of geology there were two rival hypotheses concerning the formation of the rocks of the earth, viz, the Plutonic and the
Neptunic. The battle between these doctrines raged for a generation
before the Neptunists gained the ascendancy; but it is now recognized
that by far the greater part of the rocks open to observation were deposited in the seas, and that only a subordinate part were extruded in
molten condition from the bowels of the earth. Yet a vestige of the
Plutonic hypothesis has persisted until to-day, particularly in Germany,
but to some extent in this country, in the form of a belief that the volcanic rocks of the earth represent a more or less definite series ranging
and gradually changing from the Archean to the Pliocene—that the lavas of the Paleozoic were unlike those of the Mesozoic, and these again
unlike those of the Cenozoic, and that the successive differences constitute a record of the earth's history, susceptible of an interpretation only
less definite than that afforded by the succession of organic life. This
belief (which must not be confounded with Richthofen's induction concerning the succession of rocks among the lavas of a particular province
and period, and Dutton's admirable explanation of the law of that succession) was so seriously shaken when the results of the investigation of the
Washoe rocks of Nevada by Hague and Iddings were published[*] that
it has now been largely abandoned by German students and teachers.
So an American discovery has, within the biennial period, and in at
least one foreign country, practically revolutionized thought concerning the succession and significance of volcanic rocks as geologic chronometers.

Although sometimes unquestionably connected with general deformation, seismism or earthquake movement is known to accompany volcanic action in many cases. During the biennial period the most important contribution ever made to seismology—a contribution which
revolutionized earlier conceptions and placed the entire science upon a
new and firm foundation—emanated from the American geologist Dutton, as the outcome of his studies of the Charleston earthquake of 1886.
The contribution includes two distinct conceptions: (1) It was found
on examining the means hitherto employed for ascertaining the depth
of earthquake foci that all involve sources of error of such magnitude
that the resulting determinations are worthless; and so a method was

---

[*] Bull. U. S. Geol. Survey, No. 23, 1886.

devised which is dependent, not upon the always uncertain data hitherto employed, but upon observations of intensity which can be verified by independent observers even weeks or months after a great shock, and in which the errors in judgment of the observer have comparatively little effect upon the result. In this method the various observations upon intensity are first mapped, and a center (which is the epicentrum of the volcanic area) from which the intensities diminish in all directions is found by simple inspection; the intensity observations are then assembled and plotted in the order of their distance from this center upon a diagram in which the ordinates represent intensities and the abscissa distance from the epicentrum; when it is found that in all cases there is a point of inflection in the intensity curve at a distance from the epicentrum depending upon the depth of the centrum (or focus) which can thus be determined by a simple formula. This method of determining the depth of earthquake foci is eminently satisfactory, and is unquestionably destined to supplant all others in every case in which it is applicable. By means of it the focus of the Charleston earthquake was shown to be about 12 miles beneath the surface.* (2) Hitherto the determinations of the velocity of earthquake transmission have been so variable that the more cautious seismologists looked upon them with suspicion. Now, owing partly to the extended use of standard time throughout the United States, the time observations upon the Charleston earthquake over the 850,000 square miles affected are satisfactory beyond all precedent; these observations have been carefully reduced and discussed (and in this work Dutton had the assistance of Newcomb), and a coefficient for the velocity of earthquake transmission, incomparably more trustworthy than the earlier determinations, has been deduced. The mean result of the various observations gives a velocity of $5,184 \pm 80$ meters per second. This coefficient, like the method of determining the depth of earthquake foci, is unquestionably destined to supplant all others, and so seismologists are now armed with new means of prosecuting further researches upon the most mysterious of terrestrial phenomena. But Dutton's contributions are no less important to the geologist than to the seismologist in that they coincide with experiment and observation upon the elasticity, rigidity, density, and other properties of solid and homogeneous rocks, and so throw light upon the condition of the sub-crust of the earth far beyond the depths which direct examination can ever reach.

ALTERATION.

The products of the alteration of rocks by the various agencies to which they are subject are multifarious: The soils are formed by the disintegration and decay of rocky strata; the sediments of seas and lakes are first consolidated into rock, and sometimes subsequently

---

* Bull. Phil. Soc. Wash., 1888, vol. x, p. 17.

transformed from the clastic or amorphous to the crystalline form; mineral veins and ore deposits result from alterations due to heat, pressure, and other conditions; gases are set free in the processes of alteration of original sediments, and are sometimes accumulated in the rocks in great volume; and so a large share of those geologic phenomena which are of general economic interest result from processes of alteration of the rocks of the earth. The products of many of these processes belong rather to lithology and chemistry, or to the arts, than to geology; but some of them fall within the legitimate field of the latter science.

Several years ago E. W. Hilgard proposed a classification of the soils of certain Southern States by the conditions of their genesis; but circumstances prevented the application of this classification to the soils of the country at large. During the past year Powell has adopted and extended this genetic classification of soils, and proposes to apply it to the entire country. Thus far the classification and the plan for its application has been published only in brief; * but it may be added that soil investigation has already been commenced in several divisions of the U. S. Geological Survey, and that a number of soil maps have been prepared and are shortly to be published. Agricultural geology is the geology of the future; and although great progress in the study and classification of soils has not yet been made, it is of interest to note that the work has been definitely commenced during the biennial period, and that important results will doubtless soon appear.

Two notable events in geologic progress during recent years are (1) the discovery by Becker that enormous masses of crystalline rocks in the Sierra Nevada Mountains, hitherto supposed to be Archean, are, instead, matamorphosed sediments of Cretaceous age; and (2) the elucidation of the genesis of the iron ores of the Lake Superior region by Irving and Van Hise; but these events primarily belong rather to the domain of lithology than geology.

In the history of the subjugation of natural forces for human weal there is no more interesting episode than that of the utilization of the unstable carbon compounds as fuels and illuminants. Wood and various woody plants have been used as fuel, and animal fats and vegetal oils as illuminants from time immemorial; and there is scarcely a savage tribe to which they are unknown. The advance from the use of wood and charcoal to the burning of mineral coals was an easy one, and was probably made gradually and independently in many centers both during historic and pre-historic time. The last step in the utilization of potential energy stored up in mineral substances was far longer and was taken within our own memory; and, in consequence of the ready communication of recent years between distant lands, was taken in many parts of the world at about the same time. It is true that

* Science, 1888, vol. XII, p. 150.

natural-gas vents were known to and were for ages venerated by the fire-worshipers, whose cult they inspired; it is also true that springs of mineral oil have been known from history's dawn, and that the oil was utilized sometimes as fuel or illuminant, though more commonly as a medicine or lubricant; and it is equally true that natural oils and tars were extracted by primitive means and used for primitive purposes by barbarous Oriental peoples long before their fame spread to the Occident; but it is only within a few years that these natural products have been utilized so extensively as to materially modify the course of human progress.

Pari passu with the industrial development accompanying the utilization of rock gas, geologic science made an unparalleled stride within a few months. During the last thirty years Hunt, Newberry, Peckham, Leslie, and several other geologists in this country, and Binney, Coquand, Daubrée, Lartet, and others abroad have indeed made important contributions to our knowledge concerning the constitution and origin of petroleum and its associates; and the exploitation of the Pennsylvania-New York fields afforded valuable additional data relating to these minerals. Nearly four years ago Prof. I. C. White enunciated and vigorously maintained the theory—now recognized as a fundamental law in gas prognostication—that gas, oil, and brine are accumulated in the order of their weight within inverted basins and troughs formed by flexure of the rocky strata. The importance of these contributions to our knowledge of the lighter bitumens must not be under-estimated; yet when exploitation for gas began in Ohio in 1886, the geologist literally sat at the feet of the prospecter gathering such crumbs as fell from his hands, and found himself utterly unable either to guide efforts or predict results. Less than two years later the laws governing the distribution and accumulation of gas and oil were so fully developed that the rock-gas problem claimed a solution as satisfactory as that of the well-known artesian water problem; and to day the geologist predicts the success or failure of a prospect bore for gas or oil about as readily and reliably as he can prognosticate artesian water, or coal. Greater advance was probably never before made in so limited time in any economically important branch of knowledge. The solution of the problem of rock gas and petroleum marks an era in science no less than in industry. Vast sums of money, reaching sometimes into the millions, were spent by prospecters in gathering data; but the credit for the solution of the problem belongs chiefly to three individuals—I. C. White, of the University of West Virginia; Edward Orton, State geologist of Ohio; and A. J. Phinney, a practicing physician and amateur geologist of Muncie, Indiana.

GLACIATION.

The general tendency of glaciation is to obliterate surface irregularity both by grinding down elevations and by filling up depressions, and thus to supplement hydric gradation; but glaciation may also accent-nate pre-existing irregularities of surface, certainly by moraine-build-ing and probably by basin-cutting, and must therefore be set apart as a unique agent in the modification of the external configuration of the globe. The study of living glaciers was commenced many years ago by reason of the novelty of the subject and the paradoxical behavior of an apparently rigid substance when accumulated in large mass; but it was soon ascertained that glaciers are among the most potent of the geologic agencies, and during recent years they have been studied chiefly with the object of interpreting the frequently obscure records of glaciation during past ages.

Among the most important researches upon modern glaciers made during recent years are those of Holst upon the great mer de glace of central Greenland, which have recently been summarized by Lindahl.[*] These researches are of special value to students of the glacial phenomena of America, since a considerable part of the mer de glace of Greenland apparently occupies plains comparable in general features with those of the Upper Mississippi Valley and the valley of the Great Lakes, while most of the glaciers hitherto studied are constricted ice streams flowing in mountain-bound valleys, whose behavior is determined largely by the conditions these valleys impose. In the mountainous parts of Greenland, as in the Alps and the northern Rockies the ice is indeed crevasse-torn, diversified by bowlders and other débris derived from projecting mountain tops, and sometimes broken by moulins, into which small streams cascade; but over the plains the ice is generally continuous, and free from rocky or earthy superficial deposits (other than the kryokonite which has so long puzzled students of Greenland geology), though sometimes intersected by considerable superglacial streams. Kryokonite was collected in considerable quantity by Holst, carefully examined, and found to contain nothing but the ordinary components of non-eruptive crystalline rocks in finely comminuted condition—quartz, orthoclase, plagioclase, two or three varieties of mica, hornblende, garnet, magnetite, and doubtful traces of titanite and epidote; but no metallic iron, nor the slightest trace of augite, olivine, or glass were found. In short, the chemical composition and mechanical constitution or kryokonite of Greenland is almost exactly identical with that of the loess so extensively developed in and along the flanks of glaciated regions generally. Holst's observations agree exactly with the conclusion previously reached by most American students of the loess, i. e., it is the finest flour of the ice-mill, which was swept into the glacial streams, and slowly deposited in rivers, lakes, and morasses as the flow became sluggish or ceased.

Another notable study of living glaciers has been made by G. F. Wright about Glacier Bay, in southern Alaska.[†] The observations

* Am. Naturalist, 1888, vol. XXII, pp. 589-98, 705-13.
† Am. Jour. Sci. 1887, vol. XXXIII, pp. 1-18.

upon the rate of flow of Muir glacier, which embouches into the head of the bay, are particularly interesting. The cross-section of the ice stream is about 3,500,000 square feet (5,000 feet wide by about 700 feet deep), and the mean flow is about 40 feet per day (70 feet in the center and 10 feet near the margin) in the month of August. The Muir glacier is now retreating, but it has evidently oscillated considerably during recent times, and in some of its advances it has encroached upon and buried beneath its ground moraine and aqueoglacial deposits, whole forests of full-grown trees, whose remains occasionally appear about the shores of the bay.

It was an early notion that during glacial times great ice-caps formed about the poles and extended far toward the equator; and during one stage in the development of geologic science mathematicians sought to compute the effects of these hypothetic ice-caps, first, upon the volume of the oceans from which they were drawn, second, upon the isostatic terrestrial crust on which they were heaped, and third, upon the center of gravity of the earth as a whole. The students of more recent years have, however, settled down to the more temperate conviction that great polar ice-caps never existed, and that during the glacial period the ice flowed radially from certain "centers of dispersion" (so called by Lyell). This view has recently received strong support from a new quarter: Within the last decade the Canadian geologists have shown that the striæ which form the unmistakable trail of glaciers extend from the Laurentide plateau southwesterly toward Lake Superior and the Red River, westerly toward Lake Winnipeg, and northerly and even northeasterly toward Hudson's Strait,[*] proving that these highlands were the center of dispersion for the mer de glace by which northeastern United States was overflowed. These Canadian observations have continued until within the last year or two, and have settled forever the fate of the ice-cap hypothesis. During the past two years, too, parallel observations have been made in the northwestern part of the American continent: G. M. Dawson and other officers of the Geological Survey of Canada have ascertained that the striæ of the Mackenzie Valley extend in northerly directions, proving that the northern Rockies also formed an independent center of ice dispersion.[†] Dawson's publication upon the glacial phenomena of Canada is of special interest to American geologists in that it contains definite recognition of the glacial theory, essentially in the form long held in America but rejected in Canada.

The various American observations upon glacial striæ have just been assembled, graphically depicted upon a remarkably instructive map, and discussed at length by the foremost living authority upon glacial

* Ann. Rep. Geol. Survey of Canada, 1885, p. 14 dd.
† Geol. Mag. Decade 3, 1888, vol. V, pp. 347-50,

matters, President Chamberlin.* These American observations agree with those made on the other side of the northern lakes and the forty-ninth parallel; and it is now possible to map approximately the area glaciated during the Pleistocene, and to represent moreover the form and direction of movement of each principal lobe and tongue of the Mer de Glace during some period of its existence.

The last-named geologist has also recently described the phenomena of the Driftless area of the Upper Mississippi—a tract of over 15,000 square miles, which was completely encompassed, though never over-swept, by the ice, and at one time partly or wholly submerged beneath the waters of an ice-bound lake; and from moraines, aqueo-glacial grav-els, and other products of the combined action of water and ice found about the periphery of the tract, he has deduced a history of the Pleisto-cene more extended and refined than any previously recorded. The epochs in this history are: (1) The Transition Epoch, not yet satisfac-torily distinguished from the Pliocene; (2) the Earlier Glacial Epoch, comprising an episode of glaciation, an episode of deglaciation and veg-etal accumulation, and a second episode of glaciation accompanied by deposition of the loess; (3) the Chief Interglacial Epoch, with vegetal accumulation, etc.; (4) the Later Glacial Epoch, comprising at least three episodes of glaciation and moraine-building and two of deglacia-tion and vegetal accumulation; (5) the Champlain Epoch of marine and lacustral sedimentation; and (6) the Terrace Epoch, which grad-uates into the present. †

The history of the Pleistocene and of its relations to the Tertiary has recently been read in a slightly different way from a different series of deposits (including the Columbia formation) by McGee: The geologic history recorded in the Columbia deposits and terraces and in the ero-sion and alteration which both have suffered is almost wholly supple-mentary to that read by most geologists in the later glacial deposits, and multiplies many times the length of the Pleistocene as commonly conceived. Collectively the two series of deposits indicate that the Pleistocene consisted of two, and only two, great epochs of cold (the later comprising two or more sub-epochs); that these epochs were sep-arated by an interval three, five, or ten times as long as the post-glacial interval; that the earlier cold endured much the longer; that the ear-lier cold was the less intense, and the resulting ice sheet stopped short (in the Atlantic slope) of the limit reached by the later; that the ear-lier glaciation was accompanied by much the greater submergence, ex-ceeding 400 feet at the mouth of the Hudson and extending 500 miles southward, while that of the later reached but a tithe of that depth or southing; and that during the long interglacial interval the condition of land and sea was much as at present. ‡

---

* 7th Ann. Rep. U. S. Geol. Surv. 1888, pp. 155-248.
† 6th Ann. Rep. U. S. Geol. Survey, p. 212.
‡ Am. Jour. Sci., 1888, 3d series, vol. xxxv, p. 465.

There is no subject in geology of wider popular and scientific interest than that of the relation between human chronology and geologic history, and for two generations geologists have sought to determine the remoteness of the latest episode of geology—the last ice invasion—in terms of written history. Up to about a dozen years ago the current estimates of the duration of the post-glacial epoch generally ran from 100,000 to 150,000 or 200,000 years; but about that time a number of American geologists began to make shorter estimates, based on new data, generally ranging from five or six thousand to ten or fifteen thousand years; and since that time the one hundred thousand year and the ten thousand year estimates for the post-glacial period have both had their advocates, though of late the ten thousand year men have been in the ascendant. The chronometers were various, and many of them manifestly unreliable. Probably the most reliable of them all is that afforded by the gorge of the Mississippi between Fort Snelling and St. Anthony's Falls, in Minnesota, to which attention was directed several years ago by N. H. Winchell. The gorge is walled by the friable St. Peter sandstone and a thin cap of firm Trenton limestone by which the sandstone is protected above, and the relations of the gorge to the adjacent glacial deposit are such as to prove that it was excavated by the retrogression of the falls from the present confluence of the Mississippi and Minnesota Rivers at Fort Snelling to their present position. This distance is about 8 miles. Now the gorge was first visited and mapped by Hennepin in 1680; the position was again recorded by Carver in 1756, by Pike in 1805, by Long in 1817, by Keating in 1823, by Featherstonehaugh in 1835, and by engineers of the U. S. Army in 1856; while the present position is known and comparison of the several maps indicate the rate of retrogression of the falls during the two hundred and seven years between 1680 and the time of the latest survey. If this rate be assumed to have been constant from the close of the glacial period to the present, the entire period covered by the retrogression was about eight thousand years.* This agrees with Gilbert's primary estimate of the period of excavation of the Niagara gorge.

One of the most interesting and important lines of investigation in glacial geology undertaken within recent years is that so successfully pursued by Chamberlin upon the terminal moraines built by the Pleistocene ice sheet during certain stages of its existence. The same phenomena have also been studied in this country by Upham, Cook, Wright, Lewis, Salisbury, Todd, Leverett, and others, and the number, extent, and significance in glacial geology of the American moraines have been brought out in an eminently satisfactory manner by these students.

---

* Final Reports Geology of Minnesota, vol. 2, pp. 313-41.

It has been a constant surprise to American glacialists that parallel phenomena were not recorded by the geologists of Europe; and it was a source of something more than surprise to European geologists that the Americans should find so remarkable phenomena in one of two regions of practically identical Pleistocene history, while none such were found in the other. So one of the most interesting events of the last year to American and European glacialists is the discovery of several well-developed terminal moraines in north Germany by the American geologist Salisbury during a visit to that country.* These moraines agree in all leading characteristics with those of this country; and the discovery will unquestionably open a new field of research, and a new vista opening into the past history of the world in Europe, as the earlier discovery did a decade past for this country.

Among the results of the detailed work of American glacialists during the last decade is the discovery that the great mer de glace of the Pleistocene was not a homogeneous and uniform ice field moving in the same direction in all its parts, but rather a series of great tongue-like lobes extending in different directions and to various lengths upon the interior plains of North America; and some of the most interesting lines of investigation of glacial phenomena pursued by Chamberlin and his contemporaries relate to the forms, positions, and inter-relations of these lobes, and to their connection with the system of terminal moraines extending from Long Island to Montana, to the drift sheet bordered by these moraines, and to the aqueoglacial deposits into which both moraines and drift sheets merge. Thus, during the last decade, glacial geology has passed far beyond that initial stage of segregation in which objective phenomena are simply assembled and described to form a basis of study, and well into that stage of differentiation which accompanies a wider growth of knowledge.

One of the students of the American ice-lobes was Lewis, and when he visited Great Britain, two years ago, his practiced eye and trained judgment at once perceived evidences of similar lobation of the ice sheet which plowed over the British Isles during the Pleistocene. So in another way the seed of American thought has borne fruit in Europe and Eastern science has been stimulated by the introduction of Western methods, and another tittle of the intellectual debt of the new continent to the old abated.

RÉSUMÉ.

Several important conceptions in geologic science have sprung into being in America during the past two years; many old conceptions have been modified and extended; and some conceptions hitherto diverse have been brought into harmony; and so, in a third way, knowl-

---

* Am. Jour. Sci. 1888, vol. XXXV, pp. 401-7.

edge has been extended. A few of the leading events in the foregoing history of the growth of conception are worthy of special distinction :

First in importance, by reason of its broad philosophic bearing, must be mentioned the transition from a purely objective or empiric classification in geology to the more logical, simple, comprehensive, and natural classification by processes or by fundamental principles and laws—a transition commenced some years since, but now so well advanced as to be a legitimate subject of permanent record.

Second in importance must be ranked the birth of the New Geology, which interprets geologic history from the records of degradation as the old geology interpreted history from the records of deposition, and thus greatly extends the domain of the science.

Next in importance must be placed the invention of a method of determining the depth of earthquake centers and the determination of the velocity of earthquake transmission, which together have not only revolutionized seismology and placed it upon a solid foundation, but have enlightened geologists as to the constitution of the sub-crust of the earth. These three steps in progress are epoch-marking, and the last in particular must be credited wholly to the biennial period just closed.

Important place must be given to the recognition and definition of a great geologic group—the Algonkian—by which the known geologic column is greatly extended and known geologic history greatly expanded. Like this discovery in kind are the recognition of a sub-group of rocks corresponding to a part of the geologic column—the Lower Cretaceous—hitherto recognized in Europe, but not on the American continent, and the correct determination of the succession of the subordinate divisions of the Silurian and Cambrian in the structurally complex and bitterly contested field beyond the Hudson. To the student of stratigraphy these events are epoch-marking.

Turning now from the subject matter of the science and the growth of knowledge with respect to this subject matter, and toward the means by which the science is developed, another epoch-marking event appears in the organization of the Geological Society of America, by which investigation will inevitably be stimulated and knowledge advanced more rapidly than ever before; and in the same category must be placed the establishment of a national geologic periodical, the American Geologist. And the birth of State geologic surveys in Arkansas and Texas must also be mentioned.

Many other notable steps have been taken with respect both to the means and the ends of geology; but even if there were none other these great strides would render the period 1887, 1888 memorable.

NECROLOGY.

In another and more painful way the biennial period, and particularly the year 1888, is memorable; for the mortality among geologists was unusual:

JAMES C. BOOTH, one time State geologist of Delaware, died at Philadelphia, March 21, 1888, aged seventy-eight years.

ALBERT D. HAGER, once an assistant on the geological survey of New Hampshire, died at Chicago, July 29, 1888.

FERDINAND V. HAYDEN, geologist and explorer, long director of the U. S. Geological and Geographical Survey of the Western Territories, died at Philadelphia, December 22, 1887, aged fifty-nine years.

ROLAND DUER IRVING, professor of geology in the State University of Wisconsin, and geologist on the U. S. Geological Survey, died at Madison, May 30, 1888, aged forty-five years.

HENRY CARVILL LEWIS, an active student of glacial phenomena on both sides of the Atlantic, one time a geologist on the second geological survey of Pennsylvania, died at Manchester, England, July 21, 1888, aged thirty-five years.

AUGUSTUS R. McCUTCHEN, since 1883 geologist and editing clerk of the State department of agriculture of Georgia, born October 31, 1836, died at Atlanta, November 20, 1887, aged fifty-one years.

AMOS H. WORTHEN, long State geologist of Illinois, died at Warsaw, May 6, 1888, aged seventy-five years.

CHARLES E. WRIGHT, State geologist of Michigan, died at Marquette, March 22, 1888, aged forty-five years.

NORTH AMERICAN PALEONTOLOGY FOR 1887 AND 1888.

By HENRY S. WILLIAMS.

INTRODUCTION.

In writing this report some modifications from the plan heretofore adopted have been made. The report attempts to consider only such works as refer to the Paleontology of North America. It has been found impossible in the present state of the science to classify the literature on biological lines entirely, as is done in the excellent Annuaire Géologique of Carez and Douvillé (22). I have consulted several reports of a similar nature, from which I have adopted some suggestions. Among these are the previous reports of Mr. Marcou (156, 157), the geological record by Messrs. Whitaker and Dalton (277), by Messrs. Topley and Sherborn (244), Bulletin No. 44 of the U. S. Geological Survey, by N. H. Darton (60); Les Progrès de la Géologie, by M. Margerie (158); the Annuaire Géologique of Carez and Douvillé (22), and the preceding volumes of the same work by Dr. Dagincourt (57); the Neues Jahrbuch of Messrs. Baur, Dames, and Liebische (11).

One feature I have added which has not been attempted by any of these publications so far as I have ascertained. I have quoted the names of new species and genera proposed in the various publications, and in each case have noted the page and, wherever illustrations have been given, the number of the plate and figure, in order that the report may bring before working paleontologists a list of the new species which can be referred to when the original publications are not accessible.

The reviews of the various publications have been necessarily brief, and are printed separately from the bibliographical list. The contents are arranged in the following order:

General Paleontology:
    Cambrian.
    Silurian, lower and upper.
    Devonian.

General Paleontology—Continued.
    Carboniferous and Permian.
    Mesozoic.
    Cenozoic.

Special Paleontology:
  Invertebrates:
    Protozoa, Sponges, and Eo-
    zoon.
    Corals.
    Crinoids.
    Molluscoida.

Special Paleontology—Continued.
  Mollusca.
  Arthropoda.
  Vertebrates.
Vegetal Paleontology.
List of abbreviations.
Bibliography.

This arrangement has been found necessary because the publications, as before stated, are not capable of classification on purely biological lines. So long as it is necessary for the paleontologist to report upon all the collections obtained in the course of a reconnaissance, or during the year's work of a geological survey, as means of defining the stratigraphical divisions of geology, fossils of all kinds are liable to be considered in the same treatise, and it is only where specialists take up the consideration of the fossils in their biological grouping, that we have a literature differentiated in this way. Some works will be referred to the biological sections which are not thorough treatises from the biological point of view, while others are placed in the geological sections because the treatment is confined to the fossils of one system or to the study of the characteristics of the fossils as they appear in some particular zone.

THE CAMBRIAN.

N. S. Shaler (236), and again in conjunction with August F. Foerste (237), has discussed the geology and the fauna of the Cambrain district of North Attleborough and Bristol County, Massachusetts. The following species are described as new:

Obolella ? p. 27, pl. i, f. 2.
Lamellibranch ? p. 28, pl. i, f. 5.
Stenotheca curvirostra, p. 30, pl. i, f. 8.
Pleurotomaria (Raphistoma) attleborensis. p. 30, pl. ii, f. 11.
Hyolithes quadricostatus, p. 31, pl. ii, f. 15.
Salterella curvatus, p. 34, pl. ii, f. 22.
Microdiscus belli-marginatus, p. 35, pl. ii, f. 19.
Paradoxides walcotti, p. 36, pl. ii, f. 12. The author adds " Paradoxides tenellus, Billings, is in size like this species, but very distinct. It is interesting to find a Paradoxides in the Olenellus Cambrian, since its occurrence there diminishes the importance of the Paradoxides Cambrian as a Paradoxides division."
Ptychoparia mucronatus, p. 37, pl. ii, f. 21.
Ptychoparia attleborensis, p. 39, pl. ii, f. 14.

C. D. Walcott (258) discusses the age of the roofing slate of Granville, Washington County, New York. The thin-bedded limestones, imbedded in the gray and purple slates of Middle Granville, have yielded fossils which the author identifies with species of the Olenellus or Georgian fauna of the Cambrian. The red slates, in a note, are said to be of the Hudson River formation. In a second paper (265) the same author presents an important revision of former views in regard to the order of succession of the Cambrian faunas of North America. The discovery of an unbroken section in Manuel's Brook, Conception Bay, Newfoundland, extending from the Archæan Gneiss upward through the Olenellus and to the Paradoxides fauna, confirms the order for these faunas previously recognized in Sweden. The author announces the following revised classification of the Cambrian, showing this to be the true order of succession of the several terranes of the Cambrian in North America:

(1) Lower Cambrian (Georgia, Prospect, Terra Nova terranes) with the Olenellus fauna ; (2) Middle Cambrian (St. John, Avalan and Braintree terranes) with the Paradoxides fauna ; (3) Upper Cambrian (Potsdam, Knox, Tonto, Belle Isle, etc., terranes) with the Dicellocephalus or Olenellus fauna. This article is an abstract of remarks made by the author before the International Geological Congress in London, in the course of discussion on the Cambrian system, on September 18, 1888.

R. P. Whitfield (298) records the discovery of fossils from the Birdseye limestone at Fort Cassin, Vermont, on the eastern shore of Lake Champlain. The paper is an extract from Bulletin No. 8, of the American Museum of Natural History, not yet published.

C. Rominger (228) describes as new species certain fossils from Mount Stephens, Northwest Territory of Canada, as follows:

> *Ogygia klotzi,* p. 12, pl. i, f. 1.
> *Ogygia serrata,* p. 13, pl. i, f. 2, 2a.
> *Embolimus spinosa* (gen. et sp. nov.), p. 15, pl. i, f. 3.
> *Embolimus rotundata,* p. 16, pl. i, f. 4, 5.
> *Conocephalites cordilleræ,* p. 17, pl. i, f. 7.

He also recognizes the forms *Monocephalus salteri,* Bill., *Bathyurus, Agnostus, Obolella,* and a *Theca* resembling *T. primordialis,* Hall. *Bathyurus ?,* p. 18, pl. I, f. 8. *Agnostus ?,* p. 18, pl. I, f. 1 (compare *A. integer,* Barr).

Mr. Walcott (264) criticises this paper, and Mr. Rominger replies to the criticism in the American Geologist, vol. I, pp. 356–359. (See also note, Am. Geol., vol. I, p. 61.)

In the article by C. D. Walcott (264) an account is given of fossils derived from the same locality as that from which Mr. Rominger's fossils came. Mr. Walcott compares the species with the Nevada fauna of the Cambrian, the order of sequence of which is already known, and from his comparison concludes that " the Mount Stevens fauna should be referred to about the horizon of the upper portion of the Middle Cambrian fauna." (This determination is prior to Mr. Walcott's discoveries in]Newfoundland). (See 265.) Of the new genus and five new species described by Mr. Rominger, Mr. Walcott shows that the name *Embolimus* is preoccupied by Westwood ; that *Embolimus spinosa,* Rominger, 1887, was previously described as *Olenoides spinosus* by Walcott in 1886, (Bull. U. S. Geol. Survey, No. 30, p. 184, pl. xxv, f. 6), and is therefore a synonym, and that *Embolimus rotundata,* Rominger, 1887, is identical with his species *Bathyuriscus Howelli* of the same Bulletin (p. 216, pl. xxx, f. 2, 2*a*), and is also a synonym. The species *Olenoides spinosus* was recognized previously as generically distinct from *Olenoides*, and Mr. Walcott therefore proposes (p. 168) the name *Zacanthoides* (gen. nov.) for this and congeneric species. By comparison of specimens he also found that Rominger's *Ogygia serrata* is a synoym for *Olenoides Nevadensis*, Meek, and "that *Conocephalites Cordillerœ* Rom. = *Ptychoparia Cordillerœ* Rom., sp , and *Ogygia ? ? Klotzi* Rom. are new to the previously known Cambrian fauna."

W. B. Dwight (76, 77, 78) announces the discovery of the Olenellus fauna of the Cambrian in the Wappinger Valley limestone of Dutchess County, New York.

Henry Hicks (106), in the Geological Magazine, reviews the recent work done by C. D. Walcott and G. F. Matthew in the study of the faunas of the Cambrian rocks of North America.

Charles Lapworth (144) publishes evidence of the presence of the lower or Olenellus fauna in Shropshire, England, and gives tables of European series to parallel the American tables of the faunas of the Cambrian prepared by Mr. Walcott.

G. F. Matthew has contributed a number of interesting papers in regard to the Paleontology of the Cambrian (167, 169, 170, 171, 172, 173, 174, 175). The subjects of the papers published in the American Journal of Science (171) and in the Canadian Record of Science (169) are apparently more fully discussed in the paper (167) which appears in the Transactions of the Royal Society of Canada for 1887. In these various papers the author discusses the discovery and the characters of a large Trilobite which is described as new (in the Am. Jour. Sci., vol. XXXIII, p. 389) under the name *Paradoxides regina*, from Band Ic, St. John group, St. John, New Brunswick. This species is figured of the natural size in the Transactions of the Royal Society ; a small cut illustrates it in the American Journal article. This is said to be the largest Paradoxides at present known. Its size and that of other large Trilobites are given in the Royal Society paper, and this one is estimated to be 45 by 35 centimeters in length and width. The front part of the glabella is wanting in the specimen.

In the first part of this article (173) the author gives reasons for the opinion that the tracks observed in the oldest Cambrian rocks of Sweden, and called by Dr. Otto Torell *Arenicolites gigas*, and afterwards changed to *Psammichnites gigas*, which are also found in the Acadian rocks, are tracks of a gigantic marine worm.

In the latter part of this paper the author tabulates the Trilobites of the first stage of the Acadian series, and indicates their relationship to each other, and the geological position and range of each species. These Trilobites are classified in four groups; the first, *Agnostus* and *Microdiscus*—eyeless and with short thorax; second, *Conocoryphinœ*—eyeless and with long thorax; third, *Ptychoparidœ* and *Ellipsocephalidœ*—the smaller forms with eyes; fourth, the *Paradoxides*. This table is found also in the Royal Society paper (167).

In the paper (169) in the Canadian Record of Science the author discusses the characters of *Ptychoparidæ* and *Ellipsocephalidæ*, which are dwelt upon more at length in the paper, above referred to, in the Transactions of the Royal Society. From the study of the head-shield of the young of several genera, the author concludes that they have the following relative rank to each other, those which show the more primitive features coming first, viz: (1) *Ellipsocephalia*, (2) *Agraulos*, (3) *Liostracus*, (4) *Ptychoparia*, (5) *Solenopleura*.

In the fuller paper in the Transactions of the Royal Society (167) the author describes the following species:

> *Paradoxides regina*, p. 119, pl. iii (nat. size).
> *Ellipsocephalus*, sp. ? p. 129, pl. ii, f. 8 *a–c.*
> *Agraulos* (?) *Whitfieldianus*, p. 130, pl. ii, f. 1 *a–f.*
> var. *compressa*, p. 131, pl. i, f. 1 *g–i.*
> *Strenuella* (?) *Halliana*, p. 132, pl. i, f. 2 *a–m.*
> *Solenopleura Acadica*, var. *elongata*, p. 159, pl. ii, f. 6.

Plates i and ii illustrate series of young forms of the following genera: *Agraulos, Liostracus, Ptychoparia, Solenopleura,* and *Ellipsocephalus.*

The tabulation of the trilobites of the acadian is given as in the paper (173) above referred to, and the author separates *Microdiscus* from *Agnostus*, considering the former to be in advance, in degree of development, of *Agnostus*, to present more variations of form, and to possess a greater range of variability in the number of rings in the axis of the pygidium. The third and fourth groups show a change in the eye lobe; the fourth group completes this change earlier in its development than does the other. The granulated test is regarded as indicative of the earlier species of *Paradoxides*. The author remarks upon the very great importance of the early stages of *Agraulos, Liostracus,* and *Solenopleura,* "as showing the plastic condition of the organism in the initial metamorphoses. One has only to note in the series of embryonic and larval forms how different the embryos are from the adult; and yet to observe also how soon the generic and even the specific types become visible in the larval head shield, to be satisfied that the main potentiality of development is in the embryo and the embryonic stages of the organism."

The period 1887 and 1888 is notable for the accumulation and clear presentation of facts to show the impropriety of the retention in our geological nomenclature of the name "Taconic system" of Emmons.

The discusion of the subject has been continued for half a century, and many of the ablest geologists of the country have been engaged in it, starting with Messrs. Dewey, Eaton, and Emmons. It was originally proposed by Emmons as a subdivision including the rocks lying below the "Champlain Division" of the "New York system" and above the Primordial rocks. Messrs. H. D. Rogers, E. Hitchcock, Mather,

James Hall, Vanuxem, Hunt, Marcou, Barrande, and Logan were the chief disputants in the early part of the discussion, and in its later stages the more prominent participants were Dana, Billings, Hall, Hunt, Hitchcock, W. B. Dwight, Dale, Bishop, Ford, C. D. Walcott, with a number of other writers, who as advocates or opponents, have defended or opposed those more immediately engaged in the investigations.

The original idea was the erection of a new system stratigraphically anterior to the then prominent " New York system" (1842), and at first fossils did not enter into the consideration, but the character and the stratigraphical position of the rocks were alone considered, the supposition being that the " Taconic system " was an unfossiliferous series of rocks lying above the Primordial, but below the fossiliferous Palæozoic rocks. Early in the discussion fossils were discovered, which caused the " Taconic system" to come into competition with the " Cambrian system " of Sedgwick, but it was not until comparatively recently that the rocks of the so-called " Taconic system " were known to contain fossils of the Lower Silurian or " Champlain Division" of the early New York geologists. The investigations of the last few years, mainly by the discovery of fossils, have conclusively shown that the rocks included in the "Taconic system " of Emmons are stratigraphically partly anterior but in a large measure newer than the Potsdam sandstone; that they are disturbed, metamorphosed, faulted, and do not constitute a continuous series of rocks, but several interrupted masses. The impropriety of retaining the name has been elucidated by the evidence of fossils, by showing that the rocks called " Taconic " by Emmons do not constitute a geological system, as the term is applied by geologists, in that they are made up of rocks belonging to several geological horizons, separated by breaks in the series, and that " the system" as conceived by Emmons is not pre-Potsdam, but contains some rocks as much above as others are below that horizon. Hence, if the term " Taconic system " were to be adopted, if used in the original sense, it would not be applicable to any other known series of rocks; if modified to fit it to modern facts, it would not be applicable to the Taconic area.

Although defended by strong advocates on the geological side, the settlement of the problem is due chiefly to palæontology, and the prolonged extension of the dispute has resulted from the absence of the palæontological evidence which has come to light chiefly through the investigations of Messrs. Dwight, Dana, Ford, Bishop, and Walcott.

During the years 1887 and 1888 the following papers of a more or less palæontological nature were written upon this subject. Mr. J. P. Bishop (17) had shown in 1886 by fossils that the fossiliferous limestones occurring in Columbia County, on the western border of the Taconic slates, were of the age of the Hudson River shales.

C. D. Walcott (257, 260, 262) gives an account of the fossils discovered in the lowest quartzites, in the limestones, and in the Upper Taconic of Emmons.

In the paper in the American Journal of Science (260) he describes the following new species characteristic of the fauna of the so-called "Taconic" of Emmons.

Lingulella Granvillensis, p. 188, pl. i, f. 15–15c.
Linnarssonia Taconica, p. 189, pl. i, f. 18–18d.
Orthis Salemensis, p. 190, pl. i, f. 17–17a.
Hyolithellus micans, var. *rugosa*, n. var., p. 191, pl. i, f. 10.
Modiolopsis (??) *prisca*, p. 191, pl. i, f. 19.
Leperditia (I) dermatoides, p. 192, pl. i, f. 13–13a.
Aristozoe rotundata, p. 193, pl. i, f. 9.
Microdiscus connexus, p. 194, pl. i, f. 4–4b.
Olenoides Fordi, p. 195, pl. i, f. 5–5b.
Solenopleura (?) *tumida*, p. 196, pl. i, f. 2–2a.
Ptychoparia Fitchi, p. 197, pl. i, f. 6.
Ptychoparia (?) (*subgenus* ?) *clavata*, p. 198, pl. i, f. 3.

In the "Lower Taconic" (262) he records the discovery of *Hyolithes*, *Nothozoe Vermontana*, and *Olenellus Asaphoides* in the quartzites, and *Maclurea*, *Murchisonia*, and *Raphistoma* in the eastern limestone.

Raphael Pumpelly (223) communicates a note on the fossils of Littleton, New Hampshire. These fossils were reported by T. Nelson Dale, and were determined by C. D. Walcott and C. Rominger, by whom they were referred to the Niagara age, while Billings determined other fossils, derived from the same formations by C. H. Hitchcock, to be of Helderberg age. In a note in the American Journal, vol. XXXVI, p. 255, it is stated that C. H. Hitchcock referred these fossils to the Niagara group. (See Whitfield, Amer. Journ. Sci., vol. XXV, p. 369.)

In 1888 Mr. Walcott (262) and Professor Dana (59) showed the impropriety of continuing the use of the name "Taconic system," and Mr. Marcou (154, 155) defended the usage of "Taconic." In the meeting of the International Congress at London the facts regarding the discovery of fossils of the faunas of the Lower Silurian appeared as conclusive argument against the recognition of the "Taconic System," and the terms "Cambrian," "Lower Silurian," and "Upper Silurian" were accepted for the three lower systems of the Palæozoic.

THE SILURIAN, LOWER AND UPPER.

Henry M. Ami has published several brief articles on the Paleontology of the Paleozoic rocks in Canada (3, 4, 5, 6, 7, 8, 9). In vol. I of the Ottawa Naturalist (3) the author refers to the occurrence of *Siphonotreta Scotica*, Davidson, in association with a fauna of the Utica formation in a band of impure limestone on the banks of the Rideau River, near Ottawa. In the transactions of the Field Naturalists' Club (8) he gives further account of the Utica fossils from Rideau, and notes their position in the section which he examined along Crichton street. Several species are recorded as new to the locality, and two, marked as new species, are referred to *Ambonychia* and *Metoptoma*. In the article in the Canadian Record of Science (9) he discusses the fossils from the

Utica formation at Point-à Pic. No new species are named, but a representative of the genus *Siphonotreta* is described in detail and compared with *Siphonotreta Scotica* of Davidson and *S. micula*, McCoy.

T. W. Edwin Sowter (243) offers some notes on the Chazy formation at Aylmer, Province of Quebec. He proposes the following new forms, giving brief descriptions, but no specific names:

> *Murchisonia* n. sp., p. 13.
> *Euomphalus* —— sp. ? p. 14.
> *Pleurotomaria* n. sp., p. 14.
> *Pleurotomaria* (*Scalites*) n. sp., p. 14.
> *Metoptoma* n. sp., p. 14.

S. W. Ford (88) comments upon certain fossils discovered in Quebec. The fossils were sent the author by A. R. C. Selwyn, director of the Canadian Survey, and the study of them indicates to the author a horizon equivalent to the "Levis" formation of the Canadian geologists.

Charles Lapworth (143,145) gives an account of some Graptolites discovered in Kicking Horse Pass, Manitoba, British Columbia, and on the south side of the St. Lawrence and on the north shore of the island of Orleans, and from near Quebec.

A. F. Foerste has added considerably to the list of species from the Paleozoic of Ohio. In the paper (80) in the Bulletin of Denison University, vol. II (1887), the author has described the following species . from the Clinton group of Ohio:

> *Acidaspis Ortoni*, p. 90, pl. viii, f. 1 (described and figured as *Acidaspis*, vol. I, p. 101, pl. xiii, f. 23).
> *Proetus determinatus*, p. 91, pl. viii, f. 2, 3, 3a (= *Bathyurus* vol. I, p. 103, pl. xiv, f. 5.)
> *Calymene Vogdesi*, p. 95, pl. viii, f. 12, 13, 14, 15, 16 (= *Calymene*, vol. I, p. 109, pl. xiii, f. 24).
> *Phacops pulchellus*, p. 99, pl. viii, f. 4, 20, 21 (= *Arionellus*, vol. I, p. 114, pl. xiv, f. 3).
> *Encrinurus Thresheri*, p. 101, pl. viii, f. 26.
> *Dictyonema pertenue*, p. 107, pl. viii, f. 27 a–b.
> *Dictyonema scalariforme*, p. 108, pl. viii, f. 28, 29.

In Part III of the same bulletin (81) he describes the Bryozoa [Polyzoa] of the Clinton group of Ohio; several genera and species are figured and described, and the following new species are named, described, and figured: (In his nomenclature he has followed the classification of E. O. Ulrich.)

> *Hemitrypa Ulrichi*, p. 152, pl. xv, f. 2; pl. xvii, f. 2.
> *Pachydictya emaciata*, p. 162, pl. xv, f. 8; pl. xvii, f. 8.
> *Pachydictya bifurcata*, var. *instabilis*, p. 164, pl. xv, f. 10.
> *Pachydictya turgida*, p. 164, pl. xv, f. 11; pl. xvii, f. 11.
> *Pachydictya obesa*, p. 165, pl. xv, f. 12.
> *Prasopora parmula*, p. 170, pl. xv, f. 14; pl. xvii, f. 14.
> *Monotrypella confluens*, p. 172, pl. xvi, f. 4; pl. xvii, f. 15.
> *Callopora magnopora*, p. 173, pl. xvi, f. 5; pl. xvii, f. 16.
> *Callopora Ohioensis*, p. 174, pl. xvi, f. 6; pl. xvii, f. 17.

In vol. III, Part II (1888), of the same bulletin he publishes (84) some notes on the Paleozoic fossils, and describes the following new species :

Lichas Halli, p. 118, pl. xiii, f. 4.
Encrinurus Browningi, p. 122, pl. xiii, f. 7.
Encrinurus Mitchelli, p. 124, pl. xiii, f. 2, 3, 20.
Phacops serratus, p. 126, pl. xiii, f. 1.
Cyathophyllum australa, p. 128, pl. xiii, f. 12, 13, 14.
Cyathophyllum patula, p. 129, pl. xiii, f. 9, 10, 11.
Endophyllum ——, p. 131, pl. xiii, f. 16, 17.

U. P. and Joseph F. James contribute an article (130) in the Journal Cincinnati Society of Natural History, on the Monticuliporoid Corals of the Cincinnati group, with a revision of the species. The work consists principally of a critical re-arrangement of the species heretofore described, of which a great number have been described by E. O. Ulrich. The authors attempt to make no new species, and the only new form described is *Monticulipora hospitalis*, var. *neglecta* (var. nov.), vol. XI, p. 27, pl. i, f. 3.

F. J. H. Merrill (179) reports the discovery of fossils in a limestone on the Green Pond Mountain of New Jersey, which he identifies as belonging to a Lower Helderberg fauna. Rocks of the Paleozoic (from Oneida to Hamilton) epochs are recognized.

Fred. H. Newell (200a) describes the following new species of Niagara Cephalopods from northern Indiana:

Gomphoceras Wabashensis, pp. 470–473, 3 wood-cuts.
Gomphoceras linearis, pp. 473–475, 2 wood-cuts.
Gomphoceras angustum, pp. 475–476, 1 wood-cut.
Gomphoceras projectum, pp. 476–478, 4 wood-cuts.
Hexameroceras delphicolum, pp. 479–481, 4 wood-cuts.
Hexameroceras cacabiformis, pp. 481–483, 3 wood-cuts.
Ascoceras Indianensis, pp. 484–485, 4 wood-cuts.

E. N. S. Ringueberg (225) reports the following new species from the Niagara shales of western New York :

Buthotrepis gregaria,'p. 131, pl. vii, f. 1.
Inocaulis anastomatica, p. 131, pl. vii, f. 2.
Dendrocrinus celsus, p. 132, pl. vii, f. 3.
Mariacrinus warreni, p. 133, pl. vii, f. 4.
Orthis acutiloba, p. 134, pl. vii, f. 5.
Hyolit[h]es subimbricatus, p. 135, pl. vii, f. 7.
Plumulites gracilissimus, p. 136, pl. vii, f. 8.

In another paper (226) the same author gives lists of the species recognized in the following zones, which he has studied. To these zones he applies the names the Niagara Transition group, the Niagara shales, and the Homocrinus band.

The following species are described and figured by George B. Simpson (240) in a paper entitled " Descriptions of new species of fossils from the Clinton, Lower Helderberg, Chemung, and Waverly groups, found in the collections of the Geological Survey of Pennsylvania," which was read at the meeting of the American Philosophical Society, December 5, 1888. (Not published before January, 1889.—H. S. W.)

Acervularia communis.	*Orthis subcircula.*
Aviculopecten æqualata.	*Platyceras brevis.*
Chonetes punctata.	*Platyceras dorsalis.*
Cladopora rectilineata.	*Platyceras inæqualis.*
Cyrtina triplicata.	*Platyceras mitelliformis.*
Goniophora curvata.	*Platyceras striata.*
Leptodesma leiopteroides.	*Platyceras varians.*
Leptodesma parallela.	*Ptychopteria obsoleta.*
Lyriopecten alternatus.	*Rhynchonella (Stenocisma) lævis.*
Meristella incerta.	*Rhynchonella medialis.*
Modiolopsis subrhomboidea.	*Rhynchonella striata.*
Modiomorpha rigidula.	*Syringothyris angulata.*
Nuculu sinuosa.	*Syringothyris randalli.*
Nucula subtrigona.	*Tellinomya (Palaeoneilo) cuneata.*
Orthis pennsylvanica.	*Tellinomya (Palaeoneilo) diminuens.*

THE DEVONIAN.

Robert Bell (15) in his Report G of the Annual Report of the Geological Survey of Canada for 1886, notes the occurrence of fossiliferous limestones in the valley of the At-ta-wa-pish-kat and Albany Rivers. These fossils were submitted to Prof. J. F. Whiteaves, the paleontologist of the Survey, who identified them as indicating Devonian faunas (pp. 27, G-33, G). The species reported are mainly corals and brachiopods; Mr. Whiteaves thinks them of a Lower Devonian horizon. No new species are defined.

S. Calvin (21) records the fact of the appearance of a coral-bearing zone intercalated between two brachiopod zones in the Hamilton rocks in western Ontario, and remarks upon the different form assumed by the *Spirifera mucronata* of the first and third zones. The same author (20) describes a new genus and species of tubicolar Annelida from the Hamilton period, Roberts's Ferry, Iowa; these are *Streptindites* (gen. nov.), p. 27, and *S. acervulariæ* (sp. nov.), p. 27. No illustrations are given.

J. M. Clarke (28) gives an account of the Annelid teeth from the Devonian of Ontario County, New York. Twenty-nine specimens of these teeth are figured, twenty-two of which express varieties of form appearing in the Black Shale of Naples, and are regarded as varieties of the form described by Hinde under the name of *Polygnathus dubius.* The other forms are referred to the genera *Arabellites, Prioniodus, Œnonites,* and *Ennicites.* These forms have heretofore generally gone under the name of "Conodonts."

James Hall (97) adds another volume to the valuable contributions to the paleontology of New York State. This volume (VI) contains the corals and Bryozoa [Polyzoa] from the Lower Helderberg, Upper Helderberg, and Hamilton groups. There are described one hundred and three species from the Lower Helderberg, one hundred and fifty-four from the Upper Helderberg, and one hundred and twenty-one from the

Hamilton, of which all but fifty-five species are illustrated. Many of them have been described or figured, or both, in either the twenty-sixth, or the thirty-second, report of the State Museum of Natural History, or in the reports of the State geologist for 1882 and for 1884, and the following new genera, subgenera, species, and varieties are described:

Ptychonema, n. s. g., p. xiv.
Bactropora, n. g., p. xv.
Callotrypa, n. s. g., p. xvi.
Cœlocaulis, n. s. g., p. xvi.
Favicella, n. g., p. xviii.
Coscinella, n. g., p. xix.
Ceramella, n. g., p. xix.
Stictoporina, n. s. g., p. xx.
Thamnotrypa, n. g., p. xxi.
Ptychonema, n. g., p. 14.
Genus *Trematopora*.
Orthopora, n. s. g., p. 16.
Genus *Callopora*.
Cœlocaulis, n. s. g., p. 23.
Callopora (Cœlocaulis) mediopora, p. 23, pl. xiv, f. 18; pl. xxiii, f. 11–13.
Callotrypa, n. s. g., p. 24.
Callopora (Callotrypa) striata, p. 26, pl. xi, f. 38–41; pl. xxiii, f. 13, 14.
Fistulipora triloba, p. 29.
Lichenalia serialis, p. 32, pl. xiii, f. 17, 18; pl. xv, f. 6.
Paleschara? tenuis, p. 36.
Stictopora obsoleta, p. 37, pl. xxiii a, f. 22.
Stictopora granatula, p. 38, pl. xi, f. 16; pl. xxiii a, f. 17.
Fenestella Noe, p. 47, pl. xiii, f. 19–22.
Fenestella Spio, p. 47, pl. xix, f. 16.
Fenestella (Hemitrypa) biserialis, var. *exilis*, n. var., p. 57, pl. xxii, f. 14, 15.
Fenestella (Polypora) stricta, p. 59, pl. xix, f. 1, 2.
Fenestella (Polypora) obliqua, p. 64, pl. xviii, f. 8, 9.
Fenestella adornata, p. 66, pl. xxii, f. 7, 8.
Monotrypa? spinosula, p. 67, pl. xvi, f. 25.
Paleschara concentrica, p. 67, pl. xvi, f. 24.
Thamnotrypa, n. g., p. 101.
Fenestella verrucosa, p. 110, pl. xlii, f. 11; pl. xlvi, f. 22, 24.
Fenestella biseriata, p. 113, pl. xlii, f. 16–18.
Fenestella proceritas, p. 115, pl. xlvi, f. 32, 35, 36.
Fenestella tuberculata, p. 116, pl. xlvi, f. 25, 26, 33, 34.
Fenestella clathrata, p. 117.
Fenestella (Unitrypa) acaulis, var. *inclinis*, n. var., p. 132.
Fenestella (Unitrypa) projecta, p. 132.
Fenestella (Unitrypa) transversa, p. 132.
Fenestella (Unitrypa) nana, p. 133.
Fenestella (Unitrypa) ficticius, p. 137, pl. lii, f. 11–15.
Fenestella (Unitrypa) acclivis, p. 138, pl. lii, f. 16–23.
Fenestella (Unitrypa?) consimilis, p. 142, pl. liv, f. 7–9.
Loculipora, Rominger MS. (gen. nov.), p. 144.
Fenestella (Loculipora) circumstata, p. 144, pl. liv, f. 22–25.
Fenestella (Hemitrypa) biordo, p. 149.
Fenestella (Polypora) carinella, p. 151, pl. xlii, f. 1, 2.
Fenestella (Polypora) rustica, p. 169, pl. xliii, f. 10–13.
Fenestella (Ptiloporella) inequalis, p. 171.

A valuable synopsis of the genera, occupying sixteen pages, has been prepared by Charles E. Beecher. The original drawings were all made by George B. Simpson, whose name appears on the title-page, and the author says (p. 10) that "credit is due him for the preparation of a large part of the specific descriptions."

Prof. Charles Barrois (10) presents a review of the above volume in the "Annales" of the "Société Géologique du Nord."

James Hall (98) published in 1888 another valuable contribution to the paleontology of New York State. Although many of the species figured have been described before, the new descriptions and diagnoses of the species, and better illustrations than have ever appeared before, will be of great value to the student of paleontology. One hundred and forty-four species of Crustacea are described and illustrated, ninety-seven of them Trilobites, the whole included under twenty-eight genera. The author acknowledges the assistance of Mr. John M. Clarke "in the preparation of the matter for the press and in the critical study of the material." A useful synopsis of genera, occupying forty-four pages, precedes the descriptive part of the work. The following new forms are described:

Genus *Dalmanites:*
  Subgenus *Hausmannia*, n. s.-g., p xxxi.
    Coronura, n. s.-g., p. xxxii.
    Corycephalus, n. s.-g., p. xxxiv.
Genus *Lichas:*
  Subgenus *Ceratolichas*, n. s.-g. p. xl.
Genus *Mesothyra*, nov. gen., p. lvi, pl. xxxii.
Genus *Rhinocaris*, nov. gen., p. lviii.
Genus *Schizodiscus*, nov. gen., p. lxii.
Genus *Protobalanus*, nov. gen., p. lxii.
Genus *Strobilepis*, nov. gen., p. lxiii.
Bronteus Tullius, p. 12, pl. viii, f. 34–36.
Phacops cristata, var. *pipa*, n. var., p. 18, pl. viiia, f. 5–18.
Hausmannia, n. s.-g., p. 28.
Dalmanites (Hausmannia) concinnus, var. *serrula*, n. var., p. 30, pl. xia, f. 12.
Dalmanites (Hausmannia) phacoptyx, p. 31, pl. xia, f. 23–26.
Coronura, n. s.-g., p. 33.
Dalmanites (Cryphæus) comis, p. 41, pl. xvia, f. 1.
Dalmanites (Cryphæus) Barrisi, p. 48, pl. xvia, f. 18.
Corycephalus, n. s.-g., p. 55.
Dalmanites (Corycephalus) pygmaeus, p. 56, pl. xi, f. 5–8.
Dalmanites anchiops, var. *sobrinus*, n. var., p. 62, pl. ix, f. 11.
Acidaspis callicera, p. 69, pl. xvib, f. 1–13.
Acidaspis Romingeri, p. 71, pl. xvib, f. 15–18.
Acisdaspis, sp., p. 71, pl. xvib, f. 14.
Lichas (Conolichas) hispidus, p. 77, pl. xixa, f. 14, 17, 18.
Lichas (Hoplolichas) hylæus, p. 81, pl. xixb, f. 1, 2.
Lichas (Arges) contusus, p. 83, pl. xixb, f. 3–6.
Ceratolichas, n. s.-g., p. 84.
Lichas (Ceratolichas) gryps, p. 84, pl. xixb, f. 7–13.
Lichas (Ceratolichas) dracon, p. 85, pl. xixb, f. 14–17.

Lichas (Dicranogmus) ptyonurus, p. 86, pl. xixb, f. 19–21.
Proëtus, sp. ? p. 94, pl. xxii, f. 5, 6.
Proëtus curvimarginatus, p. 94, pl. xxii, f. 13–19.
Proëtus latimarginatus, p. 97, pl. xxii, f. 7–12.
Proëtus folliceps, p. 101, pl. xxiii, f. 3–8.
Proëtus microgemma, p. 109, pl. xxii, f. 33, 34.
Proëtus stenopyge, p. 110, pl. xxii, f. 27.
Proëtus ovifrons, p. 110, pl. xxii, f. 31, 32.
Proëtus delphinulus, p. 111, pl. xxiii, f. 1, 2; pl. xxv, f. 6.
Proëtus tumidus, p. 113, pl. xxiii, f. 9.
Proëtus jejunus, p. 124, pl. xxv, f. 7.
Proëtus Nevadæ, p. 129, pl. xxiii, f. 19.
Phaëthonides arenicolus, p. 134, pl. xxv, f. 12, 13.
Phaëthonides varicella, p. 135, pl. xxiv, f, 29–31.
Phaëthonides gemmæus, p. 136, pl. xxiv, f. 32–36.
Phaëthonides cyclurus, p. 137, pl. xxiv, f. 26–28; pl. xxv, f. 11.
Cyphaspis stephanophora, p. 142, pl. xxiv, f. 2–6.
Cyphaspis diadema, p. 144, pl. xxiv, f. 13.
Cyphaspis hybrida, p. 144, pl. xxiv, f. 14.
Cyphaspis ornata, var. *baccata*, n. var., p. 146, pl. xxiv, f. 22, 23.
Cyphaspis craspedota, p. 148, pl. xxiv, f. 15–20.
Cyphaspis cœlebs, p. 151, pl. xxiv, f. 1.
Echinocaris condylepis, p. 173, pl. xxix, f. 14–17.
Elymocaris capsella, p. 181, pl. xxxi, f. 4.
Mesothyra, n. g., p. 187.
Mesothyra spumœa, p. 193, pl. xxxii, f. 8, 9; pl. xxxiv, f. 2.
Mesothyra (Dithyrocaris?) Veneris, p. 193, pl. xxxiii, f. 3.
Rhinocaris, n. g. (J. M. C.), p. lviii.
Rhinocaris columbina, p. 195, pl. xxxi, f. 16–21.
Rhinocaris scaphoptera, p. 197, pl. xxxi, f. 22, 23.
Schizodiscus, n. g. (J. M. C.), p. 207.
Schizodiscus capsa, p. 207, pl. xxxv, f. 1–9.
Protobalanus, n. g. (R. P. Whitfield), p. 209.
Protobalanus Hamiltonensis, p. 209, pl. xxxvi, f. 23.
Palæocrusia, n. g. (J. M. C.), p. 210.
Palæocrusia Devonica, p. 210, pl. xxxvi, f. 24–26.
Strobilepis, n. g. (J. M. C.), p. 212.
Strobilepis spinigera, p. 212, pl. xxxvi, f. 20–22.
Turrilepas flexuosus, p. 215, pl. xxxvi, f. 1.
Turrilepas cancellatus, p. 216, pl. xxxvi, f. 2.
Turrilepas squama, p. 217, pl. xxxvi, f. 5–8.
Turrilepas nitidulus, p. 218, pl. xxxvi, f. 4.
Turrilepas foliatus, p. 218, pl. xxxvi, f. 15.
Turrilepas tener, p. 219, pl. xxxvi, f. 9–14.

A supplement (99) to vol. v, pt. ii, by the same author, this publication is bound up with volume VII (98); it contains descriptions and illustrations of Pteropoda, Cephalopoda, and Annelida. A valuable discussion of the characters of *Cornulites* and other tubercolar Annelida occupies pages 8 to 24. The descriptions of the Cephalopoda (pp. 25 to 44), are by C. E. Beecher, and are here published for the first time, although the figures illustrating them were previously published with the names in the Fifth Annual Report of the State Geologist in

1886. The following new genera, species, and varieties appear in this volume:

Tentaculites Niagarensis (Hall), var. Cumberlandiæ, n. var., p. 5, pl. cxiv, f. 3-6.
Tentaculites acula, p. 6, pl. cxiv, f. 15-17.
Tentaculites Dexithea, p. 6, pl. cxiv, f. 18, 19.
Hyolithes heros, p. 7, pl. cxiv, f. 24-27.
Styliola spica, p. 7, pl. cxiv, f. 28.
Coleolus Herzeri, p. 7, pl. cxiv, f. 29.
Pharetrella, nov. gen., p. 7.
Pharetrella tenebrosa, p. 7, pl. cxiv, f. 30, 31.
Cornulites immaturus, p. 18, pl. cxv, f. 40.
Cornulites, sp. ?, p. 19, pl. cxvi, f. 24, 25.
Cornulites chrysalis, p. 20, pl. cxvi, f. 26-28.
Cornulites cingulatus, p. 20, pl. cxvi, f. 29.
Cornulites tribulis, p. 20, pl. cxvi, f. 30.

James Hall (95) publishes in the Sixth Annual Report of the State Geologist descriptions of Fenestellidæ of the Hamilton group. Eighteen species were previously described, but not figured, in the Thirty-sixth Annual Report of the New York State Museum, 1884, and are here re-described and figured. Two new species from the Hamilton are described, one of which is figured; two new species are from the Waverly of Ohio; the new species are as follows:

Fenestella albida, p. 48, pl. vii, f. 1-7, Waverly group, Richfield, Summit County, Ohio.
Fenestella hemicycla, p. 55, pl. vii, f. 12-16, Darien, New York, and West Williams, Canada.
Fenestella aperta, p. 58, pl. iv, f. 1-5, Waverly group, Richfield, Ohio.
Fenestella spissa, p. 59 (no figure), Hamilton, West Bloomfield, New York.

Samuel G. Williams (304) contributes a paper with the title "The Tully limestone, its distribution and its known fossils." The author offers a list of over a hundred species, the majority of which are common in the Hamilton shales immediately below the Tully limestone. The indefinite notion the author has of the limits of the Tully limestone is shown by his statement on page 20, that the estimate of the thickness varies "according as one includes or excludes the impure mixed top and bottom portions." This easily explains the length of the list of "known" Tully species. The transition from the richly fossiliferous fauna of the upper layers of the Hamilton to the comparatively barren Tully limestone is so sharp that it is not safe to include even the species found in the shale adhering to the bottom of the heavy blocks as "known fossils" of the Tully fauna.

C. S. Prosser (222) read an interesting paper before the American Association for the Advancement of Science on the Upper Hamilton of Chenango and Otsego Counties; the order and composition of the faunas of these rocks have been carefully studied by the author.

Charles R. Keyes (135) describes the following two new fossils from the Devonian of Iowa:

Conocardium altum, p. 26, pl. xii, f. 4a, 4b, Iowa City, Iowa.
Cyrtoceras opimum, p. 26, pl. xii, f. 5, Johnson County, Iowa.

Clement L. Webster (272–276) has communicated several papers on the Paleontology of the Devonian rocks of Northern Iowa. Unfortunately he has named and published descriptions of several supposed new species. Among the species reported (276) as "known to occur in the Rockford shale and the rocks a few feet below" are *Spirifera disjuncta* Sow. and *Rhynchonella venustula*, Hall. Having never before heard of the occurrence of these species in the Devonian of the interior, the writer requested a loan of the specimens so named; the author kindly sent specimens for examination of the former, which proved to be not *Spirifera disjuncta*, but the form which appears to be known in Iowa under the name *Spirifera Parryana*, Hall, a form quite distinct from *Sp. disjuncta*, although associated with it in some beds in New York. This casts doubt upon the other identifications. The specific names published by the author with descriptions, but without illustrations, are as follows (all from the Rockford shales of Iowa, and all in the American Naturalist, vol. XXII) :

Rhynchonella subacuminata, p. 1015.
Athyris minutissima, p. 1015.
Paracyclas validalinea, p. 1016.
Platystoma mirus, p. 1016.
Platystoma pervetus, p. 1016.
Naticopsis rarus, p. 1016.
Turbo strigillata, p. 1016.
Turbo (?) incertus, p. 1017.
Holopea tenuicarinata, p. 1017.
Cyclonema brevilineata, p. 1017.
Cyclonema subcrenula, p. 1018.
Spirifera substrigosa, p. 1101.
Atrypa hystrix, var. elongata, n. var., p. 1104.
Atrypa hystrix, var. planosulcata, n. var., p. 1104.

J. F. Whiteaves (291) gives a list of the fossils from the Hamilton formation of Ontario, and describes the following new species :

Homocrinus crassus, p. 95, pl. 12, f. 2.
Dolatocrinus Canadensis, p. 99, pl. 12, f. 3, 3a, 3b, and 3c.
Pentremitidea filosa, p. 104, pl. 14, f. 1, 1a, 1b.
Lingula Thedfordensis, p. 111, pl. 15, f. 1.
Spirifera subdecussata, p. 114, pl. 15, f. 3, 3a.
Platyostoma plicatum, p. 118, pl. 13, f. 6.

H. S. Williams (301) presents a paper in which the various types of the Devonian system in North America are classified and defined. This paper was read at the New York meeting of the American Association for the Advancement of Science, August, 1887, and is a part of the "Report on the Upper Paleozoic (Devonic)," published by the American Committee of the International Congress of Geologists, and presented to the London session in September, 1888. The author shows that the rocks of the Devonian system present at least four types of stratigraphical order and composition, and that the paleontological history recorded in the four areas is distinct, both in the composition of the faunas as a whole and in their subdivisions into separate temporary faunas; that in different regions the same order of sequence of genera and species in general takes place, but that for the Devonian system, at least, the stratigraphical lines of demarkation separating one temporary fauna from the next, are comparatively local and not uniform for different regions of America.

The same author (302) gives an extended discussion, in Bulletin No. 41 of the U. S. Geological Survey, of the fossil faunas of the Upper Devonian of western New York. This paper is not merely a list of the species of the Upper Devonian, but the author attempts to ascertain, by a comparative study of the species and of the faunas of the successive geological stages, the laws of variation or modification affecting the species and faunas in their passage upward through the series and in their relations to geographical distribution. Few new species are described, but frequent reference is made to the modifications expressed in the characters of species as they are traced upwards in the rocks (historically), and from region to region during the same stage (geographically). These variations are also expressed by the separate tabulation of the species forming the fauna of each fossiliferous zone. The following new forms are described and figured:

Dipterus Nelsoni, Newberry, MS., p. 62, pl. iii, f. 1.
Dipterus (?) *lævis*, Newberry, MS., p. 63, pl. iii, f. 2.
Pterinopecten (?) *Atticus*, p. 35, pl. iii, f. 10, 11.
Ptychopteria (?) *mesocostalis*, p. 35, pl. iii, f. 9.
Lunulicardium lævis, p. 39., pl. iii, f. 6, 8.
Aptychus (of Goniatites), p. 35, pl. iii, f. 3, 4.
Lucina Wyomingensis, p. 44, pl. iii, f. 13.
Lucina Varysburgia, p. 44, pl. iii, f. 14.
Arenicolites duplex, p. 46, pl. iv, f. 9.
Rhynchonella Allegania, p. 87, 88, pl. iv, f. 1-8.

The name *Spiraxis* proposed by Professor Newberry (Ann. N. Y. Acad. Sc., vol. III, 1885, pp. 217–220, pl. XVIII,) for a peculiar screw-like fossil occurring in the sandy deposits of the Upper Devonian, was observed to be preoccupied by C. B. Adams, 1850, for a genus of Gasteropoda, and the author of the above paper (302) having occasion to record the occurrence of two species of the genus in the Wolf Creek conglomerate, proposes the name *Prospiraxis* as a substitute (p. 86) for the generic name of these peculiar fossils.

THE CARBONIFEROUS AND PERMIAN.

Charles S. Beachler (13, 14) contributes two short papers on the Lower Carboniferous beds of Crawfordsville, Ind.; nothing of particular palæontological interest is communicated.

E. W. Claypole (33) offers a few notes on the discovery of specimens of *Dadoxylon* and other genera of fossil wood in the Carboniferous rocks of Ohio.

C. L. Herrick (105) contributes a number of parts of a continuous article illustrating the palæontology of Licking County, Ohio. These

are published in the Bulletin of the Denison University Laboratory of
Science, and consist of descriptions of the geology, outcrops, structure,
etc., of the Waverly rocks of Licking County, and descriptions with
figures of the forms of fossils discovered in the rocks. He has collected
a valuable series of the Waverly fossils which the illustrations help to
make familiar to scientists. He has described a large number of
new species, and an examination of the descriptions and figures leads
one to think that many of them might better have been called varieties
of already described forms, or left without specific names until more
perfect specimens were discovered and fuller comparisons made with
already described species. The following are the new species described
in volume II, 1887:

> *Bellerophon (sub-cordiformis)*, p. 18, pl. ii, f. 7, *a, b, c.*
> *Entolium attenuatum*, p. 24, pl. i, f. 11.
> *Aviculopecten scalaris*, p. 26, pl. i, f. 8.
> *Aviculopecten sorer*, p. 27, pl. i, f. 7, pl. iii, f. 16.
> *Crenipecten Foerstii*, p. 28, pl. iii, f. 9, 9a.
> *Solenomya (?) meekiana*, p. 30, pl. iv, f. 9.
> *Solenomya subradiata*, p. 30, pl. iii, f. 8.
> *Gervillia (?) ohioense*, p. 36, pl. iv, f. 13, pl. iii, **f. 12.**
> *Schizodus affinis (?)*, p. 41, pl. iv, f. 22, 22a.
> *Schizodus sub-circularis*, p. 41, pl. iv, f. 24.
> *Schizodus (?) spellmani*, p. 42, pl. iii, f. 14.
> *Lingula tighti*, p. 43, pl. iv, f. 5.
> *Stricklandinia (?) subquadrata*, p. 49, pl. i, f. 14, 14a.
> *Phillipsia trinucleata*, p. 64.

And in the list of additional fossils from the coal measures at Flint
Ridge, *Pleurophorus immaturus* (sp. ? n.) is briefly described, p. 145,
and figured (pl. xiv, fig. 17).

In volume III, 1888, the following from the sub-Carboniferous and
Waverly are described:

> *Nautilus (?) bisulcatus*, p. 20, pl. xi, f. 16.
> *Phillipsia præcursor*, p. 29, pl. xii, f. 1.
> *Chonetes tumidus*, p. 36, pl. ii, f. 21.
> *Orthis Vanuxemi*, Hall, var. *pulchellus*, var. n., p. 38, pl. v, f. 9 (?=var. of
>   Michelina).
> *Spirifer winchelli*, p. 46, pl. v, f. 28, pl. ii, f. 16.
> *Spiraferina depressa*, sp. n. ? p. 47, pl. x, f. 3.
> *Aviculopecten perelongatus*, p. 50.
> *Aviculopecten (granvillensis*, sp. n.), p. 50, pl. x, f. 8, pl. xii, f. 11.
> *Aviculopecten cooperi*, p. 51, pl. xii, f. 16, 17.
> *Crenipecten sub-cordiformis*, p. 53, pl. vii, f. 4, 5.
> *Crenipecten senilis*, p. 54, pl. iii, f. 1.
> *Aviculopecten (Lyriopecten?) cancellatus*, p. 54, pl. xii, f. 7.
> *Linatulina (?) ohioensis*, p. 55, pl. ii, f. 20, pl. iii, f. 10.
> *Streblopteria media*, p. 56, pl. iii, f. 8, 9.
> *Streblopteria squama*, p. 57, pl. vii, f. 14.
> *Streblopteria gracilis*, p. 57, pl. vii, f. 12.
> *Pterinopecten cariniferus*, p. 58, pl. xii, f. 8, 9, 42.
> *Pteronites (Leptodesma)? obliquus*, p. 58, pl. vii, f. 7 ; pl. iv, f. 20.
> *Leptodesma (?) scutella*, p. 59, pl. iv, f. 16.

Posidonomya (Streblopteria) fragilis, p. 59, pl. vi, f. 1.
Promacra (?) *truncatus*, p. 60, pl. iii, f. 30.
Leioptera ortoni, p. 60, pl. vii, f. 1.
Leioptera halli, p. 61, pl. vii, f. 31.
Leiopteria, sp., p. 62, pl. iii, f. 6.
Modiola waverliensis, p. 63, pl. i, f. 9 ; pl. iv, f. 10 ; pl. vii, f. 29.
Schizodus newarkensis, p. 64, pl. x, f. 1.
Schizodus chemungensis var. (?) *æqualis*, H., p. 64, pl. i, f. 25 ; pl. ix, f. 20.
Sanguinolites (Gomophora) senilis, p. 66, pl. ix, f. 28.
Allorisma cooperi, p. 72, pl. vi, f. 10.
Allorisma convexa, p. 74, pl. xii, f. 27.
Macrodon (?) *triangularis*, p. 74, pl. viii, f. 8.
Nuculana (Leda) spatulata, p. 79, pl. ix, f. 11 (12 ?) ; pl. vii, f. 35.
Nuculana (Leda) similis, p. 78, pl. iv, f. 15.
Palæoneilo ellipticus, p. 80. Three varieties.
Arca ornata, p. 83, pl. ix, f. 18.
Goniodon, gen. nov., p. 84. *G. ohioensis*, p. 84, pl. xii, f. 23, 24, 25.
Pleurotomaria (Cyclomena ?) *strigillata*, p. 86, pl. i, f. 10 ; pl. ii, f. 25·
Natiscopsis (?), sp. n., p. 87, pl. xii, f. 37.
Bellerophon, sp , (?) p. 90, pl. xii, f. 36.
Dentalium granvillensis, p. 92.
Schizodus (Protoschizodus) palæoneiliformis, p. 96, pl. xii, f. 44.

In volume IV, 1888, the following are described from the same form·
ations :

Lingula atra, p. 16, pl. x, f. 30.
Lingula gannensis, p. 17, pl. iii, f. 2, 3.
Lingula meeki, p. 18, pl. x, f. 31.
Lingula waverlyensis, p. 18, pl. iii, f. 1.
Productus raricostatus, p. 19, pl. iii, f. 19 ; vol. III, pl. iii, f. 28 ?.
Productus (Newberryi, var. ?) *annosus*, var. n., p. 20, pl. iii, f. 17.
Productus rushvillensis, p. 22, pl. iii, f. 15.
Productus nodocostatus, p. 23.
Athyris ashlandensis, p. 24, pl. iii, f. 6.
Terebratula (?) *inconstans*, sp. n. (cf. *T. lincklæni*, H.), p. 24, pl. xi, f. 18 ; pl. iii,
     f. 8, 9.
Rhynchospira (?) *ashlandensis*, p. 25, pl. iii, f. 16.
Spirifer (Martinia) tenuispinatus, p. 27, pl. ii, f. 4.
Spirifer deltoideus, p. 27, pl. ii, f. 7.
Allorisma cuyahoga, p. 28, pl. x, f. 34.
Allorisma consaguinata, p. 29, pl. xi, f. 13.
Leiopteria nasutus, p. 29, pl. xi, f. 30.
Avicula (?) *sub-spatula*, p. 30, pl. v, f. 11 ; vol. III, pl. iii, f. 6.
Edmondia sulcifera, p. 30, pl. v, f. 1, 2.
Lyriopecten nodocostatus, p. 32, pl. xi, f. 5.
Pterinopecten (?) *ashlandensis*, p. 33, pl. xi, f. 4.
Grammysia ovata, p. 35, pl. iii, f. 12.
Grammysia famelica, p. 35, pl. vi, f. 5.
Schizodus (chemungensis, var.) *prolongatus*, p. 36, pl. vi, f. 1, vol. III, pl. ix, f. 20.
Macrodon newarkensis, p. 36, pl. iv, f. 19.
Macrodon striato-costatus, p. 37, pl. vi, f. 7 ; pl. xi, f. 37.
Macrodon, sp., p. 38, pl. xi, f. 28.
Cypricardinia (Microdon ?) *scitula*, p. 38, pl. vi, f. 8.
Oracardia, gen. n., p. 41.
Oracardia ornata, p. 41, pl. iv, f. 8, 9, 10.

Oracardia cornuta, p. 42, pl. iv, f. 6.
Conocardium alternistriatum, p. 42, pl. xi, f. 24 ; pl. v, f.7 ?.
Palæoneilo consimilis, p. 43, pl. iv, f. 14.
Palæoncilo ignota, p. 44, pl. iv, f. 15.
Palæoneilo (Nucula ?) curta, p. 44, pl. iv, f. 4.
Flemingia (?) stulta, p. 45, pl. vii, f. 10.
Conularia gracilis, p. 48, pl. viii, f. 2 ; vol. III, pl. vi, f. 13.
Conularia micronema, Meek, var. n., p. 49, pl. viii, f. 4.
Phillipsia serraticaudata, p. 52, pl. i, f. 8, a–d.
Phillipsia (?) consors, p. 53, pl. i, f. 16, a, b, c.
Prœtus minutus, p. 56, pl. i, f. 7, a, b.
Phœthonides occidentalis, p. 57, pl. i, f. 10, a, b.
Phœthonides spinosus, p. 58, pl. i, f. 4, 5.
Phœthonides (?) immaturus, p. 59, pl. 1, f. 9, 15.
Cythere ohioensis, p. 60, pl. viii, f. 8 ; vol. III, pl. iii, f. 19.
Leioptera (?) newberryi, p. 114, pl. xi, f. 31 ; vol. III., pl. vii, f. 36.
Avicula (?) recta, p. 115, pl. x, f. 13.
Solenomya (?) cuyahogensis, p. 115, pl. x, f. 1.
Schizodus harlamensis, p. 117, pl. vi, f. 2.

W. F. Cooper (37) has prepared a tabulated list of the fossils of the Waverly of Ohio to accompany the above report.

A. F. Foerste (83) presents descriptions of species, old and new, of the Polyzoa ("Bryozoa") of Ohio. The following new species are described, vol. II, (1887):

Rhombopora multipora, p. 72, pl. vii, f. 1., a, b, c.
Glauconome whitii, p. 78, pl. vii, f. 4, a, b, c.
Chainodictyon (gen. nov.), p. 81.   C. laxum, p. 81, pl. vii, f. 8, a, b, c.
Fenestella limbatus, p. 83, pl. vii, f. 10, a, b, c, d.
Fenestella limbatus, var. remotus, p. 84, pl. vii, f. 11, made a new species, p. 87.
Stenopora ohioensis, p. 85, pl. vii, f. 12, a, b, c, d, e.

E. O. Ulrich (246) contributes to the same bulletin a list of the Bryozoa of the Waverly group in Ohio, with descriptions of the following new forms (vol. IV, 1888):

Fenestella herrickana, p. 63, pl. xiii, f. 2–2d.
Fenestella meekana, p. 64, pl. xiii, f. 1, 1b.
Fenestella albida, var. Richfieldensis, p. 66, pl. xiii, f. 3–3c.
Fenestella foliata, p. 67, pl. xiii, f. 4.
Fenestella subflexuosa, p. 68, pl. xiii, f. 6.
Fenestella cavernosa, p. 69, pl. xiii, f. 7–7b.
Polypora impressa, p. 72, pl. xiii, f. 8, 8a.
Pinnatopora intermedia, p. 74, pl. xiv, f. 1.
Pinnatopora simulatrix, p. 75, pl. xiv, f. 3.
Pinnatopora curvata, p. 76, pl. xiv, f. 4.
Pinnatopora subangulata, p. 76, pl. xiv, f. 2.
Pinnatopora minor, p. 77, pl. xiv, f. 7, 7a.
Tœniodictya interpolata, p. 80, pl. xiii, f. 9, 9a.
Cystodictya zigzag, p. 81, pl. xiii, f. 11, 11a.
Cystodictya simulans, p. 81, pl. xiii, f. 10.
Cystodictya angusta, p. 82, pl. xiv, f. 20.
Streblotrypa major, Ulrich, p. 84, pl. xiv, f. 10.
Streblotrypa obliqua, p. 85, pl. xiv, f. 9.
Streblotrypa hertzeri, p. 85, pl. xiv, f. 8.
Streblotrypa amplexa, p. 86, pl. xiv, f. 13.

Streblotrypa multporata, p. 87, pl. xiv, f. 11.
Streblotrypa striata, p. 87, pl. xiv, f. 12, 12a.
Streblotrypa regularis, p. 88, pl. xiv, f. 14.
Streblotrypa (? *Leioclema*) *denticulata,* p. 88, pl. xiv, f. 18, 19.
Rhombopora ohioensis, p. 90, pl. xiv, f. 4.

Charles R. Keyes has added three papers (134, 136, 141) to the literature of the Carboniferous. In the first, on the fauna of the Lower Coal Measures, three new species are described:

Chonetes lævis, p. [8] 229, pl. xii, f. 3, *a, b.*
Pleurotomaria modesta, p. [17] 238, pl. xii, f. 2, *a, b.*
Macrocheilus humilis, p. [18] 239, pl. xii, f. 1.

F. A. Sampson (229) describes the Subcarboniferous series at Sedalia, Missouri, and Lieut. A. W. Vodges (251) describes two new species from the same:

Phillipsia sampsoni, pp. 248, 249, and two wood-cuts, p. 249.
Griffithides (?) *sedaliensis,* p. 249.

In another paper (250) Lieutenant Vodges reviews the genera and species of North American Trilobites; the following four genera are recognized: *Proetus,* Steininger; *Phillipsia,* Portlock; *Griffithides,* Portlock, and *Brachymetopsis,* McCoy. The author gives a diagnosis of each genus and discusses the various species and synonymy, with their distribution in North America. The original description of the species is given in many cases, with a careful specific diagnosis for each species. Six species of *Proetus,* twelve species of *Phillipsia,* five species of *Griffithides,* and one species of *Brachymetopsis* are recognized. The generic characters are illustrated in the plates.

THE MESOZOIC.

William B. Clark (27) finds evidence in the fossils discovered in Anne Arundel and Prince George Counties, Maryland, to establish the persistence of the Cretaceous strata across the State, from the Delaware line on the northeast to the Potomac River on the southwest, and lists of the species with localities are given. The same author (24) remarks upon the discovery of an *Arcestes* (n. sp.), *Arcestes rhæticus,* p. 119, figured in a former paper (25), in the Rhætic beds of the northern Tyrol. This is taken as evidence for regarding the Rhætic as more closely allied with the Trias than with the Lias. The same author (26) presents lists of species collected from several localities in the southern counties of Maryland, representing the Eocene and Miocene faunas; no new species are described.

R. T. Hill has published three papers (108, 109, 110) of considerable value in expounding the knowledge of the geology of Texas, particularly of the Cretaceous system. The paper (110) on the Geology of the Cross-timbers contains a table (pp. 298-299) of a geological section of the Cretaceous across the State of Texas, in which are indicated the characteristic fossils of each zone. In another paper (109), on the

Texas section of the American Cretaceous, the author gives lists—of fossils of the upper division of the Texas Cretaceous (pp. 294, 295), of the middle division of the Texas Cretaceous (pp. 297, 299), of the upper or Washita division of the Lower Cretaceous (pp. 302, 303), of the Fredericksburgh division (p. 305). The author notes the fact of an apparent continuity of interlocking faunas throughout the series, but with the exception of *Gryphœa pitcheri*, Mort., not a single species is known to pass from the Comanche series into the upper formations. He further observes that the fauna of the Comanche series presents closer resemblance to those of Europe and tropical America than to other Cretaceous faunas of the United States.

Mr. W J McGee (177–178) contributes two papers, mainly stratigraphical and structural, on the formations of the Middle Atlantic slope; no extended palæontological facts are given, but the author mentions occasionally the species characteristic of the formations.

Eugene A. Smith, in conjunction with Lawrence C. Johnson (241), published a valuable contribution to the knowledge of the Tertiary and Cretaceous strata of Alabama. The bulletin deals mainly with geological facts, but there is frequent reference to the species of fossils characterizing the strata discussed.

C. A. White (278), commenting upon the age of the coal found in the region traversed by the Rio Grande, refers it to the age of the Laramie or Fox Hill formations. The same author (282) describes three new genera and three new species from the Cretaceous, which are as follows:

(*Crassitellidæ*),
Stearnsia (gen. nov.), p. 32, with, as type, *S. Robinsi* (n. sp.), p. 33, pl. ii, f. 7–9.
(*Aviculidæ*),
Dalliconcha (gen. nov.), p. 34, with, as types, the following species: *D. invaginata* (n. sp.), p. 35, pl. ii, f. 4, 5, and *Gervillia ensformis*.
Aquilaria (gen. nov.), p. 35, with, as type, *A. Cumminsi* (n. sp.), 37, pl. ii, f. 1–3.

C. A. White (283) gives an account of the results of examinations of the Texas Cretaceous, with R. T. Hill as field assistant. The fossils have not been fully studied, but enough is done to make clear the relations of the various deposits to those of other sections. The Comanche series are older than any Cretaceous deposits exhibited in any other American section. A complete faunal break occurs at the top of the Comanche. The upper series may be satisfactorily correlated with Cretaceous formations of western and upper Missouri.

C. A. White (285) has published a number of new species from South America, which, though not strictly appropriate to a list of North American Palæontology, are compared with American species. The author has 3 new genera and 158 new species, divided as follows: Conchifera, 58; Gasteropoda, 73; Polyzoa, 1; Cephalopoda, 9; Fresh-water Mollusca, 5; Echinodermata, 12. The same author (288) reports on the fossils from Hardin County, Iowa. These were examined by the author and found to possess close affinities with the Mollusca fauna of the Fox

Hills group. Two of them are identical with Fox Hills species. *Lispodesthes* (?) *haworthi* (n. sp.) is described and figured (pp. 224–225). Another paper (287) discusses the Puget group of Washington Territory. Twelve species are recognized from these rocks, eight of which are regarded as new, and are named but not described. They are—

Cyrena brevidens.	*B. dubia.*
Corbicula Willisi.	*Psammobia obscura.*
C. Pugetensis.	*Sanguinolaria* (?) *caudata.*
Batissa Newberryi.	*Teredo Pugetensis.*

Study of the fossils leads the author to agree with J. S. Newberry and Bailey Willis as to the equivalency and probable contemporaneity of the Puget group with the Laramie. In another paper (286) Mr. White discusses the relation of the Laramie group to other and later formations and considers the greater part of the Laramie as of Cretaceous age, the upper strata representing a gradual transition from the Cretaceous to the Tertiary period.

J. F. Whiteaves (292, 294, 295) contributes three papers on the Palæontology of the Mesozoic.

The first (295), on some fossils from the Cretaceous and Laramie rocks of the Saskatchewan, is an appendix to Mr. J. B. Tyrrell's report, and the following new species are described:

Cyprina subtrapeziformis, p. 155e.
Solecurtus (*Tagelus*) *occidentalis*, p. 157e.
Marteria tumidifrons, pp. 157e–158e.
Hydatina parvula, pp. 158e–159e.
Palæastacus (?) *ornatus*, pp. 161e–162e.

In the second paper (294), which is an appendix to G. M. Dawson's report, some Mesozoic fossils from British Columbia are described. The new species are as follows:

Aulacoceras Charlottense, p. 109b, Triassic.
Celtites (?) *Vancouverensis*, p. 110b, Triassic.
Placenticeras occidentale, p. 113b, Cretaceous.

In the third paper (292) the following new species from the Triassic of British Columbia are described:

Spiriferina borealis, p. 128, pl. 17, f. 1.
Terebratula Liardensis, p. 130, pl. 17, f. 2, 2a, 2b, 2c.
Monotis ovalis, p. 132, pl. 17, f. 4.
Halobia occidentalis, p. 134, pl. 17, f. 5, 6.
Trigonodus (?) *productus*, p. 135, pl. 17, f. 7, 7a, 7b.
Margarita triassica, p. 136, pl. 17, f. 8, 8a.
Nautilus Liardensis, p. 137, pl. 18, f. 1, 1a.
Popanoceras McConnelli, p. 138, pl. 18, f. 2, 2a, b, 3, 3a.
Acrochordiceras (?) *Carlottense*, p. 141, pl. 19, f. 1.
Trachyceras Canadense, p. 142, pl. 18, f. 4, 4a.
Arniotites, Hyatt (gen. nov.), p. 144.
Dorikranites, Hyatt (gen. nov.), p. 145.
Badiotites Carlottensis, p. 148, pl. 19, f. 5.

R. P. Whitfield (297, 299) remarks upon the fossils of the New Jersey Cretaceous. In the article in the American Naturalist (299) a synopsis of the number of species in each zone of the Cretaceous rocks of New Jersey is given, and also an account of the number of New Jersey species occurring in the corresponding beds of other States.

THE CENOZOIC.

Aug. Heilprin (102) discusses the classification of the Post-Cretaceous department. This is mainly a geological paper, but the author makes some timely remarks upon the value of faunas for determining chronology. He says: "The absolute succession of equivalent faunas, or faunas of a practically identical facies, which has been demonstrated for the greater part of the world, clearly establishes the claims of the faunal element as the *guide propre* in the determination of chronology." In another paper (103) Mr. Heilprin presents additional lists of species of Miocene Mollusca of New Jersey, and the following new species are described:

> *Murex Shilohensis*, p. 404, no figure.
> *Pleurotoma pseudeburnea*, p. 404, no figure.
> *Triforis terebrata*, p. 405, no figure.
> *Pecten Humphreysii*, var. *Woolmani* (new var.), p. 405.

Otto Meyer has produced several papers during the two years (182, 183, 184, 185, 186, 187). In the paper (183) on the "Invertebrates from the Eocene of Mississippi and Alabma," the following new species are described:

> *Odostomia Boettgeri*, p. 51, pl. iii, f. 4.
> *Turbonilla major*, p. 51, pl. iii, f. 3.
> *Dentiterebra* (gen. nov.), p. 51.
> *Dentiterebra prima*, p. 52, pl. iii, f. 2.
> *Pleurotoma Aldrichi*, p. 52, pl. iii, f. 7, 7a, 7b.
> *Tornatella volutata*, p. 52, pl. iii, f. 11.
> *Unicardium* (?) *Eocense*, p. 53, pl. iii, f. 14, 14a.
> *Mikrola* (gen. nov.), p. 53.
> *Mikrola Mississippiensis*, p. 53, pl. iii, f. 16, 16a, 16b.

Crucibulum antiquum, Meyer, Bull. 1, Geol. Survey Ala., 1886, p. 68 pl. I, f. 11, is found after cleaning to be a *Balanus* with preserved operculum. The names of a few additional Foraminifera of the Eocene of Mississippi and Alabama are given on p. 65. In the paper on the Miocene invertebrates from Virginia (185) the author presents a list of the smaller Mollusca identified in the sand adhering to the larger species, collected from the Miocene beds near Yorktown. The following new species are described:

> *Cæcum stevensoni*, p. 139, f 4.
> *Cæcum virginianum*, p. 139, f. 3.
> *Pyramis promilium*, p. 140, f. 1.
> *Astarte orbicularior*, p. 141, f. 6.
> *Semele* (?) *virginiana*, p. 143, f. 10.

In the paper (186) on the "Upper Tertiary Invertebrates from the west side of Chesapeake Bay," the author gives a list of twenty-five species discovered inside a large *Balanus concavus* Bronn ; one new species is described : *Aligena sharpi*, sp. nov.. p. 171, and wood cut. In the article (187) on the two books of Conrad on Tertiary shells, the author gives information in regard to imperfections which have appeared in various copies of T. A. Conrad's " Fossil Shells of the Tertiary Formations," and " Fossils of the Tertiary Formations."

C. L. Webster (272) has written an article on the geology of Johnson County, at the close of which, p. 419, is given a list of eighteen species of land and fresh-water shells, collected from the Loess of Johnson County by Prof. B. Shimek, of Iowa City, five of which are said not to occur as living forms in the county at the present time.

B. Shimek (239) publishes notes on the fossils of the Loess at Iowa City ; a list of twenty-five species is given with comments, but no species are described.

R. Ellsworth Call (19) defines a new Post-Pliocene Limnæid, referring it to the genus *Pompholyx*, Lea, and describing it under the name *Pompholopsis whitei* (subgen. et sp. nov.), p. 147, f. 1-3, from Tassajara Hills, California. Comparison is made of this genus with the genera *Carinifex*, Binney, *Pompholyx*, Lea, and *Vorticifex*, Meek.

T. H. Aldrich (1), in a paper in the Journal of the Cincinnati Society of Natural Science (vol. x, pp. 78–83), describes the following new species :

> *Dosinia mercenaroidea*, p. 82, no figure.
> *Sigaretus (Sigaticus) Clarkeanus*, p. 83, no figure.
> *Physa choctavensis*, p. 83, no figure.
> *Physa elongatoidea*, p. 83, no figure.
> *Mathilda Claibornensis*, p. 83, no figure.

Angelo Heilprin (100) has published in the Transactions of the Wagner Free Institute an account of his explorations of the west coast of Florida. Several new species are described as follows :

Pliocene ("Floridian") Caloosahatchie, Florida:

> *Fusus Caloosaënsis*, p. 68, pl. i, f. 1.
> *Fasciolaria scalarina*, p. 69, pl i, f. 2.
> *Melongena subcoronata*, p. 70, pl. i, f. 3, 3a.
> *Fulgur rapum*, p. 71, pl. ii, f. 4.
> *Turbinella regina*, p. 74, pl. iii, f. 5.
> *Vasum horridum*, p. 75 and p. 132, pl. iv, f. 6, 6a, pl. xvi a, f. 72.
> *Mazzalina bulbosa*, p. 76. pl. ii, f. 7.
> *Voluta Floridana*, p. 77, pl. v, f. 8.
> *Mitra lineolata*, p. 79, pl. ii, f. 9, 9a ; p. 133, pl. xvia, f. 74.
> *Columbella rusticoides*, p. 81, pl. viii, f. 9*.
> *Conus Tryoni*, p. 82, pl. v, f. 10 ; p. 133, pl. xvib, f. 75.
> *Strombus Leidyi*, p. 84, pl. vi, f. 11 ; p. 7, f. 11a.
> *Siphocypræa* (subgen. nov.), p. 86.
> *Cypræa (Siphocypræa) problematica*, p. 87, pl. iv, f. 12, 12a, 12b ; p. 133, pl. xvia, f. 73.
> *Turritella perattenuata*, p. 88, pl. viii, f. 13.

Turritella apicalis, p. 88, pl. viii, f. 14, 14*a*.
Turritella cingulata, p. 89, pl. viii, f. 15.
Turritella mediosulcata, p. 89, pl. viii, f. 16.
Turritella subannulata, p. 89, pl. viii, f. 17,
Cerithium ornatissimum, p. 90, pl. viii, f. 18, 18*a*.
Panopæa cymbula, p. 91, pl. ix, f. 20.
Panopæa Floridana, p. 91, pl. x, f. 21.
Panopæa navicula, p. 91, pl. x, f. 22.
Semele perlamellosa, p. 92, pl. xi, f. 23.
Venus rugatina, p. 92, pl. xi, f. 24, 24*a*.
Cardium Floridanum, p. 92, pl. xi, f. 25, 25*a*.
Hemicardium columba, p. 93, pl. xi, f. 26, 26*a*.
Chama crassa, p. 93, pl. xii, f. 27, pl. xiv, f. 27.
Lucina disciformis, p. 94, pl xi, f. 28.
Arca scalarina, p. 94, pl. xii, f. 29.
Arca crassicosta, p. 96, pl. xiii, f. 30, 30*a*.
Arca aquila, p. 97, pl. xii, f. 31.
Arcoptera (subgen. nov.), p. 98.
Arca (*Arcoptera*) *aviculæformis*, p. 98, pl. xiii, f. 32, 32*a*.
Spondylus rotundatus, p. 99, pl. xiv, f. 33.
Pecten solarioides, p. 99.
Ostrea meridionalis, p. 100, pl. xiv, f. 35, 35*a*.
Pecten pernodosus, p. 131, pl. xvib, f. 69, 69*a*.
Cardium Dalli, p. 131, pl. xvia, f. 70.
Cerithidea scalata, p. 131, pl. xvib, f. 71.

From the silex-bearing marl (Miocene) of Ballast Point Hillsboro Bay:

Wagneria (gen. nov.), p. 105 (near *Orthaulax* Gabb).
Wagneria pugnax, p. 106, pl. xv, f. 36, 36*a*.
Murex larvæcosta, p. 106, pl. xv, f. 37.
Murex crispangula, p. 107, pl. xv, f. 38.
Murex tritonopsis, p. 107, pl. xv, f. 39.
Murex trophoniformis, p. 107, pl. xv, f. 40.
Murex spinulosa, p. 108, pl. xv, f. 41.
Latirus Floridanus, p. 108, pl. xv, f. 42.
Turbinella polygonata, p. 108, pl. xv, f. 43.
Vasum subcapitellum, p. 109, pl. xv, f. 44.
Voluta musicina, p. 109, pl. xv, f. 45.
Voluta (*Lyria*) *zebra*, p. 110, pl. xv, f. 46.
Mitra (*Conomitra*) *angulata*, p. 110, pl. xv, f. 47.
Conus planiceps, p. 110, pl. xv. f. 48, 48*a*.
Cypræa tumulus, p. 111, pl. xvi, f. 49, 49*a*.
Natica amphora, p. 112, pl. xvi, f. 50.
Natica streptostoma, p. 112, pl. xvi, f. 51.
Turritella pagodæformis, p. 112, pl. viii, f. 52.
Turritella Tampæ, p. 113, pl. viii, f. 53.
Turbo crenorugatus, p. 113, pl. xvi, f. 54.
Turbo heliciformis, p. 113, pl. xvi, f. 55.
Delphinula (?) *solariella*, p. 113, pl. xvi, f. 56.
Pseudotrochus (gen. nov.), p. 114.
Pseudotrochus turbinatus, p. 114, pl. xvi, f. 57.
Cerithium præcursor, p. 114, pl. xvi, f. 58.
Pyrazisinus (subgen. nov.), p. 115 (near *Potamides* Brongn.).
Pyrazisinus campanulatus, p. 115, pl. xvi, f. 59.
Partula Americana, p. 115, pl. xvi, f. 60.

Cytherea nuciformis, p. 116, pl. xvi, f. 61.
Lucina Hillsboroensis, p. 117, pl. xvi, f. 62.
Crassatella deformis, p. 117, pl. xvi, f. 63.
Cardita (Carditamera) serricosta, p. 117, pl. xvi, f. 64.
Arca arcula, p. 118, pl. 16, f. 65.
Leda flexuosa, p. 119, pl. xvi, f. 66.

From north of Ballast Point:

Cerithium Hillsboroensis, p. 124, pl. viii, f. 67.
Cerithium cornutum, p. 124, pl. viii, f. 68.

Recent Floridian fauna, not fossil :

Tropidonotus taxispilotus ? var. *Brocki*, p. 129, pl. xvii, f. *a, b, c.*
Ictalurus okecchobeensis, p. 129, pl. xviii.
Aplysia Willcoxi, p. 130, pl. xix, f. *a, b, c.*

William H. Dall (58) publishes some interesting notes on the Geology of Florida, giving accounts of the results of explorations undertaken by instruction of the Director of the U. S. Geological Survey in 1885 and 1887. The paper discusses the geological structure and stratigraphical sequence of deposits, and the author refers casually to the occurrence of species of fossils in the deposits studied. " In referring to the age of the deposits," he says, "while the old terms Miocene, Pliocene, etc., may be used for the sake of convenience, it must be clearly understood that, as at present defined, they are only of relative value and indicative at most of stratigraphical succession in a very limited sense. As determined by their invertebrate fauna, the Pliocene, for instance, of South Europe, is probably older than the strata called Pliocene in America ; at all events it is highly improbable that they represent synchronous geological epochs. The method of determining which name should be used for a particular division of the Tertiary; by taking percentages of the supposed extinct species, is, on the face of it, impracticable, illogical, and misleading. Our knowledge of the Tertiary in America is still so fragmentary and imperfect as to render a synchronic subdivision of all the Post-Cretaceous strata impossible for the present."

L. C. Johnson (132) speaks upon the structure of Florida. Several fossils are identified, indicating Eocene age for the underlying rock (of the Vicksburg group); this is covered in places by the " Nummulitic limestone," and upon this rest the Miocene and more recent rocks.

J. G. Cooper (35, 36) has published lists of California shells in the Proceedings and Bulletins of the California Academy of Science, and the Annual Report of the State Mineralogist of California.

Lester F. Ward (269) presents the evidence as to the age of the Potomac formation derived from the study of the work of Professor Fontaine upon this remarkable flora. He tabulates the species, comparing them with those known and described from other deposits whose geological position is well known, and " from this exhibit it appears that no Jurassic species occurs in the Potomac formation, although it con-

tains a large number of strongly Jurassic types. The Wealden furnished the largest number of identical species, the Cenomanian next,
and the Urgonian next. Of allied species, although the largest number occurs in the Oolite, the Cenomanian, Urgonian, and Wealden each
furnish many. Taking the identical species, and considering the Wealden as Cretaceous, the flora would appear to be decidedly Cretaceous, but if this showing is considered in the light the Jurassic types
cast upon it, it is difficult to believe it to be higher than Wealden or
Neocomian." But he says at the close that in case the stratigraphical
and animal remains should require such reference, "the plants do not
present any serious obstacle to reference of the Potomac formation to
the Jurassic."

C. A. White (280) publishes a very interesting article on the inter-
relation of contemporaneous fossil faunas and floras, an addition to the
literature already contributed by him in this line. The present paper
considers the relationship between the invertebrate faunas and floras
and the vertebrate faunas preserved in the range of deposits from the
Laramie group to the Bridger, inclusive. He considers that sedimentation was continuous during the whole time, and that there was for the
whole time, and within the region where the Laramie and Bridger deposits were being made, an unbroken continuity of invertebrate and
plant life. "If these conditions actually existed we must necessarily
conclude that the Puerco and Wasatch mammalian faunas were both
suddenly and independently introduced into the region where they are
now found from some other region where they previously existed," and
he concludes that "the Wasatch fauna existed somewhere contemporaneously with the Puerco mammalia from which it differs so much, and also
contemporaneously with the Laramie dinosaurs, from which it differs far
more widely." In the latter part of the paper the author presents reasons for considering it necessary to study the history of continental and
fresh-water faunas and floras distinctly from the marine faunas, and
that until evidence is obtained positively identifying faunas of the two
types of deposits, they should be classified separately.

The same author (289) in a note to the editors of the American Naturalist announces that he has found that Mr. Cummins was entirely
correct in his reported discovery of Mesozoic and Paleozoic types of invertebrates commingled in one and the same layer of the Permian. The
deposits in which this discovery was made are in Baylor, Archer, and
Wichita Counties, Texas.

Three papers by J. W. Dawson (62, 63, 70), although not of a paleontological nature, are of interest to paleontologists. The author compares the Eozoic and Paleozoic deposits of eastern North America with
the European series of deposits, and also with those of the Arctic basin.
He finds the geological series up to the Trias-Juras, and after an interval again in the Quaternary, to be closely related on the borders of the
Atlantic on both sides, and far northward into the Artic regions, and

the series of deposits of the maritime provinces of eastern North America much more closely corresponding with those of western Europe than with those of the interior of the American continent.

PROTOZOA AND SPONGES.

Sir William Dawson and George Jennings Hinde (72) describe some new species of fossil sponges from Little Métis, Province of Quebec Canada. The following new species are proposed:

> *Protospongia tetranema*, Dawson, p. 52–53, f. 1, and further described and discussed by Hinde, pp. 63–65.
> *Hyalostelia metissica*, Dawson, p. 54, and Hinde's comments, p. 65.
> *Cyathophycus quebecensis*, Dawson, p. 54, Hinde's comments, pp. 65–67.
> *Buthotrephis pergracilis*, Dawson, p. 55.

G. J. Hinde (114) discusses the spicules and structure of *Archæocyathus minganensis*. The author concludes that the sponge spicules found in association with this fossil are not part of its structure, and that the so-called "branching spicula" are siliceous replacements of the tissue of its outer wall; but he does not conclude that the *Archæocyathus* is allied to the siliceous sponges. He is of the opinion that the fossil was originally calcareous.

C. D. Walcott (259) explains and defends his reference of *Archæocyathus profundus* of Billings to Meek's genus *Ethmophyllum*, as proposed in his recent publication, Thirtieth Bulletin of the U. S. Geological Survey.

Joseph F. James (123) discusses the Protozoa of the Cincinnati group.

George J. Hinde (111) considers the species *Hindia fibrosa* of Roemer to be identical with *Astylospongia inornata*, Hall, 1863, and that the genera *Hindia* and *Astylospongia* are closely allied.

P. M. Duncan (74) makes a critical reply defending his establishment of the genus *Hindia*, claiming that Roemer was ignorant of the characters which indicate the relationship of his species to the sponges.

Anthony Woodward (307) published a supplement to his "Bibliography of the Foraminifera" (Fourteenth Annual Report of the Geological Survey of Minnesota, pages 167–311) in the Journal of the New York Microscopical Society, January, 1888. The imperfections of this work called forth the severe criticism of Mr. Charles D. Sherborn (Nature, vol. 37, pp. 583–584, 1888), who published in London an exhaustive treatise (238) on the "Bibliography of the Foraminifera, recent and fossil, from 1565 to 1888."

James Hall (94) gives some interesting statistics in regard to the *Dictyospongidæ*. They are recorded as ranging geologically from the Utica slate to the Sub-carboniferous, and geographically are reported from the States of New York, Pennsylvania, Ohio, and Indiana. A list of forty species is given and a map of Steuben County on which are marked the localities where *Dictyophyton* has been found.

H. Mis. 142——19

Eozoon canadense has received some attention during the two years under consideration. Sir William Dawson (66, 69) has brought the dis-cussion of the nature of *Eozoon canadense* up to the present time. In the paper (69), issued by the Peter Redpath Museum of McGill Uni-versity, the author presents an exhaustive review of the characters of *Eozoon*, dis cusses the objections to its animal nature, and gives (on p. 91) a summary of the arguments in support of the animal nature of *Eozoon canadense*, the chief points of which are as follows:

"1. It occurs in masses in limestone rocks, just as Stromatoporæ oc-cur in the Palæozoic limestone.

"2. While sometimes in confluent and shapeless sheets or masses, it is, when in small or limited individuals, found to assume a regular rounded, cylindrical or more frequently broadly turbinate form.

"3. Microscopically it presents a regular lamination, the laminæ being confluent at intervals so as to form a network in the transverse section. The laminæ have tuberculated surfaces or casts of such tu-berculated surfaces, giving an acervuline appearance to those laminæ which are supposed to be the casts of chambers.

"4. The original calcareous laminæ are traversed by systems of branching canals, now filled with various mineral substances, and in some places coarse and in many others becoming a fine tubulated wall. The typical form of these canals is cylindrical, but they are often flat-tened, especially in the larger stems.

"5. In some specimens, large vertical tubes or oscula may be seen to penetrate the mass.

"6. On the sides of such tubes, and on the external surface the lam-inæ subdivide and become confluent, thus forming a species of porous epidermal layer or theca.

"7. Fragments of *Eozoon* are found forming layers in the limestone, showing that it was being broken up when the limestones were in pro-cess of deposition.

"8. The great extent and regularity of the limestones show that they were of marine origin, and they contain graphite, apatite, and obscure organic (?) fragments other than Eozoon.

"9. The ordinary specimens of *Eozoon* are mineralized with hydrous silicates (serpentine, etc.) in the same manner with Silurian and other specimens filled with glauconite, etc. These hydrous silicates also oc-cur in the same limestones in concretions, bands, etc., in such a manner as to prove that they were deposited contemporaneously.

"10. In some cases the canals and chamberlets are filled with cal-cite and dolomite, in the manner of ordinary calcareous fossils, and this filling can often be distinguished from the original calcareous wall by a minutely granular or porous structure in the latter.

"11. The specimens of *Eozoon* have been folded and faulted with the containing limestones, showing that they are not products of any sub-sequent segregation.

"12. Similar testimony is borne in the fact that the masses of *Eozoon* are crossed by the veins of chrysotile which traverse the limestones and are of later origin.

"13. The whole of the forms and structures seen in *Eozoon* correspond with those to be expected in a gigantic and highly generalized Rhizopod secreting a calcareous test, and possessing, as might be anticipated in such early organism, structures in some degree allied to such later forms as Stromatoporæ and calcareous sponges, which in the Eozoic it functionally represented."

This book will be of great value to students of palæontology, especially to those connected with the universities and called upon to discuss the order of the appearance of life in the Geological Series. Sir William Dawson, who has championed the organic nature of *Eozoon* for so many years, finds no reason to change his views, although very able antagonists have presented the arguments against its organic nature.

Dr. Selwyn, the director of the Canada Survey (235) refers to Sir William Dawson's paper in the Geological Magazine (66), and expresses his dissent from the views expressed by the author "in correlating any of the so-called Upper Laurentian Anorthosites of the vicinity of St. Jerome or elsewhere with the Huronian rocks west of Lake Superior." The massive Anorthosites he continues to regard as clearly intrusive, and that the so-called Norian or Upper Laurentian formation has, as such, no existence in Canada.

L. P. Gratacap (92) has recorded his recognition of Eozoonal rock on Manhattan Island.

CORALS.

P. M. Duncan (75) describes a new genus of Madreporaria under the name of *Glyphastræa*, of which the type species is *Septastræa Forbesi*, Edwards and Haime, from the Tertiary deposits of Maryland. He gives an amended description of the species, pages 29, 30, with figures illustrating it, plate iii, figs 1–16.

G. J. Hinde (112) presents a minute and exhaustive study of the distinguishing characters and nomenclature of the genus *Septastræa*, D'Orb., revises the generic definition, gives a list of the species with notes upon their characters, and in a plate illustrates them. He criticises the previously-mentioned paper of Duncan's and considers the original species *Septastræa Forbesi*, Edw. and H., which was used as the type of Duncan's genus *Glyphastræa* to be generically identical with the type species of D'Orbigny's genus *Septastræa*.

C. A. White (290) describes a new genus, *Hindeastræa* (page 362) of which the type species is a new species, *H. discoidea*, page 363, figs. 1, 2, 3, 4, 5, from the Ripley group (Cretaceous) of Kaufman County, Texas.

The paper of D. R. Moore (189) on Fossil Corals of Franklin County, Indiana, I have not seen.

Miss Mary E. Holmes (116) has prepared a paper beautifully illustrating the "morphology of the carinæ upon the septa of rugose corals,"
presented as a thesis for the degree of doctor of philosophy in the University of Michigan. A short notice of this paper is given in the American Geologist, vol. I, p. 61. I have seen the drawings, but have not
read the paper.

CRINOIDS.

Wachsmuth and Springer (252) publish part III, the final number, of
their Revision of the Palæocrinoidea. This consists of section 2, pp.
139-334, and an index, pp. 303-334, which, I understand, was not published in the Proceedings of the Academy of Natural Science. Although
section 2 of part III was presented to the Academy in 1886, it was not
published until 1887. This completes the grand work in which is given
a thorough diagnosis of each genus with citation of the known species,
and full bibliographic references for the Palæcrinoidea.

Part III is devoted to the discussion of the classification and relations of the Brachiate Crinoids, and the conclusion of the generic descriptions. The following new genera and species are described:

> Stenocrinus (syn. Heterocrinus in part), p. 207, type "Heterocrinus heterodac-
> tylus," Hall, 1843.
> Ohiocrinus (Heterocrinus, Hall, in part), p. 208 (Heterocrinus laxus, Hall, type
> of the genus).
> Atelestocrinus, p. 221, pl. 6, f. 4, and pl. 9, f. 4, Low. Carb., Iowa.
> Atelestocrinus delicatus, p. 223, Low. Carb., Iowa.
> Atelestocrinus robustus, p. 223, pl. 9, f. 4, Low. Carb., Iowa and Tennessee.
> Zeacrinus nodosus, p. 243, pl. 6, f. 3, Low. Carb., Tennessee.
> Stemmatocrinus Trautscholdi, p. 256, pl. 9, f. 7, 8, Low. Carb., Tennessee.

C. A. White (279) gives a review of this book. The same authors,
Wachsmuth and Springer (253), discuss the Summit plates in Blastoids, Crinoids, and Cystids. (This paper is reviewed by C. A. White,
281.) This paper consists of a review and criticism of the opinions of
Etheridge and Carpenter as expressed in the "Catalogue of the Blas-
toidea in the Geological department of the British Museum (Nat.
Hist.), with an account of the morphology and systematic position of
the group, and a revision of the genera and species. By Robert Etheridge and P. Herbert Carpenter. Quarto. Pages i-xvii, and 1-322,20
plates, London, 1886." The part discussed is found, particularly, in
chapter IV, pages 66-74 inclusive. Messrs. Wachsmuth and Springer
have prepared plates which accompany the paper illustrating the ventral aspects of species of the following genera: Sphæronites, Cyathocri-
nus, Stephanocrinus, Haplocrinus, Caryocrinus, Juglandocrinus, Talarocri-
nus, Elæcrinus. In another paper (255) the same authors discuss the
characters of Crotalocrinus, and in (254) the structure of the ventral
surface of Taxocrinus.

S. A. Miller (188) names and defines the new genus, Siphonocrinus,
page 263, adopting as the type species Glyptocrinus nobilis, Hall (20th

Report N. Y. Mus. Nat. Hist., p. 362, pl. x, f. 9, 10). The author refers to the same genus the species *Eucalyptocrinus armosus*, McChesney (= *Glyptocrinus armosus*, Hall).

The late U. P. James (131) published a reprint of the description of *Agelacrinus Holbrooki*, U. P. James, page 25, with a figure.

W. R. Billings (16) published the following new genus and species from the Trenton formation of Ottawa and neighborhood: *Ottawacrinus*, gen. nov., and *O. typus*, sp. nov., p. 49, *Calceocrinus furcillatus*, sp. nov., p. 51, *C. rugosus*, sp. nov., p. 53.

THE MOLLUSCOIDA.

A few papers have been written on the Polyzoa and Brachiopods which do not fall into any of the other divisions of this report.

C. Rominger (227) describes a new form of Bryozoa from the drift of Ann Arbor, Michigan, under the name of *Patellapora stellata*, sp. nov., p. 11, pl. i, f. 10.

Joseph F. James has a short note (125) on the value of the internal sections of corals when used for specific characters, considering them to be of small value because of the great variation they show, and of the different forms presented according to the relation of the plane of the section to the individual cells.

A. F. Foerste (82) and E. O Ulrich (249) reply to Mr. James's criticism, defending the methods in use by Mr. Ulrich and Mr. Ford.

J. F. James (128) presents a paper " on the *Monticulipora* a coral, not a Polyzoan." He had already published an elaborate review of the Trenton Monticuliporoidæ (130). In the present paper the author reviews the characters of the family Monticulporoidæ of Nicholson, including the genera *Monticulipora* and *Ceramopora*, and defends the view of Nicholson in placing them among the Coelenterata near the Helioporidæ, as opposed to the classification of E. O. Ulrich, who classes them with the Polyzoa, " Bryozoa."

H. A. Nicholson (202) writes on certain anomalous organisms which are concerned in the formation of the Palæozoic limestones. In the course of the paper he defines them under the names *Mitcheldeania gregaria*, n. sp., p. 16, f. 1, 2, and *Solenopora filiformis*, n. sp., p. 21, f. 4.

The characters of the genus *Girvanella*, Nicholson and Etheridge, 1880, are also discussed, and comparisons are made with related American forms. In another paper (201) Professor Nicholson comments upon new or imperfectly known species of Stromatoporids. No new species are described, but some American species are figured with descriptions and notes upon their characters.

E. O. Ulrich (248) discusses the genus *Sceptropora* with remarks upon *Helopora*, Hall. The author describes and figures a new genus and species of Lower Silurian Polyzoan, under the name *Sceptropora facula*, gen. et sp. nov , pp. 228,229, obtained from Manitoba, and also from two localities in Illinois. He considers the systematic position of the new genus as near that of the genus *Helopora* in the family *Arthrostylidæ* (Ulrich). This family name is based upon the new generic name *Arthrostylus*, which, in a foot-note, the author erects in place of *Arthronema*, Ulrich, which he finds preoccupied. Illustrations are given of the internal characters of *Helopora*, also of the characters of the family to which it belongs.

James Hall (93), at the end of the forty-first report of the Trustees of the New York State Museum of Natural History, published *Tectulipora* nov. subgen., *Fenestella (Tectulipora) loculata*, n. sp., and *Fenestella frequens*, n sp., pl. ix, f. 12–15. The pages are not numbered, but as bound would be 496 for all but the last, which is 497. On pl. x the figures 14,15 are called in explanation of plate " *Fenestella nexilis*, n. sp.", and on pl. xiv, figures 10–12 are called *Fenestella varia*, n. sp."

Norman Glass (90) has written a paper on the principal modifications of the spirals in the fossil Brachiopoda. The author notes the position of the spirals in the shell, comments upon the attachments of the spirals to the hinge-plate of the dorsal valve, and on the loop or the connection of the spirals with each other in the various genera of spiral-bearing Brachiopoda.

H. S. Williams (300) discusses the characters of the representatives of the family Strophomenidæ at its first prominent appearance in the Trenton. He analyzes the characters and shows their relationship to each other. The characters which became at a later stage generic differentia were found in a plastic state at the first stage. The specific differentia expressed throughout the life history of the family appeared to be more plastic in the early than in the later species. In the later stages of the history of the family the specific characters are more sharply accentuated, but except in this way they scarcely exceed in variety those appearing at the first stage of existence of the family.

THE GASTEROPODA.

Charles R. Keyes has written several papers (137, 138, 139, 140) in regard to *Platyceras* and its relations to the Crinoids upon which it is found attached. In one of the papers (138) four new species of *Platyceras* are described and figured from the Lower Carboniferous beds of Iowa. They are as follows:

> *Platyceras capax*, p. 241, f. 14, 15.
> *Platyceras obliquum*, p. 241, f. 12, 13.
> *Platyceras latum*, p. 242, f. 10, 11.
> *Platyceras formosum*, p. 242, f. 8, 9.

In the other three papers the author gives an interesting account of the mode of attachment of *Platyceras* to the dome of Crinoids. The association of the front part of the shell with the anal opening suggests the probability that the Gasteropod lived upon the excreta of the Crinoid. The attachment appears to have continued long, and probably during the life of the *Platyceras*, and this is regarded as sufficient explanation for the considerable variation of the Gasteropod in its "general form, configuration of the aperture, and the surface markings." In spite of the clear recognition of this plasticity of form the author has been unable to resist the temptation to name and define in terms of these plastic characters the four new species above mentioned.

THE CEPHALOPODA.

Alpheus Hyatt (121) has presented a valuable paper, strictly biological, in which he discusses the value of embryological characters in the definition and classification of the Cephalopoda. He proposes a new nomenclature for the stages of development of the embryo, and applies the classification in distinguishing the various stages represented by the fossil Cephalopoda. In a brief review it is impossible to give the substance of this paper, and those interested are referred to the article itself, which is fully as interesting as the important works on similar subjects which Professor Hyatt has already published. Professor Hyatt also read a paper before the National Academy, at the Boston meeting, on the primitive forms of Cephalopods (119), an abstract of which is given in the American Naturalist, as above cited. It is difficult to express in briefer words the contents of this valuable paper. The author discusses the phylogenetic relations of the Palæozoic and later Cephalopods, particularly in respect to their characters of curving, from the straight coiled form, as seen in *Orthoceras*, to the close coiled Nautilian form.

In the report of Contributions to Canadian Palæontology, by Professor Whiteaves (292), two generic descriptions are communicated by Professor Hyatt (120) from the Triassic rocks of British Columbia. The names are—

Arniotites, Hyatt, gen. nov., p. 144, type *Balatonites arietiformis*, Mojsisovics.

Dorikranites, Hyatt, gen. nov., p. 145, type *Balatonites Bagdoanus*, Mojsisovics.

Arthur H. Foord (86) publishes a note on the genus *Actinoceras* with particular reference to specimens in the British Museum showing the perforated apex of the Siphuncle; the specimens illustrated are from the Trenton and Black River rocks of the United States, British North America, and Arctic America. The same author (87) writes on the genus *Piloceras* Salter, as elucidated by examples lately discovered in North America and Scotland. The bibliography of the genus is referred to, the internal structure is described and illustrated, and the characters discussed, based upon study of Scotch and American specimens.

ARTHROPODA.

A. S. Packard published in 1887 several memoirs which were read before the National Academy of Sciences in 1885, and their contents have already been reported in the scientific journals.

The first (218a) "On the Syncarida, a hitherto undescribed synthetic group of extinct Malacostracous *Crustacea*" (vol. III, pp. 123–128, and two plates) discusses the characters of the species *Acanthotelson stimpsoni*, Meek and Worthen, and *A. eveni*, M. and W. Some new facts in regard to them have come to light through the study of additional specimens from the collections of R. D. Lacoe and J. C. Carr. The author defines one new species from Mazon Creek, *Acanthotelson* (?) *magister*, p. 127, pl. ii, f. 4, 5. In a foot-note (p. 128) some new characters, observed on a larger specimen from Brainwood, Illinois, are made the basis of a brief definition of and the proposal of a new generic name, *Belotelson* (the entire name *Belotelson magister*), for the species.

In the second paper (218*b*) " On the Gampsonychidæ, an undescribed family of fossil Schizopod Crustacea " (pp. 129–133, pl. iii), the study of specimens of *Palæocaris typus*, Meek and Worthen, has induced the author to compare them with the genus *Gampsonyx*, " and the result has led to the formation of a family or higher group for the genera, which should probably stand at the base of the Schizopoda, while also serving to bridge over the chasm existing between the Thoracostracous suborders Syncarida and Schizopoda."

In the third paper (218*c*) " On the Anthracaridæ, a family of Carboniferous Macrurous Decapod Crustacea," pp. 134–139, pl. iv, the author presents new facts regarding the species *Anthrapalæmon gracilis*, Meek and Worthen, from study of which and comparison with other forms he erects for it and kindred forms the family *Anthracaridæ*.

A fourth paper (218*d*) is " On the Carboniferous Xiphosurous fauna of North America," pp. 143–157, pls. v, vi, vii. This paper defines and figures *Cyclus Americana* Packard, *Dipeltis diplodiscus* Packard, *Prestwichia danæ*, Meek, *Prestwichia longispina* Packard, and *Belinurus lacoeï* Packard. In a note on the validity of the genus *Euproöps*, the author expresses the opinion " that the apparent differences between *Prestwichia* and *Euproops*, as stated by Messrs. Meek and Worthen, did not exist in nature." In a foot-note, p. 150, the author discusses the characters of *Prestwichia eriensis* Williams, and presents reasons for the opinion that the species is not a *Prestwichia*, and for it he proposes the name and briefly defines the new genus *Protolimulus*. A synopsis of North American Xiphosura is given, p. 150; the name Synziphosura is proposed for the suborder, including *Bunodidæ* Packard, *Hemiaspidæ* Zittel (restricted), *Pseudoniscidæ* Packard, and *Neolimulidæ* Packard.

The term Podostoma is proposed on page 156 for the class which includes the two orders (I) *Merostomata*, with the suborders *Xiphosura*, *Synziphosura*, and *Eurypterida*, and (II) *Trilobita*.

The two articles recorded under the same author's name (218*e*, 220) are reviews of the monographs above discussed. The first one (218*e*) is an abstract prepared by the author on the class Podostomata, and contains the substance of the latter part of the fourth paper above referred to (218*d*). The article (220) on Fossil Arthropods, in the American Naturalist, is a brief notice by the editor of the four papers just mentioned.

S. H. Scudder (233) communicates a brief note on Dr. Woodward's paper in the Geological Magazine, "On British Carboniferous Cockroaches."

J. M. Clarke (31) has published in the Journal of Morphology a beautiful and exhaustive memoir on the eyes of the common Devonian Trilobite, *Phacops rana* Green. He discusses the subject under the following sections : " The character of the visual area;" " The composition of the visual node," showing the arrangement of the lenses; " The structure of the lens ;" " The multiplication and diminution in the number of lenses;" "The development of the lens ;" " The structure of the sclera;" " The modes of preservation of the visual surface."

August F. Foerste (83*a*) communicates some notes on the discovery of two new species in the Trenton limestone of Minnesota. These species are *Illænus (Nileus) minnesotensis* sp. nov., p. 478, f. 1, and *Illænus Herricki*, sp. nov., p. 497, f. 2, the latter of which he compares with *Illænus pterocephalus* Whitfield, of the Niagara strata of Wisconsin. Figure and description are also given of *Illænus ambiguus* Foerste, from the Niagara group of Pennsylvania.

E. G. Chapman (23) publishes a short paper on the classification of Trilobites.

E. N. S. Ringueberg (224) read a paper on a Trilobite track which presents the ten pairs of impressions of the feet in groups, separate from each other, from which he concludes that the mode of progression was by a series of jumps.

VERTEBRATA.

G. F. Matthew (166, 168) describes an interesting fish from the Silurian at Nerepis Hills, King's County, New Brunswick, under the name *Diplaspis Acadica*, (gen. et sp. nov.) page 69 (of No. 166), and this species he regards as allied to *Pteraspis*, but distinct. The species was originally described as *Pteraspis* (?) *Acadica* by the author, in the Canadian Record of Science, 1886, pages 251, 252 and 323–325, and was taken from shales considered to be of an Upper Silurian age.

J. S. Newberry (199) discusses the characters of the genus *Edestus*, and describes the jaw of a gigantic species called *Edestus giganteus* (sp. nov.), page 121, plate vi., f. 1. The paper by Miss Hitchcock (115) is a discussion of the relations of this genus. Professor Newberry has also published several papers on fossil fishes from the Devonian and Carboniferous (191, 194, 195, 197, and 198). In the paper on *Titanichthys* (195) a general description of the bones is given, illustrated with diagrams and drawings (which are not reproduced in the paper), and the name *Titanichthys Clarkii* (sp. nov.) was given to the species in honor of the discoverer, Dr. William Clark. The note in the American Geologist by E. W. Claypole (31) refers to this same specimen. In the paper (198), which is but an abstract, Professor Newberry describes briefly and gives the names of the following new species and genus: *Cladoaus Kep-leri*, pp. 178,179; *Actinophorus* (gen. nov.) p. 179; *A. Clarkii*, p. 179; *Dinichthys curtus*, p. 179; *D. tuberculatus*, p. 179. In the paper (197) a new species is briefly noticed under the name *Rhizodus anceps*, p. 165, discovered by William McAdams in the St. Louis limestone at Alton, Illinois.

A paper was read by J. F. Whiteaves (293) in May, 1888, before the Royal Society of Canada, entitled "Illustrations of the Fossil Fishes of the Devonian rocks of Canada." (If this is published, a copy has not yet reached me. March 30, 1889.)

Edward D. Cope (41), in connection with a brief notice of the Part on Fishes of Zittel's Manual of Paleontology, takes occasion to give a synopsis of his own views on the subject of the classification of the lowest vertebrata, in anticipation, as he informs the reader, of a fuller memoir with illustrations.

J. W. Hulke (118) discusses the characters of *Ornithopsis*, H. G. Seeley, and *Omosaurus*, R. Owen, pointing out the propriety of following the classification of Professor Marsh, and places *Ornithopsis* in the group Sauropoda, and *Omosaurus* in the group Stegosauria. He questions whether the specimens in the Leeds collection called *Omosaurus* should not with justice be referred to the genus *Stegosaurus*, Marsh.

R. Lydekker (153), in an article in the Geological Magazine, makes some corrections in his Catalogue of Fossil Reptilia, suggested by conversations with O. C. Marsh during a visit to the Dinosaurian and other collections in the British Museum.

O. C. Marsh (164) describes one new genus and five new species of Dinosaurs from the Potomac formation in Prince George's County, Maryland :

> *Pleurocœlus nanus*, gen. et sp. nov., p. 90–92, f. 1–6.
> *Pleurocœlus altus*, sp. nov., p. 92.
> *Priconodon crassus*, gen. et sp. nov., p. 93, f. 7–9.
> *Allosaurus medins*, sp. nov., p. 93.
> *Cœlurus gracilis*, sp. nov., p. 94.

The same author (162, 163) describes the principal characteristics of the skull and dermal armor of *Stegosaurus*, illustrating them by numerous figures.

The paper by E. D. Cope (53) is a short notice of the paper just mentioned. E. D. Cope (38) discusses the characters of the Dinosaurian genus *Cœlurus* of Marsh. He regards the genus as Dinosaurian, allied to *Megadactylus*, Hitchcock, and describes the following new species: *Cœlurus longicollis*, p. 368, and *Cœlurus Bauri*, p. 368.

H. G. Seeley (234) discusses the characters of a vertebrate from the Wealden Beds of the Isle of Wight, called *Thecospondylus Daviesi*, Seeley, and compares it with *Cœlurus fragilis* of Marsh.

G. Baur (12) gives some points upon the classification and relations of the Ichthyopterygia. He concludes that "the Ichthyopterygia were developed from land-living reptiles which very much approach the Sphenodontidæ;" he classifies them in three families, viz: (1) Mixosauridæ, Baur (including the genus *Mixosaurus*, Baur); (2) Ichthyosauridæ, Bonaparte (including the genus *Ichthyosaurus*, Koenig, etc.); (3) Baptanodontidæ, Marsh (including *Baptanodon*, Marsh).

F. W. Cragin (55) describes, without figures, *Trinacromerum* (gen. nov.) and *T. Bentonianum* (sp. nov.), pp. 405–407. This species is said to belong to the order Sauropterygia, to resemble the genus *Baptanodon*, Marsh, and it may be identical generically with *Piratosaurus*, Leidy. The author promises a fuller paper with illustrations in the "Bulletin of the Washburn College Laboratory of Natural History, Topeka, Kansas."

E. D. Cope (52) announces the discovery of the remains of the genus *Goniopholis*, and describes a new species under the name of *G. Lucasii*, p. 1107 (no figure). In the paper (39) on American Triassic Rhynchocephalia, he describes, more fully than in the original article, *Typothorax coccinarium*, Cope, and from the study of new material he concludes that the species is allied closely to the genus *Ætosaurus* of Fraas. In another paper (43), the same author describes the following new species from the Trias of North America:

> *Episcoposaurus horridus*, p. 213; the genus of this species is also new and is contrasted with *Belodon*. (No illustrations.)
> *Tanystrophæus Willistoni*, p. 227. (No figure.)

Additional characters are described for the following species:

> *Eupelon durus*, Cope.
> *Typothorax coccinarum*, Cope.
> *Belodon buceros*, Cope.
> *Belodon scolopax*, Cope.
> *Tanystrophæus longicollis*, Cope.
> *Tanystrophæus Bauri*, Cope.

Henry F. Osborne (204) compares and contrasts the two genera *Dromatherium*, Emmons, and *Microconodon*, Osborne, and finds reason for considering them quite distinct types of animals. The *Dromatherium* he regards as distinct from any known mammal, recent or fossil, presenting some reptilian features, while the *Microconodon* is a more recent type and approaches in the form of its teeth some of the Jurassic mammals. The genus *Microconodon* was described by the author in the Proceedings of the Philadelphia Academy of Natural Science for 1886, page 362. It is founded upon the specimen in the collection of the Academy of Natural Science at Philadelphia, which was originally named *Dromatherium* by Emmons. The type of *Dromatherium* is *D. sylvestre*, Emmons, 1857, the original specimen belonging to the museum of Williams College. In this paper both specimens are figured.

O. C. Marsh (159) gives a most valuable contribution to our knowledge of Mesozoic mammals, and describes with illustrations the following new species and genera:

1. *Allodon fortis*, p. 331, pl. vii, f. 7-15.
2. *Ctenacodon potens*, p. 333, pl. viii, f. 2, 3, 7, 8, 9.
3. { *Asthenodon* (gen. nov.), p. 336, pl. ix, f. 6, 7.
   { *Asthenodon segnis*, p. 336, pl. ix, f. 6, 7.
4. *Laodon venustus*, p. 337, pl. ix, f. 5.
5. { *Enneodon* (gen. nov.), p. 339, pl. x, f. 4.
   { *Enneodon crassus*, p. 339, pl. x, f. 4.
6. *Enneodon affinis*, p. 339.
7. { *Menacodon* (gen. nov.), p. 340, pl. x, f. 5, 6.
   { *Menacodon rarus*, p. 340, pl. x, f. 5, 6.
   Priacodon (gen. nov.), p. 341, pl. x, f. 9, (type *Tinodon ferox*, Marsh, 1880), pl. x, f. 9.
8. { *Paurodon* (gen. nov.), p. 342, pl. x, f. 7, 8.
   { *Paurodon valens*, p. 342, pl. x, f. 7. 8.

These are distributed among the following families, viz, 1 and 2 in Plagiaulacidæ, 3 and 4 with *Dryolestes* in Dryolestidæ, 5 and 6, and *Diplocynodon* and *Docadon* in the family Diplocynodontidæ, 7 in the family Spalacotheridæ, the genus *Tinodon* in the family Tinodontidæ, *Triconodon* and the new genus *Priacodon* in the family Triconodontidæ, and 8 in the family Paurodontidæ.

The author regards none of the known Mesozoic mammals as truly herbivorous. The Triassic mammals belonging to the two families Dromatheridæ and Microlestidæ are quite distinct from any of the Jurassic forms. With a few exceptions the Mesozoic mammals best preserved are manifestly low generalized forms without any distinctive marsupial characters (p. 344). They are distributed by the author in the three orders, *Pantotheria* (Marsh, 1880), *Altotheria* (Marsh, 1880), and *Marsupialia;* the families Plagiaulacidæ and Microlestidæ alone being referred to the latter order. The paper (160) in the Geological Magazine appears to be a republication of the above.

H. F. Osborne (203, 210) published an abstract of a paper on Mesozoic mammalia in the Proceedings (203), which is published in full in the Journal (210) of the Academy of Natural Science, Philadelphia. The author classifies the Mesozoic mammals primarily into two groups: (I) The suborder *Multituberculata*, Cope, 1884; (II) A suborder, possibly equivalent to *Polyprotodonta*, called by him "*proto-Marsupialia*," p. 10. In the suborder *Multituberculata* are included the families, 1. Plagiaulacidæ, Marsh; 2. Bolodontidæ.

In the suborder "*proto-Marsupialia*" are arranged in several subgroups the following families:

Carnivorous sub-group, A. (1) Triconodontidæ (Marsh); (1a) Phascolotheridæ (Owen); (2) Spalacotheridæ (Owen), ("equivalent to Tinodontidæ, Marsh"). Omnivorous sub-group, B. (4) Peralestidæ (and ? Paurodontidæ, Marsh), and Diplocynodontidæ (Marsh). Insectivorous subgroup, (3) Amplotheridæ, C. (5) Stylodontidæ (Marsh). Herbivorous sub-group, D. (6) Athrodontidæ, of which the genus *Athrodon* (gen. nov.) is based upon the maxilla of *Stylodon pusillus* (Owen).

The *Multituberculata* are regarded as a sub-order of the *Marsupialia*, while the second sub-order presents no characters associating them with known Marsupialia.

Osborne (215) gives additional observations upon the structure and classification of Mesozoic mammals, and offers the following summary, pp. 300–301, of the principal features of this contribution:

"The principal features of the present contribution are the following: (1) Additional characters of *Amphilestes* and the probable determination of the premolar-molar formula. (2) Additional characters of *Phascolotherium*, suggesting a division between molars and premolars. (3) A review of the *Amphitylus* dentition. (4) The union of *Leptocladus dubius* and *Spalacotherium minus* with *Peramus*, and determination of the mandibular dentition of the latter genus. The molars are trituber cular. (5) The discovery also of apparently tritubercular molars in *Amphitherium* and probable determination of the premolar-molar formula (confirming Owen's views); (6) confirming Lydekker's suggestion of the probable union of *Peralestes* with *Spalacotherium*, and of *Peraspalax* with *Amblotherium*; (7) the probable union of *Peraspalax*, *Amblotherium*, *Achyrodon*, *Phascolestes*, *Stylodon*, and *Curtodon* into two or three genera with a substantially similar molar structure; (8) the correction of the writer's former views as to the family separation of the *Peralestidæ* and probably of the *Curtodontidæ*.

"The general result of the renewed and more extended study of these mammals has thus been, first to reduce the number of genera and eliminate two of the families proposed in the memoir; second, by the discovery of the molar structure of *Amphitherium* and *Peramus*, to substantially reduce the number of molar types among the English genera to two, viz, the *triconodont* in *Amphilestes*, *Phascolotherium*, *Triconodon*, and probably *Amphitylus*, and the *tritubercular* in all the remaining genera.

"This latter result is of great interest in its bearing upon the theory that the molar teeth of all the mammalia have either passed through the tritubercular stage, or have been arrested at one of the steps in tooth development leading to this stage."

Osborne (213) gives a short abstract of the full paper (214), which was published in the December number of the American Naturalist, 1888. The author proposes the following nomenclature for the cusps of the upper molars:

> *Protocone*, for the antero-internal cusp.
> *Hypocone*, for the postero-internal cusp, or sixth cusp.
> *Paracone*, for the antero-external cusp.
> *Metacone*, for the postero-external cusp.
> *Protoconule*, for the anterior-intermedial cusp.
> *Metaconule*, for the posterior-intermedial cusp.

For the lower molars the termination *e* is changed to *id* in the first four names for the corresponding cusps, thus, *Hypocone* for the upper, *Hypoconid* for the lower. The term *Epiconid* is applied to the postero-internal cusp.

Osborne's paper (214) in its original form was read before the Geological section of the Bath meeting of the British Association in September, 1888, and also before the National Academy of Sciences, in New Haven, November, 1888. An abstract was published in the American Naturalist (see 213), and 214 is the full paper. The author defines "the stages of Trituberculy as seen in different types" of the mammalian teeth in their order of succession as follows: I. Haplodont type (Cope), not yet discovered. I, A. Protodont tubercular type; example, *Dromatherium*. II. Triconodont type (Osborne); example, *Triconodon*. III. Tritubercular type (Cope); example, lower molars of *Spalacotherium* and *Asthenodon*.

Osborne (211) gives a review of Mr. Lydekker's arrangement of the Mesozoic mammals.

E. D. Cope (50) discusses Rütimeyer's classification with some remarks upon the American types found in Switzerland. Mr. Cope (40, 45, 47) adds some new facts regarding the vertebrate fauna of the Puerco series. In the first paper (40) the new species *Psittacotherium megalodus* is described, without figure, on page 469, and the species *P. multifragum* is referred to. In the last paper (47) the author reviews his studies of the Puerco epoch, while in the extended paper (45) the following species and one new genus are described, without illustration:

Chelydra crassa, p. 306.
Onychodectes, (gen. nov.), p. 317.   *O. tisonensis*, p. 318.
Mioclænus bathygnathus, p. 321.
Mioclænus pentacus, p. 325.
Mioclænus gaudrianus, p. 326.
Mioclænus lydekkerianus, p. 328.
Mioclænus filholianus, p. 329.
Mioclænus floverianus, p. 330.
Mioclænus zittelianus, p. 334.
Mioclænus turgidunculus, p. 334.
Chriacus schlosserianus, p. 338.
Chriacus ruetimeyeranus, p. 340
Chriacus stenops, p. 341.
Chriacus inversus, p. 342.
Triisodon biculminatus, p. 343.
Dissacus navajovius, p. 344.
Haploconus corniculatus, p 349.
Periptychus brabensis, p. 354.

The vertebrate fauna of the Puerco series has reached the number of one hundred and six species, among which are represented Crocodilia, Testudinata, Rhynchocephalia, Ophidea, Aves, Marsupialia, Bunotheria, Taxeopoda, and Amblypoda.

H. F. Osborne (212) notes the discovery, by M. Filhols, of the identity of *Chalicotherium* and *Macrotherium*.

E. D. Cope (51) states that he has found evidence of the presence of the pineal eye in some ancient vertebrates, and calls attention to the bearing of this fact upon the relationship of the vertebrates with the tunicates. In the plates published with this paper illustrations are given of *Bothriolepis Canadensis*, the skull of *Mycterops ordinatus*, *Diadectes phascolinus*, and the cranium or brain cases of *Belodon buceros*, and *Alligator Mississippiensis*. The announcement of this discovery in early reptilian vertebrates evidently suggested the following papers : H. F. Osborne (205, 206) upon reading Owen's description of *Tritylodon* of the Upper Triassic of South Africa, in which the author refers to a vacuity between the parietals which "if natural, represents a fontanelle, or it may be interpreted as a pineal or parietal foramen; it may however be due to posthumous injury," infers from this the remarkable hypothesis that "the primitive mammal of the family to which this belongs had a pineal eye of some functional value." But examination of the specimen itself by Dr. George Baur brought out the fact that no parietal foramen exists in *Tritylodon* (208). Thus suddenly the pineal eye of the primitive mammal is knocked out.

Mr. Cope (46) gives some new facts regarding the shoulder girdle and extremities of *Eriops*, and (44) presents a number of tables expressing the supposed phylogenetic relations of the several genera of artiodactyla, tracing them through the various stages of the Tertiary. The next (54) is apparently a modified form of this same paper. In another paper (42) the author describes a part of the mandible of a large cat from the Upper Miocene beds of Phillips County, Kansas, which is named *Machærodus*, and specific name *catocopis*. No figures are given.

Mr. Osborne (209) finds the name *Athrodon*, proposed in the paper (203) above referred to, preoccupied by Sauvage, and he proposes *Kurtodon* as a substitute.

A memorandum (89) of a paper read at the meeting of the Academy of Science in Paris, July 30, 1888, by M. Albert Gaudry, is given in a note, Nature, vol. XXXVIII, p. 384, in which the author records the relative dimensions of some of the larger Tertiary and Quaternary mammals; *Dinotherium giganteum* is given the first place, and *Mastodon Americanus* of the Quaternary of the United States is given the fourth place.

Mr. Cope (48) announces the discovery of a fragment of the carapace of *Glyptodon* in Nueces County, southern Texas, in beds which have yielded *Equus crenidens*, Cope. The discovery was made by William Taylor, and the specimen is described and named *Glyptodon petaliferous* (sp. nov.), pp. 345, 346.

J. A. Allen (2) describes from the Miocene of Charleston, South Carolina, *Squalodon Tiedemanni* (sp. nov.), p. 35, pls. v, vi.

J. M. Clarke (29, 30) announces the discovery of elephant bones associated with charcoal and pottery at Attica, Wyoming County, New York.

James Hall (96) notes the discovery of an elk (*Elaphus Canadensis*) [*sic*] in the town of Farmington, Ontario County, New York. The title is as above, but it does not appear whether the author intends to indicate the species found to be the red deer (*Cervus elaphus*, Linn.), or the wapiti (*Cervus Canadensis*, Erxl.), or the true moose.

Joseph Leidy (147) announces the discovery of a new species of *Hippotherium*, which is described and figured, p. 310, under the name *Hippotherium plicatile*.

O. C. Marsh (165) briefly describes a new fossil Sirenian from California, proposing the name *Desmostylus hesperus* (gen. et sp. nov.), pp. 95, 96, figs. 1, 2, 3, Tertiary, Alameda County, California. The same author (161) describes several new fossil mammals as follows :

> *Bison alticornis* (sp. nov.), p. 323, f. 1, 2, Denver group, near Denver, Colorado.
> *Accratherium acutum* (sp. nov.), p. 325, f. 3, 4, Pliocene, Phillips County, Kansas.
> *Brontops robustus* (gen. et sp. nov.), p. 326, f. 5, 6, Lower Miocene, near White River, Nebraska.
> *Brontops dispar* (sp. nov.), p. 328, f. 7, 8, Lower Miocene, Dakota.
> *Menops varians* (gen. et sp. nov.), p. 328, f. 9, 10, Lower Miocene, Dakota.
> *Titanops curtus* (gen. et sp. nov.), p. 330, f. 11, Lower Miocene, Colorado.
> *Titanops elatus* (sp. nov.), p. 330, f. 12, Miocene, Dakota.
> *Allops serotinus* (gen. et sp. nov.), p. 331, Miocene, Dakota.

Mr. W J McGee (176) notes the discovery of *Ovibos cavifrons* from the Loess of Iowa.

W. B. Scott and H. F. Osborne (230) give a preliminary account of the fossil mammals of the White River formation in the Museum of Comparative Zoology collected by Samuel Garman in Nebraska and Dakota. The following new species and genera are described :

> *Hyotherium Americanum* (sp. nov.), p. 155, no figure.
> *Minodus tichoceras* (sp. nov.), p. 159, sketch 2 of figs. 5, 6.
> *Minodus dolichoceras* (sp. nov.), p. 160, sketch 3 of figs. 5, 6.
> *Minodus platyceras* (sp. nov.), p. 160, fig. of horns, f. 4.
> *Metamynodon planifrons* (sp. nov.), pp. 165-169, f. 7, 8, 9.
> *Hyracodon major* (sp. nov.), p. 179, no figures.
> *Hyracodon planiceps* (sp. nov.), p. 170, no figures.

The genus *Menodus*, Pomel, is defined p. 157, and the following genera are recorded as synonyms, viz, *Titanotherium*, Leidy, *Megacerops*, Leidy, *Brontotherium*, Marsh, (? *Symborodon* Cope), *Diconodon*, Marsh. Restorations are given on plate i of *Hoplophoneus primævus*, Leidy, one-fourth natural size. and on plate ii of *Menodus Proutii*, Leidy, one-sixteenth natural size. *Amynodon*, Marsh, 1877, is defined on p. 164, and the author's genus *Orthocynodon* (Scott and Osborne, 1883) is considered to be a probable synonym. The new genus *Metamynodon* is named and described, p. 165, founded upon the new species *M. planifrons*, pp. 165-169, f. 7, 8, 9, and the genus is referred to the Amynodontidæ.

The same authors report upon vertebrate fossils of the Uinta formation (231), a list of species is given, and the following new species and genera described :

> *Amphicyon* (?) *vulpinum*, p. 255, no figure.
> *Plesiartomys sciuroides*, p. 256, no figure
> *Protoreodon parvus*, gen. et sp. nov. (? *Agriochœrus*, Marsh), (figure of the upper molar series).
> *Leptotragulus proavus*, gen. et sp. nov., pp. 258, 259, no figure.
> *Hyrachyus obliquidens*, p. 259.
> *Prothyracodon intermedium*, gen. et sp. nov., p. 260, no figure.
> *Isectolophus annectens*, gen. et sp. nov., p. 260, no figure.

Richard Owen (217) presents the evidence of the existence in America of mammals of the " Plastic Clay " period.

Madame Pavlow (221) gives an account of comparative study of the history of the Ungulates of America and Europe.

Alexander Winchell (305) announces the discovery of bones of the extinct *Platygonus compressus* in Ionia County, Michigan. The author states that the bones are being arranged into four skeletons in the museum of the University of Michigan, and will be described and illustrated at some future time.

E. D. Cope (46a) describes the following new genus and species from the John Day Miocene of North America :

> *Bothrolabis*, Cope, (gen. nov.), p. 66, type *B. rostratus*, Cope; *B. rostratus* (sp. nov.), pp. 77–79. The author states (p. 63) that lithographic plates of this species have been printed, but are unpublished. E. D. Cope (54a, 43a) discusses the mechanical origin of the dentition of mammals. The author attempts (54a) to show why the *Amblypoda*, having at the start apparently the same mechanical condition with the Carnivora, did not eventually produce the same result. He thinks that the divergence of mammalian dentition into two types, the tritubercular and the quadritubercular, has been due to the adoption of different food habits. " The tritubercular," he says, " is the primitive, and is adapted for softer food, as flesh, so that the primitive Mammalia were carnivorous, or nearly so. The mastication of hard food was impossible until the molars of the two series opposed each other, and this was not accomplished until the quadritubercular or superior molar was produced."

VEGETAL PALÆONTOLOGY.

Sir William Dawson (67) describes the Sporocarps of the Erian Shale. The circular specimens, originally described as *Sporangites Huronensis*, Dawson, are referred to the *Protosalvinia Huronensis*, Dawson, page 138. The bifurcate form is described under the name *Sporocarpon furcatum*, page 139, and is illustrated in fig. 1, *a*, *b*, *c*, *d*.

A remarkable specimen of Devonian *Lepidodendron* is briefly described by C—— (56). Mention is made of the discovery of a large portion, 15 feet long, of the stem of a *Lepidodendron primævum*, Rogers (?), from the arenaceous Portage Shales of Naples, Ontario County,

H. Mis. 142——20

New York, deposited in the New York State Museum at Albany. The cicatrices of the leaves are well preserved in the specimen, and present considerable difference in form and arrangement on different parts of the stem.

Leo Lesquereux (151) describes several Carboniferous forms from near Gadsden, Alabama. The following are the new species: *Rhabdocarpus Russellii*, p. 86, pl. xxix, f. 10, and *Stigmaria Russellii*, p. 87, pl. xxix, f. 11.

J. S. Newberry (196 and 200) describes some specimens of fossil plants from San Juancito, Honduras, brought by Charles M. Rolker, and other specimens sent by T. H. Leggett. In the first paper these had been identified by the author, and were announced as representatives of a Rhætic or Upper Triassic flora. In the article in the American Journal (260) fourteen species are mentioned, the following of which are new: *Otozamites linguiformis*, p. 344, f. 9, 10; *Encephalastos* (?) *denticulatus*, p. 346, f. 5; *Sphenozamites robustus*, p. 347, f. 12–14; *Sphenozamites* (?) *grandis*, p. 347; *Anomozamites elegans*, p. 348, f. 6–8; *Noggerathiopsis* sp., p. 350.

An abstract, very brief, is given in the Proceedings of the American Association of a paper read by Professor Newberry (192) on the Cretaceous Flora of North America.

Sir William Dawson (64, 68, 71) discusses the characters of the Cretaceous plants of the western territories of Canada and other parts of British America.

The flora of the Laramie group is discussed by L. F. Ward (266), and a short review of the same by Leo Lesquereux (149) is given. Professor Ward (266) describes a considerable number of new species, and illustrates others which have previously been described. The descriptions were first published in this bulletin (266). The figures, however, with the specific names were issued in connection with the author's paper in the Sixth Annual Report of the U. S. Geological Survey for 1884 and 1885, entitled "Synopsis of the Flora of the Laramie Group," pages 399–518, sixty-five plates, as explained in the "Explanatory Remarks," pages 9–12 of the bulletin. The following new species are described and beautifully illustrated:

Spiraxis bivalvis, p. 14, pl. i, f. 3.
Populus specio\a, p. 20, pl. v, f. 4–7.
Populus amblyrhyncha, p. 20, pl. vi, f. 1–8; pl. vii, f. 1–3.
Populus daphnogenoides, p. 20, pl. vii, f. 4–6.
Populus oxyrhyncha, p. 21, pl. viii, f. 1, 2.
Populus craspedodroma, p. 21, pl. viii, f. 3.
Populus Whitei, p. 22, pl. viii, f. 4.
Populus hederoides, p. 22, pl. viii, f. 5.
Populus anomala, p. 23, pl. viii, f. 7.
Populus Grewiopsis, p. 23, pl. ix, f. 1.
Populus inæqualis, p. 24, pl. ix, f. 2.
Quercus bicornis, p. 24, pl. ix, f. 3.
Quercus Carbonensis, p. 25, pl. ix, f. 6,   ·

? *Credneria daturæfolia*, p. 97, pl. xlii, f. 4 ; pl xliii, xliv, xlv.
Coculus Haydenianus, p. 100, pl. xlvii, f. 1–4 ; pl. xlvii, f. 1.
Lioriodendron Laramiense, p. 102, pl. xlviii, f. 2.
Magnolia pulchra, p. 103, pl. xlviii, f. 3, 4.
? *Diospyros obtusata*, p. 105, pl. xlix, f. 5.
Viburnum perfectum, p. 109, pl. lii, f. 3, 4 ; pl. liii, f. 1.
Viburnum macrodontum, p. 110, pl. liii, f. 2.
Vibernum limpidum, p. 110, pl. liii, f. 3–6.
Vibernum perplexum, p. 111, pl. liv, f. 2, 3.
Viburnum elongatum, p. 112, pl. liv, f. 4, 5.
Viburnum oppositinerve, p. 112, pl. lv, f. 1, 2.
Vibernum erectum, p. 112, pl. lv, f. 3.
Viburnum Newberrianum, p. 113, pl. lvi, f. 1–6.
Viburnum betulæfolium, p. 114, pl. lvii, f. 4.
Viburnum finale, p. 115, pl. lvii, f. 5.

Professor Ward has also contributed several reviews of current literature on Palæobotany (267, 268–270, 271), which have appeared in the American Journal of Science.

Mr. Lesquereux (152) describes fossil plants from Golden, Colorado; all the species are of the Tertiary age, and mostly of the Lower Miocene. The following are the new species described and named, but not illustrated :

Pteris undulata, p. 43.
Geonomites graminifolius, p. 44.
Palmocarpon lineatum, p. 44.
Piper Heeru, p. 44.
Betula fallax, p. 45.
Betula Schimperi, p. 45.
Alnus rugosa, p. 45.
Alnus carpinifolia, p. 45.
Quercus celastrifolia, p. 46.
Quercus coloradensis, p. 46.
Quercus Whitei, p. 46.
Populus tenuinervata, p. 48.
Ulmus antecedens, p. 49.
Ficus Berthoudi, p. 49.
Ficus Andræi, p. 50.

Protoficus Zeilleri, p. 50.
Styrax Laramiense, p. 51.
Cissus corylifolia, p. 52.
Cissus duplicato-serrata, p. 52.
Pterospermites grandidentatus, p. 53.
Pterospermites, species, p. 53.
Negundo decurrens, p. 54.
Celastrus Gaudini, p. 54.
Paliurus Coloradensis, p. 55.
Cratægus Englehardti, p. 56.
Cratægus myricoides, p. 56.
Cratægus betulæfolia, p. 56.
Pterocarya retusa, p. 56.
Rhamnus creatus, p. 55.

F. H. Knowlton (142) describes some specimens of silicified wood from Arizona under the names of *Araucarioxylon Arizonicum*, and under the generic name *Cressinoxylon*.

N. L. Britton (18) has described an Archæan plant from the white crystalline limestone of Sussex County, New Jersey, under the name *Archæophyton Newberryanum*, and although its characters are very imperfect, Mr. Britton regards it as the remains of a plant.

Joseph Le Conte (146) discusses the interesting flora of the coast islands of California. This same article appeared also in the American Geologist, vol. I, and in Bulletin No. 8 of the California Academy of Sciences. The author considers the flora of these islands as representing somewhat nearly the character of the flora of the whole country during the Pliocene times, and that the islands were separated from the mainland during the Quaternary period.

Leo Lesquereux (150) in a paper (compiled and prepared for publication by F. H. Knowlton, assistant curator of Botany and Fossil Plants U. S. National Museum), has described a number of new species of plants from various localities in North America of Upper Mesozoic and Cenozoic age:

> *Myrica elænoides*, p. 12, pl. iv, f. 5. Lower Eocene, Kentucky.
> Miocene, John Day Valley, Oregon:
>   *Acacia Oregoniana*, p. 14, pl. v, f. 4.
>   *Acer Bendirei*, p. 14, pl. v., f. 5; vi, f. 1; vii; f. 1; viii, 1.
>   *Acer dimorphum*, p. 15, pl. ix, f. 1.
>   *Rhus Bendirei*, p. 15, pl. ix, f. 2.
>   *Andromeda* (?) (*Leucothæ*) *crassa*, p. 16.
>   *Carpites fragariæformis*, sp. nov., p. 16 (no description).
>   *Salix Engelhardti*, p. 17, pl. viii, f. 2.
>   *Quercus Horniana*, p. 17, pl. v, f. 6.
>   *Quercus pseudolyrata*, var. *brevifolia*, n. var. (no description), pl. x, f. 2.
>   *Quercus pseudolyrata*, var. *latifolia*, n. var. (no description), pl. xii, f. 1.
>   *Quercus pseudolyrata*, var. *obtusiloba*, n. var. (no description), pl. x, f. 3.
>   *Ficus* (?) *Oregoniana*, p. 18, pl. ix, f. 3.
>   *Smilax Wardii*, p. 19, pl. xiii, f. 1.
> From Wasco County, Oregon (?), Eocene:
>   *Salix Schimperi*, p. 21, pl. xiii, f. 5.
>   *Phyllites Wascoensis*, p. 22, pl. xiv, f. 3.
>   *Equisetum Hornii*, p. 23, named without figure "*Carpites cinconæ*, n. sp.," p. 21.
>   *Persea punctulata*, p. 26, pl. xiv, f. 1. Alameda County, California (?), Miocene.
>   *Persea Dilleri*, p. 27, pl. xiii, f. 2–4. Shasta County, California (?), Miocene.
>   *Ficus Shastensis*, p. 28, pl. xi, f. 3. Shasta County, California, Miocene.
>   *Aralia Lasseniana*, p. 28, pl. xiv, f. 5. Lassen County, California (?), Eocene.
>   *Oreodaphne lithæformis*, p. 30, pl. xiv, f. 4. Lassen County, California (?), Eocene.
>   *Zamites Alaskana*, p. 32, pl. x, f. 4. Cape Lisbourne, Alaska (?), Neocomian.
>   *Chondrites filiciformis*, p. 32, pl. xvi, f. 1. Cape Lisbourne, Alaska (?), Neocomian.
>   *Diospyros Virginiana* L., var. *Turneri*, n. var., p. 35. Contra Costa County, California (?), Pliocene.
>   *Cratægus Marcouiana*, p. 36, pl. xiv, f. 2; xv, f. 1, 2,
>   *Cratægus Marcouiana*, var. *subintegrifolia*, n. var., p. 36, pl. xiv, f. 2 (no description). "Fossil Point, P. Y. Sheet."

"The Geological History of Plants," of J. W. Dawson, presents in a very readable form an account of the plants which have appeared in the past and are now extinct, describing their historical sequence and the characters presented by the faunas of each age. The notes to the several chapters contain much of value to the special student of Palæontology. A note "On examination of *Protaxites*, by Professor Penhallow," is inserted at the end of chapter II. At the end of chapter III are found notes "On the Classification of *Sporangites*," p. 84; "On the Nature and Affinities of *Ptilophyton*," p. 86; "On Tree Ferns of the Erian Period," p. 90; "On Erian Trees of the Genus *Dadoxylon*, Unger," p. 96; "On Scottish Devonian Plants of Hugh Miller and others," p. 98; "On the Geological Relations of some Plant-bearing Beds of Eastern Canada," p. 103; "On the Relations of the so-called 'Ursa Stage' of Bear Island with the Palæozoic Flora of North America." At the end of chapter IV twenty-seven pages of fine print are devoted to a note "On Characters and Classification of Palæozoic Plants." In an appendix there are eight pages giving "A Comparative View of the successive Palæozoic Floras of Northeastern America and Great Britain," and a few pages on "Heer's latest results in the Greenland Flora." The volume is particularly complete in its account of the plants of the Devonian of North America, in which field the author is the chief authority.

Leo Lesquereux (148) has prepared for the annual report of the Geological Survey of Pennsylvania a short treatise on the "Characters and Distribution of Palæozoic Plants," in which the plants of the Carboniferous system are chiefly discussed. The author also considers the evidences offered by plant remains of the physical conditions under which the deposits were formed, and the relations the several geographical tracts of North America in which coal measures appear bore to each other during the Carboniferous age.

BIBLIOGRAPHY OF NORTH AMERICAN PALÆONTOLOGY, 1887, 1888.

LIST OF ABBREVIATIONS.

Amer. Geol.—American Geologist. Minneapolis.
Amer. Journ.—The American Journal of Science and Arts. New Haven.
Amer. Nat.—American Naturalist. Philadelphia.
Annals.—Annals and Magazine of Natural History. London.
Ann. N. York Acad. Sci.—Annals of the New York Academy of Sciences. New York.
Ann. Rep. Geol. Surv. Canad.—Annual Report of the Geological Survey of Canada. Ottawa, Canada.
Ann. Rep. Geol. Surv. Penn.—Annual report of the Geological Survey of Pennsylvania. Philadelphia.
Ann. Rep. Min. Calif.—Annual Report of the State Mineralogist of California.
Ann. Rep. New York State Mus.—Annual Report of the New York State Museum of Natural History. Albany.
Ann. Rep. State Geologist N. Y.—Annual Report of the State Geologist to the Legislature of the State of New York. Albany.
Ann. Soc. Géol. Nord.—Annales de la Société Géologique du Nord. Lille.
Arch. do Mus. Nacional do Rio de Janeiro.—Archivos do Museum Nacional do Brazil. 4to. Rio de Janeiro.
Bul. Amer. Mus.—Bulletin of the American Museum of Natural History. New York.
Bull. Calif. Ac. Sci.—Bulletin of the California Academy of Science. San Francisco.
Bull. Denison Univ.—Bulletin of Denison University. Granville, Ohio.
Bull. Mus. Comp. Zool.—Bulletin of the Museum of Comparative Zoology at Harvard College. Cambridge, Massachusetts.
Bull. N. Brunswick Nat. Hist. Soc.—Bulletin of the New Brunswick Natural History Society. St. John, New Brunswick.

Bull. State Univ. Iowa.—Bulletin of the Laboratory of Natural History of the State University of Iowa. Iowa City.

Bull. Soc. Imp. Nat. Moscou.—Bulletin de la Société Impériale des Naturalistes de Moscou. Moscow.

Bull. U. S. Geol. Surv—Bulletin of the United States Geological Survey. Washington.

Canad. Rec. Sci.—Canadian Record of Science. Montreal.

Circ. Univ. Baltimore.—Johns Hopkins University Circulars. Baltimore.

Geol. Mag.—The Geological Magazine, or Monthly Journal of Geology. London. ·

Geol. Nat. Hist. Surv. Minn.—Geological and Natural History Survey of Minnesota. Minneapolis.

Journ. Cincinn. Soc. Nat. Hist.—The Journal of the Cincinnati Society of Natural History. Cincinnati.

Journ. Morph.—Journal of Morphology. Boston.

Journ. N. Y. Micr. Soc.—Journal of the New York Microscopical Society. New York.

Nature.—Nature, a weekly illustrated Journal of Science. 4to. London.

N. Jahrb.—Neues Jahrbuch für Mineralogie, Geologie, und Paläontologie. Stuttgart.

Ottawa Nat.—The Ottawa Naturalist. The Transactions of the Ottawa Field Naturalists' Club. Ottawa, Canada.

Phil. Trans. Roy. Soc.—Philosophical Transactions of the Royal Society of London. 4to. London.

Proc. A. A. A. S.—Proceedings of the American Association for the Advancement of Science. Salem, Massachusetts.

Proc. Amer. Phil. Soc.—Proceedings of the American Philosophical Society held at Philadelphia for Promoting Useful Knowledge. Philadelphia.

Proc. Boston Soc. Nat. Hist.—Proceedings of the Boston Society of Natural History. Boston.

Proc. Calif. Ac. Sci.—Proceedings of the California Academy of Natural Sciences. San Francisco.

Proc. Ac. Nat. Sci. Philad.—Proceedings of the Academy of Natural Sciences of Philadelphia. Philadelphia.

Proc. Staten Island Nat. Hist. Assoc.—Proceedings of the Staten Island Natural History Association.

Proc. U. S. Nat. Mus.—Proceedings of the U. S. National Museum. Washington.

Quart. Journ. Geol. Soc.—The Quarterly Journal of the Geological Society of London. London.

Rep. Brit. Assoc.—Report of the British Association for the Advancement of Science. London.

Science—Science. 4to. New York.

Trans. Amer. Phil. Soc.—Transactions of the American Philosophical Society held at Philadelphia for Promoting Useful Knowledge. 4to. Philadelphia.

Trans. Nov. Scot. Inst.—Proceedings and Transactions of the Nova Scotian Institute of Natural Science. Halifax, Nova Scotia.

Trans. R. Soc. Canada.—Transactions of the Royal Society of Canada. 4to. Montreal.

Trans. Vassar Bros. Inst.—Transactions of Vassar Brothers' Institute. Poughkeepsie, New York.

22. CAREZ, L., and DOUVILLÉ, H. Annuaire Géologique universel, revue de Geologie et Paléontologie, dirigée par Dr. L. Carez pour la partie Géologique, et H. Douvillé pour la partie Paléontologique, avec le concours de nombreux Géologues Français et étrangers. Fondé par le Dr. Dagincourt. Tome IV, Paris Comptoire Géologique de Paris, 15, Rue de Tournon. (Introduction dated "Paris, 15 déc. 1888.") Index Bibliographique, pp. 1-124. Revue de Géologie pour l'année 1887, dirigée par Dr. L. Carez, pp. 127-672. Revue de Paléontologie pour l'année 1887, dirigée par H. Douvillé, pp. 673-871.

(The literature for this part is divided biologically, and is reviewed separately, the Vertebrates and Arthropoda, by Dr. E. Trouessart; the Cephalopoda, by M. Em. Haug; the Gasteropoda, by M. Connann; the Lamellibranchs, by M. H. Douvillé; the Brachiopoda, by M. D. P. Oehlert; the Bryozoa, Anthozoa, Spongia, and Protozoa, by M. G. F. Dollfus; the Echinodermata, by M. Gauthier; and Vegetal Palæontology, by M. Zeiller.)

23. CHAPMAN, E. J. On the Classification of Trilobites. Canadian Rec. Sci., vol. II, p. 431. 1887. Montreal.

24. CLARK, WILLIAM B. A new Ammonite, which throws additional light upon the geological position of the Alpine Rhœtic. Amer. Jour. Sci., vol. 36, pp. 118-120. 1888. New Haven.

25. ———— On the geology of a region in northern Tyrol, together with descriptions of new species of fossils. The Johns Hopkins Univ. Circular No. 65. 1888. Baltimore.

26. ———— On three geological excursions made during the months of October and November, 1887, into the southern counties of Maryland. The Johns Hopkins Univ. Circular No. 65, with map. April, 1888. Baltimore.

27. ———— Discovery of fossil-bearing Cretaceous strata in Anne Arundel and Prince George's Counties, Maryland. The Johns Hopkins Univ. Circular No. 69. 1888. Baltimore.

28. CLARKE, J. M. Annelid Teeth from the lower portion of the Hamilton group and from the Naples shales of Ontario County, New York. 6th Ann. Rep. State Geologist, N. Y., pp. 30-37, pl. A'. 1887. Albany.

29. ———— A communication on Elephantine bones found at Attica, Wyoming County, New York, with no title. 6th Ann. Rep. of State Geol., pp. 34-35. 1887. Albany.

30. ———— Report on bones of *Mastodon* or *Elephas*, found associated with charcoal and pottery at Attica, Wyoming County, New York. 41st Ann. Rep. of Trustees of State Mus. Nat. Hist., pp. 388-390. pl. of sections. 1888. Albany.

31. ———— "The structure and Development of the visual area in the Trilobite Phacops rana, Green." Jour. of Morph., vol. II, No. 2, pp. 253-270, pl. XXI. November, 1888. Boston.

32. ———— "Paleontology of New York, vol. VII," as accredited on title page. 1888. Albany. (See Hall, James.)

33. CLAYPOLE, E. W. Preliminary note on some fossil wood from the Carboniferous rocks of Ohio. Proc. A. A. A. S., vol. 35, pp. 219-220. 1887. Salem.

34. ———— Note on fossil fishes from Berea, Ohio, collected by Dr. William Clark. Amer. Geol., vol. II, No. 1, pp. 62-64. 1888. Minneapolis.

35. COOPER, J. G. California Pulmonata, Recent and Fossil. Proc. and Bull. of Cal. Acad. Sci., Bull. II, pp. 355-497, and Proc. 2d ser., vol. I, p. 11. March, August, December, 1887. San Francisco.

36. ———— Catalogue of California Fossils. Ann. Rep. of State Mineralogist, (California,) pp. 221-30. 1888. Sacramento.

37. COOPER, W. F. Tabulated list of Fossils known to occur in the Waverly of Ohio. Bull., Denison Univ., vol. IV, pt. 1, pp. 123-129. December, 1888. Granville, Ohio.

38. COPE, E. D.   The Dinosaurian genus *Cœlurus*.   Amer. Nat., vol. 21, pp. 367–369. 1887.   Philadelphia.

39. ——— Note on "American Triassic Rhynchocephalia."   Amer. Nat., vol. XXI, p. 468.   May, 1887.   Philadelphia.

40. ——— Note: Some new Tæniodonta of the Puerco.   Amer. Nat., vol. XXI, p. 469. June, 1887.   Philadelphia.

41. ——— "Zittel's Manual of Palæontology."   Amer. Nat., vol. XXI, pp. 1014–1019. 1887.   Philadelphia.

42. ——— A sabre-tooth Tiger from the Loup Fork Beds.   Amer. Nat., vol. XXI, pp. 1019–1020.   1887.   Philadelphia.

43. ——— A contribution to the history of the Vertebrata of the Trias of North America.   Trans. Amer. Phil. Soc., vol. XIV, pp. 209–228, pl. I, II.   April, 1887. Philadelphia.

43a. ——— The mechanical origin of the sectorial teeth of Carnivora.   Proc. A. A. A. S., p. 254.   1887.   Salem, Mass.

44. ——— The Classification and Phylogeny of the Artiodactyls.   Trans. Amer. Phil. Soc., vol. XV, pp. 377–400.   October, 1887.   Philadelphia.

45. ——— Synopsis of the vertebrate fauna of the Puerco series.   Trans. Am. Phil. Soc., vol. XVI, pt. II, pp. 298–361, pls. IV, V.   January, August, 1888.   Philadelphia.

46. ——— "On the shoulder girdle and extremities of *Eryops*."   Trans. Amer. Phil. Soc., vol. XVI, pt. 2, pp. 362–367.   July, 1884.   Philadelphia.

46a. ——— On the Dicotylinæ of the John Day Miocene of North America.   Proc. Amer. Phil. Soc., vol. XXV, pp. 62–88.   1888.   Philadelphia.

47. ——— The vertebrate fauna of the Puerco Epoch.   Amer. Nat., vol. XXII, pp. 161–163.   1888.   Philadelphia.

48. ——— *Glyptodon* from Texas.   Amer. Nat., vol. XXII, pp. 345–346.   1888.   Philadelphia.

49. ——— Note: "Topinard on the latest steps in the genealogy of Man."   Amer. Nat., vol. XXII, pp. 660–663.   July, 1888.   Philadelphia.

50. ——— Rütimeyer on the classification of Mammalia, and on American types recently found in Switzerland.   Amer. Nat., vol. XXII, pp. 831–835.   September, 1888.   Philadelphia.

51. ——— The Pineal eye in extinct vertebrates.   Amer. Nat., vol. XXII, pp. 914–917, pl. 15, 16, 17, 18.   October, 1888.   Philadelphia.

52. ——— *Goniopholis* in the Jurassic of Colorado.   Amer. Nat., vol. XXII, pp. 1106–1107.   1888.   Philadelphia.

53. ——— A Horned Dinosaurian Reptile.   Amer. Nat., vol. XXII, p. 1108.   1888. Philadelphia.

54. ——— The Artiodactyla.   Amer. Nat., vol. XXII, pp. 1079–1095.   1888.   Philadelphia.

54a. ——— On the mechanical origin of the dentition of *Amblypoda*.   Proc. Amer. Phil. Soc., vol. XXV, pp. 80–88.   1888.   Philadelphia.

55. CRAGIN, F. W.   Preliminary description of a new or little known Saurian from the Benton of Kansas.   Amer. Geol., vol. II, pp. 404–407.   December, 1888. Minneapolis.

56. C———.   A noteworthy specimen of Devonian *Lepidodendron*.   Science, vol. IX, p. 516.   1887.   New York.

57. DAGINCOURT, Dr.   Annuaire Géologique universel, Revue de Géologie et Paleontologie, dirigée par Dr. L. Carez pour la partie géologique, et H. Douvillé pour la partie Paleontologique, avec le concours de nombreux Géologues Français et Etrangers.   Publié par le Dr. Dagincourt.   Tome III.   777 pages Geology, 235 Paleontology of 1886, 1887.   Paris.

58. DALL, WILLIAM H.   Notes on the Geology of Florida.   Amer. Jour. Sci., vol. XXXIV, pp. 161–170.   September, 1887.   New Haven.

59. DANA, JAMES D. A brief history of Taconic ideas. Amer. Jour. Sci., vol. XXXVI. page 410–427. 1888. New Haven.

60. DARTON, NELSON H. Bibliography of North American Geology for 1886. Bull. 44, U. S. Geol. Survey, 1887, 8vo. 94 pp. 1888. Washington.

61. DAVIS, G. Origin of life and species, and their distribution; a new theory. 52 p. 1888. Minneapolis.

62. DAWSON, Sir J. WILLIAM. On the relations of the Geology of the Arctic and Atlantic basins. Brit. Asso. Rep. of 56th meeting, 1886, p. 638. 1887. London.

63. —— On the correlation of the geological structure of the maritime provinces of Canada with that of western Europe. (Abstract.) Canadian Rec. Sci. vol. II, pp. 404-406, 1887. Montreal; also Science, vol. IX, pp589-591. 1887. New York.

64. —— Note on fossil wood and other plant remains from the Cretaceous and Laramie formations of the western territories of Canada. Trans. Royal Soc. Canada. Vol. V, pp — —. May, 1887. Montreal.

65. —— The geological history of Plants. The International Sci. series, 8vo, 290 pp. 1888. New York. D. Appleton & Co.

66. —— Note on new facts relating to Eozoon Canadense. Geol Mag. (new ser.), Dec. III, vol. V, pp. 49-54, Pl. IV. February, 1888. London.

67. —— On Sporocarps, discovered by Prof. E. Orton in the Erian shale of Columbus, Ohio. Canadian Rec. Sci., pp. 137-140. 1888. Montreal.

68. —— Cretaceous Floras of the Northwest Territories of Canada. Amer. Nat., vol. XXII, pp. 953-959. 1888. Philadelphia.

69. —— Specimens of Eozoon Canadense and their geological and other relations. Peter Redpath Mus., McGill Univ. Notes on specimens, pp. 107, 8vo, Dawson Bros., September, 1888. Montreal.

70 —— "On the Eozoic and Paleozoic rocks of the Atlantic coast of Canada, in comparison with those of western Europe and of the interior of America." Quart. Journ. Geol. Soc., pp. 797-817, November, 1888. London.

71. —— and DAWSON, G. M. VI. On Cretaceous plants from Port McNeal, Vancouver Island. Trans. R. Soc. Canada, vol. 6, sec. 4, pp. 71,72. 1888. Montreal.

72. —— and HINDE, GEORGE JENNINGS. New species of fossil sponges from Little Metis, Province of Quebec, Canada. (Preliminary note on new species of sponges from the Quebec group at Little Metis, pp. 49,59, by Sir J. William Dawson. Notes on sponges from the Quebec group at Metis, and from the Utica shale, pp. 59-68, by George Jennings Hinde.) Canad. Rec. Sci., vol. III, pp. 49-68. 1888. Montreal.

73. DOUVILLÉ, H., and CAREZ, L. (See Carez, L., and Douvillé, H.)

74. DUNCAN, P. MARTIN. A reply to Dr. G. J. Hinde's communication "On the genus Hindia, Duncan, and the name of its typical species." Ann. and Mag. Nat. Hist., ser. 5, vol. XIX, pp. 260-264. 1887. London.

75. DUNCAN, P. M. On a new genus of Madreporaria—Glyphastraea—with remarks on the Glyphastraea Forbesi, Edw. & H., sp., from the Tertiaries of Maryland. Quart. Journ. Geol. Soc., vol XLIII, pp. 24-32, pl. III. February, 1887. London.

75a. —— (Abstract.) Geol. Mag., n. s., dec. III, vol. IV, pp. 43, 44. 1887. London.

76. DWIGHT, W. B. Primordial rocks of the Wappinger Valley Limestone. Trans. Vassar Bros. Inst. for 1885-'87, vol. IV, pp. 130-141. 1887. Poughkeepsie.

77. —— Primordial rocks of the Wappinger Valley Limestone and associated strata. Trans. Vassar Bros. Inst. for 1885-'87, vol. IV, pp. 206-214. 1887. Poughkeepsie.

78. —— Art. III: Recent explorations in the Wappinger Valley Limestone of Dutchess County, New York. No. 6: Discovery of additional fossiliferous Potsdam strata and Pre-Potsdam strata of the Olenellus group, near Poughkeepsie, New York. Amer. Journ. S., vol. XXXIV, pp. 27-32. July, 1887. New Haven.

79. FALLENBURG, E. DE. Note on "Fossil trunk of a tree in hydromica or sericitic gneiss." Amer. Journ. S., vol. XXXIII, p. 158. February, 1887. New Haven.

80. FOERSTE, A. F. The Clinton group of Ohio. Bull. Denison Univ., vol. II, pt. I, pp. 89-110. May, 1887. Granville, Ohio. (Continued from vol. I.)

81. —— The Clinton group of Ohio. Part III. Bryozoa. Bull. Denison Univ., vol. II, pt. II, pp. 149-176, pls. XVI, XVII, XVIII. 1887. Granville, Ohio.

82. —— Recent methods in the study of Bryozoa. Science, vol. X, pp. 225, 226. 1887. New York.

83. —— Flint Ridge Bryozoa. Bull. Denison Univ., vol. II, pt. I, Appendix III, pp. 71-88. May, 1887. Granville, Ohio.

83a. —— Notes on Illæni. 15th Ann. Rep. Geol. Nat. Hist. Survey Minn., pp. 478-481, figs. I, II, III. 1887. Minneapolis.

84. —— Notes on Paleozoic Fossils. Bull. Denison Univ., vol. III, pt. II, pp. 117-133. 1888. Granville, Ohio.

85. —— Notes on a geological section at Todd's Fork, Ohio. (Illustrated.) Amer. Geol., vol. II, pp. 412-419. December, 1888. Minneapolis.

86. FOORD, ARTHUR H. Note on the genus Actinoceras, with particular reference to specimens in the British Museum, showing the perforated apex of the Siphuncle. Geol. Mag. (new ser.), dec. III, vol. V, pp. 487-489, and wood-cuts. 1888. London.

87. —— On the genus Piloceras, Salter, as elucidated by examples lately discovered in North America and Scotland. Geol. Mag., n. s., dec. III, vol. IV, pp. 541-546. 1887. London.

88. FORD, S. W. Notes on certain fossils discovered within the city limits of Quebec Trans. N. Y. Acad. Sci., vol. VII, pp. 2-5. 1888.

89. GAUDRY, ALBERT. "On the gigantic dimensions of some fossil mammals." Nature, vol. XXXVIII, p. 386. 1888. London.

90. GLASS, Rev. NORMAN. On the principal modifications of the spirals in the fossil Brachiopoda. Geol. Mag. (n. s), dec. III, vol. V, pp. 77-80. 1888. London.

91. GRATACAP, L. P. Preliminary list of Paleozoic fossils found in the drift of Staten Island. Proc. Staten Island Nat. Hist. Assoc. January, 1887.

92. —— The Eozoonal rock of Manhattan Island. Amer. Journ., vol. XXXIII, pp. 374-378. May, 1887. New Haven.

93. HALL, JAMES. Description of new species of Fenestellidæ of the Lower Helderberg, with explanations of plates illustrating species of the Hamilton group, described in the report of the State geologist for 1886. 41st. Ann. Rep. State Mus. Nat. Hist., pp.-(two pages not numbered following p. 390) and pls. VIII to XV. 1888. Albany.

94. —— Note on the occurrence of the Dictyospongidæ in the State of New York. 6th Ann. Rep. State Geologist, N. Y., pp. 36-38, and map. 1887. Albany.

95. —— Descriptions of Fenestellidæ of the Hamilton group of New York. 6th Ann. Rep. of State Geologist, N. Y., pp. 41-70, 7 plates. 1887. Albany.

96. —— "Note on the discovery of the skeleton of an Elk (Elaphus [sic] Canadensis) in the town of Farmington, Ontario County, New York." 6th Ann. Rep. State Geologist, N. Y., p. 39. 1887. Albany.

97. —— Corals and Bryozoa. Text and plates, containing descriptions and figures of species from the Lower Helderberg, Upper Helderberg, and Hamilton groups, by James Hall, State geologist and palæontologist, assisted by George B. Simpson. Geol. Surv. State of N. Y., Palæontology, vol. VI, pp. I-XXVI, 1-298, pls. I-LXVI. 1888. Albany.

98. —— Text and plates, containing descriptions of the Trilobites and other Crustacea of the Oriskany, Upper Helderberg, Hamilton, Portage, Chemung, and Catskill groups, by James Hall, State geologist and palæontologist, assisted by John M. Clarke. Geol. Surv. State of N. Y., Palæontology, vol. VII, pp. i-lxiv, 1-236, 41 plates, I-XXXVI. 1888. Albany.

99. HALL, JAMES. Supplement, containing descriptions and illustrations of Pteropoda, Cephalopoda, and Annelida, by James Hall, State geologist and palæontologist. Geol. Surv. State of N. Y., Palæontology, vol. v, pt. II, pp. 1–42, pls. CXIV–CXXIX, and two extra plates. 1888. Albany.

100. HEILPRIN, ANGELO. "Explorations on the west coast of Florida and in the Okerclobee Wilderness," forming vol. I of the Trans. Wagner Free Inst. of Sci. 1887. Philadelphia.

101. ———The geographical and geological distribution of animals. International Sci. Series. 12mo. 436 pp. (D. Appleton & Co.) 1887. New York.

102. ——— The classification of the Post-Cretaceous deposits. Proc. Acad. Nat. Sci. Philadelphia, pp. 314–322. 1887. Philadelphia.

103. ——— The Miocene Mollusca of the State of New Jersey. Proc. Acad. Nat. Sci. Philadelphia, pp. 397–405. 1887. Philadelphia.

104. ——— The geological evidences of evolution. 100 pp. 12mo. With illustrations. 1888. Philadelphia.

105. HERRICK, C. L. A sketch of the geological history of Licking County, Ohio, accompanying an illustrated catalogue of carboniferous fossils from Flint Ridge, Ohio. Bull. Sci. Lab. Denison Univ., vol. II, pp. 5–70, 144–148, 1887; vol. III, pp. 13–110, 1888; vol. IV, pp. 11–130, 1888. Granville, Ohio.

106. HICKS, HENRY. The Cambrian rocks of North America. Geol. Mag.(n. s.), dec. III, vol. IV, pp. 155–158. 1887. London.

107. H[ICKS], L. E. Note. Diatomaceous earth in Nebraska. Amer. Jour. Sci., vol. XXXVI, p. 86. 1888. New Haven.

108. HILL, R. T. Present condition of knowledge of the geology of Texas. Bull. 45, U. S. Geol. Survey. 8vo. 95 pp. 1887. Washington.

109. ——— The Texas section of the American Cretaceous. (Published by permission of the director of the U. S. Geological Survey.) Amer. Jour. Sci., vol. XXXIV, pp. 287–309. October, 1887. New Haven.

110. ——— The topography and geology of the Cross Timbers and surrounding regions in northern Texas. Amer. Jour. Sci., vol. XXXIII, pp. 291–303, with map. 1887. New Haven.

111. HINDE, GEORGE JENNINGS. On the genus *Hindia*, Duncan, and the name of its typical species. Ann. and Mag. Nat. Hist., 5th ser., vol. XIX, pp. 67–79. 1887. London.

112. ——— On the history and characters of the genus *Septastræa*, D'Orbigny (1849), and the identity of its type species with that of *Glyphastræa*, Duncan (1887). Quart. Journ. Geol. Soc., vol. XLIV, pp. 200–227. pl. IX. May, 1888. London.

113. ——— On the chert and siliceous schists of Permo-Carboniferous strata of Spitzbergen, and on the characters of the sponges therefrom, which have been described by Dr. E. von Dunikowski. Geol. Mag. (new ser.), Dec. III, vol. v, p. 24. June, 1888. London.

114. ——— Note on the spicules described by Billings in connection with the structure of *Archæocyathus Minganensis*. Geol. Mag., Dec. III, vol. v, No. 5, pp. 226–228. 1888. London.

115. HITCHCOCK, FANNY R. M. On the homologies of *Edestus*. Amer. Naturalist, 1887, pp. 847, 848. Philadelphia.

116. HOLMES, MARY E. The morphology of the carina upon the septa of rugose corals; 16 plates. (Presented as a thesis for the degree of doctor of philosophy in the University of Michigan, Ann Arbor. June, 1887.)

117. HONEYMAN, Rev. D. A revision of the Geology of Antigonish County, in Nova Scotia. Proc. and Trans. Nova Scotia Inst. Nat. Sci., vol. VI, p. 308. 1887. Halifax.

118. HULKE, J. W. Note on some Dinosaurian remains in the collection of A. Leeds, esq., of Eyebury, Northamptonshire. Quart. Journ. Geol. Soc., vol. XLIII, pp. 695–702. 1887. London,

119. HYATT, ALPHEUS. Primitive forms of Cephalopods. Amer. Nat., vol. XXI, pp. 64-66. 1887. Philadelphia.

120. —— (A note on and description of *Arniotites* and *Dorikranites* (gen. nov.), in an article by J. F. Whiteaves "On some fossils from the Triassic rocks of British Columbia," in) Contrib. to Canad. Pal'y, pp. 127-149. 1888. Ottawa.

121. —— Values in classification of the stage of growth and decline with propositions for a new nomenclature. Proc. Bost. Soc. Nat. Hist., vol. XXIII, pp. 396-407. 1888. Salem. (Also in Science, No. 260, p. 41, Jan., 1888. New York; and in Amer. Nat., vol. 22, October, 1888. Philadelphia.)

122. —— Evolution of the Faunas of the Lower Lias. Proc. Bost. Soc. Nat. Hist., vol. XXIV, pp. 17-31. (1889.) (Read, but not published in 1888.)

123. JAMES, JOSEPH F. Protozoa of the Cincinnati group. Jour. Cin. Soc. Nat. Hist., vol. IX, pp. 244-252. January, 1887. Cincinnati.

124. —— Note: Chalcedonized fossils. Science, vol. X, p. 156. September, 1887. New York.

125. —— F. Note: Sections of fossils [corals]. Science, vol. X, p. 180. October, 1887. New York.

126. —— Index to the journal of the Cincinnati Society of Natural History, vols. I to X inclusive, including index to part I of "Proceedings" of the Society (all published). Jour. Cin. Soc. Nat. Hist., vol. II, pp. 1-33. April, 1888. Cincinnati.

127. —— Letter: Nomenclature of some Cincinnati group fossils. Amer. Geol. vol. I, p. 333. May, 1888. Minneapolis.

128. —— *Monticulipora* a Coral, not a Polyzoan. Amer. Geol., vol. I, pp. 386-392. June, 1888. Minneapolis.

129. —— American fossil Cryptogamia. Amer. Nat., vol. XXII, pp. 1107-8. 1888. Philadelphia.

130. JAMES, U. P., and JOSEPH F. JAMES. On the Monticuliporoid corals of the Cincinnati group, with a critical revision of the species. Jour. Cin. Soc. Nat. Hist., vols. X-XI, pp. 118-141, 158-184, 15-48. 1887-1888. Cincinnati.

131. JAMES, U. P. "Genus *Agelacrinus* Vanuxem." Jour. Cin. Soc. Nat. Hist. [reprint], vol. X, p. 25. 1887. Cincinnati.

132. JOHNSON, L. C. The structure of Florida. (Read before the A. A. A. S., New York, August, 1887.) Amer. Jour. Sci., vol. XXXVI, pp. 230-236. 1888. New Haven.

132a. JOHNSON, LAWRENCE C. (*See* Smith, Eugene A., and Johnson, Lawrence C.)

133. KEMP, JAMES F. Fossil plants and rock specimens from Worcester, Massachusetts. Trans. N. Y. Acad. Sci., vol. IV, pp. 75, 76. 1887. New York.

134. KEYES, C. R. On the fauna of the lower coal measures of central Iowa. Proc. Acad. Nat. Sci. Phila., part II, pp. 222-246. July, 1888. Philadelphia.

135. —— Description of two new fossils from the Devonian of Iowa. Proc. Acad. Nat. Sci. Phila., part II, pp. 247-248, pl. XII. July 31, 1888. Philadelphia.

136. —— On fossils from the lower coal measures at Des Moines, Iowa. Amer. Geol., vol. II, pp. 23-28. July, 1888. Minneapolis.

137. —— On the attachment of *Platyceras* to Palæocrinoids, and its effects in modifying the form of the shell. Proc. Amer. Phil. Soc., vol. XXV, pp. 231-241. October, 1888. Philadelphia.

138. —— Descriptions of four new species of *Platyceras* from the Lower Carboniferous of Iowa. Proc. Amer. Phil. Soc., vol. XXV (pp. 13-15), pp. 241-243, pl. [No. 128]. 1888. Philadelphia.

139. —— Attachment of Platycerata to fossil Crinoids. Amer. Nat., vol. XXII, pp. 924, 925. 1888. Philadelphia.

140. —— On the sedentary habits of *Platyceras*. Amer. Jour. Sci., vol. XXXVI, pp. 269-272. October, 1888. New Haven,

141. KEYES, C. R. The coal measures of central Iowa, and particularly in the vicinity of Des Moines. Amer. Geol., vol. II, pp. 396–404. December, 1888. Minneapolis.

142. KNOWLTON, F. H. Silicified wood of Arizona. Proc. U. S. Nat. Mus., p. 1. 1888. Washington.

143. LAPWORTH, CHARLES. Fossils from Kicking Horse Pass, Manitoba. Science, vol. IX, p. 320. 1887. New York. (See Ann. Rept. Geol. and N. H. Surv. Canada, 1886, vol. II, 220–240.)

144. —— On the discovery of the Olenellus fauna in the Lower Cambrian rocks of Britain. Geol. Mag. (new ser.), dec. III, vol. V, pp. 484–487. 1888. London.

145. —— Preliminary report on some Graptolites from the Lower Palæozoic rocks on the south side of the St. Lawrence, from Cape Rozier to Tartigo River, from the north shore of the island of Orleans, one mile above Cape Rouge, and from the Cave Fields, Quebec. Trans. Roy. Soc. Canada for 1886, vol. V, p. 167. 1887. Montreal.

146. LE CONTE, JOSEPH. The Flora of the Coast Islands of California in relation to recent changes of Physical Geography. Amer. Jour. Sci., vol. XXXIV, pp. 457–460. December, 1887. New Haven.

147. LEIDY, JOSEPH. Fossil bones from Florida. Proc. Acad. Nat. Sci. Philad., part III, p. 309. 1887. Philadelphia.

148. LESQUEREUX, LEO. On the character and distribution of Palæozoic plants. Geol. Surv. Penn., Ann. Rep. for 1886, part I, pp. 457–522. 1887. Philadelphia.

149. —— Note on Prof. L. F. Ward's Synopsis of the Flora of the Laramie group. Amer. Jour. Sci., vol. XXXIV, pp. 487–488. December, 1887. New Haven.

150. —— Recent determinations of fossil plants from Kentucky, Louisiana, Oregon, California, Alaska, Greenland, etc., with descriptions of new species. Proc. U. S. Nat. Mus., pp. 11–38, pl. IV–XVI. 1888. Washington.

151. —— List of fossil plants collected by Mr. I. C. Russell, at Black Creek, near Gadsden, Alabama, with descriptions of several new species. Proc. U. S. Nat. Mus., vol. XI, pp. 83–87, pl. XXIX. 1888. Washington.

152. —— Specimens of fossil plants collected at Golden, Colorado, 1883, for the Museum of Comparative Zoology, Cambridge, Massachusetts, examined and determined by Leo Lesquereux. Bull. Mus. Comp. Zool., vol. XVI, No. 3, Geol. Sect., vol. II, pp. 43–59. December, 1888. Cambridge, Massachusetts.

153. LYDEKKER, R. British Museum catalogue of fossil reptilia, and papers on the Enaliosaurians. Geol. Mag. (new ser.), dec. III, vol. V, pp. 451–453. 1888. London.

154. MARCOU, JULES. Palæontologic and stratigraphic "principles" of the adversaries of the Taconic. Amer. Geol., vol. II, pp. 10–23, 67–88. 1888. Minneapolis.

155. —— The Taconic of Georgia, and the report on the geology of Vermont. Mem. Bost. Soc. Nat. Hist., vol. IV, pp. 105–131, pl. 13. March, 1888. Boston.

156. MARCOU, J. B. Review of the progress of North American Palæontology for the year 1886. Amer. Nat., vol. XXI, pp. 532–544. 1887. Philadelphia.

157. —— Review of the progress of North American Palæontology for the year 1887. Amer. Nat., vol. XXII, pp. 679–691. 1888. Philadelphia.

158. MARGERIE, EMM. DE. Les Progrès de la Géologie. Congrès Bibliographique International (Extrait du Compte rendu des Travaux), p. 42. 1888. Paris.

159. MARSH, O. C. American Jurassic Mammals. Amer. Journ. Sci., vol. XXXIII, pp. 327–348, pl. 7–10. April, 1887. New Haven.

160. —— American Jurassic Mammals. Geol. Mag. (new ser.), dec. III, vol. IV, pp. 241–247, and 289–299, pl. VI–IX June, 1887. London.

161. —— Notice of new Fossil Mammals. Amer. Journ. Sci., vol. XXXIV, pp. 323–331. October, 1887. New Haven.

162. MARSH, O. C. Principal characters of American Jurassic Dinosaurs. Part IX. The Skull and Dermal armor of *Stegosaurus*. Amer. Journ. Sci., vol. XXXIV, pp. 413-417. November, 1887. New Haven.

163. —— The Skull and Dermal armor of *Stegosaurus*. Geol. Mag. (new ser.), dec. III, vol. V, pp. 11-15, pls. I, II. 1888. London.

164. —— Notice of a new genus of *Sauropoda* and other new *Dinosaurs* from the Potomac formation. Amer. Journ. Sci., vol. XXXV, pp. 89-94. 1888. New Haven.

165. —— Notice of a new fossil Sirenian from California. Amer. Journ. Sci., vol. XXXV, pp. 94-96. 1888. New Haven.

166. MATTHEW, G. F. A preliminary notice of a new genus of Silurian fishes. Bull. New Bruns. Nat. Hist. Soc., No. 5, pp. 69-73. 1887. St. John's, New Brunswick.

167. —— Illustrations of the fauna of the St. John's group. No. IV, Pt. I: Description of a new species of *Paradoxides* (*Paradoxides regina*). Pt. II: The smaller Trilobites with eyes, *Ptychoporida* and *Ellipsocephalida*. Trans. Roy. Soc. Canada, sect. IV, vol. X, pp. 115-166, pl. I, II, III. 1887. Montreal.

168. —— Additional note on the Pteraspidian fish found in New Brunswick. Canad. Rec. Sci., vol. II, p. 323. 1887. Montreal.

169. —— On the smaller-eyed Trilobites of division I, with a few remarks on the species of the higher divisions of the group. Canad. Rec. Sci., vol. II, p. 357. 1887. Montreal.

170. —— Illustrations of the fauna of the St. John's group. No. IV. On the smaller-eyed Trilobites. Canad. Rec. Sci., vol. II, p. 432. 1887. Montreal.

171. —— The great Acadian *Paradoxides*. Amer. Journ. Sci., vol. XXXIII, pp. 388-390. May, 1887. New Haven.

172. —— On the kin of *Paradoxides* (*Olenellus?*) *Kjerulfi*. Amer. Journ. Sci., vol. XXXIII, pp. 390-392. May, 1887. New Haven.

173. —— On *Psammichnites* and the early Trilobites of the Cambrian rocks in eastern Canada. Amer. Geol., vol. II, pp. 1-9. 1888. Minneapolis.

174 —— On a basal series of Cambrian rocks in Acadia. Canad. Rec. Sci., vol. III, No. 1, pp. 21-29. 1888. Montreal.

175. —— On the classification of the Cambrian rocks in Acadia. Canad. Rec. Sci., vol. III, No. 2, April, 1888. Montreal.

176. McGEE, W J. *Ovibos cavifrons* from the Loess of Iowa. Amer. Journ. Sci., vol. XXXIV, pp. 217-220. September, 1887. New Haven.

177. —— The Columbia formation. Proc. A. A. A. S., vol. XXXVI, pp. 221-222. 1888. Salem, Massachusetts.

178. —— Three formations of the Middle Atlantic slope. Amer. Journ. Sci., vol. XXXVI, pp. 120-143, 328-330, 367-388, 448-466. 1888. New Haven.

179. MERRILL, F. J. H. Green Pond Mountain group. Geol. Surv. of New Jersey, Rep. of the Geologist, 1886, pp. 112-122. New Brunswick, New Jersey. (Abstract), Science, vol. IX, pp. 595-596. 1887. New York.

180. —— Note on the Green Pond Mountain group of New Jersey. Trans. N. Y. Acad. Sci., vol. VI, p. 59. 1887. New York.

181. —— Index to current literature relating to American geology. School of Mines Quart., vol. VIII, pp. 285-375; vol. IX, pp. 85-87. 1887. New York.

182. MEYER, OTTO. Beitrag zur Kenntniss der Fauna des Altertertiärs von Mississippi und Alabama. Bericht über der Senckenbergische naturforschende Gesellschaft in Frankfurt am Main, pp. 1-22, pls. I, II. 1887.

183. —— Invertebrates from the Eocene of Mississippi and Alabama. Proc. Acad. Nat. Sci. Philad., pp. 51-56. 1887. Philadelphia.

184. —— Some remarks on the present state of our knowledge of the North American Eastern Tertiary. Amer. Geol., vol. II, pp. 88-94. 1888. Minneapolis

185. Meyer, Otto. On Miocene invertebrates from Virginia. Proc. Amer. Phil. Soc., p. 135. 1888. Philadelphia.

186. —— Upper Tertiary invertebrates from the west side of Chesapeake Bay. Proc. Acad. Nat. Sci. Philad., pt ii, pp. 170–171. 1888. Philadelphia.

187. —— Bibliographical notes on the two books of Conrad on Tertiary shells. Amer. Nat., vol xxii, pp. 726–727. 1888. Philadelphia.

188. Miller, S. A. A new genus of Crinoids from the Niagara group. Amer. Geol., vol. i, No. 5, pp. 263–264. 1888. Minneapolis.

189. Moore, David. Fossil corals of Franklin County, Indiana. Bull. Brookville Soc. Nat. Hist., No. 2, p. 50. 1887. Indiana.

190. Nason, Frank L. On the location of some vertebrate fossil beds in Honduras, Central America. Amer. Jour. Sci., vol. xxxiv, pp. 455–457. November, 1887, New Haven.

191. Newberry, J. S. On Devonian and Carboniferous Fishes. (Abstract.) Proc. A. A. A. S., vol. xxxv, p. 216. 1887. Salem.

192. —— On the Cretaceous Flora of North America. (Abstract.) Proc. A. A. A. S., vol. xxxv, p. 216. 1887. Salem.

193. —— Fauna and Flora of the Trias of New Jersey and the Connecticut Valley, (Abstract.) Trans. N. Y. Acad. Sci., vol. vi, pp. 124–128. 1887. New York.

194. —— Cœlosteus, a new genus of fishes from the lower Carboniferous limestone of Illinois. (Abstract.) Trans. N. Y. Acad. Sci., vol. vi, pp. 137, 138. 1887. New York.

195. —— Description of a new species of Titanichthys. (Abstract.) Trans. N. Y. Acad. Sci., vol. vi, pp. 164, 165. 1887. New York.

196. —— Triassic plants from Honduras. Trans. N. Y. Acad. Sci., vol. vii, pp. 113–115 1888. New York.

197. —— Notes on a new species of Rhizodus from the St. Louis limestone at Alton, Illinois. Trans. N. Y. Acad. Sci., vol. vii, p. 165. 1888. New York.

198. —— On the fossil fishes of the Erie shales of Ohio. (Abstract.) Trans. Acad Nat. Sci., vol. vii, pp. 178–180. 1888. New York.

199. —— On the structure and relations of Edestus, with a description of a gigantic new species. Ann. N. Y. Acad. Sci., vol. iv, pp. 113–122, pls. iv, v, vi. 1888. New York.

200. —— Rhætic plants from Honduras. Amer. Journ. Sci., vol. xxxvi, pp. 342–351, pl. viii. 1888. New Haven.

200a. Newell, Fred. H. Niagara Cephalopods from northern Indiana. Proc. Bost. Soc. Nat. Hist., vol. xxvi, pp. 460–486. 1888. Boston.

201. Nicholson, H. A. On some new and imperfectly known species of Stromatoporides, part iii. Ann. and Mag. Nat. Hist., ser. 5, vol. xix, pp. 1–17, pls. i–iii. 1887. London.

202. —— On certain anomalous organisms which are concerned in the formation of the Palæozoic limestones. Geol. Mag., new series, decade iii, vol. v, pp. 15–24. 1888. London.

203. Osborne, H. F. On the structure and classification of Mesozoic mammalia. (Abstract.) Proc. Acad. Nat. Sci. Philad., pt. ii, pp. 282–292. 1887. Philadelphia.

204. —— The Triassic mammals, Dromatherium and Microconodon. Proc. Amer. Phil. Soc., No. 125, pp. 109–111, pl. xxiv. 1887. Philadelphia.

205. —— A pineal eye in the Mesozoic mammalia. Science, vol. ix, p. 92. 1887. New York.

206. —— The pineal eye in Tritylodon. Science, vol. ix, p. 114. 1887. New York.

207. —— The origin of the tritubercular type of mammalian tentition. Science, vol. x, p. 300. 1887. New York.

208. —— No parietal foramen in Tritylodon. Science, vol. ix, p. 538. 1887. New York.

209. OSBORNE, H. F. Note upon the genus *Athrodon*. Amer. Nat., vol. XXI, p. 1020. 1887. Philadelphia.

210. —— On the structure and classification of Mesozoic mammalia. Journ. Acad. Nat. Sci. Philad., vol. IX, No. 2, pp. 186-265. July, 1888. Philadelphia.

211. —— A review of the Lydekkers' arrangement of the Mesozoic mammalia. (Cat. Foss. Mamm. Brit. Mus., pt. v, 1887.) Amer. Nat., vol. XXII, pp. 232-236. 1888. Philadelphia.

212. —— Chalicotherium and Macrotherium. Amer. Nat., vol. XXII, pp. 729, 730. 1888. Philadelphia.

213. —— The nomenclature of the mammalian molar cusps. Amer. Nat., vol. XXII, pp. 926-928. 1888. Philadelphia.

214. —— The evolution of the mammalian molar teeth to and from the trituber-cular type. Amer. Nat., vol. XXII, pp. 1067-1079. October, 1888. Philadelphia.

215. —— Additional observations upon the structure and classification of the Mesozoic mammalia. Proc. Acad. Nat. Sci. Philad., pp. 292-301. October, 1888. Philadelphia.

216. —— and SCOTT, W. B. (*See* Scott, W. B., and Osborne, H. F.)

217. OWEN, RICHARD. American evidences of Eocene mammals of the "Plastic Clay" Period. Brit. Assoc. A. S., 1886, vol. LV, p. 1033. London.

218a. PACCARD, A. S. On the Syncarida, a hitherto undescribed synthetic group of Malacostracous Crustacea. Mem. Nat. Acad. Sci., vol. III, pp. 123-128, pls. I, II. 1887. Washington.

218b. —— On the Gampsonychidæ, an undescribed family of Schizopod Crustacea. Mem. Nat. Acad. Sci., vol. III, pp. 129-133, pl. III. (Read 1885.) 1887. Washington.

218c. —— On the Anthracaridæ, a family of Carboniferous Macrurous Decapod Crustacea. Mem. Nat. Acad. Sci., vol. III, pp. 135-139, pl. IV. (Read 1885.) 1887. Washington.

218d. —— On the Carboniferous Xiphosurous Fauna of North America. Mem. Nat. Acad. Sci., vol. III, pp. 143-157, pls. V, VI, VII. (Read 1885.) 1887. Washington.

218e. —— On the class Podostomata, a group embracing the Merostomata and Tri-lobites. Annals and Mag. Nat. Hist., 5th series, vol. XIX, pp. 164, 165. 1887. London.

219. ——. Discovery of the thoracic feet in a Carboniferous Phyllocaridan. Proc. Amer. Phil. Soc., vol. XXIII, p. 380. 1887. Philadelphia.

220 —— Fossil Arthropods. Amer. Nat., vol. XXI, p. 1100. 1887. Philadelphia.

221. PAVLOW, MARIE. Étude sur l'histoire paléontologique des Ongulés en Amérique et en Europe. Bull. Soc. Imp. Nat. Moscou, No. 2, p. 443. 1887. Russia.

222. PROSSER, C. S. The Upper Hamilton of Chenango and Otsego Counties, New York. (Abstract.) Proc. A. A. A. S., vol. XXXVI, p. 210. 1887. Salem, Massachusetts.

223. PUMPELLY, RAPHAEL. On the fossils of Littleton, New Hampshire. Amer. Journ. Sci., vol. XXXVI, pp. 79, 80. January, 1888. New Haven.

224. RINGUEBERG, E. N. S. A Trilobite track, illustrating one mode of progression of the Trilobites. Proc. A. A. A. S., vol. XXXV, p. 228. 1887. Salem, Mass.

225. —— Some new species of fossils from the Niagara shales of western New York. Proc. Acad. Nat. Sci. Philad., pt. II, pp. 131-137, pl. VIII. 1888. Philadelphia.

226. —— On Niagara shales of western New York; a study of the origin of their subdivisions and their faunæ. Amer. Geol., vol. I, pp. 263-271. May, 1888. Minneapolis.

227. ROMINGER, C. Descriptions of a new form of Bryozoa. Proc. Acad. Nat. Sci. Philad., pt. I, p. 11. 1887. Philadelphia.

228. —— Description of Primordial fossils from Mt. Stephens, Northwest Territory of Canada. Proc. Acad. Nat. Sci., pp. 12-19. 1887. Philadelphia.

229. SAMPSON, F. A.   Notes on the Subcarboniferous series at Sedalia, M. Trans N. Y. Acad. Sci., vol., VII pp 246,217. 1888. New York.

230. SCOTT, W. B., and OSBORNE, H. F.   Preliminary account of the fossil mammals from the White River formation contained in the Museum of Comparative Zoölogy. Bull. Mus. Comp. Zool , vol. XIII, No. 5, p 151. 1887. Cambridge.

231. ——— ——— Preliminary report on the vertebrate fossils of the Uinta formation. collected by the Princeton expedition of 1886. Proc. Amer. Phil. Soc., pp. 255–264. 1887. Philadelphia.

232. SCUDDER, S. H.   Notice of "Fossil Insects." Science, suppl., vol IX, p. 426. 1887. New York.

233. ——— Note on some British Carboniferous cockroaches. Proc. Bost. Soc. Nat. Hist., vol. XXIII, pp. 356–359. 1887. Boston.

234. SEELEY, H. G.   On *Thecospondylus Daviesi* (Seeley), with some remarks on the classification of the Dinosauria. Quart. Journ. Geol. Soc., vol. XLIV, pp. 79–87. February, 1888. London.

235. SELWYN, ALFRED R. C.   "On new facts relating to Eozoon Canadense." Science, vol. XI, p. 146. 1888. New York.

236. SHALER, N. S.   On the geology of the Cambrian district of Bristol County, Massachusetts. Bull. Mus. Comp. Zoöl., vol. XVI, No. 2, pp. 13–42. October, 1888. Cambridge.

237. SHALER, N. S., and FOERSTE, A. F.   Preliminary descriptions of North Attleborough fossils. Bull. Mus. Comp. Zool., vol. XVI, No. 2, Geol. Series, vol. II, pp. 27–41, pl. I, II. 1888. Cambridge, Massachusetts.

238. SHERBORN, CHAS. D.   A bibliography of the Foraminifera, recent and fossil, from 1865 to 1888, with notes explanatory of some of the rare and little known publications. (See notice, Amer. Journ. Sci., vol XXXVI, p. 295.) 1888. New Haven.

239. SHIMEK, B.   Notes on the fossils of the Loess at Iowa City, Iowa. Amer. Geol., vol. I, No. 3, pp. 149–152. 1888. Minneapolis.

240. SIMPSON, GEORGE B.   Descriptions of new species of fossils from the Clinton, Lower Helderberg, Chemung, and Waverly groups, found in the collections of the geological survey of Pennsylvania. Trans. Amer. Phil. Soc. (read December 5, 1888.) Philadelphia.

241. SMITH, EUGENE A., and JOHNSON, LAWRENCE C.   Tertiary and Cretaceous strata of the Tuscaloosa, Tombigbee, and Alabama Rivers. Bull. 43, U. S. Geol. Survey, pp. 1–189. 1887. Washington.

242. SMITH, H. P.   "*Bison latifrons*." Journ .Cincinn. Soc. Nat. Hist., vol. X, No.1, p. 19. Cincinnati.

243. SOWTER, T. W. EDWIN.   Preliminary Notes on the Chazy formation at Aylmer, Province of Quebec. Ottawa Nat., vol. II, No. 1, pp. 11–15. April, 1888. Ottawa, Canada. (*See* Ami, H. M , and Sowter, T. W. E.)

244. TOPLEY, WILLIAM, and SHERBORN, CHARLES DAVIES.   The Geological Record for 1880–1884 (inclusive). A list of publications on geology, mineralogy. and palæontology, published during those years; together with certain references omitted from previous volumes. Edited by William Topley, F. R. S., F. G. S., and Charles Davies Sherborn, F. G. S.   Vol. I. Stratigraphical and descriptive geology, pp. i– xl and 1–544. 1888. London.

245. ULRICH, E. O.   Silurian and Devonian fossils. Amer. Nat., vol. XXI, p. 69. 1887 Washington.

246. ——— A list of the Bryozoa of the Waverly group in Ohio, with descriptions of new species. Bull. Denison Univ., vol. IV, pt. I, pp. 61–96, pls. XIII, XIV. December, 1888. Granville, Ohio.

247. ——— A correlation of the Lower Silurian horizons of Tennessee and of the Ohio and Mississippi Valleys with those of New York and Canada. Amer. Geol., vol. I, No. 2, pp. 100–110, 179–190, 305–315; vol. II. pp. 39–44. February, 1888, etc. Minneapolis.

248. ULRICH, E. O. On *Sceptropora*, a new genus of Bryozoa, with remarks on *Helopora*, Hall, and other genera of that type. Amer. Geol., vol. I, pp. 228–234. April, 1888. Minneapolis.

249. —— Letter: Reply to Mr. J. F. James about nomenclature of some Cincinnati group fossils. Amer. Geol., vol. I, pp. 333–335. May, 1888. Minneapolis.

250. VODGES, ANTHONY W. The genera and species of North American Carboniferous Trilobites. Annals N. Y. Acad. Sci., vol. IV, pp. 69–105, pl. II, III. 1888. New York.

251. —— Description of two new species of Carboniferous Trilobites. Trans. N. Y. Acad. Sci., vol. VII, pp. 247–250. June, 1888. New York.

252. WACHSMUTH, CH., and SPRINGER, F. Revision of the Palæocrinoidea. Pt. III. Proc. Acad. Nat. Sci. Philad., pp. 64–227. (March 30, 1886.) 1887. Philadelphia.

253. —— —— The summit plates in Blastoids, Crinoids, and Cystids, and their morphological relations. Proc. Acad. Nat. Sci. Philad., pt. I, pp. 82–114. March, 1887. Philadelphia.

254. —— —— Discovery of the ventral structure of *Taxocrinus*, and the consequent modifications in the classification of the Crinoidea. Proc. Acad. Nat. Sci. Philad., pp. 337–363, pl. XVIII. 1888. Philadelphia.

255. —— —— *Crotalocrinus*, its structure and zoölogical position. Proc. Acad. Nat. Sci. Philad., pp. 364–390, pl. XVIII. 1888. Philadelphia.

256. WALCOTT, C. D. Notice of second contribution to the studies of the Cambrian faunas of North America. Amer. Journ. Sci., vol. XXXIII, p. 150. February, 1887. New Haven.

257. —— Note on "The Taconic System." Amer. Journ. Sci., vol. XXXIII, pp. 152, 153. February, 1887. New Haven.

258. —— Cambrian age of the roofing slates of Granville, Washington County, New York. Proc. A. A. A. S., vol. XXXV, pp. 220, 221. 1887. Salem, Massachusetts.

259. —— Note on the genus Archæocyathus of Billings. Amer. Journ. Sci., vol. XXXIV, pp. 145, 146. August, 1887. New Haven.

260. —— Fauna of the "Upper Taconic" of Emmons, in Washington County, New York. Amer. Journ. Sci., XXXIV, pp. 187–199. September, 1887. New Haven.

261. —— Section of Lower Silurian (Ordovician) and Cambrian strata in central New York, as shown by a deep well near Utica. (Abstract.) Proc. A. A. A. S., vol. XXXVI, pp. 211, 212. December, 1887. Salem, Massachusetts.

262. —— Discovery of fossils in the Lower Taconic of Emmons. (Abstract.) Proc. A. A. A. S., vol. XXXVI, pp. 212, 213. December, 1887. Salem, Massachusetts.

263. —— The Taconic System of Emmons, and the use of the name Taconic in geologic nomenclature. Amer. Journ. Sci., vol. XXXVI. pp. 229–242, 307–327, 394–401, and map. March, 1888. New Haven.

264. —— Cambrian fossils from Mount Stephens, northwest territory of Canada. Amer. Journ. Sci., vol. XXXVI, pp. 161–166. September, 1888. New Haven.

265. —— The stratigraphical succession of the Cambrian faunas of North America. Nature, vol. XXXVIII, p. 551. 1888. London and New York.

266. WARD, LESTER F. Types of the Laramie flora. Bull. 37, U. S. Geol. Survey. 8vo. 344 pp., incl. 57 double-page plates. 1887. Washington.

267. —— On the organization of the fossil plants of the Coal Measures. Part XIV. The true fructification of the Calmites, by W. C. Williamson. (Briefly reviewed by L. F. W.) Amer. Journ. Sci., vol. XXXVI, pp. 71, 72. 1888. New Haven.

268. —— A review of "Einleitung in die Palæophytologie vom botanischen Standpunkt aus. Bearbeitet von H. Grafen zu Solms-Laubach." Amer. Journ. Sci., vol. XXXVI, p. 72. 1888. New Haven.

269. —— Evidence of the fossil plants as to the age of the Potomac Formation. Amer. Journ. Sci., vol. XXXVI, pp. 119–131. August, 1888. New Haven.

270. WARD, LESTER F. "On the organization of the fossil plants of the Coal Measures. Pt. XIII. By W. C. Williamson, LL. D., F. R. S. Phil. Trans Roy. Soc. London, vol. CLXXVIII. 1887." (Notice.) Amer. Journ. Sci., vol. XXXVI, p. 256. 1888. New Haven.

271. —— Note on Nya anmarkningar om Williamsonia af A. G. Nathorst. (Ofversigt af Kongl. Vetenskaps Akademiens Forhandlingar, June, 1888, No. 6.) Amer. Journ. Sci., vol. XXXVI, p. 391. 1888. New Haven.

272. WEBSTER, CLEMENT L. Notes on the geology of Johnson County. Amer. Nat., vol. XXII, pp. 408-419. 1888. Philadelphia.

273. —— Notes on the Rockford Shales. Amer. Nat., vol. XXII, pp. 444-446. May, 1888. Philadelphia.

274. —— Description of new and imperfectly known species of Brachiopods from the Devonian rocks of Iowa. Amer. Nat., vol. XXII, pp. 1100-1104. 1888. Philadelphia.

275. —— Description of new species of fossils from the Rockford shales of Iowa. Amer. Nat., vol. XXII, pp. 1013-1018. 1888. Philadelphia.

276. —— A description of the Rockford shales of Iowa. Proc. Dav. Acad. Nat. Sci., vol. V, pp. 100-109. (1888?) Davenport, Iowa.

277. WHITAKER. W., and DALTON, W. H. The Geological Record for 1879, pp. i-xxxiv and 1-418. 8vo. Taylor and Francis. 1887. London.

278. WHITE, C. A. On the age of the coal found in the region traversed by the Rio Grande. Amer. Journ. Sci., vol. XXXIII, pp. 18-20. 1887. New Haven.

279. —— Remarks on the revision of the Palæocrinoidea of Wachsmuth and Springer. Amer. Journ. Sci., vol. XXXIII, pp. 154-157. 1887. New Haven.

280. —— On the inter-relation of contemporaneous fossil faunas and floras. Amer. Journ. Sci., vol. XXXIII, pp. 364-374. 1887. New Haven.

281. —— Review of Wachsmuth and Springer's "Summit plates in Blastoids, Crinoids, and Cystids, and their morphological relations." Amer. Journ. Sci., vol. XXXIV, p. 232. 1887. New Haven.

282. —— On new generic forms of Cretaceous Mollusca, and their relation to other forms. Proc. Acad. Nat. Sci. Philad. for 1887, pp. 32-37, pl. II. Philadelphia.

283. —— On the Cretaceous formations of Texas, and their relation to those of other portions of North America. Proc. Acad. Nat. Sci. Philad. for 1887, pp. 39-47. 1887. Philadelphia.

284. —— Review of Charles D. Walcott's Second Contribution to the studies on the Cambrian faunas of North America. (Bull. 30, U. S. Geol. Surv., pp. 225, 32 plates, Washington, 1886.) Neu. Jahrb. fur Min., Geol. und Pal., Band II, Seit. 361-363. 1887. Stuttgart.

285. —— Contributions to the Palæontology of Brazil, comprising descriptions of Cretaceous invertebrate fossils, mainly from the Provinces of Sergipe, Pernambuco, Para, and Bahia. 4to. 274 pp., 28 pl. Arch. do Mus. Nacional do Rio de Janeiro, vol. VII. 1888. Rio de Janeiro. (Published in English and Portuguese.)

286. —— On the relation of the Laramie group to earlier and later formations. Amer. Journ. Sci., vol. XXXV, pp. 432-438. 1888. New Haven.

287. —— On the Puget group of Washington Territory. Amer. Journ. Sci., vol. XXXVI, pp. 443-450. 1888. New Haven.

288. —— On the occurrence of later Cretaceous deposits in Iowa. Amer. Geol., vol. I, pp. 221-227. 1888. Minneapolis.

289. —— In a note to the editors, Dr White announces that he has "found that Mr. Cummings was entirely correct in his reported discovery of Mesozoic and Palæozoic types of Invertebrates commingled in one and the same layer of the Permian in Baylor, Archer, and Wichita Counties, Texas." Amer. Nat., vol. XXII, p. 926. 1888. Philadelphia.

290. —— On Hindeastræa, a new generic form of Cretaceous Astræidæ Geol. Mag., dec. III, vol. V, No. 8, pp. 362, 363. 1888. London.

291. WHITEAVES, J. F. On some fossils from the Hamilton formation of Ontario, with a list of the species at present known from that formation and province. Geol. and Nat. Hist. Surv. of Canada, Contri. to Canad. Pal., vol. I, pp. 91–126, and plate. 1887–1888. Ottawa, Canada.

292. —— On some fossils from the Triassic rocks of British Columbia. Geol. and Nat. Hist. Surv. Canada, Contri. to Canad. Pal., vol. I, pp. 127–149, and plate. December, 1888. Ottawa, Canada.

293. —— Illustrations of the Fossil Fishes of the Devonian rocks of Canada. Part I. Trans. Roy. Soc. Canada for 1886, sect. IV, p. 101. May, 1888. Montreal.

294. —— Notes on some Mesozoic Fossils from various localities on the coast of British Columbia, for the most part collected by Dr. G. M. Dawson in the summer of 1885. Geol. and Nat. Hist. Surv. Canada, Ann. Rep. (new ser.), vol. II, 1886, pp. 108B–114B. 1887. Montreal.

295. —— On some fossils from the Cretaceous and Laramie rocks of the Saskatchewan and its tributaries, collected by Mr. J. B. Tyrrell in 1885 and 1886. Geol. and Nat. Hist. Surv. Canada, Ann. Rep. (new ser.), vol. II, 1886, pp. 153E–166E. 1887. Montreal.

296. —— (See Bell, Robert.)

297. WHITFIELD, R. P. Remarks on the molluscan fossils of the New Jersey marl beds, contained in vols. 1 and 2 of that [sic] Palæontology, and on their stratigraphical relations. (Abstract.) Proc. A. A. A. S., vol. XXXV, p. 215. 1887. Salem, Mass.

298. —— Notice of geological investigations along the eastern shores of Lake Champlain, conducted by Prof. H. M. Seeley and Pres. Ezra Brainard, of Middlebury College, with descriptions of the new fossils discovered. (Abstract.) Proc. A. A. A. S., vol. XXXV, pp. 215, 216. 1887. Salem, Mass.

299. —— New Jersey Cretaceous. Amer. Nat., vol. XXI, p. 66. 1887. Philadelphia.

300. WILLIAMS, H. S. The Strophomenidæ : a palæontological study of the method of the initiation of genera and species. (Abstract.) Proc. A. A. A. S., vol. XXXV, pp. 227, 228. 1887. Salem, Mass.

301. —— On the different types of the Devonian System in North America. Amer. Jour. Sci., vol. XXXV, pp. 51–59. January, 1888. New Haven.

302. —— Fossil faunas of the Upper Devonian ; the Genesee section, New York. Bull. 41, U. S. Geol. Surv., 8vo, 121 pp., 4 pl. 1888. Washington.

303. WILLIAMS, S. G. Note on the Lower Helderberg rocks of Cayuga Lake. 6th Ann. Rep. State Geologist for the year 1886. 1887. Albany.

304. —— The Tully limestone, its distribution, and its known fossils. 6th Ann. Rep. of N. Y. State Geologist for 1886, pp. 12–29, and map. 1887. Albany.

305. WINCHELL, ALEXANDER. Extinct Peccary in Michigan. Amer. Geol., vol. I, p. 67. 1888. Minneapolis.

306. WINCHELL, N. H., assisted by UPHAM, WARREN. The Geology of Minnesota; vol. II of the Final Report. The Geol. and Nat. Hist. Surv. of Minnesota for 1882–1885, pp. i–xxiv and 1–695, 42 pls., and 32 figures. 1888. Minneapolis.

307. WOODWARD, ANTHONY. Supplement I to the Bibliography of the Foraminifera, recent and fossil, including Eozoon and Receptaculites. (Printed in the Fourteenth Annual Report of the Geological and Natural History Survey of Minnesota, pp. 167–311, 1885.) Jour. N. Y. Micr. Soc. January, 1888. New York.

PETROGRAPHY FOR 1887 AND 1888.

By GEORGE P. MERRILL, *Curator in the National Museum.*

The years 1887 and 1888, covered by this report, have been years of unprecedented activity and progress in that branch of geological science to which the name petrography is now commonly applied. Accessions to the ranks of workers, both in America and abroad, have been rapid and constant, and the science now holds a place in the curricula of our leading institutions of learning.* Prior to 1880, although beginnings had been made by Wadsworth at Harvard, Hawes at Yale, and Julien at Columbia College, yet the science was still practically unrecognized and almost unheard of in the majority of American colleges and universities. At the present date it however holds a recognized place in the curricula of Colby, at Waterville, Maine; Harvard and Amherst, Massachusetts; New Haven, Connecticut; Cornell and Columbia, New York; Johns Hopkins, at Baltimore, Maryland; State University, at Minneapolis, Minnesota; State Mining School, at Houghton, Michigan; State University, at Madison, Wisconsin; and in the University of California, at Berkeley, in that State. At many other institutions, the subject is referred to incidentally in the regular courses of geology and mineralogy, or is taken up to some extent by post-graduate students working for the higher degrees.

A pleasing and encouraging feature of this stage of work is the freedom from prejudice and pre-conceptions manifested by most classes of students, and it is doubtful if any branch of science has shown a more hopeful and healthful condition of affairs than that existing to-day among petrographers. The disposition or desire at first manifest to claim for the new departure all manner of possibilities, to solve immediately the problems of rock classification, formation, durability, and alteration, has already given way to a broader, more philosophic spirit; and petrographers in general are disposed to hold opinions and convictions in abeyance, to regard each new discovery in but the light of one new fact from among the chaos of which, when sufficient may have accumulated, may be picked out the general principles governing rock history and the history of the globe.

---

* For a very complete account of methods and aims of petrography, the American reader is referred to the neat little pamphlet of 35 pages, by Dr. George H. Williams, entitled Modern Petrography, D. C. Heath & Co , Boston.

It is a necessary consequence to the late development of the science that a great amount of detailed study be given to rock structure and composition as revealed not only by the microscope and chemical analyses, but by their field relations as well, and that therefore the published papers should be given up largely to what may seem to the outsider the dry, uninteresting and perhaps immaterial iteration and re-iteration of details in even their most minute forms. To enter upon a discussion or to note even in abstract the contents of all these papers would be useless and out of place here, and in the body of this paper I shall strive to show only the general tendencies of these, to point out if possible the ultimate conclusions towards which they seem to be leading, leaving a majority of the papers to be enumerated in the bibliography.

NEW PUBLICATIONS.

Early in 1887 there appeared the second volume of the second edition of Professor Rosenbusch's works on petrography, entitled "Mikroskopische Physiographie der massigen Gesteine," the first volume, "Mikroskopische Physiographie der Mineralien und Gesteine," having appeared in 1885. The entire work comprises 1,541 pages, with 32 full-page plates showing microstructures of rocks and minerals, and 177 wood-cuts in the text. The two volumes together form a most accurate and exhaustive résumé of the sum of petrographic knowledge up to date of issue, and their appearance marks a decided epoch in the history of the science of petrology. Under the title of "Hülfstabellen zur mikroskopischen Mineralbestimmung in Gesteinen," the same authority has issued a compact little work giving in tabular form the crystallographic, optical, and, general physical and chemical properties of all the common rock-forming minerals. It is of interest to note that upwards of one hundred and seventy varieties are recognized. The arrangement is admirable, and the book can not fail to be of great assistance to all students and workers. An event second in importance only to the issue of Professor Rosenbusch's work has been the translation and abridgment of volume I by Mr. J. P. Iddings, of the U. S. Geological Survey, and its publication by Wiley & Co., New York. As prior to this there was no comprehensive work on the subject in the English language, the importance to English-speaking students of this translation can scarcely be over-estimated.

Mr. J. J. H. Teall has published, under the name of "British Petrography," an admirable work, which, though treating only of British eruptive rocks, is the most systematic and comprehensive work of its kind that has yet been published in the English language. Its size is large octavo, with some 450 pages of text and 47 colored plates, showing microscopic structure in both ordinary and polarized light. The work is not a mere popular compilation of old and well-known facts, but is quite abreast of the times and thoroughly scientific, though at the same time written in such style as to be intelligible to those who are not experts in this particular branch of the subject. The American as

well as the British student is to be congratulated upon its appearance.
Other new works in book form, but which the present writer not having seen can speak of only by title, are noted in the bibliography.

ADVANCE WORK.

While a very large portion of the work of the past two years, as in
years before, has been purely descriptive of the mode of occurrence,
structure, mineral and chemical composition of rocks, yet the subject of
the origin of rocks and the causes of their structural variability have
been by no means ignored, as will be noticed.

THE PHYSICAL AND CHEMICAL CONDITIONS OF CRYSTALLIZATION.

For many years there has been a growing feeling among geologists
that the importance attached, particularly among German authorities,
to geological age as a criterion in rock classification was greatly over-
estimated, and the fact that neither mineral composition nor structure
are necessarily dependent upon age is now very generally conceded.
In his latest work, to be sure, Professor Rosenbusch has not wholly dis-
carded the age qualification, owing to the fact that it is, as a rule, only
among the most ancient rocks that the deep-seated portions have been
rendered accessible by erosion, while on the other hand it is often only
among the more recent that the effusive portions have escaped erosion
or alteration and hence are accessible for investigation. The now well-
known researches of Messrs. Hague and Iddings upon the rocks of the
Comstock Lode. Nevada,* showing that the "degree of crystallization developed in igneous rocks is mainly dependent upon the conditions of heat
and pressure under which the mass has cooled and is independent of
geological time," have received abundant confirmatory evidence, and it
seems now a well-established fact that under similar circumstances crystallization and structure may be the same regardless of geological age.
More recent discoveries and studies in this same general line have been
productive of very interesting results. In a paper entitled "On the latest volcanic eruption in California and its peculiar lava,"† Mr. J. S. Diller has described a very interesting type of rock, evidently a true basalt, but unique in carrying primary porphyritic quartz, associated with
olivine, a condition of affairs ordinarily considered on chemical grounds
as not likely to occur. The peculiarity is explained on the supposition
that the quartz was the first mineral to separate out from the magma,
and its crystallization took place under great pressure at such depth
and under such conditions of physical and chemical equilibrium as are
as yet largely conjectural. Mr. Diller has been followed by Mr. Iddings
with a paper on the "Origin of quartz in basalt,"‡ in which, by a series of
analyses of quartz-bearing and quartzless basalts from New Mexico and

---

* Bull. U. S. Geol. Survey, No 17, 1885.
† Am. Jour. of Science, January, 1887.
‡ Ibid, September, 1888

California, it is shown that the presence or absence of free quartz is not necessarily dependent upon the chemical composition of the magma, but that forms in which the mineral is abundant may yield on bulk analysis as low percentages of silica as those in which it is quite lacking. It is also shown that a rock from the Yellowstone Park having a composition almost identical with that of Diller's quartz basalt has the mineralogical composition and structural features of a quartzose diorite. Mr. Iddings's conclusions are that these quartzes are primary crystallizations from the molten basaltic magma and exhibit no definite relations to its chemical composition, their production being referred to certain physical conditions attending some earlier period of the magma's existence. He is inclined to regard their formation as influenced by water vapor at a great pressure.

This same authority has also published* some interesting notes on the nature and origin of the lithophysæ and the lamination of acid lavas as displayed in the obsidian of the Yellowstone Park. The lythophysæ he regards as of aqueo-igneous origin, as having been produced by the action of absorbed gases upon the molten glass, from which they were liberated during the process of cooling and consequent crystallization. The differences in consistency and phases of crystalization producing the laminated structure are regarded as "directly due to the amount of vapors absorbed in the various layers of the lava and to their mineralizing influence."

In this connection a recent paper by Dr. A. Lagorio,† of the University of Warsaw, is of the greatest interest. The author gives the results of several years' chemical investigation on the nature of the glassy ground mass and crystallized portions of eruptive rocks and arrives at some new and important conclusions. These, in brief, are as follows: He considers the "normal glass," in which are dissolved all the substances going on crystallization to form the crystalline secretions of a rock, to be a silicate of the composition of $K_2O\ 2\ SiO_2$ (p. 508). From this the dissolved oxides and silicates separate out in the order of their solubility and the relative condition of saturation, the sodium-bearing minerals, as a rule, separating out at an earlier stage than those in which potassium is the predominating alkali. The order of crystallization from the normal magma, as above given, would thus be as follows: Oxides, pure iron silicates, magnesian silicates, iron magnesian, magnesian lime, magnesian potash, lime, lime soda, soda, and finally the potash silicates and free quartz. The writer states further that the minerals forming the second generation of crystals are never absolutely identical in composition with those of the first, and are dependent for their formation not upon a recurrence of like conditions, but rather upon the composition of the residual magma.

---

* Am. Jour. Sci., 1887, XXXIII, pp. 36–45.

† Ueber die Natur der Glasbasis sowie der Krystallisationsvorgänge im eruptiven Magma. Min. u. pet. Mitth., 8. B., VI. II., 1887, p. 421.

These results, though extremely suggestive, are not, it will be observed, in exact accordance with 'those arrived at by Messrs. Diller and Iddings, to whose papers we have already referred. The results obtained by these gentlemen, coupled with what is already known regarding the phenomena of crystallization, seem to show that structural features, and to a certain extent the universal composition of eruptive rocks, are dependent upon (1) the chemical composition of the magma and (2) the varying conditions of heat and pressure under which this magma existed prior to and during the course of its eruption. A mineral which separates out under certain temporary conditions of heat and pressure may, under changed conditions, be partially or wholly resorbed, and the condition of chemical equilibrium be so changed as to give rise to crystalline secretions of quite different nature.

Mr. G. F. Becker, in a paper treating of the texture of massive rocks,[*] and drawing his illustrations from the magnificent exposure offered by Mount Davidson and the Comstock Lode, Nevada, argues on chemical and theoretical grounds that the structural differences existing between holocrystalline porphyritic and granular rocks are due not to condition of cooling, but rather to original differences in composition and fluidity of the magma. Granular structure, excepting in rare cases, is due to imperfect fusion and fluidity of the magma. Porphyritic structure, on the other hand, is the normal structure of rocks cooling gradually from a high temperature and consequent state of very perfect fluidity. When the two types of structure are associated it is argued that this is due to a lack of homogeneity in chemical composition and to temperatures sufficient to fuse portions, but not the entire mass. Granular rocks as a rule, he argues, have formed at lower temperatures than porphyries of precisely the same chemical composition. Granular structure is therefore characteristic of rocks formed by the metamorphism of sediments and porphyritic structure characteristic of those crystallizing from homogeneous fluid magmas. These conclusions are based largely on a new law of thermo-chemistry advanced by Mr. Becker in a previous paper.[†] In this same connection may be mentioned the researches of Professor Judd, who, in a very interesting and important paper in the Geological Magazine for January, 1888,[‡] calls attention, first, to the great dissimilarity in chemical composition of rocks classed as enstatite or hypersthene andesite, the silica percentages in extreme cases varying nearly 20 per cent., and shows that this difference is due mainly to the relative proportions of the crystalline constituents to the glassy base. Then, treating wholly of the glassy lavas of Krakatoa, he shows that the obsidian, containing a considerable percentage of volatile matter, swells up and fuses at approximately a white heat, while the stony

---

[*] Am. Jour. of Sci., 1887, xxxiii, p. 50.

[†] Am. Jour. of Sci., 1886, xxxi, p. 120.

[‡] The Natural History of Lavas as illustrated by the materials ejected from Krakatoa. J. W. Judd. Geol. Mag., January, 1888, vol. v, p. 1.

lavas and pitch-stones remain unchanged. In the field this distinction is shown by the pumiceous condition of the obsidian and massive form of the stony lava and pitch-stone. From these and the facts that the porphyritic constituents of the obsidian occur in "glomero-porphyritic" forms he argues that this obsidian is but a refused portion of the older Krakatoa lavas, and, after a discussion of Dr. Guthrie's experiments on the influence of water in lowering the fusion points of mineral substances, proceeds to argue that this refusion and perhaps the volcanic eruption of Krakatoa itself was brought about through the admission of water in the mass of mixed silicates buried at depths below the surface. The mass of anhydrous rock might be in a solid state at a comparatively high temperature, while the same rock rendered hydrous through the gradual percolation of water would ultimately fuse and give rise to all the phenomena of the eruption. As expressed by Guthrie, "the phenomena of fusions is nothing more than an extreme case of liquefaction by fusion," it being impossible to tell where liquefaction leaves off and fusion begins.

CONTACT METAMORPHISM.

Several fine illustrations of contact metamorphism have been described during the two years covered by this report and mention may here be made of a few of the more interesting and important.

Dr. G. H. Williams * concludes an admirable series of papers on the rocks of the "Cortland series," near Peekskill, N. Y., with a description of their contact metamorphisms or phenomena produced by eruptive rocks on the adjacent schists and limestones. The eruptive, or dike rocks in this case are norites, gabbros, peridotites, mica or mica-hornblende diorites, pyroxenites, and hornblendite. The schists are highly crystalline schistose rocks consisting of quartz and feldspar, with both muscovite and biotite together with tourmaline, magnetite, and zircon. Approaching the line of contact the schists become more and more puckered and contorted and filled with lens-shaped "eyes" of quartz containing garnets and other contact minerals. In the schists themselves are developed staurolite, sillimanite, cyanite, and garnet, the amount of metamorphism being directly proportional to the nearness to the line of contact. At contact the schistose structure is almost completely obliterated and the rock becomes hard and massive, appears more or less fused with the mica diorite, is highly garnetiferous, and consists of a great variety of minerals, including staurolite, sillimanite, pyroxene, green hornblende, diallage, scapolite, and sphene. Briefly expressed, the progressive change, approaching the line of contact consist in a gradual decrease in the amount of silica and the alkalies with a corresponding increase in iron and alumina, this being accompanied by a disappearance of the quartz and muscovite and the development of biotite, sillimanite, staurolite, cyanite, and garnet. In fragments of the schist taken up by the erup-

---

* Am. Jour. of Science, October, 1888, p. 254.

tive were found a still greater variety of metamorphic minerals, including sillimanite, cyanite, garnet, staurolite, tourmaline, pleonaste, corundum, margarite, ripidolite, rutile, sphene, ilmenite, zircon, magnetite, augite, scapolite, zoisite, and epidote.

The limestones in the vicinity were by the same agencies bleached and frequently rendered more closely crystalline, while lime-bearing pyroxenes and hornblendes, zoisite, sphene, and scapolite are developed. In the narrow dikes the nature of the erupted rock was also modified. The iron and emery beds along the southern and eastern portions of Cortland the area are regarded as a result of this same metamorphic action upon pre-existing material.

Cohen* has described a case of contact metamorphism in which an ochre yellow, fine-grained, and imperfectly schistose sandstone, consisting essentially of quartz and minute colorless mica laminæ and clayey matter colored by iron hydroxide, has been changed by contact with a dike of diabase. Approaching the contact the sandstone becomes greenish gray in color and the schistosity becomes obliterated. The green color is due to the development of a greenish, strongly pleochroic and doubly refracting chloritic mineral, which increases in quantity as the line of contact is approached. The stone also assumes a slightly higher specific gravity and the fracture becomes choncoidal. With the increase of the chloritic mineral there begin also to appear small flecks of a brown magnesia mica. The earthy (trüben) material disappears, as does also the small amount of calcareous matter observed, having apparently gone to form the new mica. As the zone of immediate contact is approached, the rock becomes darker till finally grayish black, and the choncoidal fracture more perfectly developed. The microscope shows it to still consist of the secondary chlorite and brown mica together with the original constituents. At contact the stone is a typical hornfels or lydian stone of a clear black color and shelly fracture, but with no new minerals developed, although the structural arrangements are somewhat changed. Analyses of samples in which the biotite laminæ were beginning to be developed, of the grayish black variety with shelly fracture and of the typical hornstone, showed that the composition had in all cases remained practically unchanged, that the changes were not due to any addition of material from the dike. In contact metamorphisms described by Stecher† the sandstones and shales have have exercised a very considerable influence upon the olivine diabases cutting them. The material of the dikes was found to be more acid near the contact line, due presumably to the siliceous material dissolved from the sandstone and shale. Olivine in quite perfect crystals occurs near the contact but gradually diminishes in quantity as one recedes till it is wholly lacking in the center. This is accounted for by Stecher on the supposition that the material of the dike cooled most quickly on

---

* Neues Ja'hrb., 1887, Beil.-Band. 1. Heft, p. 251.
† Min. u. pet. Mittheil., IX. B., II. and III. Heft, pp. 145–205.

the edges and preserved the olivine which had formed prior to its injection. The inner portion remaining longer liquid and becoming more acid from the dissolved silica of the shales, redissolved the olivines.

Barrois* has shown from a study of the contact phenomena of the granites of Morbihan that two forms of metamorphism occur, both structural, the one due to rapid cooling and the second to mechanical agencies. In the first there is a transition from even granular to porphyritic or aplitic forms. In the second a schistose form is produced only at the periphery of the mass and due wholly to powerful mechanical agencies.

Greim† has described in great detail an occurrence of contact phenomena between the olivine diabase near Weilburg, in Hesse-Nassau, and the adjacent schists. Here the diabases remain practically unchanged, but that they are of finer texture at the contact, while the schists, composed originally of quartz, white mica, and hematite with lenticular beds of calcite, are converted into a compact rock with an isotropic groundmass in which are quartz, andalusite, spinel, and a chloritic mineral. The change has taken place with a very decided increase in the amount of soda and iron, supplied apparently by the diabase.

Rüdemann‡ has described an interesting case of contact metamorphism in phyllites and clay slates at Reuth, near Gefrees, Bavaria. The erupted rock is a biotite granite and in itself has suffered no other than structural modifications and a slight increase in the proportional amount of biotite. At contact both phyllites and slates are converted into a hard, compact, blue-black hornfels consisting of a crystalline-granular aggregate of quartz, deep reddish brown mica (biotite), a little muscovite, and andalusite. This zone, some 120 paces in width, is succeeded by a second some 380 paces in width of andalusite mica schist and this by a spotted mica schist (Knoten-Schiefer) some 500 paces wide. Lastly the least altered rock, the chiastolite schist zone, some 400 paces wide, derived from the clay slates, or a biotite rock (Garben-Schiefer) from the phyllite. It is noticeable that in all these cases the chemical composition of the altered rocks is the same as that of the unaltered beds from which they are derived, no new material having been supplied by the erupted mass, though Rüdemann would account for the formation of the hornfels by the action of the heated waters accompanying the eruption upon the materials of the slates and phyllites. The line of contact between the granite and hornfels, it should be noted, is in all cases perfectly sharp and distinct. The entire width of the metamorphosed zone was in the case of the phyllites some 1,700 paces, and in that of the clay slates some 1,400.

DYNAMIC METAMORPHISM.

Our knowledge on the subject of dynamic metamorphism has likewise been very materially increased. The question of the origin of the foli-

---

* Ann. de la Soc. Géol. du Nord, November, 1887.
† Neues Jahrb., 1888 1. B., 1. Heft.
‡ Neues Jahrb., v, Beil.-Band, p. 643.

ated structure in gneisses and schists, together with its relation to the original bedded structure, where such existed, has received a good share of attention, particularly from British petrographers, and some very interesting and instructive results have been obtained. That a massive eruptive rock of the composition of gabbro may through dynamic agencies undergo structural changes, including a paramorphism of its pyroxenic constituent, and give rise to schistose dioritic forms, was first conclusively shown in America by the researches of Williams[*] on the gabbros in the vicinity of Baltimore, Maryland, and for several years there has been a growing feeling among petrologists that the schistose structure in many of the so-called metamorphic rocks (meaning metamorphosed sedimentary deposits) was not due to or in any way connected with an original bedding, but that these rocks were in reality of eruptive origin. That this is to a certain extent a correct supposition may now be considered as settled beyond dispute so far as it is applied to certain limited areas. How general this mode of origin may have been and how far it is applicable to the great group of distinctly banded Archæan schists and gneisses is as yet largely conjectural, and few would care to claim it as universal. That such structures are in any way indicative of bedding and consequent sedimentary origin has been vigorously combated by Lawson,[†] who finds similar structures in rocks of undoubted eruptive origin in the Rainy Lake region of Canada. Lawson, however, regards the structure as due to pressure supplied not by orographic movements but by expansion in the erupted mass itself during the process of consolidation, a view which is somewhat at variance with that held by other investigators. Teall[‡] has shown that the banded rocks of the Lizard district include granite, diorite, and gabbro; are, in short, rocks of igneous origin, and their banded structure due to the deformation to which the original rock masses have been subjected. Bonney,[§] too, has given it as his opinion that the foliated glaucophane schist of the Isle de Groix is an eruptive altered by pressure. His conclusions from a study of this rock, together with the gneisses of the district around Quimperlé and the gneisses, granites, and amphibolites of the Roscoff and Morlaix districts, were to the effect that while both igneous and stratified rocks have undergone a certain amount of pressure metamorphism, the igneous rocks being converted into gneisses and schists, yet many of them evidently possessed a true foliation prior to the earth movements. Callaway[‖] has likewise contended in favor of the igneous origin of many of the gneisses and schistose rocks of the Malvern Hills; proof to this effect being afforded by

---

[*] Bull. U. S. Geol. Survey, No. 28, 1886.

[†] Gneissic Foliation and Schistose Cleavage in Dikes, Proc. Can. Inst. of Toronto, 1886, p. 115.

[‡] Geol. Mag., November, 1887, p. 484.

[§] Quar. Jour. Geol. Sci., August, 1887, Vol. XLIII. p. 301,

[‖] Ibid., 1887, p. 517.

the intense contortion of included granitic veins and by other mechanical effects recognized in the rocks when studied by the microscope. Messrs. Fox and Teall* have in like manner accounted for the local development of actinolite schists out of the intrusive greenstones on some of the outlying islands of the Lizard.

But some of the most remarkable results of dynamic metamorphism are those described by members of the Scottish Geological Survey† as occurring in the northwest highlands of that country. In the Archæan areas of this region it is shown (I) that a great series of igneous rocks, including gabbros, peridotites, palæo-picrites, and quartz diorites, in which pegmatite and segregation veins had formed, have, owing to mechanical movements, developed a foliated structure and become converted into gneisses; (II) that basic dikes injected into these rocks subsequent to their foliation have been by similar movements converted— (1) the dolerites into diorites and hornblende schists, (2) the peridotites into talcose schists, (3) the microcline mica rocks into mica schists, and (4) the granites into granitoid gneisses, these gneisses being still further foliated by subsequent movements. This change in the dike rocks is in part molecular and in part chemical. The molecular change of augite into hornblende has afforded the transition of diabase into diorite. Where lines of movement coincide with the margins of one of the dolerite dikes it has usually happened that portions of the outer part, it may be but a few inches or feet, are converted into a hornblende schist, and a further stage of change is met when a broad dike is traversed by several lines of shearing, in which case lenticular or eye-shaped masses of diorite are formed, around which curve in wavy lines beautiful bands of hornblende schist. In the final stages the eyes disappear, and the whole of the original dike is converted into a zone of hornblende schist "consisting mainly of hornblende and secondary feldspar, with a small quantity of mica. This alteration has been attended with the formation of segregations of vitreous quartz, and in the extreme cases by a complete reconstruction of the adjacent gneisses. The latter alteration includes a production of secondary foliations and a more or less complete reconstruction of the rock, the opalescent quartz granites having become elongated and also clear and vitreous; black mica having been developed out of the original hornblende, a white mica out of the original feldspar, and a recrystallization of hornblende in the form of actinolite needles having taken place, together with a beautiful development of secondary feldspars.

Igneous rocks intrusive in Cambrian and Silurian strata are described as having likewise undergone metamorphism, in one case a porphyritic felsite being converted into a fine-grained schist, quartzite into soft sericite schist, fine-grained diorites in limestones being represented by green hornblende and chlorite schists. Pegmatite is described as de-

---

* Quar. Jour. Geol. Soc., May, 1888, XLIV, p. 309.
† Ibid., August, 1888, XLIV, p. 378.

veloped in bands sometimes 100 yards across out of an eruptive igneous mass during the process of its conversion into micaceous gneiss.

B. Lotti[*] claims to have traced the white and veined saccharoidal marbles of Carrara and the adjacent Apennines back into their unchanged forms containing fossils characteristic of the Upper Trias and Muschelkalk. This metamorphism is ascribed wholly to the orographic movements accompanying the uplifting of the mountain range. The same agencies transformed the argilo-siliceous beds into mica-chloritic, ottrelitic or other crystalline schists comparable with those of Archæan age.

MISCELLANY.

The study of the interesting group of Peridotites assumed an almost sensational aspect early in 1887 through the announcement by the late H. Carvill Lewis[†] to the effect that the diamond-bearing rock of the Kimberly, South Africa, mines was a peridotite containing numerous fragments of a highly carbonaceous shale, and that the diamonds were doubtless secondary crystallization products due to the action of the molten rock upon the amorphous carbon contained by them. In view of the fact that Mr. J. S. Diller[‡] had but recently described a somewhat similar peridotite cutting carbonaceous shales in Elliott County, Kentucky, the suggestion offered by Mr. Lewis's paper seemed of sufficient promise to warrant the sending of Messrs. Diller and Kunz once more to the latter locality in the hopes of finding confirmatory results.

The fact that no diamonds were here found is ascribed to the paucity of the shale in carbonaceous matter, Mr. Whitfield's analyses showing but 0.681 per cent. of this material against 37.521 per cent. in the shale of Kimberly. §

Close upon the heels of this discovery comes the announcement of the discovery by Professors Latschinof and Jerofeief of diamonds in a meteoric stone found at Krasnosbbodsk, government of Penza, Russia.

If more proof were needed that serpentine never occurs as an original deposit, but is always a product of the alteration of other minerals, this has been abundantly furnished in two rather striking instances in this country. A heavy dark dull green serpentinous rock occurring in the Onondaga salt group at Syracuse, New York, and which had been investigated by Dr. Hunt ‖ and pronounced by him as an undoubted aqueous deposit, as typically illustrative and confirmatory of his theory

---

* Bull. Soc. Géol. de France, 1888, 3rd, 16th, p. 406.

† Geol. Mag., January, 1887, p. 22.

‡ Bull. U. S. Geol. Survey, No. 38, 1887.

§ Science, 1887, p. 140. It should be noted that R. Cohen, as long ago as 1884 (Proc. Man. Lit. and Philos. Soc., October 7, 1884, p. 5), proposed the igneous theory for the origin of diamonds, while Maskelyne still earlier announced that the diamonds of both Kimberly and Borneo occurred in altered peridotic rocks (Daubree, Ann. des Mines, 1876, IX, p. 130.)

‖ Am. Jour. Sci., XXVI, p. 263; also Min. Physiology and Physiography, p. 447.

of the purely chemical origin of the mineral, has been investigated by
Dr. George H. Williams and proven beyond doubt to be an altered
peridotite, and eruptive. The second and equally striking case of the
secondary origin of the mineral has been furnished by the present
writer,* who investigated the well-known serpentine locality, Montville,
New Jersey. The stone occurs here associated with a coarsely crystallized dolomite in such a way as to at once declare an origin from some
other source than from an igneous rock. The mineral proved here to
be also metasomatic, "a product of indefinite substitution and replacement," after a non-aluminous pyroxene near diopside in composition.
The occurrence is so strikingly like that of the serpentines associated
with calcareous rocks, as described by Dr. Hunt, and also the serpentine of the well-known eozoon, as to render it almost a foregone conclusion that in all these cases the serpentinous material is of similar origin.

The number of mineral species recognized as occurring either as accidental or essential constituents in rock masses is naturally found to
increase as the rocks are studied in greater detail and as methods and
instruments are brought to greater perfection. Professor Rosenbusch,
in his Hulfstabellen zur Mikroskopischen Mineralbestimmung, gives
upwards of one hundred and seventy varieties, of which the optical and
micro chemical properties are sufficiently well known for their determination in the thin section. Among the more interesting occurrences of
the rarer or little noticed of these may be mentioned the following:

The rare manganese epidote or piedmontite has been described by
Prof. Bundjiro Koto † as a characteristic constituent of certain schists
of unexpectedly wide distribution in the Archæan system of Japan.
The typical piedmontite schist is described as consisting essentially
of piedmontite associated with fine quartz grains and with accessory
muscovite, greenish-yellow garnet, rutile, feldspar (probably orthoclase),
blood-red iron glance, and also opaque crystals of the same mineral.
The glaucophane rocks also carry it to some extent. The same mineral
has also been noted by Professor Haworth as occurring sparingly in the
quartz porphyries of southwestern Missouri in the United States. The
allied mineral allanite, first noted as a common constituent of many
granites by Messrs. Cross and Iddings, has been observed by Cross ‡
as a constituent of the quartz porphyries of the Leadville region, and
has also been described by W. H. Hobbs § in the form of parallel inter-
growth with epidote, as a characteristic constituent of a granite porphyry
from Ilchester, Maryland. Graeff ‖ has noted the presence of laavenite
in the elæolite syenites of Brazil. Cohen ¶ calls attention to the fact

---

* Proc. U. S. Nat. Mus., 1888, p. 105.

† Quar. Jour. Geol. Soc., August, 1887, No. 171, p. 474.

‡ Geol. and Mining Industry of Leadville, Colorado, p. 329.

§ Johns Hopkins Univ. Circular, April, 1888.

‖ Neues Jahrb., 1887, I B., 2 Heft, p. 201.

¶ Neues. Jahrb., 1887, II B., p. 178.

that andalusite, a mineral considered as normally a product of contact metamorphism in the crystalline schists, is in microscopic forms a by no means rare constituent of the true granites. Williams [*] describes for the first time in this country the presence of pleonast (hercynite) as occurring in the norites of the Hudson River region, New York, and also perowskite as a microscopic constituent of the altered peridotite at Syracuse, in the same State. A more interesting discovery than any of the above is that of the occurrence of leucite, hitherto found only in recent lavas, in some paleozoic eruptions of Brazil, as announced by Derby.[†] Schmidt has noted for the first time the alteration of olivine in a melaphyr from the Swiss Alps into a bastite-like substance. Williams [‡] has noted the occurrence of rutile secondary after ilmenite in a decomposed diabase from the Big Quinnesec Falls of the Menominee River, Wisconsin. That, however, these are in fact alteration products Cathrein denies.[§] This last-named authority has also described [||] an interesting case of the occurrence of plagioclase pseudomorphous after garnets in a garnet amphibolite from the Swiss Alps. The mineral cordierite, as an essential constituent of rock masses, has for the first time in America been observed by Hovey[¶] in a gneiss occurring near Guilford, Connecticut.

The secondary enlargement of the mineral particles of fragmental rocks as described by Törnebohm, Sorby, Irving, and Van Hise, has become a matter of almost daily observation. Such growths are not, however, confined to clastic rocks. Becke has described a case of secondary enlargements of the hornblende in massive eruptive rocks, and Van Hise [**] has described a like secondary growth of hornblende upon both hornblende and augites in certain Wisconsin diabases. Lastly, the present writer has described [††] a case of the secondary enlargement of augites by fresh deposition of augitic material in a peridotite from Little Deer Isle, on the coast of Maine.

NECROLOGY.

The science has suffered greatly through the deaths of Dr. Max Schuster, of the University of Vienna; of Prof. R. D. Irving, U. S. Geological Survey, Madison, Wisconsin; of Prof. H. Carvill Lewis, Philadelphia, Pennsylvania., and Dr. Theodor Kjerulf, of Christiania, Norway.

---

[*] Neues Jahrb., 1887, II B , p 267.
[†] Quar. Jour. Geol. Soc., 1887, Vol. XLIII, No. 171.
[‡] Neues Jahrb., 1887, II B., p 263.
[§] Ibid., 1888, II B., 2 Heft, p. 151.
[||] Ibid., 1887, I B , 2 H., p. 147.
[¶] Am. Jour. Sci , July, 1888, p 57.
[**] Ibid., May, 1887, p. 385.
[††] Ibid , June, 1888, p 438; also Proc. U. S. Nat. Mus., 1888, p. 191.

BIBLIOGRAPHY OF LITHOLOGY, 1887, 1888.

I.—SPECIAL TREATISES. BOOKS

DANA, J. D. Manual of Mineralogy and Lithology. 4th ed. 518 pp. 8vo. Wiley & Co.

IDDINGS, JOSEPH P. Microscopical Physiography of the rock-making minerals and aid to the microscopical study of rocks. H. Rosenbusch. Translated and abridged for use in schools and colleges. pp. 333. 8vo. Twenty-six plates of photomicrographs.

MAWER, W. Primer of Micro Petrology. London, Office of Life-Lore. 1888.

MICHEL-LÉVY, A., and A. LACROIX. Les Minéraux des Roches. Paris. Librairie Polytechnique. Baudry & Co. 1888.

RUTLEY, FRANK. Rock-forming minerals. Thomas Thurby. London, 1888. 8vo. pp. 252.

ROSENBUSCH, H. Mikroskopische Physiographie der massigen Gesteine. Stuttgart, 1887. 877 pp. and 6 plates showing micro-structures.

—— Hülfstabellen zur mikroskopischen mineralbestimmung in Gesteinen. Stuttgart, 1888.

II.—CURRENT LITERATURE.

(a) RELATING TO CONDITIONS OF CRYSTALLIZATION.

BECKER, GEORGE F. The Washoe Rocks. Bull. Cal. Acad. Sci., No. 6, January, 1887, vol. II, pp. 93–120.

—— The Texture of Massive Rocks. Am. Jour. Sci., 1887, vol. XXXIII, p. 50.

DILLER, J. S. The latest volcanic eruption in northern California, and its peculiar lava. Am. Jour. Sci., 1887, vol. XXXIII, p. 45.

The rock described is a basalt, carrying primary quartzes.

IDDINGS, J. P. The nature and origin of Lythophysæ, and the lamination of acid lavas. Am. Jour. Sci., 1887, vol. XXXIII, p. 36.

—— Obsidian Cliff, Yellowstone National Park. 7th Ann. Rep. U. S. Geol. Survey, J. W. Powell in charge, pp. 249–295. Ten full-page plates, showing macro and macro-structures and four figures in text. Gov't Printing Office, 1888.

A very important paper, dealing with the chemical composition and structure of obsidians, mainly of the Yellowstone Park. There is shown to be in these obsidians a gradual passage from pumiceous to lithodal and porphyritic, rhyolitic, and often more or less spherulitic forms. The obsidian cliff flow is especially remarkable for its extent and thickness, being equaled only by certain Mexican occurrences. So far as known, it is the only occurrence in which a columnar structure is developed. The absolute freshness of the rock, and absence of secondary alteration products, affords excellent opportunity for the study of the phenomena of crystallization. The results obtained have been in part alluded to in Mr. Iddings's paper on the origin of lithophysæ, etc., already noted.

—— On the origin of Primary Quartz in Basalt. Am. Jour. Sci., September, 1888, vol. XXXVI, pp. 208–221.

JUDD, JOHN W. The Natural History of Lavas as illustrated by the material ejected from Krakatoa. Geol. Mag., January, 1888, p. 1.

LAGORIO, A. Ueber die Natur der Glasbasis sowie der Krystallisationsvorgänge im eruptiven Magma. Min. und pet. Mittheilungen, VIII. Band, VI. Heft, p. 421.

WILLIAMS, GEORGE H. Holocrystalline granitic structure in eruptive rocks of Tertiary age. Am. Jour. Sci., 1887, vol. XXXIII, 3d, p. 315.

(b) CONTACT METAMORPHISM.

GREIM, G. Die Diabas-Contactmetamorphose zu Weilburg a. d. Lahn, pp. 1–31. One plate. Neues Jahrb., 1888, I. Band, 1st Heft.

HARKER, ALFRED. Woodwardian Museum. Notes on some Anglesey Dykes. Geol. Mag., September, 1887, p. 409.

Describes the rocks as Augite-andesites, and Dolerites. A dike of the latter rock at Plas-Newydd is described as having at contact converted a bed of calcareous shale into "a kind of lydianite, containing calcite and clusters of garnet and analcime crytals."

RICHARDS, GARY F. Lithological note on Contact Phenomena in South Carolina. Bull. Denison University, Parts I and II, vol. IV, 1888, pp. 5–10.

STECHER, ERNST. Contacterscheinungen an schottischen Olivindiabasen. Min. u. pet. Mittheilungen, IX, Band, II u. III Heft, pp. 145–205. One plate showing microstructure.

WILLIAMS, GEORGE H. The contact metamorphism produced in the adjoining Mica-schists and Limestones by the Massive Rocks of the "Cortlandt Series" near Peekskill, New York. Am. Jour. Sci., October, 1888, vol. XXXVI, pp. 259–269. One plate showing micro-structures.

(c) REGIONAL METAMORPHISM.[*]

BARROIS, C. Modifications et Transformations des Granulites du Morbihan, Lille, 1887. Annales Soc. Géol. du Nord, XV, 1887.

BONNEY, T. G. Notes on the structures and relations of some of the older rocks of Brittany. Quar. Jour. Geol. Soc., August, 1887, vol. XLIII, No. 171, p. 301.

Discusses the structures of the crystalline shists and their probable origin ; their age, to what extent crystalline and sedimentary rocks are affected by intrusive masses and the resemblance of such secondary structures to gneisses and schists commonly regarded as of Archæan age. The rocks carry, besides glaucophane, abundant garnets, epidote, green hornblende, white mica, quartz, sphene, rutile, and hematite. They are commonly schistose in structure and occasionally banded, the banding being produced by a predominance of epidote or sometimes glaucophane. The rocks are sometimes extraordinarily rich in glaucophane, though the individual crystals are not generally large. The writer agrees with Dr. Barrois, that the crystallization of the mineral has taken place since the foliation of the rocks, as they show no signs of strain or fracture. The garnets, on the other hand, existed prior to the foliation, as witnessed by their shattered condition. The rock appears interstratified with the adjacent schists ; but, nevertheless, Professor Bonney is inclined to regard it as an eruptive, altered by pressure. He has further described the gneisses of the district around Quimperlé with especial reference to their original and secondary structures, and the gneisses, granites, and amphibolites of the Roscoff and Morlaix district. His conclusions are that while both igneous and stratified rocks have undergone a certain amount of pressure metamorphism, the igneous rocks being converted into gneisses and schists, yet many of the Brittany gneisses and schists were evidently true foliated rocks anterior to the earth movements. Contact metamorphism produced by igneous rocks on the Paleozoic sediments does not produce rocks which resemble the presumable Archæan gneisses and schists.

——— On some results of Pressure and of the Intrusion of Granite in Stratified Palæozoic Rocks near Morlaix, in Brittany. Quar. Jour. Geol. Soc., No. 173, February, 1888, vol. XLIV, p. 11.

---

[*] Here are also, for convenience' sake, included all papers bearing on the subject of the origin of the gneisses and crystalline schists.

CALLAWAY, C. A preliminary inquiry into the Genesis of the Crystalline Schists of the Malvern Hills. Quar. Jour. Geol. Soc., No. 171, August, 1888, vol. XLIII, p. 525.

——— On Parallel Structure in rocks as indicating a sedimentary origin. Geol. Mag., July, 1887, p. 351.

——— On the alleged conversion of crystalline schists into igneous rocks in County Galway. Quar. Jour. Geol. Soc , No. 171, August, 1888, vol. XLIII, p. 517.

Contends that the ancient gneisses of Galway (Ireland) display evidence of having been formed in part from mixtures of diorite and granite, similar to the more modern " diglomerates."

The above-quoted author has also contended (same journal, p. 536) that many of the gneissic and schistose rocks of the Malvern Hills are formed out of igneous materials and owe their foliated structure to regional pressure, as proven by the intense contortion of granitic veins and by the mechanical effects recognized in the rocks under the microscope.

DANZIG, E. Ueber die eruptive Natur gewisser Gneisse sowie des Granulites im sächsischen Mittelgebirge. Kiel, 1888. Inaug.-Dis.

FOX, HOWARD. On the Gneissic Rocks off the Lizard, with notes on the specimens by J. J. H. Teall. Quar. Jour. Geol. Soc., No. 174, May, 1888, vol. XLIV, p. 309.

GEIKIE, A. Report on the recent works of the Geological Survey in the Northwest Highlands of Scotland, based on the field notes and maps of Messrs. B. N. Peach, J. Horne, W. Gunn, C. T. Clough, L. Hinxman, and H. M. Caddell. Quar. Jour. Geol. Soc., No. 175, August, 1888, vol. XLIV, p. 378.

HUNT, T. STERRY. On crystalline schists. Nature, September 27, 1888, p. 519.

LE VERRIER, M. Structure des gneiss. Note de M. Le Verrier, présentée à M. Fouque. Comptes Rendus, October 29, 1888, p. 669.

LOTTI, B. Sur les roches métamorphosées pendant les âges Tertiaires dans l'Italie centrale. Bull. Soc. Géol. de France, 1888, 3d series, vol. XVI, p. 406, No. 6.

LORY, CH. On the constitution and structure of the crystalline schists of the Western Alps. (Abstract of Professor Lory's original paper, by Dr. F. H. Hatch.) Nature, September 20, 1888, p. 506.

MARR, J E. On some effects of pressure on the Devonian sedimentary rocks of North Devon. Geol. Mag., May, 1888, p. 218.

MCMAHON, C. A. Note on the foliation of the Lizard Gabbro. Geol. Mag., February, 1887, p. 74.

——— The Gneissose Granite of the Himalayas. Geol. Mag., May, 1887, p. 212.

Describes with some detail the macroscopic and microscopic structure of this granite, and which he contends could not have assumed its marked gneissic structure through merely mechanical agencies. Regards it as produced by a forcing up of a semi-plastic granite porphyry mass through faults in the overlying rock where it was subjected to enormous pressure. Before final consolidation took place, minor and subsidiary eruptions took place, which forced new supplies of granitic material into fissures formed in the previously injected rocks, and this fresh material consolidated under conditions somewhat different from those of the first eruptions.

MICHEL-LÉVY, A. Sur l'origine des terrains cristallins primitifs. Bull. Soc. Géol. de France, 1888, 3d series, vol. XVI, p. 102, No. 2.

OLDHAM, R. D. The Gneissose Rocks of the Himalayas. Geol. Mag., October, 1887, p. 461.

REUSCH, H. Geologische Beobachtungen in einem regional metamorphosirten Gebiet am Hardangerfjord in Norwegen. Neues Jahrb., 1887, Beil.-Band, 1st Heft, pp. 52–67 ; thirteen wood-cuts in text.

Has studied the effects of pressure on sedimentary and massive rocks, and shows how in conglomerates a schistose structure may be produced which is quite distinct from the bedding due to sedimentation.

TEALL, J. J. H. On the origin of certain banded Gneisses. Geol. Mag., November, 1887, p. 484.

Contends that the gneissic rocks of the Lizard District (the granulitic series of Professor Bonney) are of igneous origin, and owe their banded structure to dynamic agencies.

(d) RELATING TO METHODS OF WORK.

BECKE, F. Unterscheidung von Quarz und Feldspath in Dünnschliffen mittelst Färbung. Min. und pet. Mittheilungen, Zehnter Band, I. Heft, 1888, p. 90.

Treats the uncovered section with hydrofluoric acid. Quartz is dissolved, while the feldspar is converted into an amorphous fluosilicate of alumina. This, when treated with aniline, absorbs the color, while the quartz remains clear.

McMAHON, C. A. On a mode of using the Quartz-Wedge for estimating the strength of the Double Refraction of Minerals in thin slices of rock. Geol. Mag., December, 1888, p. 548.

SMEETH, W. F. Apparatus for separating the mineral constituents of rocks. Sci. Proc. Roy. Dub. Soc., May, 1888, vol. VI, pp. 58-60.

—— On a method of determining the specific gravity of substances in the form of powder. Sci. Proc. Roy. Dub. Soc., May, 1888, vol. VI, p. 61.

STRENG, A. Ueber einige mikrospisch-chemische Reaktionen. Neues Jahrb. Min., Geol., etc., 1888, II. Band, 2. Heft, p. 142.

(e) MISCELLANEOUS.

ADAMS, FRANK, and A. C. LAWSON. On some Canadian Rocks containing scapolite, with a few notes on Rocks associated with the Apatite Deposits. Canadian Record of Sci., No. 4, 1888, vol. III, pp. 186-201.

AUGE, M. Note sur la Bauxite, son origine, son âge et son importance géologique. Bull. Soc. Géol. de France, 1888, 3d series, vol. XVI, p. 345, No. 5.

BAILEY, W. S. Notes on the microscopical examinations of rocks from the Thunder Bay Silver District. Rep. Geol. and Nat. Hist. Survey of Canada, 1887, Appendix I, pp. 115 H to 122 H.

—— Summary of Progress in Mineralogy and Petrography in 1887. From monthly notes in the American Naturalist.

—— Summary of Progress in Mineralogy and Petrography in 1888. From monthly notes in the Am. Naturalist.

These summaries are issued by Mr. Bailey in pamphlet form at the end of each year; they consist of the same notes published by him monthly in the American Naturalist, and form a very essential part of the literature to those not having access to many of the periodicals and other publications.

—— On some peculiarly spotted rocks from Pigeon Cove, Minnesota. Am. Jour. Sci., May, 1888, pp. 388-393.

BERTRAND, MARCEL. Sur la distribution géographique des roches éruptives en Europe. Bull. Soc. Géol. de France, 1888, 3d series, vol. XVI, No. 7, p. 573.

BEYER, OTTO. Der Basalt des Grossdehsaer Berges und seine Einschlüsse sowie ähnliche vorkommnisse aus der Oberlausitz. Min. und pet. Mittheilungen, X. Band, I. Heft, p. 1. One plate with eight figures showing micro-structures.

BLACK, J. F. On the occurrence of Glaucophane-bearing Rock in Auglesey. Geol. Mag., March, 1888, p. 125.

—— On the Monian System of Rocks. Quar. Jour. Geol. Soc., No. 175, August, 1888, vol. XLIV, p. 463.

BONNEY, T. G. The foundation stones of the earth's crust. Nature, November 22, 1888, p. 89.

—— Note on the structure of the Ightham Stone. Geol. Mag., July, 1888, p. 297.

—— Notes on a part of the Huronian series in the neighborhood of Sudbury (Canada). Quar. Jour. Geol. Soc., No. 173, February, 1888, vol. XLIV, p. 32.

BONNEY, T. G. Note on specimens from Mysore, collected by G. Attwood. Quar. Jour. Geol. Soc., No. 175, August, 1888, vol. XLIV, p. 651.

Describes the rocks as eclogites, hornblende and mica schists, felstones and porphyrites. One color-plate showing micro-structure of flattened garnets.

—— Note on specimens of the Rauenthal Serpentine. Geol. Mag., February, 1887, p. 65.

Mr. Bonney is disposed to question Mr. Teall's statement that this serpentine is an altered hornblende rock, but regards it rather as derived from a rock in which olivine was an essential constituent.

BORNEMANN, J. G. Der Quarzporphyr von Heiligenstein und seine Fluidalstructur. Zeitschrift deuts. geol. Gesell., XXXIX, Band, 4. Heft, p. 793.

—— Ueber Schlackenkegel und Laven. Ein Beitrag zur Lehre vom Vulkanismus. Jahrb. der k preus. geol. Land- u. Bergakademie zu Berlin, 1887, p. 230.

BORNEMANN, L. G., Jr. Ueber einige neue Vorkommnisse basaltischer Gesteine auf dem Gebiet der Messtischblätter Gerstungen und Eisenach. Jahrb. der k. preus. geol. Land- u. Bergakademie zu Berlin, 1887, p. 291.

BOSE, PARAMATHA, NATH. Notes on the igneous Rocks of the districts of Raipur and Balaghat, Central Provinces. Rec. Geol. Soc. of India, vol. XXI, P. 2d, 1888, p. 56. One plate, two figures, showing micro-structures.

The rocks are described as felsites, basaltic rocks, and tuffs.

BOSSCHA, J. Ueber den Meteorit von Karang Modjo oder Magetan auf Java. Neues Jahrb., Beil. Band, 1st Heft, pp. 126–144, 1887. Three plates showing macro- and micro-structures.

BRADY, HENRY B. Note on the so-called "Soapstone" of FiJi. Quar. Jour. Geol. Soc., No. 173, February 18, 1888, vol. XLIV, p. 1.

BÜCKING, H. Mittheilungen über die Eruptivgesteine der Section Schmalkalden (Thüringen). Jahrb. der k. preus. geol. Land- u. Bergakademie zu Berlin, 1887, p. 119.

CAMERLANDER, CARL VON. Zur Geologie des Granulitgebietes von Prachatitz am Ostrande des Böhmer Waldes. Jahrb. der k. k. geol. Reichsanstalt, 1887, XXXVII, 1st, pp. 117–142.

CATHREIN, A. Ueber den Proterobas von Leogang. Neues Jahrb. Min., Geol., etc., 1887, I. Band, Erstes Heft, p. 113.

—— Beiträge zur Petrographie Tirols. Neues Jahrb., 1887, I. Band, II. Heft, pp. 147–172.

Describes from the Tyrolian Alps a series of six rocks, comprising: (1) Staurolite mica schists, (2) garnet amphibolites, (3) pyroxenic serpentines, (4) tourmaline granite, (5) porphyrites, and (6) pitchstone porphyry. The garnet amphibolite is interesting mainly from its pseudomorphs of plagioclases after garnets. The serpentines are derived from diallage, bronzite or enstatite, and are appropriately named pyroxene serpentine. The porphyrites are classed as hornblende, uralite, mica, and garnet porphyrites; the last are characterized by the occurrence of numerous reddish brown garnets, the largest of the dimensions of a hemp-seed, and with channeled and rounded faces shown to be due to oscillatory combinations of dodecahedral with icositetrahedral forms. The pitchstone porphyry presents a micro-crystalline or micro-felsitic ground-mass with fluidal struct. ure with orthoclase and oligoclase porphyritically developed and more rarely quartz and biotite. It occurs in the form of independent dikes and stocks, often of considerable size, cutting the prevailing quartz-porphyry and presenting sharply defined borders without transitions between the two anywhere discernable.

—— Ueber primäre Verwachsung von Rutil mit Glimmer und Eisenerz. Neues Jahrb. Min., Geol., etc., 1888, II. Band, 2. Heft, p. 151.

—— Ueber Chloritoidschiefer von Grossarl. Min. und pet. Mittheilungen, VIII. Band, III. und IV. Heft, p. 331.

CHELIUS, C. Die lamprophyrischen und granitporphyrischen Ganggesteine im Grundgebirge des Spessarts und Odenwalds. Neues Jahrb. Min , Geol., etc., 1888, II. Band, Erstes Heft, p. 67.

CLARKE, F. W., and MERRILL, GEORGE P. On Nephrite and Jadeite. Proc. U. S. Nat. Museum, 1888, p. 115.

COHEN, E. Andalusitführende Granite. Neues Jahrb Min., Geol , etc., 1887, II. Band, p. 178.

Calls attention to the occurrence of microscopic andalusite in the granites of Klause and Rauhmünzach in the Schwarzwald; in Rochesson, Department of Vosges; Moszlavina, Croatia; and other localities.

COLE, GRENVILLE A. J. The Rhyolites of Wuenheim, Vosges. Geol Mag., July, 1887, p. 299.

——— On some additional occurrences of Tachylyte. Quar. Jour. Geol. Soc , No. 174, May, 1888, vol. XLIV., p. 300.

Describes the occurrence of tachylyte in Ardtun, in Mull; Kilmelfort, in Argyle; Bryansford, County Down, in Ireland; and among certain older rocks of the Welsh border. One plate, with six figures, showing micro-structures.

COLLINS, J. H. On the Geological History of the Cornish Serpentinous Rocks. Geol. Mag., May, 1887, p. 220.

Concludes that these are altered olivine, hornblende, or augite rocks.

CHRUSTCHOFF, K. VON. Beweis für den ursprünglich hyalin-magmatischen Zustand gewisser echter Granite und granitartiger Gesteine. Neues Jahrb. Min , Geol., etc., 1887, I. Band, zweites Heft, p. 208.

CROSBY, W. O. Quartzites and Siliceous concretions. Tech. Quarterly, May, 1888, pp. 377–407.

Discusses the origin of the secondary silica in quartzites and of the chalcedonic nodules in calcareous rocks.

——— Geology of the Outer Islands of Boston Harbor. Proc. Boston Soc. Nat. History, 1887, vol. XXIII, p. 450.

CROSS, WHITMAN. Geology and Mining Industry of Leadville, Colorado. Appendix A. Petrography, Monograph XII, U. S. Geol. Survey, pp. 319–358. Two full-page plates showing micro-structure.

The rocks described are quartz-porphyries, diorites, porphyrites, rhyolites, trachytes, and andesites. One of the more interesting rocks of the series is the nevadite variety of the rhyolite. The sanidins of this rock often show a beautiful satin-like luster, which is shown to be "due to the interference of light in passing films of air between the extremely thin plates," into which the crystals are divided by a series of partings parallel to the lustrous surface. Drusy cavities in the rock contain topaz in very perfectly developed forms. The andesites are in part hypersthenic, as previously described in Bull No. 1, U. S. Geological Survey. The quartz porphyries frequently carry the mineral allanite.

CROSS, WHITMAN. Notes on the Henry Mountain Rocks. Geol. and Min. Industry of Leadville, Colorado. Mono. XII, U. S. Geol. Survey, pp. 359–362.

The rocks are hornblendic and augitic porphyrites and are briefly noted for purposes of comparison with the rocks of the Leadville region

——— Notes on Phonolite from Colorado. Proc. Colo Sci. Soc., 1887, pp. 167–174.

This paper is of particular interest as describing the second occurrence of phonolite yet known in the United States * The rock has not as yet been found in situ., but in the form of bowlders of "local origin," and "apparently derived from the hills to the southward," and on the eastern slope of the Hayden divide.

---

* The only other known locality for this rock in the United States is the Black Hills of Dakota, where it was described by Caswell in 1880.

CROSS, WHITMAN On some eruptive rocks from Custer County, Colorado. Proc. Colo. Sci. Soc., 1887, pp. 228–250.

The rocks described are, (1) rhyolites, with primary corroded garnets; (2) trachytes, apparently allied to the so-called sanidin-oligoclase trachytes of the Siebengebirge in Germany; (3) syenites; (4) peridotites, containing essential hornblende and hypersthene, with accessory biotite, plagioclase, apatite, pyrrhotite, and sillimanite; (5) augite diorite, containing olivine; (6) sanidin bearing andesite, in which the oligoclase crystals are nearly always surrounded by a zone of orthoclase.

DALMER, KARL. Die Quartztrachyte von Campiglia und deren Beziehungen zu granitporphyrartigen und granitischen Gesteinen. Neues Jahrb. Min., Geol., etc., 1887, II Band, p. 206.

DERBY, ORVILLE A. On nepheline rocks in Brazil, with special reference to the association of phonolite and foyaite. Quar. Jour. Geol. Soc., No. 171, August, 1887, vol. XLIII, p. 457.

Describes the geological occurrence and, to a certain extent, the lithological characters of some peculiarly interesting nepheline and leucite rocks in the provinces of Rio de Janeiro, São Paulo, and Minas-Geraes, Brazil. The more striking features of the paper are the conclusions reached regarding the relations of the phonolites and foyaites (elæolite syenite), the phonolite not only showing inclusions of foyaite, but also the foyaite containing inclusions of phonolite, all appearances indicating that they are both portions of the same magma; that, in short, the phonolite occurs as a peripheral facies of the foyaite. A second remarkable feature is the occurrence of leucite in rocks of undoubted paleozoic age. The full significance of these discoveries may be best comprehended by those not specialists in this line of work if it be stated that the elæolite syenites are deep-seated or plutonic rocks of paleozoic age, and of which the phonolites have been considered the effusive tertiary or post-tertiary equivalents. Moreover the mineral leucite up to this time has been found as a constituent only of post-tertiary lavas. The two discoveries, it will be observed, having a very important bearing upon the subject of rock history and classification, and bringing once more proof of the utter impossibility of relying upon mineral composition or structure as a guide to geological age. The conclusions reached by Dr. Derby may be best understood by quoting the author's exact words. He feels convinced of, (1) the substantial identity as regards mode of occurrence and geological age of the Caldas phonolites and foyaites; (2) the connection of the latter through the phonolites with a typical volcanic series containing both deep-seated and aerial types of deposits; (3) the equal, if not greater, antiquity of the leucite rocks as compared with the nepheline rocks, whether felsitic as phonolite, or granitic as foyaite; and (4) the probable paleozoic age of the whole eruptive series.

DILLER, J. S., and GEORGE F. KUNZ. Is there a diamond field in Kentucky? Science, September, 1887, vol. X, p. 140.

ELSDEN, J. VINCENT. Notes on the Igneous Rocks of the Lleyn Promontory. Geol. Mag., July, 1888, p. 303.

FOUQUE, M. Sur les nodules de la granulite de Ghistorrai prés Fonni (Sardaigne). Bull. Soc. Française Minéralogie, February, 1887, vol. X, p. 57.

The nodules occur in a granulite consisting of quartz, orthoclase, oligoclase, and both white and black mica. They are rounded in outline and consist of an irregular nucleus of the same composition and structure as the inclosing rock surrounded by a shell composed of concentric layers of albite and biotite.

——— Pétrographie de l'Hérault. Les porphyrites de Gabian. Note de MM. P. De Rouville et Auguste Dilage, presented by M. Fouque. Comptes Rendus, October 22, 1888, p. 665.

FOX, HOWARD, and ALEX. SOMERVAIL. On the occurrence of Porphyritic Structure in some rocks of the Lizard district. Geol. Mag., February, 1888, p. 75.

FRANTZEN, W. Untersuchungen über die Gliederung des unteren Muschelkalks in einem Theile von Thüringen und Hessen und über die Natur der Oolithkörner in diesen Gebirgsschichten. Jahrb der k. preus. geol. Land und Bergakademie zu Berlin, 1887, p. 1. Three full-page plates showing micro-structures.

FRIEDEL, C. Sur un gisement de diamants et de saphirs d' Australie. Bull. Soc. Française Minéralogie, February, 1888, vol. XI, p. 64

GERHARD, ALFRED EDGAR. Beitrag zur Kenntniss der sogenannten " Sodagranite." Inaugural-Dissertation. Leipzig, 1887, thirty-live pages.

GILL, A. C. Petrographical notes on a Rock Collection from Fernando Noronha. A preliminary notice. Johns Hopkins Univ. Circular, April, 1888, p. 71.

GORGEN, ALEX. Sur la production artificielle de la zincite et de la Willemite. Bull. Soc. Française Minéralogie, January, 1887, vol. X, p. 36.

GÖTZ, J. Ueber Andalusit aus den krystallinen Schiefern von Marabastad, Transvaal. Neues Jahrb , 1887, I. Band, zweites Heft, p. 211.

GRAEFF, FRANZ FR. Mineralogisch-petrographische Untersuchung von Elaeolithsyeniten von der Serra de Tingua, Provinz Rio de Janeiro, Brasilien. Neues Jahrb. Min., Geol., etc., 1887, II, Band, p. 222.

Describes the micro-structures and mineral composition of the nepheline-bearing rocks of Brazil, the field relations of which were described by O. A. Derby in Quar. Jour. Geol. Soc. for August, 1887.

—— Laavenit im brasilianischen Elaeolithsyenit. Neues Jahrb. Min., Geol., etc., 1887, zweites Heft, p. 201.

GRATACAP, L. P. The Eozoonal Rock of Manhattan Island. Am. Jour. Sci., 3d, 1887, vol. XXXIII, pp. 374-378.

Describes the serpentine as secondary after a mineral of the amphibole group.

GRESLEY, W. S. Notes on Cone in Cone. Geol. Mag., January, 1887, p. 17.

GURICH, G. Beiträge zur Geologie von West-Afrika. Zeitschrift der deut. geol. Gesell , January, 1887, XXXIX. B., 1. Heft, p. 96.

Describes foyaits from the Isle de Los and from Tumbo. These all carry orthoclase, elæolite, hornblende, and magnetite, while more or less sporadically occur sodalite, cancrinite, augite, ægerine, lavenite, astrophyllite, zircon, and spene. Other rocks described are an olivine gabbro from Freetown, diabase and diorite, olivine diabase, amphibolite, sandstone, and gneiss from various points.

GYLLING, HJALMAR. Zur Geologie der cambrischen Arkosen-Ablagerung des westlichen Finland. Zeitschrift deuts. geol. Gesell., 4. Heft, XXXIX, p. 770.

HARKER, ALFRED. Additional note on the Blue Hornblende of Myndd Mawr. Geol. Mag., October, 1888, p. 455.

Calls attention to the probability of a blue hornblende found in the quartz porphyry proving to be riebeckite.

—— Woodwardian Museum notes on some Anglesey Dykes. Geol. Mag., June, 1888, p. 267.

—— On the Eruptive Rocks in the neighborhood of Sarn, Caernarvonshire, Quar. Jour. Geol. Soc., No. 175, August, 1888, vol XLIV, p. 442.

Describes the rocks of the area as (1) granites and granitic gneiss, (2) gabbro diorite and gneissic diorite, (3) diabase, (4) hornblende diabase, (5) hornblende picrite, and (6) dolerite.

HARTLEY, W. N. The Black Marbles of Kilkenny. Sci. Proc. Roy. Dub. Soc , April, 1887, vol. V, p. 486.

Gives results of chemical analyses.

HATCH, FREDERICK H. On the spheroid-bearing Granite of Mullaghderg, County Donegal. Quar. Jour. Geol. Soc., No. 175, August, 1888, vol. XLIV, p. 548.

Describes the spheroids as composed of a nucleus of oligoclase, biotite, and over 12 per cent. magnetite with a peripheral shell of radiating feldspars, chiefly oligoclase, a little quartz, and possibly orthoclase. Size of spheroids about 3 by 4 inches. The granite itself is described as a "sphene-bearing hornblende granite."

HATCH, FREDERICK H. On a Hornblende Hypersthene Peridotite from Losilwa, a low hill in Taveta District, at the S. foot of Kilimanjaro, East Africa. Geol. Mag., June, 1888, p. 257.

HAWORTH, ERASMUS. A contribution to the Archæan Geology of Missouri. Am. Geol. Mag., 1888, p. 280.

Describes the eruptive rocks in the vicinity of Pilot Knob and Iron Mountain, Missouri. These consist of (1) granite, (2) porphyries and porphyrites, (3) diabases and diabase porphyrites. The quartzes of the granites show often a decided approach to an idiomorphic structure and the orthoclases, in places, secondary enlargements. Topaz was found in slides from near the mineral veins. A large share of the rocks is described as quartz porphyries and porphyrites, in some of which occurs the rare manganese epidote piedmontite.

—— A contribution to the Archæan Geology of Missouri. Johns Hopkins Univ. Cir., April, 1888, p. 70.

HENDERSON, G. G. Note on the composition of a Carbonaceous Sandstone. Trans. Geol. Soc. of Glasgow, 1886-'87-'88, vol. VIII, part II, p. 276.

HERRICK, C. L., W. G. TIGHT, and H. L. JONES. Geology and Lithology of Michipicoten Bay. Results of the Summer Laboratory session of 1886. Bull. Soc. Laboratories, Denison Univ., 1887, parts 1 and 2, vol. II, p. 119.

—— E. S. CLARKE, and J. L. DEMING. Some American Norytes and Gabbros. Am. Geol., June, 1888, p. 339.

HETTNER, A., and G. LINCK. Beiträge zur Geologie und Petrographie der Columbianischen Anden. Zeitschrift deuts. geol. Gesell., XL, Band, 2, Heft, p. 205.

HIBSCH, J. E. Ueber einige minder bekannte Eruptivgesteine des böhmischen Mittelgebirges. Min. u. pet. Mittheilungen, 9. B., II., u. III., pp. 232-262. Six figures in text.

HILL, E. The Rocks of Sark, Herm, and Jethou. Quar. Jour. Geol. Soc., No. 171, August, 1888, vol. XLIII, p. 322.

The principal features are a mass of Archæan gneissoid rocks consisting of quartz, feldspars, dark green or black hornblende and microscopic apatites and sphenes. This is overlaid by a hornblendic schist consisting of alternating bands of very pure hornblende and feldspathic material with occasional quartzes. This rock often shows false bedding and is regarded as a possibly metamorphosed volcanic ash. This in its turn is overlaid by a mass of granitic or syenitic igneous rock. The whole subsequently cut by a series of dikes including quartz-felsite, diabases, and kersantites.

HINDE, GEORGE JENNINGS. On the chert and siliceous schists of the Permo-Carboniferous strata of Spitzbergen, and on the characters of the sponges therefrom, which have been described by Dr. E. von Dunikowski. Geol. Mag., June, 1888, p. 241.

—— On the organic origin of the chert in the Carboniferous limestone series of Ireland, and its similarity to that in the corresponding strata in North Wales and Yorkshire. Geol. Mag., October, 1887, p. 435.

The paper is largely controversial. The author shows apparently conclusively that the cherts in question are formed mainly from the siliceous residues of sponges.

HOBBS, WILLIAM H. On the rocks occurring in the neighberhood of Ilchester, Howard County, Maryland. Being a detailed study of the area comprised in sheet No. 16 of the Johns Hopkins Univ. Circular, April, 1888, p. 69. (A preliminary notice; the full paper, with map and plates, in course of preparation.)

Describes the rocks as hypersthene gabbro locally altered into gabbro diorite, olivine hyperite, diorites, pyroxenite, and granite containing abundant accessory allanite.

HOLLAND, P., and E. DICKSON. Examination of quartzites from Mills Hill, Pontesbury. Proc. Liverpool Geol. Soc., 1887-'88, vol. V, part IV, pp. 380-384.

HOVEY, E. O. A cordierite gneiss from Connecticut. Am. Jour. of Sci., July 18, 1888, vol. XXXVI, p. 57.

Reports from the vicinity of Guilford, Connecticut, a cordierite gneiss. This is the first to be reported in the United States. The rock consists essentially of quartz, biotite, cordierite, and some plagioclase.

HUBBARD, LUCIUS L. Beiträge zur Kenntniss der Nosean-führenden Auswürflinge des Laacher Sees. Min. und pet. Mittheilungen, VIII. Band, v. Heft, p. 356.

HUGHES, T. MCKENNY. On some brecciated rock in the Archæan of Malvern. Geol. Mag., November, 1887, p. 501.

HUTTON, F. W. The eruption of Mount Tarawera. Quar. Jour. Geol. Soc., No. 170, May, 1888, vol. XLIII, p. 178.

Gives an account of the eruption of June 10, 1886. The materials ejected are classed as augite andesites and rhyolites.

—— On a hornblende biotite rock from Dusky Sound, New Zealand. Quar. Jour. Geol. Soc., No. 176, November, 1888, vol. XLIV, p. 745.

HYLAND, J. SHEARSON. Ueber die Gesteine des Kilimandscharo und dessen Umgebung. Min. und pet. Mittheilungen, X. Band, III. Heft, p. 203.

JOLY, J. On the occurrence of Iolite in the Granite of County Dublin. Geol. Mag., November, 1888, p. 517.

JONES, E. J. Examination of Nodular Stones obtained by trawling off Colombo. Rec. Geol. Soc. of India, part 1st, 1888, vol. XXI, p. 35.

JUDD, J. W. On the Volcanic Phenomena of the eruption [of Krakatoa] and on the Nature and Distribution of the ejected materials. The Eruption of Krakatoa and subsequent Phenomena. Report of the committee of the Royal Society, London. Trübner & Co., 1888.

KRATZER, F. Geologische Beschreibung der Umgebung von Rican. Jahrbuch de k. k. geol. Reichsanstalt, 1888, XXXVIII, 3rd, pp. 355–416. Two plates showing microstructure.

KEMP, J. F. Rosetown extension of the Cortlandt Series. Am. Jour. Sci., October, 1888, vol. XXXVI, pp. 247–253.

—— The Dikes of the Hudson River Highlands. Am. Nat., August, 1888, p. 691.

Describes dikes of basic rocks somewhat resembling the Camptonite of New Hampshire.

KENDALL, PERCY F. Preliminary notes on some occurrences of Tachylyte in Mull. Geol. Mag., December, 1888, p. 555.

KINAHAN, G. H. Arenaceous Rocks, Sands, Sandstones, Grits, Conglomerates, Quartz-Rocks, and Quartzites. Sci. Proc. Roy. Dub. Soc., July, 1887, vol. V, pp. 507–618.

Gives many interesting facts relative to the composition, occurrence, and economic value of these materials.

—— Slates and Clays, with Introduction and Building notes by R. Clark. Sci. Proc. Roy. Dub. Soc., May, 1888, vol. VI, p. 69.

The paper is a continuation of those previously given on Irish economic geology.

—— On Irish Arenaceous Rocks. Supplementary note to paper given in Sci. Proc. Roy. Dub. Soc., vol. VI, p. 507. Treats of the rocks wholly from an economic standpoint. Sci. Proc. Roy. Dub. Soc., February, 1888, vol. VI, pp. 6–13.

—— Marbles and limestones. Sci. Proc. Roy. Dub. Soc., April, 1887, vol. V, pp. 489–496. Continued in January number, p. 372.

KIŠPATIĆ, M. Die Glaucophangesteine der Fruskagora in Kroatien. Jahrb. der k. k. geol. Reichsanstalt, 1887, XXXVII. 1st, pp. 35—46.

KLEIN, CARL. Optische Untersuchung zweier Granatvorkommen vom Harz. Neues Jahrb. Min. Geol., etc., 1887., I. Band, zweites Heft, p. 200.

—— Petrographische Untersuchung einer Suite von Gesteinen aus der Umgebung des Bolsener Sees. Sitz. der kön. preus. Akad. der Wiss. zu. Berlin, February, 1888, v, 2nd, pp. 91–121

The rocks described are an olivine-bearing trachyte, from Torre Alfina and San Lorenzo; olivine-bearing andesitic trachyte, from Sassara and Mont Alfina;

KLEIN, CARL—Continued.

trachyte, from Bolsena and Monte di San Magno; trachyte tuff, from Valle Vidona; leucite tephrite, leucite basanite, and augite andesite with accessory olivines. The rocks are described in detail with a large number of complete analyses.

KOTO, BUNDJIRO. On some occurrences of Piedmontite Schist in Japan. Quar. Jo. Geol. Soc., No. 171, August, 1888, vol. XLIII, p. 474.

KROUSTCHOFF, K. de. Nouvelles synthèses du quartz et de la tridymite. Bull. Soc. Française Minéralogie, January, 1887, vol. X, p. 31.

—— Note sur une inclusion d'une encrite à enstatite dans le basalte de Wingendorf près de Laban, en Silésie. Bull. Soc. Française Minéralogie, December, 1887, vol. X, p. 329.

—— Notice sur la granulite variolitique de Fonni, près de Ghittorrai, Sardaigne. Bull. Soc. Française Minéralogie, April and May, 1888, vol. XI, p. 173.

LACROIX, A. Note sur un mode de reproduction du Corindon. Bull. Soc. Française Minéralogie, vol. X, March, 1887, p. 157.

—— Note sur la composition pétrographique des roches de Blekka et Dalane (Norwège.) Bull. Soc. Française Minéralogie, March, 1887, vol. X, p. 152.

—— and BARET, CH. Sur la pyroxenite à wernerite du Point-du-Jour, prés Saint-Nazaire (Loire-Inférieure.) Bull. Soc. Française Minéralogie, July, 1887, vol. X, p. 288.

LAUNAY, L. DE. Note sur les Porphyrites de l'Allier. Bull. Soc. Géol. de France, 1888, 3rd Series, No. 2, vol. XVI, p. 84.

LAWSON, ANDREW C. Geology of the Rainy Lake Region, with remarks on the classification of the crystalline Rocks, west of Lake Superior. Preliminary note. Am. Jour. Sci., 1887, vol. XXXIII, p. 473.

—— Note on some diabase dykes of the Rainy Lake Region. Am. Geol., April, 1888, p. 199.

LEMBERG, J. Zur Kenntniss der Bildung und Umbildung von Silicaten. Zeitschrift deut. geol. Gesell., XXXIX. Band, 3. Heft, p. 559.

LEWIS, H. CARVILL. On a Diamantiferous Peridotite, and the Genesis of the Diamond. Geol. Mag., January, 1887, p. 22

Calls attention to the fact that the South African diamonds occur in portions of a peridotite in contact with highly carbonaceous shales.

—— The Matrix of the Diamond. Geol. Mag, March, 1888, p. 129.

Describes the porphyritic peridotite in which the South African diamonds occur. The principal mineral constituents are bronzite, chrome diallage, smaragdite, biotite perowskite, pyrope, titanic and chromic iron. Rutile is mentioned as occurring as a secondary constituent through the alteration of olivine into serpentine. The structure is porphyritic and brecciated; suggests the varietal name of *Kimberlite*.

LOEWINSON-LESSING, F. Die mikroskopische Beschaffenheit des Sordawalits. Min. und pet. Mittheilungen, IX. Band, 1. Heft, p. 61.

Shows that the so-called Sordawalite of Nordenskjöld is not a true mineral species, as heretofore supposed, but a vitreous eruptive rock—*diabase nitrophyrite*, according to the author. Four figures showing micro-structure.

—— Zur Bildungsweise und Classification der klastischen Gesteine. Min. u. pet. Mitth., B. IX, VI, p. 528.

LORETZ, H. Ueber das Vorkommen von Kersantit und Glimmerporphyrit in derselben Gangspalte, bei Untermenbrunn im Thüringer Walde. Jahrb. der k. preus. geol. Land- und Bergakademie zu Berlin, 1887, p. 100.

LUDWIG, E., and G. TSCHERMAK. Der Meteorit von Angra dos Reis. Min. und pet. Mittheilungen, VIII. Band, IV. Heft, p. 341.

The stone is described as consisting of augite, 93.28 per cent.; olivine, 5.45 per cent.; pyrrhotite, 1.27 per cent., and is anomalous in showing, on analysis, 24.51 per cent. of CaO. The name *Angrite* is proposed for this new variety of meteoric stones.

MACHADO, JORDANO. Beitrag zur Petrographie der südwestlichen Grenze zwischen Minas Geraes und S. Paulo. Min. und pet. Mittheilungen, IX. Band, IV u. V. Heft, p. 318.

The rocks described are nepheline syenites, quartz-diorites, olivine diabase, gneiss, and sedimentary rocks. Twelve colored figures, showing micro-structure, and map.

MERRILL, GEORGE P. Concerning the Montville Serpentine. Science, June, 22, 1888.

—— On the Fayette County Meteorite. (*See* Whitfield & Merrill.) Am. Jour. Sci., August, 1888, vol. XXXVI, p. 113.

—— On Nephrite and Jadeite. (*See* Clark & Merrill.) Proc. Nat. Museum, 1888, p. 115.

—— Note on the secondary enlargement of Augites in a Peridotite from Little Deer Isle, Maine. Am. Jour. Sci., June, 1888, pp. 488–490.

—— On the San Emiglio Meteorite. Proc. U. S. Nat. Museum, 1888, p. 161.

—— On the Serpentine of Montville, New Jersey. Proc. U S. National Museum, 1888, p. 105.

MEUNIER, STANISLAUS. Détermination lithologique de la Météorite de Fayette County, Texas. Comptes Rendus, December 17. 1888, p. 1016.

MICHAEL, PAUL. Ueber die Saussurit Gabbros des Fichtelgebirges. Neues Jahrb. Min., Geol., etc., 1888, 1. Band, 1. Heft, pp. 32–64. One plate.

MICHEL-LÉVY, A., and A. LACROIX. Sur le granite à amphibole de Vaugneray (Vaugnerite de Fournet) Bull. Soc. Française Minéralogie, January, 1887, vol. X, p. 27.

This rock, variously described under the names of *Vaugnerite, Micaceous diorite,* and *Kersanton,* is, after a microscopic study, referred by the above authorities to the group of hornblende granites.

—— Note sur les roches éruptives et cristallines des Montagnes du Lyonnais. Bull. Soc. Géol. de France, 1888, 3d series, No. 3, vol. XVI, p. 216.

—— Note sur un basalte riche en zéolithes des environs de Perrier (Puy-de-Dôme). Bull. Soc. Française Minéralogie, February, 1887, vol. X, p. 69.

MIDDLEMISS, C. S. Crystalline and Metamorphic Rocks of the lower Himalaya Garhwal and Kumaon. Sec. III. Rec. Geol. Soc. of India, 1888, vol. XXI, p. 1st, pp. 11–28. Three full-size plates, showing micro-structure.

MÖLLER, ED. Petrographische Untersuchung einiger Gesteine der Rhön. Neues Jahrb. Min., Geol., etc., 1888, 1. Band, zweites Heft, pp. 81–116, with one plate of twenty-three figures.

The rocks are described as sanidin-rich tephrites, phonolites, nepheline basalts.

MORTON, G. H. Microscopic characters of the Millstone Grit of southwest Lancashire. Proc. Liverpool Geol. Soc., 1886-87, vol. V, p. 111, pp. 280,253.

—— The microscopic characters of the Cefn-y-fedw Sandstones of Denbighshire and Flintshire. Proc. Liverpool Geol. Soc., 1886-'87, vol. V, part III, pp. 271–279.

MÜGGE, O. Ueber "Gelenksandstein" aus der Umgegend von Delhi. Neues Jahrb. Min., Geol., etc., 1887, 1. Band, zweites Heft, p. 195.

OSANN, A. Ueber Sanidinite von São Miguel. Neues Jahrb. Min., Geol., etc., 1888, 1. Band, zweites Heft, p. 117.

—— Beitrag zur Kenntniss der Labradorporphyre der Vogesen. Habilitationsschrift zur Erlangung der Venia Docendi der hohen philosophischen Facultät der Universität Heidelberg, vorgelegt von Dr. A. Osann, Assistent am mineralogischen Institut. Abhandlungen zur geologischen Special-Karte von Els.-Lothr., Band III, Heft II, 1887. Inaug. Diss.

PATTON, H. B. Die Serpentin- und Amphibolgesteine nördlich von Marienbad in Böhmen. Min. u. pet. Mittheilungen, 9. B , II. u. III. Heft, pp. 89–144. With two wood-cuts in the text.

POHLMANN, R Einschlüsse von Granit im Lamprophyr (Kersantit) des Schieferbruches Bärenstein bei Lehesten in Thüringen. Neues Jahrb. Min., Geol., etc., 1888, II. Band, 2. Heft, p. 87.

Pošepny, F.   Ueber die Admolen von Pribram in Böhmen.   Min. und pet. Mittheilungen, 1888, x. Band, iii. Heft, p. 175.

Raisin, Catherine A.   Notes on the Metamorphic Rocks of South Devon.   Quar. Jour. Geol. Soc., No. 172, November, 1887, vol. xliii, p. 715.

——— On some rock specimens from Somali Land.   Geol. Mag., September, 1888, p. 414.

Describes these rocks as porphyrites, hornblende diabase, granite, gneisses, talc schists, epidote schists, quartzite, grits, sand and lime stones.

——— On some rock specimens from Socotra.   Geol. Mag., November, 1888, p. 504.

Rowe, A. W.   On the rocks of Essex Drift.   Quar. Jour. Geol. Soc., No. 171, August, 1888, vol. xliii, p. 351.

The rocks were studied with a view, if possible, of ascertaining their original source. They are identified as granite syenite, quartz porphyries, quartz trachytes, trachytes, dolerites, granulites, crystalline schists, quartzites and quartz rocks, sandstones, limestones, and fragments of silicified woods.

Rudolph, Fritz.   Beitrag zur Petrographie der Anden von Peru und Bolivia.   Min. und pet. Mittheilungen, ix. Band, iv. u. v. Heft, p. 269

The rocks described are andesites of the pyroxene or hornblende varieties.

Rutley, Franc.   On Perlitic Felsites, etc.   Quar. Jour. Geol. Soc., No. 176, November, 1888, vol. xliv, p. 740.

Describes an obscure perlitic structure occurring in certain felsitic rocks of the Herefordshire Beacon; suggests, further, the probability that felsites resulting from the devitrification of obsidian, quartz felsites, aplite, arkose or feldspathic grits may on decomposition pass into rocks composed mainly of quartz and kaolin and thence by further alteration into epidosite.

——— On the rocks of the Malvern Hills.   Quar. Geol. Jour. Soc., No. 171, August, 1888, vol. xliii, p. 481.

Sandberger, F.   Bemerkungen über den Silbergehalt des Glimmers aus dem Gneisse von Schapbach und des Augits aus dem Diabase von Andreasberg am Harze.   Neues Jahrb. Min., Geol., etc., 1887, i. Band, erstes Heft, p. 111.

Sauer, A.   Ueber Riebeckit, ein neues Glied der Hornblendegruppe, sowie über Neubildung von Albit in granitischen Orthoklasen.   Zeitschrift deuts. geol. Gesell., xl. Band, i. Heft, p. 138.

Schmidt, C.   Diabasporphyrite und Melaphyre vom Nordabhang der Schweizer Alpen.   Neues Jahrb. Min., Geol., etc., 1887, i. Band, erstes Heft, p. 58.

Describes a diabase porphyrite and melaphyr presenting certain interesting features. The porphyrite occurs, cutting Eocene strata in its three typical varieties, as a dense, dirty, grayish green, in places dark violet mottled or veined rock carrying small nests of calcite. In the thin section it is pronouncedly porphyritic, with long, slender plagioclases, which from their small extinction angles are supposed to be oligoclase. The groundmass consists of augite and feldspars, sometimes grouped in tuffs or with a tendency toward spherulitic structure. The feldspars contain inclosures of the amorphous base, often showing a mere vein of feldspar substance. The second variety is of a gray green color, and badly altered, only the feldspars being recognizable while the base has gone over to chloritic material, and granules of opacite, calcite, and chlorite abound. The third variety is a reddish brown dense rock which the microscope shows to consist of a confused aggregate of oligoclase leistens with interstitial irregularity developed augites. The stone therefore presents all the characters of the pre-Tertiary porphyrites, although, as above noted, of post-Eocene age. The melaphyr is also of interest as containing olivine, which has undergone alteration into a bastite-like substance, here noted for the first time.

——— Ueber den sogenannten Taveyannaz-Sandstein.   Neues Jahrb. Min., Geol., etc., 1888, ii. Band, erstes Heft, p. 80.

SHERBORN, C. DAVIES. On a limestone with Concentric Structure, from Kulu, North India. Geol. Mag., June, 1888, p. 255.

SMOCK, JOHN C. Building stone in the State of New York. Bull. No. 3, N. Y. State Mus. of Nat. History, 1888, 8vo, pp. 152; printed for the Museum.

The volume gives an account of (1) the geological position and geographical distribution of the building stone in this State; (2) descriptive note of quarry district and quarries.

SOMERVAIL, ALEX. On a remarkable Dyke in the Serpentine of the Lizard. Geol. Mag., 1888, p. 553.

STRENG, A. Ueber die in den Graniten von Baveno vorkommenden Mineralien. Neues Jahrb. Min., Geol., etc., 1887, I. Band, erstes Heft, p. 98.

STRUVER, J. Ueber Gastaldit und Glaukophan. Neues Jahrb. Min., Geol., etc., 1887, I. Band, zweites Heft, p. 213.

TATE, A. NORMAN. Iron as a coloring matter of Rocks. Proc. Liverpool Geol. Soc., 1886-'87, vol. V, part III, pp. 287-289.

TERMIER, M. Note sur trois roches éruptives interstratifiées dans le terrain houiller du Gard. Bull. Soc. Géol. de France, 3d series, 1888, No. 7, vol. XVI, p. 617.

TÖRNEBOHM, A. E. Ueber das bituminöse Gestein vom Nullaberg in Schweden. Neues Jahrb. Min., Geol., etc., 1888, II. Band, erstes Heft, p. 1, with 12 wood-cuts.

VAN HISE, C. R. Note on the enlargement of hornblendes and augites in Fragmental and Eruptive Rocks. Am. Jour. Sci., 1887, vol. XXXIII, p. 385.

VON FOULLON, H., and VICT. GOLDSCHMIDT. Ueber die geologischen der Inseln Syra Syphmos u. Tinors. Jahrb. d. k. k. geol. Reichsanstalt, 1887, XXXVII, 1st, pp. 1-34.

The rocks described are gneisses, glaucophone, hornblende, "strahlstein," and augitic schists, with secondary serpentine after the hornblende schists.

WETHERED, EDWARD. On insoluble residues obtained from the Carboniferous Lime stone series at Clifton. Quar. Jour. Geol. Soc., No. 174, May, 1888, vol. XLIV, p. 186.

WHITFIELD, J. E., and G. P. MERRILL, The Fayette County Meteorite. Am. Jour. Sci., August, 1888, vol. XXXVI, pp. 113-119. Two figures in text.

Gives results of chemical and microscopic examinations of a chondritic olivine enstatite stone from above-named locality.

WILLIAMS, GEORGE H. On the Serpentine of Syracuse, N. Y. Science, March, 1887, vol. IX, p. 232.

—— The Norites of the "Cortlandt Series" on the Hudson River, near Peekskill, New York. Am. Jour. Sci., 1887, vol. XXXIII, 3d, p. 135-144, also 191-199.

The rocks described are norites proper, hornblende norite, mica norite, hyperite or augite norite, and pyroxenite.

—— On the chemical composition of the orthoclase in the Cortlandt norite. Am. Jour. of Sci., 1887, vol. XXXIII, p. 243.

—— On the Serpentine (Peridotite) occurring in the Onondaga Salt-group, at Syracuse, New York. Am. Jour. Sci., Aug., 1887, vol. XXXIV, p. 137.

Shows that this rock, considered by Dr. Hunt (Min. Phys., pp. 443-447) as originating as an aqueous precipitate, is in reality an altered peridotite.

—— The massive rocks and contact phenomena of the "Cortlandt Series," near Peekskill, New York. Johns Hopkins Univ. Circular, April, 1888, p. 63.

Abstract of a series of papers in course of publication in the American Journal of Science.

—— Rutil nach Ilmenit in verandertem Diabas-Pleonast (Hercynit) in Norit vom Hudson-Fluss, Perowskit in Serpentin (Peridotit) von Syracuse, New York. Neues Jahrb. Min., Geol., etc., 1887, II. Band. p. 263.

WORTH, R. N. Some Detrital Deposits associated with the Plymouth Limestone, Trans. Roy. Geol. Soc. of Cornwall, vol. XI, part III, pp. 151-162,

WULF, HEINRICH. Beitrag zur Petrographie des Hererolandes in Südwest-Afrika. Min. und pet. Mittheilungen, VIII. Band, III. u. IV. Heft, p. 193.

Describes the rocks as granite, diorite, basalt, gneiss, mica and diorite schists, amphibolite, augite, gneisses bearing scapolite and wallastonite, augite schists, and granular limestones.

WÜLFING, E. A. Untersuchung eines Nephelinsyenit aus dem Mittleren Transvaal, Süd-Afrika. Neues Jahrb. Min., Geol., etc., 1888, II. Band, erstes Heft, p. 16.

YOUNG, JOHN. Quartz as a Rock-Forming Mineral. Trans. Geol. Soc. of Glasgow, 1886–'87, 1887–'88, vol. VIII, part II, p. 278.

RECENT PROGRESS IN DYNAMIC METEOROLOGY.

By Cleveland Abbe.

PREFACE.

The previous summaries of progress in meteorology that I have published since 1871 have each in its turn more or less imperfectly covered the whole field of meteorology, but it has not seemed wise for me in the present summary to endeavor to compass a science which is now so rapidly enlarging in all directions. Several reasons have led me to this conclusion, among which I may mention, first, the fact that the American Journal of Meteorology, published at Ann Arbor, Mich., and which is now in its fifth year, has, since the publication of my summary for 1884, endeavored to keep its American readers fully acquainted with the progress in all branches of our subject, while the German Zeitschrift, published at Hamburg, and which is now in the sixth year of its succession to the Austrian Zeitschrift, accomplishes the same object for German readers in the most exhaustive manner, and is of course widely circulated in this country. Again, as regards recent progress in instrumental meteorology, American readers will perhaps find a sufficiently complete statement of the present condition of that subject in my Treatise published in December, 1888, as part II of the annual report of the Chief Signal Officer for 1887. Finally, as my own studies have during the past year been almost wholly directed to the dynamical phenomena that are offered to us in the movements of the atmosphere, and as these are undoubtedly by far the most important questions that come before the practical meteorologist, and are those about which most numerous inquiries are made (or rather by means of which innumerable popular questions must be answered), I have in the present summary endeavored to give an account of the important works that have appeared up to December, 1888, on the movements of storms and the general motions of the atmosphere, reserving for a next report some equally important papers that have come to hand since that date.

Some of these memoirs are so important and so little accessible to American readers, that not content with a popular summary, I have prepared full translations of them, which will be printed in the present, or a following Report, in the confident hope and expectation that American mathematicians, physicists, and meteorologists may thus be stimulated to prosecute further studies in the directions indicated by the most success-ful European students. At first sight these original memoirs and even the popular summaries may appear mathematical and repugnant to the ordinary meteorological observer, but meteorology, like astronomy, em-ploys a wide range of talent. If the observer and the computer are needed in both, so also are the physicist and mathematician; in both cases we have to do not merely with the superficial phenomena of nature, but also with the fundamental laws that underlie these and a process of severe thought is needed in the discovery and the applica-tion of these laws. It seems to have been conceded by all that meteoro-logical phenomena, at least those which depend on the motions of the atmosphere, are too difficult to be unraveled at present, but during the past few years the application of thermo-dynamics has been so helpful, and the study of fluid motions, whether discontinuous or steady, has made such advances as to justify the belief that we may begin to build a lasting superstructure of dynamic and rational deductive meteorology. But such a work needs the co-operation of many minds.

The fundamental factors in meteorology and climatology are the forces of heat and gravity; the figure, rotation, and inequalities of the earth; the circulation of vapor, and its latent heat; all this is summed up in "the thermo dynamics and hydro dynamics of our atmosphere."

For ages mankind has relegated to evil and good spirits, to chance, to instinct or will, to the stars, the planets, the comets, and the moon, to the fates, to sun-spots, to electricity, and to every other form of su-perstition the explanation of our complex phenomena, because, in our despair, we were not able to comprehend the possibilities of the simple laws of mechanics. The labors of hydraulic engineers in handling the turbulent flow of rivers; of astronomers in treating the motion of the planets; of chemists in unraveling the mysteries of compound bodies; of physicists in explaining the phenomena of light, heat, and electricity; of mathematicians in resolving the difficulties attending the treatment of complex functions, were all needed as preparatory to successful attacks upon the laws of the motions of the atmosphere. May the pres-ent summary be the means of enlisting the co-operation of universities and their patrons, professors and their students, in a work that prom-ises results so important to human welfare.

The few memoirs that I have summarized in the following pages as having important bearings on our knowledge of the atmosphere and its storms are to be classified as follows:

I. Laboratory experiments on fluid motion.

1. Helmholtz and Kirchoff.	5. Colledon and Weyher.
2. Oberbeck.	6. Reynolds.
3. Vettin.	7. Hagen.
4. Bezold.	8. Kummer.

II. Statistics of actual storms,

9. Loomis,

III. Theoretical hydro-dynamics applied to the motion of the air.

IV. Thermo-dynamics of atmospheric phenomenon.

V. Prediction of storms and weather.

I.—LABORATORY EXPERIMENTS ON FLUID MOTION.

The imitation in laboratory experiments of natural motions of the atmosphere offers an instructive and fascinating field for research. Among those who have contributed to this subject are:

(1) *Helmholtz*, in 1857, first solved analytically the problems of vortex motion, and in 1868 those of jets, both being illustrations of general propositions in discontinuous motions. Kirchhoff immediately followed with solutions of other cases, and since then W. Thomson, J. J. Thomson, Rayleigh, Hicks, and other English writers, Oberbeck, Planck, Zöppritz, Bertrand, Boussinesq, Saint Vincent, and others, have added to these conquests of analysis. The experimental illustrations and verifications of their results have been especially due, as regards jets in liquids, to Savart 1833, Bidone 1838, Rayleigh 1879, Oberbeck 1877, Reynolds 1883, and as regards jets and whirls in air to Vettin 1857 to 1887, Colladon and Weyher 1887.

(2) *Oberbeck.*—As long ago as 1877 this mathematician, by careful experiments, reproduced the results analytically obtained by himself and predecessor, all of which will be found in the appended translation of his memoir on discontinuous motions. These jets in water have a close analogy to the columns of warm air that rise in the atmosphere.

(3) *Vettin*, of Berlin, whose work began 1856, and whose first publication was in Poggendorff's Annalen of 1857, met with an opposition from Dove, that seems to have inspired him with the resolution to observe and experiment until all doubt was settled. Consequently, we owe to Vettin a remarkable series of observations on clouds and most instructive experiments, illustrating the whole convective process by which heat and moisture are carried by the air from the ground to the upper atmosphere, and inversely the dryness, cold and motion of the upper air brought down to us. Vettin's latest contributions are in the volumes of the Meteorologische Zeitschrift for 1887.

(4) *Bezold*, who, in 1886, was called from Munich to Berlin to take charge of the reorganized Meteorological Institute of Prussia, has pub-

lished the account of some carefully executed experiments on vortices and other motions in water, illustrating points in the movements in the air.

(5) *Colladon and Weyher.*—As to experimental work in circular vortices nothing has been more interesting than that done on a large scale in 1887 by Colladon at Geneva, and Weyher at Paris.

Colladon used a simple apparatus for producing vortices and artificial whirlwinds and water-spouts both in water and in air. A more effective apparatus was constructed by Weyher, in which a great variety of interesting vortical phenomena were produced, illustrating what might happen in the free atmosphere if only the conditions were the same. He established a drum, rapidly revolving about a vertical axis, which therefore set in motion the surrounding air of the room or other inclosure. If the drum is at the top of the inclosure, the air thrown out from it descends along the sides of the room, while, in the center immediately below the drum, a rapid spiral or corkscrew movement exists inward and upward. Water contained in a vessel in the middle of the room is set in motion by the air, and some drops are even carried upward through the ascending core, thus approximately imitating the lower end of a water-spout, and showing how spouts and tornadoes originating in the clouds settle downwards to the earth. Many modifications of his apparatus have been made by Weyher, illustrating many problems in vortex motion, and which are valuable for the comparison with the analytical formulæ of hydro-dynamics, but which have only indirect bearing on meteorological phenomena. They, however, serve to remove from the mind any difficulties that may have been experienced by those who hesitate to admit the importance of vortex motion in meteorology.

(6) *Reynolds.*—Among the investigations into the motions of fluids, that made by Prof. Osborne Reynolds, on "the two modes of motion of water," has had a peculiar interest for me and seems generally to be regarded as one that has contributed decidedly to our knowledge of the conditions under which steady motion and eddying or vortex and wave motions take place. Reynolds's paper is published in the London Philosophical Transactions of 1883. In his annual address, November 30, 1888, Professor Stokes says of it: "The dimensions of the terms in the equations of motion of a fluid, when viscosity is taken into account, involve, as has been previously pointed out, the conditions of dynamical similarity in geometrically similar systems in which the motion is regular; but when the motion becomes eddying it seemed no longer to be amenable to mathematical treatment. But Professor Reynolds has shown that the same conditions of similarity hold good as to the average effect even when the motion is of the eddying kind; and moreover that if in one system the motion is on the border between steady and eddying, in another system it will also be on the border, provided this system satisfies the above conditions of dynamical as well as geometri-

cal similarity. The resistance to the flow of water in channels and conduits usually depends mainly on the formation of eddies, and though we can not determine mathematically the actual resistance, yet the application of the above proposition leads to a formula for the flow in which there is a most material reduction in the number of constants, for the determination of which we are obliged to have recourse to experiment."

(7) *Hagen.*—No experimental work has been done on the absolute resistance of the air to bodies moving through it superior to that of the eminent hydraulician H. Hagen, of Berlin; a translation of whose memoir will be given in the series previously referred to, because of the frequent inquiries that are made of me as to his results.

But in applying Hagen's observed pressures to other surfaces, or other angles of incidence than those used by him, great mistakes are liable to be made, and the student should consult the chapter on anenometers and wind pressure in the "Treatise on Meteorologial Apparatus," Report of the Chief Signal Officer for 1887, part II, or the excellent memoir of St. Venant, quoted below, if he would avoid serious errors.

(8) *Kummer.*—Allied to the problem of resistance, treated of by Hagen, for plates normal to the wind, is that of plates inclined to the wind, which is one that is specially important in problems relating to gunnery, sailing, flying, and the construction of windmills. On this matter Kummer has made a serious of experimental determinations of the center of pressure for a thin flat plate when struck by the wind at special angles of incidence.

Although his revised results were published in 1876 in the Berlin Abhandlungen yet they seem unknown in America, and I have therefore re-arranged them in the following table. Kummer's final measurements were made on six stiff glass plates of the following shapes and dimensions :

Plate.	Length	Breadth.
	Millimeters	*Millimeters.*
A........	90	90
B........	180	90
C........	180	60
D........	180	30
E........	180	20
F........	·180	10

The center of pressure is the point at which the plate must be supported in order to remain quietly balanced when the wind is blowing upon it at a given inclination. These points are always in front of the center of figure, or between it and the windward edge.

The distance between the two centers is given in the column ζ; the angle between the wind and the plate is given in the column a. At first thought one would be inclined to convert the ζ, as given in millimeters, into decimal fractions of the whole length of the plate, and apply the corresponding angles to similar plates of any size.

This can be done in the case of the square plate A, by simply multiplying its sides and its ζ by two, and thus obtaining the column 2A, as if for a square 180^{mm} on a side. If the reasoning were correct then the α in the column 2A should be comparable with those extrapolated from B and C, but the relation between them is not simple, so that care must be taken in applying this data to other cases.

Center of pressure for inclined rectangles.

A.		G.	a					
ζ	a		2A.	B.	C.	D.	E.	F.
mm	°	mm	°	°	°	°	°	°
0	90	0	90	90	90	90	90	90
1	84	2	84	85	85	86	87	86
2	77	4	77	78	77	83	85	82
3	70	6	70	68	66	77	82	78
4	62	8	62	58	56	69	75	74
5	52	10	52	52	53	66	70	71
6	41	12	41	48	52	63	65	68
7	31	14	31	45	51	61	61	64
8	28	16	28	43	50	59	60	X
9	26	18	26	41	49	57	59	
10	25	20	25	39	48	55	58	
11	24	22	24	37	46	53	55	
12	22	24	22	35	43	50	X	
13	21	26	21	33	38	45		
14	19	28	19	28	27	X		
15	18	30	18	23	13			
16	16	32	16	16	11			
17	14	34	14	13	9			
18	13	36	13	10	X			
19	12	38	12	9				
20	10	40	10	8				
21	8	42	8	7				
22	7	44	7	X				
23	5	46	5					
24	X	48	X					

X indicates that the angle is indeterminate or that the plate oscillated so much as to show that it was in a state of unstable equilibrium.

II.—STATISTICS OF ACTUAL STORMS.

(9) *Elias Loomis, on the form, extension, movement, and temperature phenomena of barometric maxima and minima.*—The first and second chapters of the revised edition of Loomis's contributions to meteorology, although printed in New Haven in 1885 and 1887, respectively, for private distribution in Europe mostly, will not be generally accessible to American readers until they appear in permanent form in the forth-

coming volume IV of the Memoirs of the National Academy of Science. As an early copy of the private edition has fallen into the hands of Drs. Van Bebber and W. Koeppen, the latter has given a condensed review of both chapters more perspicuous than the mass of details given in the original. We shall do our readers a favor by laying this before them; and the more so inasmuch as the labor bestowed by Koeppen and his occasional criticisms as reviewer enhance the value of his work. This constitutes a most condensed summary of the results to dynamic meteorology of the statistics published daily by the U. S. Signal Service.

BAROMETRIC MAXIMA.—The isobars around a barometric maximum are of irregular, more or less elliptical, form. The ratio of the greatest to the least axis of the ellipse, as determined by Loomis from three years' observations for North America, for Europe and the Atlantic Ocean, is, respectively, 1.91 for 238 cases in North America, and 1.84 for 252 cases in Europe and on the Ocean. In a third of all these cases this ratio was more than 2. The same number is also found by Loomis for the ratio of the similar axes in areas of barometric minima. The direction of the longest axis with reference to the meridian is also demonstrated to vary very little in the two regions, being as shown in the accompanying table:

	North America.	Europe and the Atlantic Ocean.
Maxima	N. 44° E ...	N. 75° E.
Minima	N. 36° E ...	N. 35° E.

The more easterly direction of the axes of the minima on the ocean and in Europe is by Loomis attributed to the frequent formation of a ridge of high pressure which in the colder half of the year connects the area of high pressure in Asia and the Azores. Three fourths of the above cases are of this kind.

Loomis subjects to a special investigation the especially intense barometric maxima. He collects these in three tables, of which the first one (Loomis No. XL) contains all cases in which, during the years 1872 to 1884, a pressure of over 30.85 inches (783.6 millimeters) occurs at any station of the United States on the charts of the Signal Service; the second table (Loomis LVI) contains the cases in which, during the years 1874, 1876, and 1881, an isobar of 785 millimeters occurs on the Hoffmeyer charts, and their continuation by the Seewarte; the third table (Loomis LVIII) contains those cases in which, during the interval from 1877 to the beginning of 1884, an isobar of 31 inches (787.4 millimeters) occurs on the charts of the International Bulletin of the Signal Service, which comprehends the whole northern hemisphere.

The *annual distribution* of these cases is given by the following tabular summary; in which, of the double numbers, the first one gives the num-

ber of separate occasions on which high maxima occur, each one being
separated from the other by intervening times of low pressure; the
second number [in brackets] gives the number of charts on which they
occur.   With respect to these numbers it is necessary to remember that
for the United States (series *a*) there are three charts daily, but for
Europe and the Atlantic Ocean (series *b*) two, and for the northern
hemisphere one each day (series *c*).

(*a*) United States and Canada..1[3]	10[73]	8[64]	14	91]	16[80]	3[26]	52[337]
(*b*) Europe and Atlantic Ocean.2[4]	6[14]	4[14]	3[12]	5[20]	4[18]	24[82]
(*c*) Northern hemisphere.. ....1[1]	6[8]	13[34]	10[29]	4[4]	5[5]	37[81]

In the other months of the year such high barometric readings do not
occur.

As concerns the *geographical distribution over the surface of the earth*,
the maxima occurred as follows :   ·

Series (*a*).—Eighty-two per cent. west of 90° longitude (west of Greenwich), and the greater part north of 46° north latitude.

Series (*b*).—Three-fourths were in Asia and only two on the Atlantic
Ocean.*

Series (*c*).—Of these eighty-one charts, seventy-four show the maximum over Europe and Asia, six over North America, and one on the
ocean west of Ireland.   The station with the highest pressure occurred
in Europe or Asia, always between latitude 50° and 60° north, with one
exception, when it was at Taschkent; in thirty-two cases it was at
Jenisseisk (latitude 58°.5 north); in nine cases at Barnaul (53° north),
and in seven cases at Nertschinsk (51° north), and the other seven at
Semipalatinsk (50°.5 north).   Within Europe proper such extreme
maxima were observed only in European Russia, and the centers occurred either at Wjatka, Kazan, Moscow, or Warsaw, the two latter
only once each.   Such high pressures occur very decidedly only in the
centers of the continent and in the colder seasons of the year.

For such of the areas of high pressure as could be followed for many
days the following results are given :

Series (*a*).—An average movement toward south 40° east, or, if we consider only the movement east of the Rocky Mountains, south 57° east,
with a velocity of 21 English miles per hour (eight degrees of a great
circle per day); the average movement of the maxima is therefore directed more southerly than that of the minima.

Series (*b*).—In fourteen cases of long-continued high areas there were
eleven where the last position lay more southerly than the first, and

---

* On nineteen of these eighty-two charts, the highest isobar is 790, on five charts
it is 795, and on one chart (January 1, 1876) it is 800 millimeters; on this day the
maximum was at Omsk; in the year 1877, for which the Hoffmeyer charts were not
printed, there occurred a still higher barometer, on December 16, namely, 806.5 as
reduced to sea-level, or unreduced 784.5, which is the highest atmospheric pressure
that Loomis has found anywhere charted.

eight where the last was more easterly than the first, as opposed to three and five cases, respectively, where the movement was toward the north or west.

Series (*c*).—For the maxima in this series, Loomis remarks that apparently, by reason of small variations of the pressure of the air, the centers appear to show rapid movements to and fro, but that in general, in the fourteen cases where the isobar of 31 inches continued for at least two days, the position on the last day did not differ materially from that on the first.

The *relative size* of the barometric maxima in the United States was investigated by Loomis for the maxima of Series (*a*) (Loomis Table XII), with the assistance of the charts of the International Bulletin, but only since October, 1877, because the weather charts for the United States only did not cover enough ground to fully present these extended phenomena. The mean value of the smallest diameters of these regions of extraordinary high pressures measured between the isobars of 762 millimeters is 2,587 miles, which is equal to the width of the American continent at 40° north latitude. The mean distance of the centers of low pressures from the centers of maxima was 2,371 miles on the east side of the maxima and 2,381 miles on the west side; the value of the lowest isobars in these measurements was 29.19 inches = 741.4 millimeters on the east side, and 29.57 inches = 751.1 millimeters on the west side; so that therefore the gradient was twice as great on the east side as on the west side. If we reduce the adopted superior limit from 30.85 to 30.4, we find that the mean diameter of the maxima between 1877 and 1884 that rise above this limit amounts to 1,406 miles, and that the barometer in these is on the average 0.40 inch above its normal value. For the maxima above 30.85 these values become, respectively, 2,587 miles and 0.75 inch. Since 0.75 : 0.40 = 2,587 : 1,380, therefore the diameters of the maxima are approximately proportional to their altitudes measured from the normal value.

Series (*b*).—The mean diameter of the maxima of this series for which the isobar 760 millimeters is taken, is at least 2,740 miles, therefore larger than in the United States. The lowest isobar on the west side was on the average 739 millimeters—only in two cases was it less than 730—whereas this is a frequent case on the Atlantic Ocean; therefore here also an uncommon high pressure does not imply a remarkably low pressure in the neighborhood. The mean distance of the center of high pressure from that of low pressure on the west amounted to 2,280 miles, which indicates a somewhat greater gradient on the European side of the ocean than on the western or American side.

Series (*c*).—The mean diameter of the maxima of this series is 3,800 miles in the north-south direction under 55° of north latitude, and 4,900 miles in the east west direction.

The temperature relations of the barometric maxima are quite thoroughly investigated by Loomis. In the cold season of the year the maxima are characterized by very low temperature. For those in North America the following table gives from twelve years' observations the pressure and the departures of temperature for the stations that showed the highest pressure at the time:

Barometric pressure.		Temperature departure.	
Inches	Millimeters	Fahrenheit.	Centigrade.
30. 5–30. 6	747–772	—18. 0	—10. 0
30. 6–30. 7	772–798	—20. 3	—11. 3
30. 7–30. 8	798–823	—23. 8	—13. 2
30. 8–30. 9	823–848	—26. 3	—14. 6
30. 9–31. 0	848–874	—26. 8	—18 2
31. 0–31. 1	874–899	—28. 9	—18. 8

This shows that the higher the pressure by so much greater is the cold. The maxima of pressure and of cold, however, do not as a rule occur at the same time and place, but lie on the average 400 miles apart, and the greatest temperature departure ordinarily lies north of the highest barometer. (This which holds for North America does not obtain in Europe.—W. K.) The temperature depression at the center is greater when the center lies west of 87° W. longitude than when it lies east thereof; for pressures of 30.85 inches the temperature depression is in the first case 28.8° F. (or 16° C.); for the second case it is 24° F. (or 13.3° C.). In three-fourths of all the cases in series (*a*) the thermometer at the center fell below 0° F. (or—17.8° C.). In twelve cases it fell to—30° F. (or—34.5° C.). For the maxima of the series (*b*) for Europe, after excluding the two cases of the ocean, the mean temperature fell to —25.4° C., and the mean for the three winter months fell to—28.9° C. For the maxima of the series (*c*), in so far as they occur over Europe and Asia, the departure from the normal was somewhat less, averaging — 19° F., or—10 6° C., and the mean temperature was about the same, namely—28° C.

For the average of all cases, whenever the thermometer at Jenisseisk, between 1876 and 1882, went below—36° C., the barometer stood 7.8 millimeters above its normal value, but only in one of these cases did the pressure exceed 787 millimeters. Therefore, extraordinary low temperatures are generally accompanied by high, but seldom by extremely high, barometric pressures.

In the *warmer season* of the year the temperature in the center of the maxima is also generally below the normal, but only a little below. For the average of the cases where the pressure in the United States during 1873 to 1880 exceeds 30.35 inches (or 770.9 millimeters) the temperature was 8.3° F.=4.7° C. below the normal, and here also for places west of 87° longitude the depression is greater, *i. e.*, 6.6° C., than for places on the east of that meridian, where it is 3.8° C.

In the interior of the United States the highest temperature of the summer usually occurs with a pressure that is decidedly below the mean value, but, on the other hand, on the Atlantic coast it occurs with a normal pressure. For the North Atlantic Ocean and Europe-Asia Loomis deduces from seven years' observations the mean thermometric departures at the time of the monthly maxima of temperature for the months of June, July, and August, and for a number of stations. The average of the three months is given in the following table:

Station	Departure		Station.	Departure	
	°	°		°	°
Godthaab	+0.7	....	St. Petersburg	+2.4	....
Stykkisholm......	2.2	....	Archangel	0.8	....
Thorshaven	4.2	....	Moscow	0.1	....
Parsonstown	3.5	....	Kazan	0.9	....
Oscott	2.3	....	Akmolinsk	....	—3.1
Copenhagen	0.1	....	Barnaul	....	2 6
Paris	.. ..	—1.0	Jenisseisk	....	3.2
Brussels	....	2.2	Turuchansk	....	1.2
Vienna	....	2.8	Irkutsk.............	....	3.6
Warsaw	....	0.9	Pekin...............	....	—2.0
Lemberg............	....	—2.3			

Therefore equally as in North America, so also in the interior of the Europe-Asiatic continent, the greatest summer temperature occurs with a barometric pressure that is some millimeters below the normal value, while on the ocean and also rarely in the northern parts of the continents, southward to Moscow and Kazan, the greatest summer temperatures occur, with relatively high pressure.

BAROMETRIC MINIMA.—In order to make the comparison more complete between the areas of high and low pressure, Professor Loomis has also supplemented his work on the latter subject by a new collocation of data, and his Tables XLIX and L give a summary of the minima under 29 inches (736.6 millimeters) for the years 1873 to 1884 for the United States and Canada. His Table LVII gives a similar summary for the minima under 725 millimeters for the years 1873 to 1876 and 1880 and 1881 over the Atlantic Ocean and Europe according to the Hoffmeyer charts and the new synoptic charts, published jointly by the Danish Institute and the Seewarte. This is the same material quoted, respectively, as series a and b in the table of maxima given in the first part of this summary. The arrangement of the data taken from the International Bulletin of the Signal Service (series c) is carried out in a different manner by Loomis as regards the minima, in that he has in Table LXIX given only the minima under 29 inches for the Pacific Ocean, and in Table LXIV those under 29.6 inches (751.8 millimeters), and only for the winter season for the Asiatic continent. The number and annual distribution of these comparatively deep minima, is as shown in the following table, which gives the number of charts that show such minima:

Series.	Locality.	January.	February.	March.	April.	May.	June.	July.	August.	September.	October.	November.	December.
a	United States and Canada	14	16	25	10	4	1	0	2	2	7	26	24
b	Europe and Atlantic Ocean.	33	12	22	6	2	0	0	1	1	22	19	19
c_1	Pacific Ocean	19	10	4	4	2	0	0	0	2	4	7	22
c_2	Asia	35	43	......	......	......	......	......	......	......	......	......	38

Only the first of these series, depending upon twelve years of records, can have any pretense of accurately presenting the normal annual rate. The remarkable double maximum of frequency with a diminution in the middle of winter will probably remain even in long series of observations, and has its origin in the development of the continental area of high pressure in January and February. The small number of depressions under 29 inches in the Pacific Ocean is doubtless in part due to the insufficient data from this ocean for the first year, but Loomis shows that even in the last three years (summer of 1881 to the summer of 1884), where the number of observations was nearly sufficient, only nineteen cases below 736 millimeters occurred in the year, whilst on the Atlantic Ocean twenty-eight cases occurred annually below 725 millimeters on the average of four years; in the Pacific Ocean the barometer sank below this latter limit only five times in three years, so that such deep depressions occur sixteen times more frequently over the Atlantic than over the Pacific Ocean. This result is confirmed by another consideration: On the average of five years' observations at Stykkisholm, in Iceland, the barometer fell below 725 millimeters on 6.8 days annually, but in three years' observations in the Aleutian Islands only on one day annually. The lowest depression reported from the Pacific Ocean during seven years is 719 millimeters, but in the North Atlantic such depressions occur on the average about thirty times annually.

As concerns the location of these barometric minima, Loomis finds that of one hundred and thirty-one in the first (a) series, one hundred and twelve occurred on the Atlantic coast, and only nineteen in the interior of North America; that, therefore, the neighborhood of the ocean is an almost indispensable condition for these deep depressions. He presents the location of the one hundred and thirty-seven minima of series (b) on a chart that shows that three-fourths of the total number occurred on the Atlantic Ocean or its coast, and that of the remaining cases ten occurred within 100 miles distant from the coast; seven at 100 to 150 miles; and only one, January 15, 1881, at Moscow, occurred more than 150 miles from the coast. Within the area of the ocean more centers of depression occurred in the neighborhood of the coast than in its central portions, and four regions of greater frequency are especially recognizable; namely, Southern Greenland, west coast of Iceland, the islands north of Scotland, and the North Cape. This confirms in general the results that Köppen attained and presented graphically for all depressions without considering the depths (Zeitschrift Oesterreichisches Gesellschaft für Meteorologie, July, 1882).*

Of the one hundred and sixteen winter days that show a barometric pressure in Asia below 752 millimeters, fifteen show such depressions simultaneously at many places; so that we have one hundred and thirty-one separate cases that are distributed as follows: Thirty-seven on the eastern coast of Asia and in Japan; seventy-seven on the western border of Asia, namely, at Ekaterinburg, and seventeen in the interior of Asia, at Akmolinsk, Barnoul, or Jenisseisk. The minima of the first group seem to originate in the Pacific Ocean or on the coast. None of them appear to have come from the interior of the continent, or from a region north of latitude 62°, so that the numerous depressions that pass from west to east over the eastern part of North America seem to find no analogue in Eastern Asia. The minima of the second and third groups appear to progress from Northern Europe along a path directed somewhat south and east, and none of them pass eastward over Jenisseisk, unless perhaps some of them are deviated northeastward beyond the region occupied by the station.

The highest isobar in the neighborhood of these depressions was on the average, in series (a) 30.29 inches (769.4 millimeters) on the west side, and 30.35 inches (770.9 millimeters) on the east side; in the series (b) the isobars of 785 millimeters and upwards occurred only twice on the west side, and twice on the east side of the depressions; the maxima in the neighborhood of the deep minima therefore seldom attain exceptional heights—a confirmation of what is above said for the maxima. The mean distance of the centers of these maxima from those of the depressions was in series (a) 2,130 miles on the east side of the depression, and 1,985 miles on the west side. The mean diameter of the depressions (namely between the isobars of 760 to 770 millimeters) Loomis has determined to be for the depressions of series (a) from the years 1877 to 1884, 2,139, but for series (b) 2,365 miles.

The mean of the temperatures at the centers of such barometric depressions as were lower than 737 millimeters, was 6°.4 Fahr.,=3°.6 C., above the normal in the United States for the years 1873 to 1877; but the greatest excess of temperature did not occur here, but about 300 miles farther southerly or easterly, and on the average, for the cases that allowed of a satisfactory determination, amounted to 22°.3 Fahr., or 10°.3 C.

---

*Journal of the Austrian Meteorological Society, July, 1882. See also the charts compiled by me for Walker's Statistical Atlas of the United States, Washington, 1874.

These deep depressions belonged, as we have seen, almost exclusively to the colder period of the year; in order to investigate the temperature of the summer depressions, Loomis has brought together the depressions with a central pressure less than 29.4 inches (746.7 millimeters) for June, July, and August of the three years 1873, '74, '77. For these the average departure of the temperature from its normal value was $+6°.5$ Fahr., or $3°.6$ C. at the center of the depression and $+20°$ Fahr. $= 11°.1$ C. at the above-mentioned warmest point, therefore almost the same as in the winter depressions.

For the minima of series (b) Loomis has determined only the temperature at the center, not its departure from the normal value; the former is $+4°$ C. ($39°.2$ Fahr.), which is very high for the season and the latitude of most of these minima.

Loomis has subjected to a thorough investigation the relation of the wind to the gradient. First, he selected from Hoffmeyer's synoptic charts eighty-one on which there appeared especially well-developed cyclones or anti-cyclones. For meteorologists who desire to submit to a special proof some notable examples, he calls attention to the cyclones of January 12, and December 21–22, 1875; January 22 and March 9 and 10, 1876; and the anti-cyclones of December 30–31, 1875, and January 1–2 and 13, 1876. Loomis says nothing as to his interpretation of the arrows indicating the strength of the wind on Hoffmeyer's charts; under the assumption that he has properly considered the half-degree marks on the wind arrows of Hoffmeyer's charts, we can consider the mean strength of the wind deduced by him and given according to the "1 to 6" scale as correct Beaufort degrees, since the wind estimates of both German and English navigators, on which these charts are based, are alike made on the Beaufort scale; on the other hand, if he has counted the half-degree marks as full scale degrees, then all his figures for mean wind force, when they are uneven figures, are too large by one, and therefore his mean values for the whole series will be too large by one-half of a Beaufort degree.

Loomis's results from Hoffmeyer's charts are summarized in the following table; the measurements were generally made on that side of the center where the strongest gradients and winds were found. The mean latitude of the centers of the cyclones was $58°.8$ north, and that of the anticyclones $49°.7$ north.

Loomis's wind and barometric gradients on the North Atlantic Ocean.

Isobars			Winds		Location		
Consecutive numbers.	Distance in degrees of great circle	Gradients in milli meters per degree	Wind force, Beaufort scale	Inclination to Isobars.	Distance to central pressure	Geographical latitude.	Temperature centigrade.
Cyclones.	°	*Mm.*	°	°	°	*Km.*	°	°
715–720...	1 20	4.17	6.70	64.6	2.49	277	58.0	+2.1
720–725 ..	1.29	3.87	6.80	63.5	3.74	415	57.6	2.2
725–730 ..	1.35	3.71	6.78	62 1	5.06	562	57.2	2.2
730–735 ..	1.39	3.60	6.76	60.1	6.42	714	56.8	2.2
735–740...	1.42	3.52	6.78	58.1	7.83	870	56.4	2.3
740–745....	1.45	3.45	6.82	56.7	9.26	1029	55.9	2.7
745–750...	1.48	3.37	6.82	56.3	10.73	1192	55.5	3.2
750–755...	1.54	3.24	6.68	55.9	12.24	1360	55.0	3.5
755–760...	1.61	3.10	6.32	55.2	13.82	1536	54.5	+3.8
Anti cyclones.								
760–765 ..	1.70	2.95	5.54	53.1	13.84	1537	54.0	+1.5
765–770 ..	1.82	2.75	4.78	49.3	12.08	1342	53.4	−4.0
770–775 ..	1.98	2.53	4.28	45.6	10.18	1131	52.9	−9.0
775–780 ..	2.16	2.31	3.78	42.1	8.11	901	52.2	−13.6
780–785 ..	2.37	2.11	3.40	39.4	5.84	649	51.5	−18.1
785–790....	2.60	1.92	3.04	37.9	3.36	373	50.7	−22.4

In order to determine the same quantities also for the storms of the United States, Loomis has chosen thirty-six charts for cyclones and thirty-six for anti-cyclones out of the twelve thousand published by the Signal Office since November, 1871, which gave him the following table of results. The mean latitude of the centers of these cyclones was 44°.7 north, that of the anti-cyclones 45°.1 north.

Loomis's wind and barometric gradients within the United States.

Isobars.			Wind.		Locality.		
Consecutive numbers.	Distance in degrees of great circle.	Gradients in milli meters per degree	Velocity meters per second	Inclination to Isobars	Distance to central pressure.		Temperature centigrade
Cyclones.	°	*Mm.*	*Miles.*	°	°	*Km.*	°
731.5–734.0	1.36	3.73	12.20	53.2	2.24	249	−2.2
734.0–741.7	1.51	3.36	11.80	51.7	3.68	409	−2.1
741.7–746.7	1.65	3.08	11.44	50.2	5.26	584	−1.9
746.7–751.8	1.75	2.90	11.09	49.0	6.96	773	−1.7
751.8–756.9	1.82	2.80	10.64	47.6	8.74	971	−1.9
756.9–762.0	1.87	2.72	10.28	46.7	10.58	1176	−3.2
Anti-cyclones.							
762.0–767.1	1.94	2.61	9.66	45.6	9.59	1065	−6.2
767.1–772.1	2.05	2.48	9.03	44.8	7.59	843	−10.1
772.1–777.2	2.20	2.31	8.18	43.0	5.46	607	14.1
777.2–782.3	2.43	2.09	7.20	40.8	3.15	350	17.4

These two tables contain a wealth of data for future deductions, but as to the results that Loomis draws from them, Köppen promises a fut. ure communication.

III.—THEORETICAL HYDRO-DYNAMICS APPLIED TO THE MOTION OF THE AIR.

(10) *Köppen*, whose skill in studying the mechanism of storms and in handling masses of data has so frequently been shown, has contributed to the Meteorological Zeitschrift of December, 1888, a study "On the form of the isobars in reference to their dependence upon altitude and the distribution of temperature." Assuming that isotherms and isobars have been given by the daily weather chart, he then gives a most convenient and rapid method of computing tables and deriving the isobars for any elevation, such as 2,500 meters, by an inspection of the tabular figures. Such upper isobars were first published for a given storm by Möller in the Annalen für Hydrog., April, 1882. The importance of such upper isobars had been urged by me in 1871-'72, and sample maps were drawn preparatory to their daily use, but subsequently the introduction of departures and variations of departures in pressure and temperature as auxiliary to sea-level isobars and surface isotherms was decided on by General Myer. Köppen's diagrams of ideal systems are very suggestive.

(11) *Ferrel.*—In 1886 there appeared a treatise by Prof. William Ferrel, "Recent Advances in Meteorology," being Appendix 71, or part II, of the Annual Report of the Chief Signal Officer for 1885. This treatise was originally designed as professional paper of the the Signal Service, No. 17, but the abolition of that series of papers by order of the Secretary of War caused a change in the method of publication.

An abstract of the contents of this book was delivered in lectures by Professor Ferrel to the second lieutenants of the Signal Corps, but the abolition of the Signal-Service school of instruction at Fort Myer has prevented its further use in that direction. The complete volume being easily obtained in this country, I need give only a short account of it.

In this work Ferrel has collected the results of recent investigations by many authors, adding to them many of his own demonstrations, and combining the whole into a systematic treatise on meteorology under the following seven chapters: (1) The constitution and physical properties of the atmosphere; (2) the temperature of the atmosphere and the earth's surface; (3) the general motions and pressure of the atmosphere; (4) cyclones; (5) tornadoes; (6) observations and their reductions; (7) ocean currents and their meteorological effects. In the first chapter, after the sections on chemical constituents, pressure and weight, there comes a section on the diffusion and arrangement of the constituents, including the vapor atmosphere, followed by the ordinary applications to the atmosphere of the thermo-dynamics of adiabatic processes. In his section on the diathermancy and transparency of the

air Ferrel gives especial attention to the effect of wave length upon the
law of diminution in a complex bundle of rays, such as those from the
sun, and shows that his formula and constants hold good for the visual,
the thermal, and the chemical effects of the solar rays. (A special memoir by him on radiation is published in the American Journal of Science,
July, 1889.)

In chapter 2, on temperature of the atmosphere, Ferrel gives an ex
pression for the mean diurnal intensity of the sun's radiation developed
into a series as a function of the sun's declination and the observer's
latitude, which expression he also further converts into a series de.
pending on the time and the observer's latitude. With this he then
combines the effect of the absorption by the earth's atmosphere, and
proceeds to discuss the conditions that determine the temperature at
any place and any time for a body of any shape and co-efficient of absorption and radiation. The important results obtained in this chapter
depend principally upon the radiation observations of Prevostaye and
Desains, Melloni, Langley, Dulong, and Petit, and are applicable to the
temperature of bodies at the earth's surface, the temperature shown by
thermometers and those shown by solar radiation apparatus. Especial
attention is given to the nocturnal cooling by radiation. (The late publications by Maurer, H. F. Weber, Angot and Zenker could of course
not be utilized by Ferrel.)

In chapter 3 Ferrel deduces the general motions and pressure of the
atmosphere, beginning with the equations of absolute motion on the
earth at rest, whence follows his law that all bodies in motion are deflected to the right in the northern hemisphere. Combining these equations with the equation of continuity, certain general relations are deduced expressed by differential equations.

Ferrel's method of solution of these equations consists in successive
approximations, beginning with the simplest cases of no friction and no
disturbance of the normal distribution of temperature, he finally proceeds in section 4 of chapter 3 to give a special solution for the actual
case of the earth, which although only approximate yet within the limits
indicated, appears to agree well with observed phenomena; this solution is summed up in the two following formulæ for the connection between the barometric gradient (G) expressed in millimeters per degree
of the great circle of the meridian from north to south, the angular distance (θ) from the north pole or 90 degrees minus the latitude; the velocity (v) of the east-west motions of a particle of air; the total velocity (s)
of the particle; the temperature (τ) on which the density of the air depends; the inclination (i) of the wind to the parallel of latitude; the
observed barometric pressure (P) and the normal sea level barometric
pressure (P_0). The resulting formula for the barometric gradient measured on the meridian, as given on page 207 of his "Recent Advances," is

$$G = \frac{0.1571 \; v \cos \theta}{\cos^2 i (1 + 0.004 \; \tau)} \cdot \frac{P}{P_0} = \frac{0.1571 \; s \cos \theta}{(1 + 0.004 \; \tau) \cos i} \cdot \frac{P}{P_0}$$

Substituting this value of G in the general differential equation of motion, Ferrel deduces the following expression for v for the mean temperature condition of the earth where h is the altitude, and G^1 the full gradient at the earth's surface; the last term is negligible as expressing the effect of inertia and friction due to meridional motions:

$$v = \frac{6.37\ (1+0.004\ \tau)}{\cos \theta} G^1 - \frac{0.0001690\ A_2 \sin \theta}{1+0.004\ \tau} h + \frac{\frac{du}{dt}+F_u}{\cos \theta\ (2n+v)}$$

The coefficient A_2 represents the principal term in Ferrel's previous development of the solar diurnal variation of temperature in a harmonic series that obtains for the whole year and the whole earth. Instead of attempting to compute the temperature (τ) Ferrel has preferred to compile from charts of temperature and pressure the actual average values of temperature and pressure and wind velocity for each five degrees of latitude for January, July and the whole year, for the northern and southern hemispheres. The introduction of these observed temperatures and pressures enables him to compute the value of v which on comparison with the observed velocity shows a very excellent agreement. The process is simply a refinement upon the numbers already published by him in 1858, and is, I think, equivalent to the statement that if among the many direct solutions of the equations of motion possible when the boundary conditions are given, we, without a previous knowledge of these boundary conditions, select that special solution that we find existing on the earth's surface as indicated by our observed temperatures and pressures, then the resulting computed velocity agrees with the observed velocity of the wind. After explaining the annual oscillations of winds and calms, rain and cloud, Ferrel passes to chapter 4 on cyclones. In this is given an elementary mechanical theory of the gyration of a small portion of the atmosphere near the earth's surface at any latitude, the resulting equations (7) on page 238 being, of course, entirely similar to the general equations 13 on page 188 for the general cyclonic motion of the atmosphere about the earth's axis.

The treatment of these equations is naturally very similar to that for the general motion of the atmosphere, and if Ferrel's methods seem prolix and inelegant, as compared with the beautiful work of Oberbeck and Helmholtz, it must be remembered that he expressly states this treatise to have been written for persons who have a slight acquaintance with the mathematical progress of the past thirty years, and that he has therefore adopted such elementary and simpler methods as could be easily comprehended by those who graduate from minor colleges and scientific schools, while at the same time he has also expressly avoided analytical refinements that are not demanded in the present crude state of meteorological knowledge. In fact, like all his other treatises, this also impresses one with the conviction that Ferrel aims to be a practical

meteorologist rather than an elegant analyst. He is satisfied with showing that the larger features of atmospheric motion are abundantly
explicable by known laws of mechanics and that, therefore, the ultimate details of these phenomena will undoubtedly be also thus explained, and this conviction is that which is needed in order to attract
to this study those who wish to devote themselves to "exact science."

The formulæ for cyclones are treated approximately for the case of no
friction and uniform temperature; then for the case of a difference of
temperature between the central and exterior parts, the warm center
being a cyclone, the cold center the anti-cyclone; finally, the solution is
indicated for the case of the existence of both friction and temperature
disturbances. In the next section on the progressive motion of cyclones,
Ferrel states, on page 259, that "the principal cause of the progressive
motion is the general motion of the atmosphere;" but he also adds that
"the velocity of progress is much greater than the general motion of the
atmosphere," and his short discussion of this subject suffices, we think,
to show that the cyclonic progress is only to a small extent actually due
to the general atmospheric motion, and is mainly due to those causes
that determine the distribution of vapor and precipitation around "the
center of power," as he terms it. By this precipitation and redistribu-
tion of heat, the cyclone center is, as Ferrel states, continually renewed
a little in advance of its former position. My own view differs from his
only in the relative effect attributed by us to the general movement of
the atmosphere on the one hand, and the tendency to the formation of
new aspiration centers on the other. Ferrel gives special prominence
to the former, but I to the latter; possibly he is correct for high southern or northern latitudes, but my own view agrees best with my experience in the temperate zones; it appears to agree closely with the excellent work of John Eliot in India, and is peculiarly applicable to many
abnormal storm-paths that I have had occasion to predict. I notice
that Ferrel, on page 260, quotes the lake region of North America as
possibly attracting cyclones by reason of the aqueous vapor furnished
by them: but would it not be more rational to infer that the course of
our great storms is determined by larger forces than the slight excess
of evaporation over the lakes as compared with surrounding forest and
prairie; that in fact the lakes are *the result* of the precipitation that
occurs from the atmosphere above them? Evaporation and moist air
are not of themselves able to produce a storm; we must have cold or
dry air ready to flow in beneath, and our present lake region (as well as
our ancient glaciated region) is so evidently located precisely in the
spot where cold northerly and warm southerly winds conspire with the
orography of the continent to produce precipitation and storms, that I
must consider the lakes (and glacial epoch) as the result of the orography, and as exerting by their evaporation only a very slight reflex action
principally appreciable in the re-distribution of local rains and snow
and slightly higher temperatures in their immediate neighborhood. On

page 282 Ferrel shows that the formula expressing the relation between the barometric gradient (G) and the velocity of the winds is very much the same for the pressures and winds around a cyclone center as for the pressures and winds about the polar axis of the earth, and is expressed by a quadratic equation $s^2 + as = b\,G$. As the cyclone moves from the land to the ocean the so-called friction term would, *a priori*, be expected to suffer a decided change, and the actual amount of such change is indicated by the data collected by Loomis. Adopting his results Ferrel deduces a correction to his formula based upon the principle "that the frictional resistance of any stratum of air moving over the earth's surface comes both from the earth's surface and from the stratum above it," and again, "that the direction of motion of the air of the stratum above differs considerably in a cyclone from that at the surface of the earth." To me it seems that there is here not a sufficient distinction between the small and negligible friction called viscosity, which acts both from above and below upon any intermediate stratum, and the resistances due to impact and convection, both which operate principally from below upward; still the general effect is undoubtedly, as Ferrel says, to make the gradient that accompanies a given velocity of the wind at the earth's surface greater than that accompanying the same velocity of wind over the sea or at higher altitudes. Similarly the gradient is less in summer than in winter.

The chapter on tornadoes deals in a very interesting manner with the different types of cyclones in which the horizontal movement is less conspicuous than the vertical movement; the formation of water-spouts is explained as a special case of tornado action, and examples are computed showing the dimensions of the spout as depending on the humidity of the air. In a section on the force of the wind and supporting power of ascending currents, Ferrel gives merely the old approximate formulæ for the resistance of the air varying as the square of the velocity and the square of the cosine of the angle of incidence, and applies the resulting numerical resistances to the explanation of the formation of large drops of water, cloud-bursts, hail-stones, and the destructive effects of tornado winds. Stokes's explanation of the effect of viscosity seems to have been overlooked. On page 314 he explains the effective force of the wind against an obstacle, or in the production of drafts up chimneys, as due "not simply to the inertia of the air but to the dragging effect of the air through friction upon the columns of air in the front and rear of the obstacle." I presume that this "drag" is intended to refer to viscosity or so-called internal friction of gases, and apparently the same use of the word is made by Hagen in his explanation of the fact that the pressure against a thin plate depends upon the size and shape and especially upon the sharp angles of the plate. It is a sufficient answer to this introduction of viscosity to state that the value of the viscous resistance can be easily computed with sufficient accuracy to show that it is not an important factor in these experiments on large bodies. The true explanation of Hagen's results and of the production of drafts by wind transverse to the chimney flue is found in the study of the pressure within discontinuous spaces and the vortices attending the flow of liquid past any resisting body. The same criticism applies to Ferrel's explanation of the pumping of the barometer, in so far as he implies that friction drags away the air.

In his sixth chapter Ferrel gives an excellent exposition of harmonic analysis as applied to periodic phenomena, which is followed by the fundamental principles of thermometry, actinometry, hygrometry, barometry, and anemometry. Among the new things, we notice that he introduces here the analytical portion of his investigations upon the psychrometric formula, the numerical portion of which is published by him in full as an appendix to the annual report of the Chief Signal Officer for 1886. In regard to the reduction of the barometer to sea-level he recommends, on page 398, the use of monthly normals for the upper and lower station. In order to diminish the diurnal temperature effect he has since then acceded to the present practice of the Signal Service in the use of mean daily temperatures.

In 1886, to the great regret of his colleagues, Professor Ferrel announced that, conformably to a long-cherished resolution, he should celebrate his seventieth birth-day by resigning official public office and retiring to his homestead in Kansas City, Missouri. The leisure thus secured, we learn, has been used in the preparation of a "Popular Treatise on the Winds," which will be published in 1889 and be doubly welcomed by the student of meteorology.

(12) *Sprung.*—In 1885 Dr. A. Sprung published his Lehrbuch der Meteorologie. Shortly afterward he moved to Berlin, and as instructor in the university and as assistant under Professor Bezold has exerted a strong and good influence on the progress of meteorology.

His Lehrbuch is by far the best treatise extant on dynamic meteorology, and I have included it in this section of theories of atmospheric motion, because Dr. Sprung has devoted two-thirds of his Treatise to the exposition of the views that have been worked out by the mathematicians whose names are already so familiar to my readers. It is scarcely necessary to say that the volume contains nearly all that had been satisfactorily established in dynamic meteorology at that time. Those who have not access to—or time to consult—the original memoirs should by all means study this volume.

Of the other general treatises those that bear especially on storms are:

(13) *Greely.*—"American weather," by Gen. A. W. Greely, in which the statistics of American storms are quoted to substantiate the theory of their progress by transportation in the general drift of the atmosphere.

(14) *Scott.*—"Elementary meteorology," by R. H. Scott, in which only a small section is devoted to storms.

(15) *Blanford.*—"A practical guide to the climates and weather in India, Ceylon, and Burmah, and the storms of Indian seas," by H. F. Blanford. This volume, published in 1889, marks the retirement of Mr. Blanford as meteorological reporter to the Government of India, in which position, since 1875, he has undoubtedly accomplished the greatest works ever undertaken in meteorology. Wilde's Repertorium and Annalen, Mascart's four annual volumes of observations and memoirs, Neumayer's annual Ergebnisse and Archiv, are the principal works to be named in comparison with Blanford's annual reports and Indian memoirs.

In the present work Blanford devotes only a moderate portion to storms, and summarises the results that have been attained in India by Piddington, Willson, Pedlar, Meldrum, and especially the great work of John Eliot.

So far as could be seen from the scattered records available up to the end of 1876, cyclones are most frequent in the Bay of Bengal in May and October, and least frequent, being almost unknown, in February and very rare in July; but with the more perfect data furnished by the Government weather office Mr. Eliot has compiled a list of cyclones for the ten years 1877–'86, which entirely alters this supposed annual distribution, and makes the distribution almost uniform from June to November. The Indian storms generally move toward northwest or west-northwest, and with very few exceptions the direction is toward some point in the northwest quadrant.

The incurvature of the winds for storms in the northern part of the Bay of Bengal is about 35 degrees, with a slight increase as we go southward. The barometer does not fall for the approaching cyclone until long after the wind and skies show that the center of the storm is close at hand and only when the winds become strong and squally, nor does it fall rapidly until the winds have increased to hurricane force and the center is distant less than 50 miles. The most important indications of the approach of a storm are therefore to be found in the observation of the sky and clouds.

The storms of the Arabian Sea, on the west coast of India, have been studied by Mr. F. Chambers. The storms that cross India as they move westward deteriorate greatly before they reach the Arabian Sea, but then at once begin to increase. The stormy months are April, May, June, and November, but the records are rather fragmentary, and the results will probably be changed by future study. The system of storm signals for the Bay of Bengal is under the control of the Calcutta office, and consists of a simple warning or danger signal at all ports except Calcutta, where a much more elaborate system is used. There is an independent system of storm warnings for the Arabian sea-coast by the office at Bombay.

(16) *Davis.*—"Whirlwinds, cyclones, and tornadoes," by William M. Davis. This little book is the result of a series of lectures for the

Lowell Institute in Boston. The author is professor of geology and meteorology in Harvard College. The work is written in a very popular and easy style, and deserves to be read and used in elementary schools.

(17) *Abercromby.*—"Weather," by Hon. Ralph Abercromby, London, 1887. As the name implies, this book deals with the weather, its causes and changes, as distinguished from the statistics of climate. Neither formula nor numerical tables interrupt the reader, as the object of the author is to sketch the general principles of the science and give a picture of the methods ordinarily adopted in predicting the weather.

The present book reads as though it had its origin in the thought, "Farmers and sailors have always foretold the weather by the sky and cloud; why may not the meteorologist do the same?"

He therefore devotes one-fourth of the book to clouds and cloud prognostics, and, again, fifty pages to types of weather. The last eighty pages are given to the rules and methods of weather predictions or (as the English call them) forecasts. His whole system, as he says (pp. 430), "depends neither on theory nor calculation, but solely on observation and experience, and success depends on natural aptitude and the experience of many years' study."

To this we add, that these same statements apply to work in astronomy, chemistry, etc., and that he who makes forecasts merely by means of generalization relative to types of weather and clouds, is sure to suffer from the neglect of a deeper study into causes and laws of operation, but to those who have mastered these mechanical laws the additional information given in Abercromby's book would be of value.

(18) *Eliot.*—The report by John Eliot in 1876 on the Backergunge cyclone, and his report of 1879 on the Madras cyclone, marked an important step in the progress made, by one of the ablest meteorologists. He tells us he began his inquiry with a strong bias towards the hypothesis that cyclones originate between belts of parallel opposing winds, but that this proved so unsatisfactory that he rejected it and adopted the condensation theory, which accounts satisfactorily for the entire range of atmospheric action that constitute an extensive and intense cyclonic storm in the Bay of Bengal. At the close of his work on the Madras cyclone, and after refuting some views as to cyclone formation that Dr. Hann had advanced, Eliot sums up his own conclusions, from which we make the following extract:

"The invariable antecedents of powerful cyclones at the two transition periods, April and October, are (*a*) approximate uniformity of pressure over and around the coast of the Bay of Bengal; (*b*) light and variable winds or calms over a considerable portion of the bay; (*c*) little or no rain-fall over the coast region as well as in the bay; (*d*) hence the weather is sultry; (*e*) hence the sea is smooth; (*f*) the amount of aqueous vapor accumulates and finally gives rise to peculiar sky effects;

(*g*) the immediate antecedent is heavy rain-fall, concentrated over a portion of the bay; (*h*) accompanied by a strong indraft, which is most marked from the Indian Ocean at the entrance of the bay; (*i*) this indraft from the Indian Ocean gives rise to strong winds and heavy rains at the stations on the south and west coast of Ceylon."

Of the preceding items (*a*) (*b*) (*c*) are invariable and necessary antecedents, but the source of the energy is the item (*g*), condensation of vapor and precipitation of rain, or, as stated in the Backergunge report, the primary cause of cyclone formation is the production and ascent of a large quantity of vapor, which is condensed with the liberation of its latent heat over the place of its production instead of being carried away to some distant region.

This independent confirmation of the views for which Espy lived and died, as well as the numerous other generalizations not quoted by us, after having been clearly apprehended by their author, were found repeated in other storms, and were confirmed in his subsequent memoir "On the cyclonic storms of November and December, 1886, in the Bay of Bengal." Eliot states that there is a marked difference in the characteristics of the storms of one year and of another, which is explicable on the same hypothesis as that which explains the variations in the southwest monsoon rain-fall. These variations are apparently periodic in Bengal, and when the Bengal branch of the monsoon current becomes strong the Bombay branch becomes weak.

Pending the appointment of a successor to Mr. Blanford, Eliot, as officiating reporter, has published the report of 1887 on the Meteorology of India. On page 209 he refers to certain storms in Bengal known as northwesters, which are occasionally as destructive as the tornadoes of the United States, but his description does not enable us to conclude as to whether they were of the nature of twisting tornadoes, or the straight-line Derecho, described by Hinrichs, in Iowa.

On page 251 Eliot says the great majority of cyclonic rain-storms march across the Bengal coast in the direction of the belt of lowest pressure at the time of their formation. As the chief characteristic of such a barometric trough is light and variable winds, it will be seen that this principle virtually coincides with the rule of cyclonic storms in the Bay of Bengal, which march in the direction of least relative air motion immediately antecedent to the formation of the cyclone.

On page 271 Eliot states that "the persistency of the pressure anomolies (for weeks and months) is almost certainly due to the fact that an abnormal variation of pressure in a moving mass of air necessarily gives rise to or accompanies the modification of its motion and in consequence of well-known properties of fluid motion this changed or modified air motion tends to perpetuate the pressure variation which gave rise to it."

If I correctly understand this sentence I should apply it to the flow of air over an obstacle where the change of motion produces a change of pressure or *vice versa* a change of pressure produces a change in the motion; for example: Standing waves are produced at the surface of a stream which tend to perpetuate themselves; the atmosphere is thrown into a system of undulations by mountain ridges, plateaus, and continents (which undulations may also be horizontal deviations on a grand scale) and into periodic recurrences due to their own inertia and therefore as Eliot says, tending to reproduce themselves until broken up by outside disturbances. This is the explanation of the special seasons of droughts, storms, and rains that we experience in America, and it doubtless obtains equally in India.

(19) *Sir William Thomson.*—Thompson has published a series of papers sparkling with his customary brilliancy on fluid motions; these are scattered through the Philosophical Magazine, the proceedings of the societies at London, Edinburgh, and Glasgow, and the reports of the British Association. These papers will cover theoretical questions as to the stability of fluid motions, the formation of standing waves, the discontinuous space in the rear of an obstacle, the laminar flow of liquids, the turbulent flow of water, and other matters bearing on atmospheric phenomena. These papers have apparently been drawn out as notes for the forthcoming third volume of his mathematical and physical papers, and when collected will be recognized as completing our views on many subjects.

(20) *Oberbeck.*—In 1882 Oberbeck published in Wiedemann's Annalen a mathematical development based on the correct hydrodynamic formulæ, of the theory of horizontal atmospheric currents.

A full translation of this important memoir will be included in the series of papers formerly referred to; but the following popular statement of his results is given here as published by Oberbeck himself in the proceedings of the second German Geographical Congress:

Starting from the generally known results of recent meteorological observations in so far as these relate to the distribution of pressure and the direction and force of the wind, the author explains that one of the most important problems of the mathematical theory of the motion of fluids is to explain quantitatively the connection of the above-named phenomena. The recently published investigations of Guldberg and Mohn (Ètudes sur les mouvements de l'atmosphère, Christiania, 1876 and 1880), are to be considered as a specially successful attempt in this direction. It must be of interest also for the larger number of geographers to know the most important results to which the Norwegian scientists have attained.

In order to understand the horizontal movements of the atmosphere it is important for a moment to consider their causes. As such we consider the differences of pressure at the surface of the earth as observed with the barometer. But whence do these arise? This question has been answered a long time since. It is heat which is to be considered as the prime cause of the disturbance of equilibrium in the atmosphere.

Because of the slight conductivity of the air the process of warming can progress only slowly from below upwards, so that, as is well known, the temperature of the air steadily diminishes as we ascend. The heated air expands. The pressure becomes less. If the heating takes place uniformly over a large area there will be at first no reason for horizontal currents. But vertical currents can certainly be brought about by this means. If we imagine a circumscribed mass of air transported into a higher region without any increase or diminution of its heat its temperature will sink because it has expanded itself proportionately to the diminished pressure. If its temperature is then equal to that prevailing in the upper stratum it will remain in equilibrium at this altitude as well as below. The atmosphere in this case exists in a state of indifferent equilibrium. If its temperature is lower the mass of air will again sink down; in the reverse case it will rise higher. The air in these cases is then in stable or unstable equilibrium respectively. In the latter case any vertical movement initiated by some accidental disturbance will not again disappear, but rapidly assumes increasing dimensions. The current will also continue uniform for a long time.

This is the explanation given by Espy, 1831, William Thomson, 1861, and Reye, of Strasburg, 1868, of the ascending air currents in the whirlwinds of the tropics.

The winds of our (temperate) zone also presuppose such ascending currents whose origin must have been quite similar. The ascending current is in general restricted to a definite region that we can designate as the base. Since the ascending current consists of warmer air, therefore above this base the pressure sinks.* A barometric depression is inaugurated there. The pressure increases from this region outward in all directions. The isobars therefore surround the region of ascending atmospheric currents in closed curves. At greater heights the upper cooled air flows away to one side, and in other regions gives occasion to descending currents of air. At the earth's surface itself the air flows towards the depression; its influence thus extends over an area much greater than that of the base. If we neglect the curvature of the earth's surface over this larger area we find there simple horizontal movements. Mathematical computations should now reveal to us the nature of such horizontal movements. To this end all the causes of motion or the forces that come into consideration are first to be collected together.

The differences of pressure have already been several times spoken of; these are measured by the gradient, and it gives for any point the direction and amount of the greatest change in pressure. In horizontal movements the effect of gravity can be omitted.

---

* Thus in the original;—but the thoughtful reader will perceive that in this "popular" presentation Oberbeck has not escaped the repetition of a popular error. The fall of pressure, due to the warming of the air, is quite inappreciable; the observed barometic depression is due to cyclonic motions.

On the other hand, attention must be given to the rotation of the earth on its axis, since we are only interested in the paths of the winds on the rotating earth. This influence can be taken account of if we imagine at every point of the mass of air a force applied which is perpendicular to the momentary direction of motion and is equal to the product of the double angular velocity of the earth, the sine of the latitude, and the velocity of the point. On the northern hemisphere this influence causes a continuous departure of the path towards the right-hand side. Since the movement takes place directly on the earth's surface the direct influence of that surface, namely, the friction, remains to be considered. Its influence diminishes with the distance from the earth's surface. Furthermore, it depends on the nature of the earth's surface, whether sea or lands, plains or wooded mountains. For this computation Guldberg and Mohn have made a convenient assumption in that they introduce the friction as a force which opposes the movement and is equal to the product of a given factor and the velocity. This factor can have different values according to the nature of the earth's surface.

All these forces are to be introduced into the general equations of motion of the air. If however one desires solutions of these general equations for special cases there is still needed a series of assumptions.

Let there be only one single vertical current of air present. The totality of all the atmospheric movements depending upon this one vertical current is called a wind system. If the strength of the ascending current is variable or if the basis itself changes its place then the wind system is variable. In the first case the system stands still, in the second case it is movable.

If, on the other hand, the ascending current of air retains its strength and location without change, or, which is the same, if the isobars for a long time retain their position then the wind system is invariable.

It is evident that the last case is by far the most simple. We will therefore begin with its consideration.

In order to execute the calculation the location of the isobars must be known. Even in this respect also in a preliminary way one must limit himself at first by simple assumptions. Let the isobars be either parallel straight lines or concentric circles.

In the first case the computation leads to the following simple results:

(1) The parallel isobars are equally distant from each other. The gradient is therefore everywhere of equal magnitude.

(2) The paths of the wind consist of parallel straight lines. The strength of the wind has everywhere the same value.

(3) The direction of the wind forms an angle with the gradient whose tangent is equal to the quotient of the factor arising from the earth's rotation divided by the friction-constant.

The deviation of the wind from the gradient is therefore greater in proportion as friction is smaller. If the earth's surface were perfectly smooth the wind would blow in the direction of the isobars,

This result following directly from the computation and at first surprising finds its confirmation in a variety of observations. For example in England we observe a deviation of 61 degrees for land winds but of 77 degrees for sea breezes. From this it follows that the friction on the land is more than twice as great as on the sea.

Conditions of pressure like those here considered frequently occur. In the regions of the trade winds and monsoons they ordinarily prevail either during the whole or about half of the year.

The circular isobars to the consideration of which we now pass produce systems of wind that can be considered as the simplest types of cyclones and anti-cyclones according as the pressure in the interior is a minimum or maximum. We confine ourselves here to the consideration of cyclones.

As already remarked, these are not conceivable without an ascending current of air, whose area in our case is defined by a circle. Outside of this horizontal movements prevail exclusively; inside of it there is also the vertical movement to be considered. Therefore the computations for the outer and inner regions are different. In this way we obtain the following results:

(1) The pressure increases from all sides outward from the center; the gradient increases also from the center out to the limit of the inner region; from there on it diminishes, and at a great distance becomes inappreciable.

(2) The wind-paths in both regions are curved lines, logarithmic spirals, which cut the isobars everywhere at the same angle or make everywhere the same angle with the radial gradient. Therefore the movement of the air can be considered as consisting of a current toward the center and a rotation around the center, the direction of the latter is counter clock-wise. This departure from the gradient is of different magnitudes in the outer and inner regions. For the former the departure has the same value as for straight isobars, that is to say, it depends alone upon the rotation of the earth and the friction. For the inner region the departure is greater, and depends besides upon the intensity of the ascending current of air. If both regions were separated from each other by a geometrical cylindrical surface, then the wind-paths in these would not continuously merge into each other, but would form an angle with each other. This, of course, can never occur in nature. We must therefore assume a transition region in which the wind is continuously diverted from one into the other direction. At any rate accurate and comparative observations of the wind direction in the inner and outer region of a cyclone would be of great interest. From these one could draw a conclusion as to the limitation of the ascending current of air. This limit is, moreover, also notable in that at it the winds reach their greatest force.

There is no arrangement that has been discussed theoretically as yet, except the straight line, circular, and nearly circular forms of the isobars.

We have as yet only spoken of the invariable systems of wind. In fact, however, their duration is relatively short. No sooner is a depression formed than it fills itself up. Furthermore, the central region of depression generally does not remain long in the same place, but progresses often with great velocity, drawing the whole system of winds with it. We must look to the density of the horizontal current flowing in toward the ascending current of air as the cause of these changes. The system of winds remains unchanged only when, as has hitherto been silently assumed, the temperature and density of the horizontal and vertical currents are alike. If the inflowing air is warmer, the depression increases in depth, in the opposite case it becomes shallower.

Finally, if the inflowing air is not of the same temperature on all sides, but is on the one side of higher and on the other side of lower temperature than the ascending air, then it will on the one side be strengthened and its area increased, on the other side enfeebled and its area diminished. The consequence of this is that the current of air or the region of depression moves along. The cyclone progresses. Since in the cyclones of our zone the air entering on the east side comes from more southern, therefore in general warmer, regions, while the air entering on the west side comes from the north and is generally colder, therefore the cyclone progresses from west to east or from southwest to northeast. This is in fact the path of most cyclones in northern Europe. For a moving cyclone the isobaric curves must have a different shape than for a stationary. Therefore one can inversely, from the shape of the isobars, infer the direction of motion. If the region of ascending air has a circular form the computation can be rigorously executed. Without going into the details of this interesting problem in this place, I will only remark that the isobars consist of closed curves similar to an ellipse. There is one direction from the center outwards, in which the isobars are most crowded together, while in the opposite direction they are furthest apart. The movement of the cyclone is in a direction at right angles to this line. With the solution of this problem we now stand about at the limits of what analysis has thus far accomplished. Still there is hope that it will make further progress so far as concerns the relations between the pressure and the motion of the air at the earth's surface.

(21) *Oberbeck.*—Oberbeck has added to his memoir of 1882 a further investigation on the general movements of the atmosphere, which was published in full in two communications to the Academy of Sciences at Berlin in the year 1888. (See Sitzungsberichte, 1888, XIV, p. 383–395.) On account of their importance I have, as in his former memoirs, given a complete translation of these in the collection of translations previously noticed; but to those who do not care to follow the mathematical investigation the following résumé of his results is given mostly as expressed in a popular paper by Oberbeck himself and originally contributed by him to the Naturwissenschaftliche Rundschau of June 9, 1888.

" The systematic and successful labors of meteorological observers in the last decade has given a series of empirical laws for the motion of the air that have already become of great importance for meteorology and for weather predictions, and promise to become still more so in the future.

" In general the active forces that constitute the principal causes of these phenomena of motion have been correctly appreciated, but so far as I know we have not yet been successful in bringing them into such a systematic connection that we have been able to deduce therefrom a mechanics of the atmosphere or a theory that reproduces the most important points in the phenomena of motion.   However, very noteworthy attempts in this direction have already been made by different parties.

" The oldest investigations upon this point are due to the American meteorologist, William Ferrel.   They are contained in a large number of memoirs, only a part of which is accessible to me; but from the memoirs that are known to me I think I may conclude that the most important results to which Ferrel has attained are collected together by himself in a work recently published (Recent Advances in Meteorology, Washington, or Appendix 71 to the Annual Report for 1885 of the Chief Signal Officer), so that the following remarks relate to this work:

" Ferrel starts, in reality, with the equations of motion of a free heavy point or a small free mass, and endeavors, by the addition of further terms, to accommodate these equations to the motion of a fluid, but without finally attaining the correct form of the hydrodynamic equations.   As effective forces he introduces the attraction of the earth, the consideration of the differences of density of the air (in consequence of differences of temperature), the effects resulting from the rotation of the earth, and, finally, the resistances of friction.

" From the general equations he derives special solutions, in which, first, the friction is neglected, and the additional assumption is made that the currents in the directions of the small circles (parallels of latitude) materially exceed in strength or velocity the movements in the meridian that would take place on a motionless earth, in consequence of the differences in temperature between the tropics and the polar zones.

" But such an assumption, in my opinion, ought not to be made without further considerations.   Rather is it the province of theory to demonstrate its correctness, and to show for what reasons east and west currents are stronger than the north and south currents.   The complete neglect of friction leads, as not otherwise to be expected, to formulæ that make the velocity at the poles become infinitely great, whence follows that the atmospheric pressure will there be zero.   The consideration of friction, as to the method of whose action no special assumption is made, has the result of mollifying these incorrect results and accommodating the phenomena of motion to the recognized special distribution of pressure on the earth surface.

" The motions in the atmosphere have been further treated of by C. M. Guldberg and H. Mohn. (Studies on the Motions of the Atmosphere, Christiania, part I, 1876, part II, 1880.) These authors both start with the correct hydrodynamic equations. The motions are by them directly recorded in differences of pressure. Furthermore, the resistance is assumed to be proportional to the velocity of the wind then prevailing. It is very probable that this assumption is appropriate for the lowest strata of the atmosphere. The calculations of the above-named scholars will, therefore, lead also to results that agree with observations in general for the movement of the air in the neighborhood of the earth's surface, especially when we carry through the computations somewhat more accurately, as was done by me a short time ago. (See Wiedemann Annalen, 1882, vol. XVII, p. 128, reproduced in No. 7 of the accompanying translations; compare also A. Sprung, Treatise on Meteorology, pp. 142–151.) On the other hand, there can certainly be no doubt that the above-given assumption as to the nature of the frictional resistance is entirely inappropriate for the upper strata of air. A general comprehensive theory of cyclones, in which the upper and the lower currents are considered, and in which, furthermore, the fundamental cause of cyclones, namely, local differences of density in the atmosphere, occupies the foreground, can certainly not be attained by using the above-mentioned assumption as to resistance.

"The problem of the progressive movement of cyclones, so remarkably important but at the same time so very difficult, can indeed only first find a satisfactory solution when (1) the constitution of a stationary cyclone is sufficiently well known (2) the currents in the upper strata of the atmosphere are established with some degree of certainty.

"The above mentioned investigations are presented in a clear and comprehensive form in the treatise on meteorology by A. Sprung, Hamburg, 1885.

"Especially would I call attention to the judgment of the author as to W. Ferrel (page 198 and notes on pages 200 and 202), with which I entirely agree.*

"Since that publication the motions of the atmosphere have been treated by W. Siemens, introducing the fundamental proposition of the conservation of energy. (Siemens, On the Conservation of Energy in the Atmosphere of the Earth. Sitzungsberichte of the Berlin Academy, 1886, p. 261). This author, without special analytical developments, makes the existence of strong currents in the direction of the parallels of latitude very probable, and ascribes to them a predominant influence on even the wind systems of the temperate zones.

---

* Sprung's criticism is but little more than the opinion of a regret that Ferrel has not fully solved the equation of continuity, but as he has adopted the special solution that is offered by the mean distribution of temperature and pressure in the earth, I do not see that any error has been introduced thereby.—C. A.

"From all this it seemed to me worth the trouble to investigate to what results a new treatment of the problem of atmospheric movements in the most general analytical method would lead.

"The starting point necessarily is the equations of motion of hydro-dynamics, as to whose reliability, so far as is known to me, no manner of doubt has been expressed. The ultimate cause of the movements con-sists in differences of density of air that is subject to the attraction of the earth.

"The influence of the rotation of the earth, according to the laws of mechanics, can be expressed by a deviating force, so that after its intro-duction the earth can be considered as at rest. Furthermore, frictional forces are to be introduced, since without them the atmospheric currents under the continuous influence of accelerating forces will attain infinitely great velocities. The resistances opposing the atmospheric movements in all cases consist of a series of influences of various origins, and in part also, variable in amount. If a rapidly moving mass of fluid penetrates into a quiet fluid it experiences a sensible resistance almost like that of a solid body moving in the quiet fluid. If, on the other hand, a definite portion of a fluid comes continuously under the influence of a motive force, then "fluid jets" are formed, or, as they were first called by Helmholtz, "discontinuous currents," which glide through the quiet fluid with rela-tively slight friction.* Two neighboring currents running parallel to each other, with different velocities, will always affect each other in such a way that the more rapid is retarded, the slower current is accelerated. This interchange is much favored when between the two larger main currents smaller side currents are produced by means of local causes, which bring about a partial mixture of the two streams. All these phenomena, especially that last mentioned, indicate in my judgment that we shall take account of the most important resisting influences if we follow the assumption first expressed by Newton, that the mutual influence of the rapidly moving parts of a fluid is proportional to the difference of their velocities. Hence it at once follows that a current, in which all parts move parallel and with equal velocities, experiences in general no friction. On the other hand, wherever currents of different velocity occur near each other the friction has an effect which is especi-ally strong at the boundary of the currents.

"Since I also adopt the just mentioned law of friction for the atmos-pheric currents, I would expressly designate this as an hypothesis. I thereby in nowise assume that the process is so simple as it is in the experiments for the determination of the coefficient of friction, i. e., viscosity or internal friction, in which everything is so arranged inten-tionally that the velocities of the fluid remain very small.

---

* H. von Helmholtz, Ueber discontinuirliche Flussigkeitsbewegungen, Berlin, Mo-natsb., 1868. Reprinted in Helmholtz, Wissenschaftliche Abhandlungen, Vol. I, p. 146. Compare also Oberbeck, Wiedem. Ann., II, S. 1, on the same subject.

"Hence the numerical value of the coefficient of the friction of the air (or viscosity), as found experimentally, can in nowise be used for the computation of the influence of friction in the atmosphere. Rather will the number that for brevity is here called 'friction coefficient,' be much larger than the above-mentioned coefficient.

"The influence of the earth's surface on the air streaming over it can be easily expressed according to this theory of friction. According to the nature of the earth's surface the neighboring particles of air are either forced to adhere to it or else move over it with greater or less retardation.

"The density of the air as is well known depends upon the pressure and the temperature. For increasing distance above the earth's surface the density diminishes rapidly, and at an altitude of 20 kilometers it has a density of only one-tenth of that which prevails at the earth's surface. The consideration of this circumstance would greatly increase the difficulty of the calculation. I have temporarily ignored the diminution of density at great altitudes. But in the explanation of the final result one would have to take into consideration this point. Since as above mentioned, the density of the air is inappreciably small at altitudes which are slight in comparison with the horizontal dimensions of the atmosphere, therefore the movements that occur at those altitudes can in general exert only a slight influence on the currents in the lower stratum. We can therefore from a dynamic point of view consider the atmosphere as bounded at a moderate altitude by a spherical surface on which the air slides freely.

"The calculation executed on the basis of this assumption leads to the following result: *If we imagine a definite distribution of temperature over the earth's surface or over a special portion of it to continue for a long time,* then permanent currents of air exist, that can be calculated from the distribution of temperature if it be considered as given.

"Now the contrast in temperature of the hot and cold zone is the principal force that, with slight modifications in the different seasons of the year, causes a system of currents that includes the greatest part of the earth's surface.

"A form of expressing this distribution of temperature that is very convenient for computation consists in the utilization of the following expression:

$$T = A + B \ (1 - 3 \cos^2 \theta)$$

In this θ is the angle that the line connecting any point of the atmosphere with the center of the earth makes with the axis of the earth so that $90° - \theta$ is the geographical latitude of the point in question. Under this assumption analysis furnishes the following values for the three components of the currents at any point of the atmosphere, viz, V for the vertical component taken positive upwards, N the horizontal component taken positive toward the north, and O the horizontal component taken as positive toward the east.

$$V = C \ (1-3 \cos^2 \theta) f$$
$$N = -6 \ C \cos \theta \sin \theta . \ \varphi$$
$$O = D \ [\sin \theta \ (1-3 \cos^2 \theta) \ \dot{g} + 6 \cos^2 \theta . \ \gamma]$$

"In these expressions f, φ, g, γ are functions of the distance of the point in question in the atmosphere above the earth's surface. They depend also upon the condition of the atmosphere at its two boundary surfaces (the concentric spherical surfaces above and below). At both these two boundary surfaces the vertical component V, and therefore also f, must disappear. Furthermore, φ, g, γ, must disappear at the earth's surface if we assume that there the atmosphere adheres to it.

"The function φ is zero for a certain definite altitude—that is to say, at this altitude the meridional current changes its sign; below it is directed toward the south, but above it is directed toward the north. The function g is everywhere negative; the function γ is everywhere positive, but always zero at the earth's surface.

"The two constants C and D unfortunately do not admit of direct numerical computation, and that for two reasons: First, the unknown value of the friction constant for atmospheric currents enters into them. Again, they contain the whole difference in temperature between the equator and the pole. But it is allowable to assume that only a certain fractional part of this difference of temperature is the actual effective cause of the currents, since in the higher strata the difference of temperature is certainly considerably smaller.

"In other respects the above expressions give a clear picture of the currents. The vertical current (V) is an ascending one from the equator up to 35° 16′ north and south latitudes, but thence to the poles it is directed downwards. The meridional currents (N) are 0 at the equator and at the poles; they attain their greatest value at 45° latitude.

"In consequence of the earth's rotation there arises the current O along the circles of latitude, which consists of two branches, O_1 depending on the function g, and O_2 depending on the function γ. O_1 is, from the equator to 35° 16′ north and south latitudes, directed toward the west; there this current changes its sign, and in the higher latitudes is easterly. O_2 represents a current directed toward the east; everywhere at the earth's surface it is zero (corresponding to the value of the function γ), but, on the other hand, at higher altitudes it attains a very considerable value. Both the movements O_1 and O_2 along the small circles of latitude disappear at the pole. Moreover, the current O_2 is zero at the equator, and attains its greatest value at the latitudes 54° 44′ north and south.

"We would especially call attention to the fact that these results depend essentially upon the assumption as to the distribution of temperature. A change in the location of the maximum of temperature (as for instance, its transfer into the northern hemisphere), would cause a corresponding change of all the currents.

"The accompanying sketch, Fig. 1, gives a picture of the atmospheric currents as they would result from the adopted distribution of temperature. This presents the earth's surface in the Mercator projection. The curves u and u represent the currents of air in the lower strata; the curves o and o in the upper strata of the atmosphere. At the equator and at the poles the vertical currents serve as the means of transition of the lower currents into the upper, and *vice versa*. The lower current can, under favorable circumstances, come to be observed at the earth's surface. In fact, the diagram presents in its u curves in the tropics the trade winds as they prevail over the Pacific and Atlantic Oceans, and also the west wind as it prevails beyond the fortieth degree of latitude. From the agreement of the wind paths in this diagram with those actually

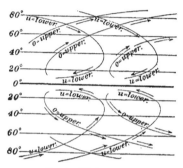

FIG 1 — Wind currents.

observed, the important conclusion can be drawn that in general the currents u and o_1 are of the same order of magnitude. Hence, it follows that o_2 or the upper easterly current must be of materially greater intensity than the lower currents. The upper wind paths agree in the tropics with the anti-trade. In higher latitudes the west wind must principally prevail in the upper regions.

"In the very highest strata of air the currents must again diminish in strength; this is to be concluded from the fact that the two quantities C and D contain the density of the air as a factor which enters in its first power into C, but in its second power into D. •

"To this general presentation of the currents of air the detailed computation of the distribution of pressure is still lacking by this execution, perhaps some unimportant modifications of the results here communicated may be attained."

(22) *Oberbeck.*—In his third communication on this subject (the second of 1888), Oberbeck passes from a consideration of the *motions* of the atmosphere to that of the general distribution of *pressure* that results from the movements, which themselves result from the distribution of temperature, or more properly of density. In this case he again deals with the hypothetical atmosphere of uniform density and depth adhering to the earth but gliding under the upper layers and adopts the approximate law of temperature of the air as above given. His general solution of the equations leads to the formula:

$$p = \text{constant} + m \cos^2\theta - n \cos^4\theta.$$

In the southern hemisphere we have conditions that approximate those here adopted more nearly than in the northern, and having shown that the observed pressures agree with the preceding result, Oberbeck then utilizes the terms m and n to separate the motions in latitude and longitude. This process is more general than that which Ferrel executed in the case of the solutions given by him in 1859 in the Mathematical Monthly, so that the equations can be adapted to a wide range of constants in the law of distribution of temperature at the earth's surface. Oberbeck proceeds to apply it to the extreme seasonal change in the atmosphere as well as to the assumed mean. The whole memoir will be given in my selected translations.

(23) *Helmholtz.*—In May, 1888, Helmholtz submitted to the Berlin Academy the memoir on atmospheric movements that I have given in full in the accompanying translations. He first shows that the results of laboratory experiments on a small scale can not be directly applied to larger atmospheric movements because of the fact that the inertia and density of the masses, the forces of viscosity and gravitation, and the linear dimensions, length, area, volume, angle and time, are not all enlarged in the necessary ratios, so that certain results, especially viscosity, become inappreciable in large natural phenomena. He then studies the conditions of stability among masses having discontinuous motions; thus if two ring vortices encircle the earth having different latitudes and temperatures, stable equilibrium is possible only when the warm ring is on the polar edge of the colder ring. If they have the same latitude then the warmer must be above the colder. The unrolling of the vortex-cylinders and rings destroys their integrity and motions, mixes their own and the surrounding air together, determines the actual average distribution of temperature and moisture in the atmosphere, and is the important step in the history of all atmospheric phenomena. Helmholtz announces his intention of further developing this subject.

(24) *Diro Kitao* —Comparable with the elegant analysis of Helmholtz and Oberbeck, and, in fact, reminding us remarkably of the work of Kirchhoff, is the memoir by Kitao (professor of physics and mathematics in the Imperial Academy of Agriculture of the University of Tokio), entitled " Contributions to the theory of the movement of the terrestrial atmosphere and of whirlwind storms."

A few years ago, Professor Kitao returned from studying in Germany, and Japan is to be congratulated on possessing two such mathematicians as Kikuchi and Kitao, the former as able a pupil of the English school as the latter is of the German.

Kitao's memoir is published in two parts, in vol. I, 1887. and vol. II, 1889, of the Journal of the College of Science of the University Tokio, and a further continuation is promised. But for its great length his work would have been included in the appended collection of translations, but awaiting its completion and eventual translation I can now only call the attention of students to this extensive analytical memoir.

(25) *General treatises on fluid motion.*—To complete our list of recent
works bearing directly on the mechanics of the atmosphere, we should
include a few general treatises on fluid motion that are specially worthy
of the study of meteorologists.

I do not note any general works by French authors, but have reason
to expect such in the near future, judging from the introductions and
notes in recent publications by Poincaré, Boussinesq, Duhem, and
Mathieu. Our list is as follows:

G KIRCHHOFF. Vorlesungen über mathematische Physik. Mechanik. Dritte Auf-
lage. Leipsig, 1883. [Chapters 15–26, or one-half of this volume, is devoted to
fluid motions.]

A. B BASSET. A treatise on hydro-dynamics, with numerous examples. Vols. I and
II [a third is expected], Cambridge (England), 1888.

W. S. BESANT. A treatise on hydro-mechanics. Fourth edition, Part I, hydrostat-
ics. Cambridge (England), 1883. [Part II, hydro-kinetics, is promised.]

M. DE SAINT VENANT. Résistance des Fluids [edited by Boussinesq]. Institut de
France, Tome XLIV. Paris, 1887.

IV.—THERMO-DYNAMICS OF ATMOSPHERIC PHENOMENA.

(26) *Introductory.*—The application of the laws of thermo-dynamics
to the movements of the atmosphere was first made in a crude manner
by Espy and Joseph Henry before the development of this branch of
physics had been attempted by Clausius, Sir William Thomson, and
others. The memoir of Thomson in 1861; Reye, 1864 and 1872; that
of J. H. Lane (American Journal of Science and Arts, July, 1870); that
of Charles Chambers (see the Meteorology of the Bombay Presidency,
1878); the short paper by Hann (Z. O. G. M., 1874); the memoirs of Prof.
William Ferrel (see especially his Meteorological Researches, 1877, 1881,
1883, and his Recent Advances, 1885; those of Guldberg and Mohn,
1876–'78), and the treatise of Sprung (Meteorologie, 1885), have all of
them given analytical expressions for this application of thermo-dynamics, so that the whole subject of adiabatic changes should now be
familiar to all meteorologists. The works of these authors have now
been most admirably supplemented by two memoirs by Hertz and Bezold, respectively, who have developed graphic methods that render the
entire process of cooling and warming easy of computation and clear
of comprehension, as also very expeditious.

The memoir of Hertz is confined to the determination of adiabatic
changes, but the memoir of Bezold includes the consideration of changes
that are not strictly adiabatic, but in which the quantity of heat within
a mass of air actually changes by reason of mixtures, precipitations,
and radiations.

It is evident to the most superficial thought that the quantity of
heat within a given mass of air actually is continually in a state of
change and that too not only by reason of its gain of heat from the sun
by day and its loss by radiation at night, but especially by the process
of mixture that is continually going on. On the one hand cold and dry

airs are being mixed with warm and moist; on the other hand aqueous vapor with latent heat is being added to the air by evaporation from the ground, and again being taken from the air, but leaving its heat behind by the process of formation of rain, hail, and snow. Therefore the ascent and descent of atmospheric currents is by no means an adiabatic process, and it is the aim of Bezold to so present graphically the changes that take place in ascending and descending air as that we may at any time calculate its thermal condition.

(27) *Bezold.*—The original memoirs of Hertz and Bezold detailing their graphic methods in thermo-dynamics as applied to our atmosphere will be given in full in the promised collection of translations. The ground covered by these will be easily understood from the following analysis of Bezold's work by Lettry,[*] with slight additions by myself.

(A.) DEFINITIONS.—Let p and v be respectively the values of the volume and pressure of a unit weight, namely, a unit mass, of gas or gaseous vapor whose absolute temperature is T. Then according to the law of Boyle Mariotte-Gay-Lussac and Charles, we have

$$pv = \mathrm{RT} \quad . \quad . \quad . \quad . \quad . \quad . \quad (a).$$

Let the condition of the unit of gas be graphically represented as to pressure and volume by the ordinate and abscissa of a point; when p and v are given, the location of the point is known by the graphic construction, but equally is the temperature.T known by the equation (a); thus the location of a point in the diagram corresponds to a definite temperature of the gas. If the gaseous mass is maintained at a constant temperature then p and v may vary continuously, only fulfilling the condition that their product $p\,v$ remains constant. The locus of the continuous series of points thus defined is called an *isotherm*, and we see that the isotherm occurring for any given temperature must be a hyperbola with the axis p and v as its asymptotes, as in Fig. 2, where the co-ordinate axes are rectangular and the hyperbola is equilateral.

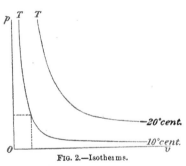

FIG. 2.—Isotherms.

If on the other hand the temperature be allowed to change, but the original amount of heat or thermal energy in a unit mass of gas is forced to remain constant, then a new relation between the pressure and volume that can co-exist is brought about and is definitely determined by the laws of thermo-dynamics; this relation is given by the equation,

$$p^k v^{k\prime} = \text{constant}$$

where k and k' are respectively the specific heat of the gas or vapor at constant volume and again at constant pressure. If, as before, the co-existing p and v are made the co-ordinates of a point, the locus of the points representing the pressure and volume for a given constant quantity of heat is called the *adiabatic* curve for that special quantity, as is shown in Fig. 3.

An isotherm and an adiabatic line may be imagined passing through any point whatever if the latter be considered as an *indicator* of a given initial state of the gas; that is to say, a point whose position is determined by co-ordinates having the initial values p_0 and v_0. The indicator point will follow the isotherm if we make the condition of the gas vary while maintaining a constant temperature; it will follow the adiabatic if the condition of the gas varies without increase or diminution of the quantity of heat contained within it.

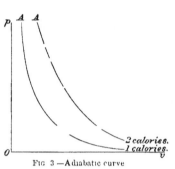

FIG 3 —Adiabatic curve

Hitherto in the application of the mechanical theory of heat to meteorology the adiabatic changes only have been considered, but Hertz has shown how to approximately consider non-adiabatic changes, and especially has Bezold freed himself from the adiabatic hypothesis, which is in fact not generally realized in nature.

Dynamic cooling.—Bezold first considers the preliminary question, Why does air cool on ascending to higher elevations? Most meteorologists explain this cooling as the transformation of molecular energy into external work done in the expansion of the gaseous mass as it comes under and acts against the diminished pressure of the upper regions. This is correct, and it is necessary to be on our guard against an erroneous explanation adopted by Guldberg and Mohn, to the effect that the work done is the elevation of the gas to the higher level; this latter explanation is not allowable, since the work of raising the gas is really done by gravity, namely, the heavier descending air pushes up the lighter rising gas.

(B.) THE DRY STAGE.—Let x be the mass of aqueous vapor (namely, not the weight nor the tension, but strictly the mass of vapor) that is associated with a unit mass, *i. e.*, a kilogram of dry air, and m the mass of the mixture; then $m = 1 + x$. Note that x differs slightly from the quantity of vapor in a kilogram of the mixture, which latter is the quantity generally given in meteorological tables.

Let p_λ and p_δ be the partial pressures of the dry air and the vapor, respectively; the total barometric pressure will be $p = p_\lambda + p_\delta$.

Let R_λ and R_δ be the constants in equation (a) for the air and vapor; that equation then gives for the mixed gas and vapor

$$p_\lambda\, v = R_\lambda\, T \qquad p_\delta v = x\, R_\delta\, T \qquad p = \frac{1}{v}(R_\lambda + x R_\delta)\, T. \quad . \quad . \quad . \quad (1)$$

Approximately, $R_\lambda = 29.272$ and $R_\delta = 47.061$ in the metric system of units.

Comparing this with the corresponding equation for dry air, we see that (1) contains the additional variable x, and that the thermal condition of the gas is not defined until we know p, v, and x. Geometrically the condition of the gas would be represented by the location of a point in space whose co-ordinates are these three variables.

Let pov, in Figs. 2 and 3, be called the "plane of co-ordinates," as that term is used by Bezold, and let x be measured perpendicular thereto; we have thus the necessary system of three rectangular co-ordinates. The value of x in ordinary meteorological problems is generally very small in comparison with p and v. For any given constant value of x the indicator point, showing the thermal condition of the air, would move in a plane parallel and very near to the plane pov. If x is zero the equation and the curve becomes the same as for dry air.

Isotherms.—If we assume that the temperature T is maintained constant, then the indicator moves along an isotherm, as above described. For a given value of x equation (1) shows that the isotherm is an equilateral hyperbola precisely like that in dry air, but situated in a plane parallel to the plane of co-ordinates. The isotherms for the same temperature T and for different values of x, when projected upon the plane pov, agree sensibly. In fact the ordinates p_1 and p_2 of the two isotherms corresponding to a given abscissa, v, and to the given quantities of aqueous vapor x_1 and x_2 are connected by the relation

$$p_1 - p_2 = (x_1 - x_2)\frac{R_\delta T}{v}$$

Since the second member of this equation is very nearly zero, since the values of x are generally less than 0.03, therefore the ordinates p_1 and p_2 are sensibly equal. One may then be content to consider in the geometrical interpretation of the facts, not the isotherms themselves, but their approximately common projection upon the plane of co-ordinates; this amounts to saying that we may consider x as constant.

The line of saturation.—The changes in the condition of the air are not reversible, and the equation (1) holds good only for certain values of v. In fact the fundamental condition of the dry stage is that the vapor pressure p_δ shall be rather less than the maximum pressure of the saturated vapor for the temperature T. Designating this maximum pressure by e it is necessary that we should have

$$p_\delta \underset{=}{\leq} e$$

or rather by replacing p_δ by its value as a function of v that we should have

$$\frac{xR_\delta T}{v} \underset{=}{\leq} e$$

that is to say

$$v > \frac{x R_\delta\, T}{e} \quad \cdots \cdots \cdots \quad (2)$$

or for the limiting case

$$v = x\, \frac{R_\delta\, T}{e} \qquad\qquad (3)$$

Each isotherm therefore commences only at a certain limiting point, whose abscissa is given by the equation (3) and whose ordinate is determined by the relation found by combining equations (1) and (3) namely,

$$p = e\, \frac{R_\lambda + x\, R_\delta}{x\, R_\delta} \quad \cdots \cdots \cdots \quad (4)$$

If the quantity x preserves a given constant value the isotherm continues to lie in its own plane as the temperature T varies; the limiting point of the isotherm, as just defined, is displaced at the same time, and describes a curve that Bezold calls *the line of saturation* or *the line of the dew-point.* (See Fig. 4.)

This curve has its concavity turned toward the side of positive p. The indicator point for air in the dry stage ought therefore always to be on the concave side of the line of saturation; if this point passes over to the convex side it indicates that the dry stage has been followed by the rain stage.

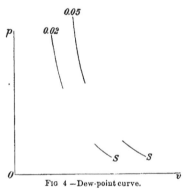

Fig 4 — Dew-point curve.

When the quantity x varies while T remains constant the projections upon the plane of co-ordinates of the isotherms corresponding to the various values of x sensibly agree with each other, as we have said, at least when one draws a diagram rather than a rigorously exact figure. On the other hand, the limiting point in this common projection on the plane of co-ordinates is not the same when we take different values of x. We find, without difficulty, that if v_1 and v_2 are the abscisses of the limiting points belonging to the quantities of vapor x_1 and x_2, respectively, we have $\frac{v_1}{v_2} = \frac{x_1}{x_2}$, that is to say, that the abscissas of the limiting point vary proportionately to x. To each value of x there corresponds a line of saturation, precisely as to each value of T there corresponds an isotherm.

Adiabatics.—The equation of an adiabatic in the dry stage is

$$(c_p + x c_p{}') \log \frac{T}{T_1} - A(R_\lambda + x R_\delta) \log \frac{p}{p_1} = 0 \quad \cdots \quad (5)$$

where c_p and c_p' designate respectively, the specific heats at constant pressure of air and of non-saturated aqueous vapor; $A=430$, approximately, is the mechanical equivalent of a unit of heat. T and p pertain to an initial state of the air, but T_1 and p_1 to a final state. Bezold gives a method of constructing by points an indefinite number of adiabatics when we know one and when we have first constructed the system of isotherms.

In the dry stage the adiabatics are appreciably independent of x, which is a very small quantity, and they can be regarded as sensibly the same as the adiabatics for dry air entirely without aqueous vapor.

Résumé.—For the dry stage the condition of the atmosphere is represented by three systems of lines that can be traced upon a diagram, whose co ordinates are p and v, which lines constitute a net-work intersecting each other over the whole plane of co-ordinates, as follows:

(1) *Isotherms* that are equilateral hyperbolas that depend, respectively, upon the values of the variable parameter T, but can for a given temperature be considered as independent of x, the quantity of aqueous vapor.

(2) *Lines of saturation*, the position of each of which depends on the variable parameter x. Each line of saturation divides the plane of coordinates into two parts; on the concave side of this curve the dry stage is represented, and on the convex side the wet stage.

(3) *Adiabatics*, which are asymptotic to the axes of p and v and intersect the two preceding systems of lines; these adiabatics are sensibly the same as those that relate to absolutely dry air.

(C.) THE RAIN STAGE.—When rain is forming let x be the quantity of saturated vapor that is associated with one kilogram of dry air, and x' the quantity of water as such suspended within this kilogram of dry air; let M be the mass of the mixture; we have the equation

$$M=1+x+x'$$

Here the tension of the vapor is determined by the temperature itself; if e designates this tension then we have the two following equations of condition as representing the relations in this stage of rain:

$$p=R_\lambda\frac{T}{v}+e \quad . \quad . \quad . \quad . \quad . \quad . \quad . \quad . \quad (6)$$

$$e=xR_\delta\frac{T}{v} \quad . \quad . \quad . \quad . \quad . \quad . \quad . \quad . \quad (7)$$

The following remarks may be made with regard to the rain stage:

(1) The quantity of water in suspension, x', is always very small; for as soon as this quantity becomes rather large the water separates from the foggy mass and falls; therefore the changes of condition are irreversible.

(2) In general, the quantity, x, of saturated vapor can only diminish. This quantity could increase with v if, in an exceptional case, the temperature remained constant, or with T, if the volume remained the same, but it would be necessary that the added vapor should be furnished by the evaporation of the water in suspension. Now, the quantity of water in suspension is very small, and this store would be quickly exhausted. The contact of the air with moist bodies or any circumstance of the same class would also tend to increase the quantity of vapor x, but still this would be an exceptional case.

(3) The equations (6) and (7) show that when x is given it suffices to know any one of the quantities e, T, v, or p in order that the others may be determined. We see also that if x is given and T varies, the indicator of the condition of the air moves along the line of saturation that is peculiar to the special value of x.

(4) Let us suppose that at the moment when the vapor becomes saturated and that one enters into the rain stage the quantity of vapor is x_a, and that at the end of a certain time this quantity is diminished to x_b. The indicator was at first on the line of saturation belonging to x_a, but it now is found on the line of saturation belonging to x_b. While x has decreased from x_a to x_b, the indicator has passed from its initial to its final position by cutting across all the lines of dew-point or lines of saturation relative to the intermediate values of x.

But the indicator can not retrace its path, because x can not increase in general. Therefore in the rain stage the indicator always describes its path in the same direction. For such paths or trajectories, described in the given direction, one can apply the principles of thermo-dynamics as if reversible changes were under consideration. Therefore the changes of condition in the case of rain can be described as " partially reversible."

Isotherms.—As the tension e of saturated vapor is constant so long as the temperature T is constant, and as on the other hand x can only decrease, the equation (7) shows that v can only decrease if T does not change. This being allowed, the equation (6) will be the equation of the isotherm for a given temperature, T, and for decreasing values of v and of x. The isotherm remains entirely throughout its whole extent on the convex side of the line of saturation belonging to x_a, the initial value of x. •

We see that the isotherm in the rain stage is still an equilateral hyperbola, and that it varies very little from the isotherm of the dry stage for the same temperature.

Adiabatics.—Strictly speaking there is no adiabatic, unless we suppose that all the condensed water remains in suspension. If all or a part of the water falls to the ground there is an exterior work performed, and consequently a loss of internal heat or calorific energy, and the definition of the adiabatic no longer applies,

If we assume that all the water formed by condensation continues in suspension, we have for the differential equation of the adiabatic

$$(c_v+x_a)dT+Td\left(\frac{xr}{T}\right)+AR_\lambda T\frac{dv}{v}=0 \quad \ldots \ldots \quad (8)$$

where c_v designates the specific heat of the air at a constant volume, x_a is the quantity of aqueous vapor at the moment when the rain stage begins, x is the quantity of aqueous vapor at any given moment during the rain stage, r is the latent heat of vaporization or quantity of heat required to vaporize a unit mass of water at the temperature T, and the pressure p or approximately, 606 at $0°$ C and varying with the temperature; A and R_λ, known constants, as before used. We have moreover $x_a=x+x'$, where x' designates the mass of condensed water that remains in suspension. We could have given another form to the preceding equation by choosing as variables p and T in place of v and T.

Integration furnishes the equation of the adiabatic under a finite form. If we pass from an initial condition designated by the subscript 1 to a final condition designated by the subscript 2 the equation of the adiabatic is

$$AR_\lambda \log \frac{v_2}{v_1}+(c_v+x_a) \log \frac{T_2}{T_1}+\frac{x_2r_2}{T_2}-\frac{x_1r_1}{T_1}=0 \quad \ldots \ldots \quad (9)$$

Pseudo-adiabatic.—When the condensed water is separated wholly or in part from the mass of air, exterior work is done, and consequently there is a loss of heat. The changes of condition in this case are called *pseudo-adiabatic* by Bezold. He gives this name especially to the curve described by the indicator when all the water that is formed falls to the ground without increasing the energy of the mass of gas and without other loss than that just mentioned ; actually the fall of rain does communicate some energy to the air.

The differential equation of the *pseudo-adiabatic* is

$$(c_v+x)dT+Td\left(\frac{xr}{T}\right)+AR_\lambda T\frac{dv}{v}=0 \quad \ldots \ldots \quad (10)$$

This equation is independent of x_a or the quantity of saturated vapor that existed at the moment when the rain stage began; it is also independent of the quantity of water formed, and consequently on our hypothesis, fallen to the ground since the beginning of the rain stage. In equation (10) x represents the quantity of saturated vapor that exists at any given moment.

Integrating this equation between an initial condition designated by the subscript 1 and a final condition designated by the subscript 2 we obtain

$$AR_\lambda \log \frac{v_2}{v_1}+c_v \log \frac{T_2}{T_1}+\int_1^2 \frac{xdT}{T}+\frac{x_2r_2}{T_2}-\frac{x_1r_1}{T_1}=0 \quad \ldots \ldots \quad (11)$$

The integration can not be completely effected so long as the relation between the variables is not given under an explicit form; but we may remark that in the third term the integral is here present only as a correction whose value is comprised between very small limits. By comparing the adiabatic and the pseudo-adiabatic that start from the same initial point we find that this latter curve is the one that most rapidly approaches the axis of v.

(D.) THE SNOW STAGE AND THE HAIL STAGE.—These are treated by Bezold in a manner entirely similar to the preceding. He gives the following examples of application of his methods.

(A) *Foehn.*—In the Foehn, moist air expanding by ascending the sides of a mountain is then compressed when it descends upon the other slope, all without any addition or diminution of its heat. The curves representing these changes of condition are therefore adiabatics.

In Fig. 5, let a be the position of the indicator for the condition corresponding to the initial condition; $Sa\,Sa$ the corresponding line of saturation; as the air expands the indicator moves correspondingly along the adiabatic ab down to the point b, where this curve reaches the line of saturation Sa. The arc ab is located really in a plane parallel to the plane pov of the diagram, and at a distance from this plane equal to the mass x_a of the vapor of water that accompanies 1 kilogram of the dry air.

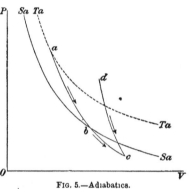

FIG. 5.—Adiabatics.

From a to b the adiabatic crosses a series of isotherms, of which the first one only, namely, the dotted line $Ta\,Ta$ is traced in the diagram, and we see that the temperature has fallen continuously. At the moment when the indicator cuts the line of saturation at b the dry stage ceases and the rain stage begins. The adiabatic ab is now continued by the pseudo-adiabatic bc, which represents the rain stage.

The air does not now cease to expand, but the temperature falls more slowly; this is why the curve bc is less steeply inclined to the axis ov and intersects continually the lines of saturation for quantities of aqueous vapor that are steadily diminishing.

However, the air arrives at the summit of the mountain and crosses it and the compression begins; at this moment the indicator of the condition of the air is at c. Then we have the following alternatives:

(1) All the water that is formed remains in suspension; in this case bc is a true adiabatic, and here the change of condition of the air is completely reversible. The indicator returns from c to b in the rain stage, and then from b to a in the dry stage. We find the same conditions as to temperature, volume, and pressure, on either side of the mountain. This case of complete reversibility always occurs when the

line of saturation has not been attained ; that is to say, when the changes
have occurred entirely within the dry stage.

(2) Or, on the other hand, and which generally happens, the water
that is formed as the indicator passes below h is separated from the rest
of the mass by falling to or towards the earth, and bc is a pseudo-adiabatic; in this case the change is irreversible, and as the air descends
along the opposite slope of the mountain the indicator follows a curve
cd other than bc, or the adiabatic of the dry stage.

We see by the consideration of Fig. 5, that the initial temperature
will be recovered at a pressure lower than the initial pressure ; that the
temperatures that are attained become higher and higher, and the excess over the former becomes greater in proportion as the air descends
and is compressed.

Moreover, the absolute quantity of the aqueous vapor has become
smaller, therefore the real line parallel to the plane pov, and of which
cd is the projection, is now much nearer to this plane than was the original line ab.

Thus we have cold and moist air on one side of the mountain becoming warm and dry air on the other.   Thus we derive all the characteristic properties of the Foehn, and explain without difficulty how it is
that these properties do not pertain to descending winds that have not
first surmounted a summit, for example, to the winds that simply descend along the slope of a plateau.

(B) *Interchange of air between a cyclone and anti cyclone, in the summer.*—The changes of condition of air within a cyclone and anti-cyclone
are analogous to those of air that has surmounted a mountain ridge.
Rain within the area of a cyclone, dry weather in a clear sky within an
anti-cyclone.   But whereas, in the case of the Foehn, these changes are
experienced within an area of small diameter, so that one can neglect
external thermal actions ; the passage from the cyclonic state to the
anti-cyclonic is, on the contrary. effected within a space so extended
that it is necessary to take account of these actions.

In summer the addition of solar heat is the prevailing power; in
winter it is the reverse ; the day-time and the night time have influences
very nearly like those of summer and winter.   In all cases the curves
representing the condition are no longer adiabatic.

Let us suppose that the air passes from the cyclonic to the anti-cyclonic condition in the summer time.   Starting from an initial condition
a in the cyclone, the temperature diminishes by expansion and the indicator of the condition of this mass of air starts to describe the adiabatic ab^1, but the diminution of temperature is retarded by the addition
of external heat and the air expands, as shown by the movement of the
indicator along the curve ab, which is less inclined than the adiabatic
ab^1.   It follows that the line of saturation is attained later than it otherwise would be, and this corresponds to a higher elevation above the
surface of the earth of the mass of air under consideration. (See Fig. 6.)

In the rain stage the curve bc of the change of condition is also less inclined than the adiabatic bc^1; at the same time it remains nearer to the line of saturation. While traversing the line bc the condensed vapor is forming clouds.

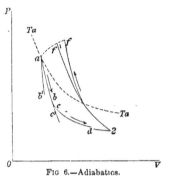

FIG 6.—Adiabatics.

If the addition of external heat continues, the air can even return to the dry stage along the curve cd; let c be this point where this occurs; the point c will at the same time be the upper limit of the lower clouds.

From b to c the absorptive power of the suspended water renders the warming by insolation relatively large. But when one has entered into the dry stage, beyond the point d, the absorptive power of the atmosphere diminishes; however, the expansion continues, and with the expansion the cooling, and at some point d, which corresponds to the height of the cirrus clouds, we enter into the snow stage. The absorption of heat, as we go from c to d, has become so feeble that the line cd can be considered as an adiabatic. From d to 2 we continue in the snow stage or the cirrus-cloud stage. At 2 the air begins to descend in the anti-cyclone

During the first portion of the period of compression the air follows a curve $2f$, corresponding very nearly to the adiabatic $2f^1$ of the dry stage, but departing from it always a little toward the higher isotherms, in proportion as we descend to the lower altitudes, where there exists an energetic absorption of heat.

The final pressure at the point f at the base of the anti-cyclone is greater than the initial pressure at the point a at the base of the cyclone. Moreover, it generally happens that the point f is situated to the right of the point a, that is to say, that v is larger than v_a, or that the air in an anti-cyclone is specifically lighter than in a cyclone. This results from the fact that the addition of external heat compensates for the influence of compression.

If the air, descending in the anti-cyclone, encounters a new depression, this is represented in the diagram by the dotted line fa, supposing everything else to be the same in the old and in the new cyclone. The line fa completes the cycle of the changes of condition.

(C) *Interchanges of air between a cyclone and anti-cyclone, in winter.*— We note at first that the curves of the changes of condition more nearly approach the axes of co-ordinates in winter than in the summer, since the temperatures remain relatively low and the higher isotherms are not attained. At the initial point a the pressure is lower and the temperature higher; at the final point d the pressure is higher and the temperature lower. The point d is therefore to the left and above the point a.

H. Mis. 142——26

Moreover, the curves of condition are in winter nearer the plane *pov* than in summer, because in winter the absolute quantity of aqueous vapor contained in the air is always smaller.

When the air rises in the cyclone, starting from the initial condition *a*, the indicator-point very nearly follows the adiabatic until it attains the upper limit of the mass of clouds; in fact, below this limit the insolation and the radiation can produce only inappreciable effects. As for the rest, in so far as the curve departs from the adiabatic, it approaches the axes, contrary to what happens in the summer time.

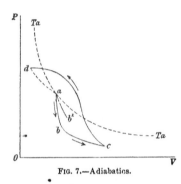

FIG. 7.—Adiabatics.

In the accompanying diagram, Fig. 7, *abc* is the curve of conditions from the initial point *a* up to the moment when the compression begins. We have supposed that the initial mass passes immediately from the dry stage *ab* to the snow stage *bc*.

It is probable that at high altitudes the compression of the descending air proceeds adiabatically, according to the adiabatic of the dry stage; but nearer the ground the radiation causes a deviation toward the co-ordinate axis *ov*. Thus one obtains a curve somewhat analogous to *cd* in Fig. 7. The curve *cd* is only a graphic representation of the well-known fact that there is an inversion in the vertical distribution of temperature during clear days in winter.

Near *d* the curve approaches the line of saturation, so that it may even intersect it; this case corresponds to the formation of fog at the surface of the ground.

Numerical data are wanting to determine whether the passage from *c* to *d* can be made in any other manner, as when the cooling exerts its action near the point *c*. The curve of condition in the plane *pov* would then possess a double point.

These examples suffice to enable us to judge of the usefulness of this graphic method, devised by Bezold, and of which, as he says, when perfected from a mathematical point of view, this method will give an excellent means of discussing the numerical data furnished by observation; it will at the same time make known in what direction other observations are to be sought to the greater profit of dynamic meteorology.

In his second memoir of November, 1888, Bezold adopts the term, "potential temperatures" as equivalent to Helmholtz's expression "thermal contents," and as the term has been applied by the latter it will, we hope, obtain general use, although it is perhaps objectionable, as involving a new modification of the much used word potential. The "potential temperature" is simply the absolute temperature that a body would assume if it were brought to a normal pressure without loss or gain of heat.

Adiabatic or pseudo-adiabatic changes of free air that do not involve evaporation either leave the potential temperature unchanged or increase it, but never diminish it. Bezold uses the term to simplify the state-ment of theorems in atmospheric circulation.

V.—PREDICTION OF STORMS AND WEATHER.

(28) *Abbe.*—In 1871 the present writer prepared a short sketch of views held by himself and other meteorologists with reference to the laws of storms and methods of weather predictions. Three editions of this sketch were published by the Signal Office under the title of "Sug-gestions as to the Practical Use of Meteorological Reports and Weather Maps." A fourth edition, under the title of "How to Use Weather Maps," was prepared in 1883 and printed without charts in 1884, but has not yet been published, and will be replaced by a more recent re-port compiled at the request of General Greely as chief signal officer. As a popular presentation of most of the principles that underlie a philosophical system of weather predictions the last ᴄhapter of the work, as printed in 1884, is perhaps worthy of the attention of the reader, and a rather full synopsis of it is here given, so that the course of the entire argument may be seen. This chapter is entitled "The Prediction of Storms and the Weather by the use of daily Weather Maps."

The weather maps first prepared at the Signal Office were based upon observations taken simultaneously at 7:35 A. M., 4:35 and 11:35 P. M., subsequently these hours were changed to 7 A. M., 3 P. M., and 11 P. M., Washington time; after the introduction of standard seventy-fifth meri-dian time the hours were 7, 3, and 10 standard time. Since July, 1888, they have been 8 A. M. and 8 P. M. standard time. The present remarks refer to the earlier series, but are very nearly applicable to the others.

The early morning map gives the condition of the atmosphere at a moment of almost perfect repose, so far as concerns the disturbing in-fluence of the direct radiation of the sun.

The mid-day map gives the condition at the moment when this dis-turbing influence is nearly at its maximum. The evening map is, as it were, an instantaneous photograph of the condition of the atmosphere while it is rapidly quieting down during the absence of the sun.

Were there no heat received from the sun the whole atmosphere, with the land and the ocean, would rapidly cool off, moisture would con-dense, winds would cease, except possibly very gentle currents, and the prediction of the weather would be reluced to the simplicity of a per-fect uniformity. The first step in the problem of weather prediction therefore is to determine the nature and amount of the disturbing in-fluences exerted from day to day by the heat of the sun, which latter is the sole ultimate cause of the origin and motion of storms.

(I) *Insolation.*—The solar radiation received at any station varies in intensity with the season and the hour of the day, depending slightly on the distance of the earth from the sun, but principally on the apparent solar altitude above the horizon and on the length of the day. The relative number of units of heat received by a horizontal surface, at the outer surface of the atmosphere, in the course of twenty-four hours is shown for each month and each latitude either graphically or in the numerical table No. I, which is here omitted as not necessary to this abstract of the course of the argument.

The relative number of units of heat received at the outer surface of the atmosphere during an entire year is shown by a similar Table No. II. According to Pouillet the total amount of solar heat received annually at the outer surface of the atmosphere is equivalent to 231,675 calories per square centimeter, or an amount of heat that would melt a layer of ice 30.89 meters thick, or evaporate into vapor a layer of water about 4 meters deep, having a temperature of 5° C. (45° F.), or 3.9 meters, having a temperature of 27° C. (80° F.). The most recent measures make the solar radiation about 20 per cent. larger than this.

The relative amounts of solar heat received at the outer surface of the atmosphere for the intervals between the three moments for which the Signal Service tri-daily weather maps are made up, are given in the numerical table, III, and are also graphically shown on charts by lines of equal amounts of solar heat received at all parts of the earth.

(II) *The results of insolation.*—The effects of solar heat before and after it reaches the earth's surface are analyzed as follows:

A portion is (1) directly and selectively absorbed in its passage through the earth's atmosphere to the surface of the earth, or to the upper surface of a layer of fog or clouds, and does molecular work in the air and vapor; the remaining portion passes directly, or after diffuse reflection, finally to the earth's surface, and either (2) evaporates moisture from the surfaces of the ocean, earth, clouds, leaves of plants, etc., or (3) it heats up these latter and all other bodies, which, in turn communicate the greater part of their heat by convection (4) and radiation (5) to the adjacent air, although (6) a little is conducted down to a depth of 50 or 100 feet, whence it returns subsequently. We will consider these in detail.

(1) *Atmospheric absorption.*—When the sun is near the zenith, about 25 per cent. (according to Pouillet) of the energy in its vertical rays is absorbed by the atmosphere before it reaches the earth's surface—the quantity absorbed is less in proportion as the air is purer and lighter, and on the clearest days, at the summit of mountains 15,000 feet high, the zenithal absorption is only about 20 per cent.; the difference is the quantity absorbed in the lowest portion of our atmosphere, and which is largely utilized in preventing the condensation of invisible aqueous vapor. The researches of Langley indicate that much more than 25 per cent. is absorbed by the atmosphere, that percentage applying only to the rays that more easily penetrate the air, and that possibly as much as 50 per cent. is the total absorption, as was indicated by Forbes in 1842.

According to Pouillet (Paris, Comptes Rendus, 1838, tome VII, pp. 24–65), a surface of 1 square centimeter exposed perpendicularly to the sun's rays at the outer limit of the atmosphere receives 0.0017633 calorie per minute (this calorie being the amount of heat required to raise 1 kilogram of water 1° C.). The same plate at the earth's surface and with the sun in the zenith would, owing to the absorption by the atmosphere, receive only 0.76 of the above, or 0.0013401 calorie per minute.

(This is the result of observation on six very clear days in 1837–'38, but observations by others have generally shown a higher value for the amount of heat originally incident on the outer surface of the atmosphere.)

Adopting 25 instead of 24 per cent. as an approximation to the absorption by our atmosphere in the clearest weather, when the sun is in the zenith, it has been shown that of the total heat received by the illuminated half of the earth and atmosphere, about 40 per cent. is absorbed by the air, and about 60 per cent. reaches the surface of the earth; this latter is the average percentage for the whole illuminated disk whose border receives at the earth's surface no transmitted heat, but whose center receives 75 per cent. of that incident on the outer atmosphere.

Therefore, in order to know the distribution over the earth's surface of the heat that penetrates the atmosphere, we must subtract this large absorption from the figures in Tables I, II, and III (omitted here for brevity, but easily found in Meech, Angot, Radau, Hennessy, and other authorities), and thus obtain the results given in Tables IV, V, and VI, as follows:

TABLE IV.—*Relative solar heat, after absorption by the atmosphere, as received at the earth's surface in one minute for varying altitudes of the sun.*

Sun's apparent altitude.	Relative solar heat received by a horizontal surface.	Relative solar heat received by a normal surface
°		
0	0.00	0.00
5	0.01	0.05
10	0.03	0.19
15	0.09	0.33
20	0.15	0.43
25	0.21	0.51
30	0.28	0.56
35	0.35	0.61
40	0.41	0.64
50	0.53	0.69
60	0.62	0.72
70	0.69	0.74
80	0.74	0.75
90	0.75	0.75

TABLE V.—*Total amount of heat received during the whole of March 21 or September 21, at the equator, by a square centimeter, exposed either horizontally or normally.*

	Calories.
1. Above the atmosphere and by a normal plate	1.2696
2. Above the atmosphere by a horizontal plate	0.8099
3. At the earth's surface by a normal plate	0.7159
4. At the earth's surface by a horizontal plate	0.5441

This last figure, 0.5441, is the unit of the following table:

TABLE VI.—*Solar heat received in twenty-four hours at various latitudes, in terms of the amount received on March 21 at the equator, by a horizontal plate at the surface of the earth.*

Date.	North latitude.					
	50°	40°	30°	20°	10°	0°
June 21	1.002	1.115	1.111	1.057	0.970	0.890
March 21 .... ⎱ September 21 ⎰	0.513	0.680	0.815	0.910	0.960	1.000
December 21...	0.086	0.225	0.393	0.565	0.740	0.900

(2) *Evaporation.*—The quantity of moisture evaporated throughout the whole globe must be equivalent to the total precipitation of rain, snow, etc., otherwise there would be a steady increase or diminution instead of the present condition of approximate equilibrium; but the local variations and irregularities in the distribution of this moisture are very great, and constitute a secondary cause of the periodical, diurnal, annual, and secular changes, variations in the weather, and especially of the non-periodical variations or the so-called storms, droughts, etc. The periodical changes in the evaporation are roughly indicated by the figures in Table VII. (Omitted.)

The Table VII, however, relates only to average periodical effects. In order to compute the special cases of evaporation that are particularly interesting in the study of the daily weather map recourse must be had to the formula of Weilenmann, or to its modifications by Stelling, and more recently by Fitzgerald or to the observations by Russell.

It is very important to keep in mind the relative amounts of evaporation going on in all portions of the country, and it is recommended to enter upon various portions of the weather map, on the scale of 10 or 100, some number expressing in a general way the probable relative activity during the coming twenty-four hours. In the compilation of such a set of numbers Tables VII, VIII, IX, X, XII (omitted) are furnished as helps to a rapid approximation.

(3) *Absorption;* (4) *Convection;* (5) *Radiation;* (6) *Conduction.*—The quality and amount of heat absorbed by the earth and afterward given

either by convection or radiation into the atmosphere from the earth's surface will vary with the nature of that surface; the relative quantities are roughly expressed in a numerical table (XIII).

The relative amounts of heat that reach the earth's surface will depend upon the percentage of cloudiness and the altitude of the sun somewhat as given in a numerical table (XIV).

(III) *Resulting density of the air.*—By a combination of the numbers given in the preceding tables and charts there may, in a rough way, be indicated by relative numbers written upon the tri-daily maps what it is expected will be the amount of heat and moisture added to any region of the lower atmosphere during the interval between any two weather charts. The effect of this heat and moisture is to forcibly alter the density of the atmosphere, hot or moist air being lighter than cold or dry air, assuming, of course, the barometric pressure to be the same in both cases. These relative densities are shown in the Table XV, for perfectly dry air (relative humidity, 0) and for perfectly saturated air (relative humidity 100).

By means of Table XV one is able finally to construct a map showing relative densities of the lower or surface air over the United States during the next eight or twenty-four hours. After much experience one becomes able to make a rapid general mental summary of these diverse influences without the labor of recording the items upon the daily maps, and this is practically the method followed in daily routine work.

Now, the normal distribution of density is that on which the general movements of the atmosphere depend, and the deviations shown by the above map of densities will give a clue to the new disturbances that will perhaps be initiated during the day. The normal distribution of temperature, pressure, and winds is shown by the monthly and annual maps. (Omitted.) Similar charts should be constructed for both hemispheres when studying international meteorology.

The Table XV, just explained, shows that the relative density of the atmosphere is much more likely to be disturbed by changes of temperature than of moisture; thus at 70° of temperature an increase of temperature by 10° diminishes the density 0.018, while at the same temperature an increase of moisture up to full saturation of the atmosphere diminishes the density 0.008. An abnormal change of temperature is therefore to be carefully looked for as a cause of further disturbance, but after a disturbance is once set up the moisture becomes the most important consideration, since its condensation alters the vertical distribution of temperature.

(IV) *Wind, Friction, and Pressure.*—The general distribution of density over the earth's surface determines the flow of the denser air of the polar regions toward and under the lighter air of the equator, and Professor Ferrel has shown that from this (and the rotation of the earth on its axis) results the general distribution of pressure prevailing throughout the atmosphere. This distribution is very much affected by the presence of oceans, continents, mountain ranges, and plateaus which determine the irregular distribution of density and the irregular resistances to the winds. Were the coefficient of friction uniform throughout the whole of the earth's surface the distribution of winds and pressure would be much simpler, but as affected by friction it is complicated, as is shown by the isobars on the charts of monthly mean values.

As the elevations throughout the United States must therefore be carefully borne in mind, because of their bearing on the question of their resistances to the motions of the atmosphere, and still more for the thermo-dynamic reasons shown further on, therefore a hypsometric map is provided. On this map may be introduced relative numbers, changing with the seasons, showing the local frictional resistance at a standard altitude, or the relative drag of the air blowing over different surfaces; approximate estimates of these numbers are given in the Table XVI.

The increase of wind velocities at various moderate heights above fields of grass, grain, etc., is given by Stevenson and by Archibald, and may be assumed to be as the square root of the altitude.

Any departure from the normal densities must be followed by a disturbance in the flow of air from the denser toward the lighter.

This disturbed movement of the air produces at once a change in the distribution of barometric pressure, which change becomes greater in proportion to the movement; the observed barometric changes are thus principally dependent upon the wind, and in daily predictions it is convenient to use the barometer as an index of what movements are going on in the atmosphere in the absence of observations of temperature and winds above or beyond the limits of our stations.

The relations between pressure and wind are given in Professor Ferrel's works, as also in those of Oberbeck and Guldberg and Mohn, from which it will be seen that a very slight difference of pressure produced by a very slight difference of density is sufficient to set the atmosphere in motion in the direction of an "initial gradient," the result of which is immediately to produce a vorticose motion and a steeper "barometric gradient" nearly perpendicular to the initial gradient and to the motion of the wind; these steep gradients accompany all storms, and are exemplified in Ferrel's "Movements on the Surface of the Earth," 1858, "Meteorological Researches, part II," 1877, and "Recent Advances," 1886.

The resistances to the motion of the atmosphere would, however, soon bring it to rest, and the abnormal isobars would soon disappear or relapse into the normal ones, were there not some force at work maintaining the disturbance of density and the abnormal motions. A successful storm prediction must depend upon the accuracy with which one can determine the amount, location, and effects of the force that maintains this disturbance.

(V) *The disturbing force.*—The disturbing force is recognized as the solar heat, either directly absorbed by the air or evolved by the condensation of aqueous vapor in the atmosphere; the former has already been considered and the latter must now be studied. This involves (1) the amount of aqueous vapor and (2) its condensation.

(1) *Amount of vapor.*—The normal distribution of vapor in the atmosphere at sea-level is suggested by the hygrometric table (XVII), which in its three sections, *a*, *b*, and *c*, gives the monthly normal values of the mean dew-point, the mean weight, and tension of vapor for a few stations in North America.

Knowing the temperature of the dew-point, one can determine the weight of the vapor contained in any volume of air, and also the tension of the vapor by the use of the accompanying table, XVIII:

TABLE XVIII.—*Tension and weight of aqueous vapor.*

Dew-point.	Tension.	Weight in 1 cubic foot.	Weight (avoirdupois) in 5,280 cubic feet.
Fahr.	*Inches.*	*Grains.*	*Pounds.*
0	0.043	0.545	0.41
10	0.068	0.841	0.63
20	0.108	1.298	0.97
30	0.167	1.969	1.48
40	0.248	2.862	2.16
50	0.361	4.089	3.08
60	0.518	5.756	4.34
70	0.733	7.992	6.02
80	1.023	10.049	8.26
90	1.410	14.810	11 17
100	1.918	19.790	14.94

The geographical distribution of moisture at the earth's surface is best shown by charts of lines of equal tension or dew-point. A comparison of such hygrometric charts for each of the daily reports shows the presence of regions where moisture is in excess or is deficient, and where a given cooling will produce precipitation.

The normal distribution of moisture in successive strata of the atmosphere is shown approximately in the second column of the following table (XIX), computed by the formula of Hann, but which is based on observations in continental areas, and may not so closely represent the conditions over the oceans:

TABLE XIX.—*Normal distribution of aqueous vapor at various altitudes above the earth's surface.*

Altitude in feet.	Relative tensions or weights.	Actual weight (grains per cubic foot) for dew-point at the surface.			
		80°	70°	60°	50°
500	1.000	10.95	7.99	5.76	4.09
2,000	0.806	8.83	6.44	4.64	3.30
4,000	0 650	7.11	5.19	3.74	2.66
6,000	0.524	5.75	4.19	3.02	2.14
8,000	0.423	4.63	3.38	2.44	1.73
10,000	0.341	3.73	2.72	1.96	1 39
12,000	0.275	3.01	2.20	1.58	1.12
14,000	0.221	2.42	1.77	1.27	0.90
16,000	0.179	1.96	1.43	1.03	C.73
18,000	0.144	1.58	1.15	0.83	0.59
20,000	0.116	1.27	0.93	0.67	0.47
22,000	0.094	1.03	0.75	0.54	0.38
24,000	0.075	0.82	0.62	0.43	0.31
26,000	0.061	0.67	0.49	0.35	0.25
28,000	0.049	0.54	0.39	0.28	0.20
30,000	0.040	0.43	0.32	0.23	0.16

The total amount of moisture present at any moment in a column of saturated air extending from sea-level up to the altitude of 6,000, 12,000, etc., feet is found from the numbers given in the preceding table, and is expressed in the following table, by the depth in inches of the corresponding layer of water that would be formed if all the moisture in such column were to fall to the earth as rain:

TABLE XXI.

Height of column in feet.	Depth of water in the atmosphere corresponding to the respective dew points at the earth's surface.			
	80°	70°	60°	50°
	Inches.	Inches.	Inches.	Inches.
6,000	1.3	1.0	0.7	0.5
12,000	2.1	1.5	1.1	0.8
18,000	2.5	1.8	1.3	0.9
24,000	2.7	2.0	1.4	1.0
30,000	2.8	2.1	1.5	1.1

Besides the observation of local dew-point, the amount of moisture in the whole layer of air above us can perhaps be directly determined, as per example, by means of the spectroscope or the cyanometer, at each station; but as these observations have not as yet been reduced to a system the Signal Service makes use of what is called a sunset observation, that is to say, the appearance of the sky at sunset is recorded as yellow, red, or green. These sky colors vary with the changing amounts of moisture through which the sun's rays pass. From these appearances an observer can form an estimate of the general hygrometric condition of large tracts of the atmosphere.

(2) *Condensation of vapor.*—When a mass of air, whether dry or moist, is, on account of its relative lightness, lifted up by the pressure of the surrounding denser atmosphere, or is drawn up by any abnormal diminution of the pressure above, or is pushed up the incline of a mountain or plateau, it is raised into a region where the barometric pressure is less than in its initial position. Consequently the rising mass must expand to an extent proportional to the diminution of pressure. In this expansion a great amount of both internal and external work is done, corresponding, respectively, with the increased separation of the gaseous molecules and the pushing aside of surrounding air; this work is done at the expense of the internal heat of the rising air, consequently the whole expanding mass of mixed air and vapor grows cooler as it rises.

The cooling process is known as a dynamic cooling, and takes place uniformly and simultaneously throughout the whole rising mass of air. It is a very different process from the much slower processes of cooling by radiation or by convection. For dry air the rate of dynamic cooling is almost the same for all pressures and temperatures, and is approximately 1° C. for every 100 meters of ascent or 1° Fahr. for 180.5 feet; for moist air the rate of diminution of temperature is a little slower, but the above value may also be used for it so long as no moisture is condensed, that is to say, so long as. the temperature does not fall below the dew-point.

From the preceding it follows that the elevation above the ground at which cloud or haze begins to be formed depends primarily upon the depression of the dew-point of the rising air below its temperature at the time when it starts from the ground.

The third column of Table XXII gives an idea of this relation between altitude and temperature.

TABLE XXII.—*Initial depression or complement of the dew-point necessary in order that cloud or haze may form in a mass of rising air at the given altitudes above the starting point.*

Altitude.	Approximate barometric pressure.	Initial depression of dew-point.	
		Dynamic cooling	Actual cooling.
Feet.	*Inches.*	° *Fahr.*	° *Fahr.*
0	30.0	0.0	0.0
1,000	28.9	5.5	3.3
2,000	27.8	11.1	6.6
3,000	26.7	16.6	9.9
4,000	25.8	22.2	13.2
5,000	24.8	27.7	16.5
6,000	23.8	33.2	19.8
7,000	23.0	28.8	23.1
8,000	22.1	43.3	26.4
9,000	21.3	49.9	29.7
10,000	20.5	55.4	33.0
11,000	19.7	60.9	36.3
12,000	19.0	66.5	39.6

Conversely, when the air is drawn or forced down from the upper regions it comes under greater pressure and is compressed and warmed at the same rate as above, namely, 1° Fahr. for 180.5 feet or 0.°55 Fahr. for 100 feet. But this latter warming (like the preceding cooling) is so largely affected by radiation of heat, absorption of solar heat, the mixing with air that has a different temperature, and by the absorption of heat in the process that is the reverse of condensation, *i. e.*, that of evaporating fog and other forms of water, that the actual average rate of cooling, as we ascend in the air, is barely one-half of the above, *i. e.*, 0.°33 Fahr. per 100 feet or 0.°6 C. per 100 meters.

The fourth column in Table XXII shows the elevation at which haze or cloud begins to be formed by the actual observed rate of cooling in an ascending mass, the initial depression of whose dew-point is known. Conversely, if we actually observe the height to which a mass of air has ascended, when it begins to become hazy or cloudy, we can from this last column deduce, at least approximately, the corresponding depression of the dew-point that obtained at its place of starting.

The cooling by ascension is therefore not a truly adiabatic process. Espy's rule of an ascent of 100 yards for each degree of depression of the dew point is thus seen to be a close approximation.

As soon as the dew-point is reached in this process of ascension and cooling the condensation of vapor is accompanied by evolution of the latent heat of steam, that is to say, of the enormous amount of heat originally required to convert the water into invisible vapor, and which has been carried from the surface of the earth up into the cloud region, where it is now ready to be set free.

This evolution of latent heat without wholly checking the rate at which the ascending air is cooling, diminishes its rate nearly in proportion to the amount of vapor condensed; therefore the interior of a cloud is warmer and lighter than the interior of a corresponding mass of clear dry air that has attained the same level. The rate at which the temperature diminishes within a mass of ascending, expanding and condensing, saturated air, such as that of which clouds are composed, depends almost wholly on thermo-dynamic adiabatic conditions, and is shown in the following table (XXIII), by Hann, for various initial pressures and temperatures:

TABLE XXIII.—*Diminution of temperature in a rising mass of saturated air, expressed in degrees Fahrenheit, for each 1,000 feet of ascent.*

Initial.		Initial temperature of saturation or dew-point.									
Approximate altitude.	Pressure.	14°	23°	32°	41°	50°	59°	68°	77°	86°	95°
Feet.	*Inch.*	°	°	°	°	°	°	°	°	°	°
—900	31	4.2	3.8	3.5	3.3	3.0	2.7	2.5	2.3	2.1	1.9
+900	29	4.1	3.8	3.4	3.3	3.0	2.7	2.5	2.2	2.1	1.9
2,900	27	4.0	3.7	3.3	3.2	2.9	2.7	2.4	2.2	2.0	
5,000	25	3.9	3.6	3.2	3.1	2.8	2.5	2.2	2.1		
7,200	23	3.9	3.6	3.2	3.0	2.7	2.4	2.2	2.0		
9,700	21	3.8	3.5	3.1	2.9	2.6	2.3	2.1			
12,100	19	3.7	3.3	3.0	2.8	2.2	2.2				
15,500	17	3.6	3.2	2.8	2.7	2.2	2.1				
18,900	15	3.4	3.1	2.7	2.5	2.2					
22,800	13	3.2	2.9	2.5	2.4						
27,300	11	3.0	2.7	2.3	2.2						
32,800	9	2.8	2.5	2.2							

NOTE —The approximate altitudes in feet are computed on the assumption of 50° Fahr. as the average temperature of the air column.

Thus we see for instance, that with a dew-point of 32° Fahr. the foggy air, which near sea-level cools 3°.5 for 1,000 feet of ascent, will, when it becomes a cloud at an elevation of about 15,500 feet or when the pressure is about 17 inches, be cooling at the rate of 2°.8 per 1,000 feet, and, in general, the higher the saturated air ascends the slower it cools. So far, then, as concerns this important cause the ascent of moist currents would continue indefinitely, but the continued loss of water by its fall as rain, and the more rapid loss of heat by surface radiation at the higher altitudes, or the absorption of solar heat by the clouds probably determines the limiting form and the height of the outer or upper surface of the clouds.

The average altitudes at which these clouds are respectively formed may be approximated from the following table (XXIV), for Berlin, by

Dr. Vettin, or may be specially calculated from the data previously given for the cooling of ascending air:

TABLE XXIV.—*Average altitude of clouds at Berlin, Germany.*

Month.	Lower cumuli.	Cumuli.	Small cumuli	Lower cirri.	Upper cirri.
	Feet.	*Feet.*	*Feet.*	*Feet.*	*Feet.*
December	4, 823	10, 433	21, 231	39, 876	68, 600
January.	4, 593	9. 908	20, 952	38, 862	67, 249
February.......	4, 790	10, 499	21, 621	39, 535	69, 614
March	5, 151	12, 107	23. 655	40, 214	74, 345
April	5, 446	12, 927	25, 066	41, 897	79, 076
May	5, 709	13, 386	25, 689	45, 283	89, 456
June	5, 873	13, 845	25, 817	48, 662	84, 483
July...........	5, 906	14, 042	25, 817	49, 673	85, 159
August	5, 879	13, 845	25, 683	48, 662	84, 145
September. ..	5, 807	13, 353	25, 073	46, 635	81, 780
October	5, 643	12, 861	23, 452	43, 931	78, 062
November	5, 236	11, 680	22, 304	41, 566	74, 007

In addition to the intrinsic lightness and ascensive power of every cloud, due to its internal moisture and heat, another powerful external influence comes into play. It has been before said that about 85 per cent. of the radiated solar heat penetrates the atmosphere to within 15,000 feet of the earth's surface. But no appreciable part of this is able to penetrate through a thick layer of cloud or fog. Consequently all the heat that falls upon the top of a cloud is retained therein instead of reaching the earth's surface, and, both by evaporating the particles of vapor and by warming the adjacent air, contributes powerfully to diminish the specific gravity of the cloud as a whole, increasing the up-draft and disturbing the vertical distribution of heat in the atmosphere. The maximum temperature thus communicated to the top of a cloud is not far from the maximum temperature attainable anywhere at the surface of the earth.

(VI) *Special suggestions.*—It will therefore be seen that invisible aqueous vapor disturbs the equilibrium of the atmosphere in the following three ways:

(1) By its evaporation and subsequent distribution throughout the air it renders the atmosphere, over certain geographical sections, specifically lighter than others.

(2) By its condensation into fog or clouds and rain or snow it transfers to distant regions the heat that had been accumulating in each particle before its evaporation at the earth's surface.

(3) In the form of fog or cloud it causes to be retained, at the upper surface of the cloud, the total amount of heat that would otherwise reach the earth, thus increasing the up-draft within a cloud, but diminishing the evaporation at the earth's surface, by which the clouds are supplied with moisture.

A philosophical prediction as to the origin, development, and movement of a storm must take account of the three items above, but in the rapid approximate work of the Signal Service indication-room there is need to avoid tables and calculations as much as possible and to seek to obtain from direct observations such indications as they will give.

The first item is already provided for in the maps showing dew-point and relative humidity. With regard to the second item, the study of the clouds and fog, the past and the prevalent rainfall, the weather, and daily range of temperature from maximum to minimum give indications as to the extent of the process of condensation at any moment, and the evolution of heat dependent thereon, and the student is guided by considerations such as the following :

(a) Fog at the earth's surface bespeaks clear dry air above, free from cloud or haze, through which radiation is taking place rapidly ; hence it implies the absence of uprising convective currents ; hence also the general prevalence of a stable equilibrium as regards vertical temperature gradient. The time of day at which the fog breaks up under the solar radiation indicates the thickness of the layer.

(b) Clear weather followed by cirrus clouds, increasing in quantity at the successive reports, and these again followed by small cumuli, indicate the advance of overlying areas of moist air or a steadily increasing amount of moisture that is being locally carried up into the air. These clouds are soon followed by larger cumuli, and these by rain and storm centers. .

(c) The range of temperature between 11 P. M. and the morning minimum (or in lieu thereof an early observation) has its maximum when radiation takes place uninterruptedly through a clear dry atmosphere, and diminishes in proportion as moisture, haze, and cloudiness increase. If therefore we make allowance for the effect of the wind in bringing to the thermometer warm or cold air we shall find this range of temperature a valuable index to the condition of the mass of air overhead. In place of this indirect process of reasoning, it is probable that *direct observations*, with proper apparatus, of *the intensity of radiation* would give better results.

(d) The slightest formation of haze in a clear sky in the evening proves that the upper layers are cooling to their dew-point. Frequently the 11 P. M. observations will give such indications as show that before 7 A. M. the sky will probably be covered with cloud, and possibly followed by rain or snow. This cooling is partly due to radiation, as the vapor is a good radiator, but it is also frequently due to a dynamical cooling of rising air currents flowing toward a distant area of low pressure. As soon as clouds form, the air beneath ceases to cool by radiation and the area that was clear at 11 P. M. is, by sunrise, covered by a layer of cloud that protects the warm air, whose buoyancy increases during the day and specially favors the formation of a local new storm center. In this way many centers originate within a few hours in Maryland, Virginia, and North Carolina in the early morning following a clear evening.

(e) A report of rain or snow-fall during any interval indicates that the process of cloud formation has gone on to its extreme limit; the quantity of rain is an index to the relative amounts of latent heat temporarily left behind in the cloud stratum to be slowly lost by radiation; hence it shows the disturbance over different parts of the country of the normal distribution of density. Where however only little rain has fallen while the cloud stratum is extensive and dense, the total disturbance due to the general warmth of air and cloud over the whole region may be equally great, but not especially intense at any one point.

(VII) *Prediction of the weather.*—The preceding considerations, which are those that guided me in my earliest predictions in Cincinnati and Washington, will enable any one to enter upon any series of charts of existing conditions a system of numbers showing the places over which the atmospheric disturbance in the cloud region is—or is likely to be— appreciable, and to judge of its relative intensity as depending on the excess or deficiency in the density of the air. From this we can reason as to the first tendency of the movements of the air or the initial wind. The consideration of the orography of the surrounding country will then give us the basis for a conclusion as to whether in any region the general movement of the atmosphere will tend to cool or warm any mass of air (especially by carrying it over rising or resisting ground and forcing it up to the higher levels or by pushing cold air under warm air), and thereby initiate a still further condensation and exaggerate the disturbances already existing, or possibly producing local rain and wholly new centers of disturbance. By thus considering as fully as possible the effects of solar heat, atmospheric moisture, orography, etc., we are able to enter upon the weather map a series of figures showing our estimate of all the disturbances likely to occur during the immediate future. In general, we find that convective disturbances of equilibrium increase from the morning map to the afternoon map, and diminish from the 11 P. M. to the 7 A. M. map; during the interval from 3 P. M. to 11 P. M. the larger disturbances, such as thunder storms, tornadoes, and hurricanes, generally attain a maximum and begin to diminish. The phenomena specially due to terrestrial radiation have their maximum effect between the 11 P. M. and 7 A. M. reports; between these hours we find, for instance, that many extensive storms begin over regions for which at 11 P. M. the reports show clear weather. As the prevailing and probable future direction and force of the wind are so important, it becomes very necessary, in dealing with a limited part of the earth's surface, to examine the reports from outlying border stations in order to ascertain the possible existence at a distance of unseen centers of disturbance; a slight abnormal fall in the barometer, or rise of temperature, or shift of winds, or increase in cloud and rain may be the indicator of a distant storm; equally frequent is it that a general rise of pressure or increase of cold northerly winds indicates the existence of an unseen low barometer and severe storm to the southwest or southeast, toward which these winds are blowing. . Perhaps the most useful rule in this respect is founded on the motions of clouds. The following generalization (announced by me in February 1872 as resulting from the study of upper and lower clouds and winds displayed on every Signal Service map and quite independent of simultaneous European studies), will, it is believed, be found to hold good for the whole northern hemisphere: "The general direction towards which any stratum of air is moving nearly horizontally, is somewhat to the right hand of the direction of motion of the stratum just above it, that is to say, the direction of the lower clouds is to the right of that of the wind at the earth's surface; the higher clouds move to the right of the lower clouds and the cirrus again to the right of the latter; these directions of motion may be so related that the cirrus shall be moving in a direction nearly opposite to that of the surface winds or the lower clouds. In general, when the lower currents are flowing in toward a storm center the upper currents are flowing out from it; or again, when the lower currents are flowing out from an area of high pressure and clear, dry weather the upper currents are flowing in towards it." It follows that when an outlying station reports the motions of the cirrus cloud, we are able to infer something as to the existence of the area of the low barometer from which the cirri are coming.

(1) *Prediction of general storms.*—When we have thus approximately estimated the probable location and amount of the disturbances in density over all portions of the United States and outlying regions, we are then to decide whether a storm already initiated will increase or diminish in intensity, and in what direction its center will move.

It may be accepted as a fundamental principle that a given disturbance will spread in the direction of those regions where processes are going on that favor similar disturbances. Thus, if a mass of heavy air, like the northers of the Mississippi Valley, is flowing in any direction under a mass of abnormally light air, it will tend to move always in the direction where the lightest air is to be found, or where the diurnal changes of heat and evaporation favor the development of abnormally light air. Or again, if a storm is already in existence and is maintained by the condensation of moisture in the cloud region, it will be continuously moving toward the region where the condensation is going on most actively. The regions where storms are being initiated or most liberally supported are generally detected (1) by observed abnormal temperature and moisture; (2) by the formation of haze, halos, cloud, and rain or snow; and (3) by a slight fall in the barometer due to movements in the atmosphere at the level of the cloud stratum. The future movements of storm centers can generally be detected by the observed changes going on in the direction of movement of the wind or clouds. All of these meteorological elements must be examined by careful comparisons of the preceding tri-daily maps in order to ascer-

H. Mis. 142——27

tain whether a given storm will increase or diminish, and especially whether it will follow some one of the average storm tracks, or whether it will make special deviation from them. The general paths pursued by storm centers and their average velocities can be used only for general climatic indications, and not for special storm predictions. Detailed maps of the direction and velocity of the movements of storm centers in the United States have been prepared; a general view of the so-called storm frequency, or, more properly, the frequency with which barometric minima (sometimes without violent winds) pass over each section of the country, is given by a chart designed and prepared by me in 1874, and published in Walker's Statistical Atlas of the United States. With these barometric minima generally come clouds, rain and snow, high winds, suddenly shifting from south and east to west and north, warm, moist, followed by colder, dry weather, and all the characteristics of very variable severe climates. A more complete chart, showing the total number of times that such barometric minima have during the ten years October, 1872, to September, 1882, passed over each degree square of the territory east of the meridian of 102° west longitude, has been prepared, and gives a basis for many climatic generalities.

The prediction of a special storm path, or its deviation from a *normal path* (if such a term is allowable) must be based upon a detailed study of all the above mentioned disturbing or controlling influences. Some of the average effects of these influences are shown in the following paragraphs:

(a) Maydell, from the study of the storms of Northern Europe, showed in 1873 that the storm path for the coming twenty-four hours forms a determinate angle with the line connecting the present place of the barometric minimum with that of the greatest rise of temperature in the past twenty-four hours. This angle is always formed on the left hand of that connecting line, supposing the face to be turned towards the point of rising temperature and the back towards the point of minimum barometer. This angle varies between zero and 90 degrees, as the extreme cases, while it is on the average in winter about 60 degrees; the summer storm tracks are classified in two groups, for which this angle is respectively 40 and 70 degrees. The angle depends to a certain extent upon the position of the center of highest temperature, being smaller according as the point lies more to the east of the barometric minimum. (See Maydell's appendix to the Bulletin for December, 1873, of the Physical Observatory at St. Petersburg.)

Maydell's rules accord with my own experience; the elevation of temperature before a storm had been long known both for England and for the United States, but the amount of angular deviation of the storm-center to the left of the rising temperature is, I think, very little in the eastern part of the United States.

(b) The region over which the greatest rain fall will take place is that towards which the storm center will have a strong tendency to move; the location where it is now raining, as shown by the map, is usually near the present location of the center of disturbance and in advance of the center of low pressure due to the movement of wind. Loomis finds that in the United States the rain area extends farther in front than in the rear of the storm; its mean extent is 500 miles in front, and for every increase in this distance the velocity of the storm movement is increased. He also finds that within the United States much more rain falls in front of the area of low pressure than in its rear; a great rain-fall in the rear retards the motion.

(c) The barometric changes, being the direct result of horizontal winds and only the indirect result of the changes in temperature, moisture, vertical movements and condensations sum up as it were the result of all preceding disturbances. Loomis finds that the velocity of progress of a storm is independent of the amount of the central depression of the barometer. The average velocity of movement of centers of low pressure in the United States is about 26 miles per hour; the pressure rises faster in the rear of fast-moving storms; thus, if the pressure in the rear rises 20 per cent. faster than the mean, the storm moves 7 miles per hour faster; if it rises 20 per cent. slower, the storm moves 7 miles per hour slower. This is evidently a direct result of the fact that the center of indraft up toward the clouds is propagated (not moved bodily) forward faster than the lower winds can follow.

(d) J. Elliot gives the following as the favorable conditions for the formation and growth of cyclones in the Bay of Bengal, and these may, with slight modifications, be applied to the Gulf of Mexico and the West Indies:

1. The invariable antecedents of cyclones are approximate uniformity of pressure over and around the coast of the Bay of Bengal, light variable winds or calms over a considerable portion of the bay, and little or no rain-fall over the coast region, as well as in the bay; the weather is therefore sultry and the sea smoother. The amount of aqueous vapor accumulates and finally gives rise to peculiar sky effects. The immediate antecedent is heavy rain-fall concentrated over a portion of the bay accompanied by a strong indraft, most marked from the Indian Ocean at the entrance of the bay. This indraft from the Indian Ocean gives rise to strong winds and heavy rains at the stations on the south and west coasts of Ceylon.

2. The source of the energy is the condensation of vapor and precipitation of rain; or the primary cause of cyclone formation is the production and ascent of a large quantity of vapor, which is condensed with the liberation of its latent heat over the place of production, instead of being carried away to some distant region. (See J. Eliot's report on the Madras cyclone of May, 1877, and similar conclusions in his account of the southwest monsoon storm of 1883.)

(2) *Prediction of local storms.*—The tornado is an exaggeration of the mild thunder storm, especially in that the revolving cloud that is some-

times seen high up at the base of the thunder storm now reaches down to the earth, and the violent winds due to its up-draft cause great destruction. These storms occur usually in the broad currents of warm, moist southerly winds that prevail on the south and east sides of an area of low pressure or general storm center; they are in fact whirls within whirls, and may be expected as likely to occur when on the morning weather map the depression of the dew-point is reported as only a few degrees, and southerly winds cover the country, blowing toward a storm center in the northwest, or lake region.

(The preceding paragraph as written in 1883 expresses a generalization familiar to me since boyhood and in agreement with views of Espy and many writers; the conviction of its general truth had led me in 1871 and 1872 to frequently publish in the official daily weather predictions the paragraph, " Conditions are favorable for severe local storms." Any discussion as to the original author of this generalization would carry us back to the first weather charts of Leverrier 1858, Henry 1850, Espy 1838, Loomis 1838, and Kaemtz 1835, and Brandes 1828.)

The number of tornadoes likely to occur in any State in any one year is shown approximately by the figures in the sixth column of the following table, as copied from Finley's " Character of Six Hundred Tornadoes," first edition, 1882 (the second edition April 1884, would not materially change these figures); but the relative geographical distribution is only fairly shown by adopting some such unit of area as 100 miles square or 10,000 square miles, for which unit we find the annual average frequency given in the seventh column. The last column of this table should replace the misleading statement of the number of tornadoes on record in any State, without considering the area of the State or the number of years and observers involved in getting together the lists.

Table of frequency of tornadoes in each State.

State or Territory.	Area in units of 10,000 square miles.	Finley's record.		Tornadoes from 1874 to 1881, inclusive (eight years complete)		
		Total number of tornadoes.	Length of record (years).	Finley's numbers.	Annual average per State.	Annual average per 10,000 square miles.
Alabama.......... ...	5.1	14	42	12	1.5	0.29
Alaska	51.7	....	....	....	....	....
Arizona	11.4	2	1	2	0.2	0.02
Arkansas...	5.2	8	4	8	1.0	0.19
California...	15.8	1	1	1	0.1	0.01
Colorado	10.4	1	1	1	.0.1	0.01
Connecticut...	0.5	6	87	2	0.2	0.40
Dakota ..:..........	15.1	9	7	9	1.1	0.07
Delaware.	0.2	....	....	....	....	....
District of Columbia	0.0	....	....	....	....	......:..
Florida	5.9	5	7	5	0.6	0.10
Georgia	5.8	33	78	29	3.6	0.62

*Table of frequency of tornadoes in each State—*Continued.

State or Territory.	Area in units of 10,000 square miles.	Finley's record.		Tornadoes from 1874 to 1881, inclusive (eight years complete)		
		Total number of tornadoes.	Length of record (years).	Finley's numbers.	Annual average per State.	Annual average per 10,000 square miles.
Idaho	8.6					
Illinois	5.5	54	28	50	6.2	1.13
Indiana	3.4	27	29	24	3.0	0.88
Indian Territory	6.9	1	1	1	0.1	0.01
Iowa	5.5	31	28	26	3.2	0.58
Kansas	8.1	62	23	55	6.9	8.85
Kentucky	3.8	6	27	5	0.6	0.16
Louisiana	4.1	11	6	11	1.4	0.34
Maine	3.5	3	8	3	1.4	0.40
Maryland	1.1	7	6	8	1.0	0.91
Massachusetts	0.8	9	9	7	0.9	1.12
Michigan	5.6	14	27	13	1.6	0.29
Minnesota	8.4	21	7	21	2.6	0.31
Mississippi	4.7	13	59	9	1.1	0.23
Missouri	6.5	44	68	40	5.0	0.77
Montana	14.4	1	1	1	0.1	0.01
Nebraska	7.6	14	7	14	1.8	0.24
Nevada	11.2	1	1	1	0.1	0.01
New Hampshire	0.9	5	60	3	0.4	0.44
New Jersey	0.8	5	42	5	0.6	0.75
New Mexico	12.1	1	1	1	0.1	0.01
New York	4.7	35	51	20	2.5	0.53
North Carolina	5.1	18	49	14	1.8	0.35
Ohio	4.0	28	49	21	2.6	0.05
Oregon	9.5					
Pennsylvania	4.6	18	28	17	1.9	0.46
Rhode Island	0.1	1	1			
South Carolina	3.4	17	80	13	1.6	0.47
Tennessee	4.6	18	52	15	1.9	0.41
Texas	27.4	18	7	18	2.2	0.08
Utah	8.4					
Vermont	1.0	2	2	2	0.2	0.20
Virginia	6.1	9	8	9	1.1	0.17
Washington	7.0					
West Virginia	2.3	1	1	1	0.1	0.04
Wisconsin	5.3	11	7	11	1.4	0.26
Wyoming	9.8	1	1	1	0.1	0.01

When we consider the narrowness and shortness of the destructive portion of the paths of most "tornadoes," we see that even in Kansas and Iowa the probability that any given spot will be visited by one is at the rate of less than 1 per cent. per century, or less than the chance of death by lightning or railroad accident, or other casualty.

These storms move along nearly with the prevailing general current of air at the cloud level, but deflecting somewhat as influenced by the supply of moist air and by local topography; they die out when friction or dry air cuts off the moisture or when the supply wind blows down grade. They apparently owe their characteristics to an upward draft of air toward the dark masses of cloud that are overhead, and within which the processes of condensation of moisture, evolution of latent heat, and uprising of lighter air are going on with intensity. The details of the mechanism of these storms are fully given by Ferrel in his "Meteorological Researches, part II," Washington, 1880 (and in his "Recent Advances," Washington, 1886).

The relative frequency of occurrence of tornadoes in the United States for each month is shown by the following table, as given by Finley, who has however possibly included a few storms that should more properly have been classed as destructive thunder storms:

Monthly frequency of tornadoes.

January	7	July............	90
February	21	August..........	47
March	37	September......	50
April	97	October.........	15
May	81	November. ...	22
June...........	112	December	9

(3) *Special local predictions.*—Beside the predictions of storms the next most important item is the prediction of the separate elements of the weather that affect local human industries; especially hoar-frost, heat, wind, and rain.

(a) *Frost.*—Severe frosts occur only when the atmosphere is clear; they are in great part the effect of radiation of heat from the surfaces of plants and the earth. Their prediction depends principally upon the questions, how many degrees will the temperature of the surface of leaves of plants fall by radiation; if it falls to 32° or less, then will the atmospheric moisture condense into fog or cloud before or after the radiating surface of the plants cools down to that freezing temperature? If on the evening map there are entered, first, a series of relative numbers showing the prospective clearness of the sky; second, a series showing the time that will elapse before sunrise; then a series showing the probable diurnal range of temperature, an estimate can be made of the fall in temperature for each section of the country before the next sunrise. If now these latter figures are compared with the map showing the depression of the dew-point at 11 P. M., those regions will be perceived over which fog and clouds are likely to be formed; the remaining or clear regions are the only ones in which dew is to be feared, and of these only those are in imminent danger of frost at which the dew-point is below 32°.

The probable diurnal range of temperature is best found by studying the actual fall between 11 P. M. and 7 A. M., as reported during the preceding few clear days from the stations in the neighborhood in question. The preceding rule takes no account of the wind, which if fresh or brisk, will generally prevent or nullify the severity of the frost. Areas of cold dry air frequently flow southward and spread as northers over large regions of the country, confining themselves especially to the low lands and river valleys. Within these areas of clear, cold, dry air, and especially on their advancing fronts, the process of freezing is often accelerated by the combination of convection with radiation, and in such cases the destruction to vegetation is particularly severe; therefore, in the prediction of frosts, attention must be especially directed to such areas. The rate at which these advance is of course greater when the cold air flows down a gentle incline, such as that of the Mississippi Valley. When such cold areas reach the Gulf of Mexico the lowest stratum of air moves more rapidly, and after overrunning a large portion of the Gulf, banks up the atmosphere on the Mexican shore, and causes extensive rains, which sometimes initiate cyclones, and return as such to the northward. This phenomenon was clearly perceived and verbally explained to my fellow-laborers in 1871-'72 in the Signal office; the parallelism between the Norther, the Bore, the Pampero, and similar winds was also then dwelt on ; the flow of cold air and the formation of gulf storms were even then clearly predicted.

(*b*) *Rain.*—For convenience in establishing general rules for the prediction of rains, they may be divided into four classes, as follows:

(1) Merely local rains depending almost wholly upon the rapid ascent of small masses of over-heated moist air; these occur almost entirely between 9 A. M. and 6 P. M., and are oftentimes simultaneous in isolated localities over a great extent of the country. They are liable to occur whenever the 7 A. M. map shows a high dew-point and clear or nearly clear weather, and when the winds are or are about to be such as will carry the surface air up a gentle slope; they occur with southerly winds in the Gulf States or southeast winds on the Atlantic coast; they occur on the latter coast rarely with winds between west and northwest, since such winds are carrying the air downwards toward the sea and warming it by compression.

(2) Local rains, on a larger scale, generally accompanied by lightning, and known as thunder storms, occurring in the afternoon between 3 and 10 o'clock, and due to the uplifting of large masses of moist air from the low lands by the underflow of denser (*i. e.* cooler or drier) air. This convective process begins most easily in mountainous regions, where the afternoon radiation, during the declining sun, proceeds more rapidly than in the low lands ; in fact the downflow of cold dry air from the mountains is a periodical phenomena tending to take place regularly at all times of the year. The decision of the question as to whether rain will follow or not depends upon the balance between the mass of cooled air over the mountains and the adjacent moist air. The question can generally be decided by considering the time of day at which the formation of heavy cumuli begins. If, *e. g.*, at Washington this occurs later than 5 P. M. rain is not likely, if before 3 P. M. rain is probable.

Such storms generally show themselves as well under way on the 3 P. M. map. The geographical distribution of frequency of this class of storms for the United States was illustrated by me in the map for August, 1874, published in the Signal Service Monthly Weather Review for that month.

The paths pursued by these thunder storms trend eastward or northeastward, as in Europe, see Mohn and Hildebrandsson. They may be classed as (1) those that attend a very low pressure, and (2) those that start on the advancing edge of areas of cool, dry air or high barometer, and (3) those that occur within and on the rearward side of high areas. Quite a number of them may exist simultaneously, for instance, along the whole eastern slope of the Appalachian range, all moving in nearly parallel lines northeastward until they die out in the early morning hours, generally before they reach the Atlantic shore, but sometimes extending a little ways out to sea.

(3) Light general rains occurring between 1 and 8 A. M., and which are apparently caused by radiation of heat from a layer of moist air some distance above the earth. Frequently when the sky is perfectly clear at 11 P. M. there prevails over a special region a general strong southerly current feeding a storm center to the northward, but not as yet followed by any condensation in this special region. It would seem that the nocturnal radiation of heat from the moist and hazy sky now comes in powerfully to supplement the dynamic cooling, which latter process depends on ascension, and therefore, of course, is less active during the night than during sunshine; accordingly haze and cloud form after 11 P. M. and light general rains or snow fall in the early morning hours, and are reported on the 7 A. M. map; these are liable to be stopped by the sun's heat as soon as that is sufficient to counteract the radiation, but when this heat first falls on the cloud top it stimulates the convection and the precepitation. The only means of anticipating the occurrence of this class of rains consists in a close observance of all the antecedent phenomena in order to estimate the probable relative temperature and moisture of the air overhead ; the only observations bearing on this subject, as shown by the 11 P. M. map, are a slight tendency to haze, the formation and disappearance of loose clouds, a slight check in the temperature, and especially the reports of halos around the moon, to which, according to Montigny, it is important to add the observation of the scintillation of the stars.

(4) Extended heavy rains. These generally attend either areas of low pressure, where great masses of air apparently have slow ascending and vorticose movements, or prevailing winds that carry great masses of moist air up mountain or plateau slopes to higher levels; these rains are therefore due principally to dynamic cooling, and are well illustrated by easterly storms of the Atlantic coast, the northerly storms of the Central American and Mexican coasts, and the southerly winds of the Gulf States. Their prediction is implied in the prediction of a general storm as before treated of.

CHEMISTRY FOR 1887 AND 1888.

By F. W. Clarke.

GENERAL AND THEORETICAL.

Atomic weights ; oxygen.—The composition of water and the relation between the atomic weights of hydrogen and oxygen have been discussed during the year by Cooke and Richards, Scott, Keiser, Morley, and Lord Rayleigh.

Cooke and Richards adopted the following plan : Hydrogen, purified with extraordinary care, was weighed in large glass globes which had previously been exhausted by means of a Sprengel pump. It was then burned by passing it over heated copper oxide, and the water so formed was weighed. Three series of experiments, numbering sixteen in all, were made, and distinguished from each other by the use of hydrogen derived from different sources. First, hydrogen was used which had been evolved from zinc and sulphuric acid ; secondly, hydrogen was obtained by electrolysis ; and in the third series the gas was derived from the action of potassium hydroxide upon aluminium foil. In this way the errors due to possible impurity in hydrogen from only one source were sought to be avoided. The mean results by series were as follows, when H=1 :

Series I, five experiments..................	O=15 954 ; $\pm$ .0048
Series II, five experiments.....................	15.953 ; $\pm$ .0022
Series III, six experiments.....................	15.952 ; $\pm$ .0035
Average of the sixteen experiments.............	15.953 ; $\pm$ .0017

The quantity of hydrogen burned in each experiment was a little over 0.4 gramme. The only possible impurity in it was nitrogen, which was looked for spectroscopically, but not found. Its absence however could not be certainly proved, and its effect, if present, would be to render the apparent atomic weight of oxygen too low ; in other words, its presence would lead to possibly erroneous conclusions relative to "Prout's law." (Proc. Amer. Acad., XXIII, 149.)

The investigations of Alexander Scott relate to the composition of water by volume. It is well known that oxygen and hydrogen, as actually measured at ordinary temperatures and pressures, do not rigidly conform to Boyle's law. They vary from it in opposite directions ; and this fact must be taken into account before we can deduce their relative

425

atomic weights from their relative densities.   Scott, in his experiments, has paid especial attention to the following points:

(1) The preparation of purer gases.

(2) The use of larger volumes.

(3) The measurement of both gases in the same vessel.

(4) The analysis of the residue left after explosion of the mixed gases, and determination of the impurity in each experiment.

Twenty-one experiments were made, giving as the most probable ratio 1.994 volumes of H to one volume of O.   Hence, if the density of O in terms of H is 15.9627, its atomic weight becomes 16.01.   (Proc. Roy. Soc., XLII, 396.   Chem. News, LVI, 173.)

Morley's paper (Am. Chem. Journ., X, 21) is essentially a discussion of Scott's work, with an outline of proposed methods for the settlement of the problems under consideration.

Lord Rayleigh (Chem. News, LVII, 73) has re-determined the density ratio between H and O, and finds it to be 1 : 15.884.   The application of this ratio to atomic-weight discussions depends upon investigations like those of Scott.   Rayleigh also calls attention to a source of error in the process of weighing gases, which arises from the fact that a glass globe when exhausted of air, is sensibly condensed by atmospheric pressure; that is, its capacity when empty is perceptibly less than when full. This error affects Regnault's density determinations.   Cooke and Richards (Am. Chem. Journ. X, 191) recognize the importance of Rayleigh's observations, and apply them to the correction of their own results. They determine the magnitude of the error produced in their own glass globes, and find that it reduces their value for the atomic weight of oxygen from 15.953 to 15.869.   This is the lowest value yet assigned to that constant.

Keiser attempts to ascertain the composition of water directly by weighing hydrogen occluded in palladium, expelling it by heat, burning it over copper oxide, and weighing the water so formed.   Three preliminary experiments (Berichte, XX, 2323) gave in sum a value for oxygen of 15.8722.   In a later paper he gives in detail his process, together with his final results.   Ten combustions were made, with 6.5588 grammes of hydrogen in all, giving values for O ranging from 15.943 to 15.958, or, in sum, 15.9482.   He shows that the hydrogen weighed was presumably pure, and that no nitrogen was occluded with it.   His final figure agrees quite nearly with the earlier determination of Cooke and Richards. (Am. Chem. Journ., X, 249.)

Fluorine.—The atomic weight of this element, which has hitherto been determined by the conversion of fluorides into sulphates, Christenson has verified by a new method.   When the double fluoride of ammonium and manganese, Am_2MnF_5, is added to a mixture of potassium iodide and hydrochloric acid, it liberates iodine, which may be titrated with sodium thiosulphate.   One molecule of the salt, as above formulated, sets free one atom of iodine.   Four determinations were made, giving in mean, if H=1, N=14.01, I=126.54, and Mn=55.0; F=18.94. (Journ. Prakt. Chem. (2), xxxv, 551.)

Zinc.—Morse and Burton redetermine the atomic weight of zinc by the oxidation of the metal. Pure distilled zinc was treated with nitric acid, and the residue from the evaporated solution after gentle heating was strongly ignited in a muffle. Fifteen experiments gave figures ranging from Zn=65.091 to Zn=65.119, or in mean, Zn=65.106 when O=15.96. The same method with slight differences of detail had previously been used by Erdmann, and was recently criticised by Marignac, who claimed that oxide of zinc was dissociated at high temperatures, and also that it retained oxides of nitrogen. Morse and Burton show these objections to be groundless. (Am. Chem. Journ., x, 311.)

Reynolds and Ramsay estimate, with many elaborate precautions, the amount of hydrogen evolved upon the solution of pure zinc in an acid. Twenty-nine experiments were made, of which twenty-four were rejected. The remaining five when fully corrected give concordant values, making the atomic weight of zinc in mean, Zn=65.4787,±.06135. The weight of the hydrogen measured was computed by means of Regnault's data. (Journ. Chem. Soc., December, 1887.)

Zinc, iron, and aluminum.—The equivalents of these metals as roughly redetermined by students in his laboratory have been published by J. Torrey, jr. In each case the metal was dissolved in an acid, and the hydrogen set free was measured. The mean results are as follows, when H=1.

> Fifteen experiments .... Zn=64.952.
> Fourteen experiments .... Fe=55.777.
> Thirteen experiments .... Al=27.049.

The values obtained in the individual determinations are not sharply concordant, and the work is chiefly interesting from the stand-point of the teacher. It illustrates the possibility of training students in the verification of important constants. (Am. Chem. Journ., x, 73.)

Copper.—Richards has published two papers on the atomic weight of this element. When metallic copper is placed in a solution of silver nitrate, metallic silver is precipitated, and when the solution is ice cold the reaction is sharply quantitative. In the first paper six experiments are given, in which the silver was dried at 150° C. From them, if Ag=107.675, we can deduce the value Cu=63.437. In the second paper Richards states that the silver of his earlier series of weighing still retained traces of moisture. Five additional determinations were therefore made, in which the silver before weighing was heated to incipient redness. These gave in mean, Cu=63.450; ±.0006. (Proc. Amer. Acad., xxii, 346, and xxiii, 177.)

Silicon—Thorpe and Young re-determine the atomic weight of silicon by means of the bromide. That compound was decomposed by water, and after evaporation to dryness the residual silica was weighed. Nine experiments were made, giving from Si = 28.243 to Si = 28.429; in mean, Si $= 28.332$. Meyer and Seubert's values for O and Br. were used in calculating. (Journ. Chem. Soc., June, 1887.)

Thorium.—From eight analyses of the sulphate, Krüss and Nilson find in mean Th $= 231.869$, when O $= 15.96$ and S $= 31.98$. (Berichte, XX, 1665.)

Osmium.—The atomic weight of osmium has had peculiar interest from the fact that the value ordinarily assigned to it was out of harmony with the periodic law. The constant has been re-determined by Seubert, who analyzed after usual methods the osmichlorides of ammonium and potassium. His results may be computed in the form of eight ratios, which give values for Os varying from 189.72 to 192.00. The mean of all is Os $= 191.12$; which Seubert regards as still slightly too high. Meyer and Seubert's figures for Ag, K, N, and Cl were used in the calculations, with H $= 1$. (Berichte, XXI, 1839.)

Platinum.—Dittmar and McArthur, from experiments of a complex kind upon the chloroplatinates of potassium, ammonium, and rubidium, conclude that Seubert's determination, Pt $= 194.8$, is too low, and that 195.5 is more nearly the correct value. (Trans. Roy. Soc. Edinburgh, XXXIII, 561.)

Seubert replies to the foregoing paper, and maintains his own figures. He also calls attention to the fact that his results had been fully confirmed by Halberstadt. (Berichte, XXI, 2519.)

Ruthenium.—Redetermined by Joly, who gives Ru $= 101.5$, without particulars. (Compt. Rend., CVII, 997.)

Gold.—Krüss determines the atomic weight of gold by means of five ratios, representing the neutral chloride, Au Cl$_3$, and the salt K Au Br$_4$. The chloride was reduced by sulphurous acid, the gold was weighed as metal, and the chloride as silver chloride. Eight such experiments gave in mean Au $= 196.622$. The double bromide gave the following ratios:

> K Au Br$_4$: Au, nine experiments .... Au $= 196.741$.
> 4 Ag Br: Au, five experiments .... Au $= 196.743$.
> Br$_3$: Au, four experiments...................... Au $= 196.619$.
> K Br: Au, four experiments .... Au $= 196.697$.

The final value, representing thirty experiments, was Au $= 196.697$, H being taken as unity, with Stas' values for Ag, Cl, K, and Br. (Berichte, XX, 205.)

The same constant was also measured by Thorpe and Laurie, who likewise made use of the double salt K Au Br$_4$. Three ratios were taken: First, the salt was decomposed by heat, and the residual Au, and K Br, were both weighed. Secondly, the K Br from the former series was titrated with silver solution, giving the ratio Au : Ag. Thirdly, the Ag Br found in the last reaction was also weighed, giving the ratio Au : Ag Br. Taking H $= 1$ and Stas' figures for Ag, K, and Br, we have:

> From Au : K Br, eight experiments................ Au $= 196.876$.
> From Au : Ag, nine experiments .... Au $= 196.837$.
> From Au : Ag Br, eight experiments .... Au $= 196.852$.
> Mean of all..................................... Au $= 196.852$.

(Journ. Chem. Soc., June, 1887.)

Over these two sets of determinations, which differ in mean by nearly 0.2, some controversy has arisen. For details, see Thorpe and Laurie (Berichte, xx, 3036, and Journ. Chem. Soc., December, 1887), and Krüss, (Berichte, xx, 2365, and xxi, 128). Meanwhile Mallet has published a preliminary note, without particulars, concerning a determination which he has made. He gets a direct ratio between gold and hydrogen, giving for gold a value somewhat higher than that obtained by Thorpe and Laurie. (Chem. News, No. 1452.)

The determination of molecular weights.—Early in 1888 Victor Meyer called attention to Raoult's method for ascertaining molecular weights, pronouncing it to be the most important advance in that field of work since the announcement of Dulong and Petit's law. The method, in principle, is as follows: When any substance is dissolved, the freezing point of the solvent is lowered; and that depression of freezing point is directly related to the molecular weight of the body in solution. If we divide the observed depression of freezing point for each substance examined by the weight of the substance dissolved in 100 grammes of water, we get a coefficient of depression which gives, when multiplied by the molecular weight, a constant quantity. The latter constant is independent of concentration, and has approximately uniform value for all similarly constituted bodies in any given solvent. It is called the *molecular depression;* and differs for different solvents; but in glacial acetic acid it seems to have one value for all substances. Water, acetic acid, and benzene seem to be the only solvents of general applicability. If now it is desired to know the molecular weight of a soluble body to which vapor-density methods are inapplicable, we have only to determine its coefficient of depression and compute from that the sought for value. The method, as a physical process, is not sharply accurate; but it is close enough to decide between the lowest empirical formula assignable to a substance and the various multiples thereof. Although the original investigation was published by Raoult in 1883, it attracted little attention until Meyer's paper appeared; but since then it has been widely noted, and the method extensively applied. (See Meyer, Berichte, xxi, 536, and Auwers, *ibid.*, xxi, 701.) Auwers also describes a convenient form of apparatus, and so too does Beckmann. (Zeit. Phys. Chem., ii, 638.)

In illustration of the use of Raoult's method, the following researches out of many may be cited:

Ramsay, working with an acetic acid solution, finds the molecular weight of liquid nitric peroxide to be 92, at a temperature of about 16°. Hence its formula is N_2O_4, and it seems, furthermore, to undergo no dissociation upon dilution. (Journ. Chem. Soc., LIII, 621.)

Brown and Morris, using aqueous solutions, get depression values for dextrose, cane sugar, maltose, lactose, and arabinose corresponding to their accepted molecular weights. For raffinose the simplest empirical formula, $C_{18}H_{32}O_{16} . 5H_2O$, corresponds to the results obtained by Raoult's method. (Journ. Chem. Soc., LIII, 610.)

Paterno and Nasini with aqueous solutions find that citraconic, mesaconic, and itaconic acids have the same coefficients of depression, and are therefore strictly isomeric. A like statement holds of malic and fumaric acids. (Berichte, XXI, 2156.)

Louïse and Roux, in order to determine the constitution of aluminum compounds, investigated aluminum ethyl, propyl, and isoamyl by Raoult's method, with ethylene bromide as the solvent. The results agree with the formulæ Al_2X_6, in which X stands for the alcohol radicle. Compare the diverse results obtained by other chemists with the vapor-density method. (Compt. Rend., CVII, 600.)

The depression produced in the freezing point of benzene by various phenolic substances was studied by Paterno. Phenol behaves abnormally, but ethylphenol, acetylphenol, two nitrophenols, tribromphenol, picric acid, paracresol, methyl salicylate, thymol, nitro thymol, nitrosothymol, naphthol, and benzylphenol all gave normal results, both in benzene and in acetic acid. (Berichte, XXI, 3178.)

Density of gases and vapors.—In discussing the atomic weight of oxygen attention was called to Lord Rayleigh's observation that the volume of a glass globe when full differs from the volume of the same globe when empty. This observation affects all of Regnault's determinations of the weight of gases, and the results of the latter have been corrected by Crafts, who had access to Regnault's original apparatus, excepting the glass globe actually used, which had been destroyed. Another globe of the same lot, however, was available, and presumably identical for all practical purposes with it. The following are the specific gravities as given by Regnault and as corrected by Crafts, air being taken as unity.

	Regnault.	Crafts.
N	.97137	.97138
H	.06927	.06949
O	1.10564	1.10562
CO_2	1.52910	1.52897

The actual correction was 3 milligrammes added to the weight of each gas as given by Regnault at 760 millimeters pressure. (Compt. Rend., CVI, 1662.)

J. Mensching and Victor Meyer find that at high temperatures the vapors of phosphorus and arsenic are not in agreement with the supposed molecules P_4 and As_4, but that at a white heat they approximate to P_2 and As_2. For antimony the molecule Sb_4 does not exist, the probable molecule being either Sb_2 or Sb_1. (Berichte, XX, 1833.)

Biltz, redetermining the vapor density of sulphur, under various conditions, obtains values ranging from 7.937 down to 4.734. He concludes, hence, that the commonly accepted view that free sulphur in vapor is S_6 is not correct, and that the true formula is S_2. (Berichte, XXI, 2013.)

With reference to the chlorides of iron, chromium, indium, gallium, and aluminum, various determinations have been made, with varying results. First, as to aluminum, whose chloride has hitherto been written, on the strength of Deville and Troost's researches, $Al_2 Cl_6$, which corresponds to a density of 9.20. According to Nilson and Petterson the density at 440° is 7.789, at 758° it is 4.802, and above that temperature, from 1117° to 1260°, it is fairly constant at from 4.247 to 4.277. The value 4.600 corresponds to the molecule $AlCl_3$, which is required by the trivalency of aluminum, as indicated by the periodic law. (Zeitsch. Physikal. Chem., I, 459.)

On the other hand, Friedel and Crafts, at temperatures ranging from 218° to 433°, find a vapor density of 9.24, agreeing with Deville and Troost's determination. They get no evidence of dissociation into any simpler molecules. (Compt. Rend., CVI, 1764.)

Conformable with these data Louïse and Roux, working with aluminum methyl and aluminum ethyl, get values corresponding to the general molecules $Al_2 R_6$. For the same compounds Buckton and Odling long ago found densities according with $Al R_3$. Both compounds, according to Louïse and Roux, decompose at high temperatures, yielding aluminum, hydrogen, and hydrocarbons. (Compare also the data obtained by the same authors by Raoult's method, as cited in the preceding article. (Compt. Rend., CVI, 73 and 602.) ·

Altogether the evidence seems to prove the existence of Al_2R_6 molecules, which split up at high temperatures into two of $Al R_3$.

Ferric chloride, if Fe_2Cl_6, requires a vapor density of 11.2. If $FeCl_3$, its value should be 5.6. Grünewald and V. Meyer obtain the following values: At 448°, 10.487; at 518°, 9.569; at 606°, 8.383; at about 750°, 5.389 to 5.528, with evidence of dissociation; at about 1050°, 4.915 to 5.307, and similar figures at higher temperatures. At 448° it vaporizes completely undecomposed, and even then its vapor density is too low for Fe_2Cl_6. That compound, therefore, they believe does not exist; and regard the lower symbol, $FeCl_3$, to be the true one. At the higher temperatures it splits up to some extent into $FeCl_2$ and free chlorine. (Berichte, XXI, 687.)

To this investigation, as to Nilson and Petterson's on aluminum chloride, Friedel and Crafts reply. They determine the vapor density of ferric chloride in presence of free chlorine, in order to prevent any decomposition, and find a figure agreeing with Fe_2Cl_6. Their data are for temperatures from 321° to 342°. (Compt. Rend., CVII, 302. Compare Biltz, Berichte, XXI, 2766.)

Ferrous chloride, redetermined by Nilson and Petterson, at temperatures varying from 1300° to 1500°, has a density of 4.292 to 3.340. Theory for $FeCl_2$, 4.375. Earlier work by V. Meyer seems to indicate a more complex molecule at lower temperatures. (Journ. Chem. Soc., LIII, 827.)

Nilson and Petterson also have determined the vapor density of chromic and chromous chlorides. For the former, at 1200° to 1300°, it agrees closely with the molecule $CrCl_3$. At 1065° a higher value was found, but not at all approximating to Cr_2Cl_6. The latter probably can not exist in the gaseous state. For chromous chloride the data give a density considerably too high for $CrCl_2$; but the compound vaporizes with difficulty, and the density diminishes with rise of temperature. $CrCl_2$ is probably the true formula. (Journ. Chem. Soc., LIII, 828.)

Gallium.—According to Nilson and Petterson the trichloride of this metal has a vapor density which at 350° is 8.846, at 606° is 6.144, and at 1,000–1,100° is 5.185. Ga_2Cl_6 requires 12.16. $GaCl_3$ requires 6.08. The latter value is probably correct. They also describe a dichloride whose vapor density agrees with the symbol $GaCl_2$. (Journ. Chem. Soc., LIII, 822.)

In this case also Nilson and Petterson are partly controverted by Friedel and Crafts, who find the tri-chloride of gallium, as measured at 273°, to be Ga_2Cl_6. Above this temperature it begins to dissociate, perhaps into 2 $GaCl_3$. (Compt. Rend., CVII, 306.)

For indium, Nilson and Petterson re-examined the trichloride, and also describe two new compounds, a mono- and dichloride, respectively. The vapor densities of the three compounds indicate molecules of $InCl_3$, $InCl_2$, and $InCl$. (Journ. Chem. Soc., LIII, 816.) The density of the trichloride is also given by Biltz, who finds it concordant with $InCl_3$. (Berichte, XXI, 2766.) All of the foregoing data relative to the iron-aluminum group are well summarized by Sydney Young, who gives them in tabular form in Nature for December 27, 1888. His note is discussed by Brauner in the same journal for January 31, 1889.

The vapor density of tellurium tetrachloride has been studied by Michaelis. It boils at 380°, and up to 448° it distills undecomposed. Even at 530 it is scarcely dissociated at all, and its density indicates a molecule of $TeCl_4$. Hence tellurium is at least quadrivalent. (Berichte, XX, 1780.)

Refrigerating mixtures.—The freezing mixtures containing solidified carbon dioxide have been carefully studied by Cailletet and Colardeau, who give the following determinations of temperature:

	° C.
Solid carbon dioxide	− 60
Solid carbon dioxide in vacuo	− 76
Solid carbon dioxide in ether	− 77
Same mixture in vacuo	− 103

The following all represent ordinary pressures:

	°
Solid carbon dioxide in methyl chloride	−82
Solid carbon dioxide in sulphur dioxide	−82
Solid carbon dioxide in amyl acetate	−78
Solid carbon dioxide in phosphorus trichloride	−76
Solid carbon dioxide in absolute alcohol	−72
Solid carbon dioxide in ethylene chloride	−60

In the three compounds last named the carbon dioxide was manifestly less soluble than in the others. Hence a smaller reduction of temperature as compared with that of the original solid. (Compt. Rend., CVIII, 1631.)

Hydrates of gases.—Villard finds that when certain gases mixed with aqueous vapor are condensed in Cailletet's apparatus, crystalline hydrates are produced, which decompose spontaneously at the following temperatures: Of CH_4, at $21.^{\circ}5$; of C_2H_6, at 12°; of C_2H_4 at $18.^{\circ}5$; of C_2H_2, at 14°; of N_2O, at 12°. Nitrogen, hydrogen, carbonic oxide, nitric oxide, cyanogen, ammonia, propylene, butylene, and allylene gave no crystals under similar conditions. (Compt. Rend., CVI, 1602.)

The formation of alloys.—The claim made by Spring that Wood's alloy could be formed from its component metals by means of pressure has led Hallock to investigate the subject from another point of view. One part cadmium, one part tin, two parts lead, and four parts bismuth, in fine filings, were mixed in a glass tube of about five millimeters interior diameter, closed at one end. The mixture was packed in the tube by gentle pressure with an iron wire, and the whole was then suspended in a water bath and exposed to a temperature of 98° to 100°. Within two days the entire mass was fluid, the alloy having formed at a temperature 130° below the melting point of its most fusible constituent.

The well-known alloy of sodium and potassium, which is liquid above 6° C., can be produced with great case at ordinary atmospheric temperatures. When freshly cut surfaces of the two metals are gently pressed together, liquefaction begins at the points of contact, almost instantly, and spreads rapidly to completion. In short, it seems probable that all alloys may be made from their components at temperatures little, if any, in excess of their own melting points. (Zeitschr. Physikal. Chem., II, 379.)

The same alloy of sodium and potassium has also been investigated thermo-chemically by Joannis, who prepared it by the usual method of melting the two metals together under petroleum. The calorimetric data given by the action of water upon this alloy, led Joannis to conclude that the only true compound among the sodium-potassium alloys is represented by the formula NaK_2. (Ann. de Chim. Phys. (6), XII, 358.)

The dehydration of metallic hydroxides by heat.—By experiments on the temperature and rate of dehydration of hydrates corresponding to sixteen metals, Carnelley and Walker conclude that Henry's views concerning the polymerization of metallic oxides are mainly true. They find that when a precipitated hydrate is heated, it gradually loses water with the successive formation of a large number of definite hydrates, each of which is further decomposed on a small rise in temperature, with the formation of a compound containing a smaller proportion of water. As the elimination of water proceeds, the residual molecule becomes larger and more complex, until at last a highly complex molecule of anhydrous oxide is left, of which the formula is some multiple of that generally received. For the oxides of silicon, titanium, and tin the coefficient of polymerization must be at least ten, while oxide of zirconium must be at least $Zr_{24}O_{48}$, and antimonious oxide at least $Sb_{20}O_{30}$. The most infusible oxides are probably those in which the highest polymerization is reached.

The authors also connect the phenomena of dehydration with the periodic curve, and reach the following conclusions:

(A.) As regards oxides belonging to the same group. In the case of *odd* members the temperature of complete dehydration diminishes as the atomic weight of the positive element increases. For *even* members the reverse is true.

(B.) As regards oxides belonging to the same period, as from Li to F, or from K to Br. Here the temperature of complete dehydration seems to diminish from the beginning to about the middle of the period, and then to increase as we approach its end. To this rule there are only three apparent exceptions, and to the former rules there are none. (Journ. Chem. Soc., LIII, 59.)

The interaction of zinc and sulphuric acid.—The ordinary reaction between commercial zinc and dilute sulphuric acid is familiar to every one, and it is also well known that the hydrogen evolved is sometimes contaminated with sulphur dioxide and sulphuretted hydrogen. Taken altogether the re-actions are somewhat complicated, varying with different qualities of zinc and different concentrations of acid. An interesting qualitative study of the problem has been made by Muir and Adie, who used six different forms of zinc, ranging from the commercial granulated metal, through re-distilled zinc, to platinized zinc foil and zinc especially purified. The acid varied from H_2SO_4 to H_2SO_4, $100H_2O$ approximately.

In all the re-actions hydrogen was evolved, and zinc sulphate with sometimes free sulphur was the only solid product. Sulphur was liberated only at relatively high temperatures, and by acids not less concentrated than H_2SO_4, $2H_2O$, and its separation is always accompanied by evolution of sulphur dioxide and sulphuretted hydrogen; although the quantity of the latter was sometimes extremely small. When the specially purified zinc was used, hardly any sulphur was set free, but with platinized foil it appeared in large quantities; its formation being possibly due to the mutual action of sulphuretted hydrogen and hot sulphuric acid.

The purer the zinc the smaller become the quantities of sulphur dioxide and sulphuretted hydrogen evolved at ordinary temperatures, and when the acid is so dilute as H_2SO_4, $12H_2O$, hydrogen is almost the sole gaseous product. The proportions of the other two gases vary with purity of the zinc, concentration of acid, and temperature. With platinized foil and concentrated acids, sulphur dioxide is generated at a lower temperature than sulphuretted hydrogen, but the latter is produced the more freely of the two when the acid is dilute. With commercial zinc and H_2SO_4, $2H_2O$, little sulphur dioxide or sulphuretted hydrogen appears at 100°; at 165° both gases are produced freely; at 180° torrents of the latter gas nearly free from the former are evolved.

With the specially purified zinc and the same concentration of acid both gases are given off in quantity at 165°. The dependence of the production of these gases upon temperature and concentration seems to indicate that they are not altogether generated by any reducing action of nascent hydrogen upon sulphuric acid. The authors regard the interaction in the case of pure zinc and acid as chiefly chemical, and ascribe the products evolved by less pure zincs to secondary electrolytic changes. Doubtless the actual re-actions are more complex than can be shown by any system of equations at present. (Journ. Chem. Soc., LIII, 47.)

Absorption spectra of the rare earths.—Krüss and Nilson, studying the rare earths from thorite, wöhlerite, cerite, fergusonite, euxenite, etc., have discovered various anomalies in their absorption spectra which they ascribe to a greater elementary complexity than has commonly been recognized. In place of the so called erbium, holmium, thulium, didymium, and samarium, they assume the existence of more than twenty elements, each of the above-named substances giving spectra which vary for each substance with differences of origin. For example, in the earths from thorite, all the lines ascribable to holmium were seen, but all faintly except one. That one, which was strong, is ordinarily one of the faintest. The lines which are commonly strongest were barely visible. Of earths from fergusonite a series of fractionations was made, and in these similarly curious anomalies were noted. In certain portions some lines belonging to a given element would appear, and others would be wanting, and thus the supposed element was shown to be presumably a mixture. For details, with wave lengths of the lines, the original paper must be consulted. (Berichte, xx, 2134.)

To the foregoing conclusions of Krüss and Nilson, Bailey objects. As regards the relative intensity of absorption lines, he holds that the several spectra in a mixture of earths modify each other, the proportioned quantity of each earth affecting the problem decidedly. A strong absorption band may hide a weaker one, and furthermore, differences of dilution with respect to any given oxide will influence its spectrum. Variations may also be due to the presence of reagents; as for instance, as nitrate solutions were studied, an excess of nitric acid. (Berichte, xx, 2769.)

To Bailey's objections, Krüss and Nilson publish a rejoinder, in which, with other evidence, they state that their solutions contained only neutral nitrates of the earths. (Berichte, xx, 3067.) Later, Bailey replies, leaving the question still in doubt. (Berichte, xx, 3325.) The discussion is continued in Berichte, xxi, pp. 585, 1521, and 2019, and further spectral investigations by Kiesewetter and Krüss appear in the same volume, p. 2310. In the latter paper the earths from keilhauite and gadolinite are studied with results analogous to those given in the first of the above-cited publications.

Elements and meta elements.—In his address as president of the Chemi-

cal Society, in March, 1888, Crookes discusses at some length the nature
of the chemical elements, and considers the nature of the many doubtful bodies contained in the so-called rare earths. Recognizing the
differences between the modifications of supposed elements developed
by fractional precipitation many times repeated, he does not regard
them as equal in rank to the broader differences which distinguish well-
characterized elementary bodies, and proposes the term "meta-elements" as one well adapted to indicate their peculiar nature. In general, he proposes to substitute for the word "element," as commonly
used, the expression "elementary group," the meta-elements being the
closely similar components. In the original evolution of the elements
from "protyle" he conceives that there was a massing tendency of the
primeval atoms about certain nodal points in space. A cluster of particles, so formed, is a mass of that element whose atomic weight it represents, while the outlying particles of the cluster, varying in weight
form the average, and varying almost imperceptibly in properties, are
meta-elements. He further discusses the main problem in the light of
the periodic law, and replaces the ordinary tabular expression by a
lemniscate spiral, along which the atomic weights of the elements are
distributed.

INORGANIC.

The waters of the Yellowstone Park.—In Bulletin No. 47 of the U. S.
Geological Survey there is an elaborate investigation by Gooch and
Whitfield upon the waters of the Yellowstone Park. Forty-three of
these waters, mostly representing geysers and hot springs, were thoroughly analyzed, and found to be of remarkable interest. All of the
geyser waters are highly siliceous; all contain notable quantities of
borates; all carry weighable amounts of arsenic and of lithia. In no
case was iodine detected, and bromine was found but rarely in very
small amounts. The main constituents, apart from the substances already named, were the usual sulphates, carbonates, and chlorides of
lime, magnesia, and the alkalies. None of the waters are markedly
chalybeate. As regards concentration, all are comparatively weak,
most of them carrying under 2 grammes of solid contents to the liter,
and not one reaching 4 grammes.

One of the springs, the Devil's Ink Pot, is probably unique among
mineral waters. It contains 3.3871 grammes of dissolved matter in the
kilogramme of water, and of this 2.8185 grammes are ammonium sulphate. It also contains free sulphuric, boric, and hydrochloric acid,
some alum, a little sulphuretted hydrogen, and several metallic sulphates. No suggestion is offered concerning the origin of this water.
The bulletin contains full details as to the methods of analysis employed, and will be found valuable by other analysts on the score of
suggestiveness.

The chlorides of iodine.—According to Stortenbeker the only solid chlorides of iodine are the trichloride, and two modifications, α and β of the monochloride. The α compound crystallizes in long, red needles, melting at 27°.2, while the β modification forms brownish red lamellæ, which fuse at 13°.9. All these bodies can exist below their points of fusion in liquid mixtures containing an excess of either element, and varying in composition with temperature. ·In the gaseous state only the molecule ICl. is possible, and it dissociates slightly at 80°; the trichloride dissociates completely in passing from solid to gas. (Rec. Trav. Chim., VII, 152.)

The valency of boron.—Lorenz, from a study of the oxychlorides, concludes that boron is trivalent. Neither of the compounds BOCl nor $BOCl_3$ could be prepared; but a substance $B_8O_{11}Cl_2$, analogous in all respects to several well-known salts of trivalent antimony, was obtained. (Am. Chem., CCXLVII, 226.)

The same subject is also discussed by Georgievicz from other points of view; but with the same final conclusions. He points out as evidence of the trivalency of boron the isomorphism of euclase and datolite, and also describes a reaction by which when iodine is boiled with a solution of borax, sodium iodate is formed. (Journ. Prakt. Chem. (2), XXXVIII, 118.)

The preparation of boron.—The following method is proposed by S. G. Rawson: A mixture of $3\frac{1}{2}$ parts of boron trioxide and 11 parts of calcium fluoride is treated in a flask with strong sulphuric acid. On gently warming, a steady stream of boron fluoride is evolved, which is then passed through a glass tube on which several bulbs have been blown. In each bulb a small piece of potassium is placed, and these are heated successively. Decomposition ensues with formation of potassium fluoride and liberation of boron. Finally, the mass is thrown on a filter and washed with water, boron remaining behind. Amorphous silicon may be easily prepared in a similar way. (Chem. News, LVIII, 283.)

According to Hampe amorphous boron may also be prepared by the electrolysis of fused borax between electrodes of platinum and gas carbon. The free boron accumulates about the negative pole, and may be separated from slag by means of water and hydrochloric acid. (Berichte, XXI, ref. 827.)

The manufacture of aluminum.—Under the patents of Mr. H. G. Castner, of New York, the manufacture of aluminum has been begun at Oldbury, near Birmingham, England. The process revolves itself into four stages. First, sodium is produced from caustic soda by reduction by means of iron carbide in steel retorts at a temperature of 800°. From 6 pounds of caustic soda and 5 pounds of carbide 1 pound of sodium is obtained at a cost of about 18 cents. A residual product is crude carbonate of soda of commercial value. Second, chlorine is prepared by the Weldon process, the necessary hydrochloric acid being supplied by the makers in return for the crude carbonate of soda above mentioned. Third, by passing the chlorine over a heated mixture of alumina, salt, and carbon, a double chloride of aluminum and sodium is produced. Fourth, the aluminum is extracted by heating, in appropriate furnaces, 80 pounds of the aforesaid double chloride, 25 pounds of sodium, and 30 pounds of cryolite, the latter serving as a flux. The charge is maintained for two hours at a temperature of 1,000°, and yields about 8 pounds of aluminum containing not over 2 per cent. of impurities. The present cost of the metal is from $10 to $12 a pound, and under this process it is estimated that the price can be reduced to about $1.25. (Chem. News, LVIII, 64.)

Some products of the Cowles electric furnace.—The following observations are due to Prof. C. F. Mabery.

First, as to the reduction of aluminum from corundum : When that mineral, mixed with charcoal, is submitted to the action of an electric current in the furnace it fuses and reduction proceeds rapidly. The liberated metal, vaporized, partly condenses in the upper layer of charcoal, while part escapes into the air and is burned. The mixture of carbon and metal contains from 10 to 50 per cent. of the latter. If silicon is present in the ore it is also reduced and the silicon alloys with the aluminum in variable proportions up to 10 per cent. of the former. With clay a similar reduction takes place, and when the alloy obtained is treated with hydrochloric acid, crystalline or graphitoidal silicon is left behind. The slags which are produced usually contain some metallic aluminum, rarely iron, and almost no silicon. When corundum is reduced in presence of iron, the latter retains aluminum to a greater or less extent. One product, which seems available for foundry purposes and for introducing aluminum into steel, contains from 6 to 10 per cent. of aluminum. It resembles in appearance a hard, fine-grained white iron.

Secondly, as to the reduction of silicon. Sand is more easily reduced in the furnace than corundum. It first fuses, and reduction immediately follows, yielding crystallized silicon. Copper mixed with the charge dissolves the silicon up to 14 per cent., giving a bronze of remarkable strength. The product obtained when silicon is reduced in the absence of metals contains more or less of an amorphous greenish substance of vitreous luster, which always occurs between the unreduced sand and the free silicon. In composition it appears to be the hitherto unknown silicon monoxide, SiO. Its specific gravity is 2.893, or somewhat higher than quartz. (Am. Chem. Journ., IX, 11.)

Alum in baking-powders.—In a series of experiments upon baking-powders used in the United States, Professor Mallet has reached the following conclusions : The greater part of the aluminous powders contain alum, acid calcium phosphate, sodium bicarbonate, and starch. They give off very different proportions of carbon dioxide, and therefore require to be used in different amounts. Generally there is an excess of the alkaline ingredient in these powders, but sometimes the reverse is true. On moistening the powders they yield small amounts of calcium and aluminum in soluble form. After bread-making the powders containing acid calcium phosphate leave most of their aluminum behind as phosphate, but when alum alone has been used the phosphate is replaced by hydroxide. In baking, the interior of the loaf does not exceed a temperature of 100° C., at which temperature neither the ·aluminum phosphate nor the hydroxide is completely dehydrated. Both of these compounds in doses not much exceeding the quantities found in bread produce an inhibitory effect upon indigestion, this point having been determined by personal experiments. That effect is probably due to the fact that a part of the alumina unites with the acid of the gastric juice and is taken into solution, while the remainder of the hydroxide or phosphate precipitates the peptic ferment in insoluble form. Partial precipitation of some of the organic matter of food may also be brought about by the aluminum compounds in question. From all the evidence Mallet concludes that not only alum itself, but also the residues which it leaves in bread, are unwholesome. (Chem. News, LVIII, 276, 284.)

Aluminum in plants.—It is commonly believed and asserted that flowering plants do not contain aluminum as a normal constituent, although one or two exceptions have been admitted. But Yoshida, on examining carefully selected and washed seeds of the pea, bean, rice, wheat, barley, millet, and buckwheat, finds alumina present in the ash in every case. The quantities found range from 0.053 per cent. in the ash of the pea, *Soja hispida*, up to 0.272 per cent. in the ash of millet, *Panicum italicum*. In the pea the cotyledons contain no alumina, while the ash of the hull or skin contains 0.268 per cent. The figure given above relates to the whole pea. (Journ. Chem. Soc., LI, 748.)

Silicon in iron and steel.—Thomas Turner, after a long and laborious investigation, announces the following conclusions as to the influence of silicon upon the properties of iron and steel :

Ingot iron containing silicon in all proportions up to 0.5 per cent. rolls well and does not show any signs of red-shortness ; it welds perfectly with all proportions of silicon, and, with the somewhat doubtful exception of the 0.5 per cent. specimen, it is not brittle when cold. With less than about 0.15 per cent. of silicon, the limit of elasticity, the breaking load, the extension, and the reduction of area are but little, if at all, affected by the proportion of silicon present. With over 0.15 per cent. the limit of elasticity and breaking load are increased, though the effect of silicon in this respect is not nearly so marked as that of carbon. But the ductility is distinctly reduced and rendered more irregular by the presence of much silicon. The fracture is also rendered more granular or crystalline, and is less regular in character. (Journ. Chem. Soc., LIII, 824 ; continued from LI, 129.)

The chemical structure of the natural silicates.—Under this heading Clarke has summarized his views upon silicate structure, which vary somewhat from those which have been hitherto generally held. After arguing in favor of simplicity of structure, he discusses a number of the common aluminous silicates, and shows that the more complex of them are easily represented as substitution derivatives of normal salts, aluminum itself being regarded as trivalent. Thus, from the normal orthosilicate of aluminum, xenolite, the species fibrolite, topaz, muscovite, paragonite, eucryptite, dumortierite, grossularite, prehnite, and natrolite are simply derived, and in a way which accords well with their actual occurrences and alterations in nature. The paper concludes with the general hypothesis that all double salts are substitution derivatives of normal compounds. (Am. Chem. Journ., x, 120.)

In a later number of the same journal (x, 405) E. A. Schneider shows that the differences in the behavior of silicates toward hydrochloric acid are in the same order as the differences pointed out in Clarke's formula.

The constitution of the clays.—By a careful study of the thermal phenomena attending the dehydration of many clays, Le Chatelier arrives at the conclusion that they represent only five compounds, as follows:

Halloysite	$2 SiO_2 Al_2O_3 . 2H_2O . aq.$
Kaolin	$2 SiO_2 Al_2O_3 . 2H_2O$
Allophane	$SiO_2 Al_2O_3 . aq.$
Pyrophyllite	$4 SiO_2 Al_2O_3 . H_2O$
Montmorillonite	$4 SiO_2 Al_2O_3 . H_2O . aq.$

Of these the last one is doubtful. (Zeitschr. Phys. Chem., I, 396.)

Hydroxychlorides of titanium.—According to Koenig and Otto von der Pfordten, dry, gaseous hydrochloric acid does not act upon titanium tetrachloride. On the other hand, concentrated aqueous hydrochloric acid acts upon the chloride, forming a series of hydroxy-derivatives, which may be represented as follows: $TiCl_4$; $TiCl_3OH$; $TiCl_2(OH)_2$; $TiCl(OH)_3$. These compounds are called by the authors chlorides of titanic acid, and all are solids. The monochloride is stable in the air; the dichloride is very hygroscopic; the trichloride somewhat so. (Berichte, XXI, 1708.)

Titanic acid in soils.—J. F. McCaleb has examined fourteen samples of soil from central Virginia, together with one from Alabama and one from Nevada, finding titanic oxide present in all in percentages ranging from 0.33 to 5.42. Although this wide distribution of titanium was reasonably to be expected, it seems not to have been hitherto observed. (Am. Chem. Journ., x, 36.)

Germanium.—Several papers upon this interesting new metal have appeared, which identify it completely with the predicted "ekasilicium" of Mendelejeff. For the specific heat of the metal, between $0°$ and $440°$, Nilson and Pettersson find 0.0757, which gives an atomic heat of 5.33. They also find normal values for the vapor density of $GeCl_4$, GeI_4, and GeS. (Berichte, xx, ref. 134.)

By Winkler several compounds of germanium are described, notably a germanium chloroform, $GeHCl_3$; germanium ethyl, $Ge(C_2H_5)_4$, and a germanium ultramarine. The double fluorides of germanium are strictly analogous to those of the other elements of the same group. (Journ. Prakt. Chem. (2), XXXVI, 177.) The potassium germanifluoride, K_2GeF_6, is also studied by Nilson and Pettersson, who show its analogies with the silicofluoride. Crystallographic measurements by Paykull show it to be isomorphous with ammonium silicofluoride. (Berichte, XX, 1696.) In euxenite Krüss discovers about one-tenth of 1 per cent. of germanium oxide. (Berichte, XXI, 131.)

Hydrazin.—The compound N_2H_4, hydrazin or amidogen, of which many derivatives have long been known, has at last been isolated by Curtius. When diazoacetic ether is treated with hot, strong potash lye the potassium salt of a new acid is formed. When this salt is treated with a mineral acid the new diazo acid is set free, which upon digestion with dilute sulphuric acid deposits superb colorless crystals of hydrazin sulphate. The latter by warming with caustic alkali solutions readily yields up free hydrazin as a colorless, perfectly stable gas having a peculiar odor slightly suggestive of ammonia. It dissolves easily in water to a strongly alkaline solution, which acts as a powerful reducing agent, precipitates alumina and other like bases from their salts, and unites readily with acids. (Berichte, XX, 1632.)

The chloride of nitrogen.—This compound, which is perhaps the most violent explosive known, has been recently investigated by Gatterman. As obtained by the action of chlorine upon sal ammoniac solution, it was found to be indefinite in composition and to contain various admixtures of chloramines. From this mixture the pure NCl_3 was prepared by first washing thoroughly with water in a separatory funnel and then saturating for half an hour with a stream of chlorine. The oil so obtained was thoroughly washed, dried, and analyzed and, was found to be definite in composition. By careful manipulation it was prepared about thirty times without explosion, and its reputedly capricious explosibility was found to be due to the action of light. By flashing upon it the light from burning magnesium it exploded violently. On careful heating up to 90° it remains unchanged, but exploded with great force when the temperature reached 95°. (Berichte, XXI, 751.)

In a note upon the foregoing paper Mallet calls attention to the fact that nitrogen iodide, which is not sensitive when wet, when dry also detonates by exposure to bright sunlight. (Chem. News, LVIII, 64.)

Thiophosphoryl fluoride.—According to Thorpe and Rodger, when phosphorus pentasulphide is heated with lead fluoride in a leaden tube a gas is formed which analysis shows to be thiophosphoryl fluoride, PSF_3. It is also produced by several other re-actions, and is a transparent, colorless, liquefiable gas. In contact with air it spontaneously ignites, burning at a jet with a pale yellowish-green flame tipped with blue. It dissolves in water, to some extent in ether, not at all in alcohol or benzene. It has no action on mercury. (Jour. Chem. Soc., LIII, 766.)

Amorphous antimony.—This modification of antimony, discovered by Gore, is prepared by Hérard by heating antimony to dull redness in a current of nitrogen. The grayish vapors condense at the cool end of the tube in which the operation is performed, to an amorphous powder. Its specific gravity is 6.22 and it melts at 614°, while ordinary crystalline antimony fuses at 440° and has a density of 6.73. (Compt. Rend., CVII, 420.)

Decomposition of antimony sulphide by water.—Elbers finds that when antimonious sulphide is boiled with water it is slowly decomposed with evolution of sulphuretted hydrogen. In this way 0.05 gramme of sulphide was converted into oxide in fourteen hours, giving a liquid of faintly alkaline re-action. (Jour. Chem. Soc., LVI, 108, from Chem. Zeitung, XII, 355.)

Hydrochlorates of chlorides.—Three of these hitherto doubtful salts, well crystallized, are described by Engel. They are $(SbCl_3)_2. HCl. 2H_2O$; $SbCl_5. 5HCl. 11H_2O$; $(BiCl_3)_2. HCl. 3H_2O$. A similar copper salt, $CuCl_2. 2HCl. 5H_2O$, also crystallized, is described by Sabatier. (Compt. Rend., CVI, 1724 and 1796.) The fluohydrates of potassium fluoride, $KF.2HF$ and $KF.3HF$, lately discovered by Moissan, may be analogous in constitution. (Compt. Rend., CVI, 547.)

Pentathionic and hexathionic acids.—When sulphuretted hydrogen is passed into an aqueous solution of sulphurous acid a milky liquid is formed in which an acid called pentathionic acid is commonly believed to exist. Its existence, however, having been called in question by Spring, the question has been re-investigated by Debus with affirmative results. According to Spring the pentathionic acid is merely a physical solution of sulphur in tetrathionic acid, and the pentathionates are mixtures of tetrathionates with free sulphur.

The original liquid from which pentathionic acid is obtained is known as Wackenroder's solution, and is a highly complex and unstable mixture. Its properties were thoroughly studied by Debus, who explains the anomalies which have troubled Spring and others, and who discovers in it, besides tetra- and penta-thionic acids, still a new compound, hexathionic acid, $H_2S_6O_6$. He obtained well-crystallized and definite pentathionates of potassium and copper, and also the potassium salt of hexathionic acid, establishing the existence of both acids beyond all reasonable question. He also found in the Wackenroder solution rather large quantities of free sulphur in a new colloidal modification, soluble in water. (Journ. Chem. Soc., LII, 278.)

A new sulphur acid.—Villiers, studying the action of sulphur dioxide upon sodium thiosulphate, finds that when the gas is passed into an ice-cold solution of the latter salt a new sulphur acid is generated. If the solution, after saturation, be allowed to stand for a few days and then is evaporated in vacuo over sulphuric acid, crystals of the sodium salt, $Na_2S_4O_8$, are obtained. It crystallizes from water with $2H_2O$. From the first mother liquor on further evaporation sodium trithionate crystallizes out. For the new acid the name disulphopersulphuric is proposed. (Compt. Rend., CVI, 851 and 1354.)

Tellurium.—According to Berthelot and Fabre the transformation of amorphous tellurium into the crystalline variety is attended by an absorption of heat. In this particular it is the opposite of selenium. Fabre finds that in its different modifications tellurium has sensibly the same specific heat. Telluride of magnesium is easily prepared by heating magnesium in dry hydrogen, and passing over it an excess of tellurium vapor. It is a white, flaky substance, which, treated with acidulated water, yields telluretted hydrogen, and the latter gas is so unstable as to decompose immediately in contact with moist air. Its heat of formation is negative. A number of metallic tellurides were prepared and studied by Fabre thermo-chemically. Their heats of formation were all positive, but less than in the case of the corresponding selenides. (Ann. Chim. Phys. (6), XIV, 93, 110.)

Solution of iron in caustic soda.—When a strong current of air is forced into a hot, concentrated solution of caustic soda contained in an iron vessel, or in which finely divided ferric hydroxide is suspended, noticeable quantities of iron are dissolved without coloration. At ordinary temperatures the liquid remains clear and colorless for several days, but ultimately becomes turbid and discolored, depositing ferric hydroxide. This color or turbidity disappears upon heating. Zirmité, who describes the phenomenon, attributes it to the possible formation of a sodium perferrate, $NaFeO_4$. (Journ. Chem. Soc., LVI, 105; from Chem. Zeitung, XII, 355.)

Luteocobalt permanganate.—This salt, with several of its derivatives intermediate between it and the chloride or bromide of luteocobalt, is remarkable for being violently explosive, both upon heating and by percussion. It forms many highly crystalline double salts of considerable stability. (T. Klobb, Ann. Chim. Phys. (6), XII, 5.)

Electrolytic precipitation of copper.—According to Soret, dilute solutions of copper, except with very weak currents, yield a spongy precipitate of metal. The nature of the deposit depends not only on the intensity of the electric current and on the concentration of the solution, but also on the proportion of free acid which may be present. The electrolytic copper always contains hydrogen, its amount depending upon the temperature of the solution and its acidity. That hydrogen is simply occluded, not combined; and it sometimes contains traces of carbonic anhydride and carbonic oxide. (Compt. Rend., CVII, 733.)

New platinum bases.—Dr. H. Alexander describes a number of compounds, analogous to the platosamines, in which hydroxylamine replaces ammonia. The platodioxamine, of which the chloride, $PtCl_2.4NH_3O$, corresponds to the chloride of Reiset's base, forms a large series of salts, in which alkalies precipitate an insoluble hydroxide, $Pt(OH)_2.4NH_3O$. In this reaction the hydroxylamine base differs from all the other platinum bases so far known. (Ann. Chem., CCXLVI, 239.)

By Blomstrand a remarkable series of platinum bases containing organic radicles and sulphur are described. In one memoir he discusses the sulphin bases of methyl and ethyl, and in a second paper, jointly with Rudelius and Löndabl, the propyl, isopropyl, butyl, isobutyl, and benzyl bases are considered. The platoethylsulphin chloride, $Pt=(S(C_2H_5)_2Cl)_2$, may be cited as a representative of these new compounds. (Journ. Prakt. Chem. (2), XXXVIII, 345 and 497.)

Influence of impurities upon gold.—Roberts-Austen, of the British mint, investigating the influence of small impurities upon gold, attempts to correlate his observations with the periodic law. Those metals whose atomic volumes exceed that of gold, when alloyed with the latter element, diminish its tenacity. Silver, having nearly the same atomic volume as gold, hardly affects its toughness at all. So far as the experiments go, the toughness of gold is not lessened by any element which stands below it in Meyer's curve, while all the elements above gold in the curve tend to make it brittle. (Berichte, XXI, ref. 508.)

Salts of gold —In the periodic system gold may be placed with almost equal propriety either in line with the alkaline metals or in column with the iron and platinum groups. Chemically, its relations suggest the first-named grouping; physically, it is nearer platinum. In a former paper Krüss has shown that aurous oxide, like the alkalies, is completely soluble in water, and now Hoffmann and Krüss find a like statement to hold good of aurous sulphide, which, when freshly prepared, dissolves easily to a clear brown solution, from which it is precipitated by hydrochloric acid and various salts. The trisulphide, Au_2S_3 appears not to exist, in spite of the common belief in its favor, but a sulphide, Au_2S_2, is easily obtainable. The so-called trisulphide of chemical literature is a mixture of this auro-auric salt with free sulphur. (Berichte, XX, 2369 and 2704.)

In experiments upon the halogen compounds of gold Krüss and Schmidt conclude that Thomsen's auro-auric salts, Au_2Cl_4 and Au_2Br_4, do not exist. When chlorine or bromine acts directly upon gold the normal auric compound is produced. (Berichte, XX, 2634.)

ORGANIC.

Higher paraffins from brown coal.—In the oil distilled from brown coal Krafft has identified a number of the higher homologues of methane. He has isolated the members of the series from $C_{17}H_{36}$ to $C_{21}H_{48}$ inclusive, and finds them to be identical with the normal paraffins prepared synthetically. Seven of them are described in detail. (Berichte, XXI, 2256.) In other papers Krafft studies aromatic compounds involving pentadecyl and hexadecyl groups, such as hexadecyl benzene, etc. (*Ibid.*, pp. 2265, 3180.)

The origin of petroleum.—Although petroleum is generally believed to be of organic origin, some writers, and notably Mendelejeff, have sought to show its derivation from inorganic material. Evidence as to its animal origin is now furnished by the researches of C. Engler, who studied the distillation of fish oil under favorable conditions. In a large apparatus made for manufacturing purposes he distilled 492 kilogrammes of menhaden oil, at a temperature of 350° to 400°, and under a pressure of two atmospheres. Combustible gases were given off, and a liquid distillate was obtained in two layers; the upper watery, the lower oily, in character. The latter amounted to 299 kilogrammes, was brownish, and had a strong green fluorescence. In brief, it resembled crude petroleum; and on fractional distillation it yielded pentane, hexane, heptane, octane, and nonane, all of the normal series, together with some secondary hydrocarbons. It was essentially an artificial petroleum.

As fish oil is mainly a mixture of triolein, tristearin, etc., Engler made further experiments upon a similar distillation of these compounds, although on a very much smaller scale, and obtained confirmatory results. The fact that petroleum contains no free carbon, which is cited as evidence against its organic origin, he disposes of by showing that if all the oxygen in the glycerides of fatty oils should combine with part of their hydrogen to form water, the residue would still contain 87 per cent. carbon and 13 per cent. hydrogen, which is almost exactly the average composition of natural petroleum. (Berichte, XXI, 1816.)

Metallocyanides of ethyl.—The ferrocyanide, $(C_2H_5)_4$ $FeCy_6$, is described by Freund, who prepared it by acting upon silver ferrocyanide with ethyl iodide. Recrystallized from chloroform it forms large rhombic crystals. Freund also makes some observations on von Than's alleged platinocyanide of ethyl. (Berichte, XXI, 931 and 937.)

Oxymethylene and formaldehyde.—Tollens and Mayer, attempting to determine the molecular weight of oxymethylene by Raoult's method, find that upon solution in water it is converted into formaldehyde. The latter, in dilute solution, did not undergo polymerization, even after six months' standing, nor was it expelled upon heating; this fact being explained by its transformation, in concentrated solution, into a polymer $(CH_2O)_2$. Upon standing, this di- or paraformaldehyde quickly dissociates at ordinary temperature into formaldehyde. The oxymethylene, which is with difficulty soluble, is probably metaformaldehyde $(CH_2O)_3$. (Berichte, XXI, 1566 and 3503.)

Diacetyl.—By acting upon nitrosomethylacetone with a solution of sodium bisulphite, H. v. Pechmann has prepared a compound which appears to be diacetyl, $CH_3.CO.CO.CH_3$. It is a volatile liquid boiling at 87° to 88°, having a yellowish-green color, and an odor like crude acetone. Its vapor resembles chlorine in tint. Homologues of nitrosomethylacetone, similarly treated, yield homologues of diacetyl. (Berichte, XX, 3162.)

In a later paper Pechmann and Otte describe acetyl-butyryl, acetyl-isobutyryl, acetyl-isovaleryl, acetyl-isocaproyl, and acetyl-crotonyl. (Berichte, XXI, 2140.)

The fatty acids of the drying oils.—Norton and Richardson, in an investigation of linoleic acid prepared from linseed oil, have come to the conclusion that it is a mixture. About three-fourths of the original sample proved to be volatile, distilling under reduced pressure at 290° C. Ricinoleic acid exhibits a similar volatility, the non-volatile residue amounting to about one-fourth of the sample, and solidifying upon cooling. The volatile parts of the two acids appear to be identical, and to agree with the formula $C_{20}H_{36}O_2$. Further investigation is promised. (Am. Chem. Journ., X, 59)

Tests for fats and oils.—This subject has been elaborately studied by Prof. H. W. Wiley, in the laboratory of the United States Department of Agriculture. On account of the increase in the use of cotton-seed oil as an adulterant of other oils, and in the manufacture of imitation lard and butter, he has paid special attention to its detection, and finds that Bechi's test for it is the most trustworthy. That test is based upon the fact that of all the fatty oils, cotton-seed oil alone is able to reduce salts of silver. First, a solution of silver nitrate in water is prepared, to which a large proportion of alcohol and ether is added. Secondly, a mixture of amyl alcohol and rapeseed oil is provided. On adding to a suspected oil, first the silver solution and then the amyl alcohol preparation, and heating upon the water bath, the cotton-seed oil is readily detected. If it is present a color varying from brownish to black is developed, in consequence of the deposition of metallic silver.

With the aid of Abbe's refractometer, he has also studied the refractive indices of many fats and oils, finding such wide differences between them as to justify the use of the instrument in the discovery of adulterations or the identification of samples. (Journ. Anal. Chem., II, 275 and 277.)

The composition of Japanese bird-lime.—This substance, which is prepared like European bird-lime from a species of holly, is extensively used in Japan for catching birds and insects. According to Divers and Kawakita it contains, apart from mechanical impurities, such as bark and dirt, some lime salts, caoutchouc, and a number of interesting organic compounds. Upon saponification with alcoholic potash it yields the potassium salts of palmitic acid and of a semi-solid acid not farther identified, a resinoid substance, and two crystalline alcohols. The latter are named mochylic and ilicylic alcohols and melt at 234° and 172°, respectively. Mochylic alcohol is represented by the formula $C_{26}H_{46}O$, while ilicylic alcohol is $C_{22}H_{38}O$. The ilicic alcohol, obtained by Personne from European bird-lime is $C_{25}H_{44}O$, and, being made from a different species of holly, is probably a distinct compound. The three alcohols are homologous, and belong in a series having the general formula $C_nH_{2n-6}O$. The resinoid constituent of Japanese bird-lime has the composition $C_{26}H_{44}O$, differing from mochylic alcohol by having two atoms less of hydrogen. (Journ. Chem. Soc., LIII, 268.)

A solid hydrocarbon in plants.—Helen C. de S. Abbott and H. Trimble, in the petroleum ether extract from *Cascara amarga* and *Phlox Carolina*, have discovered a solid, crystalline hydrocarbon, melting at 196°. In composition it is represented by the formula $C_{11}H_{18}$, or some multiple thereof. (Berichte, XXI, 2598.)

The synthesis of closed carbon chains.—During 1887 and 1888, W. H. Perkin, jr., has published a number of papers extending his earlier researches upon compounds containing closed carbon chains. In some of these papers he appears in joint authorship with other investigators.

By acting upon ethyl malonate in presence of sodium with trimethylene bromide a number of tetramethylene derivatives were formed, but the hydrocarbon itself could not be prepared. In the same reaction some pentamethylene derivatives were also produced. By other processes compounds involving hexa- and hepta-methylene were obtained. Some work was also done on trimethylene derivatives, and also on the synthesis of aromatic compounds having closed carbon chains. (See Perkin, Journ. Chem. Soc., LI, pp. 1, 240, 702, 849, and LIII, 1; Colman and Perkin, *ibid.*, LI, 228, and LIII, 185; Freer and Perkin, *ibid.*, LI, 820, and LIII, 202, 215.) The aromatic compounds were also studied by Kipping, *ibid.*, LIII, 21. None of these papers are suited for detailed abstraction.

A new general method of synthesis for aromatic compounds.—Friedel and Crafts, continuing their researches upon the re-actions of aromatic hydrocarbons in presence of aluminum chloride, find that the latter re-agent causes benzene and its homologues to take up readily various elements, radicles, and acid anhydrides. Thus, when dry oxygen is passed into a mixture of benzene with aluminum chloride, it is slowly absorbed; and upon treating the mass with water phenol is formed. Toluene, similarly treated, yields cresol. The benzene and chloride mixture easily takes up powdered sulphur, with evolution of hydrochloric and sulphydric acids, and afterwards, with water, gives phenyl mercaptan, phenyl sulphide, and diphenylene disulphide. With carbonic anhydride the same fundamental mixture yields benzoic acid, with sulphur dioxide it gives benzylsulphurous acid, and so on through a long list of similar reactions. In every case, however, treatment with water is necessary to complete the re-action.

In all these syntheses, according to the authors, the first step appears to be the formation of a peculiar organo-metallic compound, as follows:

$$C_6H_6 + Al_2Cl_6 = C_6H_5.Al_2Cl_5 + HCl.$$

This compound, $C_6H_5.Al_2Cl_5$, being formed, it is readily acted upon by various agents, as, for example, by the paraffin chlorides, in which case hydrocarbon derivatives are produced with regeneration of aluminum chloride, thus:

$$C_6H_5.Al_2Cl_5 + CH_3Cl = C_6H_5.CH_3 + Al_2Cl_6.$$

This order of syntheses is discussed in previous papers. In the present essay the reactions are but little more complex. In the first case, in which oxygen is taken up to form phenol, the equations are as follows:

$$C_6H_6+O+Al_2Cl_6=C_6H_5.O.Al_2Cl_5+HCl,$$

an oxygenated compound being formed which, upon treatment with water, is destroyed and phenol is generated.

$$C_6H_5.O.Al_2Cl_5+H_2O=C_6H_5OH+Al_2Cl_5(OH).$$

The definite addition compounds of aromatic hydrocarbons and aluminum chlorides which were some time ago described by Gustavson, Friedel and Crafts were unable to prepare. Instead they obtained variable mixtures. They describe, however, a definite aluminum-phenyl, which serves as a starting point for still other syntheses. (Ann. Chim. Phys. (6), XIV, 433.)

The application of aluminum chloride to organic syntheses in the fatty series has also been studied by Combes (*ibid.*, XII, 199), with reference to diphenyl by Adam (*ibid.*, XV, 224), and in connection with naphthalene derivatives by Roux (*ibid.*, XII, 289).

Inosite.—This substance, isomeric with glucose, has been elaborately studied by Maquenne. With acids it yields ethers which prove it to be a hexatomic alcohol, while with reducing and oxydizing agents it gives derivatives belonging in the aromatic series. Its constitution, therefore, seems to be "hexagonal" like that of benzene; but the evidence leads Maquenne to suppose that it contains no double bonds and is to be regarded rather as a derivative of hexamethylene. As existing in plants it is perhaps an intermediary between the fatty and the aromatic compounds, and one of the sources from which the natural benzene derivatives originate. (Am. Chim. Phys. (6), XII, 80.)

Perseite.—Maquenne, in a new research upon this carbohydrate, finds by Raoult's method that its molecular weight is represented by the formula $C_6H_{14}O_6$. It acts as a hexatomic alcohol, and its hexacetate, hexnitrate, etc., are described. (Compt. Rend., CVI, 1235.)

In a later paper Maquenne revises his former conclusions, and shows that perseite is really a heptavalent alcohol of formula $C_7H_{16}O_7$. On treatment with boiling hydriodic acid it yields heptine, C_7H_{12}. (Compt. Rend., CVII, 583.)

Graminin and phlein.—Two new carbohydrates, isomeric with inulin, are given the above names by Ekstrand and Johanson. The first is derived from the rhizomes of *Trisetum alpestre*; the second from *Phleum pratense*. (Berichte, XXI, 594.)

Cadaverin.—This base, derived from putrefaction, has been identified by Ladenburg as pentamethylenediamine. Both cadaverin and the synthetic compound form the same double salt with mercuric chloride. (Berichte, XX, 2217.)

Putrescin.—This compound, analogous to cadaverin, has been identified with tetramethylenediamine by Udránzky and Bawmann. (Berichte, XXI, 2938.)

Identity of the naphtenes with the aromatic hexhydrides.—In 1883 Markownikoff and Ogloblin obtained from Caucasian petroleum a series of hydrocarbons isomeric with the aromatic hexhydrides, to which they gave the name of naphtenes. Konovaloff, studying the hexhydropseudocumene, which he prepared synthetically from pseudocumene, finds it to be in all respects identical with nononaphtene, and concludes that the supposed naphtenes, as an independent series of hydrocarbons, do not exist. (Berichte, XX, ref. 570.)

Action of pyridine on metallic salts.—The observations of Jorgensen upon metallic pyridine compounds have been extended to a number of new cases by Lang. When pyridine in excess is added to a solution of zinc chloride, a voluminous white precipitate is formed. This dissolves in boiling water with which pyridine has been mixed and crystallizes out in long silky needles having the composition $ZnCl_2 . 2C_5H_5N$. It is recrystallable from boiling alcohol, but water decomposes it into free pyridine and a basic chloride.

From an alcoholic solution of copper chloride pyridine precipitates magnificent bluish-green needles of $CuCl_2.2C_5H_5N$. With copper sulphate dissolved in water, pyridine produces a heavy, light green precipitate, which dissolves in excess of the reagent. From the latter solution alcohol throws down the compound $CuSO_4.C_5H_5N.3H_2O$, which is essentially the normal sulphate with two of its water molecules replaced by one of the organic base. Cuprous chloride treated with pyridine in absence of air reacts so strongly that the mixture becomes boiling hot. Upon cooling the solution, crystals of $Cu_2Cl_2.4C_5H_5N$ are deposited. With great excess of pyridine, six molecules are taken up, forming the salt $Cu_2Cl_2.6C_5H_5N$ in long, greenish-yellow needles.

With an alcoholic solution of cadmium chloride, pyridine precipitates the salt $CdCl_2.2C_5H_5N$. A similar salt, highly crystallized, is also formed by cadmium iodide. With mercuric chloride a compound $HgCl_2.C_5H_5N$ is produced. Anhydrous cadmium chloride absorbs three molecules of pyridine with evolution of heat. Other salts of cobalt chloride, ferrous sulphate, and nickel sulphate with pyridine were also prepared.

(Berichte, XXI, 1678.)

Pyridin and piperidin.—In a paper of nearly a hundred pages, Ladenburg presents the collected results of recent investigations made partly by himself and partly by students under his direction, concerning the preparation and properties of the pyridin, and piperidin bases. The compounds were partly synthetic, and in part derived from tar oil, and embrace pyridin, three methylpyridins, two ethylpyridins, isopropylpyridin, two dimethylpyridins, three methylethylpyridins, diethylpyridin, and the corresponding members of the piperidin series.

H. Mis. 142——29

(Ann. Chem., CCXLVII, 1.) Some higher homologues of the same series, synthetically prepared, are also described by Jaeckle. (*Ibid.*, CCXLVI, 32.)

A new base from tea.—Under the name theophylline, A. Kossel describes a new alkaloid which occurs with caffeine, but in very small quantities, in tea. Its formula, $C_7H_8N_4O_2$, makes it isomeric with theobromine and paraxanthine; from which bases, however, it distinctly differs. Unlike theobromine, it crystallizes with one molecule of water, and in crystalline form it is unlike either of its isomers. It melts at 264°, while paraxanthine melts at above 280°, and theobromine sublimes without fusion at 290°. Its salts crystallize well. As it is convertible into caffeine by methylization, it is doubtless a dimethylxanthine, but the position of its methyl groups is not yet determined. (Berichte, XXI, 2164.)

Some homologues of cocaine.—Starting from cocaine as methyl-benzoyl-ecgonine, F. G. Novy has prepared the corresponding ethyl, propyl, and isobutyl compounds, of which the first had already been described by Merck. In each case benzoyl-ecgonine was heated in a sealed tube with the proper alkyl iodide and the corresponding alcohol. The new alkaloids and their salts crystallize easily, and all possess like cocaine strong anæsthetic properties. (Am. Chem. Journ., X, 145.)

Isatropyl cocaine.—This alkaloid, discovered by Liebermann, was obtained as a bye-product in the extraction of cocaine from coca leaves. It is amorphous, forms amorphous salts, and has the composition represented by the formula $C_{19}H_{23}NO_4$. Upon prolonged treatment with hydrochloric acid it is easily split up into methyl alcohol, ecgonine, and two isomeric isatropic acids, $C_9H_8O_2$. In constitution it is probably a cocaine, in which the benzoic radicle is replaced by one from isatropic acid. Physiologically, the new alkaloid is highly poisonous, differing from cocaine and atropine, and acting mainly on the heart. (Berichte, XXI, 2342.)

The alkaloids of areca nut.—From the areca or betel nut Jahns has obtained two new alkaloids. The first, arecoline, $C_8H_{13}NO_2$, is a colorless, oily liquid of strong alkaline reaction, which boils at about 220°. Its salts are easily soluble, and mostly crystallizable. It appears to be the physiologically active principle of the nut, and to be near pelletierine in its properties. The second alkaloid, arecaine, $C_7H_{11}NO_2.H_2O$, forms colorless, easily soluble crystals, whose solution reacts neutral. It loses its water at 100°, melts at 213°, and chars upon stronger heating. Physiologically it is inactive. Probably it is related to betaine. (Berichte, XXI, 3404.)

Atropine and hyoscyamine.—Ladenburg, investigating the isomerism of these two alkaloids, concludes that it is "physical" in character, and that they are related to each other like tartaric and racemic acids, atropine being the inactive compound optically. The actual transformation of one into the other is yet to be accomplished, the supposed change heretofore having been deceptive, on account of impurities in the atropine examined. (Berichte, XXI, 3065.)

Coloring matter from Drosera Whittakeri.—From the tubers of this South Australian plant Rennie has isolated a magnificent red coloring matter which dyes silk brilliantly. It crystallizes easily from solution in hot alcohol or glacial acetic acid, and has the formula $C_{11}H_8O_5$. From experiments upon the oxidation and reduction of the compound, Rennie infers that it may be a trihydroxy-methylnaphthaquinone. (Jour. Chem. Soc., LI, 371.)

The supposed identity of rutin and quercitrin.—These two tinctorial substances approximate to each other so nearly in properties and composition, that the question of their identity or distinctness has not hitherto been settled. By the action of strong acids both are decomposed into quercetin and isodulcite, they dye similar colors, and have many properties in common. Schunck now points out a number of differences in physical characteristics and reactions, and by careful analyses shows that whereas quercitrin contains two molecules of isodulcite to one of quercetin, rutin has three of isodulcite to one of quercetin. The differences and similarities are thus easily explained. (Jour. Chem. Soc., LIII, 262.)

The fluorides of the paraffin radicles.—Several of these compounds have been prepared and described by Moissan, partly in co-operation with Melsans. They are produced by acting on silver fluoride with the paraffin iodides, and up to isobutyl fluoride they are gaseous at ordinary temperatures. Methyl fluoride is a colorless gas of extreme stability, which is saponifiable only with difficulty. It can be liquefied in Cailletet's apparatus. The ethyl compound liquefies at -48, under normal pressure, and isobutyl fluoride becomes liquid at $+16^\circ$. The gases are combustible, and burn with a blue flame. (Compt. Rend., CVII, 260, 992, 1155.)

The action of fluoride of silicon upon organic bases.—By acting upon aniline, orthotoluidine, paratoluidine, diphenylamine, dimethylaniline, and chinoline with silicon fluoride, Comey and Jackson have prepared a series of compounds which they designate silicotetrafluorides. In these compounds the nitrogen appears to be quinquivalent, one of its bonds being satisfied by fluorine and another by silicon. (Am. Chem. Jour., X, 165.)

Other organic fluorine compounds, substitution derivatives of the aromatic series, are described by Wallach and Heusler. Among them are difluobenzene, parafluoanilin, fluonitrobenzene, parafluophenol, fluopseudocumene, fluodiphenyl, etc. (Ann. d. Chem., CCXLIII, 219.)

Organo-metallic compounds.—The question as to the valency of bismuth is settled by the researches of Michaelis and Polis on bismuth triphenyl. This compound unites directly with two atoms of chlorine or bromine, to form halogen salts in which the metal is definitely pentavalent. (Berichte, XX, 54.)

On the other hand Marquardt has studied the trimethyl, triethyl, triisobutyl, and triisoamyl compounds of bismuth. These only form salts by replacement of the alkyl radicle, which are compounds of the di- and monoalkyl compounds, the bismuth remaining triad throughout. (Berichte, XX, 1516, and XXI, 2035.)

The tetraphenyl and tetratolyl lead compounds have also been studied by Polis. The derivatives of lead tetraphenyl are salts of the diphenyl compound, being formed by replacement and not by addition. (Berichte, XX, 717 and 3331.) .

By Marquardt and Michaelis we have a research upon tellurethyl. When zinc ethyl acts on tellurium tetrachloride, the monochloride of tellurium triethyl is formed. Tellurium tetrethyl probably does not exist. Tellurium diethyl is also described. (Berichte, XXI, 2042.)

By Michaelis and Weitz trianisylarsine and its compounds and also triphenetylarsine are described. In these bodies the arsenic remains trivalent throughout. (Berichte, XX, 48.)

A silico-organic compound of a new type.—When silicon tetrabromide or tetrachloride is added to an excess of aniline diluted with three or four volumes of benzene, silicotetraphenylamide is produced. By distilling off the excess of benzene on a water bath, and crystallizing the residue from solution in warm carbon disulphide, magnificent colorless prisms of the new compound are obtained. According to the discoverer, Prof. J. Emerson Reynolds, its formula is $Si(NHC_6H_5)_4$, and it seems to be the first well-defined compound in which silicon is in direct and exclusive union with amidic nitrogen. About 50 grammes of it were shown at the meeting of the British Association at Bath. (Chem. News, LVIII, 272.)

The action of micro-organisms upon nitric acid.—Upon cultivating thirty-two species of micro-organisms in sterilized solutions containing nitrates, Percy Frankland found a great difference in their power of reducing nitric to nitrous acid. Sixteen or seventeen of the species produced the reduction more or less completely, while the remaining fifteen or sixteen were quite destitute of the power. In no case did the reducing action lead to the formation of any noteworthy amount of ammonia. With two of the more powerful organisms the quality of nitrate reduced to nitrite in a given time was found to depend on the proportion of organic matter—peptone and sugar—present in the solution; the peptone exerting far more influence than the sugar. None of the organisms examined were capable of oxidizing ammoniacal nitrogen—present as ammonium chloride—to nitric or nitrous acids. (Journ. Chem. Soc., LIII, 373.)

The same subject is also discussed by Warington, who made numerous experiments with pure cultures. He studied their action upon urea, upon milk, and upon nitrates, using in all twenty seven micro-organisms, many of them being well known as pathogenic. Considering his own results in connection with those of Frankland and others, as regards the nitrifying power of organisms, he concludes that no one who has worked with isolated bacteria has obtained more than a mere trace of nitric or nitrous acid in ammoniacal solutions. On the other hand, the mixed organisms present in arable soil produce distinct and complete nitrification in ammoniacal liquids containing twenty-five parts of nitrogen in the million. ⁻ Of twenty-five organisms studied, sixteen reduced nitrates with considerable vigor, and seven were entirely destitute of reducing capacity. The reduction was from nitrates to nitrites, and not to nitrogen. (Journ. Chem. Soc., LIII, 727.)

The chemistry of fish.—Atwater has published in the form of a preliminary notice the results of his elaborate analyses of the flesh of American food-fishes. One hundred and twenty-two specimens belonging to fifty-two species were examined, together with two European fishes, and an account of the methods of analysis is included in the statement. The results are given in the form of elaborate tables which are not suitable for abstraction. (Amer. Chem. Journ., IX, 421, and X, 1.)

MINERALOGY FOR 1887 AND 1888.

By EDWARD S. DANA.

GENERAL WORK IN MINERALOGY.

The wide interest felt during the last few years in the general subject of microscopical mineralogy, and the advance made in this field, are well shown by the number of new works that have recently appeared which are devoted to this line of research. It has been in the allied department of petrography that the work has been most actively done and the progress made, but the result has been to bring about a most important advance in the instruments and methods of study applied to mineralogy proper. The works of Rosenbusch and Zirkel, (1873,) were the pioneers in this direction, and since then the workers have been many and the progress made rapid. A second edition of the work of Rosenbusch was published in 1885, and now an English edition [1] has been given to students in this country and England by J. P. Iddings. In this translation the original work appears in somewhat abridged form, but not so much so as to diminish its value, while making it rather more convenient of use. All that is essential has been retained, including the large number of fine plates of microphotographs. Another work of similar character is that of Rutley. [2] The methods of studying minerals with the microscope are given systematically, with the characters especially of those species which enter into the formation of rocks. A book of rather wider scope and more profound character is that of Michel-Lévy and Lacroix. [3] The first author has already made important contributions in this field, and the Mineralogie micrographique by Fouqué and M.-Lévy (1879) is one of the most exhaustive memoirs that has been published. In the present volume the author introduces some of the results of his former labors; for instance, on the variation of the

---

[1] Microscopical Physiography of Rock-making Minerals, and aid to the Microscopical study of Rocks, by H. Rosenbusch. Translated and abridged for use in schools and colleges, by Joseph P. Iddings. 333 pp., 26 plates. New York, 1886. J. Wiley & Sons.

[2] Rock-forming Minerals, by Frank Rutley, F. G. S. 252 pp. London, 1888. Thomas Murby.

[3] Les Minéraux des Roches: (1) Application des méthodes minéralogiques et chimiques à leur étude microscopique, par A. Michel-Lévy; (2) Données physiques et optiques, par A. Michel-Lévy et Alf. Lacroix. 334 pp. Paris, 1888. Baudry & Cie.

angle of extinction in crystal sections cut in different directions, and other related subjects. The first part is thus theoretical ; the second gives a concise summary of the characters, chiefly physical, of rock-making mineral species. This part of the work contains many original observations by the authors of the optical constants, indices of refraction, absorption, and so on. Rosenbusch has also issued a set of tables giving in compact form the microscopical characters of all important minerals;[1] these will be found of great practical use by the worker in this line of research.

Related to the works mentioned is that of Teall on British Petrography, an extended and well illustrated volume, but too exclusively petrographical to call for more than simple mention. Other important petrographical works are those of Rosenbusch (Die massigen Gesteine, 1887) and Roth (Allg. und chemische Geologie, vol. 2, 1887).

The work of Goldschmidt[2] on Crystallography and the forms of crystalline minerals is without question the most extended which has ever been undertaken in this field. The author has developed a new system of crystallographic notation, simply related to those in common use, and designed to exhibit especially the relations of the forms of a crystal as given in the projection. In connection he has developed a method of calculation adapted to this notation, and further has given a thorough discussion of the various systems that have been in use from the earliest time down. This forms the first half of the first volume, after which begins the work proper, namely, the catalogue for each species of all the planes that have been observed with the literature, the letters and other notation of different authors, the equations for transformation, and so on. The species are arranged alphabetically, and the whole work is to consist of three large volumes. The working mineralogist will profit to no small degree from the author's labors, though the fact that neither figures nor angles are given, and that theoretical considerations have often led to a variation from the commonly accepted method for the orientation of the crystals of a species will restrict its usefulness.

Several volumes on local mineralogy have recently appeared. The Russian Mineralogy[3] of von Kokscharof has now entered upon its tenth volume, and although the veteran author celebrated his fiftieth anniversary of active service in 1887 he is still carrying forward his labors with vigor. The present state of knowledge in regard to the mineralogy of India is well presented by F. R. Mallet,[4] in a volume devoted to this

[1] Hülfstabellen zur mikroskopischen Mineralbestimmung in Gesteinen. Stuttgart, 1888.

[2] Index der Krystallformen der Mineralien, vol. I, 1886; vol. II, Nos. 1-4, 1888; vol. III, Nos. 1-3, 1888.

[3] Materialien zur Mineralogie Russlands, von N. von Kokscharow, 1888, vol. 10, pp. 1-224,

[4] A Manual of the Geology of India, part IV, Mineralogy (mainly non-economic), by F. R. Mallet, 179 pp., with 4 plates. Calcutta, 1888.

subject, and forming volume IV of the Geology of India. Except in certain special directions, the mineral wealth of this country is but partially developed, and much remains to be done, particularly on the scientific side. Progress will be stimulated and directed by this excellent volume. A large volume has been prepared by Liversidge[1] on the mineralogy of New South Wales, being an extension of earlier publications, by the author on the same subject. It is a handsomely published work, with a large colored map of that part of Australia, and giving a detailed scientific account of the local mineralogy. The paragraphs on the discovery and occurrence of gold, diamonds, tin ore, and similar subjects will be consulted with especial interest.

The volumes on the mineral resources of the United States for 1886 and 1887,[2] the fourth and fifth of the series, are too well known in character and scope to need to be described at length. They have been edited by David T. Day, with the assistance of various persons in special fields, and present very fully the present state of the development of the economic minerals and mineral industries of this country. The tabulated list of localities at which useful minerals are being and have been mined, prepared by A. Williams, and notes on localities of precious stones, by G. F. Kunz, may be mentioned as of particular mineralogical interest.

A mineralogical report for California for 1886 has been issued by H. G. Hanks, and two other volumes for 1887 and 1888, by William Irelan, jr. Scacchi has published a list of the large number of species that have been identified or newly discovered—and in great part by himself—at the wonderfully active laboratory of Vesuvius. A list of the large number of minerals from the neighborhood of New York City has been published by the late B. F. Chamberlin. Some other mineralogical works to be noted are the following: The Manual of Mineralogy and Lithology, fourth edition (1887), by James D. Dana. The Grundriss der Edelstein-kunde, by Paul Groth (1887). A Chapter in the History of Meteorites, by the late Walter Flight (1887). The Mineral Physiology and Physiography, by T. Sterry Hunt, presents the author's theoretical views as to mineral classification and relationship. A new mineralogical periodical was commenced in 1887, called Rivista di Mineralogia e Cristallografia Italiana, edited by R. Panebianco, at Padua.

CRYSTALLOGRAPHY AND PHYSICAL MINERALOGY.

Some important additions have been made to our knowledge of the species which fall in the tetartohedral divisions of the hexagonal system. Cinnabar, which was long ago shown by Des Cloizeaux to belong to the

---

[1] The Minerals of New South Wales, etc., by A. Liversidge, 326 pp., with a map. London, 1888. Trübner & Co.

[2] Mineral Resources of the United States, calendar year 1886, 813 pp., issued in 1887; calendar year 1887, 832 pp., issued in 1888. David T. Day. U. S. Geological Survey. J. W. Powell, Director.

trapezohedral-tetartohedral division like quartz, with the consequent power of circular polarization, has been recently studied by A. Schmidt,[1] and later by H. Traube,[2] on the morphological side. The material examined was from Mount Avala, near Belgrade, in Servia, and the crystals have afforded a considerable number of new forms, especially among the trapezohedrous. These trapezohedral planes are largely developed, thus exhibiting this character of the species. On the rhombohedral side the tetartohedral species, tourmaline,[3] dolomite,[4] and phenacite[5] have been studied by Ramsay, Becke, and Penfield, respectively. The tetartohedral character of tourmaline was shown in 1871 by the Russian mineralogist, Jerofeieff, who published a long paper upon the Russian species. This paper, however seems to have been for the most part overlooked by later writers. Solly (1884) describes a crystal from Pierrepont, New York, with tetartohedral development of planes, and Ramsay shows that there is no question in regard to this point. The crystals examined by him were from Ramfos and Snarum, in Norway, and exhibited the tetartohedral character in the distribution of the planes and the asymmetric form of the etching figures.

Becke's monograph upon dolomite is an important contribution to our knowledge of that species, giving a number of new forms, chiefly of the tetartohedral character, that is rhombohedrous of the third series, and establishing the right or left handed character of all these planes, as has not been attempted before. He also describes the vicinal planes, and the various methods of twinning with a large number of figures. Other crystals of dolomite, also exhibiting these tetartohedral forms have been described by A. Sella in a paper upon crystals of the rare magnesium fluoride, sellaite,[6] named in honor of his father Quintino Sella.

The phenacite crystals of Mount Antero, Colorado, are described and figured by Penfield; they are interesting since a tetartohedral form, that is, a rhombohedron of the third series is often the predominating form and terminates the crystals sometimes alone. An earlier account of these crystals was given by Des Cloizeaux. A somewhat related subject is the crystallization of the two ruby silvers, pyrargyrite and proustite, studied exhaustively on the historical side a few years ago by Rethwisch and now receiving new contributions from the original work of Miers.[7] He decides upon slightly different angles for the fundamental rhombohedron from those of Rethwisch (viz, 71° 22′ pyrargyrite, 72° 12′ proustite) and questions his conclusion as to the relation of this angle to the composition. The study of the fine series of specimens in the British Museum has enabled him to add upwards of twenty new forms

[1] Zeitscher. Krvst., vol. XIII, 433.
[2] Ibid., vol. XIV, 563.
[3] Bihang Svensk. Vet. Ak. Handl., vol. XII, p. 2.
[4] Min. petr. Mitth., vol. X, 93.
[5] Amer. Journ. Sci., vol. XXXIII, 130, XXXVI, 320.
[6] Mem. Accad. Lincei, vol. IV, read November 13, 1887.
[7] Mineralogical Magazine, 1888, vol. VIII, p. 37.

to the already long catalogue for the two species, and others that are not certain. He also distinguishes between the characteristic forms of pyrargyrite and proustite, not often attempted before, and develops the hemimorphic nature of the two species.

A study of some specimens of polianite from Platten, Bohemia,[1] has led to the interesting conclusion that the anhydrous MnO_2 crystallizes in the tetragonal system and is isomorphous with rutile (TiO_2) cassiterite (SnO_2) and zircon (SiO_2, ZrO_2). The fact that the hard, gray manganese ore, polianite, was distinct from the soft pyrolusite was long ago insisted upon by Breithaupt, and his view is thus fully sustained. Flint has extended his earlier crystallographic studies and has given valuable contributions on scolecite, braunite, hausmannite, and other species from Sweden. The crystals of rutile,[2] apatite, and beryl, of Alexander County, North Carolina, are described by Hidden and Washington and shown to have a number of interesting features. Some of the species of the chrysolite group have been studied by Bauer[3] and the relation between their forms and composition brought out. The species especially considered are chrysolite, hyalosiderite, and the magnesium silicate forsterite. Crystals of kaolinite,[4] rarely obtained in a form allowing of study, have been described by Allan Dick and their form measured and figured by H. Miers. A monoclinic parameter is assigned to them, viz:

$$a : b : c := 0.5748 : 1 : 4.7267; \ \beta = 83° \ 11'$$

The kaolinite from Colorado[5] was recently referred to the triclinic system of Reusch on the basis of an optical examination. The subject of the crystallization of ullmannite has been reviewed by Klein,[6] and it is shown that both kinds crystallizing in the pyritohedral and tetrahedral divisions of the isometric system are identical in composition, as proved by analyses by Jannasch. An inaugural address by Herschenz gives an account of the Harz barite, with a number of new forms. Düsing[7] adds many other new planes for crystals of various localities; many of them seem to be vicinal planes. The inexhaustible species epidote has been taken up anew, the Swedish mineral by Flink,[8] that from the Austrian Alps by Gränzer,[9] and again by Zimanyi,[10] and that from Elba[11] by Artini. The result of these memoirs is to add a number of new forms to the already very long list. The absorption phenomena of epidote have been studied by Ramsay.[12] Becke[13] continues a former line of investigation in describing the etching figures on pyrite, sphalerite,

---

[1] Amer. Journ. Sci., 1888, vol. XXXV, 243.

[2] Ibid., 1887, vol. XXXIII, p. 501.

[3] Jahrb. Min., 1887, vol I, 1.

[4] Min. Mag., 1888, vol. VIII, p. 15.

[5] Jahrb. Min., 1887, vol. II, 70.

[6] Ibid., 169.

[7] Zeitschr. Kryst., vol. XIV, 481.

[8] Bib. Svensk.Vet. Ak. Handl vol. XII, pt. 2.

[9] Mem. Accad. Lincic, 1887, vol. IV, November 13.

[10] Min. petr. Mittb., vol. IX, 361.

[11] Földtani Közlöny, vol. XVIII, 443.

[12] Zeitschr. Kryst., vol XIII, 97.

[13] Min. petr. Mitth, vol. IX, p. 1.

galena, and magnetite. Of more general physical character may be
mentioned the work of Hastings[1] on the double refraction of calcite;
remarkable as of a higher grade of accuracy than any experiments of
the same kind before made, and which prove the law of Huyghens to
be true to less than one part in five hundred thousand. In other words,
it is concluded that there is no known method by which an error in it,
if it is not absolutely true, can be discovered. Bäckstrom[2] has contributed a paper on the thermo electricity of crystals. An excellent discussion of the molecular structure of crystals has been given by Groth, in
his address before the Munich Academy. A paper read by J. W. Judd[3]
before the Mineralogical Society of Great Britain is also an interesting
discussion of the development of a lamellar structure in quartz crystals
by mechanical means. Abstracts of a number of other papers of 1887–
'88 referring more or less closely to mineral physics are given in Groth's
Zeitschrift, vol. xv, p. 298 *et seq.*

CHEMICAL MINERALOGY.

Riggs has investigated anew the composition of tourmaline,[4] and with
improved methods has made a series of analyses, twenty in all, of the
widely different varieties from typical localities. The following ratio is
established: $Si : B : R^1 : O = 1 : \frac{1}{2} : \frac{2}{3} : 5$ and the formula $R_9BO_22SiO_4$
where R^1 is the univalent equivalent of the bases with the oxygen-excess
incorporated in an $Al=O$ group. If an $O-H$ group is assumed the formula is written, $R_{10}BO_22SiO_4$. The typical kinds are then

Lithia tourmaline.....$12SiO_2$. $3B_2O_3$ $4H_2O$. $8Al_2O_1$. $2(Na,Li)_2O$.
Iron tourmaline ......$12SiO_2$. $3B_2O_1$. $4H_2O_3$. $7Al_2O_1$. $4FeO.Na_2O$.
Magnesia tourmaline..$12SiO_2$. $3B_2O_1$. $4H_2O$. $5Al_2O_3$. $2\frac{2}{3}MgO.\frac{4}{3}Na_2O$.

Wülfing[5] has made the analyses of Riggs the basis of a series of calculations designed to throw light upon the composition. He concludes
that the various varieties can be regarded as isomorphous mixtures in
different proportions of the molecules

$$Si_{12}B_6Al_{16}Na_4H_8O_{63} \text{ and } Si_{12}B_6Al_{10}Mg_{12}H_6O_{63}.$$

Clarke has added some analyses[6] to those previously published of
different kinds of mica, including a muscovite from North Carolina, and
a number of iron micas from different points. The same author has
studied the nickel ores of Oregon,[7] which are similar to those of New
Caledonia in composition. He concludes that the parent mineral was
a nickel-bearing olivine. Whitfield[8] contributes a series of analyses of
some borates, colemanite, ulexite, ludwigite, axinite, etc., using recent im-

[1] Amer. Jour. Sci., 1888, vol. xxxv, 60.
[2] Œfversigt. k. Vet. Akad. Förhandl.. No. 8, 1888.
[3] Min. Mag., 1888, vol. viii, 1.
[4] Amer. Journ. Sci., 1888, vol. xxxv, 35.
[5] Min. petr. Mitth., 1888, vol. x, 161.
[6] Amer. Journ. Sci., vol. xxxiv, 133.
[7] *Ibid.*, vol. xxxx, 483.
[8] Amer. Jour. Sci., 1887, vol. xxxiv, p. 281.

proved methods in determining the boron. Penfield and Sperry[1] have also worked in the same line, and their analyses of howlite prove that it is in fact a silicoborate, not a mixture as had been suggested before, and having the composition $H_5Ca_2B_5SiO_{14}$.

Jannasch[2] has analyzed a series of heulandites from different localities and proved that they contain considerable amounts of strontium (up to 3.6 per cent.) which must have been overlooked by earlier analysts. Linck[3] has made an examination of some iron sulphates from Chili on both the chemical and crystallographic side, adding a new species (quenstedtite, see beyond) and also new points about copiapite, coquimbite and roemerite, halotrichite and fibroferrite. The work of Frenzel and Darapsky in the same direction is mentioned on a later page.

Eakins[4] gives descriptions and analyses of two sulphantimonites from Colorado, one of which is a freieslebenite containing only lead; the other has the composition $3PbS.2Sb_2S_3$. An inaugural dissertation by Carl Hersch is devoted to the discussion of the water in the zeolites with numerous analyses. Another by Vogel gives a number of analyses of vesuvianite from different localities, without, however, attempting to establish a new formula. Still another by Noelting discusses the relations of the "Schalenblende" to the ordinary isometric sphalerite and the hexagonal wurtzite. He finds that wurtzite is generally present, and probably in many cases has been formed by molecular rearrangement from the original sphalerite.

An important series of papers by Julien[5] discusses at length the relations of the different minerals coming under the general head of iron pyrites, pyrite, marcasite, and pyrrhotite, especially as regards their occurrence together. The varying physical characters of pyrite, specific gravity, color, and especially resistance to change, are found to be due to the presence of marcasite—the less stable compound—with it in different proportions. This is shown to have important applications as affecting the durability of building stones containing iron pyrites. The alteration of pyroxene into serpentine has been minutely studied by Merrill[6] for the locality at Montville, New Jersey. The jade articles in the Washington Museum have been studied chemically and microscopically by Clarke and Merrill.[7]

The synthetic formation of minerals has been further studied by some of the French chemists, who have already done such important work in this direction. Among the various contributions in this field are the formation of crocoite, celestite, anglesite, hydrocerussite, by Bourgeois; of pharmacolite, by Dufét; of zincite, franklinite, magnetite, tephroite, rhodonite, wollastonite, barite, celestite, anhydrite, pyrolusite, by Gorgeu; quartz and tridymite, by Kroustchoff; of pyro-

---

[1] *Ibid*, p. 220.
[2] Ber. Chem. Ges., Berlin, vol. xx, 346.
[3] Zeitschr. Kryst., vol. xv, 1.
[4] Amer. Jour. Sci., 1880, vol. xxxvi, 450.
[5] Ann. New York Acad. Sci.
[6] Proc. U. S. Nat. Museum, p. 105, 1888.
[7] *Ibid.*, p. 115.

morphite, mimetite, campylite, by Michel; of pyrochroite, by de Schulten. Papers upon the above subjects will be found in volumes IX and X of the Bulletin of the French Mineralogical Society.

A paper of especial interest on this class of topics is that of Doelter[1] on the synthesis of the micas by fusing together various silicates with metallic fluorides. Thus the fusion of an aluminous hornblende or augite with sodium or magnesium fluoride yielded a magnesia mica (meroxene); from an aluminous augite, with little iron, a mica resembling phlogopite was obtained, and from glaucophane a magnesia mica containing a considerable amount of soda. By fusing together the silicate $K_2Al_2Si_2O_8$ with potassium or sodium fluoride in potassium fluosilicate, muscovite was obtained. With magnesium silicate a mica near phlogopite was the result, and if iron silicate was also used a brown mica near meroxene was obtained. The same potassium silicate, with lithium silicate and potassium or sodium fluoride, yielded a mica with large axial angle. When pennine was fused with potassium silicate a product resembling phlogopite was the result; a magnesium garnet under like conditions, a meroxene mica low in iron. Andalusite fused with the fluorides of potassium, of silicon, and aluminium yielded a muscovite, and by the addition of lithia and iron, a mica near zinnwaldite. From vesuvianite mica was seldom obtained, the common result being scapolite. The author also describes his results in obtaining the calcium silicate, wollastonite, by fusing together $CaSiO_3$ with calcium and sodium fluorides. There have also been recent contributions to the same subject by Hautefeuille[2] and by Kroustchoff.[3]

NEW MINERAL OCCURRENCES.

A point of much interest is the discovery of a diamond-like form of carbon in the meteoric stone of Novo-Urei, Penza, Russia, which fell September 22, 1886. This is described by Jerofeieff and Latschinoff.[4] The meteorite was not unusual in general appearance, having a dark-gray color and consisted chiefly of olivine, augite, and nickeliferous iron. In the course of the analysis, however, it was found that from 2 to $2\frac{1}{2}$ per cent. was not attacked by acids; nearly two-thirds of this proved to consist of amorphous carbon, and the remainder in the form of light-gray grains was also nearly pure carbon. These grains had a specific gravity of 3.1, and a hardness sufficient to scratch corundum, so that the conclusion was reached that they were true diamond, perhaps in a massive form like the carbonado. The occurrence of graphitic carbon in isometric form in an Australian iron is mentioned under the description of cliftonite beyond.

The rare aluminium silicate, dumortierite, remarkable for its fine blue

---

[1] Min. petr. Mitth., 1888, vol. x, 67.
[2] C. R., vol. civ., 508.
[3] Min. petr. Mitth., vol. ix, 55.
[4] Verhandl. Russ. Min. Ges. at St. Petersburg, vol. xxiv, 263.

color and strong pleochroism has been noted at a number of localities since its original discovery, near Lyons; these are Brignais, department of the Rhone, France; Wolfshau, in Silesia; near Tvedestrand, in Norway; Harlem, New York, and Clip, Yuma County, Arizona. The equally rare mineral bertrandite, a beryllium silicate, first found near Nantes, has since been identified at Pisek, Bohemia, by Scharizer,[1] and in Colorado with the beryl and phenacite of Mount Antero by Penfield.[2] This last occurrence of phenacite deserves special note, since it has added materially to our knowledge of the species as noted before. Another new locality of phenacite has also been discovered in the region of. Stoneham, Maine,[3] a few miles west, just across the State line in New Hampshire, in North Chatham.

Låvenite, a mineral recently (1885) described, from the island Låven, on the Norwegian coast, has been identified at several widely separated localities, thus in the elæolite syenite of Brazil, and the foyaite of West Africa. Attention has been called by Judd[4] to the occurrence of leucite in Australia, and G. H. Williams[5] shows that the rare calcium titanate perofskite occurs in the serpentine of Syracuse, New York. Kunz[6] describes a variety of oligoclase remarkable for its glassy transparent character; it is from Bakersville, North Carolina. It has been analyzed by Clarke, and later by Penfield,[7] and the latter finds further that it is abnormal in its optical character, giving an extinction angle on the base of $+40°$ instead of $+1$.

The Mammoth mine, Utah, has recently afforded a series of rare copper arseniates, most of which had not before been known from this country These were first noted by Richard Pearce, and since have been described by Hillebrand[8] on the chemical, and Washington on the physical side. Among the species identified are olivenite, clinoclasite, pharmacosiderite, mixite, erinite, tyrolite, chalcophyllite, brochantite, scorodite. Scorodite is also shown by Hague[9] to be a hot spring deposit in the Yellowstone Park.

Crystals of rhodochrosite, of a beautiful pink color, and perfectly transparent, have been obtained from the John Reed mine, Lake County, Colorado; it is perhaps the finest occurrence of the species. The western United States have also recently yielded fine specimens of azurite, cuprite, malachite, vanadinite, wulfenite, from Arizona; hauksite, colemanite, trona, from California, and many others.

The recent demand for some of the rare chemical elements for technical purposes has led to the discovery that the supposed relatively rare minerals, zircon and monazite, occur on a large scale in the rocks and soil of North Carolina. During six months in 1887–1888, no less than 25

[1] Zeitschr. Kryst., vol. XIV, 33.
[2] Amer. Journ. Sci., vol. XXXVI, 52.
[3] Kunz, Amer. Journ. Sci., vol XXXVI, 222, 472.
[4] Min. Mag., vol VII, 194.
[5] Amer. Jour. Sci., vol. XXXIV, p. 137.
[6] Amer. Jour. Sci , vol. XXXVI, 222.
[7] Ibid., p. 324.
[8] Amer. Jour. Sci., vol. XXXV, 298.
[9] Ibid, vol. XXXIV, 171.

tons of zircons were obtained from the Green River mines, Henderson County, North Carolina; the mining was carried on under contract with W. E. Hidden. The same mineralogist has described[1] the rare yttrium phosphate, xenotime, from a number of new localities in North Carolina, and also from New York (Manhattan Island).

Some of the most important mineral discoveries of the past two years are contained in the following descriptions of new species.

NEW MINERALS.

Amarantite.—See Hohmannite.

Arseniopleite.—A new manganese arseniate, belonging to a group of minerals to which a considerable number of new species have been added recently. It occurs in cleavable masses or nodules, often forming small veins, with rhodonite and hausmannite, in a crystalline limestone at the Sjö mine, Grythyttan, Sweden. Its color is reddish brown. It has been investigated optically by Bertrand and found to be uniaxial with nega-tive double refraction, and probably is to be referred to the rhombo-hedral system. An analysis yielded the following:

As_2O_5	Sb_2O_3	MnO	Fe_2O_3	PbO	CaO	MgO	H_2O	Cl.
44.98	trace	28.25	3.68	4.48	8.11	3.10	4.54	trace = 97.14.

Deducting impurities and correcting it according to the state of oxi-dation of the manganese it becomes Mn_2O_3 7.80, MnO 21.25. (Described by L. J. Igelström in Bull Soc. Min., 1888, vol. XI, 39.)

Auerlite.—A new thorium mineral of peculiar interest because it seems to occupy an intermediate position between the silicates and phos-phates. It was discovered by W. E. Hidden, in Henderson County, North Carolina, occurring in disintegrated granitic rocks associated with zircon and implanted upon it in parallel position. It is found in pris-matic tetragonal crystals like zircon in form and angle. It has a pale yellow to orange or deep red color. The hardness is 2.5 to 3, and the specific gravity 4.42 to 4.77, the orange-red crystals having the higher density. The luster is wax-like and it is brittle and easily crumbled. An analysis by J. B. Mackintosh gave the following results:

SiO_2	P_2O_5	ThO_2	Fe_2O_3	CaO	MgO	Al_2O_3 etc.	H_2O,CO_2
7.64	7.46	70.13	1.38	0.49	0.29	1.10	11.21 = 99.70

The water and carbon dioxide are present in about the ratio of 10: 1. Assuming the homogeneity of the material, which its appearance seemed to justify, the mineral is a hydrous silicate and phosphate of thorium. It will be remembered that the cerium phosphate, monazite, uniformly contains more or less thorium silicate about which there has been some difference of opinion as to whether it is an impurity or not; this new mineral throws light upon the question. It is named after Dr. Carl Auer von Welsbach. (Described by Hidden and Mackintosh in Amer. Journ. Sci., 1888, XXXVI, 461.)

---

[1] Amer. Journ. Sci., 1888, vol. XXXVI, 380.

Awaruite.—A kind of nickeliferous native iron found in the drift of the Gorge River, which empties into the Awarua, or Big Bay, on the west coast of the middle island of New Zealand. It is believed to have been derived from a peridotite, now altered largely into serpentine, and is associated with gold, platinum, cassiterite, chromite, magnetite. Its hardness is about 5, and the specific gravity 8.1. The composition is expressed by the formula $FeNi_2$, as shown by an analysis by W. Skey, viz:

Ni	Fe	Co	S	SiO$_2$
67.63	31.02	0.70	0.22	0.43 $=100$

This terrestrial nickeliferous iron is closely allied to the similar meteoric mineral which has been called octibbehite, found in Oktibbeha, County, Mississippi. (Described by G. H. F. Ulrich in Amer. Journ. Sci., 1887, XXXIII, 244.)

Barkevikite, etc.—In a preliminary account of the results of an extended study of the minerals of the augite-syenite and elæolite-syenite veins of Southern Norway, W. C. Brögger has given brief accounts of a number of new species. Full descriptions are promised later. The names of these are, *barkevikite, calciothorite, melanocerite, nordenskiöldine, rosenbuschite.* They are characterized briefly as follows:

Barkevikite is a mineral belonging to the amphibole group, and most closely related to arfvedsonite; it is distinct, however, in optical characters.

Calciothorite is a hydrous silicate of thorium and calcium, and it is inferred, as seems very probable, that it is an alteration product of an original thorium silicate (ThO_2SiO_2) isomorphous with zircon. Thorite, orangite, eucrasite, freyalite, are other hydrous silicates that probably have had a similar origin.

Melanocerite is a complex silicate of the cerium metals, yttrium and calcium, with other substances in small amounts, including 3 per cent. boron trioxide. It occurs in dark-brown crystals, belonging to the rhombohedral-system, and tabular in habit.

Nordenskiöldine, named after the Swedish mineralogist and explorer, A. E. Nordenskiöld, is a mineral of remarkable composition, viz, a borate of tin and calcium, $CaO.SnO_2.B_2O_3$. It has a sulphur-yellow color; its hardness is 5.5 to 6, and its specific gravity 4.20. It appears in tabular rhombohedral crystals.

Rosenbuschite, named after Professor Rosenbusch, of Heidelberg, is a silicate of calcium and sodium with zirconium, titanium, and lanthanum in small amount. It belongs to the monoclinic system and its crystals are near wollastonite and pectolite in angle, and it is accordingly called a zirconium-pectolite. The color is orange-gray; the hardness is 5 to 6, and the specific gravity 3.30.

This account is given in the Geol. Förening Förhandlingar (Stockholm), 1887, vol. IX, 247, and an abstract is given in Groth's Zeitschrift, 1888, vol. XV, 103. In the latter place hiortdahlite is mentioned as another new mineral from the same region but not described.

Barysil.—A new lead silicate from the Harstig mine, Pajsberg, Sweden. It is referred to the hexagonal system, has basal cleavage, white color, hardness equal to 3, and a specific gravity of 6.11 to 6.55. An analysis afforded:

SiO_2	PbO	MnO	. FeO	CaO	MgO	Ign
16.98	77.84	3.49	0.16	0.41	0.58	0.66=100.12

The formula is accordingly $3PbO.2SiO_2$. It occurs in iron ore with calcite, yellow garnet, tephroite, and galena. The name has reference to its high specific gravity. (Described by A. Sjögren and Lundström in the Œfversigt Vet. Akad. Förhandlingar, 1888, XLV, 7.)

Belonesite.—The study of a mass of ancient volcanic rock enveloped in the Vesuvian lava of 1872 has led to the discovery of two species to which Scacchi has given the names belonesite (belonesia) and criphiolite (crifiolite). Belonesite, as the name suggests, occurs in needlelike crystals. These are white and transparent, and are referred to the tetragonal system. The material was insufficient for an analysis, but qualitative tests led to the conclusion that it is a molybdate of magnesium.

Criphiolite occurs in small tabular crystals belonging to the monoclinic system. They are covered by apatite so as to be concealed by it, whence the name given to the species. The color is honey-yellow; the specific gravity 2.674. An analysis gave: P_2O_5 48.91, MgO 33.58, CaO 14.60. Loss 2.91=100. The examination showed that fluorine was probably present, and the amount is estimated as nearly equal to 7 per cent. The mineral is hence near wagnerite in composition. (Described by A. Scacchi in Mem. Accad. Napoli, 1887, vol. I, No. 5.)

Bementite.—A new manganese silicate from the prolific locality at Franklin Furnace, New Jersey. It occurs in stellate aggregations, having a foliated structure and in aspect closely resembling some pyrophyllite. The color is a pale grayish-yellow; it is soft and friable; the specific gravity is 2.981. An analysis yielded:

SiO_2	MnO	FeO	ZnO	MgO	H_2O
39.00	42.12	[3 75]	2.86	3.83	8.44 = 100

This yields the formula $2(H_2,Mn)O,SiO_2$. It is found that the water goes off at a temperature above 200°. Bementite is named after Mr. Clarence S. Bement, of Philadelphia, by G. A. Koenig. (Proceedings Acad. Nat. Sci., Philadelphia, 1887, p. 311.)

Beryllonite.—A new beryllium phosphate from Stoneham, Maine. A preliminary description announces that it occurs in colorless crystals and cleavage fragments. The crystals are highly modified, and belong to the orthorhombic system, with a prismatic angle of about 120°. The hardness is 5.5; the specific gravity 2. A qualitative analysis by H. L. Wells shows it to be an anhydrous phosphate of beryllium and sodium.

The same region has afforded a number of rare minerals, including the beryllium phosphate, herderite, and the beryllium silicate, phenacite. (Described by E. S. Dana in Amer. Journ. Sci., 1888, vol. XXXVI, p. 290).

Bückingite.—Announced by G. Linck as a new iron sulphate from Tierra Amarilla, near Copiapó, Chili. A further study has proved it to be identical with roemerite, and in a later paper he describes it under this name. The material has allowed of a more perfect crystallographic and chemical investigation than has hitherto been possible. (Jahrb. für Min., Vol. I, 213, 1888; Zeitschr. für Kryst., 1888, vol. XV, p. 22).

Calciothorite.—See Barkevikite.

Calciostrontianite.—A name given by Cathrein to a calcium-bearing strontianite from Brixlegg, Tyrol, and corresponding to the mineral "from Massachusetts" called by Thomson in 1836 emmonite, after Prof. E. Emmons.

Cliftonite.—A form of graphitic carbon found in the meteoric iron of Youndegin, West Australia (discovered 1884). It occurs in minute cubic crystals imbedded in the iron, and separated by dissolving the iron in acid. The average thickness of the larger crystals is one-hundredth of an inch. The cubic planes predominate, but dodecahedral faces were also noted. They are black in color; the hardness is 2.5, and the specific gravity 2.12. They were proved chemically to be pure carbon, and they resemble graphite in most of the characters except form and greater hardness. These observations are of interest in view of the recent discovery of carbon, having the hardness of the diamond in a meteoric stone (noted above), and also the earlier observations of Haidinger on isometric crystals of carbon, supposed to be pseudomorph after pyrite in the Arva iron. Cliftonite is named after Prof. R. B. Clifton, of Oxford, by L. Fletcher, in the Mineralogical Magazine, 1887, vol. VII, p. 121.

Cristobalite.—A form of silica in minute octahedal crystals found at the tridymite locality of Cerro San Cristobal, near Pachuca, Mexico. They are associated with tridymite in cavities in andesite. It is not certain whether they represent an allotropic form of silica, or as seems more probable a pseudomorph after some mineral in isometric octahedrons. A cubic form of silica (melanophlogite) was found by Lasaulx on the sulphur of Girgenti. Cristobalite is described by G. vom Rath in the Jahrb. Min., 1887, vol. I, 198.

Dahllite.—A mineral of remarkable composition, since it contains both calcium phosphate and calcium carbonate; it is in fact the first case in which a phosphate and carbonate occur in the same species. The natural suggestion that the carbonate is present as impurity only, in the form of calcite, is regarded by the describers as inapplicable, since their microscopic examination convinced them of its homogeneity. Dahllite occurs as a rather thin crust, having a rounded lustrous surface and a fibrous structure, the fibers being perpendicular to the underlying base of massive reddish apatite. In color it is pale yellowish white or reddish yellow; it is translucent and resembles chalcedony. It is optically, uniaxial and negative. The hardness is about 5 and the specific gravity 3.053. An analysis yielded the following results:

P_2O_5	CO_2	CaO	FeO	Na_2O	K_2O	H_2O
38.44	6.29	53.00	0.79	0.89	0.11	1.37 = 100.89.

This leads to the formula $4\,Ca_3\,P_2O_8 + 2\,Ca\,CO_3 + H_2O$. The locality where it has been found, though only very sparingly, is the apatite region in the parish of Bamle, Norway. Named after —— by W. C. Brögger and Backström in the Œfversigt Vet.-Akad. Förhandlingar, Stockholm, 1887, p. 493.

Dihydro-thenardite.—A sodium sulphate, allied to thenardite, but, as the name suggests, containing two molecules of water. It crystallizes in the monoclinic system. It forms a thin bed on the shores of Lake Gori, Tiflis, Russia. (Described by Markovnikoff in Journ. Russ. Phys. Chem., and an abstract in the Berichte deutsch. Chem. Ges. Berlin, 1887, p. 546).

Edisonite.—A rare mineral consisting of titanium dioxide and (if distinct from rutile) the fourth form in which this oxide is known to occur in nature. The original specimen was found in 1879 by W. E. Hidden at the Whistnant gold mine, Polk County, North Carolina, in the concentrations of placer washings. It was associated with zircon, xenotime, rutile, monazite, and a number of other species. It has a bronze-yellow or golden-brown color, a resinous to adamantine luster and a yellowish white streak. The hardness is about 6 and the specific gravity 4.26 to 4.28. The symmetry of the form is that of an orthorhombic crystal and the crystallographic study by Des Cloizeaux (Bull. Soc. Min., 1886, vol. IX) shows that it does not vary very widely from the tetragonal type, and in angle bears a certain relation to rutile; he calls it, in fact, a dimorphous form of rutile. A qualitative examination by Damour showed it to be essentially TiO_2 in composition and a more thorough analysis by Penfield, undertaken later, has confirmed this and proved the absence of all other substances except a trace of iron. Named after Mr. Thomas A. Edison, by W. E. Hidden, in Amer. Journ. Sci., October, 1888, vol. XXXVI, p. 272.

Eudidymite.—A new silicate of sodium and beryllium from the island Obere Arö in the Langesundfjord, Norway. In his preliminary account Brögger describes it as occurring in tabular monoclinic crystals having the axial ratio $a : b : c = 1.7107 : 1 : 1.1071$, $\beta = 86° 14\frac{1}{2}'$. The crystals are twins with the basal planes as twinning plane, which is also the direction of cleavage. The color is white and the luster vitreous or pearly. The hardness is 6 and the specific gravity 2.553. The optic axes lie in the plane of symmetry and the acute positive bisectrix makes an angle of 58° 30′ with the vertical axis in the acute angle of β. The first analysis by Flink made the mineral contain aluminium instead of beryllium. This was corrected by Nordenskiöld, whose analysis gave

SiO_2	BeO	Na_2O	H_2O
73.11	10.62	12.24	3.79 = 99.76.

The formula is consequently H_2O, Na_2O, BeO, $3SiO_2$, or HNa BeSi_3O_8. It is associated with analcite, natrolite, and apophyllite. (Brögger in Nyt Mag. f. Vid., vol. XXXI, 196, 187; Nordenskiöld in Geol. Förening. Förhandl. 1887, vol. IX, 434.)

Facellite or *Phacellite.*—Described by E. Scacchi (Rend. Accad. Napoli, December, 1888) as a new mineral from Monte Somma; it is, however, evidently identical with the mineral from the same locality called by Mierisch kaliophilite (Tschermak's Mineral. petrograph. Mittheilungen, vol. VIII, p. 160). It occurs in acicular crystals which are optically uniaxial, and probably belong to the hexagonal system. They are colorless, have a hardness of 6, and a specific gravity of 2.493. An analysis yielded :

SiO_2	Al_2O_3	K_2O	Na_2O
37.73	33.09	29.30	0.37 $= 1\lrcorner 0.49$.

This agrees closely with the formula $KAlSiO_4$ or K_2O, Al_2O_3, $2SiO_2$, which is that given to kaliophilite. It falls into the same group with nephelite which has an analogous formula, and also the lithium silicate eucryptite.

Griqualandite.—A name given by G. Grant Hepburn to a variety of the silicified crocidolite from South Africa; well known under the name of tiger-eye. He regards it as a silicate of iron, but it is obviously not a distinct mineral but an indefinite mixture of silica and hydrated iron sesquioxide. (Chemical News, May, 27, 1887.)

Fiedlerite.—*See* Laurionite.

Heliophyllite.—A new chloro-arsenate of lead occurring with rhodotilite (see below) at Pajsberg, Sweden. It has a pale sulphur-yellow color, and a foliated structure showing one distinct cleavage yielding thin plates. These show an acute bisectrix in the polariscope with symmetrical axial figure, from which it is safely concluded that it belongs to the orthorhombic system. The hardness is 2, the specific gravity 6.886; on the cleavage surface the luster is adamantine, elsewhere vitreous. An analysis yielded:

As_2O_3	PbO	MnO, FeO	Cl
11.69	80.70	0.54	8.00 $= 100.3$; deduct O 1.80 $= 99.13$.

This corresponds to the formula $Pb_4As_2O_7 + 2PbCl_2$, which requires As_2O_3 12.03, PbO 81.28, Cl 8.63 $= 101.94$ (deduct 1.94 $= 100$). This mineral has essentially the composition of Nordenskiöld's ecdemite from Långban, but differs in form and is probably identical with a mineral noted as occurring with ecdemite and at that time referred to the orthorhombic system. (Described by G. Flink in Œfversigt Vet. Akad. Förhandl. Stockholm, 1888, p 574.)

Hiortdahlite.—*See* Barkevikite.

Hohmannite.—In specimens of copiapite from Caracoles, Bolivia, Frenzel has identified a new iron sulphate, and perhaps two new species. The mineral, named hohmannite after the discoverer, occurs in brownish red fibrous aggregates having the optical characters of a triclinic species. The hardness is 3, and the specific gravity 2.24. Associated with it is the other iron sulphate called amarantite, which is in aggregates of minute prismatic crystals. These are orange-red in color, and in cleavage and optical characters they approach hohmannite. They are, however, less readily attacked by water. The composition of the two minerals is the same, viz: $Fe_2O_3 2SO_3 + 7H_2O$, the analyses being as follows:

	SO_3	Fe_2O_3	H_2O
Hohmannite:	33.84	35.58	30.00 = 99.50
Amarantite:	35.58	37.26	27.62 = 100.46

An earlier analysis of hohmannite gave somewhat different results but was made on less pure material. There is little doubt, therefore, that both minerals are to be united under the above name. (Min. petr. Mitth., 1887, vol. IX, 397, 428.)

Horsfordite.—A new copper antimonide, analogous to the copper arsenide, algodonite, and the silver antimonide, dyscrasite. It is a massive mineral, resembling native silver in color, with a high luster on a fresh surface but soon tarnishing. The hardness is 4 to 5, and the specific gravity 8.812. The mean of three analyses gave:

Sb	Cu
26.86	73.37 = 100.23.

The formula lies between Cu_5Sb and Cu_6Sb, the analytical results agreeing very closely with $Cu_{11}Sb_2$. It forms an extensive deposit near Mytilene in Asia Minor. It is named after Professor Horsford by A. Laist and T. H. Norton in Amer. Chem. Journ., vol. x, p. 60, 188–.

Inesite.—A hydrated silicate of manganese and calcium, probably the same mineral as that called rhodotilite by Flink (see below). It occurs in fibrous radiated forms, of a flesh-red color, in the Dillinburg region, Germany. Hardness, 6 to 7; specific gravity, 3.103. An analysis gave:

SiO_2	MnO	CaO	FeO	MgO	Al_2O_3	H_2O
43.92	38.23	8.00	0.69	0.28	0.29	8.49 = 99.90.

Described by A. Schneider in Zeitschr. deutsch. geolog. Ges., 1888, vol. XXXIX, p. 829.

Ignatieffite.—A name given by K. K. Flug to a variety of aluminite from Bachmut in southern Russia. It occurs in considerable quantity in reniform concretionary forms and though impure may have technical value. (Verh. Russ. Min. Ges., St. Petersburg, vol. XXIII, p. 116.)

Långbanite.—A mineral of unusual composition, a silico-antimonate of manganese and iron. It occurs in hexagonal prismatic crystals, often complex in form and resembling apatite. It has an iron-black color, a metallic luster and conchoidal fracture. The hardness is 6.5, the specific gravity 4.918. An analysis yielded:

Sb_2O_5	SiO_2	MnO	FeO
15.42	10.88	64.00	10.32 = 100.62.

The author regards this as corresponding to a manganese silicate (Mn_5 SiO_7) and antimonate of iron ($Fe_3Sb_2O_8$) in about the ratio of $4:1$. Långbanite is found at Långban, Sweden, in granular limestone with schefferite, magnetite, and rhodonite. (Described by G. Flink, in the Zeitschrift f. Kryst., 1887, vol. XXIII, p. 1.)

Lansfordite.—A white translucent mineral having a crystalline structure and vitreous luster. The hardness is 2.5, the specific gravity 1.54 to 1.69. An analysis by Keeley gave:

CO_2	MgO	H_2O
18.90	23.18	57.79 = 99.87.

Of the very large amount of water contained 26.3 per cent. were lost over sulphuric acid at the end of a week. The formula deduced is $3MgCO_3$, $Mg(OH)_2 + 21H_2O$. It occurs as a stalactitic growth in the anthracite coal mine of Lausford, near Tamaqua, Schuylkill County, Pennsylvania. (Described by F. A. Geuth in Zeitschr. f. Kryst., vol. XIV, p. 255.)

Laubanite.—A new zeolitic mineral resembling stilbite from the basalt, near Lauban, Silesia. It occurs in fine fibrous radiated snow-white aggregates, sometimes spherical in form. The hardness is 4.5 to 5; the specific gravity 2.23. An analysis gave:

SiO_2	Al_2O_3	FeO	CaO	MgO	H_2O
47.84	16.74	0.56	16.17	1.35	17.08 = 99.76.

This corresponds to $2CaSiO_3$, $Al_2(SiO_2)_3$, $6H_2O$, which brings it near to laumontite. (Described by H. Traube in Jahrb. Min., 1887, vol. II, 64.)

Laurionite.—A mineral of comparatively recent origin, having been formed as the result of the action of sea-water upon the ancient lead slags at Laurion, Greece, where there were lead and zinc mines worked by the Greeks before the Christian era. Laurionite occurs in white prismatic crystals related to mendipite in form, and has a hardness of 3.5. An analysis by Bodewig gave:

Pb	O	Cl	H_2O
79.38	3.17	13.77	3.68 = 100.

This gives the formula $Pb(OH)_2$, $PbCl_2$.

Associated with the laurionite is another mineral in tabular monoclinic crystals and having the same qualitative composition. It is inferred to be also an oxy-chloride of lead and has been named *Fiedlerite* after Baron Fiedler. (Described by G. vom Rath in Sitzungsber. Nied. Ges. Bonn., June 6, 1887.)

Mangano-tantalite.—A member of the tantalite-columbite group of minerals from the gold washings in the Ural. It has the form and habit of common columbite, but the specific gravity is 7.37, and the color, though nearly black, is orange-red in thin splinters. The following analysis by Blomstrand shows it to be pure tantalate of manganese:

Ta_2O_5	Nb_2O_5	SnO_2, WO_3	MnO	FeO	CaO	ign
79.81	4.47	0.67	13.88	1.17	0.17	[0.17] = 100.33.

This mineral is of interest because it shows that the same form belongs alike to the tantalate and niobate of iron and manganese, although the mineral ordinarily called tantalate does not conform to this very closely. (Described by A. Arzruni in Verb. Russ. Min. Ges., St. Petersburg, vol. XXIII, 181.)

Martinite.—A pseudomorphous mineral having the form of gypsum, but consisting chiefly of calcium phosphate; it is from the guano of the Island of Curaçoa. It appears in aggregates of minute rhombohedrons, white or yellowish in color. The specific gravity is 2.894. An analysis gave:

P_2O_5	CaO	H_2O	Organic	Insol
47.67	46.78	4.52	0.75	0.20 = 99.92.

For this the formula is $2Ca_3(PO_4)_2$, $4 CaHPO_4 + H_2O$. (Described by J. H. Kloos in Samml. Mus. Leiden, ser. 2, vol. I; abstract in Jahrb. Min., 1888, vol. I, 41 ref.)

Mazapilite.—Stated on the basis of a preliminary examination to be an arsenite of calcium and iron. It occurs in deep red to black crystals, having a hardness of 7, and a specific gravity of 3.567. It is from the mining district of Mazapil, Zacatecas, Mexico. (G. A. Koenig in Proceed. Acad. Nat. Sci., Philadelphia, July 3, 1888.)

Melanocerite.—*See* Barkevikite.

Metalonchidite.—A varity of marcasite from the St. Bernhard mine, near Hausach, Baden. It is peculiar in containing 2.7 per cent. of arsenic, with some nickel and lead, and hence approaches Breithaupt's lonchidite. (Described by F. Sandberger in Oesterreich. Zeitschr. Berg. Hütt., 1887, vol. XXXV.)

Metastibnite.—A form of antimony sulphide, like stibnite in composition, but of a bright red color, like the corresponding compound obtained in the laboratory. It occurs sparingly as an amorphous red deposit at Steamboat Springs, California. (Described by G. F. Becker in Monograph XIII, U. S. Geological Survey.)

Nordenskiöldine.—*See* Barkevikite.

Paposite.—A hydrous iron sulphate from the Union mine near Paposa, Atacama. It occurs in dark red crystalline masses, having a fibrous radiated structure. The formula obtained by Darapsky is $2Fe_2O_3$, $3SO_3 + 10H_2O$, so that it approaches closely to fibroferrite. (Bol. Soc. Min. Santiago, No. 92, October, 1887, in Jahrb. Min., 1889, vol. I, 23 ref.)

Pseudobiotite.—An alteration product of the biotite from the crystallized limestone of the Kaiserstuhl. The mean of two analyses gave:

SiO_2	TiO_2	Al_2O_3	Fe_2O_3	Mn_2O_3	MgO	K_2O	H_2O
35.91	1.115	15.18	10.85	0.89	22.80	2.90	10.77 = 100.45.

It is not to be regarded as a definite compound. (Described by A. Knop in Zeitschr. f. Kryst., 1887, vol. XII, 607.)

Rhodotilite.—A mineral occurring with heliophyllite (see above) at the

Harstig mine, Pajsberg, Sweden. It occurs in massive forms, having a columnar or fibrous structure, and shows two unequal cleavages inclined at an angle of 82½ degrees. On the basis of an optical examination it is referred to the triclinic system. The color is rose-red and the luster silky. The hardness is 4 to 5, and the specific gravity 3.03. An analysis yielded:

SiO₂	MnO	FeO	CaO	MgO	PbO	H₂O
43.67	37.04	1.11	8.38	0.15	0.77	7.17=99.29.

This gives as the formula $2(MnCa)SiO_3 + H_2O$, which brings it in composition near the hydrorhodonite of Igelström which is $MnSiO_3 + H_2O$. In form and appearance it bears some resemblance to wollastonite and pectolite. It is the most recently formed of the minerals of the Harstig mine, filling cavities between calcite crystals. (Described by G. Flink, in Œfversigt Vet. Akad. Förhandl., Stockholm, 1888, p. 571.) See Inesite, above.

Riebeckite—A mineral belonging to the amphibole group, from the island of Socotra, where it was collected by Dr. E. Riebeck, after whom it is named. It appears in slender prismatic crystals, having the characteristic cleavage imbedded in granite. The color is black. An analysis, after deducting 7.12 per cent. zircon, yielded:

SiO₂	Fe₂O₄	FeO	MnO	CaO	MgO	Na₂O	K₂O
50.01	28 30	9.87	0.63	1.32	0.34	8.79	072 = 99.98.

It is thus like the pyroxene ægirite, essentially a silicate of iron sesquioxide and soda, and is regarded as occupying the same place among the amphiboles. The mineral arfvedsonite has occupied this position, but recent analyses have made it contain chiefly iron protoxide, and if these are sustained, riebeckite cannot be united with it. (Described by A. Sauer in Zeitschr. deutsch. Geol. Ges., 1888, vol. XL, 138.)

Rosenbuschite.—*See* Barkevikite.

Sulphohalite.—A mineral consisting of the sulphate and chloride of sodium. It was discovered by W. E. Hidden on the bankside of Borax Lake, San Bernardino County, California, and thus far is extremely rare. It appears in rhombic dodecahedrous, which are transparent and of a faint greenish-yellow collor. The hardness is 3.5, and the specific gravity 2.489. An analysis by J. B. Mackintosh yielded:

SO₃	Cl	Na₂CO₃
42.48	13.12	1.77

or calculating the chlorine and sulphur as combined with sodium only:

Na₂SO₄	NaCl	Na₂CO₃
75.41	21 62	1.77=98.80.

This corresponds to $3Na_2SO_4 \cdot 2NaCl$. The name sulphohalite is given in allusion to the unusual composition of the mineral. (Described by W. E. Hidden and J. B. Mackintosh in Amer. Journ. Sci., 1888, vol XXXVI, p. 463.)

BOTANY FOR 1887 AND 1888.

By F. H. KNOWLTON, M. S., *Assistant Curator in the National Museum.*

The years 1887, 1888 have witnessed the publication of a very large amount of material, considerably in excess of that of many former years, without there being published anything of special moment. The results that have been presented may be regarded simply as a continuation of the various lines of investigation that have occupied attention during later years. Since the field of systematic botany has been so thoroughly worked up, more and more attention has been shown to the investigation of problems of histology, physiology, and embryology. Notwithstanding the many avenues open for the publication of material of this character, several new periodicals have been inaugurated: Malphigia, The Annals of Botany, Pittonia, Garden and Forest, etc. The constantly increasing attention that has been given of late years to the study of *Bacteria* has resulted in the production of such a mass of material that it can no longer be considered under the head of botany, and must be relegated to the special journals and works devoted to the subject.

The compiler desires to make special acknowledgment for valuable assistance to the Journal of the Royal Microscopical Society, in which Prof. A. W. Bennett has given so complete a digest of current botanical literature.

VEGETABLE ANATOMY AND PHYSIOLOGY.

The structure of the vegetable cell-wall has been much investigated of late years, and many of the mooted questions had seemingly been set at rest, but the latest observations may possibly render some of them doubtful. Elliott (Trans. Bot. Soc. Edinb. XVII) has given an interesting résumé of recent researches in this direction. Beginning with the presentation of the theory of growth by opposition as defined by Pringsheim, and the theory of intussusception as presented by Nägeli, von Mohl, and others, he traces the growth of ideas as modified by the researches of Schmitz, Strasburger, Wiesner, Klebs, Schneck, and others, and concludes that the present state of our knowledge warrants the following conclusions: (1) Growth of the cell-wall may be affected by deposition from the protoplasm of the cell; (2) the cell-wall, however, always contains, during the life of the cell, living protoplasm, which is

475

united to the cell-protoplasm; (3) this intramural protoplasm appears in some cases capable of growth on its own account; (4) possibly the cell-wall is formed in the same way as the starch grain. Pechi (Atti Soc. Tosc. Sci. Nat., VIII) has very recently studied the thickening of cell-walls in the leaf-stalk of *Aralia*. During the early stage of growth the thickening takes place mainly in the angles, but later distinct layers of cellulose are formed within each cell, which soon becomes lignified. From this the author concludes that in the earlier stages the thickening is mainly by intussusception, and during the later stages probably by opposition. On the other hand, Noll (Abhandl. Senckenburg Naturf. Gesell. XV) concludes, from an experimental application of staining reagents, that growth takes place chiefly by opposition, and the part played by intussusception is unproved. Krabbe has also studied the structure and growth of the cell-wall (Pringsheim's Jahrb. f. Wiss. Bot., XVIII). He investigated especially the process of increase in thickness in the walls of the bast cells of the *Apocynaceæ* and *Asclepiadaceæ*, and found them to be composed of lamellæ, which are themselves made up of lamellæ. These lamellæ apparently arise by fresh formations from the protoplasm. Intussusception he regards as playing only a subordinate part, and must be confined to the innermost lamellæ. Zimmermann has an exhaustive treatise, "Die Morphol. u. Physiol. d Pflanzenzelle," which forms the third volume of Schenck's "Handbuch der Botanik." It treats very fully of the structure and chemical composition, as well as the physiology of the cell.

The morphological and chemical composition of protoplasm has been treated of at great length by Schwarz (Beitr. z. Biol. d. Pflanzen, B. v). He has given many details of the action of various reagents upon protoplasm and its various modifications, only a few of which may be here enumerated. The varying acid or alkaline reaction of cell-sap he attributes to the substances in solution in it, such as pigments. The protoplasm he has found to be always alkaline in reaction, as also is the cytoplasm, nucleus, chromatophores, and in some cases the protein-grains. The chlorophyl the author regards as having a fibrillar structure composed of what he calls chloroplastin. The nucleus is composed of several substances, among which he recognizes chromatin, pyrenin, linin, and paralinin. The cytoplasm is made up of three substances: (1) the cell-sap, (2) the microsomes, insoluble in water and the cytoplasm; (3) the cytoplastids. All the nuclear substances, with the exception of chromoplastin and cytoplastin, are soluble in concentrated potash-lye, or a 10 per cent. solution of sodium chloride.

"The influence of light upon protoplasmic movement," in Journ. Linn. Soc. Lond., XXIV, is the title of a long paper by Moore. The well-known circumstance of the chlorophyll grains becoming collected into masses in sunlight and being more or less dispersed in darkness has been very fully re-investigated, and the conclusion reached is that these displacements are more the result of illumination than heat. Frank applied the term *epistrophe* to the distribution of the grains upon the free walls of the cells, and *apostrophe* to the arrangement on the side walls. Apostrophe produced by strong illumination Moore proposed to call *positive* and that produced by weak illumination, *negative.* He coins the word *phytolysis* for the whole of these phenomena. He also re-investigated the question as to whether the grains are drawn along passively with the streaming plasma, or whether they possess the power of independent motion. He finally adopts the conclusions of Sachs, Pfeffer, and others, that they are drawn along passively.

The nucleus has been the subject of numerous experiments and studies. Thus Zacharias (Bot. Zeit. XLV.) has investigated its structure and concludes that the cell-nucleus of both plants and animals is composed of two distinct substances, which he calls *plastin* and *nuclin*, which remain undissolved after treatment with artificial gastric juice. The nuclin forms the colorable filament loups of the nucleus that remain after treatment with artificial gastric juice or hydrochloric acid, sharply defined and shining in appearance. It also readily absorbs certain pigments, especially methyl-green. Plastin, on the other hand, is an essential constituent of the entire protoplasmic cell-contents, and differs from nuclin in its action under reagents. The prevalent theory that the vital properties of the cell are derived from the nucleus has been confirmed by Klebs (Biol. Centralbl.), who plasmolysed living cells of *Zygnemia* with a solution of sugar. The effect of the plasmolysis was to cause the cell-contents to contract and separate into two halves, each containing one of the two chlorophyll bodies, while the whole of the nucleus was contained in one of the halves. The half cell containing the nucleus soon regained its activity and surrounded itself with a new cell-wall. The half-cells destitute of nucleus, while they retained their vitality for a considerable time and even produced an abundance of starch, never started to grow, and could not secrete a new cell-wall. Zacharias has still more recently studied the part taken by the nucleus in cell-division (Ber. deutsch. Bot. Gesell. v.). He confirms the earlier observations that the cell protoplasm does not penetrate into the nucleus during its division. Haberland (*op. cit.*), has studied the position of the nucleus in mature cells and reaches the conclusion that their position is not arbitrary, but depends on its function as the bearer of the idioplasm which governs development. The young condition of the vacuoles has been investigated by Went (Arch. Néerland, XXI.). He finds, contrary to the general opinion, that minute vacuoles are present in the youngest cells, for example, in the growing point. He also found vacuoles in oöspheres, pollen-grains, and cambium-cells. Halsted has recorded (Bot. Gaz. XII.) the finding of three nuclei in pollen-grains of *Sambucus racemosa.*

Chlorophyll has also been made the subject of recent investigation. Tschirch has given (Ber. deutsch. Bot. Gesell., v) a résumé of recent studies on the composition of chlorophyll, and concludes that iron is not a necessary constituent. He gives $C_{28}H_{47}N_3O_6$ as the formula for phyllocyanic acid. Schunck has also studied the chemistry of chloro-phyle (Proc. Roy. Soc. Lond., XLII). Hansen states (Arbeit. Inst., Würzburg, III) that the orange-red pigment reported to have been observed in leaves is only an aggregation of the yellow chlorophyll pigment, which has an orange tint when present in dense masses. Epi-dermal chlorophyll has been further studied by Moore (Journ. Bot., XXV) and the preparation of pure chlorophyll described by Macchiati (Malpighia, I), Peyron (Compt. Rend., CV), has devised an instrument with which he has investigated the hourly variation in the action of chlorophyll, finding that the function at different hours in the day is proportional to the intensity of light.

Numerous other cell-contents have been studied. Hillhouse (Midi. Nat., X and XI) has investigated the function of tannin, and finds that it is not used in the process of growth after its production, and it can not therefore be regarded as a food material. Fribosin is described by Zopf (Ber. deutsch. Bot. Gesell., V) as a new cell-content, found in the conidia of *Podosphæra*, *Sphærotheca* and *Erysiphe*. The formation of oxalate of lime in leaves has been investigated by Schimper (Bot. Zeit., XLVI), and the formation of calcium oxalate by Wakker (see Bot. Cen-tralbl., XXXIV). In regard to the acid secretion from the roots of plants Molisch states (Sitzb. K. K. Zool. Bot. Gesell., Wien, XXXVII), that it attacks organic substances even more powerfully than inorganic, and not only dissolves them but induces other important chemical changes.

The use of histological elements as a means of classification has been further investigated during the year, and while no comprehensive dic-tum can yet be laid down, substantial progress has been made, and the prospect is that when all plants have been thoroughly investigated distinctive characters will be detected. Hildebrandt, for example, has examined a large number of species of *Ambrosieæ* and *Senecionideæ* (Beitr. Z. vergleich. Anat. der Ambros. u. Senec. Inaug. Diss.) and con-cludes that they may be very clearly distinguished by the histological elements. Jäunicke (Bot. Centralbl., XXXI) also concludes that the three genera of the *Geraniaceæ* examined by him can be distinguished from one another by characters derived from the structure and distribution of the vascular bundles in the leaf and flower-stalks. Juel (Bot. Centralbl., XXXIII) has studied the anatomical structure of the *Marcgraviaceæ*, and Solereder (see Bot. Centralbl., XXXIII) has discussed "The systematic value of the perforation in the walls of vessels," and Wible has a paper "Zur Diagnostic des coniferen Holzer." On the other hand, Plitt (Beitr. z. vergleich. Anat. d. Blattstieles d. Dikotyledonen) has examined the petiole or leaf-stalk of two hundred and eighty-three plants in thirty natural orders for characters of systematic value and the results were mainly negative, and Saupe (Flora, LXX) has investigated the wood of *Leguminoseæ*, and finds that the division into the sub-orders *Papilion-aceæ Cesalpinieæ* and *Mimoseæ* does not correspond to structural differeuces in the wood. He finds, however, that the species of most of the tribes, such as *Genisteæ*, *Dalbergieæ*, etc., do exhibit common characters. and in a few genera, *e. g.*, *Cassia*, *Cercis*, *Podalyria*, *Sophora*, the species may be distinguished by histological characters. The structure of the *Chenopodiaceæ* has been worked out in an elaborate manner by Professor St. Gheroghieff (Bot. Centralbl., xxx and xxxi), and he finds that many species may be distinguished by the histological elements of stem or roots.

The further contributions to this same general subject have been unusually numerous. A few only may be mentioned by title: Daguillon, "Structure of the Leaves of Certain Coniferæ" (Bull. Sec. Bot. France, xxxv); Flot, "Aerial Stems" (*l. c.*); Baillon. "Ovules of Plantago" (Bull. Mens. Soc. Linn., Paris, 1887); Penzig, "Anatomy and Diseases of the Aurantiaceæ" (Rome, 1887); Halsted, "Trigger-hairs of the Thistle-flower" (Torr. Bull., xv); Schenck, "Anatomy of Water Plants" (Uhl-worm u. Haenstein's Bibliot. Bot., i); Coulter and Rose, "Development of the Fruit of Umbelliferæ" (Bot. Gaz., xii).

The literature relating to the fertilization of flowers has been particularly extensive, and during the year much valuable information has been obtained. Thus Hildebrandt (Bot. Zeit., xlv), has studied the fertilization of Oxalis, and particularly the trimorphic forms. For example, in *Oxalis Bowiei* the short-styled form was found to be only imperfectly fertile when polinated with its own pollen, and the seedlings from this form produced only mid-styled plants, while the short-styled crossed with the mid-styled produced mid-styled plants exclusively. Many other equally interesting results were brought out. Burck (Ann. Jard. Bot. Buitenzorg, vi), who has been working on heterostylism and self fertilization, announces the finding of transition forms between dimorphic and trimorphic flowers in species of *Conarius*, *Averrhoa*, etc. Robertson, (Bot. Gaz., xii), describes the method of fertilization of *Calopogon parviflorus*, asserting that it is accomplished by small bees; Lindman (Bot. Centralbl., xxxii), describes methods for fertilization of certain Alpine plants, and Magnus (Bot. Contralbl., xxxiii), has studied the pollination of *Silene inflata*. Jordan's paper, "Beitr. z. physiologischen Organography d. Blumen" (Ber. deutsch. Bot. Gesell., v), is one of the most extensive. He studied flowers representing three classes, viz: *Actinomorphic* honey-flowers, *Actinomorphic* pollen flowers, and *Zygomorphic* honey-flowers. He found in all an evident adaptation for cross fertilization by aid of insects. The polination of *Zannichellia palustris* is described by Roze (Morot's Journ. Bot., i). The single stamen is located at the base of the cupuliform perigyne, which includes from one to six pistils, is at first almost sessile, but just before flowering the filament elongates and carries the anther above the pistils and the pollen in falling is caught by the funnel-shaped stigmas. MacLeod (Arch. de Biol., vii), has added a sort of appendix to the great work of Müller on the fertilization of flowers.

Of other papers on the same subject may be mentioned the following: Robertson, "Insect Relations of Certain *Asclepiads*" (Bot. Gaz., XII); Arcangeli, "Flowering of *Euryale ferox*" (Atti Soc. Tosc. Sci .Nat , VIII); Nicotra, "Pollination of *Serpias*" (Malpigdia, I); Oliver, "Pollination of *Pleurothallis ornatus*" (Nature, XXXVI); Webster, "Fertilization of *Epipactis latifolia,*" (Bot. Gaz., XII); Bateson, (Ann. Bot., I), "Effect of Cross-Fertilization on Inconspicuous Flowers."

Wortman has studied the rotation of tendrils and finds that the movement is similar to the movement of climbing stems, being however much more irregular. The movement in some species is not always uniform, that is, a part of a tendril may rotate to the right and another part of the same tendril rotate to the left. Gardner (Proc. Roy. Soc., Lond., XLIII), has continued his exceedingly interesting experiments on the pulvinus of *Mimosa pudica*. He examined sections cut under an aqueous solution of eosin, and found that the coloring matter penetrated and acted upon the protoplasm of the outer cells of the convex side of the pulvinus, while the specially irritable tissue on the other side was left unstained. Electricity was then employed and the extreme delicacy of the irritable tissue was manifest. In conclusion, Gardner states that in his opinion the protoplasm of plant as well as animal cells is capable of active contraction, and the movements of all irritable plant organs is due to a definite contraction of the protoplasm. Vines (Rep. Brit. Assoc. Adv. Sci., 1887) has extended these experiments upon Mimosa, and finds that atropin causes the closing of the leaves or an effect similar to darkness, while physoatigmin produces the opposite effect or that of light.

Elliott has given (Trans. Bot. Soc. Edinb., XVII) a valuable résumé of opinion in regard to the movement of water in plants. The old view of Sachs, Unger, and others, that the water travels in the walls of the lignified tissues, is proved by the later experiments of Van Tieghem, Elfving, and others to be wrong, since in branches of *Taxus* in pigment solution, the walls of the cells remain uncolored, while the cavities of the cells are full of coloring matter. The weight of opinion inclines to regard the path of the water as through the cell cavity. The part taken by the medullary rays in the movement of water has been re-examined by Janse (Pringsheim's Jahrb. f. Wiss. Bot. XVIII), and the theory propounded by Godlewski is confirmed by his experiment. The living parenchymatous elements of the wood undoubtedly take an important part in the movement of water. The investigations were made mostly with conifers, but the author thinks that it would be the same in dycotyledons. "The Literature of Transpiration," by Burgerstein (Verhandl. k. k. Zool. Bot. Gesell. Wien, XXXVIII) is important. He has collected a list of two hundred and thirty-six works, of greater or less magnitude, published between 1672 and 1886. No less than sixteen languages are represented. Henslow also has a paper on "Transpiration as a function of living protoplasm," in Journ. Linn. Soc. Lond. Bot. XXIV. Wiesner has a paper in Bot. Zeit. XLV. Christison, who has conducted a series of experiments to ascertain the relative monthly increase in the girth of trees (Trans. Bot. Soc. Edinb., XVII), concludes that in Scotland the commencement of the growing season in deciduous trees is in April, and reaches its maximum in June; that of evergreens is earlier, attaining its maximum in May. The end of the growing season is for both about the end of August. The "Growth and origin of multicellular plants" has been studied by Masser (Journ. Bot. XXV).

CHEMISTRY OF PLANTS.

Some exceedingly interesting and valuable results have lately been brought out in regard to the sources of nitrogen in plants. The long-current statement that plants necessarily absorb their nitrogen in a combined form seems to require modification. Indeed Lawes and Gilbert some time ago pointed out that the ordinary sources of supply in the soil will account for only a fraction of the amount used by plants. H. Marshall Ward (Ann. Bot. I) has given a valuable résumé of "Some Recent Publications Bearing on the Sources of Nitrogen in Plants," the first of these, the now well-known paper by Frank, published in 1875, announcing the discovery of a symbiosis between the roots of certain plants, notably *Cupuliferæ*, and a fungus. These fungoid growths surround the roots by a dense mycelial web. A part of the hyphæ penetrate the epidermal cells of the root, while the rest act as or take the place of root hairs, there being in these trees no root hairs developed. The fungus, it will thus be seen, is essential to the life of the host, for by its aid alone is it able to take up the nutritive material of the soil. Later, in 1886, Hellriegel, director of the agricultural experimental station at Bernberg, in conducting an extensive series of experiments to ascertain the sources of the supply of nitrogen, reached results that throw very considerable light upon the question of symbiosis as described by Frank. He cultivated Gramineæ in soil destitute of nitrogen and shut off from all possible sources of supply except the free air. After the supply of nitrogenous materials stored up in the seed had been exhausted the plants ceased to grow, and unless furnished with a fresh supply, all died. There can thus be no doubt that they are unable to utilize free nitrogen from the air. On the other hand, peas cultivated under precisely similar conditions continued to grow. The only time at which the growth was stopped was when the supply in the seed was exhausted, when there was a brief period of cessation of growth, but this was soon overcome and the plants again became healthy and vigorous. The question is, Whence came the nitrogen which allowed a growth of this kind? The only answer is that it must have come from the air, and evidently the Leguminoseæ possess powers not enjoyed by the Graminæ. Hellriegel noticed that the plants that quickest recovered and were the most vigorous were those in which the roots exhibited the largest number of the well-known tubercular swellings, which, as was then known, were caused by what were called bacteria. Little stress was placed by Hellriegel on the observations of Frank, but as Ward has shown in his paper "on the tubercular swellings on the root of Vicia Faba" (Phil. Trans., 1887), there is a clear relation between the presence of this fungus and the power of fixing pure nitrogen, enjoyed by Leguminous plants. A further contribution to the same subject is given by Lawes and Gilbert in Proc. Roy. Soc. XLIII.

"The Comparative Chemistry of Higher and Lower Plants," by Miss Abbott (Am. Nat., XXI), is a very suggestive paper, although still lacking confirmation in many particulars. It is claimed by the author that a progression in chemical complexity can be traced *pari passu* with the progression in structural differentiation. Of the other papers of more or less interest may be mentioned the following: Staco, "Plant Odors" (Bot. Gaz., XII); Schimper, "Ueber Kalkoxalatbildung in den Laubblättern" (Bot. Zeit. 46 Jahrg).

Krasser, "Ueber den microchemiochen nachweis von Eiweiss körpern in den Pflanzlichen Zellhaut" (Bot. Zeit 46); "On the Nature and Toxic Principle of the Aroideæ," by Pedder and Warden (Journ. Asiatic Soc. Bengal, LVII). The authors here found that the irritating effect on tongue, stomach, etc., of the *Aroideæ* is a purely mechanical one. The cells of the Arums are filled with needle-shaped crystals of oxalate of lime and by mechanical action produce the deleterious effects; "The Ash of Tillandsia usneoides, by Palmer (Am. Nat. XX).

TECHNOLOGY.

The constantly increasing attention that is being given to the microscopical study of plants has given rise to a copious literature of the subject, which has been considerably added to during the year. Detmer's "Das Pflanzenphysiologische Praktikum" is perhaps the most important work that has appeared. The work is evidently the result of the author's personal experience in teaching physiology, and is a very carefully written account of all the manipulations required to illustrate the ordinary facts of plant physiology. The details are very minutely given. "Manipulations de Botanique, guélle pour les travaux d histologie végétale," by Girod, is also a valuable work. "The application of the paraffin—imbedding method in Botany," by Moll (Bot. Gaz., XIII), is a very interesting paper detailing accounts of the sucessful imbedding and cutting of the most delicate vegetable tissues, such as the growing point of roots and stems, flower buds, etc. The application of zoological methods to botany has only recently been successful, since the last edition of Strasburger's "Botanische Praktikum" contains no mention of it. Schönland has also contributed observations on the process of imbedding (Bot. Centralbl, XXX, and Bot. Gaz., XIII), and Campbell also has a short note in Bot. Gaz., XIII. Bumpus has described (Bot. Gaz., XII) a simple and inexpensive self-registering auxanometer, and Barus (*op. cit*) has described a registering auxanometer. Goodall (Am. Journ. Sci. XXXV) has described a combination auxanometer and clinostat. Campbell has recorded some interesting experiments (Bot. Gaz., XII) regarding the successful staining of the nuclei of living cells. A 0.1 per cent. solution of dahlia, a violet-purple pigment, was made and this diluted with from fifty to one thousand parts of water. The object, as for example the stamen hairs of *Tradescantia*, on being immersed in this solution for a time had the nuclei very deeply stained. The ordinary protoplasmic movements were not interfered with in any way. Campbell has also another note on the absorption of analine colors by living cells (Bot. Gaz., XII), a continuation of investigations first made by Pfeffer. Welling has a short paper in The Microscope, VIII, on staining and mounting plant sections, and Doherty (Am. Month. Mic. Journ., IX) has given extensive notes on the staining of animal and vegetable tissues.

TEXT-BOOKS.

The following text-books have appeared during the year : " Elements of Botany," by Gray ; " Botanische Practicum," second edition, by Strasburger ; " Course of Practical Instruction in Botany," Part II, by Bower and Vines ; " Elements of Botany " by Bastin ; " A Manual of Botany," fifth edition, by Bently ; " Hand-Book of British Flora," fifth edition, Bentham and Hooker ; " A Primer of Botany " by Knight; " Schule-Botanik " by Krause ; " Botanique Élémentaire " by Maugin ; " Lehrbuch zum botanischen Untersicht " by Schramm ; " Elementary Practical Biology (vegetation)," by Shore.

DIATOMS.

The *Diatomaseœ* collected by the *Challenger* expedition have been worked up by Castracane and presented as volume II of the Botany of the expedition. He first reviews the biology of diatoms, and writes of geographical and bathymetrical distribution. He proposes the terms " valval " and " zonal " to take place of the confusing terms " side-view " and " end-view." Several new genera and a host of new species are described. The classification followed is that proposed in 1872 by H. L. Smith ; Costracane has also a note (Atti. Accad. Pontif. Nuovi Linc. XXXVIII), recording the finding of diatoms in the stomachs of *Echini* and *Holothureœ* dredged from a depth 2,511 to 5,274 meters. Imhof claims (Biol. Centralbl., VI, that he has detected the pores through which protoplasmic filaments are protruded in the valves of certain large species of Surirella. Kain and Taylor have given (Torr. Bull., XIV) a list of the diatoms found at Tampa Bay, Florida. Smith has a note on diatom structure in Journ. Quek. Mic. Club, III, and Schütt (Bot. Ziet., XLCII), " Ueber die Diatomeengattung Chætoceros,"

ALGÆ.

The most important American work is the long-promised "Fresh-water Algæ of the United States," by Francis Wolle. It is complemental to the author's "Desmids of the United States," which was published in 1882, and makes two handsome volumes, one of text and one of plates. The atlas contains 151 plates and over 2,300 illustrations, drawn from nature by the indefatigable author himself. The classification adopted is, so far as applicable, that employed for the Marine Algæ, viz: Rhodophyceæ, chlorophyceæ, and cyanophyceæ, the melanophyceæ not being represented. The classification, however, is unexplained and the exact views of the author are difficult to ascertain. The subject of polymorphism among algæ is given a prominent place.

Bennett (Journ. Linn. Soc., Lond., XXIV) has recently proposed some modifications in the existing systems of classification of Algæ, based largely on retrogression or degeneration, which, according to the author is manifested by more or less suppression of reproduction or vegetative organs. He traces the various forms of vegetable life to three lines of descent, represented by three distinct kinds of cell-contents, viz: Colorless, blue-green, and pure green. The first, originating in the bacteria, includes all the fungi; the second type consists of unicellular organisms, in which the cell-contents is composed of pale, blue-green endochrome without distinct chlorophyll-grains, starch-grains, or nucleus. The third series, and the only one which has developed into higher forms of vegetable life, is characterized by cells containing chlorophyll-grains, starch-grains, a nucleus, and usually a true cellulose wall.

The last published part of Agardh's classification of algæ (Lunds Univ. Arsskr., XXIII) refers to the *Siphoneæ*. He divides the whole group into six families: (1) Bryopsideæ; (2) Spongodieæ; (3) Udoteaceæ; (4) Valoniaseæ; (5) Caulerpeæ; (6) Dasycladeæ. "Physiol. u. alogologische Studien," by Hansging, Prag., 1887, is a collection of the author's papers published before on various algological topics. Mme. A. Webea van Bosse has described (Nat. Verh. Holland. Maatsch der Wettenschappen, Haarlam, 1887), the curious discovery of algæ parasites in the hairs of sloths. Two new genera and three new species are characterized. Potter (Journ. Linn. Soc., Lond., XXIV) has given observations on the curious algæ growing on the shell of the European tortoise. Janse (Plasmolytische Versuch. an Algen, Bot. Centralbl., XXXII) shows that the living protoplasm in various algæ is permeable to dilute solutions of mineral salts and cane sugar. The plasmolysis completely disappears in two hours, and after four days the cells have regained their former turgidity. "Zur Entwicklungsges einiger Confervaceen," by Langerheim, is an interesting paper on the development of confervaceæ. The sensitiveness of *Spirogyra* to shock is described by Coulter (Bot. Gaz., XII). He finds that when the filaments are cut through with a sharp instrument, eight or ten cells nearest the point of laceration show remarkable changes in their protoplasmic contents, the bands of chlorophyll being broken. Cooke's finely illustrated work on "British Desmids" has reached parts 7–10. Oliver has a valuable paper "On the Obliteration of Sieve-tubes in Laminarieæ" (Ann. Bot., I); Holmes has a short note (Trans. Bot. Soc., Edinb., XVII), on the fructification of *Sphacelaria radicans* and *S. olivacea*; Scott, "On Nuclei in Oscillaria and Tolypothrix," (Journ. Linn. Soc., Lond., XXIV); Nordstedt, "The fresh-water Algæ of New Zealand," (see Bot. Centralbl., XXXI); Piccone, "Dessemination of Algæ by Fish" (Nuov. Giorn. Bot., Ital., XIX).

CHARACEÆ.

Dr. Allen has given the results of his long-continued studies of those little-known plants in his "Characeæ of America," part I. This part is devoted to the introduction, morphology, and classification, the descriptive portion being reserved for a final part. The key to the classification is translated from Nordstedt, with additions of American species detected since its original publication. The Characeæ are world-wide in distribution and number in all something over two hundred forms, distributed as follows: *Nitella*, 93 species and varieties; *Tolypella*, 13; *Lamprothamnus*, 4; *Lichnothamnus*, 3; *Chara*, 102. The same author has given (Torr. Bull., XIV) notes on Characeæ, in which several new forms are described: *Nitella Muthnata* from the Feejee Islands; *N. Morongii*, from Nantucket, and *Tolypella* (afterwards changed to *Nitella*) *Macounii*, from the Niagara River. Vines has a short note on *Apospory in Characeæ* in Ann. Bot., I. Knowlton (Bot. Gaz., XII) has described a fossil species of *Chara* (*C. compressa*) from the Wasatch group at Wales, Utah. This is the second American species found fossil, the other (*C. glomerata Lx.*) being from the Green River group at Florissant, Colorado.

FUNGI.

The activity in the investigation of fungi still continues unabated, and although few large works have appeared during the year, much material, in the form of short papers containing descriptions of new species, revision of genera, etc., has been contributed.

The most important general work is the continuation of Saccardo's "Sylloge Fungorum." De Bary's excellent work has been translated by Garnsey under the title of "Comparative Morphology and Biology of the Fungi, Mycetoza and Bacteria." It is indispensable to all elementary students of these groups, and is the best working book that we have. Burrell and Earll's "Parasitic Fungi of Illinois, the Eresipheæ," is one of the most valuable American publications. It describes about forty species and reduces many so-called species to synonyms of well-known forms. Cohn's "Kryptogamen Flora v. Schlesein, Pilze," for which Schrœter is preparing the fungi, has reached the second part. It concludes the description of the Myxogastres, and

embraces the Schigomycetes, Zygomycetes, and Oomycetes. Rabenhorst's "Krypogamen Flora v. Deutschland u. s. w., Pilze," has
reached parts 27 and 28, being the last contribution from the lamented
Winter. Part 27 completes the Sphaeriaceæ and includes the small
sub-order Dothideaceæ. Part 28 commences the Hysteriaceæ and embraces the families Hysterineæ, Hypodermiæ, and Dichaenaceæ.
" Cooke's Illustrations of British Fungi" has now reached parts 46 to 48.

Martin's "Enumeration and Description of the Septorias of North
America" (Journ. Mic., III) includes one hundred and eighty-eight species
of Septoria, eight of Pleospora, twenty of Rhabdospora, and eight of
Phlyctæna. He also gives a convenient index to the species and a list
of the host-plants. "The Synopsis of North American Species of
Xylaria and Poronia," by Ellis and Everhart (l. c., III), describes thirty
species of Xylaria and two species of Poronia. The same authors have
a "Synopsis of the North American Species of Hapoxylon and Num-
mularia (l. c., IV). Phillips' "Manual of British Discomycetes," recently
published as a volume of the International Scientific Series, will be
useful to American as well as English students, as many of the species
described are common to both countries. The work describes nine
orders, forty-nine genera and about six hundred species. The genus
Phleospora has been monographed by Berllase (Nuov. Giorn. Bot. et al.,
XX), who makes out about one hundred and five species, and DeToni
(Rev. Mycol., July, 1887) has a "Revisio Monographica Geasteris e.
Tribu Geasteromycetum." He recognizes forty-eight species, and Morgan, who reviewed the paper in Am. Nat., XXI, describes two additional
species from Nebraska. "Les Hymenomycetes D'Europe," by Potouillard, is also a valuable work. As this is the first volume of "Materiaux pour L'Historie des Champignons," it is devoted to general
anatomy and classification.

Of exsicati, Ellis' "North American Fungi" has reached centuries
20 and 21, and Roumeguere's "Fungi selecti exiscati præcepue Galliæ
et Algereæ" has passed through centuries XLII–XLV.

Farlow and Trelease have done a most valuable work in compiling
"A list of Works on North American Fungi," which is issued by the library of Harvard College. The report of the botanist of the State of
New York, Peck, in "Fortieth Ann. Rept. N. Y. State Mus. Nat. Hist.
for 1886," contains descriptions of about forty new species.

As it is impossible to attempt anything like a complete enumeration
of all the work that has been done, the following list of articles that
have appeared in American periodicals, with a few of the more important foreign papers, will convey some idea of its magnitude. The
following have appeared in the Journal of Micology from July, 1887, to
June, 1888: Calkins, "Notes on Florida Fungi;" Ellis and Everhart,
" New Kansas Fungi, Additions to Hypocreaceæ, New Species of Fungi
from various localities, New Iowa Fungi, Additions to Ramularia;"
Tracy and Galloway, " Notes on Western Erysipheæ and Peronospo-

reæ, Notes on Western Uredineæ, New Western Uredineæ;" De Toni, "Revision of the Genus Doassausia;" Forster, "Agarics of the United States, genus Panus;" Pammel, "Some Mildews of Illinios."

"The growth of Tulostoma mammosum" and "Ash-rust," by Bessey, have appeared in Am. Nat.. XXI; "Character of Injuries produced by Parasitic Fungi upon the host Plants," by Seymour (Am. Nat., XXI); "Æcidium on Juniperus Virginiana," by Farlow (Bot. Gaz., XII); "Uncinula polychæta B. and C.," by Tracy and Galloway (l. c., XII); "Iowa Peronosporeæ and a dry season," by Halsted (l. c., XII); "The identity of Podosphæra minor Howe, and Microsphæra fulvofulcra Cooke," by Miss M. Merrey (l. c., XII); "The Mycologic Flora of the Miami Valley, Ohio," by Morgan (Journ. Cin. Soc. Nat. Hist., X); "Contributions to the Botany of the State of New York," by Charles H. Peck (Bull. N. Y. State Mus. Nat. Hist., vol. I, No 2); the Bulletin from the Botanical Department Iowa State Agricultural College contains several short articles on Fungi by Professor Halsted; "Fungi of the Pacific coast," by Harkness (Bull. Cal. Acad. Sci.); "Polyporus sanguineus and other Fungi of the White Cedar," by P. H. Dudley (Journ. N. Y. Mic. Soc.).

A few of the papers in foreign periodicals are: Trail, "Revision of Scotch Shpæropsideæ and Melanconieæ" (Scotch Nat., July 18, 1887); Mouten, "Ascomycetes observ aux cnverous de Liege" (Bull. Soc. Roy. Bot. d Belgique); Boruet, "Du Parasitisme der Touffles" (Rev. Mycol., 1887); Barclay, "Descriptive list of Uredineæ in the neighborhood of Simla, Western Himalaya" (Journ. Asiatic Soc. Bengal, LVI). In *Greviliea* Cooke has several articles: "New Australian Fungi," "New British Fungi," "Some Exotic Fungi." Massee has also an article (l. c.) on "British Pyrenomycetes." Points in the comparative anatomy of *Uredineæ* are presented by Dietel in Bot. centralbl XXXII; Classification of *Agaricineæ* is taken up by Potouillard (Morot's Journ. d Bot., II); Polymorphism of the *Hyphomycetes*, by Gasperini (Atti Soc. Tosc. Nat., VI); "On the type of a new order of Fungi," by Massee (Journ. Roy. Mic. Soc., 1888, pt. 2); "Fungi of Finland," by Rostrup (Bot. Tidsskr., XV); "Experimental Observations on certain British Heterœcious Uredineæ," by Plowright (Journ. Linn. Soc. Lond. XXIV); "Revision of the genus Bovista," by Massee (Journ. Bot., XXVI); "Fungi Japonici Nonnulli," by Spegazzine and Ito (Journ. Linn. Soc. Lond., XXIV).

DISEASES OF PLANTS.

In speaking of the fungus diseases of plants under a separate heading the impression should not be conveyed that they differ from fungi in general. It is simply a convenient way of treating of those forms that are especially injurious to cultivated plants. The extent of the annual injury done to agricultural interests by the attacks of parasitic fungi is little appreciated by the community at large. Even when it is understood that the injury is caused by parasitic plants, so little is known of their nature and conditions of growth that no very effective remedial measures can be employed against them. It is only by care-fully studying their life history that methods of prevention or cure can be suggested. Various governments, but especially those of France and the United States, have undertaken systematic investigations of the life history of the injurious forms. Prof. P. Viala, as the represent-ative of French interests, has visited this country and studied the wild grapes and the various fungi found affecting them.

The section of vegetable pathology of the U. S. Department of Agri-culture, under Prof. F. Lamson Scribner, has accomplished valuable work in this direction. His report (Ann. Rep. Dept. Ag., 1887), which embraces about seventy-five pages, is illustrated by seventeen plates, and deals with the diseases of the vine, the potato blight and rot, straw-berry-leaf blight, apple scab, rust of beets, leaf rust of cherry, plum, peach, etc., cotton-leaf blight, anthracnose of the raspberry and black-berry, smut of Indian corn, corn rust, etc. The Department has also issued a Bulletin (No. 5) containing a report on experiments made in 1887 on the treatment of the downy mildew and black rot of the grape-vine. In a former Bulletin (No. 2) the life history of these highly de-structive parasites had been treated, and in this, the best method for controlling them are described and discussed.

" Les Maladies de la Vigne" is the title of a large work by Professor Viala. A long list of species is enumerated, among which one hundred and fifty species are regarded as accidental, one hundred as saprophytic, and twenty-five as parasitic. The larger portion of the work is devoted to a few well-known destructive forms, such as *Peronospora viticola*, *Oidium Tuckeri*, etc. " Le Black Rot et le Coniotherium diplodiella" is a well-written pamphlet of eighty pages by Viala and Ravaz. M. Prieilleux (Compt. Rend., CV) has an article on the grape disease (*Conotherium diplodiella*). He concludes that it is a true parasite. Gasperini (Atti Tosc. Soc. Sci. Nat., VIII) describes a new disease of lemons, a species of Aspergillus. Vuillemin (Morot's Journ. Bot., I) writes of the "Disease affecting cherry and plum trees." The disease of tomatoes (*Dactylium roseum*, var.,) is described by W. G. Smith in Gard. Chron., August, 1887. "A new fungus disease of the vine" is characterized by Scribner and Viala in Agricult. Sci., September, 1887. The species is named *Greeneria fulginea*, and is both saprophytic and parasitic. It is reported to be very destructive to fruit in some parts of North Carolina. "The curl of peach leaves" is described by Knowles in Bot. Gaz., XII.

LICHENS.

The much-needed help to the study of the North American Lichens has been furnished by Willey's "Introduction." Although a pamphlet of only fifty-eight pages, it contains chapters on the collecting and mount-ing of Lichens; on their structure and organs; their geographical dis-tribution. There is a key to the seventy-six genera, enumerated as inhabitants of North America, and also a list of all the species, with an indication of their habitat. The work is accompanied by ten plates, illustrating the spores of each genus as well other parts, such as gonidia, apotheceine, spermogones, pycnides, etc. The much-discussed question of the autonomy of Lichens still remains a mooted point. Thus Willey, in the above paper, concludes that "for the present and for practical purposes the Lichen remains a Lichen," while Forssell, "Beitr. z. Kennt. d. Anatomie u. Systematic d. Gloeslichtenen" (Nov. Act. Reg. Soc. Scient. Upsal, VIII), describes a new family of the class Ascolichens with the gonidia belonging to the Chroococcaceæ, and Massee (Phil. Trans., CLXXVIII), under the name Gastrolichens, describes a form produced by the union of a fungus belonging to the order Trichogastres with a uni cellular alga. Möller has furnished the results of the cultivation of Lichen-forming Ascomycetes without algæ (Unters. Bot. Inst. k. Akad. Munster-in-Westfalen, 1887). Recognizing the fact that light on this subject can only be obtained by cultivating gonidia alone or synthetically combining spores and gonidia, he has turned his attention to the culture of spores. Contrary to the common statement that hyphæ coming from germinating Lichen spores necessarily die in a short time if gonidia are not supplied, he found that if germinated in a suitable culture medium the hyphæ produced "small characteristic thalli without any trace of gonidia whatever." These he had at the time of writing kept alive three months, and although they had not produced apothecia there were indications that these were being formed. He also concluded that the spermatia are not male reproductive organs, as has been supposed by some.

Of the shorter papers Willey has described a new species (*Dermatiscum Catawbanse*) from —— (Torr. Bull., XIV); Knowlton has enumerated (Bot. Gaz. XIII) several species found attached to some of the stone idols lately brought to the U. S. National Museum from the Easter Islands, and Eckfeldt and Calkins have published a "Lichen Flora of Florida" (Journ. Micology's, III), enumerating three hundred and thirty species, a few of which are new. Bonnier's "La Constitution des Lichens" (Journ. d. Botanique, 1887) is an interesting paper.

HEPATICÆ.

The distribution of the Italian species of Hepaticæ is considered by Massalongo (Atti Congr. Naz. Bot. Critt., Parma, September, 1887), and Underwood has written of some undescribed forms from California (Bot. Gaz., XIII). He describes five species that had been sent by Bo lander in 1866 to Dr. Gottsche but were never published. Goebel has an interesting paper (Ann. Jard. Bot., Buitenzorg, VII), in which he describes some curious appliances for storing water in the epiphytic Jungermannicæ of Java. Trabus has a paper in Rev. Bryol., 1887, "Mousses et Hépatiques nouvelles d'Algérie."

MOSSES.

Of the larger systematic works Braithwait's "British Moss Flora" has reached part x, completing volume I, and Rabenhorst's "Crypto-gamen-Flora v. Deutschland u. s. w." has reached numbers 7 and 8, being still occupied with the Acrocarpæ. Both of these publications still maintain the uniform high character of the earlier parts. Philibert has a short paper (Rev. Bryol., XIV) on the fructification of Grimmia Hartmanni, in which he concludes that it should be placed among the true Grimmia and near to *G. contorta* Wahl. The same author has also another paper (*l. c.*) "Contrib. à la flore mycologique de la Grèce. Arcangeli (Atti Soc. Tosc, Nat., V) states that a useful character for some species of moss "can be drawn from the fact that in some forms the nervation of the leaves ends in a small projecting point or tooth and in addition to this presents another small tooth pointing downwards below the opical tooth." Species of *Rhyncostegium* and *Brachythecium* are enumerated. Several hybrid mosses are described by Sanio (Hedwigia, XXVI), and the "Anatomy and Development of the Sporostegium of Mosses," by Vaizey in Journ. Linn. Soc., Lond., XXIV. In the "Sphagnaceæ of North America" (Bull. Soc. roy. de Bot. Belgique, XXV), Cardot proposes some changes in our species. He admits sixteen species and nine varieties as compared with twenty seven species in Lesquereux and James' "Manual." "Die Entwick. d. Sporogone v. Andreæ u. Sphagnum," by Waldner, is a valuable contribution to our knowledge of the development of the sporogonium of these genera, and the paper is further enriched by systematic notes by Müller. Variations in *Sphagnaceæ* are described by Jansen (Rev. Bryol, XIV).

FERN-ALLIES.

Baker's "Hand-book of the Fern-Allies" is by far the most valuable contribution that has appeared during the year on the systematic study of the related members of the Pteridophyta. It is similar in its method of treatment to the author's well-known "Synopsis Filicum." It includes descriptions of 565 species, distributed at follows: *Equisetaceæ*, 20 species; *Lycopodiaceæ*, 98 species; distributed among *Phylloglossura*, 1, *Lycopodium*, 94; *Tmesipteris*, 1; *Psilotum*, 2; *Selaginellaceæ*, 383 species, of which *Selaginella* has 334, and *Isoetes*, 49; *Rhizocarpeæ*, 64 species, distributed among *Salvinia*, 13; *Azolla*, 5; *Marsillia*, 40, and *Pilularia*, 6.

In the *Equicetaceæ* Buchtien has given a short paper (Uhlworm u. Haenlein Biblioth. Bot., VIII), in which he points out the difference between the male and female prothalli. "Some words on the life-history of Lycopods" (Ann. Bot., I) by Treub, is a suggestive paper. He has studied the prothalli of four species before unknown, of which number three belong to the *Phlegmaria* type, and one to the *cernuum* type. The *annotinum* type, the third into which Lycopodium is divided, is still imperfectly known. This genus, as is well known, played an important part in past geological time, and the modern forms are seemingly but poor representations, but as Treub suggests, it is more than probable that when the life-history of each form is made out some important generalizations in connection with what is known of the fossil form will be possible. Goebel is also working in similar lines and has recently described (Bot. Zeitg., XLV) the prothallium of *L. inundatum*, confirming previous observations that it belongs to the *cernuum* type.

The genus *Isoetes* which is generally much neglected by botanists is treated geographically by Underwood (Bot. Gaz., XIII). It embraces fifty-three well-marked species of world-wide distribution. Europe has thirteen species; Africa, ten; Asia, six; Australia, eight; South America, six; and North America, nineteen species, two of which are here described as new.

FERNS.

About the usual annual amount of work seems to have been done on the ferns without, however, producing anything of particular moment. Bower (Trans. Linn. Soc., Lond., 2d ser., II) has described and discussed at considerable length the discovery of apospory in ferns. This phenomenon, which is simply a transition by direct vegetative process, and without the assistance of spores, from the sporophore to the oophore, was first defined by Pringsheim and Stahl in 1876, but has only recently been detected in ferns. Goebel (Ann. Jard. Bot., Buitenzorg, VII), has given a long paper describing the germination of several little-known species, among them *Vittaria*, *Trichomanes*, and *Hymenophyllum*. The same author has a paper, "Ueb. künstliche Vergründung d. Sporophyll v. Onoclea Struthiopteris" (Ber. deutsch. Bot. Gesell., V) describing the conversion of fertile sporophylls of *Onoclea* into barren green fronds. The development of the sporangium of the Polypodiaceæ is described by Kündig (Hedwigia, XXVIII), and the "Dehiscence of the Sporangium of Adiantum pedatum," by Miss Lyon (Torr. Bull., XIV). Campbell's paper "On the development of the Ostrich Fern Onoclea Struthiopteris" (Mem. Boston Soc. Nat. Hist., IV) is a very carefully prepared paper on the histology and development.

Baker has given several descriptive papers: "A further collection of ferns from West Borneo." (Journ. Linn. Soc., Lond., XXIV); "On a collection of ferns from San Domingo" (Journ. Bot., XXVI), in which several new species are characterized. Beddome has a short paper enumerating a collection made in Perak and Penang (Journ. Bot., XXVI), and Forbes, (*l. c.*) has described a single new species (*Polypodium Annabellæ*) from New Guinea. *Nephrolepis acuta* is reported from the vicinity of Miami River, Florida, by Holden (Torr. Bull., XIV). Rabenhorst's "Kryptogamen Flora v. Deutschland u. s. w." has reached parts 8 to 10 of the vascular cryptogams. It completes the *Polypodiaceæ* and includes descriptions of the German species of *Osmundiaceæ*, *Ophioglossaceæ* and *Rhizocarpeæ*, and commences the *Equisetaceæ*. Each species is care-fully illustrated. Underwood's "Our Ferns and their Allies" has now reached a third edition. It describes about one hundred and sixty-five species and several varieties of ferns as native of North America, north of Mexico. One of the most important additions to the "fern-allies" is the genus *Salvinia* reported from Missouri.

ANTHOPHYTA.

The number of papers of more or less magnitude that have appeared during the year are very great, and considerably in excess of the pro-duction of most former years. In America, while most of the papers have been short, many of them are of considerable value.

The most extensive papers have been numbers XIV and XV of Watson's "Contributions to American Botany." The first of these, issued in 1887, is largely taken up with a list of the plants selected by Dr. Ed-ward Palmer in the State of Jalisco, Mexico, in 1886. The *Gamopetalæ* were determined by Dr. Gray; the *Juncacaceæ* and *Cyperaceæ* by Britton; the *Gramineæ* by Vasey, and the *Filices*, by Eaton. The whole collec-tion includes about six hundred and seventy-five species, with a consid-erable proportion of species new to science. The last part of the paper contains descriptions of over forty new species of American plants from various localities. Part XV, issued May, 1888, contains an enumeration of new American plants with revisions of *Lesquerella* (old *Vesicaria*) and of the North American species of *Draba*. Of *Draba*, thirty-two species and several varieties are described. It also contains descrip-tions of over fifty new species of Mexican plants, chiefly collected by Pringle in the mountains of Chihuahua, and descriptions of a few plants of Guatemala. Gray's last paper, which was presented to the Academy of Arts and Sciences after his death, by Watson, consists of notes upon the *Rutaceæ* and *Vitaceæ*, the study of which he had taken up immedi-ately on his return from his last European trip.

The Smithsonian Institution has issued a second edition of Gray's "Synoptical Flora of North America," *Gamopetalæ*, which forms vol-ume XXXI of its Miscellaneous Collections. In this form it is distribu-ted to libraries and institutions of learning in all parts of the world, as well as to many of its private correspondents, to whom it is known that it would be of special value.

Of the foreign works Hillebrand's "Flora of the Hawaiian Islands" is one of the most extensive and valuable. Insular floras have always a peculiar interest, and "few are more interesting than the Hawaiian Islands." The work describes 844 species of Phanerogams, belonging to 335 genera, and 155 Pteridophytes, representing 80 genera, being a total of 999 species. Of this number it is thought that 115 species have been introduced since the discovery by Captain Cook in 1779, and 24 species by natives before this time. There remains 860 species as original residents, of which number 653, or over 75 per cent., are endemic.

About 250 of these endemic species belong to endemic genera. Of the dicotyledons more than 85 per cent. of these species are endemic. The "Flora Miquelonenis," by M. M. Delamare, Renauld, and Cardot is another insular flora. The Island of Miquelon, which is just off the south shore of Newfoundland, has been very carefully explored and the results here presented. About 46 per cent. of the species observed are American. Mueller still continues his indefatigable labors on the Australian flora. His "Iconography of Australian species of Acacia and cognate genera" has reached decade 11 and is similar in appearance to his well-known "Euccliptographia." Forbes and Hemesley have inaugurated a most valuable work, "An Enumeration of all the plants known from China proper, Formosa, Hainan, Corea, the Luchu Archipelago, and the Island of Hong Kong, together with their distribution and synonomy." It is published in the Jour. Linn. Soc., Lond., and has now reached part V, taking it through the Compositæ. The "Botany of the Roraima Expedition of 1884," by F. im Thurn, assisted by Oliver, Ridley, Baker, and others (Trans. Linn. Soc., Lond., 2d ser., II), is another valuable paper. It enumerates three genera and fifty-three species new to science. Of similar scope is the "Enumeration of the plants collected by Mr. H. H. Johnston on the Kilima-Najaro expedition of 1884," by Oliver and other of the officers of the Kew Herbanium, and the "Botany of the Afghan Delimitation Commission," by Aitchison, both of which appear in Trans. Linn. Soc., Lond., 2d ser., II. King's "The species of Ficus of the Indo-Malayan and Chinese countries" is a magnificent contribution, in two large volumes, to our knowledge of the perplexing genus Ficus. Over two hundred species are described and two hundred and twenty-five plates devoted to their illustration. The synonomy, distribution, etc., are very completely presented. The continuation of De Candolle's Prodromus, under the title of "Monographeæ Phanerogamarum," still progresses. The present volume by Planchon is devoted to the Ampelideæ. In the volume of the "Prodromus," issued in 1824, that contained the Ampelideæ, only one hundred and eight species were known, while the present monograph includes three hundred and ninety species. Some of the radical changes in nomenclature proposed by Planchon are not likely to meet with universal acceptance. The paper "Serjania Sapindacearum Genus monographica descriptum," by Radelkofer (Trans. Roy. Bav. Acad., 1875) is now supplemented by two hundred pages and nine plates.

"Biologia Centrali-Americana," by Hemsley, has reached part XXII; the "Flora of British India," by Hooker, has reached part XIV, completing the Euphorbiacæ; and the "Flora Italiana" of Parlatore, continued by Caruél, has reached vol. VII. Of Hooker's "Icones Plantarum," parts I-III, vol. VIII, have appeared during the year. Each contains twenty-five plates of new or little known species.

The shorter American notes and papers have been exceedingly numerous. We may mention the following:

"New or rare plants," by Dr. Gray (Bot. Gaz., XIII), is the best contribution of the Nestor of American botany. It enumerates only four
species. The Botanical Gazette, XII, has an account of "An excursion
to the Platte," by Thompson; "Proteogyne in Datura meteloides," by
Schneck; "Fertilization of Calopogon parviflorus," by Robertson. Vol.
XIII contains "Notes on North American willows," by Bebb; "Notes
on the Flora of James Bay," by Macoun; "A New Water Lily" (*Castalia
Leibergi*) from the Northwest; "Phacelia heterosperma, n. sp.," by
Parish; "Notes on Carex, No. IX," by Bailey; "Notes on some Illinois
Grapes," by Schneck (six species are enumerated); "Prunus pumila in
North Carolina," by Memminger; "Notes on Western Umbelliferæ," by
Coulter and Rose; "Erigeron Tweedyi, n. sp.," from Southwestern Mon-
tana, by Canby; "Undescribed Plants from Guatemala," by Smith.

The Torry Bulletin, vol. XIV, contains many articles. Among them
are "Bibliographical notes on well-known plants," by Green; "A
supposed new genus of Anacardiaceæ (*Sycocarpus*)," by Britton, "The
Genera Echinocystis Migarrhiza and Echinopepon," by Watson; "A
new variety of *Aralia nudicauli L.*," by Apgar; "Note on Sarracenia
variolaris," by Pierce; vol. XV, contains the following:

"Sherardia arvensis," by Meehan; "Remarks on the Group Caro-
lineæ of the genus Rosa," by Best, describes *Rosa humilis* Marshall, and
the varieties *lucida* and *villosa;* "Studies in the Typhaceæ," by Morong;
"Re-discovery of *Nymphæa elegans*, Hook., by Stearns, reports this
beautiful species from Waco, central Texas, where it has remained
unique since it was first collected by Wright in 1849; "New or Noteworthy North American Phanerogams," by Britton; and Bebb has an
article on "White Mountain Willows."

A number of papers on grasses and cyperaceæ have appeared, of which
we may mention "Grasses of North America for Farmers and Students," by W. J. Beal. It contains chapters "on the structure, form,
and development of the grasses, power of motion, plant growth, classification, native grazing lands, grasses for cultivation, early attempts to
cultivate grasses, testing seeds, grasses for pastures and meadows,
preparation of the soil, care of grass land, etc." It will be followed by
a second volume, which will contain descriptions of the North American
species. Flint's well-known "Grasses and Forage Plants," has been
revised and a new edition published during the year. Vasey has papers
on "Redfieldia, a New Genus of Grasses," "New Western Grasses," and
"New or Rare Grasses," in Torr. Bull., and a "Synopsis of the Genus
Panicum," in Bot. Gaz., XIII. Scribner has notes on "New or Little-
known Grasses," in Torr. Bull., XV, and Beal on "The Rootstocks of
Leersia and Muhlenbergia," in Am. Nat., XXII. *Websteria*, a new genus
in *Cyperaceæ*, is described by Wright (Torr. Bull., XV), from Valusia
County, Florida. The plant is entirely submerged.

The American Naturalist has short articles, by Bessey, on "The Eastward Extension of *Pinus ponderosa*, var. *scorpulorum*," "The Western

Extension of the Black Walnut," "Still another Tumble-weed (*Cyclo-doma platyphyllum*)," and the "Grass Flora of the Nebraska Plains." Also a note on "An Overlooked Function of Many Fruits." He thinks that the "greening" of young fruits, such as those of Ulmus, Negundo, etc., is to aid in the development of the embryo, since at the time when it is forming there are no leaves. The American Naturalist has also a long paper on "Evolution in The Plant Kingdom," by Coulter, and a note by Ed. Palmer on "The Effect on Vegetation of the Variable Rainfall of Northwest Mexico." Sturtevant has continued his notes on the "Origin of Garden Vegetables."

Parry (Bull. Cal. Acad. Sci., II) has a valuable paper on the California Menzanetas, "A partial revision of the Uva-urse section of the genus Arctoetaphylos," as represented on the North American Pacific coast. He enumerated thirteen species, of which one is extra limital, and several are either new or newly characterized. Curran (*op. cit.*) has a note on the "Priority of Dr. Kellogg's Genus Marah over Megarrhiza."

Pittonia is the name of a botanical publication that has been begun by Edward Lee Green, of the University of California. It consists of a series of papers, usually short, devoted mainly to Western plants, descriptions of new species, critical notes, etc. Following is a list of the most important articles: No. 1, "Some West American species of Trifolium;" "Some West American Asperifoleæ;" "The species of Zauscheria;" "A New Genus of Asteroid Compositæ (*Hazzardia*);" "New Species, mainly California." No. 2, "A Curious Collinsia;" "Some West American Asperifoleæ, II;" "Miscellaneous Species, New or Rare;" "A Botanical Excursion to the Island of San Miguel;" "Catalogue of the Flowering Plants of the Island of San Miguel." No. 3, "West American Phases of the Genus Polentilla;" "Some American Polemoniaceæ;" "New or Noteworthy Species;" "Echinocystis § Megarrhiza;" "Biographical Notice of Dr. Albert Kellogg." No. 4, "New Species from Mexico;" "New or Noteworthy Species, II;" "Botanical Literature, Old and New;" "The Botany of Cedros Island;" "List of Cedros Island Plants;" "On Some Species of Dodecathion."

The shorter foreign papers have also been exceedingly numerous, but only a few of them can be mentioned: Baker's "Synopsis of Tilandsie" was continued into 1888, and completed in the June number of the Journ. Bot. Two hundred and forty-one species are enumerated, a large proportion of which are new to science. Dietz (Abhandl. Naturwiss. Ver., Bremen, IX) has investigated *Sparganium* and *Typha*, and concludes that that they should be placed under distinct families; *Sparganium* having nearest affinities to the *Pandanaceæ* and *Typha* to the *Aroideæ*. Hooker has described, under the name of *Hydrothrix*, a remarkable new genus of *Pontederiaceæ* (Ann. Bot., I). Ridley (Journ. Linn. Soc., Lond., XXIV) describes a new genus of *Orchidaceæ* from the Island of St. Thomas, West Africa. Ward's article on "Fruits and Seeds of Rhamnus (Ann. Bot., I) is devoted to an investigation of the sources of coloring-matter in certain species. "A Second Series of New Species of Ficus from New Guinea," and "Some New Species of Ficus from Samatra," by King (Journ. Asiatic Soc., Bengal, LVI), are additions to the great work on Ficus mentioned before. Huxley has an interesting paper (Journ. Linn. Soc., Lond., XXIV) on Gentians, their variations, relationships, etc. Ito (*op. cit.*) has described a curious species of *Belanophora* new to the Japanese flora. "The Nomenclature of Nymphæa" is reviewed by Brittin (Journ. Bot., XXVI). It is shown that the species of *Nymphæa*, Smith, 1808–'09, must be transferred to *Castalia*, Salisbury, 1805, and the species of *Nuphar*, Smith, 1808–'09= *Nymphæa*, Salisbury, 1805. Bennett has an account of the British species of *Epilobium* (Trans. Bot. Soc. Edinb., XVII). Twelve species and several forms are enumerated.

ANTHROPOLOGY FOR 1887 AND 1888.

By OTIS T. MASON.

INTRODUCTION.

The record of progress in anthropology during the years 1887 and 1888 includes publications of general and of special significance. For the sake of convenience, following the suggestion of Dewey in his decimal classification of knowledge, this summary will commence with the encyclopædic portion of anthropology. To render this portion more easy of reference, the following order may be observed :

(0) General treatises, including addresses, courses of lectures, bibliographies, dictionaries, encyclopædias, collections of materials for study, general discussions, classifications of anthropology.

(1) Societies, their history, scope, and enterprises, and a list of their publications.

(2) Journals, proceedings, transactions, organs of associated bodies.

(3) Periodicals, like the Revue d'Anthropologie, etc., devoted to the subject of anthropology at large.

(4) Congresses, caucuses, general assemblies for some special occasion, Compte-rendus.

(5) Laboratories and apparatus of research, in which the whole ground is covered. Special laboratories, such as Francis Galton's, for sociological inquiries, or Wundt's, in psycho-physics, should be described under their appropriate head.

(6) Museums and collections. A properly arranged account of all collections, with their specialties, would save much tiresome hunt and enlarge the results of our work.

(7) Galleries or collections of anthropological illustrations. Little has been done to perfect this side of anthropology.

(8) Libraries, catalogues of books on anthropology, check-lists, and similar devices for ready reference, classifications of books.

(9) Instructions to collectors.

Works on the general subject of the natural history of man have been published in the two years covered by this summary by Herr Schaaff-hausen, Serrurier and de Quatrefages, Hovelacque and Hervé, Canestrini, Friedrich Ratzel, Johannes Ranke, O. T. Mason, J. Lippert, E. Morselli, and Sayce.

H. Mis. 142——32

There is as yet no catalogue or list of anthropological societies avail-able. The greatest journals, such as Archiv, Correspondenz-Blatt, Revue d'Anthropologie, and Archivio, furnish each résumés of meetings held and of work done, which might be easily combined into a general directory. It is understood that Mr. Henry Phillips, of Philadelphia, will undertake a work of this kind for our own country.

The journals and kindred publications of societies, periodicals pub-lished for subscription, and Comptes-rendus of societies, fall into the same general scheme, and may be considered together. There is a growing desire for information about what the world is doing in this most interesting of all sciences. In spite of all that has been said or may be said, there will always be most excellent treatises printed in out-of-the-way places. Friendship, and the good prices paid by popular magazines, will allure good material away from its legitimate home. Nevertheless, with our present system of bibliographical appendices, a few publications can be mentioned that unitedly include about all that is worthy of notice.

The American Anthropologist. Washington.
The American Naturalist. New York.
Annual Report of the Peabody Museum. Cambridge.
Annual Record of Progress. Smithsonian Report.
Archiv für Anthropologie. Braunschweig.
Archivio per l'Antropologia. Firenze.
Association Francaise pour l'Avancement des Sciences.
Athenæum. London.
Ausland. Stuttgardt.
Bibliotheque Anthropologique. Paris.
Bulletins de la Société d'Anthropologie. Paris.
Comptes-rendus du Congrès International d'Anthropologie et d'Archeologie préhis-torique. In various cities.
Correspondenz-Blatt der deutschen Gesellschaft für Anthropologie, etc. München.
Journal of the Anthropological Institute of Great Britain and Ireland. London.
Journal of the Royal Asiatic Society of Great Britain and Ireland. London.
Mittheilungen der Anthropologischen in Wien.
Nature. London.
The Popular Science Monthly. New York.
Proceedings of the American Association for the Advancement of Science.
Proceedings of the U. S. National Museum. Washington.
Report of the British Association for the Advancement of Science.
Report of the Smithsonian Institution. Washington.
Revue d'Anthropologie. Paris.
Science. New York.
Verhandlungen der Berliner Gesellschaft für Anthropologie, Ethnologie und Urge-schichte. Berlin.

In our own country there are but two cities where the whole ground of anthropology is sought to be covered, Cambridge and Washington. In the former city the Peabody Museum, re-enforced by the library of Harvard University and the lectures delivered under its auspices, occu-pies all the fields of research. In Washington the Congressional Li-brary, the Smithsonian Institution, the National Museum, the Army

Medical Museum, the Library of the Surgeon-General, with its Index-Catalogue and the Index Medicus; the Bureau of Ethnology, and the Anthropological Society of Washington, not to speak of a dozen other contributory departments and bureaus; all these, taken together, furnish a band of workers, a body of material, and a series of publications that will compare favorably with those of London, Paris, and Berlin.

There are museums, societies, and other means of study in Salem, Worcester, New York, Philadelphia, Baltimore, Cincinnati, St. Louis, Davenport, Milwaukee, and San Francisco not to be overlooked. Dr. Brinton, of Philadelphia, was the first anthropologist in our country to bear the title of professor in a regular university.

The State historical societies are all more or less busy in gathering the material for local history.

Among foreign resources of study, in addition to the old societies now approaching manhood's years, a fact worthy of special notice is the establishment at Leyden, under favorable auspices, of the Internationales Archiv., devoted especially to the interchange of information and courtesies between museums. The editor, Mr. J. D. E. Schmelz, has been very active in gathering summaries of information about many public collections.

Under the head of congresses must be included the anthropological section of the American Association, of the British Association, of the French Association, the German Allgemeine Versammlung der deutschen Gesellschaft für Anthropologie, Ethnologie und Urgeschichte, the Congrès des Américanistes, and the International Congress of Anthropology and Prehistoric Archæology.

A systematic bibliography of anthropology has not yet been attempted. The nearest approach to the subject is the Smithsonian summaries and the lists given in the German Archiv. Excellent special lists will be noticed under their appropriate heads, which, if brought together, would nearly complete the work. It is to be hoped that all bibliographers will adopt the order and plan pursued by the authors of the Index-Catalogue of the Surgeon-General's Library. This would avoid confusion in transferring titles from one work to another. For instance, Fauvelle (Dr.) Des causes d'erreur en anthropologie. Bull. Soc. d'anthrop. de Par., 3. s., x, 263-275; or, in case of a published volume, Hovelacque (Abel). Précis d'anthropologie (Bibliothèque anthropologique). Paris (1887), Delahaye et Lecroisnier, 365 pp., 20 figs. 8vo.

In quoting from a magazine, journal, or other serial the order should be: (1) author; (2) title of extract; (3) journal, always abbreviated by the Surgeon-General's code; (4) town, publisher, series, volume, date, number of pages, maps, plates, and figures, and, finally the size.

In giving the title of a printed book the same order of author and title are to be observed. Then comes the place of publication, the date in parenthesis, the publisher, the pages, etc., as in extracts from journals. If there be more than one volume it is sometimes the plan to treat each volume as a separate thing, after giving the publisher, until the mo. is reached.

A glance at the bibliography accompanying this summary will exhibit the abbreviations for longer words, and the following table will suffice for single-letter abbreviations:

a., aan, alla, auf, aus, aux, etc.	o., och. oder, over.
b., bei, bij, etc.	p., par, pei, pel, pour.
d., das, degli, del, der, die, din, etc.	Q., Quarterly.
E., east.	R., Raekke, Reeks.
e , ein, eine, einer, etc.	r., reale.
f., för, for, fra, für, etc.	S., Surgery, Surgical.
g , gorli.	s., series; e. g., 1 s., 2 s., etc.; n. s., new
h., het.	series; sulla.
J., Jornal, Journal.	t., tegen, ter, till, tot, etc.
K., Kaiserlich, Königlich, Koninklijke.	n., und.
K. K., Kaiserlich Königlich.	ü., über.
l., las, les, los, etc.	v., van, vid, von, voor, vor, etc.
M., Medical, Medicine, Medico, etc.	V. p., various places of publication.
m., mit.	v. s., various sizes.
N., n., Nene, new, nouveau, nuova, nya, North, etc.	W., west.
	z., zur.
n. F., neue Folge.	

In the Bulletin of the Anthropological Society of Lyon, E. Chantre gives a list of the laboratories and public collections in Italy relating to man. (1887, 163-165.)

There are already a number of excellent guide-books for investigators, but Dr. Emil Schmidt added one more, entitled Anthropologische Methoden, Anleitung zum Beobachten und Sammeln für Laboratorium und Reise. (Leipzig (1888). 333 p., figs., 8vo.)

BIOLOGY OF MAN.

Progress in human biology has been along many lines. The one most persistently followed is that supposed to lead to the source of the species. In the method of man's appearance on earth there are two sets of phenomena to be distinguished, the establishment of the fact of his origin and the proper answer to the question, How did this fact come to be. M. Topinard well states the latter case in the following words: There are two general processes of evolution, the one by the transfiguration of species, according to Broca, the other by transformation, according to Darwin. Darwin's method is by natural selection, Lamarck's method is by adaptation to external circumstances of an organism stimulated by internal needs.

The Précis d'anthropologie of Hovelacque and Hervé gives a fresh impetus to the polygenic theory of man's origin. The evolution theory is accepted, but men were evolved in more than one center and from more than one pair. This revived the suggestion made some years ago of two races of men originating at the north and the south-pole, respectively. The polygenic origin of our race is also advocated in M. Debierre's

L'Homme avant l' Histoire. Following up Professor Flower's attempt to summon the teeth as a witness to the various types of mankind, Dr. Fauvelle employs the dental system to teach the ancestral origin of our race. Indeed, there needs to be stated only the titles of a few important papers to show the many gates through which anthropogenists hope to enter the successful answer. Such, for instance, are " The morphological place of man in the mammalian series," by Paul Albrecht; " The origin, races, and antiquity of man," by B. Platz; "A new theory of heredity," by C. Weigert; "The latest phases of heredity," by A. M. Selling; "Can the existence of a tendency to change in the form of the skeleton of the parent result in the actuality of that change in the offspring," by W. Arbuthnot Lane; " The modern theories of generation and heredity," by E. G. Balbiani; " The heredity of crime, alcoholism, etc.," by G. Algeri; "The history of transformism," by A. Giard; "Origin of the fittest," by E. D. Cope; " Evolution and creation," by J. H. Hardwicke; "Lessons upon man according to the doctrine of evolution." But the most useful treatise upon this point is that of Dr. Topinard, the lecture of March 21, 1888, before L'École d'anthropologie, entitled, Les dernières étapes de la genealogie de l'Homme, and published in Revue d'anthropologie in the mouth of May in the same year.

In Nature (XXXVI, 268; 341) is reviewed one of the most thought inspiring works that have come within our notice during the two years under consideration, Mr. G. J. Romaine's paper before the Linnæan Society (see also Nineteenth Century, No. CXIX, 1887, 59–80) on physiological selection. The author is entirely in harmony with Mr. Darwin about the intent and extent of natural selection as the preserver of forms, but looks to other causes to create the variations to be selected and conserved. "If," says he, " variation should be such that while showing some degree of sterility with the parent form, it continues to be as fertile as before within the limits of the varietal form, it would neither be swamped by intercrossing nor die out on account of sterility." In human evolution of varieties there have been going on exactly such excluding forces, shutting off to inbreeding color, clan, caste, nationality, religion, and the like. A paper read by Dr. Burnett before the Washington Anthropological Society on the Melungeons in the southern Alleghanies is a case in point. Neither white nor black nor Indians, these people live encysted, like the Basques of the Pyrenees and little contaminated by mixture.

One of the first convictions of the elder anthropologists of the last century was that man comes within the domain of scientific consideration only so fast as we can apply to him processes of counting, weighing, and tabulation. The progress of anthropometry has been along the lines of refined apparatus and the subjecting of new parts of the body to the metric processes. Anthropometry applied to the living also to a large extent replaces the measuring of the skeleton. Rate of growth, stature, size, weight, proportion, vigor, strength of muscle and breathing, personal identity, these are the subjects of measures innumerable. Professor Hitchcock, of Amherst College, has published an anthropometric manual giving the average and physical measurements and tests of male college students and methods of securing them, prepared from the records of the department of physical education and hygiene in Amherst College in the years 1881-'82 and 1886-'87 inclusive.

Mr. Francis Galton describes an anthropometric laboratory as a place where a person may have any of his various faculties measured in the best possible way at a small cost, and where duplicates of his measurements may be preserved as private documents for his own future use and reference. Such an institution would contain apparatus both of the simpler kind used for weighings and measurings and for determinations of chest capacity, muscular strength, and swiftness, and that of a more delicate description used in what is technically called psychophysical research, for determining the efficiency of each of the various senses and certain mental constants. Instruction might be afforded to those who wished to make measurements at home, together with information about instruments and the registration of results. An attached library would contain works relating to the respective influences of heredity and nurture. These would include statistical, medical, hygienic, and other memoirs in various languages, that are now either scattered through our different scientific libraries or do not exist in any of them. Duplicates of the measurement but without the names attached would form a growing mass of material accessible to statisticians.

From conversation with friends Mr. Galton gathers that the library might fulfill a welcome purpose in becoming a receptacle for biographies and family records, which would be in two classes, the one to be preserved as private documents accessible only to persons authorized by the depositor, and the other as ordinary books, whether they were in manuscript or in print. (Nature, 1887, 112.) In addition to Galton's catalogue of apparatus, Fisher, Venn, Bloxam, and Sargent have published lists of apparatus, with directions.

The philosophical instrument makers publish catalogues of anthropometric apparatus. These are applied to new sets of phenomena every year. Among the notable publications in this direction are Galton's paper on the head-growth of students at Cambridge; the weight of new-born children, by Farago; relation of the hand to stature in Asiatics, by Muguier; reports on laboratory work, by Bloxam and Garson; anthropometric data based on the measurement of three thousand students, by Tuckerman; child-growth, by Zelenski, Lansberger, Chaille, Lorey, Tetherston, and Stephenson.

Coördinated with cranial measurements are cephalic measurements. Ever since Broca's day earnest efforts have been made to perfect this coördination. On the cephalic measurements in France have appeared Collignon's charts of the repartition of the index; C. Arbo has studied the same question in Norway, and A. Fallot publishes a note upon the index of the Provençals.

With reference to the external characteristics of the human body, none attracts so much attention as color of the skin, hair, and eyes. Both in Germany and in France commissions have been appointed by the Government to report on this subject. In certain lines of investigation this must lead to excellent results. Admitting that all variations in our species are the composite result of a struggle between the environment and the species, it is incontrovertible that these changes will take place more rapidly at those points where the battle rages most fiercely, at the most exposed points, where sunlight and heat and actinism, where humidity and aridity, heat and cold, and the like have made their fiercest attacks upon us. The most eminent anthropologists have not been unmindful of this. DeCandolle, Pommerol, Hansen, Variot, Flinker, and Topinard, in many papers, have brought together the results of the public inquiries and pointed out the way to better methods.

Longevity is the subject of several publications that have appeared. There are several factors which enter into the count of race vitality, namely, fecundity, longevity, and energy or vigor, both bodily and mental. There are vague accounts of long-lived individuals, but it is only recently that means have been adopted for verifying the statement as regards individuals and for reaching definite conclusions respecting the life periods of races, communities, or peoples.

M. Turquan and M. Tissandier have collected the statistics of macrobians. Signor Corradi and Signor Trussardi have written treatises on longevity in relation to history, to anthropology and hygiene. Other papers on the same subject have appeared by Ornstein, Humphrey, and Ledyard. On the subject of vigor Signor Zoja has investigated methods of measuring the muscular force of various races.

Further researches in this same line are the study of chest types in man, the Mongolian eye, physiognomie, prehension, right-handedness, erectness of posture, the senses of savages, bodily size and stature, vital statistics, the preservation of vigor, weight, hairiness, and baldness.

There is a mooted question concerning the relative advantage of savagery and civilization as regards vitality. On May 24, 1888, George Harley read an essay before the London Anthropological Institute on the relative recuperative powers of man living in a rude, and man living in a highly civilized, state, in which he brought forward a number of hitherto unpublished though mostly well-known facts, demonstrating that the refining influence of civilization had not been altogether the unalloyed boon we so fondly imagine it to have been. For the cases cited went far to demonstrate the fact that while man's physique as well as his mental power had increased during his evolution from a barbaric state into a condition of bienseance, his recuperative capacity, on the other hand, has materially deteriorated. In fact, it appears from the examples cited that every appliance adding to man's bodily comfort as well as every contrivance either stimulating or developing his mental faculties, while increasing his personal enjoyment, materially diminishes his animal vitality, rendering him less able to resist the effects of lethal bodily injuries, or recover from them as well and as quickly as his barbaric ancestors, or his less-favored brethren. (Nature, 1887, p. 143.)

The body in disease as well as in health may be interrogated about the origin of man and the methods of his physical history. Dr. Matthews writes about diseases among our Indians; Max Bartels upon the rate of healing; McKee and Tecce upon the results of cousin marriages. In the same direction are the studies of abnormal forms, monstrosities, such as microcephals, maternal impressions upon the offspring, platycnemism, pygmies, splanchnology, tailed men, the defective classes, supernumerary organs.

This leads us to the anatomy of the cadaver and the examination of exhumed skeletons. The pelvis, the thorax, the long bones of the arm and of the leg, the scapula, the teeth, and other parts of the mouth, the nose, the orbit, have all been thoroughly studied by Rollet, Fauvelle, Collignon, Bertillon, Giacomini, Prochownick, Runge, Manouvrier, Dwight, Ribbe, Pohlman, Harderup, Riccardi, Testut, Matthews, Beddoe, and Daubes. Upon these studies it is proposed to build a correct account of our racial history and of our origin.

But the great mass of anthropological anatomists still expend their labor upon the skull and the brain, separately and in relation to each other. Under cranial measurements and cranial indices consult the papers of A. B. Meyer, Sergi and Moschen, Sanson, Emil Schmidt, J. G. Garson, O. Fraenkel, Legge, Mies, Dight, Laloy and Benedikt, Topinard and Shufeldt. Upon the evolution of the brain, its mass, its convolutions, its intimate and comparative structure and functions we have to consult the papers of Pozzi, Simms, Topinard, Fauvelle, Manouvrier, Hervé, Bechtereu, Benedikt, Rolleston, Sergi, Houzé, Collignon, Arbo, Fallot, and Luys.

In this same connection the question of topography in the brain and cranio cerebral topography have been discussed by Dr. Cunningham, of the Royal Irish Academy, by Dr. S. Brown, and by Dr. Bonnafort.

To follow up this wide subject with any degree of thoroughness the reader must consult carefully Archiv für Anthropologie and Revue d'Anthropologie. The Index Medicus and the Index-Catalogue of the Surgeon-General's Library leave nothing to be desired in the bibliography of human biology in the widest acceptation of the term, and relieve this summary from repeating a long list of biological journals.

PSYCHOLOGY.

Following closely after biology and entangled with it beyond hope of extrication is the modern psychology, which within its proper area includes many investigations into the origin of mind, the study of animal intelligence, of the faculties of the mind, of the diseases, abnormalities, and idiosyncrasies of mind, of unusual states of mind exhibited in ecstasy, hypnotism, and mind reading ; psychophysics and the physical substratum of mental operations, and various other recondite problems not amenable to classification.

The first series of investigation to consider relates to what Madame Clemence Royer calls L'evolution mentale dans la sérié organique. It has at present a speculative rather than a practical manifestation. But the inquiry about the Unseen from which our spirits come and to which they return continues to excite the pens of such philosophers as Huxley, Gladstone, Du Bois-Reymond, Virchow, and Quatrefages.

A more practical form of investigation is that which treats mentality as a branch of nature with its individual growths from the egg, in its genera and species, relation to environment, and so forth. And so we follow with pleasure and without embarrassment M. Pietrement in his study of hunting dogs, Romanes in his matchless studies in the intelligence of animals. Sir John Lubbock long ago conducted important investigations along the same line, and the studies of Professor Cooke are still fresh in our memories. The most interesting query started by Lubbock inquires into the existence of other organs of sense than ours. The natural history of intelligence, by which is meant the attempt to apply the study of origin, growth, development, chorology, etc., to mental processes has received great encouragement from the observation of animals. In our own country George and Elizabeth Peckham have experimented on spiders and wasps, and in England Sir John Lubbock published a volume on the senses, instincts, and intelligence of animals, with special reference to insects.

The genius of the investigation may be apprehended in the following paragraph :

" We find in animals complex organs of sense, richly supplied with nerves, but the function of which we are as yet powerless to explain. There may be fifty other senses as different from ours as sound is from sight, and even within the boundaries of our own senses there may be endless sounds which we can not hear, and colors as different as red from green, of which we have no conception. These and a thousand other questions remain for solution. The familiar world which surrounds us may be a totally different place to other animals. To them it may be full of music which we can not hear, of sensations we can not conceive. To place stuffed birds and beasts in glass cases, to arrange insects in cabinets and dried plants in drawers, is merely the drudgery and preliminary of study ; to watch their habits, to understand their relations to one another, to study their instincts and intelligence, to ascertain their adaptations and their relations to the forces of nature, to realize what the world appears to them ; these constitute, as it seems to me, at least, the true interests of natural history, and may even give us the clue to senses and perceptions of which at present we have no conception."

The faculties of the mind are studied in the same manner as the mind itself. The phenomena of consciousness and unconsciousness, of sensation, of perception and apperception; of instinct, memory, emotion, reason, and volition in healthy exercise are taken up as so many rocks, or plants, or animals, and their natural history scrutinized. And this is true regardless of the metaphysical basis of the study; the most pronounced materialists and spiritualists have caught the inspiring motive of the naturalist. In this line reference may be made to Wilbrand, Osterman, James, McCosh, Bowne, Dewey, Ladd, Burnham, Féré, Fouilleé, Scholz, Nelson, Hall, and writers in Mind and other journals of psychology.

Just as some of the richest results in mineralogy have been realized from the study of allotropism, in botany and zoology from abnormalities, so in mind study the utmost diligence is exercised in observing the phenomena of mental deformities and eccentricities. In the first number of the American Journal of Psychology, William Noyes discusses paranoia. Further researches in the same line are Routh on overwork and premature mental decay, G. H. Savage on homicidal mania, Grissom on the history and poetry of insanity, Tenchini on the brains of delinquents, Foy on idiosyncrasies, Stevenson on genius and mental disease, and Duval, Ploix, and Dally on aphasia. Indeed, both in France and Italy, congresses, societies, and journals are devoted to this side of anthropological research.

The scientific psychologist has pursued his researches still further. There have been hanging around the suburbs of knowledge many descendants of aboriginal philosophy. One of these offspring is belief in the possibility of occult contact with the spirits of men and a spirit world of the dead. This whole subject, to study which the English Society for Psychical Research was organized, is ably reviewed by Prof. Stanley Hall in the first number of the American Journal of Psychology (128–146). He says: "Thus far not only the formation of such a society, but the boldness of its plan, with its committees on apparitions and haunted houses, and on the claims of Mesmer and Reichenbach, and the degree to which the difficulties and the dangers of the proposed investigations were realized, were all such as to commend it not only to every psychologist, but to every true and intelligent friend of culture and religion. While those who regard the baser forms of modern spiritualism as the refined and concentrated embodiment of all the superstitions of a remote and barbarous past, and the claims of those who pretend to mediate between the living and their friends who are dead as a nameless crime against the most sacred things of the soul, must feel a deep interest in such work, there is another class, perhaps still larger, and with an interest still deeper. This class consists of those who, in these days of unsettlement in religious beliefs, hope to find amid superabundant *aberglaube* a nucleus of certainty for at least the doctrine of immortality. The most absolute idealists are not so satisfied with the speculative method which works by exhausting thought possibilities as not to welcome the most empirical refutation of materialism and mechanism. Even Mr. Meyer's "phantasmagoric efficacy," his "telepathic percolation," or veritable ghosts of those dying or dead or even in great danger, are not unwarrantable in establishing his "solidarity of life which idealism proclaims," or "the universal mind in which all minds are one." But the impartiality attainable in most fields of scientific research is impossible here. A rigorously unbiassed and yet an intelligent jury, could probably not be found in this country or in England, so many and subtle and remotely ancestral are the conscious, and far more the unconscious, prepossessions which enter like Schopenhauer's primacy of the will, making us all lynx-eyed to all that favors one side and bat-eyed for all that favors the other. It is this inexpungable bias, evolved from a state of savage superstition, which enters into our judgment and prevents a just critical estimate of evidence. Gurney's phantasms of the living, Sinnett's hypnotism in the Orient, Herter's discussion of the nature of hypnotism, such are the works that are constantly appearing upon this corner of anthropology.

Psychology is now clearly within the area of anthropology, having its laboratories and instruments of precision, its systematic experiments and its organized corps of observation. Prof. G. Stanly Hall says, "Several departments of science have touched and enriched psychology, bringing to it their best methods and their clearest insights." Among those whose studies have contributed to this end are teachers of psychology in higher institutions of learning, biologists and physiologists; anthropologists who are interested in primitive manifestations of psychological laws; physicians who give special attention to mental and nervous diseases; men who, like Mr. Galton, have applied more exact methods to the problem of human feelings, will, and thought.

The establishment in our country of a journal devoted solely to psycho-physics is a noteworthy event, and the fact that Prof. G. Stanley Hall will have charge of the American Journal of Psychology is a sufficient guaranty of its great scientific value.

In the first number of this publication Dr. Lombard and Professor Jastrow both explain with great clearness the psycho-physic law and illustrate its operation. Professor Jastrow, in his paper on star magnitudes, very clearly explains the action of the psycho-physical law in the first number of the American Journal by referring to Bernouille's illustration of the distinction between the value and the emolument of money. The emolument, or pleasure-giving power, of an additional sum of money is shown to be the logarithm of the wealth of an individual. By widening the conception of the wealth to the general one of a physical stimulus of any kind, and putting sensation in general for the particular sensation caused by an increase in money, we have the psycho-physic law. For the particular illustration of this law Professor Jastrow compares the star magnitudes as they have been arranged by means of the eye with the results of mechanical photometers.

Some interesting experiments on the reciprocal influence of organs of sense have been recently made by Herr Urbanschitsch, of Vienna. His general conclusion is that any sense-excitation has for result an increase of acuteness of other senses. Thus sensations of hearing sharpen the visual perceptions. If colored plates are placed at such a distance that one can hardly distinguish the colors, and various sounds are then produced, the colors become generally more distinct the higher the sounds. Similarly, one can, while a sound affects the ear, read words which one could not read before. Again, the ticking of a watch is better heard when the eyes are open than when they are closed. Red and green increase auditive perceptions, but blue and yellow weaken them. Several musicians, however, were agreed that red, green, and yellow and blue caused an intensification of sound about one-eighth; while violet had a weakening effect. Taste, smell, and touch are under like laws. Light and red and green colors increase their delicacy; while darkness, blue and yellow diminish it. Under the influence of red and green, taste extends from the anterior border of the tongue to the whole surface. On the other hand, a strengthening of smell, taste, or touch exalts the other sensitive perceptions. Specially interesting is the reciprocal influence of touch and the sense of temperature. If one tickle the skin with a hair and plunge the hand in hot water the tickling sensation ceases; on the contrary, if the hand be placed in cold water and a part of the body tickled the temperature is felt more vividly. Herr Urbanschitsch finds in this reciprocal action an explanation of supposed double consecutive sensations on excitation of one sense. (Nature, 1887, p. 157.)

The two sources of information which are absolutely indispensable to the student of psycho-physics are Wundt's "Physiologische Psychologie" and "Hall's American Journal of Psychology." In addition to these "Mind," "Brain," "Philosophische Studien" and "Pflüger's Archiv" are to be consulted. In our own country we have at Johns Hopkins University, in Professor Cattell's laboratory, in Philadelphia, in the Army Medical Museum at Washington, apparatus for psycho-physical experiments. Works of eminent authority in this line of research must be sought under the names, Cattell, Cowles, Donaldson, Fauvelle, Galton, Hall, Hodge, Hyslop, Jackson, Jastrow, König, Lombroso, Krauss, Krouer, Ladd, Lombard, Thompson, Vigna, Wolfe, and Wundt.

In the study of mind many subsidiary and leading questions arise not included in any of the classes above noticed. Such would be the paper of G. J. Romanes on the mental differences of men and women, of Mantegazza, on psychic atavism, of Nicolas, upon automatism in voluntary actions, and that most interesting discussion in Nature by Max Müller, Francis Galton, H. S. Wortley, H. Picton, G. J. Romanes, and J. J. Murphy (XXXVI, 28, 100, 101, 124, 125, 171, 172, 249), upon the pos sibility of thoughts without words. The same question was raised some years ago in the Anthropological Society of Washington, by Professor Porter, of the Deaf Mute College. This correspondence is all printed as an appendix to "Three introductory lectures on the science of thought" by Max Müller. (London, 1888, 8vo.)

ETHNOLOGY.

What was previously said of psychology may be repeated concerning ethnology ; it is at bottom a biological science. That is, when we say "race" we ought to mean blood, not language, nor nationality, nor a region of country, certainly not arts or institutions.

It is true that the science includes all about a certain breed or stock of mankind; indeed, it is the anthropology of men taken by breeds. The ethnologist and the ethnographer are biologists to start with, but they cover the entire area of the natural history of man. The latter works out the anthropology of a single stock or breed. The latter is concerned with anthropology arranged with blood or consanguineous groups for his primary concept. Strictly speaking we apply the term ethnogra· pher to a student of a nation or any other agglommeration of human beings, but this ought not so to be.

As the first question in anthropology is the origin of man so the first question in ethnology is the origin and boundaries of races. The search for primitive man, therefore, is at the same time the search for primitive men.

The second inquiry, which trenches on archæology, and is indeed the motive of the archæologist's researches, is what races of men have lived on the earth and what may be the relation of the present races to them. Upon this question M. de Quatrefages and Marquis de Nadaillac are our chief authorities ; while for general treatises on the species at large the reader must consult Snell, Kriegel, Achelis, Maladini, Robert Brown, Featherman, and various translations and adaptations of Von Hellwald. The seventh volume of the Standard Natural History is reprinted with an appendix which very much adds to its value. Prof. A. H. Keane in his published classifications and in his reviews in Nature continues to be the best English authority on general ethnology.

The biological inquiry into color of hair, eyes, and skin, into pilosity and other anthropometric characteristics is mainly with reference to the subject of race.

In the Journal of the Anthropological Institute (xvi, 370–379) Mr. R. S. Poole shows the Egyptian classification of the races of man.

The question of racial healing or medical ethnography is considered by Tiffany and Verrier.

In all anthropological journals will be found more or less ethnography. In Paris is published Revue d'Ethnographie. The Journal of the Royal Asiatic Society of London is a rich mine of information, and a complete index of all its volumes will be found at the close of the volume for 1888,

No student of ethnography can overlook the publications of the National geographical societies of England, France, Belgium, Russia, Petermann's Mittheilungen, and kindred works.

Special works on ethnography have appeared in great numbers, and the only way to bring the reader into relationship with them is to present a list by continents of those which have come under the writer's notice.

A.—EUROPE.

Aryans, origin, primitive seat, achievements: Morris, Taylor, Hale.
Basques: Lucien Bonaparte.
Brittany: Carquet and Topinard.
Canary Islands: Edwards, Keibel.
Celts: D. Arbois de Jubainville.
Friesland: A. Folmer,
German Alps: Steub.
Gypsies: Crofton, and J. of Gypsy Lore.
Ireland: McDowall.
Lake Dwellers: Messikommer.
Mediterranean Races, non-Aryan, non-Semitic: Glennie.
Neanderthal and Canstadt: Julin.
Norse bibliography: Carpenter.
Russia: A. Castaing, W. Youferou.
Spain, an outcast race in: Pop. Sc. Mouth., xxxii, 546.
Sweden: Montelius.
Transylvania: G. le Comte Kuun.

B.—AFRICA.

Algiers, French Africa: M. Wahl.
Bobos: M. Tautain.
Central African Stocks: Ludwig Wolf, Emin Pasha.
Congo, Lower: R. C. Phillips.
Danakils: L. Faurot.
Egyptians: Virchow, Tomkins, Flinders Petrie.
Gold Coast Peoples: A. B. Ellis.
Gypsies in Sus and the Sahara: Haliburton.
Hottentots, or Khoi Khoi: Ch. Ploix.
Kabyles, of Grand Kabylie: Fr. Drouet.
Liberia: J. Büttekofer.
Madagascar: Max Leclerc.
Manjaques: T. Galibert.
Negro race in America: Corson, Armstrong.
Niger River and Señegal: Chambers, J. Ancelle.

Senegambia: Vigne.
Somalis: P. Pauletschke.
Southern Africa: G. Schils.
Tanganjika Tribes: Houzé.
Tripolitania, Cyrenaica, and Fezzan: Hamy and Borsau.
Tunis: R. Collignon.
West Africa: V. Jacques and E. Storms, E. Decazes, A. Corré.

C.—ASIA.

Afghans: L. Rousselet.
Ainos: F. V. Dickins, Basil Hall Chamberlain, R. Collignon, J. K. Goodrich,
Babylonian Races: G. Bertin.
Cambodia: E. Mamel.
Caucasus: R. von Erckert, E. Chantre.
Central Asia: Henry Lansdell.
China: G. E. Simon, H. J. Allen.
Chinese in America: Stewart Crulin.
Corea: W. R. Carles.
Dardistan: C. E. de Ujfalvy.
Formosa: Terrien de la Couperie, G. Taylor.
Hittites: W. W. Moore, Thomas Tyler, C. R. Conder.
India: E. A. Lawrence, George Campbell, " W. W. Hunter, Gustav Oppert, Bugaigne.
Japan: Wm. E. Griffis, J. D'Autremer, Henry Knollys, Kr. Bahnson.
Jews of the East: A. K. Glover.
Kashgar and the passes of Tian Chan: N. Seeland.
Manipur: G. Watt.
Persia: E. Duhousset, S. G. W. Benjamin, Houssay.
Siam, Bibliography of: E. M. Satoa.
Tadjiks or Galtchas: Ch. E. de Ujfalvy.
Turks in China: J. Deniker.
Yakuts: Albert Roussy.

One of the most celebrated feats of reconstructing the civilization of ancient nations is the history of the discovery of Hittites. In January,

1888, Mr. Thomas Tyler delivered a course of lectures upon this people in the British Museum,

A few years ago all we knew of the Hittites was contained in a few vague references in the First and Second Book of Kings. In the true sense of the word empire, it is doubtful whether a Hittite empire ever existed. Says Mr. Tyler: " Most likely there were in Asia Minor many states or even single cities which were usually to a great extent independent, and the peoples of which were not, perhaps, altogether homogeneous in race, but which, under pressure of the necessity of war, formed a federation. That the Hittites spoken of in the Old Testament are to be identified with the Khita of the Egyptian monuments and with the peoples of the land of Khatti in the Assyrian records, is coming out more and more clearly."

The primitive home of the Aryans seems now to be less definitely fixed than formerly. The studies of Pott, Lassen, and Max Müller made the highlands of Asia to be the cradle of the Aryans. Dr. Latham, even at that time, urged that the Asiatic hypothesis was mere assumption based on no shadow of proof. Recently the European theory has been entertained by Gugei, Cuno, Penka, and Schrader.

The commingling of blood, language, social organization, beliefs, and activities in the Malayan area is elucidated by Dr. Fridrich's paper in the miscellany relating to Indo China. He noticed the continued existence of Hindooism in Java and other parts of Malaysia, and says that it is essential to a proper understanding of the condition of the Malayan tribes that the influence which Hindoo civilization has exerted on them should be investigated.

At a meeting of the Asiatic Society of Japan, reported in the Japan Weekly Mail of November 19, Mr. Batchelor read a paper on Kamui or Gods of the Ainos. The author is not convinced that the Ainos are dying out.

D.—OCEANICA.

Australia : Dominic Daly, J. Fraser, E. M. Carr, S. Gason.
Borneo : Dominic Daly.
Celebes : d'Estrey Meyners.
Malays : F. Grabowski.
Maldives : M. Habelandt.
Maori : J. Errington de la Croix.
New Britain : B. Danks, H. H. Romilly.
New Caledonia : E. Verrier, M. Glaumont.

New Guinea : Prince Roland Bonaparte, a series of reports; Chalmers, G. L. Bink.
New Hebrides : A Hagen and A. Pigneau.
Philippines : Ollivier Beauregard.
Polynesians : E. Tregear.
Samoa : Wm. B. Churchward.
Sandwich Islands : Ed. Arning.
Solomon Islands : H. B. Guppy, F. Elton, C. M. Woodford.
Surinam : R. Virchow, H. Ten Kate.

E.—NORTH AMERICA.

The very best—and only reliable—study of the tribes of North America is that of the Bureau of Ethnology of the Smithsonian Institution, an account of which has been given to the American association by Maj.

J. W. Powell. Dr. D. W. Brinton has also published notes on American ethnology. The following works have special reference:

Aztecs: H. W. Haynes, Lucien Biart.
Beothucs: Lady Edith Blake.
British Columbia: Franz Boas.
California peninsula: H. Ten Kate.
Canada: E. Hamy. (It must also be kept in mind that the British association appointed a special committee to study the Indians of the Dominion of Canada.)
Delaware or Lenape: D. G. Brinton.
Eskimo: H. Rink, Sören Hansen, A. H. Keane, Emile Petitot.
Kwakiutl: Franz Boas.
Missisaquas: A. F. Chamberlain.
Mandans: Dr. Washington Matthews.
Selish Indians of Puget Sound: M. Eells.

F.—MIDDLE AMERICA.

Antilles: Leon de Rosny.
Caribs: Pere de la Borde.

Central America: Leon Laloy.
Costa Rica: Wilhelm Herzog.
Maya: F. A. de Rochefaucould.
Mexico: C. Breker, A. Baker, Alf. Chavero.
Panama: A. Pinart.
Toltecs, were they a historic nation: D. G. Brinton.

G.—SOUTH AMERICA.

Amazon tribes: J. F. Smith.
Botocudos of Espiritu Santo and Minas Geraes: P. Ehrenreich.
Fuegians: Dr. Hyades, G. Sergi.
Guiana: H. A. Condreau, H. Ten Kate.
Paraguay: Dr. Stewart.
Peru: O. Ordinaire.
Venezuela: A. Ernst.

LANGUAGE.

By many anthropologists language is placed among the biological sciences. Such liberties with the term, however, would consign the whole study of man to the realm of biology. In reality the true starting point of anthropology is the study of invention, the consideration of all those devices, institutions, ways and means through which our race has made its progressive journey.

Among the inventions or institutions that lie at the foundation of culture, the most universal in time and place is language, or devices for the communication of thought.

The science of glossology is the anthropology or natural history of speech. It therefore is concerned with origins, with classifications, with life histories, with variation under stress, with as many questions as would be asked about plants or animals.

Indeed, the very first problem that confronts us is this: How far have the animals anticipated us in speech; to what extent have they been our teachers, and what suggestions of their activities and natural qualities have helped in forming the vocabularies of the world.

Close on the heels of this inquiry comes the subject of gesture-language, to the study of which Col. Garrick Mallery has devoted so many years of patient research. The result of his labors, with references to further authorities, are to be found in the publications of the Bureau of Ethnology.

Upon the biological side have appeared such works as Handman upon the human voice and language in physiological psychology, Loewenberg's physiological researches on nasal vowels, Marique upon the larynx, organ of phonation, in its relations with the cerebral centers of language and ideation, Aranjo on the metamorphoses of a sound, Bell's university lectures on phonetics, Jacobi on the special liability to the loss of nouns in aphasia, Horatio Hale on the development of language. The Index-Medicus should be faithfully consulted for papers on the anatomy, abnormalities, diseases, and peculiarities of the vocal organs.

Other productions of general interest are Tregear's ancient alphabets, Newell on the color of words, Brinton on the language of palaeolithic man, Stevenson on place names, Horatio Hale on the development of language.

In this connection reference is again made to the controversy in Nature originated by Max Müller, concerning the dependence of reason upon speech.

The study of an individual language may be termed glossography, just as the study of a separate people is styled ethnography. The two, indeed, are often confounded. If language and race were conterminous a list of all the languages of the world would be at the same time a list of all the peoples or breeds of mankind. Just so far as they are not conterminous is confusion introduced into the enumerations of the languages of the different continents. The complaint is made by critics of great lists, such as Cust's for Africa and Polynesia, that this or that term is not of a language, but of a government.

Moreover, the author who writes about a people generally includes a chapter on their language. It is safe, therefore, for the glossologist to look carefully over the ethnographic titles for material. Furthermore, the accompanying list of works that have been noticed will be useful.

Europe.—The old Runic writing of the North : Oscar Montelius. Color names among English gypsies: W. E. A. Aron. An old Basque test: J. Vinson. The Basque language : V. Stempf. Restitution of the European mother language: Paul Reynaud.

Africa.—Kabail vocabulary: U. Newman. Algerian grammar and lexicon: J. Vinson. Introduction to glossology and literature of the African languages: A. F. Pott.

Asia.—Semitic languages in the Encyclopædia Britannica: Cyrus Adler. Sanscrit texts from Tonkin: G. Dumoutier. The yellow languages : E. H. Parker. Japanese: The Manchus, by the same. The Japanese and the adjacent continental languages : Joseph Edkins. Hittite monuments: Wm. H. Ward. Some useful Hindu books: G. A. Grierson. Formosan language: J. Vinson. Chinese, three papers on : Joseph Edkins. Grammar of the Chinese in San Francisco: H. Cordier. Pre-Chinese language in China: Terrien de la Couperie. Sakuntala : Gerard Deveze.

Polynesia.—The Oceanic languages, Semitic: D. Macdonald. Api grammar: S. H. Ray.

America.—The thorough work of Mr. J. C. Pilling in cataloguing the entire literature of North American aboriginal languages will leave nothing further to be desired. The original plan of including all works under a single alphabetical list has been abandoned, and the author takes up each of the stocks separately. Two monographs have appeared in the new series, "Bibliography of the Eskimo Language" and "Bibliography of the Siouan Language," both issued by the Bureau of Ethnology and printed at the Government Printing Office. Each of the other stocks will receive similar treatment. When the work shall be completed it will leave nothing to desire as a pointer to all sources of information on America.

Mr. A. S. Gatschet has worked up the linguistic families in Southeastern United States. Further publications on North American speech mixture in French Canada: A. M. Elliott. Timucua grammar: Raoul de la Grasserie. The hieratic manuscripts of Yucatan: Pousse. Tarascan texts: H. de Charency. Ancient Nahuatl poetry: Daniel G. Brinton. On the Chane Abal tribe and dialect of Chiapas: By the same. The Ixil language: O. Stoll. The Maya language: San Buenaventura. The Chiapanec language: L. Adam. The Alaquilae language: D. G. Brinton.

The Revue de Linguistique, American Journal of Philology, Internationale Zeitschrift für algemeine Sprachwissenschaft, Journal of the Royal Asiatic Society, Transactions of the Philological Associations, Zeitschrift der morgenländische Gesellschaft, and the journals mentioned under general anthropology, must be the authorities on glossology.

TECHNOLOGY.

The arts of mankind are the material on which to base the natural history of invention. Each art has had its humble birth and has grown to maturity by the constant increase of complexity. The process of inventing itself has had an organic growth, commencing with what might be called an unicellular process and ending with a most complicated set of co-ordinated actions, as numerous and intricate as the parts of the human body. Between a childish or a savage acting on suggestion, a no-sooner-said-than-done performance, and the inventing of the Bell telephone, with all the thinking, experimenting, petitioning, pleading, correspondence, examination, and litigation involved is a very long way. Between the two lie all human mental activities, growing more and more complex as we proceed.

Anthropology is concerned with every human activity and industry, for the purpose of obtaining their testimony to human history. The history of man and of his mind are indeed more clearly written in things than in words.

There are two or three distinct ways of treating technological material, based on the order of the ruling concepts, art, race, region. A study might be governed by certain groups of arts for the principal concept, as in all Mr. E. B. Tylor's writings; or by certain regions of the globe, where the conditions are unique, as in the writings of A. Bastian; or we could study out the industries of a race, a nation, a sect, wherever in time or place they may have lived.

One of the most profitable series of investigations into the origin of form and decoration in the arts is a series of papers by W. H. Holmes, published by the Bureau of Ethnology. Mr. Holmes finds a little fragment of pottery in the fields around Washington. This tells him that the aborigines knew the ceramic art. By pressing on the surface a piece of artist's clay he gets the impress of woven texture. This tells that these aborigines were weavers, and it is very easy to see what kind of weavers they were. It also tells how they decorated pottery. Thus, by piecing art to art, fragment to fragment, the author is able to reconstruct the daily life of an extinct people; to ascertain how the inventive faculty has caught up one suggestion of dame nature after another, and then technic laziness has reduced the full form to conventionalisms and abbreviations. Herr Schaaffhausen has caught up the same idea and published "Entwickelung des menschlichen Handwerks und den Einfluss des Stoffes auf die Kunstform."

Next to the subject of invention and the stimulus thereto by means of patents the subject of learning a trade, of industrial training, demands the careful study of the anthropologists. It is easy to follow up the methods of our own day, but our chief inquiry is how things came to be as they are. Such papers as that of G. P. Morris on industrial training two centuries ago will be hailed with pleasure by comparative technologists.

The only way to illustrate and to study this branch of anthropology is by means of the museum, the gallery or cabinet of drawings, and the specifications. If one would follow up an art he must collect material, he must supply himself with many pictures, he must have his card catalogue or files of ready reference, and all these must be movable and interchangeable.

In the U. S. National Museum there are many series of objects installed to show the natural history of invention, such as naval architecture, land transportation, fishing, music, pottery, cutlery, weapons. These are of especial interest to craftsmen, who find no difficulty in reading the history of their daily occupations.

It is not necessary to enumerate the names of all the arts about which books have been written in 1887-'88. A glance at the list of titles proves that some one has been fascinated with nearly every occupation of mankind. The unit chapter on this subject, the technographic unit is an art of a people. If these be well written they may be allowed to tell their story in two directions, either as a part of the whole history of a people or as a part of the whole history of an art. If Mr. Sato has written a work on Japanese farming, it may be filed away under farming or under Japanese, according to the ruling motive in the mind of the general student; the same is true of the hundreds of technographic chapters that have been written.

The reader may consult with profit The American Manufacturer, Annales des Ponts et Chausseés, Patent-Office Reports, Report of the Department of Agriculture, L'Art, English Mechanic, Journal of the Society of Arts, Scientific American and Supplement.

ARCHÆOLOGY.

Leaving the question of anthropogeny to the biologists the archæologist will still be concerned with primitive man. He desires to know where our race made its début on this planet, how long ago it was, and what was the intellectual and material stock in trade of that first man.

For the study of what M. Collignon calls L'homme avant l'Histoire there is constantly collecting fresh material.

The geologist and the palæontologist are the first to take the stand. Mr. W J McGee, of the U. S. Geological Survey, whose especial department is the quaternary period, has addressed himself to the stratigraphic question, while the palæontology has been discussed by Marcellin Boule, and the cotemporaneity of the mammoth and man by J. M. Clarke and H. Howorth, MM. de Puydt and Lohest.

On the subject of the antiquity of man we have a paper by L. Guignard, relating to France; by A. R. Wallace, on the antiquity of man in America; by E. Rivière, on the antiquity of man in the Alps.

There has been a question agitated between geologists, palæontologists, and archæologists whether in cave and other explorations we are to regard the form and finish of implements, the associated animal remains, or the condition of the strata, to be the best guide to a knowledge of the age of the deposit. The case has been pretty thoroughly reviewed by Henry Hicks and Worthington G. Smith. (Nature, XXXVII 105, 129, 202.)

A fresh classification of archæology is marked by the appearance in England of a new journal, the Archæological Review. The range and divisions of the subjects are: (1) Institutional archæology, which extends the domain of archæology into that of sociology. Indeed, every branch of anthropology may thus have its archæology. (2) Anthropological archæology. This is a bad title. It is meant to include biological and technological subjects, the remains of man and of his arts. (3) Folk-lore. The society would include in this the origin of language, all kinds of tales, rhymes, myths, and lore, and the beginnings of philosophy. (4) Literature; that is, the oldest literatures. The society has promised to do one good thing, for which, well done, they will receive the gratitude of all students. They will index all English archæological publications prior to 1886 and current English and foreign archæological periodicals, and will issue special indexes to different branches of archæological research.

The British Association for the Advancement of Science has regular standing committees on prehistoric remains and the preservation of ancient monuments. The former committee has been busy in mapping and describing all the monuments of the country; the latter in petitioning both Parliament and the local proprietors to preserve the most celebrated remains. A brief of the reports will be found in Nature, XXXVII, 93, 94.

The same is also true in France and Germany. Movements are on foot for the cataloguing of all museums, for the systematic and co-operative survey of remains and the preservation of such monuments as have historic interest.

The Royal Academy of Sciences in Austria has appointed a prehistoric commission, which has already issued its first report. In our own country the subject of archæology is also receiving a systematic treatment. Fortunately for the final result the two principal institutions engaged in extended work are pursuing different methods.

Prof. Cyrus Thomas, of the Bureau of Ethnology, commences with a census of all the mounds, earth-works, and other aboriginal remains in the United States. In the Ohio Archæological and Historical Quarterly Mrs. Thomas presents a bibliography on this subject, but the plan of the Bureau has been more extended than this. The whole area has a card catalogue, by means of which it is possible to construct maps of large or small spaces and to exhibit the number and distribution of each class. The most valuable portion of Professor Thomas' task, and that which exhibits the great advantage of combined labor, is that he is able to work by the side of another staff of men who are studying the distribution of Indians over this continent at the time when they were first visited by white men. Laying the map of the distribution of linguistic stocks on the top of his own map of the mounds, and so forth, he has a starting point for deciding who were the Mound-builders.

The Peabody Museum, or, strictly speaking, its curator, Professor Putnam, educated in comparative anatomy under the elder Agassiz, has addressed himself to another problem, namely, the careful dissection of graves, mounds, and remains so as to know exactly how they were constructed, what relics are deposited in them, and what modern modes of burial they most resemble. Of course, the final result will be reached by combining the two investigations.

It is impossible to mention the names of authors who have reported special researches in archæology.

To follow the subject abroad it is only necessary to study the English Archæological Review, Antiqua, the French Materiaux pour l'Historie de l'Homme, and the bibliographical appendix to the Archiv für Anthropologie.

In our own country the annual reports of the Peabody Museum, the reports of the Archæological Institute of America and its ally the American Journal of Archæology, the American Antiquarian, Proceedings of the American Antiquarian Society, the reports of the Smithsonian Institution and of the Bureau of Ethnology, the American Anthropologist, the Ohio Archæological and Historical Journal, Anales del Museo Nacional de Mexico, and the proceedings of a few State and local societies give publicity to about all that is worthy of permanent record.

SOCIOLOGY.

Sociology is the natural history of society, and studies the formation and growth of human compacts that have survived and become varieties or species. It also investigates the life history of societies, their customs and principles.

To repeat the titles of all sociological papers that appeared in 1887–'88 would require a space equal to Pool's Index to periodical literature. To show the variety of topics and not to exhaust the subject, a list of catch-words is given, with the authors to consult respecting each. It may not always be the most eminent authority. Suffice it to say, the subject has been of sufficient prominence to arrest some one's attention.

Administration: W. Wilson.

Altruism: C. W. Smiley.

America: Justin Winsor, narrative and critical history.

Antagonism as a social force: Sir W. R. Grove.

Anthropophagy: Richard Andree, O. Beauregard, A. Bordier, Ch. Letourneau, Marquis de Nadaillac, Friedrich Ratzel.

Australian sociology: A. W. Howitt.

Charities: Herbert B. Adams.

Child-life: A. C. Fletcher.

Circumcision: P. Lafargue, A. Reverdin, J. G. Harvey, Ch. Letourneau.

Civilization, Hindu: E. W. Hopkins.

Colonization: G. Rolland.

Commerce: A. E. Bateman, Rene de Maricourt, Leone Levi.

Communal life: W. M. Beauchamp.

Contact as a modifying force: Sabatier.

Coöperation: Amos G. Warner.

Copyright: F. A. Seely.

Deformation of the body: N. Rudinger, R. Virchow, T. Ungern-Sternberg, M. A. Rust.

Degeneracy: G. Barron.

Depopulation in France: G. de Lapouge.

Diminution in size of families: G. Lagneau.

Dying out of aborigines; M. Eells.

Economic disturbances: D. A. Wells.

Economic science: Yves Guyot.

Emigration: Rudolf Disselhorst.

Equality and inequality: H. D. Chapin.

Ethnic selection: Dr. Dally.

Evolution by competition: J. W. Powell.

The family: Carlos Soler y Arques.

Family names: Herbert A. Giles.

Food statistics: Karl Keleté.

Games and amusements: Richard Andree, Franz Boas, J. T. Bent, H. S. Halbert, Andrew Hebbert.

Governments, local: J. G. Bourinat. (The whole Johns Hopkins series of historical and political studies are excellent examples of scientific work in this line.)

Guilds in China: D. J. McGowan.

Heirship in Africa: B. Nicholson.

Inheritance: W. Detmer, M. Nussbaum.

Intoxication: Dr. Dormet.

Labor: T. E. Kebbel, O. Pringsheim.

Life tables: William Ogle.

Love, or romantic love and personal beauty as factors in social life and history: H. T. Fink.

One of the latest subjects to be brought within the area of scientific study is romantic love. It is well known that the many stories about the young savage "wooing his dusky mate" are the creations of the novelist's imagination. The conditions of society, with rare exceptions,

were not such as to favor the romantic passion even in Greece and
Rome. The highest expressions of sexual devotion are to be found in
the ancient literature of Semitic peoples. Mantegazza was the first to
write seriously upon the subject. Since his celebrated papers the literature has rapidly multiplied. (Nature, XXXVII, 149.)

The part played by both love and beauty in social selection may be
studied in connection with Romanes on physiological selection. Another method of inquiry is to follow up the natural history of the process of love-making from its simplest to its most complex forms.

Man and the state: Albert Shaw.
Marriage: Leopold von Schroeder, Lori-
 mer Fison, Raj Coomar Roy, D. R.
 McAnally, Benjamin Danks, F. Gal-
 ton, Y. V. Athalgie, E. B Tylor.
Masks and masquerading: L. Serrurier.
Matriarchy: K. Friedrichs.
Money and the mechanism of exchange:
 Désiré Charnay, Benjamin Danks.
Morality: T. H. Huxley, George P. Best,
 Ch. Letourneau.
Mortuary customs: Adele M. Field, James
 Moony.

Nationality in its scientific aspect: B. J.
 Stokvis.
Overcrowding of population: J. Ichen-
 haeuser.
Penance: O. H. Howarth.
Police: W. A. Dun.
Political economy in America: Richard
 T. Ely.
Politics: G. de Lapouge.
Poverty: William G. Sumner, Ferdinand
 Maurice.

Professor Huxley has said respecting the effect of modern civilization in repressing the spirit of militancy among men, "that though
the restraints imposed by civilization have altered the methods by
which the struggle for existence is carried on, they have not made it
less real or less bitter." In other words, great enterprises and the results of world compelling inventions are achieving great social victories
and defeats as influential as those wrought by decisive wars. Note the
influence on the trade of England and the Mediterranean, first, by the
voyage of Vasco da Gama, and second, by the Suez Canal. Parliamentary writers have taken up the same line of inquiry and have brought
politics within the area of anthropology.

Primitive law and custom: R. Dareste,
 C. Staniland Wake.
Prisons of the world: E. Gautier.
Prostitution of minors: V. Augagneur.
Punishment, its genesis and function:
 Angelo Vaccaro.
Revenues: H. G. Keene.
Salaries and wages: G. J. Goschen.
Savagery and childhood: John Johnson,
 jr., Sir John Lubbock.
Schools and school life: E. P. Gould.
Secret societies: H. Cordier.
Sexes, their relation to government: E.
 D. Cope.
Socialism: E. W. Bemis.

Social selection: G. de Lapouge.
Societies: A. Bordier.
Sociology, the science of: Guillaume de
 Greef, J. H. Gubbins, G. L. Gomme,
 F. W. Blackmar.
Statistics: M. de Foville.
Strikes, the social problem of: V. Miret.
Succession in authority: G. d'Aguanno.
Suicide and natality: E. Durkheim.
Tattooing among prostitutes: De Alber-
 tis, G. Vanot and Morau, G. Salsalto.
Trades unions: E. W. Bemis.
Widowhood: G. L. Gomme.
Woman: M. Letourneau, H. Ploss, Emily
 Pfeiffer, H. Thulie.

In every one of the journals devoted to the subject at large sociological papers are published. Furthermore, the great English quarterlies, the North American Review, the Forum, even the monthlies, weeklies, and dailies, are witness of the absorption of the public mind in this department of anthropology.

Like every other investigation, the attempt to study crime in a scientific manner began with crude and false methods. For instance, the comparison of states or nations based on arrests led to a positively inverted result; because in highly organized communities a great many acts are considered to be criminal that are not noticed in worse communities. Even in the case of prison statistics, General Walker says, "The number of persons in prison on a given date affords a very delusive measure of the comparative morality of different sections of the country having different codes of laws and different social standards. For instance, a very large part of the persons who are at any time in prisons and jails in the State of Massachusetts, are there for drunkenness or for the illegal sale of liquors. In another State, the man who sells liquor is a public benefactor. So far, then, the paucity of prison lists simply represents the toleration of vice, if not of crime."

The Italian criminologists were not slow to notice this and apply the facts in rectifying deductions about heredity, atavism, primitive man, and the descent of man, based on the anthropometry of arrested persons and convicts in general. If a good but poor man die in a debtor's prison one would scarcely look for the promise of his misfortune in his cranium. Even deductions based on special crimes, as theft or murder, must not omit the history of the man on account of the times, the various external stimuli that have helped, perhaps forced, against his will, the man to the action. This subject has been thought worthy of a special world's convention, which has published Actes du I congrés internationale d'anthropologie criminelle in Rome, November, 1885, and issued in Turin in 1887. The following mentioned works will also help to the public interest and the variety of treatment which the subject has elicited.

Human criminality from the point of view of comparative anatomy : Paul Albrecht. Atlas of criminality, the new anthropometry and criminality, and bibliographie penitentiaire of different countries since the beginning of the century : Luigi Anfosso. Criminal anthropology in Corsica : A. Bournet. Degereration and criminality : Ch. Féré. The thieves' oracle in Java : G. Beyfuss. Thermometric variations and criminality : E. Ferri. The external ear, a study in criminal anthropology : L. Frigerio. Anomaly of the criminal : R. Garofalo. Criminal anthropology : S. Gache. The penal code and frenopathology : J. Giné y Partagas. Corporeal and mental peculiarities of criminals : von Hölder. Crime—a social study : Henri Joly. Criminal anthropology and punishment : H. Kurella. The criminal in his anthropological, medical, and judicial relations : Cesare Lombroso. The characters of delinquents :

A. Marro. Anatomical observations on the brains and skulls of criminals: G. Mingazzini. The actions of criminals: Pitré. The principle of causation in criminal science: F. Puglia. Notes on crime and accidents in Norfolk at the time of Edward I: W. Rye. Studies upon a century of crime: V. Rossi. Criminology: M. Tarde. The frontal crest in criminals: Tenchini. Criminal anthropology: Paul Topinard. Creating criminals: Amos G. Warner. The essential elements which should be present in criminal statistics and the means of rendering them comparable: E. Younes.

Close on the heels of crime attends, the punishment, and the one has had as varied a history as the other. Upon this subject has appeared crucifixion in the ancient east by George Rawlinson. Judicial executions: J. J. Z. Marshall. The prison world: E. Gautier. Genesis and function of legal penalties: Angelo Vaccaro.

The police system of various countries and all the paraphernalia of arrest should also find a place in this department of sociology.

Chinese civilization has a sympathizing exponent in the volume of M. Simon. The most civilized state, according to this author, is that " in which on a given area, the largest possible number of human beings are able to procure and distribute most equally amongst themselves the most well-being, liberty, justice, and security." Upon this scale China is pronounced to be the most highly civilized country in the world. " Its history shows the phenomena of heredity in regular succession, neither modified nor obstructed by change of medium, with the evolution of events and ideas—an evolution as regular as that of living beings freely proceeding unshaken and untroubled by any exterior influence, by which its direction might have been altered, or its development retarded ; and it is here that we find the deep and original interest of China, and perhaps also the secret of her extraordinary longevity."

PHILOSOPHY, MYTHOLOGY, AND FOLK-LORE.

Among the lowest tribes of men all lore and myth is an attempt to explain phenomena. This was long ago pointed out by Peschel. Among the higher races we may study metaphysics, ethics, folk-lore, and religion as somewhat separate problems. Even here they are much intertwined. The philosophy of living in this world has never been able to disengage itself from a world beyond, a spirit world, acquainted with ours, influencing it, and often believed to dominate over the life beyond.

For the purpose of scientific investigation, religion is here defined to include the following topics:

(1) Social organization in view of the spirit world ; in general terms, the clergy and laity of a people. This we may call the *Church*.

(2) The beliefs of a people about the spirit world embodied in their sacred books, national epics, myths, and folk-lore. This we may call the *Creed*.

(3) Conduct in view of the ecclesiastical organization. It includes sacred precincts, edifices, regalia, paraphernalia of worship, fêtes, processions, selemn services, rites, sacrifices, holidays. In a single word, it is the *Cult* of a people.

From this definition it will readily be seen that all religions may enter the area of scientific inquiry, and, again, that it is very difficult to keep philosophy, or the explanation of the universe, religion, or creed and cult and folk-lore, which is the literature and custom of the unlettered, apart in the laboratory.

It is an evidence of progress that there is in Paris a Musée des Religions, publishing Revue de l'Histoire des Religions. In the sixteenth volume of this periodical, Theodore Reinach has a paper on Les classifications des religions et la rôle de l'Histoire des religions dans l'enseignement public. Julien Vinson has also in Revue de Linguistique (XXI, 361–364) a paper entitled "Les religions actuelles, leurs doctrines, leur · evolution, leur histoire." Anthropological mythology also receives the attention of B. Platner in the New Englander (1888), and the ghost theory of the origin of religion is discussed in Bibliotheca Sacra for the same year.

The whole subject of the basis of morality is being reviewed in the most learned of our periodicals in America, in England, and on the continent. The North American Review, the Forum, the Contemporary Review, the Nineteenth Century, the Revue Politique et Litteraire, the Revue des deux Mondes must be faithfully studied by one who would keep posted on the questions raised. Reviewing the ethical treatises of Schuman and Best, Mr. Romanes enforces the sufficiency of the Darwinian hypothesis to explain the moral sense in all its protean forms as proximately due to natural causes. In Popular Science Monthly, W. S. Lilly discusses materialism and morality (XXX, 474–493), and Prof. A. P. Peabody speaks of classic and semitic ethics in Andover Review (X, 361–376). All of the theological periodicals discuss ethical questions, basing human duty on divine injunction. In addition to the publications of the Musée Guimet and the journals and proceedings of the great anthropological societies, the student must consult for the study of comparative religion the Journal of the Royal Asiatic in London and the transactions, etc., of the branches in India and China. At the close of the volume of the Journal for 1888 (vol. XX, pt. 4; appendix, pp. 1–218) will be found an excellent index to the whole series.

In the classified index appended to Archiv für Anthropologie each year is a separate collection of titles relating to this branch of anthropology.

The Revue d'Anthropologie and Revue d'Ethnographie also give each quarter a list of publications, among which are many bearing on religion.

The most fascinating department of our science is folk-lore. It is so familiar to every intelligent person from childhood; it is imbedded in every mind, and furnishes the starting point for every department of knowledge.

To this subject are now devoted several journals, namely:

Folk-Lore Journal. London.
The Journal of American Folk-Lore. Cambridge.
Journal of the Gypsy-Lore Society. London.
Les Litteratures Populaires de toutes les Nations, twenty-seven volumes. Orleans.

Melusine. Paris.
Le Museon. Louvain.
Bibliographie des Traditions. Paris.
Archæological Review. London.
Revue des Traditions Populaires, Paris.

The English Folk-lore Society has made the greatest possible advance in systematizing its work by the tabulation of folk-tales. This works a great economy in two ways. First, two or more persons do not waste their time by working on the same author. A list of collections is published and the name of the tabulator is appended to each volume. Second, and this is the greatest improvement, there is a form of tabulation prescribed by the society, consisting of the title of the story, the dramatis personæ, an abstract of the story, giving its leading incidents and leaving out vain repetitions, an alphabetic list of incidents, and so much bibliography as will enable the future student to follow up the matter for himself. It can be readily seen how much labor is spared to the comparative folk-lorist by this economic scheme.

HEXIOLOGY.

The surroundings of a people, the play of the environment on the people, and their effect on the nature of things around them Mivart calls hexiology.

In the U. S. National Museum is a room, the function of which is to show how vegetable and animal products have been made contributory to human weal and happiness. A few titles of books and papers along this line of research will show how important to us is this branch of study.

The French have a société d'acclimatation, patronized by the Government, publishing a large series of journals, and consulted with reference to colonization. Attention may also be called to the following: The animal economic products of India: J. R. Murray. L'influence du milieu sur les peuples de l'Asie Centrale: M. de Ujfalvy. On tropical and subtropical climate and the acclimatization of the fair races in hot countries: D. H. Cullimore. Origin of the domestication of the horse: R. S. Huidekoper. Le cheval sauvage de la Dzoungaril: Dr. Fauvelle. Equidae de la période quarternaire: Ed. Piette. The metals of ancient Chaldaea: P. E. Berthelot. On nephrite and jadeite: F. W. Clarke and G. P. Merrill. Food and fibre plants of the North American Indians: J. S. Newberry. Nouvelle recherches sur le type sauvage.

In this brief record, doubtless many titles of great value are omitted.

Nevertheless, enough are given to show how many avenues of scientific research lead up to man as their object. It will be possible in future summaries to systematize the subject still further. Several journals of special function are now giving bibliographies in their own departments so that we shall have only to combine their work to perfect the record.

BIBLIOGRAPHY OF ANTHROPOLOGY FOR 1888.

ABBOT, C. C. Evidences of the antiquity of man in eastern North America. Vice-President's address, American Association, August, 1888.

ACHELIS, T. Die Principien und Aufgaben der Ethnologie. Arch. f. Anthrop., Brnschwg., XVII, 265-277.

Actes du 1er Congrès international d'anthropologie criminelle, Rome, novembre 1885. Biologie et sociologie. Turin (1887). 549 pp., charts and plates. 8vo.

ADAM, L. La langue chiapanèque. Observations grammaticales, vocabulaire méthodique, textes rétablis. Wien (1887), Hölder. viii, 117 pp. 8vo.

ADAMCIEWICZ, A. Ueber die Nervenkörperchen des Menschen. Wien, 1888. 20 pp., 3 tables. 8vo.

ADAMS, HENRY C. Public debts. An essay in the science of finance. New York: Appleton, 1888, xi+407 pp. 8vo.

ADAMS, HERBERT B. Notes on the literature of charities. Baltimore: Johns Hopkins Studies in Hist. and Polit. Sc., s. 5, viii+48 pp. 8vo.

ADLER, CYRUS. The views of the Babylonians concerning life after death. Andover Rev., 1888 (July), x, 90-101.

—— Discussion on the study of modern oriental languages. Trans. and Proc. Mod. Lang. Ass., 1887, III, 18.

—— Semitic languages in the Encyclopaedia Britannica. Proc. Am. Phil. Ass., 19th session. Burlington, Vt., 1887. 14-17 pp.

ALBRECHT, PAUL. Noch einmal die Chorda dorsalis im "prächordalen" Schädel. Rückänsserung auf einen Angriff des Dr. Carl Gegenbaur in Heidelberg. Hamburg: P. Afbrecht. 10 pp. 8vo.

—— Sur la place morphologique de l'homme dans la série des mammifères, ainsi que sur la criminalité de l'homme au point de vue de l'anatomie comparée. Actes Congr. internat. crim., 1885, Rome, I, 104-115.

ALLEN, HERBERT J. Is Confucius a myth? J. China Br. R. A. S., XXI, 193-198.

—— Ta-Ts'in and dependent states. Id., 204-213.

ALLIS, O. H. Man's aptitude for labor in an erect position; with an inquiry into the agencies that predispose to a very universal preference for the right leg and arm. Tr. Coll. Phys. Phila., 3. s., IX, 35-62.

ALLOTTE, L. Primordialité de l'écriture dans la genèse du langage humain. Paris, 1888. 8vo.

ALSBERG, M. Anthropologie mit Berücksichtigung der Urgeschichte des Menschen. Stuttgart (1887). Liefg. 3. pp. 85-112. 8vo. Ill.

ALVIELLA, GOBLET D'. Histoire religieuse du feu. Biblioth. Gilon, No. 173. Verviers, 1887. 12mo.

American Anthropologist. Organ of the Anthropological Society of Washington. Vol. I in 1888. By the Society. Quarterly.

American Antiquarian and Oriental Journal. Chicago, 1887. Vol. IX. Six numbers a year.

American Antiquarian Society. Worcester, Mass. (See Proceedings.)

American Association for the Advancement of Science. (See Proceedings.)

American Journal of Archæology and of the History of Fine Arts. Boston: Ginn & Co. Vols. I-IV, 1885-'88. (The journal is the official organ of the Archæological Institute of America and of the American School of Classical Studies at Athens.) Quarterly.

American Journal of Philology. Baltimore : The editor, Basil L. Gildersleeve. Vol. I–IX, 1880-'88. Quarterly.

American Journal of Psychology. Baltimore: N. Murray. Vol. I, No. 1, in November, 1887. Quarterly.

American Naturalist. An illustrated monthly, devoted to the natural sciences in their widest sense. New York: Leonard Scott. Vol. XXI in 1887. Monthly.

Anales del Museo Michoacano. Morelia : Escuela de Artes. Vol. I in 1888.

Anales del Museo nacional de México. México: Escalante. IV.

ANCELLE, J. Les explorations au Sénégal et dans les contrées voisines depuis l'antiquité jusqu'à nos jours. Paris (1887), xl, 445 pp., chart. 12mo.

ANDERSON, WILLIAM. Pictorial arts in Japan. Rev. in Nature, XXXV, 591.

ANDREE, RICHARD. Das Zeichnen bei den Naturvölkern. Mittheil. d. anthrop. Gesellsch., Wien, XVII, 98–106, 3 pl. ; Verhandl. d Berl. Gesellsch. f. Anthrop., 1888, 410–412.

—— Die altmexikanischen Mosaiken. Intern. Arch. f. Ethnog., 1888, I, 214–215.

—— Die Anthropophagie. Leipzig : Veit. vi+105 pp. 8vo.

—— Ueber die Spiele in ihrer ethnographischen Bedeutung. Cor.-Blatt d. deutsch. Gesellsch. f. Anthrop., Brnschwg., XIX, 53.

ANFOSSO, LUIGI. Atlante geografico della criminalità. Studi e ricerche. Torino. 1 pl., 5 maps. fol.

—— Il segnalamento dei delinquenti ed il nuovo antropometro popolare. Arch. di psichiat., Torino, IX, 363–374, 1 pl.

Annales de l'Extrême-Orient. Vol. III in 1888.

Annales du Musée Guimet. Paris : E. Leroux. Vols. I–XII. 4to.

Annual report of the Peabody Museum. Cambridge, Mass. (F. W. Putnam, director.)

Anthropologische Gesellschaft in Wien. Mittheilungen. Quarterly

Anthropology. Miscellaneous papers relating to anthropology. (From the Smithsonian Report for 1885.) Washington (1887). 44 pp. 8vo.

Antiqua. Unterhaltungsblatt für Freunde der Alterthumskunde. Special-Zeitschrift für Prähistorie und einschlägige Gebiete. Zürich : F. Lohbauer. Vol. VI in 1888. Monthly.

ANUTCHINE, D. N. Bows and arrows. Archæological and ethnological study. Moscow: Mamóntoff, 1887, 75 pp. 4to. [In Russian. Reprint from Transactions of Tiflis Archæol. Congress.]

—— Ueber die Reste des Höhlenbähren und des Menschen aus Transkaukasien. Bull. Soc. impériale d. naturalistes de Moscou, 1887, pp. 374–377.

ARANJO, FERNANDO. Les métamorphoses d'un son. Rev. de ling., Par. (1888), XXI, 145–159.

ARBO, C. La carte de l'indice céphalique en Norvège. Rev. d'anthrop., Par., 3. s., II, 257–264.

Archæological and Ethnological Papers of the Peabody Museum. Harvard University. Cambridge : By the Museum. Vol. I, No. 1, in 1888.

Archæological news from all parts of the world. Am. J. Archæol., III, 136–204.

Archæological Review. Ed. by G. L. Gomme. London : David Nutt. Published in monthly parts. Vol. I in 1888.

Archives de l'anthropologie criminelle. Paris. Founded in 1886.

Archives des missions scientifiques, 3. sér., XIII. Published in Paris in 1887.

Archiv für Anthropologie. Herausgeg. u. redig. v. L. Lindenschmit u. J. Ranke. Braunschweig (1888), pp. 1–369, u. Verzeichniss der anthropologischen Literatur, pp. 1–194. 16 Tafeln. Band IV. Vierteljahrsheft, I–IV.

Archivio per l' antropologia e la etnologia. Organo della Società italiana di antropologia, etnologia e psicologia comparata. Firenze : Salvadore Landi. Vol. XVII in 1887. Quarterly.

Archivio per lo studio delle tradizioni popolari. Palermo. Vol. VI in 1887. Quarterly.

ARMSTRONG, S. C. The future of the American negro. Proc. Nat. Confer. Char., Bost., XIV, 167-170.

ARNING, ED. Ethnographie von Hawaii. Verhandl. Berl. Gesellsch. f. Anthrop., 1887, 129-138.

AKON, W. E. A. Color names amongst the English gypsies. Nature, XXXVI, 599.

ASPELIN, J. R. Die Freunde der finnischen Handarbeit. [Rev. in Intern. Arch. f. Ethnog., 1888, I, 109.]

Association française pour l'avancement des sciences, session de Toulouse. 2e section : Anthropologie. [Rev. in Rev. d'ethnog., Paris, VI, 492-502.]

ATHALGIE, Y. V. On betrothal among the Maharashtra Brahmanas. J. Anthrop. Soc., Bombay, I.

AUBERT, Dr. Notes sur le département de l'Ain (Doubes, Bresse et Bugey). Rev. d'anthrop., Par. (1888), 3. s., III, 456-468.

AUBRY, PAUL. Bonnet de derviche tourneur. Bull. de la Soc. d'anthrop., Paris, 3. s., X, 260.

—— Présentation de costumes russes. Bull. de la Soc. d'anthrop., Paris, 3. s., X, 709-710.

AUGAGNEUR, V. La prostitution des filles mineures. Arch. de l'anthrop. crim., Paris, III, 209-228. 1 ch.

Ausland (Das). Stuttgart. Weekly.

AVERY, JOHN. Notes from the far East. Am. Antiquarian, IX. Series of articles.

AXON, WM. E. A. The use of beef and spirituous liquors in India. Am. Antiquarian, IX, 199-201.

AYA, M. Sur un cas de microphthalmic. Bull. de la Soc. d'anthrop., Paris, 3. s., X, 548.

A., E. History of civilization. The ancient world, or dawn of history. Cincinnati, 1888. Central Publishing House. [Rev. in Am. Antiquar. Mendon, Ill. (1888), X, 396.]

BABCOCK, W. H. Here and there in Maryland. Am. Antiquarian, IX, 203-207.

—— Notes on local names near Washington. J. Am. Folk-Lore, N. Y. (1888), I, 146-147.

BABELON, ERNEST. Review of Greek and Roman numismatics. Am. J. Archæol., III, 75-86.

BACKHOUSE, T. W. The natural history of the Roman numerals. Nature, XXXVI, 555.

BAHNSON, KR. S. Bing's japan. Ausstellung in Copenhagen. Rev. in Intern. Arch. f. Ethnog., 1888, I, 161-162.

—— Sépultures d'hommes et de femmes de l'âge de bronze. Mém. d. antiq. du Nord, 1888.

—— Ueber ethnographische Museen. Mitth. d. anthrop. Gesellsch. in Wien, n. F., VIII, 109-164. Also, Archeol. Rev., Lond., II, 1 ; 73 ; 145.

BACER, A. The aboriginal races of the state of Vera Cruz. Proc. Roy. Geog. Soc., IX, 568-574,

BALBIANI, E.-G. Les théories modernes de la génération et de l'hérédité. (Résumé,. Rev. phil., Paris, 1888, XXVI. 529-559.

BALDWIN, C. C. Col. Charles Whittlesey. Am. Antiquarian, IX, 111-113.

BALFOUR, HENRY. Exhibition of arrows from the Solomon Islands. J. Anthrop, Inst., Lond. (1888), XVIII, 30.

—— The evolution of a characteristic pattern on the shafts of arrows from the Solomon Islands. J. Anthrop. Inst., Lond. (1888), XVII, 328-332, 1 pl.

BARROIL, G, Le Tabou. Lecture faite au Cercle philologique de Florence, année 1888. Rev. d'anthrop., Par. (1888), 3. s., III, 627,

—— Una gita fra i Calabro-Albanesi. Arch. per l' antrop., Firenze, XVII, 257-270,

BARRON, G. The constitutional characteristics of dwellers in large towns as relating to degeneracy. Lancet, London, II, 758-760. Pop. Sc. Month., XXXIV, 324-330,

BARTELS, M. Culturelle und Rassenunterschiede in Bezug auf die Wundkrankheiten. Ztschr f Ethnol , Berl., 1888, XX, 169-183.

BARTHÉLÉMY, M.-A. Une légende nanienne (traduite du pehlevi). Rev. de Ling., Par. (1888), XXI, 314-339.

BASTANZI, G. Superstizioni religiose nelle provincie de Treviso e di Belluno. Arch. per l' antrop , Firenze, XVII, 271-310.

BASTIAN, A. Die Welt in ihren Spiegelungen unter dem Wandel des Völkergedankens. Prolegomena zur einer Gedankenstatistik. Berlin, Mittler und Sohn, 1887. 1 vol., 8vo.

—— Ethnologisches Bilderbuch mit erklärendem Text. Zugleich als Illustrationen zu dem Werke: Die Welt in ihren Spiegelungen unter dem Wandel des Volkergedankens. Berlin (1887), qu fol., 25 Tafeln, davon 6 in Farbendruck u. 3 in Lichtdruck m. 23 pp., Text.

—— Neue Erwerbungen des Museums für Völkerkunde. Verhandl. d. Berl. Gesellsch. f. Anthrop , Berl., 1888, 266.

—— Notice sur les pierres sculptées du Guatémala, récemment acquises par le Musée Royal d'Ethnog. de Berlin, trad. de l'allemand par J. Pointet Ann. du Musée Guimet, X, 263-305, 1887.

BAT, NESCATCHA. Basque Cookery. Rev. de Ling , Par. (1888), XXI, 287-294.

BATEMAN, A. E. Our statistics of foreign trade, and what they tell us. Jour. Roy Statis. Soc. Lond., L, 653-658.

BAXTER, SYLVESTER. The old new world· an account of the explorations of the Hemenway southwestern archæological expedition in 1887-'88, under the direction of Frank Hamilton Cushing. Salem, Mass. (1888), 1 vol., 40 pp., 6 illus.

BAYE, J. DE. L'archéologie préhistorique. 1 vol., 8vo., 51 figs. In Bibl. scientif. contemp., Paris, 1888, J.-B. Baillière et fils Rev. d'anthrop., Par. (1888), 3. s., III, 592-596.

BEAL, S. The narrative of Fahien [the Chinese Buddhist pilgrim to India (A D. 400)], J. R. A. S., XIX, 191-206, pl.

BEAUCHAMP, W. M. Aboriginal communal life in America. Am. Antiquarian, IX, 343-349.

—— Onondaga tales. J Am. Folk-Lore, N. Y., I, 44-48.

—— Onondaga customs. Id., 195-203.

BEAUREGARD, OLLIVIER. Anthropologie et philologie· Aux Philippines. Bull. de la Soc d'anthrop., Par., 3. s., X, 482-515.

—— Calvitie précoce. Bull. de la Soc d'anthrop.. Par., 3. s., X, 642-643.

—— L'anthropophagie à Madagascar. Bull Soc d'anthrop de Par., 3. s., XI, 234-237.

BECHTEREU, W. Le cerveau de l'homme dans ses rapports et connections intimes. Arch. slaves de biol., Paris, IV, 249-296, 1 pl.

BECKWITH, THOMAS Mounds in Missouri. Am. Antiquarian, IX, 228-232.

BEDDOE, J. On the stature of the older races of England, as estimated from the long bones. J. Anthrop Inst , Lond., XVII, 202-209.

Beiträge zur Anthropologie und Urgeschichte Bayerns. Organ der Münchener Gesellschaft für Anthropologie, Ethnologie und Urgeschichte. München· Theodor Riedel, vol. VIII, in 1888.

BELL, ALEXANDER MELVILLE University lectures on phonetics. Werner: New York. 78 pp. 8vo.

BELL, E. On the distinction between romanesque and gothic. Archæol. Rev., Lond., 1888, II, 237-251.

BEMIS, E W. Old-time answers to present problems as illustrated by early legislation of Springfield, Mass. New Englander and Yale Rev., Feb., 18~7,

—— Socialism. The Overland Monthly, March, 1888,

—— The iron octopus; Evils of our railroad system. Cosmopolitan; Rochester, Feb., 1888.

BEMIS, E. W. Trades union benefit features. Political Science Quarterly. June, 1888.

BENEDICT, M. Drei Chinesen-Gehirne. Med. Jahrb., Wien, n. F., II, 121–133.

—— Die klinischen Resultate der Kraniometrie und Kephalometrie. Internat. klin. Rundschau, Wien, II, 1601–1604.

—— Kraniometrie und Kephalometrie. Wien (1888), 172 pp., ill., 8vo.

BENJAMIN, S. G. W. Persia and the Persians London: Murray, XVII+507 pp., 8vo.

BENT, J. T. The Pisan game. Archæol. Rev., Lond., II, 57–60.

BENTON, G. Mahommedism in Africa. N. Am. Rev., Feb. (1888), p. 222.

BÉRANGER, Dr. Doigts supplémentaires sur le bord cubital de chaque main. Bull. de la Soc. d'anthrop. Par., 3 s., X, 600–603.

BÉRENGER, FÉRAUD, Dr. Note sur la légende grecque d'Ibicus chez les Provençaux de nos jours. Rev. d'anthrop., Par. (1888), 3. s., III, 192–196.

—— Note sur les castellets (petits amoncellements de pierres) de la montagne de la Saint-Baume en Provence. Rev. d'anthrop, Par. (1888), 3. s, III, 49–58.

—— Note sur une légende de Semiramis en Provence. Rev. d'anthrop., Par., 3. s., II, 559–569.

—— Note sur un vestige du culte de la Terre mère (Phallisme) en Provence. Rev. d'anthrop., Par. (1888), 3. s., III, 560–567.

BERGAIGNE, A. L'ancien royaume de Campâ dans l'Indo-Chine. J. Asiatique (Rev. d'Ethnog , XVI, 167).

BERLIN, A. F. Fraudulent relics. Am. Antiquar., Mendon, Ill. (1888), X, 316–318.

BERNARD, P. Considérations médico-légales sur la taille et le poids depuis la naissance jusqu'à l'âge adulte. Arch. de l'anthrop. crim., Par., II, 213–225.

BERNER, H. Til fælde af Skafocefali med anthropologiske Bemærkninger. Norsk Mag. f. Lægevidensk, Christiania, 4. R., II, 625–635.

BERTHELOT, M. P. E. The metals of Ancient Chaldea. Pop. Sc. Month., XXXII, 220–225, 1887

BERTHOLON et LACASSAGNE. Quelques renseignements sur les habitants de la Kroumiric. Bull. de la Soc. d'anthrop. de Lyon, VI, 71–80, 1887.

BERTILLON, A. De la morphologie du nez. Rev. d'anthrop., Par., 3. s, II, 158–169.

BERTILLON, Mlle. JEANNE. L'indice encéphalo-cardiaque. Bull. Soc. d'anthrop., Par., 3. s., XI, 149–158.

BERTIN, G. The races of the Babylonian Empire. J. Anthrop. Inst., Lond. (1888), XVIII, 104–120, 1 pl.

BEST, GEORGE P. Morality and utility. London (1887): Trübner.

BEYFUSS, G. Diebes Orakel in Java. Verhandl. d. Berl. Gesellsch. f. Anthrop., Berl., 1888, 278–283.

BEZZENBERGER, A. Ueber die Sprache der preussischen Letten. Göttingen: Vandenhoeck. 12mo

BIANCHI, S. Ricerche anatomiche sul processo innominato dell' osso occipitale. Bull. d. r. Accad. med. di Roma, XIII, 51–64.

—— Sul modo di formazione del terzo condilo e sui processi basilari dell' osso occipitale nell' uomo. Arch. per l' antrop., Firenze, XVII, 345–358.

BIART, LUCIEN. The Aztecs, their history, manners, and customs. (Trans. by J. L. Garnier.) Chicago: McClurg.

Bibliographie pénitentiaire pour les différents pays depuis le commencement du siècle. Actes Cong. pénitent. internat. de Rome, 1885, II, pt. 2, 7–388.

Bibliothèque anthropologique. (H Thulie La Femme. M. Duval: Darwinism. Ch. Letourneau: L'évolution de la morale. Hovelacque et Hervé Précis d'anthropologie.) Paris: Delahaye.

BICHLER, J. Zum Volksglauben. Wien. med. Wchnschr., XXXVII, 373; 407; 453; 557.

BICHLER, L. Bijdragen tot de Taal-Land-en Volkenkunde van Nederlandsch-Indie, uitgegeven door het Koninklijk Instituut. 's Gravenhage: Martinus Nijhoff, 5. s., III in 1888.

BINDER. Das Morel'sche Ohr; eine psychiatrisch-anthropologische Studie. Arch. f. Psychiat, Berl., 1888-9, XX, 514-564.

BINK, G.-L. Réponses faites au questionnaire de sociologie et d'ethnographie. Nouvelle-Guinée, spécialement au golfe de Geelwink (côte de Dorlh et île de Rhoon). Bull. Soc d'anthrop. de Par., 1888, 3. s., XI, 386-410.

BINET, A. Le fétichisme dans l'amour Rev. Philosophique, Paris, XXIV, 143-167 ; 252-274. Also, separate, 306 pp , 12mo.

BISCHOFF, T. Ueber die Sambaquys in der Provinz Rio Grande do Sul (Brasilien). Zeitschr. f. Ethnol., Berl., XIX, 176-198.

BLACKMAN, F. W. Social phenomena of the Early Hebrew. Overland Monthly. April, 7 pp.

BLAKE, Lady EDITH. The Beothucs of Newfoundland. XIXth Cent., Lond., XXIV. 899-918.

BLAKE, W. W. The metals of the Aztecs. Am. Antiquarian, IX, 164-167.

BLONDEL, SPIRE. L'art capillaire chez les peuples primitifs. Rev. d'ethnog., Paris, VI, 414-427.

———— L'art capillaire daus l'Inde, à la Chine et au Japon. Id , VI, Paris, 1888; pp. 422-448

BLUMNER, HG. Technologie und Terminologie der Gewerbe und Künste bei Griechen und Römern. Leipzig (1887)· Teubner, IV. Bd , 1 u. 2. Abth., xi+629 pp , figs., 8vo.

BOAS, FRANZ. American Folk-Lore Publication Society. Rev. in Internat. Arch. f. Ethnog., 1888, I, 110.

———— Census and reservations of the Kwakiutl Nation. Bull. Am. Geog. Soc., XIX, 225-232.

———— Chinook Songs. Am. Folk-Lore Journal. I, New York, 220-226.

———— Die religiose Vorstellungen und einige Gebrauche der centralen Eskimos. Petermann's Mittheil., XXXIII, 302-315.

———— Ethnol. of Br. Columbia. Proc. Am. Phil. Soc. (1887).

———— Gleanings from the Emmons collection of ethnological specimens from Alaska. Am. Folk-Lore Journal, New York, I, 215-219

———— Myths and legends of the Catloltq. (Second paper.) Am. Antiquar., Mendon, Ill. (1888), X, 366-373.

———— On certain songs and dances of the Kwakiutl of British Columbia. J. Am. Folk-Lore, N. Y., I, 49-64 (1888).

———— The Central Eskimo. VI. Ann. Rept. Bur. Ethnol., 1888, pp. 399-669, 157, figs., maps, pl. ii.

———— The game of cat's-cradle. Internat. Arch f. Ethnog , Leiden, 1888, I, 229-230, 5 ill

———— Poetry and music of some North American tribes. Science, IX, 383

———— The occurrence of similar inventions in areas widely apart. Science, vol. IX, May 20, p. 485.

BOBAN, M. Collection d'instruments en silex de l'Amérique du Nord. Bull de la Soc. d'anthrop., Paris, 3 s., X, 649-652.

Body weight of the force in the Imperial Navy. Sei-i-Kwai M. J., Tokyo, VI, 93, 1 diag.

BOLAU, H. Der Elephant im Krieg und Frieden und seine Verwendung in unseren afrikanischen Colonien. Hamburg (1887). 8vo.

BOLTON, H. CARRINGTON. The counting-out rhymes of children. J Am Folk-Lore, N Y., I, 31-37, 1888.

BONAPARTE, Prince ROLAND. La Nouvelle-Guinée. ive notice. Le Golfe Huon. Paris, 1888. Privately printed, 62 pp., 4 maps, 4to

BONAPARTE, Prince ROLAND.   La Nouvelle-Guinée.   iii° notice.   Le fleuve Augusta.
Paris, 1887.   Privately printed, 16 pp., 1 map 4to.

BONAPARTE, L.-L.   Un texte basque du xvii° siècle.   Rev. de Ling., Par. (1888), XXI,
183–186.

BONAR, JAMES.   Letters of David Ricardo to Thomas Robert Malthus   [Rev. in Jour.
Roy. Statis. Soc., London, L, 739–742.]

BONNAFORT, M.   Sur les localisations cérébrales.   Bull. Soc. d'anthrop . Paris, 1887,
3. s., X, 783–784.

BONNEMÉRE, L.   Cimetière préhistorique de Saint-Ellier.   Bull. Soc. d'anthrop. de
Par , 1888, 3. s., XI, 239–243.

—— La baguette des sourciers vendéens.   Bull. de la Soc. d'anthrop., Paris, 3. s., X,
780–782.

—— Les pierres de serpent.   Bull. de la Soc. d'anthrop., Paris, 3. s., X, 290–294.

—— Une amulette bretonne.   Bull. de la Soc. d'anthrop., Paris, 3. s., X, 374–375;
704–705.

BOOTHBY, H. E.   Ancient canals in Nevada.   Am. Antiquar., Ill. (1888), X, 380–281.

BORDE, PÉRE DE LA.   History of the origin, customs, religion, etc., of the Caribs of
Antilles, Timehri, Br. Guiana.   (Nature, XXXVI, 309.)

BORDIER, A.   La vie des sociétés.   Par., 1887, C. Reinwald, 374.   L'anthropophagie.
Bull Soc. d'anthrop , Paris, 3. s , XI, 62–71.

BÓRNHARDT, A.   Ueber die Bezeichnung der Korperbeschaffenheit durch Ziffern.   St.
Petersb med. Wchnschr., 1888, n. F., V, 413–416.

BORSARI, FERDINANDO.   La letteratura degl' Indigeni americani.   Napoli : Pierro
(1888), 76 pp., 12mo.

BOSELLI e LOMBROSO.   Nuovi studi sul tatuaggio nei criminali.   Arch. di psichiat.,
etc., Torino, VIII, 1–11, 2 pl.

BÓTTICHER, E.   Die Cultusmaske und der Hochsitz des Ohres an ägyptischen, assy-
rischen und griechisch-römischen Bildwerken.   Arch. f. Anthrop., XVI, 523–592.

BOUCART, M. A.   Une visite aux ruines de Xochicalco.   Rev. d'ethnog., Paris, VI,
439–443.

BOUINAIS, A., & PAULUS, A.   La France en Indo Chine.   Paris : Challamel aîné, 1886.
[Rev. in Nature, XXXV, 221.]

BOULE, MARCELLIN.   Essai de paléontologie stratigraphique de l'homme.   Rev. d'anthrop., Par. (1888), 3. s., III, 129–144; 172–297; 385–411; 647–680.

—— Puits préhistoriques d'extraction du silex de Mur-de-Barrez (Aveyron).   Matériaux, 3. s., IV, 5–21.

BOURINOT, J. G.   Local government in Canada.   Baltimore· Murray, 72 pp., Johns-Hop-
kins Univ. Studies in Hist and Polit. Sc., 5. s., V–VI.

BOURNET, A.   Une mission en Corse.   Notes d'anthropologie criminelle.   Paris, 1888,
G. Steinheil, 31 pp., 8vo.

BOURKE, JOHN G.   Compilation of notes and memoranda bearing upon the use of
human ordure and human urine in rites of a religious or semi-religious character
among various natives.   Washington, pp. 56.   [Rev. in Arch per l' anthrop., Firenze (1888), XVIII, 290.]

BRAMBACH, W. A. LOQUIN.   Folk-lore et musique basques.   Rev. de Ling., Par. (1888),
XXI, 160–173.

BRECCER, C.   Beiträge der Ethnographie Mexico's.   Internat Arch. f. Ethnog., Leiden, 1888, I, 212, 214, ill.

BRINTON, D. G.   Ancient Nahuatl poetry, containing the Nahuatl text of twenty-seven
ancient Mexican poems, with a translation, introduction, notes, and vocabulary.   Brin-
tón's Library of Aboriginal Literature.   No. VII.   Phila., Brinton, 1887, 1 vol., 8vo.

—— A review of the data for the study of the prehistoric chronology of America.
Proc. Am. Ass. Adv. Sc., XXXVI, 283–301.

BRINTON, D. G.   Critical Remarks on the Editions of Diego de Landa's Writings.   [Rev. in Rev. d'Ethnog., Paris, VI, 167.]

———— Foot-prints in Nicaragua.   Proc. Am. Philos. Soc., 1887, 437–444.

———— Lenapé conversations.   J. Am. Folk-Lore, N. Y., I, 37–43 (1888).

———— Linguistique Américaine.   Rev. de Ling , Par. (1888), XXI, 54–56.

———— Notes on American ethnology.   Rev. in Am. Antiquar., Chicago, IX, 115–116.

———— On the Chane-Abal (four-language) tribe and dialect of Chiapas   Am. Anthropologist, I, 77–96

———— On the so-called Alaguilac language of Guatemala.   Proc. Am. Phil. Soc., 366–377. 1887.

———— Rejoinder to M. Gatschet.   Rev. de Ling., Par. (1888), XXI, 340–341.

———— The Editions of Diego de Landa's Writings.   Proc. Am. Phil. Soc , XXIV, 1–7.

———— The language of Palæolithic man.   Phila. (1888), MacCalla & Co., 3–16 ; Proc. Am. Phil. Soc., Phila., 1888, XXV, 212–225

———— Were the Toltecs an Historical Nationality?   Proc. of Am. Philos Soc., 1887, July to Dec., VI, 455–462.

The British Association for the Advancement of Science in 1888, at Bath.   The Anthropological papers read were as follows:

> Report of the Committee on the Prehistoric Race in the Greek Islands.
> Report of the Committee on the Development of the human body.
> Report of the Committee on the Erratic inscribed blocks of England, etc.
> Report of the Committee on Provincial Museums in the United Kingdom.
> Report of the Committee on the Tribes of Northwest Canada
> Report of the Committee on Prehistoric inhabitants of the British Isles
> Address of the Vice-President, Section H, Gen Pitt-Rivers.
> Report of the Committee to investigate the effects of different occupations on the development of the human body
> Dwelling in Towns and Degeneracy.   By G. B Barron.
> The Physique of the Swiss   By Dr. Beddoe.
> On Color blindness.   By Carl Grossmann
> On Human bones discovered at Woodcuts, etc   By Dr Beddoe.
> Human Remains from Wiltshire   By J. G. Garson
> On a method of investigating the Development of Institutions.   By Edward B. Tylor.
> Australian Message-sticks.   By A W. Howitt
> Social regulations in Melanesia   By R. H Codrington.
> Funeral Rites, etc , of the Nicobar Islands   By E H. Man.
> Shell-Mounds of Choptank river.   By R Elmer Reynolds.
> Marriage Customs of the New Britain Group   By B. Danks.
> Totem clans and star worship   By George St Clair.
> The survival of Corporal penance   By Osbert H Howarth.
> Notes on Chest types   By G W Hamilton
> Necklaces and prehistoric commerce   By Miss A. W. Buckland.
> The definition of a nation.   By J Park Harrison
> Sun myths in modern Hellas.   By J Theodore Bent
> Ancient inhabitants of Canary Islands   By J Harris Stone.
> Ancient stronghold at Worlebury.   By H G Tomkins.
> Celtic earthworks in Hampshire.   By T. W. Shore.
> King Orry's Grave   By Miss A W. Buckland.
> Anthropometric laboratory at Manchester   By George W Bloxam and J. G. Garson.
> The early races of Western Asia   By Maj C. R Conder.
> Discoveries in Asia Minor.   By J. Theodore Bent
> The Hyksos or Shepherd Kings of Egypt   By H. G Tomkins.
> Pelasgians, Etruscans, and Iberians   By J Stuart Glennie

BROCA, P   Mémoires d'anthropologie.   Publiés avec une introduction et des notes par S. Pozzi.   Paris (1888), 94 figs.   8vo.

BROOKS, W. K.   Francis Galton on the persistency of type.   Rev. in Am. Jour. of Psychology.   Baltimore, I, 173–179.

BROWN, JOHN ALLEN   On some small highly specialized forms of stone implements, found in Asia, North Africa, and Europe.   J. Anthrop. Inst., Lond., (1888), XVIII, 134–139.

BROWN, JOHN ALLEN. Palæolithic man in the northwest of Middlesex. Vol. IV, 227 pp., 9 pl. London: McMillan. [Rev. in Matériaux, 3. s., iv, 431]

BROWN, ROBERT. The peoples of the World. London: Cassell & Co. 6 vols., illustr.

BROWN, S. Experiments on special sense localizations in the cortex cerebri of the monkey. Med. Rec., N. Y., XXXIV, 113-115.

BROWNING, OSCAR. Aspects of Education; a study in the history of Pedagogy. Mon. Ind. Educ. Ass., N. Y. (1888), I, 131-176.

BRUGSCH, H. Gräber im Kaukasus. Verhandl. d. Berl. Gesellsch. f. Anthrop., Berl., 1888, 308.

—— Zwei bearbeitete Silex altägyptischen Ursprungs. Verhandl. d. Berl. Gesellsch. f. Anthrop., 1888, 209

BRUHL, G. Die Culturvolker Alt-Amerika's. N. Y., Benziger Bros., 516 p., 8vo.

BRYAN, S. Nature and functions of a complete symbolic language. "Mind" (1888).

BRYCE, JAMES. The predictions of Hamilton De Tocqueville, Balt.: Johns Hopkins Studies in Hist. and Polit. Sc., 5. s., IX.

BUCHNER, H. Wie verhalt sich die Disposition verschiedener Völkerracen zu den verschiedenen Infectionsstoffen, und welche praktischen Consequenzen ergeben sich daraus fur den Verkehr der verschiedenen Racen ? Wien. med. Bl., X, 1205-1207.

BUCCLAND, A. W. Gen. Pitt-Rivers's Explorations. J. Anthrop. Inst., Lond. (1888), XVIII, 200-204.

—— Some recent Publications of the Bureau of Ethnology, Washington, D. C., U. S. A. [Rev. in J. Anthrop. Inst., Lond. (1888), XVIII, 96-98.

—— Tattooing. J. Anthrop. Ins., Lond. (1888), XVII, 318-328, 1 pl.

Bulletin de la Société d'anthropologie de Bruxelles. Bruxelles (1887), tome IV, 1885-'6, 8vo.

Bulletin de la Société d'anthropologie de Lyon. (1888) tome VI, 1887.

Bulletins de la Société d'anthropologie de Paris. Paris. [Organ of Paris Anthropological Society]

Bulletin de la Société de géographie. Paris: Soc. de Géog., 7. s., vol. IX, in 1888, quarterly.

Bulletin de la Société d'Ethnographie. 2e série, 1887. Alliance scientifique universelle-Institution Ethnographique, Société d'Ethnographie, Société Oriental, Société Sinico-Japonaise, Société Africaine, Société Américaine de France, Société Océanienne. Paris· Sc. d'Ethnographie, 2. s., vol I in 1887. Monthly.

Bulletin de l'Institut Égyptien. (No 14 in 1886.)

Bulletin et mémoires de la Société archéologique du département d'Ile-et-Vilaine. Paris, 1888, 211 pp, 8vo.

Bulletino della Commissione Archeologica Communale di Roma. Roma: R. Accad. dei Lincei xvith year in 1888. Monthly.

Bulletino di paleontologia italiana 2. s., III, 23d year [Filled with Italian Archæology.]

Bulletin of the American Geographical Society. New York: Printed for the Society. XIX in 1887. Quarterly.

Bulletin of the California Academy of Sciences. San Francisco, II, 1887.

Bulletin of the Essex Institute. Salem, Mass. Vols. 1-18.

BUMM. Ueber die Genital und Beckenverhältnisse der Hottentottinnen. Sitzungsb. d. phys.-med. Gesellsch. zu Wurzb., 6.

BURNHAM, W. H. Memory, historically and experimentally considered. Am. J. Psychol., Balt., 1888-9, II, 39-90.

BUSCHAN, G. Ueber prähistorische Gewebe und Gespinnste. Arch. f. Anthrop., Braunschwg., 1888-9, XVIII, 235-262.

BÜTTIKOFER, J. Die Eingebornen von Liberia. Internat. Arch. f. Ethnog., I, 33-48, 77-91, tab. IV, V.

—— Die Vey Sprache. [Rev. in Intern. Arch. f. Ethnog., 1888, I, 108.]

CALDWELL. R. On demonology in southern India. J. Anthrop. Soc., Bombay, I.

CAMPBELL, GEORGE. The races of India. Rev. in J. Anthrop. Inst., Lond (1888), XVII, 289-290.

CAMPBELL, S. G. Zulu witch doctors. Glasgow Med. J., 4 s.

Canadian Record of Science (The), Montreal. Quarterly. Replaces the Canadian Naturalist. Vol I, in 1887

CANAL. Marnia (Lalla-Marghnia.) Rev de l'Afrique francaise, 213-227, 1887, figs.

CANDOLLE, ALPHONSE DE Les types brun et blond au point de vue de la santé. Rev d'anthrop., 3 s., II, 265-274.

——— Nouvelles recherches sur le type sauvage de la pomme de terre. Arch. sc. phys. et nat., 3. s, XV, No 5. Biblioth. universelle. Genève, 15 mai, 1886.

CANESTRINI, G. Anthropologia. 2 ed. Milano (1888), 232 pp., 12mo.

CAPPELLI, G. La calotta cranica di Donizetti. Arch ital. per le mal. nerv., Milano, XXIV, 135-153.

CARGUET ET TOPINARD. Contribution a l'anthropologie de la Basse-Bretagne, la population de l'ancien pagus Cap Sizun (pointe du raz). Rev. d'anthrop , Par. (1888), 3 s., iii,159-168.

CARLES, W. R. Life in Corea. London, 1888, MacMillan. Ill. and maps.

CARPENTER, W. H. Old Norse bibliography. Mod. Language Notes, Feb. (See Johns. Hopkins Circulars, No. 57.)

CASTAING. Croyances sur la vie d'outretombe chez les anciens Péruviens. Arch. Soc. Amér. de France. No 2.

——— Les populations de la Russie. Le Muséon. Louvain, VI, 31-49.

CASTELFRANCO, POMPEO. Les villages lacustres et palustres et les terremares. Rev. d'anthrop., Par. (1888), 3 s , III, 568-587; 607-619; 707-719.

——— Paléoethnologie italienne. Les fonds de Cabane. Rev. d'anthrop., Paris, 1887, 182-200.

CATAT, LOUIS Les habitants du Darien méridionel. Rev. d'ethnog., Paris, 1888, VII, 397-421, 6 ills.

CATTELL, J. McK. The time it takes to think. Nineteenth Cent., Lond., XXII, 827-830

CAUVIN. Anatomie et physiologie anthropologiques des Hindous. Mém. Soc. d'anthrop., Paris, 2 s., III, 430-442.

CENTORIZE, RAFFAELE L' uomo preistorico sul Monte Gargano e sulle rive del Lago di Lesina in Capitinata, Sanseverino, 1888, 41. [Rev. in Arch. per l' antrop., Firenze (1888), XVIII, 281-282]

CHAILLE, S. E. Infants, their chronological progress. N. Orl M. and S. J., n. s., XIV, 893-912 Also, reprint.

CHALLEMEL. Superstitions médicales. J. de méd et chir. prat., Paris, 1888, lix, 479. Also, Gaz. hebd d. sc. méd , Bordeaux, 1888, IX, 495-497

CHALMERS, JAMES. Pioneering in New Guinea. Religious Tract Society. Nature. XXXVI, 255.

CHAMBERLAIN, A. F. Notes on the history, customs, and beliefs of the Mississagua Indians J. Am Folk-Lore, N Y. (1888), I, 150-160

CHAMBERLAIN, BASIL HALL. Note on the Japanese Go-hei, or paper offerings to the Shinto Gods. J. Anthrop. Inst , Lond (1838), XVIII, 27-29, 1 pl.

——— The language, mythology, and geographical nomenclature of Japan viewed in the light of Ainu studies Mem Lit College Imp Univ. Jap., Tokyo, Japan, 1887. [Rev. in Nature, XXXVI, 25]

CHAMBES. Les populations indigènes entre le Haut-Sénégal et le Haut-Niger. Rev. san. de Bordeaux, IV, 112, 177

CHANTRE, E. Les laboratoires et les collections anthropologiques publiques de l'Italie en 1886. Bull. Soc. d'anthrop., Lyon, 163-165.

CHANTRE, E.   Recherches anthropologiques dans le Caucase.   Bull. d. l. Soc. d'anthrop.,
    Par., 1888, 3 s., XI, 198-221.   *Also*, Paris, 1885-7, Reinwald, 5 vols., 130 pl., 4to.
    [*Rev.* in Rev. d'ethnog., VI, 470-489.]
CHAPIN, H. D.   Social and physiological inequality.   Pop. Sc. Month., XXX, 757-765,
    1887.
CHARENCY, H. DE.   Textes en langue tarasque.   *Rev.* in Rev. d'ethnog., Paris, VI, 491.
CHARNAY, DÉSIRÉ.   A propos de Tamoanchan.   Rev. d'ethnog., Paris, VI, 347-350.
——— Expédition au Yucatan.   Bull. d. l. Soc. d'anthrop., Paris, 3. s., X, 65-78.
——— Monnaie de cuivre en Amérique avant la conquête.   Bull. d. l. Soc. d'anthrop.,
    Paris, 3. s., X, 237-240.
——— The ancient cities of the new world, being voyages and explorations in Mexico
    and Central America from 1857 to 1882.   New York: Harpers.   209 ill., map,
    8mo.
CHARVET.   Essai de reconstitution d'époque et d'origine d'un mors de bride antique
    conservé au musée de Naples.   Bull. d. l. Soc. d'anthrop. de Lyon, VI, 179-182, pl.
    VI-X, 1887.
CHATELLIER, P. DU.   Tumulus emblématiques de l'Amérique du Nord.   Matériaux,
    3. s , Paris, 1887, IX, 274-280, pl.
CHAUVET, G.   Étude préhistorique   Les débuts de la gravure et de la sculpture.
    Melle· Lacuve, 1887, br. in-8, fig.
CHAVERO, ALF.   Historia antigua y de la Conquista.   México á través de los siglos.
    Vol. I.   México: Ballesca, pl. and figs., 4to.
CHUDZINSKI ET MANOUVRIER.   Étude sur le cerveau de Bertillon.   Bull. d. l. Soc.
    d'anthrop., Paris, 3. s , X, 558-591.
——— Buste d'une jeune Cynghalaise.   Bull. d. l. Soc. d'anthrop., Paris, 3. s., X, 146-
    148.
——— Sur un os surnuméraire du pied.   Bull. d. l. Soc. d'anthrop., Paris, 3. s., X, 603-
    605.
——— Quelques notes sur la splanchnologie des races humaines.   Rev. d'anthrop.,
    Paris, 3. s., II, 275-290.
CHURCHWARD, WILLIAM B.   My consulate in Samoa.   London: Bentley & Son.
CLAIRIN, EM.   Notice biographique de Jean-Charles Geslin.   Vitry-le-François, 1887,
    br., 8vo.
CLARKE, F. W., and G. P. MERRILL.   On Nephrite and Jadeite.   Proc. U. S. Nat. Museum, 1888, Wash., 115-130, 1 pl.
CLARKE, J. M.   Report on bones of Mastodon or Elephas found in association with human relics in the village of Attica, Wyoming Co., N. Y., 1888.   Albany, James B.
    Lyon, p. 7.
CLARKE, W. B.   Supernumerary auricles.   Illust. M. News, Lond., 1888, I, 321.
CLELAND, J.   Rational teratology.   Brit. Med. J., II, 346-348.
CLÉMENT, E.   Ethnographie et démographie lyonnaises.   Lyon méd., LVI, 361; 394;
    591.
CLERKE, A. M.   Homeric astronomy.   Nature, XXXV, 585-588.
CLERMONT-GANNEAU C.   Deux inscriptions inédites de la Phénice propre.   Ann. du
    musée Guimet, X, 503-516, et pl. XIX-XX (1887).
CLOSMADEUC, DE M.   Fouilles sous le dallage du monument intérieur de Gavr'inis,
    Morbihan).   Bull. d. l. Soc. d'anthrop., Paris, 3. s., X, 10-13
COCKBURN, J.   On palæolithic implements from the drift gravels of the Singrauli Basin, South Mirzapore.   J. Anthrop. Inst., Lond., XVII, 57-65.
CODRINGTON, R H.   A Folk-tale from New Hebrides.   Archæol Rev., Lond., II, 90.
COLAJANNI, NAPOLEONE.   La sociologia criminale.   1 vol.   Catania, 1889, 1 vol., pp.
    505, e una grande tavola.   [Rev. in Arch. per d'antrop., Firenze (1888), 288-290.]
COLLIGNON, RÉNÉ.   Carte de répartition de l'indice céphalique en France.   Bull. d. l.
    Soc. d'anthrop., Paris, 3. s., X, 306-312.

COLLIGNON, RÉNÉ. Étude sur l'ethnographie générale de la Tunisie Bull. de Géog. hist. et descriptive, 1886, Nos. 1-5. Paris: Leroux.

—— L'inscription de temïa découverte par le capitaine Lefèvre; contribution à l'étude des Ainos. Rev. d'ethnog, VII, Paris, 1888, pp. 449-454, 1 ill.

—— La nomenclature quinaïre de l'indice nasal du vivant. Rev. d'anthrop., 3. s., III, 8-9.

—— E. Houzé. La taille, la circonférence thoracique et l'angle xiphoïdien des Flamands et des Wallons (avec une carte). Rev. d'anthrop., Par. (1888), 3. s., III, 359-361.

—— E. Morselli. Leçons sur l'homme suivant la théorie de l'évolution (Lezioni su l' uomo secondo la teoria dell' evoluzione.) Cours professé à l'Université de Turin, 1887-1888. Rev. d'anthrop., Par. (1888), 3. s., III, 373-374.

—— Les âges de la pierre en Tunisie. Matériaux, 3. s, IV, 171-204, maps and plates. Bull. Soc. d'anthrop., Paris, 3. s., X, 460-461.

—— L'homme avant l'histoire, par Ch. Debierre. J. B. Baillière (1888), 1 vol., in-12. Rev. d'anthrop. (1888), 3 s., III, 77.

—— Vianna de Lima: L'homme selon le transformisme, 1 vol. de la Bibl. de philosophie contemporaine. Paris, F. Alcan, 1888. Rev. d'anthrop., Par. (1888), 3. s., III, 477-479.

—— G. J. Romanes. L'intelligence des animaux, 2 vol. de la Bibl. scientifique internationale. Paris, F. Alcan. Rev. d'anthrop., Par. (1888), 3 s., III, 736-740.

—— Répartition de la couleur des yeux et des cheveux chez les Tunisiens sédentaires. Rev. d'anthrop., 3. s, II, 1-8.

COMBEMALE, F. La déscendance des alcooliques. Montpel. (1888), Coulet, 213 pp., 8vo.

CONDER, C. R. Hittite ethnology. J. Anthrop. Inst., Lond., XVII, 137-158.

Congrès international d'anthropologie criminelle. Rome, 1885. Actes published in Rome, 1886-1887.

Congrès international d'anthropologie et d'archéologie préhistoriques. Compte rendu de la 8. session à Budapest, 1876. Budapest (1887). Vol. II, partie 2. in 8vo. L'ouvrage complet (2 vols.) M.

Congrès international des Américanistes. VIe session. Turin. Président, Ariodante Fabretti. Matériaux, 3. s., IV, 39-41.

CONS, H. Le bassin du Niger. Union géog. du nord de la France. Bull. XIII, 128-143, 1887.

COOC, PIZARRO. Effigy mounds on the Kickapoo River. Am. Antiquarian, IX, 175-177.

COPE, E. D. Origin of the Fittest. London: Macmillan & Co., 1887. Reviewed in Nature, XXXVI, 505. D. Appleton & Co., 486 pp., 5 pl.

—— The relation of the sexes to government. Pop. Sc. Month., XXXIII, 721-730.

COPLAS. A la engarnacion y nacimiento de Nuestro Señor Jesu Christo. Rev. de Ling., Par. (1888), XXI, 64-65.

CORDIER, H. La grammaire chinoise du Père Francisco Varo. Paris: Maison neuve, 1887, br. in-8

—— Les sociétés secrètes chinoises. Rev. d'ethnog., VI, 52-72.

CORRADI, A. Della longevità in relazione alla storia, all' antropologia ed all' igiene. Ann univ. di med. e chir., Milano, CCLXI, 161-199 Also, transl.: Rev. internat. d. sc. méd, Par., IV, 405-414.

CORRE, A. Les peuples du Rio Nunez, W. Africa. Mém. Soc. d'anthrop., Paris, 2 s., III, 42-73.

Correspondenzblatt der deutschen Gesellschaft für Anthropologie, Ethnologie und Urgeschichte. Munich: Johannes Ranke. Vol. XVIII in 1887, monthly, 4to.

CORSON, E. R. The future of the colored race in the United States, from an ethnic and medical standpoint. N. York M. Times, XV, 193-201.

CORTINA, CARLO A. Cesare Lombroso e la nuove dottrine posıtiviste in rapporto al diritto penale. Torino. 1888, Petrini, 28 pp., 8vo.

COSMOS, GUIDO CORA'S. Torino. Guido Cora. Vol ıx, 1886–'88.

Cosmos, Revue des sciences et de leurs applications. Paris: By the Journal. Founded in 1850, 37th year in 1887, weekly, 8vo.

COUDREAU, H. A. La France équinoxıale. Voyage à travers les Guyanes et l'Amazonie. Paris, Challamel, 1887, 2 vols., 8vo.

———— La Haute-Guyane. Rev. d'ethnog., VII, Paris, 1888, pp 455–481.

COURTES, L. Le musée Guimet. Rev. d'anthrop., 1887, 476–482.

COURTNEY, Miss. "Cornish Folk-Lore." Folk-Lore Journal. (Vol. V, Part II.) 1887.

COWLES, EDWARD. Insistent and fixed ideas. Am J. Psychol., 222–270.

CRANE, T. F. The diffusion of popular tales. J. Am. Folk-Lore. New York, I, 8–15 (1888).

CREMER, MAX. Ueber das Schätzen von Distanzen bei Bewegung von Arm und Hand. Wurzb., 1887, A. Menninger, 36 pp., 8vo.

CULLIMORE, D. H. On tropical and subtropical climates, and the acclimatisation of the fair races in hot countries. Med. Press and Circ., London, n s., XLVI, 436, 461.

CUYER, ÉDOUARD. Forme d'une région du poignet dans la supination et la pronation. Différence de saille des métacarpiens sur le squelette et sur l'écorche. Bull d. l. Soc d'anthrop., Par., 1888, Par., 421–430, 9 figures.

CULIN, STEWART. China in America: A study in the social life of the Chinese in the eastern cities of the United States. Phila., 1887, 16 pp , 1 map. 8vo.

CUMMING, Miss C. F. GORDON. Strange medicines Pop. Sc. Month., XXXI, 750–767.

CUNNINGHAM, ————. Development of the brain and cranio-cerebral topography. Royal Irish Academy of Medicine, May, 1888

CUNYNGHAME, H. The present state of education in Egypt. J. R. A S., XIX, 223.

CURR, E. M. The Australian race, its orıgın, languages, customs, place of landing in Australıa, and the routes by which it spread ıtself over that continent. Melbourne (1888), 46 pp., w. color map. 4 vols.

CURRAN, W. The senses of savages. J. Anat. and Physıol., Lond., XXI, 558–570.

CURTIN, J. Paper on folk-lore of Ireland. Anthrop. Soc. of Washıngton, 1888. Nature, p 473. (Vol. 37.)

CUST, R. N. Lınguistic and oriental essays from 1847–1887. London: Trübner, xiv+ 548 pp. 8vo.

———— Orıgınal vocabularıes of five west Caucasıan languages. J. Roy. Asiat Soc., Lond., XIX, 145 (1887).

———— The modern languages of Oceanica. J. R. A. S., XXI, 369–392.

CUYER, ÉDOUARD. Sur un allongement anormal du cubitus et sur la présence d'un muscle rond pronateur chez un cheval. Bull. d. l. Soc. d'anthrop., Paris, 3. s., X, 701–704.

———— Sur un os surnuméraire du corps humaın. Bull. d. l. Soc. d'anthrop., Paris, 3. s., X, 303–306

D'ACY, E. De l'emmanchement des silex tailles du type généralement connu sous le nom de type de Saınt-Acheul ou de Chelles. Bull. d. l. Soc. d'anthrop., Par., 3. s., X, 158; 219–223.

D'AGUANNO, GIUSEPPE. Concetto ed orıgine del diritto di successione. Studii di sociologia comparata. Milano-Torıno, 1888, pp. 38. [Rev. in Arch. per l' antrop., Firenze (1888), XVIII, 287–288]

DALLY, M. Aphasie congénitale chez un enfant de quatre ans et demi. Bull. d. l. Soc. d'anthrop., Paris, 3. s., X, 320–323.

———— De la sélection ethnique et de la consanguinité chez les Grecs anciens. Rev. d'anthrop., Paris, 3. s , II, 408–444.

DALY, DOMINIC D. Digging, squatting, and pıoneerıng life in the northern territory of South Australia London: Sampson Low, 1887. Rev. in Nature, XXXVI, 363.

DALY, DOMINIC D. Native life in British Borneo. Pop. Sc. Month., N. Y., XXXIV, 246–251.

DANFORTH, GRACE. A law of heredity, or possibly maternal impressions. Texas Cour. Rec Med., Dallas, 1888–9, VI, 79–81.

DANCS, BENJAMIN. The shell-money of New Britain J. Anthrop. Inst., Lond (1888), XVIII, 305–317.

—— Marriage customs of the New Britain group. J. Anthrop. Inst., London, 1888–9, XVIII, 281–294.

D'ARBOIS DE JUBAINVILLE. Papers on the Celts Revue Celtique, VII, 2; 129.

DARESTE, M. Compte rendu de l'autopsie d'un veau, presénté dans la séance du 24 février. Bull. d. l. Soc. d'anthrop., Paris, 3. s., X, 185–186.

—— Coutume contemporaine et loi primitive J. des savants, March and May, 1887.

—— - Les veaux à tête de bouledogne. Bull d. l. Soc. d'anthrop , Paris, 3. s., X, 375–383.

DAUBÉS, M. GUYOT. Variations in human stature. Pop. Sc. Month., XXXI, 314–323, ill , 1887.

DAVEGNO, F. Le superstizioni de Portofino (Liguria, riviera di levante). Arch. per. l' antrop., Firenze, 1888, XVIII, 83–90.

DAVIS, J A. Fœtal measurements. Univ. M. Mag., Phila., I, 101.

DE ALBERTIS. Le tatouage sur 300 prostituées liguriennes. Arch d. psichiat., sc. pen. ed antrop., 1888, IX, fasc. 6.

—— Cas de tatouage chez une femme. Actes Cogr. internat. d'anthrop. crim., 1885, Rome, I, 456–458

DEANS, JAMES. The feast of Ne-kilst-luss, the raven god. A tradition of the Queen Charlotte Haidas. Am. Antiquar., Mendon, Ill. (1888), X, 383.

—— The raven's place in the mythology of Northwestern America. Am. Antiquar., Mendon, Ill. (1888), X, 273–278.

—— What befell the slave-seekers. J. Am. Folk-Lore, N. Y. (1888), I, 123–124.

DEBIERRE, CH L'homme avant l'histoire. Paris (1888), Baillière.

DECAZES, E. L'Ouest Africain. Bull. Soc. Norm. Géog., Rouen.

DEHOUSSET. De l'index et de l'annulaire. Bull. Soc d'anthrop. de Paris, 1888, 3. s., XI, 449–451.

DELISLE, F. Note sur une fouille faite au champ du double-d'or. Bull. de la Soc. d'anthrop., Paris, 3. s , X, 774–777.

DELPINO, FEDERICO. Il passato, il presente e l' avvenire della psicologia. Bologna, 1888. [Rev. in Arch. per. l' antrop., Firenze (1888), XVIII, 290–291.

DEMPSTER, MISS. The folk-lore of Sutherlandshire. The Folk-Lore Jour., Lond. (1888), VI, pt IV, 215–252. •

DENICER, J. Émile Schmidt. Methodes anthropologiques; instructions pour collectionner et observer en voyage et au laboratoire. (Anthropologische Methoden; Anleitung zum Beobachten und Sammeln fur Laboratorium und Reise.) Leipzig, 1888, in-8 vo, 3 pp , avec figs. Rev. d'anthrop , Par. (1888), 3. s., III, 611–616.

—— Le préhistorique en Allemague Rev. d'anthrop., Par (1888), 3 s., III, 59–72.

—— Les populations turques en Chine et plus spécialement les Daldes. Bull. de la Soc. d'anthrop., Paris, 3. s., X, 206–210.

—— Rapport de la commission pour l'étude des echantillons de cheveux rapportés par M. de Ujfalvy de son voyage dans l'Inde. Bull d. l. Soc d'anthrop , Paris, 3 s., X, 516–518

DEPÉRET, CHARLES. Note sur la Faune de Vertébrés Miocènes Matériaux, 3. s., IV, 53–56.

DESCHAMPS, ALBERT. Les névroses et le pessimisme. Paris, 1888, Doin, 38 pp , 18mo.

DESCHMANN, K. Bronzesachen von der Kulpa. Verhandl. d. Berl. Gesellsch f. Anthrop., Berlin, 1888, 246.

DESHMUKH, M. G. On the habits of a Jain Ascetic. J. Anthrop. Soc. Bombay, I.

DETMER, W.   Zum Problem der Vererbung.   Thiermed. Rundschau, Halle, II, 121–124,́
133–135, 203–215.

Deutsche anthropologische Gesellschaft.   XVII. general meeting in Stettin, 10–12 Aug.,
Correspondenz-Blatt, XVII, 33–94.

DEÉVZE, GÉRARD.   Çakuntala, traduction de la version tamoule.   Rev. de Ling., Paris,
XX, 352–376; XXI, 48–53.

DEWEY, JOHN.   Psychology.   Rev. in Am. Journal of Psychology.   Baltimore, I, 146–
159.

DICKENS, F. V.   Aino hairiness and the urvolk of Japan.   Nature, XXXV, 534.

────· The story of the old Bamboo Hewer.   J. R. A. S., XIX, Art. I.

Dictionnaire des sciences anthropologiques.   Publié sous la direction de MM. Ad. Bertillon, Condereau, etc. etc.   Paris.

Dictionnaire Universel, Paris.

DIGHT, C. F.   Measurements from skulls of the seventh century,   J. Am. Med. Ass.,
Chicago, VIII, 205.

Discussion sur la craniométrie.   Bull. d. l. Soc. d'anthrop., Paris, 3. s., X, 659–687.

DISSELHORST, RUDOLF.   Studien über Emigration.   Halle a. S.,́ 1887, 22 pp., 8vo.

DOLBESCHEFF, W. J.   Archaologische Forschungen im Bezirk des Terek (Nordkaukasus).   Zeitschr. f. Ethnol., Berl., XIX, 101–118.

DONALDSON, HENRY H.   On the relation of neurology to psychology.   Am. J. Psychol.,
I, 209–221.

DÖNITZ, W.   Vorgeschichtliche Gräber in Japan.   Verhandl. d. Berl. Gesellsch. f. Anthrop., 1887, 114–126.

DONNET. Dr.   De l'intoxication professionnelle des dégustateurs de vins et de liqueurs.
Rev. in Am. Jour. of Psychology, Baltimore, I, 194–195.

DORSEY, J. OWEN.   Abstracts of Ponka and Omaha myths.   J. Am. Folk-Lore, N. Y.
(1888), i, 74–78; 204–208.   Omaha songs.   Ibid., 209–214.

──── A Teton Dakota ghost story.   J. Am. Folk-Lore, N. Y. (1888), I, 68–72.

──── Books on Myths and Mythology.   Am. Antiquarian, IX, 40, 41; 173, 174.

──── Osage traditions.   VI. An. Rept. Bur. Ethnol., 1888, pp. 373–397, 1 fig.

──── Songs of the Heucka Society.   J. Am. Folk-Lore, N. Y. (1888), I, 65–68.

──── The Orphan Myth.   Am. Antiquarian, IX, 95–97.

DRAMANT, Mrs.   The Folk-Lore of Guillim.   Antiquary, London, XV, 149–155.

DRAPER, LYMAN C.   Forman's journey down the Ohio and Mississippi in 1789–90́.
[Rev. in Am. Antiquar., Chicago (1888), X, 396.]

DRAUTREMER, J.   L'Ile de Kiou Siou.   Bull. Soc. d'Ethnog., Paris, 2. s. I, 88–98.

DREWS, R.   Ueber das Mongolenauge als provisorische Bildung bei deutschen Kindern
und uber den Epicanthus   Arch. f. Anthrop., Braunschwg., 1888–9, XVIII. 223–233.

DROUET, FR.   Grande Kabylie.   Excursion chez les Beni-Yenni.   Bull. Soc. Normande
de Géog., 212–240, 1887.

DUHOUSSET, E.   Les races humaines de la Perse.   Rev. d'ethnog., Paris, VI, 400–413.

DUKA, THEODORE.   An essay on the Brāhūī Grammar, after the German of the late Dr.
Trumpp, of Munich.   J. R. A. Soc., n. s.,XIX, 59, 1887.

DUMONTIER, G.   Le Nam-giao de Hanoi.   Rev. d'ethnog., Par., VI, 181–184.

──── Les textes Sanscrits au Tonkin   Rev. d'ethnog., VI, 23–38.

──── Notes sur le bouddhisme tonkinois.   L'enfer.   Rev. d'ethnog., Paris, 1888, VI,
285–301.

DUN, W. A.   The police standard of Cincinnati.   Cincin. Lancet, n. s, XVIII, 131–135;
767–769.

DURAFFOURG, V.   Béja et ses environs.   Bull. Soc. de Géog. de Lille, VII, 214–240,
1887.

DURAND, M.   Ethnologie du Rouergue.   Bull. Soc. d'anthrop., Par , 3. s., XI (1888),
138–156.

DUREAU, A.   Le bec-de-lièvre.   Rev. in Rev. d'anthrop.,́ Paris, 3. s., II, 290–292.

DUR(HEIM, É. Suicide et natalité. Rev. phil., Paris, XXVI, 446-463.

DUVAL, MATHIAS. Installation d'un laboratoire de transformisme au parc de Mont-souris. Proposition de Clémence Royer. Bull. d. l. Soc. d'anthrop., Paris, 3. s., X, 525-526.

—— L'aphasie depuis Broca. Bull. d. l. Soc. d'anthrop., Paris, 3. s , X, 743-771.

DWIGHT, T. The range of variation of the human shoulder-blade. Am. Naturalist, Phila., XXI, 627-638, 2 pl.

ED(INS, J. Connection of Japanese with the adjacent continental languages. Tr. As. Soc. Japan, XV, 96-102.

—— Origin of Chinese words in natural sounds. Ztschr. f. allg. Sprachwissensch., III, 276-285.

—— Philological importance of geographical terms in the Shi-ki. J. China Br. R. A. S., XXI, 199-203.

—— Priority of labial letters illustrated in Chinese phonetic. J. R. A. S., XIX, 207-222.

EDWARDS, BLANCHE. Fracture intra-utérine des deux tibias et syndactylie ou ectro-dactylie concomitante. Bull. d. l Soc. d'anthrop., Paris, X, 299-302.

EDWARDS, C. L. Winter roosting colonies of crows. Am. J. Psychol., I, 436-459.

—— Rides and studies in the Canary Islands. London: Unwin. 380 pp., 8vo.

EELLS, M. Decrease of population among the Indians of Puget Sound. Am. Anti-quarian, IX, 271.

—— The Indians of Puget Sound. Am. Antiquarian, IX, 1-9; 97-104; 211-219 (1887).

EHRENREICH, P. Ueber die Botocudos der brasilianischen Provinzen Espiritu Santo und Minas Geraes. Ztschr. f. Ethnol., Berl., XIX, 1; 49, 2 pl.

ELLIOTT, A. M. Speech mixture in French Canada. Am. J. Philol., VIII, 133-157.

ELLIS, A. B. The Tshi-speaking peoples of the gold coast of West Africa; their re-ligion, manners, customs, laws, language, etc. London (1887), 340 pp.. 8vo.

ELTON, F. Notes on natives of the Solomon Islands. J. Anthrop. Inst., Lond., XVII, 90-99.

ELY, RICHARD T. Political economy in America. N. A. Review, Feb.; also Labor Organizations, The Forum, March.

EMERSON, E. Man in relation to the lower animals. Pop. Sc. Month., N. Y., XXXIII, 751-754.

EMIN, PASHA. Collection of letters and journals. Central Africa Edited by Schwein-furth, Ratzel, Felkin & Harlaub. London (1888), Geo. Philip & Son. Nature, XXXVI, 563.

Εφημερις Αρχαιολογικη. Journal of the Archæological Society in Athens, 1886, vol. I.

v. EREKERT R. Der Kaukasus und seine Völker Nach eigener Anschauung. Mit Text-abbildungen und Lichtdrucken, kurzen tabellarischen Resultaten linguistischer und anthropologischer Forschungen, und einer ethnographischen Karte des Kaukasus. Leipzig (1887), Frohberg. 385 pp. 8vo

ERMAN, A. Das frühzeitige Auftreten von Eisen in Aegypten. Verhandl. d. Berl. Ge-sellsch. f. Anthrop., 1888, 180.

ERNST, A. Rio Tigre und Rio Conejo. Verhandl. d. Berl. Gesellsch. f. Anthrop., Berl., 1888, 274-278.

—— Ueber einen Motilonen-Schädel aus Venezuela. Verhandl. d Berl. Gesellsch. f. Anthrop.. Berl., 296-301.

ERRERA, LEO. Pourquoi dormons-nous? Bull. Soc. d'anthrop. de Bruxelles, V, 249-281; Rev. Scient., Paris, XL, 105-111.

ERRINGTON DE LA CROIX, J. La tombe Maori au Musée du Trocadero. Nature, Par., XV, 297-299.

ESTHENAUER, M. Chevelure en vadrouille. Bull. d. l. Soc. d'anthrop., Paris, 3. s., X, 418.

ESTREY, MEYNERS D'. Tribus aborigènes du centre de Celebes. Les Topautunuasu. [Rev. in Rev. d'Ethnog., Paris, VI, 163–164.

Ethnographische Studien uber Alt-Serbien. Mitth. d. anthrop. Gesellsch. in Wien, n. F., VIII, 182–190.

Ethnologische Mittheilungen aus Ungarn. Zeitschrift für die Volkskunde der Bewohner Ungarns und seiner Nebenlander. Budapest: Redaction. 1st year, 1887–'88 4to.

EVANS, A. J. Stonehenge. Archæol. Rev., Lond., 1888–'89, II, 312–330.

Exposition de M. Joseph Martin, au Musée du Trocadero. [Rev. in Rev. d'Ethnog., Paris, VI, 503–506.

Exposition rétrospective du travail et des sciences anthropoliques. (See plan and organization of this exposition to be held in 1889, in Matériaux, 3. s., IV, 480–486.)

FALLOT, A. Note sur l'indice céphalique de la population provençale et plus particulièrement Marseillaise. Rev. d'anthrop., Paris, 3. s., II, 129–135.

FARAGO, G. Az ujszülott gyermekek nehany reflex. [Some reflections on new-born children (as to weight).] Gyogyaszat, Budapest, XXVII, 205.

FARNELL, L. R. The origin and earliest development of Greek sculpture. Archæol. Rev., Lond., II, 167–194.

FAUROT, L. Observations ethnographiques dans l'île de Kamarane. Rev. d'ethnog., Paris, VI, 433–438.

—— Observations ethnographiques sur les Danakils du golfe de Tadjoura. Rev. d'ethnog., Paris, VI, 57–66.

FAUVELLE, Dr. De la direction de la crinière comme caractéristique du type cheval. Bull. de la Soc. d'anthrop., Paris, 3. s., X, 706–707.

—— De la philosophie au point de vue anthropologique. Mém. Soc. d'anthrop. de Paris, 2. s., III, 376–390.

—— Des causes d'erreur en anthropologie. Bull. de la Soc. d'anthrop., Paris, 3. s., X, 263–275.

—— De l'importance des caractères de l'appareil masticateur en anthropologie. Bull. Soc. d'anthrop. de Paris, 1888, 3. s., XI, 463–471.

—— Des mystifications dans les sciences anthropologiques. L'Homme, Par., IV, 651–657.

—— Le cheval sauvage de la Dzoungarie. Bull. d. l. Soc. d'anthrop., Paris, 3. s., X, 188–193.

—— Le système nerveux, la nervosité et l'intelligence considérés au point de vue physico-chimique. Bull. d. l. Soc. d'anthrop., Paris. 3. s., X, 462–482.

—— Quelques considérations sur l'évolution phylogénique des hémisphères cérébraux de l'homme. Bull. d. l. Soc. d'anthrop., Paris, 3. s., X, 104–118.

—— Qu'est-ce que la psychologie physiologique. Bull. d. l. Soc. d'anthrop., Paris, 3. s., X, 119–128.

—— Recherche sur l'origine ancestrale de l'homme à l'aide du système dentaire. L'Homme, Par., IV, 545–552.

—— Sur un point fixé pouvant servir de repère dans les mensurations crâniennes. Bull. Soc. d'anthrop. de Par., 3. s., XI, 55–62.

FAVIER, HENRI. Le recrutement militaire dans les cantons de Saint-Omer. Rev. d'anthrop., Par. (1888), 3. s., III, 42–48.

FEATHERMAN, A. Social History of the Races of Mankind. Division II: Papuo-and Malayo-Melanesians. London (1887). 518 pp. 8vo. [Rev. by A. H. Keane, in Nature, XXXVI, 147.]

FÉRÉ, CH. A contribution to the pathology of dreams and of hysterical paralysis. Rev. in Am. Jour. of Psychology, Baltimore, I, 192.

—— Dégénérescence et criminalité. Rev. phil., Par., XXIV, 337–377.

—— Note sur les conditions physiologiques des émotions. Rev. phil., Par., XXIV, 561–581.

FERRI, E. Variations thermométriques et criminalité. Arch. de l'anthrop. crim., Par., II, 3-22.

Festschrift zur Begrüssung des XVIII. Kongresses der deutschen anthropologischen Gesellschaft in Nurnberg. Nurnberg (1887), v. Ebners; 12 tables, 31 figures.

FIELD, ADELE M. Chinese marriage customs. Pop. Sc. Month , N. Y., XXXIV, 246-251.

—— Chinese mortuary customs. *Ibid.*, XXXIII, 569-596.

FELLENBERG, E. VON. Alte Schweizer-Hauser. Verhandl. d. Berl. Gesellsch. f. Anthrop., Berlin, 1888, 312-316.

—— Jadeit bei Borgo nuovo. Verhandl. d. Berl. Gesellsch. f. Anthrop., Berlin, 1888, 316.

Fifth national convention of the bureaus of statistics of labor in the United States. [Rev. in the Jour. Roy. Statis. Soc., London, L, 735.]

FINC, H. T. "Romantic Love and Personal Beauty." London: Macmillan & Co., 1887, 2 vols. [Rev. in Nature, XXXII, 149.]

FINSCH, O. Canoes und Canoebau in der Marshal-Inseln. Verhandl. d. Berl. anthrop. Gesellsch., 22-29, 1887, 8vo. --

—— Hausbau, Hauser, und Siedelungen an der Südostköste von Neu-Guinea. Mittheil. d. anthrop. Gesellsch. in Wien, XVII, 1-15.

FISHER, C. H. Adjustable frames for taking facial measurements. Med. Rec., N. Y., XXXIV, 522.

FISKE-BRYSON, LOUISE. Women and nature. N. York M. J., XLVI, 627.

FISON, LORIMER. The new Norcia marriage laws. J. Anthrop. Inst., Lond. (1888), XVIII, 68-70.

FLEMMING, W. Eine Karte des menschlichen Auges. Braunschweig, 1887. Am. J. Psychology, Baltimore, I, 196.

FLETCHER, ALICE C. Glimpses of child-life among the Omaha tribe of Indians. J. Am. Folk-Lore, N. Y. (1888), I, 115-123.

FLINCER, A. Ueber den Farbensinn der Thiere. Wien med. Wochenschr , XXXVII, 273-277.

FLINT, E Paleolithics in Nicaragua. Am. Antiquar , Mendon, Ill. (1888), X, 381, 382.

FLOWER, WILLIAM HENRY. Description of two skeletons of Akkas, a Pygmy race from Central Africa. J. Anthrop. Inst., Lond. (1888), XVIII, 3-19, 3 pl., also 73-91.

Folk-Lore Journal. Published by the Folk-Lore Society. London: Elliot Stock, for the Folk-Lore Society, bimonthly, vol. VI in 1887

FOLMER, A. Eene bijdrage tot de ethnology van Friesland. Nederl. Tijdschr. v. Geneesk ,. Amst , XXIII, 401-439

FORBUSH. The Hindu doctrine of death and immortality. Unitar. Rev., Apr., 1888, 319-330.

FORRER, R. The copper age in Europe. Am Antiquar., Mendon, Ill. (1888), X, 318-321.

FORTIER, ALCÉE. Customs and superstitions in Louisiana. J. Am. Folk-Lore, N Y. (1888), I, 136-140.

—— Louisianian nursery-tales. J. Am. Folk-Lore, N. Y. (1888), I, 140-145.

FOUILLÉE, ALFRED. The language of the emotions. Pop. Sc Month., XXXI, 814-824.

FOVILLE, M. DE. The abuse of statistics. Jour. Roy. Statis. Soc. London, L, 703-708.

FOWKE, GERARD. Brer Rabbit and Brer Fox. J Am Folk-Lore, N. Y. (1888), I, 148-149.

—— The manufacture and use of aboriginal stone implements. 20 pp , 8vo. (n. d.)

FOY, G. M. Idiosyncrasy. Dublin J. M Sc , LXXXIV, 197-202.

FRADENBURGH, I N. Living religions, or the great religions of the Orient, from sacred books and modern customs. New York, 1888, IV, 508 pp., 12 mo

FRAEN<EL. M. O. Etwas über Schädel-Asymmetrie und Stirnnaht. Neurol. Centralbl., Leipz., VII, 438-442.

FRAIPONT, J., et BRACONNIER. La poterie en Belgique de l'âge du mammouth. Rev. d'anthrop., 3. s., III, 385-407.

—— et M. LOHEST. La race humaine de Néanderthal ou de Canstadt en Belgique (1887). (Lille, Bull. Scient.), 18 pp., 8vo

—— Le tibia dans la race de Néanderthal, étude comparative de l'incurvation de la tête du tibia, dans ses rapports avec la station veiticale chez l'homme et les anthropoïdes. Rev. d'anthrop., Par. (1888), 3. s., III, 145-158.

—— Nouvelle exploration des cavernes d'Engis Soc. Géol. de Belg., reported in Matériaux, 3. s., IV, 163-165.

FRAN<LIN, CHRISTINE L. A method for the experimental determination of the horopter. Am. J. Psychol., I, 99-111.

FRAZER, JOHN. The aborigines of Australia; their ethnic position and relations. J. Trans. of Victoria Inst., Lond., 1888, XXII, 155-181.

FRAZER, J. G. Folk-lore at Balquhidder. Folk-Lore Jour., Lond. (1888), VI, IV, 268-271.

—— Totemism Edinburgh, Adam and Chas. Black. I vol, 1887. 16mo.

FREICHEL. Pferdekopf und Storchschnabel in Westpreussen. Verhandl. d. Berl. Gesellsch f. Anthrop., Berl., 1888, 295-297.

FREMANTLE, CANON. Theology under changed conditions. Pop. Sc. Month., XXXI, 171-187.

FRESHFIELD, D W. The Suanetians and their home. Pop. Sc. Month., N. Y., 1888-9, XXXIV, 380-385.

FRIEDRICHS, K. Zur Matriarchaftsfrage. Zeitschr f. Ethnol., Berlin, 1888, XX, 211-216.

FRÉRÉ, CH. Contribution to the pathology of dreams and of hysterical paralysis. Paris 1887.

FRIGERIO, L. Caso di porencefalia posteriore destra da cause traumatica. Ann. univ., di med. e chir., Milano, CCLXXIX, 46-52.

—— L'oreille externe; étude d'anthropologie criminelle. Arch. de l'anthrop crim., Paris, III, 438-481.

FRITSCH, A. Principien de Organisation der naturhistorischen Abtheilung des neuen Museums in Prag (1888). 8vo.

—— Bemerkungen zur anthropologischen Haaruntersuchung. Verhandl. d. Berl. Gesellsch. f Anthrop., 1888, 187-199.

FROTHINGHAM, A. L. The development and character of Mohammedan education. Proc. Am. Orient. Soc , Oct., 1888, 114-116.

FROTHINGHAM, A. L , Jr. A proto-Ionic Capital and Bird-worship. Am. J. Archæol., III, 57-61.

FULLER, E. M. Pedigree in health and disease. Tr. Maine M. Ass., Portland, 189-210.

FURTWÄNGLER, A. Studien über die Gemmen mit Künstlerinschriften. Jahrb. d. k. deutsch. archæol. Inst. Berlin, III, 193-224.

GACHE, S. Antropologia criminal. An. d. Circ. méd. argent., Buenos Ayres, X, 404-414.

GAIDOZ, H., et PAUL SÉBILLOT. Bibliographie des traditions et de la littérature populaire des Frances d'Outre-Mer Rev. de Ling., Par. (1888), XXI, 105-144.

GAILLARD, F. Du tumulus de Kerlescan à Carnac, de son acquisition et de sa restauration. Bull. de la Soc. d'anthrop., Paris, 3 s., X, 687-693.

—— Les dolmens de Kergo en Carnac. Bull. Soc. d'anthrop , Paris, 1888, 3. s., XI, 430-433.

—— Observations sur le complément de la restauration du tumulus de Kerlescan. Bull. d. l. Soc. d'anthrop , Par., 1888, 461-463.

GALIBERT, T. Au pays des Manjaques. Ann. de l'Extr. Orient et de l'Afrique, 65-74, 143-149, 180-185.

GALLIPPE, V. La droiterie et la gaucherie, sont-elles fonction de l'éducation ou de l'hérédité? Compt. rend. Soc. de biol., Par., 8. s., IV, 519-529. *Also*, Gaz. d. hôp., LX, 953; 1062.

GALTON, FRANCIS. Anthropometric statistics from Amherst College, Mass. J. Anthrop. Inst., London, XVIII, 192-199.

———— Co-relations and their measurement, chiefly from anthropometric data. Proc. Roy. Soc., Lond , 1888, XIV, 135-145.

———— Exhibition of an ancient Peruvian gold breast-plate. J. Anthrop. Inst., Lond., 1888-9, XVIII, 274.

———— Human variety. Nature, Lond., 1888-'89, XXXIX, 296-300.

———— List of Anthropometric apparatus. Cambridge Scientific Instrument Co. Nature, 1887, pp. 615, vol. 36.

———— Note on Australian marriage system. J. Anthrop. Inst., Lond. (1888), XVIII, 70-72.

———— On head growth in students at the University of Cambridge. J. Anthrop. Inst., Lond. (1888), XVIII, 155-156. 1 pl. *Also*, Nature, XXXVIII, 14.

———— Personal identification and description. J. Anthrop Inst., Lond. (1888), XVIII, 177-191, 8 ills. *Also*, Nature, Lond., XXXVIII, 173; 201.

GARDNER, JOHN LESLIE. The Legends of Jamched Quetzalcoatl. Am. Antiquar., Mendon, Ill. (1888), X, 285-291.

GARDNER, PERCY. Catalogue of Greek Coins. [Vol. X, Cat. Greek Coins in Brit. Mus.] London: Longmans, etc., lxiv+250 pp., 8vo.

GARMAN, SAMUEL. An Andean Medal. Bull. Essex Inst. (1888), XX, 1-4, 2 ills.

GAROFALO, R. L'anomalie du criminel. Rev. phil., Par., XXIII, 225-261.

GARSON, J. G. Observations on Recent Explorations made by General Pitt-Rivers at Rushmore. Nature, XXXVI, 600.

———— Skulls from the Hindu Kush district. J. Anthrop. Inst., Lond. (1888), XVIII, 20-26.

GASON, S. The Dieyerie tribe, South Australia J. Anthrop. Inst., Lond. (1888), XVIII, 94-95.

GATSCHET, A. S Bibliography of Gatschet's writings in Pilling's Bibliographies, Bureau of Ethnology, Washington.

———— Elephants in America. Am. Antiquarian, IX, 202.

———— Ethnologic notes. American Antiquarian Bi-monthly.

———— Linguistic families in southeastern United States. Science, April 29, 1887.

———— Réplique à D. G. Brinton, au sujet de son article. "Linguistique Américaine." Rev. de Ling., Par. (1888), XXI, 199-208.

GAULTIER DE CLAUBRY, J. Note sur le vocabulaire des couleurs chez les Arabes d'Algérie. Bull. Soc. d'anthrop., Paris, 3 s , IX, 698-701, 1886.

GAUTIER, E. Le monde des prisons. Arch de l'anthrop. crim., Paris, 1888, 3. s., III, 417; 541.

GERLAND and RATZEL. Controversy concerning the limit of the regions within which the boomerang is used in Australia. Internat. Arch. f. Ethnog., 1888, I, 61.

GIACOMINI, CARLO. Annotazioni sulla anatomia del negro. Appendice alle tre prime memorie VIII Esistenza della ghiandola d'Harder in un Boschimane. Duplicitàe della cartilagine della plica semilunaris. Muscolo ciliare nei negri. Distribuzion. del pigmento del globo oculare. Torino, 1887, E. Loescher, 23 pp., 2pl 8vo. [Repr. from Atti d. r. Accad. d sc. di Torino, 1887, XXII.]

GIARD, A. Histoire du transformisme. Rev. scient., Paris, 1888, XLII, 689-699.

GIFFEN, ROBERT. The recent rate of material progress in England. Jour. Roy. Statis. Soc., London, L. 615-647.

GIGLIOLI, ENRICO H. Ossa umane portate come ricordi o per ornamento e usate come utensili od armi. Arch. per l'antrop., Firenze (1888), XVIII, 201-213.

——— Mask from Boissy Island, N. E. New Guinea; and queries on the lizard in the folklore of Australasia. Internat. Arch. f. Ethnog., Leiden, I, 184-187.

GILBERT. J. H. Results of experiments at Rothansted on the growth of root-crops. Royal Agricultural College, Cirencester. Agric. Students' Gazette, new series, III, pt. V, 1-50.

GILES, HERBERT A. Family names in China. J. China Br. J. R. A. S., XXI, n. s, 255-288.

GINÉY PARTAGAS, J. El codigo penal y la frenopatologia Correo méd. Castellano, Salamauca, V, 406, 421, 436, 449, 468, 483, 499, 513, 529, 548.

GIROD, P., et ELIE MASSÉNAT. Art paléolithique. Sur une sculpture en bois de renne, de l'époque Magdalénienne représentant deux phallus réunis par la base. Compt. rend. Acad. d. sc. Paris, 1888, CVII, 1027.

GITTEÉ. Sur les moyens de recueiller le Folk-lore. Bull. Soc. d'anthrop., Bruxelles, V, 331-345.

GLAUMONT, M. Ethnogénie des insulaires de Kunie. Rev. d'ethnog., Paris, VI, 336-342.

——— Usages, mœurs et coutumes des Néo-Calédoniens. Rev. d'ethnog., XVI, 73-141.

GLENNIE, J. S. STUART. The Non-Aryan and Non-Semitic white Races. Nature, XXXVI, 598.

Globus. Illustrirte Zeitschrift fur Länder-und Völkerkunde. Braunschweig, vol. LI and LII in 1887.

GLOVER, A. K. The Jews of the extreme eastern diaspora, and the Jews of the Chinese Empire (Jews of China Proper). The Menorah, July, 1888, pp. 10-19.

GODFREY, J. Psychological and pathological influences of self-consciousness. Am. Pract. and News, Louisville, n. s, IV, 129-131.

GOEHLERT, V. Statistische Betrachtungen über biblische Daten; ein Beitrag zur Volkskunde des Alterthums. Ztschr. f. Ethnol., Berl., XIX, 83-93.

GOMME, G. L. On the evidence for Mr. McLennan's theory of the primitive human horde. J. Anthrop. Inst., Lond., XVII, 118-133.

——— On the Village Community at Ashton and Cote, in Oxfordshire. Archæol. Rev., Lond., II, 29-44.

——— The primitive human horde. Anthrop. Inst., Lond., (1888), XVII, 356-357.

——— Widowhood in manorial law. Archæol. Rev., Lond., II, 184-197.

GOODRICH, J. K. Ainu family-life and religion. Pop. Sc. Mo., N. Y. (1888), XXXIV, 81-92, 2 ills.

GOODYEAR, W. H. The lotus in ancient art. Critic, Apr, 1888, p. 209.

GORDON, C. A. Notes from the history of medicine and of medical opinion from the earliest times. Med. Press and Circ., Lond., n. s., XLIII, 25; 44; 69.

GOSHEN, G. J. The increase of moderate incomes Jour. Roy. Statis. Soc., Lond., L, 589-612.

GOTTHEIL, R. A Syriac geographical chart. Proc. Am. Orient. Soc., May, 1888, 16-20.

GOUBAUX, A. Des aberrations du sens génésique et de l'hybridite chez les animaux. N. Arch. d'obst. et de gynéc., Paris, III, 455-480.

GOUINLOCK, W. C. Hats as a cause of baldness. Pop. Sc. Month., XXXI, 97-100.

GOULD, ELIZABETH P. School life in China. Education, 1888, VIII, 557-562.

GOW, J. M. Notes on cup-marked stones, etc., Perthshire. Archæol. Rev., Lond., II, 102-104.

G. P. F. Notice sur la campagne contre le marabout Mahmadou Lamine. Union géog. du nord. l. France. Bull., VIII, 236-251, 1887.

GRABOWSCY, F. Opfergebrauche bei den Ngadju in Borneo. Internat. Arch. f. Ethnog., I, 130-134.

——— Das Betelkauen bei den malaischen Völkern. *Ibid.* 188-191.

GRASSERIE, RAOUL DE LA. Esquisse d'une grammaire du Timucua, langue de la Floride Rev. de Ling., Par. (1888), XXI, 295–313.

GREEF, GUILLAUME DE. Introduction à la Sociologie, pt. I. Bruxelles : Gustave Mayolez.

GREGOR, WALTER. Some Folk-lore from Achterneed. Folk-Lore Jour., Lond. (1888), VI, pt IV, 262–265.

GROSS, V. La paléoethnologie en Suisse. Rev d'anthrop., Paris, 1888, 3. s., III, 720–735.

—— Pferdegebiss aus Hirschhorn und Knochen. Verhandl. d Berl. Gesellsch. f. Anthrop , 1888, 180

GRIERSON, G A Some useful Hindi Books J R A. S.,XIX, art IV.

GRIFFIS, WILLIAM E. The Mikado's Empire. History of Japan from 660 B C. to 1872 A. D. New edition New York Harper, ill., 8vo.

—— Japanese Art, Artists, and Artisans, with illustrations from drawings by a Japanese artist. Scribner's Monthly Mag , Jan., 1888.

—— Japanese ivory carving. Harper's Mag., Apr , 1888, 7 ill.

GRIMALDI, A. Il pudore. Manicomio, Nocera, IV, 57–80.

GRISSOM Insanity in history and poetry. N E Med Month , VII, 565–583.

GRUNWEDEL. Acht Schadelschalen der Aghôri. Verhandl d Berl. Gesellsch. f. Anthrop., Berlin, 1888, 307.

GUBBINS, J H. The feudal system in Japan under the Tokugawa Shoguns. Tr. As. Soc. Japan, XV, 131–142.

GUIGNARD, L Antiquité de l'homme dans le Loir-et Cher, Chartres, 1888, 16 pp.,8vo.

GUPPY, H. B. Solomon Islands and their natives. Longmans Nature, XXXVI, 454.

—— The Solomon Islands and their natives. London Sonnenschein.

GURNEY, EDMUND, and others. Phantasms of the living. London Trübner, 1886. Rev., in Nature, XXXV, 290.

GUSS, A. L. Tribal affinity of Shickalamy and his son Logan. Am. Antiquar., Chicago, IX, 108–111.

GUYAU, L. Irreligion de l'avenir Paris· Alcan, xxviii+479 pp. (See review in Rev. de l'hist d relig , XVI, 317–351.)

GUYOT-DAUBES M. Les anomalies dactyles. Rev. d'anthrop., Par (1888), 3. s., III, 534–559

—— Variations in human stature. [Transl. from La Nature, Par.] Pop Sc. Month., N Y., XXXI, 314–323

GUYOT, YVES. La science économique, Paris. Rev in Jour. Roy Statis Soc., London, L, 730–732.

GROVE, Sir W R Antagonism. Pop Sc Month., N Y., XXXIII, 608–624

GURLITT, W. Die Hügelgraber von Loibenberge in Steiermark. Mitth. d anthrop. Gesellsch. in Wien., n. F VIII, 202–204.

—— Das Urnenfeld von Borstendorf in Mahren Ibid, 201.

HABEL, S. Sculptures de Santa Lucia Cosumalwhuapa dans le Guatémala, Ann. du Musée Guimet, X, 121–259, pl. VIII-XV, 1887.

HABERLANDT, M. Die Cultur der Eingebornen der Maledicen. Mitth d anthrop Gesellsch. in Wien. Sitzungsb , 1888, 29–37, figs.

—— Zum Ursprung des Bogens. Mittheil. d anthrop Gesellsch in Wien, XVII, 116.

HAGEN, A. La colonie de Porto-Novo et le roi Toffa Rev. d'ethnog., Par., VI, 81–116

—— et A. PIGNEAU Les Nouvelles Hébrides, études ethnographiques. Rev. d'ethnog., Paris, 1888, VII, 302-362, 1 map

HALBERT, H S. The Choctaw chungkee game Am Antiquar., Mendon, Ill. (1888), X, 283–284.

HALE, E. M A prehistoric amphitheater in Florida. Am Antiquar , IX, 207–210.

H. Mis. 142——35

HALE, HORATIO. Les origines d'une ancienne monnaie. Rev. in Rev. d'anthrop. Paris, 3. s., II, 372-373.

—— Huron folk-lore. J. Am Folk-Lore, I, 177-183.

—— Les sacrifices du chien blanc chez les Iroquois. Rev. in Rev. d'anthrop., Paris, 3. s, II, 373.

—— The development of language. Proc. Canadian Inst., Toronto, 3. s., VI, 92-134.

—— The Aryans in science and history. Pop. Sc. Month., N. Y., 1888-9, XXXIX, 672-686.

HALÈVY, J. Recherches Bibliques, x. Le XIV° chapitre de la Genèse. Rev. des Études Juives, XV, 161-202, 1887.

HALIBURTON, R. G. Gypsies and an ancient Hebrew race in Sus and the Sahara. Nature, XXXVI, 599.

HALL, ALFRED J. A grammar of the Kwakiutl language. Trans. Roy. Soc., Canada, Montreal (1888), VI, 59-105.

HALL, G. STANLEY, and MOTORA YUZERO. Dermal sensitiveness to gradual pressure changes. Am. Jour. of Psychology, Baltimore, I, 72-98.

HAMBLETON, G. W. The experimental production of chest types in man. Lancet, Lond., II, 610.

HAMDY-BEY, M. J. Sur une nécropole royale découverte à Saida. Rev. d'ethnog., Paris, VI, 444-456.

HAMMOND, C. M. The prolongation of human life. Pop. Sc. Month., N. Y., XXXIX, 92-101.

HAMY, E. T. Decades americanæ. Mémoires d'archéologie et d'ethnographie américaine. Rev. d'ethnog, Paris, VI, 150-160.

—— Decades americanæ. Peintures ethnographiques d'Ignacio de Castro. Rev. d'ethnog., VII, 142-151; Mém. d'archéol. et d'ethnog américaines. Ibid., VI, 150-160.

—— Études ethnographiques et archéologiques sur l'exposition coloniale et indienne de Londres. Rev. d'ethnog., Par., V, passim; VI, 185-227.

—— Note sur une statue ancienne du Dieu Çiva, provenant des ruines de Kamphengphet, Siam Rev. d'ethnog., Paris, 1888, XII, 363-372, 1 pl

—— Notice sur les fouilles exécutées dans le lit de la liane en 1887 pour l'établissement du nouveau viaduc du chemin de fer. Rev. d'anthrop., Par. (1888), 3. s., III, 257-271.

—— Sur un envoi d'Emin-Bey. Bull. de la Soc d'anthrop, Paris, 3. s., X, 605.

—— Tête momitiée provenant de la tribue des Jivaros (République de l'Équateur). Bull. d. l. Soc. d'anthrop., Paris, 3. s, X, 148.

HAMY, E. et F. BORSARI. Geografia ethnologica e storica della Tripolitania, Cirenaicae Fezzau. Napoli, L. Pierro, 1888, 1 vol. in-8. Rev. in Rev. d'ethnog., VII, Par., 1888, p. 486, 1 ill.

HAMY, E. et Fr MOREAU. Notice sur des silex tailles recueillis en Tunisie. Paris, Quentin, 1888, br. in-8, 3 pl., chrom. 1 carte. Rev. in Rev. d'ethnog., VII, Par., 1888, pp. 483-485, 4 ills.

HAMY, E. et J C. B. Voyage au Canada, dans le nord de l'Amérique septentrionale, fait depuis l'an 1751 à 1761 (publié par. M. l'abbé H. R. Casgrain, Quebec, Brousseau, 1887, 1 vol. in-8. Rev. in Rev. d'ethnog., VII, Par., 1888, p. 483.

HANDELMANN, H. Zu der Krote von Crobern. Cor.-Bl. d. deutsch. Gesellsch. f. Anthrop., etc., Brnschwg., 1888, XIX, 57.

HANDMANN, R. Die menschliche Stimme und Sprache in psychologischer Beziehung. Munster (1887), 230 pp. mit 27 Figuren, 8vo.

HANRIOT et C. RICHET. Présentation d'un spiromètre Compt rend. Soc. de biol., Par, 8 s. IV, 405.

HANSEN, SÖREN. Danische Untersuchungen in Grönland. Rev. in Intern. Arch. f. Ethnog., 1888, I, 76.

HANSEN, SÖREN. Dr. Henry Rink's, "The Eskimo Tribes." [Rev. in Intern Arch. f. Ethnog., 1888, I, 74-75.

——— et TOPINARD. La couleur des yeux et des cheveux en Danemark. Rev. d'anthrop., Par. (1888), 3 s., III, 39-41

HANTZSCHE, J. C. Der alte Kanal von Gulga. Festschr. des Vereins f. Erdkunde zu Dresden (1888), 217-224.

HARDERUP, V. Proposal for an international signification of the teeth. Presented to the iv. Intern Med. Cong., Washington, 1887. Kristiania, 1887, Cammer, 8vo.

HARDWICKE, H. J. Evolution and Creation. Lond., 1887, 180 pp., 51 pl., 8vo.

HARDY, M. Paléo-ethnologie. Découverte d'une sépulture de l'époque quaternaire à Raymonden, commune de Chancelade (Dordogne). Compt. rend. Acad. d sc., Paris, 1888, CVII, 1025.

HARLEY, GEORGE. Comparison between the recuperative bodily power of man in a rude and in a highly civilized state London (1887), Harrison & Sons. 6-12.

Harvard University Bulletin. Edited by Justin Winsor. Camb, Mass., vols. IV and V. [Classified lists of accessions to library, including all departments of anthropology.]

HARVEY, J. G. Circumcised by a maternal impression. Med Rec., N.Y., XXXIV. 535.

HASSELMANN, F. Ueber altägyptische Textilfunde in Oberägypten. Cor-Bl. d. deutsch. Gesellsch. f. Anthrop., Brnschwg, XIX, 45-81.

HAYNES, HENRY W. Some Aztec questions. Am. Antiquar., Chicago, IX, 107-108

HEDGE, F. H. Mahommedan mysticisms. Unitarian Rev, May, 1888, XXIX, 410-416.

HEGER, F. Die Ethnographie auf der Krakauer Landesausstellung, 1887. Mitth. d. anthrop, Gesellsch. in Wien, n F., VIII, 190-201.

HELFRICH, O. L., W R. WINTER, en D M. J. SCHIFF. Het Hasan-Hosein of Taboet-Feest te Benkoelen Intern Arch. f. Ethnog, 1888, I, 191-196, 1 pl.

HELLWALD, F. VON. Haus und Hof in ihrer Entwickelung mit Bezug auf die Wohnsitzen der Volker. Lipsia, 1888, 1 vol., 581 pp., 222 ills. [Rev. in Arch. per l'antrop., Firenze, 1888, XVIII, 283]

HENNIGHAUSEN, LOUIS P. The redemptioners and the German Society of Maryland. An historical sketch. Balto. (1888), Theo. Kroh & Sons, 1 vol., 1-22.

HENRI, M., and LOUIS SIRET. The early age of metal in the southeast of Spain. J. Anthrop. Inst, Lond. (1888), XVIII, 121-132, 1 pl.

HENSHAW, H. W. Perforated stones from California. Wash., Gov. Print, 1887, bi. 16 figures, 8vo.

HERING, E. Ueber die Theorie des simultanen Contrasts von Helmholtz. Pflüger's Arch., 172, 1887.

HERMANN, ANTON Ethnologische Mittheilungen aus Ungarn. Zeitschrift fur die Volkskunde der Bewohner Ungarns und seiner Nebenlander Budapest, Selbstverlag der Redaction, 1887, 4. [Rev. in Arch f Anthrop, Brnschwg. (1889), XVIII, 286.]

HÉRON. Funérailles de M. O. Rayet. Discours Paris, Soc. nat antiq, 1887, 8vo

HERTER, C. A. Hypnotism, what it is and what it is not. Pop. Sc Month, N Y., XXXIII, 755-777.

HERVÉ, GEORGES. Crâne de gorille. Bull. Soc. d'anthrop., Par, 3 s., XI (1888), 181.

——— La circonvolution de Broca chez les Primates. Bull Soc. d'anthrop., Par., 3. s, XI, 275-315. Also separate Delahaye, 164 pp, 4 pl, 8vo

HERZOG, WILHELM Die Verwandtschaftsbeziehungen der costaricensischen Indianer-Sprachen mit denen von Central und Sud Amerika. Arch f. Anthrop, XVI. 623-627.

HIBBERT, ANDREW School plays and games. Antiquary, XV, 52-54.

HICKS, HENRY "The Faunas of the Ffynnon Beuno Caves and of the Norfolk Forest Bed" Geological Magazine, 1887, March Reviewed in Nature, XXXVI, 259

HILL, S. A. The life statistics of an Indian province. Nature, Lond., XXXVIII, 245-250.

HINS, EUGÉNE   L'opinion que les langues romanes dérivent du latin, a-t-elle un fonde-
ment historique? Rev. Linguis., Paris, XX, 325-351.

HINSDALE, G   Menneskets Holdning, fysiologisk og klinisk betragtet. Norsk Mag.
f Lægevidensk , Christiania, 4 R., II, 782-787

HITHCOCK, E , and H. H. SEELYE   Amherst College   An anthropometric manual, giving the average and physical measurements and tests of male college students and
method of securing them   Prepared from the records of the department of physical education and hygiene in Amherst College during the years 1861-2 and 1886-7,
inclusive   Amherst, 1887, J. E. Williams, 26 pp., 2 tab., 8vo.

——— Anthropometric statics from Amherst College, Mass , U. S A   J Anthrop.
Inst., Lond. (1888), XVIII, 192-199

——— and H H Seelye   Statistics bearing upon the average and typical student in Amherst College, 1888   J Anthrop Inst , Lond (1888), XVII, 357-358

HODGE, C F   Some effect of stimulating ganglion cells   Am. J Psychol., I, 479-486.

HODGETTS, J F   The smith and wright   Antiquary, XVI, 1-4. 96-100

HOERNES, M.   Die Graberfelder an der Wallburg von St. Michael, bei Adelsberg in
Krain. Mitth. d. anthrop. Gesellsch. in Wien, 1888, n. F., VIII. 217-249, 4 pl.

——— Einige Notizen und Nachträge zu älteren Erwerbungen und Mittheilungen der
anthropologischen Gesellschaft. Ibid. (Sitzungsb., 86.)

——— Ferner Zusätze zu alteren Mittheilungen der anthropologischen Gesellschaft.
La Tène-Funde. Ibid. [Sitzungsb., 94-96.]

——— La paléoethnologic en Autriche-Hongrie. Rev. d'anthrop , 3. s., III, 333-347.

——— Die altesten Beziehungen zwischen Mittel- und Süd-Europa. Mitt. d. anthrop.
Gesellsch., Wien, n. F., VIII, 57-61.

HOFFDING, HARALD. Psychologie in Umrissen auf Grundlage der Erfahrung. Leipzig (1887), Fues's Verlag, vi+463 pp., 8vo.

HOFFMAN, W. J. Folk-lore of the Pennsylvania Germans   J Am. Folk-Lore, N. Y.
(1888), I, 125-135

HÖFLER, M. Volksmedicin und Aberglaube in Bayern's Gegenwart und Vergangen-
heit. Beitr. z. Anthrop., Munchen (1888), VIII, 37-38.

——— Ueber Votiv-Gaben. Beitr. z. Anthrop., Munchen (1888), VIII, 39-40

HOLDER, M. DE. Moulages des type crânieus du Wurtemberg offerts. Bull. d. l. Soc.
d'anthrop., Paris, 3. s., X, 640-641.

——— Ueber die korperlichen und geistigen Eigenthümlichkeiten der Verbrecher.
Arch. f. Anthrop., Bruschwg , 1888-'89, XVIII, 205-221.

HOLL, M. Ueber die in Tirol vorkommenden Schadelformen   (Dritter Beitrag.)
Mitth. d anthrop Gesellsch. in Wien, n. F., VII, 129-152.

HOLME, R. F. A journey in the Province of San Paulo, Brazil. Proc. Roy. Geog. Soc.,
IX, 108-114.

HOLMES, W. H. Ancient art of the Province of Chiriqui. VI. Ann. Rept. Bur. Ethnol.,
1888, pp. 3-252, 285 figs., 1 map.

——— A study of the textile art in its relation to form and ornament. VI. Ann. Rept.
Bur. Ethnol., 1888, pp. 189-252, 73 figs.

——— The use of gold and other metals among the ancient inhabitants of Chiriqui,
Ithmus of Darien. Wash , Gov. Print, bi., 22 figs., 1887, 8vo.

HOPKINS, E. W. Inquiry into the conditions of civilization in the Hindu Midde Age,
from the point of view of the ruling power or warrior caste. Proc. Am. Orient. Soc.,
1888, 8.

HOROWITZ, VCT. J. Marokko. Das Wesentlichste und Interessanteste über Land und
Leute. Leipzig (1887), Friedrich, III, 215 pp., 8vo.

HORSLEY, VICTOR. Trephining during the Neolithic period in Europe. J. Anthrop.
Inst., XVII, 100-106.

HOUGH, WALTER. An Eskimo strike-a-light from Cape Bathurst, British-America. Proc. U. S. Nat Mus , Wash. (1888), XI, 181-184

—— Notes on the ethnology of the Congo. American Naturalist, vol. XXI, Aug., pp. 689-693.

HOUSSAY, FR Les peuples actuels de la Perse. Bull Soc d'anthrop., Lyon, V, 101-147.

—— Les races humaines de la Perse. [Extr. du Bull. de la Soc. d'anthrop. de Lyon] Lyon, Pitrat, fig , pl., 1887, 8vo

HOUTSMA, M. TH. Réponse à la question sur une statuette ithyphallique. [Rev. in Inter. Arch. f. Ethnog., 1888, I, 235.]

HOUZÉ, E. Comparaison des indices céphalométrique et crâniométrique, indices céphaliques de Belgique. Bull Soc. d'anthrop de Brux., V, 397-407.

—— Les tribus occidentales du Lac Tanganjika. Bull Soc d'anthrop. de Bruxelles, V, 43-65.

HOVELACQUE ABEL. La grammaire indo-européenne d'après Fr Müller Rev de Ling , Par. (1888) XXI, 91-104, 27-47.

—— et HERVÉ, G Précis d'anthropologie (bibliothèque anthropologique). Paris, A. Delahaye et Lecrosnier, 1 vol., 20 fig , 1887, 8vo [Cf., Natue, XXXVI, 1198

—— Sur la juxtaposition de charactères divergents à propos de crânes Birmans. Rev. d'anthrop., Par (1888), 3 s , III, 681-683

HOVEY, H. C. Eyay Shah· a sacrificial stone near St Paul. Am. Antiquarian, IX, 35, 36.

HOWARTH, H. H The survival of corporal penance. J. Anthrop. Inst., Lond., XVIII, 275-281. 2 pl.

HOWITT, A. W. Further notes on the Australian class system. J. Anthrop. Inst., Lond (1888), XVIII, 31-68, 1 pl.

HOWORTH, H. H. The mammoth and the flood. London Sampson Low, 564 pp , 8vo.

HUIDEKOPER, R. S Origin of the domestication of the horse J. Comp. Med and S., Phila., IX, 377-389.

HUBBARD, D. A. The religious of Zoroaster Unitarian Rev., 1888, 112-139.

HULL, EDWARD. Sketch of geological history, being the natural history of the earth and of the pre-human inhabitants London (1887), C W Deacon.

HUMPHRY, G M. Additional report on centenarians. [Brit M. J., Lond., I.] Collect. Invest Rec., Lond , III, 83-85.

—— Centenarians. Brit. Med J., Lond., I, 502, 564, 612.

—— The habits and family history of centenarians. Pop Sc Month., XXX, 618-630, 1887.

HUNTER, W. W. Religions of India. Our day. Boston, 1888, 378 pp

HURGRONJE, C. S. Ethnographisches aus Mekka. Internat. Arch f. Ethnog., Leiden, I, 116-154, 4 pl

HUTCHINSON, J Skeleton of a short-limbed dwarf, aged thirty-five, from the Norfolk and Norwich Museum. Lancet, Lond , 1888, II, 1230.

HUTH, ALFRED HENRY. The marriage of near kin considered with respect to the laws of nations, the results of experience and the teachings of biology. 2 ed. Lond., 1887, Longmans, Green & Co , 485 pp., 9 tab.

HUXLEY, T H. Science and morals. Pop Sc Month., XXX, 493-506, 1887.

HYADES. Ethnographie des Fuégiens Bull Soc d'anthrop , Par., 3 s , X, 327-345.

HYSLOP, J H. The new psychology. New Princeton Review, n s , VI, 155-171.

ICHENHAEUSER, J. Ein Beitrag zur Uebervolkerungsfrage. Berlin, 1888, Heuser, 84 pp., 8vo.

IHERING, H V. Die Verbreitung der Ankeräxte in Brasilien. Verhandl d. Berl. Gesellsch f Anthrop , 1888, 217-221.

ILJINSKI, A. Feasibility of preserving condition of women for an indefinite time. Moskoa, 1888, Iverskaja, 241 p., 8vo.

Index-catalogue of the Library of the Surgeon-General's Office. Washington Government Print Vol IX — MEDICINE to NYWELT.

Index Medicus. A monthly classified record of the current medical literature of the world. Boston G. S Davis. Vol. IX, monthly.

Indian affairs Report of commissioner, Washington Government Print.

Indian Annals and Magazine of Natural Science. Ed. by J. Murray, Bombay. Monthly. No. 1 issued in May, 1887. 8vo.

The Indian Antiquary. Bombay Vol. XVII in 1888.

Internationales Archiv für Ethnographie. Edited by J. D. E. Schmelz. Leyden: Trap. [Vol. I of this illustrated quarto published in 1888. Especially devoted to museums.]

Internationale Zeitschrift für allgemeine Sprachwissenschaft.

International meeting respecting the cranial indices. Corr.-Blatt, XVII, 17-22.

IRELAND, W. W. Herrschermacht und Geisteskrankheit. Studien aus der Geschichte alter und neuer Dynastien Autorisirte Uebersetzung. Stuttgart: Robert Lutz, 1887, 8. [Rev. in Arch. f. Anthrop., Brnschwg. (1889), XVIII, 288-289.]

IVES, S. E. Japanese magic mirror. J. of the Franklin Institute, 1888, 324 pp.

JACKSON, J. H. Remarks on the psychology of joking. Lancet, London, II, 800. Also: Brit. M. J., Lond., II, 870.

JACOB, G. Eiserne Hohlschüssel von dem kleinen Gleichberge bei Römhild. Arch. f. Anthrop., Brnschwg., 1888-9, XVIII, 283.

JACOBI, M. PUTNAM. Note on the special liability to loss of nouns in aphasia. J. Nervous and Mental Disease, N. Y., 1887

JACOBS, J. Experiments on prehension. Mind, 1887. Notes on prehension in idiots, by Francis Galton. [Rev. in Am. J. Psychology, I]

JACQUES, V., et STORMS, E. Notes sur l'ethnographie de la partie orientale de l'Afrique équatoriale. Bull. Soc. d'anthrop. de Brux., V, 91-202.

———— L'ethnographie préhistorique dans le sud-est de l'Espagne. Bull. Soc. d'anthrop. de Brux , VI, 210-236.

JAGOR, T. Indische Zahnbürsten. Verhandl. d. Berl. Gesellsch. f. Anthrop., Berlin, 1888, 412.

Jahrbuch der königlichen deutschen archaeologischen Institute. Berlin. Founded in 1886.

JAMES, WILLIAM. Some Human Instincts. Pop. Sc. Month., XXXI, 666-681, 1887.

———— The perception of space. Mind., London, XII, 1; 183.

JANES, LEWIS G. Egyptian doctrine of the future life. Unitarian Rev., 1888, 33-48.

JANKE, H. Die willkurliche Hervorbringung des Geschlechts bei Mensch und Hausthieren. Berlin, 1887, XIX, 495 pp., 8vo

JARDINE, JUSTICE. Kattywar. Sassoon Mechanic Institute, Bombay, 25-29.

JASTROW, JOSEPH. A critique of psycho-physic methods. Am J. Psychol., I, 271.

———— Eye-mindedness and ear-mindedness. Pop. Sc. Month , N. Y., XXXIII, 597-608.

———— The psycho-physic law and star magnitude. Am. J. Psychol., Baltimore, I, 112-127.

JASTROW, MORRIS. Babylonian cemeteries. Harper's Weekly, 1888.

JENTSCH, H. Alterthümer aus dem Gubener Kreise und von Magdeburg Verhandl. d Berl. Gesellsch. f. Anthrop., Berlin, 1888, 283-287.

———— Niederlausitzer Alterthümer. Verhandl. d. Berl. Gesellsch. f. Anthrop , Berlin, 1888, 253-256.

JESSUP, R. B , Jr. Monstrosities and material impressions J. Am. Med Ass., Chicago, XI, 519.

JOEST, WILHELM. Waffe, Signalrohr oder Tabakspfeife ? Intern. Arch. f. Ethnog., 1888, I, 176 184.

———— Tätowiren, Narbenzeichnen und Körperbemalen. Ein Beitrag zur vergleichenden Ethnologie. Berl , 1887, A. Asher & Co , 136 pp , 11 col. pl., fol.

Johns Hopkins University Studies in Historical and Political Science. Herbert B. Adams, editor. Baltimore: N. Murray. Series I-VII, 1883-1888.

JOHNSON, JOHN, Jr. The savagery of boyhood. Pop. Sc. Month., XXXI, 796–800.

JOLY, HENRI. Le crime; étude sociale Paris. 1888, 392 pp , X, 18mo.

JONES, JOSEPH. Vital capacity of the lungs in health and disease. N. Orleans (1888), 8 pp.; 8vo ; also Contribution to teratology. *Id.*, 41 pp , 8vo.

JOUAN, H. Les légendes des îles Hawaii (îles Sandwich) et le peuplement de la Polynésie. Extr. des Mém. Soc nat des sc. nat et math. de Cherbourg, 1887, br., 8vo.

Journal (The) of American Folk-Lore. Boston and New York. Houghton & Co., quarterly. Issued by the American Folk-Lore Society. Vol I, in 1888.

Journal of the Anthropological Institute of Great Britain and Ireland. Vol. XVI, nos. 3, 4 to vol. XVIII, nos 1, 2 in 1887 and 1888, quarterly. London · Trübner and Co

Journal of the Anthropological Society of Bombay. Vol 1, monthly, published in 1887.

Journal of the Asiatic Society of Bengal Calcutta · G. R. House. Vol. LVII. Part I, Philogical; part II, Nat. History, in 1888.

Journal of the China Branch of the Royal Asiatic Society. Shanghai: Kelly and Welsh, vol. XXIII, new series, in 1888. Bi-monthly.

Journal of the Cincinnati Society of Natural History. Vol. IX. in 1887. By the Society.

Journal of the Gypsy Lore Society Vol. 1. No. 1, in July, 1888, printed by T. and A. Constable, Edinburgh. Quarterly.

Journal of the Manchester Geographical Society. Manchester For the Soc., vols 1–4, 1885–1888. (Contents of the 4 vols. Vol. IV, 3d page of cover.)

Journal of the Military Service Institution. New York : By the Institution. Vol. IX in 1888. Bi-monthly.

Journal of the Royal Asiatic Society of Great Britain and Ireland. London · Trübner, new series, vol XX in 1888. Quarterly. (At the end of this vol. is an index to the Transactions and all the Journals of both series, covering 217 pages)

Journal of the Royal Statistical Society. London, 1887. Pub. quarterly. Ed. Stanford. 8vo.

Journal of the Society of Arts. London : George Bell & Sons. Vol. 36 in 1888.

Journal of the Transactions of the Victoria Institute, or Philosophical Society of Great Britain. London By the Institute. Vol. XXII in 1888.

JUBAINVILLE, H. d'ARBOIS DE. Littérature épique de l'Irelande. Rev. de Ling., Par. (1888), xxi, 352–360.

JULIN, C. La race humaine de Néanderthal ou de Constadt en Belgique, par Julien Fraipont et Max Lohest. Bull scient dép. du nord, etc., Par., 2. s , x, 28–45.

JUS, H. Les oasis du souf du département de Constantine (Sahara Oriental). Rev. in Rev. d'ethnog , Par., VI, 164–165.

—— Stations préhistoriques de l'Oued Rir. Rev. d'ethnog , Paris, VI, 343–346

KARR, H. W. SETON. Shores and Alps of Alaska. London (1887) Sampson Low. Rev in Nature, XXXVI, 220

KARUSIO, A. Pregiudizi popolari putignanesi (Bari). Arch. per l' antrop., Firenze, XVII, 311–332.

KEANE, A. H. The Eskimo. [Rev. of Dr. Rink.] Nature, XXXV, 309.

—— The Necropolis of Ancon, in Peru. A. Asher & Co., 1880–'87, vols. 3 (141 colored plates).

KEBBEL, T. E. The agricultural laborer; a summary of his position. [Rev. in Jour. Roy. Statis. Soc. London, L, 743.]

KEENE, H G. On the revenues of the Moghul Empire. J. R. A. S., XIX, 495–499.

KEIBEL. FRANZ. Die Urbewohner der Canaren Ein anthropologischer Versuch. Strassb., 1887, Heitz & Münchel, 60 pp., 11 tabl., 3 pl., 8vo

KELETI, KARL. Die Ernährungs-Statistik der Bevölkerung Ungarns auf physiologischer Grundlage bearbeitet. [Rev in Jour. Roy. Statis. Soc. London, L, 742–743.

KELLNER & MORI Food of the Japanese. German Asiatic Soc. of Japan. (Heft 37.) *Also:* Ztschr. f. Biol., München u. Leipz., n F., VII, 102–122.

KELLOG. The ghost theory of the origin of religion. Bibliotheca Sacra, April.

KERN, H., and Dr. N. ANUCHIN. Bow and arrow. [Rev. in Intern Arch. f. Ethnog., 1888, I, 167-170, 2 ills.

KINAHAN, G. HENRY. An inscribed rock surface at Mevagh, Rosguile, County Donegal, Ireland. J. Anthrop. Inst., Lond. (1888), XVIII, 170-171

—— Barnes' inscribed dallâns, County Donegal. J. Anthrop. Inst , Lond. (1888), XVIII, 171-174, 1 pl.

—— Irish folk-lore notes. Folk-Lore Jour., Lond. (1888), VI, pt. iv, 265-267.

KINGSLEY, N. W. Illustrations of the articulations of the tongue. Internat. Ztschr. f. Sprachw. III, 225-248.

KLEIN. Zur älteren Geschichte der Stadt Bonn. Cor.-Bl. d. deutsch. Gesellsch. f. Anthrop., etc., Brnschwg.. 1888, XIX, 84-98.

KNOLLYS, HENRY. Sketches of life in Japan. London : Chapman & Hall (1887), Ill.

KOBELT, W. Les dolmens de Guyotville, Algérie. Rev. d'ethnog., Paris, VI, 133-149.

KONIG, A., und E BRODHUN. Experimentelle Untersuchungen über die psychophysische Fundamentalformel in Bezug auf den Gesichtssinn. Berlin, Mitth. Akad. (1888), 15 pp., mit 3 Abbildungen, 8vo

KÖROSI, JOSEF Resultate der am 1. Juli 1836 durchgeführten Conscription der Bevölkerung Budapests. Uebersetzung aus dem Ungarischen. Berl., 1887, Puttkammer & Mühlbrecht, 48 pp , 4to.

Kosmos. Zeitschrift für die gesammte Entwicklungslehre. Stuttgart Dr. B. Vetter.

KRAHULITZ, J. Prähistorische Gräber und Ansiedlungen bei Eggenburg in Niederösterreich. Mitt. d. anthrop. Gesellsch. in Wien, XVII, 65.

—— Urgeschichtliche Funde und Fundplätze in Niederösterreich. Mitth d. anthrop. Gesellsch. in Wien, 1888, n. F., XIII. [Sitzungsb., 85.]

KRAUSS, A. Di alcuni strumenti musicali della Micronesia e della Melanesia regalati al museo nazionale d' antropologia e di ethnologia dal Dott. Otto Finsch. Arch. per l' antrop , Firenze, XVII, 41; XVIII, 161-162.

—— Cesare Lombroso's Werk in seinem Verhältniss zur Gegenwart und Zukunft der gerichtlichen Psychopathologie Friedreichs Bl. f gerichtl. Med., Nürnb., 1888, XXXIX, 251-328.

KRAUSS, F. Das Bauopfer bei den Südslaven Mittheil. d. anthrop Gesellsch., Wien, 16-23. Also · Sitzungsb., 65. Das Schamanentum der Jakuten. Ibid., 165-182.

—— South Slavic moon-myths Pop. Sci. Mouth., N. Y., 1888-'89, XXXIV, 615-618.

KRIEGL. G. L Die Volkerstämme und ihre Zweige. Ediz. 5 per cura di F von Hellwald. Basilea, 1887. [Rev. in Arch. per l' antrop. (1888), XVIII, 282.]

KRONER, EUGEN. Das körperliche Gefühl. Ein Beitrag zur Entwickelungsgeschichte des Geistes. Breslau, 207, 1887 [Rev in Am. J. Psychol., Balt., I, 182, 183.]

KÜCHENMEISTER, F. Die verschiedenen Bestattungsarten menschlicher Leichname vom Anfange der Geschichte bis heute. Vierteljschr. f gerichtl. Med , Berl., n. F., XLIX, 84-104.

KUHN, HEINRICH. Mein Aufenthalt in New Guinea. Festchr. des Vereins f. Erdkunde zu Dresden (1888), 117-151. 5 figs. 1 pl.

KUNTZ, GEO. F. Gold and silver ornaments from mounds of Florida. Am Antiquar., 1887. 9 pp., with 9 illustrations, 8vo.

—— Meteoric iron from Arkansas, 1886. Proc. U. S. Nat. Museum, Wash (1887), 598-605, 2 pl., 2 figs., 1 map.

—— Mineralogical notes. Am J. of Sc., XXXVI (1888), 222-224, 2 ill.

—— Precious stones, gems and decorative stones in Canada and British America. Rep. Geol. Surv., Ottawa, Canada (1887), 1-16.

—— Precious stones. U. S. Geol. Surv., Wash. (1888), 555-579.

—— On two masses of meteoric iron. Am. J. of Sc. (1888), XXXVI, 275-277, 1 pl.

KUNZ, G. F. Gold ornaments from United States of Colombia. (Am Antiquar., 1887.) 4 pp., with 1 pl. and 3 illustrations, 8vo, IX, 267–270

KURELLA, H Criminelle Anthropologie und positives Strafrecht. Centralbl. f. Nervenh , Leipz., XI, 534–575.

KUUN, Le Comte G Étude sur l'origine des nationalités de la Transylvanie. Rev. d'ethnog , Paris, VI, 223–272

LABORDE, M. Étude expérimentale sur les poisons de flèche des Négritos (Sakayes) de la presqu'île malaise et des Wakamba (Zanguebar) Bull. Soc. d'anthrop , Par., 3. s , XI (1888), 194–196.

LACOMBE, M. Sur une coutume funéraire du midi de la France. Bull de la Soc. d'anthrop., 3. s., X, 780.

LACOUPERIE, TERRIEN Formosa notes on mss., races, and languages, including notes on nine Formosan mss , by E. Colborne Baber J Roy. Asiat Soc., Lond., XIX, 413 (1887).

—— Les langues de la Chine avant les Chinois. Le Muséon, Louvain, VI, 100–112; 143–155, 464–491.

—— "Miryeks, or Stone men of Corea." J. Roy. Asiat.Soc., n. s., XIX, 1887, 553.

LADD, GEO T. Physiological Psychology. London (1887) Longmans, Green & Co., 1887 [Rev. in Nature, XXXVI, 290; Am. J. Psychol,. Balto , I, 159–164]

LAFARGUE, P. La circoncision, sa signification sociale et religieuse. Bull. Soc. d'anthrop. de Par., 3. s., X, 420–436.

LAFAYE, GEORGES. Les découvertes en Grèce au point de vue de l'Histoire des religions. Rev. de l'Hist. des Relig., XVI, 189–202.

LAGNEAU, M. G. Planche et prospectus des premiers âges du métal dans le sud-est de l'Espagne Bull. de la Soc. d'anthrop., Par., 3. s., X, 419.

—— Étude démographique de la diminution ou de l'accroissement des familles. Bull. Acad. de méd., Paris, 1888, 2. s., IXX, 498–514

LACE, R. Double supernumerary auricle. Illust. M News, London, 1888, I, 322.

LALOY, LÉON. Bulletin de la Société d'anthropologie de Vienne. (Mittheilungen der anthropologischen Gesellschaft in Wien; tomes XVII (1887) et XVIII (1888, 1er fascicule). Rev. in Rev. d'anthrop., Par. (1888), 3 s., III, 741–744

—— and MORIZ BÉNÉDIKT. Crâniométrie et céphalométrie. (Kraniometrie und Kephalometrie; Vorlesungen gehalten an der Wiener allgemeinen Poliklinik. Wien und Leipzig, 1888.) Rev. d'anthrop., Par. (1888), 3 s., III, 621-623.

—— Indiens de l'Amérique Centrale Bull. Soc d'anthrop , Par., 3. s , XI (1888), 224–225.

—— and H SCHAAFFHAUSEN. La physiognomique. (Archiv f. Anthrop , XVII, No. 4.) Rev. d'anthrop., Par. (1888), 3. s , III, 495–496.

—— Revue d'ethnologie de Berlin. (Ztschr fur Ethnol., année 1887, No. VI, année 1888, Nos I et II. Rev. d'anthrop., Par. (1888), 3 s., III, 617–621.

LAMPREZ, J. J. Horned men in Africa. Further particulars of their existence. Brit. M. J., Lond., II, 1273

La Nature. Genoa. Ed by Prof. A. Isset.

LANDOIS, H , und B VORMANN. Westfälische Todtenbäume und Baumsargmenschen. Arch. f. Anthrop , Brnschwg., XVII, 339–362.

LANDSBERGER Das Wachsthum im Alter der Schulpflicht. Arch f. Anthrop., Brnschwg., XVII, 229–264

LANE. W. ARBUTHNOT Can the existence of a tendency to change in the form of the skeleton of the parent result in the actuality of that change in the offspring? J. Anat. and Physiol., XXII, 215

LANGDON, F. W. Mound crania from St. Francis County, Arkansas. Am. Antiquar , Mendon, Ill. (1888), X, 377–378

LANGKAVEL, B. Pferde und Naturvölker Internat Ztschr l. Ethnog., I, 49–60

LANNOIS, M.   De l'oreille au point de vue anthropologique et médico-légal   Arch. de l'anthrop. crim., Par., II, 336; 389.

LANSDELL, HENRY.   Through Central Asia.   London Sampson Low, 1887.   (Rev. in Nature, XXXVII, 221.)

LAPOUGE, G. de.   De l'inégalité parmi les hommes.   Rev. d'anthrop., Par. (1888) 3. s., III, 9-38.

——— La dépopulation de la France.   Rev d'anthrop., 3. s , III, 69-80.

——— L'anthropologie et la science politique.   Rev. d'anthrop , Paris, II, 136-157, 1887.

——— Les sélection sociales.   Rev. d'anthrop., 3. s., III, 519-550.

——— L'Hérédité dans la science politique.   Rev. d'anthrop., 3. s., III, 169-191.

——— Méthodes de réproduction.   Paris, Didot, 1888.   [Rev. in Rev. d'anthrop., IV, 1889, Par., 86]

LAURENT, E.   Les dégénérés dans les prisons.   Arch. de l'anthrop. crim., Paris, 1888, III, 564-588.

LAWRENCE, EDWARD A.   Among the villages of South India.   Andover Rev., 1888, 284-293.

LA ROCHEFOUCAULD, F. A. DE.   Palenque, et la civilization Maya.   Paris (1888): Ernest Leroux. 1 vol., pp. 192, illustr.   [Rev. in Am. Antiquar., Mendon, Ill. (1888), X, 393.]

LAYARD, GRANVILLE.   Through the West Indies.   London Sampson Low, 1887.   (Rev. in Nature, XXXVII, 199.)

LE BON, GUSTAVÉ.   Les premières civilisations.   Paris, 1888, 824 pp. 4to.

LE CLERC, MAX.   Les peuplades de Madagascar.   Rev. d'ethnog , VI. 1

——— Les pygmées à Madagascar.   Rev. d'ethnog., Paris, VI, 323-335.

——— Notes sur Madagascar   Rev. in Rev. d'ethnog., Paris, VI, 463-469.

LEDGARD, W. E.   Remarkable case of longevity.   [102.]   Lancet, Lond., II, 947.

LEDOUBLE.   Les anomalies des muscles   Mém. Soc. d'anthrop., Paris, 2. s., LII, 369-375.   [Rev. d'anthrop., 3 s., II, 551-558, III, 429-455.

LEFÉBURE, E.   L'œuf dans la religion égyptienne.   Rev. de l'Hist. Relig., Paris, XVI, 16-25.

——— Un des procédés du démiurge égyptien.   Ann. du musée Guimet, X, 553-558, 1887.

LEGGE, F.   Sul significato morfologico dell' osso prebasioccipitale e sulla presenza dell' os jugale nel cranio umano.   Bull. d. r. Accad. d. med. di Roma, XIII, 90-110.

LELAND, CHAS. G.   Practical education.   London: Whittaker & Co (Paternoster Square).

LEMIRE, M. CH.   Les tours Kiams de la province de Biuh-Diuh.   Rev. d'ethnog., Paris, VI, 215-222. 383-394.

LEMOINE, M.   Derniers temps de l'âge du bronze.   Matériaux, 3. s., IV, 367.

Le Muséon, Revue internationale.   Études de Linguistique, d'Histoire et de Philsosophie.   (Société des Sciences et Lettres.   Société Orientale.   Quarterly.   Louvain. Vol. VI.

LEON, NICHOLAS.   Anales del museo Michoacan.   Redactor: Morelia, Mexico, 1887-'8.   [Rev. in Am. Antiquar., Mendon, Ill. (1888), X, 395.]

——— Apuntes para la historia de la medicina en Michoacan.   2. ed. Morelia. 8vo.

LE PLONGEON, AUGUSTUS.   The Egyptian Sphinx.   Am. Antiquar., Mendon, Ill. (1888), X, 358-363.

——— and A. D.   The monuments of the Mayas and their historial teachings.   Brooklyn (1887).   8vo.   With photographs.

LETOURNEAU, CH.   La femme et l'anthropophagie en Polynésie.   Bull. Soc. d'anthrop. de Par., 3. s., XI (1888), 133-136.

——— La phallotomie chez les Spartiates el les Abyssins.   Bull. Soc. d'anthrop. Paris, 3. s., XI, 25.

LETOURNEAU, CH Les mensura'·ons du cou en Bretagne et en Kabylie. Bull. Soc. d'anthrop Paris, 1888, 3. s, XI. 458-461.

—— Sur l'anthropophagie en Amérique. Bull. Soc. d'anthrop , 3. s., X, 777-780.

—— Survivances de la propriété communautaire dans le Morbihan. Bull Soc. d'anthrop., Par., 1888, 475-477.

LEUTMANN, H. Graphic pictures of native life in distant lands. Trans. by G Philip, London, 1888, 5 pp., 12 pl , 8vo.

LEVI, LEONE. On the progress of commerce and industry during the last fifty years. J Roy. Statis. Soc , London, L 659-668

LEWIS, A. L The " Longstone " at Mottistone, Isle of Wight. J. Anthrop. Inst., Lond. (1888), XVIII, 192.

LEWIS, H. C. [et al]. Account of some so-called "spiritualistic" seances. Proc. Soc. Psych. Research, Lond , IV, 338-380.

LEWIS, T. H. Effigy mounds in Iowa. Snake and snake-like mounds in Minnesota. [Rev. in Rev. d'ethnog., Paris, VI, 246.]

—— Incised boulders in the Upper Minnesota Valley Am. Naturalist, XXI, 639-642.

—— The "Old Fort " earthworks of Greenup County, Kentucky. Am. J Archæol., Baltimore, 1887, 1-8, ill.

—— Quartz-workers of Little Falls, Minn. Am. Antiquai., Chicago, IX, 105-107.

LIEBLEIN, J. Les quatre races dans le ciel inférieur des Égyptiens. Ann. du Musée Guimet, Paris, X, 547-550.

LILLY, W. S. Materialism and morality. Pop. Sc. Month., XXX, 474-493, 1887.

LILLIEHÖÖK, C B. Om Tonga-öarna Ymer, 1888, Stockholm, XVIII, 87-93.

LIPPERT, J. Kulturgeschichte der Menschheit in ihrem organischen Aufbau. Stuttgart (1887), Schlauss, 2 vols , 8vo.

LISSAUER, A Die prähistorischen Denkmäler der Provinz Westpreussen und der angrenzenden Gebiete. Herausgegeben von der Naturforschenden Gesellschaft zu Danzig Leipzig (1887), 110 pp , ch., 5 pl., 4to.

LITHGOW, R. A D. From generation , a prelude to the study of heredity. Prov Med. J., Leicester, VI, 116, 157, VII. 13, 61, 100, 156, 214, 253, 306, 342, 445, 493.

LITTLE, A. J. Through the Yang-tse Gorges. London (1888), Sampson Low.

LODOLI, E. Relazione fra lunghezza della mano e sviluppo fetale. Boll. d. sez. d. cult. d. sc med. Accad. d fisiocrit. di Siena, V, 19-23.

LOESCHCKE, G. Relief aus Messene. Jahrb d. k. deutsch archæol. Inst., Berlin, III, 189-193, 1 pl.

LOESCHE, PECHNEL. Maske mit Federkleid. [Rev. in Intern. Arch f. Ethnog., 1888, I, 197.]

LOEWENBERG, B. Physiological researches on nasal vowels. Tr. Internat. Med. Cong., IX, Washington, 1887, III, 870-873

LOMBARD, W. P. The variations of the normal knee-jerk and their relation to the activity of the central nervous system. Am. J. Psychol., Baltimore, I, 5-71.

LOMBROSO, CESARE. Die Verbrecher in anthropologischer, ärztlicher und juristischer Beziehung. In deutscher Bearbeitung von Dr. M O. Fraenckel. Mit Vorwort von Dr. jur von Kirchenheim. Hamburg, 1887, J. F. Richter, 594 pp , 8vo.

—— L'art chez les délinquents Arch. d. psichiat , sc. pen. e antrop. crim., 1888, IX.

—— Nuovo carattere speciale degli epilettici e analogia coi criminali. Arch di psichiat , etc., Torino, VIII, 520, 1 pl.

—— Photographies composites de criminels Rev. scient , Paris, XLI; 731·

LONGO, Dr. La médicine arabe en Algérie. Rev. de l'Afrique Fr., 15 mars, 1888, 116-119.

LORANGE, A. Forteguelse over Bergens Museums Tilvæxt af Oldsager ældre Reformationen. Kristiania, 1887. [Rev. in Internat Arch f. Ethnog., I, 29 31.]

LORET, V La tombe d'un ancien égyptien. Ann. du Musée Guimet, Paris, X, 519-543.

LOREV, C.   Ueber Gewicht und Massnormal entwickelter Kinder in den ersten Lebens-jahren   (Vorschlag zu Sammelbeobachtuugen.)   Jahrb. l.   Kinderh , Leipz., n. F., XXVII, 339, 1 tab.

LOYE, P.   Contribution à l'étude du nœud vital chez l'homme.   Compt. iend. Soc. de biol., Paris, 8. s., V, 581–585.

LUBBOCK, Sir JOHN.   L'homme préhistorique.   Paris, 1888, 3ᵉ éd., 228 pp., 8vo.

—— On the senses, instincts and intelligence of animals.   London : Kegan Paul & Co.

—— Problematical organs of sense.   Pop. Sc. Month., N. Y., XXXIX, 101–107.

—— Une conférence sur les sauvages.   Rev in Rev. d'anthrop., Paris, 3. s , II, 369–372.

LUYS.   Nouvelle méthode de céphalométrie.   Bull. Soc. d'anthrop., Par., 3. s., X, 48–54.

LYON, D. G.   The Pantheon of Assurbanipal.   Proc. Am. Orient. Soc., 1888, 94–95.

MCANALLY, D. R.   About the wedding-ring.   Pop. Sc. Month., XXXII, 71–76, 1887.

MACCAULEY, CLAY.   The Seminole Indians of Florida.   Rep. Bur. Ethnol., 1883–'84. pp. 469–531, 1 pl., 18 figs.

MCCHARLES, A.   The mound-builders of Manitoba.   Am. J. Archæol., III, 70–74.

MCCOSH, JAMES.   Psychology.   The motive powers.   New York . C. Scribuer's Sons, 273 pp., 8vo.

MACDONALD, D.   The Oceanic languages Semitic.   Tr. and Proc. Roy. Soc., Victoria, Melbourne, 1887, XXIV, 1–41.

MACDOWALL, A. B.   Facts about Ireland   "Nature," 1888, p. 474, vol. 37.

MCFARLAND, R. W.   Ancient work near Oxford, Ohio.   Ohio Archæol. Hist. Quart., I, 265–271.

MCGEE, W. J.   Palæolithic man in America; his antiquity and environment.   Pop. Sc. Month., N. Y., XXXIX, 20–36.

—— Three formations of the Middle Atlantic Slope.   Am. J. Sc., New Haven, 1888, XXXV. 120–466, 2 pl.

—— Paleolithic man in America.   Pop. Sc. Month., Nov., 1888, 20–36.

MCGOWAN, D. J.   Chinese guilds, or chambers of commerce, and trades unions.   J. China Br R. A. S , XXI, D s , 133–192.

MCKEE, E. S.   Cousin marriages unobjectionable.   South Cal. Pract , Los Angeles, III, 417–420.

MACKENZIE, JOHN.   Austral Africa.   London, 1887, Sampson Low, 2 vols   [Rev. in Nature, XXXVII, 5.]

MCLEAN, J. P.   Aboriginal history of Butler County.   Ohio Archæol. Hist Quart., I, 64.

Magazine of American History.   Ed , Mrs. M. J. Lamb, N. Y   20th volume, 1887–'88.

MAGNAN, Docteur.   Trois cas de conformation vicieuse des organes génitaux· atrophie testiculaire, cryptorchidie, pseudo-hermaphrodisme mâle.   Bull. de la Soc. d'an-throp., Paris, 3. s., X, 88–103.

MAHOUDEAU, P.-G.   Coupes de circonvolution cérébrales   Bull. d l. Soc d'anthrop., Paris, 3. s., X, 771–774.

—— Sur les groupements des grandes cellules pyramidales dans la région motrice des membres.   Bull Soc. d'anthrop., Par., 1888, 380–386.

MALADINI.   Studi etnografici.   Milano Rebeschini, 380 pp., 8vo.

MALLERY, G.   Indian Pictographs.   Am. Antiquar., 1888, p. 327.

MANOUVRIER, L , et DOUTREBENTE.   Étude d'une idiote microcéphale (Nini, morte à 55 ans).   Bull. d. l. Soc. d'anthrop., Paris, 3. s., X, 241–259.

—— et G. HERVÉ.   La circonvolution de Broca.   Paris, Lecroisnier, 1888.   Rev. d'an-throp., Par (1888), 3. s., III, 589–592.

—— La platycnémie chez l'homme et chez les singes   Bull. Soc d'anthrop., Par., 3. s , X, 128–141; Mém Soc. d'anthrop., Paris, 2. s., III, 469; 548.

MANOUVRIER, L., et G. HERVÉ. Le prognathisme et sa mesure. Matériaux, 1887, 487-492.

—— Les caractères du crâne et du cerveau. Sur l'interprétation de la quantité dans l'encéphale et dans le cerveau en particulier Mém Soc. d'anthrop, Paris, 2. s., III, 137-328

—— Sur la capacité du crâne chez les assassins comparée à celle d'hommes quelconques et d'hommes distingués. Actes Cong. internat. d'anthrop. crim, Rome, I, 115, 147.

—— Sur la taille des Parisiéns. Bull. Soc. d'anthrop., Par., 3. s, XI (1888), 156-178.

MANTEGAZZA, P. Gli atavismi psichici. Arch per l' antrop, Firenze, 1888, XVIII, 69-82.

—— Inchiesta sulle superstizioni in Italia. Arch. per l' antrop., XVII, 53.

MANTEGAZZA, PAOLA, und MORIZ BENEDIKT. Kraniometrie und Kephalometrie, etc. Wien und Leipzig (1888), 1 vol., 172 pp., 36 figs [Rev in Arch per l' antrop., Firenze (1888), XVIII, 277-278]

MARCANO, M. Station précolombienne des vallées d'Aragua (République du Vénézuéla). Bull. Soc. d'anthrop., Par, 3 s., XI (1888), 225-234.

MARCHAND. Schädel mit überzähligem Schneidezahn. Anat. Anz.. Jena, III, 726-728.

MARGRY, P. Mémoires et documents pour servir à l'histoire des origines françaises des pays Outre-Mer. Paris Maisonneuve. Vol V, 697 pp, 8vo. 1887-8, 8vo.

MARICOURT, RÉNÉ DE. Un mode de trafic. Bull. d. l Soc. d'anthrop., Paris, 3. s., X, 262

MARINO, F. Contributo allo studio della fossetta occipitale e della cresta frontale nel cranio umano (normali, pazzi, delinquenti e razze inferiori). Arch per l' antrop., Firenze, XVII, 243-255.

—— Sulle ossa interparietali e preinterparietali nel cranio umano. Arch. per l' antrop., Firenze, 1888, XVIII, 101-120, 2 pp.

MARIQUE. Le larynx, organe de la phonation dans ses rapports avec les centres cérébraux du langage et de l'idéation. Bull Soc d'anthrop, Bruxelles, V, 226-248.

MARQUER. Les établissements français en Océanie. Bull. Soc. Bretonne de Géog., 20-62, 1887. [Rev. in Rev. d'ethnog., Par., VI, 489-490]

MARRO, A. I caratteri dei delinquenti. Roma: Bocca, 487 pp, 22 tab

MARSHALL. J. J. DE Z. Judicial executions. Brit. Med J, Lond, II, 779-782.

MARTIN, C. T. Witchcraft in the sixteenth century. Archæol Rev., London, 1888, II, 280-283.

MARX, M. Note sur les tombeaux de Ter-duc et de Minh-mang. Rev. d'ethnog., Paris, VI, 428-432.

MASON, D. Notes from the North Highlands. Archaeol. Rev., London, II, 45-50.

MASON, O. T. Méthode de classification dans les musées d'ethnographie. Rev. d'ethnog., Par., VI, 239-242.

—— The occurrence of similar inventions in areas widely apart. Science, vol. IX, June 3, p 534.

MASPERO, G. L'archéologie égyptienne Paris (1887), 318 pp, ill., 12mo.

—— Egyptian souls and their works. New Princeton Rev., 1888, 23-36.

—— Le rituel du sacrifice funéraire. Rev. de l'Hist. d. Religions, XVI, 159-188. Also review of Naville's Book of the Dead, id., 265-315.

—— Rapport à l'Institut égyptien sur les fouilles et travaux exécutés en Égypte pendant l'hiver de 1885-1886. Extr. du Bull d. l'Institut égyptien. Le Caire: Barbier, 1887, br. in-8.

MASSA, ACIRA TOMII. Le shintoisme, sa mythologie, sa morale. Ann. du musée Guimet, X, 309-320, pl. XVI, 1887.

Matériaux pour l'histoire primitive et naturelle de l'homme Paris Ch. Reinwald, Vol XXI, 3. s., IV, in 1887 Monthly.

MATHER, FREDERIC G. Celebrated clocks. Pop. Sc. Month., XXX, 640-651, 1887.

MATTHEWS, W.   An apparatus for determining the angle of torsion of the humerus. J. Anat. and Physiol., Lond., XXI, 536–538

——— Further contribution to the study of consumption among the Indians.   Trans. Am. Climatological Ass., Phila., 1888, 1–20.

——— The Mountain Chant.   Rep. Bur. Ethnol., 1883–'84, 379–467, 9 pl., 10 figs.

——— The prayer of a Navajo shaman.   Am. Anthropologist, April, 1888.   Vol. I.

——— Two Mandan chiefs.   Am. Antiquar., Mendon, Ill., 1888, x, 269–272, 2 ills.

MATTISON, J. B.   The ethics of the opium habitués.   Brooklyn Med. J., II, 125–130.

MAUGHS, G. M. B.   The Hottentot Venus.   St. Louis Cour. Med , XVII, 117–122.

MAUNOIR, CH.   Les travaux de la Société de Géographie et sur les progrès des sciences géographiques pendant l'année 1886.   Bull. Soc. Géog., Paris, 7. s., VIII, 5–117.

MAUREL, E.   Anthropologie et ethnographie du Cambodge   Mém. Soc. d'anthrop., Paris, 2. s., III, 442–468.

——— De la cyrtographie, stéthométrie et stéthographie   Bull gén. de thérap., etc., Par., CXIII, 399; 451.   Also: Bull. Soc. d'anthrop. de Par., 3. s , x, 345–368.

——— Étude sur la longueur comparée des deux premiers orteils dans les races mongoles. Bull. Soc. d'anthrop. de Paris, 1888, 3. s., 437–447.

MAURICE, FERNAND.   La réforme agraire et la misère en France.   [Rev. in J. Roy. Statis. Soc., London, L, 744.]

MAZZUCCHI, PIÓ.   Note di viaggio di S. Sommer.   Arch. per l' antrop., Firenze (1888), XVIII, 215–276.

Mélanges asiatiques tirés du Bulletin de l'Académie impériale des sciences de St.-Pétersbourg   Eggers & Co., tome IX, 1887

MÉLUSINE.   Revue de mythologie, littérature populaire, traditions et usages.   Fondée par H. Gaidoz et E. Rolland, 1877–1887.   Dirigée par Henri Gaidoz.   Monthly. 12 pp., 4to, Paris, Le Chevalier.

MAZZUCCHI, P.   Leggende, pregiudizi e superstizioni del volgo nell' alto Polesine. Arch. per l' antrop., Firenze, XVII, 333–344.

MEISNER, Dr.   Die Körpergrösse der Wehrpflichtigen im Gebiete der Unterleibe, insbesondere in Holstein.   Arch. f. Anthrop., Brnschwg. (1888), XVIII, 101–133, 1 table.

Memoirs of the Boston Society of Natural History.   Boston: Samuel H. Scudder, vols. I–III.

MENANT, J.   Forgeries of Babylonian and Assyrian Antiquities.   Am. J. Archæol., III, 14–31, pl., 11 figs.

MENARD DE SAINT-MAURICE, E.   Les poteries des sépultures indiennes du Chiriqui. Paris, 1888, 16 pp., 4to.

MERCIER, CHARLES.   Coma.   Brain, Jan., 1887.   [Rev. in Am. J. of Psychology, 185–187.

MERCIER, E.   Les Mozabites.   Rev. d. l'Afrique française, 253–258, 1887.

MESSIKOMMER, H.   Beitrag zum geistigen Leben der Bewohner der Pfahlbauten. Internat. Arch. f. Ethnog., Leiden. 1888, I, 227–229.

METZLER, GUSTAV KARL.   Statistische Untersuchungen über den Einfluss der Getreidepreise auf die Brotpreise und dieser auf die Löhne.   [Rev. in Jour. Pop. Statis. Soc., London, L, 732–734.

MEYER, A. B.   Abhandlungen und Berichte des k. zoologischen und anthropologisch-ethnographischen Museums zu Dresden.   235 pp., 4to.

MEYER, E. H.   Indogerman myths.   Achilles.   Berlin: Dümmler, xvii+710 pp., 8vo.

MEYNERS D'ESTREY, D. C.   Tribus aborigènes du centre de Célèbes.   Les Topantunuasu.   Rev. de Géog., Paris, Feb.–Mar.

MEYNERT, T.   Die anthropologische Bedeutung der fontalen Gehirnentwicklung, nebst Untersuchungen über den Windungstypus des Hinterhauptlappens der Säugethiere und pathologische Wägungsresultate der menschlichen Hirnlappen. Wien (1887), 48 pp., 8vo.

—— Mechanik der Physiognomik. Wien. med. Presse, XXVIII, 1293; 1325; 1357; 1365; 1400; 1438; 1471. *Also, transl.*. Rev. scient., Par., XL, 545; 554.

MIES, JOSEF. Abbildungen von sechs Schädeln mit erklärendem Text. München, 1888, 7 pp., 6 photos, 8vo.

—— Beschreibung und Anwendung eines neuen kraniometrischen Instrumentes. München, 1888, 30 pp., 2 pl.

—— Ein neuer Schädelträger und Schädelmesser. Anat. Anz., Jena, III, 728–739.

—— Methode, die Schädel-und Gesichts-Indices bildlich darzustellen. Verhandl. d. Berl. Gesellsch. f. Anthrop., Berl., 302–304.

—— Zusätze zu den Erklärungen der einliegenden linearen Darstellung von Schädel- und Gesichts Indices. München, 1888, 1 p., 1 pl.

MILLS, T. WESLEY. Comparative psychology; its objects and problems. Pop. Sc. Month., N. Y., 1887, XXX, 651–660.

Mind. Quarterly Review of Psychology and Philosophy.

MINGAZZINI, G. Osservazioni anatomiche sopra cervetti e crani di delinquenti communicate al Congres o medico di Pavia. Arch. di psichiat., etc., Torino, VIII, 521–523; also, Riv. sper. di freniat. Reggio-Emilia, XIV, 1–48, 1 pl.

MIRET V. Essai sur la sociologie, à propos de la protestation des employés des postes, des télégraphes et des chemins de fer. Paris, 1888, 16 pp., 8vo.

MIREUR, H. Le mouvement comparé de la population à Marseille, en France et dans les états de l'Europe. Paris, 1888, 396 pp, 8vo.

Mittheilungen der anthropologischen Gesellschaft in Wien. XVII. Band; n. s., VII. Band, Wien: Hölder.

Mittheilungen der prähistorischen Commission der kais. Akademie der Wissenschaften, 1887, Nr. 1, Wien (1888), 40 pp., m. Ill. Chart.

Mittheilungen des anthropologischen Vereins in Schleswig-Holstein. Heft I: Ausgrabungen bei Immenstedt, 1879–82. Kiel (1888), 32 pp., m. 1 Tafel u. 3 Figuren, 8vo.

MONCELON, L. Un peuple qui s'éteint. L'Homme, Par., IV, 97–104.

MONDIÈRE, M. Rapport sur le concours du prix Godard. Bull. de la Soc. d'anthrop., Paris, 3. s. X, 725–730.

MONTALTI, A. Cranio di un ladro. Sperimental, Firenze, LIX, 392–397.

MONTÉ. The development of Fencing. Antiquary, XV. 55–61.

MONTELIUS, OSCAR. Bronsåldern i Egypten. Ymer, 1888, Stockholm, XVIII, 3-49, 63 figs.

MONTELIUS, OSCAR. Das Alter der Runenschrift im Norden. Arch. f. Anthrop., Brnschwg. (1888), XVIII, 151–170, 26 figs.

—— The civilization of Sweden in heathen times. Trans. by F. H. Woods. London and New York, MacMillan & Co., 214 pp.

—— Ueber die Einwanderung unserer Vorfahren in den Norden. Arch. f. Anthrop., Brnschwg., XVII, 151–160.

MONTYEL, E. MARANDON DE. De la dégustation des vins en Bourgogne. An. méd. psychol., 1887. [Rev. in J. Psychol., I, 195.]

—— Du diagnostic médico-légal de la Pyromanie par l'examen indirect. Arch. de neurologie, 1887. [Rev. in Am. J. of Psychology, I, 191.]

Monumenti inediti del instituto. Published by the German government in Italian at Rome. Dating about 50 years ago, still continued. Professors Hulbeg and Hanson.

MOONEY, JAMES. Myth of the Cherokees. J. Am. Folk-Lore (1888) I, 97–108.

—— The funeral customs of Ireland. Proc. Am. Phil. Soc., Phila., 1888, XXV, 243–296.

—— The medical mythology of Ireland. Phila., McCalla, jr., 1887, 8vo.

MOORE, W. W. The Hittite Empire. Presbyt. Quart., 1888.

MORAN, H. et VARIOT, G. Étude microscopique et expérimentale sur les tatouages européens. Bull. d. l. Soc. d'anthrop., Paris, 3. s, X, 730–736.

MORGAN, E. DELMAR. Prejevalsky's Journeys and Discoveries in Central Asia. Proc. Roy. Geog. Soc., IX, 213-232. [The next two papers treat of neighboring regions.]

MORGAN, E. L Ceremonies observed at the age of puberty, etc., amongst the Calispel Indians. Virginia M. Month., Richmond, XIV, 853-858.

MORICI, DOMENICO. L' imitazione considerata nella vita sociale e nelle affezioni nervose. Palermo, 1888, 218 pp., 12mo.

MORRIS, C. Aryan race; its origin and achievements. Lond., 1888, 8vo.

MORRIS, GEO. P. Industrial training two centuries ago. Pop. Sc. Month., XXXI, 608-612, 1887.

MORSELLI, E. Antropologia generale. Lezioni sul uomo secondo la teoria dell' evoluzione dettate nella R. Università di Torino. Torino (1888), 4to.

———— Sul peso dell' encefalo en rapporto con i caratteri craniometrici negli alienati. Rev. sper. di freniat., Reggio-Emilia, XIII, 365-392.

MORTILLET, A. DE. Hache en pierre de la Guadeloupe. Bull. d. l. Soc. d'anthrop., Paris, 3. s., X, 46.

———— Rubans de Saint-Amable. Bull. d. l. Soc. d'authrop., Paris, 3 s., X, 705-706.

———— Silex tailles. Bull. d. l. Soc. d'authrop., Paris, 3. s., X, 417-418

MORTILLET, G. DE. Anthropophagie mythique. Bull. Soc. d'anthrop., de Paris, 3. s., XI (1888), 182-183.

———— Découverte protohistorique en Portugal. Ibid., 47-52.

———— Les sépultures de Solutre. Bull. d. l. Soc. d'anthrop. de Lyon (1888), VII, 1-8.

———— Menhirs mammelles de Sardaigne. Bull. Soc. d'anthrop. de Par., 3. s.. XI (1888), 257-259.

MOTT, F. W. Intellectual evolution and its relation to physiological dissolution. Edinb. M. J., XXXII, 871-879.

MOURIER, J. L'état religieux de la Mingrélie. Rev. de l'Hist. d. Relig., XVI, 84-100.

MUCH, M. L'âge du cuivre en Europe et sou rapport avec la civilisation des Indo-Germains. Vienna. [Reviewed in Matériaux, 3. s., IV, 232-242. See Id., 261.]

MUGNIER. Étude sur la main et la taille d'indigènes Asiatiques. Mém. Soc. d'indigènes. Ann. d. l'Extrème Orient., III, 391-429.

MÜLLER, JOHANNES. Zur Anatomie des Chimpansegehirns. Arch. f. Anthrop., Brnschwg., XVIII, 173-185.

MÜLLER, MAX. Three introductory lectures on the science of thought, * * with an appendix which contains a correspondence on thought without words, between F. Max Müller, Francis Galton, the Duke of Argyll, George F. Romanes, and others. London, 1888, 8vo.

MUMMENTHEY, K. Das Südeiland unter besonderer Berücksichtigung seiner Stein- und Erd-Denkmäler. Cor.-Bl. d. deutsch. Gesellsch. f. Anthrop., etc., Brnschwg., 1888, XIX, 127-129.

MUNCK, M. DE. Recherches sur les silex éclatés sous l'influence des agents atmosphériques et sur ceux retouchés et taillés accidentellement. Bull. Soc. d'anthrop de Bruxelles, reported in Matériaux, 3. s., IV, 158-163.

MUNK, J. Physiologie des Menschen und der Säugethiere. Berlin (1887), 2. Aufl., VIII, 592 pp. ill., 8vo.

MUNZ, I. Ueber die jüdischen Aerzte im Mittelalter. Berlin, Dreimer. 8vo.

MURDOCH, JOHN. On the Siberian origin of some customs of the Western Eskimos. Am. Anthrop., Washington, I, 325-336.

MURRAY, JAMES A. The animal economic products of India. The Indian Annals, I, 25, 26, sq.

MURRELL, T. E. Peculiarity of the structure and diseases of the ear in the negro. Tr. Internat. Med. Cong , IX, Washington, III, 817-824.

Museo nacional de México. See Anales.

Muséon, Le. Revue Internationale. Études de l linguistique d'histoire et de philosophie. Publiées par des professeurs de différentes universités. [Société des sciences, Société orientale, vol. VII, in 1888, quarterly.

MYER, ISAAC. Qabbalah. The philosophical writings of Solomon Ben Yehudah Ibn Gebirol, or Avicebron, and their connection with the Hebrew Qabbalah and Sepher-Ha-Zohar. Phila , 1888, Isaac Myer, 1 vol., pp. 497. Illust., 8vo. [Rev. in Am. Antiquar., Mendon,Ill. (1888), x, 394-395.]

M. Le papier au Japon. Rev. d'ethnog., Paris, VI, 152-155.

NADAILLAC, M. DE. A propos du procès-verbal. Bull. d. l. Soc. d'anthrop., Paris, 3. s., x, 81-86.

—— Étude sur l'anthropophagie. Paris, Hennuyer, 20 pp. Extr. from Bull. Soc. d'anthrop., Jan., 1888.

—— et HENRI et LOUIS SIRET. Les premiers âges du métal dans le sud-est de l'Espagne. Texte 1 vol. in-4°; Atlas, 1 vol. in-fol Anvers, 1887. Revue des questions scientifiques, Bruxelles, 1888; Rev. d'anthrop., Par. (1888). 3. s., III, 597-604.

—— Le bâton de commandement de Montgaudier. Bull. d. l. Soc. d'anthrop., Paris, 3. s , x, pp. 7-10, 1887.

—— La pêche préhistorique. Review of Rau, Matériaux, 3. s , IV, 93-110.

—— La poterie de la Vallée du Mississippi. Matériaux, 3. s., IV, 373-383.

—— L'origine et le développement de la vie sur le globe. Paris (1888), E. de Soye, 74 pp.

—— Megalithic Monuments. Pop. Sc. Month., XXX and XXXI, 39-44.

—— Mœurs et monuments des peuples préhistoriques. Paris (1888), Masson, 120 figs , 8vo. Rev. d'anthrop., 3. s., III, 354-358. [Rev. in Am. Antiquar. and Orient. J., Mendon, Ill., 1888, x, 395.

—— Observations sur les temps préhistoriques. Bull. Soc. d'anthrop. de Brux., v, 282-287.

—— Sur un cas de surdi-mutité et de cécité congénitales (d'après le Jour. Science, de New York). Bull. Soc. d'anthrop., Par., 3. s., XI (1888), 221-223.

NANE, J. Die Bronzezeit in Cypern. Cor.-Bl. d. deutsch. Gesellsch. f. Anthrop., Bruschwg., 1888, XIX, 123-127.

Nature. A weekly illustrated journal of science. London : Macmillan & Co., vols. 37 and 38, in 1888.

NEHRING. Das sogenannte Torfschwein. Verhandl. d. Berl. Gesellsch. f. Anthrop., 1888, 181-187.

—— Bos primigenius, insbesondere über seine Coexistenz mit dem Menschen Ibid., 22-231.

—— Knochenharpune aus dem Moor von Barnow. Verhandl. d. Berl. Gesellsch. f. Anthrop., Berlin, 1888, 343.

—— Vereinzelte gefundene Hornkerne des Bos primigenius. Verhandl. d. Berl. Gesellsch. f. Anthrop., Berl., 1888, 341-343.

NELSON, J. A Study of Dreams. Am. J. Psychol., Balt., 1, 367-40x.

NEWBERRY, J. S Food and fiber plants of the North American Indians. Pop. Sci. Month., N. Y., XXXII, 31-46.

NEWELL, N. E. The Color of Words. Pop. Sci. Month., XXXII, 257-261, 1887.

NEWELL, W. W. Myths of Voodoo Worship and Child Sacrifice in Hayti. J. Am. Folk-Lore, N. Y., I, 16-30 (1888).

New England Historical and Genealogical Register. Boston. Vol. XLII, 1888

NEWMAN, U. Kabail Vocabulary, supplemented by aid of a new source. London Trübner, 1 vol., 8vo.

NICHOLSON, B. Heirship of the youngest among the Kafirs of Africa. Archæol. Rev., London, II, 163-166.

NICOLAS, AD. L'Automatisme dans les actes volontaires Mém Soc d'anthrop , Paris, 2. s., III, 329-368.

—— Sur les avantages de l'adoption d'une langue internationale. Bull. et mém. Soc. de méd prat. de Paris, 1888, 757-766

—— Sépultures de Gadague. Bull. Soc. d'anthrop. de Par., 1888, 3 s , XI, 411-415.

NICOLS, A. Wild life and adventure in the Australian Bush. London, 2 vols., 8vo.

NIPPERDEY, H. Fetish faith in Western Africa. Pop. Sc. Month., XXXI, 801-803.

NORDENSKJOLD, Baron de. Observations sur les ruines nordiques du Grönland. Rev. d'ethnog., XVI, 1-22.

Notes and Queries. The Bizarre. A monthly magazine of History, Folk-lore, &c., Manchester, N. H., Gould, vol. V, in 1888.

NOYES, WILLIAM. Paranoia. Am. J. Psychol., I, 460-478.

NUSSBAUM, M. Ueber Vererbung. Bonn, 1888, 8vo.

NUTT, A. Celtic Myth and Saga. Archæol. Rev., II, 110-142, 1888.

D'ODIARDI, E. S. New pneumo-dynamometer and spirometer. Lancet, London, II, 623.

OGLE, WILLIAM. Summary of several male life tables. Jour. Roy. Statist. Soc., London, L, 648-652.

Ohio Archæological and Historical Quarterly. Vol. I, no. 1, June, 1887. Columbus: Smythe.

OLSHAUSEN. Ueber den Moorfund von Mellentin, Neumark. Verhandl. d. Berl. Gesellsch. f. Anthrop., Berlin, 1888, 273.

—— Zwei neue Gemmen vom Alsentypus. Verhandl. d. Berl. Gesellsch. f. Anthrop., Berl., 1888, 247-249.

OPPERT, GUSTAV. On the original inhabitants of Bharatavarsa or India. London, (1888), Trübner & Co., 1-108.

ORDINAIRE, O. Les sauvages du Pérou. Rev. d'ethnog., Par., VI, 265-322.

Orientalische Bibliographie. Herausgegeben von Prof. Dr. A. Müller, in Königsberg. Berlin: Reuther, Bd. I, 1-4, 1887-1888, 8vo.

ORMEAUX, A. L. DES. Usage des bâtons de bois de Rennes. Rev. d'ethnog., XVI, 39-51.

ORNSTEIN, B. Makrobiotisches aus Griechenland. Arch. f. Anthrop., Brnschwg., 1888-9, XVIII, 193-204.

—— Ein Fall übermässiger Behaarung. Archiv f. Anthrop., XVI, 507-510.

—— Ueber den griechischen Riesen Homer Spyridon Tingitsoglu, Amenates genatt. Arch. f. Anthrop., Brnschwg., XVII, 277-278.

ORTVAY, THEODOR. Ursprung der ungarländischen und nordeuropäischen prähistorischen Steinwerkzeuge. Mittheil. d. anthrop. Gesellsch. in Wien, XVII, 29-65.

OSTERMANN, HEINRICH. Die Symmetric im Fühlraum der Hand. Würzb. (1888), Stabel, 28 pp., 8vo.

OTTOLENGHI, S. L' olfatto nei criminali. Gior. d. r. Accad. di med. di Torino, 1888. 3. s., XXXVI, 427-436. Also : Arch. di psichiat., etc., Torino, 1888, IX, 495-499.

—— Un cretinoso ladro. Arch. di psichiat., etc., Torino, VIII, 180-184.

—— Il recambio materiale nei delinquenti-nati; sunto. Arch. di psichiat., Torino, IX, 375-379.

Outcast (An) race in the Pyrenees. [Transl. from : Das Ausland.] Pop. Sc. Month., N. Y., XXXII, 546-549.

OVERMAN, H. W. Fort Hill, Ohio. Ohio Arch. & Hist. Quarterly, I, 260-264.

PAINTER, C. C. A change of policy requires a change of methods. Proc. Lake Mohonk, Conf. Friends of Inds. Philadelphia (5th meeting), 3-24.

PALLARY, P. Les dolmens du Puig-Noulous (Pyrénées-Orientales). Bull. Soc. d'anthrop. de Lyon, VI, 95-100, fig.

—— Monuments mégalithiques de l'arrondissement de Mascara. Bull. Soc. d'ethnog., Paris, 2. s., I, 57-68.

PARIS, G. Tombeaux en pierre trouvés à Luxeuil. Bull. d. l. Soc. d'anthrop., Paris, 3. s., X, 261.

PARKER, EDWARD HARPER. The yellow languages. Tr. As. Soc. Japan, XV, 13-49; the Manchus, ibid., 83-92 ; the Manchu relations with Corea, ibid., 93-95.

—— Manchu relations with Thibet. J. China Br. R. A. S., XXI, n. s., 289-304.

—— The relation between the Japanese language and the languages of the neighboring continent. Trans. Asiatic Soc. of Japan, (Vol. XV, Part L.)

PATRICK, G. T. W. A further study of Heraclitus. Am. J. Psychol., I, 557-690.

PATY DE CLAM, A. DU. Le Triton dans l'antiquité et à l'époque actuelle. Réponse à la brochure de M. Rouire. Toulouse, 1 vol., 7 l., 1887, 8vo.

PAULITSCHKE, PHILIPP. Beiträge zur Ethnographie und Anthropologie der Somâl, Galla und Hasari. Leipz., zweite Ausgabe, 1888, VIII, 105.

Peabody Museum of American Archæology and Ethnology, in connection with Harvard University. XXII. Ann. Rept., Cambridge, 1888, Vol. IX, No. 2.

PEACOCK. Original vocabularies of five West Caucasian languages. J. R. A. Soc., n. s., XIX, 145, 1887.

—— The church porch. Archæol. Rev., Lond., 1888, II, 283.

—— The dedications of churches. Archæol. Rev.. Lond., 1888, II, 268-279.

PECKHAM, GEORGE. Mental habits and peculiarities of insects. Nat. Hist. Soc., Wisconsin.

—— and ELIZABETH G. Some observations on the mental powers of spiders. J. of Morphology. Boston: Ginn & Co., I, 383-419; also on the special senses of wasps in Proc. Nat. Hist. Soc., Wis., 1887, 91-140.

PEEK, CUTHBERT E. Exhibition of terra cotta tablets from Babylonia. J. Anthrop. Inst., Lond. (1888), XVIII, 102-103.

PEET, S. D. Archæology in Ohio. Rev. in Am. Antiquar., Chicago, IX, 114.

—— Are there any dragons in America? Am. Antiquar., IX, 179-182.

—— Early books which treat of the mounds. Am. Antiquar., IX, 239-247.

—— Houses and house-life among the prehistoric races. Am. Antiquar., Mendon, Ill. (1888), X, 333-357, illus.

—— Some problems in connection with the stone age. Am. Antiquar., IX, 280-295.

—— The cross in America. Am. Antiquar., Mendon, Ill. (1888), X, 292-315, illus

—— The serpent-symbol. Am. Antiquar., IX, 133-163

—— Village life and clan residences among the emblematic mounds. Am. Antiquar., IX, 10-34 (ninth paper), 67-94.

—— Who were the effigy builders? To what age and race did they belong? Am. Antiquar., Chicago, IX, 67-94.

PELI, G. Sul preso della callotta cranieuse rispetto della sua capacità in quaranta sani e in trecento cinquanta infermi di mente. Arch. ital. per le mal. nerv., Milano. XXIV, 130-135.

PELL, O. C. Domesday measures of land. Archæol. Rev., Lond., 1888-9, II, 353-360.

PELLEW, GEORGE. Fetichism or anthropomorphism. Pop. Sc. Month, XXX, 514-520. 1887.

Pennsylvania Magazine of History and Biography. Phila Hist. Soc. Penn., vol. XII, in 1888.

PENTA, P. Le popolazioni della campania. Riv. d' ig. prat. e sper., Napoli, 1888, I, 49-63.

PEREZ, BERNARD La psychologie de l'enfant. L'art et la poésie chez l'enfant. Paris, 1888, 1 vol. in-8, p. 308. [Rev. in Arch. per l' antrop., Firenze (1888), XVIII, 287.]

PERRIER, EDMOND. Le transformisme. Paris (1888), Bailhère 344 pp., 88 figs. [Bibl. Scient. Contemp.] Rev. d'anthrop, 3 s., III, 474-477.

PETERMANN'S (Dr. A.) Mittheilungen a. J. Perthes' Geographischer Anstalt, Gotha: Justus Perthes. Band 34 in 1888, 4to, monthly, with Ergänzungshefte.

PETITOT, ÉMILE. Les Grands Esquimaux, ouvrage accompagné d'une carte et de sept gravures, d'après les croquis de l'auteur. Rev. in Rev. d'ethnog., VI, 245-246.

—— Traditions indiennes du Canada Nord Ouest. Paris, 1887, XVIII, 521 pp., 16mo.

PETITOT, ÉMILE. La femme aux métaux, légende nationale des Dènè Conteaux-jaunes du Grand Lac Des Esclaves. 1888, Meaux, 5-24.

PETRI, ED., and D. ANUTCHIN. Bogen und Pfeil. Rev. in Intern. Arch. f. Ethnog., 1888, I, 115.

PETRI, ED., and D. ANUTCHIN. Ethnogr. Museum der kais. Akad. der Wissenschaften, St. Petersburg. Rev. in Intern. Arch. f. Ethnog., 1888, I, 162.

PETRIE, W. M. F. The earliest racial portraits. Nature, Lond., 1888-9, XXXIX, 128-130.

PFEIFFER, EMILY. Women and works. An essay treating on the relation to health and physical development of the higher education of girls, and the intellectual or more systematised effort of women. Lond., 1887, Trübner & Co., 186 pp.

PHILIPPI, R. A. Verzierte Knochenscheiben aus alten Gräbern von Caldera. Verhandl. d. Berl. Gesellsch. f. Anthrop., Berl., 1888, 318.

PHILLIPS, H., Jr. First contribution to the folk-lore of Philadelphia and its vicinity. Proc. Am. Phil. Soc., Phila., 1888, XXV, 159-170. (& sep.)

—— Folk-lore of the Germans. Rev. in Am. Antiquar., Chicago (1888), X, 395-396.

—— Notes on European archæology. Rev. in Am. Antiquar., Chicago, IX, 116-117.

PHILLIPS, R. C. The lower Congo: a sociological study. Anthrop. Inst., Lond., XVII, 214-237 (1888).

PHILPOTT, H. J. Social sustenance. Pop. Sc. Month., XXXI, 45-50, 228-233; 1887.

PICK, E. Memory and its doctors. New York, 1888, 54 pp., 16mo.

PIEHL, KARL. Bronsålder i Egypten. Ymer, 1888, Stockholm, XVIII, 94-102.

PIÉTREMONT, C.-A. Le patois Briard du Canton d'Esternay. Rev. Linguis., Paris, XX, 289-314; XXI, 7-26 (1888).

—— L'origine et l'évolution intellectuelle du chien d'arêt. Bull. Soc. d'anthrop., Paris, 1888, 3. s., XI, 320-373.

PIETTE, ED., Équidés de la Période Quaternaire. Matériaux, 3. s., IV, 359-366.

—— Le Kertag Quaternaire. Bull. de la Soc. d'anthrop., Paris, 3. s., X, 736-743.

—— The error of Buffon in thinking that the reindeer lived in the Pyrenees in the xivth century and the causes of his committing it. Matériaux, 3. s., IV, 407.

PIGORINI. Pointes de flèches ovoïdes d'Italie regardées comme archéolithiques. (Cuspidi di salce ovoidali dell' Italia giudicate archeolitiche da A. de Mortillet.) Bull. di paleontologia italiana. Anno XIV, Nos. 1 et 2, 1888. Rev. d'anthrop., Par. (1888), 3. s., III, 371-372.

PILATTE, Dr., SIDNEY, NOUMÉA. Voie du Sud, souvenirs et impressions de voyage. Bull. de la Soc. de géogr. de Marseille, XI, 337-364, 1887.

PILLING, J. C. Bibliography of the Eskimo language. Wash., Gov. Print, br. 1887, 8vo, 116 pp.

—— Bibliography of the Iroquoian languages. Wash. (1888), Gov. Print, 208 pp.

—— Bibliography of the Siouan language. Wash., Gov. Print, br. 1887, 8vo.

PILLOY. Une trépanation à l'époque Franque. Mat. pour l'hist. primit. et nat. de l'homme, 3. s., IV, 263-273, 407-420. Bull. Soc. d'anthrop., Paris, 3. s., IX, 668; 686.

PINART, A. Les Indiens de l'état de Panama. Rev. d'ethnog., Par., VI, 33-56, 117-132.

PINCOTT, FREDERICK. The Tri-Ratna [Budha, Dharma, and Sangha conjoined]. J. R. A. S., XIX, 238-246.

PITRE et LOMBROSO. Les gestes des criminels. Arch. d. psichiat., sc. penale ed antrop., 1888, IX.

PITT-RIVERS, Lieut. Gen. An ancient British settlement excavated near Rushmore, Salisbury. J. Anthrop Inst., Lond. (1888), XVII, 190-201.

—— Excavations in Cranborne Chase near Rushmore, on the borders of Dorset and Wilts, 1880-1888; (printed privately), 1888, 287 pp., 159 pl., 4to.

PJATNITZKI, I. [Case of caudal extremity in man. Tumor coccygeus]. Med. Obozr., Mosk., 1888, XXIX, 963-968.

PLATNER, B. Anthropological Mythology. New Englander & Yale Rev., 1888.

PLATZ, B. Der Mensch, sein Ursprung, seine Rassen und sein Alter. Würzburg (1887), Liefg. 6. u. 7, pp. 321-448, 8vo.

PLEURY, I. DE. Découverte d'un tour à tuiles romain au village de Chez-Ferroux, commune de Vieux Cérier. Paris, 1888, 11 pp., 4 pl., 8vo,

PLOIX, C. L'Atlantide. Rev. d'anthrop., Par., 3. s., II, 291-312.

—— Les Hottentots ou Khoikhoi et leur religion. Rev. d'anthrop, Paris, 3. s., II, 570-589 (1887), 270-289.

—— et JULIEN VINSON. Les religions actuelles, leurs doctrines, leur évolution, leur histoire. Paris, 1888, édit., Delahaye et Lecrosnier, 1 vol. de 600 pages. Rev. d'anthrop., Par. (1888), 3. s., III, 202-204.

—— De l'aphasie. Bull. Soc. d'anthrop., Par., 3. s., XI (1888), 243-257.

—— Du nom de l'ours, en grec ancien et en sanscrit. Bull. d. l Soc. d'anthrop. Paris, 3. s., X, 316-320.

PLOSS, H. Das Weib in der Natur-und Völkerkunde. Anthropologische Studien. 2. Aufl. Nach dem Tode des Verfassers bearbeitet und herausgegeben von Max Bartels. Leipz., 1887, I. Grieben, 596 pp., 4 pl.; 727 pp., 3 pl., 8vo.

POGORELSKI, M. Circumcisio ritualis Hebræorum. Die rituelle Beschneidungsceremonie der Israeliten. St. Petersb. med. Wchnschr., 1888, n. F., v, 333-343.

POHLMAN, J. The human teeth viewed in the light of evolution. Med Press, West N. York, Buffalo, II, 245-250.

POLAK, J. E. Die Metalle nach persischen Quellen. Mitth. d. anthrop. Gesellsch. in Wien, 1888.

POLAKOWSKY, H. Altertumer aus Costa-Rica. Festschr. des Vereins f. Erdkunde zu Dresden (1888), 205-214, 3 figs.

POMMEROL, F. De la couleur des cheveux et des yeux en Limagne. Bull. d. l. Soc. d'anthrop.. Paris, 3. s , x, 383-397.

—— Le culte de Faramis dans les traditions populaires de l'Auvergne. Bull. Soc. d'anthrop., Par., 3. s., X, 398-415.

Popular Science Monthly. New York: D. Appleton & Co., vols XXXIII and XXXIV in 1888.

POOLE, R. S. The Egyptian classification of the races of man. J. Anthrop. Inst., Lond., XVI, 370-379.

POTT, A. F. Einleitung in die allgemeine Sprachwissenschaft zur Litteratur der Sprachenkunde Afrikas. Ztschr. f. allg. Sprachwissenschaft, III, 249.

POUCHET, G. La prétendue évolution du sens des couleurs. Rev. scient., Paris, 1888, XLII, 464-467.

POUSSE. Les manuscrits hiératiques du Yucatan. Arch Soc. Amér. de France, No. 1.

POWELL, J. W. Competition as a factor in human evolution. Am. Anthrop. Soc., Wash., 1888, I, 297-323.

—— Report of the Director of the Bureau of Ethnology. 1883-'84, XVII-LIII; 1884-'85.

POZZI, S. Les caractères distinctifs du cerveau de l'homme, au point de vue morphologique. Bull. de la Soc. d'anthrop., Paris, 3. s., X, 784-802.

Preliminary report of the Commission appointed to investigate Modern Spiritualism. Phila.: Lippincott, 159 pp., 8vo.

PRENGRUEBER. A. Anthropométrie; médecine légale. La détermination de l'âge des indigènes en Kabylie, basée sur les moyennes annuelles de la croissance des différentes régions du corps Alger méd., 1888, XVI, 153-185.

PRICE, J E. Roman remains in Yorkshire. Archæol. Rev., London, 1888-9, II, 330-342.

—— Roman remains in Essex Archæol. Rev., Lond., II, 92-102.

PRINGSHEIM, O. Die Lage der arbeitenden Klassen in Holland Arch. f. soziale Gesetzgeb. u. Statistik, Tubing., 1888, I, 69-82

Proceedings of the Academy of Natural Sciences of Philadelphia Phila.: By the Acad , vol. XVIII, 3d ser. completed in 1888

Proceedings of the American Antiquarian Society. Worcester, Mass. Ch. Hamilton, new series, V, in 1888.

Proceedings of the American Association for the Advancement of Science. 36th meeting in New York, 1887; 37th meeting in Cleveland, 1888.

Proceedings of the American Philosophical Society. Philadelphia, XXIV, in 1887.

Proceedings of the Asiatic Society of Bengal. Calcutta: Thomas, Monthly, 1865–1888.

Proceedings of the Canadian Institute, Toronto. Being a continuation of the "Canadian Journal" of Literature and History. 3d ser., VI in 1888, whole No. vol. XXIV. Toronto: Copp, Clark Co.

Proceedings of the nineteenth annual session of the American Philological Association, held at Burlington, Vt., July, 1887. Boston, 1888, 59 pp.

Proceedings of the Royal Geographical Society and Monthly Record of Geography London: Edward Stanford. N. ser., X, published in 1888.

Proceedings of the Royal Institution of Great Britain. London: By the Society, XII, pt. I, Dec., 1887.

Proceedings of the Royal Irish Academy. Published by the Academy. Ser. III, vol. I, No. I, published in Dec., 1888.

PROCHOWNICK, L. Beiträge zur Anthropologie des Beckens. Arch. f. Anthrop., Brnschwg., XVII, 61–139.

PROUDFIT, S. V. Note on the turtle back celt. Am. Anthrop., Wash., 1888, I, 337–339.

PUGLIA, F. El principio di casualità nella scienza criminale. Arch. di psichiat., etc., Torino e Roma, 1888, IX, 467–477.

PULLEN, CLARENCE. New Mexico; its geography, scenes and peoples. Bull. Amer. Geog. Soc., XIX, 22–47.

PUTNAM, F. W. Conventionalism in Ancient American Art, Salem (From Bull. Essex Inst.), XVIII, 155–167.

—— How bone fish-hooks were made in the little Miami Valley. 20th An. Rep. Peabody Mus., 1887, 581–586, 11 figs.

—— The Serpent Mound. The Evening Post, Cincin., June 4; also, O. Arch. and Hist. Quart., I, 187–190.

PUYDT, M. DE, et M. LOHEST. L'Homme contemporain du mammouth à Spy, province de Namur (Belgique). Crânes et ossements humains de la race de Néanderthal; l'industrie des hommes de cette race; l'industrie aux époques suivantes de l'âge du mammouth. Namur (1887), 36 pp., avec 10 planches in 8vo.

QUATREFAGES, A. DE. Espèce humaine. Extr. du Dict. encycl. d. sciences méd., XXXVI, 1–88, 1887. (Rev. scient., Par., XXXIX, 642–648.)

—— Histoire générale des races humaines. Paris: A. Hennuyer, 1887. (Rev. in Nature, XXXV, 389.) [Rev. in Rev. d'anthrop., Paris, 3. s., II, 221–223.]

—— Introduction à l'étude des races humaines. Paris: Hennuyer, 8vo. [Rev. in Matériaux, IV, 117–123.]

—— Les pygmées. Bibl. sc. contemp., Paris, 1887, J. B. Baillière, 1 vol. 357 p., fig. 31. 12mo. [Rev. in Matériaux, 3. s., IX, 425–443.]

—— Les races humaines. Rev. scient., Par., XL, 524–531.

QUEDENFELDT. Anthropologishe Aufnahmen von Morokkauern. Verhandl. d. Berl. Gesellsch. f. Anthrop., Berl. 1888, 32–37. Also: Ztschr. f. Ethnol., Berlin, 1888, 98–184.

QUELLIEN, N. Les mélodies populaires en Basse-Bretagne. Arch. d. miss. scient., 3. s, XIII, Paris.

RADIMSKY, V., and J. SZOMBATHY. Urgeschichtliche Forschungen in der Umgegend von Wies in Mittel Steiermark.

RAJ. COOMAR ROY. Child marriage in India. N. Am. Rev., 1888.

RANKE, JOHANNES. Ueber das Mongolenauge als provisorische Bildung bei deutschen Kindern. Corr. Bl. d. deutsch. Gesellsch. f. Anthrop., Brnschwg, 1888, XIX, 115–118.

—— Beiträge zur physischen Anthropologie der Bayern. Beitr. z. Anthrop., München (1888), VIII, 49–92.

—— Bibliography of German archæology and anthropology. Corr.-Blatt., XVII, 83.

RANCE, JOHANNES. Die XIX allgemeine Versammlung der deutschen Gesellschaft, f. Anthropologie, Ethnologie und Urgeschichte, zu Bonn, Aug. 1888; München, 1888; 158 pp., 4to.

—— Der Mensch Die Heutigen und die vorgeschichtlichen Menschenrassen. (Allgemeine Naturkunde, 5. Bd.) Leipzig: Bibliog.

RASERI, E. Sulla frequenza delle seconde nozze e sulla durata della vedavanza in Italia e altri stati. Giov. Soc. ital. d'ig., Milano, 1888, X, 489–497.

RATZEL, F. Völkerkunde. Band III: Die Kulturvölker der Alten und Neuen Welt. Leipzig (1888), 778 pp., mit 9 colorirten Tafeln, 1 Karte u. 225 Abbildungen, 8vo.

—— Zur Beurtheilung der Anthropophagie. Mitth. d. anthrop. Gesellsch. in Wien, XVII, 81–85.

RAU, CH. La stèle de Palenqué du musée national des États-Unis à Washington. Trad. fr. Ann. du musée Guimet. X, 3–103, fig. 1–14 et pl. I–V, 1887.

RAUFF. Die geologische Bildung des Rheinthals. Cor.-Bl. d. deutsch. Gesellsch. f. Anthrop., etc., Brnschwg., 1888, XIX, 99–103.

RAY, SIDNEY H. Sketch of Aniwa grammar. J. Anthrop. Inst., Lond. (1888), XVII, 282–289.

—— Sketch of Api grammar. J. Anthrop. Inst., Lond., 1888–9, XVIII, 295–303.

READ, M. C. The archæological exhibit for the Ohio Centennial. Ohio Archæol. and Hist. Quarterly, I, 170–173.

RAWLINSON, GEO. Crucifixion in the Ancient East. S. P. Times, 1888 (May).

RAYET, OLIVIER. Études d'archéologie et d'art. Paris, 1888, XVI, 466, pp., 8vo.

RECLUS, ÉLISÉE. Contributions à la sociologie des Australiens. Rev. d'anthrop., Paris, 3. s., II, 20–43; 692–606.

—— Les sacrifices humains chez les Khonds de l'Inde. Mém. Soc. d'anthrop. 2. s., III, 74–103.

REGALIA, E. Orbita e obliquità dell' occhio mongolico. Arch. per l'antrop., Firenze, 1888, XVIII, 121–158.

REGNAUD, PAUL. La question de la restitution de la langue-mère indo-européenne., Rev. de Ling., Par. (1888), 174.

—— La théorie des deux K Indo-Européens. Rev. de Ling., Par., XXI, 1–6 (1888).

—— Le δαίμων, histoire d'un mot et d'une idée. Rev. de l'Hist. des Religions. XVI, 156–158.

—— Sur l'étymologie du latin rex. Rev. Linguis., Paris, XX, 323–324.

REINACH, THÉODORE. Les classifications des religions et le rôle de l'histoire des religions dans l'enseignement public. (Rev. de l'Hist. des Religions, XVI, 228, from Rev. crit. d'histoire et de littérature, April.)

REISCHEL, G. Zur Statistik der Körpergrösse in den drei preussischen landrathlichen Kreisen Erfurt, Weissensee, und Eckartsberga Arch. f. Anthrop., Brnschwg., XVIII, 135–150, 1 map.

REISS, W., and A. STÜBEL. Das Todtenfeld von Ancon in Peru. Ein Beitrag zur Kenntniss der Cultur u. Industrie des Inca-Reiches. Nach den Ergebnissen eigener Ausgrabungen. Berlin (1880–87), m. 141 Farbendrucktafeln, 3 Bände.

Report of the British Association for the Advancement of Science, 1888. Bath, London: John Murray, 1889. (See British Association.)

REVERDIN, A. La circoncision chez les Juifs. Rev. méd. de la Suisse Rom., Genève, VIII, pp. 153–157.

Revue d'anthropologie. Paris: G. Masson, 16th and 17th years, 1887–'88, 3. ser., II, III, 8vo, quarterly.

Revue de l'Histoire de Religions. M. Jean Neville, director. Paris: E. Leroux, vol. XVI, No. 1, July and Aug., 1887. Annales du Musée Guimet. [Excellent bibliographers of religion and kindred subjects.]

Revue de Linguistique et de Philologie Comparée. Paris: Maisonneuve, vol. XXI, in 1888.

Revue des Traditions Populaires   Paris, vols. II and III published in 1887 and 1888.
Monthly. Organ of Société des Traditions Populaires au Musée d'Ethnographie
du Trocadere. Paris: Maisonneuve, vols I and III, 1886-1888.
Revue d'Ethnographie. Paris, Ed. E. T. Hamy; founded in 1883.
Revue Scientifique; founded in 1863. Paris: Lagrange, tome 41 and 42, 3. s., 9th
year, 1888.
REYNOLDS, HENRY L., Jr. The metal art of Ancient Mexico. Pop. Sc. Month.,
XXXI, 519-531, 1887.
—— Algonkin metal smiths. Am. Anthrop., Wash., I, 341-352.
RIANT, A. Les irresponsables devant la justice. Paris, 1888, Ballière, 320 pp., 12mo.
BIBBE, F. C. Étude sur l'ordre d'oblitération des sutures du crâne dans les races
humaines. Rev. d'anthrop., 3. s., III, 348-352.
RICCARDI, P. Intorno a due curiosi ornamenti personali in quarzo degli indigeni de-
Brasile. Arch. per l'antrop., Firenze, XVIII, 27-33.
—— Intorno a la oscillazioni giornaliene de la statura nel'uomo sano. Rassegna
di sci. med., Modena, II, 127-131.
—— Circonferenza toracica e statura studiate a seconda de l'età e del sesso in una
serie de Bolognesi. Boll. scient., Pavia, IX, 10-22.
RICHARD, O. J. Les progrès des études archéologiques aux États-Unis. Poitiers,
1888, 18 pp., 8vo.
RICHARDSON, B. W. The health of nations. London : Longmans, 1887, 2 vols.
RICHER, P. Les aveugles dans l'art. N. Iconog. de la Salpêtrière, Paris, 1888,
I, 209-212, 2 pl.
RINK, H. Resultaterne af de nyeste danske Undersøgelser i Grønland med Hensyn
til Indlandet og de svømmende Isbjerges Oprondelse. Geog. Tidskr., Kjøben,
havn, Hoffenberg, IX, 63-72.
—— The Eskimo Tribes, their distribution and characteristics, especially in regard
to laugnage, with a comparative vocabulary. Kjøbenhavn (Meddel. om Grön,
land), (1888), 176 pp., m. Karte, 8vo.
RITTER VON BRACHELLI, H. F. Statistische Skizzen der europäischen und amerika-
nischen Staaten. Rev. in Jour. Roy. Statis. Soc., London, L., 734.
RIVIÈRE, É. De l'antiquité de l'homme dans les Alpes maritimes. Paris (1887), 18
et 336 pp., avec 24 planches cromolith. et 95 figs., cart. 4to.
—— L'époque néolithique à Champigny (Seine). Bull. Soc. d'anthrop., Par., 3. s.,
XI (1888), 186-194.
—— Sur une station humaine de l'âge de la pierre, découverte à Chaville. Compt.
rend. Acad. d. sc., Par., CIV, 1117.
ROBECCHI, L. Notizie sull' Oasi di Siuwah. Arch. per l'antrop., Firenze, XVII, 224-
241, 1887.
ROBERTS, CH. La non-universalité du déluge. Réponse aux objections. Rev. d.
quest., Jan., 1887.
ROCHER, M. E. Crâne de pirate tonkinois offert. Bull. d. l. Soc. d'anthrop., Paris,
3. s., X, 638-639.
ROCKHILL, W. W. On the use of skulls in Lamaist ceremonies. Proc. Am. Orient.
Soc., 1888, 24-31.
—— The Lamaist ceremony called "making of mani pills." Proc. Am. Orient.
Soc., 1888, 22-24.
ROLLAND, G. L'Oued Rir' et la colonisation française au Sahara. Extr. de la Rev.
scientifique, Paris, 1887, Challamel aîné, br., 8vo.
ROLLESTON, H. D. Description of the cerebral hemispheres of an adult Australian
male. J. Anthrop. Inst., Lond., XVII, 32-42.
ROLLET, E. De la mensuration des os longs des membres, et de ses applications an-
thropologique et médico-légale. Compt. rend. Acad. d. sc , Paris, 1888, CVII,
957-960.
ROMANES, G. J. Mental difference of men and women. [From : Nineteenth Century.]
Pop. Sc. Month., N. Y., XXXI, 383-401 ; 654-672.

ROMANES, G. J. Physiological Selection. Nature (1887), XXXVI, 268-341.

ROMILLY, 11. H. The islands of the New Britain group. Proc. Roy. Geog. Soc., IX, 1-18.

ROSENBERG, H. VON. Een en ander over de bewoners der Menta wei-eilanden. Internat. Arch. f. Ethnog., Leiden, 1888, I, 218, 1 pl.

ROSNY, L. DE Les Antilles. Étude d'ethnographie et d'archéologie américaines. ["Mémoires de la Société d'ethnographie, Nr. 7."] Paris (1887), IV, 240 pp., 4to.

ROSSI, V. Studi sopra una centuria di criminali. Roma e Torino, 1888, Bocca, 155 pp., 8vo.

ROUSSELET, LOUIS. Les Afghans. Rev. d'anthrop., 3. s., III, 412-428.

ROUSSY, ALBERT. Les Iakontes, leurs dieux et leurs chamans. Soc. de Géog. de Gèneve, reported in Matériaux, 3. s., IV, 250-257.

ROUTH, C. H. F. Overwork and premature mental decay. IV. edition. London: Ballière, Tindall & Cox. [Reviewed in Nature, XXXVI, 507.]

Royal Asiatic Society. See Journal.

ROYCE, CHARLES C. The Cherokee nation of Indians. Rep. Bureau Ethnol., 1883-'84, 3pl., 121-378.

ROYER, CLÉMENCE. La domestication des singes. Rev. d'anthrop., Paris, 3. s, II, 170-181.

—— L'évolution mentale dans la série organique. Rev. scient., Paris, XXXIX, 749; XL, 70.

—— Projet d'installation d'un laboratoire d'expériences transformistes au parc de Montsouris. Bull. d. l. Soc. d'anthrop., Paris, 3. s.. x, 461-462.

—— Variabilité morphologique des muscles sous l'influence des variations fonctionnelles. Bull. d. l. Soc d'anthrop., Paris. 3. s., x, 643-649.

RÜDINGER, N. Ueber kunstlich deformirte Schädel und Gehirne von Südseeinsulanern (Neue Hebriden). München, 1887, G. Franz, 33 pp., 3 pl., 8vo. [Repr. from: Abhandl d. k. bayer. Akad. d. Wissensch., 1887, II. Cl., XVI.]

RUNGE, GEORGIUS. Shape of female pelvis in different races; pelvis of Russian women. St. Petersburg, 1888, R. Laferentz, 80 pp., 2 diag., 8vo

RUSDEN, H. K. Physiological selection. Nature, XXXVI, 268. (Rev. of Romanes.)

RUSSELL, J. The Cartrail or Pict's work-ditch. Blackwood's Mag., Edinb., CXLIV, 716-735.

RUST, M. A. Mutilations Gaillard's M. J., N. Y., XLIV, 26-37.

—— Remarks on certain mutilations and artificial deformities, including trepanning, foot deformities, etc. Virginia M. Month., Richmond, XIV, 171-182. Also: Gaillard's M. J., N. Y., XLIII, 538-546.

RYE, W. Notes on crime and accident in Norfolk, temp., Edward I. Archæol Rev., II, 201-215.

SABATIER. De l'éducation des peuples conquis; de l'action du peuple éducateur étudiée dans ses conditions d'efficacité et dans ses effets. L'Homme, Par., IV, 33-40.

SALMON, P. Dolmen avec tumulus et cromlech à Kertescan, commune de Carnac (Morbihau). L'Homme, Par., IV, 641-649.

—— Géographie préhistorique de la France. Matériaux, 3. s , IV, 221-227; 384-390; 421-424.

—— Les races humaines préhistoriques L'Homme, Par., IV, 321-334 (1888).

—— Précis d'anthropologie, par Abel Hovelacque et Georges Hervé. Compte rendu, Par., 1887, A. Delahaye & E. Lecrosnier, 15 pp. 8°. [Repr fr. L'Homme.]

—— Recensement des monuments mégalithiques de l'Algérie et de la Tunisie. Bull. d. l. Soc. d'anthrop. de Lyon, VI, 202-204.

SALSOTTO, G. Il tatuaggio nelle donne criminali e nelle prostitute. Arch di psichiat., etc., Torino, VIII, 102.

SAN BUENAVENTURA, GABRIEL DE. Arte de la lengua Maya, por México, 1684. Reprinted, Mexico, 18-8, 8vo. [Rev. in Am. Antiquar., Meudon, Ill. (1888) sc, 393–394.]

SANFORD, E. C. Personal equation. Am. J. Psychol., Balt., 1888–89, ii, 1–38.

—— The relative legibility of small letters. Am. J. Psychol., i, pp. 402–435.

SANSON, M. ANDRÉ. La craniologie expérimentale. Bull. d. l. Soc. d'anthrop., Paris, 3. s., x, 607–62).

SANTA-ANNA NERY, F. J. Folk lore brésilien. Paris, 16°.

SARGENT, DUDLEY ALLEN. Anthrometric apparatus, with directions for measuring and testing the principal physical characteristics of the human body. Cambridge, 1887, 141 pp., 8vo.

SATO, SHOSUKE. The Japanese farming class. Overland Monthly, Feb.

SATOW, E. M. Essay toward a bibliography of Siam. Sing. Govt. print., 103 pp. 8vo.

SAVAGE, G. H. Homicidal mania. Fortnightly Rev., n. s., xliv, 448–463.

SAYCE, A. H. Anthropology. Address before Br. Assoc. Nature, xxxvi, 511.

—— The white race of Palestine. Nature, Lond., xxxviii, 321.

SCHAAFHAUSEN, H. Der Neanderthaler Fund. Der deutschen anthropologischen. Gesellschaft, zu ihrer XIX. Allgemeinen Versammlung in Bonn gewidmet. Bonn, 1888, A. Marcus, 49 pp., 3 pl., 4to.

—— [Die anthropologische Forschung.] Cor.-Bl. d. deutsch. Gesellsch. f. Anthrop., etc., Brnschwg., 1888, XIX, 71–77.

—— Entwickelung des menschlischen Handwerks und der Einfluss des Stoffes auf die Kunstform. Cor.-Blatt, XVII, 10–12.

—— Die Physiognomik. Arch. f. Anthrop., Brnschwg., XVII, 309–338.

SCHADENBERG, A. Beiträge zur Ethnographie von Nord Suzon (Filirinen). Mitth. d. anthrop. Gesellsch. in Wien, 1888, n. F., VIII, 265–271.

SCHELLONG, O. Ueber die Herstellung einiger Ethnographica der Gegend Flnschhafen's (Kaiser Wilhemsland). Internat. Arch. f. Ethnog., Leiden, 1888, I, 220–222, 1 pl.

SCHENCK, W. L. Moustrosities and mental impressions. J. Am. Med. Ass., Chicago, 1888, XI, 646.

SCHIERENBERG. Grabfelsen am Externsteine Verhandl. d. Berl. Gesellsch. f. Anthrop., Berlin, 1888, 311.

SCHILS, G. La race jaune de l'Afrique Australe Le Muséon, Louvain, VI, 224–231; 339–449.

SCHINZ, HANS. Exploration of the German colony known as Luderitzland (southwest Africa). Nature, xxxvi, 309.

SCHLEGEL, G. A Singapore street scene. Internat. Arch. f. Ethnog., I, 121–129.

—— CH. DE HARLEZ. La religion nationale des Tartares orientaux. Rev. in Intern. Arch. f. Ethnog., 1888, I, 203–206.

SCHLIEMANN, H. Tiryns, der prähistorische Palast der Könige von Tiryns. Leipzig: Brockhaus, 198 figs., 24 tab., 1 ch., 4 plans. [Rev. in Corr.-Bl., XVII, 14–15.]

SCHMELTZ, J. D. E. Editor of the Internationales Archiv fur Ethnographie, in which he has many notices of museums, reviews of books, etc.

SCHMIDT, EMIL. Ueber alt- und neuägyptische Schädel. Beitrag zu unseren Anschauungen über die Veränderlichkeit und Constanz der Schädelformen. Arch. f. Anthrop., Brnschwg., XVII, 189–227.

SCHMIDT, O. Les mammifères dans leurs rapports avec leurs ancêtres géologiques. [Rev. in Rev. d'anthrop., Paris, 3. s., II, 293–299.]

SCHMORL, G. Ein Fall von Hermaphroditismus. Arch. f. path. Anat., Berl., CXIII, 229–244, 1 pl.

SCHNEIDER, OSCAR. Der Chamsin und sein Einfluss auf die niedere Tierwelt. Festschr. des Vereins f. Erdkunde zu Dresden, 1888, 95–113.

SCHOLZ, FRIEDRICH. Schlaf und Traum. Leipzig: Maher, 70 pp., 8vo.

SCHROEDER, LEOPOLD VON. Die Hochzeitsbrauche der Esten und einiger anderer finnisch-ugrischei Volkerschatten, etc. Berlin, 1888, 1 vol., pp. 265. [Rev. in Arch. per l'antrop., Firenze (1888), XVIII, 284-286.]

SCHUMANN. Steinkistengräber bei Blumberg an der Randow. Verhandl. d. Berl. Gesellsch. f. Anthrop., Berlin, 1888, 264.

SCHUMANN, J. C. The ethical import of Darwinism. London, 1888: Williams and Norgate, 250 pp., 8vo.

SCHWARTZ, W. Die rossgestaltigen Himmelsätzte bei Indern und Griechen. Ztschr. f. Ethnol., Berl., 1888, XX, 221-230.

Science. Weekly. New York. Vols. I-XII, 1883-1888.

SEARCY, J. T. The mental characteristics of the sexes. Alienist & Neurol., St. Louis, IX, 555-564.

SÉBILLOT, PAUL. Légendes, croyances, et superstitions de la mer. Meteors and tempests. Paris: Charpentier, 342 pp., 12mo.

—— Blason populaire de la Haute-Bretagne. Rev. Linguis. Paris, XX, 315-322.

—— Folk-lore des oreilles. L'Homme, Par., IV, 524-537.

—— Quelques traditions sur les volcans. Bull. de la Soc. d'anthrop., 3. Paris, s., X, 187, 188.

—— Superstitions des civilisés. Rev. d. tradit. populaires, April.

SEELAND, VON. Consecutive effects of diet and nutrition on the organism. Biologisches Centralblatt for the year 1887.

SEELAND, NICOLAS. La Kashgarie et les passes du Fiau-chan. Rev. d'anthrop., Par. (1888), 3. s.; III, 684-609; IV, 37-74.

SEELY, F. A. History of the International Union for the Protection of Industrial Property. Washington, 3-20.

SELER. Eine Liste der mexikanischen Monatsfeste. Verhandl. Berl. Gesellsch. Anthrop., 1887, 172-177.

SELLING, A. M. Om ärftlighetslaran i dess nyaste skeden. [Theory of heredity in its latest phases.] Hygiea, Stockholm, 1888, I, 641, 709.

SERGI, G. Antropologia fisica della Fuegia. Bull. d. r. Accad med. di Roma, IX, 52-62.

—— Anthropologie physique de la Terre de Feu. Rev. in Rev. d'anthrop. Paris, 3. s., II, 300-307. From Arch. per l' antrop, Firenze, XVIII, 25-32.

—— Crani d' Omaquaca. Bull. d. r. Accad. med di Roma, XIII, 403-416.

—— and L. MOSCHEN. Crani della Papuasia. Arch. per l' antrop., Firenze, 1888, XVIII, 91-100, 1 pl.

—— Crani peruviani antichi del Museo antropologico nella Università di Roma. Arch. per l' antrop., Firenze, XVII, 5-33.

—— La psychologie physiologique. [From the Italian.] Paris (1888), Alcan, 452 pp., 8vo.

SERRURIER, L. Dubbel masker met veeren kleed uit Cabinda. Intern. Arch. f. Ethnog., 1888, I, 154-159.

—— Histoire générale des races humaines, by A. de Quatrefages. Rev. in Intern. Arch. f. Ethnog, 1888, I, 170, 171.

—— Une statue ithyphallique. Avec deux figures dans le texte. Rev. in Intern. Arch. f. Ethnog., 1888, I, 27, 28.

—— Systematik der Neu-Guinea Pfeile. Internat. Arch. f. Ethnog., I, 1-22, ill.

SHAW, ALBERT. The American state and the American man. Contemp. Review, May, 17 pp.

SHEPARD, C. The evolution of man, and our relation to him as physicians. Tr. Mich. M. Soc., Detroit, 29-44.

SHEPARD, HENRY A. Antiquities of the State of Ohio. Cincin: Yoston & Co., ill.

SHUFELDT, R. M. Comparative data from 2,000 Indian crania in the United States Army Medical Museum. J. Anat. and Physiol., Lond., XXII, 191-214.

SHUFELDT, R. M. Contributions to the comparative craniology of the North American Indians; the skull in the Apaches. Loud., 1887, 8vo. [From: J. Anat. and Physiol., XXI, 524-535.]

—— The Navajo Tanner. Proc. U. S. Nat. Mus., Wash. (1888), 59-66, 6 pl. [Rev. in Arch. per l' antrop., Firenze, 1888, XVIII, 292.

—— Notes on certain traits of infant Navajos. Nature, XXXV, 346.

—— Observations upon the morphology of Gallus Bankiva of India (including a complete account of its skeleton) J. Comp. M. & S., N. Y. (1888), 1-34, 7 ills.

SIMÉON. La semaine chez les anciens Mexicains. Arch. Soc. Amér. de France, No. 1.

SIMMS, JOSEPH. Human brain-weights. Pop. Sc. Month., XXXI, 355-359.

SIMON, G. E. China: its social, political, and religious life. London: Sampson Low. [Translation.]

SIMONEAU, M. Ossements humains de Lizy. Bull. Soc. d'anthrop., Paris, 3. s., X, 699,700.

—— Silex tailles. Bull. Soc. d'anthrop., Paris, 3. s, X, 184,185; XI,378.

SINNETT, A.-P. Le monde occulte, hypnotisme transcendant en Orient. Paris: Carrée, XXXV, 267 pp., 8vo. [See Rev. d'hist. des relig., XVI, 372.]

SIRET, HENRI et LOUIS. Les premiers âges du métal dans le sud-est de l'Espagne. Bruxelles (1888), Centerick et Lefébure, 5-110. (Rev. de Quest. Scient., Brux.)

SIROTININ, W. Die punctiförmig regreuze Reizung des Froschrückenmarkes. [Rev. in Am. J. of Psychology, Baltimore, I, 188.]

SKERTCHLY, SYDNEY B. J. The occurrence of stone mortars in the ancient (Pliocene ?) river gravels of Butte County, California. J. Anthrop. Inst., Lond. (1888), XVII, 332-337, 1 pl.

SMILEY, CHARLES W. Altruism considered economically. Proc. Am. Ass. Adv. Sc. (1888), XXXVII, 3-22.

SMITH, J. A. Buddhism, Siddartha. Chautauquan. 1888 (May), 468.

SMITH, DE C. Witchcraft and demonism of the modern Iroquois. J. Am. Folk-Lore, Boston, I, 184-193.

SNELL, K. Vorlesungen über die Abstammung des Menschen. Leipzig (1887), R. Seydel, 216 pp., 8vo.

Société suédoise de géographie et d'anthropologie. [Complete list of papers in 1886, in Matériaux, 3. s., IV, 130-131.]

Société des traditions populaires; publishes Revue; holds its sessions in the Trocadéro Museum. Summary of publications in Matériaux, 3.s., IV, 165-169.

Society of Psychical Research. Proceedings. London.

SOLER Y ARQUÉS, CARLOS. Ideal de la familia. Madrid: Huerfanos, 403 pp.

SOLLIER, ALICE. De l'état de la dentition chez les enfants idiots et arriérés. Rev. d'anthrop., 3. s., III, 352-354.

South African food-plants. J. Soc. Arts, XXXV, 986-988.

South Kensington Museum. A list of books and pamphlets, illustrating gold and silversmiths' work and jewelry. London: Eyre & Spottiswoode, 91 pp., 8vo.

SPANG, NORMAN. Catalogue illustrating the choicest specimens in archæology, including amulets, banner stones, discoidal stones, pipes, axes, celts, spear heads, arrow points, etc. Boston: 1888, T. R. Marvin & Son, 84 pp., 8vo.

SPATUZZI, A. Relazioni tra l'igiene e l' antropologia, quesiti practici che ne derivano ed applicazioni allo sviluppo di statura. Morgagni, Napoli, XXIX, 509-512.

SPRAGUE, T. B. On the probability that a marriage entered into by a man of any age will be fruitful. Proc. Roy. Soc. Edinb., 1888, XIV, 327-346.

STARR, FREDERICK. Preservation by copper salts. Am. Antiquar., Mendon, Ill. (1888), X, 279-282.

STARR, M. ALLEN. Logical machines. Rev. in Amer. Jour. of Psychology, Baltimore, I, 165-173.

STANLEY, W. F. The stature of the human race. Nature, XXXVI, 366.

STEMPF, V. Die Sprache der basken Erstlinge von Herrn Bernard Dechepare, Rector zu Alt Sanct-Michael. Rev. de Ling., Par. (1888), XXI, 235.

STEPHEN, ALEXANDER. The Navajo shoemaker. Proc. U. S. Nat. Mus., Wash., (1888), 131-136, 7 figs.

—— Legend of the Snake Order of the Moquis, as told by outsiders. J. Am. Folk-Lore, N. Y. (1888), I, 109-114.

STEPHENSON, W. On the rate of growth in children. Tr. Internat. Med. Cong., IX, Wash., III, 446-452.

—— On the relation of weight to heigth and the rate of growth in man. Lancet, Lond., 1888, II, 560-564.

STEUB, L. Zur Ethnologie der deutschen Alpen. Salzburg (1887), 112 pp., 8vo.

STEVENSON, JAMES. The Arabs in Central Africa. J. Manchester Geog. Soc., IV, 72-87.

STEVENSON, TILLY E. The religious life of the Zuñi child. Rept. Bur. Ethnol., 1883-'84, pp. 533-555, 4 pl.

STEVENSON, W G. Genius and mental disease. Pop. Sc. Month., XXX, 663-678 (1887).

STEVENSON, W. H. The derivation of place names. Archæol. Rev., Lond., 1888-'89, II, 104-107.

STEWART, Dr. The inhabitants of Paraguay. J. Anthrop. Inst., Lond., 1888, XVIII, 174-176.

STOLL, O. Die Sprache der Ixil-Indianer. Ein Beitrag zur Ethnologie und Linguistik der Maya-Völker. Nebst einem Anhang: Wörterverzeichnisse aus dem nord westlichen Guatemala. Leipzig (1887), Brockhaus, XII, 156 pp., 8vo.

—— Ethnographische Gesellschaft, Zürich. Rev. in Intern. Arch. f. Ethnog., 1888, I, 284.

STONE, OLIVIA M. The Canary Islands. London (1887), Marcus Ward & Co., vols. 2, illustrated. [Rev. in Nature, XXXVI, 231.

STRANGE, GUY LE. The Noble Sanctuary in Jerusalem in 1470 A. D. J. R. A. S., XIX, 247-305.

STRUCKMANN, C. Urgeschichtliche Notizen aus Hannover. Arch. f. Anthrop., Bruschwg, 1888-9, XVIII, 171-175.

Strumenti musicali della Micronesia e della Melanesia. Collection of Dr. Finsch. Arch. per l' antrop., XVII, 35-41.

STÜBEL, ALPHONS. Ueber altperuanische Gewebemuster und ihnen analoge Ornamente der altklassischen Kunst. Festschr. des Vereins f. Erdkunde zu Dresden, 1888, 37-56, 30 figs.

STURTEVANT, E. LEWIS. History of garden vegetables. Am. Naturalist, XXI, 433-444.

SUCHY. Siamesische Schwestern. Sternothorakopagus. Wien. med. Wchnschr., 1888, XXXVIII, 8115.

Suite de la discussion sur l'aphasie. Bull. Soc. d'anthrop. de Par. 3. s., XI (1888), 264-274.

SULIGOWSKI, F. Kilka slow o pomiarach antropometrycznych mlodziezy gimnazyum mezkiego w Radomin. [The anthropometric measurements of pupils in the gymnasium of Radom.] Medycyna, Warszawa, XV, 512; 528; 544; 559; 641.

SUMNER, WILLIAM G. What makes the rich richer and the poor poorer. Pop. Sc. Month., XXX, 289-296, 1887.

SUTTON, J B Supernumerary auricles. Illust. Med. News, Lon., 1888, I, 320.

Svensk (En) läkare. Ar osedlighet helsosam och är sedlighet skadlig för helsan? [Is immorality healthy and is morality hurtful to health?] Helsovannen, Göteborg, II, 137-142.

SWAINSON, CHARLES. The folk-lore and provincial names of British birds. Published for Folk-Lore Soc., London (1886). Nature, XXXVI, 49.

SZOMBATHY, J. La Tène-Funde von Nassentuss in Krain. Mitth. d. anthrop Gesellsch. in Wien, 1888, n. F., VIII. [Sitzungsb., 92-94.]

TARDE, M. La criminologie. Rev. d'anthrop., Par. (1888), 3. s., III, 521-533.

TAUBNER.   Vorchristliche rechtwinklige Kreuzzeichen.   Verhandl. d. Berl. Gesellsch.
    f. Anthrop., Berl, 1888, 331–333.
TAUTAIN, M.   Le Dioula-Dongou et le senefo.   Rev. d'ethnog., Paris, VI, 395–399.
—— Quelques renseignements sur les Bobos.   Rev. d'ethnog., Par., VI, 228–233.
TAYLOR, C. FAYETTE.   Gofio: food and physique.   Pop. Sc. Month., XXXI, 224–228,
    1887.
TAYLOR, CANON ISAAC.   The origin and primitive seat of the Aryans.   J. Anthrop.
    Inst., Lond. (1888), XVII, 238–275; Nature, XXXVI, 597.
TAYLOR, G.   Formosa and its aborigines.   China Review (Nature, 1887, p. 22),
    vol. 36.
TECCE, E.   I danni della consanguineità nella riproduzione delle famiglie.   Med.
    contemp., Napoli, IV, 589–606.
TEN KATE, H.   Beitrag zur Ethnographie von Surinam.   Internat. Arch. f. Ethnog.,
    Leiden, 1888, I, 223–227, 1 pl.
—— Materiales para servir á la antropologia de la península de California.   [Transl.
    by F. Martinez Calleja, from : Bull. Soc. d'anthrop., Par.]   An. d. Mus. nac. de
    México, IV, 5–16.
—— Observations anthropologiques recueillies dans la Guyane et le Vénézuéla.
    Rev. d'anthrop., 3. s., III, 44–68.
—— Sur quelques objets indiens trouvés près de Guaymas (Mexique).   Rev. d'eth-
    nog., Paris, VI, 234–238.
—— Ueber mohammedanische Bruderschaften in Algerien.   Verhandl. d. Berl.
    anthrop. Gesellsch., 1887, 372–375.
TEPLOUCHOFF, A. E.   Moschusochse.   Arch. f. Anthrop., XVI, 519–562.
Teratology, the study of organic anomalies.
TESTUT, Dr.   Qu'est-ce que l'homme pour un anatomiste ?   Rev. scient., Jan., reported
    in Matériaux, 3. s., IV, 286–289.
TETHERSTON, R. H.   Weight of Victorian infants.   Austral. M. J., Melbourne, n. s.,
    IX, 495.
TEUCHINI, LORENZO.   Cervelli di delinquenti (superficie parieto-temporo-occipitale).
    Parma, 1887, L. Battie, 141 pp.
—— Note sur la crête frontale chez les criminels.   Actes Cong. internat. d'anthrop.
    crim., 1885, Rome, I, 449–456.
TEWES.   Alterthümer und Steindenkmäler im Osnabrückschen.   Verhandl. d. Berl.
    Gesellsch. f. Anthrop., 1888, 205–208.
THIEULLEU, M.   Meulières taillées de Fontenay-aux-Roses.   Bull. d. l. Soc. d'anthrop.,
    Paris, 3. s., X, 605–607.
—— 1. Sur une sépulture sous roche de l'âge de la pierre à Crécy-en-Brie.   2. Sur
    des silex taillés trouvés dans les sables d'alluvions sous Paris (quartier de la
    Banque.   3. Sur un atelier préhistorique de meulières taillées à Fontenay-aux-
    Roses.   Bull. d. l. Soc. d'anthrop., Paris, 3. s., X, 548–557.
THOMAS. Mrs. CYRUS.   Bibliography of the earthworks in Ohio.   Ohio Archæol. and
    Hist. Quart., I, 69–78.
THOMAS, CYRUS.   Aids to the study of the Maya Codices.   VI. Ann. Rep. Bur. Eth-
    nol., 1888, pp. 253–371, 3 figs.
—— Work in mound exploration of the Bureau of Ethnology.   Wash., Gov. Print.
    Off., br., 1887, 8vo.
—— Curious customs of the mound builders.   Am. Anthrop., 1888, I, 353–355.
—— Burial mounds of the northern section of the United States.   Ann. Rep. Bur.
    Ethnol., 1883–'84, 9–110, 6 pl., 49 figs.
THOMPSON, DANIEL GREENLEAF.   Thought and language.   Pop. Sc. Month., XXXII,
    213–220, 1887.
THOMPSON, EDWARD H.   Archæological researches in Yucatan.   Proc. Am. Antiquar.
    Soc., IV, 248–254 ; 379–385.
THWAITES, REUBEN G.   Collections of State Historical Society of Wisconsin.   Vol.
    XI.   [Rev. in Amer. Antiquar., Mendon, Ill. (1888), X, 332.

TIFFANY, L. McL. Comparison between the surgical diseases of the white and colored races. Tr. Am. Surg. Ass., Phila., v, 262-273.

TIMEHRI. Being the Journal of the Royal Agricultural and Commercial Society of British Guiana. n. s., vol. 1, in 1887, Demerara, J. Thompson. Semi-annual.

TISCHLER, O. Ueber das Gräberfeld von Oberhof. Cor.-Bl d. deutsch. Gesellsch. f. Anthrop., etc., Braunschw., 1888, xix, 118-122.

TISSANDIER, G. Les centenaires. Nature, Paris, 1887-'8, xvi, 129.

TODD, J. E. Some ancient diggings in Nebraska. Am. Antiquar., Mendon, Ill. (1888), x, 374-376.

TOMASCHEK, W. Ueber die Zinngewinnung und Bronzebereitung in Asien. Mitth. d. anthrop. Gesellsch. in Wien, 1887. Also : Die Culturzustande der Jenisejor. Ibid., n. F., viii, Sitzungsb., 63-65.

TOMKINS, H. G. Remarks on Mr. Flinders Petrie's collection of ethnographic types from the monuments of Egypt. J. Anthrop. Inst., London, 1888-'89, xviii, 206-239. 2 pl.

TOPINARD, P. Anthropologie. Leipzig (1887), Baldamus, 552 pp., 8vo. Transl. from 3d French edition.

—— Carte de la répartition de la couleur des yeux et des cheveux. Rev. d'anthrop. Paris, 3. s., ii, 1-7.

—— Crâne néolithique trépané de Feigneux (Oise). Procédé opératoire suivi. Rev. d'anthrop , Par. (1888), 3. s., iii, 243-247.

—— Têtes moulées montrant le développement du cerveau et la topographie cranio-cérébrale. Académie royale de médecine d'Irlande, mars 1888. By Prof. J. D. Cunningham. [Rev. in Rev. d'anthrop., Par. (1888), 3. s., iii, 490, 491.]

—— Description et mensuration d'une série de crânes Kirghis offert par le Dr. Secland. Rev. d'anthrop., Par., 3. s., ii, 445-475.

—— Documents sur la couleur des yeux et des cheveux. I. Asie Centrale. II. Angleterre. III. Méthode Bertillon. Rev. d'anthrop., Par. (1888), 3. s., iii, 513-520.

—— Étude sur les Hottentots observés au Jardin d'acclimatation. Bull. et Mém. Soc. de méd. prat. de Par., 1888, 657-663.

—— Grotte néolithique de Feigneux (Oise) ; crâne trépané sur le vivant et après la mort. Bull. Soc. d'anthrop. de Par., 3. s., x, 527-548.

—— Parallèle statistique des races blanche et de couleur à Washington. Rev. d'anthrop., Paris, 1888, 3. s., iii, 632.

—— Précis d'anthropologie. By Hovelacque et Hehvé. [Rev. in Rev. d'anthrop., Paris, 3. s., ii, 492-495.]

—— La carte de l'indice céphalique des Italiens. Rev. d'anthrop., Paris, 576-624, 1886 ; 1-7, 1887 ; 3. s., ii, 333-338.

—— La formule de reconstitution de la taille d'après les os longs. Rev. d'anthrop., Par. (1888), 3. s , iii, 469-471.

—— L'anthropologie criminelle. Rev. d'anthrop., Par., 3. s., ii, 658-691.

—— Le poids de l'encéphale d'après Paul Broca. Mém. Soc. d'anthrop., Paris, 2. s., iii. 1-41.

—— Les ancêtres de nos animaux dans les temps géologiques. By Albert Gaudey. Vol. petit in-8° de 296 pages, avec 49 figures. Bibl. scient. contemp., J.-B. Baillière et fils. Rev. d'anthrop., Par. (1888), 3. s., iii, 472-474.

—— Les dernières étapes de la généalogie de l'homme (leçon du 21 mars 1888). Rev. d'anthrop., Par. (1888), 3 s , iii, 298-332. Also : Pop. Sc. Month., xxxiii, 821 ; xxxiv, 171.

—— Le transformisme. By Edmond Perrier. Vol. petit in-8vo de 344 pages, avec 88 figs. Bibl. scientif. contemp., J.-B. Baillière et fils, Paris, 1888. Rev. d'anthrop , Par. (1888), 3. s., iii, 474-477.

—— L'histoire de l'anthropologie en 1788. Rev. d'anthrop., 3. s., iii, 195-201.

—— L'homme quaternaire de l'Amérique du nord. Rev. d'anthrop., Paris, 3. s., ii, 483-491.

TOPINARD, P. M. Cope sur la généalogie de l'homme. Rev. d'anthrop., Par. (1888), 3 s., III, 744–746.

—— Mensuration des crânes des dolmens de la Lozère. Rev. d'anthrop., 3. s., II, 513–518.

—— Mœurs et monuments des peuples préhistoriques. By Marquis de Nadaillac. Paris, 1888, in Bibloth. de la Nature. Édit. Masson, 120 figures, 1 vol. in-8vo. Rev. d'anthrop., Par. (1888), 3. s., III, 354–358.

—— Os longs de Spy. Bull. Soc. d'anthrop. de Paris, 1888, 3. s., XI, 376–378.

—— Un mot sur la conversion de l'indice céphalométrique en indice craniométrique. Rev. d'anthrop., Paris, 1888, 3. s., III, 641–646.

—— Trephining in neolithic times. Rev. d'anthrop., 3. s., III.

—— Statistique de la couleur des yeux et des cheveux en France. Bull. Soc. d'anthrop., Paris, 1888, 3. s., XI, 87.

—— Un mot sur la conversion de l'indice céphalométrique en indice craniométrique. Rev. d'anthrop., Par. (1888), 3. s., III, 641–646.

—— Un mot sur l'histoire de l'anthropologie en 1788. Rev. d'anthrop., Par. (1888), 3. s., III, 197–201.

TORÖK, A. VON. Ueber den Yézoer Ainoschädel. Ein Beitrag zur Rassen-Anatomie der Aino. Arch. f. Anthrop., Brnschwg., 1888–9, XVIII, 15–100, 2 pl.

—— Ueber ein Universal-Kraniometer. Internat. Monatschr. f. Anat. u. Physiol., Leipz., 1888, v, 165; 233; 277; 307, 4 pl.

—— Ueber den Yezoer Ainoschädel aus der ostasiatischen Reise des Herrn Grafen Bela Szechenyi und über den Sachaliner Ainoschädel des königl. zoologischen und anthropologisch-ethnographischen Museums zu Dresden. Arch. f. Anthrop., Bruschwg. (1888), XVIII, 15–100, 1 fig., 2 tables.

—— Wie kann der Symphysiswinkel des Unterkiefers exact gewesen werden? Arch. f. Anthrop., Bruschwg., XVII, 141–150; also, 15–100.

TRÄGER, EUGEN. Die Volksdichtigkeit. Weimar, 1888, 36 pp., 1 map, 8vo.

Tradition (La). Paris. Vol. I, published in 1887.

Transactions of the Academy of Science. St. Louis: Studley, vol. IV.

Transactions of the Asiatic Society of Japan. Yokohama: Meiklejohn, vol. XV, in 1887.

TREGEAR, E. Ancient alphabets in Polynesia. Trans. of the New Zealand Inst., XX, 353–368.

—— Polynesian folk-lore. Trans. of the New Zealand Inst., XX, 369–399.

—— The Aryo-Semitic Maori. Trans. of the New Zealand Inst., XX, 400–413.

—— The Maori and the Moa. J. Anthrop. Inst., Lond. (1888), XVII, 292–305.

TREICHEL. Bauer und Wohnung im Kreise Deutsch-Krone. Verhandl. d. Beil. Gesellsch. f. Anthrop., Berl., 1888, 292–295.

—— Eine Gesichts- und eine Spitzmützen-Urne von Strzepcz. Verhandl. d. Berl. Gesellsch. f. Anthrop., Berl., 1888, 321–323.

—— Pferdekopf und Storchschnabel in Westpreussen. Verhandl. d. Berl. Gesellsch. f. Anthrop., Berl., 1888, 295–297.

—— Schwedenschanze bei Stocksmühle, Kreis Marienwerder. Verhandl. d. Berl. Gesellsch. f. Anthrop., Berl., 1888, 290–292.

—— Westpreussische Burgwälle. Verhandl. d. Berl. Gesellsch. f. Anthrop., Beil., 1888, 257–263; 323–330.

TRIA, G. Ricerche sulla cute del negro. Gior. internaz. d. sc. med., Napoli, 1888, n. s., X, 365–369, 1 pl.

TROMP, S. W. Mededeeligen omtrent Mandan's. Internat. Arch. f. Ethnog., I, 22–26, 1 pl.

TROTTER, C. Among the Fiji Islands. Pop. Sc. Month., N. Y., 1888–9, XXXIV, 644–652.

TRUSSARDI, GIACIUTOR. La salute e la longevita considerate sotto il rapporto dell' igiene. Bergamo, 1887, Cattaneo, 169 pp., 12mo.

TUCHMANN, J. La fascination. Mélusine, mai, 1887.

TUCKER, WM. The Creator in the religions of the East. Am. Antiquar., IX, 276-280.

TUCKERMAN, F. Anthropometric data based upon nearly 3,000 measurements taken from students. Amherst, 1888, 1 l., 8vo.

TURQUAN, V. Statistique des centenaires. Rev. scient., Paris, 1888, XLII, 269-275.

TYLER, THOMAS. The Hittites, with special reference to recent discoveries. Nature, XXXVII, 511; 536; 559; 609; 590.

TYLOR, E. B. Marriage systems and laws of descent. Oxford Magazine, June, 1888. [Rev. in J. Anthrop. Inst., Lond. (1888), XVIII, 91, 92.]

—— Notes on Powhatan's mantle, preserved in the Ashmolean Museum, Oxford. Internat. Arch. f. Ethnog., Leiden, 188ϯ, I, 215-217, 1pl.

—— On a method of investigating the development of institutions; applied to laws of marriages and descent. J. Anthrop. Inst., London, 1888-9, XVIII, 245, 272.

UHLE, M. Die Sammlung Censeno. Rev. in Internat. Arch. f. Ethnog., 1888, I, 234, 235.

—— Ethnologische Erfahrungen und Belegstücke. Dr. Otto Finsch. I. Rev. in Internat. Arch. f. Ethnog., 1888, I, 244-246.

UFFOLZ, PAUL. Trente observations anthropologiques recueillies à Hue sur des An-namites du Nord. Bull. Soc. d'anthrop., Par., 1888, 319.

—— Pfeilschlenderhaken? Internat. Arch. f. Ethnog., Leiden, 1888, I, 209-211, ills

—— Wurfstock von Australien. [Rev. in Internat. Arch. f. Ethnog, 1888, I, 196.]

—— Ueber die ethnologische Bedeutung der malaischen Zahnfeilung. Berlin (1887), R. Friedländer und Sohn, 18 pp. mit 20 Figuren in Holzschnitt, 4to.

—— Ueber die Wurfhölzer der Indianer Amerikas. Mittheil. d. anthrop. Gesellsch., Wien, XVII, n. s. VII, pl. iv.

—— Ueber Pfeile aus der Torresstrasse. Internat. Arch. f. Ethnog., Leiden, 1888, I, 173-176.

UJFALVY, CH. E. DE L'influence du milieu sur les peuples de l'Asie centrale. Bull. d. l Soc. d'anthrop., Paris, 3. s., X, 436-457.

—— Nouvelles de la dernière expédition française dans l'Asie centrale. Bull. d. l. Soc. d'anthrop., Paris, 3. s., X, 459, 460.

—— Quelques observations sur les Tadjiks des montagnes, appelés aussi Galtchas. Bull. d. l. Soc. d'anthrop. de Paris, 3. s., IX, 15-43, 1887.

—— Quelques observations sur les peuples du Dardistan. L'Homme, Par., IV, 161-169.

UNDSET, I. Le préhistorique scandinave, ses origines et son développement. Rev. d'anthrop., Par., 3. s., II, 313-332.

UNGERN-STERNBURG, T. Deformirte Schädel aus dem Lande der Taulu, Nordkauka-sus. Verhandl. d. Berl. Gesellsch. f. Anthrop., Berl., 1888, 406-410.

VACCARO, ANGELO. Genesi e funzione delle leggi penali. Ricerche sociologiche. Roma, 1889, 1 vol., pp. 238. [Rev. in Arch. per l'antrop., Firenze (1888), XVIII, 238.]

VANCE. AP. M. A child with a tail. Weekly Med. Rev., St. Louis, 1888, XVIII, 540.

VAN MAUSVELT, C. G Afneming van ligchaamsgewigt in den winter. Nederl. Tijdschr v. Geneesk., Amst., XXIII (2. d.), 465-469.

VARIGNY, H. DE La sélection physiologique. Rev scient., Paris, XXXIX, 449-456.

VARIOT, G, et MORAU. Étude microscopique et expérimentale sur les tatouages européens. Bull. Soc. d'anthrop., Paris, 3. s., X, 730-735.

—— Note sur la Nigritie du chien comparée à celle de l'homme. Bull. Soc. d'an-throp, Par., 3. s., XI (1888), 183-186.

—— Nouveau procédé de destruction de tatouages. Compt. rend. Soc. de biol., Paris, 1888, 8. s., V, 636-638.

VATER. Bei Spandau ausgegrabene Schädel. Verhandl. d. Berl. Gesellsch. f. An-throp., Berl, 1888, 249-253.

VAUVILLE, M. Note sur les sépultures d'une galerie couverte fouillée en septembre 1887, sur la commune de Montigny-l'Engrain, près Vic-sur-Aisne. Bull. d. l. Soc. d'anthrop., Paris, 3. s , x, 710-713.

———— Sépultures à incinérations de l'époque de la pierre polie, sur la commune de Montigny-l'Engrain (Aisne). Bull. Soc. d'anthrop. de Paris, 1888, 3. s., xi, 455-458.

VENN, JOHN. Cambridge Anthropometry. J. Anthrop. Inst. Lond. (1888), xviii, 140-154.

Verhandlungen der Berliner Gesellschaft für Anthropologie, Ethnologie und Urgeschichte. Red. von Rud. Virchow, Berlin, A. Asher & Co. Monthly.

Verhandlungen der anthropologischen Gesellschaft in Wien. See Mittheilungen.

VERNEAU, R. Crânes de l'allée couverte de Montigny-l'Engrain ; la race de furfooz à l'époque des dolmes. Bull. d. l. Soc. d'anthrop., Paris, 3. s., x, 713-725.

———— Instruments en pierre des Îles Canaries. Bull. Soc. d'anthrop., Paris, 3. s., x, 652-656.

———— La taille des anciens habitants des Îles Canaries. Rev. d'anthrop., Paris, 3. s., ii, 641-657.

———— L'industrie de la pierre chez les anciens habitants de l'Archipel Canarien. Rev. d'ethnog., Paris, vi, 361-382.

———— Mission scientifique dans l'Archipel Canarien. Paris (1887), Impr. nationale, 4 pl., 41 figs., 8vo. (Rev. d'ethnog , xvi, 156-162.)

———— On the stature of the ancient inhabitants of the Canary Islands. Revue d'anthrop., Paris (1887), 3. s., vol. ii, p. 16.

———— Rapport sur une mission dans l'Archipel Canarien. Arch. d. missions scient., Paris, 3. s., xiii.

VERRIER, E. Anthropologie, ethnographie et pathologie comparée des Néo-Calédoniens; avenir du métissage dans la colonie. Bull. Soc. d'ethnog., Paris, 2. s., i, 231-240.

———— Ethnographie médicale des peuples de race jaune. J. de méd. de Par., xiii, 735, 1-10 ; xii, 591-612.

———— Ethnographie, nature, histoire et géographie de la lèpre. Bull. Soc. d'ethnog., Paris, 2. s., 5-13, map.

VETH, P. J. Brief aan de Redactie naar aauleiding van Dr. Laugkavel : "Pferde und Naturvölker." [Rev. in Internat. Arch. f. Ethnog., 1888, i, 159-161.]

———— Opmerkingen naar aauleiding van het opstel "Het Hasau-Hosein of Taboetfeest te Benkoeleü." Rev. in Internat. Arch. f. Ethnog., 1888, i, 230-233.

VIANNA, A. L'homme primitif actuel. Rev. scient., Par., xl, 621-629.

VIANNA DE LIMA, A. L'homme selon le transformisme. Paris (1888), Alcan. [Bibl. philos. contemp.] Rev. d'anthrop., 3. s., iii, 477-479.

VIERLING, A. Prähistorische Hügel an der Waldnah und Luhe. Corr.-Bl. d. deutsch· Gesellsch. f. Anthrop., Bruschwg., 1888, xix, 49-51.

VIGNA, C. Importanza fisiologica e terapeutica della musica. Atti d. Cong. d. Soc. freniat. ital., 1887, Milano, 1888, v, 99-105.

VIGNÉ. Les peuplades des rivières du sud de la Sénégambie et les erreurs des ethnographes. Rev. scient., Paris, 1888, xlii, 450-464.

VINSON, JULIEN. Contes et légendes du Caucase, traduits par J. Mourier. Paris, Maisonneuve et Ch. Leclerc, 1888 (iv), 112 pp., in-12°. Rev. de ling.. Par. (1888), xxi, 188-189.

———— Contes populaires recueillis dans la Grande-Lande, le Born, les Petites Landes et le Marensin, par Félix Arnaudin. Paris et Bordeaux, 1887, in-12° de 312 pp. Rev. de ling., Par. (1888), xxi, 190.

———— De la langue des Formosans. Rev. de ling., Par. (1888), xxi, 191-197.

———— Dupleix, ses expéditions et ses projets. par H. Castonnet des Fosses. Paris, Challamel et Cie, 1888. 68 pp. in-8vo. Rev. de ling., Par. (1888), xxi, 364.

Vinson, Julien. Le folk-lore de l'île Maurice, par C. Boissac. Paris, Maissonneuve et Ch. Leclerc (les littératures populaires de toutes les nations, t. xxvii), (viii), xix. 467 pp. in-12mo. Rev. de ling., Paris (1888), xxi, 189-1890.

—— Les étapes d'un petit algérien dans la province d'Oran, par Jules Renard. Paris, Hachette et Cⁱᵉ, 1888, pet. iv, 228 pp. et 40 grav. in-8vo. Rev. de ling., Par. (1888), xxi, 284.

—— Les religions actuelles, leurs doctrines, leur évolution, leur histoire. Paris, Delahaye, 600 pp., 8vo. [Bibl. Anthrop.]

—— Les religions actuelles, leurs doctrines, leur évolution, leur histoire, par Julien Vinson. Paris, Delahaye et Lecrosnier, 1888, viii-xxiv, 624 pp., in-8vo. Rev. de ling., Par. (1888), xxi, 361-364.

—— Manuel algérien, grammaire, chrestomathie et lexique, par A. Mouliéras. Paris, 1888, viii, 288 p. in-8vo. Rev. de ling., Par. (1888), xxi, 283.

—— Manuel de langue kabyle (dialecte zouaoua), par René Basset. Paris, 1887, xvi, 88-70 pp. in-8vo. Rev. de ling., Par. (1888), xxi, 281-283.

—— Nyare bidrage till kænnedom om de svenska landsmaolen ock svenskt folklif, 1886-1888. Rev. de ling., Par. (1888), xxi, 284, 285.

—— Le spiritisme (fakirisme occidental), par le docteur Paul Gibier. Paris, O. Doin, 1887 (iv), 398 pp. in-12mo. Rev. de ling., Par. (1888), xxi, 75-87.

—— Suomalais-ugrilaisen seuran aikakauskirja, Journal de la Société Finno-Ongrienne, t. iii et iv. Helsingfors, 1888, iii, iv, 175 pp.; iv, xxx, 352 pp. Rev. de ling.,,Par. (1888), xxi, 285.

—— Un vieux texte basque du xviiᵉ siècle. Rev. de ling , Par. (1888), xxi, 57-63.

Virchow, R. Alte Bauerhäuser in Deutschland und der Schweiz. Verhandl. d. Berl. Gesellsch. f. Anthrop.. Berl., 1888, 297-305.

—— Anthropologie Aegyptens. Cor.-Bl. d. deutsch. Gesellsch. f. Anthrop., Brnschwg., 1888, xix, 105-112.

—— Chemische Untersuchung von altägyptischer Augenschwärze. Verhandl. d. Berl. Gesellsch. f Anthrop., Berl., 1888, 340.

—— Deformirter Schädel aus dem Lande der Taulu, Nordkaukasus. Verhandl. d. Berl. Gesellsch. f. Anthrop., Berl., 1888, 406-410.

—— Die menschlichen Ueberreste aus der Bilsteiner Höhle bei Warstein in Westfalen. Verhandl. d. Berl. Gesellsch. f. Anthrop., Berl., 1888, 335.

—— Land und Leute malten und neuen Aegypten. Berlin, 1888. Opuscolo Dalle Verhandl. d. Ges. f. Erdkunde. [Rev. in Arch. l'anthrop., Firenze (1888), xviii, 283.]

—— Metallcimer (Mörser) von Lübtow bei Pyritz, Pommern. Verhandl. d. Berl-Gesellsch. f. Anthrop., Berl., 1888, 338-340.

—— Schädel von Dualla von Kamerun. Verhandl. d. Berl. Gesellsch. f. Anthrop., Berl., 331-334.

—— Sendung aus Surinam. Verhandl. d. Berl. Gesellsch. f. Anthrop., Berl., 1888, 405, 1 pl.

—— Ueber den Transformismus. Arch. f. Anthrop , Brnschwg. (1888), xviii, 1-14.

—— Vorhistorische Zeit Aegyptens. Verhandl. d. Berl. Gesellsch. f. Anthrop., Berl., 1888, 344-394.

—— Wetzmarken und Näpfchen an altägyptischen Tempeln. Verhandl. d. Berl. Gesellsch. f. Anthrop.. Berl., 1888, 214-217.

Virey, Ph. Études sur le papyrus Prisse, le livre de Kaquimna et les leçons de Ptah-Hotep. Bull. d. l'École d. Hautes Études, No. 70. Paris, Vieweg, 1887, br. 8vo. Volkskunde. Ghent. Vol. i, in 1888.

Wahl, M. Alger. Rev. de l'Afrique française, 43-52, 83-91, 115-122, 1887, fig.

—— Les congrégations dans l'Islam. Rev. de l'Afrique française, 1887, 286-292.

Wace, C. Staniland. Origin of Totemism. Nature, xxxvi, 599.

WACE, C. STANILAND. The primitive human horde. J. Anthrop. Inst., Lond. (1888), XVII, 276-282; XVIII, 99.

WALDEYER. Das Rückenmark des Gorilla verglichen mit dem des Menschen. Cor.-Bl. d. deutsch. Gesellsch. f. Anthrop., etc., Brnschwg., 1888, XIX, 112.

WALDT, A. Die Kulturgegenstände der Golden und Giljaken. Internat. Arch. f. Ethnol., Leiden, I, 92-107, 2 pl.

WALCER, F. A. Oriental entomology. J. Trans. of the Victoria Inst., Lond. (1888), XXII, 191-225.

WALLACE, ALFRED RUSSEL. Oceanic Islands. Bull. Am. Geog. Soc., XIX, 1-21.

—— The antiquity of man in North America. Nineteenth Cent., Lond., XXII, 667-679.

WALLACH, H. The Guanchos. J. Anthrop. Inst., Lond., XVII, 158-165.

WARD, LESTER F. Our better halves. Forum, N. Y. (1888), VI, 266-275.

WARD, WM. HAYES, and A. P. FROTHINGHAM. Unpublished and imperfectly published Hittite monuments. Am. J. Arch., III, 62-69.

WARNER, AMOS G. Three phases of cooperation in the West. Am. Economic Assoc., II, No. 1, March.

—— C. D. Creating criminals. Forum, N. Y. (1888), VI, 235-240.

—— F. Methods of examining children in school as to their development and condition of brain. Brit. Med. J., Lond. (1888), II, 483.

WARREN, J. J. Les idées philosophiques et religieuses des Jaïnas, trad. du hollandais par J. Pointet. Ann. du Musée Guimet, X, 323-411.

Was America known to Europeans before Columbus? [Rev. in Am. Antiquar, Mendon, Ill. (1888), X, 328.]

WATTEVILLE, A. DE. Sleep and its counterfeits. Pop. Sc. Month., XXXI, 597-608, 1887.

WATT, G. The aboriginal tribes of Manipur. J. Anthrop. Inst., Lond., XVI, 346-370.

WEBER, F. On melody in speech. Pop. Sc. Month., XXX, 778-788, 1887.

WEBER, FR. Die Besiedlung des Alpengebietes zwischen Inn und Lech und des Innthales in vorgeschichtlicher Zeit. Beitr. z. Anthrop.. München (1888), VIII, 22-36.

WEIGERT, C. Neuere Vererbungstheorien. Schmidt's Jahrb., Leipz., CCXV, 89; 193.

WEIR, T. S. Note on sacrifices in India as a means of averting epidemics. J. Anthrop. Soc., Bombay, I, 35-39.

WEISBACH, A. Körpermessungen in der Bukowina. Mitth. d. anthrop. Gesellsch. in Wien, 1888, n. F. VIII [Sitzungsb., 83.]

WELCCER, H. Cribra orbitalia. Arch. f. Anthrop., Brnschwg., XVII, 1-18, pl. Zur Kritik des Schillerschädels, id., 19-60, 3 pl.

WELLS, DAVID A. The economic disturbances since 1873. Pop. Sc. Month., XXXII, 1-17, 433-451, 577-597, 1887.

WIEDEMANN, A. Maâ, déesse de la vérité, et son rôle dans le Panthéon égyptien. Ann. du Musée Guimet, X, 550-573, 1887.

WILBRAND, HERMANN. Die Seelenblindheit als Herdescheinung und ihre Beziehungen zur Homonymen Hemianopsie zur Alexie und Agraphie. Wiesbaden, 192, 1887, 8vo. (Rev. Am. J. Psychol., I, 183, 184.)

WILCEN, G. A. Lhamanism among the people of the Indian Archipelago. La Haye: Nyhoff, 71 pp., 8vo. See Rev. de l'Hist. des religions, XVI, 123.

—— Ueber das Haaropfer und einige andere Traugebräuche bei den Völkern Indoneseins. Rev. Colon. Internat., and separate by T. H. de Bussy, Amsterdam, VI, 71 pp., 8vo.

WILCINS W. J. Modern Hinduism. Being an account of the religion and life of the Hindus in Northern India. London (1887), 488 pp., 8vo.

WILSON, ANDREW. Studies in life and sense. London: Chatto & Windus, 1887; Nature, XXXVI, 316.

WILSON, THOMAS. Archæology in Western Europe. Am. Antiquarian, IX, 335-342.

Wilson, Thomas. Epitome of prehistoric archæology in Western Europe. [Extr. Am. Antiquarian, Nov., 1887], 52 pp., 8vo.

―――― Survival of the Stone Age. Am. Antiquar., Mendon, Ill. (1888), x, 379, 380.

―――― Description of exhibit made by the department of prehistoric anthropology in the National Museum at the Ohio Valley and Central States Exposition in Cincinnati, Ohio, 1888, pp. 33.

―――― Megalithic monuments of Brittany. American Naturalist, July, 1888. [Rev. in Arch. per l' antrop., Firenze (1888), xviii, 278, 279.]

Winsor, Justin. Narrative and critical history of America. Boston: Houghton, Mifflin & Co. 7 vols., 8vo. Vols. v and vi in 1887, vol. vii in 1888, and vol. i in 1889.

Winternitz, M. Der Sarpabali, ein altindischer Schlagencult. Mitth. d. anthrop. Gesellsch. in Wein, 1888, n. F., viii, 25-52.

Witter, G. F. Heredity. Rep. Bd. Health Wisconsin, Madison, x, 167-181.

Woldt, A. Die Kultusgegenstande der Golden und Giljaken. Internat. Arch. f. Ethnog., i, 92-107.

Wolfe, H. K. Untersuchungen über das Tongedächtniss. Rev. in Am. Jour. of Psychology, Baltimore, i, 185, 186.

Wolf, Ludwig. Volksstämme Central-Afrika's. [Paper read before the Berlin Anthrop. Soc., Dec., 1886.]

Woodford, C. M. Paper on the Solomon Islands. Roy. Geog. Soc., 1886-'7; Nature, xxxvii, 546.

Worsaae, J. J. A. The pre-history of the North. translated by T. and F. Moreland Simpson. (London: Trübner & Co , 1886.) [Rev. in Nature, xxxvi, 79.]

Wratislaw, A. H. The lame fox. The Folk-Lore Jour., Lond. (1888), vi, pt. iv, 252-262.

Wright, Caroline R. Worship of the Dervishes in Cairo, Egypt. Christian Advocate, N. Y., 1888 (July), p. 491.

Wright, G F. Importance of the study of archæology in Ohio. Ohio Archæol. and Hist. Quart., i, 55-60.

―――― The relation of the Glacial period to the archæology of Ohio. Ohio Archæol and Hist. Quart., i, 174-186. Also: Preglacial Man in Ohio, 257-259.

Wundt, W. Grundzüge der physiologischen Psychologie. 2 Bände. Leipzig (1887), Engelmann, 210 Holzschn., 8vo

―――― Ueber Ziele und Wege der Völkerpsychologie. Rev. in Am. Jour. of Psychology, Baltimore, i, 193, 194.

Wzn, C. M. Pleyte. Het ethn. Mus. v. h. Kon. Gen. Natura Artis Magistra te Amsterdam. Rev. in Internat. Arch. f. Ethnog., 1888, i, 28, 29.

Youferow, Wl. Dolmens dans la Russie méridionale. Bull. Soc. d'ethnog., Paris, 2. s., 13-19.

Yvernes, E. Des éléments essentiels qui doivent figurer dans la statistique criminelle et des moyens de les rendre comparables. Bull. de l'Inst. internat. de Statist., Rome, 1888, iii, 71-79.

―――― Le mélange des races qui a produit la nationalité russe actuelle. iv, 20, 21.

Zaborowski. Les peuples préhistoriques et les peuples actuels du Caucase. Rev. scient., Par., xl, 811-815.

Zampa, Raffaello. Il tipo umbro. Arch. per l' antrop., Firenze (1888), xviii, 175-197.

Ziesberger, David. Essay of an Onondaga grammar, or a short introduction to learn the Onondaga Almaqua tongue. Penn. Mag. of Hist. and Biog., Phila. (1888), xii, 65-75.

Zeisberger's Indian Dictionary. English, German, Iroquois; the Onondaga and Algonkin; the Delaware. Printed from the original manuscript in Harvard College Library. Cambridge: John Wilson & Son, Publishers.

Zeitschrift für Ethnologie. Organ der Berliner Gesellschaft für Anthropologie, Ethnologie und Urgeschichte. Berlin: A. Asher & Co., vol. XIX in 1887; vol. XX in 1888. Zeitschrift für Volkskunde, Leipzig. Founded at the end of 1888. Zeitschrift für Völkerpsychologie und Sprachwissenschaft, Leipzig.

ZELENSCI, M. [Scientific method of ascertaining weight of body (of infants), and its importance in indicating health or diseased organism.] Trudi Obsh. Russk. vrach. v Moskve, ii, 1st ed., 18–29.

ZOJA, G. Misure della forza muscolare dell' uomo. Arch. per l' antrop., Firenze, XVII, 43–51.

——— Intorno al mucrone dell' angolo della mandibola del Sandifort. Arch. per l' antrop., Firenze (1888), XVIII, 169–173.

MISCELLANEOUS PAPERS.

CHRONOLOGY OF THE HUMAN PERIOD.*

By J. WOODBRIDGE DAVIS.

The earliest exact date we have is that of the victory of Corœbus, the runner, at the Olympian festival, July 21, B. C. 776. Beyond this, uncertainty grows from years into decades and from decades into centuries until, in the earliest existing traditions, it becomes supreme; and yet man's history is not half told.

Of the vast preceding ages from which no word has come, the chronology is necessarily based upon traces of the events themselves. So the best results we can expect from an exploration of this dark region of time are a meager knowledge of events, a fairly accurate knowledge of successions, and a very inaccurate knowledge of durations.

There is however an artificial difficulty in the way of the student of archæology, namely, the several scales used in the division of prehistoric time. A like difficulty pertaining to the era of written records has been overcome by means of formulæ for the translation of dates from one scale to another. But no systematic attempt seems to have been made to correlate the various scales applied to the measurement of the older Quaternary.

For instance, the antiquity of a certain "find" is rated by reference to the geological event then taking place; of another, according to a scale indicated by the successive disappearances of wild animals from a particular district. Other scales are based upon the progress in human arts and customs, the successive domestication of animals, etc. Each author relies especially upon one or two of these modes of reckoning with occasional references to some of the others. Except to experts, this is confusing.

On this account the chart appended was prepared for private use. Here it is attempted to exhibit the principal scales in their chronological inter-relations. This was accomplished by collecting and arranging all the cross-references occurring in many of the best works, chiefly those of Worsaae, Morlot, Gastaldi, Lartet and Christie, Lubbock, Lyell and Dawkins.

(*From the School of Mines Quarterly, No. 4, vol. x.)

HUMAN CHRONOLOGY. (With reference to Europe).

	GEOLOGICAL DATA.			CIVILIZATION DATA.			
Periods.	Events.	Extinct or emigrated mammalia. (Latest abundant occurrence.)	Depots. (Earliest examples.)	Implements.	Interments.	Husbandry, etc.	Architecture.
Historic, About 1000 B. C.	Alluvium,		Books, Inscriptions, Traditions.	Steel (hardened iron), Iron.	Cumbent.	Agriculture.	Refined architecture from Asia and Africa.
Prehistoric.	Denud'ats, ..ke deposits, Deltas, Glacial moraines, Peat bogs, Raised beaches, Sunken beaches	Aurochs. Urus.	Existing tumuli, Lake deposits, Deltas, Ancient beaches, Moraines, Peat-bogs. Coast finds, Shell mounds.	Bronze (hardened copper), (No trace of copper age in Europe). Polished stone or Neolithic. Unpolished stone.	By cremation. In sitting posture.	Cattle, Horses, Utensils, etc. No agriculture, Dog domesticated, First traces of pottery.	Circular wooden huts, Pile dwellings, Picts houses, Pits, Wheems, Cromlechs, Circles, Cairns, Tumuli.
Late pleistocene (terraces).	Land elevation. Cold climate.	Reindeer, Irish elk.	Caves and	Rudely shaped stone.		No agriculture and	Caves.
Mid-pleistocene (Champlain).	Land depression. Warm climate.	Hippopotamus, Woolly-haired rhinoceros, Mammoth.	River drifts.	A few simple flint flakes.		No domestic animals.	
Early pleistocene (glacial).	Land elevation	Cave lions. Hyena. Cave bear.					

Palæolithic (label spanning implements)

Traces of man's existence uncertain.

Recent — Post-pleiocene — Quaternary

The chart explains itself. All the items occurring together in one column between two horizontal lines, represent the characteristics of the period embraced by those lines. It has been found useful for determining the relation in time of events originally referred to different scales, and it also serves to divide the human period into smaller parts than can any single scale.

The chart relates to Europe only, the most thoroughly investigated of the continents. Even so, its divisions are not contemporaneous for all that land. The dawn of written history in Britain breaks eight or nine centuries after that of Greece. The polished stone and the bronze ages must have rolled over Europe in slowly moving waves. The advancement of the other arts and the domestication of animals similarly spread from men to men, retarded by mountain chains and salty channels. But if these scales were applied to America, the later stone age alone must be shifted downward at least five thousand years.

WERE THE OSAGES MOUND BUILDERS?

By Dr. J. F. SNYDER, *Virginia, Cass County, Illinois.*

A reported instance of mound building by the Osage Indians, near the close of the last century, has been cited by numerous writers on American ethnology in proof of the otherwise well-authenticated fact that the custom of erecting mounds over their distinguished dead was practiced by some of our Indian tribes down to comparatively recent times. The instance referred to was related by Dr. Beck, in his "Gazetteer of Missouri and Illinois." When writing of the Osage River he says: "Ancient works exist on this river as elsewhere. The remains of mounds and fortifications are almost everywhere to be seen. One of the largest mounds in this country has been thrown up on this stream, within the last thirty or forty years, by the Osages, near the great Osage village, in honor of one of their deceased chiefs. This fact proves conclusively the original object of these mounds, and refutes the theory that they must necessarily have been erected by a race of men more civilized than the present tribes of Indians." *

This was written in 1822. In the fall of 1834, Mr. Featherstonhaugh, the noted English geologist, when in the vicinity of St. Louis, Missouri, heard a similar statement in regard to the erection of a large mound, by the Osages, in the same locality, which he relates as follows: "We therefore walked into the country a mile and a half, to a Major Sibley's, to whom I had a letter. - - - He had resided many years amongst the western Indians as agent of the United States, and had been one of the commissioners appointed to lay out the Traders' Road to Santa Fé, in New Mexico. We soon got into conversation about the lofty mounds I had seen, when he stated that an ancient chief of the Osage Indians (corrupted by the French from Whashash) informed him, whilst he was a resident amongst them, that a large conical mound (which he, Major Sibley, was in the habit of seeing every day whilst he resided amongst them) was constructed when he was a boy. That a chief of his nation, who was a distinguished warrior, and greatly beloved by the Indians, and who was called Jean Defoe by the French, unexpectedly

---

* A Gazetteer of the States of Illinois and Missouri. By Lewis C. Beck. Albany N. Y., 1823, p. 308.

died whilst all the men of his tribe were hunting in a distant country. His friends buried him in the usual manner, with his weapons, his earthen pot, and the usual accompaniments, and raised a small mound over his remains. When the nation returned from the hunt this mound was enlarged at intervals, every man assisting to carry materials, and thus the accumulation of earth went on for a long period until it reached its present height, when they dressed it off at the top to a conical form. The old chief further said that he had been informed and believed that all the mounds had a similar origin.."*

It is altogether probable that these two accounts relate to the same mound, and that Dr. Beck's source of information regarding it is the same as Mr. Featherstonhaugh's. The "ancient chief" may have purposely imposed upon Major Sibley's credulity in this matter: at any rate his reliability as a historian of his people is somewhat shaken by his further statement that "the tradition had been steadily transmitted • down from their ancestors; that the Whashash (Osages) had originally emigrated from the east in great numbers, the population being too dense for their hunting-grounds. He described the forks of the Allegheny and Monongahela Rivers, and the Falls of the Ohio, where they had dwelt some time, and where large bands had separated from them, and distributed themselves in the surrounding country, etc." † The Osages, it is well known, are a branch of the Dakotas, and migrated to Missouri from the north, or northwest; and perhaps the only members of that tribe who have at any time visited the headwaters of the Ohio were the few who joined the force that defeated General Braddock in 1755, and the peaceful delegations that have since visited Washington City.

The first mention of the Osages in history is by Father Marquette, who heard of them when descending the Mississippi in 1673; and in his map of the regions discovered by him he locates them as the "Ouchage." on the Missouri River, about the present site of Jefferson City. We have then no definite account of these Indians until 1719, when Du Tissenet, a young Canadian-Frenchman, was sent with a party, by M. DeBienville, then -governor of Louisiana, to explore the western wilderness in search of ores and precious metals. Du Tissenet's expedition set out from Kaskaskia, and, traversing southern Missouri, followed the Osage River—which he so named—to its northwestern sources in Kansas. He visited the Osages at their "Great Village" near the confluence of the Little Osage and the Marmiton, in what is now Vernon County, in Missouri, and which was then the central point of their country. During the next year, 1720, Renault, with his lieutenant, La Motte, and party, including five hundred negro slaves, arrived at Fort Chartres, and at once sent out exploring parties in all directions in

---

*Excursion through the Slave States, etc. By G. W. Featherstonhaugh, F. R. S., F. G. S., Two vols., London, 1844, vol. I, pp. 286, 287.

† *Ibid*, pages 287, 288.

quest of precious ores. They opened lead mines in the vicinity of Potosi, at Mine a Renault and Mine La Motte, which have been, more or less, in operation to the present day; and established trading posts and intimate commercial relations with the Osages. In 1806 Lieutenant Pike, on his expedition to the mountains, found the Osages at their "Great" and "Little" villages, where they had entertained Du Tissenet eighty-seven years before; both travelers locating the larger or main village in what is now Blue Mound Township, Vernon County, Missouri. Several years before Lieutenant Pike's visit—in 1787—Pierre Chouteau had established, near the Great Village, a fortified trading post which he named Fort Carondelet in honor of the Baron De Carondelet.

The topographical features of the country bordering the Osage River are in many respects very peculiar and strangely attractive. In the greater part of its course the river has cut its way through ledges of massive magnesian limestone which tower above the beautiful stream in domes and terraces and knobs that seem to have been designed by skillful architects. Professor Swallow says of these bluffs, about the junction of the Niangua and Linn Creek with the Osage, they "slope back into knobs and ridges, which are frequently surrounded by numerous natural terraces so regular and uniform that they appear like the work of human hands. These terraces are formed by the decomposition of the strata of magnesian limestone which form the bluffs."[*] Farther back from the river, remarks the same writer, "The prairie of this region is characterized by what are called knobs or mounds; they are somewhat variable in size and form, but usually present the appearance of a truncated cone. The tops of these mounds are usually flat, and covered by a thin soil, underlaid by a durable stratum of sandstone or limestone, which crops out on all sides near the top, prevents the wearing away of the upper edges, and preserves the well defined angle between the top and sides; while the stratum of shale or clay, which forms the lower part, is easily decomposed and carried away by aqueous agencies. The sides rise with a gentle declivity, at first, but become more and more abrupt until they are nearly perpendicular at the top. The most of these mounds belong to the coal measures; but those near Bolivar are in the Chemung group, the upper beds of the vermicular sandstone and shales forming the top, and the underlying shales the lower part of them."[†] Of the mounds mentioned by Professor Swallow, near Bolivar, one of the largest was almost in sight at my front door. It stood, in bold relief, near the middle of a cultivated field, a truncated pyramid, 20 feet high, with level top 20 by 50 feet in dimensions, and with angles and sides true

---

[*] Geological Report of the Southwest Branch, etc., by G. C. Swallow, State geologist, St. Louis, Mo., 1859, p. 22.

[†] First and second reports of the Geological Survey of Missouri, by G. C. Swallow, State geologist, Jefferson City, 1855.

and regular; the complete duplicate *in appearance* of many artificial mounds to be seen east of the Mississippi.*

The region at the head of the Osage River, particularly the district lying between its main branches, the Marais des Cygnes and the Little Osage, is mostly prairie, rising in graceful undulations and ridges, and isolated conical mounds, with broad valleys between, eroded by aqueous or glacial action, combining in landscapes of charming interest and beauty.

Prof. G. C. Broadhead, late State geologist of Missouri, in treating of the geology of Vernon County, remarks: "It is here diversified by clusters of mounds, reaching more than 100 feet above the general surface of the prairie. Blue Mound is 150 feet high, and can be seen for a long distance. Timbered Hill, near the mouth of Marmaton and Little Osage is a round, isolated mound, 170 feet above the Marmaton, and over 100 feet above the surrounding plain. Being several miles from other marked elevations, it is seen for many miles off. North of the Little Osage a series of mounds extends east and west along the county line at an elevation of over 100 feet above the gently stretching valley at their base. - - - Further west, in range 32, we find the mounds rising still higher. These mounds continue on southward through the county, interrupted sometimes for several miles by the streams. From Moundville a high ridge or series of mounds connected, trends off to the south line of the county, rising near the northern and middle line to 140 feet above the lower valleys, or 80 to 100 feet above Moundville Valley. - - - The occasional occurrence of these mounds gives a charming variety to the landscape. Many of them can be seen at a long distance, and from their summits the views are often very fine. - - - Undoubtedly this county has been subjected to glacial agency at some former period of time. Its results may be seen in isolated mounds and deep valleys between. The amount of erosion must have been of great force and of long continuance, if we view the mounds and long stretches of distance from one to the other. When protected by the upper series of limestones, the erosion was not complete; but if these limestones were much broken, or entirely absent, leaving the sandstones exposed, the waters would rush down with resistless force, and bear away all the softer material."†

In a foot-note on page 82 of his exhaustive monograph on "The Mounds of the Mississippi Valley Historically Considered," Prof. Lucien Carr, in discussing the trustworthiness of a book purporting to have been written by one J. D. Hunter, ("Memoirs of a Captivity," etc., London, 1828,) remarks: "To go no further than the instances quoted in the text, we find undoubted evidence that the Osages have, within the present century, built both stone heaps and burial mounds."

---

* These dimensions are not exact, but given from memory, the writer not having seen the mound since 1860.

† Report of the Geological Survey of the State of Missouri, Garland C. Broadhead, State geologist, Jefferson City, 1874, pp. 120, 121.

So far as history can aid us in tracing the Osages we are satisfied that at the period of Marquette's descent of the Mississippi, in 1673, they occupied one or both banks of the Missouri River, at and above the mouth of the Osage; and that they established the central villages of their tribe at the head of the Osage River about the year 1700, or a few years before that date, and remained there until their removal, in 1826, farther west. That, in that time, they erected stone heaps occasionally over the graves of their dead—to preserve the bodies from the ravages of wild beasts—is true, for some of the stone heaps, attesting the fact, are still to be seen there. But they built no earthen mounds. In all the region of their occupancy of the immediate valley of the Osage River there is not an artificial mound of earth to be found ; and it is not reasonable to suppose that such monuments, if erected, should in the lapse of less than a century have so completely disappeared. Professor Broadhead, who carefully explored the entire valley of the Osage in prosecuting the geological survey of Missouri, in a private letter replying to my inquiries, says: " I have seen no artificial sepulchral mounds on the Osage River. With the exception of pictographs, on the rocks, about 25 miles above its mouth, I found but few, if any, prehistoric remains anywhere on that river."

Robert I. Holcombe, esq., who ranks little below Parkman in American historical research, after spending many months at or near the site of the "Great Osage village," when writing of that locality in his " History of Vernon County, Missouri," says: "It does not seem that the mysterious race of beings termed the Mound Builders ever dwelt here in any considerable numbers or for any considerable period. But few traces of their occupation remain, if they ever existed. In some parts of the county there are a few small elevations resembling the sepulchral mounds of the Mound Builders; but it can not be asserted that they are not natural. If any examination has been made, it has not disclosed any noteworthy archæological specimens, and few, if any, flint arrow-heads, lance heads, stone axes, or fragments of pottery have been found."[*]   After calling Mr. Holcombe's attention specially to this branch of inquiry he informed me, in the course of our correspondence, that in all the region he had examined he had not seen an artificial earthen mound; and had met but few, if any, evidences of a pre existent "stone age." Of the many residents on and near the Osage, from its mouth to its sources, to whom I have addressed my inquiries, not one has seen an artificial earthern mound there, and but few have found aboriginal stone implements of any description in that region. All agree that such evidences of prehistoric occupancy are almost totally absent.

E. B. Morerod, M. D., an old resident of Vernon County, Missouri, an intelligent and scholarly man, who had devoted much time and thought to the study of American history and antiquities, and who per-

---

[*] History of Vernon County, Missouri. St. Louis. Brown & Co. 1887, pp. 87, 88.

sonally inspected every locality on the upper Osage that had been inhabited by the Osage Indians, with the view of collecting reliable materials for his "Centennial History of Vernon County" (published in 1876), and to secure, if possible, relics of ancient Indian art for the Philadelphia Exposition of that year, in writing to me says: "As far as my knowledge extends there are but very few evidences of prehistoric man existing in Vernon County. Excepting a few flint arrow-points, I do not know of a stone implement of any kind, neither grooved ax, celt, or ornament, ever having been found here. Nor is there an artificial sepulchral mound in our county, though we have many magnificent natural mounds of geological origin. Absence of Indian burials here has often suggested to my mind the query, what did the Osages do with their dead? We know that they were a numerous tribe, and that this district was the central point of their territory for nearly, or quite, a century and a quarter; yet although I have searched all over the sites of the Big and Little Osage villages, and in every direction throughout the county, I have failed to find any indication of Indian burying grounds, or any isolated graves that could, with any degree of certainty, be attributed to the Indians. I am therefore of the opinion that with the exception of their distinguished men, these Indians cremated their dead. In my search for Indian relics here, in 1876, all that I found were brass and pewter ornaments, glass beads, fragments of gun flint-locks, broken iron and copper utensils, and crockery of French make. There are no Indian graves here on the crest of our ridges and bluffs, or on the top of our natural mounds, as is the case elsewhere throughout the Mississippi Valley, with but one known exception. A very noted chief of the Osages, named Pah-hus kah, or Pawhuska, but called by the early French "Cheveux Blanche," said to have been killed in a skirmish with the whites, was buried on the top of the big Blue Mound, and over his grave a large stone heap was erected by his people. Dr. Badger, an old settler here, says that on his arrival, in 1844, this stone heap was a very conspicuous landmark and could be seen from a great distance. At that time it was 8 or 9 feet high and about the same in diameter at its base. When I first saw it, in 1867, there was still a portion of it plainly to be seen from the prairie in all directions; but in 1876 there was not a vestige of it remaining."

Of the death and burial of this chief Mr. Holcombe says, "The exact date of the death of old White Hair can not here be given. He died at his village in the northern part of this county, however, and was buried on the summit of Blue Mound, in a stone sepulcher made for the occasion. It is probable that this was about the year 1824. His grave was afterward broken into by white vandals in search of treasure."[*]

To the foregoing statements it may not be inappropriate to add the results of my own personal observations. During my residence of eight years in southwestern Missouri, 1853–1861, I traversed the entire valley

---

[*] History of Vernon County, Missouri, p. 142.

of the Osage River, from its junction with the Missouri to the extreme heads of the Little Osage and of the Marais des Cygnes, and was familiar with its entire southern water-shed west of the Niangua. And, though always a persistent relic hunter, I never found, or saw, or heard of having been found by others, in that time, or since, in all that region, exceeding a dozen flint arrow-points, and not one stone ax, or celt, or other implement in stone, or ornament of bone or shell, or any fragments of Indian pottery. The only burials presumably Indian I met with were on the east bank of Sac River, near the village of Orleans, in Polk County, Missouri. The perpendicular rocky cliff rises from the river bottom at that place 75 or 80 feet, and is capped with shelly subcarboniferous limestone, overgrown with briars and stunted bushes. On the verge of this precipice I found, in 1853, five small cairns a few feet from each other, constructed of rough stones rudely laid up, in dimensions 3½ feet high and 3 or 4 feet in diameter. On opening them each was found to contain the fragments of a single human skeleton, much decayed, and broken in small pieces by the falling in of the loose stone covering. From the relative position of the bones, I inferred that the body had been placed upon the bare rock, in a squatting position, with the face to the west overlooking the river, and that the broken rocks of the surface had been piled up around it to protect it from destruction by wolves and vultures. The only work of art I discovered in or about the five stone heaps was a well-worn gun-flint with one of the skeletons. I saw no artificial earthen mounds there of any description.

In treating specially of the history of Blue Mound Township, Mr. Holcombe says on page 539 of his " History of Vernon County:" "In many other graves in the mound [Blue Mound] there have been found mingled with human bones tomahawks, knives, arrow-points, shell implements and ornaments, bone ear rings, beads of various materials, sizes, and shapes, and other curious articles. Some of these relics are apparently of such antiquity as to lead almost to the thought that the graves containing them may be those of the Mound Builders, or of some other prehistoric race; but this is not at all probable. The graves are undoubtedly those of Osages, who, as is well known, were in this country as early at least as the year 1700."

I have not learned Mr. Holcombe's authority for the statement he makes in regard to the discovery of " arrow-points, shell implements, and ornaments, bone ear-rings," etc., found in the graves on Blue Mound. My investigations have failed to verify it. By persons who have resided in that immediate vicinity at an early day I am informed that in years past, quite a number of graves were distinctly seen on the slopes of the Blue Mound; but as in dimensions, construction, and relative position they exhibited the usual characteristics of an ordinary cemetery, and as none of them were opened to determine the question,

H. Mis. 142——38

it was not known whether they inclosed the remains of Indians or white persons. And as to the relics, it is now not known that any of them were actually found in the graves; but they were found on the surface of the ground there, and subsequently turned up *by* the plow about the base of the mound, as well as about the sites of the Big and Little Osage villages—as Dr. Morerod states—and are to this day occasionally found there. But the "tomahawks" are made of iron, and the ear-rings of brass; and if any implements or ornaments of bone or shell have been found associated with them, the reasonable conclusion is that they, too, were of French or English manufacture.

Systematic investigation by adepts may yet discover the mortuary customs of the Osages. Their cemeteries have perhaps not yet been found. They died, of course, but as yet we are ignorant of the disposition of their corpses. The suggestion of Dr. Morerod that they practised cremation is scarcely tenable, for the negative reasons that no mention of such an extraordinary custom is made by Dr. Tissenet, Rénault, or Lieutenant Pike; and that none of the crematories, or ancient fire-hearths ("altars"), have yet been found in the original Osage territory. In the absence of more accurate knowledge upon this point, it is not a violent presumption that these Indians—as the Pawnees, Dakotas, and other tribes of the plains have since been accustomed to do—placed their dead upon pole-scaffolds on the prairies, and in the branches of trees in the woods, as their final disposition, where the remains decayed, and in time were dispersed by the elements.

Hunter, in his "Captivity," p. 300, says, of the Osages, "at or soon after burial, they cover the grave with stones, and for years after occasionally resort to it, and mourn over or recount the merits and virtues of its silent tenant." This was not perhaps their general custom; but, in regard to the burial of Old White Hair, is strictly true. Mr. Holcombe confirms it in his statement: "For many years up to 1870 the Osages made annual pilgrimages to the site of their ancient towns in this county, and of the graves of their ancestors and the tomb of the renowned chieftain, Pawhuska, on Blue Mound. Gathering about the mighty mound containing the ashes of their progenitors, they called to mind their virtues and lifting up their voices wept loudly and bitterly. Many citizens of the county have often heard them at their lamentations. The Osages themselves called the Blue Mound the "Crying Mound" because it was to them a place of mourning and weeping."* I have seen it nowhere stated that the Osages conducted their lamentations at any other locality excepting the Blue Mound, which towered above their principal village; and this fact alone is a strong basis for for the supposition that about the apex of this majestic natural elevation these Indians interred all of their distinguished chiefs; thus disposing of them, when dead, and of their common people's corpses by different methods. We know that old White Hair was buried there,

---

* History of Vernon County, pp. 142, 143.

and it is reasonably certain that this was the mound pointed out to Major Sibley, by the "old Chief," as the burial place of "Jean Defoe." *

The singular absence of stone and bone implements in the valley of the Osage can only be explained by the hypothesis that prior to its occupancy by the Osage Indians it was a neutral ground, only occasionally visited by hunting parties of Indians residing on the Missouri, to the north, and on the Arkansas, to the south; in both of which localities evidences of long-continued tenancy before the knowledge of metals are quite abundant. It is altogether probable, too, that when the Osages abandoned their territory on the Missouri and removed to the headwaters of the Osage River—about the close of the seventeenth century—they had secured fire-arms and European implements and utensils, and had adopted many of the methods of life of their French visitors.†

The manners, customs, and practices of these Indians before their migration to the mounds and streams of Vernon County can now only be conjectured; but there is no reason to doubt that in every respect they were identical with those of other pre-Columbian Indians of the Northwest. We are assured, however, that after that event in their history they no longer employed stone as a material for weapons and tools; and they erected no mounds of earth as monuments over their dead, or for any other purpose.

Dr. Beck, author of the "Gazetteer" before mentioned, may have inspected the Osage River personally before he published the statement that "Ancient works exist on this river, as elsewhere," and that " remains of fortifications and mounds are almost everywhere to be seen" there. And, if he did, it is not astonishing that he was led into such an error upon viewing the beautiful, faultless domes and terraces carved upon the great rocky cliffs of the Osage and the Niangua by the capricious elements; or the isolated natural mounds in the prairie region beyond—enduring monuments, not of a by-gone people, but of a vastly remote glacial force. For when he wrote—sixty-seven years ago—archæology had not become a science, and geology was but in its infancy.

Nor is it surprising that Major Sibley, an intelligent and educated officer of the Government, who resided for some years at the base of the great Blue Mound, should have accepted, without doubt or question,

*The name of this chief is here probably incorrectly written. At the period of Lieutenant Pike's visit, in 1806, *Cheveux Blanche* was the head chief of the Big Osages, and his son, Jean La Fou—as Pike wrote the name in his journal and official reports—was the second chief in authority. I have thought this orthography may possibly also be erroneous; because I remember, when a boy at my home near St. Louis, hearing the "*engagers*," recently returned from the Indian country, often mention a chief whom they called Jean Le Fou—"Mad," or "Crazy John"—on account of his peculiar eccentricities. It may be that Jean Defoe, Jean La Fou and Jean Le Fou were identical.

†As early as 1673 Marquette found Indians on the Mississippi, below the Ohio, well supplied with guns, powder, glass bottles, iron hoes, knives, hatchets, etc.

the extraordinary account of its recent erection by the Indians he was
then residing amongst, as told to him by the " Old Chief." For to him
glacial agency was unknown. Superstition had not yet abdicated to
systematized investigation ; and society paid silent homage to the marvellous and mysterious.

THE PROGRESS OF SCIENCE AS EXEMPLIFIED IN THE ART OF WEIGHING AND MEASURING.*

By Prof. WILLIAM HARKNESS, *U. S. Naval Observatory.*

Two centuries ago the world was just beginning to awaken from an intellectual lethargy which had lasted a thousand years. During all that time the children had lived as their parents before them, the mechanical arts had been at a stand-still, and the dicta of Aristotle had been the highest authority in science. But now the night of mediæval-ism was approaching its end, and the dawn of modern progress was at hand. Galileo had laid the foundation for accurate clocks, by discover-ing the isochronism of the simple pendulum; had proved that under the action of gravity, light bodies fall as rapidly as heavy ones; had invented the telescope and with it discovered the spots on the sun, the moun-tains on the moon, the satellites of Jupiter, and the so-called triple character of Saturn; and, after rendering himself immortal by his advo-cacy of the Copernican system, had gone to his grave, aged, blind, and full of sorrows. His contemporary, Kepler, had discovered the laws—which while history endures, will associate his name with the theory of planetary motion; and he also had passed away. The first Cassini was still a young man, his son was a little child, and his grandson and great-grandson, all of whom were destined to be directors of the Paris Observatory, were yet unborn. The illustrious Huyghens, the discov-erer of Saturn's rings, and the father of the undulatory theory of light, was in the zenith of his powers. The ingenious Hooke was a little younger, and Newton, towering above them all, had recently invented fluxions, and on the 28th of April, 1686, had presented his Principia to the Royal Society of London and given the theory of gravitation to the world. Bradley, who discovered nutation and the aberration of light; Franklin, the statesman and philosopher, who first drew the lightning from the clouds; Dollond, the inventor of the achromatic tel-escope; Euler, the mathematician who was destined to accomplish so much in perfecting algebra, the calculus, and the lunar theory; Laplace, the author of the Mécanique Céleste; Rumford, who laid the founda-

---

*Presidential address delivered before the Philosophical Society of Washington, December 10, 1887. (Bulletin Phil. Soc., vol. x, pp. xxxix–lxxxvi.)

tion of the mechanical theory of heat; Dalton, the author of the atomic theory upon which all chemistry rests; and Bessel, the greatest of modern astronomers,—these and others almost as illustrious, whom we can not even name to-night, were still in the womb of time.

Pure science first felt the effects of the new intellectual life, and it was more than a century later before the arts yielded to its influence. Then came Hargreaves, the inventor of the spinning-jenny; Arkwright, the inventor of the cotton-spinning frame; Watt, who gave us the condensing steam-engine; Jacquard, the inventor of the loom for weaving figured stuffs; Murdock, the originator of gas-lighting; Evans, the inventor of the high-pressure steam-engine; Fulton, the father of steam navigation; Trevithick, who ranks very near Watt and Evans in perfecting the steam-engine; and Stephenson, the father of railroads. If now we add the names of those who have given us the telegraph, to wit, Gauss, the eminent physicist and the greatest mathematician of the present century; Weber, Wheatstone, and Henry, all famous physicists, and Morse, the inventor and engineer, we have before us the demi-gods who have transformed the ancient into the modern world, given us machinery which has multiplied the productive power of the human race many fold, annihilated time and space, and bestowed upon toiling millions a degree of comfort and luxury which was unknown to kings and emperors of old.

The discoveries and inventions of the last two centuries have so far exceeded all others within historic times, that we are amply justified in calling this an age of amazing progress, and under the circumstances a little self-glorification is pardonable, perhaps even natural. The weekly and monthly records of scientific events which appear in so many newspapers and magazines are the immediate result of this, and the great increase of ephemeral scientific literature has led multitudes of educated people to believe that such records represent actual progress. The multiplication of bricks facilitates the building of houses, but does not necessarily improve architecture. Similarly, the multiplication of minor investigations improves our knowledge of details, but rarely affects the great philosophic theories upon which science is founded. The importance of human actions is measured by the degree in which they affect human thought, and the only way of permanently affecting scientific thought is by modifying or extending scientific theories. The men who do that, are neither numerous, nor do they require weekly paragraphs to record their deeds; but their names are honored by posterity. Even in this golden age the advance of science is not steady, but is made by spasmodic leaps and bounds. Mere scientific brick-making, commonly called progress, is always the order of the day until some genius startles the world by a discovery affecting accepted theories. Then every effort is directed in the new line of thought until it is measurably worked out, and after that brick-making again resumes its place. While the progress in two centuries has been immense, the progress in a week or a month is usually almost nil. Optimism has its uses in many departments of human affairs, but science should be cool and dispassionate, having regard only for the truth. To make a trustworthy estimate of the actual state of the whole vast realm of science would be a task beyond the powers of any one man; but perhaps it will not be amiss to spend the time at our disposal this evening in briefly reviewing the recent progress and present condition of the fundamental processes upon which the exact sciences rest;—I allude to the methods of weighing and measuring.

Physical science deals with many quantities, but they are all so related to each other that almost every one of them can be expressed in terms of three fundamental units. As several systems of such units are possible, it is important to select the most convenient, and the considerations which guide us in that respect are the following:

(1) The quantities selected should admit of very accurate comparison with other quantities of the same kind.

(2) Such comparisons should be possible at all times and in all places.

(3) The processes necessary for making such comparisons should be easy and direct.

(4) The fundamental units should be such as to admit of easy definitions and simple dimensions for the various derived units.

Scientific men have long agreed that these requirements are best fulfilled by adopting as the fundamental units, a definite length, a definite mass, and a definite interval of time. Length is an element which can be very accurately measured and copied, but it must be defined by reference to some concrete material standard, as for example, a bar of metal, and as all substances expand and contract with changes of temperature, it is necessary to state the temperature at which the standard is correct. A standard of mass, consisting of a piece of platinum, quartz, or other material not easily affected by atmospheric influences, probably fulfills the conditions set forth above better than any other kind of magnitude. Its comparison with other bodies of approximately equal mass is effected by weighing, and as that is among the most exact of all laboratory operations, very accurate copies of the standard can be made, and they can be carried from place to place with little risk of injury. Time is also an element which can be measured with extreme precision. The immediate instruments of measurement are clocks and chronometers, but their running is checked by astronomical observations and the ultimate standard is the rotation of the earth itself.

It is important to note that the use of three fundamental units is simply a matter of convenience and not a theoretical necessity, for the unit of mass might be defined as that which at unit distance would generate in a material point unit velocity in unit time; and thus we should have a perfectly general system of measurement based upon only two fundamental units, namely, those of space and time. Such a system is quite practicable in astronomy, but can not yet be applied with

accuracy to ordinary terrestrial purposes. According to the law of
gravitation

$$\text{Mass} = \text{Acceleration} \times (\text{Distance})^2$$

and as in the case of the earth we can measure the quantities on the
right-hand side of that equation with considerable accuracy, we can satisfactorily determine the earth's mass in terms of the supposed unit.
That suffices for the needs of astronomy, but for other scientific and
commercial purposes a standard of mass having a magnitude of about
a pound is necessary, and as two such masses can be compared with
each other from five to ten thousand times more accurately than either
of them can be determined in terms of the supposed unit, three fundamental units are preferable to two.

The Chaldeans, Babylonians, Persians, Greeks, and Romans all seem
to have had systems of weights and measures based upon tolerably definite standards, but after the decline of the Roman Empire these stand
ards seem to have been forgotten, and in the beginning of the sixteenth
century the human body had so far become the standard of measurement that the units in common use, as for example, the foot, palm, etc.,
were frequently taken directly from it. The complete table of measures
of length was then as follows: The breadth (not the length) of four
barley corns make a digit, or finger breadth; four digits make a palm
(measured across the middle joints of the fingers); four palms are one
foot; a foot and a half is a cubit; ten palms, or two feet and a half, are
a step; two steps, or five feet, are a pace; ten feet are a perch; one
hundred and twenty-five paces are an Italic stadium; eight stadia, or
one thousand paces, are an Italic mile; four Italic miles are a German
mile; and five Italic miles are a Swiss mile It was then the practice
to furnish standards of length in books by printing in them lines a
foot or a palm long, according to the size of the page, and from these
and other data it appears that the foot then used on the continent of
Europe had a length of about ten English inches.

In England the first attempts at scientific accuracy in matters of
measurement date from the beginning of the seventeenth century, when
John Greaves, who must be considered as the earliest of the scientific
metrologists, directed attention to the difference between the Roman
and English foot by tolerably accurate determinations of the former,
and also attempted the investigation of the Roman weights. He was
followed by Dr. Edward Bernard, who wrote a treatise on ancient
weights and measures about 1685, and towards the end of the century
the measurements of the length of a degree by Picard and J. D. Cassini
awakened the attention of the French to the importance of rigorously
exact standards. In considering the progress of science with respect
to standards of length, we may safely confine our inquiries to the English yard and the French toise and meter, for during the last two hundred years they have been almost the only standards adopted in scientific operations.

The English measures of length have come down from the Saxons, but the oldest standards now existing are the exchequer yards of Henry VII (1490)* and Elizabeth (1588).† These are both brass end measures, the former being an octagonal rod about half an inch in diameter, very coarsely made, and as rudely divided into inches on the right-hand end and into sixteenths of a yard on the left-hand end; the latter, a square rod with sides about half an inch wide, also divided into sixteenths of a yard and provided with a brass bed having end pieces between which the yard fits. One end of the bed is divided into inches and half inches. Francis Baily, who saw this Elizabethan standard in 1836, speaks of it as " this curious instrument, of which it is impossible, at the present day, to speak too much in derision or contempt. A common kitchen poker, filed at the ends in the rudest manner by the most bungling workman, would make as good a standard. It has been broken asunder, and the two pieces have been dove-tailed together, but so badly that the joint is nearly as loose as that of a pair of tongs. The date of this fracture I could not ascertain, it having occurred beyond the memory or knowledge of any of the officers at the Exchequer. And yet, till within the last ten years, to the disgrace of this country, copies of this measure have been circulated all over Europe and America, with a parchment document accompanying them (charged with a stamp that costs £3 10s. exclusive of official fees) certifying that they are true copies of the English *standard*."‡

In the year 1742 certain members of the Royal Society of London, and of the Royal Academy of Sciences of Paris, proposed that in order to facilitate a comparison of the scientific operations carried on in the two countries, accurate standards of the measures and weights of both should be prepared and preserved in the archives of each of these societies. This proposition having been approved, Mr. George Graham, at the instance of the Royal Society, had two substantial brass rods made, upon which he laid off, with the greatest care, the length of three English feet from the standard yard kept at the Tower of London. These two rods, together with a set of troy weights, were then sent over to the Paris Academy, which body, in like manner, had the measure of a French half toise set off upon the rods, and keeping one, as previously agreed, returned the other, together with a standard weight of two marcs, to the Royal Society. In 1835, Baily declared this copy of the half toise to be of little value, because the original toise-étalon was of iron and the standard temperature in France differed from that in England.§ In his opinion the French should have sent over an iron half toise in exchange for the English brass yard, but this criticism loses much of its force when it is remembered that in 1742 neither England nor France

* 50, p. 34, and 5, pp. 51, 52. (The numbers cited in the foot-notes refer to those of the Bibliography at the end of the article.)
† 50, p. 25.
‡ 37, p. 146.
§ 37, p. 37.

had fixed upon a temperature at which their standards were to be regarded as of the true length. On the return of the rod from Paris Mr. Graham caused Jonathan Sisson to divide the English yard and the French half toise each into three equal parts, after which the rod was deposited in the archives of the Royal Society, where it still remains.[*] Objection having been made that the original and legal standard yard of England was not the one at the Tower, but the Elizabethian standard at the Exchequer, the Royal Society requested Mr. Graham to compare his newly made scale with the latter standard, and on Friday, April 22, 1743, he did so in the presence of a committee of seven members of the Royal Society. In the following week the same gentlemen compared the Royal Society's scale with the standards at Guildhall and the Tower, and also with the standards of the Clock-makers' Company. These comparisons having shown that the copy of the Tower yard upon the Royal Society's scale was about 0.0075 of an inch longer than the standard at the Exchequer, Mr. Graham inscribed upon the Royal Society's scale a copy of the latter standard also, marking it with the letters Exch., to distinguish it from the former, which was marked E. (English), and from the half toise which was marked F. (French).[†]

In the year 1758 the House of Commons appointed a committee to inquire into the *original* standards of weights and measures of England; and under instructions from that committee, the celebrated instrument maker, John Bird, prepared two brass rods, respecting which the committee speak as follows in their report: "And having those rods, together with that of the Royal Society laid in the same place, at the receipt of the Exchequer, all night with the standards of length kept there, to prevent the variation which the difference of air might make upon them, they the next morning compared them all and by the means of beam compasses brought by Mr. Bird found them to agree as near as it was possible."[‡] One of these rods was arranged as a matrix for testing end measures, and the other was a line measure which the committee recommended should be made the legal standard of England, and which has since been known as Bird's standard of 1758. Respecting the statement that after lying together all night the rods were *all* found to agree as near as it was possible, Baily says: "This is somewhat remarkable, and requires further explanation, which unfortunately can not now be accurately obtained. For it is notorious that the measure of the yard of the Royal Society's scale differs very considerably from the standard yard at the Exchequer: - - - Owing to this singular confusion of the lengths of the measures, which does not appear to have been unravelled by any subsequent Committee, it has happened that the Imperial standard yard - - - has been assumed nearly $1 \div 140$ of an inch longer than the ancient measure of the kingdom."[§] There is little difficulty in surmising what Bird did. The Exchequer standard consisted of a rod and its matrix. The Royal

<hr>

[*] 7, pp. 185–'8.   [†] 8, pp. 541–556.   [‡] 13, p. 434.   [§] 37, p. 43.

Society's committee assumed the rod to be the true standard of 36 inches, and upon that assumption Graham's measurements gave for the length of the matrix 36.0102 inches, and for the length of the Royal Society's yard 36.0075 inches. The Parliamentary Committee of 1758 probably assumed the standard to consist of the rod and matrix together, which seems the better view; and by laying the rod in its matrix and measuring to the joint between them Bird would have got a length of about 36.0051 inches. The mean between that and 36.0075 would be 36.0063, which differs very little from the length of Bird's standard resulting from Sir George Shuckburgh's measurements. Thus the committee's statement is justified, and there has been no falsification of the ancient standards.

On December 1, 1758, Parliament created another committee on weights and measures which in April, 1759, repeated the recommendation that Bird's standard of 1758 should be legalized, and further recommended that a copy of it should be made and deposited in some public office, to be used only on special occasions.[*] The copy was made by Bird in 1760, but owing to circumstances entirely unconnected with the subject, no legislation followed for sixty-four years.

The Royal Commission appointed during the reign of George III to consider the subject of weights and measures made its first report on June 24, 1819, and therein recommended the adoption of the standard of length which had been used by General Roy in measuring the base on Hounslow Heath;[†] but in a second report, made July 13, 1820, they wrote: "We - - - have examined, since our last report, the relation of the best authenticated standards of length at present in existence, to the instruments employed for measuring the base on Hounslow Heath, and in the late trigonometrical operations :—But we have very unexpectedly discovered, that an error has been committed in the construction of some of these instruments.[‡] We are therefore obliged to recur to the originals which they were intended to represent; and we have found reason to prefer the Parliamentary standard executed by Bird in 1760, which we had not before received, both as being laid down in the most accurate manner, and as the best agreeing with the most extensive comparisons, which have been hitherto executed by various observers, and circulated through Europe; and in particular with the scale employed by the late Sir George Shuckburgh."[§]

Accordingly, when in 1824, Parliament at length took action, Bird's standard of 1760 was adopted instead of that of 1758. The former being a copy of a copy, its selection as a national standard of length seems so singular that the circumstances which brought about that result should scarcely be passed over in silence. Bird had a very accurate brass scale 90 inches long, which he used in all his dividing operations, whether upon circles or straight lines, and which Dr. Maskelyne said was 0.001 of an inch shorter on three feet than Graham's Royal Society yard E.* In the year 1792, or 1793, the celebrated Edward Troughton made for himself a 5 foot scale, which conformed to Bird's, and which he afterwards used in laying down the divisions of the various instruments that passed through his hands. This was the original of all the standard scales he ever made, and at the beginning of the present century he believed these copies, which were made by the aid of micrometer microscopes, to be so exact that no variations could possibly be detected in them either from the original or from each other. Among the earliest of the scales so made by Troughton was the one used by Sir George Shuckburgh in 1796–'98 in his important scientific operations for the improvement of the standards. Subsequently, the length of the meter was determined by comparison with this scale and with the supposed fac-simile of it made by Troughton for Professor Pictet, of Geneva; and thus it happened that on the continent of Europe all measures were converted into English units by a reference to Sir George Shuckburgh's scale. The Royal Commission of 1819 believed Bird's standard of 1760 to be identical with Shuckburgh's scale, and they legalized it rather than the standard of 1758, in order to avoid disturbing the value of the English yard which was then generally accepted for scientific purposes.

There are yet four other scales of importance in the history of English standards, namely: The brass 5-foot scale made for Sir George Shuckburgh by Troughton in 1796; two iron standard yards, marked 1A and 2A, made for the English Ordnance Survey department by Messrs. Troughton and Simms in 1826–'27, and the Royal Society's standard yard, constructed by Mr. George Dollond, under the direction of Captain Henry Kater, in 1831.

Bearing in mind the preceding history, the genesis of the present English standard yard may be thus summarized: In 1742 Graham transferred to a bar made for the Royal Society a length which he intended should be that of the Tower yard, but which was really intermediate between the Exchequer standard yard of Elizabeth and its matrix. That length he marked with the letter E, and although destitute of legal authority, it was immediately accepted as the scientific standard and was copied by the famous instrument-makers of the time with all the accuracy then attainable. Thus it is in fact the prototype to which all the accurate scales made in England between 1742 and 1850 can be traced. Bird's standard of 1758 was compared with the Exchequer standard and with the Royal Society's yard E, and was of a length between the two. Bird's standard of 1760, legalized as the Imperial standard in June, 1824, was copied from his standard of 1758. After becoming the Imperial standard, Bird's standard of 1760 was compared with Sir George Shuckburgh's scale by Captain Kater in 1830, and by Mr. Francis Baily in 1834; with the Ordnance yards 1A and 2A in 1834 by Lieutenant Murphy, R. E., Lieutenant Johnson, R. N., and Messrs.

F. Baily and Donkin; and with Kater's Royal Society yard by Captain Kater in 1831. On October 16, 1834, the Imperial standard (Bird's standard of 1760) was destroyed by the burning of the houses of Parliament, in which it was lodged, and very soon thereafter the Lords of the Treasury took measures to recover its length. Preliminary inquiries were begun on May 11, 1838, and on June 20, 1843, they resulted in the appointment of a commission to superintend the construction of new Parliamentary standards of length and weight; among whose members the Astronomer Royal (now Sir George B. Airy), Messrs. F. Baily, R. Sheepshanks, and Prof. W. H. Miller were prominent. The laborious investigations and experiments carried out by that commission cannot be described here, but it will suffice to say that for determining the true length of the new standard Mr. Sheepshanks employed a provisional yard, marked upon a new brass bar designated "Brass 2," which he compared as accurately as possible with Sir George Shuckburgh's scale, the two Ordnance yards, and Kater's Royal Society yard. The results in terms of the lost Imperial standard were as follows:

Brass bar 2 = 36.000084 from comparison with Shuckburgh's scale, 0-36 inch.
　　　　　　 36.000280 from comparison with Shuckburgh's scale, 10-46 inch.
　　　　　　 36.000303 from comparison with the Ordnance yard, 1A.
　　　　　　 36.000275 from comparison with the Ordnance yard, 2A.
　　　　　　 36.000229 from Captain Kater's Royal Society yard.

　　Mean = 36.000234

Respecting this mean Mr. Sheepshanks wrote: "This should be pretty near the truth; but I prefer 36.00025, if in such a matter such a difference be worth notice. I propose, therefore, in constructing the new standard to assume that—

"Brass bar 2 = 36.00025 inches of lost Imperial standard at 62° Fahr."

And upon that basis the standard now in use was constructed.[*]

Turning now to the French standards of length, it is known that the ancient *toise de maçons* of Paris was probably the toise of Charlemagne (A. D. 742 to 814), or at least of some Emperor Charles, and that its *étalon* was situated in the court-yard of the old Châtelet, on the outside of one of the pillars of the building. It still existed in 1714, but entirely falsified by the bending of the upper part of the pillar. In 1668 the ancient toise of the masons was reformed by shortening it five lines; but whether this reformation was an arbitrary change, or merely a change to remedy the effects of long use and restore the étalon to conformity with some more carefully preserved standard, is not quite clear.[†] These old *étalons* were iron bars having their two ends turned up at right angles so as to form *talons*, and the standardizing of end measures was effected by fitting them between the *talons*. Being placed on the outside of some public building, they were exposed to wear from constant use, to rust, and even to intentional injury by ma-

---

[*] 45, p. 664.　　　　　　　　　　[†] 1, p. 536 and 2, p. 395.

licious persons. Under such conditions every étalon would sooner or later become too long and require shortening.

Respecting the ancient toise of the masons there are two contradict. ory stories. On December 1, 1714, La Hire showed to the French Academy what he characterized as "a very ancient instrument of mathematics, which has been made by one of our most accomplished workmen with very great care, where the foot is marked, and which has served to re-establish the toise of the Châtelet, as I have been informed by our old mathematicians."[*] Forty-four years later, on July 29, 1758, La Condamine stated to the Academy that "We know only by tradition that to adjust the length of the new standard, the width of the arcade or interior gate of the grand pavilion, which served as an entrance to the old Louvre, on the side of the rue Fromenteau, was used. This opening, according to the plan, should have been twelve feet wide. Half of it was taken to fix the length of the new toise, which thus became five lines shorter than the old one."[†] Of these two contradictory state· ments that of La Hire seems altogether most trustworthy, and the ordinary rules of evidence indicate that it should be accepted to the exclusion of the other.

In 1668 the étalon of the new toise, since known as the *toise-étalon du Châtelet,* was fixed against the wall at the foot of the staircase of the grand Châtelet de Paris, by whom or at what season of the year is not known. Strange as it now seems, this standard (very roughly made, exposed in a public place for use or abuse by everybody, liable to rust, and certain to be falsified by constant wear) was actually used for adjusting the toise of Picard, that of Cassini, the toise of Peru and of the North, that of La Caille, that of Mairan—in short, all the toises employed by the French in their geodetic operations during the seventeenth and eighteenth centuries. The lack of any other recog- nized standard made the use of this one imperative; but the French academicians were well aware of its defects and took precautions to guard against them.

The first toise copied from the étalon of the Châtelet for scientific purposes was that used by Picard in his measurement of a degree of the meridian between Paris and Amiens.[‡] It was made about the year 1668, and would doubtless have become the scientific standard of France had it not unfortunately disappeared before the degree measure· ments of the eighteenth century were begun. The second toise copied from the étalon of the Châtelet for scientific purposes was that used by Messrs. Godin, Bouguer, and La Condamine for measuring the base of their arc of the meridian in Peru. This toise, since known as the *toise du Pérou,* was made by the artist Langlois under the immediate direc· tion of Godin in 1735, and is still preserved at the Paris Observatory.[§] It is a rectangular bar of polished wrought-iron, having a breadth of 1.58 English inches and a thickness of 0.30 of an inch. All the other

[*] 2, p. 395.   [†] 17, p. 484.   [‡] 6, Art. 4, p. 15.   [§] 17 p. 487, and 53, p. C. 2.

toises used by the Academy in the eighteenth century, were compared with it, and ultimately it was made the legal standard of France by an order of Louis XV, dated May 16, 1766. As the toise of Peru is the oldest authentic copy of the toise of the Châtelet, the effect of this order was simply to perpetuate the earliest known state of that ancient standard.

The metric system originated from a motion made by Talleyrand in the National Assembly of France, in 1790, referring the question of the formation of an improved system of weights and measures, based upon a natural constant, to the French Academy of Sciences; and the preliminary work was intrusted to five of the most eminent members of that Academy,—namely, Lagrange, Laplace, Borda, Monge, and Condorcet. On March 19, 1791, these gentlemen, together with Lalande, presented to the Academy a report containing the complete scheme of the metric system. In pursuance of the recommendations in that report the law of March 26, 1791, was enacted for the construction of the new system, and the Academy of Sciences was charged with the direction of the necessary operations. Those requisite for the construction of a standard of length were:

(1) The determination of the difference of latitude between Dunkirk and Barcelona.

(2) The re-measurement of the ancient bases which had served for the measurement of a degree at the latitude of Paris, and for making the map of France.

· (3) The verification by new observations of the series of triangles employed for measuring the meridan, and the prolongation of them as far as Barcelona.

This work was intrusted to Méchain and Delambre, who carried it on during the seven years from 1791 to 1798, notwithstanding many great difficulties and dangers. The unit of length adopted in their operations was the toise of Peru, and from the arc of $9° 40' 45''$ actually measured, they inferred the length of an arc of the meridian extending from the equator to the pole to be 5,130,740 toises. As the meter was to be one ten millionth of that distance, its length was made 0.5130740 of a toise, or, in the language of the committee, 443.296 lines of the toise of Peru at a temperature of $13°$ Reaumur ($16\frac{1}{4}°$ C. or $61\frac{1}{4}°$ Fahr.).[*]

Before attempting to estimate how accurately the standards we have been considering were inter-compared it will be well to describe briefly the methods by which the comparisons were effected. In 1742 Graham used the only instruments then known for the purpose,—namely, very exact beam compasses of various kinds, one having parallel jaws for taking the lengths of the standard rods, another with rounded ends for taking the lengths of the hollow beds, and still another having fine points in the usual manner. The jaws, or points, of all these instruments were movable by micrometer screws having heads divided to show

[*] 22, pp. 432, 433, and 642.

the eight huudredth part of au inch directly, aud the tenth of that
ʝuautity by estimatiou; but Mr. Graham did not consider that the
measurements could be depended upon to a greater accuracy thau one
sixteen-huudredth of an inch.*

Troughton is generally regarded as the author of the application of
micrometer microscopes to the comparison of standards of leugth, but
the earliest record of their use for that purpose is by Sir George
Shuckburgh in his work for the improvement of the standards of
weight aud measure, in 1796–'98.† Siuce then their use has been general; first, because they are more accurate than beam compasses, aud
second, because they avoid the iujury to standard scales which necessarily results from placing the points of beam compasses upon their
graduations. As the objective of the microscope forms a magnified
image of the staudard, upou which the micrometer wires are set by the
aid of the eye-piece, it is evident that in order to reduce the effect of
imperfections in the micrometer, the objective should have the largest
practicable magnifyiug power. To show the progress in that direction
the optical constants of the microscopes, by means of which some of the
most important standards have been compared, are given in the accompanying table:

Date	Observer	Power of micro-scope.	Mag-nifying power of objective	Equiva lent focus ot eye-piece	Value of one revo-lution of microme-ter screw.
				Inches.	*Inches.*
1797	Sir George Shuckburgh	14	1.7	1.50	0.01000
1817	Captain Henry Kater	18	(2.3)	....	.00428
1834	Francis Baily.............................	27	(2.0)	....	.00500
1834	Lieutenant Murphy, R. E....	....	(2.0)	....	.00500
1850	R. Sheepshanks	....	(2.8)	....	.00358
1864	General A. R. Clarke, R. E...............	60	4.	0.67	.00287
1880	Prof. W. A. Rogers, 1 inch objective	....	(12.7)	....	.00079
	Prof. W. A. Rogers, ½ inch objective	....	(28.6)	....	.00035
	Prof. W. A. Rogers, ¼ inch objective	....	(52.7)	....	.00019
1883	International Bureau.....................	90	7.5	0.83	0.00394

NOTE.—The magnifying power of Sir George Shuckburgh's microscope seems to be
referred to a distance of 12 inches for distinct vision. The powers inclosed in paren-
theses are estimated upon the assumption that the respective micrometer screws had
one huudred threads per inch.

In the memoirs of the Freuch Academy, nothing is said respecting the
method adopted by the Academiciaus for comparing their various toises;
but in his astrouomy, Lalande states that the comparisons were effected
partly by beam compasses, and partly by superposing the toises upon
each other aud examiuing their euds, both by touch and with magnify-
ing-glasses; they being all end standards.‡ For the definitive adjust-
meut of the length of their meters, which were also end standards, the
Freuch Metric Commission used a lever comparator by Lenoir.

* 8, pp. 545–'6.   † 21, p. 137.   ‡ 19, p. 8.

In 1742 Graham used beam compasses, which he considered trust-worthy to 0.00062 of an inch, in comparing standards of length; but at that time the French Academicians made their comparisons of toises only to one twentieth or one thirtieth of a line, say 0.00300 of an inch, and it was not until 1758 that La Condamine declared they should be compared to 0.01 of a line, or 0.00089 of an English inch " if our senses aided by the most perfect instruments can attain to that." * Half a century later, ten times that accuracy was attained by the lever comparator of Lenoir, which was regarded as trustworthy to 0.000077 of an inch.†

The heads of micrometer microscopes are usually divided into one hundred equal parts, and if we regard one of these parts as the least reading of a microscope, then in 1797, Sir George Shuckburgh's microscopes read to one ten thousandth of an inch; and the least reading of microscopes made since that date has varied from one twenty thousandth to one thirty-five thousandth of an inch. A few investigators, among whom may be mentioned Prof. W. A. Rogers, of Colby University, have made the least reading of their microscopes as small as one ninety thousandth of an inch, but it is doubtful if there is any advantage in so doing. At the present day the errors committed in comparing standards arise, not from lack of power in the microscopes, but from the difficulty of determining sufficiently exactly the temperature of the standard bars, and the effect of flexure upon the position of their graduations. In order to ascertain the length of a three-foot standard with an error not exceeding 0.000020 of an inch, its temperature must be known to 0.06° Fahr. if it is of brass, or to 0.09° Fah. if it is of iron. To get thermometers that will indicate their own temperature to that degree of accuracy is by no means easy, but to determine the temperature of a bar from their readings is far more difficult. Again, we imagine the length of our standards to follow their temperature rigorously, but what proof is there that such is the case? If we determine the freezing point of an old thermometer, then raise it to the temperature of boiling water, and immediately thereafter again determine its freezing point, we invariably find that the freezing point has fallen a little; and we explain this by saying that the glass has taken a set, from which it requires time to recover. Is it not probable that an effect similar in kind, although less in degree, occurs in all solids when their temperature is varying? When we look at the highly polished terminals of an end standard we are apt to regard them as mathematical surfaces, separated by an interval which is perfectly definite, and which could be measured with infinite precision if we only had the necessary instrumental appliances; but is that a correct view? The atomic theory answers emphatically, No. According to it, all matter consists of atoms, or molecules, of a perfectly definite size, and with definite inter-

---

* 17, p. 483.   † Base du Système Métrique. T. 3, pp. 447-462.

vals between them; but even if that is denied, the evidence is now overwhelming that matter is not homogeneous, but possesses a grain of some kind, regularly repeated at intervals which can not be greater than one two millionth nor less than one four-hundred millionth of an inch. Accordingly, we must picture our standard bar as a conglomeration of grains of some kind or other, having magnitudes of the order specified, and all in ceaseless motion, the amplitude of which depends upon the temperature of the bar. To our mental vision the polished terminals are therefore like the surface of a pot of boiling water, and we recognize that there must be a limit to the accuracy with which the interval between them can be measured. As a basis for estimating how near this limit we have approached it will suffice to say that for fifty years past it has been customary to state comparisons of standards of length to one one-millionth of an inch. Nevertheless, most authorities agree that although one one-hundred thousandth of an inch can be distinguished in the comparators, one twenty-five thousandth of an inch is about the limit of accuracy attainable in comparing standards. Possibly such a limit may be reached under the most favorable circumstances, but in the case of the yard and the meter, which are standard at different temperatures, the following values of the meter by observers of the highest repute render it doubtful if anything like that accuracy has yet been attained.*

		Inches.
1818.	Captain Henry Kater	39. 37079
1866.	General A. R. Clarke	39. 37043
1883.	Prof. William A. Rogers	39. 37027
1885.	General C. B. Comstock	39, 36985

The earliest standard of English weight of which we have any very definite knowledge is the mint pound of the Tower of London. It weighed 5,400 troy grains, and the coinage was regulated by it up to the year 1527, when it was abolished in favor of the troy pound of 5,760 grains. Contemporaneously with the tower pound there was also the merchant's pound, whose exact weight is now involved in so much doubt that it is impossible to decide whether it consisted of 6,750 or of 7,200 grains. The tower pound and the troy pound were used for weighing only gold, silver, and drugs, while all other commodities were weighed by the merchant's pound until the thirteenth or fourteenth century, and after that by the avoirdupois pound. It is not certainly known when the troy and avoirdupois pounds were introduced into England, and there is no evidence of any relation between them when they first became standards. The present avoirdupois pound can be clearly proved to be of similar weight to the standard avoirdupois pound of Edward III (A. D. 1327–1377), and there is good reason for believing that no substantial change has occurred either in its weight or in that of the troy pound since their respective establishment as standards in England.

---

* See Note C, at the end of the Address.

The oldest standard weights now existing in the English archives date from the reign of Queen Elizabeth, and consist of a set of bell-shaped avoirdupois weights of 56, 28, and 14 pounds, made in 1582, and 7, 4, 2, and 1 pounds, made in 1588; a set of flat circular avoirdupois weights of 8, 4, 2, and 1 pounds, and 8, 4, 2, 1, $\frac{1}{2}$, $\frac{1}{4}$, $\frac{1}{8}$, and $\frac{1}{16}$ ounces, made in 1588; and a set of cup-shaped troy weights, fitting one within the other, of 256, 128, 64, 32, 16, 8, 4, 2, 1, $\frac{1}{2}$, $\frac{1}{4}$, $\frac{1}{8}$ (hollow), and $\frac{1}{8}$ (solid) ounces, also made in 1588.* All these standards were constructed by order of Queen Elizabeth, under the direction of a jury composed of eighteen merchants and eleven goldsmiths of London; the avoirdupois weights being adjusted according to an ancient standard of 56 pounds, remaining in the Exchequer from the time of Edward III; and the troy weights being adjusted according to the ancient standard in Goldsmiths' Hall.†

In view of the fact that the weight mentioned in all the old acts of Parliament from the time of Edward I (A. D. 1274–1307) is universally admitted to be troy weight, the Parliamentary Committee of 1758, appointed to inquire into the original standards of weights and measures in England, recommended that the troy pound should be made the unit or standard by which the avoirdupois and other weights should be regulated; and by their order three several troy pounds of soft gun metal were very carefully adjusted under the direction of Mr. Joseph Harris, who was then assay master of the mint. To ascertain the proper mass for these pounds the committee caused Messrs. Harris and Gregory, of the mint, to perform the following operations in their presence:‡

First. In the before-mentioned set of troy weights, made in 1588, which were then the Exchequer standard, each weight, from that of 4 ounces up to that of 256 ounces, was compared successively with the sum of all the smaller weights; and by a process for which no valid reason can be assigned § it was concluded from these weighings that the troy pound composed of the 8 and 4 ounce weights was $1\frac{1}{2}$ grains too light.

Second. The aforesaid 8 and 4 ounce weights of the Exchequer were compared with five other authoritative troy pounds, four of which belonged to the mint and one to Mr. Freeman, who, like his father before him, was scale-maker to the mint, and from the mean of these weighings it appeared that the sum of the Exchequer 8 and 4 ounce weights was one grain too light.

The committee adopted the mean between the latter result and that which they had deduced from the Exchequer weights alone,§ and accordingly Mr. Harris made each of his three troy pounds $1\frac{1}{4}$ grains heavier than the sum of the Exchequer 8 and 4 ounce weights; but sixty-six years were destined to elapse before Parliament took action respecting them.

---

* 13, p. 430.   ‡ 13, p. 437.
† 13, pp. 435 and 443–448.   § See Note B, at the end of the Address.

The commissioners appointed in 1818 to establish a more uniform system of weights and measures repeated the recommendations of the committee of 1758,* and as the avoirdupois pound which had long been used, although not legalized by any act of the legislature, was very nearly 7,000 troy grains, they recommended that 7,000 such troy grains be declared to constitute a pound avoirdupois.† These recommendations were embodied in the act of Parliament of June 17, 1824, and thus one of the troy pounds made in 1758 became the Imperial standard. That standard, like Bird's standard yard, was deposited in the Houses of Parliament and was burned up with them in October, 1834.

The present English standard pound was made in 1844–'46 by Prof. W. H. Miller, who was one of the members of the commission appointed in 1843 to superintend the construction of the new Parliamentary standards of length and weight destined to replace those destroyed in 1834. A number of weights had been very accurately compared with the lost standard; namely, in 1824 or 1825, by Captain Kater, five troy pounds of gun metal, destined respectively for the use of the Exchequer, the Royal Mint, and the cities of London, Edinburgh, and Dublin; and in 1829, by Captain v. Nehus, two troy pounds of brass and one of platinum, all in the custody of Professor Schumacher, and a platinum troy pound belonging to the Royal Society. The first step for recovering the mass of the lost standard was manifestly to compare these weights among themselves, and upon so doing it was found that for the brass and gun-metal weights the discrepancies between the weighings made in 1824 and 1844 amounted to 0.0226 of a grain,‡ while for the two platinum weights the discrepancies between the weighings made in 1829 and 1845 was only 0.00019 of a grain.§ With a single exception, all the *new* brass or gun-metal weights had become heavier since their first comparison with the lost standard, the change being probably due to oxidation of their surfaces, and on that account the new standard was made to depend solely upon the two platinum weights. For convenience of reference these weights were designated, respectively, Sp (Schumacher's platinum) and RS (Royal Society). A provisional platinum troy pound, T, intermediate in mass between Sp and RS, was next prepared, and from two hundred and eighty-six comparisons made in January, February, July, and August, 1845, it was found that in a vacuum‖

$$T = Sp + 0.00105 \text{ grain},$$

while from 122 comparisons made in January, July, and August, 1845,

$$T = RS - 0.00429 \text{ grain}.$$

By combining these values with the results of the weighings made in 1824–'29, namely,

$$Sp = U - 0.52956 \text{ grain},$$
$$RS = U - 0.52441 \text{ grain},$$

where U designates the lost standard—the comparison with Sp gave

$$T = U - 0.52851 \text{ grain},$$

---

* See 26, 27, and 28.   † 28, pp. 4–5.   ‡ 40, p. 772.   § 40, p. 941.   ‖ 40, pp. 819–20.

while those with RS gave

$$T = U - 0.52870 \text{ grain.}$$

To the first of these expressions double weight was assigned, because the comparisons of T and U with Sp were about twice as numerous as those with RS. The resulting mean was therefore

$$T = U - 0.52857 \text{ grains} = 5759.47143 \text{ grains,}$$

and from that value of T the new standard avoirdupois pound of 7,000 grains was constructed.

From sometime in the fifteenth century until the adoption of the metric system in August, 1793, the system of weights employed in France was the *poids de marc*, having for its ultimate standard the *pile de Charlemagne*, which was then kept in the mint, and is now deposited in the Conservatoire des Arts et Métiers. The table of this weight was

Grains.

72 grains	= 1 gros	=	72
8 gros	= 1 once	=	576
8 onces	= 1 marc	=	4608
2 marcs	= 1 livre	=	9216

The origin of the pile de Charlemagne is not certainly known, but it is thought to have been made by direction of King John (A. D. 1350–1364). It consists of a set of brass cup-weights, fitting one within the other, and the whole weighing fifty marcs. The nominal and actual weights of the several pieces are as follows : *

	Marcs.	Grains.
Boîte de 20 marcs	20	+ 1.4
Pièce de 14 marcs	14	+ 4.5
de 8 marcs	8	— 0.4
de 4 marcs	4	— 2.1
de 2 marcs	2	— 1.0
de 1 marc	1	— 0.7
Marc devisé.	1	— 1.7
	50	± 0.0

In determining the relation of the poids de marc to the metric weights, the committee for the construction of the kilogram regarded the entire pile de Charlemagne as a standard of fifty marcs, and considered the individual pieces as subject to the corrections stated. On that basis they found

$$1 \text{ kilogram} = 18827.15 \text{ French grains} †$$

and, as a kilogram is equal to 15432.34874 English troy grains,‡ we have

$$1 \text{ livre, poids de marc} = 7554.22 \text{ troy grains.}$$
$$= 489.506 \text{ grams.}$$

The metric standard of weight, called a kilogram, was constructed under the direction of the French Academy of Sciences simultaneously with the meter, the work being done principally by Lefèvre-Gineau and Borda. It was intended that the kilogram should have the same

---

* 20, pp. 270-'71.   † Base du Système Métrique, T. 3, p. 638.   ‡ 44, p. 893.

mass as a cubic decimeter of pure water at maximum density, and the experimental determination of that mass was made by finding the difference of weight in air and in water of a hollow brass cylinder whose exterior dimensions at a temperature of 17.6° C. were, height = 2.437672 decimeters, diameter = 2.428368 decimeters, volume = 11.2900054 cubic decimeters. The difference of weight in question was first measured in terms of certain brass weights, by the aid of which the platinum kilogram of the archives was subsequently constructed, special care being taken to apply the corrections necessary to reduce all the weighings to what they would have been if made in a vacuum.*

The best results hitherto obtained for the weight of a cubic decimeter of water, expressed in terms of the kilogram of the archives, are as follows : †

Date.	Country.	Observer.	Weight of a cubic decimeter of water at 4° C.
			Grams.
1795....	France	Lefèvre-Gineau.....................	1000.000
1797.. ⎱ 1821.. ⎰	England	Shuckburgh and Kater	1000.480
1825....	Sweden	Berzelius, Svanberg, and Akermann...	1000.296
1830....	Austria	Stampfer.........................	999.653
1841....	Russia	Kupffer...........................	999.989
		Mean....................	1000.084

These results show the extreme difficulty of determining the exact mass of a given volume of water. The discordance between the different observers amounts to more than one part in a thousand, while good weighings are exact to one part in eight or ten millions. Without doubt two weights can be compared at least a thousand times more accurately than either of them can be reproduced by weighing a specified volume of water, and for that reason the kilogram, like the English pound, can now be regarded only as an arbitrary standard of which copies must be taken by direct comparison. As already stated, the kilogram is equivalent to 15432.34874 English troy grains, or about 2 pounds 3 ounces avoirdupois.

In consequence of the circumstance that the mass of a body is not affected either by temperature or flexure, weighing is an easier process than measuring; but in order to obtain precise results many precautions are necessary. Imagine a balance with a block of wood tied to its right-hand pan and accurately counterpoised by lead weights in its left-hand pan. If with things so arranged the balance were immersed in water the equilibrium would be instantly destroyed, and to restore

---

* Base du Système Métrique, T. 3, pp. 574-'5
† This table has been deduced from the data given by Professor Miller in 44, p. 760.

it all the weights would have to be removed from the left-hand pan, and some of them would have to be placed in the right-hand pan to overcome the buoyancy of the wood. The atmosphere behaves precisely as the water does, and although its effect is minute enough to be neglected in ordinary business affairs, it must be taken into account when scientific accuracy is desired. To that end the weighing must either be made in a vacuum, or the difference of the buoyant effect of the air upon the substances in the two pans must be computed and allowed for. As very few vacuum balances exist, the latter method is usually employed. The data necessary for the computation are the latitude of the place where the weighing is made and its altitude above the sea-level; the weights, specific gravities, and co-efficients of expansion of each of the substances in the two pans; the temperature of the air, its barometric pressure, and the pressure, both of the aqueous vapor, and of the carbonic anhydride contained in it.

Judging from the adjustment of the pile de Charlemagne, and the Exchequer troy weights of Queen Elizabeth, the accuracy attained in weighing gold and silver at the mints during the fourteenth, fifteenth, and sixteenth centuries must have been about one part in ten thousand. The balance which Mr. Harris of the London mint used in 1743 indicated one-eighth of a grain on a troy pound, or about one part in 50,000; while that which he and Mr. Bird used in their observations upon the Exchequer weights, for the Parliamentary Committee of 1759, was sufficiently exact "to discern any error in the pound weight to the 230,400th part of the weight."* In 1798 Sir George Shuckburgh had a balance sensitive enough to indicate 0.01 of a grain when loaded with 16,000 grains, or about one part in 1,600,000. The balance used by Fortin in 1799, in adjusting the kilogram of the archives, was not quite so delicate, its sensitiveness being only the one-millionth part of its load; but in 1844, for the adjustment of the present English standard pound, Professor Miller employed a balance whose index moved about 0.01 of an inch for a change of 0.002 of a grain in a load of 7,000 grains.† He read the index with a microscope, and found the probable error of a single comparison of two avoirdupois pounds to be one twelve-millionth of either, or about 0.00058 of a grain. At the present time it is claimed that two avoirdupois pounds can be compared with an error not exceeding 0.0002 of a grain; and two kilograms with an error not exceeding 0.02 of a milligram.

The mean solar day is the natural unit of time for the human race, and it is universally adopted among all civilized nations. Our ultimate standard of time is therefore the rotation of the earth upon its axis, and from that rotation we determine the errors of our clocks and watches by astronomical observations. For many purposes it suffices to make these observations upon the sun, but when the utmost precision is desired it is better to make them on the stars. Until the close

---

* 12, p. 456.   † 44, pp. 762 and 943.

of the seventeenth century quadrants were employed for that purpose, and so late as 1680 Flamsteed, the first English astronomer royal, thought himself fortunate when he succeeded in construting one which enabled him to be sure of his observed times within three seconds.* About 1690 Roemer invented the transit instrument, which soon superseded the quadrant, and still remains the best appliance for determining time. Most of his observations were destroyed by a fire in 1728, but the few which have come down to us show that as early as 1706 he determined time with an accuracy which has not yet been very greatly surpassed. Probably the corrections found in the least square adjustment of extensive systems of longitude determinations afford the best criterion for estimating the accuracy of first-class modern time observations, and from them it appears that the error of such observations may rise as high as ± 0.05 of a second.

During the intervals between successive observations of the heavenly bodies we necessarily depend upon clocks and chronometers for our knowledge of the time, and very erroneous ideas are frequently entertained respecting the accuracy of their running. The subject is one upon which it is difficult to obtain exact information, but there are few time-pieces which will run for a week without varying more than three-quarters of a second from their predicted error. As the number of seconds in a week is 604,800, this amounts to saying that the best time-pieces can be trusted to measure a week within one part in 756,000. Nevertheless, clocks and chronometers are but adjuncts to our chief time-piece, which is the earth itself, and upon the constancy of its rotation depends the preservation of our present unit of time. Early in this century Laplace and Poisson were believed to have proved that the length of the sidereal day had not changed by so much as the one hundredth part of a second during the last twenty-five hundred years, but later investigations show that they were mistaken, and so far as we can now see, the friction produced by the tides in the ocean must be steadily reducing the velocity with which the earth rotates about its axis. The change is too slow to become sensible within the life-time of a human being, but its ultimate consequences will be momentous.

Ages ago it was remarked that all things run in cycles, and there is enough truth in the saying to make it as applicable now as on the day it was uttered. The Babylonian or Chaldean system of weights and measures seems to be the original from which the Egyptian system was derived, and is probably the most ancient of which we have any knowledge. Its unit of length was the cubit, of which there were two varieties, the natural and the royal. The foot was two-thirds of the natural cubit. Respecting the earliest Chaldean and Egyptian system of weights no very satisfactory information exists, but the best authorities agree that the weight of water contained in the measure of a cubic

---

* Account of the Rev. John Flamsteed. By Francis Baily. pp. 45–'6. (London, 1835. 4to. pp. lxxiv + 672.)

foot constituted the talent, or larger unit of weight, and that the six-tieth or fiftieth parts of the talent constituted, respectively, the Chaldean and Egyptian values of the mina, or lesser unit of commercial weight. Doubtless these weights varied considerably at different times and places, just as the modern pound has varied, but the relations stated are believed to have been the original ones. The ancient Chaldeans used not only the decimal system of notation, which is evidently the primitive one, but also a duodecimal system, as shown by the division of the year into twelve months, the equinoctial day and night each into twelve hours, the zodiac into twelve signs, etc., and a sexagesimal system by which the hour was divided into sixty minutes, the signs of the zodiac into thirty parts or degrees, and the circle into three hundred and sixty degrees, with further sexagesimal subdivisions. The duodecimal and sexagesimal systems seem to have originated with the Chaldean astronomers, who, for some reason which is not now evident, preferred them to the decimal system, and by the weight of their scientific authority impressed them upon their system of weights and measures. Now observe how closely the scientific thought of to day repeats the scientific thought of four thousand years ago. These old Chaldeans took from the human body what they regarded as a suitable unit of length, and for their unit of mass they adopted a cube of water bearing simple relations to their unit of length. Four thousand years later, when these simple relations had been forgotten and impaired, some of the most eminent scientists of the last century again undertook the task of constructing a system of weights and measures. With them the duodecimal and sexagesimal systems were out of favor, while the decimal system was highly fashionable, and for that reason they subdivided their units decimally instead of duodecimally, sexagesimally, or by powers of two; but they reverted to the old Chaldean device for obtaining simple relations between their units of length and mass, and to that fact alone the French metric system owes its survival. Every one now knows that the meter is not the ten-millionth part of a quadrant of the earth's meridian, and in mathematical physics, where the numbers are all so complicated that they can only be dealt with by the aid of logarithms, and the constant π, an utterly irrational quantity, crops up in almost every integral, mere decimal subdivision of the units counts for very little. But in some departments of science, as, for example, chemistry, a simple relation between the unit of length (which determines volume), the unit of mass, and the unit of specific gravity is of prime importance, and wherever that is the case the metric system will be used. To engineers such relations are of small moment, and consequently among English-speaking engineers the metric system is making no progress, while, on the other hand, the chemists have eagerly adopted it. As the English yard and pound are the direct descendants of the Chaldean-Babylonian natural cubit and mina, it is not surprising that the yard should be only 0.48 of an inch shorter than the double cubit, and the avoirdupois pound only 665 grains lighter than the Babylonian commercial mina; but, considering the origin of the metric system, it is rather curious that the meter is only 1.97 inches shorter than the Chaldean double royal cubit, and the kilogram only 102 grains heavier than the Babylonian royal mina. Thus, without much exaggeration, we may regard the present English and French fundamental units of length and mass as representing, respectively, the commercial and royal units of length and mass of the Chaldeans of four thousand years ago.

Science tells us that the energy of the solar system is being slowly dissipated in the form of radiant heat; that ultimately the sun will grow dim; life will die out on the planets; one by one they will tumble into the expiring sun; and at last darkness and the bitter cold of the absolute zero will reign over all. In that far-distant future imagine some wandering human spirit to have penetrated to a part of space immeasurably beyond the range of our most powerful telescopes, and there, upon an orb where the mechanical arts flourish as they do here, let him be asked to reproduce the standards of length, mass, and time with which we are now familiar. In the presence of such a demand the science of the seventeenth and eighteenth centuries would be powerless. The spin of the earth which measures our days and nights would be irretrievably gone; our yards, our meters, our pounds, our kilograms would have tumbled with the earth into the ruins of the sun and become part of the débris of the solar system. Could they be recovered from the dead past and live again? The science of all previous ages mournfully answers, No; but with the science of the nineteenth century it is otherwise. The spectroscope has taught us that throughout the visible universe the constitution of matter is the same. Everywhere the rythmic motions of the atoms are absolutely identical, and to them, and the light which they emit, our wandering spirit would turn for the recovery of the long-lost standards. By means of a diffraction grating and an accurate goniometer he could recover the yard from the wave length of sodium light with an error not exceeding one or two thousandths of an inch. Water is everywhere, and with his newly recovered yard he could measure a cubic foot of it, and thus recover the standard of mass which we call a pound. The recovery of our standard of time would be more difficult; but even that could be accomplished with an error not exceeding half a minute in a day. One way would be to perform Michelson's modification of Foucault's experiment for determining the velocity of light. Another way would be to make a Siemen's mercury unit of electrical resistance, and then, either by the British Association method or by Lord Rayleigh's modification of Lorenz's method, find the velocity which measures its resistance in absolute units. Still another way would be to find the ratio of the electro-static and electro-magnetic units of electricity. Thus all the units now used in transacting the world's business could be made to re-appear, if not with scientific, at least with commercial, accuracy, on the other side of an abyss of time and space before which the human mind shrinks back in dismay. The science of the eighteenth century sought to render itself immortal by basing its standard units upon the solid earth, but the science of the nineteenth century soars far beyond the solar system and connects its units with the ultimate atoms which constitute the universe itself.

Note A.

The appended table exhibits the principal comparisons hitherto made of the more important early English standards of length. The significations of the reference numbers, and the authorities for the descriptions of the standards, are as follows:

No. 1. Standard yard of Henry VII (1490); an end measure formed of an octagonal brass rod half an inch in diameter.

No. 2. Standard yard of Queen Elizabeth (1588); an end measure formed of a brass rod six-tenths of an inch square.

No. 3. Matrix to Queen Elizabeth's standard yard (1588); of brass, $1\frac{1}{2}$ inches wide, 1 inch thick, and 49 inches long.

No. 4. Standard ell of Queen Elizabeth (1588); an end measure of brass, six-tenths of an inch square.

No. 5. Standard yard of the Clock-makers' Company (1671); a matrix formed by two pins in an octagonal brass rod half an inch in diameter.

No. 6. Standard yard at the Tower; a line measure marked on a brass bar seven-tenths of an inch square and 41 inches long.

No. 7. Graham's Royal Society scale (1742); a line measure, on a brass bar half an inch wide, one-quarter of an inch thick, and 42 inches long. Line marked E. Mem. Roy. Ast. Soc., vol. 9, p. 82.

No. 8. Ditto. Line marked Exch.

No. 9. Ditto. Paris half toise; marked F.

Numbers 1 to 9 are described in the Philosophical Transactions, 1743, pp. 547–550.

No. 10. Bird's standard yard of 1758; a line measure, on a brass bar 1.01 inches square, and 39.06 inches long. Mem. Roy. Ast. Soc., vol. 9, p. 80.

No. 11. Bird's standard yard of 1760; a line measure, on a brass bar 1.05 inches square, and 39.73 inches long. Mem. Roy. Ast. Soc., vol. 9, pp. 80–82.

No. 12. General Roy's scale; a line measure, upon a brass bar 0.55 of an inch broad, about 0.22 of an inch thick, and 42.8 inches long; divided by Bird. Phil. Trans., 1785, p. 401, and Measurement of Lough Foyle Base, p. 73.

No. 13. Ramsden's bar, used in the trigonometrical survey of Great Britain. Phil. Trans.. 1821, p. 91, and Measurement of Lough Foyle Base, pp. 73–74.

No. 14. Sir George Shuckburg's scale (1796); a line measure, upon a brass bar 1.4 inches broad, 0.42 of an inch thick, and 67.7 inches long. Space compared, 0 inch to 36 inches. Phil. Trans., 1798, p. 133, and Mem. Roy. Ast. Soc., vol. 9, pp. 84–85.

No. 15. Ditto. Space compared, 10 inches to 46 inches.

No. 16. Ordnance yard 1A (1827); a line measure, upon an iron bar 1.45 inches broad, 2.5 inches deep, and rather more than 3 feet long. Measurement of Lough Foyle Base, pp. 71, 82, and [28].

No. 17. Ordnance yard 2A (1827). Similar to 1A. Same authorities.

No. 18. Captain Kater's Royal Society yard (1831); a line measure, upon a brass plate 0.07 of an inch thick. Phil. Trans., 1831, p. 345.

No. 19. The Royal Astronomical Society's standard scale (1834); a line measure, upon a brass tube 1.12 inches exterior diameter, 0.74 of an inch interior diameter, and 63 inches long. The central yard was the space compared. Mem. Roy. Ast. Soc., vol. 9, p. 69.

No. 20. "Colonel Lambton's standard;" a line measure, upon a brass plate 0.92 of an inch broad, 0.21 of an inch thick, and 66½ inches long; strengthened by an edge bar of nearly the same breadth, but only 0.08 of an inch thick. Phil. Trans., 1821, p. 88, and Mem. Roy. Ast. Soc., vol. 9, pp. 82–83.

The authorities for the comparisons given in the various columns of the table are as follows:

Column A. Comparisons by Mr. George Graham. Phil. Trans., 1743, pp. 187 and 547–550.

Column B. Comparisons by Sir George Shuckburgh. Phil. Trans., 1798, pp. 167–181.

Column C. Comparisons by Captain Kater. Phil. Trans., 1818, p. 55, and 1821, p. 91.

Column D. Comparisons by Captain Kater. Phil. Trans., 1830, p. 377, and 1831, p. 347.

Column E. Comparisons by Francis Baily, esq. Mem. Roy. Ast. Soc., vol. 9, p. 145.

Column F. Comparisons by Francis Baily, esq. Mem. Roy. Ast. Soc., vol. 9, p. 120.

Column G. Values adopted by R. Sheepshanks, esq. Phil. Trans., 1857, p. 661.

The values used by Mr. Sheepshanks in 1848 to determine the length of the present Imperial standard yard were Nos. 14 D, 15 F, 16 and 17 G, and 18 D.

It will be observed that several different units are employed in the various columns of the table, and care must be taken to allow for that circumstance when comparing numbers not situated in the same column.

COMPARISONS OF THE FUNDAMENTAL ENGLISH STANDARDS OF LENGTH.

Ref. No.	A.	B.	C.	D.	E.	F.	G.
	Inches.	Inches.	Inches.	Inches.	Inches.	Inches.	Inches.
1....	35.9929	35.966	....	....	....	....	....
2....	36.0000	35.993	....	....	....	....	....
3....	36.0102	....	....	....	....	....	....
4....	45.0494	44.964	....	....	....	....	....
5....	35.9790	....	....	....	....	....	....
6....	36.0111	....	....	....	....	....	....
7....	36.0075	36.0013	36.002007	....	36.001473	....	....
8....	36.0000	35.9933	....	....	35.993684	....	....
9....	38.355	38.3561	....	....	....	....	....
10....	....	36 00023	36.000802	....	....	....	....
11....	....	....	36.000659	36 000000	35.999624	36.000000	36.000000
12....	....	....	36.001537	....	....	....	....
13 ...	....	....	36.003147	....	....	....	....
14....	....	....	36.000642	36.00009	36.000185	....	....
15....	....	36.0000	....	....	35.999921	36.000058	....
16....	....	....	....	....	....	....	35.999716
17....	....	....	....	....	....	....	35.999892
18....	....	....	....	35.99938	....	....	....
19....	....	....	....	....	36.000000	....	....
20....	....	....	36.000000	....	....	....	....

NOTE B.

By direction of the Parliamentary Committee of 1758, and in the presence both of that body and of Mr. Farley, deputy chamberlain, Messrs. Harris and Gregory, of the London mint, compared the several standard troy weights of the Exchequer, with the following results:

4-ounce weight = All smaller weights — ½ grain.
8-ounce weight = All smaller weights + ½ grain.
16-ounce weight = All smaller weights + ¼ grain.
32-ounce weight = All smaller weights + 2 grains.
64-ounce weight = All smaller weights + 3 grains.
128-ounce weight = All smaller weights + 14 grains.
256-ounce weight = All smaller weights — 21 grains.

The weighings which yielded these results were made at the London mint; the instruments employed being "a very curious and exact pair of scales, belonging to Mr. Harris, and the scales used at the Mint for the weighing of gold." After recording the results in their report* the committee continued as follows:

Therefore beginning the Difference from the sixteen Ounce Weight, and carrying it on to the greatest Troy Weight in the Exchequer, the total Difference will be eight Grains and one-half.

The fourth Part of which is two Grains upon sixteen Ounces, which is a Grain and a half upon the twelve Ounces or Pound Troy.

* 13, p. 437.

Then the eight and four Ounces Troy of the Exchequer were compared with the following Weights:

First, With the Pound Troy used at the Mint in weighing of Gold, which was heavier than that at the Exchequer one Grain.

Secondly, With the eight and four Ounces at the Mint of the 6th of Queen *Anne,* 1707, which was heavier than that at the Exchequer half a Grain.

The eight and four Ounces of Queen *Elizabeth* 1588 at the Mint, was heavier than that at the Exchequer three Quarters of a Grain; another of the same Year of Queen *Elizabeth* at the Mint, stampt with a Tower, a Thistle and Crown, and EL and Crown, was heavier than that at the Exchequer one Grain.

Mr. *Freeman* produced a four and eight Ounce of the 6th of Queen *Anne* 1707, by which he makes Weights for Sale, which was heavier than the same Weights at the Exchequer one Grain and three Quarters: Therefore, upon an Average of all these Weights, the Pound Troy should be one Grain heavier than the Weights at the Exchequer, and that added to the Grain and a half, which, upon the former Experiments, the Weights at the Exchequer are too light a Medium taken from thence, makes the proper Increase of the Exchequer Pound Troy to be one Grain and one Quarter.

And it is to be observed, that the Pound Troy Weight at the Mint, which is now used for Gold, and the eight and four Ounces at the Mint, marked with a Tower, and in the Time of Queen *Elizabeth,* are both one Grain heavier than the eight and four Ounces of the Exchequer.

And considering that the Exchequer Weights have been used ever since the 30th of Queen *Elizabeth,* 1588, one hundred and seventy Years, to size other Weights by, it is highly probable, that the Difference may have been occasioned by the frequent Use of the Standard.

Your Committee endeavored to compare the Troy Weights with the original Standard at *Goldsmith's Hall,* from whence it is said, in the aforesaid Verdict of the 29th and 30th of *Elizabeth,* that the Weights now at the Exchequer were made, and for that Purpose sent to *Goldsmith's Hall* for the said Weights; but were informed that no such were to be found there, the Goldsmiths having no Weights older than those at the Exchequer.

The committee's statement respecting the way in which the correction of $1\frac{1}{2}$ grains was deduced from the weighings of the Exchequer weights is very obscure, and the result is not justified by generally accepted principles. If we put x for the sum of all the weights smaller than 4 ounces, then the results of the weighings made by the committee may be written in the form:

$$
\left.
\begin{array}{rcl}
\text{4 ounce divided} &=& 1\,x \\
\text{4 ounce weight} &=& 1\,x - \tfrac{1}{4}\ \text{grain.} \\
\text{8 ounce weight} &=& 2\,x + \tfrac{1}{4}\ \text{grain.} \\
\text{16 ounce weight} &=& 4\,x + \tfrac{1}{4}\ \text{grain.} \\
\text{32 ounce weight} &=& 8\,x + 2\tfrac{1}{4}\ \text{grains.} \\
\text{64 ounce weight} &=& 16\,x + 5\tfrac{1}{2}\ \text{grains.} \\
\text{128 ounce weight} &=& 32\,x + 22\ \text{grains.} \\
\text{256 ounce weight} &=& 64\,x + 9\ \text{grains.}
\end{array}
\right\} \qquad (1)
$$

Before proceeding further we must decide in what sense these weights are to be regarded as standards, and perhaps the most natural course

will be to regard the entire set as a standard of 512 troy ounces. In
that case the summation of the several columns gives

$$512 \text{ ounces} = 128\,x + 39 \text{ grains.}$$

whence

$$x = 4 \text{ ounces} - 0.3047 \text{ grain} \qquad (2)$$

and by substituting that value in the equations (1) we obtain the corrections to the several weights given in the second column of Table I.

TABLE I.—CORRECTIONS TO THE EXCHEQUER STANDARD TROY WEIGHTS OF 1588,
DERIVED FROM THE WEIGHINGS MADE BY MESSRS. HARRIS AND CHISHOLM.

Denomination of Weight.	Apparent correction in 1758.	Committee's correction in 1758	Chisholm's correction in 1873	Loss by wear in 115 years.
	Grains.	*Grains.*	*Grains.*	*Grains.*
4 ounces divided	— 0.30	— 0.42	— 1.69	— 1.27
4 ounces	0.55	0.67	0.68	0.01
8 ounces.......................	0.36	0.58	1.09	0.51
16 ounces......................	0.97	1.42	3.84	2.42
32 ounces......................	— 0.19	1.08	3.82	2.74
64 ounces......................	+ 0.62	— 1.17	— 5.04	3.87
128 ounces.....................	+ 12.25	+ 8.67	+ 4.28	4.39
256 ounces.....................	— 10.50	— 17.67	— 53.58	— 35.91
Sums..........................	± 0.00	— 14.34	— 65.46	— 51.12

From equations (1) and (2) we have

$$4 \text{ ounces} = 4\text{-oz. weight} + 0.5547 \text{ grain.}$$
$$8 \text{ ounces} = 8\text{-oz. weight} + 0.3594 \text{ grain.}$$

whence it follows that the sum of the 8 and 4 ounce weights, which
constituted the Exchequer standard troy pound, was too light by
0.9141 of a grain. As the mean correction obtained from the four
weights belonging respectively to the Mint and to Mr. Freeman, agrees
closely with this result, the true correction to the Exchequer standard
must have been very approximately 1 grain; and in adopting $1\frac{1}{4}$
grains the committee seem to have augmented the weight of the troy
pound by about one-quarter of a grain. The corrections which result
to the Exchequer troy weights upon the committee's assumption that
the sum of the 8 and 4 ounce weights was $1\frac{1}{4}$ grains too light are given
in the third column of Table I; while the fourth column contains the
corrections found by Mr. Chisholm in 1873,[*] and the fifth column shows
the loss of weight which occurred between 1758 and 1873. In view of
the fact that these weights were constantly used for comparing local
standards during a period of no less than two hundred and thirty-seven
years, from 1588 to 1825, their excellent preservation is very remarkable.

In the report of the committee of 1758 there is another set of comparisons of the Exchequer troy weights,[†] said comparisons having
been made on April 14, 1758, in accordance with the directions of

---

[*] 50, p. 21.   [†] 13, p. 435.

the committee, by Mr. Freeman and Mr. Reed, expert scale-makers, in the presence of Mr. Farley, deputy chamberlain. They are as follows:

$\frac{1}{8}$-ounce hollow $= \frac{1}{8}$-ounce solid $+ \frac{1}{4}$ grain.
$\frac{1}{4}$-ounce weight $=$ All smaller weights $- \frac{1}{4}$ grain.
$\frac{1}{2}$-ounce weight $=$ All smaller weights $- \frac{1}{4}$ grain.
1-ounce weight $=$ All smaller weights $- \frac{1}{2}$ grain.
2-ounce weight $=$ All smaller weights $- \frac{1}{2}$ grain.
4-ounce weight $=$ All smaller weights ± 0 grains.
8-ounce weight $=$ All smaller weights ± 0 grains.
16-ounce weight $=$ All smaller weights ± 0 grains.
32-ounce weight $=$ All smaller weights $- 2$ grains.
64-ounce weight $=$ All smaller weights ± 0 grains.
128-ounce weight $=$ All smaller weights $+ 15$ grains.
256-ounce weight $=$ All smaller weights $- 24$ grains.

In these equations the symbol ± 0 is used to indicate the relation which the committee expressed by saying that the weights "very nearly agreed."

Regarding the entire set of weights as a standard of 512 ounces, and putting x for the mass of the $\frac{1}{8}$-oz. solid weight we have

$$
\left.
\begin{array}{ll}
\frac{1}{8}\text{-ounce solid} & = \quad 1x. \\
\frac{1}{8}\text{-ounce hollow} & = \quad 1x + \frac{1}{4}\text{ grain.} \\
\frac{1}{4}\text{-ounce weight} & = \quad 2x. \\
\frac{1}{2}\text{-ounce weight} & = \quad 4x. \\
1\text{-ounce weight} & = \quad 8x. \\
2\text{-ounce weight} & = \quad 16x. \\
4\text{-ounce weight} & = \quad 32x + \frac{1}{2}\text{ grain.} \\
8\text{-ounce weight} & = \quad 64x + 1 \text{ grain.} \\
16\text{-ounce weight} & = \quad 128x + 2 \text{ grains.} \\
32\text{-ounce weight} & = \quad 256x + 2 \text{ grains.} \\
64\text{-ounce weight} & = \quad 512x + 6 \text{ grains.} \\
128\text{-ounce weight} & = \quad 1024x + 27 \text{ grains.} \\
256\text{-ounce weight} & = \quad 2048x + 15 \text{ grains.}
\end{array}
\right\} \qquad (3)
$$

Summing the various columns

$$512 \text{ ounces} = 4096x + 54 \text{ grains}$$

whence

$$x = \tfrac{1}{8} \text{ ounce} - 0.01318 \text{ grains,} \qquad (4)$$

and by substituting that value in the equations (3) we obtain the corrections given for the several weights in the second column of Table II. The third column contains the corrections which result upon the committee's assumption that the sum of the 8 and 4 ounce weights was $1\frac{1}{4}$ grains too light; and the fourth and fifth columns contain corrections given by Mr. Chisholm in his seventh annual report.[*] Mr. Chisholm does not explain how he obtained the corrections quoted in the fourth column of the table, but their close agreement with those in the third column renders it almost certain that they were computed from the comparisons made by Messrs Freeman and Reed. As the committee of 1758 used Mr. Harris's weighings *to the exclusion of those by Messrs. Freeman and Reed*, the adoption of the opposite course by Mr. Chisholm is perhaps explained by the circumstance that in his report on the Exchequer standards[†] *he has quoted the weighings by Messrs. Freeman and Reed and has attributed them to Mr. Harris.*

[*] 50, p. 21.   [†] 46, p. 11.

In addition to being less exact, the weighings by Mr. Freeman differ from those by Mr. Harris principally in the sign of the correction to the 32-ounce weight; the former stating that the 32-ounce weight was lighter than the sum of all the smaller weights and the latter that it was heavier. To ascertain which was right we have only to compare the resulting systems of corrections with those found by Mr. Chisholm in 1873. Table I shows that according to Mr. Harris's weighings all the weights have grown lighter during the interval from 1758 to 1873, while Table II shows that according to Mr. Freeman's weighings some have grown lighter and others heavier, and that by quantities which cannot be attributed to accidental errors in the weighings. In view of these facts there can be no doubt that the committee of 1758 was right in using only Mr. Harris's weighings, and it seems equally certain that the numbers in Table I should be adopted to the exclusion of those in Table II.

TABLE II.—CORRECTIONS TO THE EXCHEQUER STANDARD TROY WEIGHTS OF 1588, DERIVED FROM THE WEIGHINGS MADE BY MESSRS. FREEMAN AND CHISHOLM.

Denomination of Weight.	Apparent correction in 1758.	Committee's correction in 1758.	Corrections given by Mr. Chisholm—	
			For 1758.	For 1873.
	Grains.	Grains.	Grains.	Grains.
¼ ounce solid	— 0.01	— 0.03	0.0	— 0.06
¼ ounce hollow	+ 0.49	+ 0.47	+ 0.5	+ 0.40
½ ounce	— 0.03	— 0.06	0.0	— 0.21
½ ounce	0.05	0.11	0.0	0.36
1 ounce	0.11	0.23	0.0	0.45
2 ounces	— 0.21	0.46	— 1.0	1.01
4 ounces	+ 0.08	0.42	0.5	0.68
8 ounces	0.16	0.83	0.75	1.09
16 ounces	+ 0.31	1.68	1.75	3.84
32 ounces	— 1.38	5.36	5.5	3.82
64 ounces	— 0.75	8.70	— 9.0	— 5.04
128 ounces	+13.50	2.40	+ 3.0	+ 4.28
256 ounces	—12.00	— 43.81	—45.0	—53.58
Sums	± 0.00	—63.62	—61.0	—65.46

From comparisons of their troy pound with their avoirdupois pound, and with the 2-marc weight sent to them by the French Academy in 1742, the Royal Society of London found*—

(1) That the English avoirdupois pound weighed 7,004 troy grains:

(2) That the French *livre*, consisting of 2 marcs, weighed 7,560 troy grains:

And for three-quarters of a century the latter value was universally accepted. Further, when the metric system came into being the kilo-

*7, page 187. It is usual to designate 1742 as the date of the exchange of standards, but the remark of Cassini de Thury (5, p. 135) shows that the true date must have been prior to April, 1738. In his paper of November, 1742, Graham makes only the indefinite statement that the exchange was "proposed some time since."

gram was declared to consist of 18,827.15 French grains, of which the
livre contained 9216; * or, in other words, the kilogram was declared
equal to 2.04288 livres, whence, *with the Royal Society's value of the livre*,
the English equivalent of the kilogram was computed to be 15,444 troy
grains.

During some experiments at the London mint in March, 1820, it was
found that the French livre belonging to that institution weighed only
7,555 troy grains. This discovery led to an examination of the Royal
Society's standards of 1742, which had been carefully preserved, and it
was found that their livre agreed with that at the mint, but their Troy
pound was nearly 4 grains lighter than the Imperial standard of 1758,
and their avoirdupois pound weighed only 7,000 troy grains instead of
7,004.† Thus it was rendered almost certain that the accepted English
equivalent of the kilogram was about 10 grains too large, and, to remove
all possible doubt, a direct comparison of the English and French standards of weight was effected in 1821,‡ through the co-operation of the
respective governments, and then it was definitively ascertained that
the weight of the kilogram is only 15,433 troy grains.

The facts respecting the Royal Society's standards of 1742 are as
follows:

(1) The weighings recorded in the Philosophical Transactions, 1743,
pages 553 and 556, give

$$\text{R. S. troy pound} = \text{Exch. (8 ounces + 4 ounces)} - \tfrac{1}{2}\text{ grain} \qquad (5)$$
$$\text{R. S. troy pound} = \text{Mint (8 ounces + 4 ounces)} - 2\tfrac{3}{8}\text{ grains} \qquad (6)$$

whence

$$\text{Exch. (8 ounces + 4 ounces)} = \text{Mint (8 ounces + 4 ounces)} - 1\tfrac{7}{8}\text{ grains} \qquad (7)$$

(2) The weighings by Mr. Harris for the Parliamentary Committee
of 1758 give §

$$\text{Exch. (8 ounces + 4 ounces)} = \text{Mint (8 ounces + 4 ounces)} - \tfrac{1}{2}\text{ grain} \qquad (8)$$

whence by (6),

$$\text{R. S. troy pound} = \text{Exch. (8 ounces + 4 ounces)} - 1\tfrac{7}{8}\text{ grains} \qquad (9)$$

In equations (6) and (8) the weights at the mint were those of the
sixth of Queen Anne, 1707.

(3) In the Philosophical Transactions, 1742, page 187, it is stated that
the Paris 2-marc weight weighs 7560 troy grains. As the true weight
of 2 marcs is 7554.22 grains, this implies that the Royal Society's troy
pound was too light by 5.78 (5760 ÷ 7560) = 4.40 grains.

In the Philosophical Transactions, 1742, page 187, it is stated that
the Royal Society's avoirdupois pound weighed 7004 troy grains, while
the comparisons made in 1820 show that its weight was then only 7000
such grains. This implies that the Royal Society's troy pound was too
light by 4.00 (5760 ÷ 7000) = 3.29 grains.

Finally, the comparisons of 1820 showed that the Royal Society's
troy pound was "nearly 4 grains too light."

The mean of these three independent results shows that the Royal

---

* Base du Systèm Métrique, T. 3, p. 638.   ‡ 31, pages 19–22.
† See 40, vol. 1, p. 140, and 31, p. 19.   § 13, p. 437.

Society's troy pound was 3.9 grains lighter than the Imperial standard of 1758; whence

$$\text{R. S. troy pound} + 3\ 9 \text{ grains} = \text{Standard of 1758} \tag{10}$$

but

$$\text{Standard of 1858} = \text{Exch. (8 ounces} + 4 \text{ ounces)} + 1\tfrac{1}{4} \text{ grains} \tag{11}$$

and therefore

$$\text{R. S. troy pound} = \text{Exch. (8 ounces} + 4 \text{ ounces)} - 2\tfrac{5}{8} \text{ grains} \tag{12}$$

Considering the indefiniteness of the data respecting the weighings made in 1820, equations (9) and (12) agree fairly well, but equation (5) is very discordant, as are also equations (7) and (8). All the evidence seems to point to an error of about $1\frac{1}{2}$ grains in equation (5); and if instead of (5) we write

$$\text{R. S. Troy pound} = \text{Exch. (8 ounces} + 4 \text{ ounces)} - 2 \text{ grains} \tag{5'}$$

(7) will become

$$\text{Exch. (8 ounces} + 4 \text{ ounces)} = \text{Mint (8 ounces} + 4 \text{ ounces)} - \tfrac{3}{8} \text{ grain} \tag{7'}$$

and then all the equations will be reasonably accordant.

NOTE C. [Subsequently added.]

Assistant O. H. Tittmann, of the U. S. Coast and Geodetic Survey, in charge of weights and measures, has recently shown that the discrepancies in the values assigned to the meter in terms of the yard depend mainly upon errors either in the assumed lengths or in the assumed coefficients of expansion of the standards employed.[*] By a skillful use of the data published by the various observers, combined with the known coefficient of expansion of the iron committee meter, "CM," of the U. S. Coast and Geodetic Survey, he has succeeded in determining the absolute expansions of the standards in question, and by means of these expansions he has referred all the observations to the said committee meter and to the present British Imperial yard. From the data thus reduced to a common standard he has obtained the very consistent results given in the fourth column of the following table. The values in the third column are those published by the observers themselves, and it is now evident that they really depend upon several different British and metric units. As there is no means of referring the standard used by Prof. W. A. Rogers to the committee meter, his result could not be included in the table.

LENGTH OF THE METER EXPRESSED IN ENGLISH INCHES.

Date.	Authority.	Published value.	Value in terms of British Imperial yard and of the committee meter, CM.
1817–32	Hassler	39.380917	39.36994
1818	Kater	39.37079	39.36990
1835	Baily	39.369678	39.36973
1866	Clarke	39.370432	39.36970
1885	Comstock	39.36985	39.36984
Indiscriminate mean			39.36980

[*] See 73 and 74.

LIST OF THE PRINCIPAL AUTHORITIES CONSULTED IN THE PREPARATION OF THE FOREGOING ADDRESS.

NOTE.—The abbreviation "E. P. P." is used to designate English Parliamentary Papers. Some of these papers are of folio size and others of octavo size, but in the official sets they are all bound up indiscriminately in volumes of folio size, measuring 13 by 8½ inches.

Throughout the preceding pages authorities in this list are usually cited by number and page. For example, "30, p. 91" would indicate page 91 of Captain Kater's account of his comparisons of various British standards of linear measure, contained in the Philosophical Transactions for 1821.

1. PICARD, M. l'Abbé. De mensuris. Divers ouvrages. Mém. de l'Acad. Roy. des Sciences, 1666-1699, tome 6, pp. 532-549. Paris, 1730.

2. HIRE, M. DE LA. Comparaison du pied antique Romain à celui du Châtelet de Paris, avec quelques remarques sur d'autres mesures. Mém. de l'Acad. Roy. des Sciences, 1714, pp. 394-400. Paris, 1717.

3. FOLCES, MARTIN. An account of the standard measures preserved in the Capitol at Rome. Phil. Trans., 1735-'36, pp. 262-266.

4. MAUPERTUIS. La figure de la terre, déterminée par les observations de MM. de Maupertuis, Clairaut, Camus, le Monnier, - - - Outhier, - - - Celsius, - - - faites par ordre du Roy au cercle polaire. Paris, 1738. 16mo., pp. xxviii + 184.

5. CASSINI DE THURY. Sur la propagation du son. (On p. 135 has statement respecting standards of length exchanged between the French Academy and the English Royal Society.) Mém. de l'Acad. Roy. des Sciences, 1738, pp. 128-146. Paris, 1740.

6. Degré du méridien entre Paris et Amiens, déterminé par la mesure de M. Picard et par les observations de MM. de Maupertuis, Clairaut, Camus, le Monnier, - - - Paris, 1740, 16mo, pp. lvj + 116.

7. GRAHAM, GEORGE. An account of the proportions of the English and French measures and weights, from the standards of the same, kept at the Royal Society. Phil. Trans., 1742, pp. [185-188].

8. GRAHAM, GEORGE. An account of a comparison lately made by some gentlemen of the Royal Society, of the standard of a yard, and the several weights lately made for their use; with the original standards of measures and weights in the Exchequer, and some others kept for public use, at Guild-hall, Founders-hall, the Tower, etc. Phil. Trans., 1743, pp. [541-556].

9. CASSINI DE THURY. La méridienne de l'Observatoire royal de Paris, vérifiée dans toute l'étendue du royaume par de nouvelles observations. Paris, 1744. 8vo, pp. 292 + ccxxxvj.

10. REYNARDSON, SAMUEL. A state of the English weights and measures of capacity, as they appear from the laws as well ancient as modern; being an attempt to prove that the present avoirdupois weight is the legal and ancient standard for the weights and measures of this Kingdom. Phil. Trans., 1749-'50, pp. 54-71.

11. CONDAMINE, M. DE LA. Nouveau projet d'une mesure invariable, propre à servir de mesure commune à toutes les nations. Mém. de l'Acad. Roy. des Sciences, 1747, pp. 489-514. Paris, 1752.

12. BOUGUER, CAMUS, CASSINI DE THURY PINGRÉ. Opérations faites par ordre de l'Académie pour mesurer l'intervalle entre les centres des Pyramides de Villejuive & de Juvisy, etc. Mém. de l'Acad. Royale des Sciences, 1754, pp. 172-186. Paris, 1759.

13. Lord CARYSFORT. Report from the Committee appointed to inquire into the original standards of weights and measures in this Kingdom, and to consider the laws relating thereto. (Dated 26th May, 1758, and agreed to by the House June 2, 1758.)

Printed on pp. 411-451 of Reports from Committees of the House of Commons, which have been printed by order of the House, and are not inserted in the Journals. Reprinted by order of the House. Vol. 2. Miscellaneous subjects. (June 10, 1737, to May 21, 1765). Reprinted in 1803. Folio, $16\frac{3}{4}'' \times 10\frac{3}{4}''$. pp 468.

14. Lord CARYSFORT. Report from the Committee appointed (upon the first day of Dec., 1758) to inquire into the original standards of weights and measures in this Kingdom, and to consider the laws relating thereto. (Dated 11th April, 1759, and agreed to by the House April 12, 1759.) Printed on pp. 453–463 of Reports from Committees of the House of Commons, which have been printed by order of the House, and are not inserted in the Journals. Reprinted by order of the House. Vol. 2. Miscellaneous subjects. (June 10, 1737, to May 21, 1765). Reprinted in 1803. Folio, $16\frac{3}{4}'' \times 10\frac{3}{4}''$. pp. 468.

15. MASKELYNE, Rev. NEVIL (Astronomer Royal). The length of a degree of latitude in the province of Maryland and Pennsylvania, deduced from the foregoing operations (by Messrs. Chas. Mason and Jeremiah Dixon); by the Astronomer Royal. Phil. Trans., 1768, pp. 323-325.

16. NORRIS, HENRY. An inquiry to show what was the ancient English weight and measure according to the laws or statutes prior to the reign of Henry the Seventh. Phil. Trans., 1775, pp. 48-58.

17. CONDAMINE, M. DE LA. Remarques sur la toise-étalon du Châtelet, et sur les diverses toises employées aux mesures des degrés terrestres & à celle du pendule à secondes. Mém. de l'Acad. Roy. des Sciences, 1772, 2ᶜ partie. pp. 482-501. Paris, 1776.

18. ROY, Major-General WM. An account of a measurement of a base on Hounslow Heath. (Four large folding plates.) Phil. Trans., 1785, pp. 385-480.

19. LA LANDE, JÉRÔME LE FRANÇAIS. De la grandeur et de la figure de la terre. Astronomie, tome 3, pp. 1-47. (3ᵉ édition; Paris, 1792.)

20. BORDA, COULOMB, LEGENDRE, LAPLACE, PRONY et BRISSON. Rapport sur la vérification de l'étalon qui doit servir pour la fabrication des poids républicains. Annales de Chimie, Paris, 1797, tome 20, pp. 269-273.

21. SHUCKBURGH EVELYN, Sir GEO. An account of some endeavors to ascertain a standard of weight and measure. Phil. Trans., 1798, pp. 133-182.

22. VAN-SWINDEN, TRALLÈS, LAPLACE, LEGENDRE, MÉCHAIN, DELAMBRE, et CISCAR. Rapport sur la détermination de la grandeur de l'arc du méridien compris entre les parallèles de Dunkerque et Barcelone, et sur la longueur du mètre qu'on en déduit. Base du Système Métrique Décimal, tome 3, pp. 415-433. Paris, 1810. 4to.

23. KATER, Capt. HENRY. An account of experiments for determining the length of the pendulum vibrating seconds in the latitude of London. Phil. Trans., 1818, pp. 33-102.

24. KATER, Capt. HENRY. On the length of the French mètre estimated in parts of the English standard. Phil. Trans., 1818, pp. 103-109.

25. Experiments relating to the pendulum vibrating seconds of time in the latitude of London. 41 pp. (E. P. P.) Accounts and papers. Session, 27 Jan.—10 June, 1818. Vol. 15. Folio, $13\frac{1}{4}'' \times 8\frac{1}{4}''$. This is a verbatim reprint of Captain Kater's papers in the Phil. Trans., 1818, pp. 33-109.

26. BANKS, CLERK, GILBERT, WOLLASTON, YOUNG, and KATER. First report of the commissioners appointed to consider the subject of weights and measures. (Dated 24 June, 1819). 17 pp. (E. P. P.) Report from commissioners. Session, 21 Jan.—13 July, 1819. Vol. 11. Folio, $13\frac{1}{4}'' \times 8\frac{1}{4}''$.

27. CLERK, GILBERT, WOLLASTON, YOUNG, and KATER. Second report of the commissioners appointed by His Majesty to consider the subject of weights and measures. (Dated July 13, 1820). 40 pp. (E. P. P.) Reports from commissioners. Session, 21 April to 23 Nov., 1820. Vol. 7. Folio, $13\frac{1}{4}'' \times 3\frac{1}{2}''$.

28. CLERK, GILBERT, WOLLASTON, YOUNG, and KATER. Third report of the commissioners appointed by His Majesty to consider the subject of weights and measures.

(Dated March 31, 1821). 6 pp. (E. P. P.) Reports from committees. Session, 23 Jan. to 11 July, 1821. Vol. 4. Folio, $13\frac{1}{4}'' \times 8\frac{1}{2}''$.

29. Report from the Select Committee on Weights and Measures. (Dated May 28, 1821). 7 pp. (E. P. P.) Reports from committees. Session, 23 Jan. to 11 July, 1821. Vol. 4. Folio, $13\frac{1}{4}'' \times 8\frac{1}{4}''$.

30. KATER, Capt. HENRY. An account of the comparison of various British standards of linear measure. Phil. Trans., 1821, pp. 75–94.

31. Report from the Select Committee of the House of Lords - - - (on petition from Glasgow relative to) - - - the bill entitled "An act for ascertaining and establishing uniformity of weights and measures" - - - together with the minutes of evidence taken before said committee. (Dated 2 March, 1824). 35 pp. (E. P. P.) Reports from committees. Session, 3 Feb. to 25 June, 1824. Vol. 7. Folio, $13'' \times 8\frac{1}{2}''$.

32. KATER, Capt. HENRY. An account of the construction and adjustment of the new standards of weights and measures of the United Kingdom of Great Britain and Ireland. Phil. Trans., 1826, part 2, pp. 1–52

33. KATER, Capt. HENRY. On errors in standards of linear measure, arising from the thickness of the bar on which they are traced. Phil. Trans., 1830, pp. 359–381.

34. KATER, Capt. HENRY. An account of the construction and verification of a copy of the imperial standard yard made for the Royal Society. Phil. Trans., 1831, pp. 345–347.

35. Minutes of evidence taken before the select committee on bill to amend and render more effectual two acts of the 5th and 6th years of the reign of his late Majesty King George the 4th, relating to weights and measures. 67 pp. (E. P. P.) Reports from committees. 1834. Vol. 18, part 1. Folio, $13'' \times 8\frac{1}{2}''$.

36. Report from the select committee on the weights and measures act; together with the minutes of evidence. (Dated 17 June, 1835). 60 pp. (E. P. P.) Reports from committees. Session, 19 Feb. to 10 Sept., 1835. Vol. 18. Folio, $13'' \times 8\frac{1}{2}''$.

37. BAILY, FRANCIS. Report on the new standard scale of this (the Royal Astronomical) Society. (Gives also a history of English standards of length.) Mem. Roy. Ast. Soc., 1836. Vol. 9, pp. 35–184.

38. AIRY, Sir GEO. B. Extracts of papers, printed and manuscript, laid before the Commission appointed to consider the steps to be taken for restoration of the standards of weight and measure, and the subjects connected therewith. Arranged by G. B. Airy, esq., Astronomer Royal. Printed by order of the Lords Commissioners of the Treasury. London, 1840. 4to, 155 pp. (Consists of a vast number of brief extracts giving the opinions of many experts upon various points connected with the construction and use of standards of weight and measure, and the advantages and disadvantages of various systems of such standards.)

39. AIRY, BAILY, BETHUNE, HERSCHEL, LEFEVRE, LUBBOCK, PEACOCK, SHEEPSHANKS. Report of the commissioners appointed to consider the steps to be taken for restoration of the standards of weight and measure. (Dated 21 Dec., 1841). 106 pp. (E. P. P.) Reports from commissioners. Session, 3 Feb. to 12 Aug., 1842. Vol. 25. Folio.

40. KELLY, PATRICK. The universal cambist: being a full and accurate treatise on the exchanges, coins, weights, and measures of all trading nations and their colonies. By P. Kelly, LL. D. 2d edition. London, 1835. · 2 vols., 4to. Vol. 1, pp. xl + 422; vol. 2, pp. xxiv + 380.

41. YOLLAND, Capt. WM. An account of the measurement of Lough Foyle base in Ireland, with its verification and extension by triangulation; etc., etc. Published by order of the Hon. Board of Ordnance. London, 1847. 4to, pp 154 + [117].

42. AIRY, ROSSE, WROTTESLEY, LEFEVRE, LUBBOCK, PEACOCK, SHEEPSHANKS, HERSCHEL, MILLER. Report of the commissioners appointed to superintend the construction of new parliamentary standards of length and weight. (Dated March 28, 1854) 23 pp. (E. P. P.) Reports from commissioners. Session, 31 Jan. to 12 Aug., 1854. Vol. 19. Folio $13'' \times 8\frac{1}{2}''$.

43. Abstract of "Report of the Commissioners appointed to consider the steps to be taken for restoration of the standards of weight and measure " 16 pp. (E. P. P.) Reports from commissioners. Session, 12 Dec., 1854 to 14 Aug., 1855. Vol. 15. Folio, 13" × 8½".

44. MILLER, Prof. W. H. On the construction of the new imperial standard pound and its copies of platinum; and on the comparison of the imperial standard pound with the Kilogramme des Archives. Phil. Trans., 1856. pp. 753-946.

45. AIRY, Sir GEO. B. Account of the construction of the new national standard of length, and of its principal copies. Phil. Trans., 1857. pp. 621-702.

46. Copies "of a letter from the Comptroller General of the Exchequer to the Treasury, dated 3 June, 1863, transmitting a report on the Exchequer standards of weight and measure, dated 27 April, 1863, by Mr. Chisholm, chief clerk in the office of the Comptroller-General of the Exchequer; together with a copy of his report:" and, of a memorandum by the Astronomer Royal, dated 24 April, 1862, containing notes for the Committee on Weights and Measures, 1862. 51 pp. (Contains a complete descriptive list of all the old Exchequer stanards; a discussion on the moneyer's pound; and a history of English legislation on weights and measures.) (E. P. P.) Trade (Generally). Session, 4 Feb. to 29 July, 1864. Vol. 58. Folio.

47. CLARKE, Capt. A. R. Comparisons of the standards of length of England, France, Belgium, Prussia, Russia, India, Australia, made at the Ordnance Survey Office, Southampton. Published by order of the Secretary of State for War. London, 1866. 4to, pp. 287.

48. CLARKE and JAMES. Abstract of the results of the comparisons of the standards of length of England, France, Belgium, Prussia, Russia, India, Australia, made at the Ordnance Survey Office, Southampton, by Capt. A. R. Clarke, R. E., F. R. S., &c., under the direction of Col. Sir Henry James, R. E, F. R. S., &c., Director of the Ordnance Survey. With a preface by Col. Sir Henry James, R. E., F. R. S., &c. Phil. Trans., 1867, pp. 161-180.

49. CLARKE, Lt. Col. A. R. Results of the comparisons of the standards of length of England, Austria, Spain, United States, Cape of Good Hope, and of a second Russian Standard, made at the Ordnance Survey Office, Southampton. By Lieutenant-Colonel A. R. Clarke, C. B., R. E., F. R. S., &c., under the direction of Major-General Sir Henry James, R. E., F. R. S., &c., Director-General of the Ordnance Survey. With a preface and notes on the Greek and Egyptian measures of length by Sir Henry James. Phil. Trans., 1873, pp. 445-469.

50. CHISHOLM, HENRY WILLIAMS. Seventh annual report of the Warden of the Standards on the proceedings and business of the standard weights and measures department of the Board of Trade. For 1872-'73. 8vo, pp. 105. (Contains: Appendix IV. Account of the standard weights and measures of Queen Elizabeth. pp. 10-26: Appendix V. Account of the standard weights and measures of Henry VII. pp. 27-34: Appendix VI. New standard weights and measures constructed and legalized from the reign of Queen Elizabeth to George IV. pp. 35-40.) (E. P. P.) Reports from Commissioners. Session, 6 Feb. to 5 Aug., 1873. Vol. 38.

51. CHISHOLM, H. W. On the science of weighing and measuring, and standards of measure and weight. By H. W. Chisholm, warden of the standards. 16mo, pp. xvi+192. London: Macmillan & Co., 1877.

52. HILGARD, JULIUS E. Report on the comparison of American and British standard yards. Report of the Superintendent of the U. S. Coast Survey, 1877. Appendix No. 12, pp. 148-181. 4to.

53. WOLF, C. Recherches historiques sur les étalons de poids et mesures de l'Observatoire, et les appareils qui ont servi à les construire. Annales de l'Observatoire de Paris. Mémoires, tome 17, pp. C.1-C.78. (Published in 1883.)

54. WOLF, C. Résultats des comparaisons de la toise du Pérou au mètre international, exécutées au Bureau international des Poids et Mesures par M. Benoît. Comptes Rendus, 3 Avril 1888. Tome 106, pp. 977-982.

55. Annual reports of the Warden of the Standards on the proceedings and business of the standard weights and measures department of the Board of Trade. 8vo. (Printed as English Parliamentary Papers and contained in the volumes of "Reports from Commissioners.")

No. of Report.	Date.	No. of pages.	Volume of Reports from Commissioners.
1st	1866–'67	19	1867, Vol 19.
2d	1867–'68	13	1867–'68, Vol. 27.
3d	1868–'69	18	1868–'69, Vol. 23.
4th	1869–'70	25	1870, Vol. 27.
5th	1870–'71	46	1871, Vol. 24.
6th	1871–'72	203	1872, Vol. 35.
7th	1872–'73	105	1873, Vol. 38
8th	1873–'74	138	1874, Vol. 32.
9th	1874–'75	58	1875, Vol. 27.
10th	1875–'76	68	1876, Vol. 26.
11th	1876–'77	12	1877, Vol. 33.
12th	1877–'78	12	1878, Vol. 36.

56. Reports of the commissioners appointed to inquire into the condition of the Exchequer (now Board of Trade) standards. Presented to both Houses of Parliament by command of Her Majesty. Folio. (Printed as English Parliamentary Papers, and contained in the volumes of "Reports from Commissioners.")

No. of Report.	Date.	No. of pages.	Volume of Reports from Commissioners.
1st	24 July, 1868	8	1867–'68, Vol. 27.
2d	3 Apr., 1869	133	1868–'69, Vol. 23.
3d *	1 Feb., 1870	159	1870, Vol. 27.
4th †	21 May, 1870	438	1870, Vol. 27.
5th	3 Aug., 1870	265	1871, Vol. 24.
General Index		101	1873, Vol. 38.

* On the abolition of troy weight.
† On the inspection of weights and measures, etc.

57. ADAMS, JOHN QUINCY. Report upon weights and measures, by John Quincy Adams, Secretary of State of the United States. Prepared in obedience to the resolution of the Senate of the 3d of March, 1817. Washington: printed by Gales & Seaton. 1821. 8vo, pp. 245. (Contains report of F. R. Hassler on comparisons of English and French measures. pp. 153–170.)

58. ALEXANDER, J. H. Report (made to the governor of Maryland) on the standards of weight and measure for the State of Maryland; and on the construction of the yard-measures. Baltimore, Dec. 13, 1845. 8vo, pp. iv + 213.

59. HASSLER, FERDINAND RODOLPH. Papers on various subjects connected with the survey of the coast of the United States. Trans. Amer. Philosophical Society (Philadelphia), 1825, vol. 2, new series, pp. 232–420.

60. HASSLER, F. R. Comparison of weights and measures of length and capacity. Reported to the Senate of the United States by the Treasury Department in 1832, and made by Ferd. Rod. Hassler. 22d Congress, 1st session, Ho. of Reps., Doc. No. 299. Washington, 1832. 8vo, 122 pp., with 4 folding plates. (Contains a paper by Tralles giving important details, not published elsewhere, respecting the original iron meters of the Commission des Poids et Mesures of 1799.)

61. HASSLER, F. R. Report from the Secretary of the Treasury, transmitting the report of F. R. Hassler, Superintendent of the Coast Survey, and of the fabrication of standard weights and measures. 25th Congress, 2d session, Senate, Doc. No. 79. Washington, 1837. 8vo, 16 pp. (Explains method adopted for determining subdivisions of the troy pound.)

62. HASSLER, F. R. Report upon the standards of the liquid capacity measures of the system of uniform standards for the United States; with description of a new original barometer, and of the balance for adjusting the half bushels by their weight of distilled water. By F. R. Hassler. 27th Congress, 2d session, Senate, Doc. No. 225. Washington, 1842. 8vo, 26 pp. and 3 folding plates.

63. McCULLOH, R. S., and BACHE, A. D. Reports from the Secretary of the Treasury, of scientific investigations in relation to sugar and hydrometers, made, under the superintendence of Prof. A. D. Bache, by Prof. R. S. McCulloh. 30th Congress, 1st session, Senate, Ex. Doc. No. 50. Washington, 1848. 8vo, pp. 653.

64. BACHE, Prof. ALEXANDER D. Report to the Treasury Department on the progress of the work of constructing standards of weights and measures for the customhouses, and balances for the States, and in supplying standard hydrometers to the custom-houses, from 1 Jan., 1848, to 31 Dec., 1856. 34th Congress, 3d session, Senate, Ex. Doc. No. 27. Washington, 1857. 8vo, 218 pp. with 6 folding plates. (Contains descriptions of yard dividing engine, and various comparators.)

65. ROGERS, Prof. W. A. On the present state of the question of standards of length. (Contains a bibliography.) Proceed. Amer. Acad. of Arts and Sciences (Boston), 1879-80. Vol. 15, pp. 273-312.

66. ROGERS, Prof. W. A. On two forms of comparators for measures of length. 8vo, 12 pp. American Quarterly Microscopical Journal, April, 1879.

67. ROGERS, Prof. WM. A. Studies in metrology. 5 plates. (Contains description of the Rogers-Bond universal comparator.) Proceed. Amer. Acad. of Arts and Sciences, 1882-'83. Vol. 18, pp. 287-398. 8vo.

68. ROGERS, Prof. W. A. An examination of the standards of length constructed by the Société Génevoise. Proceed. Amer. Acad. of Arts and Sciences, 1884-'85. Vol. 20, pp. 379-389. 8vo.

69. ROGERS, Prof. W. A. A study of the centimeter marked "A," prepared by the U. S. Bureau of Weights and Measures for the Committee on Micrometry. 8vo, 23 pp. Proc. Amer. Society of Microscopists. Vol. 32, p. 184.

70. ROGERS, Prof. WM. A. On a practical solution of the perfect screw problem. 8vo, 44 pp. Trans. Amer. Soc. of Mechanical Engineers. Vol. 5.

71. ROGERS, Prof. W. A. A critical study of the action of a diamond in ruling lines upon glass. 8vo, 17 pp. Proc. Amer. Society of Microscopists. Vol. 32, p. 149.

72. Travaux et mémoires du Bureau International des Poids et Mesures, publiés sous l'autorité du Comité International, par le Directeur du Bureau. Paris. 4to. Tome 1, 1881, 391 pp.; T. 2, 1883, 413 pp.; T. 3, 1884, 348 pp.; T. 4, 1885, 421 pp.; T. 5, 1886, 416 pp.

73. TITTMANN, O. H. On the relation of the yard to the meter. Bulletin No. 9, U. S Coast and Geodetic Survey. June 15, 1889. 4to., 8 pp.

74. TITTMANN, O. H. The Shuckburgh scale and Kater pendulum. Nature, April 10, 1890. Vol. 41, p. 538.

75. WALKER, Gen. J. T. On the unit of length of a standard scale by Sir George Shuckburgh, appertaining to the Royal Society. Proceedings Roy. Soc., Feb. 13, 1890. Vol. 47, pp. 186-189.

76. LEHMANN, Dr. On the nature and distribution of the Babylonian metrical system. Nature, Dec. 19, 1889. Vol. 41, pp. 167-168.

DETERMINATION OF THE MEAN DENSITY OF THE EARTH BY MEANS OF A PENDULUM PRINCIPLE.

By J. WILSING.

Translated and condensed by Prof. J. HOWARD GORE, Ph. D.[*]

Four different methods have been used in the determination of the mean density of the earth. The·first is based upon the measurement of the deflection of the plumb-line in the neighborhood of great mountain masses; the second upon the determination of the length of the second's pendulum at various distances from the earth's center. According to the third and fourth methods, the attraction of a body of known mass, usually of a globular shape, is ascertained by means of the torsion balance, or directly with an ordinary balance and compared with the constants of gravity.

The first attempts towards the solution of this problem were by Maskelyne, receiving a new discussion at the hand of Hutton a few years later. Maskelyne's results depended upon the measurement of the deflection of the plumb line caused by the attraction of Schehallien, in connection with an approximated value for the density of the mountain. This estimated density, derived from the superficial strata alone, was so subject to uncertainties that the result can be regarded as nothing more than a rough approximation. Later and more general investigations have shown that local deflection may arise from a variety of co-existing or conspiring causes, so that the attraction of elevations can be accounted for by the presence of depressions or interior defects in the earth's mass. In such a case, a value for the attracting mass which is deduced from the exterior configuration alone, must lead to incorrect results. Similar objections can be applied to the method of pendulum swinging, which was made use of by Carlini and Airy, and more recently by von Sterneck and Albrecht.

Hence the invention by Coulomb of the torsion balance and its application by Cavendish to the problem in question marked a great advance towards its accurate solution. The great sensitiveness of this instrument makes its possible to render measurable the attraction of balls of a few hundredweight, the mass of which can easily be ascer-

* From Publicationen des astrophysikalischen Observatoriums zu Potsdam, vol. VI, Potsdam, 1887, 1888.

tained by weighing, so that the determination of the density of the earth enters into the realm of laboratory investigation. However, this sensitiveness which eliminates the uncertainty in the computation of the attracting forces has, as a consequence, some disadvantages which were first mentioned by Francis Baily while engaged upon the same problem. These drawbacks consist chiefly of a limited inertia and stability against accidental disturbances, especially temperature changes and the variations in the twisting force of the supporting thread. In the interesting investigations of A. Cornu and J. B. Baille the disturb. ances just referred to seem to have been essentially eliminated. Unfortunately it is not possible to form an opinion regarding the accuracy of the results from the short report that is given in Compt. Rend., 1878, LXXXVI, pp. 699–702. At all events measurements with the torsion balance must be regarded as especially difficult.

For this reason the fourth method, the determination by the means of a balance of the change in weight of a body caused by the proximity of a second body of known mass, has the preference. It is true, however, that the ordinary balance is not sufficiently sensitive to measure the attraction of bodies as small as those employed in the torsion balance. Jolly, who first made use of this method, utilized a ball of lead of 120 hundredweight. At this time Messrs. König and Richarz are working at Jolly's method, using a parallelopiped block of lead of 2,000 hundredweight. Since it is necessary to actually determine the weight of these large bodies, a task rendered difficult on account of their size, the measurement of their attraction requires the transposition of them while being weighed. Jolly had four scale pans, two of which were fastened below the others by a wire 21 meters long; he determined the increase in the weight of a glass vessel filled with mercury which was caused by its transfer to the lower scale pan under which was the attracting ball of lead. This transfer caused a loss of time, and necessitated a frequent stoppage of the balance, a condition which might seriously affect the results since the change in the relative positions of knife-edge and its resting place would bring about a deformity in the former, causing a disturbance in the oscillation of the balance.

I have sought to overcome these difficulties by turning the instrument through 90°, that is, by replacing for a horizontal balance a vertical one or a pendulum whose knife-edge is above the center of gravity and very near to it, upon the hypothesis that the sensitiveness of the apparatus could be materially increased if it forms a rigid system and is protected from flexure by being supported with its length vertical. Then it is possible to succeed with smaller and more easily handled masses, and to prosecute the observations without difficulty while the necessity to stop the instrument during the progress of the work is entirely avoided. A trial apparatus was constructed in which the time of oscillation was prolonged to the desired extent, giving results so harmonious that a final pendulum was completed in 1885 by Repsold.

The pendulum consists of a drawn brass tube 1ᵐ long, 4.15ᶜᵐ in diameter, and 0.16ᶜᵐ thick, which is strengthened near its middle by means of a frame, C E F D. At this place are two mortises on opposite sides of the tube, E F, rectangular in shape, 9ᶜᵐ long and 2ᶜᵐ wide, for the insertion of the resting place or bed L for the knife-edge S which is firmly fastened to the pendulum. The upper portion of this bed is a slightly concave piece of agate of 6ᶜᵐ in length and 1ᶜᵐ in width securely attached to the supporting brass. The knife-edge, also of agate, has the same length as its bed. Its cross-section is an equilateral triangle with sides 1.7ᶜᵐ long. The edge is not perfectly sharp, and on account of the concavity of the bed rests on it only near the end. The slits just referred to serve as a guide to the knife-edge and also admits the air into the interior of the tube so that there may be a quick and equable response to all temperature changes. The ends of the tube are closed by means of brass caps which carry conical pins. Upon these pins balls of brass, A, are attached by means of screws. The pins are prolonged beyond the balls and one of them carries three small movable screws, N, whose determinations will be given later; at the other end corresponding to this additional weight a brass disk of equal weight is screwed on so that the symmetry of the apparatus is preserved. Through the upper end of the pendulum rod perpendicular to the length of the knife-edge there is a slender screw, G H, 7ᶜᵐ long, which serves in adjusting the position of the center of gravity. Directly before and behind the knife-edge circular mirrors of 3.5ᶜᵐ diameter are attached, with whose assistance the swinging of the pendulum can be observed. In order to avoid magnetic interferences, brass is used throughout the entire instrument.

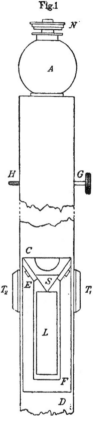

Fig.1

DESCRIPTION OF THE OBSERVING-ROOM.

The observing-room, 4ᵐ square, is situated in the basement of the west wing of the observatory. As the walls are very thick and the room, being on the southern side directly under the cupola, is protected from the direct rays of the sun, the changes in the temperature are very slight.

In the middle of the room there was a rigid pillar of brick with its foundation 3 feet deep. On its south side is the cast-iron bracket which supports the pendulum, so arranged that when once placed in a perpendicular position it can be securely held so. The whole is protected from air disturbances by means of a wooden box covered with cloth and fastened directly to the pillar. The front of the box can be taken off, so as to remove or replace the pendulum, while an opening, provided with a cover, in the top allows the weights to be moved at will. On the sides in front of the mirrors, already described, are small square windows closed with glass. Later this box was covered with a coat of white lead.

The telescope with which the oscillations were observed had an opening of 8^{cm} and 80^{cm} focal distance. It was fastened on a brick pillar in communicating passage. The scale utilized in the observations was on glass; it was 50^{cm} in length, and was placed at a distance of 500^{cm} from the mirror. The magnifying power of the telescope was such that the tenth of a millimeter could be approximated, and after some practice the twentieth, a value which represented about a second of arc. The graduation error in the scale was never greater than 0.01^{mm}.

THE ATTRACTING MASSES.

Until now balls of lead have been universally used. But on account of the softness of lead it is almost impossible to secure a geometric body homogeneous in its structure; besides, the continued suspension would bring about, through the action of gravity, deformities. For these reasons, notwithstanding its small specific gravity, the preference was given to cast-iron, and for practical convenience and the possibility of a more exact figure the cylindrical shape was chosen. They were cast under pressure, and upon a subsequent weighing and examination for specific gravity they appeared practically identical.

These masses, each of which weighed 325 kilograms, were so hung by a wire rope over a system of pulleys that they always balanced one another, and could be easily moved, one up, the other down. The length of the rope was so adjusted that when one of the cylinders was directly opposite the upper end of the pendulum the other would be on the opposite side and directly on a line with the lower end. In order to obviate any lateral motion and consequent shaking, each cylinder was provided with guiding rollers which ran up tracks attached to uprights, firmly held in their proper places. This and similar precautions were so well taken that during the entire series of observations no jarring was observed.

ARRANGEMENT OF THE OBSERVATIONS.

When the pendulum was put in motion, before the cylinders were put in place, it was noticed if the amplitude was bisected by the vertical through the point of support. If not, the screw in the upper end, already referred to, was made use of, aided, if necessary, by a change in the position of the thin plates on the top of the rod.

The position of equilibrium was next determined by placing, for instance, the eastern weight near the upper end of the pendulum, observing a series of four consecutive elongations, then changing the weights, observe another series of four elongations. Both series were, with few exceptions, separated from one another by a complete double swing. The observations were repeated, so as to have two or three sets of four readings for each day. The arc of oscillation gradually decreased to a fixed limit, since the series were so arranged that the transfer of the weights could be made to follow that phase of oscillation in which the change in the direction of the force causes a retardation of its motion. The amplitude of the arc was between three degrees and a few minutes, with about 45′ as an average.

With the determination of the position of equilibrium that of the duration of the oscillation is closely allied. The time of the transit of a division of the scale over the wire of the telescope could be estimated within 0.1 second. These transits were usually observed on three divisions. If the times of transits of the same phase were observed, the difference would give an approximate value for the time of a double oscillation; which, however, must be corrected for the decreased arc owing to the resistance of the air.

For the reduction of the observations there is still needed a determination of the sensitiveness of the pendulum. This is also found from the period of oscillation, by changing the position of the supplemental weights attached to the upper end of the pendulum. Each observed period in combination with the normal period gave the moment of inertia and the distance of the center of gravity from the knife-edge.

In all the observations a chronometer giving stellar time was used, and was compared both before and after each series with the standard clock of the observatory. Barometric readings were made, as well as those for temperature, which were taken from thermometers placed in various parts of the room.

Laplace noticed, and Bessel proved by experiments, that the shape of the knife-edge supporting a pendulum exerted an appreciable effect upon the period of oscillation and the diminution in the amplitude. Since this period furnishes an important element in all reductions, it was necessary to investigate the effect of the dulling of the knife-edge. At the same time the resistance of the air and its resulting interference were investigated.

The computation of the moment of inertia was divided into parts, taking up first the moment for the mean position of the instrument as previously determined, using in this connection the moment of a material line coincident with the axis of the pendulum rod and perpendicular to the line joining the centers of the attracting masses. The attraction of the masses is:

$$2\pi f m\, g\, \delta(\sqrt{(a-h)^2+R^2} - \sqrt{(a+h)^2+R^2}+2h)$$

in which mg is the weight of the ball, f a constant, δ, $2h$, and R the specific gravity, height, and radius of the cylinder, and a the distance of the middle point of the ball to the center of the cylinder. If l is the distance of the center of the ball from the knife-edge, the moment will be:

$$2\pi f m g \delta l\,(\sqrt{a-h)^2+R^2} - \sqrt{(a+h)^2+R^2}+2h)$$

The effect of the screws and the rollers serving as guides for the cylinders was next investigated and allowance therefor duly made, likewise for such other parts as were not of an eliminating character. After making all corrections that presented themselves the result was the desired moment for the normal position of the pendulum. The next thing was to find what change was produced upon this moment by giving to the pendulum a certain position; that is, when the pendulum is at a known point, as shown by the reading of the reflection on the scale. By combining both elongations certain terms in the computation disappeared, thus simplifying the labor. If $2\varphi(a)$ represents the moment in the normal position of the pendulum, regarding a as the distance from the origin, b the linear deviation of the middle of the ball, e the deviation, likewise expressed in linear measure, caused by attraction, the moment will be expressed by $\varphi(a+b-e)$ for the first position of the weights and $\varphi(a-b-e)$ for the second. The sum of both is $2\varphi(a-e)+b^2\varphi''(a-e)$, but since $\varphi''(a-e)=0$, the resulting moment can be expressed by $2\varphi(a)-2e\varphi'(a)$, a value which can be accepted as sufficiently accurate when it is considered that e never exceeds two millimeters.

Although the attraction of the cylinders upon the instrument is theoretically determined with sufficient precision, yet the accuracy of the final result is limited by the closeness with which the constants are known. Therefore it is preferable to eliminate from the final result those constants which can not be ascertained with the desired accuracy. This can be done in the following simple manner:

Suppose a series of observations with the complete apparatus gave for the mean density $\varDelta$, and a second series after diminishing the weights on the upper end of the pendulum gave $\varDelta_{//}$; the difference between these two values rests upon a false value for the specific gravity of the pendulum, not regarding errors of observation for the present. If X is the error in the moment arising from this cause, the true value can be derived from $\varDelta = \varDelta_{/} + \dfrac{x}{m_{/}}$, $\varDelta = \varDelta_{//} + \dfrac{x}{m_{//}}$, in which $m_{/}$ and $m_{//}$ are obtained from the observations. In this manner the attraction of the weights upon the pendulum-rod appears to be perfectly eliminated from the final result. It is conditioned upon the value accepted as the attraction of the balls alone, in which no uncertainty is involved, while the agreement $\varDelta_{/}$ and $\varDelta_{//}$ furnishes a thorough control over the experiments.

Correction for the resistance of the air was applied, and a law for the decrease in the amplitude sought. This was found to be proportional to the first power of the velocity, a result which agrees with the expression found by Cornu and Baille for the effect of the air upon the torsion balance.

The constants were determined with great care, and in each case the units of weight and measure were compared with the standards, while the specific gravity was ascertained from some metal taken from the same crucible from which the weights were cast. The relative position of the weights and pendulum balls during the observations was an important factor, as was also the radius vector of each of the balls, and they were most carefully investigated. It was found that after the first few days there was no appreciable change in the length of the wire rope supporting the weights, so that the employment of the mean relative position could not introduce dangerous errors. The length of the pendulum balls from the knife-edge, the principal element entering into the computation of the moments, was measured by a standard catheto-meter belonging to the Prussian commission of standards. The distance of the knife-edge from the scale was ascertained by means of direct measurement and by triangulation with results quite harmonious. In the determination of all the constants the effort was made, and successfully it is believed, to keep the error within one unit in the third decimal place.

Just here it might be mentioned that, taking every possible element into consideration, the resulting moment of the pendulum with the balls for both positions of the weights was 10.3106δ, while without the balls it was 4.3578δ, in which δ represents the specific gravity of the weights.

DISCUSSION OF THE OBSERVATIONS AND RESULTS.

The observations consisted of the determination of the duration of oscillation and the equilibrium position of the pendulum, for which a series of fourteen observations were made with the balls on the pendu lum and twelve with the balls removed. They were begun with a large amplitude and continued until the arc passed over was only six or ten minutes. In both cases a continuous decrease in the time showed itself, which could not be explained by the usual reduction to the smallest swings. Hence the time was taken for two double swings when the amplitude was at an average value, and two or more times taken on each side of this value. These observations were adjusted graphically, a method which answered in this case in consequence of the regularity in the values. The theoretical time was compared with the observed, and the discrepancy reduced to a minimum. Knowing the equilibrium position of the pendulum, and the distance of the ball from this point, at each elongation a simple subtraction gave the distance of the ball from the attracting body.

The formula used in the final computation was:

$$g = \text{a constant } \Delta \frac{4}{3}\pi R\left[1+\sigma-\left(\frac{5}{2}\sigma-\varepsilon\right)\cos^2\varphi\right]$$

in which Δ is the desired density, R the polar radius, σ the ratio of the equatorial centrifugal force to the polar$\left(\dfrac{1}{289.06}\right)$ ε the ellipticity of the earth $\left(\dfrac{1}{299.15}\right)$ and φ the geographicall atitude ($52\degree\ 23''$). This gave with the balls $\varDelta_{\prime}=5.651\pm0.017$ and without $\varDelta_{\prime\prime}=5.731\pm0.020$. As already intimated the discrepancy·is to be ascribed to the inaccuracy in the determination of the weight of the pendulum, so, using the formulæ already given :·

$$\varDelta=\varDelta_\prime+\frac{x}{m_\prime},\ \varDelta=\varDelta_{\prime\prime}+\frac{x}{m_{\prime\prime}},\ \text{from which}\ \varDelta=\frac{m_\prime\varDelta_\prime-m_{\prime\prime}\varDelta_{\prime\prime}}{m-m_{\prime\prime}}$$

the reduced observations gave

$$m_\prime=4.6268\pm0.0136$$
$$m_{\prime\prime}=1.9269\pm0.006$$

from which the mean density $\varDelta=5.594\pm0.032$.

The probable error of the final result might have been reduced by increasing the number of observations. Still it seemed better while testing this new method not to accumulate too much material or more than was needed to reach a reasonably accurate result. But since the experiments here made point to the possibility of a better solution of this problem, it is intended to carry the observations further, and by a new determination of the constants to secure results independent of their first determination.

CONCLUSION.

For the purpose of comparison, the previously-found values for the mean density might properly be given here.

Maskelyne found from local deflection at Schehallien, 4.713 ; Colonel James, at Arthur's Seat, 5.14 ; Carlini and Airy received from pendulum determinations 4.837 and 6.623, and in more recent times Mendenhall and von Sterneck, 5.77.

Cavendish (5.48), Reich (5.49, in the revision 5.58), Baily (5.66, after correction by Cornu and Baille, 5.55), Cornu and Baille (5.56) used the torsion balance, finally Joily (5.692), Poynting (5.69) utilizing the ordinary balance. The result here found is considerably smaller than those found by Jolly's method, and slightly larger than the values which the torsion balance gave, especially the corrected value of Baily. I think, however, that the correction here referred to as made by Cornu and Baille admits of criticism. As in the present case, Baily observed in each position of the weights four stationary points. He also used the time when the balance was stationary at its greatest elongation for changing the weights, so that the last observation of each series might at the same time be the first of the next series. With most of his observations the difference between two consecutive elongations on the one side did not agree with the corresponding difference on the other, and furthermore this difference was always greater on the side where the first reading was. Cornu and Baille concluded that this lack of symmetry was owing to the presence of a constant error which was not eliminated in the subsequent adjustments. However, it is not equally apparent that the tendency of this error is to increase the final result. According to their belief the irregularity referred to in the diminution of the amplitude is owing to unsteadiness which was caused by the change of the weights, and therefore influences the first reading of each series. But it is not easy to see how the disturbance, which was so regular, can be explained in this manner, especially since Baily has expressly referred to the perfect isolation of the masses, and their easy motions free from jar. He did not explain with equal clearness the way in which he obviated such disturbances as might arise from change of temperature, disturbances which, at the beginning of his observations, caused serious difficulties. The supposition of a difference of temperature, scarcely shown by a thermometer, between the masses and the balance inclosed in a thick box seems justified, and such differences are sufficient to explain the disturbances of a system swinging with such a slight inertia. They would be analogous to the irregularities which have been observed in these experiments to exist between the temperature of the two sides of the pendulum-rod and which were in direct dependence upon the algebraic sign of the motion of the zero point from the source of heat. The disturbances which showed themselves in Baily's series of observations were regarded as a change of sign in the course of the zero point, which produced such an effect that the observed deflection grew regularly with the time since the transfer of the weights to their new position. The plan of computing the position of equilibrium from the last three numbers of each series, a method which leads to a much smaller value, was set aside by Cornu and Baille for one which will increase the error in the reduction of Baily's work. It would have been too much to expect for this reason a smaller value for the mean density of the earth from Baily's observations than would have resulted from the avoidance of this error, a remark intensified by the deviation of his result from those deduced by others from the torsion balance. Unfortunately it is not possible to reach from the observations any conclusion regarding the two opposing hypotheses, since no readings are given of a long series without changing the weights.

The observations here given have shown that the pendulum is a most excellent instrument for the determination of gravity, a problem which for a time it did not seem competent to solve. It is to be hoped that its somewhat restricted domain may be extended. In this connection there may be mentioned the determining of inner friction, a matter of great importance in the mechanical theory of gas. Since the resistance of the air in the case of a sensitive pendulum causes a rapid decrease in the amplitude of the arc, the amount of retardation is so considerable that an accurate determination of the desired quantity can best be secured from a few observations. The results might be modified by an appreciable change in the sensitiveness, atmospheric pressure, or temperature. Stokes has discussed the case in which an infinitely long cylindrical rod oscillates so that its axis remains parallel. The solution of this is closely related to that of a rod swinging about a fixed axis in a closed box, if in addition to the conditional equations which are to be fulfilled on the surface of the rod certain others are introduced. In this way Stokes reduced Baily's experiments with the rod-shaped seconds pendulum. In the foregoing case the pendulum-rod was hollow, into which the air could enter unrestricted. This condition complicated the problem ; however only a few changes in the construction of the pendulum would be necessary in order to render Stokes's theory applicable.

May the apparatus whose application to a special case is here shown, prove itself useful in physical investigations in other realms.

In "Publicationen des Astrophysikalischen Observatoriums," vol. VI (the preceding part of this abstract), I have given a series of observations which I prosecuted with a peculiarly constructed pendulum for the purpose of determining the mean density of the earth. The discussion of these observations led to satisfactory results, but the experiments justified the expectation that a greater accuracy might be reached by an elimination of certain obstacles, partly of an accidental nature, and especially by a more thorough protection against the influence of temperature change. The results of the observations made after the application of the contemplated improvements gratified the anticipations, since the probable error in the latter set of experiments is only one-third of that obtained by the former. The axes of the cylinders, which were directed towards the center of the balls attached to the pendulum, during the first experiments made an angle with the plane of oscillation in order to secure a sufficient proximity of the balls to the attracting masses. This state of affairs complicated the numerical computation of the situation of the pendulum with respect to the masses, since besides the measurement of the separation of their surfaces from the middle point of the apparatus it was necessary to accurately ascertain the difference of direction which the axes of the masses made with the plane of oscillation. The supports were so changed that the axes could be brought precisely into the plane of the pendulum. This simplification made it possible to secure such a position as to allow a more ready and accurate measurement of the distance of the masses from the apparatus, and at the same time it served to keep it in that position. On both sides of the pillar which supported the instrument places were attached for the support of a contact lever rotating about a vertical axis. One arm of this lever, terminating in a sharp point, rested against the back of the attracting mass, while the other arm swept over a short scale divided into millimeters, provided with a registering apparatus so that its position could be readily ascertained. Since the lengths of the arms were as 1: 4, a change in the situation of the cylinder could be estimated to a tenth of a millimeter without difficulty. In case of a contrary movement of the mass, the pin of the lever would keep in contact with it through action of a pressure weight on the lever. The guides on the sides were renewed and made stronger so as to counteract all swinging motions of the masses.

While the changes and improvements just referred to were being made to secure a more accurate and ready determination of the constants, protection against the ill effects of sudden and irregular changes in temperature in the neighborhood of the apparatus was so complete as to obtain a closer agreement in the results of the experiments. The door and window were also tightened and the wooden coverings coated with paint. The box containing the pendulum was covered with tinfoil and white-lead, and the attracting masses were likewise subjected to a covering of tin-foil so as to free them from the action of the lamp which illuminated the scale. To still further secure the apparatus from sudden changes of temperature during a series of observations all operations were conducted without entering the room, employing electricity to mark the correct height of the cylinders when their positions were changed.

With the precautions just referred to, it was possible not only to keep the temperature of the room constant during a series of observations, but also to eliminate, so far as the thermometer would show, the effect of the warmth of the lamp, which was apparent during the first set of experiments.

A disturbance was however noticeable, caused by a temporary horizontal stratification of temperature, which in the neighborhood of the apparatus was interrupted by the changing of the masses whose temperatures were unequal. I sought to compensate the operation of this interruption by so attaching lead disks of the same diameter as the cylinders that they remained in every position opposite the masses, in this way securing at each change the same temperature throughout any horizontal cross-section of the pendulum.

The order of observing is essentially the same as during the former series; however, instead of having a pause in the middle of the set, with four readings on each side, or before and after, the eight or ten readings of the elongations of the pendulum were consecutive, in this way making it possible to discuss the observations of a day as equably distributed over the period of observation. In the determination of the time of oscillation of the pendulum after the removal of the extra weight on its upper end a better method was adopted by computing the desired quantity directly from the means of two series of observations separated from one another by a considerable interval.

In the first experiments I computed numerically the attraction of the masses upon the pendulum rod. The result was important, especially as a control or check upon the experiments, but on account of the uncertainty in the computation of certain constants which entered into the work, it was not to be compared with the latter results which were obtained by an empirical elimination. In these computations this control could be dispensed with, thus relieving one of the numerical work which the determination of the moments of the pendulum required. On the other hand it was desirable to make surer the empirical elimination or ascertaining of these constants by increasing and modifying the observations. I have therefore made a series of observations, using on the pendulum balls of lead the same size but heavier than the brass balls, which, combined with the series made without any balls, gave another result independent of the result obtained when the brass balls were used.

In all other respects the method of reduction was the same as during the first determination.

The value found for the mean density is 5.579 ± 0.012.

AMERRIQUES, AMERIGHO VESPUCCI, AND AMERICA.

By Jules Marcou.

INTRODUCTION.

The Amerriques tribe of Indians, now few in number, are confined to their mountains, called Sierra Amerrique, which form the cordillera between Lake Nicaragua and the Mosquito coast, in the province of Chontales, Nicaragua.

By a combination of circumstances, not rare, in what pertain to the first discoveries made in the New World, the name of *Amerrique* was not printed or perhaps even written in documents until 1872, when the late Thomas Belt, a naturalist of genius, during an exploration of Nicaragua, heard of the name and used it in his excellent and very remarkable book "The Naturalist in Nicaragua," London, 1874. De Humboldt says: "Les pays découverts les premiers sont aujourd'hui oubliés et presque déserts." (See "Examen critique de l'histoire de la géographie du nouveau continent," vol. III, p. 381, Paris, 1839.)

SIERRA AMERRIQUE AND THE AMERRIQUES.

I quote all I have been able to gather on the subject:

"At a short distance to the west (of Fairbairn's ranch, 2 leagues from Libertad, Nicaragua), rise the precipitous rocks of the Amerrique range, with great perpendicular cliffs, and huge isolated rocks and pinacles. The name of this range gives us a clue to the race of the ancient inhabitants. In the highlands of Honduras, as has been noted by Squiers, the termination of *tique* or *rique* is of frequent occurrence in the name of places, as *Chaparristique, Lapaterrique, Llotique, Ajuterique,* and others. The race that inhabited this region were the Leuca Indians. · · · I think that the Leuca Indians were the ancient inhabitants of Chontales, · · · and that they were partly conquered, and their territories encroached upon by the latter before the arrival of the Spaniards." Now the Chontales Indians are confined to the western part of the province of that name (departamento de Chontales), west of the cordillera or Amerrique range; while all the eastern part, as far as the Mosquito coast (Reserva Mosquita), is inhabited by uncivilized Indians called *Caribisi* or Caraïbs, and also Amerriques, Carcas, and Ramas Indians—*tribus de aborigenes no civilizados*—as they are called on maps of Nicaragua.

On Fairbairn's Ranch : " There are many evidences of a large Indian population having lived at this spot, and their pottery and fragments of their stones for bruising maize have been found in some graves that have been opened." - - - " There are many old Indian graves, covered with mounds of earth and stones." (See "The Naturalist in Nicaragua," p. 154.) At page 324, Belt refers again to the cordillera, saying : "About noon we came in sight of the Amerrique range, which I recog nized at once, and knew that we had reached the Juigalpa district."

As regards gold, Belt, the engineer of the Chontales Gold Mining Company, during his four years' residence in Nicaragua, was particularly well posted as to the location of the mines ; and he says : " Gold mining at Santo Domingo is confined almost entirely to auriferous quartz lodes, no alluvial deposits having been found that will pay for working. - - - The gold does not occur pure, but is a natural alloy of gold and silver, containing about three parts of the former to one of the latter. - - - The small town of Libertad is the principal mining centre of Chontales. There are a great number of gold mines in its vicinity."

The absence of paying *placers*, or auriferous alluvial gravels, in the valleys of the Rios Mico and Carca, the two main affluents of the Rio Blewfields, shows that they had been worked out in the old Indian time.

The following letter from Mr. Belt, written a short time before his premature death,* is interesting, because it gives his impression after reading my first paper on the " Origin of the name America," published in the Atlantic Monthly for March, 1876 :

LONDON, April 8, 1878.

M. JULES MARCOU,
        Salins, Jura, France:

MY DEAR SIR : I am much obliged to you for your kind letter and the copy of your most ingenious speculation respecting the origin of the name " Amérique."

The Amerrique range in Nicaragua was well known to me, and the curious coincidence with the name of the continent had often struck me, but only as a coincidence.

I hope your suggestion will receive the attention it deserves, and that the origin of the name will be thoroughly inquired about. Should it turn out as you believe, you will have cleared up a most interesting point.

I am, dear sir, yours very truly,

THOMAS BELT.

In 1887, by a happy circumstance, I was able to communicate with Senator Don José D. Rodriguez, of Managua (Nicaragua), who lived for

---

*Thomas Belt, born in Newcastle-upon-Tyne, 1832, died at Kansas City (Kansas), the 21st of September, 1878.

many years in the dsitrict of Chontales, and who was also a personal friend of Thomas Belt. Here are extracts from two of his letters to me:

WASHINGTON, D. C., *December* 29, 1887.

- - - The word *Amerrique* is pronounced as Mr. Thomas Belt wrote it by the natives of the tribe, with whom I have conversed. These Indians seem to have been formerly a powerful tribe. At a distance from the sierra (range), in the level ground, there are extensive spaces which were at one time cemeteries and undoubtedly belonged to these Indians. It is certain that towards the south other tribes inhabited that region. It is, moreover, easy to note that they kept up, from a very ancient date, a communication with the Atlantic coast, cultivating probably friendly relations with the once war-like tribe of the Moscos, who held the country from about Laguna de Caratasca (Honduras) and the Cape Gracias à Dios to a little south of the Laguna de Perlas and the rio Blewfields. At the present day the Amerriques are few in number, but I do not feel able, at the moment, to give any sufficient reason for the fact. They are not molested by any one and they live at their ease in their mountains, but it is evident that no long time will elapse before they disappear entirely, perhaps by absorption into other tribes. - - - Mr. Thomas Belt, to whom you refer, must have had occasion to know the mountains and the Indians of that name during a journey which he made over the cordillera to Matagalpa and Segovia. I served under the order of that gentleman in the mines of Chontales, and enjoyed the honor of his friendship and confidence.

WASHINGTON, *January* 12, 1888.

- - - I can assure you that the insinuation, ascribed to Mr. Peralta, that the name Amerrique was invented by my deceased friend, Mr. Thomas Belt, is an entirely gratuitous one. The mountain range and the tribe of the Amerriques have existed in Nicaragua for centuries which it is beyond our power to determine; and these facts may be verified at any moment. Moreover, Mr. Belt was a serious person, who would never have lent himself to a deception.

This protest of Senator J. D. Rodriguez was brought out by the position taken by a few opponents, who claimed that because the map-makers have not inscribed the name Amerrique on any of the maps known until now, the name Amerrique applied to a chain of mountains of Nicaragua was created out of Mr. Belt's "inner consciousness." Don Manuel M. de Peralta, minister of Costa Rica at Washington, wrote a letter to the President of the Republic of Nicaragua, Don Ad. Cárdenas, asking if there really is in "el departamento de Chontales" a chain of mountains known by the name of Amerique, Amerrique, or Americ. The answer not only confirmed the existence of the Sierra Amerrique, but also of a tribe of Indians called "los Amerriques"; and that the spelling of the name was as Mr. Belt wrote it: *Amerrique*, with two *r*'s.

From those well-authenticated facts, we can be fully confident that there are still in existence the remnants of an Indian tribe calling themselves *Amerriques*, formerly powerful, and extending over a great part of the ground between the Lake of Nicaragua and the Atlantic coast.

The mountains to which they are now confined are called *Amerrique* range, or Sierra *Amerrique;* and they have occupied for centuries the richest gold area of the region. The gold mines are numerous and are worked even to this day, on a great scale, round Libertad, Santo Domingo, and Juigalpa, where great quantities of the precious metal have been and are still extracted. The name Juigalpa (Huzgalpa) means the country of gold; and the name of the Mosquito coast in the Indian language is Tauzgalpa, or Taguzgalpa. *Galpa* means gold, so that the true name of the country between the Cape Gracias á Dios to the Rios Rama and San Juan, instead of being Mosquito coast or Mosquita, is, according to the aborigines, *Gold Coast.*

Now let us see about the first explorations by European navigators of the coast of the central part of the New World.

FIRST VOYAGE OF VESPUCCI.

From the beginning we are confronted by the most contested of Vespucci's voyages, May, 1497, to October, 1498. Las Casas, Herrera, Charlevoix, Robertson, Tiraboschi, Muñoz, Navarette, and Washington Irving declare that the author of the "Quatuor Navigationes" has forged his first voyage. Alexander de Humboldt, after calling his so-called first voyage *prétendu*, tries to show an *alibi* for Vespucci, who, according to his opinion, was then in Sevilla and at San Lucar superintending the arming of a fleet for the third voyage of Cristoforo Colombo, from April, 1497, to May, 1498; and accordingly in a material impossibility of having then accomplished his first voyage, which finally he calls "*problematic* voyage of a contested date,"[*] admitting as proved that the date of May 10 or 20, 1497, is false.

F. A. de Varnhagen is the only person who has accepted and maintained by excellent arguments and proofs drawn from the three historians, Pierre Martyr d'Anghiera, Oviedo and Gomara, the authenticity of the first voyage. After a careful study of all the objections, I have come to the same conclusion with Varnhagen, who correctly says, that "if the first voyage is not true, all fall to the ground;" and also, "if we admit that Vespucci has been guilty of not telling the truth in regard to such an important voyage, then we must treat him as a forger and an imposter, and accept nothing of all that he says in his four voyages." In fact, if the first voyage is a fable, or even only "problematic," Vespucci is a fabulist and an imposter who can not be trusted. But I do not believe it is the case. Vespucci, according to the great admiral, Cristoforo Colombo, was a good man (*es mucho hombre de bien*), unfortunate in his commercial enterprise, but eagerly looking out to get a reputation of being a great discoverer and traveler, what I have called him before, a *tan fino*, in Italian (*Nouvelles recherches*, p. 80, Paris, 1888.)

---

[*] *Examen critique*, vol. IV, p. 292.

According to Varnhagen the chiefs of this expedition of 1497 were V. Y. Pinson and J. D. de Solis; they first saw the land in the vicinity of the Cape Gracias à Dios, and after two days' sailing, in following a sandy coast, they stopped at a small harbor near the Laguna de Caratasca, Honduras. They met there a great many Indians of the Caraïbes type, some of whom possessed a few gold ornaments, which they got from some neighboring tribes. As we know now that the Amerriques Indians had relations with the Caraïbes of the coast as far as the Laguna de Caratasca, we have here the first contact of the Spaniards with the Indians possessing a little gold on the coast of Central America; and it is possible that the name *Amerrique* was then spoken of as a tribe of Indians and a country rich in gold, for it is the only gold area of that part of the coast of Honduras.

THE LAST VOYAGE OF COLOMBO.

Cristoforo Colombo in his fourth and last voyage sighted the Cape Gracias à Dios the 14th of September, 1502, followed all along the Mosquito coast, until he stopped at Quiriviri (Huerta Island), now Booby Island, opposite the Indian village of Cariaï at the mouth of the Rio Rama. He staid there ten days, from the 25th of September until the 5th of October. There he repaired his vessels and let his crews recruit after their very fatiguing navigation from Cuba.

The Indians were friendly and there was a great deal of communication and intercourse between them and the one hundred and fifty seamen composing the crews of his four caravels (schooners). Colombo in his *Lettera rarissima* says that at Cariaï he heard of gold mines in the province of Clamba; that he took with him two Indians who conducted him to another place called Carambaru, where the aborigines are always naked and carry round their necks mirrors in gold, which they declined to exchange on any account. At Cariaï, the Indians named several places where gold mines existed; the last named being Veragua, 25 leagues distant.

As de Humboldt says, that letter is not clear; it is written in a melancholy mood, and characterized by many obscurities and want of order, due to many injustices and deceptions to which Colombo was subjected at the end of his life. Colombo was then an old man, almost infirm, when he wrote the letter at Jamaica, the 7th July, 1503, just after returning from the rich gold region of Veragua; being badly treated by the governor, Ovando, his mind was more or less affected by his suffering, and it is not strange if he did not give all the details and all the names of the countries rich in gold, as well as the names of the Indian tribes with which he came in contact.

However, from his letter, we can say almost to a certainty that Cariaï was at the mouth of the Rio Rama, that Colombo heard there of the tribe of Amerriques as possessing a good deal of gold, which the Spaniards were so anxious to get; that he took with him two Indians with

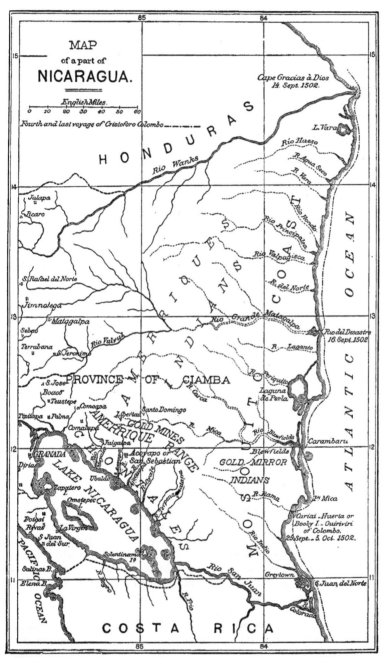

MAP
of a part of
NICARAGUA.

English Miles.

0　10　20　30　40　50　60

Fourth and last voyage of Cristoforo Colombo

HONDURAS

Cape Gracias à Dios
14. Sept. 1502.

L. Vara

Rio Hueso

R. Agua Seco

R. Vera

Julapa

Ocaro

Rio Wanks

Rio Hondo

Rio Principala

Rio Valpagisca

S. Rafael del Norte

R. del Norte

Jimnotega

Matagalpa

Rio Grande de Matagalpa

Sebaco

Rio Valvu

R. Laganto

Rio del Desastre
16. Sept. 1502

Terrabana

S. Jeronimo

PROVINCE OF CIAMBA

S. Jose

Boaco

Teustepe

Comoapa

Santo Domingo

R. Garci

Ririquito

Laguna
de Perla

Tipitapa

Palma

Libertad

R. Mica

Comalapa

GOLD MINES

Jugalpa

GOLD MIRROR

Rio Blewfields

Carambaru

GRANADA

Acoyapo or
San Sebastian

Blewfields

Diria

GOLD. MIRROR
INDIANS

LAKE NICARAGUA

Ubaldo

R. Rama

Zapatero

Omotepec

Potosi

Rivas

La Virgen

R. Mica

S. Juan
del Sur

Cariai - Huerta or
Booly I. - Ouirivivi
o' Colombo.
25 Sept. - 5 Oct. 1502.

Solentinama

Rio Negro

Rio San Juan

Greytown

S. Juan del Norte

Salinas B.

Elena B.

PACIFIC OCEAN

R. Rio

R. Colorado

COSTA RICA

ATLANTIC OCEAN

whom he went to Carambaru, another land. Carambaru in all probability, as we shall see if we consult a map of the coast, was at or near
the mouth of the Rio Blewfields and there he found Indians wearing
round their necks mirrors in gold which they declined to trade away.

Those Indians can not be any others than the Amerriques, who then
inhabited the gold area of the province of Ciamba, occupying all the
placeres of the Rios Mico and Carca, the two main affluents of the Rio
Blewfields. Being not successful in his endeavor to get their gold mirrors, Colombo was not well disposed to speak much of those Indians,
and he did not give their name nor the name of the country from which
they got the gold, speaking only of the province of Ciamba and the village of Carambaru, without localizing the area of gold in the Sierra
Amerrique, as he did for Veragua.

But because Colombo did not write the name Amerrique in his letter
to the King and Queen of Spain it does not follow that he did not hear it;
and it would be against all that we know of discoverers of gold regions
if the name Amerrique was not heard and afterwards repeated by Co
lombo and the one hundred and fifty men of his crews. If Colombo
is the only man who ever wrote anything about that eventful and difficult voyage, all his hundred and fifty companions spoke at their return
of what they saw and heard during the voyage; and it is to them, and
probably also to Colombo, that is due the spread among the people of
the name *Amerrique* as a country rich in gold and of Indians of that
name possessing gold mirrors as their only article of dress. The name
passed from mouth to mouth, first among seamen, and then it penetrated into the continent of Europe so fast that in less than twelve
years the name *Amerrique* was generally used to designate the New
World, according to a contemporary, John Schoener, of Bamberg.

That the name came from the masses of the people and not from the
few scholars who could read and write Latin is admitted by everybody.
Officially the name was " Las Indias " and " New World." Until 1520
we do not possess a single map with the name *America*, and if any existed with that name, they have been lost and destroyed, since their
number must have been extremely limited; and they can not be quoted
as having spread the name among the people, who then did not know
how to read, for we must always have in mind that it was the beginning of the sixteenth century and that the number of people able to
read and write was very small and formed a special class far above the
common people and having only occasional contact with the masses.

In résumé, Colombo and his one hundred and fifty companions saw
Indians on the Mosquito coast wearing gold mirrors round their necks
and otherwise naked. They had long talks with them in regard to
countries and peoples where the gold existed in their neighborhood.
We know now that those Indians were the Amerriques Indians, that they
live still in the most productive gold area of that region, and that the
Sierra Amerrique is, according to Thomas Belt, the most conspicuous

land-mark between Lake Nicaragua and the Atlantic coast. After the last voyage of Colombo of 1503 the name *Amerrique* spread so fast in Europe among the sailors and common people that in 1515 it was generally adopted and used to designate the New World. Such are facts which seem well established.

Now we come to the singular and rather mysterious christening of the New World at St. Dié, in Lorraine.

CONFUSION OF VESPUCCI'S CHRISTIAN NAME.

The Christian name of Vespucci is an example of confusion unique in history. Being an Italian, it was to be expected that his first name would be given exactly by his countrymen; on the contrary, they are the authors of all the confusions. As far back as 1503, or 1504 at most, the Italians Lorenzo Pier Francisco di Medicis, of Florence, and Giovanni del Giocondo, of Verona, call Verpucci *Albericus,* a Christian name well known ; and even since, until a few years ago, Italians, and more especially Florentins, have persisted in calling him *Alberico* and even *Albertutio.* I made diligent researches to know exactly Vespucci's Christian name. In a country like Tuscany and its capital Florence, where so many erroneous and forged documents have appeared on Vespucci in manuscripts, letters, printed books, and even inscriptions engraved on marble that I was obliged to be very careful before accepting any name that it should be well authenticated by indisputable documents. After many researches I did not find anything certain until the appearance of the first letter of Vespucci to Laurentio Petri de Medicis, with the name *Albericus Vesputius,* in 1504 or 1505. And in my second paper, "Nouvelles Recherches sur l'Origine du nom d'Amérique" (Bulletin Soc. de Gèographie, p. 66, Paris, 1888), I say : "As long as the Christian name of Vespucci has not been submitted to a very minute and exact control, we must remain in doubt as to which is the true one, *Alberico* or *Amerigo.'* - - - "The question has a certain importance, although its solution does not touch the vital and most important part of the origin of the name America, which remains undecided between the poetical license of Jean Basin and the indigenous name in the New World of *Amerrique.* The decision of this point will involve Vespucci more or less according to the help which he may have given, perhaps without knowing it, to the christening at St. Dié."

It is true that I inclined then toward *Alberico* instead of *Amerigo* for the Christian name of Vespucci, and in my second paper I have given reasons which seemed to sustain that view ; saying, however, several times in speaking of *Amerigo,* that it was either his true Christian name, or only a surname or nickname.

Diligent researches were continued to find proof if *Amerigo* was truly an Italian Christian name; for a learned Italian friend, who then lived at Florence, wrote me that the name, unknown to him as a Christian name, even after the celebrity given the name by Vespucci, was not used in Italy.

HAMERICUS IN DANTE AND AMERIGO IN MACHIAVELLI.

My son, Dr. Philippe B. Marcou, succeeded last year (1888) in finding twice the name *Hamericus* and *Amerigo*; first in Dante Allighieri, " De Vulgaris eloquentia," liber secundus, caput vi, and in the Comedia di Nicolo Machiavelli, in his *Opere*, vol. nono, Milano, 1805, where he has, as his first personage, *Amerigo, vecchio Padrone*, and as his last, *frate Alberigo*; besides he speaks at page 45 of the same volume in *Novella piace volissima di Nicollo Machiavelli*, of a " figliuola d' Amerigo Donati." In Danté we have two provencal poets of the name *Hamericus*, written with an *h*, as a family name written in provencal or *langue d'oc*, " Aimeric." Even now the name Emeric is a family name in Provence.

Danté inhabited Provence for some time, and was well acquainted with two Provencal poets, Emeric of Belinoi and Emeric of Péguilain; and in translating the family name of Emeric into Hamericus, its Latin form, it does not follow that he regarded Emeric as the Provencal name of the Florentine Amerigho; and we can not quote Danté as having translated the name Amerigho or Amerigo into Hamericus.

AMERIGO IN SPAIN IN 1495.

A short time after I received a letter from Don Márcos J. de la Espada, the most learned Americanist of Spain, and who knows more about the Archives de Indios than anybody else. The letter, dated Madrid, 22 de Marzo de 1889, says: " Por el consta que Amerigo Vespucci se llameba y se llamabe *Amerigo* en las libros de cuentes y despachos de armadas á Indias perde el año de 1495."

The oldest document made public in Spain before this was a receipt dated January 12, 1496, with only the name Vespuche, and no Christian name. The first time we have the Christian name of Vespucci, in well-authenticated documents, is in the two letters of Cristoforo Colombo of the 5th and 25th of February, 1505, written two years after the return of Colombo from his last voyage. Now since the discovery of Señor de la Espada we have the Christian name Amerigo in 1495, consequently before any of the voyages of Vespucci to the New World, and before the fourth voyage of Colombo to Nicaragua and Veragua. It is most important, for the *Libros de gastos de armadas* of the archives *de la casa de contractation* at Sevilla, are justly regarded as an excellent authority for everything relating to the first voyages of discoveries of the New World or Las Indias.

AMERIGHO IN THE ARCHIVES OF MANTOVA IN 1492.

Lately I have received from Rome a paper: "Come veramente si chiamasse il Vespucci, e se dal nome di lui sia venuto quello del Nuovo Mondo, nota del socio Gilberto Govi" (Rendiconti della R. accademia dei Lincei, vol. IV, pp. 297–307, seduta del 18 nov. 1888, Roma, 4to). The author, Signor G. Govi, has the good fortune to publish the only

truly authentic letter of Vespucci that had yet been found in Italy. It was discovered by Signor Davari conservatore dell 'archivio Gonzoga di Mantova, and although very short—only seven lines—is most important for it is wholly written by Vespucci, who was, as I have said before, an excellent calligraphist. The date is : *Sybilie die xxx decembris M°CCCC°LXXXXII* (Sevilla, the 30 Dec., 1492), and consequently before the return of Colombo from his first voyage. The very distinct signature is :

> Ser. Amerigho Vespucci mer-
> chante fiorentino for
> . Sybilia.

I have received a photograph of the letter and its address, by the courtesy of an Italian friend; and I here give the *fac-simile* of it, as well as of the signature to a letter of Vespucci to the Cardinal Archbishop of Toledo, dated Sevilla, 9 December, 1508, which was published in *fac-simile* by the Spanish Government in 1878. Those two letters are the only authentic ones we possess; and the signatures are too important in the question of the origin of the name America not to be carefully studied.

Now we have, without any possible doubt, the Christian name of Vespucci, written by himself *Amerigho* with only one *r* and an *h* at the last syllable, in 1492; and *Amerigo* with only one *r* and no *h* in the *Libros de cuentes y despachos de armadas a Indias* in 1495.

Gilberto Govi[*] thinks that it is the Italian Fra Giovanni del Giocondo, who translated and changed too freely *Amerigho* into *Alberico*. It is only a personal opinion, without any base to rest upon, for the original letter of Vespucci to Lorenzo Pierfrancisco de Medicis is unknown. Generally, translators do not alter and change the signatures of authors; and so long as we have no positive proof to the contrary, we must say that Vespucci used for his Christian name, in 1502 or 1503, the name *Alberico* or *Alberigo*. But as his second letter to Piedro Soderini, written in 1504, is signed *Amerigo*, it is evident that he did not make use of the name *Alberico* for any length of time. There are certainly strong suspicions that he made use of it, not only in his first letter to Medicis, but also because Gomara, a Spanish historian of great reputation, in his General History of the Indies of 1551, uses both names, saying *Americo* or *Alberico* Vespucci, showing that in Spain the name of Al-

---

[*] Govi died suddenly at Rome, in June, 1889, a few months only after his communication to the Accademia dei Lincei. He was a physicist-mathematician of talent.

berico must have been known quite well during the first part of the sixteenth century, although we do not know a single example of the name having been used in any official authentic Spanish document relating to Vespucci.

COSMOGRAPHIÆ INTRODUCTIO.

Thanks to the discoveries and researches of Alex. de Humboldt, D'Avezac, and a few others, we know a great deal about the *Cosmographiæ Introductio* of the Vosgian gymnasium of St. Dié, in which is found the first announcement of the name America as the name of the New World. The interested reader will find all the descriptions, dissertations, and conclusions of the extraordinary value attached to this now very celebrated small quarto volume in the "Examen critique," by Alex. de Humboldt, 5 vols., Paris, 1839; "Martin Hylacomilus Waltzemuller," by D'Avezac, Paris, 1867; and "Nouvelles recherches sur l'origine du nom d'Amérique," by Jules Marcou, Paris, 1888, in Bulletin Soc. géographie.

The only addition to our knowledge about the printing press of St. Dié, is that it was removed in 1512 to Strasburg, from whence, very likely, it came; and that the same types used for the *Cosmographiæ Introductio* were used at Strasburg in 1512 and 1513 to finish the printing of the Ptolemey's Geography of 1513, two-thirds of it having been printed at St. Dié between 1505 and 1510, as D'Avezac has proved. So, instead of calling it the Strasburg's Ptoléme, it ought to be called the Vosgian Gymnasium Ptoléme, or at least the St. Dié and Strasburg's Ptoléme.

M. Ed. Meaume has lately proved the existence of a fourth edition, or more properly speaking, fourth issue, of the *Cosmographiæ Introductio* of St.-Dié, which had been considered by d'Avezac and Mr. H. Harisse as an amalgamated copy, composed with parts taken from the first and third issue or edition. (See "Recherches critiques et bibliographiques sur Améric Vespuce et ses voyages," par Ed. Meaume, Chapitre iii, "La *Cosmographiæ Introductio*, étude bibliographique sur les quatre premières éditions—Saint-Dié, 1507, p. 83, in "Mémoires de la Société d'Archéologie, Lorraine," 3ième série, vol. XVI, Nancy, 1888)

The late M. Meaume thought that this reprint or last issue was made in 1508, although dated, like the third edition, 29th August, 1507. It is very probable that Waltzemüller (Zlacomylus) tried a second time to place secretly his name as the author of the book instead of the collective name of the Vosgian Gymnasium; but being promptly detected, the issue was stopped at once, just as Gauthier had stopped the distribution of the first issue. This explains the great rarity of the fourth issue or edition. Only four copies are now known: the one called the Chartener's copy of Metz, now in the possession of M. Langlard, of Nancy; the second copy, described by Mr. Harisse in his "Bibliotheca Americana Vetustissima," under No. 47, p. 92, belonging to the Lenox's

Library of New York; the third copy is in the Mazarine Library in Paris (an incomplete copy, having only the first thirty-eight leaves); and the fourth copy is preserved in the city library of Besançon.

After having been deterred twice from naming himself as the sole author of the St. Dié book, Waltzemüller got up a special edition of his own, which he had printed at Strasburg in 1509. Very likely these proceedings caused an estrangement and a final breach between the *castigator* (proof-reader) Zlacomylus and the Vosgian Gymnasium, and this was the main reason for the stopping of the St. Dié's Ptolemey edition, and its transfer to Strasburg in 1512, where it was issued at last in 1513.

"LE QUATTRO GIORNATE."

After his success with the publication of his first letter to Lorenzo Pierfrancisco de Medicis, Vespucci took special precautions to have all his voyages well known in different parts of Europe. In his letter to Soderini, of 1504, he speaks of a book written by him under the title " Le Quattro Giornate," which was never published, and the manuscript of which had escaped all researches until this day. But he wrote a résumé of it, dated Lisbonne, September 4, 1504, taking special care to address it, first, to the King of Spain ; second, to his friend the Goufalonier of Florence; and third, to King René, duc of Lorraine.

The copy addressed to Ferdinand of Spain was never published, and until now has not been found in the archives of Spain. Probably it was written in Spanish, and with a dedication to the King. The copy addressed to Soderini was published in 1506, at Pescia, near Florence, by Piero Paccini, under the title, " Lettera di Amerigo Vespucci delle isole nuovamente trovate in quatro suoi viaggi," in an Italian rather incorrect, containing a quantity of Spanish words and phrases, as might be expected from a man like Vespucci, who had lived at least twelve years in Spain or among Spaniards. It was dedicated to His Magnificence Signor Pietro Soderini, Perpetual Gonfalonier of the Il- lustre Republic of Florence, but without the name, giving only his title of " Magnifice Domine," and " Vostra Mag."

The third copy was addressed to René, King of Sicily and Jerusalem and Duc of Lorraine. It was published in 1507, at St. Dié, by the *Gymnasium Vosagense*, under the title " Quattuor Americi Vesputii Navigationes," in Latin, translated by the Canon Jean Basin, from a French version. That French version was never published, or, if published, no copy of it has ever been found ; and the manuscript is un- known, very likely lost and destroyed. It is dedicated to the " Illus- trissimo Renato Jherusalem et Sicilio Regis ;" but for some unexplained reason the dedication to Soderini was copied entirely, with only the name of the good King René put instead of " Magnifice Domine," and "T. M." (tua majestas) instead of " Vostra Mag.," which has been ren- dered by the translator from Italian into French as " Vestra Majestas" or " Votre Majesté." It has been the custom to say that Jean Basin made the change, in his Latin version, as a sort of poetical license. But it is very doubtful, for King René received the French manuscript, and very likely the person who sent it made the dedication, as it is the custom when you address Royalty. Besides, René gave the manuscript to his secretary, Gaultier Lud, and finally Lud delivered it to Jean Basin; and it is too much to suppose that Jean Basin took upon himself to alter the manuscript to such an extent, for it would have raised protests from both Lud and the good and honest King René.

Who did send the manuscript to King René is not known with certainty. Alexander de Humboldt thought it was Vespucci himself, and everything favors the same conclusion. Vespucci was desirous of notoriety as a great traveller and discoverer. He addressed his first letter to a Medicis, after placing the relation of his third voyage in the hands of the King, Don Manuel of Portugal; and he addressed his second letter first to the King, Don Ferdinand of Spain, and second to the Perpetual Gonfalonier of Florence, instead of Lorenzo Pierfrancscio de Medicis, who was dead. Evidently Vespucci sought the good opinions of the great of the earth, and to acquaint them with what he did as a navigator and discoverer. Not knowing French, he had his manuscript translated, and the translator did it literally, only by an oversight of Vespucci he wrote the dedication to the illustrious King René, and substituted for *Vostra Mag.*, "Votre Majesté." Very likely Vespucci intended to make some changes in the term of the dedication used for Soderini, but by some mistake or misunderstanding, or from being at some distance from the translator,—if the translation was made in Florence, which is probably the case.* Vespucci was not able to see that the dedication to King René was correct, and the elegant poet, Jean Basin, simply translated into Latin the French version without any explanation or rectification, not knowing if Vespucci really had occasion to know King René in his youth.

No trace of a correspondence between Vespucci and King René has been found. We are reduced to conjecture. Vespucci was interested to enrol among his admirers such an important personage as the good King René, known as a Mecœnas and a seeker for geographical news, for it is known that he had sent Ringman twice to Italy in order to control the texts of Ptoleme and procure the best copies it was possible to collect. There is no doubt that Vespucci was well informed of what was going on in the world. He knew that Lorenzo Pierfrancisco de Medicis was dead, and that his first letter had been published in Latin in Paris; and he wanted his second letter to be also published in Latin in central Europe.

It is possible that King René received the French translation of the four voyages of Vespucci from another source; only then it is difficult

---

* The translation of the second letter of Vespucci into French was made at Florence, by some one well acquainted with the family of Vespucci, for the translator has added that Soderini and he were pupils at the school kept by the uncle of Vespucci; a fact which is not indicated in the Italian edition.

to account for the position taken by Jean Basin and the whole Vosgian Gymnasium, that Vespucci was the discoverer of the New World, a position which can not have been taken lightly and without the knowledge and consent of King René. It was well known that Cristoforo Colombo was the discoverer; and the members of the Vosgian Gymnasium can not have ignored the fact, because the first voyage of Colombo had been published not only in Paris, but also in Strasburg in 1497; and Ringman, who had inhabited Paris and had been twice in Italy, must have been well acquainted with all the history of the first voyage of Colombo.

The reference of the discovery of the New World to Vespucci by the Vosgian Gymnasium of St. Dié in 1507 is a very suspicious act, which can not be explained, except that a conspiracy existed after the death of Colombo to reduce, and even obliterate, the great celebrity attached to his memory, and that Vespucci was a party to, or at least helped secretly, the undertaking. The members of the Vosgian Gymnasium were not in a position to decide so bluntly, as they did, that Vespucci was the discoverer of the New World; and it is impossible to explain the position they have taken, without supposing that they had recourse to underhand influences, and a special desire to create a rival and an adversary to Colombo.

The second letter of Vespucci is written in a very careful way, in order to escape all associations with any of the other navigators. He has taken a special care not to name a single commander or chief of the expeditions in which he was engaged, and any one not well acquainted with all the first voyages to the New World will easily be deceived, and be led to believe that he was in command himself. As I have said before, his two published letters are the work of a very shrewd man, a *tan fino* in Italian. It is unique in maritime voyages that a man who was a subordinate does not give the name of the chief of his expeditions. That he may have passed over one of those names may be understood and regarded as a forgetfulness of no great consequence, but that all four are passed silently over is a case of willful negligence.

Vespucci certainly addressed the manuscripts of his voyages to the Kings of Spain and Portugal, to a Medicis and to the Perpetual Gonfalonier of Florence; and it is reasonable and natural to suppose that he did send them also to King René, Duc of Lorraine. The other supposition, that King René received the French translation of the four navigations of Vespucci from another source can not be accepted, unless it was proved by authentic facts and documents, which is not the case.

Humboldt says: "Vespucci was in correspondence with René II" [*] Unhappily nothing has been found yet in the archives of Lorraine on the subject, and we are reduced to probabilities and inductions.

---

[*] Examen Critique, Vol. IV, p. 107.

AMERIGE, AMERICUS, AND AMERICA.

However this may be decided, the Vosgian Gymnasium published in April, 1507, a Latin translation of the résumé of the four voyages of Vespucci, and in the introduction, *Cosmographiæ Introductio*, is the christening of the New World under the name of *America*, in honor of Americus (*Amerige*) Vespucius, who discovered it.

It took many years to prove that Vespucci was not the discoverer of the *terra firma* of the New World and consequently had no valid claim to its name, and the numerous and voluminous discussions and controversies on this subject have lasted until this century.

Jean Basin, the translator from the French into Latin of the "Quatuor navigationes" of Vespucci, instead of retaining the word *Amerige* for the Christian name of Vespucci, as it was in the manuscript, turned it into *Americus*. He knew perfectly well that it was a very free translation, not easy to accept without an explanation, and consequently he took the precaution to print in two places of this small book the word *Amerige* very conspicuously opposite *Americus*, in order to show that by Americus he means the Christian name of Vespucci. The French translator from the original Italian text did not translate *Amerigo* by *Americ*, or *Emeric*, or *Aïmeric*, but by *Amerige*; it was only in 1515, when a French translation by Mathurin Du Redouer of the third voyage of Vespucci appeared in Paris, that Amerigo was translated into Emeric and not Amerige; and strange to say, Redouer translated it from the celebrated collection of Vicenza of 1507, in which the Christian name of Vespucci is *Alberico*; showing what confusion Vespucci and his friends had already created by using indiscriminately the word Amerigo and Alberico, two different names in Florence, where Machiavelli in his *Comedia* uses both for two entirely different personages called Amerigo and Alberigo.

TRIPLE ERRORS IN THE CHRISTENING OF ST. DIÉ.

The Vosgian Gymnasium first attributed the discovery of the New World to Vespucci in 1507, two years after the death of Colombo, and during the life of Vespucci, who did not die until 1512. Vespucci did not rectify the error, and no document exists which shows any steps taken by him to decline the honor. This absence of protestation on his part has a tendency to sustain the idea that it was he who suggested to King René and the Vosgian Gymnasium that he was the discoverer of the New World, for both René and the Gymnasium knew beyond any possible doubt the great discovery of 1492 by Cristoforo Colombo, and the only excuse in their favor which can be given is, that Vespucci claimed to have discovered the *terra firma*, the discoveries of Colombo being confined to the islands, and that he succeeded in impressing on those far away Lorrainers that fallacious idea.

As to the christening of the New World with the name *Americus*, in honor of Americus Vespucius, the Vosgian Gymnasium has gone out of all rules, not only in giving the Christian name of a traveller or navigator to a great country, but also in spelling his name, transforming *Amerige* or *Amerigo* into *Americ*. It is a well known rule that names given to any great country newly discovered are either the family name, if in honor of the discoverer, or the Christian name of some members of royal reigning families. We can quote: "Strait of Magellan, Hudson Bay, Vancouver Island, Juan Fernandez Island, Colombia and Columbia, Washington, Van Diemen Land or Tasmania; Cook, Laperouse, Torres, and Davis Straits; Baffin Bay, Parry Islands, Kerguelen Islands, Heard Islands, Crozet Islands, Tristan do Cunha Island, Kermadec Island, Bougainville Island, Lord Howe Island, Fernando do Noromha Island, Grinnell Land, Wilkes Land, etc.; and on the other side: Carolina, Maryland, Virginia, Georgia, Victoria, Philippine Islands, Queen Charlotte Islands, Charlestown, Charles River, Cape Charles, Jamestown, James River, Isabel Island, Port Adelaide, Terre Louis Philippe, Franz Joseph Land, etc.

If the explanation of the Vosgian Gymnasium is accepted the only exception to the rule is a continent covering a hemisphere,—that is to say the greatest geographical fact existing, and that in the face of a fact admitted by everybody, even the Vosgian Gymnasium in the Ptoléme of 1513, that Cristoforo Colombo discovered the New World.

The name Amerigho, or Amerigo, or Amerige, which are the three variations in spelling known until 1507, would give in Latin: *Amerigonius, Amerighius, Amerigo*, or even *Amerige*, but not *Americus*. Jean Basin, in making such a *lapsus lingæ*, must have been influenced and entirely directed by the aboriginal name of *Amerrique*, which reached Europe four years before, and had time to spread as a name of a country and a tribe of Indians rich in gold, for in 1503 Colombo and his one hundred and fifty seamen returned from Cariai and Carambaru on the Mosquito Coast. Being assured by some one, perhaps directly by Vespucci himself, or indirectly through Laurent Phrisius (Fries) of Metz, an attaché to the service of the Duc of Lorraine; the canon Jean Basin, —an enthusiast like all poets, and a master in the art of eloquence and fine writing,—perceiving the analogy between the christian name of Vespucci, *Amerigho*, and more especially *Amerige*, and the somewhat popular name of *Amerrique*, Basin thought that a part of the New World was already named after the Christian name of Vespucci, and instead of proposing to call the New World *Vespuccia*, as he ought to have done, he called it *America*. A poetical creation due to a too great imaginative power. Beside the erroneous notion of the discovery of the New World by Vespucci, Basin committed another error, that the name *Amerrique* must be derived from Amerige, creating a confusion which was absolutely inexplicable, without the knowledge we have now of the existence of a tribe of Indians called *Amerriques*, inhabiting a country rich in gold, and carrying round their necks mirrors of gold at the time of Colombo's visit in 1502.

The Vosgian Gymnasium is responsible for the christening, but it is certain that no one of the other members, except Basin, had any enthusiasm about it, or even any sympathy with it, for no one of them uses the word America in any of their publications. The proof-reader (*castigator*) Martin Hylacomylus (Waltzemüller) wrongly credited as the God-father of the New World, was not a partisan of the name *America*, for he does not use it in any of his publications, not even on his map of the New World of the Ptoleme of 1513, called only *Terra nove*, without the name America anywhere. The canon Gauthier Lud, secretary of the Duc of Lorraine, did not use it in his: *Speculi orbis declaratio*, etc., 1507, and Ringmann, the Vosgian poet and professor of cosmography (geography) at St. Dié and afterward at Basel, never quoted it.

The only publication in which the name America is found, after the proposition of the Vosgian Gymnasium in 1507, is in the "Globus mundi," 1509, Strasburg, without name of author, but which is attributed to Jean Basin, the translator of the "Quatuor Navigationes," and the true God-father of the New World, and there it is found only *once* in the chapter *De Descriptio Terræ*.

IN 1515 THE NAME AMERICA IS ALREADY POPULAR.

John Shœner, of Bamberg, in his "Luculentissima quædam terræ totius descriptio, etc.," published in 1515, makes the important and significant remark that the name America was already accepted, used, and popular. How can the name have been popular in 1515, when it has been impossible to find it printed on a single map, and in no other books than the small and extremely rare pamphlets of the *Cosmographiæ Introductio* and the *Globus mundi?* To be sure, some maps with the name America may have existed then; but not one of them has reached us, all having been destroyed, for the preservation of maps is more difficult than the preservation of pamphlets, especially when the maps are on a large scale. Only during the first quarter, and even half, of the sixteenth century all the printed maps were small, on account of the material difficulties in their engraving and the writing of names on them; and their preservation was facilitated by their publication in books in which they were inserted, like the Ptolemeys. Large-scale maps existed then in manuscript, and besides the map of Juan de la Cosa of 1500, the map of Sebastian Cabot of 1544, and many others now existing in the archives of Europe, we know with certainty that many more have been destroyed or lost, among them all the maps of Vespucci and the first map of Sebastian Cabot.

The only dated map we possess now with the name *America*, is the one of Apianus (Pierre Bienewitz), inserted in the "Polyhistor" of Solinus, 1520. The Ptoleme of 1522, of Strasburg, gave the same map, with the name America. Laurent Frisius or Phrisius of Metz, is the editor, and at the reverse of the folio numbered 100, he names Martin Ilacomylus as the author of the map, and even of all the maps of that new edition. But Ilacomylus had been dead for some time, and it is almost certain that the name America was not put there by him, but more likely by Laurent Phrisius himself, who was probably the medium between Vespucci, Pierre Martyr d'Anghiera, and the Duc of Lorraine.

It is plain that the name America can not have been popular in 1515, except that it has passed from mouth to mouth among illiterate people, as the masses were then. Shoener was a contemporary, well acquainted with the discoveries of the New World, and it is impossible to accept the idea that its popularity was an error on his part.

VESPUTIA AND CABOTIA.

Let us make a few suggestions in order to show the absolute impossibility of referring to the christian name of Vespucci the origin of the name America. If the rule to give the family name of the discoverer to a new country had been followed—although Vespucci was not the discoverer—Jean Basin and the Vosgian Gymnasium would have called the New World *Vesputia*. Does any one entertain for an instant the idea that the proposition of the Vosgian Gymnasium would have stood any chance of being accepted, or even been the object of any discussion? or controversy? The proposition to call the northern part of the New World *Cabotia*, in honor of Cabot, although sustained by the well proved fact that Sebastian Cabot first discovered North America—at least scientifically, for the Norsemen certainly anticipated his discovery by several centuries—was never accepted and not even discussed.

AMERIGIA AND ALBERICIA.

If we say that the Vosgian Gymnasium and its leader Jean Basin, in the matter of christening the new continent, were conscious that it was well to diverge from the rule of using family names, and that it was best to use the Christian name—although without a single precedent, even in antiquity—why did they choose a name so different from the christian name of Vespucci, for if they followed the orthography of the different names before them, they ought to have called the New World *Amerigia* (for Amerige), *Amerigonia* (for Amerigo), or *Albericia* (for Albericus). To write those names and pronounce them aloud suffices to show that they were not likely to be used by a majority of those who were accustomed in one way or another, as traders, seamen, adventurers, colonists, statesmen, or religious men, to speak of the new continent.

POETICAL LICENSE OF JEAN BASIN.

The assimilation of the Christian name of Vespucci, Amerige or Amerigho, to the gold-mirror Indians Amerriques, or their country Sierra Amerrique, is simply a fiction, in which Jean Basin took the name of an Indian tribe and of a country of the New World and placed it on Vespucci, either as a poetical license or as a sort of joke without any consequence.

Unhappily the matter has been taken very seriously, more so than the originator even thought of; for the Vosgian Gymnasium took very quietly the correction that Vespucci was not the discoverer, and they were prepared to do the same as to their naming of America from Amerigho Vespucci; only the matter was considered as too trifling by those interested in the question, such as the son of Colombo, to require a correction. The attribution of the discovery to Cristoforo Colombo was considered sufficient; and that the name of Amerrique has nothing to do with Vespucci was so evident and such a matter of course that nobody cared to correct the vagary of a Vosgian poet.

The name Amerrique continued to be used among the people, just like the names Chrysé, El Dorado, Quivira, etc., and the map makers wrote the name America as they pleased, on many places of the new continent, without following in the least the proposition of the Vosgian Gymnasium, which passed entirely unnoticed until found out more than three centuries after by Alexander de Humboldt. If the geographers who constructed maps during the sixteenth century had thought that the New World was named from the Christian name of Vespucci, as that name varied according to the numerous pamphlets of his third voyage and his "Quatuor Navigationes" into Alberico, Amerigo, Amergio, Almerigo, Albertutio, Damerigho, Armenico, Morigo, some of them would have certainly used such names as Albericia, Amerigia Amerigonia, Amergia, Almerigia, Albertutia, Armenica, Morigia. But the name America is ne varietur, without a single case of different spelling, showing that Amerrique was in general circulation, and that they made use of it without thinking if it was in honor of Vespucci or not. "Le mot était dans l'air," as the French say for all popular expression, and all the variations of the Christian name of Vespucci have not the slightest influence on it.

Little by little the aboriginal name of Amerrique and its derivative America took possession, first of the maps, and afterwards of all the chancelleries and state departments of all Europe, the Spanish one included, without much thought about the injustice committed toward Colombo, or any desire on their part to raise Vespucci above the very small position he occupied as third rate navigator.

The whole is an example of a sort of process of infiltration, coming from the masses where it unconsciously originated, entirely outside of the doing of a few Latinists lost in their books and manuscripts, and which eventually covered half of the earth's surface, carrying pêle-mêle partisans and adversaries of Colombo and Vespucci, sure that in the end truth will prevail over all false pretensions, obscurities, and errors.

After all the incorrect reference of the name of the New World to Amerigho Vespucci has lasted a little less than four centuries, even less than the forgetfulness which has kept in the background the discoveries of the Norsemen Bjarni and Leif Ericksen, at the end of the tenth century; a small number of years when compared to the past human history and its great future. The fourth centenarian anniversary of the greatest event for the human race will be celebrated without the feeling that the name of the New World is derived from a third-rate navigator, without any claim to such an honor and to the detriment and great injustice of the great discoverer, Colombo; but that it originated simply from a tribe of Indians and a mountain range of the new continent itself. The name Amerrique is equal to and of as much poetical beauty as Niagara, Ontario, Canada, Monongahela, Mississippi, Missouri, Arkansas, Alabama, Dakota, Mexico, Nicaragua, Guatemala, Cuba, Panama, Veragua, Chimborazo, Peru, Venezuela, etc.

VESPUCCI CHANGES THE SPELLING OF HIS CHRISTIAN NAME.

When Vespucci received a copy of the "Cosmographiæ Introductio" of St. Dié, at the end of 1507, he must have been more than gratified: for not only in it he is qualified as the discoverer of the New World, which very likely he wanted to be, but more, the name of *Amerrique* was attributed to him, and that name was extended to the whole of the new country. An ambitious man has seldom seen his desires so well fulfilled.

If Vespucci had been "es mucho hombre de bien" as Colombo thought, he would have taken proper steps to correct the very great errors committed by the Vosgian Gymnasium, and referred to Cristoforo Colombo as the true discoverer of the New World; but notwithstanding that Vespucci lived five years more, he did nothing of the kind, and instead we see he did all he could to sustain the scheme of naming the New World after him, by correcting the orthography of his Christian name. Until then he wrote *Amerigho*, as is proved by his letter of 1492, the earliest authentic autograph of him that we possess, while his other letter of the 9th of December, 150 :, addressed to the Archbishop of Toledo, he signs *Amerrigo*, with a double r and the suppression of the h. (See page 657.) That modification in the orthography of his Christian name is "the end of the ear which sticks out" (*le bout de l'oreille qui perce*). Seeing the analogy of Amerigho and Amerrique, he did all he could to bring his name as near as possible to the aboriginal name, without identifying it entirely; for a complete identification might have been detected at once, for there were still alive quite a number of Colombo crews of one hundred and fifty seamen; and very cunningly he signed himself Amerrigo, with a most attractive and prominent flourish (paraph), using it until his death in 1512, as is seen in two or three other signatures of him after 1508, preserved in the Casa de Contractation at Sevilla, and all written with the double r and the dropping of the h.

The Spanish historian J. B. Muñoz, is the first who has observed the double r in the signatures found by him in Spain; that strange and unique spelling attracted his attention, without his being able to assign

any reason for it. Muñoz was convinced that some intentional falsification existed in regard to the voyages of Vespucci; and he was as well
as the other historian, M. F. de Navarrete, a believer in some sort of
fraud on the part of the Florentine. Alexander de Humboldt not knowing what to do with the double r, thought it might be "a proof of eru-
dition" on the part of Vespucci, quoting the opinion of Professor von
der Hagen of Berlin that "when in Italian Vespucci uses the double
r in signing *Amerrigo*, it is by assimilation of two consonants, it is
Amerrigo for *Amelrigo* (name of a bishop of Como in 865)." The main
difficulty in accepting such an explanation is that Vespucci did not
use it when he wrote in Italian and to Italians, as is proved by his letter of Mantova, but only to Spaniards and in Spanish. After the many
researches of all sorts made in the archives and in published books and
documents, it is certain that the spelling of Amerigo with two r's is
subsequent to the christening of St. Dié in 1507. It is the most dam-
aging discovery made against Vespucci, which can not be satisfactorily
explained in any other way than to bring his Christian name as near as
possible to the Indian name of *Amerrique*.

SCHOENER VERSUS VESPUCCI.

By a strange occurrence, not rare however in the first discoveries of
lands and aborigines of the new continent, the name of the Indian tribe
and of their country was not printed in any pamphlet or book or written on any map that we know of. It escaped the researches of all the
Americanists; even of Alexander de Humboldt, and it seems that
everything conspired to make good the triple errors of Jean Basin,
accepted and consolidated by Vespucci as much as he safely could.

It may be that Vespucci wrote on some manuscript map Tierra di
Amerriques, and that it was read *Tierra di Amerigo*, as Schoener has
accused him of doing in 1535. Johannes Schoener, born in 1477, at
Carlstadt, Lower Franconia, in Bavaria, died at Nuremberg in 1547.
He was an excellent geographer and well acquainted with all the discoveries made during his time, as is amply proved by Dr. Franz Wieser,
in his important book: "Magalhaes-Strasse und Austral-Continent auf
den Globen des Johannes Schoener," Innspruck, 1881. Certainly Schoener can not be considered as a detractor of Vespucci. He seems to
have acted with great honesty of purpose, saying only the truth of what
he heard about him; for in 1515, in his "Luculentissima," etc., he is
very friendly to Vespucci, saying that he discovered the New World in
1497 and that the name America was generally accepted and already
in great use. But when he was convinced of the great injustice done
to Cristoforo Colombo, the true discoverer, he did not hesitate to say
that he knew that Vespucci had written his name upon some maps.

There is no doubt that maps made by Vespucci existed at that
time; for we know of their existence through his contemporaries Pierre
Martyr d'Anghiera and his nephew and heir, Juan Vespucci. Only, as
I have said before, it may be that instead of ₋wᵣᵢₜᵢₙg *Tierra di Amerigo*

upon them, he wrote *Tierra di Amerriques*, and that Jean Basin and others made the mistake which led Schoener to make the accusation. I believe that there is no reasonable doubt that there was some sort of shrewd underhand practice by some one in the whole matter of the attribution of the discovery of the New World to Vespucci, and in the maintenance of the name Americ as his Christian name, when it is Amerigho. Without going so far as to regard Vespucci as an impostor, it is difficult not to admit that he was a great diplomatist, what we call now a shrewd politician, a *tan fino* in Italian, and that there are reasons enough to consider him as a sort of mystificator.

COLOMBO AND VESPUCCI.

Cristoforo Colombo has the honesty and simplicity of a seaman who has passed all his life before the mast; believing easily that others were " hombre de bien," if they had the reputation of being honest merchants.

Amerigho Vespucci has been during the greatest part of his life a " fiorentino merchante," as he called himself, educated for the trade at Florence and accustomed to all the little underhand ways of traders. He was considered at Sevilla as an " hombre de bien " in trade, and his failure of success as a merchant confirms that view to a certain extent.

Unfortunate in his speculations, he took at the end of his life to seamanship, as an astronomer, chart maker, captain, and pilot, and finally he was appointed piloto major. He never had command of a single expedition, and was after all a very secondary man in Spain or Portugal where there were such great navigators as Colombo, Vasco de Gama, Pinson, de la Cosa, Hojeda, Pedro de Ledesma, de Solis, Juan and Sebastiano Caboto, Diego de Lepe, the Cortereal, Cabral, de Bastidos, Vergara, Coelho, etc.

But it is evident that ambition to be known as a great discoverer and a navigator of renown took hold of Vespucci, soon after entering into his new life; and he addressed his voyages to the King of Spain, the King of Portugal, a Medicis in Paris, the perpetual gonfalonier of Florence, and finally to the good René, King of Sicily and Duc of • Lorraine. The style of Vespucci is rather diffuse and pretentious, "*il vise à l'effet*," according to de Humboldt. He leans constantly towards exaggeration, and boasts of having received patent letters from the King of Portugal. The most exhaustive researches into the books, which are all preserved in the archives of the Torre do Tombo, containing all the patent letters delivered by the kings of Portugal, have failed entirely to show any trace of these; and even the name of Vespucci has never been found in a single document in Portugal.

Everything pertaining to Vespucci, as a traveller and a navigator, must be received with some apprehension that it is either much exaggerated or even untrue. We must remember that Vespucci was a Florentine, a friend of a Medicis and of Soderini; a trader until forty-eight years old; that he was living during a period when it was possible to be a cheat and at the same time regarded as a "*hombre de bien.*" It was a time which it is difficult to understand now, because the society of the fifteenth century lived among troubles of all sorts, which influenced all the ideas and relations of men; and the honesty of men during that period can not be compared with our actual ideas on the subject. With Cristoforo Colombo everything is clear and explained easily, while on the contrary with Amerigho Vespucci everything is obscure, or even clashes with well-known facts, and all the time his defenders or friends are obliged to have recourse to suppositions and to throw the blame upon others without the slightest proof and against plain facts. It is going too far to say with de Humboldt that Vespucci is "the victim of a concourse of fortuitous circumstances," and of "the exaggerations of unskillful and dangerous friends," for it is evident that Vespucci himself did all he could to create those circumstances, and during his life he never did anything to correct his "unskillful and dangerous friends" of St. Dié, Strasburg, and Metz.

A name for a continent covering a whole hemisphere can not come as a spontaneous generation, and as Pasteur says, "spontaneous genera-tion" does not èxist in nature nor in philology. There is always a source and a base, and until the re-discovery of a tribe of Indians called Amerriques, formerly powerful, and who have always lived in a coun-try rich in gold and close to the coast explored first by Colombo and afterward by Vespucci, it was impossible to give a rational and satis-factory explanation of the christening of the New World. A writer has said with great pertinence, "The attribution of the name America to Vespucci has been respected especially because there was no other solution to oppose to it."

After almost four centuries it is impossible to expect that every fact should be sustained by authentic documents and indisputable proofs. Many of the archives have been destroyed, and we are reduced often—too often—to suppositions and probabilities. That the publication of the "Cosmographiæ Introductio" of St. Dié was directed against the reputation of Cristoforo Colombo is an undeniable fact, and that some secret lay at the bottom of it is plain enough. Nothing is truly known as to how the French manuscript came into the hands of King René, nor what part Vespucci took in the matter. We are reduced to in-ferences from the known facts of Vespucci sending his accounts of his voyages in all directions. His admirers and partisans are obliged to make more suppositions and have given less probable explanations than his adversaries, and the custom adopted of throwing upon others all the manifest and glaring errors in order to take off all blame from Vespucci is only a "*dessein coupable d'agrandir artificieusement le mérite de Vespucci,*"* at the expense of the veracity and knowledge of some of his contemporaries.

---

*Examen critique, vol. v, p. 187

The name was not "accidentally created in the Vosges,"[*] as de Humboldt thought; but the application to Vespucci of the indigenous name Amerrique was wrongly made there. The name is not a creation of the Vosgian Gymnasium, but only an erroneous assimilation to the Christian name of a man having some similarity with it, against all the rules of priority of discovery and of naming a great country in using the Christian name of a Piloto instead of his family name. After the mistake had been made Vespucci took care to make it good by altering the autography of his Christian name, changing his signature of 1492, *Amerigho*, into *Amerrigo* after 1507 and until his death.

All the discussions among Americanists come entirely from their ignorance of the existence of a tribe of Indians who call themselves *Amerriques*, and who inhabit the Sierra *Amerrique* and the country rich in gold, between Lake Nicaragua and the Mosquito coast. They were confronted by such difficulties that it is a true chaos of dates, names, pretentions of all sorts, patriotic rivalries, and futile explanations unworthy of the characters and profound science of some of their number. If Varnhagen and d'Avezac, and more especially de Humboldt, had known the existence of the Amerriques, the Sierra Amerrique, and the gold region of the vicinities of Cariai and Carambaru, of the *lettera rarissima* of Colombo, they would have given a very different explanation, and instead of giving such weak and inadequate reasons as they did they would have thrown a great deal more light upon the matter than I have been able to do, for I have no pretention of being an Americanist, and even less a scholar, being only a practical travelling geologist.

RÉSUMÉ.

We have the following authentic facts:

(1) On the 30th of December, 1492, Vespucci wrote a letter from Sevilla, preserved at Mantova, in the Archives Gonzaga, signed *Amerigho* Vespucci, merchante fiorentino in Sybilia.

(2) In the last voyage of Christoforo Colombo he staid from the 25th of September to the 5th of October, 1502, with his 150 companions, at Cariaï (Rio Rama) and Carambaru (Rio Blewfields) among Indians wearing gold mirrors round their necks. The localities of the mouth of the Rios Rama and Blewfields are so near the country occupied now by the the *Amerrique* Indians and the Sierra *Amerrique*, and the proved existence there of an area of gold mines, altogether make it certain that Colombo and his 150 seamen heard the name Amerrique and used it at their return to designate some of the Indian tribes and a country rich in gold.

(3) First letter of Vespucci to Lorenzo Pier Francisco di Medicis, published at Paris, in 1504 or 1505, with the name *Albericus* Vesputius.

(4) Second letter of Vespucci to Pietro Soderini, published at Pescia, near Florence, in 1506, with the name *Amerigo* Vespucci.

***

[*]Examen critique vol. v, p. 175.

(5) Jean Basin, of St. Dié, uses the names of *Amerige* and *Americus* in translating from the French into Latin the second letter of Vespucci, entitled, *Quatuor navigationes;* and the Vosgian Gymnasium proposes in 1507 to name the New World America, in honor of its discoverer *Amerige* Vespucci.

(6) On the 9th of December, 1508, Vespucci wrote a letter to the Archbishop of Toledo, lately published in fac-simile by the Spanish Government, signed *Amerrigo* Vespucci, Piloto mor (major).

(7) From 1508 until 1512, the date of his death, two or three signatures of Vespucci have been found in Spain, all written with the double *r* and without the letter *h. Amerrigo* instead of *Amerigho* of 1492, showing a willful alteration in the spelling of his Christian name, after the christening of the New World in his honor, at St. Dié, in 1507.

(8) In 1515, Shoener says that the name *America* is generally used to designate the New World.

(9) The first map, with an authentic date, on which the name *America* has been found, is the map of Apianus, in the Polyhistor of Sollnus in 1520.

(10) In 1533, twenty-one years after the death of Vespucci, Schoener, an astronomer and geographer of good standing and just reputation, accuses Vespucci of having written his name on charts; but he did not say how the name was spelled. The Americanist Henry Harrisse thinks that Shoener "had fastened on the memory of Vespucius the odious charge of having artfully inserted the words *Terra di Amerigo* in charts which he has otherwise altered."* Vespucci may have inserted *Terra di Amerriques*, an exact name, very closely allied to the new spelling of his Christian name *Amerrigo*, and which has led Schoener to make the accusation. The exact expressions used by Schoener are: "Americus Vesputius maritima loca Indiæ superiores ex Hispaniis navigio ad occidentem perlustrans, eam partem quæ superioris Indiæ est, credidit esse Insulam quam a suo nomine vocari instituit" (In: *Joanis Schoeneri Carolostadii opusculum geographicum ex Diversorum libris*, etc., etc., Norica, Novembris xxxiii).

No maps made by Vespucci have been found, although we know that he made some.

One thing is certain, it is that Vespucci did not discover the New World, and another fact is also certain, that *Amerrique* is an indigenous name. From the central part of the continent, just about the middle, the name *Amerrique* or *Amérique* in French or *America* in Latin extended first southward and then northward, until finally we have the *Three Americas.*

Geographically the name Amerrique has never varied, the Latin name *America* and the French *Amérique* have always been spelled without any changes among the letters on all the maps and charts; while, on the contrary, the Christian name of Vespucci had varied from Amerigho to

---

* Bibliotheca Americana Vetustissima, p. 304.

Amerrigo, according to his own signature, and has taken all the forms and combinations imaginable between Albericus and Morigo.

To conclude, I shall quote a sentence taken from the life of Louis Pasteur: "All new discoveries bring into the ideas generally used until then, a change which is accepted by some with joy, while others resist, because it deranges all their old habits." (*M. Pasteur, Histoire d'un savant*, etc., p. 341, Paris, 1883); which applies exactly to this case. Almost all Americans and all the Spaniards have accepted with joy the idea that the New World was not named for Vespucci, who has no claim whatever to such an honor, but that the beautiful name of *Amerrique* belongs to a tribe of Indians and to a range or sierra of the central part of the continent, discovered and first explored.by Cristoforo Colombo. A few Americanists, disturbed in their old habit of proclaiming in books, in pamphlets, or in speeches, that the new continent has been called after Amerigho Vespucci, do not like it, for it is disagreeable to them to see all they have published or said replaced by something more rational and natural, of which they had not the smallest idea, or even thought of for one instant, and their resistance is natural enough. I expected it from the time I wrote my first paper on the *Origin of the Name America*, published in March, 1875, in *the Atlantic Monthly ;* and nothing that has been said by a few critics and reviewers in the United States, in Italy, and in Germany has surprised me. But time will show who is right and I trust fully to the good sense of the people.

The name of the New World was taken from the mountain range and Indian tribe at the center of the continent, and brought into general use by the people who had been there, and the people will now see who has the correct view as to the origin of the name.

H. Mis. 142——43

PROGRESS OF ORIENTAL SCIENCE IN AMERICA DURING 1888.

BY CYRUS ADLER, PH. D.

The study of oriental science has had a remarkable development in America during the past decade, and has at the same time taken on an almost entirely new aspect. Under the lead of Professor Whitney, and of the men whom he inspired, the Indian branch of oriental studies has in the past given—and still continues to give—many valuable contributions to science, and holds an almost unique position towards the Old World in the circle of philological study.

Investigation in the field of Semitic languages and archæology, on the other hand, was carried on mostly by the way, and in spite of a few valuable contributions the publications in that line were, as a rule, not important. The year 1883 marks a new era for these studies in America with the establishment of regular courses in Semitic languages (including Assyrian inscriptions) at two of our great universities, Harvard and Johns Hopkins. Most of the other important seats of learning have followed this departure, so that in 1886 it was already possible for the eminent French archæologist, M. Joachim Menant, to say that the most serious efforts in this line are now concentrated in America.*

The year 1888 was one of great moment to oriental science in this country. Possibly no stronger evidence of the interest had for these studies could be afforded than the determination of the publishers of the series of text-books known as *Porta Linguarum Orientalium* to put an English translation on the American market; a confirmatory incident is the selection of an American member of the board of editors of the *Zeitschrift für Orientalische Bibliographie*, Prof. R. J. H. Gottheil, of Columbia College.

A number of gentlemen of Philadelphia equipped and sent out a party to explore and conduct excavations in Mesopotamia, under the auspices of the University of Pennsylvania. Considerable difficulty was experienced in procuring from the Turkish authorities the requisite

---

* *Les Langues Perdues de la Perse et de l'Assyrie.* Assyrie, par M. Joachim Menant. Paris, Leroux, 1886, p. xiv.

permission to dig, and at the close of the year the party proceeded southward to Niffer. It is likely that work will be continued during the coming year.*

The American Oriental Society, at its meeting in Philadelphia, took a step which may lead to important results. A resolution was adopted and a committee appointed to obtain information and make a report in May, 1889, on the feasibility and utility of the preparation of a catalogue of oriental manuscripts in America. Such a catalogue, if it could be made complete, would be of the greatest service to American oriental scholars, whose chief drawback lies in the fact that their materials for work are scattered over the entire country.

· The University of Pennsylvania has acquired a collection of cuneiform originals (briefly described by Dr. Robert F. Harper in *Hebraica*, Vol. v, pp. 74–76), and also a collection of casts of Assyrian objects in the British Museum.

The National Museum is steadily pursuing its policy of collecting copies of Assyrian and Babylonian objects preserved in this country. An exhibit of specimens in the field of Biblical Archæology was set up in the Government exhibit at the Centennial Exposition of the Ohio Valley held at Cincinnati. An interesting collection of casts of Assyrian and Egyptian objects has been received from the Berlin Museum and a working oriental library is being collected in the Smith-sonian Institution for the use of the oriental section, and of oriental scholars visiting Washington.

Possibly the first German journal in the field of oriental philology, to be published with the aid of an American learned body is the *Beiträge zur Assyriologie und Vergleichenden Semitischen Sprachwissenschaft*, which will appear *mit Unterstützung der Johns Hopkins Universität zu Baltimore*, edited by Prof. Friedrich Delitzsch, of Leipzig, and Prof. Paul Haupt, of Baltimore.

American scholars have contributed to most of the important journals in the field of oriental science published abroad, and a number of for-eign scholars, among whom may be mentioned Canon Cheyne, of Ox-ford, Prof. G. Maspero, Mr. W. M. Flinders Petrie, Mr. Theo. G. Pinches of the British Museum, Prof. George Rawlinson, Prof. A. H. Sayce of Queens College, Oxford, Dr. Hugo Winckler, of Berlin, and the late Prof. William Wright, of Cambridge, have sent contributions to Ameri-can journals.

The range of topics covered by American orientalists comprises : As-syro-Babylonian language, art, history, and religion ; Armenia ; Budd-hism and Sanskrit ; China ; Cyprus ; Egypt ; Hittites ; Japan ; Jews and Judaism (so far as they bear on the history of the orient); modern oriental languages; Mohammedanism and Arabic ; Old Testament and Hebrew ; Pedagogics ; Persia; Samaritan ; Siam ; Semitic Philology ; Syriac.

---

* Compare *Philadelphia Ledger*, June 14, 1888; *New York Evening Post*, June 22, 1888 ; *New York Independent*, June 28, 1888.

The present report is the first attempt made in this country to present in brief the work of oriental scholars during one year. It is necessarily imperfect partly because of its novelty and for lack of assistance on the part of scholars throughout the country. Many of the papers mentioned in the bibliography could not be described because they were not accessible.

ASSYRIOLOGY.

Cyrus Adler showed that two classes of Assyrian verbs weak in the third stem consonant, and usually confounded, were capable of sharp differentiation; criticised the neglect of Assyrian in the article on Semitic languages in the Cyclopædia Britannica, and suggested that a certain class of Syriac verbs (the saphel) might not be organic forms; described the views of the Babylonians concerning life after death; some of the oriental objects in the National Museum, among them an Ethiopic version of the Gospels in the Grant collection; the German expedition to southern Babylonia; the Tell-Amarna tablets in the British Museum; and announced to the American Oriental Society, on behalf of the Semitic Seminary of the Johns Hopkins University, the purpose to publish a complete edition of the life and writings of Edward Hincks, subjoining a tentative bibliography of Hincks's works.

Edgar P. Allen offered some new translations of the inscription of Tiglath-pileser I. In columns ɪ 31-2, ɪ 25, and vɪɪɪ 34 he reads *zêr šangûti*; and in ɪɪ 66 *gammarêa irḫûti*, "swift veterans;" he also made a conjecture which, if established, would present the unique instance of an Assyrian king mentioning an unsuccessful campaign.

Francis Brown explained why the religious poetry of the Semitic cuneiform monuments is Babylonian rather than Assyrian; translated a number of Babylonian penitential psalms, and drew comparisons with the corresponding portions of the Old Testament. He pointed out the identification of the names of the kings mentioned in Genesis, chapter xɪv, discussed the question of the capture of Samaria, disputing Delitzsch's opinion that it was captured by Shalmaneser, and attempted to harmonize the statements of the Bible (Is., xxxvii, 38), Alexander Polyhistor, and the Babylonian chronicle with reference to the murderer of Sennacherib. He gave notes on the Tell-Amarna tablets, discovered in 1887 in middle Egypt. One of the most surprising facts brought to light by these new tablets is the extent to which the cuneiform character and the Babylono-Assyrian language were employed in Western Asia.

Robert F. Harper published text and translation of the cylinder of Esarhaddon, and described his visit as a member of the University of Pennsylvania exploring party to Zinjirli, where a German expedition under Dr. Human has been excavating with most valuable results.

Paul Haupt described modern researches in Assyria and Babylonia; the development of the Assyrian writing; published the text of the twelfth tablet of the Nimrod Epic; re-collated the whole of the poem; gave a new translation of the first column of the Deluge tablet on the basis of recently found fragments; discussed the dimensions of the Babylonian ark (=120 half cubits, 110 feet, for both the depth and width, and 600 half cubits, 540 feet, for the length); and developed a theory of the Assyrian prefix *na*.

Morris Jastrow discussed the Assyrian word *kudûru*, which he connected with the ring of the sun-god and the biblical and later Hebrew *kaddur;* reviewed Part I of Delitzsch's Assyrian dictionary, offered translation of some passages in the monolith inscription of Shalmaneser II, and described ancient Babylonian cemeteries.

M. L. Kellner gave a new translation of the standard inscription of Asurnazirpal, and compared and discussed the Babylonian and Old Testament accounts of the Deluge.

David G. Lyon showed the development of the Assyro–Babylonian religious conceptions by a collection of the prayers appended to the royal inscriptions. He proved from a statistical study of the Pantheon of Asurbanipal (668–626 B. C.) that this king mentions most frequently Assur, the national god, and Istar, the goddess of war, and that he exhibited a marked tendency to invoke a group of twelve deities, not the same, however, which preside over the twelve months. He also called attention to some parallels between the Assyrian inscriptions and the Old Testament.

S. H. McCollester described his trip from Bagdad to Babylon and Mosul, the site of ancient Nineveh, with an account of the excavations, explorations, and discoveries made there.

J. A. Paine gave a discussion of the eclipse in the seventh year of Cambyses, based on T. G. Pinches's paper, "An astronomical or astrological tablet from Babylon" (*Babylonian and Oriental Record*, August, 1888). This tablet is either the original or a copy of the text from which Ptolemy (in the Almagest) derived his information of the fifth eclipse which he enumerates (July 16, 523 B. C.). In this text we meet for the first time the Assyrian word *iriḫu* Hebrew *iâreaḥ* "moon."

Theophilus G. Pinches, of the British Museum, contributed to the *New York Independent* an article entitled, "An old Babylonian letter," being a translation and commentary on a tablet in the British Museum, S+375.

Zenaide A. Ragozin wrote a brief history of Media, Babylonia, and Persia, from the fall of Nineveh to the Persian war. Especial attention is given to the religion of the Parsees.

A. H. Sayce described in the *New York Independent* the literary correspondence between Asia and Egypt in the century before the Exodus, being an account of some of the Tell-Amarna tablets.

S. Alden Smith has carried on his studies in Assyrian letters, publishing a number of new texts; described Assyrian report tablets and the progress of Assyrian study, and criticized Delitzsch's Assyrian dictionary.   •

William Hayes Ward concludes that there is no clear evidence, on Assyrian and Babylonian seals, of human sacrifice. He considers the so-called gate god a conventionalized form of the sun-god coming out of the gates of the east.

Hugo Winckler translated in *Hebraica* a cuneiform text describing the building of Nebuchadnezzar's artificial reservoir. One inscription records that the royal canal was built because the river Euphrates had departed from the city of Sippar.

D. A. Walker gave a historical sketch of the reign of the Assyrian king Asurbanipal.

BUDDHISM AND SANSKRIT.

A. H. Edgreen wrote a criticism of Van den Gheyn. His conclusion is that of the thirteen roots which have been referred to the eighth class of verbs in Sanskrit five are fictitious, and the remainder must be referred to the fifth class.

T. B. Forbush described the Hindu doctrine of death and immortality. The early Hindus had no dread of death. The future life was a joyous one, when all good people reap the reward of virtue. The terrible conception of hell is no part of the primitive Vedic faith. The fundamental postulate of Hindu ontology is that the soul is eternal. It is not born, it can not die, and is itself changeless. At different times it wears different garments; sometimes it assumes the form of a man, sometimes the disguise of an animal, and sometimes it is clad in the robes of a spirit of light.

James T. Hatfield edited a Vedic text on omens and portents from two MSS. in the British Museum.

E. W. Hopkins continued his inquiry into the conditions of civilization in the Hindu middle age from the point of view of the ruling power or warrior caste, and discussed the quantitative variations in the Calcutta and Bombay texts of the Mahabharata.

A. V. W. Jackson called attention to a new reference in the Avesta to "the life-book" hereafter.

S. H. Kellogg discussed the origin of certain Rajput forms of the substantive verb in Hindi.

David Ker described Burmah's mighty river and the capital cities of the past, the old caverns, site and great temple of Moulmein, Lower Burmah; a trip by rail up the Himalaya; temples and Buddhist shrines that have been used as fortresses in times of war; the street scenes and play-houses of Rangoon, the Liverpool of Burmah, and the famous Shway Dagohn of Rangoon, the golden pagoda of Burmah; also a trip among the Circassian mountains.

Edward A. Lawrence gave an account of his visit among the missionary stations in South India. Churches and Christian worship are described. The population of South India is largely aboriginal, of Dravidian stock. The social institutions are primitive and interesting to the student of early customs.

Henry C. Lea in a note on Emerson and the Katha Upanishad referred to a notice of Mr. W. S. Kennedy calling attention to a passage in the "Katha Upanishad" which furnished Mr. Emerson the initial thought in his mysterious stanzas on "Brahma."

H. W. Magoun treated of the *Asuri Kalpa*, a witchcraft practice of the Atharva-Veda. *Asuri* is the black mustard of India, and it was used in this rite to make an image of some person whom it was desired to overcome or destroy by magical practices. Mr. Magoun prints text, critical notes, extracts from the Scholiast, translation and a commentary.

Raj Coomar Roy corrected various misapprehensions concerning child-marriage in India. The boys and girls, though married in infancy, are never allowed to live together until the girl reaches puberty. This being the case, and marriage ordained by God, it fulfills the twofold object of the procreation of children, and a remedy against sin; it even fulfills a third object, viz, mutual society. There is great ignorance among Europeans in regard to the position of Hindu women, which is by no means that of slavery.

W. W. Rockhill described the Lamaist ceremony of "making of mani pills." During the entire process no one is permitted to approach who has used meat, spirits, garlic, tobacco, or other impure objects. The process is sometimes one hundred days in length (consisting of a very careful preparation of the pills, which are made of flour and scented water), followed by a period of meditation and prayer. He discussed the use of skulls in Lamaist ceremonies, which is at present twofold: (1) as an offering to Tsepamed, who is represented as holding in his hands a skull filled with ambrosia; (2) as a receptacle for the wine or other liquid offered to the gods.

Justin A. Smith gave a summary of the ancient literature of the East. He treats of romance and drama, the Pankatantra, the Sakoontalâ ot Kalidasa, and Hindu fiction in general; of Hindu epic and mythology, the Mahâbhârata and the Râmâyana; of the Iranian scriptures, the Zend-Avesta of Zarathustra, adding notes on Persian and Iranian history; of the Shah-Nameh and the Bundehesh; of Buddhism and the teachings of Buddha; and of Chinese literature, especially the works of Confucius and Mencius.

W. D. Whitney wrote a review of the second volume of Eggeling's translation of the Catapatha Brahmana, and brought out a new edition of his Sanskrit grammar.

CHINA.

W. S. Ament discussed the ancient coinages of China. Starting with the assertion that the Chinese were the inventors of coined money, he investigated, specifically, (1) the composition of Chinese coins; (2) the mode of their casting; (3) their inscriptions; (4) their form.

Adele M. Fielde described some Chinese mortuary customs. The obsequies of a parent are reckoned the most troublesome affair in human experience among the Chinese, and, therefore, when they wish to declare the extreme vexatiousness of any piece of work, they say, "It is more trouble than a funeral." Infants are buried summarily, without coffins, and the young are interred with few rites; but the funerals of the aged, of both sexes, are elaborate in proportion to the number of the descendants and to their wealth.

Elizabeth P. Gould describes the result of Yung Wing's efforts to raise the standard of education in his native country during the last thirty years. It was through his influence that students were sent to America to be educated. One of these was Yan Phou Lee, whose biography is given on the basis of his book, "When I was a boy in China."

W. A. P. Martin gave an account of diplomacy in ancient China. The doctrine of extraterritoriality was unknown; no agent was a minister plenipotentiary, and the sovereign always held himself free to disavow the acts of his representative; there were no resident ministers, only *envoyés extraordinaires*. He made a translation of the devotional portion of a pictorial sheet engraved and published by the Buddhist high priest in charge of the Pas-ên Temple; found traces of the philosophic ideas of Descartes in the Chinese thinkers of the eleventh century, and the same views among them concerning filial duty that are advanced by Plato.

S. A. Stern described domestic customs in Japan and China, the business habits of the people, their dress and amusements.

H. W. Warren described a journey on the Yang-tze-kiang, with some geographical and social notes. Canton, he says, is a thoroughly English place. The architecture is imposing and solid. It is a little London planted in the distant East.

CYPRUS.

W. H. Goodyear described the Cypriote sculptures in the Metropolitan Museum; and in a note to the *Critic*, April 18, corrects some misapprehensions in the *Critic's* notice of his paper published in the *American Journal of Archæology* on the Egyptian origin of the Ionic capital and the anthemion.

EGYPT.

The various articles on the Tell-Amarna tablets, discussed under Assyriology, all bear more or less on Egyptian history.

Lysander Dickerman discussed Groff's discovery of the names of Jacob and Joseph on the Egyptian monuments, holding that Groff's inference was not warranted.

William N. Groff, who continues his residence abroad, speaks of *q. l. y. i.* on an Egypto-Aramean papyrus, which he identifies with the Egyptian *Kelbi*, a sort of wine; published in hieroglyphic the romance of the two brothers, with a translation and commentary; discussed the

pronouns in Egyptian, and discovered the names of Jacob-El and Joseph-El, in lists of defeated nations, transported to Egypt in the time
of Tuthmosis III, about 1700 B. C.

Lewis G. Janes reviewed Edward Naville's edition and translation
of the Egyptian Book of the Dead. A careful study of this book, with
an unbiased scrutiny of the monuments and inscriptions, reveals coincidences of notable change and development in the Eyptian doctrine of
the future life. Mr. Janes follows the development from the archaic
period down to the days of St. Paul.

G. Lansing, in two articles on Egypticity and Authenticity of the
Pentateuch, discussed the Biblical narratives of the lives of Joseph and
Moses (Genesis xxxix, *et seq.*) with reference to the local hints and linguistic usages; in other words, the Egyptian cast and character of the
narraratives. He concludes that the narratives *must* have been written
at or near the time the events narrated occurred.

G. Maspero studied the Egyptian words which seem to apply to the
human soul and the places it inhabited after death. He pointed out
that the views of the Egyptians with reference to death and a future
state underwent many changes.

Ch. E. Moldenke edited the first part of a new edition of the so-called
tale of two brothers, or the D'Orbiney papyrus.

Howard Osgood made an English translation of M. Philippe Virey's
French translation of the Papyrus Prisse, "The Oldest Book in the
World;" described society, ethics, and religion in Egypt before 2000
B. C.

Aug. de Plongeon recalled the fact that the Egyptian Sphynx is
a riddle still unsolved and its age unknown. He directed attention
to certain striking analogies existing between the Egyptian Sphynx
and the leopard with human head that crowns the mausoleum of Prince
Coh at Chichen-Itza (Yucatan).

C. A. Siegfried described a tour from Tripoli to Alexandria. Tripoli
is a typical Arabian town with all the evils of Moslem misrule, wretch-
edness, and neglect. From Tripoli to Egypt is an agreeable change.
The social and mercantile condition of Alexandria is described. He
gives an account of his experience of a journey to the Dalmatian coast
and Montenegro, describing the political, social, and archaeological
features of the country.

Cope Whitehouse discussed the map of Joseph the Fayumi and the
Raian Basin, in the light of the survey made during 1887-'88.

E. L. Wilson described " the great Pyramid " of Cheops, narrates the
incidents of an ascent and descent; pictures the views from its summit
and hills, discusses its history and the curious speculations to which it
has given origin; he wrote an illustrated paper on the temples of Egypt.
No perfectly preserved Egyptian temple is in existence, but by studying the various parts in the existing examples an adequate idea can
be obtained of what one of these structures must have been in its completeness.

HITTITES.

William Hayes Ward restored and described some imperfectly published Hittite monuments from Carcemish (Jerablûs), which appeared in the *London Graphic* December 11, 1880. These monuments had been rephotographed by the Wolfe expedition to Babylonia.

JAPAN.

S. Beale described Japanese pictures at the British Museum. Japan possesses works of art which from its own particular point of view equal any school of European painting; this art is the outcome of that of China. It dates back to the fifth century A. D. All pictures are essentially decorative; light and shade are unknown quantities, and linear perspective completely ignored. He also gave an account of Japanese ivory carvings; showed the potent influence of tobacco in the decorative art of that country. Every domestic occurrence is represented in ivory, and many of their classic romances are illustrated in the bronze, porcelain, and lacquer work.

William Elliot Griffis described Japanese artists and artisans; with illustrations from drawings by a Japanese artist. Among things unexpected in Japan, none strikes the visitor or resident more than the enviroment of art and its maker; the critic and historian, who is yet to write the story of art in Japan, will discriminate between what is borrowed and what is original. The folding fan, the arts of lacquering, sword-making, cloissonné on porcelain, and some of the methods of decorating are of native origin. Other works of art are mostly imported.

E. H. House gives a history of the tariff in Japan. The first effective commercial treaty with Japan was negotiated in 1858 by Townsend and Harris, upon terms which in general were not disadvantageous to the unsophisticated people with whom they were dealing. If they had taken the precaution to insure the absolute termination of the treaty at a proper date, all would have resulted as they desired, but under the circumstances it has proved disastrous to Japan and proportionately favorable to the western powers. He also discussed foreign jurisdiction in Japan. The authors of the early treaties never intended to supersede the laws of Japan by those of their own nations. The inflation of arrogant pretense, the multitude of entangling and bewildering complications, the aggregation of gross abuses, and the offensive domination over the national rule which have been exercised in later years have no other basis than the narrow foundations of mutual assistance, stipulated in the treaties of Harris and Townsend. The "diplomatic co-operative policy" of European nations has put Japan in ties which hold her in political and moral enslavement.

S. E. Ives describes a Japanese magic mirror. It is a circular, metallic hand-mirror, having figures in relief upon its back; the reflecting surface is highly polished, and reflects the face as well apparently as do mirrors of silvered glass, but when it is used to reflect the direct rays of a powerful light upon a screen the reflection shows the figures that are at the back of the mirror. This peculiarity is explained by the fact that there are irregularities in the convexity of the mirror which cause an irregular reflection of the sun's rays.

H. H. S. Thompson wrote on the women of Japan. They pride themselves on the fact that nine of the sovereigns of Japan have been women; that the chief deity in their mythology is a woman, and that the keeper of the "divine regalia" is a virgin priestess. They say the women of the early centuries had great mental and physical vigor, and filled offices of public trust with dignity and honor. There are many heroines whose names are renowned in Japanese classics, while instances of woman's valor, fortitude under suffering, and greatness in the hour of persecution abound. The Japanese woman has a place all her own in the world of letters. The evils in the position of women in Japan are traceable to Buddhism.

JEWS AND JUDAISM.

S. Adler discussed the various forms of benedictions in use in ancient times among the Jews. They fall into three classes: (1) After a physical enjoyment; (2) on special occasion or at particular localities; (3) before fulfillment of a religious duty.

B. Felsenthal showed that the popular Sabbath hymn *Leha dodi* was not composed by Judah ha-Levi, as Heine supposed, but was written by Solomon Alkabitz ha-Levy, who lived in the sixteenth century and died in the city of Safed, in Northern Palestine. He also showed that the pronunciation of *Jehovah* for the name of God was first employed in Germany in the sixteenth century.

A. K. Glover described the Jews of India. They are all offshoots of Judah and not of the ten tribes. He also gave an account of the Jews of the Chinese Empire.

R. J. H. Gottheil continues his translation of Karpeles's History of Jewish Literature.

M. Jastrow, jr., treated of several Jewish grammarians of the middle ages. Hayyûg lived about the middle of the tenth century in Cordova, though born in Fez. He wrote two grammatical works on Hebrew verbs. In his studies he started from Arabic principles. From his treatises his pupil, Ibn Ḡanâh, worked out his elaborate grammatical system. Dônâsh ben Labrat's only distinction is that he is the opponent of Saadia Gaon and of Menaḥem b. Sarûg. He is the author of two sharp polemical essays, the one containing a pointed criticism of Saadia's Arabic translation of the Bible, the other an attempt to discountenance Menaḥem's standing as a grammarian.

Alexander Kohut discussed the etymology of a number of talmudical words.

H. C. Trumbull, in his history of the origin and development of the Sunday school, devotes the first chapter to a history of the ancient Jewish schools.   •

The doctrines of the resurrection and of a world of the dead are found among the oldest heathen religions of Chaldea and Egypt. Howard Osgood maintains against negative critics that the same doctrines are taught in the Pentateuch, especially in the narrative of Cain and Abel.

B. Pick discussed the Old Testament, passages applied Messianically by the ancient synagogue, in Jeremiah, Lamentations, Ezekiel, Daniel, and the twelve minor prophets. His work consists in the collection of quotations from the Midrashim with reference to the promised Messiah. He maintains (*Christ and the Essenes*) against Giusburg and Frankel that whatever points of resemblance critical ingenuity may emphasize, the teaching of Christianity was in a direction opposed to that of Essenism, and that the latter could have had no intentional connection with the origin of Christianity. In describing the Therapeutæ, of Egypt, a peculiar sect of Jewish ascetics, he points out agreements and disagreements between this sect and the Essenes. The characteristics of the two are so different that they can not be identical. Against Grætz he maintains the genuineness of Philo's Tracta, and contends that the Therapeutæ were Jews.

Aaron Wise discussed the origin of Jewish angelology and demonology. He holds that it could not have arisen at the time of the Babylonian captivity, but antedates it.

MISCELLANEOUS.

I. N. Fradenburg has undertaken to show the connection of certain living religions of the Orient with the Jewish faith, and the connection of certain others with Christianity. He treats of (1) the great reformer of Asia, Buddha; (2) the old philosopher, Las-the, the contemporary of Confucius; (3) Confucius, his life, teachings, and his religious system; (4) Brahmanism and Hinduism, its caste, doctrines, precepts, and speculations.

I. H. Hall gave a note on a Rhodian jar in the Boston Museum of Fine Arts; on one handle is the eponym and name of Doric month, and on the other the name of the manufacturer, owner, or exporter.

L. describes the Musée Guimet in Paris, which contains a collection intended to teach the history of the characteristics of oriental religions. The Christian and the Hebrew forms of worship are excluded; there is no other collection of the kind nearly so large, or so well adapted for the study of the development of oriental and ancient civilization.

Allan Marquand described an archaic patera from Kourion, belonging to the Cesnola collection; the central medallion is missing; the center zone represents a banquet scene; the scene figured upon the patera seems to be the autumnal Adonis festival, in which honor was paid to both Adonis and Aphrodite.

A. P. Peabody compared classic and Semitic ethics. Semitic morality has a ground or standard of right, and therefore a reason for conduct, of which we find no trace in the ethical philosophers of Greece and Rome. Acts are judged by their intrinsic and inherent nature, not by their bearing on some ultimate end ; a fatal deficiency in the morals of the classic ages was the relation of the sexes and the lack of purity and permanence of domestic institutions.

S. D. Peet compared animal worship and sun worship in the East and in the West. The worship of the sun was prevalent in different parts of the world at a very ancient date. It was preceded by animal worship; but it is more powerful and more extensive than animal worship and grew out of it. The customs, habits, and language of the races of northern Asia are compared, especially the Ostyaks, with those of the aborigines of America. He discussed American religions and the Bible, and thinks that there are many things which go to show that there must have been a historic connection between the original religions of America and the teachings of the Bible.

S. B. Platner, reviewed *Myth, Ritual, and Religion* of Andrew Lang. A method of explaining the irrational in mythology has been here worked out far more comprehensively and satisfactorily than by any other writer.

MODERN ORIENTAL LANGUAGES.

Cyrus Adler showed the importance of the study of modern oriental languages for a knowledge of the ancient tongues and for the improvement of our consular service and increase of trade with the East.

MOHAMMEDANISM AND ARABIC.

The question, Why am I a Moslem? is answered by Ibn Ablis. There is a universally wrong conception of Mohammedanism among Western nations, but the more the religion of the Moslem is investigated the more does it claim the respectful homage of those who study its teachings. The Islam does not persecute any more than did or does Christianity. Notwithstanding his extensive travels in the East and West, the writer still clings to the five great duties of the true Moslem, and the six great dogmas of faith ; in them he finds all that is needed to discipline the human soul to that condition which is expressed in the word "Moslem"—" one who is resigned." " I am a Moslem because I recognize in Islam one of the many avenues through which the Creator of the universe leads his people to the temple of truth."

G. Benton discussed Mohammedanism in Africa, with reference to Canon Isaac Taylor's statements, implying that Mohammedanism in Africa is an almost unmingled and beneficial success, while Christianity there is an undoubted failure. The replies of Canon McColl Bosworth Smith show that Canon Taylor was partly right. The superior success of Mohammedanism in Africa is due to the fact that it agrees better with the material and practical which it is within the power of the crude African mind to accept.

Theodore Child gave a description of a visit to Constantinople. He narrates his treatment by the custom-house officers, his visit to the bazar, with notes on the municipal and social life of Stamboul. Guide-books are of very little help to the visitor of Stamboul, at least, to a man who really wants to know the life and social condition of the city.

A. L. Frothingham sketched the development and character of Mohammedan education. The contrast between the liberal and the progressive Arab of the Khalifate, and the intolerent and fanatical part of the East, are not to be lost sight of in a judgment of the culture of Mohammedanism. He traces the development and character of Arabian culture as influenced by the civilization of Byzantium, Syria, and Persia; gives the curriculum of studies; names the three institutions of instruction (school, college, and mosque), and points out the strong moral element in their education.

F. H. Hedge, in an article on Mohammedan Mysticism, affirms that the recent account of the superior success, as compared with the Christian, of Mohammedan missions in Africa confirms the former estimate of the prophet of Islam, whose claims were for the first time vindicated by Thomas Carlyle in 1840, and M. Barthilemy St. Hilaire in 1865. Mohammed borrowed much of his religion from Judaism, but, notwithstanding that this is the dominant element, he favored an un-Jewish mysticism. He compares Mohammed's life with that of David. The two most obnoxious features of his religion, fatalism and the sensual character of his paradise, are found in the belief held by some branches of the Christian church, and, on the whole, are grossly misunderstood. He furnishes the biography of a saintly woman, Rabia, and closes with a few extracts from Tholuck's Anthology of Eastern Mystics (1825).

Thomas P. Hughes discussed the Moslem's Bible, or Koran. Two hundred and one millions receive and venerate the Koran as the word of God. It is read more devoutly, more extensively, by the Moslems than the Christian Bible by the Christians. The Moslem takes religion seriously. The Koran contains some eighty thousand words, arranged in one hundred and fourteen chapters, called soorahs. The finest collection of ancient MSS. is in the library at Cairo. Whosoever can recite the whole Koran from memory is diguified with the title of hafiz, or protector of the faith. The early chapters are merely poetic effusions. The Koran is not an historic book; five periods can be distinguished in its composition.

E. P. Sanguinetti related his impressions of Constantinople; his journey to Batna, one of the French military outposts; an excursion to the tomb of Sidi Okbar; an Arab marriage, and his experiences in the Arab markets.

Lawrence M. Simmons gave a brief statement of the views of Philippi and Wright on the separation which may take place between the so-called defined and defining noun in Arabic, followed by a translation from the celebrated "Watchfire" of the late Nasif Al-Yazigi, showing the treatment of this subject by a native grammarian.

C. H. Toy described some phonetic peculiarities of Cairo Arabic, especially the Egyptian mute *Gym*, palatal *q*, and the pronunciation of the dentals. In the Cairo pronunciation the old Arabic *th* and *dh* become *t* and *d*; in some cases the Cairo fricatives pass into sibilants.

George Washburn summarized the articles of the Mohammedan creed. Islamism has for its base faith in the unity of God and in the mission of his dearest servant Mohammed. The book of God which descended last from Heaven is the sacred Koran. The first of the prophets was Adam and the last Mohammed; the greatest of all is Mohammed, etc.

Caroline R. Wright described the worship of the dervishes of Cairo. The preliminary prayers over, the curtain of the entrance door is raised, and giaours are admitted to the sanctuary. At this moment the chief dervish and other dervishes were prostrate, with their heads on the ground in the direction of *meihrab*, and for nearly half an hour they continued kneeling, praying and bowing, rocking to and fro, reciting the Koran in a twanging nasal tone. Then follows the howling of the litany, with its unison refrain *Allah-hou, Allah-hou.*

OLD TESTAMENT AND HEBREW.

Benjamin Wisner Bacon presented in tabular form the results of the principal schools of higher Biblical criticism, including fragments and portions assigned to editors, interpolators, compilers, and glossators. His classification is: Priestly Law Book, P^2; Ephraimite Narrative, F; Judean Narrative, J; Law of Holiness, P^1.

E. C. Bissell published a work on *Biblical Antiquities*, for popular use. It embraces the main facts under the classification of domestic, civil, and sacred antiquities.

W. G. Blakie has published the first and second books of Samuel. They belong to the series called the Expositor's Library, based on the plan of giving the substance of scripture in a running commentary or connected narrative, which furnishes all needful explanations.

C. A. Briggs continued his studies on the forms of Hebrew poetry. The *tetrameters* are measured by four beats of the accent, and are often divided by a cæsura into two halves. Examples are Psalm xlvi, 13; 2 Samuel i, 19–27; Exodus xv; Psalm lxxxix. *Tetrameters* are not so numerous as the pentameters. The *pentameter* is measured by five beats of the rythmical accent; the cæsura usually comes after the third beat. Examples are Lamentations iii; Psalm cxix; Jonah ii; Psalms cxx, cxxxiv (the dirge of Babylon); Isaiah xlvii. The hexameter is a double trimeter. Instances of *hexameter* are Proverbs xxxi, 12 ff; Psalm cxxxvii; Isaiah lx, and Jeremiah viii, 9.

T. K. Cheyne offers an emandation to Job iii, 14, and translates " to build up ruined places."

Howard Crosby asserts that the revised Old Testament is too much a new edition of the old authorized version, and illustrates this by a passage from the book of Job (xxviii, 1-12), which, of all the Old Testament writings, needed the most thorough revision. Against Cheyne he shows that the Cyrus inscription, and the statements contained in Isaiah xliv, 28, and xlv, 1-13, do not really contradict each other. Cyrus may have treated Bel, and Nebo, and Merodach with the greatest courtesy, and yet have sent the Jews back as a wise piece of policy.

James D. Dana discussed the cosmogony of Genesis in reply to Canon Driver (Defense and Critique, *Andov. Rev.*, 1887). He favors the stand taken by Guyot, and holds that the fiats of Genesis did not produce completed results, but initiated slowly developing processes.

T. G. Dashiel maintains that the Old Testament teaches practically the doctrine of eternal existence.

Samuel Davidson. Notes on the Psalms: ii, 12; iv, 3; vi, 2; viii, 2; xii, 7; xvi, 3, render: as to the saints who are in the land and the nobles, all my pleasure is in them; xviii; xix; xxii, 17; xxv, 11; xxix, 2; xxxii, 9, With bit and bridle their youth must be bound; they do not come near thee otherwise; xxxvi, 13; xxxvii, 38; xxxix, 3; xlii, 5; xlv; xlviii, 3; li; lii; lv; lvi; lvii; lviii, 2; lx, 6; lxiv, 7; lxv, 6; lxvi; lxviii; lxix; lxx; lxxii; lxxiii, 4; lxxiv, 19; lxxvi, 5, and lxxvii, 11, 17-20.

W. N. Davis characterized the *Chokmah* or Hebrew philosophy. It dates its development from the age of Solomon. It differs from the Greek philosophy in taking for granted the existence of an omniscient, omnipotent, and omnipresent God. Hebrew wisdom is inseparable from morals; wisdom and right living are synonomous terms. The best specimens of the *Chokmah* are found in Ecclesiastes and Job. In discussing Job xix, 25-7, he holds there is no evidence that the word "redeemer," used in Job xix, 25, can be applied to Christ, "the Redeemer." The word *Goel* used here is avenger, blood relative. He explains what a *Goel* is and translates verse 25. "I know that my Goel lives and my vindicator will arise upon the earth; (26) and after my sin is thus destroyed, and without my flesh (body) I shall see God."

Marcus Dod's edition of the Book of Genesis belongs to the series called "The Expositor's Bible."

G. C. M. Douglas reviews *The prophecies of Isaiah*, by T. K. Cheyne; and *Isaiah, his life, and times, and writings*, by S. R. Driver. Douglas does not agree with the position of either Cheyne or Driver, and gives his reason at length; there is nothing to justify us in disbelieving the universal and unbroken tradition which attributes them to Isaiah, the alleged reasons being misconceptions.

J. F. Genung discussed the interpretation of the Book of Job. Many of its difficulties are due less to original fault than to crude interpretation of them. The so-called debate-theory, with its assumed main subject, "the mystery of God's providential government of men," does not result in an exposition so homogeneous as we could wish; it does not reach the heart of the book. The problem of the book is doth Job fear

God for naught? And the solution of it is Job himself, the man Job. The poem is an epic, not a drama. It is the epic of the inner life; as such its significance extends far beyond national bounds to the universal heart of humanity.

W. H. Green proposed a new nomenclature for the Hebrew tenses; he prefers preterit and future as designations of the Hebrew tenses to perfect and imperfect, and holds that these tenses primarily and properly denote the time of action, and not simply its mode as complete or incomplete. He has re-edited his Hebrew grammar, first published twenty-seven years ago; it has been revised throughout and the syntax entirely recast.

W. R. Harper published Elements of Hebrew Syntax and discussed the Pentateuchal question; he presented a detailed analysis of the Hexateuch, in parallel columns, giving not only the chapters and verses by sections as they are divided by critics, but also the topics of which each section treats. An introductory note states the points (7) agreed upon by the two schools. Then follow the facts and considerations urged in favor of the analysis of Genesis i, 1,–xii 5, in sections.

Edward P. Humphrey (in *Sacred History, from the Creation to the Giving of the Law*) defends the traditional view of the Mosaic records. The difficulties which are supposed to embarrass the Mosaic account of the creation he classes as follows: (1) All those questions in which the meaning of the text is fully ascertained and opposing sciences are immature. (2) The problems in which natural science is mature and the Bible is not understood. (3) Where the results of science are incomplete and proper explanation of the Bible is not yet reached.

M. Jastrow, sr., discussed the transposed stems in Talmudic, Hebrew, and Chaldaic, especially the reduplicated stems, the so-called pilpels and palpels of verbs and nouns.

K. Kohler criticised the arrangement and method of Jastrow's Talmudic dictionary, especially the tendency to give up derivations from the Greek and find Semitic etymologies.

Thomas Lauris rendered Genesis xli, 32, " the dream was told or *set forth* to Pharaoh twice."

G. F. Moore gave a sketch of the history of Semitic studies in this country from the settlement of New England to about 1875. The author describes the state of learning among the Puritans, and its gradual decadence; then, at greater length, the revival of Biblical science in the early part of this century, with brief biographical notices of Stuart and other leading representatives of this movement; and gives, finally, without any attempt at exhaustiveness, a survey of the more recent literature. A second article is to contain a fuller account of the work, of the last ten years. He pointed out some seeming evidence that the supralinear system of vowels originated under Arab influence.

Henry Preserved Smith reviewed Victor Rysoels *The text of Micah*, part I (1887). The book is one of real importance. The text of Micah's prophecies is corrupt and must be corrected from the ancient versions. He also discussed the value of the Targum to Jeremiah: in seventy passages, the Targum helps us to determine the text of the book of Jeremiah. In fixing our Old Testament text we must not ignore this version.

W. O. Sproull holds that the native language of Abraham was Aramaic, since he emigrated from Ur of the Chaldees to the land of Canaan (Genesis, xi, 31). It is probable, however, that he knew Hebrew before he came into the land of Canaan, for there is no indication that he had any difficulty in conversing with its inhabitants.

A. W. Thayer calls attention to the fact that Professor Graetz, of Breslau, has prepared a revised text of the Massoretic Bible, which is now awaiting publication.

PEDAGOGICS.

At the fall meeting of the American Oriental Society, Francis Brown A. L. Frothingham, jr., W. H. Green, W. R. Harper, Paul Haupt, Morris Jastrow, jr., D. G. Lyon, C. H. Toy, and W. H. Ward discussed the history of Semitic studies in this country, and offered suggestions for the future. The remarks were collected and published in *Hebraica* with an introduction by Morris Jastrow, jr.

PERSIA.

Morris Jastrow discussed the plan of the Palace of Artaxerxes Mnemon, compared it with the description of the Palace of Ahasuerus in the book of Esther, and accepts M. Dieluafoy's conclusion, that the palace he discovered at Susa is the one described in the book of Esther.

SAMARITAN.

G. F. Moore described a fragment of a manuscript of the Samaritan Pentateuch deposited by Grant-Bey in the Library of Andover Seminary. The fragment contains Ex. viii, 16—xxx, 28; it is of the thirteenth century, and apparently a part of the codex described by Rosen, *Zeitschrift der Deutschen Morgenländischen gesellschaft*, xviii, 586.

SEMITIC PHILOLOGY.

E. P. Allen answered G. F. Moore's objections to his former paper on Semitic sounds and their transliteration. Allen's theory is that the so-called Semitic emphatic consonants are distinguished by a combination of mouth position with the glottal catch.

G. F. Moore questions the theory that the distinctive characteristic of the emphatic consonants is a combination of glottal catch with mouth articulation.

SYRIAC.

Robert H. Beattie described the recent changes in life in Syria and the new opportunities they bring to American scholarship and industry.

Syriac literature has been enriched by the discovery and description of a number of unedited texts.

Isaac H. Hall described a manuscript recently acquired by the Union Theological Seminary of New York, consisting of the service of obsequies, and introduced by the ritual of the washing of the dead, publishing portions of the text with translation; a manuscript of the Peshitto four Gospels, the property of Beloit College, Wisconsin, accompanied by a manuscript of the traditions of the Apostles, text and translation of which are given.

R. J. H. Gottheil published a manuscript containing a fragment of a Porphyry in the Berlin Library; a Syriac geographical chart; text of Berlin manuscript tract on the Syriac conjunctions and a collation of a text of a portion of the Targums in a map or manuscript in the Library of the Temple Emanuel, New York.

G. F. Moore called attention to the fact that four of the British Museum Hebrew manuscripts with the Targum recently acquired from Yemen are in this same hand, and together form a complete Bible; also to the excellent character of the Targum text.

The *New York Tribune* of August 12, 1888, gave a description of a Syrian commencement and the scenes attendant on the closing of the American College at Beirut.

BIBLIOGRAPHY OF ORIENTAL LITERATURE IN THE UNITED STATES
DURING 1888.

ADLER, CYRUS. Semitic Languages in the Encyclopædia Britannica. *Proc. Amer. Phil. Assn.*, XIX session, pp. xiv–xvii.

—— Discussion on the study of modern oriental languages. *Trans. Mod. Lang. Assn.*, vol. III, p. xviii.

—— Review of Friedr. Delitzsch, Prolegomena eines neuen hebraisch-aramäischen Worterbuchs. *American Hebrew.* Jan. 20.

—— A Babylonian Expedition. *American* (Philadelphia). March 24.

—— Announcement of a proposed complete edition of the works of Edward Hincks, with a biographical introduction and portrait of the author. Presented on behalf of the Semitic Seminary of the Johns Hopkins University. *Proc. Amer. Orient. Soc.* May, pp. xxii–xxvii.

—— Note on the collection of Oriental Antiquities in the U. S. National Museum at Washington. *Proc. Amer. Orient. Soc.* May, pp. xxvii–xxviii.

—— Note on Babylonian Inscriptions discovered at Tell-Amarna and now in the British Museum. *American* (Philadelphia) June 16.

—— The views of the Babylonians concerning life after death. *Andover Review,* July, vol. X, pp. 92–101.

—— Assyrian verbs tertiæ infirmæ. *Proc. Amer. Orient. Soc.* Oct., pp. xcviii–c.

——The U. S. National Museum exhibit of Oriental Antiquities at the recent Cincinnati Exposition. *Proc. Amer. Orient. Soc.* Oct. pp. i–lii.

—— Note on the proposed edition of the life and writings of Edward Hincks. *Proc. Amer. Orient. Soc.* Oct., pp. ci–civ.

ADLER, S. Benedictions. *Jewish Conference Papers.* (New York, 1887), p. 358.

ALEXANDER, JOSEPH II. Who was Melchizedek? *Presbt. Quart.* Jan.

ALLEN, EDGAR P. Some additions and corrections to Lotz's Tiglath-Pileser. *Proc. Amer. Orient. Soc.,* Oct., pp. civ–cviii.

—— On the Semitic emphatic consonants. *Proc. Amer. Orient. Soc.,* Oct., pp. cviii–cxii.

ALLEN, J. H. A word on Islam. *Unitar. Rev.,* May, p. 463.

AMENT, W. S. The ancient coinage of China. *Amer. Journ. of Archæol.,* vol. IV, pp. 284–290 and pl. xii, xiii.

Anonymous. A Persian funeral. *Christian Leader,* May 10, p. 7.

—— China then and now. *N. Y. Evangelist,* June 14, p. 2.

—— Babylonian excavations. *N. Y. Evening Post,* June 22.

—— A Mohammedan tract. *Christian Intelligencer,* May 16.

—— Why am I a Moslem? *North Amer. Rev.,* April, pp. 378–389. (Attributed to I'bn Ablis).

—— To dig in Babylon; the proposed expedition. *Philada. Ledger,* June 14 (editorial).

—— Wonders of Egypt; ruins of the city of Bubastis. (Cairo correspondence to the *N. Y. Tribune.*) Copied in the *Cincinnati Commercial Gazette,* June 24.

—— A Syrian commencement; scenes at the American College at Beirut, from an occasional correspondent. *N. Y. Tribune,* Aug. 12.

BAILEY, J. Sabbath commentary. A Scriptural exegesis of all the passages in the Bible that relate, or are supposed to relate in any way, to the Sabbath doctrine. New York, American Sabbath Tract Soc.

BEALE, S. Japanese pictures in the British Museum. *American Architect,* Apr. 21, p. 190.

BEATTIE, ROBERT H. Recent changes in Syria (some false impressions corrected). *Christian at Work,* May 24, p. 596.

BENTON, G. Mohammedanism in Africa. *North Amer. Rev.,* Feb., p. 222.

BERENSON, H. Mohammed, was he an imposter? *Harvard Monthly,* p. 8.

BISSELL, E. C. Joshua xxii, 9–34, and the Israelitish Cultus. *Jour. of the Soc. of Biblical Lit. and Exegesis,* Dec., 1887.

—— Biblical Antiquities: A hand-book for use in seminaries, Sabbath schools, and families, and by all students of the Bible. Philada. Amer. S. S. Union. (Rev. by J. P. Taylor in the *Andover Rev.,* Dec.)

BLAKIE, W. G. The First Book of Samuel. New York, Armstrong. (Reviewed *Chr. Union,* Oct. 18, p. 423; T. W. Chambers, *Presbt. Rev.,* Oct.)

—— The Second Book of Samuel. New York, Armstrong.

BLISS, FRED. J. The Mohammedan Lent; scenes during Ramadan. (Correspondence from Beirut.) *N. Y. Evening Post,* July 11.

BRIGGS, C. A. The Hebrew tetrameter. *Hebr.,* vol. IV, pp. 65–74.

—— The Hebrew pentameter. *Hebr.,* vol. IV, pp. 129–139.

—— The Hebrew hexameter *Hebr.,* vol. IV, pp. 201–205.

BROWN, FRANCIS. Recent explorations in Egypt. *Jour. Am. Geogr. Soc. N. Y.,* vol. XIX, pp. 164–193.

—— The religious poetry of Babylonia. *Presbt. Rev.,* Jan., IX, pp. 69–87.

—— The Babylonian "List of Kings" and "Chronicle." *Presbt. Rev.,* Apr., IX, pp. 293–300.

—— Babylon and Egypt, B. C. 1500. *Presbt. Rev.,* July, IX, pp. 476–482.

—— Ur-Kasdim. *Jour. Soc. Bib. Lit. and Exeg.,* Dec.

—— Semitic study in the Theological Seminary. *Hebr.,* vol. V, pp. 86–88.

BROWSKI, L. C. Nineve und seine Ruinen. *Sonntagsblatt der N.-Y. Staatszeitung,* Sept. 30.

BRUNNOW, R. E. Eine assyrisch-aramäische Bilingue. *Zeit. für Assyriologie,* III, pp. 238–242.

BRUNNOW, R. E. The twenty-first volume of the Kitab Al-Aghani, being a collection of biographies not contained in the edition of Bulaq; edited from manuscripts in the Royal Library of Munich. Pt. I-text. Leyden, Brill.

—— A classified list of all simple and compound ideographs (cuneiform) occurring in the texts hitherto published, with their Assyrian equivalents. Part II. Leyden, Brill.

CARPENTER, FRANK G. At the Chinese capital : strange sights that are seen in the home of the Mikado. N. Y. World, Oct. 28.

—— The Buddhists of Japan. Interesting talk with the high priest of a strange religion. N. Y. World, Dec. 9.

CHEYNE, T. K. On Job III. 14. Hebraica, vol. IV, p. 123.

CHILD, T. Constantinople. Atlantic Monthly, Jan., p. 72.

COLSTON, R. E. Stone-Pasha's work in geography. Jour. Am. Geogr. Soc. of N. Y., vol. XIX, pp. 48–50.

CORCORAN, J. A. The Syrian Church office book. Amer. Catholic Quart., Jan., p. 28.

CROSBY, HOWARD. A passage from Job. Critic, Jan. 21, p. 25.

—— Dr. Cheyne on Isaiah (the Cyrus inscription). Old Testam. Stud., VII, p. 186.

CURTISS, S. IVES. Recent Old Testament studies in America. Expositor, Jan., p. 78–80 ; Feb., p. 154–157.

CUTTER, GEORGE W. Constantinople. Christian Register, June 14, p. 371.

—— Abdul Hamid. Christian Register, July 12, p. 445.

—— The Armenians Christian Register, Nov. 8, p. 338.

—— Thebes. Christian Register, Mar. 22.

—— Tangier, Morocco. Christian Register, Jan.

—— El-Azhar. Christian Register.

—— The Jews of the Orient. Christian Register.

—— The Sea of Galilee. Christian Register, p. 325.

—— Letters from the Nile. Congress (Wash.), April and May, pp. 47, 64.

—— Jerusalem. Congress May, p. 74.

—— Buda-Pesth. Congress, July, p. 108.

DANA, JAMES D. Cosmogony of Genesis. Andov. Rev., Feb., vol. IX, pp. 197–200; see also Biblioth. Sac., vol. XLV, pp. 356–365.

DASHIEL, T. G. Immortality in the Old Testament. North Amer. Rev., Feb., p. 224.

DAVIDSON, SAMUEL. Notes on the Psalms. Hebr., vol. IV, pp. 158–166.

DAVIES, W. W. The Chokhma. S. S. Times, Aug. 11.

—— Is the Book of Jonah historical ? Methodist Review, LXX, Nov., pp. 827–844.

—— Exegesis of Job, XIX. 25–27. Homiletic Review, Oct.

—— The Levirate marriage. Christian Advocate, Dec. 13.

DAVIS, VARINA ANNE. Serpent myths. North Amer. Rev., Feb., pp. 161–171.

DICKERMAN, LYSANDER. The names of Jacob and Joseph in Egypt. O. T. Student, VII, pp. 181–185.

DODS, MARCUS. The book of Genesis. New York, Armstrong. (Rev. in the Amer. Heb., Nov. 9.)

DOOLITTLE, T. S. Will India become Mohammedan or Christian ? Christian at Work, May 10, p. 539.

DOUGLAS, G. C. M. The two Isaiahs, the real and the imaginary. Presbyt. Rev., Oct., pp. 602–637.

EDGREEN, A. H. On the propriety of retaining the VIII verb class in Sanskrit. Univ. Studies, pub. by the Univ. of Nebraska, vol. I, pp. 17–30.

—— Det gamla Indiens bildsprak och bildsprak i allmanhet. Nordisk Tidskrift, Stockholm.

FELSENTHAL, B. How old is Jehovah ? Menorah, April, pp. 355–358.

—— How old is Lekbah Dodi ? Menorah, July, pp. 38–46.

FIELD, ADELE M. Some Chinese mortuary customs. Pop. Sci. Month., Sept., pp. 569–596.

FISCHER, EUSTACE W. India. *Journ. Amer. Geogr. Soc. of N. Y.*, vol XIX, pp. 337–355.

FORBUSH, T. B. The Hindu doctrine of death and immortality. *Unitarian Rev.*, Apr., pp. 319–330.

FRADENBURGH, J. N. Living religions; or, the great religious of the Orient from sacred books and modern customs. New York, pp. 508.

FROTHINGHAM, A. L., Jr. Archæological news. *Amer. Jour. Archæol.*, pp. 69–125; pp. 191–219.

—— The development and character of Mohammedan education. *Proc. Amer. Orient. Soc.*, Oct., pp. cxiv–cxvi.

—— The existence of America known early in the Christian era. *Amer. Jour. Archæol.*, IV, p. 456.

GARLAND, JAMES A. An odd bit of China. (Record of a visit to Canton.) *N. Y. Mail and Express*, June 18.

GARNER, J. LESLIE. Omar Khayam: The strophes. From the Persian, with introduction and notes. Milwaukee.

GEIKE, CUNNINGHAM. The Mount of Olives. *S. S. Times*, May 5.

GENUNG, J. F. The interpretation of the Book of Job. *Andov. Rev.*, Nov., pp. 437–466.

GLOVER, A. K. The Jews of India. *Menorah*, March, pp. 239–249.

—— The Jews of the Chinese Empire. *Menorah*, Apr., pp. 359–365; May, pp. 431–441; June, pp. 520–524; July, pp. 10–19.

GOODENOW, S. B. Bethsaida. *Bibl. Sacra.* Oct., p. 729–732.

GOODYEAR, W. H. Cypriote sculptures in the Metropolitan Museum of Art. *Catholic World*, Jan., p. 489.

—— The Lotus in ancient art. *Critic*, Apr. 28, p. 209.

GOTTHEIL, RICHARD J. H. A tract on the Syriac conjunctions. *Hebr.*, vol. IV, pp. 167–173.

—— A Syriac fragment. *Hebr.*, IV, pp. 206–215.

—— Kalilag Wedamnag in Syriac literature. *Hebr.*, vol. IV, p. 251.

—— A Syriac geographical chart. *Proc. Amer. Orient. Soc.*, May, pp. xvi–xx.

—— A manuscript containing parts of the Targum. *Proc. Amer. Orient. Soc.*, Oct., pp. xlii–li.

—— Translation from the German of Karpeles' History of Jewish literature. *Menorah.*

GOULD, ELIZABETH P. School-life in China. *Education*, May, vol. VIII, pp. 557–562.

GREEN, W. H. On the Hebrew tenses. *Proc. Amer. Orient. Soc.*, Oct., p. xxxiv.

—— Semitic studies in this country. *Hebraica*, vol. V, pp. 89, 90.

—— A Hebrew grammar. New edition. New York.

GRIFFIS, WILLIAM ELLIOT. Japanese art, artists, and artizans; with illustrations from drawings by a Japanese artist. *Scribner's Magazine*, Jan., pp. 108–121.

—— Japanese ivory carving. *Harper's Magazine*, Apr., pp. 714–719.

GROFF, WILLIAM N. Note sur le mot *q. u. l. i.* en papyrus égypto-araméen du Louvre. *Journ. Asiat*, VIII, p., 305 ff.

—— Étude sur le papyrus d'Orbiney. Paris, Ernest Leroux.

— —— Étude sur le pronom de la 1e personne du singulier en égyptien. *Rev. égyptol.* v. 4, pp. 145–152.

—— Diverses études. I. Le pronom en égyptien. II. Note sur Jakob-el et Joseph-el (le Beth-Jakob et le Beth Joseph de la Bible). Paris, Leroux.

—— Le décret de Canope. *Rev. Égypt*, VI, pp. 13–21.

—— Les deux versions démotiques du décret de Canope. Textes, étude comparative, traductions, commentaires historique et philologique. Paris, Leroux.

GROSSMAN, L. Abraham Ibn Ezra. The Basis of Faith, translated from the Hebrew. *Amer. Israelite*, Aug. 17, ff.

—— The origin of the Americans and the Lost Ten Tribes. "Hope of Israel," of Menasseh ben Israel, translated from the Spanish. *Amer. Jew's Annual*, pp. 69–89.

HALL, ISAAC H. On a manuscript of the Peshitto Four Gospels. *Proc. Am. Or. Soc.*, Oct., pp. li–lix.

—— On a manuscript of the Peshitto New Testament, with the Tradition of the Apostles. *Proc. Am. Or. Soc.*, Oct. pp. lix–lxxxv.

—— Who were the Philistines ? *S. S. Times*, Dec. 1.

—— The Nestorian Ritual of the Washing of the Dead. *Hebr.*, IV, pp. 82–86.

—— Specimens from the Nestorian Burial Service. *Hebr.*, IV, pp. 193–200.

—— Lamps and oil vessels (in the Orient). *S. S. Times*, Apr. 7.

—— On a Rhodian jar in the Boston Museum of Fine Arts. *Proc. Am. Or. Soc.*, May, p. xi.

—— The Syriac Ritual of the Departed. *Proc. Americ. Or. Soc.*, May, pp. xi–xii.

—— On a Nestorian liturgical manuscript from the last Nestorian church and convent in Jerusalem. *Proc. Am. Or. Soc.*, May, pp. xii–xvi.

—— A Syriac Apostolic MS. in the library of the A. B. C. F. M., at Boston. *Journal of the Society of Biblical Literature and Exegesis.*

HAMM, J. L. Mohammedanism. *Lutheran Quarterly.*, Apr., p. 270.

HARPER, ROBERT FRANCIS. Transliteration and translation of Cylinder A of the Esarhaddon inscriptions (I, 45–47). *Hebr.*, IV, pp. 99–117.

—— Cylinder B of the Esarhaddon inscriptions (III, 15–16) transliterated and translated. *Hebr..* IV, pp. 146–157.

—— Babylonian letter. The Joseph Shemtob collection of Babylonian antiquities, recently purchased for the University of Pennsylvania. *Hebr.*, V, 74–76.

HARPER, WILLIAM R. Elements of Hebrew syntax. Charles Scribner's Sons, New York.

—— The Pentateuchal question (1). Genesis i. 1–12, 5. *Hebr.*, V, pp. 18–73.

—— Semitic studies in the University. *Hebr.*, V, pp. 83–85.

HARRIS, J. RENDEL. The Harmony of Tatian in the Arabic version. *S. S. Times*, May 26.

HARRISON, WILSON J. China and its progress. *Bull. Amer. Ggr. Soc.*, XX, 4, p. 401.

HART, VIRGIL C. Western China. A journey to the great Buddhist center of Mount Omei. Boston, Ticknor. Rev. *N. Y. Times*, Dec. 17.

HAUPT, PAUL. Modern researches in Assyria and Babylonia. *Johns Hopkins Univ. Circular*, VII, 64, p. 461.

—— On the Assyrian writing. *J. H. U. Circ.*, VII, No. 4, p. 41.

—— Explanation concerning a remark in the notes of the Prolegomena to a comparative Assyrian grammar. *Proc. Am. Or. Soc.*, May, p. xxviii.

—— Die zwölfte Tafel des babylonischen Nimrod-Epos. *Beiträge zur Assyriologie und vergleichenden semitischen Sprachwissenschaft*, Heft 1, Leipzig, 1888. pp. 48–79.

—— Ergebnisse einer erneuten Collation der Izdubar Legenden. *Beiträge zur Assyriologie*, etc., pp. 94–152.

—— Ueber das assyrische Nominalpräfix na. *Beiträge zur Assyriologie.* pp. 1–20.

—— On some passages in the Cuneiform Account of the Deluge (with special reference to the first column of the tablet). *J. H. U. Circ.*, VIII, No. 69, pp. 17–18.

—— On the dimensions of the Babylonian Ark. *Proc. Am. Or. Soc.*, Oct., pp. lxxxix–xc.

—— Semitic studies in this country. *Hebr.*, V, p. 89.

HEDGE, F. H. Mohammedan mysticism. *Unitarian Rev.*, May, XXIX, pp. 410–416.

HERZBERG, W. Jerusalem of to-day. *Menorah*, March, April.

HOLCOMB, Mrs. H. H. Bits about India. Philad. Presbyt. Board of Publ., pp. 272.

HOPKINS, E. W. Inquiry into the conditions of civilization in the Hindu Middle Age from the point of view of the ruling power or warrior-caste. *Proc. Am. Or. Soc.*, May, p. viii. ff.

—— Quantitative variations in the Calcutta and Bombay texts of the Mahābhārata. *Proc. Am. Or. S.*, Oct., p. v–vi.

HOUSE, E. H. The tariff in Japan. *New Princ. Rev.*, Ja. 66–77.

House, E. H.   Foreign jurisdiction in Japan.   *Ibid.*, Mar., 207-218.
Hovey, A.   Biblical eschatology.   Philada., Amer. Baptist Pub. Soc., pp. 192.
Hubbard, D. G.   The religion of Zoroaster.   *Unit. Rev.*, Feb., pp. 112-139.
Hughes, Th. P.   Missions to Muslims.   *Andov. Rev.*, Jan., IX, pp. 1-17.'
—— The Muslim's Bible.   *Andov. Rev.*, May, IX, pp. 466-474.
—— Islam and Christianity in India.   *Contemp. Rev.*, Feb., vol. LIII, pp. 161-168.
—— The Muslim's Faith.   *Andov. Rev*, July, X, pp. 23-36.
Hulbert, Henry W.   Bethlehem of Judea.   *Independent* (N. Y.), Dec. 20.
—— At the Temple of Bast.   *N. Y. Tribune*, May 31.
—— Education in Egypt.   *Evening Post* (N. Y.), Aug. 15.
—— Wortabet's Arabic-English Dictionary.   *Hebr.*, Oct., vol. V, pp. 92-93.
Humphrey, Edward P.   Sacred History from the Creation to the Giving of the Law.   New York, Armstrong.
Itt, Boon.   Sketches in Siam : a day in the country.   *The Williams Literary Monthly*, July.
Ives, F. E.   Japanese Magic Mirror.   *Journal of the Franklin Institute*, Apr., p. 324.
Jackson, A. V. Williams.   A new reference in the Avesta to " the Life-book " hereafter.   *Proc. Am. Or. Soc.*, Oct., pp. xx-xxi.
—— A hymn of *Zoroaster* : Yasna 31.   Translated with comments.   Stuttgart.
Janes, Lewis G.   Egyptian doctrine of the future life.   *Unit. Rev.*, Jan., pp. 33-48.
Jastrow, M., Sr.   On transposed stems in the Talmudic, Hebrew, and Chaldaic.   *Proc. Am. Or. Soc.*, Oct., pp. xl-xlii.
—— Scènes de chasse dans le Talmud.   *Revue des Ét. juives*, XVII, pp. 146-149.
Jastrow, Morris, Jr.   Delitzsch's Assyrian Dictionary, Part I.   *Proc. Am. Phil. Ass.*, XIXth session, Burlington, Vt., July, 1887, pp. xii-xiv.
— —— Mohammedanism.   Abstract of a series of public lectures.   *Publ. Ledger*, Mar. 14.
—— Babylonian cemeteries.   *Harper's Weekly*, May 12.
—— Yehûdâ Hayyûg and his work.   *Proc. Am. Or. Soc.*, May, pp. xxi-xxii.
—— Jewish grammarians of the Middle Ages. V. Dônâsh Ben Labrat.   *Hebr.*, IV, pp. 118-122.
—— Some notes on " The Monolith Inscription of Salmaneser II."   *Hebr.*, IV, pp. 244-246.
—— The Pott Library.   *Proc. Am. Or. Soc.*, Oct., pp. iii, iv.
—— On a fragment of Hayyûg's treatise on weak verbs.   *Proc. Am. Or. Soc.*, Oct., pp. xxxviii-xl.
— —— On the Assyrian Kudûru and the ring of the Sun-god in the Abu-Habba tablet.   *Proc. Am. Or. Soc.* Oct., xcv-xcviii.
— —— The present status of Semitic studies in this country.   *Hebr.*, V, 77-79.
— — The Palace of Artaxerxes Mnemon and the Book of Esther.   *S. S. Times*, Nov. 17, p. 772.
—— Persian art from Susa.   *N. Y. Times*, Dec. 9.
Keene, H. G.   Omar Khayyam.   *Eclectic Magaz.* (N. Y.), Jan., p. 104.
Kellner, M. L.   The standard inscription of King Asshurnazirpal of Assyria.   (Cambridge, Mass.)
—— The Deluge in the Izdubar Epic and the Old Testament.   *Church Rev.*, Nov.
Kellogg, S. H.   On the origin of certain Rajput forms of the substantive verb in Hindi.   *Proc. Am. Or. Soc.*, Oct. pp. xvii-xx.
Ker, David.   Burmah's mighty river.   *N. Y. Times*, June 21.
—— Moulmein's Old Caverns.   (Correspondence from Moulmein, in Lower Burmah.)   *Ibid.*, July 1.
—— Among the Circassian Mountains.   *The Cosmopolitan*, vol. 2 April, p. 131-136.
—— The Liverpool of Burmah : Rangoon, its street scenes and its play-house.   *N. Y. Times*, Sept. 2.
—— Burmah's golden pagoda : the famous Shway Daghon of Rangoon.   *N. Y. Times*, Sept. 7.

KER, DAVID. By rail up the Himalaya. *N. Y. Times,* July 30
—— Temples used in war times: Buddhist shrines that have been fortresses. *N. Y. Times,* Sept. 16.
—— Petroleum in Burmah: primitive and expensive methods in use, etc. *N. Y. Times,* Oct. 14.
KOHLER, K. Jastrow's Talmudic Dictionary. *Hebr.,* v, 1–6.
KOHUT, ALEXANDER. Talmudical-Rabbinical Analecta. *Jewish Conference Papers* (New York, 1887), p. 360.
—— Ethics of the Fathers. IVth series (in the *American Hebrew,* New York).
L. Object-lessons in Oriental faiths and myths. *Science,* July 13, XII, p. 24.
LAIRD, H. P. Analysis of the Song of Solomon. *Reformed Quarterly Review,* Jan., p. 1.
LANSING, G. The Pentateuch—Egypticity and Authenticity. *Expositor,* Sept. and Oct. (219–231 and 307–317.)
—— The Pentateuch—Egypticity and Authenticity (Part 2.) *Evangelical Repository,* Jan.
—— Summering in Egypt. *The Christian Union* (N. Y.), Nov. 1.
LAURIE, TH. Genesis 41: 22. *Presb. Rev.,* July. IX, pp. 474–476.
—— The name of God and the cuneiform inscriptions. *Bibliotheca Sacra.* July, XLV, pp., 515–518.
LAWRENCE, EDWARD A. Among the villages of South India. *Andover Review,* March, pp. 284–293.
—— Self support of the native churches in India. *Andover Review,* Sept., pp. 263–283.
LEA, HENRY C. Emerson and the Katha Upanishad. *Critic,* Feb. 11, p. 70.
LOVEJOY, W. W. Will the Jews again have a national history? *Epis. Recorder,* April 19.
LOWELL, PERCIVAL. A visit to Shirane San. *Appalachia,* v, June 2, pp. 87–108.
—— The soul of the Far-East (an essay on the impersonality of the Far-Orientals), Houghton, Mifflin & Co., Boston, Dec.
LYON, D. G. Six lectures on ancient Assyrian life, delivered at the Lowell Institute, Boston, Mass. *Boston Evg. Record,* Feb. 15 and 18; *Boston Post,* Feb. 22, 25, 29, and Mar. 3.
—— The Pantheon of Assurbanipal. *Proc. Am. Or. Soc.,* Oct., pp. xciv–xcv.
—— Assyrian and Babylonian Royal Prayers. *Proc. Am. Or. Soc.,* Oct., pp. xcii–xciv.
—— Semitic studies in this country. *Hebr.,* v, 90–91.
—— Notice of Schodde's "The Book of Jubilees." *Bib. Sac.* July, p. 542.
—— The American Oriental Society (report of the recent meeting in Philadelphia). *Independent,* Nov. 15, pp. 14–15.
—— American Orientalists. *Boston Evening Transcript,* Nov. 19.
MACLEAN, J. P. The word Hell in various languages. *Universalist Quarterly,* Oct.
—— Gælic elements in the Hebrew language. *Ibid.,* Apr., p. 173.
MAGOUN, H. W. The Asuri-Kalpa, a witchcraft practice of the Atharva-Veda. *J. H. U. Circ.,* VII, No. 66, pp. 81–82.
—— On the Asuri-Kalpa. *Proc. Am. Or. Soc.,* Oct., pp. xiii–xvii.
MARQUAND, ALLAN. The Proto-Doric character of Paphlagonian tombs. *Proc. Am. Or. Soc.,* Oct., pp. xxxi, xxxii.
—— An Archaic Patera from Kourion. *Am. Journ. Archæol,* June, pp. 169–171
MARTIN, W. A. P. The Cartesian Philosophy before Descartes. *Jour. Peking Orient. Soc.*
—— Diplomacy in Ancient China. Read before the Oriental Society of Peking, Oct.
—— Plato and Confucius: a curious coincidence. *Proc. Amer. Or. Soc.,* Oct., pp. xxxi–xxxiv.
—— Translation of the devotional portion of a pictorial sheet. *Journ. of the China Branch o th Ro al Asiatic Societ.* vol. XXIII.

MASPERO, G. Syria before the invasion of the Hebrews according to the Egyptian Monuments. *N. Y. Independent*, Jan. 12.

—— Egyptian Souls and their Worlds. *New Princ. Rev.*, July, pp. 23–36.

MATHEWS, SHAILER. The rhetorical value of the study of Hebrew. *O. Test. Stud.* VII, pp. 276–280.

MCCOLLESTER, S. H. Delhi, India, Modern and Ancient. *Christian Leader*, April 26 and May 3.

—— From Bagdad to Babylon. *Christian Leader*, May 24.

—— The Nineveh of to-day. *Christian Leader*, June 14.

MCELRONE, HUGH. The literature of America. *S. S. Times*, Aug. 18, p. 515.

—— An Arabian Utopia. *S. S. Times*, Sept. 29, p. 611.

MITCHEL, S. S. Prizes from the Faiyum papyri and portraits that light up the past. *N. Y. Times*, July 1.

MOLDENKE, CH. E. The tale of the two brothers. A fairy tale of ancient Egypt. Being the D'Orbiney papyrus in hieratic characters in the British Museum. To which is added the hieroglyphic transcription, a glossary, critical notes, the translation, and a list of hieratic characters with their hieroglyphic equivalents, pronunciation, determinative values, etc. Part 1. The hieratic text. New York.

MOORE, G F. Alttestamentliche Studien in Amerika. I. Geschichtliches. *Zeitschrift für die alttestamentliche Wissenschaft*, pp. 1–42.

—— Emphatic consonants in the Semitic languages. *Proc. Am. Or. Soc.*, May, pp. xxx–xxxiii.

—— Note on the Targum manuscripts in the British Museum. *Proc. Am. Or. Soc.*, Oct., p. xxxviii.

—— On a fragment of the Samaritan Pentateuch in the library of Andover Seminary. *Proc. Am. Or. Soc.*, Oct., pp. xxxv–xxxvii.

—— Note on the origin of the supralinear system of vowel points in Hebrew. *Proc. Am. Or. Soc.*, Oct., pp. xxxvii–xxxviii.

MOORE, W. W. The Hittite Empire. *Presbyt. Quart.*, Jan.

MYER, ISAAC. Qabbalah. The philosophical writings of Solomon Ben Yehuda Ibn Gebirol or Avicebron and their connection with the Hebrew Qabbalah and Sepher ha-Zohar; with remarks upon the antiquity and contents of the latter, and translations of selected passages of the same. Also, an ancient lodge of initiates, translated from the Zohar, and an abstract of an essay upon the Chinese Qabbalah, contained in the book called the Yih King, a translation of part of the mystic theology of Dionysius the Areopagite, and an account of the construction of the ancient Akkadian and Chaldean universe, etc., accompanied by diagrams and illustrations. Philadelphia, 1888. 8vo, 449 pp., with 39 illustrations and 11 diagrams.

NORTH, LEIGH. The literature of Japan. *The Churchman* (N. Y.), Apr. 21, p. 491.

OGDEN, WILLIAM BUTLER. Four days in Petra. *Bull. of the Geog. Society*, June 30, xx, pp. 137–153.

OSGOOD, HOWARD. The Oldest Book in the World. *Bibliotheca Sacra*, Oct., XLV, pp. 629–668.

—— The Resurrection in the Pentateuch. *Baptist Quarterly Review*, Oct., x, pp. 425–436.

—— A reasonable hypothesis of the origin of the Pentateuch. "Moses and his Recent Critics." Funk & Wagnalls, New York, pp. 369–403.

PAINE, J. A. Was the Exodus-Pharaoh drowned in the Red Sea? *Examiner*, Aug. 16, 23, 30.

—— The Pool of Serpents. *N. Y. Independent*, Sept. 13, p. 1169.

—— The eclipse of the seventh year of Cambyses. *Proc. Am. Or. S.*, Oct., pp. xc–xciii.

—— The three Walls of Jerusalem : The Wall of Jeremiah as relating to Calvary. *Christian at Work*, Nov. 29.

PEABODY, A. A.   Classic and Semitic ethics. *Andover Review*, Dec., x, pp. 561-576.
PEET, STEPHEN D.   Animal worship and sun worship in the East and the West compared. *Amer. Antiquarian*, Mar., pp. 69-95.
—— American religious and the Bible. *O. T. Student*, June, pp. 320, 322.
—— The Shaman in Northern Asia. *Amer. Antiq.*, x, pp. 326-327.
PETRIE, W. M. F.   The Grand Tour three thousand years ago. *Harper's Mag.*, July, LXXVII, pp. 297-307.
PICK, BERNHARD.   Old Testament passages Messianically applied by the ancient synagogue. Jeremiah, Lamentations, Ezekiel, Daniel, and the twelve minor prophets. *Hebr.*, IV, 3, pp. 176-185.
—— Old Testament passages Messianically applied by the ancient synagogue. Zachariah, Malachi. *Hebr.*, IV, pp. 247-249.
——, Jerome as an Old Testament student. Part III. *Lutheran Church Review*, pp. 137-149, 272-293.
—— Christ and the Essenes. *Lutheran Quarterly Review*, pp. 217-245.
—— The Therapeutæ. *Ibid.*, pp. 321-341.
PINCHES, T. G.   An old Babylonian letter. *N. Y. Independent*, Aug. 23, p. 1071.
PLATNER, B. S.   Anthropological mythology. *New Englander and Yale Rev.*, Jan., pp. 44-53.
PLONGEON, AUG. DE.   The Egyptian Sphynx. *Am. Antiquar.*, Nov., pp. 360-364.
POST, GEORGE E.   Among the mountains north of Palestine (with maps). *N. Y. Evangelist*, May 10; July 5 and 12.
PRINCE, J. DYNELEY.   Archæology in Turkey. *The Independent* (N. Y.), Dec. 6, p. 1572.
RAGOZIN, ZENAIDE A.   The story of Media, Babylon, and Persia from the fall of Nineveh to the Persian war. G. P. Putnam's Sons, New York, pp. 448.
RAWLINSON, GEO.   Crucifixion in the Ancient East. *S. S. Times*, May 19.
—— Walled cities in the Ancient East. *S. S. Times*, Oct. 13.
ROCKHILL, W. W.   On the use of skulls in Lamaist ceremonies. *Proc. Am. Or. Soc.*, Oct., pp. xxiv-xxxi.
—— The Lamaist ceremony called " Making of mani pills." *Proc. Am. Or. Soc.*, Oct., pp. xxii-xxiv.
ROY RAJ COOMAR.   Child marriage in India. *N. A. Review*, Oct., pp. 415-423.
SANGUINETTI, E. P.   Impressions of Arabs in burnoose and saddle. *Harper's Magazine*, June, p. 75.
SAYCE, A. H.   Literary correspondence between Asia and Egypt in the century before the Exodus. *N. Y. Independent*, June 28, p. 801.
—— The way of the Philistines. *Ibid.*, Aug. 2.
SCHAUFFLER, W. G.   Autobiography. Edited by his sons; with an introduction by E. A. Park. New York.
SCHODDE, GEORGE H.   Cuneiform tablets at Tell-Amarna. *Harper's Weekly*, Sept. 20.
SCHWARTZ, J.   A newly discovered key to Biblical chronology. (No. I) *Bibliotheca Sacra*, Jan., vol. XIV, pp. 52-83; (No. II) *Ibid.*, July, vol. XIV, pp. 137-465.
SEWALL, B.   Christianity against Mohammedanism. *New Englander and Yale Review*, Feb., pp. 88-101.
SIEGFRIED, C. A.   Tripoli to Alexandria. *The Nation*, Jan. 12, pp. 26, 27.
—— The Dalmatian coast and Montenegro. *Ibid.*, Sept. 6, pp. 188, 189.
SIMMONS, LAWRENCE M.   On the separation which may take place between the so-called defined and defining noun in Arabic. *Hebr.*, IV, pp. 87-91 (see *Hebr.*, IV, pp. 250, 251).
SMITH, HENRY PRESERVED.   The text of Micah. *Hebr.*, IV, pp. 75-81.
—— The Targum to Jeremiah. *Hebr.*, IV, pp. 140-145.
SMITH, J. A.   An ancient literary epoch. *Chautauquan*, Jan., pp. 205-208.
—— Eastern apologue, romance, and drama. *Ibid.*, Feb.
—— Epic and mythology. *Ibid.*, Mar.

SMITH, J. A. The Iranean Scripture (Zendavesta). *Ibid.*, April.

———— Siddartha. *Ibid.*, May.

———— Literature of the Chinese. Confucius and Mencuis. *Ibid.*, June.

SMITH, S. A. Assyrian letters. Part II. (12 plates). *Proc. Soc. Bibl. Archæol.*, Jan., x, 10, pp. 155- 176.

———— Assyrian letters. Part IV. (9 plates). *Ibid.*, Apr. 6, x, pp. 305-315.

———— Assyrian letters from the Royal Library at Nineveh transcribed, translated, and explained. Leipzig, Pfeiffer, 64 pp.

———— Assyriological notes. *Ztschr. f. Assyriol.*, III, pp. 100-102.

———— The progress of Assyrian study. *Independent*, June 7, p. 721.

———— Assyrian Report documents. *Ibid.*, Aug. 9, p. 1007.

———— An unpublished text of Assurbanipal. *Rev. d'assyriol. et d'archéol. orient.*, II, pp. 20-22.

———— Why that "Assyrisches Wörterbuch" ought never to have been published. Leipzig, E. Pfeiffer, pp. 16

SMITH, W. TAYLOR. The monuments illustrating the early life of Moses. *Pulpit Treasury*, Jan.

SOUTH, EDWARD L. Mohammed and his work. *The Student*, Germantown, Pa., VIII, 6 (3), pp. 178-181 ; 7 (4), pp. 203-206.

SPROULL, W. O. The native language of Abraham. *Hebr.*, IV, p. 186.

STAPFER, EDMUND. Palestine in the time of Christ. New York: A. C. Armstrong & Son. (Translated by Annie H. Holmden.)

STRONG, JAMES. The Tabernacle of Israel in the Desert. *Christian Advocate*, Aug. 16, p. 545.

THAYER, A. W. A revised text of the Hebrew Bible. *Unit. Rev.*, July, pp. 58-69.

THOBURN, J. M. India and Malaysia. *Christian Advocate*, Sept. 13, p. 607.

THOMAS, J. H. The characteristics of Hebrew poetry. *Presbyt. Quart.*, July.

THOMPSON, H. H. S. The women of Japan. *Overland Monthly* (San Francisco), Feb., pp. 173-178.

TOY, C. H. Semitic studies in this country. *Hebr.*, V., p. 92.

———— On some phonetic peculiarities of Cairo Arabic. *Proc. Am. Or. Soc.*, Oct., pp. cxii, cxiv.

TRUMBULL, H. CLAY. The Sunday-school; its origin, missions, methods and auxiliaries. Yale lectures. Philadelphia, John D. Wattles.

———— The Ten Commandments as a Covenant of Love. Philadelphia, John D. Wattles.

WALKER, ANNA A. Mountains in sacred history. *Christian at Work*, May 24, p. 587.

WALKER, DEAN A. The Assyrian King Assurbanipal. *O. T. Student*, Oct. and Nov., VIII, pp. 57-62, and pp. 96-101. .

WARD WILLIAM HAYES. A new Babylonian expedition from America. *N. Y. Independent*, June 28, p, 811 (editorial).

———— Nebuchadnezzar in Egypt. *Ibid.*, Apr. 26, p. 529.

———— The oldest libraries : *Book-News* (Philadelphia), Jan., pp. 225-227.

———— Notes on Oriental antiquities. VII. Two stone tablets with hieroglyphic Babylorian writing. (Plates IV, V.) *Am. J. of Archæol.*, March, IV, pp. 34-41.

———— On so-called "Human-Sacrifice Seals. *Proc. Am. Or. Soc.*, May, pp. xxviii-xxx.

———— Unpublished or imperfectly published Hittite monuments. III. Reliefs at Carchemish.—Jerablus. (Plates VIII, IX.) *Ibid.*, June, IV, pp. 172-174.

———— Retrospect and Prospect (for Semitic studies in this country). *Hebr.*, V., pp. 80-82.

———— A Babylonian cylindrical object. *Proc. Am. Or. S.*, Oct., pp. lxxxviii-lxxxix.

———— The Babylonian Caduceus. *Proc. Am. Or. S.*, Oct., pp. lxxxv-lxxxviii.

———— Was there a Babylonian Gate-God ? *Acad.*, July 28, vol. XXXIV, p. 60 ff.

WARREN, H. W. Yang-tze-Kiang *Chautauquan*, Apr., p. 419 ff.

WARREN, W. F. As to a Tertiary Eden. *N. Y. Independent*, June 28.

WARREN, W. F. Proctor's latest researches.—"The Star-Story of the Flood." *Zion's Herald*, Boston, Sept. 26.

WASHBURN, GEORGE. Mohammedan doctrine. *N. Y. Independent*, Feb. 9.

WHITEHOUSE, COPE. Map of the Raian Basin. *Proc. Geogr. Soc. Lond.*, x, p. 811.

—— The River of Joseph, the Fayum and Raian Basins. *Ib.*, p. 733.

WHITNEY, W. D. On the second volume of Eggeling's Translation of the Catapatha-Brāhmana. *Proc. Am. Or. Soc.*, Oct., pp. vi–xi.

—— Sanskrit grammar, second edition (thoroughly revised). Leipzig.

WILSON, EDWARD L. The Great Pyramid. *Scribner's Magazine*, Jan., pp. 41–63.

—— From Dan to Beersheba. *Century Magazine*, Apr., pp. 815–833.

—— Sinai and the Wilderness. *Ibid.*, July, pp. 323–340.

—— The Temples of Egypt. *Scribner's Magazine*, Oct., pp. 387–409.

—— From Sinai to Shechem. *Century Magazine*, Dec., pp. 193–208.

WINCKLER, HUGO. Nebuchadnezzar's artificial reservoir. *Hebr.*, IV, pp. 174–175.

WISE, AARON. The origin of Jewish angelology and demonology. *Jewish Conference Papers* (1887), p. 40.

WISNER, BENJAMIN BACON. Pentateuchal analysis. *Hebr.*, IV, 4 pp. 216–243.

—— Pentateuchal analysis; priestly and prophetic codes in the Pentateuch; the Law of Holiness, etc. *Hebr.*, V, pp. 7–17.

WRIGHT, CAROLINE R. Worship of the Dervishes in Cairo, Egypt; *Christian Advocate* (N. Y.), July 26, pp. 491.

WRIGHT, WILLIAM. Oriental numbers and battles. *S. S. Times*, Nov. 24.

YOUNG, S. L. Among the Fellahs in Egypt. *S. S. Times*, Jan. 14.

—— Children of the East. *Ibid.*, Mar.

—— Floating Capital. *Ibid.*, June.

—— Pearl of the East. *Ibid.*, Dec.

—— Dome of the Rock. *Christian Observer*, Feb. 15.

—— Crown of the City. *Ibid.*, May.

—— Marriage bells in far-off lands. *Ibid.*, Sept. 30.

—— In Morning Land. *Ibid.*, Nov. 21.

—— Temple and Templars. *Herald and Presbyterian*, Jan. 8.

BIOGRAPHICAL MEMOIRS.

SPENCER FULLERTON BAIRD.*

By ROBERT RIDGWAY.

MR. PRESIDENT AND MEMBERS OF THE AMERICAN ORNITHOLO-GISTS' UNION: When asked by the worthy president of our union to prepare a memorial address upon the life and services to ornithology of our great teacher and leader, Professor Baird, it was with many misgivings that the invitation with which I was thus honored was accepted; for, glad as I am to render what tribute I can to the revered memory of a departed and beloved friend, the sense of my own inability to do justice to such a subject has almost deterred me from the attempt.

The preparation of an address which shall consist essentially of new matter is rendered particularly difficult by the circumstance that there has already been published by Prof. G. Brown Goode, in Bulletin 20 of the U. S. National Museum, an excellent biography of Professor Baird, giving in detail a history of the principal events and chief results of his life, together with a complete bibliography of his publications. Since the present memoir is intended to deal more particularly with Professor Baird as an ornithologist, the reader is referred for more general information to Professor Goode's admirable "Biographical Sketch," from which are taken most of the chronological data and the occasional quotations in the following prelude to what I have to offer from my own personal knowledge of the life, labors, attainments, and personal qualities of one who in history must hold a place at the head of American naturalists, and in the hearts of those who knew him a place which none other can fill.

Spencer Fullerton Baird was born in Reading, Pennsylvania, February 2, 1823. In 1834 he was sent to a Quaker boarding school at Port Deposit, Maryland, and the following year to the Reading grammar school. In 1837 he entered Dickinson College, graduating in 1840, at the age of seventeen. The next several years were spent in making

---

*Read before the Fifth Meeting of the American Ornithologists' Union. From The Auk, January, 1888, vol. v, No. 1.

natural history studies, and in the study of medicine, including a
winter's course of lectures at the College of Physicians and Surgeons,
in New York, in 1842, though he never formally completed his medical
course. "In 1845 he was chosen professor of natural history in Dickinson College, and in 1846 his duties and emoluments were increased
by election to the chair of natural history and chemistry in the same
institution. July 5, 1850, he accepted the position of Assistant Secretary of the Smithsonian Institution, and October 3, at the age of
twenty-seven years, he entered upon his life work in connection with
that foundation—'the increase and diffusion of knowledge among
men.'"

Mr. Goode informs us that "his ancestry upon one side was English, upon the other Scotch and German. His paternal grandfather
was Samuel Baird, of Pottstown, Pennsylvania, a surveyor by profession, whose wife was Rebecca Potts." The Bairds were from Scotland,
while the Potts family came from England to Pennsylvania at the close
of the seventeenth century. "His great grandfather on the mother's
side was the Rev. Elihu Spencer, of Trenton, one of the war preachers
of the Revolution, whose patriotic eloquence was so influential that a
price was set on his head by the British Government; his daughter
married William M. Biddle, a banker, of an English family for many
generations established in Pennsylvania, and identified with the bank-
ing interests of Philadelphia. Samuel Baird, the father of the subject
of this sketch, established himself as a lawyer at Reading, Pennsylvania,
and died when his son was ten years old. He was a man of fine culture,
a strong thinker, a close observer, and a lover of nature and out-of-door
pursuits. His traits were inherited by his children, especially by his
sons Spencer and William. The latter, who was the elder, was the first
to begin collecting specimens, and as early as 1836 had in hand a collection of the game-birds of Cumberland County. His brother soon
became his companion in this pursuit, and six years later they published
conjointly a paper entitled 'Descriptions of two species, supposed to be
new, of the Genus *Tyrannula* Swainson, found in Cumberland County,
Pennsylvania.'"*

Early in 1838 Professor Baird became acquainted with Audubon,
"with whom he was for many years in correspondence, and who, in
1842, gave to him the greater part of his collection of birds, including
most of his types of new species." In 1841 a very intimate friendship was
begun with George N. Lawrence, of New York, with John Cassin of
Philadelphia, in 1843, and Thomas M. Brewer, of Boston, in 1845. These
close friendships continued through life, though of these ornithologists
only the first named survives him, the others having died before Professor Baird. They were all at one time or another associated with him
in his ornithological work.

---

* These species are now known as *Empidonax flaviventris* Baird and *E. minimus*
Baird.

Although his elder brother had anticipated him by a few years in beginning the formation of a collection, he soon "diverged into other paths," and became a lawyer in Reading, Pennsylvania,* leaving to him the field of ornithology, which he cultivated so assiduously that when the catalogue of his collection† was closed, at number 3696, almost every species of bird occurring, regularly or otherwise, in eastern and central Pennsylvania was represented, and in most cases by series of specimens showing the different stages and phases of plumage. This collection, deposited there by Professor Baird when he entered upon his duties as Assistant Secretary of the Smithsonian Institution, is still in the National Museum, of whose ornithological treasures it forms an important element, so many of its specimens having served as the types of Professor Baird's descriptions in his "Birds of North America" and subsequent works. In it are "specimens of birds prepared by these boys forty-five [now nearly fifty] years ago by a simple process of evisceration, followed by stuffing the body-cavities full of cotton and arsenical soap".—a method probably adopted by them before they had learned the art of skinning birds.

Although his collection was made at a time when the art of taxidery 'v is generally supposed to have been far behind its present status, especially so far as this country is concerned, the excellent preparation of the specimens, their very precise labelling and perfect preservation, show Professor Baird to have been in every respect the peer of any ornithological collector of the present period. Exposed for more than thirty years to constant handling and everything that could effect their deterioration, they are still in a most excellent state of perservation, and none have lost their labels. I have never known a specimen of Professor Baird's preparation to be attacked by insects, a statement which I am able to make regarding few other collections of which I possess the knowledge to speak. The force of these observations may be better appreciated when it is considered that probably no other collection of skins has ever received so much handling as that made by Professor Baird, every standard work on North American birds published since 1850 having been based essentially upon it, so far as eastern species are concerned. Not only are the specimens prepared and preserved in a manner equalled by only the best of our living collectors, but their labels are fastened with unusual security, and contain very precise data, including scientific name (with authority), sex, age, locality, and date; and usually, on the reverse side, the total length and stretch of wings, measured before skinning.

The formation of so large and varied a collection of course in-

---

* Mr. Goode informs us that "at the time of his death, in 1872," he "was United States, collector of internal revenue at Reading."

† This catalogue constitutes Volume I of the series of National Museum "Register of Specimens," now filling twenty-one volumes, and containing more than 112,000 separate entries.

volved such a vast amount of field work as to remove Professor
Baird from the *limbo* of so-called "closet-naturalists." How pleasant
and instructive to him must have been his out-of-door studies of birds
may be inferred from the extent of his excursions, which are thus described by Mr. Goode:

"In 1841, at the age of eighteen, we find him making an ornithological excursion through the mountains of Pennsylvania, walking four
hundred miles in twenty-one days, the last day sixty miles between daylight and rest.* The following year he walked more than 2,200 miles.
His fine physique and consequent capacity for work are doubtless due
in part to his outdoor life during these years."

Considering Professor Baird's great interest in the study of birds, the
number of his ornithological publications is astonishingly small, amounting to only seventy-nine different titles (see Mr. Goode's Bibliography,
pp. 250-253). It is, therefore, strikingly evident that his publications
must have possessed unusual merit to earn for him so great a reputation
as an ornithologist. This reputation was indeed established by the first
of his separate works, usually known and quoted as "The Birds of North
America," though not published under this title until two years after its
publication by the Government as volume IX of the "Report of Explorations and Surveys, to ascertain the most practicable and economical
route for a Railroad from the Mississippi River to the Pacific Ocean."
With the publication, in 1858, of this great quarto volume of more than
one thousand pages, began what my distinguished colleague, Professor
Coues, has fitly termed the "Bairdian Period" of American ornithology—
a period covering almost thirty years and characterized by an activity
of ornithological research and rapidity of advancement without a parallel
in the history of the science. Referring to this great work, in his "Bibliographical Appendix" to "Birds of the Colorado Valley" (page 650),
Professor Coues says: "It represents the most important single step ever
taken in the progress of American ornithology in all that relates to the
technicalities. The nomenclature is entirely re-modelled from that of the
immediately preceding Audubonian period, and for the first time brought
abreast of the then existing aspect of the case. - - - The synonymy of the work is more extensive and elaborate and more reliable
than any before presented; the compilation was almost entirely original,
very few citations having been made at second-hand, and these being
indicated by quotation marks. The general text consists of diagnoses
or descriptions of each species, with extended and elaborate criticisms,
comparisons, and commentary. - - - The appearance of so great a
work, from the hands of a most methodical, learned, and sagacious
naturalist, aided by two of the leading ornithologists of America (John
Cassin and George N. Lawrence), exerted an influence perhaps stronger
and more widely felt than that of any of its predecessors, Audubon's

---

* Professor Baird informed the writer that he had once, in a pedestrian contest,
walked forty miles in eight consecutive hours.

and Wilson's not excepted, and marked an epoch in the history of American ornithology. The synonymy and specific characters, original in this work, have been used again and again by subsequent writers, with various modifications and abridgment, and are in fact a large basis of the technical portion of the subsequent ' History of North American Birds,' by Baird, Brewer, and Ridgway. Such a monument of original research is likely to remain for an indefinite period a source of inspiration to lesser writers, while its authority as a work of reference will always endure."

Thus are graphically described the distinctive features of what Mr. Leonhard Stejneger has truthfully termed the Bairdian School* of ornithology, a school strikingly characterized by peculiar exactness in dealing with facts, conciseness in expressing deductions, and careful analysis of the subject in its various bearings;—methods so radically different from those of the older "European School" that, as the esteemed member whom we have just named has already remarked,† conclusions or arguments can be traced back to their source and thus properly weighed, whereas the latter affords no basis for analysis. In other words, as Mr. Stejneger has, in substance, said, the European School requires the investigator to accept an author's statements and conclusions on his personal responsibility alone, while the Bairdian furnishes him with tangible facts from which to take his deductions.

The dominant sources of Professor Baird's training in systematic ornithology are not difficult to trace; in fact, the bases of his classifications are so fully explained or frequently mentioned in his various works as to leave nothing to mere inference. He studied carefully the more advanced systems of his time, and with unerring instinct selected from them their best features, and combined them, together with original ideas, into a classification which was an improvement on its predecessors. Thus, the classification presented in the "Birds of North America" (1858) is based essentially upon the systems of Sundevall ("Ornithologiskt System," 1835 and 1843), Cabanis ("Ornithologische Notizen," 1847), and Keyserling and Blasius ("Wirbelthiere Europas," 1840). The nomenclature was fixed by methods adopted from G. R. Gray ("List of the Genera of Birds," etc., 1841–'42), to the abandonment of which must be attributed most of the subsequent changes in generic names. In the "Review" (1864–'66) and "History of North American Birds" (1874), a further concession is made to the classifications of Sundevall and Cabanis by commencing with the Order Passeres and Family Turdidæ instead of the Raptores. The same systems were the foundation of Liljeborg's "Classification of Birds," formally adopted by the Smithsonian Institution (through Professor Baird) in 1866, by Messrs. Sclater and Salvin (with certain emendations and amplifica-

---

*Proc. U. S. Nat. Mus., vol vii, 1884, p. 76.   † *Ibid.*, p. 77.

tions) in 1873, and with still further modifications by the American
Ornithologists' Union, in 1886.

The distinctive features of the "Bairdian School" were still further
developed by the publication, in 1864-'66, of the "Review of American
Birds," a work of unequalled merit, displaying in their perfection Professor Baird's wonderful powers of analysis and synthesis, so strongly
combined in his treatment of difficult problems. Unfortunately for
ornithology this work was but fairly begun, only a single volume (an
octavo of 450 pages) being published. The cause of its discontinuance
is not definitely known to the present writer, but it may have been the
intervention of the "Ornithology of California," * a work based on the
manuscript notes of Dr. J. G. Cooper, but edited by Professor Baird,
who also superintended its publication, and the "History of North
American Birds," † material for which was already being arranged, besides other literary work and the increasing pressure of administrative
duties. Whatever the cause, however, its discontinuance is to be
regretted, since its completion would have given us an invaluable guide
to the study of Neotropical birds. I have it on good authority
that no single work on American ornithology has made so profound an
impression on European ornithologists as Professor Baird's "Review;"
and, by the same authority, I am permitted to state that he—a European
by birth and rearing—became an American citizen through its influence.

In the preface to the present writer's latest work on American
ornithology‡ the author is proud to mention that the book was "orgi-
nally projected by Professor Spencer F. Baird, - - - whose works
represent the highest type of systematic ornithology and have furnished
the model from which the younger generation of ornithologists have
drawn their inspiration ;" and that his friendly advice and suggestions
had rendered comparatively easy the performance of a task which under
less favorable auspices would have been far more difficult of accomplishment—acknowledgments which but faintly express the author's obligation to his tutor.

---

*Geological Survey of California. J. D. Whitney, State Geologist. Ornithology.
Vol. I. Land Birds. Edited by S. F. Baird, from the manuscript and notes of J. G.
Cooper. Published by authority of the legislature, 1870. A royal octavo volume of
592 pages, illustrated by numerous wood-cuts, some colored by hand.

†A History of North American Birds, by S. F. Baird, T. M. Brewer, and R. Ridgway.
Land Birds, illustrated by 64 colored plates and 593 wood cuts. Boston : Little,
Brown & Company, 1874. 3 vols., small quarto. Vol. I, pp. i-xxviii, 1-596, i-vi,
cuts, and pll. i-xxvi; vol. II, 3 pll. pp. 1-590, i-vi, cuts, and pll. xvii-lvi; vol. III, 3 pll.,
pp. 1-560, i l., i-xxviii, cuts, and pll. lvii-lxix.

‡A Manual of North American Birds, by Robert Ridgway. Illustrated by 464
outline drawings of the generic characters. Philadelphia : J. B. Lippincott Company, 1887. Royal octavo. Frontispiece (portrait of Professor Baird), pp. i-xi, 1-631,
pll. i-cxxiv.

The history of this work, briefly stated, is as follows :

Before the printing of the "History of North American Birds" had been completed,
Professor Baird had under way a smaller but very useful work, consisting of the ana-

In commenting upon the value of Professor Baird's contributions to scientific literature, Professor Goode remarks that "no one not living in the present can form an accurate idea of the personal influence of a leader upon his associates and upon the progress of thought in his special department, nor can such an influence as this well be set down in words. This influence is apparently due not only to extraordinary skill in organization, to great power of application and concentration of thought constantly applied, and to a philosophical and comprehensive mind, but to an entire and self-sacrificing devotion to the interests of his own work and that of others."

But it is not only through his published works and personal influence with his associates and pupils that Professor Baird was powerful in the development and advancement of ornithology in America. His position as head of the Smithsonian Institution and the National Museum gave him peculiar opportunities for putting into practical shape his plans for a thorough exploration of little known portions of the continent. "To his influence with the Government authorities is due the excellent field-work done in connection with nearly all the Government surveys and the Signal Service Bureau, from the first inception of the various Pacific Railroad surveys to the present time."* If the exploration of a particular field suggested itself to him, he rarely failed to find, sooner or later, means to accomplish the object in view; no opportunity for making use of, or securing the co-operation of, other departments of the Government in maintaining explorations which he had himself instigated or organized was ever neglected, and for such opportunities he was constantly alert. His success in thus promoting the cause of science was, however, by no means wholly due to the importance of his official positions, his personal zeal and influence often accomplishing what might not otherwise have been successful.

The sterling qualities of mind and heart which were so conspicuous in Professor Baird's character were as well known and as highly appreciated abroad as at home. As an illustration of this fact, I quote the

lytical or synoptical tables of the larger work, improved and somewhat enlarged by the introduction of brief diagnoses of the nests and eggs of the different species, together with the English names. This book, of which there exists only a single copy, and that not perfect, was completed early in 1874. Its title is "Outlines of American Ornithology, by S. F. Baird and R. Ridgway. Part I, Land Birds." For some reason the work was never published, and the electrotype plates were destroyed. This work, in which the present writer had some share, was the embryo which, after twelve years' incubation, finally developed into the more comprehensive "Manual of North American Birds," in the preparation of which, however, Professor Baird took no active part, though it is scarcely necessary to say that he was much interested in its progress, even almost to the close of his life, which ended shortly after the work had been printed, but before it could be published. It has been a matter of deep regret to the author that Professor Baird could not have had a share in the preparation of the book, and still more that he could not have lived to enjoy the satisfaction of seeing it published.

* Editorial in The Auk, October, 1887, p. 358.

following obituary notice in "Nature" for August 25, by Mr. R. Bowdler Sharpe, senior assistant, Department of Zoology, in the British Museum, well known as an ornithologist of eminence:

"By Englishmen who knew Professor Baird personally, the loss must be especially felt, but there are many who never had met him in the flesh, to whom the news of his decease must come as that of a dear friend. As one of the latter class we venture to express our sympathy with our scientific brethren in America on the decease of one of their most eminent and respected colleagues. As chief of the Smithsonian Institution, Professor Baird possessed a power of conferring benefits on the world of science exercised by few directors of public museums, and the manner in which he utilized these powers has resulted not only in the wonderful success of the United States National Museum under his direction, but in the enrichment of many other museums which were in friendly intercourse with the Smithsonian Institution. We know by experience that the British Museum is indebted beyond measure to Professor Baird, and we need only to refer to the recent volumes of the 'Catalogue of Birds' to show how much our National Museum owes to the sister museum in America for hearty co-operation. We had only to write and express our wants, and immediately every effort was made, by Professor Baird's instructions, to supply all the desiderata in our ornithological collection, and this without the slightest demand for an equivalent exchange, though, of course, in the case of the British Museum every effort was made to reciprocate the good feeling shown by the great American museum. There must be many private collectors in this country who will endorse our acknowledgments to Professor Baird for the unrivalled liberality which he has always shown in the advancement of the studies of every ornithologist who invoked his aid. - - - We may add that during an experience of twenty years we have never heard from any ornithologist, European or American, a single unkind word concerning Professor Baird, either in his public or private capacity. This is something to say in this age of jealousies and backbitings."

Indeed, it may with truth be said that so widespread, so nearly universal has been his influence that few there are, if any, among his contemporaries who have not had occasion to record their sense of obligation for his aid, his counsel, or his noble example. We all delight to acknowledge him our great teacher, and in doing so do honor to ourselves.

A very marked trait of Professor Baird's character was his aversion to personal controversy, which was so decided that under no circumstances could he be drawn into one. It was his invariable rule to answer his critics by a dignified silence, no matter how great the provocation to reply, or how strong a case his side presented; and in every instance known to the writer it has transpired that the ground taken or the statements made by Professor Baird have stood the test of time. "One of his striking characteristics was that he would never quarrel and never have anything to do with the quarrels of others. He was always for peace." *

As a public officer, no man was more conscientiously devoted to his duty or faithful in its performance; and he administered the complicated affairs of three distinct and important establishments with an ability which commanded admiration, although it was plainly to be seen that the responsibilities were too great for any single person to bear. His capacity for work was enormous, and he was constantly occupied. He enjoyed work, and it was not his industry which hurt him; but the harassing cares of his public trusts and the weight of their responsibility were too much for even his powerful physique to endure, and he gave way under the strain.

No man was more easily approached than Professor Baird, or greeted a new acquaintance more cordially. His reception of young persons— especially those with an inclination for natural history, was particularly charming, at once relieving them from embarrassment and captivating them by his unassuming manners, his geniality, and frankness.

Trusting that he does not introduce too prominently his own personality into this memoir, the writer offers the following brief outline of his personal acquaintance with Professor Baird, as being of probable interest to members of the Union, and as giving an insight into the character of his lamented friend.

Until near the middle of the year 1864, the writer, then a lad in his fourteenth year, was unacquainted with the name of any living naturalist, or with any books on natural history except such general or superficial compilations as Goldsmith's 'Animated Nature,' a history of the United States (author forgotten) which included a chapter or two on the natural history, and Goodrich's 'Animal Kingdom'—works which, although supplying much valuable information to the general reader, were of course wholly inadequate to the wants of a special student. A lady resident in the town learned of his difficulties, and suggested that by writing to the Commissioner of Patents in Washington he might be able to obtain the correct names of birds, supplementing her fortunate suggestion by the gift of an envelope bearing the printed address of a former Commissioner of Patents. A letter was written, and with it was inclosed a colored drawing, life size, of a pair of Purple Finches ("Roseate Grosbeak, *Loxia rosea*," of the incipient ornithologist) perched upon a dry stalk of the great ragweed (*Ambrosia trifida*), the seeds of which in winter constitute the principal food of the bird in that locality. An answer was awaited with great impatience, but in due time was received, the following being an exact copy:

" No. 5664.]   "SMITHSONIAN INSTITUTION,
" *Washington, D. C., June* 23, 1864.

" DEAR SIR: The present Commissioner of Patents (Mr. Holloway, not Mr. Bishop) has sent me your letter, as more conversant with the subject of North American birds than himself. I have read it with

---

* Prof. Otis T. Mason, in Washington *Evening Star* of August 20.

interest and much pleasure, as showing an unusual degree of ability as an artist, and of intelligent attention to a scientific subject. I had no difficulty in recognizing the bird you sent, and was much pleased to see that you had given all the essential features of form and color with much accuracy.

"The bird is the Purple Finch (*Carpodacus purpureus*). I send you a catalogue of the birds of North America and some other pamphlets.* If you can procure the ninth volume of the Pacific Railroad Reports, you will find descriptions of all the North American birds, by myself.

" I will be glad to hear from you and to render you any aid by naming your drawings, or in any other way. You must learn the scientific names of the birds, and thus be able to talk and write about them with persons not knowing the English names used in your part of the country.

" Let me know what kind of eggs you have.

"Very truly yours,
"Spencer F. Baird.
"Assistant Secretary Smithsonian Institution.

" Robert Ridgway,
  Mt. Carmel, Illinois.

The above letter was a revelation to the recipient, who, in his isolation, was ignorant of the existence of any one but himself engaged in the study of birds. He had read of Audubon and Wilson, and Nuttall, and Bonaparte, but these he knew were all dead. The profound impression produced by the letter and the hope that it gave, may be imagined. From this commencement arose a correspondence which to the present writer was a constant source of delight and instruction, and to which he looks back with feelings that cannot be expressed. It was not until the early part of 1867, nearly three years later, that the writer obtained a copy of the text of " Birds of North America" (volume IX, Pacific Railroad Report), and it therefore became necessary for him to continue the sending of drawings and descriptions in order to obtain the much-desired identifications. In replying to the writer's numerous letters of this character, Professor Baird always wrote most kindly and encouragingly, replying to multitudinous queries as fully as the arduous duties of his official position would allow. To mention all the useful hints which he gave would require to much space here, but the following are selected as samples:

" I would advise you to spend most of your leisure time in practising drawing of birds and mammals from nature and from life, so as to acquire a facility in seizing a temporary attitude and transferring it to paper. Make these sketches continually whenever you have the opportunity, so as to secure the more practice. A certain number of these drawings you may work up in their minutest details, and it will be a good exercise to draw the feathers of a single wing, as well as bill, feet, etc., and skulls of mammals. The object should be in drawing

---

* These were the various circulars of instruction for collecting and preserving specimens of natural history, published by the Smithsonian Institution, and well known to naturalists in this country.

form to secure artistic elegance and at the same time a minute, almost microscopic, accuracy in matters of detail, as far as they can be represented.

" The drawings you have sent are too fragmentary to show what your present abilities as an artist are, and I would rather see some full-sized figures." - - -

" It will not be necessary to spend much time in practising coloring, as this is rather a mechanical work, easily acquired by practice. The first object should be to obtain the highest perfection in drawing the form and in filling out minute details." (From a letter dated December 24, 1865.)

In a letter dated January 13, 1867, he gave this valuable advice as to writing field-notes : " Let me give you one hint in regard to making notes on the specimens. *Never write on both sides of the same leaf.* In this way it will be possible to cut apart your notes into slips and assort with others of same purport, so as to re-arrange systematically. Do this for your own notes as well as those you send me : You will often realize the advantage of so doing."

It is unnecessary here to go into details concerning events subsequent to the beginning of this correspondence. Suffice it to say that in all his relations with Professor Baird the writer remembers, with deepest gratitude and reverence, his uniform great kindness of heart, his genial manners, his wise counsels, and his steadfast friendship; and, with others who were so fortunate as to have enjoyed the privilege of his acquaintance, he mourns a departed friend and teacher, whose loss is irreparable.

PROCEEDINGS AT A MEETING COMMEMORATIVE OF THE LIFE AND
SCIENTIFIC WORK

OF

SPENCER FULLERTON BAIRD,

Held January 11, 1888, *under the joint auspices of the Anthropological, Biological, and
Philosophical Societies of Washington.*

INTRODUCTION.

On August 19, 1887, Spencer Fullerton Baird, Secretary of the Smithsonian Institution, Director of the U. S. National Museum, and U. S. Commissioner of Fish and Fisheries, died at Wood's Holl, Massachusetts, his post of duty in the last-named office. His death at once excited throughout the world feelings and expressions of profound regret. At that time nearly all of his Washington associates in scientific pursuits were absent from the city, on field duty or in vacation, and were thus unable to jointly testify to the affection and respect in which he was held by them.

And especially the scientific societies of Washington, none of which meet during the summer months, were unable to immediately take any action in the matter or to give organized expression to the sentiments of their members.

With the resumption of meetings, however, it was determined that such expression should be given with all ceremonial completeness, and as the senior of the Washington scientific societies, and the one with which Professor Baird had been most closely connected, the Philosophical Society took the initial steps in arranging a joint meeting with the Anthropological and Biological Societies, a meeting which might enable the members and their friends to testify not only their profound respect for this foremost scientific leader, but also their affectionate regard for the man.

The appended invitation and programme, which was mailed to all members of the Philosophical, Anthropological, Biological, and Chemical Societies, and of the Cosmos Club, sets forth the form taken in those arrangements.

WASHINGTON, *January* 4, 1888.

SIR: The Philosophical Society in conjunction with the other scientific societies of the city will hold a meeting on Wednesday evening, January the eleventh, in commemoration of the life and services to science of the late SPENCER FULLERTON BAIRD, Secretary of the Smithsonian Institution, Director of the National Museum, and United States Commissioner of Fish and Fisheries.

Members of the societies, and ladies and gentlemen whom they may desire to invite, will assemble in the lecture-room of the Columbian University, on the southeast corner of H and Fifteenth streets, at a quarter past eight o'clock.

Your presence on this occasion is earnestly desired.

C. E. DUTTON,
ROBERT FLETCHER,
J. H. KIDDER,
Committee of Management.

Opening of the meeting, by the president of the Philosophical Society.

Professor Baird as Administrator, Mr. W. B. Taylor, of the Smithsonian Institution.

Professor Baird in Science, Mr. W. H. Dall, president of the Biological Society.

The Personal Characteristics of Professor Baird, Mr. J. W. Powell, president of the Anthropological Society.

Mr. Garrick Mallery, president of the Philosophical Society, called the meeting to order at the time and place above named.

RELATIONS BETWEEN PROFESSOR BAIRD AND PARTICIPATING SOCIETIES.

By Mr. GARRICK MALLERY, *President of the Philosophical Society.*

LADIES AND GENTLEMEN: During several winters before 1871, a club, with commingled social and scientific purposes, used to meet in this city at the houses of its members. A single paper on some scientific subject was read, usually by the host of the evening, following which was a discussion. Supper was always provided. The title of the club only related to the night of meeting, Saturday, and the organization was so loose that several of the survivors among the regular participants at the meetings do not now remember whether they were actual members, or indeed that there was a definite membership. As the city of Washington emerged from the condition of a Southern village, and the benign policy of the Government increased the number and force of the scientific institutions at the capital, the need of an organization which should bring scientific men together on an equal footing and give more time to papers and their discussion became manifest. To meet this want the attendants of the Saturday-Night Club, on March 13, 1871, formed the Philosophical Society of Washington, its object, in the words of the call, being "the free exchange of views on scientific subjects and the promotion of scientific inquiry among its members."

The term "philosophical," as the first president of the society, Joseph Henry, stated in his first address, was chosen after considerable deliberation, "not to denote, as it generally does in the present day, the unbounded field of speculative thought, which embraces the possible as well as the actual of existence, but to be used in its restricted sense to indicate those branches of knowledge that relate to the positive facts and laws of the physical and moral universe."

Of the forty-three gentlemen who signed the call twenty-one are now dead. Professor Baird was prominent among the founders, and served continuously as a member of the general committee from the organization to November 10, 1877; and from that date until his death, on August 19 last, he was a member of the committee on publications.

The first communication of a scientific paper to the Society was made by him on March 18, 1871. The most important and extended original

717

papers communicated by him were "On the decrease of fish on the southern coast of New England," presented March 23, 1872, and "On the artificial propagation of the cod, describing the measures and process adopted at Gloucester, Massachusetts, and the success thus far obtained," presented March 1, 1879.

The last-mentioned occasion is memorable to me, and some account of it will be interesting to the younger members of the Society, few of whom ever heard Professor Baird's voice raised in its hall. I happened to join him on his way to the meeting, and during the walk he spoke of the struggle at that moment between the sense of duty requiring him to take his part in the proceedings of the Society and his repugnance to making any formal address. This modesty—indeed timidity —in an eminent writer and thinker, whose lightest words were sure of eager attention in a society composed mainly of his personal friends and wholly of his admirers, was the more remarkable because his address, presented a few minutes later, was most pleasing in its delivery as well as instructive in its substance. He spoke without notes, and, though his style was conversational and in no degree oratorical, his appropriate words in their rapid flow expressed his thoughts clearly, completely, and in orderly sequence.

During the same walk, Professor Baird mentioned with earnest commendation the usage of the Society by which the perfect equality of members is recognized through the omission of all official and professional titles. This was not a merely unwritten custom but was founded on a binding resolution, appearing in the minutes of June 6, 1874. The Society is probably the only non-esoteric body in the United States in which the titles of judge and general, professor and doctor, governor, senator, and even honorable member are forbidden; the simple and dignified Mr., the modern form of magister, being the only address allowed. Perhaps the plethora of titles and the burdensome hierarchical gradations in Washington compelled this measure of relief.

The Anthropological Society was founded February 17, 1879, its defined object being "to encourage the study of the natural history of man, especially with reference to America." Professor Baird warmly approved of the organization of this society, took constant interest in it, and, at the time of his death, was the only honorary member residing in the United States on its rolls.

The Biological Society was organized December 3, 1880, "to encourage the study of the biological sciences," and Professor Baird was the only honorary member ever elected by it. He did not take an active part in the proceedings of either of the last-mentioned societies but gave them material assistance. Both of them met at first in the Regents' room of the Smithsonian Institution, placed by him at their disposal, and he provided for the stereotyping and circulation of their volumes of transactions, a benefaction which the Philosophical Society had earlier enjoyed.

President Henry, in his address before mentioned, stated that in no other city in the United States was there, in proportion to the number of its inhabitants, so many men actively engaged in pursuits connected with science as in Washington. In the seven following years the number of persons in the city engaged in scientific work was nearly doubled, and most of them joined the Philosophical Society, so that in the year 1878 it had become recognized as the most efficient scientific body on this continent with a membership confined to a single locality. The criteria of this superiority were not only the large membership and regular attendance of members, but the number, quality, and variety of the papers presented and discussed. This abundance, and, as was proved by the later successful establishment of differentiated societies as an overflow, this superabundance of scientific papers occupied every moment of the meetings, so that the members as such had no opportunity to become acquainted with one another or to interchange views, except in the formal discussions following the papers announced in the printed programs. There was no provision for social introduction or intercourse. This appreciated want, the converse of the inadequacy of the Saturday-Night Club, resulted in the foundation of the Cosmos Club on December 13, 1878, in the organization of which all the members of the Philosophical society were invited to join. It is needless to descant upon the unique character of the Cosmos Club in its membership and objects, its vital connection with science, literature, and art, and its immediate but enduring success. The remark, however, is pertinent that in the winter of 1878 an unprecedented agitation, excited by impending national legislation, perturbed the scientific circles of the Capital, during which the proposition to form the club was attacked with virulence as a scheme in the selfish interest of a few individuals, and one fraught with machiavelian political designs; but when Professor Baird manifested his approval of the plan by accepting the first presidency of the club after its formal organization, confidence in him was so dominant that suspicion was allayed and opposition disappeared. To him profound thanks are due for the timely establishment of the most important institution in the conjoint social and scientific life at Washington.

But by his work in the organization of these several societies and of the Cosmos Club Professor Baird was, as in his other fields of labor, a benefactor and not a participant in the benefits secured to others. He was imbued with the cardinal principle of the Smithsonian Institution not only to establish and assist all useful agencies for the promotion of the well-being of man, but afterwards, when they had attained to successful operation, to leave them to themselves and explore new fields of beneficence. It was also his own character, apart from any formulated maxim of the Institution, that he could not rest in the personal

enjoyment of accomplished results.   He was one of the ceaseless workers, born

> " To scorn delights, and live laborious days,"

until

> " Comes the blind Fury with th' abhorred shears
> And slits the thin-spun life.   But not the praise!"

It is for us now, repressing sorrow, to join in tributes of praise to our
benefactor.

PROFESSOR BAIRD AS ADMINISTRATOR.

By Mr. WM. B. TAYLOR, *of the Smithsonian Institution.*

We are met this evening to express in a memorial service our respect for an honored fellow-member of our several societies, lately deceased, and to indulge as well in an interchange of affectionate reminiscence of a departed friend.

Spencer Fullerton Baird was born at Reading, Pennsylvania, February 3, 1823. He was graduated at Dickinson College, in Carlisle, Pennsylvania, in 1840, at the age of seventeen, and with an original fondness for natural history and the study of the out-door world, he spent several years in his favorite pursuits and in collecting animal specimens for preservation. In 1845, at the youthful age of twenty-two, he was elected Professor of Natural History in his *alma mater*—Dickinson College.

Three years later, in 1848, while still pursuing with ardor the study of nature, he applied for and obtained from the Smithsonian Institution (then recently established) its first modest grant for the promotion of original research. This was to be applied to the exploration of bone caves, and to the development of the local natural history of southeastern Pennsylvania. The transaction appears to have been the occasion of first bringing the young professor to the favorable notice of the Smithsonian Director, Professor Henry, and of initiating between the two a mutual respect and friendship that continued throughout their several lives.

The early history of the Smithsonian Institution was signalized by a long struggle—both in the Board of its Regents and in the halls of Congress, between the votaries of literature, and those of science, for the disposal of the Smithson fund. During this period, in 1850, when it was seen that the income of this institution was not to be absorbed in the building up of a great national library, Professor Henry asked of the Regents authority to appoint an Assistant Secretary in the department of natural history to take charge of the Museum, and to aid in the publication and other interests of the establishment. A resolution authorizing such an appointment being adopted, Henry selected Professor Baird, of Dickinson College, as the one well fitted for the place.

H. Mis. 142——46

The appointment was unanimously confirmed by the Board July 5, 1850, and Professor Baird being notified, at once accepted and entered upon his new duties. He deposited in the Museum his own valuable collections, comprising an extensive series of the skins of various mammals (European as well as American), a large number of bird skins (unmounted), representing about five hundred American species and half as many European species, a rich variety of birds' nests and birds' eggs, more than five hundred glass jars, tin vessels, and kegs containing alcoholic specimens of reptiles and fishes, and a number of vertebrate skeletons and of fossil remains.

The new Assistant Secretary was truly in his element, and showed himself pre-eminently "the right man in the right place." In Henry's Fourth Annual Report (that for 1850), after recording the appointment of his Assistant, he adds: "He entered on his duties in July last and, besides being actively engaged in organizing the department of natural history, he has rendered important service in conducting our foreign exchanges and attending to the business of the press."

The Smithsonian system of exchanges was instituted for the purpose of facilitating the reciprocal transmission between the Old World and the New of the memoirs of learned socities, and this system has become an essential agency in the interchange and diffusion of knowledge, and in the more rapid advancement of scientific discovery, by a wider and prompter co-operation. Previous to this inauguration such distant scientific information was so rarely and inconveniently accessible largely through the delays and harassments of customs exactions, that important principles had not unfrequently been re-discovered abroad or at home, and sometimes with a considerable interval of time, to subsequently disturb and dispute a coveted and settled priority.

By the urgent zeal of the Smithsonian Director, representing to foreign powers that only gratuitous distribution of the literary and scientific memoirs of societies or of individuals (not usually found on sale) was undertaken by the Institution, and that no commercial enterprise calculated in any way to interfere with the legitimate operations of trade was attempted, one port after another was opened to its packages, until in the course of a few years, the announcement was made that the Smithsonian exchanges were allowed to pass through every custom-house on earth, unopened and unquestioned.

Creditable as this special liberality is, it has not yet, unfortunately, been applied to the customary channels of book lore, and the quest for knowledge is still held by a majority of civilized nations as an indulgence very proper to be taxed. Our own legislators have also made our higher education a source of revenue; possibly with a view to the "incidental protection" of American science by the heavy tariff laid on the foreign and imported article.

The advantage to the cause of science from this Smithsonian system of international exchange of intellectual products, free of duty, and with the freight expenses assumed by the Institution, can scarcely be too highly appreciated. In the early promotion of this beneficent scheme, Professor Baird became an energetic agent and sympathetic coadjutor of the Smithsonian Secretary. The remarkable development of this service may be sufficiently indicated by a glance at the amount of material transmitted through this Institution, on each tenth year for thirty years, showing something like a geometrical ratio of increase. The total weight of books, pamphlets, and charts distributed in 1855 was about 6 tons; in 1865, about 9 tons; in 1875, about 20 tons; and in 1885, about 85 tons. With the rapid growth of the exchange operations, the active and comprehensive faculties of Professor Baird seemed but to find a better field of exercise.

At the same time, the accumulating collections of the Museum—increased in 1858 by the transfer from the Patent Office to the Smithsonian Building of the interesting contributions from the earlier national exploring expeditions—demanded a large share of attention for their proper arrangement, exposition, and superintendence.* To say that this important work of organization was zealously and judiciously carried out, is to characterize but imperfectly the directive skill and energy of the Museum curator.

Of Professor Baird's work in original biologic research, of his contributions to various scientific journals and society proceedings, of his English translation of the popular "Iconographic Encyclopædia," of his editorship of the "Annual Record of Science and Industry" for eight years, and of his other publications, it is not proposed here to speak. This aspect of his intellectual life will be discussed by one in every respect far more competent to a just and discriminating presentation of the theme. The present remarks will be confined to a cursory review of Professor Baird's varied administrative work.

For a number of years a notable decline in the productiveness of our extended fisheries had been with anxiety observed; the annual yield of this important element of our food supply having in many cases fallen off one-half of its amount a quarter of a century earlier. So serious a diminution and consequent enhancement of cost of subsistence was becoming a menacing problem. Were our leading food fishes undergoing a process of slow but certain extinction? Several of the States (especially those of New England) appointed commissions of inquiry into the causes and remedies of the threatening evil but with little result.

In the stern competitive struggle that from the dawn of terrestrial palæontogeny has been ordained by nature as the feudal tenure of all existence, and from which service man himself is not exempted, the feebleness of early youth in the individuals of every race would speedily

---

* This accession of the Government deposit of ethnological and natural history specimens was estimated by Professor Baird, in his report for 1858, as comprising not more than a fourth of the material already in the Smithsonian Museum or a fifth of the aggregate amount.

terminate the biology of our planet were not provisions made for bridging over these cross lines of weakness to preserve the continuity of
species. In the lower classes of being we find the crude expedient of a
fertility so enormous as to allow of the wholesale destruction of the un-
protected eggs or of their brood, and yet leave a remnant to spare for
the chances of reaching adult age. In numerous other classes a mar-
velous sagacity is displayed by the mother in depositing her eggs where
they will be least exposed to accident or voracious attack, and where
the progeny (that she shall never see) will meet with their appropriate
sustenance. In insects this peculiar instinct—so difficult of explanation
as "inherited experience"—is perhaps most strikingly displayed. And
lastly, when we ascend to the higher classes of birds and mammals we
find the parental sentiment developed to an untiring vigilance for the
protection, and provident care for the nutrition, of the new generation
until it is able to take up for itself the battle of life.

As an illustration of the reckless prodigality of productiveness in
some of the lower families of the vertebrate branch it may be recalled
that a single salmon will lay five thousand eggs; a trout, fifteen thousand eggs; a perch, a herring, or a shad, thirty thousand eggs; a
pike, one hundred thousand eggs; a carp, four hundred thousand
eggs; a mackerel five hundred thousand eggs; a flounder, one million
eggs; a haddock, one million and a half of eggs; a halibut, two and a
half millions of eggs; a pollock, four million eggs; a codfish of medium
size, five million eggs; a large-sized cod, eight million eggs, and a tur-
bot, nine million eggs. Such numbers are simply astounding; they
can not be realized. And how great the marvel when we consider that
each of these nine million units is a potential fish, capable of development into all the perfected attributes and functions of the parent form!
Among the lower *invertebrates* may be simply instanced the oyster—
capable of producing the incredible number of twenty or thirty million
eggs, and if of large size as many as forty or fifty million eggs.

If with this amazing fertility the various kinds of fish just named
are not rapidly increasing, but are stationary or even decreasing in
numbers, how overwhelming must be their early destruction. Even
after allowing for the many millions of adult fish taken by man, it is
obvious that of many species not one in a thousand or in ten thousand
of eggs or of the newly hatched can survive to maturity. Professor
Möbius estimates that for every grown oyster upon the beds of Schleswig-Holstein more than a million have died.

To avert, if possible, the menace of increasing scarcity of fish supply
the attention of Congress was directed to the subject; the more properly since in our National Government resided the jurisdiction over our
extended sea-coasts. By a joint resolution, approved February 9, 1871,
the President was authorized and required to appoint a person of
proved scientific and practical acquaintance with the fishes of the coast
to be Commissioner of Fishes and Fisheries, with the duty to prosecute

investigations into the causes of diminution, if any, in numbers of the food-fishes of the coast and the lakes of the United States, and to report whether any and what protective, prohibitory, or precautionary measures should be adopted in the premises.

No man more suitable for this important and responsible position than Professor Baird could have been selected. He was at once appointed by President Grant and confirmed by the Senate as the Commissioner. In his first report he announced, as the result of a most careful and thorough examination, that the decrease of the shore fishes of the New England waters during the preceding twenty years was fully substantiated, and that it had been much more rapid since the year 1865.

In furtherance of his great work the resources of the Smithsonian Institution were freely placed at the disposal of the Commissioner, and in the same report he gratefully acknowledges this hearty co-operation by saying: "I am indebted to Professor Henry for permission to use the extensive collection of apparatus belonging to the Smithsonian Institution in the way of nets, dredges, tanks, etc., and thus saving the considerable outlay which would otherwise have been necessary."

The new studies into the life-history of the principal shore fishes, into the character and range of their enemies, and into their appropriate means of subsistence, requisite to an intelligent consideration of the conditions most favorable to their propagation,—involved investigations embracing the entire marine fauna of the coast, vertebrate and invertebrate. These extensive and varied researches necessarily demanded the aid of skilled assistants,—of a corps of eminent specialists in marine biology, and a corresponding division of labor.

The results of these investigations have been given to the world in hundreds of memoirs, published in the reports and bulletins of the Commission, and in the proceedings and bulletins of the National Museum. And it is quite within bounds to say that in importance, in variety, and in extent of original information thus communicated no such quantity of contribution to our knowledge of zoology has ever emanated from any other organization within the same interval of time. Many species of fishes entirely new to science have been discovered and carefully described, and the number of invertebrate forms known to inhabit the waters explored has probably been fully doubled.

It was shown, from the abundance of the lower forms of life, that the decline of the useful fishes had not resulted from any lack of their accustomed food supply, nor had it resulted apparently from any less favorable conditions of environment, nor from the prevalence of any epidemic diseases. It was therefore a consequence of excess in their destruction.

Among all the ravages of predaceous fishes it was found that the "bluefish" was the most voracious and devastating pirate of the coast. In the report it is stated: " Sometimes among a school of herring or menhaden, thousands of bluefish will be seen biting off the tail of one and then another, destroying ten times as many fish as they really need for food, and leaving in their track the surface of the water covered with the blood and fragments of the mangled fish." Fortunately this fish is itself valuable for food, and it is accordingly taken in large numbers.*

But by far the most rapacious and destructive scourge of the waters is man himself. By reckless extravagance in his methods of capture he would soon consume the capital of his abundant patrimony, were no restraints imposed upon the thoughtless improvidence of his greed. With the growth of population and demand, and the improved facilities for rapid transportation, the stimulus to inventive ingenuity occasioned the establishing of fish-traps and fish-pounds on a large scale that gathered thousands in their confines, with little regard to the probable supply of the future. As these traps and pounds were placed directly in the way of the fish to their spawning-beds, it resulted that a very large proportion of spawn fishes were taken by them, thus greatly reducing the prospects of the succeeding generation.

Whatever protective measures might be deemed expedient to check this spendthrift waste, it was seen that the most immediate and promising work of the Commissioner would be to promote the rapid multiplication of fish; and to this dominant interest the annual appropriations by Congress have been more and more largely directed.

Pisciculture is by no means a recent art, it having been extensively practiced by the Chinese for a number of centuries: and even the artificial fecundation of fish-spawn is nearly a century and a third old, having been apparently first introduced by Jacobi, a German, of Westphalia. Most of the European nations had already given attention to the practical application of fish-culture, and in different parts of our own country enterprising individuals had undertaken the operation with gratifying results.

Under the organizing direction of Professor Baird a careful study was made of existing methods, extended experiments on artificial propagation were conducted, and successive improvements in the various stages of incubation, hatching, and development introduced—each detail receiving a scientific treatment—until a scale of success has been effected far more complete and satisfactory than ever before attained. While under natural conditions but a small proportion of the spawn deposited is hatched (the greater mass being eagerly devoured by various aquatic tribes), and of the portion hatched but a small percentage escapes to reach maturity, under the careful breeding of art fully ninety per cent. of all the eggs secured are fertilized and successfully developed.

---

* In his first report, Professor Baird says: "I am myself cognizant of the capture of no less than 20,000 bluefish, representing a weight of at least 100,000 pounds, in one weir in the course of a single night."   •

Of the practical results of this great national enterprise it is unnecessary to speak. A dozen varieties of our best food-fishes have been disseminated throughout the inland waters and the sea-board of our country in increasing quantities; transported in the form of the young fry or in that of fertilized eggs to other hatching stations; and while an accurate estimate is, perhaps, at present not easily attainable, it will hardly be held an exaggeration to say that these productions are to be numbered by thousands of millions. Of these, many millions (by a most praiseworthy public courtesy) have been distributed to foreign countries—to Australia, to Brazil, to Canada, to England, to France, to Germany, to Mexico, to The Netherlands, to Scotland, and to Switzerland.

In the great International Fisheries Exhibition at Berlin in 1880 our national commission was authorized by Congress to participate. Professor Baird appointed as his deputy to personally superintend this movement Professor Goode, the present Fish Commissioner, under whose energetic direction, in a remarkably short space of time, the marvellous American exhibit was organized, transported, and installed, to the wonder and admiration of every visitor. The head of the American Commission was hailed by the President of the German Fisheries Association as the "chief fish-culturist in the world," and to him was awarded for the most complete and imposing display of all the details and accessories of his scientific art the unique first-honor prize of the exhibition, the gift of the Emperor of Germany.

But time fails to permit more than a passing glance at other fields of activity no less important in which Professor Baird employed his remarkable powers of executive management. The Smithsonian Institution from its inception had given great encouragement to explorations, and its director had zealously labored to enlist, as far as practicable, the various expeditions undertaken by the Government, in the extension of scientific research. These efforts were liberally responded to by the Executive Departments, and trained experimentalists and observers were given every facility for physical, physiographical, and biological investigations at distant points. The Institution thus became almost the Government superintendent of scientific expeditions. In all that pertained to ethnology and natural history Professor Baird became, of course, the leading spirit, and the various circulars of direction and inquiry issued by him show with what range and thoroughness he supervised this wide department, while the resulting memoirs and valuable museum accessions attest as their fruits the practical wisdom of the measures and methods adopted.

Congress having made provision for the representation by the Government in the National Centennial Exhibition to be held at Philadelphia, the President of the United States requested the Executive Departments, together with the Smithsonian Institution, to co-operate in a collection illustrative of our progress and resources. In his report of 1875, Professor Baird formulated (as requested by Professor Henry) his plans for the different details of the projected exhibit, and these being adopted were carried out to a result that made the Smithsonian display the leading attraction of the extensive Government building.

At the death of Professor Henry, in 1878, his faithful assistant and coadjutor was elected by the Regents as his successor, and his long familiarity with the different lines of active operations pursued by the Institution, made him from the start an efficient director. Another grave responsibility was thus thrown entirely upon his shoulders, and he proved himself equal to the occasion.

In 1879, Congress made an appropriation (since continued annually) for the prosecution of North American ethnology, to be expended under the direction of the Smithsonian Institution. For the administration of this important trust, Professor Baird selected one whom he knew to be peculiarly fitted by training, by zeal, and by congenial tastes, to pursue successfully the anthropologic study of our waning aborigines, and the new Bureau of Ethnology was judiciously committed to the control of the distinguished Director of the Geological Survey, Major Powell.

In the same year (that following Henry's death) an appropriation (for many years importunately besought of Congress) was made for the erection of a national museum building. In 1882 the completion of this building rendered necessary the re-organization of the Museum, with a staff of expert curators, on a scale commensurate with its importance and the abundance of its previously stored material.

Professor Baird had now become the manager of three great establishments;—the Fisheries Commission, the Smithsonian Institution, and the National Museum; either one of which was a charge sufficient to fully task the energies of a vigorous man. No wonder, with the strain of unremitted though divided attention to these exacting duties, that while unconscious himself of any unaccustomed or undue exertions, he should find even his robust and stalwart strength was slowly failing under his accumulated labors.

Informed by his medical adviser that an entire and continued rest from all intellectual exertion was necessary to restore his nervous energies to their wonted tone, he reluctantly accepted the decision. A year ago he asked from the Smithsonian Regents authority to appoint two official assistants to relieve him from the greater portion of his responsibility, and in hearty compliance with his expressed desire, the eminent astronomer and physicist, Professor Langley, was appointed assistant in charge of the Smithsonian operations, and his well-tried friend and collaborator, Professor Goode, was appointed assistant in charge of the Museum affairs.

But the relaxation came too late. After a vigorous resistance of his strong constitution to the encroachments of internal organic derangements, he finally succumbed to the Destroyer, and quietly breathed his last on the 19th of August, 1887; another example (far more frequent in the higher than in the lower fields of occupation) of sacrifice to over-work.

From even this hurried and imperfect sketch of Professor Baird's diversified administrative work it is at once apparent that he pos-sessed, in a pre-eminent degree, two great capacities;—the faculty for successful organization, and the faculty for continuous labor. As a biologist he had made a study of the entire range of organic nature— vegetable and animal; and with the accuracy of the specialist, he com-bined the larger and fuller perception of the general zoologist as to the functional and genetic inter-relations of animated being. The tenor of his mind was rather synthetic than analytic. While he ever displayed a marvellous memory for particulars, and a comprehensive grasp of details, these were apprehended more as the constituents of a general end or purpose, than as the residuals of a disjunctive conception. Clear-sighted and determined, he prevised and compassed the result in the means. Simple and unostentatious, he received with ready affability a visitor, even when most pre-occupied. What young naturalist ever applied to him for the resolution of a difficulty or un-certainty without receiving cordial attention and satisfactory enlight-enment ?

Great as were his undoubted services in the original discovery of biologic truths, it may well be doubted whether his indirect influence in the advancement of science, was not still greater, by the assistance and encouragement given to others and by his numerous official occa-sions of directing the efforts of the aspiring into channels of novel exploration, whenever the opportunities of land or naval expeditions presented themselves.

Now that the first shock of bereavement at missing one who has occupied a prominent place in the public eye, as well as in our private regard, has somewhat subsided, we but the more clearly realize that in the lamented death of Spencer F. Baird the scientific world has lost an accomplished and illustrious naturalist, the institutions over which he presided an energetic and judicious administrator, and we, assembled here, an exalted associate, a faithful counsellor, an ever open-hearted friend.

PROFESSOR BAIRD IN SCIENCE.

By Mr. WM. H. DALL, *President of the Biological Society.*

In accepting the honor of addressing you this evening on the biological work of Prof. Spencer F. Baird it is hardly necessary to state that I have felt keenly the inadequacy of my own equipment for the task. Not only does it happen that my own work has been almost entirely in departments of biology different from those which he adorned, but my early efforts were fostered by his wisdom and geniality, the period of my scientific studies has coincided with an acquaintance which ripened into affection and admiration, they have depended for their results upon opportunities largely due to the intervention of Professor Baird, and I feel that the best and truest of him is that which can not be put in words. The sense of personal loss, as with many of you, is still so keen as to accentuate the difficulty of doing justice to the theme assigned me.

I should have almost despaired of myself on this occasion were it not that others have aided me in my endeavor to set forth the debt owed by the various departments of research to Professor Baird's original investigations. To naturalists so distinguished in their specialties as Ridgway, Stejneger, Goode, Coues, Allen, Merriam, and Yarrow, I am indebted either for direct contributions toward the substance of this address or for matter in their published works which has been similarly utilized.

Professor Baird's scientific activity was exhibited in three principal directions : First, in original investigation of the zoology of vertebrates; second, in the diffusion of scientific knowledge and methods through official documents, reports, cyclopedias, and records of progress; and lastly, in the organization and administration of scientific agencies such as the National Museum or the Fish Commission, which include in their scope not merely public education or economic applications of science, but the promotion of research. Behind all these and hardly less important for science was the personal influence of the man himself, which shone through all the planes of his activity as coruscations light the facets of a gem.

Although it is very difficult to separate the phases of his work, one from another, so closely were they inter-related, my theme to-night is restricted to the impress left upon zoological science by Baird's original investigations. So great has been his reputation as an organizer, so numerous have been the publications in which he has garnered for the public the precious grain of the annual scientific harvest, that the extent and importance of his original work, except by specialists, is in danger of being overlooked.

We owe an excellent bibliography of his publications to Professor Goode. From this we learn that, up to the end of 1882, the list comprises nearly eleven hundred titles, from which, after deduction of all notices, reviews, official reports, and works edited for others, some two hundred formal contributions to scientific literature remain, many of which are works of monographic character and extensive scope.

With the exception of a single early botanical paper these relate to the vertebrates of America and, in their several branches, cover nearly the entire field. Although descriptions of species in themselves afford a poor criterion of the value of the work containing them, it is interesting to note that, among the terrestrial vertebrates, the proportion of the fauna first made known by Baird to the total number recognized at the time as North American varied from twenty-two per cent. of the whole to forty per cent. in different groups.

His method of study of new material was as far removed as possible from bookishness. In the case of the collections from Hudson Bay or the Pacific Railroad Surveys, when birds, mammals, or reptiles sometimes came to hand by hundreds, each specimen having the collector's data attached, the whole collection was thrown together, each form to be sorted out on its merits and studied in the light of a multitude of specimens.

Professor Baird's early life had included so much of exercise in the shape of long pedestrian journeys with gun and gamebag, so much familiarity with the wood-life of his favorite birds and mammals, that it would have been in any case impossible to class him with the closet-naturalist, while to this knowledge he added a genius for thorough, patient, and exhaustive research into all which concerned the subject of his study, and a wonderful inventiveness in labor-saving devices for labeling, museum work, and registration.

He had a wonderful capacity for work. He undertook and carried out successfully tasks which it would seem nobody else would have dared to attempt, or, attempting, would have been physically unable to complete. In the case of the immense volume on the mammals of the Pacific Railroad Surveys, he says in the preface, July 20, 1857:

The examination of the material was actually commenced early in 1855 and many of the articles written in that year or 1856. With the continual accession of additional specimens it became finally necessary to rewrite, alter, or extend all that had been prepared prior to the present year (1857). It is to this that the frequent want of uniformity is due, the time allowed not being sufficient in many cases to permit the reworking of the whole matter. · · · It is, perhaps, unnecessary to state that the matter of the present report is entirely original throughout. - - - It is proper to state, that owing to various circumstances, the work was necessarily passed through the press with a rapidity probably unexampled in the history of natural-history printing, allowing very little opportunity for that critical and leisurely examination so necessary in correcting a work of the kind. For most of the time the proof has been furnished and read at the rate of twenty-four to thirty-two pages per day, nearly 400 pages having been set up, read, and printed during the first half of July alone. Owing to the urgent necessity for the speedy completion of the volume, no time was allowed for the revision of the manuscript as a co·plete work, nor, indeed, of its separate portions, and, for much of the time, the preparation of much of the manuscript was only a few hours in advance of its delivery to the compositor.

The volume above referred to contains over 800 quarto pages and 42 plates. The manuscript was entirely prepared after 6 o'clock of working days which had been spent in the active administrative and executive work of the Assistant Secretary of the Smithsonian Institution, then unassisted by stenographer or other clerical supplement. Fortunately for science Baird did not always have to work under such circumstances, but the incident shows what he was capable of doing when the occasion seemed to him to warrant it. Probably no other work of equal importance, on any subject, was ever carried out under such pressure.

Mammals.—Professor Baird's contributions to a knowledge of North American mammals, though less voluminous than those relating to birds, are not less important. Previous to this time but one general work on the subject had been published, that of Audubon and Bachman on the Quadrupeds of North America, which was issued in three volumes, from 1846 to 1854.* Immediately after the completion of this great work collections began to pour into the Smithsonian Institution from the various exploring parties of the Pacific Railway surveys. This material comprised so large a number of new species, and cast so much light upon many previously doubtful points concerning the relations of species already described, that a revision of the whole subject became necessary. Hence Professor Baird at once set about the preparation of the book commonly known as the Mammals of North America. I have already alluded to the manner in which it was prepared. This great work was rapidly pushed to completion and appeared in 1857, just three years after the publication of the last volume of Audubon and Bachman's Quadrupeds. It constitutes the eighth volume of the Pacific Railroad Reports, and is a ponderous quarto of more than 800 pages, accompanied by numerous excellent plates.

Though published thirty years ago, this work still remains the standard general treatise on North American mammals. It contains no biographical matter, but consists wholly of technical descriptions. It treats of all the mammals then known from the continent of North

---

* The volume on Mammals of Richardson's Fauna Boreali Americana does not fall under this head, because it treats only of the northern portion of the continent.

America north of Mexico, except the bats and the truly pelagic forms—whales, sea-cows, and seals. The total number of known species was increased nearly twenty-five per cent.

In fullness of synonymy, and in the correct assignment of species previously described, Professor Baird was much in advance of previous workers. The descriptions, which are models of painstaking accuracy and precision, are taken from the specimens themselves, and are accompanied by long tables of measurements, the value of which more than justifies the enormous expenditure of time necessary in their preparation. Much more attention was paid to craniological characters than had been the custom with previous writers, which fact contributes largely to the permanent value of the work.

Professor Baird's long training as a careful observer, his power of concentrating his knowledge of matters under investigation, the wide scope of his information on nearly all departments of natural science, his clear perception of details, together with his excellent judgment, which was as marked in matters of minor detail as in those requiring great executive ability, enabled him to draw conclusions which subsequent accumulations of material have verified in a surprising manner; in fact, his pre-eminent superiority as a systematic zoölogist is everywhere apparent.

Birds.—When the great interest he took in birds is considered, and the long period over which his studies extended, it is somewhat surprising to find that the number of separate papers on ornithology published by Professor Baird sums up only some seventy-nine titles. It is less to their number that he owed his fame as an ornithologist than to their quality, combined with the fact that several of these publications covered practically the entire field of North American ornithology, and were of the nature of monographs.

"His reputation was, indeed, established," says Ridgway; "by the first of his separate works, usually known and quoted as the "Birds of North America," though not published under this title until two years after it had been printed by the Government as Volume IX of the Pacific Railroad Reports. With the publication of this great quarto volume, containing more than a thousand pages, in 1868, began what has been fitly termed by Dr. Elliott Coues the "Bairdian period" of American ornithology. This period, covering almost thirty years, was characterized by an activity in ornithological research and a rapidity of advancement without a parallel in the history of the science.

Of the "Birds of North America" Coues states* that "it represents the most important single step ever taken in the progress of American ornithology in all that relates to the technicalities." The nomenclature was entirely remodeled from that previously in current use, and for the first time was brought abreast of the systematic acquirements of the time. The synonymy of the work, in which is embodied the history of

---

*Bibl. app. to the Birds of the Colorado Valley, p. 650.

investigation relating to each species, is more extensive, reliable, and elaborate than any before presented. With few exceptions, citations were original, and when, as occasionally happened, they were necessarily at second-hand the fact was always indicated. The text comprised not only diagnoses and descriptions of each species, but extended and elaborate commentary, comparisons, and criticisms.

In this learned and sagacious work Professor Baird was aided by Cassin and Lawrence, two of the leading ornithologists of America. It exerted an influence perhaps strongly and more widely felt than any of its predecessors, Audubon and Wilson not excepted, and marked an epoch in the history of American ornithology. The data original to and embodied in this work have been used again and again by subsequent writers with various modifications. Such a monument of original research is likely to remain for an indefinite period a source of inspiration to other writers, while its authority as a work of reference will always endure.

The publication of this work rendered possible the studies and progress of a large number of persons, who without it would hardly have been able to enter the domain of scientific ornithology, but who, aided by the book as a standard of reference and by the genial correspondence and pregnant suggestions of its author, have made reputations of more or less distinction for valuable and permanent original investigation. The number of those who profited by this stimulation has been very large, and in this way arose what has been called* the Bairdian School of Ornithologists, a school characterized by exactitude in matters of fact, conciseness in deductive statement, and careful analysis of the subject in all its various bearings. Its work is marked by a careful separation of the data from the conclusions derived from them, so that conclusions or arguments can be traced back to their sources and duly weighed, while the writings of the older European school afford little basis for analysis. In substance, according to Dr. Stejneger, the European method required an investigator to accept an author's statements and conclusions on his personal responsibility alone, while the method originated by Baird furnishes him with tangible facts from which to make his deductions.

These distinctive features were still further developed by the publication in 1864–'66 of the "Review of American Birds," a work of unequaled merit, displaying in their perfection Professor Baird's wonderful powers of analysis and synthesis, so strongly combined in his treatment of difficult problems. Although never completed, this work has received unstinted praise from all competent to estimate it. It is said on excellent authority that no other single work on American birds has made so profound an impression on foreign ornithologists, notwithstanding the fact that circumstances prevented it from being made complete.

---

* Stejneger, Proc. U. S. Nat. Mus., 1884, VII, p. 76.

Although in his systematic work Professor Baird, like other naturalists, built partly on the scientific foundations laid by his predecessors and contemporaries, always with due acknowledgment, the high value of his work in this direction was largely due to an unerring instinct which enabled him to recognize and confirm the best features of the work of others and by adding material from his own lines of original research to combine the whole into a fabric which was a distinct advance on anything previously offered to the scientific world.

While the bent of his genius led him, in this as in other departments, to devote a main proportion of his work to the systematic biology which was the need of the time, and which, with the exploration and description upon which it is based, must always precede and lay the track for the theoretical biology more in vogue to-day, it must not be supposed that the work of Baird was confined to descriptive and systematic work. With the latter in his publications are combined a host of biographical data such as the field naturalist revels in. One of the earliest and most pregnant papers bearing on mutations of specific forms which have been contributed to the literature of evolution by American biologists is to be found in his article on the "Distribution and Migrations of North American Birds" published in the American Journal of Science in 1866.[*] In this paper, an abstract of a memoir presented to the National Academy of Sciences in 1865, are to be found the germs of much of the admirable work which has since been elaborated by other biologists on the correlation of geographical distribution and the peculiarities of the environment, with the modifications of color, size, and structure in the forms of animal life, called species.

Unlike some of his contemporaries twenty years ago, the views of Darwin excited in him no reaction of mind against the hypotheses then novel and revolutionary. His friendly reception of the new theories was so quiet and undisturbed that, to a novice seeking his advice and opinion amid the clatter of contending voices, it seemed almost as if the main features of the scientific gospel of the new era had existed in the mind of Baird from the very beginning. His thorough apprenticeship in the study of details of structure and their expression in systematic classification, as well as his cautious and judicial habit of mind, prevented him, notwithstanding his hearty recognition of evolutionary processes, from falling into those exuberancies of utterance and hypothesis characteristic of narrowness and immaturity which, within the memory of most of us, have enjoyed a sort of vogue now happily on the decline.

Batrachians and Serpents.—Professor Baird's contributions to herpetology began as early as 1849, his first paper being a revision of the North American tailed batrachians which appeared in the Journal of the Academy of Natural Sciences of Philadelphia. Excluding notices of the work of others in the Annual Record between 1849 and 1880, he

*Am. Jour. Sci. and Arts, 2nd Series, 1866, XII, pp. 78–90, 184–192, 337–347.

published fourteen papers on this branch of science beside nine of which he was the joint author with Charles Girard. His activity in original work in this, as in some other directions, came to an end with the assumption of the burden of administrative work required by the organization and development of the Fish Commission.

Many of his herpetological papers were elaborate studies. One of the most important of the early memoirs was that on the reptiles of Stansbury's expedition to the valley of the Great Salt Lake, and another, that on those collected by the United States exploring expedition under Wilkes. The catalogue of North American Reptiles in the collection of the Smithsonian Institution is a classical work, serving to the present day as a text-book for students of herpetology. In 1859 appeared his great study of the reptiles collected by the parties engaged in the explorations for a Pacific Railroad, a monument of patient research and discriminating analysis. After this his contributions to the subject were mostly short papers or announcements of new or interesting facts.

At the time Professor Baird began his studies of the amphibia little had been done for herpetology in America. The classical work of Holbrook contained little more than descriptions of Southern species, and the work of Duméril and Bibron was equally meager. Immense collections were placed in Baird's hands from the Western plains, and the work upon these was necessarily in great part original. How well this work was done is shown by the fact that, in spite of the changes which are constant in zoological classification, nearly all the species still retain the names he applied to them. The descriptions were so carefully prepared that later students have never been troubled in making their identifications.

Notwithstanding his multifarious duties in later years, Professor Baird never lost his interest in these animals, and up to the last afforded every aid and encouragement to those studying them. Much of the work done in this country by such herpetologists as Girard, Kennicott, Hallowell, Cope, and others, found in his example and encouragement the stimulus which made it possible, was built on the foundations which he laid, and owes its publication to agencies which he promoted or controlled.

Fishes. Professor Baird's contributions to ichthyological literature number some fourteen or fifteen papers, chiefly of a descriptive character, embodying the results of original research into the ichthyology of western and southwestern America and of the marine fishes of New Jersey and New York. Most of these papers were published jointly with Charles Girard.

Besides these, however, he added more than four hundred titles to the list of reviews, notices, reports, translations, and official documents relating to economic ichthyology, fish culture, and the general progress of the science. In this way he was instrumental in bringing together

H. Mis. 142——47

for the use and benefit of the English-speaking public the largest body of facts relating to fish and fisheries ever prepared and digested for such purposes by any individual or organization. Recognized by experts of foreign countries with one accord, as the most eminent living authority on economic ichthyology, America owes to his fostering care and unwearied labor the existence of a whole generation of ichthyologists, breeders of fishes, and inventors of appliances of all sorts for use in connection with the taking, preservation, and increase of these animals. So thoroughly is this understood by all who are in any way acquainted with American fish and fisheries, that to them this statement will appear a truism.

It does not enter into the purpose of this address to enumerate the economic results of the Commission which grew into such stately proportions under his skillful and progressive leadership, nor yet to enumerate the multitudinous researches in pure as well as economic biology for which this organization has furnished material and means. No more emphatic object-lesson of the vital relations existing between research, as such, and the promotion of the material interests of mankind has ever been furnished to the so-called "practical man" than that afforded by the work of the United States Fish Commission as directed by Professor Baird.

Whether germane to the subject of scientific research or not, the most narrow specialist can hardly grudge an allusion to the grandeur of the methods by which the food supply of a nation was provided, hundreds of rivers stocked with fish, and the very depths of ocean re-populated. Typically American we may call them in their audacity and their success. The fishery boards of foreign countries, first quietly indifferent, then loudly incredulous, in due time became interested inquirers and enthusiastic followers. In a few years we may fairly expect to see the food supply of the entire civilized world materially increased, with all the benefits which that implies, and this result will in the main be owing to the unremunerated and devoted exertions of Spencer F. Baird.

THE PERSONAL CHARACTERISTICS OF PROFESSOR BAIRD.

By J. W. POWELL, *President of the Anthropological Society.*

Baird was one of the learned men of the world, and, to a degree per-haps unexampled in history, he was the discoverer of the knowledge he possessed. He knew the birds of the air, from the ptarmigan that lives among everlasting snows to the humming-bird that revels among the orchids of the tropics; he knew the beasts of the forests and the prai-ries, and the reptiles that crawl through desert sands or slimy marshes; he knew the fishes that scale mountain torrents, that bask in quiet lakes, or that journey from zone to zone through the deep waters of the sea. In all this realm of nature he had a minute and comprehensive knowledge that no other man has ever acquired. What others had recorded in this field of research he knew, and to their discoveries he made a contribution of his own so bounteous, so stupendous, that he is recognized as the master of systematic zoologists.

All of Baird's scientific work is an illustration of modern inductive or scientific reasoning. The inductions or general principles of modern science are reached by the accumulation of vast stores of facts. He knew how to accumulate facts; how to reject the trivial and select the significant. Modern science is almost buried under the débris of obser-vation, the record of facts without meaning, the sands of fact that are ground from the rock of truth by the attrition of mind; but Baird could walk over the sands and see the diamonds. Then he knew how to marshal significant facts into systems, and how to weld them into funda-mental principles. In all his works there can be discovered no taint of *a priori* reasoning or syllogistic logic; for in his mind there was no room for controversy; and disputation fled before the light of his genius. Formal logic, a disease of modern thought, the contagion of *Aristotleina*, never ravaged his brain. With healthful directness, he sought the truth guided by wise inference, and told the truth in its simplicity.

Baird was an organizer of the agencies of research. When a bold explorer essayed to penetrate the seas of ice by the path of peril and in quest of fame, Baird would ever so manage that a corps of quiet scholars should be attached to the expedition to study the climate of the Arctic zone, the geology of the Arctic rocks, the flora of the Arctic lands, or the fauna of the Arctic fields; and the best knowledge we have of the igloo-dwellers, the Eskimo whose home is on the ice of the North, has been brought to us by the quiet students he succeeded in attaching to Arctic exploring expeditions, and so the love of glory was made to serve the cause of truth.

When, in the interests of international commerce, expeditions were sent to explore and survey routes of travel and transportation across Central America from sea to sea, he managed to send with them corps of scientific men whose function it was to bring from the tropics all forms of its abundant life, vegetal and animal, and the relics of the arts of the people of Central America as they are exhibited in stone and clay and gold; and the National Museum has been enriched by the results of this labor, and the boundaries of human knowledge extended thereby, and so the greed of gain was made to serve the love of truth.

When our Army was distributed on the frontiers of the land, he everywhere enlisted our scholarly officers in the service of science and he transformed the military post into a station of research; the Indian campaign into a scientific expedition. Scott, Marcy, McClellan, Thomas, and many other of the great generals of America were students of natural history and collectors for Baird. When our Navy cruised around our shores its officers were inspired with that love of nature which made every voyage of military duty a voyage of discovery in the realms of natural science; when they journeyed among the islands of the sea they brought back stores of scientific materials, and when they sailed through the littoral waters of other continents they made voyages of scientific investigation. Many of these earlier naturalists of the Navy in subsequent times became commodores and admirals.

But time would fail me to tell of the exploring expeditions and the railroad surveys throughout America, and the travels throughout the world, which he utilized in the interest of science, or of which he was the immediate projector. Of the abundant material thus gathered from all parts of the world, some has gone to enrich American institutions of learning, and some has been gathered into the National Museum;—an outgrowth of Baird's organizing genius and a splendid monument to his memory.

The hills of the land stretch not so far as the billows of the sea; the heights of the mountains are not so great as the depths of the ocean; and so the world was unknown until this greater region was explored. The treasures of the land did not satisfy the desires of

Baird ; he must also have the treasures of the sea, and so he organized a fish commission, with its great laboratories and vessels of research.

What hid'st thou in the treasure-caves and cells,
Thou hollow sounding and mysterious main ?
Pale, glistening pearls and rainbow-colored shells,
Bright things which gleam unreck'd of, and in vain.
Keep, keep thy riches, melancholy sea!
We ask not such from thee.

What the scholar asked of the sea was all its forms of life, its organisms minute and lowly, its crawling articulates, its pearl-housed mollusks, its fishes that swim in armies, and its leviathans that prowl among the waves—the life of the reedy shore, the life of the ocean-current, and the life of the deep sea. Thus with many ingenious appliances, he and his lieutenants sailed away to explore the ocean's mystery.

So the Fish Commission was an agency of research; but it was more,—he made it an agency by which science is applied to the relief of the wants of mankind,—by which a cheap, nutritious, healthful, and luxurious food is to be given to the millions of men. He affirmed that for the production of food an acre of water is more than equal to 10 acres of land, thus giving to the gloomy doctrine of Malthus its ultimate refutation, and tearing away the veil of despair from the horizon of the poor ; for, when the sea shall serve man with all the food that can be gathered from its broad expanse, the land can not contain the millions whom it is thus possible to supply.

In the research thus organized the materials for the work of other scientific men were gathered. When a great genius reads to the world a chapter from the book of nature the story is so beautiful that many are stimulated to search in the same field for other chapters of the same story. Thus it was that the publication of Baird's great works on natural history developed in America a great corps of naturalists, many of whom have become illustrious, and the stimulus of his work was felt throughout Europe. In the research which he organized the materials were furnished for this corps of naturalists; but his agency in the development of this body of workers was even more direct. He incited the men personally to undertake and continuously to prosecute their investigations. He enlisted the men himself, he trained them himself, he himself furnished them with the materials and instruments of research, and best of all, he was their guide and great exemplar. Thus it was that the three institutions over which he presided,—the Smithsonian Institution, the National Museum, and the Fish Commission— were woven into one great organization,—a university of instruction in the methods of scientific research, including in its scope the entire field of biology and anthropology. Such is Baird the investigator, Baird the organizer, and Baird the instructor, in the length breadth and height of his genius, the solidarity of a great man.

All that I have said is a part of the public record, found in the great libraries of the world; but however exalted the feeling of admiration we may entertain for Baird as a scholar and administrator, it is to his attributes as a man, as disclosed in his personal relations with friends, associates, and men of affairs, that we most fondly turn. It is in these relations that he most clearly exhibited those kindly and modest traits of character which made him so universally beloved.

As a man of affairs, Professor Baird exhibited great sagacity. His plans for the organization of scientific work were of great magnitude, and had they been presented to the administrative officers of the Government or to legislative bodies with exaggeration, or even had they been presented with the glow of an enthusiastic missionary of science, they might well have encountered opposition. But Baird had a wonderful faculty of presenting his plans with extreme modesty, and with a degree of under-statement, but suggestion of possibilities which speedily caused him to whom the appeal was made, himself to become an advocate of the Professor's measure. He had traits of character in this respect which are hard to explain, and which seem at first to be contradictory. In the advocacy of measures his modesty amounted almost to timidity; he avoided alike argumentation and ostentation, and he presented his measures with the directness of a child. Notwithstanding all this, there was such a poise of faculties, such dignity of mien, that he impressed those with whom he came in contact as a venerable and wise patriarch. He seemed devoid of personal interest or feeling, and solicitous only for the welfare of those to whom he was in fact appealing, and he conveyed the impression that he was giving benignant advice. Thus the shrinking, sensitive man, who could not even stand before a public body, such as a committee of Congress, or a scientific society, and advocate a cause, could from his seat by the fireside or at the desk, so illumine the subject with which he had to deal that men stood round him to gather his words, that nothing should be lost; for in the exposition of his subject he illumined everything with clear statement, arising from an exhaustive knowledge and full understanding of results.

As the director of the work of research in which other men were engaged, Professor Baird had marvellous insight and skill. The appliances of modern research, alike in the inorganic world and in biology, have come to be multifarious and diverse, and there is this peculiarity about them;—once used, so that the secret of nature which they were planned to unlock has been revealed, they speedily become obsolete, and immediately new keys, new apparatus, new devices are necessary. Thus to a large extent skill in research is absorbed in the skill necessary for the development of the agencies of research. A continuous line of research, prosecuted by a corps of men so that the boundaries of knowledge are carried far forward, can result only from a continuous line of inventions in the apparatus of research, and it was here that Baird exhibited his skill. His own devices were many and constant, and he was ever fertile in suggestions to his assistants. No wonder, then, that so many of the secrets of nature were unlocked through his agency. It was in the direction of this work of research that the man Baird stood forth as a giant; it was where his vast knowledge of details was most apparent; it was where his marvellous skill was most shown; it was where his insight into human character was most exhibited. With clearness he formulated his interrogatories; with aptness he selected his course of procedure; with judgment he sought the aid of others, and with suggestiveness directed their work. And, lo! his questions were speedily answered. It was in this manner that his own good hands were supplemented by the hands of many, that his own great mind was re-enforced by the best mental activity of many assistants; and thus the whole body of men under his control worked together as one organic integer for the increase and diffusion of knowledge among men.

In his work with his assistants he scrupulously provided that every one should receive the meed of honor due for successful research and be treated all with generosity. Many an investigation begun by himself was turned over to assistants when he found that valuable conclusions could be reached; and these assistants, who were his warm friends, his younger brothers, reaped the reward; and he had more joy over every young man's success than over the triumphs and honors heaped upon himself from every quarter of the globe. He was the sympathetic counsellor of many men; into his ears were poured the sorrows and joys of others, and he mourned with the mourning and rejoiced with the rejoicing. To those in need his hand was ready and his purse was open, and many were the poor who called him "blessed." Though a man of great force of character, a man of great learning, a man upon whom had been showered the honors of the scientific world, in character he was as simple as a child. He had a fund of "folk-lore," and loved the books and papers written for children. In his later years, weakened with disease and burdened with many labors, he still read "St. Nicholas" from month to month, and kept the run of every little story, and was glad to be "a child again." His life at home was pure and sweet, and full of joys, for he gave and received love and trust and tender care. But the history of his home life is sacred. Its words and acts abide in the hearts of the wife and the daughter.

For many long months he contemplated the day of parting. Labor that knew no rest, responsibility that was never lifted from his shoulders, too soon brought his life to an end. In the summer of the past year he returned to his work by the seaside, that he might die in its midst. There at Wood's Holl he had created the greatest biologic laboratory of the world; and in that laboratory, with the best results of his life-work all about him, he calmly and philosophically waited for the time of times. Three days before he died he asked to be placed in a chair provided with wheels. On this he was moved around the pier, past the vessels which he had built for research, and through the laboratory, where many men were at work at their biologic investigations. For every one he had a word of good cheer, though he knew it was the last. At the same time, along the pier and through the laboratory, a little child was wheeled. "We are rivals," he said, "but I think that I am the bigger baby." In this supreme hour he was playing with a child. Then he was carried to his chamber, where he soon became insensible, and remained so until he was no more.

"Blessed are the pure in heart, for they shall see God."

A MEMOIR OF ASA GRAY.[*]

By James D. Dana.

Our friend and associate, Asa Gray, the eminent botanist of America, the broad-minded student of nature, ended his life of unceasing and fruitful work on the 30th of January last (1888). For thirty-five years he has been one of the editors of this Journal, and for more than fifty years one of its contributors; and through all his communications there is seen the profound and always delighted student, the accomplished writer, the just and genial critic, and, as Darwin has well said, "the lovable man."[†]

Asa Gray was born on the 18th day of November, 1810, at Sauquoit, in the township of Paris, Oneida County, New York, a place 9 miles south of Utica. When a few years old his father moved to Paris Furnace, and established there a tannery; and the child, one account says, was put to work feeding the bark-mill and driving the horse, and another, riding the horse that ground the bark. "At six or seven he was a champion speller in the numerous 'matches' that enlivened the district school." At the age of eleven, nearly twelve, he was sent to the grammar school at Clinton, where he remained for two years, and the following year to the Fairfield Academy, both of the schools places where all the classics and mathemetics were taught that were required for entering the colleges of the land. But his instruction was cut short by his father's desire that he should enter the Fairfield Medical School. This school, of high repute, was established at that place in 1812 as the College of Physicians and Surgeons of the Western District of New York. Dr. James Hadley was the professor of chemistry and materia medica, and his lectures of 1825-'26, while Gray was in the academy, and 1826-'27, after he had taken up medicine, gave the young student his first instruction in science. During the following winter at Fairfield, that of 1827-'28, the article on Botany in the Edinburgh Encyclopædia attracted young Gray's attention, and excited his interest

---

[*] From the American Journal of Science, March 1, 1888. Vol. xxxv.

[†] In the preparation of this sketch I have been much aided by the papers of Professor Goodale, Professor Sargent and Prof. C. R. Barnes, the last in the Botanical Gazette for January 1, 1886

so deeply that he at once bought a copy of "Eaton's Botany" and longed for spring. As spring opened, "he sallied forth early, discovered a plant in bloom, brought it home, and found its name in the manual to be *Claytonia Virginica*, the species *C. Caroliniana*, to which the plant really belonged, not being distinguished then." From this time collecting plants became his chief pleasure. He finished his medical course, and in the spring of 1831 took his degree of Doctor of Medicine—to him the basis for a title, but not for future work.

This ended his school and college days. As Gray's scientific education was carried forward without the aid of a formal scientific school, so it was with his literary studies. He had not the benefit of university training, and yet became eminent for his graceful and vigorous English, the breadth of his knowledge, his classical taste, and the acuteness of his logical preceptions.

Before the close of the medical course he had opened correspondence about his plants with Dr. Lewis C. Beck, a prominent botanist of Albany, and had had a collection named for him by Dr. John Torrey, of New York. Moreover, about this time he delivered his first course of lectures on botany, as substitute for Dr. Beck, and made use of the fees that he received for the expenses of a botanical excursion through western New York to Niagara Falls. Gray also delivered a course of lectures at Hamilton College, Clinton, on mineralogy and botany, for Professor Hadley, in the college year of 1833–'34, a biographical sketch of Professor Hadley, of Fairfield, by his son, the eminent Professor of Greek at Yale, stating that his father, who gave up his lectures at this college in 1834, "supplied his place during the last term by a favorite pupil and much valued friend, Dr. Asa Gray, who commenced under Professor Hadley the studies which were to make him pre-eminent among the botanists of his time." Professor Hadley, the sketch says, had studied botony at New Haven, Connecticut, in 1818, under Dr. Eli Ives, an excellent botanist of that place, and mineralogy and geology under Professor Silliman.

In the autumn of 1831 Gray became instructor in chemistry, mineralogy, and botany at "Bartlett's High School," in Utica. The scientific department of the school had been under the charge of a graduate of Eaton's "Rensselaer School," at Troy—the earliest school of science in America—and Professor Eaton's practical methods of instruction in chemistry, mineralogy and botany were there followed. Great was the delight of the boys in botanical and mineralogical excursions with Mr. Fay Egerton, and their pleasure, too, in the lectures on chemistry. In 1830 the writer left the Utica High School for Yale College; and a year later, Mr. Egerton having resigned on account of his health, Gray took his place. We had then no acquaintance and knew nothing of one another's interest in minerals and plants. My minerals and herbarium went with me to New Haven; and while I was there Gray was mineralizing as well as botanizing, during his vacations, in New

Jersey and western and northern New York. His first published paper is mineralogical,—an account of his discoveries (along with Dr. J. B. Crawe) of new mineral localities in northern New York. It is contained in the twenty-fifth volume of the American Journal of Science,[*] and the title gives Utica as his place of residence. He had previously made excursions after plants, fossils and minerals in New Jersey, and in 1834 joined Dr. Torrey in botanizing, besides collecting for him in the "pine barrens" of New Jersey and other places.

In the autumn of 1834 Gray accepted the position of assistant to Dr. Torrey in the chemical laboratory of the Medical School of New York. Botany was at first his study *under* Dr. Torrey, but soon his work *with* Dr. Torrey; and here commenced their long-united labors and publications. From the first he showed himself an adept in his methods of investigation and in his terse and mature style of scientific description. During the year 1834, while Torrey was preparing his monograph on the North American sedges, the Cyperaceæ, Gray had in hand an illustrated memoir on the genus Rhynchospora, in which he doubled the number of known North American species; and another also on "New, rare, and otherwise interesting plants of northern and western New York." Both papers were read before the Lyceum of Natural History of New York in December of that year (1834), and are published in volume III of the Annals of the Lyceum. Dr. Torrey's monograph was read on the 8th of August, 1836; and in it he says that the part on the genera Rhynchospora and Ceratoschœnus was prepared by Dr. Gray, and that his descriptions are so full, that he gives only his list of the species, with such alterations as he has thought it advisable to make, and some additional matter received since the publication of his paper. During 1834, 1835, two volumes of a work on North American Gramineæ and Cyperaceæ were issued by him, (each containing a hundred species, and illustrated by dried specimens,)—now rare volumes, as only a small edition was published through private subscription. The first of these volumes, issued in February, 1834, only three years after his graduation at the Fairfield Medical School, is dedicated to his instructor and friend Dr. James Hadley. The preface acknowledges his indebtedness to Dr. Torrey and to Dr. Henry P. Sartwell, of Penn Yan. Of the species described as new in the work, the first one, No. 20, from specimens collected by Dr. Sartwell, turned out to be Nuttal's *Calamagrostis confinis*. But the next one, No. 28, *Panicum xanthophysum,* from the vicinity of Oneida Lake, stands and is the first of the thousands of good Asa-Gray species. Thus Gray's botanical investigations were well begun before his twenty-fifth year had passed.

[*] Page 346. The article is in the second number of the volume, which was issued Jaunary 1, and is without date; the one following it is dated September 6, 1833. The paper therefore was probably written in the autumn of 1833, after a summer's excursion.

In February or March of 1835 he gave his last instruction at the Utica High School. He expected to continue as Dr. Torrey's assistant the following season; but "the prospects of the Medical School were so poor that Dr. Torrey could not afford to employ him." He nevertheless returned to New York in the autumn, took the position of curator and librarian of the Lyceum of Natural History, and continued his botanical investigations. During the summer he had begun the preperation of his "Elements of Botany," and in the course of 1836 the work appeared. It showed the scholar in its science and in its style. The subjects of vegetable structure, physiology, and classification were presented in a masterly manner, though within a small compass. The book moreover showed his customary independence of judgment and clear head in various criticisms and suggestions,—later investigations sustaining them, much to his gratification.

The Wilkes Exploring Expedition came near making a profound impression on Gray's life. In the summer of 1836 the position of botanist in the expedition was offered him and accepted. But delays occurred in the time of sailing, and changes were threatened that threw uncertainties over the cruise, and for these reasons, and on account of the work on the North American Flora, of which, by invitation of Dr. Torrey, he was to be joint author, his resignation was sent in the following year. The expedition changed its commander from Commodore Patterson, over a ship-of-the-line, to Lieutenant Charles Wilkes, with a squadron of two sloops-of-war (better adapted for the purpose), besides other vessels, six in all, and sailed in August, 1838. The four years abroad would have given him an opportunity for observations and discoveries that would have rejoiced him—excursions in Madeira, the Canaries, to the Organ Mountains in Brazil, a brief look about Orange Bay near Cape Horn, excursions to the Andes of Chili and about lower Peru, over Oregon and Washington Territory, and parts of California, through numerous island groups of the South and North Pacific, in Australia and New Zealand, about Luzon in the Philippines, at Singapore, at Cape of Good Hope and St. Helena—and his open mind would have gathered in facts on the relations and geographical distribution of species that would have been to him a mine of wealth as science advanced under Darwin's lead. The place of botanist in the expedition was well occupied by the most excellent, indefatigable, and many-sided zoologist Dr. Charles Pickering, and by Mr. William D. Breckenridge, a Scotch gardener and zealous collector, and Mr. William Rich; but with Dr. Gray, devoted to the one subject, great results would have been accomplished. North American botany however would no doubt have suffered.

By October of 1838, a couple of months after the sailing of the Exploring Expedition, two parts of the projected "Flora" were already out. But so many doubtful points had been brought to light, that a study of foreign herbaria had become imperative. Dr. Gray had accepted, dur-

ing the summer, the chair of botany in the recently founded University
of Michigan, but with the condition that he should have a year abroad
for study; and the year was given to this object. All the herbaria of
Europe were carefully examined with regard to the type-specimens of
American plants, and full notes taken for use in the discrimination and
identification of species. The fortieth volume of the American Journal
(April, 1841) opens with a highly interesting paper by him, giving accounts of these herbaria, their contributors, condition, and special characters, commencing with that of Linnæus and the story of its career before
reaching the Linnean Society of London. His labors abroad involved
an immense amount of detailed and exact observation, requiring
thorough knowledge, excellent judgment, and a retentive memory; and
he came home well stored for the work which he and Torrey had in
hand.

Moreover, he made during the trip the personal acquaintance of the
leading botanists of England and the Continent, and had from all a
cordial reception.

"In Glasgow he made the acquaintance of William Jackson Hooker,
the founder of the greatest of all herbaria, the author of many works
upon botany, who had already published a large part of his "Flora
Boreali-Americana," in which were described the plants of British
North America, a work just then of special interest to the young American, because it first systematically displayed the discoveries of David
Douglas, of Drummond, Richardson, and other English travelers in
North America. At Glasgow, too, was laid the foundation for his life-
long friendship with the younger Hooker, then a medical student seven
years his junior, but destined to become the explorer of New Zealand
and Antarctic floras, the intrepid Himalaya traveler, the associate of
George Bentham in the authorship of the "Genera Plantarum," a president of the Royal Society, and, like his father, the director of the Royal
Gardens at Kew. At Edinburgh he saw Greville, the famous crypto-
gamist; while in London, Francis Boott, an American long resident in
England, the author of the classical history of the genus "Carex," and
at that time secretary of the Linnean Society, opened to him every botanical door. Here he saw Robert Brown, then the chief botanical figure in Europe, with the exception, perhaps, of De Candolle; and Men-
zies, who fifty years before had sailed as naturalist with Vancouver on his
great voyage of discovery; and Lambert, the author of the sumptuous
history of the genus "Pinus," in whose hospitable dining-room were
stored the plants upon which Pursh had based his North American
Flora. Here, too, he met Bentham and Lindley and Bauer, and all the
other workers in his scientific field.

"A visit to Paris brought him the acquaintance of the group of dis-
tinguished botanists then living at the French capital: P. Barker
Webb, a writer upon the botany of the Canaries; the Baron Delessert,
Achille Richard, whose father had written the Flora of Michaux; Mir-

bel, already old, but still actively engaged in investigations upon vegetable anatomy; Spach; Decaisne, then a young *aide naturaliste* at the Jardin des Plantes, of which he was afterward to become the distinguished director; Auguste St. Hilaire, the naturalist of the Duke of Luxembourg's expedition to Brazil, and at that time in the full enjoyment of a great reputation earned by his works upon the Brazilian flora; Jacques Gay; Gaudichaud, the naturalist of the voyage of L'Uranie and La Physicienne; the young Swiss botanist Edmond Boisser, the Spanish traveler, and later one of the most important contributors to systematic botany in his classical "Flora Orientalis;" Adrien de Jussieu, grand-nephew of Bernard, and son of Laurent de Jussieu, himself a worthy and distinguished representative of a family unequaled in botanical fame and accomplishment.

"At Montpellier Dr. Gray passed several days with the botanists Delile and Dunal, and then hurried on to Italy, where at Padua, in the most ancient botanical garden in Europe, he made the acquaintance of Visiani, at that time one of the principal botanists in Italy. At Vienna he saw the learned Endlicher, the author of a classical " Genera Plantarum;" and at Munich, Von Martius, the renowned Brazilian traveler, the historian of the palms, and the earliest contributor to that stupendous work the "Flora Brasiliensis," which bears his name; and here, too, was Zuccarini, the collaborator with Von Siebold in the "Flora Japonica." Geneva then—as at the present time, was a center of scientific activity; and there he made the personal acquaintance of the De Candolles, father and son, and worked in their unrivalled herbarium and library. He saw Schlechtendal at Halle; and at Berlin, Klotzsch, Kunth, and Ehrenberg,—familiar names in the annals of botanical science. Alphouse De Candolle and Sir Joseph Hooker alone are left of the brilliant group of distinguished naturalists who cordially welcomed the young American botanist in 1839." *

Dr. Gray also, while abroad, performed a great service for the University of Michigan in superintending the selection of works for the nucleus of its library; and the University showed its appreciation of his judgment and of the benefit to the institution, by honoring him and itself at its semi-centennial celebration the past summer by conferring on him the degree of Doctor of Laws.

Again at home, and now well equipped for conquering difficulties about American species, he went at the Flora with new vigor. The first volume was completed by Torrey and Gray in 1840 and the second in February, 1843. In the interval between these dates, during the summer of 1841, Gray spent five to six weeks in a botanical excursion through the valley of Virginia to the summits of the high mountains of North Carolina. A letter about the trip, addressed to Sir William J. Hooker, published in this Journal in 1842, first gives an account of the excursions into these regions by his predecessors, Bartram, Michaux, and

---

* From a sketch of Dr. Gray by Prof. C. S. Sargent.

John Fraser, of the last century, and John Lyon, Michaux the younger, Pursh, Nuttall, Curtis, and others, of this, mentioning their discoveries, with critical remarks on the species they observed and on their distribution; and then he describes his own journey, adding notes on the plants met with by the way and in the mountains, commencing his observations at Harper's Ferry. His journey among the North Carolina mountains included the ascent of the "Grandfather," 5,897 feet in elevation, and the Roan Mountain, 6,306 feet. This is one among a number of such excursions.

Another labor of this period was the revision of his "Elements of Botany," which, without much change of general method, he made a far more comprehensive and thorough treatise, and in 1842 issued under the title of the "Botanical Text-book." Since then successive editions have appeared with large advances, as the science required. By the fifth edition, that of 1879, the subject had so expanded that it was divided, and the work made to include only Structural Botany, covering Morphology, Taxonomy and Phytography, leaving Physiological and Cryptogamic botany to other hands. The second volume, an exposition of Physiological Botany, appeared in 1885 from the pen of his colleague, Prof. G. L. Goodale. A third volume on Cryptogamic Botany is promised by another colleague, Prof. W. G. Farlow.

Gray never entered on duty at the Michigan University, it being impossible for him to carry on his publications so far away from the New York herbaria and botanical libraries. In 1842 he was invited by the Fellows of Harvard College to the Fisher Professorship of Natural History, recently founded on a bequest by Dr. Joshua Fisher. The duties of the professorship included the delivery of a course of lectures on botany, and the direction of a small botanic garden which had been established in Cambridge in 1805, under the auspices and with the assistance of the Massachusetts Society for promoting Agriculture. Thomas Nuttall had charge of the garden from 1822 to 1828, and after that it was without a head until the appointment of Dr. Gray. The garden was still poor in funds, and had not even a herbarium to aid Gray in his botanical studies. But he entered on the duties with zeal, conducted the required lectures in the most lucid and attractive manner, freely gave the use of his study to such students as wished to learn more of the science than they could acquire from the lectures, and gathered a vast herbarium. And all the time he carried on an enormous correspondence with promptness, and answered all social demands with unfailing courtesy, besides continuing his botanical investigations and writing books and memoirs. These duties continued until 1872, when he was relieved from that of teaching and the charge of the garden. In 1864 he made the offer to Harvard College of the herbarium and library which he had gathered, already very large, on condition of their erecting a fire-proof building to contain them, which was accepted.

Botanical work was always in progress in some form. One of the very valuable parts of it consisted in his contributions to the American Journal of Science,—which were continued, with scarcely any interruption, for the love of the science and of the men engaged in it. Every important work as it was issued was here noticed, with often critical remarks, or additional facts and illustrations, or modifications of opinions, that gave them great scientific value. And not the least instructive and attractive part were the biographical sketches of deceased botanists, European as well as American; for to him the world was all one, and all botanists were akin. He was sure to criticise what he believed to be wrong; but it was done so fairly, with so evident a desire for scientific accuracy, and in so kind a spirit, that offense was rarely given. A botanist of eminence says that "these notices form the best history of the botanical literature of the last fifty years, and of the progress and development of botanical science, that has been written."

The fortieth volume of this Journal (1841) contains an admirable example of his kindly method of reviewing an author that had faults, and of his critical study among great difficulties. It is a review of the botanical writings of Rafinesque, that enthusiastic naturalist, poet, etc., with reference, not to his faults, but to the value to be attached to his numerous genera and species and their recognition in American Botany. Throughout there is a full appreciation of Rafinesque's sagacity in many of his discriminations, a fair presentation of his scientific claims, of his love of nature and greater love of self, without a harsh word for his errors or egotism; and only a citing of a sentence here and there, or a fact, that enables Rafinesque to make his own presentations as to his species and genera, with a bare mention of his "twelve new species of thunder and lightning."

The publication of the second volume of the " Flora," in 1843, ended that work. The territory of the United States afterward took larger dimensions, and new fields were to be explored before a complete "Flora" could be published. Torrey was engaged on these studies until his death in 1873; and Gray also was publishing memoirs that were contributions to the subject. Gray's various memoirs include— descriptions of the collections made by Lindheimer, in western Texas (1843-'48); by Fendler, in New Mexico (1846-'47); by Wright, near the boundary of Texas and Mexico (1849 and 1851-'52); by Thurber, along the United States and Mexican boundary (1851-'52); the Botany of various Government surveys, and other Government reports, and a portion of the Botany of California. Other papers are distributed through the publications of learned societies, especially the American Academy of Arts and Sciences of Boston, which contains hundreds of pages of them, the Proceedings of the Philadelphia and California Academies, the Boston Society of Natural History, the Linnean Society of London, etc.

Further, the plants of the Wilkes Exploring Expedition, exclusive of the ferns and those from western North America, were early sent to him for description; and in 1854 appeared his Report, in quarto, accompanied by a folio atlas, containing a hundred plates.

Gray was three times over the Rocky Mountain region to the Pacific coast. On the second trip he was accompanied by Sir Joseph Hooker; and an important paper on the "Vegetation of the Rocky Mountain Region" by them is published in the Reports of the Hayden Geological Survey for 1878. He was in Europe again in the years 1850–'51. A note from Mrs. Gray says, "He went abroad especially for the plants of the Wilkes Expedition. After traveling in Switzerland (going up the Rhine to Geneva, where he worked awhile in DeCandolle's herbarium), we went to Munich and saw Martius, and then back to England by Holland. On the first of October we went into Herefordshire to the country place of George Bentham, and spent two months there, Mr. Bentham going over with Dr. Gray the collection which had been sent out from America, a most generous piece of work." It was at this time, while at the Kew Gardens, near London, that he had the passing introduction to Darwin, alluded to in Darwin's first letter to him.*

In 1868 he crossed the ocean the fourth time, going in September and returning in November of the following year. He was hard at work over herbaria at Kew during both autumns, and worked also in Paris, Munich, Geneva, and elsewhere, but with more holiday than in any journey he took, except the last. In this visit he was twice with Darwin, first in the autumn of 1868, and then in October, 1869.

After forty years of studying and discriminating among the older species of the continent and their representatives abroad, and of describing species from late discoveries, and of work at classification, with experimental work at Flora-making during the years 1838 to 1843, he was finally ready, in 1878, with the first part of a new North American "Flora," to which he gave the name of "Synoptical Flora of North America." This first part contained the Gamopetalæ after the Compositæ. A second part was published in 1884, comprising the Caprifoliaceæ to the Compositæ inclusive, or the ground of the second volume of Torrey and Gray's Flora; so that the middle half of the entire Flora is now completed. The two parts cover 974 closely printed pages. "They are masterpieces of clear and concise arrangement, and of compactness and beauty of method, and display great learning and analytical power." The progress of the science since the time of Michaux is well exhibited in the fact that while this author knew 193 species of Compositæ when he published his Flora, Gray, seventy-five years later, describes no less than 1,636 species under 239 genera.

During these years Dr. Gray added to the resources of the instructor in Botany by the publication of his "Manual," a descriptive work including all species growing east of the Mississippi and north of Tennessee and North Carolina. It was first issued in 1848, and its fifth and last edition in 1868. The "Elementary Lessons in Botany and Vege-

---

*Darwin's Life and Letters, p. 420.

table Physiology," also, was published first in 1868, as an accompaniment to the Manual, and has had its five editions at nearly the same dates. The first volume of another companion work to the Manual was issued in 1848,—his " Genera Illustrata," containing descriptions of the genera of the United States Flora, with illustrations of great beauty by I. Sprague; and in 1849 a second volume was published, carrying the works nearly to the Leguminosæ; and here it stopped, on account mainly of the expense. His " Field, Forest, and Garden Botany," a useful flora for schools, came out in 1868; and the charming smaller volumes, " How Plants Grow " and " How Plants Behave," respectively in 1858 and 1875. The latter was prompted by Darwin's works on Insectivorous Plants, the Orchids, and Dimorphism, and both are well adapted to the young student and all uninitiated readers.

Besides the subjects of Gray's investigations already mentioned, two others of a wider philosophical character interested him deeply : one, in which he was pioneer, the other, the Origin of Species, after Darwin.

The first of these subjects was the Geographical Distribution of Plants. and particularly the species of the northern United States both within and beyond the bounds of the continent, and the bearings of the facts on variation and origin.

His first paper on the subject is contained in volumes XXII and XXIII of the American Journal of Science, the numbers for September, 1856, and January and May, 1857. It was written partly in compliance with the request of " an esteemed correspondent" for a list of American alpine plants, who, as now appears, was Darwin. Darwin's Life contains, on page 420, the letter, and shows that its date was April 25, 1855; and, also, a second letter of June 8, 1855, which opens thus: " I thank you cordially for your remarkably kind letter of the 22d ult., and for the extremely pleasant and obliging manner in which you have taken my rather troublesome questions. I can hardly tell you how much your list of alpine plants has interested me." And then Darwin puts more questions to his genial correspondent.   \

The long paper, modestly entitled " Statistics of the Flora of the United States," contains numerous tables, comparing as regards plants the northern United States with Europe on one side, and Asia and Japan on the other; the eastern part of the country with the western, and with the adjoining continents in the north temperate zone; the plants of alpine and subalpine regions in the northern United States, and their distribution southward and eastward and westward over the other continents; the distribution of species common to this country and Europe, as to size of orders and genera; also, as regards related and representative species, and the same for eastern and western America; lists of species of widely sundered habitation; with numerous other points, and abundant explanatory remarks; making thus a thorough philosophical digest of the subject of geographical distribution, having all the completeness as respects the northern United

States that the existing state of the science admitted of. He closes with a general review of the characteristics of the North American flora.

In the course of the pages, he advocates the idea of a single area of origin for a species, with dispersion at an epoch more or less ancient, to account for distribution; sustains Darwin's "surmise" as to the species of large genera having a greater geographical area than those of small genera; observes that a large per-centage of the extra European types of eastern America are shared with eastern Asia, and finds "that, curiously enough, eleven, or one-third, of our strictly alpine species common to Europe—all but one of them arctic in the Old World—are not known to cross the Arctic circle on this continent; so that it seems almost certain that the interchange of alpine species between us and Europe must have taken place in the direction of Newfoundland, Labrador, and Greenland, rather than through the polar regions" (XXIII, 73).

Two years later, in 1859, Dr. Gray had studied a collection of plants from Japan (alluded to in the former paper, XXIII, 369, as in hand), which had been collected by Mr. Charles Wright; and his memoir on the subject, read that year before the American Academy of Arts and Sciences, closes with a sequel to the subject of Geographical Distribution, bringing out conclusions of still higher interest. He starts off with the then new announcement and its evidence, that among the plants of Japan, more species are represented in Europe than over the nearer land, western North America; more in eastern North America than in either of the other two regions; and adds, that hence, there has been a peculiar intermingling of the eastern American and eastern Asia floras, which demands explanation. The explanation he finds in the idea of migrations to and from the arctic regions, determined in part, at least, by the climate of the preglacial, glacial, and postglacial eras, and that the alpine plants of the summits of the White Mountains, Adirondacks, Black Mountains, and Alleghanies are species left by the retreating glacier.

Dr. Gray returned to this subject in his presidential address, in 1872, before the American Association for the Advancement of Science,[*] and, owing to the progress that had been made in the paleontology of the continent, the arctic portion as well as the more southern, and developments elsewhere also, he was enabled to trace out the courses of the migrations of plants, the Sequoias or Redwoods and many other kinds, by positive facts with regard to the arctic and more southern floras; and showed that the distribution southward into the western United States, into eastern Europe or western Eurasia, and into Japan and Asia or eastern Eurasia, was not only dependent, as he had before put forth, on change in continental climates, but also that the particular direction southward was determined to a large extent by fitness of

---

*Am. Journal of Science, 1872 (3), IV, 282.

climate as to heat and dryness. The surprising revelations are now so generally known that this brief reference to them is all that is here needed.

Gray's comprehensive knowledge of the plants of the world, of their distribution, and specifically of the relations of North American species, genera, and orders to those of the other continents, and the precision of his knowledge, enabled him to be of much service to Darwin in the preparation of the first edition of the Origin of Species, and afterward, also, in the elaboration of Darwin's other publications. His mind was not very strongly bound to opinions about species, partly because of his natural openness to facts, his conclusions seeming always to have only a reasonable prominence in his philosophical mind, rarely enough · to exclude the free entrance of the new, whatever the source, and to a considerable extent from the difficulties he had experienced in defining species and genera amidst the wide diversities and approximate blend· ings which variation had introduced.

Darwin, in a letter to Gray written during the following summer, having in view Gray's article in this journal, and another discussion of his—published in the proceedings of the American Academy, says, "I declare that you know my book as well as I do myself, and bring to the question new lines of illustration and argument in a manner which excites my astonishment and almost my envy." "As Hooker lately said in a note to me, you are, more than *any one* else, the thorough master of the subject."

Gray's "Darwiniana," published in 1876, is composed of a number of his essays and reviews, from the American Journal of Science, the "Nation" and the "Atlantic Monthly," together with a closing chapter, written for the volume, entitled "Evolutionary Teleology." The last chapter brings out Gray's adherence to the doctrine of natural selec- tion, and also his divergence from true Darwinism. These divergences are thus expressed:

"We are more and more convinced that variation, and therefore the ground of adaptation, is not a product of, but a response to, the action of the environment. Variations, in other words the differences between individual plants and animals, however originated, are evidently not from without, but from within; not physical, but physiological." And elsewhere he has said that the variation in a species is apt to take place in particular directions and make linear ranges of varieties, as often ex· emplified among plants; which accords with the preceding conclusion, pp. 386.

Again speaking of the forms of Orchids and their connection with, and relation to, insect fertilization, he says: "We really believe that these exquisite adaptations have come to pass in the course of nature, and under Natural Selection, but not that Natural Selection alone ex- plains or in a just sense originates them. Or. rather, if this term is to stand for sufficient cause and rational explanation, it must denote or include that inscrutable something which produces, as well as that which results in the survival of, 'the fittest,'" p. 388.

Neither of these doctrines is strictly Darwinian, though not at variance with Natural Selection. They take away what has often been urged against Darwinism: the idea that the environment under Natural Selection dominates in the determination of the direction of variation, and hence that evolution comes chiefly through external conditions; and substitutes the idea that the environment works under organic control through Natural Selection. One view implies that the environment influence is superior to organic law in the process; the other, that organic law is superior to the environment. Moreover, Gray's last sentence expresses the opinion that Darwin's Natural Selection can not produce the "survival of the fittest," though "survival of the fittest" is the *result* brought about. There is an "inscrutable something" that "produces." The writer would go a little farther and say that the "survival of the fittest," under "natural selection," is survival, not the production of "the fittest;" but this substitute I have reason to believe that Gray would not accept.

Further, Gray was a theistic Darwinian, as abundantly shown in his "Darwiniana," and alike also in his "Natural Science and Religion." Here is his creed in his own words, as published in the preface to the Darwiniana: "I am scientifically and in my own fashion a Darwinian, philosophically, a convinced theist, and religiously, an accepter of the 'creed commonly called the Nicene,' as the exponent of the Christian faith."

Gray's various literary or less scientific papers, contributions mostly to the "North American Review," "Nation," and the "Atlantic Monthly," always show the clear thinker, the graceful writer, and the well-stored head, whatever the topic; and when it is scientific, his method of popularizing and illustrating his views is of the most attractive kind. His last contribution to the "Nation" was a long characteristic notice of Darwin's Life and Letters, in November, showing no waning in his faculties; on the contrary, there is manifest the same clear-headed, judicial, and sprightly reviewer, as honest as ever in his opinions and in his modesty amid Darwin's profuse (he says effusive) commendations.

The last visit to Europe was made during the past year. He went with the intention of doing but little of his herbarium work, and finding pleasure among friends old and new. Mrs. Gray, as usual, was with him. It proved to be a triumphal time to the modest botanist, for he received the honor of doctorate from each of the great universities of Britain, that of Oxford, of Cambridge, and of Edinburgh. He returned in October in excellent spirits and health—an apparent promise of some years more of work. He was soon again occupied with his "Flora," the completion of which was the earnest desire of all botanists. Yet while wishing to see its last page himself, his anxiety about it had lessened in later years, because aware that his colleague in charge of the Herbarium, Dr. Sereno Watson—one of the students that he had gathered about him—was capable of taking up the lines whenever he should lay them down.

Gray's standing among philosophers abroad, is manifested in his recent reception in Great Britain. It is further shown in his having been elected an honorary member of all the principal academies or societies of science in Europe, including the Royal Society of London and the Institute of France. He was president of the Association for the Advancement of Science in the year 1871, and has been one of the Regents of the Smithsonian Institution since 1874; and for ten years, from 1863 to 1873, he was president of the American Academy of Arts and Sciences. In 1884 his portrait in bronze, made by St. Gaudens, was presented to Harvard College.

One of the most gratifying testimonials from his fellows in science was received on his seventy-fifth birthday. To his surprise there came greetings or notes of congratulations from every American botanist, old and young, and, along with the notes, a silver vase embossed with figures of the plants more particularly identified with his name or studies. It was delightful to witness, says one of his associates, his child-like pleasure as he received the gift. Among the letters were some from friends who were not botanists. The following lines were from Mr. Lowell:

> JUST FATE: prolong his life, well spent,
> Whose indefatigable hours
> Have been as gaily innocent
> And fragrant as his flowers.

The vase is about 11 inches high exclusive of the ebony pedestal. The pedestal is surrounded by a hoop of hammered silver on which is the inscription:

> 1810 November eighteenth 1885
> ASA GRAY
> In token of the universal esteem
> of American Botanists

Among the flowers, in raised figures about the vase, the place of honor on one side is held by *Grayia polygaloides*, and on the other by *Shortia galacifolia*. On the Grayia side, the prominent plants are *Aquilegia Canadensis, Centaurea Americana, Jeffersonia diphylla, Rudbeckia speciosa* and *Mitchella repens;* and on the Shortia side, there are *Lilium Grayi, Aster Bigelovii, Solidago serotina,* and *Epigœa repens.* The lower part of the handles runs into a cluster of Dionæa leaves, which clasps the body of the vase, and their upper part is covered with *Notholœna Grayi. Adlumia cirrhosa* trails over the whole back-ground, and here and there its leaves and flowers crop out. The greetings, in the form of cards and letters, that had been sent by the givers of the vase, were placed on a simple but elegant silver plate, which had within the engraved inscription: Bearing the greetings of one hundred and eighty botanists of North America to Asa Gray, on his seventy-fifth birthday, November 18th, 1885.*

Botanists have, as their common object of interest, that part of Nature which seems by its free gift of beauty and fragrance (without a trace of self, the dominating element in the animal) fully to reciprocate affection; and there is hence a reason for that feeling of fraternity which such a gift so beautifully expresses, independently of the tribute in it to the botanist of botanists. Plants seem thus to select from among inquiring minds those which are to be their investigators, or the botanists.

Darwin first mentioned to Gray his view that "species arise like varieties with *much* extinction," in a letter to Gray of July 20, 1856.†
At this time all men of science with a rare exception believed in the permanence of species. J. D. Hooker's Flora Indica of 1855 "assumes that species are *distinct* creations."‡ Professor Huxley, in his history of the reception of Darwinian ideas, says, with the perfect fairness that always has characterized him, that " within the ranks of the biologists, at that time [1851-'58], I met with nobody [and he here includes himself] except Dr. Grant, of University College, who had a word to say for evolution; and his advocacy was not calculated to advance the cause. Outside of these ranks, the only person known to me whose knowledge and capacity compelled respect, and who was, at the same time, a thorough-going evolutionist, was Herbert Spencer. - - - But even my friend's rare dialectic skill and copiousness of apt illustration could not drive me from my agnostic position." Lyell, he shows, was leaning that way, but not himself. So it was in 1857, and in 1858 up to the publication of Darwin's and Wallace's papers of that year.§

Gray therefore knew of Darwin's views before the biologists of Britain, unless we except Lyell and J. D. Hooker. Darwin acknowledged Gray's "remarkably kind letter" on the 5th of September, 1857,‖ and was prompted by his "extraordinary kindness," and evidently by his assurances, that he had no objections to facts from any source, had great interest in the subject, and only saw some " grave difficulties" against his doctrine, to explain to Dr. Gray with detail, under six heads, the prominent facts and arguments in the theory of " Natural Selection," which he says is the "title of his book." This letter is the first exposition that Darwin had made of his theory, and hence it has proved to have great documentary value.

A letter which the writer received from Gray in the interval between Darwin's two letters, dated December 13, 1856, shows well the state of his mind at that time. He says: " On the subject of species, their nature, distribution, what system in natural history is, etc., cer-

---

* This description of the vase is from the "Botanical Gazette" of December, 1885, which contains also good figures of the vase.

† Darwin's Life and Letters, p. 437.

‡ Gray's review, Am. Journal of Science, 1856, XXI, 135, January.

§ Darwin's Life and Letters, chapter xiv of vol. I, by Professor Huxley.

‖ *Ibid*, p. 477.

tain inferences are slowly settling themselves in my mind or taking shape; but on some of the most vexed questions, I have as yet no *opinion* whatever, and no very strong *bias*, thanks partly to the fact that I can think of and investigate such matters only now and then, and in a very desultory way." *

In a letter of a year later, subsequent in date to Darwin's letter, Gray wrote me with reference to my paper on " Species," read at the meeting of the American Association in August, 1857,—which paper may be taken, perhaps, as a culmination of the past, just as the new future was to make its appearance,—pointing out to me the fatal objection to my argument.

His words (dated November 7) are worth quoting: "Taking the *cue* of species, if I may so say, from the *inorganic*, you develop the subject to great advantage for your view, and all you say must have great weight in 'reasoning from the general.' But in reasoning from *inorganic species* to *organic species*, and in making it tell where you want it, and *for what* you want it to tell, you must be sure that you are using the word *species* in the same sense in the two; that the one is really the equivalent of the other. That is what I am not yet convinced of; and so to me the argument comes only with the force of an *analogy*, whereas I suppose you want it to come as demonstration. Very likely you could convince me that there is no fallacy in reasoning from the one to the other to the extent you do. But all my experience makes me cautious and slow about building too much on analogies, and until I see further and clearer I must continue to think there is an essential difference between *kinds of animals or plants* and *kinds of matter*.

"How far we may safely reason from the one to the other is the question. If we may do so even as far as you do, might not Agassiz (at least plausibly) say that as the *species Iron* was created in a vast number of individuals over the whole earth, so the presumption is that any given species of plants or animals was originated in as many individuals as there are now, and over as wide an area; the human species under as great diversities as it now has, barring historical intermixture; thus reducing the question between you to insignificance? because, then, the question whether men are of one or of several species would no longer be a question, or of much consequence. You may answer him from *another starting point*, no doubt; but he may still insist that it is a legitimate carrying out of your principle."

In the same letter Gray prophesies as follows, from actual knowledge, it now appears: "You may be sure that before long there must be one more resurrection of *the development theory* in a new form, obviating many of the arguments against it, and presenting a more respectable and more formidable appearance than it ever has before."

---

* Gray has some important observations on the bearing of hybridization on variation, in a review of Hooker's Flora Indica in the number of the Am. Journal of Science for January, 1856, XXI, 134.

The Origin of Species was out in November, 1859. Gray received an early copy of it from Darwin, and therefore his very valuable review was ready for the American Journal of Science early in 1860.*

With regard to the sufficiency of the argument brought forward in Darwin's work, Gray says that "To account upon these principles for the gradual elimination and segregation of nearly allied forms—such as varieties, sub-species and closely related or representative species,—and also for their geographical association and present range, is comparatively easy, is apparently within the bounds of possibility, and even of probability." But as to the formation of genera, families, orders, and classes by natural selection, Gray simply states Darwin's arguments on the subject, and some objections on a few weak points, without expressing further his own views. He concludes with some remarks on the religious bearing of a theory that refers creation to natural law and declares rightly, in accordance with his firm faith to the end, that "Natural law is the human conception of continued and orderly Divine action."

It is a case of natural selection. But Dr. Gray was more to botanists than a friend and leader. He was the "Beloved Gray"—the object of their admiration and devotion on account of his goodness, his high principle, his frank independence, his unfailing cordiality, and the clearness of his intellectual vision, like that of a seer. He stands before the world as a lofty example of the Christian philosopher.

Dr. Gray was married in 1848 to the daughter of the late eminent lawyer of Boston, Charles G. Loring. His excellent and accomplished wife, who survives him, was in full sympathy with him in all his pursuits and pleasures, a bright, cheerful and helpful companion, at home and in his travels abroad.

In a letter to the writer in 1886, Gray says :

- - - I have had a week in old Oneida, which still looks natural. I am grinding away at the Flora, and shall probably be found so doing when I am called for. Very well : I have a most comfortable and happy old age.

Wishing you the same, yours ever,

A. GRAY.

November last, the month after his return from Europe, he put aside his nearly completed revision of the "Vitaceæ, or Grape-vines of North America," to write his last words about Darwin in the review of Darwin's Life and Letters, and to prepare his usual annual Necrology for this Journal. The latter manuscript lay unfinished on his table when, on the 27th of the month, a paralytic stroke put an end to work, with every prospect then that his name also would have to be added to the

---

* It occupies 32 pages in the March number, vol. XXIX, pp. 153 to 184.

list of 1887.   He lingered until the 30th of January without a return at
any time of his powers of speech, and toward evening of that day
passed quietly away.

Asa Gray's remains lie buried in the Mount Auburn Cemetery.   American botanical science, wrought out so largely in its details, its system,
and its philosophical relations, by his labors, is his monument.

MEMOIR OF ASA GRAY.*

By Prof. WILLIAM G. FARLOW.

Asa Gray was born on November 18, 1810, in Sauquoit Valley in the township of Paris, Oneida County, New York, and died on January 30, 1888, at Cambridge, Massachusetts. On the paternal side he was descended from a Scotch-Irish family who emigrated to this country in the early part of the last century. His grandfather, Moses Wiley Gray, was born at Worcester, Massachusetts, December 31, 1745, and was married in 1769 to Sallie Miller. He went in 1787 to Vermont, where his wife soon afterwards died; and when their son Moses, the father of Asa Gray, was eight years old, the father and son moved still farther west, to Sauquoit Valley, then almost a frontier settlement. Sixteen years later, Moses Gray was married to Roxana Howard, a daughter of Joseph Howard, of English descent, who, leaving his home in Massachusetts, had settled in Sauquoit Valley the same year as the Gray family. Of their family of eight children, five sons and three daughters, Asa was the first-born.

When a boy he assisted his father in the smaller duties connected with his farm and tannery; but at an early age he showed a much greater fondness for reading than for farm work, and the father soon came to the conclusion that his son would make a better scholar than farmer. Until he was about twelve years old the only education he received was what could be obtained for a part of the year in the small district school, and in the small private school at Sauquoit taught by the son of the parish pastor. He was then sent to the grammar school at Clinton, New York, where he remained for two years; and when, in the autumn of 1825, his teacher, Mr. Charles Avery, accepted a place in Fairfield Academy, young Gray followed his instructor to that place, where for four years he pursued elementary mathematical and classical studies. Connected with the Fairfield Academy was a medical school which enjoyed a high reputation, and was attended by two hundred students, a large number for that time. Dr. James Hadley, the professor of Materia Medica and Chemistry in the Medical School, also gave some in-

*Memorial address before the American Academy of Arts and Sciences; June 13, 1888.

struction in the academy, and it was probably through his influence that Gray's attention was first strongly drawn towards natural science. Apparently, he was not at first so much interested in plants as in minerals; and it was not until towards the close of his course in the academy that his passion for plants was aroused by reading the article on botany in the Edinburgh Encyclopedia, and his delight the following spring at being able to make out with the aid of Eaton's Manual the scientific name of the common *Claytonia* is now a well known story.

Following his father's wish, which probably was in accord with his own inclination, he decided to study medicine, and formally entered the Fairfield Medical School in 1829, although for two years previously, while a student in the academy, he had attended some of the medical lectures. The sessions of the medical school, like those of the academy, hardly occupied more than six months of the year, and the remainder of the time was spent in study with different physicians in the neighborhood of Sauquoit, one of whom, Dr. John F. Trowbridge, of Bridgewater, was a man of good scientific attainments. He was thus in an excellent position for collecting, and even before he graduated he had brought together a considerable herbarium, and had entered into correspondence with Dr. Lewis C. Beck, of Albany, and Dr. John Torrey, of New York, who aided him in the determination of his plants. He received his doctor's degree at Fairfield on February 1, 1831. He never, however, entered upon the practice of medicine; but after receiving his degree he became instructor in chemistry, mineralogy, and botany in Bartlett's High School at Utica, New York, and taught those subjects, for a part of the year, from the autumn of 1831 to 1835.

The first actual record of any public lectures on botany given by him is found in a circular of the Fairfield Medical School, dated January, 1832, in which the following statement is made: "Asa Gray, M. D., will give a course of lectures and practical illustrations on botany, to commence [in June] and continue the same time with the lectures on chemistry [six weeks]. Fee, $4." This course was attended apparently by ten persons; for he states that he spent the $40 earned from these lectures in making a botanical excursion to Niagara Falls. It appears to be the case however that in the previous year, just after graduation, he had given a few lectures on botany in the medical school, in the absence of the regular instructor, Dr. Beck; and a little later, he gave another course of lectures on mineralogy and botany at Hamilton College, Clinton. During other intermissions of his work at Bartlett's school, he made mineralogical and botanical excursions to different parts of New York and New Jersey; and it was while living at Utica that he published in the American Journal of Science of October, 1833, his first scientific paper on new mineral localities in northern New York, written in connection with Dr. J. B. Crawe.

In the autumn of 1833, having leave of absence from Bartlett's School, he accepted the position of assistant to Prof. John Torrey, in the chemical laboratory of the Medical School of New York. His time was here mainly occupied in botanical studies; and, besides aiding Dr. Torrey in his botanical work, he prepared and published several original papers of his own, of which his memoir on *Rhynchospora* may be said to be his first contribution to descriptive botany. His connection with Bartlett's School ended early in 1835, and, although the financial condition of the New York Medical School did not permit his continuing as assistant of Dr. Torrey, he returned to New York in the autumn of 1835, and accepted the position of curator and librarian of the Lyceum of Natural History, a position which gave him leisure for continuing his botanical studies, and to prepare his first text-book, "Elements of Botany," which appeared in 1836.

About this time a Government expedition, since known as the Wilkes Exploring Expedition, was fitting out, and the position of botanist of the expedition was offered to Dr. Gray in the summer of 1836. The expedition did not sail, however, until two years later; and meanwhile, wearied by the numerous delays and uncertainties about the management of the expedition, Dr. Gray resigned his position and settled in New York, where, in company with Dr. Torrey, he worked energetically on the preparation of the earlier parts of the "Flora," of which the first two parts appeared in October, 1838. While occupied in this work, a new State University had been founded in Michigan, and Dr. Gray accepted the chair of botany which was offered to him, with the understanding that he should be allowed to spend a year abroad in study before beginning his official duties.

The elaboration of the new "Flora" made it necessary for him to examine the types of American plants in foreign herbaria; and in November, 1838, he started on the journey which was not only to give him the means of clearing up much of the existing confusion with regard to the identity of previously described North American species, but, what was more important, was to bring him into close scientific and social relations with the botanical lights of a generation now long past, and with those who were then the young men of promise, a brilliant group, of which Sir J. D. Hooker and A. De Candolle are now almost the only survivors.

He returned to America in November, 1839, but never assumed the duties of professor at Michigan. He was absorbed in his work on the "Flora," and refreshed and stimulated by what he had seen and heard abroad, he was pushing rapidly ahead with the second volume, of which he wrote the greater portion, and at the same time printing a "Botanical Text-Book," which was to form the basis of his many subsequent text-books, when he was invited to Cambridge to fill the newly endowed chair of the Fisher Professorship of Natural History in Harvard College.

He accepted, and in 1842 took up his residence in Cambridge. The second volume of the "Flora" was completed the following year. He was at once favorably received in learned and social circles of Cambridge and Boston; and when delivering a course of lectures at the Lowell Institute, he first became acquainted with Miss Jane Lathrop Loring, daughter of Mr. Charles Greely Loring of Boston, to whom he was married on May 4, 1848. From this time his energies were devoted to building up a botanical establishment at Cambridge—for what was in existence before 1842 hardly deserves mention—and to the completion of a "Flora of North America." The number of collectors and explorers had by this time greatly increased, and the material they had brought together contained so much that was new, that it was plain that the original plan of the "Flora" must be changed, for the two volumes already published had hardly appeared when a revision seemed necessary. It was not until many years later, in 1878, that the first part of the new "Flora" appeared; and he continued to labor toward the completion of his great work until death forced him to relinquish the unfinished task.

He continued in the exercise of the active duties of lecturer and instructor until 1872, when he was relieved of this charge by the appointment of a colleague, Prof. G. L. Goodale; but he gave occasional lectures in the college for a few years longer. In 1873 he resigned his office of Director of the Botanic Garden, and Prof. C. S. Sargent was appointed his successor. He retained the title of Fisher Professor and Director of the Herbarium until his death, although he was in part relieved of the responsibilities of the latter position by the appointment of Mr. Sereno Watson as Curator of the Herbarium in 1874.

His long residence and arduous labors at Cambridge were varied and relieved by several journeys, some of which were of considerable extent, and all of which were made to contribute to the advancement of work on the "Flora," either by enabling him to examine in the field the plants which he was studying, or by examination of foreign herbaria, and consultations with leading foreign botanists. He made three trips to California, in 1872, in 1877, when he was in company with Sir J. D. Hooker, and in 1885, when he visited not only southern California and the great Colorado Cañon, but journeyed into Mexico as far as Orizaba and Cordoba. He was once in Florida, in 1875, and made, besides, several trips to the mountains of North Carolina, where he botanized at different times with his botanical friends, Sullivan, Carey, Engelmann, Canby, and Redfield.

He made in all six journeys to Europe, including the journey already mentioned and a short business trip of six weeks to Paris in the summer of 1855. On the other journeys he was accompanied by Mrs. Gray. When abroad, he always spent much of his time with the English botanists, among whom he counted many warm personal friends; and he looked forward with special pleasure to his visits at Kew, where he was welcomed by the director, Sir W. J. Hooker, and by his son and successor, Sir J. D. Hooker, for forty years his intimate friend, whose opinion in botanical matters he esteemed more highly than that of any of his contemporaries. In his second journey, from June, 1850, to August, 1851, he traveled through France, Germany, and Holland, and spent two months with Bentham at his home in Herefordshire, studying the plants of the Wilkes Expedition, upon which he was then working. The fourth journey, from September, 1868, to November, 1869, was undertaken at a time when he was much overworked, and he spent the winter in Egypt, that country being almost the only spot where there was nothing to tempt him to botanize, besides visiting Italy, France, Germany, and England. The event of the journey of September, 1880, to November, 1881, was a trip to Spain, a country where he obtained much relief from Botany.

His last journey, on which he started in 1887, was a triumphant farewell, in which were heaped upon him honors bestowed on few naturalists. He visited friends in France, Austria, and Germany; stopped at Geneva to see De Candolle, his life-long friend, older by four years than himself, and sorrowfully bade him what both must have felt to be a last farewell; then hurried back from the continent to receive the doctor's degree from the three great British Universities, and to attend the meeting of the British Association at Manchester. Here he saw many old friends, and met for the first time three of Germany's most distinguished botanists—Cohn, Pringsheim, and the lamented De Bary, whose untimely death was to come but a few days before his own. At Manchester he was brought into contact with a large number of young botanists, who were charmed with his genial manner, and astonished at his well preserved vigor of body, as well as mind. He returned to America in October, apparently in perfect health, and resumed active labor on the "Flora;" but while busied with the preparation of the *Vitaceæ* for that work, he was suddenly stricken with paralysis, on the morning of November 28, and lingered in a partially conscious condition until the evening of January 30, when he passed calmly away.

By the death of Asa Gray this academy has lost a member whose activity and zeal were unceasing, and whose brilliant talents as a scientific writer, not surpassed by those of any of the illustrious names on our roll, added much to the reputation of the society at home and abroad. Elected a corresponding member in 1841, he became an active member in 1842, on his settlement in Cambridge, and served as corresponding secretary from 1844 to 1850, and again from 1852 to 1863, and as president from 1863 to 1873. During this long membership of more than forty years his attendance was always exemplary. The storms of winter and the inclemencies of spring, which kept younger men at home, did not prevent his coming from the remote Botanic Garden regularly to attend the meetings. Although an honorary member of most of the learned societies of this country, and of many of the most prominent societies of Europe, including the Royal Society of London, the French Academy, and the Imperial Academy of St. Petersburg, of which he was one of the very few Americans who have been elected corresponding members, this Academy was the society in which he felt the greatest interest and was most at home.

There are few volumes of our Proceedings which do not contain important communications from his pen. One of the earliest of his works, the "Chloris Boreali-Americana," was printed in the third volume of the Academy's Memoirs, in 1846; and to subsequent volumes he contributed "Plantæ Fendlerianæ Novi-Mexicanæ," presented in November, 1848; "Plantæ Novæ Thurberianæ," and "Note on the Affinities of the Genus *Vavæa*, Benth., also of *Rhytidandra*, Gray," August and October, 1854; and a group of four papers, entitled "Botanical Memoirs," in 1859, including one "On the Botany of Japan, and its Relations to that of North America"—a remarkable essay on the geographical distribution of plants, which stamped the author as worthy to rank with the great botanists of the world. We need not enumerate his many papers which have appeared in the Proceedings of the Academy, for they alone would fill several volumes. It was his custom to embody the results of his preliminary studies on the North American flora in the form of notes on critical species, descriptions of novelties, and monographs of genera, and sometimes orders, of which by far the greater part first appeared in our Proceedings, usually under the heading of "Botanical Contributions," a long and very valuable series, dating from the paper "On some New *Compositæ* from Texas," presented December 1, 1846, and ending with the posthumous "Notes upon some Polypetalous Genera and Orders," presented April 19, 1888. Nor should we forget the many biographical notices in which he commemorated the lives and works of others with an appreciating discrimination, written in a manner peculiarly his own.

The botanical department of Harvard University was practically created by Asa Gray. In 1805 a small botanic garden was established at Cambridge, under the auspices and by the aid of the Massachusetts Society for Promoting Agriculture, and William Dandridge Peck was appointed director and professor of botany. In 1818 he printed a "Catalogue of American and Foreign Plants cultivated in the Botanic Garden, Cambridge," in which one thousand three hundred and nine species were enumerated; but the list included some common cryptogams found everywhere, and a large number of phænogamic shrubs and weeds, common natives of the region, hardly to be counted as legitimate members of a botanic garden. Professor Peck died in 1822, when, owing to the low state of the funds, a professor was not appointed, but Thomas Nuttall, the well-known botanist and ornithologist, was appointed curator of the garden, and later, lecturer on botany. This amiable, but very reticent naturalist—who apparently did not find his residence in Cambridge very congenial (for he describes himself as vegetating like his plants),—resigned his position in 1833, and returned to Philadelphia. The garden, such as it was, was then put under the charge of William Carter, a gardener, and the lectures on botany were given by T. W. Harris, the well-known entomologist and librarian of the college, and Dr. A. A. Gould, of Boston. Not long before 1842, the directorship of the garden was offered to Mr. George B. Emerson, of Boston, who declined the position soon afterwards accepted by Dr. Gray in connection with the Fisher professorship.

On Dr. Gray's accession there was no herbarium, no library, only one insignificant greenhouse, and a garden all in confusion, with few plants of value. In 1844 he moved into the house which had been built for Professor Peck in the Garden, and with his characteristic energy he soon brought together an herbarium and library, and arranged the Garden systematically. At the time of his marriage a small wing was added to the house, of which the lower story served as a study and herbarium until 1864. But the plants soon overran the limits of the herbarium, and finally the whole house was crammed with plants—plants in the dining-room, in the attic, in the closets, and in the bedrooms; for whatever he could spare from a salary of $1,000 at first, and $1,600 afterwards, was spent on his herbarium and library. In 1864, dreading the danger from fire to a collection kept in a wooden house, he offered to present his collections to the college, on condition that a suitable building should be erected for their reception. Through the liberality of Mr. Nathaniel Thayer of Boston, a brick building to be used as an herbarium and library was erected in 1864, at a cost of $12,000; and mainly through the agency of Mr. G. B. Emerson, a further sum of $10,000 was raised, the income of which was to be used in defraying the current expenses of the herbarium. From a letter by Dr. Gray to the president of the university, dated November 20, 1864, and a notice in the American Journal of Science, of March, 1865, we learn that the herbarium then contained at least 200,000 specimens, and the library about 2,200 botanical works, not including a good many pamphlets. There was also a set of 335 very costly illustrated works, contributed by Mr. John A. Lowell.

Since 1864 the herbarium has been constantly enlarged, principally by exchanges, of which those from the Kew Herbarium especially were of very great value; so that it is now probably twice as large as in 1864, and forms practically a National Herbarium, for it is by far the largest and most valuable herbarium in America, and is excelled in size by but few of the older and richer herbaria of Europe, as those at Kew, Paris, Berlin, the De Candolle Herbarium at Geneva, and possibly that at St. Petersburg. In the representation of the phænogams of North America outside the tropics, it is probably unequalled by any herbarium except that at Kew. The library at the time of Professor's Gray's death was roughly estimated to contain something over 5,000 volumes and 3,000 pamphlets, but these figures are probably too low. Many of the additions since 1864 are the gift of Dr. Gray. In building up this vast collection, he gave not only much of his time and thought, but also an actual sum of money, which comes well up in the thousands, and, to crown all, manifested his devotion to the welfare and perpetuation of the collection by bequeathing to the university for its support the royalties on his publications.

The Garden during his administration was improved by the addition of several greenhouses, in which were cultivated a choice selection of exotics, and the rather limited space of the Garden itself was filled with good representatives of the flora of the temperate regions, the collection of *compositæ* being especially important. In the absence of a sufficient endowment, activity on the part of the director had to replace the want of money, and he, utilizing the means at hand, succeeded in making the Garden an exceedingly important means of exchange between foreign establishments and our own botanists and collectors. European botanists who visited the Garden wondered how, from such a small and ill-endowed establishment, so much had been done in aid of other institutions. The explanation lay in the skill and energy of Dr. Gray himself.

Gray's work as a teacher extended over a period of more than fifty years, dating from the first lectures on botany at the Fairfield Medical School, in 1831 and 1832, and the publication of his "Elements of Botany," in 1836. During that period he trained up a whole race of botanists, now scattered through all parts of the United States, so that wherever he went he was greeted by those who rembered his instruction with pleasure. When at Santa Barbara in 1885, an elderly man, who seemed to be about his own age, introduced himself as a former pupil in his first class at Harvard. As a college lecturer he was not seen at his best, for his somewhat hesitating manner when he spoke extemporaneously was unfavorably contrasted with the fervid, almost impetuous utterance of Agassiz, and the clear exposition and dignified address of Jeffries Wyman, his two great contemporaries at Harvard. In his public addresses he always spoke from notes, and, especially in his later years, his strikingly expressive face commanded the attention of his hearers from the start. In the class-room he was personally much liked, and he made a strong impression on the majority of students, although, in the days when every student was forced to study botany, there were of course some who would not have cared for the subject under any circumstances. The instruction, as was natural, bearing in mind his own early training and the state of botany in this country at the time when he became professor at Harvard, was confined mainly to the morphological study of flowering plants; for he recognized that, until some advance had been made in that direction, it was out of the question dealing adequately with the more technically complicated subjects of histology, embryology, and physiology.

For the instruction which he was obliged to give, the resources of the garden and the herbarium and the ordinary college lecture-rooms at first sufficed, but at last it became necessary to provide a special laboratory and lecture-room at the garden. A liberal friend of Dr. Gray and the college presented a sum of money for this purpose, and in 1872 a wing was added to the herbarium. About this time the demand for laboratory instruction and equipment increased rapidly, and the new lecture-room and laboratory were soon found to be inadequate to meet the needs of the increasing calls for microscopic and physiological work, and they were at length abandoned. It is not surprising that Dr. Gray could not foresee how great the growth in this direction was to be even in his own life. Probably no person of his age could have foreseen it.

His herbarium was, at one period or another, the resort of nearly all the active working botanists of the country, and thither came many young men who were afterwards to aid in the development of botanical studies in the United States. His intercourse with them was always free and unrestrained by formalities of any kind, and he seemed more like a learned friend than a teacher. Passing to and fro from his own study to the herbarium he greeted all cordially, watching and criticising sharply but good-naturedly the work that was going on. No one enjoyed a hearty laugh more than he, and every now and then he would brighten the work by some anecdote from the large stock which his retentive memory ever had at hand ; always however for the purpose of emphasizing some point or illustrating some fact which he wished to bring out more clearly, but never allowing the attention of those about him to be distracted from their work. Life at the herbarium was indeed a pleasure, and the more serious work was well seasoned and spiced in the days when the agile assistant, Charles Wright, skipped about like a squirrel, his diminutive body in Cambridge, his larger mind wandering away in his beloved Cuba and the Pacific islands,—when Brewer, less continent than his teacher in the matter of anecdote, saw in every plant before him some episode of his own life in camp. The approach of Dr. Gray, heralded by his cheery laugh, or perhaps by a mild anathema against the gardener, who every morning, regardless of the intentions of nature, deluged the cacti placed in the corridor, we all understood to mean business, for, if joking was allowed, trifling was not. We learned something about botanists as well as about botany, and often wondered whether Robert Brown were really as great as he was represented ; and, on the rare occasions of a visit from a man like Dr. Torrey or Dr. Engelmann, we asked ourselves whether there was any chance that the younger generation of botanists would bear any comparison with the older. None who have worked under Dr. Gray at the herbarium will forget the deep personal interest he always manifested in their work and future prospects. He always encouraged and stimulated without holding out false hopes. To those who wished to devote themselves to botany in the years still recent, when it was scarcely possible for a botanist to live by botany alone, he used to say : " Study medicine, and if you then still want to be a botanist, go ahead. Your medicine will keep your botany from starving."

Great as was the direct influence of Dr. Gray upon the students with whom he came in contact, his influence on the development of botany in this country through the medium of his numerous text-books and manuals was even more important. His first text-book, "Elements of Botany," written when he was only twenty-six years old, shows many of the best characteristics of his later works, being written in a smooth, graceful style, with the different topics clearly and methodically arranged. The vigorous defense of the natural system of classification, which now appears superfluous, indicates that the author of 1836 was a progressive young man, who had shaken off the conservatism which prevailed among American botanists of that period. That he was young and inexperienced is occasionally shown, as in the amusing statement that "the herbarium of a diligent botanist will pass so frequently under his observation that any very extensive ravages [by insects] can hardly take place without his being aware of it in time to check the progress of the destroyers." He evidently had no conception of how large his own collection would become in a few years.

The "Elements" of 1836 developed into the "Botanical Text-Book" of 1842, in which the portion relating to systematic botany was much more fully treated than in the earlier volume. The latter editions, which appeared at intervals until 1879, are familiar to every one, for they have been the means of opening the world of botany to more than one generation of American botanists. In 1868 the "Lehrbuch der Botanik," by Sachs, appeared. That work was a genuine revelation, showing the advance which had been made by experts in the science of botany, and, although somewhat above the capacity of the common student, it was destined to produce in a few years a revolution in the method of botanical instruction.

Recognizing the new era which had opened in botany, Dr. Gray revised the plan of the "Text-Book," with a view of bringing it into accord with the more widely developed science of the day, and in 1879 issued the first volume of the revised work, in which he included the Morphology of Phænogams, Taxonomy, and Phytography, thus covering the greater part of the ground of the original "Text-Book," intrusting to his colleague, Professor Goodale, the volume on Physiological Botany, (which appeared in 1885—a worthy companion of its predecessor,) and to the writer the volume on Cryptogams. He hoped, but hardly could have expected, to write a fourth volume, on the Orders of Phænogamous Plants. It is deeply to be regretted that he was never able to write this volume, for it would have enabled him to present the general views on classification derived from a long and exceptionally rich experience. No better text-book on the subject had ever been written in the English language than Gray's "Text-Book" in the original form; and, although botanical instruction is now very different from what it used to be, it is still true that, as an introduction to the study of Phæ-nograms, the group to which beginners naturally turn their attention, the later "Structural Botany," is likely to hold its own for some time to come. In 1887, just before he started on his last European journey, he finished a small book giving in an abbreviated form the substance of the Structural Botany, as well as some chapters on Cryptogams; and for this, his latest text-book, he revived the title of his earliest work, "Elements of Botany. "

The "Manual of the Botany of the Northern United States, " of which the first edition appeared in 1847, needs no words of praise here. There are probably few members of the Academy who do not own, or have not at some time owned, a copy of this model work. Occasionally some overwise person has discovered that certain plants grow a few inches taller or bloom a few days earlier than is stated in the "Manual"; but the botanist is yet to be born who could write a more clear, accurate, and compact account of the flora of any country. The only regret is that he could not have written manuals for all parts of the country.

Dr. Gray had the rare faculty of being able to adapt himself to all classes of readers. With the scientific he was learned, to the student he was instructive and suggestive, and he charmed the general reader by the graceful beauty of his style, while to children he was simplicity itself. The little books, "How Plants Grow," and "How Plants Be-have," found their way where botany as botany could not have gained an entrance, and they set in motion a current which moved in the general direction of a higher science with a force which can hardly be estimated. His scientific friends, especially those abroad, sometimes blamed him for spending time in popular writing; but he may have understood himself and his surroundings better than they. With him botany was a pleasure as well as a business. Few wrote as easily as he, and, so long as he spent most of his time in higher work, he certainly had a right to amuse himself with writings of a popular character if he chose. As it was, he interested a multitude of readers in the subjects which he had at heart, and if he was not permitted to live to see the completion of his greatest work, "The Synoptical Flora," he at least was able to leave the work at a point where it could be continued by a trusted friend in sympathy with all his plans.

As a reviewer he was certainly extraordinary. Some of his reviews were in reality elaborate essays, in which, taking the work of another as a text, he presented his own views on important topics in a masterly manner. Others were technically critical, while some were simply concise and very clear summaries of lengthy works. Taken collectively, they show better than any other of his writings the literary excellence of his style, as well as his great fertility and his fairness and acuteness as a critic. Never unfair, never ill-natured, his sharp criticism, like the surgeon's knife, aimed not to wound, but to cure; and if he sometimes felt it his duty to be severe, he never failed to praise what was worthy. The number of his reviews and notices written during his connection with the American Journal of Science as editor and assistant editor for over thirty years, and for the North American Review, the Nation, the Atlantic Monthly, and numerous other journals, is enormous, and it almost seems as if he must have written notices of the greater part of all the botanical works he had ever read. Those intimately acquainted with him more than half believed that he was able to write good notices of books written in languages which he could not read. He was able, as if by instinct, to catch the spirit and essence of what he read, without any exertion on his part. One who wrote so much might have become monotonous. But he was never prosy, and his style was so easy and flowing, and so constantly enlivened by sprightly allusions and pleasing metaphors, that one could read what he wrote for the mere pleasure of the reading. His was one of the rare cases where Science had appropriated to herself one who would have been an ornament to any purely literary profession.

It would be presumption were we to express an opinion on the position of Gray as a scientific botanist. Fortunately for us, it is unnecessary. The greatest living systematic botanist, Sir J. D. Hooker, the one by his attainments and position fitted above all others to speak with authority on the subject, has already recorded his opinion in the following words:

When the history of the progress of botany during the nineteenth century shall be written, two names will hold high positions: those of Prof. Augustin Pyrame De Candolle and of Prof. Asa Gray. - - Each devoted half a century of unremitting labor to the investigation and description of the plants of continental areas, and they founded herbaria and libraries, each in his own country, which have become permanent and quasi-national institutions. - - - There is much in their lives and works that recalls the career of Linnæus, of whom they were worthy disciples, in the comprehensiveness of their labor, the excellence of their methods, their judicious conception of the limits of genera and species, the terseness and accuracy of their descriptions, and the clearness of their scientific language.

The accuracy of the resemblance of Gray and De Candolle, so admirably and justly expressed by Hooker, will be recognized by all botanists. Gray was the De Candolle of America, whose mission it was to bring together the scattered and crude works of the earlier explorers and botanists and the vast unwrought material of his own day, and to combine them with his surpassing skill into one grand comprehensive work which should fitly describe the flora of a continent. But while recognizing the resemblance between De Candolle and Gray in their mode of work and the purpose for which they strove, we can only marvel how it was possible for a poor farmer's boy in America, without a university education, to become the peer of one of Europe's best trained botanists.

From his training and early surroundings we might have expected him to be energetic and original, but we should not have expected to find him highly polished and cultured. His associates at Fairfield and Clinton were persons of scientific tastes, and, even if their attainments were not of the highest quality, they encouraged his fondness for natural history. But it is not easy to see how he obtained the literary training which enabled him to write with the ease and elegance found even in his earlier works, for although a man may by nature be a good observer of natural objects, a finished style comes only with training and experience. From his teacher, Avery, he could not have received much in the way of training; for Dr. Gray himself says that he did not give him the sharp drilling and testing which was needed. His residence with the Torrey family in New York first placed him in a society where literary excellence as well as scientific knowledge was prized ; and while he profited by the accuracy and strict scientific methods of Dr. Torrey, then the foremost American botanist, the frequent conversations and kindly criticism of Mrs. Torrey made good many of the literary deficiencies of his early training. He was also aided while in New York by the criticisms and suggestions made on some of his earlier manuscripts by the cultured botanist, Mr. John Carey. But he must have been an apt pupil, for, while still with Dr. Torrey, he showed that in point of clearness and accuracy he was not much inferior to his highly respected teacher, and in the second volume of the "Flora" he proved himself to be quite his equal.

The plan of the "Flora of North America" originated with Dr. Torrey; but when his pupil went to Cambridge to assume the duties of his new position, neither of them suspected the magnitude of the task which they had undertaken, nor the modifications which the plan must ultimately undergo. The pupil was now in a more fortunate position than his teacher, for Gray was henceforth able to devote himself to his favorite science, while Dr. Torrey could only employ his leisure hours in botany. The two volumes of the original Torrey and Gray "Flora" will always remain a memorial of the unbroken friendship of America's two greatest botanists, alike in the spirit which animated their work and in the reverent simplicity of their characters.

The greater part of Gray's scientific work during the thirty-five years following the completion of the second volume of Torrey and Gray's "Flora," in 1843, had a more or less direct bearing on the contemplated revision and enlargement of that work. Besides the papers printed in the Academy's publications, he wrote a very large number of monographs and notes on points connected with the determination and description of new and doubtful species. They are scattered through the proceedings of different learned societies, and the columns of the American Journal of Science, the Torrey Bulletin, Botanical Gazette, the Naturalist, and other American as well as European journals. One of his most important works was " Genera Floræ Americæ Boreali-

Orientalis Illustrata" (1848–'49), in which he intended to figure and describe all the genera of the Eastern States, with the aid of the artist, Mr. Isaac Sprague. Of this work only two of the proposed volumes were ever published, owing to the expense entailed. Other important papers were "Plantæ Wrightianæ Texano-Neo-Mexicanæ," in the Smithsonian contributions of 1852 and 1853; "Plantæ Lindheimerianæ," written in connection with Dr. Engelmann; "Reports on the Botany of the 32d, 38th, 39th, and 41st Parallel Expeditions," in connection with Dr. Torrey; *Gamopetalæ* in Watson's Flora of California, etc. An examination of the complete list of his works, which will soon be printed in the American Journal of Science, would alone convey an adequate idea of his extraordinary fertility as a writer and the wide range of his investigations.

After this long preparation of thirty-five years, the first part of the "Synoptical Flora," including the *Gamopetalæ* after *Compositæ*, appeared, in 1878. It formed the first part of the second volume; for, on the revised plan, the first volume was to include the *Polypetalæ* and *Gamopetalæ* through *Compositæ*, and the second volume the remaining Exogens and the Endogens. A second part, including from *Caprifoliaceæ* through *Compositæ*, appeared in 1884, and in 1886 supplements to both parts were issued, and the whole bound in one volume. He was at work on the *Polypetalæ*, and had nearly finished the *Vitaceæ*, when attacked by his last illness, and the unfinished volumes must now be completed by him who was his associate for many years, and, after Dr. Gray himself, the best fitted for the work.

Gray's critical knowledge of the Flora of North America not only placed him at the head of all American botanists, but also gave him a high reputation abroad. In his knowledge of the difficult order *Compositæ*, the largest of all the orders of flowering plants, and the one in which he always felt the most interest, he probably surpassed any living botanist. He was at one time urged by Bentham and Hooker to treat that order in their classic "Genera Plantarum," but, as the work involved a residence at Kew for a considerable time, he was obliged to decline the offer.

It was however more especially through his observations on the geographical distribution of plants made incidentally during the progress of his work on our own flora, that he was recognized as a naturalist of the highest type by the scientific circles of Europe. When we consider the marked capacity for studies of this nature which he afterwards exhibited, remembering the brilliant contributions to Plant Geography which resulted from the explorations of Robert Brown, Darwin, and Hooker, we can only regret that Gray did not sail as botanist of the Wilkes Expedition. The collectors of the expedition, Dr. Charles Pickering, W. D. Brackenridge, and William Rich, brought back many interesting plants, of which the Phænogams, excepting those from the Pacific coast of America sent to Dr. Torrey, were placed in

his hands for description. But Gray would have been more than a collector. He would have brought back impressions, and, recalling the
charming narrative of the illustrious naturalist of the *Beagle*, we can
imagine the pleasure with which we should have read the journal of a
botanist, written with the delicate humor and the keen appreciation of
the beautiful and curious in nature which Asa Gray possessed.

The study of the Wilkes plants, in which he was aided by Bentham's
large experience, gracefully acknowledged in his Memorial of Bentham
in the American Journal of Science of February, 1885, introduced him
to an exotic flora of large range. The work appeared in 1854 as a quarto
volume of nearly eight hundred pages, with an atlas of a hundred folio
plates.

His first paper* on the distribution of plants appeared in the American Journal of Science of September, 1856, and was followed by two
other parts the next year. It bore the title of "Statistics of the Flora
of the northern United States," and was prepared at the time he was at
work on a second edition of the "Manual,". partly in response to a request from Darwin for a list of American alpine plants. In this paper
he gave a general view of the characteristics of the North American
flora, with tables of species showing the extension of alpine plants and
the comparative distribution of Eastern and Western species, and their
relation to species of Europe and Asia, although he states that he must
defer making an extended comparison with the plants of northeastern
Asia until he has studied some recent collections from the northern
part of Japan. The most important conclusions reached in this paper
may be stated in his own words: "All our strictly subalpine species
(with two exceptions), which are common to us and to Europe, extend
northward along the central region of the continent quite to the arctic
sea-coast, while curiously enough eleven, or one-third of our strictly
alpine species common to Europe—all but one of them arctic in the
Old World—are not known to cross the arctic circle on this continent.
This, however, might perhaps have been expected, as it seems almost
certain that the interchange of alpine species between us and Europe
must have taken place in the direction of Newfoundland, Labrador, and
Greenland rather than through the polar regions." Again: "The
special resemblance of our flora to that of Europe, it is clear, is not
owing simply either to the large proportion of genera in common, or
to anything striking or important in the few genera, nearly or quite
peculiar to the two. The latter, indeed, are insignificant in our flora
and not to be compared, as to any features they impart, with the much
more numerous and really characteristic genera which are shared by
the eastern United States and eastern temperate Asia. We must

---

* In the paper "On the Botany of Japan," p 442, Gray speaks of a paper on the distribution of plants in the American Journal of Science of an earlier date than the one
here mentioned, apparently the review of Siebold's Flora Japonica, *l. c.* June 1840,
XXXIX, 175.

look for it in the species, partly in the identical ones and partly in those which closely answer to each other in the two floras." He accounts for such cases as the occurrence of *Phryma leptostachya* in the United States and Nepal as follows: "We should therefore look in one and the same direction for the explanation of these extraordinary no less than of the more ordinary cases of distribution, and should - - - refer such anomalous distribution to very ancient dispersion."

The plants from Japan to which he referred were collected by Charles Wright, botanist of the North Pacific Exploring Expedition, known as the Ringgold and Rodgers Expedition, of which Dr. Gray gave an account in a paper " On the Botany of Japan, and its Relations to that of North America and of other Parts of the Northern Temperate Zone," presented to this academy December 14, 1858, and January 11, 1859, and published April 25, 1859, in the sixth volume of the Memoirs. This memoir raised his reputation to its highest point among scientific men, and, appealing again to the authority of Sir J. D. Hooker, "in point of originality and far-reaching results was its author's *opus magnum.*" In referring to his previous paper in the American Journal, he states, with great candor, that, from the facts there brought out, " (1) that a large percentage of our extra-European types are shared with eastern Asia, and (2) that no small part of them are unknown in western North America." Mr. Bentham was the first to state the natural conclusion that the interchange between the temperate floras even of the western part of the Old World and of the New has mainly taken place via Asia. He cites Bentham's suggestion of a continuity of territory between America and Asia "under a latitude, or at any rate with a climate, more meridional than would be effected by a junction through the chains of the Aleutian and the Kurile Islands." He then proceeds to show why a connection in a more meridional latitude need not be assumed; and, fortified by the wide geological knowledge of his friend, Prof. J. D. Dana, he gives a masterly account of the relations of the floras of the north temperate regions from the Cretaceous period to the present time, accounting for the present distribution by migrations of species from the arctic regions due principally to the different climatic conditions of the pre-glacial, glacial, and post-glacial eras. The relations of the floras of eastern America and eastern Asia was a favorite topic with him, and he often spoke on the subject in public; his two most important addresses in which he referred to plant distribution being that on " Sequoia and its History," delivered as retiring president of the American Association for the Advancement of Science, in 1872, and a lecture on " Forest Geography and Archæology," read before the Harvard Natural History Society in 1878, and afterwards translated in the Annales des Sciences.

The study of plant distribution necessarily involved the question of the origin of species, and this brings us to a consideration of the relations of Gray to Darwin and Darwinism. Gray first met Darwin at Westbank, the residence of Sir W. J. Hooker, at Kew, in 1851; and their correspondence dates from a letter of Darwin, written April 25, 1855, asking for information about the alpine plants of the United States. How intimate and frequent their correspondence became, and how deeply each was interested in the work of the other is admirably shown in the "Life and Letters of Charles Darwin." The published letters present a vivid picture of the inner scientific life of these two men, both equally simple, earnest, remarkably free from prejudice, and anxious to do justice to the work of others. Many of the problems upon which Darwin was at work were those in which Gray was most interested; and he was often able to aid Darwin by his observations, and still more by his judicious and always acceptable criticisms. While the naturalist at Down was absorbed in the study of climbing plants and cross-fertilization, the greenhouses at Cambridge were also used as nurseries for the growth of climbers and the odd, irregularly flowered plants which ought to be cross-fertilized. The writer recalls the time when Dr. Gray hardly ever passed in or out of the herbarium without stroking—patting on the the back by way of encouraging them it almost seemed—the tendrils of the climbers on the walls and porch; and when, on the announcement that a student had discovered another new case of cross-fertilization in the garden, he would rush out bareheaded and breathless, like a school-boy, to see the thing with his own critical eyes.

Darwin, in a letter dated June 20, 1856, confided to Gray that he had "come to the heterodox conclusion that there are no such things as independently created species,—that species are only strongly defined varieties." In this letter he also says "I *assume* that species arise like our domestic varieties with *much* extinction." About a year after this (September 5, 1857) Darwin wrote to Gray the now famous letter, in which he propounded the law of the evolution of species by means of natural selection; and it was this letter, read at the Linnean Society July 1, 1858, on the occasion of the presentation of the joint paper of Darwin and Wallace "On the Tendency of Species to form Varieties; and on the Perpetuation of Varieties and Species by Natural Means of Selection," which fixed the date of the priority of the great discovery as due to Darwin. What were Gray's own views on the subject of evolution previous to the publication of the "Origin of Species," in November, 1859, may perhaps be inferred from some remarks which he made on January 11, 1859, when he presented his paper "On the Botany of Japan" to this academy. He then stated that "the idea of the descent of all similar or conspecific individuals from a common stock is so natural, and so inevitably suggested by common observation, that it must needs be first tried upon the problem [of distribution], and if the trial be satisfactory its adoption would follow as a matter of course." In brief, he was inclined to accept evolution, but wished more proof; and nearly three years earlier, in a letter to Professor Dana, written December 13, 1856, he had well expressed his own attitude by saying, "I have as yet no *opinion* whatever, and no very strong *bias*."

He saw what was coming however, and in a later letter to Professor Dana, anticipating the publication of the " Origin of Species," he says, "You may be sure that before long there must be one more resurrection of *the development theory* in a new form, obviating many of the arguments against it, and presenting a more respectable and more formidable appearance than it ever has before."

Gray was one of the favored three, including Hooker and Lyell, to whom Darwin sent advance sheets of the " Origin of Species " prior to its publication in November, 1859; and of his review in the American Journal of Science of the following March, Darwin wrote, "Your review seems to me admirable,—by far the best I have read." The review certainly presents most accurately, succinctly, and attractively Darwin's own views; but Gray does not even here announce that he is himself a complete convert to the doctrine, as is seen by the following citation : "What would happen if the derivation of species were to be substantiated, either as a true physical theory or as a sufficient hypothesis? The inquiry is a pertinent one just now. For, of those who agree with us in thinking that Darwin has not established his theory of derivation, many will admit with us that he has rendered a theory of derivation much less improbable than before; that such a theory chimes in with the established doctrines of physical science, and is not unlikely to be largely accepted long before it can be proved." And the similar statement in the Atlantic Monthly of October, 1860: " Those, if any there be, who regard the derivative hypothesis as satisfactorily proved must have loose notions of what proof is. Those who imagine it can be easily refuted and cast aside must, we think, have imperfect or very prejudiced conceptions of the facts concerned and of the questions at issue."

In 1876 he brought together in a volume, entitled " Darwiniana," his principal essays and reviews pertaining to Darwinism, taken from the American Journal of Science, the Nation, and the Atlantic Monthly, and added a chapter on " Evolutionary Teleology;" and in 1880 he published " Natural Science and Religion," two lectures delivered to the Theological School of Yale College, before a critical audience, who listened with the deepest interest to what was, in some points, his most advanced view of natural selection. We need not dwell on a subject about which so much has lately been written by far abler pens than ours. Briefly stated, Gray was probably the best expounder of Darwinian principles—meaning thereby those actually advocated by Darwin himself, and excluding the wild deductions attached to the original theory by those who deserve the name of Darwinissimists rather than Darwinists—although he himself regarded natural selection as a less efficient cause than it was assumed to be by Darwin.

His influence as an exponent of Darwinism was due partly to the admirable clearness and candor of his reviews and his interesting way of putting things; for his fertile imagination was constantly discovering apt similes to illustrate otherwise dry arguments. It was also due in part to his known caution and conservatism, and his professed Christian faith. If an avowed accepter " of the creed commonly called the Nicene" saw nothing in Darwinism which implied atheism, or was opposed to the idea of design on the part of the Creator, surely one might, at least, listen to his account of his development theory with safety. To his hearers at New Haven, in 1880, he said: "Natural selection by itself is not an hypothesis, nor even a theory. It is a truth—a *catena* of facts and direct inferences from facts. · · · There is no doubt that natural selection operates; the open question is, what do its operations amount to. The *hypothesis* based on this principle is, that the struggle for life and survival of only the fittest among individuals, all disposed to vary and no two exactly alike, will account for the diversification of the species and forms of vegetable and animal life, will even account for the rise, in the course of countless ages, from simpler and lower to higher and more specialized living beings." He gave it as his opinion that natural selection is, on the whole, a good working hypothesis, but does not explain how wholly new parts are initiated, even if the new organs are developed little by little. He repeated over and over again in different reviews his belief that natural selection could not account for variation, and he stated the case particularly forcibly in his "Evolutionary Teleology:" "Natural selection is not the wind which propels the vessel, but the rudder, which, by friction, now on this side and now on that, shapes the course. The rudder acts while the vessel is in motion, effects nothing when it is at rest. Variation answers to the wind. · · · Its course is controlled by natural selection. This proceeds mainly through outward influences. But we are more and more convinced that variation · · · is not a product of, but a response to, the action of the environment. Variations are evidently not from without, but from within."

But how do variations arise? According to Gray, by virtue of some inherent power imparted in the beginning by Divine agency. That granted, natural selection would in great part account for the present condition and distribution of life, so that one could be a Darwinian and Deist at the same time. Gray further believed that variation is apt to follow in certain more or less regular directions, and particularly in beneficial directions. Here he differed very widely from Darwin. The one saw design where the other could not, and it must be confessed that Gray was treading on delicate ground, scientifically if not theologically speaking, when he affirmed the direction of variation in beneficial lines. For what is meant by beneficial? Beneficial to whom? Beneficial for what purpose? In one sense, any variation which tends to enable a living being to survive in the struggle for existence is beneficial; and to say that any being or structure has survived is the same as saying that the variation from which it sprang was beneficial. But

Gray apparently uses the word beneficial in the sense of being fore-ordained to be beneficial.

Perhaps we must look to inheritance itself for an explanation of the difference in the views of Gray and Darwin. The Gray family were devout members of the Presbyterian Church, and throughout his life Dr. Gray adhered faithfully to the orthodox faith of his fathers, his own views being in harmony with those of the liberal branch rather than with those of the conservative branch of that communion. The agnostic position of Darwin may perhaps be inferred from his own description of himself and his father as belonging "nominally to [the] Church of England," an expression which leads one to believe that he was hardly to be counted a member of that or any other denomination. When a young man, Gray certainly had no leanings towards evolution. In his review of the "Vestiges of Creation," in the North American Review of 1846, he wrote: "Although ' geology fully proves' that there have been various creations, that different species were created at different periods, and that some of the humblest and simplest first appeared, while land animals, quadrupeds, quadrumana, and bimana were not introduced until after the earth was fitted for their residence, yet we are still to be convinced that they were not *then* created as perfect as they now are." But he was convinced later, when he studied the relations of the North American flora to that of Asia, and he accepted without hesitation the view that the present species are not special creations, but derived from previously existing species, at a time when the truth of the theory was scarcely recognized by any naturalists, and at a date when in the public mind a belief in evolution meant atheism. He had the courage to avow openly his convictions, but, on the other hand, never allowed his convictions to be governed by wild speculations.

But we who have known Asa Gray so many years would now recall, not the great botanist, but rather the kind-hearted, genial man, whose sympathy cheered and whose wisdom guided, whose heart was ever young, whose brain was ever active. His long life, unclouded by great sorrow and almost free from personal enmities, was inspired throughout by a faith which never faltered. Retaining to the last the energy and vivacity of youth, his intellect broadening and ripening, his character growing more and more sweet and serene, he reminds us of one of those trees which bear flowers and fruit at the same time. Industrious to an extent that few could equal, his work done, he enjoyed society with a relish, and his ready wit, his inexhaustible stock of anecdotes, and his quick and keen appreciation of the best in literature and art, made him everywhere welcome. His own house was open to all, and even those who came to pay the simple tribute of staring were not often turned away. With a graceful hospitality to which wealth could have lent no greater charm, he entertained the learned of many nations, and welcomed with special cordiality his brother botanists, a long array, including not only the experts in the science, but the poor and struggling student as well. He shared with all, the treasures of his knowledge, and not infrequently he added something from the modest competence which his industry had amassed. The words of good cheer from his lips were re-echoed in after years, and the life so honorable was not un-honored. If the numerous honorary degrees from learned societies at home and abroad testify to the esteem in which he was held as a scientific botanist, the warm congratulations of friends from all parts of the country when the memorial vase was presented on his seventy-fifth birthday show no less clearly how much he was beloved as a man. And when, during dreary weeks, his anxious friends hoped against hope, watching to catch the sound of the loved voice which would speak but could not, all felt that the message which he sought to utter must have been a benediction. But it was not needed. His life was a benediction, and as his body was borne to its last resting place the freshly-fallen snow was not more pure than his character, nor the sparkling winter air more bright and clear than his intellect.

LIST OF THE WRITINGS OF DR. ASA GRAY.*

I.—Scientific Works and Articles.

1834.

A Sketch of the Mineralogy of a portion of Jefferson and St. Lawrence Counties (N. Y.); by Drs. J. B. Crawe, of Watertown, and A. Gray, of Utica (N. Y.). Am. J. Sci., xxv, 346–350.

North American Gramineæ and Cyperaceæ (exsiccatæ). Part I, 1834; Part II, 1835.

1835.

A Monograph of the North American species of Rhynchospora. Ann. N. Y. Lyc., iii, 191–220 (reprint, 191–219), t. 1. [Hook. Comp. Bot. Mag., ii, 26–38.]

A notice of some new, rare, and otherwise interesting plants from the northern and western portions of the State of New York. Ann. N. Y. Lyc., iii, 221–238 (reprint, 220–236).

1836.

Elements of Botany. New York, 1836, 8vo, pp. xiv, 428.

1837.

Remarks on the structure and affinities of the order Ceratophyllaceæ. Ann. N. Y. Lyc., iv, 41–60.

Melanthacearum America Septentrionalis Reviso. Ann. N. Y. Lyc., iv, 105–140.

Remarks on the progress of discovery relative to vegetable fecundation: Being a preface to the translation of A. J. C. Corda's "Beiträge zur Lehre von der Befruchtung der Pflanzen" Am. J. Sci., xxxi, 308–317.

1838.

A Flora of North America: Containing abridged descriptions of all the known indigenous and naturalized plants growing north of Mexico; arranged according to the Natural System. By John Torrey and Asa Gray. Vol. i, New York, 1838–1840, 8vo, pp. xvi, 711; Vol. ii, 1841–1843, pp. 504.

1840.

Remarks chiefly on the Synonymy of several North American plants of the Orchis tribe. Am. J. Sci., xxxviii, 306–311.

1841.

Notices of European Herbaria, particularly those most interesting to the North American Botanist. Am. J. Sci, xl, 1–18. [Ann. Nat. Hist, vii, 132–140, 179–185: Hooker's Jour. Bot., iii, 353–374.]

Notice of the Botanical Writings of the late C. S Rafinesque. Am J. Sci., xl, 221–241.

* From the American Journal of Science, Vol XXXVI

1842.

Notes of a botanical excursion to the mountains of North Carolina, etc., with some remarks on the botany of the higher Alleghany Mountains. Am. J. Sci., XLII, 1-49. [Hook. Lond. Jour. Bot., I, 1-14, 217-237; II, 113-125; III, 230-242.]

The Botanical Text-Book for Colleges, Schools, and Private Students. New York, 1842, 8vo, pp. 413. Edition 2d, ib., 1845, 8vo, pp. 509; 3d, ib., 1850, 8vo, pp. 520; 4th, ib., 1853, 8vo, pp. 528; 5th, under the title, Introduction to Structural and Systematic Botany, being a fifth and revised edition of The Botanical Text-Book, New York, 1857-'58, pp. xii, 555. A second issue bears date 1860. Edition 6th, Part I, Structural Botany, or Organography on the basis of Morphology. New York, 1879, 8vo, pp. XII, 442.

1843.

Selections from the Scientific Correspondence of Cadwallader Colden with Gronovius, Linnæus, Collinson and other Naturalists. Am. J. Sci., XLIV, 85-133.

1844.

Characters of some new genera [Monoptilon, Amphipappus, Calliachyris, Anisocoma] and species of plants of the natural order Compositæ, from the Rocky Mountains and Upper California. Proc. Bost. Soc. Nat. Hist., I, 210-212 (abstract); Jour. Bost. Soc. Nat. Hist., V, 104-111, with plate.

The Longevity of Trees. N. A. Review, July, 1844, 189-238.

1845.

The Chemistry of Vegetation. N. A. Review, Jan., 1845, 3-42.

Plantæ Lindheimerianæ; an enumeration of F. Lindheimer's collection of Texan plants, with remarks, and descriptions of new species, etc. By George Engelmann and Asa Gray. Jour. Bost. Soc. Nat. Hist., V, 210-264.

1846.

Musci Alleghanienses, sive Spicilegia Muscorum atque Hepaticarum quos in itinere a Marylandia usque ad Georgiam per tractus montium A. D. mdcccxliii decerpserunt Asa Gray et W. S. Sullivant (interjectis nonnullis aliunde collectis) [Review, with notes.] Am. J. Sci., II, I, 70-81, 312.

Notice of a new genus of plants of the order Santalaceæ (Darbya) Am. J. Sci., II, I, 386-389; Proc. Bost. Soc. Nat. Hist., II, 115-116 (abstract); Jour. Bost. Soc. Nat. Hist., V, 368-351.

Scientific Results of the Exploring Expedition. N. A Review, July, 1846, 211-226.

Analogy between the Flora of Japan and that of the United States Am. J. Sci., II, II, 135-136.

Characters of some new genera and species of Compositæ from Texas. Proc. Am. Acad. I, 46-50. [Am. J. Sci., II, III, 274-276, in part.]

Chloris Boreali-Americana. Illustrations of new, rare, or otherwise interesting North American plants, selected chiefly from those recently brought into cultivation at the Botanical Garden of Harvard University. Decade I. Mem. Am. Acad., III, 1-56, tt. 1-10.

1847.

Food of the Mastodon. Am. J. Sci., II, III, 436.

Note upon Carex loliacea *Linn* and C gracilis *Ehrh.* Am. J. Sci., II, IV, 19 22.

1848.

Genera Floræ Americæ Boreali-Orientalis Illustrata. The Genera of the Plants of the United States, illustrated by figures and analyses from nature, by Isaac Sprague; superintended and with descriptions, etc., by Asa Gray. Vols. I, II, (1848, 1849), 8vo, pp. 230, 229, and 186 plates.

A Manual of the Botany of the Northern United States, from New England to Wisconsin and south to Ohio and Pennsylvania, inclusive (the Mosses and Liverworts by Wm. S. Sullivant), arranged according to the Natural System. Boston and Cambridge, 1848, 8vo, pp. lxxii, 710. [Later editions are given under dates of publication.]

1849.

Plantæ Feudlerianæ Novi-Mexicanæ: An account of a Collection of Plants made chiefly in the Vicinity of Santa Fé, New Mexico, by Augustus Fendler. Proc. Am. Acad., II, 5–9 [abstract]; Mem. Am. Acad., IV, 1–116.

On some plants of the order Compositæ from the Sandwich Islands. Proc. Am. Assoc., II, 397, 398.

On the composition of the plant by phytons, and some applications of phyllotaxis. Proc. Am. Assoc., II, 438–444.

Note on the genus Thelesperma, *Lessing*. Hook. Jour. Bot., I, 252.

1850.

Plantæ Lindheimerianæ, Part II. Jour. Bost. Soc. Nat. Hist., VI, 141–233.

1851

Characters of some Gnaphalioid Compositæ of the division Augiantheæ. Hook. Jour. Bot., III, 97–102, 147–153, 172–178.

Characters of a new genus (Dissothrix) of Compositæ-Eupatoriaceæ, with remarks on some other genera of the same tribe. Hook. Jour. Bot., III, 223–225.

1852.

Account of Argyroxiphium, a remarkable genus of Compositæ, belonging to the mountains of the Sandwich Islands. Proc. Am. Acad., II, 159, 160.

Characters of three new genera of plants of the orders Violaceæ and Anonaceæ discovered by the naturalists of the United States Exploring Expedition [Agatea, Isodendrion, Richella]. Proc. Am. Acad., II, 323–325.

Plantæ Wrightianæ Texano-Neo Mexicanæ: An account of a Collection of Plants made by Charles Wright, A. M., in an expedition from Texas to El Paso, New Mexico, in the summer and autumn of 1849. Part I. Smithsonian Contributions, III, 1–146, tt. 10.

Remarks on Menodora, Humb. and Bonpl., and Bolivaria, Cham. and Schlecht., Am. J. Sci., II, XIV, 41–45.

Note on Tetratheca. Hook. Jour. Bot., IV, 199–200.

Characters of some Southwest Australian Compositæ, principally of the subtribe Gnaphalieæ. Hook. Jour. Bot., IV, 225–232, 266–276.

1853.

Plantæ Wrightianæ Texano-Neo Mexicanæ. Part II. An account of a collection of plants made by Charles Wright, A. M., in western Texas, New Mexico, and Sonora, in the years 1851 and 1852. Smithsonian Contributions, V, 1–119, tt. 10.

Brief characters of some new genera and species of Nyctaginaceæ, principally collected in Texas and New Mexico. Am. J. Sci, II, XV, 259–263, 319–324.

On the discovery of two species of Trichomanes in the State of Alabama, one of which is new. Am. J. Sci., II, XV, 324–326.

Characters of Tetraclea, a new genus of Verbenaceæ. Am J. Sci., II, XVI, 97–98.

Note on the parasitism of Comandra umbellata, Nutt. Am. J. Sci., II, XVI, 250–251. [Ann. Nat. Hist., XII, 365–366.]

Characters of some new genera of Plants, mostly from Polynesia, in the collection of the United States Exploring Expedition under Captain Wilkes. Proc. Am. Acad., III, 48–54, 127–129.

1854.

On the age of the large tree recently felled in California. Am. J. Sci., II, XVII, 440–443.

Note on the genus Buckleya. Am. J. Sci., II, XVIII, 98–100.

Plantæ Novæ Thurberianæ. The characters of some New Genera and Species of Plants in a Collection made by George Thurber, Esq., of the late Mexican Boundary Commission, chiefly in New Mexico and Sonora. Mem. Am. Acad., n. s., V, 297–328.

On the Affinities of the Genus Vavæa, Benth.; also of Rhytidandra, Gray. Mem. Am. Acad., n. s., V, 329–336. [Hook. Jour. Bot., VII, 189–190.]

United States Exploring Expedition, during the years 1838, 1839, 1840, 1841, 1842, under the command of Charles Wilkes, U. S. N. Vol. XV. Botany. Phanerogamia. With a folio Atlas of one hundred plates. Part I. Philadelphia, 1854. 4to, pp. 775.

Mammoth Trees of California. Am. J. Sci., II, XVIII, 286–287.

1855.

The Smithsonian Institution. Am. J. Sci., II, XX, 1–21.

Botanical Report, by John Torrey and Asa Gray, upon the Collections made by Captain Gunnison, Topographical Engineers, in 1853, and by Lieutenant E. G. Beckwith, Third Artillery, in 1854. Pacific R. R. Surveys, II, 115–132, with ten plates.

Report on the Botany of the Expedition [under Captain John Pope], by John Torrey and Asa Gray. Pacific R. R. Surveys, II, 157–178, with ten plates.

Note on the Development and Structure of the Integuments of the Seed of Magnolia. Hook. Jour. Bot., VII, 243–245; VIII, 26.

1856.

A Manual of the Botany of the Northern United States: Second edition; including Virginia, Kentucky, and all east of the Mississippi; arranged according to the Natural System. (The Mosses and Liverworts by Wm. S. Sullivant.) With fourteen plates, illustrating the genera of the Cryptogamia. New York, 1856. 8vo, pp. xxiii, 739.

Note on Obolaria virginica L., Jour. Linn. Soc., I, 129–130.

For what purpose were plants created? (Addressed to Prof. Dana). Am. J. Sci., II, XXI, 428, 429.

Statistics of the Flora of the Northern United States. Am. J. Sci., II, XXII, 204–232; XXIII, 62–84, 369–403.

Wild Potatoes in New Mexico and Western Texas. Am. J. Sci., II, XXII, 284, 285.

1857.

Centrostegia. Pacific R. R. Surveys, VII (Botany), 19.

List of Dried Plants collected in Japan, by S. Wells Williams, esq., and Dr. James Morrow. Narrative of the Expedition of an American Squadron to the China Seas and Japan, performed in the years 1852, 1853, and 1854, under the command of Commodore M. C. Perry, II, 303–329.

Report of the Botany of the Expedition [under Lieutenant A. W. Whipple]. (By John Torrey. The Compositæ, Plantaginaceæ, Orobanchaceæ, Scrophulariaceæ, and Bignoniaceæ, by Asa Gray). Pacific R. R. Surveys, IV, 95–115, 117–122, with eight plates.

General Catalogue of the Plants collected on the expedition [under Lieut. R. S. Williamson and Lieut. H. L. Abbot]. (By J. S. Newberry. Ivesia, Compositæ, Hemitomes (and Monotropeæ), Scrophulariaceæ, Hydrophyllaceæ, and Gentianaceæ, by Asa Gray). Pacific R. R. Surveys, VI, 72, 73, 76-87, with six plates.

First Lessons in Botany and Vegetable Physiology. New York, 1857. 8vo, pp. 236. [There are later issues.] Revised Aug., 1868.

On the age of a large Californian coniferous tree. Proc. Am. Acad., III, 94–97.

1858.

A short exposition of the structure of the ovule and seed-coats of Magnolia. Jour. Linn. Soc., II, 106–110.

How Plants Grow: a simple introduction to Structural Botany. With a popular Flora. New York, 1858. 8vo, 233.

Note on the coiling of tendrils of plants. Proc. Am. Acad., IV, 98, 99. [Ann. Nat. Hist., III, 513, 514; Am. J. Sci., II, XXVII, 277, 278.]

Notes upon some Rubiaceæ, collected in the South Sea Exploring Expedition under Captain Wilkes. Proc. Am. Acad., IV, 33–50, 306–318.

Action of foreign Pollen upon the Fruit. Am. J. Sci., II, XXV, 122, 123.

1859.

Neviusia,, a new genus of Rosaceæ. Mem. Am. Acad., VI, 373–376, with plate.

Diagnostic characters of new species of phænogamous plants, collected in Japan by Charles Wright, botanist of the United States North Pacific Exploring Expedition. With observations upon the relations of the Japanese Flora to that of North America, and of other parts of the Northern Temperate Zone. Mem. Am. Acad., VI, 377–452. [Bibl. Univ. Archives, IX, 32–43; Canadian Naturalist, IV, 296, 297; Am J. Sci., II, XXVIII, 187–200.]

On the genus Croomia, and its place in the Natural System. Mem. Am. Acad., VI, 453–457, with plate.

Characters of Ancistrophora, a new genus of the order Compositæ, recently detected by Charles Wright. Mem Am. Acad., VI, 457, 458.

Notes upon some Polynesian plants of the order Loganiaceæ. Proc. Am. Acad., IV, 319–324.

Diagnoses of the species of Sandal-wood (Santalum) of the Sandwich Islands. Proc. Am. Acad., IV, 326, 327.

A revision of the genus Forestiera. Proc. Am. Acad., IV, 363–366.

Report of the United States and Mexican Boundary Survey made under the direction of the Secretary of the Interior, by William H. Emory. Vol. II, Part I. Botany of the Boundary. (Note on Synthlipsis, Compositæ, Scrophulariaceæ, note on Datura, conspectus of the genera of Nyctaginaceæ and the species of Mirabilis and Oxybaphus, by Dr. Gray), pp. 34, 73–107, 110–121, 154, 172–175, with five plates.

Lists of Plants collected by Emanuel Samuels, in Sonoma County, Cal., in 1856. Proc. Bost. Soc. Nat. Hist., VII, 142–145.

List of a collection of dried plants made by L. J. Xantus, at Fort Tejon and vicinity, California, near lat. 35° and long. 119°, 1857–'58. Proc. Bost. Soc. Nat. Hist., VII, 145–149.

Manual of the Botany of the Northern United States. Revised [Third] Edition; including Virginia, Kentucky, and all east of the Mississippi; arranged according to the Natural System. With six plates, illustrating the Genera of Ferns, etc. 1859, pp. XXIV, 635.

British National Museums of Natural History. Am. J. Sci., II, XXVII, 277.

Trichomanes radicans, Swartz. Am. J. Sci., XXVIII, 440, 441.

1860.

Catalogue of Plants collected East of the Rocky Mountains. Pacific R. R. Surveys, XII, part 2, 40–49, with three plates.

* Report upon the Colorado River of the West, explored in 1857 and 1858 by Lieut. Joseph C. Ives. Part IV. Botany (the orders preceding Verbenaceæ, excepting the Cactaceæ, by Professor Gray), pp. 1–20.

Potamogeton crispus, L.; Marsilea quadrifolia, L.   Am. J. Sci., II, xxx, 139, 140.
Discussion between two readers of Darwin's Treatise on the Origin of Species.
Am. J. Sci., II, xxx, 226-239. [Design versus Necessity. Discussion between two
readers of Darwin's Treatise on the Origin of Species, upon its natural theology.
Darwiniana, pp. 62-86.]

1861.

Note on the species of Nissolia. Jour. Linn. Soc., v, 25, 26.

Characters of some Compositæ in the collection of the United States South Pacific
Exploring Expedition under Captain Wilkes; with observations, etc. Proc. Am.Acad.,
v, 114-146.

Notes on Lobeliaceæ, Goodeniaceæ, etc., in the collection made by the South Pacific Exploring Expedition. Proc. Am. Acad., v, 146-152.

Enumeration of a collection of dried plants made by L J. Xantus, at Cape San
Lucas, etc., in Lower California, between August, 1859, and February, 1860. Proc.
Am. Acad. v, 153-173.

A cursory examination of a collection of dried plants made by L. C. Ervendberg
around Wartenberg, near Tantoyuca, in the ancient province of Huasteca, Mexico,
in 1858 and 1859. Proc. Am. Acad., v, 174-190

Note on the genus Graphephorum Desv., and its synonymy. Proc. Am. Acad., v,
190, 191; Ann. Bot. Soc. Canada, i, 55-57.

Notes upon a portion of Dr. Seemann's recent collection of dried plants gathered
in the Feejee Islands. Proc. Am. Acad., v, 314-321.

Characters of new or obscure species of plants of Monopetalous orders in the collection of the United States Pacific Exploring Expedition ; with occasional remarks,
etc. Proc. Am. Acad., v, 321-352; vi, 37-55.

Heath (Calluna vulgaris) in North America. Am. J. Sci., II, xxxii, 290, 291;
xxxviii, 122-124; 428, 429; xxxix, 228; xliii, 128, 129. [Calluna atlantica Seem.;
also Seemann's Jour. Bot., v, 84, 85.]

Aira caryophyllea in the United States. Am. J. Sci., II, xxxii, 291.

1862.

Plantæ Vitienses Seemannianæ. Remarks on the Plants collected in the Vitian or
Fijian Islands by Dr. Berthold Seemann. Bonplandia, x, 34-37.

Enumeration of the Plants of Dr. Parry's collection in the .Rocky Mountains in
1861. Am. J. Sci., II, xxxiii, 237-243, 404-411 ; xxxiv, 249-261, 330-341.

Notes upon the "Description of New Plants from Texas by S. B. Buckley." Proc.
Phila. Acad. Nat. Sci., 1862, 161-168.

A Report upon Mr. S. B. Buckley's "Description of Plants, No. 3, Gramineæ."
Proc. Phila. Acad., 1862, 332-337.

Additional note on the genus Rhytidandra. Proc. Am. Acad., vi, 55, 56.

Synopsis of the genus Pentstemon. Proc. Am. Acad., vi, 56-76.

Revision of the North American species of the genus Calamagrostis, sect. Deyeuxia.
Proc. Am. Acad. vi, 77-80.

Fertilization of Orchids through the Agency of Insects. Am. J. Sci., II, xxxiv,
420-429.

1863.

Darlingtonia Californica, Torr. Am. J. Sci., II, xxxv, 136,137.

Botanical Collections in the Rocky Mountains. Am. J. Sci. II, xxxv, 137.

Species considered as to Variation, Geographical Distribution and Succession.
Ann. Nat. Hist., xii, 81-97. [Darwiniana, pp. 178-204.]

Enumeration of the species of plants collected by Dr. C. C. Parry and Messrs.
Elihu Hall and J. P. Harbour, during the summer and autumn of 1862, on and near
the Rocky Mountains, in Colorado Territory, lat. 36°-41°. Proc. Phila. Acad. Nat.
Sci., 1863, 55-80.

Structure and fertilization of certain Orchids. Am. J. Sci., II, xxxvi, 292-294.

Manuel of the Botany, etc. Fourth revised Edition. To which is added Garden Botany, an Introduction to a knowledge of the common cultivated Plants. With twenty-two plates, illustrating the Grasses, Ferns. Mosses, etc. New York, 1863, pp. ci, 743.

Synopsis of the species of Hosackia. Proc. Acad. Phila., 1863, 346-352.

1864.

On Streptanthus *Nutt.*, and the plants which have been referred to that genus. Proc. Am. Acad., vi, 182-188.

A revision and arrangement (mainly by the fruit) of the North American species of Astragalus and Oxytropis. Proc. Am. Acad., vi, 188-236.

On scientific nomenclature. Am. J. Sci., II, xxxvii, 278-281. [Ann. Mag. Nat. Hist., xiii, 517-520; Seemann's Jour. Bot., ii, 188-190.]

Radicle-ism. Am. J. Sci., xxxviii, 125-126.

New Scirpi of the Northern United States: S. Canbyi, S. Clintonii. Am. J. Sci., II, xxxviii, 289-290.

1865.

Najas major, Ruppia maritima, etc., discovered at Salina, N. Y. Am. J. Sci., II, xxxix, 106-107.

Harvard University Herbarium. Am. J. Sci. II, xxxix, 224-226.

Story about a Cedar of Lebanon. Am. J. Sci., II, xxxix, 226-228.

New or little known Polynesian Thymeleæ. Seemann's Jour. Bot., iii, 302-306.

The Tennessee Yellow-Wood (Cladrastis lutea). Am. J. Sci., II, xl, 273.

Characters of some new plants of California and Nevada, chiefly from the collections of Prof. William H. Brewer and of Dr. Charles L. Anderson, with revisions of certain genera or groups. Proc. Am. Acad., vi, 519-556.

1866.

Professor Tredwell's Improvements in constructing Cannon : Address of the president of the American Academy of Arts and Sciences (Prof. Asa Gray) upon the presentation of the Rumford Medal to Professor Tredwell, November 15, 1865. Proc. Am. Acad., vii, 44-51 ; Am. J. Sci., II, xli, 97-103.

Scolopendrium officinarum in western New York. Am. J. Sci., II, xli, 417.

A new Fijian Hedycaria: H. dorstenioides. Seemann's Jour. Bot., iv, 83-84.

Note on a regular dimerous flower of Cypripedium candidum. Am. J. Sci., II, xlii, 195. [Ann. Mag. Nat. Hist., xviii, 341-342; Seemann's Jour. Bot, iv, 378-379.]

1867.

An innovation in nomenclature in the recently issued volume of the *Prodromus*. Am. J. Sci., II, xliii, 126-128. [Seemann's Jour Bot, v, 81-84.]

Manual of the Botany of the Northern United States, including the district east of the Mississippi and north of North Carolina and Tennessee, arranged according to the Natural System. Fifth edition, with twenty plates, illustrating the Sedges, Grasses, Ferns, etc. New York, 1867. 8vo, pp. 701. A second issue in 1868 has four pages of addenda.

Morphology of stamens and use of abortive organs. Am. J. Sci., II. xxliii, 273-274.

Botanical Notes and Queries. On Sambucus Canadensis, Robinia hispida, and Clerodendron Thompsonæ. Am. Nat., i, 493-494.

May apples in Clusters ; Invasions of Foreign plants. Am. Nat., i, 494-495.

1868.

Botanical Notes and Queries. On Tillandsia usneoides; Robinia hispida. Am. Nat., i, 673-674.

Monstrous Flowers of Habenaria fimbriata ; The Elder (Sambucus Canadensis) as a native plant; German Ivy, so-called, flowering under peculiar circumstances. Am. Nat., II, 38-39.

Descriptions of eleven new Californian plants. Proc. Calif. Acad., III, 101-103.

Characters of new plants of California and elsewhere, principally of those collected by W. H. Brewer and H. N. Bolander. Proc. Am. Acad., VII, 327-401.

Shortia *Torr. & Gray* and Schizocodon *Sieb. & Zucc.*, identical. Am. J. Sci., II, XLV, 402-403.

Remarks on the laws of botanical nomenclature. Am. J. Sci., II, XLVI, 74-77.

Planera aquatica, the Planer-tree. Am. Nat., II, 441.

Saxifraga Virginiensis. Am. Nat., II, 448.

Field, Forest, and Garden Botany. A simple introduction to the common plants of the United States east of the Mississippi, both wild and cultivated. New York, 1868. 8vo, pp. 386. A second revised issue, 1870. Bound with the "Lessons," this forms the "School and Field-book of Botany."

1870.

A revision of the Eriogoneæ. By Asa Gray and J. Torrey. Proc. Am. Acad., VIII, 145-200.

Dialysis with Staminody in Kalmia latifolia. Am. Nat., IV, 373, 374.

Botanical Contributions. 1. Reconstruction of the Order Diapensiaceæ. 2. Revision of the North American Polemoniaceæ. 3. Miscellaneous Botanical Notes and Characters. Proc. Am. Acad., VIII, 243-296.

1871.

On hypocotyledonary gemmation. Am. J. Sci., III, II, 63. [Ann. Mag. Nat. Hist., VIII, 220.]

Arrangement for Cross-fertilization of the flowers of Scrophularia nodosa. Am. J. Sci., III, II, 150, 151.

Characters of a new genus (Eophyton) consisting of two species of parasitic Gentianeæ: E. tenellum, E. Lobbii. Jour. Linn. Soc., XI, 22-23.

A new species of Erythronium: E. propullans. Am. Nat., V, 298-300. [Canadian Naturalist, V, 465, 466.]

Anthers of Parnassia. Am. J. Sci, III, II, 306. [Am. Nat., V, 649-650.]

Baptisia perfoliata: The arrangement of morphology of its leaves. Am. J. Sci., III, II, 462-463. [Seemann's Jour. Bot., X, 84-85.]

Drosera (Sundew) as a Fly-catcher. Am. J. Sci., III, II, 463-464.

1872.

Dismissal of the late Botanist of the Department of Agriculture. Am. Nat., VI, 39-45. [Am. J. Sci., III, V, 315-318.]

Botany for Young People. Part II.—How Plants Behave; how they move, climb, employ insects to work for them, etc. New York, 1872. Small 4to, pp. 46.

Plant Dryers. Am. Nat., VI, 107-108.

New parasitic plant of the Mistletoe family: Arceuthobium minutum. Am. Nat., VI, 166-167.

Botanical Contributions. 1. Notes on Labiatæ. 2. Determinations of a collection of Plants made in Oregon by Elihu Hall during the summer of 1871, with characters of some New Species and various Notes. Proc. Am. Acad., VIII, 365-412.

Rumex Britannica. L. Seemann's Jour. Bot., X, 211-212 (from Proc. Am. Acad., VIII, 399).

Address before the American Association at Dubuque, Iowa, August, 1872. Am. J. Sci., III, IV, 282-298; Am. Nat., VI, 577-596 ("Sequoia and its history"); Trimen's Jour. Bot., X (1872), 309-313 (extract, "Origin of the Flora of Atlantic North America"); Proc. Am. Assoc., XXI, 1-31 (with corrections and appendix). [Sequoia and its history ; the relations of North American to Northeast Asian and to Tertiary Vegetation. Darwiniana, pp. 205-235.]

Wild Double-flowered Epigæa repens. Am. Nat., vi, 429.

Acer nigrum with Stipules. Am. Nat., vi, 767.

1873.

The Horse Disease. Am. Nat., vii, 167.

Gelsemium has dimorphous flowers. Am. J. Sci., III, v, 480.

Note on apples which are half like one and half like another species. Am. Nat., vii, 236.

Fly-catching in Sarracenia. Am. J. Sci., III, vi, 149, 150 ; 467, 468 ; vii, 440–442.

Botanical Notelets. Equisetum arvense ; Cypripedium acaule ; Acer nigrum ; Anemone nemorosa or trifolia ; Dimorphism in Forsythia. Am. Nat., vii, 422, 423.

Dionæa. Am. J. Sci., III, vi, 150.

Plantæ Texanæ : a list of the Plants collected in Eastern Texas in 1872, and distributed to subscribers by Elihu Hall. Salem, 1873. 4vo, pp. 29.

Rubus deliciosus Torr.; Spiranthes Romanzoviana. Am. J. Sci., III, vi, 389, 390.

Characters of new genera and species of plants. Proc. Am. Acad., viii, 620-631.

Notes on Compositæ and characters of certain genera and species, etc. Proc. Am. Acad., viii, 631-661.

Cleistogenous Flowers in Oxybaphus nyctagineus. Am. Nat., vii, 692.

Note on movements of leaves of Drosera and Dionæa. Am. Nat., vii, 738, 739.

1874.

Yucca gloriosa ; Arundo Donax in Virginia ; Trichomanes radicans in Kentucky. Am. J. Sci., III, vii, 65.

How Trees grow tall. New York Semi-weekly Tribune, Feb. 20, Mar. 6, Mar. 13.

Insectivorous Plants. Nation, No. 457 ; pp. 216, 217 ; No. 458, pp. 232-234. [Darwiniana, pp. 289-307.]

Notes on Compositæ and characters of certain genera and species. Proc. Am. Acad., ix, 187-218.

Were the Fruits made for Man, or did Man make the Fruits? Am. Nat., viii, 116-120. (Reprinted from the "Horticulturist.")

Sphæralcea acerifolia in Illinois. Am. J. Sci., III, vii, 239.

Pachystigma Canbyi. Gray: Woodsia Ilvensis, why so named? Villars and Villarsia. Am. J. Sci., III, vii, 442, 443.

Insectivorous Plants, additional investigations. New York Semi-weekly Tribune, June 5.

Note on the origin of "May Apples." New York Semi-weekly Tribune, June 12.

A Vegetable Steel-trap. New York Semi-weekly Tribune, Nov. 6

The Office of Leaves. N. Y. Semi-weekly Tribune, Nov. 27.

Do Varieties wear out or tend to wear out? New York Semi-weekly Tribune, Dec. 8. [Am. J. Sci., III, ix, 109-114 ; Darwiniana, pp. 334-355. Noticed in Am. Nat. ix, 53.]

Contributions to the Botany of North-America.—1. A Synopsis of the North American Thistles. 2. Notes on Borraginaceæ. 3. Synopsis of North American Species of Physalis. 4. Characters of various New Species. Proc. Am. Acad., x, 39-78.

Johnson's New Universal Cyclopedia. Botany, i, 566-571. Leaf, ii, 1694. Morphology, iii, 627.

1875.

Revision of the Genus Symphoricarpus. Jour. Linn. Soc., xiv, 9-12.

Note on Nemacladus Nutt. Jour. Linn. Soc., xiv, 28, 29

A conspectus of the North American Hydrophyllaceæ. Proc. Am. Acad., x, 312-332.

Æstivation in Asimina. Am. J. Sci., III, x, 63.

Note on peas from mummies and clover from greensand marl. Nation, No. 523, p. 27.

The Potato Rot; Slitting down the Bark of Fruit Trees in Early Summer. Am. Agriculturist, July, pp. 262, 263.

A Pilgrimage to Torreya. Am. Agriculturist, July, pp. 266, 267.

The Box-Huckleberry (Gaylussacia brachycera Gray). Am. J. Sci., III, x, 155.

Spontaneous Generation of Plants. Am. Agriculturist, Oct.

Æstivation and its Terminology. Am. J. Sci., III, x, 339–344. [Trimen's Jour. Bot., xiv, 53–58.]

Menyanthes trifoliata; Botrychium simplex, with pinnated divisions to the sterile frond. Am. Nat., ix, 468.

The Botanic Garden. The Harvard Book, i, 313–315.

1876.

Miscellaneous Botanical Contributions. Proc. Am. Acad., xi, 71–104.

Burs in the Borage Family. Am. Nat. x, 1–4.

Plantain. Am. Agriculturist, Jan., p. 19.

How Flowers are Fertilized. American Agriculturist. Art. I. Campanulas or Bell Flowers, Jan., p. 22; Art. II. Compound Flowers, Feb., p. 62; Art. III. Clerodendron and Fire-weed, Apr., pp. 142–143; Art. IV. Houstonia and Partridge-berry, May, p. 182; Art. V. Dicentra or Bleeding-hearts, June, p. 222; Art. VI. Laurel, July, p. 262; Art. VII. False Indigo and Red Clover, Aug., p. 303; Art. VIII. Beans and other Flowers of the Pulse Family, Oct., pp. 382, 383; Art. IX. Ground-nut or Apios, Jan. 1877, pp. 22, 23; Art. X. The Busy Bee, Feb., pp. 62, 63; Art. XI. The Good of Cross-fertilization, Mar. p. 102; Art. XII. How Cross-fertilization benefits, May, p. 182; Art. XIII. Lady-slippers, June, pp. 222, 323.

Cheilanthes Alabamensis; Dichogamy in Epilobium angustifolium; Dimorphism in Claytonia. Am. Nat., x, 43, 44.

Comparative Zoology, Structural and Systematic. Nation, No. 578, p. 63, 64.

Seeds that float in water; Use of the hydrometric twisting of the tail to the carpels of Erodium. Am. J. Sci., III, xi, 157, 158.

Our Wild Gooseberries. Am. Nat., x, 270–275.

Tolmiæa Menziesii. Am. Nat., x, 300.

Botany of California. [Saxifragaceæ and Gamopetalæ by Asa Gray].—Vol. i, 192–208, 277–622.

Darwiniana: Essays and reviews pertaining to Darwinism. New York, 1876. 8vo, pp. 396.

Schœnolirion Torr. Am. Nat. x, 426, 427, 552, 553.

Anthers in Trillium. Same, x, 427, 428.

Notes on Acnida [Trimen's Jour. Bot., xiv, 310–312]; Large Elm; Calluna vulgaris, the Ling or Heather, rediscovered in Massachusetts. Am. Nat., x, 487–490.

Sedum reflexum, L. Am Nat., x, 553.

Nymphæa flava, Leitner. Am. J. Sci., III, xi, 416.

Heteromorphism in Epigæa. Am. J. Sci., III, xii, 74–76 [Am. Nat. x, 490–492].

Contributions to the Botany of North America.—1. Characters of Canbya (n. gen.) and Arctomecon. 2. Characters of New Species, etc. Proc. Am. Acad., xii, 51–84, with two plates.

Subradical solitary Flowers in Scirpus, Relation of Coloration to Environment. Am. J. Sci., III, xii, 467.

1877.

Date of Publication of Elliott's Botany of South Carolina and Georgia. Am. J. Sci., III, xiii, 81, 392.

Homogone and Heterogone (or Homogonous and Heterogonous) Flowers. Am. J. Sci., III, xiii, 82, 83. [Am. Nat., xi, 42.]

Notice of Darwin on the Effects of Cross and Self Fertilization in the Vegetable Kingdom. Am. J. Sci., III, XIII, 125–141.

Dextrorse and Sinistrorse. Am. J. Sci., III, XIII, 236, 237, 391.

Fertilization of Gentiaua Andrewsii. Am. Nat., XI, 113.

On some remarkable specimens of *Kalmia latifolia*, L. Proc. Bost. Soc. Nat. Hist., XIX, 75, 76 [Am. Nat., XI, 175].

Characters of some little-known or new genera of plants. Proc. Am. Acad., XII, 159–165.

Notes on the History of Helianthus tuberosus, the so-called Jerusalem Artichoke. By J. H. Trumbull and Asa Gray. Am. J. Sci., III, XIII, 347–352; XIV, 428, 429.

The Jerusalem Artichoke once more. Am. Agriculturist, p. 142. [Gardeners' Chronicle, n. ser., VII, 472.]

The Germination of the genus Megarrhiza *Torr*. Am. J. Sci., III, XIV, 21–24 [Bot. Gazette, II, 130–132].

Orchis rotundifolia *Pursh*. Am. J. Sci., III, XIV, 72. [Am. Nat., XI, 431.]

Athamantha Chinensis, L. Am. J. Sci., III, XIV, 160.

Saxifraga Virginiensis. Am. Nat., XI, 366.

Three-flowered Sanguinaria. Am. Nat., XI, 431.

Fertilization of Browallia elata. Proc. Phil. Acad., XXIX, 11, 12.

1878.

Plants May Thrive on a Meat Diet. Am. Agriculturist, Apr., p. 131.

The two wayside Plantains. Bot. Gaz., III, 41, 42.

Contributions to the Botany of North America. 1. Elatines Americanæ. 2. Two New Genera of Acanthaceæ. 3. New Astragali. 4. Miscellaneæ. Proc. Am. Acad., XIII, 361–374.

Synoptical Flora of North America. Vol. II.—Part 1. Gamopetalæ after Compositæ. New York, May, 1878. Roy. 8vo, pp. VIII, 402.—Second Edition [with Supplement, etc., in connection with vol. I, Part 2]. New York, January, 1886. Roy. 8vo, pp, VIII, 494. Reissued, with corrections, April, 1888, as Smithsonian Miscellaneous Collections, vol. XXXI.

Early Introduction and Spread of the Barberry in Eastern New England. Am. J. Sci., III, XV, 482, 483.

Forest Geography and Archæology: a lecture delivered before the Harvard University Natural History Society, April 18, 1878. Am. J. Sci., III, XVI, 85–94, 183–196. [Géographie et Archéologie forestières de l'Amerique du Nord (a French translation by Ch. Naudin). Ann. Sci. Nat., VI, VII, 126–163.]

Classification of the Botanical Collection made during the San Juan Reconnaissance of 1877, in Colorado and New Mexico. Annual Report of the Chief of Engineers for 1878. Appendix SS, pp. 1833–1840.

Some Western Plants. Bot. Gaz., III, 81.

Dr. Newcomb and the Uniformity of Nature. By a Country Reader. Independent, No. 1558, p. 1. Letters on the same subject in No. 1555, p. 16, and No. 1564, p. 15.

The Animal Poison of the Far West—"Loco" or "Crazy-weed." Am. Agriculturist, Oct., pp. 380, 381.

Does Nature forbid Providence? By "Country Reader." Independent, XXX, No. 1562, pp. 1–3.

What is a Sweet Potato? Am. Agriculturist, Nov., p. 423.

On a form of Scirpus supinus, L. Trimen's Jour. Bot., XVI, 346.

Shortia galacifolia rediscovered. Am. J. Sci., III, XVI, 483–485. [Bot. Gaz., IV, 106–108.]

Note sur le Shortia galicifolia et Revision des Diapensiacées. Ann. Sci. Nat. Bot., VI, VII, 173–179, with plate.

Diclytra, Dielytra, Dicentra; Sporting Trillium grandiflorum. Bull. Torr. Bot. Club, VI, 277, 278.

1879.

Gerardia tenuifolia, Vahl, var. asperula. Bot. Gaz., IV, 153.

Bentham on Nomenclature. Same, IV, 158-161.

Notes upon "Notes of a Botanical Excursion into North Carolina" (by J. H. Redfield). Bull. Torr. Bot Club, VI, 331-338.

Epipactis Helleborine, var. viridens (*E. viridiflora*, Reichenbach), a North American plant. Bot. Gaz., IV, 206.

Roots and "Yarbs."—In the Mountains of North Carolina. Am. Agriculturist, Sept., p. 337, 338.

Botanical Contributions.—1. Characters of some new Species of Compositæ in the Mexican Collection made by C. C. Parry and Edward Palmer, chiefly in the Province of San Louis Potosi, in 1878. 2. Some New North American Genera, Species, etc. Proc. Am. Acad., XV, 25-52.

Pertinacity and predominance of Weeds. Am. Jour. Sci., III, XVIII, 161-167.

On the Self-fertilization of Plants. Bot. Gaz., IV, 182-187.

Who finds White Partridge-berries? Bot. Gaz., IV, 190.

Duplicate Corolla of Campanula. Bot. Gaz., IV, 207.

Scutia ferrea and Reynosia latifolia. Bot. Gaz., IV, 208.

Nomenclature in Atlantic U. S. Polypetalæ. Bot. Gaz., IV, 210.

The beheading of flies by Mentzelia ornata; The Dichogamy of Spigelia Marilandica; The most Arctic timber; "Carniverous Plants." Bot. Gaz., IV, 213-215.

The Gymnospermy of Coniferæ. Bot. Gaz., IV, 222-224.

Vaccinium macrocarpon, var. intermedium; Common and Troublesome Weeds near Santa Barbara, Cal. Bot. Gaz., IV, 226.

On the Genus Garberia. Proc. Acad. Phila., 1879, 379, 380.

1880.

The Flora of Boston and its vicinity, and the changes it has undergone. Winsor's Memorial History of Boston, I, 17-22 (with autograph).

Tennessee Plants. Bot. Gaz., V, 3.

Littorella and Schizæa in Nova Scotia. Bot. Gaz., V, 4. [Gard. Chron., XIII, 4.]

Note on trapping of moths or butterflies by certain plants. Am. Nat., XIV, 50.

Natural Science and Religion: Two lectures delivered to the Theological School of Yale College. New York, 1880. 12mo, pp. 111.

The Genus Leavenworthia; Automatic Movement of the Frond of Asplenium Trichomanes. Bot. Gaz., V, 25-27.

Flora of Kerguelen's Land. Bot. Gaz., V, 39.

Notulæ exiguæ. Bot. Gaz., V, 53. 63, 75, 87, 88.

On a point of botanical nomenclature. Trimen's Jour. Bot., XVIII, 186 (from Am. J. Sci., III, XIX, 420).

Meanwhile, what should be done and how? Independent, XXXII, No. 1652, p. 1.

Action of Light on Vegetation. Am. J. Sci., III, XX, 74-76.

Contributions to North American Botany.—1. Notes on some Compositæ. 2. Some Species of Asclepias. 3. A New Genus of Gentianaceæ. 4. Miscellaneæ of the North American Flora. Proc. Am. Acad., XVI, 78-108.

Mesembrianthemum, not Mesembryanthemum. Trimen's Jour. Bot., XVIII, 243 (from Bot. Gaz., V, 89).

Botany of the Black Hills of Dakota. Report on the Geology and Resources of the Black Hills of Dakota, by H. Newton, E. M., and W. P. Jenney, E. M. [U. S. G. G. Survey R. M. R.], pp. 529-537.

1881.

The Vegetation of the Rocky Mountain Region and a Comparison with that of other Parts of the World. By A. Gray and J. D. Hooker. Bull. U. S. Geol. and Geogr. Survey of the Territories, VI, 1-77.

A Chinese puzzle by Linnæus. Trimen's Jour. of Bot., xix, 325, 326.

Review of the North American climbing species of Clematis, with compound leaves and thick or thickish erect sepals. Curtis's Botanical Magazine, cvii, under plate 6594.

1882.

Chrysogonum Virginianum, var. dentatum. Bot. Gaz., vii, 31, 32.

Githopsis. Bot. Gaz., vii, 40.

Plucheas. Bot. Gaz., vii, 45.

Ranunculus. Bot. Gaz, vii, 47.

The Relation of Insects to Flowers. The Contemporary Review, xli, 598-609. [Eclectic Magazine, xxxv, 732-739.]

The citation of botanical authorities. Trimen's Jour. Bot., xx, 173, 174.

Contributions to North American Botany.—1. Studies of Aster and Solidago in the Older Herbaria. 2. Novitiæ Arizonicæ, etc.; Characters of the New Plants of certain Recent Collections, mainly in Arizona and adjacent Districts, etc. Proc. Am. Acad., xvii, 163-230.

Parishella Californica. Bot. Gaz., vii, 94, 95.

Evolution versus Evangelical Religion. Boston Evening Transcript, Sept. 13, 1882.

Note on the Musaratic Chapel of the Cathedral of Toledo. Nation, No. 884, p. 482.

Mimulus dentatus, Nutt.; Linnæa borealis. Bot. Gaz., vii, 112.

Remarks concerning the Flora of North America. Am. J. Sci., III, xxiv, 321-331. [Reprinted in part in Bot. Gaz., vii, 129-135, 139-143.]

Note on the Lignified Snake. Bull. Torr. Bot. Clu b, ix, 152.

Synopsis of species of Nama. Godman & Salvin, Biologia Centrali-Americana; Botany, ii, 360-365.

1883.

The Lignified Snake from Brazil. Am. J. Sci., III, xxv, 79-81. [Bot. Gaz. (in part), viii, 153, 154.]

Natural Selection and Natural Theology. Nature, xxvii, 291, 292, 527, 528; xxviii, 79.

Reports as Director of the Herbarium of Harvard University. Annual Reports of the President and Treasurer, 1882-'83, p. 114, 116; 1883-'84, p. 136; 1884-'85, p. 142, 143; 1885-'86, p. 118-119; 1886-'87, p. 123.

Gonolobus Shortii. Bot. Gaz., viii, 191.

Hibiscus Moscheutos and H. roseus; Stipules in Saxifragaceæ; Vincetoxicum. Bot. Gaz , viii, 244, 245.

Condurango. Bot. Gaz., viii, 260.

Lonicera grata. Bull. Torr. Bot. Club, x, 94-95; xi, 76.

Rhododendron (Azalea) Vaseyi. Bot. Gaz., viii, 282.

Aquilegia longissima. Bot. Gaz., viii, 295.

Contributions to North American Botany. 1. Characters of New Compositæ, with Revisions of certain Genera, and Critical Notes. 2. Miscellaneous Genera and Species. Proc. Am. Acad., xix, 1-96.

Letter on publication of a letter by Dr. Torrey, etc. Bot. Gaz., viii, 317.

1884.

Antirrhina prehensilia. Bot. Gaz., ix, 53-54.

Lonicera grata. Bull. Torr. Bot. Club, xi, 76.

A revision of the North American species of the Genus Oxytropis, DC. Proc. Am. Acad., xx, 1-7.

Notes on the Movements of the Andrœcium in sunflowers. Proc. Acad. Philad., 1884, 287-288.

Synoptical Flora of North America. Vol. I, Part 2. Caprifoliaceæ—Compositæ. New York, July, 1884. Roy. 8vo, pp. 474. Second edition [with supplement, etc., in connection with vol. II, Part 1]. New York, January, 1886. Roy, 8vo, pp. 480. Reissued, with corrections, April, 1888, as Smithsonian Miscellaneous Collections, vol. XXXI.

Notes on some North American Species of Saxifraga. Proc Am. Acad., XX, 8-12.

Veatchia, nov. gen. Anacardiacearum. Bull. Calif. Acad., I, 4-5.

Gender of Names of Varieties. Am. J. Sci., III, XXVII, 396-398.

Breweria minima. Bot. Gaz., IX, 148.

Hypopitys or Hypopithys? Am. J. Sci., III, XXVIII, 238, 239.

Characteristics of the North American Flora: An address to the botanists of the Brit. Assoc for the Adv. Sc. at Montreal. Am. J. Sci., III, XXVIII, 323-340 ; Rep. Brit. Assoc., 1885.

The name Trilisa, Am. J. Sci., III, XXVIII, 402.

1885.

The Scientific Principles of Agriculture. Science, V. 76.

Notes upon the Plants collected on the Commander Islands (Behring and Copper Islands) by Leonard Stejneger. Proc. U. S. Nat. Museum, VII, 527-529.

Pine needles. Bull. Torr. Bot. Club, XII, 102.

Contributions to the Botany of North America. 1. A Revision of some Borragineous Genera. 2. Notes on some American Species of Utricularia. 3. New Genera of Arizona, California, and their Mexican Borders, and two additional species of Asclepiadaceæ. 4. Gamopetalæ Miscellaneæ. Proc. Am. Acad., XX, 257-310.

The Monterey Pine and Cypress. Science, V, 433-434.

How to reach the Grand Cañon. Science, V, 516-517.

Circular Letter to American Botanists. Published separately, Nov. 19, 1885.

Report of the International Polar Expedition to Point Barrow, Alaska. [By Lieut. P. H. Ray.] (Plants. By Asa Gray. pp. 191, 192.)

1886.

Notes on Myosurus. Bull. Torr. Bot. Club, XIII, 1- 4.

Anemone nudicaulis. Bot. Gaz., XI, 17.

Anemonella thalictroides, Spach. Bot. Gaz., XI, 39.

Contributions to American Botany. 1. A Revision of the North American Ranunculi. 2. Sertum Chihuahuense. 3. Miscellanea. Proc. Am. Acad., XXI, 363-413.

The Genus Asimina. Bot. Gaz., XI, 161-164.

Tiarella cordifolia. Bull. Torr. Bot. Club, XIII, 100, 101.

Vancouveria. Bot. Gaz., XI, 182, 183.

Corydalis aurea and its allies ; The Arillus in Asimina. Bot. Gaz., XI, 188-190.

Essay towards a revision of Dodecatheon. Bot. Gaz., XI, 231-234.

Letter to the Botanical Club of the A. A. A. S. Bot. Gaz., XI, 245, 246.

Memorando of a revision of the North American Violets. Bot. Gaz., XI, 253-256, 289-293.

Ambrosia bidentata × trifida. Bot. Gaz., XI, 338.

Note on Shortia. Am. J. Sci., III, XXXII, 473. [Note to Prof. Sargent's article on Journey of André Michaux.]

1887.

The Genus Iris. Bot. Gaz., XII, 16, 17.

Delphinium, an attempt to distinguish the North American Species. Bot. Gaz., XII, 49-54.

Contributions to American Botany. 1. Revision of some Polypetalous Genera and Orders precursory to the Flora of North America. 2. Sertum Chihuahuense; appendix. 3. Miscellanea. Proc. Amer. Acad., XXII, 270-314.

Capitalization of Botanical Names Amer. Florist, II, 294.

List of Plants collected by Dr. Edward Palmer in the State of Jalisco, Mexico, in 1886 [Gamopetalæ, by Dr. Asa Gray]. Proc Am. Acad., XXII, 416-446.

The elements of Botany for Beginners and for Schools (based upon First Lessons in Botany). New York, 1887. 8vo., pp. 226.

Coptis, section Chrysocoptis. Bot. Gaz., XII, 296, 297.

Annotations. [Nelumbo lutea and Nemacaulis.] Bull. Torr. Bot. Club. XIV, 228, 229.

Botanical Nomenclature. Britten's Journal of Botany, XXV, 353-355.

1888.

New or Rare Plants. Bot. Gaz., XIII, 73.

Contributions to American Botany. Notes upon some Polypetalous Genera and Orders. Proc. Amer. Acad., XXIII, 223-227.

II.—BOTANICAL NOTICES AND BOOK REVIEWS.

1841.

Botanical Notices. W. Griffith, Report on Tea Plant of Upper Assam; M. Guillemin, Report on Expedition to Brazil to obtain information on culture of the Teaplant; Meyen, report on Progress of Vegetable Philosophy for 1837; Hooker's Journal of Botany; Hooker's Flora Boreali-Americana; Endlicher's Genera Plantarum; Moquin-Tandon, Enumeratio Chenopodearum; Steudel's Nomenclator Botanicus; Kunze Caricography; J. E. Bowman, Fossil Infusoria in England. Am. J. Sci., XL, 165-176.

Botanical Notices. Horsefield, Bennett and Brown, Plantæ Javanicæ Rariores; Hooker's Icones Plantarum, part 7; Linnæa, vol. XIII, nos. 4, 5, 6; Wikström, on the Progress of Botany. Am. J. Sci., XL, 391-393.

Botanical Notices. William Darlington, Discourse on Gramineæ; Teschemacher, Address to Boston Natural History Society, May, 1841; A. de St. Hilaire, Leçons de Botanique; Endlicher, Genera Plantarum; E. T. Steudel, Nomenclator Botanicus; Kunze, Supplements der Riedgräser (Carices) zu Schkuhr's Monographie; Hooker and Arnott's Botany of Capt. Beechey's Voyage; A. Moquin-Tandom, Elémens de Tératologie Végétale; John Darby, Manual of Botany, adapted to the productions of the Southern States. Am. J. Sci., XLI, 365-376.

Botanical Notices. Endlicher, Euchiridion Botanicum exhibens Classes et Ordines Plantarum; Lindley, Flora Medica and Elements of Botany; Laura Johnson and A. Eaton, Botanical Teacher for North America; Hooker's Journal of Botany; Schomburgk, on the Urari or Arrow-poison of the Indians of Guiana; Archiv für Naturgeshichte; J. F. W. Johnston, Lectures on the Applications of Chemistry and Geology to Agriculture. Am. J. Sci., XLII, 182-191

Botanical Notices. H. E. Richter, Caroli Linnæi Systema, Genera, Species Plantarum uno volumine; H. W. Buek, Genera, Species, et Synonyma Candolleana; Kunth, Enumeratio Plantarum, vol. III; Loudon's Arboretum et Fruticetum Britannicum abridged; Steudel's Nomenclator Botanicus, 2d ed.; Torrey & Gray's Flora of North America, vol. II, part 2; Nuttall's edition of Michaux's Sylva Americana. Am. J. Sci., XLII, 375-377.

1842.

Botanical Notices. New edition of Michaux's North American Sylva; Loudon's Encyclopædia of Trees and Shrubs; Ledebour, Flora Rossica; London Journal of Botany; Kunze, Supplemente der Riedgräser (Carices) zu Chr. Schkuhr's Monographie, etc. Am. J. Sci, XLIII, 188-189.

Botanical Notices. Ward, On the Growth of Plants in closely glazed cases; Hooker's London Journal of Botany. Am. J. Sci., XLIII, 383-386.

Botanical Notices. Nuttall, The North American Sylva; Choisy, de Convolvu. laceis dissertatio tertia complecteus Cuscutarum, etc.; Spring, Monographie do la Famille des Lycopodiacées; Endlicher, Mantissa Botanica; Hooker's British Flora. Am. J. Sci., XLIV, 194–199.

1843.

Botanical Notices. Hooker's Icones Plantarum, vol. I, new series; Tuckerman, Enumeratio methodica Caricum quarundam; Flora Brasiliensis, fasc. 1. Am. J. Sci., XLV, 214–218.

Botanical Notices. Notice of Botanical Collections; Brand, Iodine in Phanerogamic Plants and Mosses; Wiegmann and Polsdorff, Disengagement of Carbonic Acid by the Roots of Plants. Am. J. Sci., XLV, 225–227.

Botanical Notices. Wm. Darlington, Reliquiæ Baldwinianæ; A. de Jussieu, Cours élémentaire de Botanique; F. Unger, Grundzuge der Botanik; G. W. Bischoff, Lehrbuch der Botanik; G. Fresenius, Grundriss der Botanik; Buck's Index generalis et specialis ad A. P. DeCandolle Prodromum Syst. Nat. Reg. Veg., etc.; Ledebour's Flora Rossica; C. C. Babington, Manual of British Botany; Kunze's Supplemente der Reidgräser (Carices) zur Schkuhr's Monographie; Botanische Zeitung. Am. J. Sci., XLVI, 192–208.

1844.

Botanical Notices. DeCandolle, Prodromus, vol. VIII; G. G. Walpers, Repertorium Botanices Systematicæ; C. S. Kunth, Enumeratio Plantarum, etc.; Endlicher, Mantissa Botanica; R. B. Hinds and G. Bentham, Botany of H. M. S. Sulphur in 183 –42; H. B. Fielding and G. Gardiner, Sertum Plantarum, etc.; A. de Jussieu, Cours Élémentaire de Botanique; H. F. Link, Jahresbericht für Physiologische Botanik, 1841, and Anatomia Plantarum Iconibus Illustrata. Am. J. Sci., XLVII, 198–205.

Botanical Notices. J. D. Hooker, Botany of the Antarctic Voyage of H. M. Ships Erebus and Terror in 1839–43, and Species Filicum, parts 1 and 2; E. C. Maout, Leçons Elémentaires de Botanique; Martius, Systema Materiæ Medicæ Veg. Brasiliensis. Am. J. Sci., XLVIII, 204–208.

1845.

Botanical Notices. A. Lasègue, Musée Botanique de M. B. Delessert; DeCandolle's Prodromus, vol IX, and Théorie elementaire de la Botanique. Am. J. Sci., XLIX, 171–176.

1846.

Review of "Explanations; a sequel to the Vestiges of the Natural History of Creation." N. A. Review, April, 1846, 465–506.

Botanical Notices. Vegetable Physiology; Unger, Distribution of the Vestiges of Palms in the Geological Formations; Analogy between the Flora of Japan and that of the United States; Unger, Conspectus of the Fossil Flora. Am. J. Sci., II, II, 133–136.

Botanical Notices. D. J. Browne, The Trees of America; A. Henfrey, Outlines of Structural and Physiological Botany; Delessert, Icones Selectæ Plantarum, etc. Am. J. Sci., II, II, 442–445.

1847.

Botanical Notices. F. E. L. Fischer et C. A. Meyer, Sertum Petropolitanum, etc.; Flora Brasiliensis, fasc. 6; Trautvetter, Plantarum Imagines et Descriptiones Floram Russicam Illustrantes; Hooker, Species Filicum; S. Moricand, Plantes Nouvelles ou Rares d'Amerique, fasc. 1–8; Ledebour, Flora Rossica, fasc. 7. Am. J. Sci, II, III, 146–148.

Botanical Notices. L. Agassiz, Nomenclator Zoologicus; Ruprecht, 3 papers in Beiträge zur Pflanzenkunde des Russischen Reiches; G. B Emerson, Report on Trees and Schrubs of Massachusetts; Bot. Magazine for 1847. Am. J. Sci , II, III, 302-310.

1848.

Botanical Notices. DeCandolle's Prodromus; Trans. Linn. Soc., XX, Botanical Papers by J. D. Hooker, Falconer, etc.; E. Tuckerman, Synopsis of Lichenes of New England; A. Young, A Flora of Maine; Ledebour, Flora Rossica, fasc. 8; Hooker's London Journal of Botany, No. 73. Am. J. Sci., II, V, 449-459.

1849.

Botanical Notices. A. DeCandolle, Prodromus. Am. J. Sci., II, VII, 309-311.

Botanical Notices. Fendler's Botanical Collections in New Mexico; Hooker's Journal of Botany, papers in Nos. 1, 2, 3; W. Griffith, Posthumous Papers. Am. J. Sci., II, VII, 452-454.

Notice of Dr. Hooker's Flora Antarctica Am. J. Sci., II, VIII, 161-180.

Botanical Notices. DeCandolle's Prodromus Reg. Veg., vol. XIII; T G. Lea, Catalogue of Plants near Cincinnati collected in 1834-1844; A. de Jussieu, Elements of Botany, transl. by J. H. Wilson; J. H. Balfour, Manual of Botany. Am. J. Sci., II, VIII, 300-303.

1850.

Memorials of John Bartram and Humphrey Marshall, with notes of their Botanical Contemporaries, by Wm. Darlington, LL. D. Am. J. Sci., II, IX, 85-105.

Botanical Notices. Endlicher, Genera Plantarum, part 2, and Synopsis Coniferarum. Am. J. Sci., II, IX, 148-149.

1852.

Botanical Notices. [In the form of a letter to one of the Editors.] De Candolle's Prodromus; Kunth, Enumeratio Plantarum, Vol. V; Fenzl and Endlicher, Genera Plantarum; Unger, Die Urwelt in ihren Verschiedenen Bildungsperiod; Martius, on Palms; von Esenbeck and Spinner, Genera Floræ Germanicæ Iconibus Illustrata; changes in Professorships in German Universities; Fries, Summa Vegetabil. Scandinaviæ and Monograph of Hieracium; Ledebour, Flora Rossica; Webb, Phytographia Canariensis; Weddell, Monograph of Cinchona, and Balanophoreæ vs. Rafflesiaceæ; M. Decaisne at Jardin des Plantes; Botany of the Voyage of the Bonité and the Astrolabe and Zelée; Botanists at the Jardin des Plantes; M. C. Gay, Historia Fisica et Politica de Chile; Richard, Botany in de la Sagra's Histoire Physique, etc., of Cuba: Boissier, Diagnoses Plantarum Orientalium; work of Choisy, Duby, Godet, Shuttleworth, Lehmann, Blume, DeVriese, Dozy, Molkenboer, Hooker, Babington; W. Hooker, Species Filicum, Icones Plantarum and Victoria Regia; J. D. Hooker, Rhododendrons of Sikkim Himalaya, Flora Indica, Novæ-Zealandiæ, Tasmaniæ; Bentham, Niger Flora; Webb, Spicilegia Gorgouica; Trans. Linn. Soc. of London, XX, part 3, Botanical papers; Cryptogamic Botany, works by Kunze, Gottsche, Lindenberg, and von Esenbeck, Müller, Gümbel, Schimper, Kützing, Agardh; Harvey, Phycologia, Britannica, Manual of British Algæ, etc.; Schærer's work on Lichens. Am. J. Sci., II, XIII, 42-53.

Botanical Notices. Kunze, Supplemente der Riedgräser (Carices) zu Chr. Schkuhr's Monographie, etc.; Pritzel, Thesaurus Literaturæ Botanicæ; Flora Brasiliensis, fasc. 10. Am. J. Sci., II, XIII, 421-425.

Nereis Boreali-Americana; or Contributions to a History of the Marine Algæ of North America, by Wm. Henry Harvey, M. D. Am. J. Sci., II, XIV, 1-8.

Botanical Notices. Junghuhn and De Vries, The Camphor-Tree of Sumatra; W. Hooker, Chinese Rice-Paper Plant; H. W. Ravenel, Fungi Caroliniani Exsiccati;

H. Mis. 142——51

Antonio Bertoloni, Miscellanea Botanica, parts 1-10; A. Henfrey, Vegetation of Europe. Am. J. Sci., II, xiv, 113-116.
Botanical Notices. De Candolle's Prodromus, Vol. xiii. Am. J. Sci., II, xiv, 291.
Botanical Notices. J. D. Hooker, Botany of the Antarctic Voyage, II, Flora of New Zealand; Seemann, Botany of the Voyage of the *Herald*. Am. J. Sci., II, xiv, 427, 428.

1853.

Botanical Notices. J. G. Agardh, Species, Genera et Ordines Algarum, Vol. i; L. R. Tulasne, Monographia Podostemacearum ; Seemann, Botany of the Voyage of the *Herald*, part 2; Walpers, Ann. Bot. Syst., Tom. ii. Am. J. Sci., II, xv, 131-133.
Botanical Notices. Mohl, Grundzüge der Anatomie and Physiologie der Vegetabilischen Zelle ; Schacht, Die Pflanzenzelle ; Lindley, Folia Orchidacea. Am. J. Sci., II, xv, 279-280.
Botanical Notices. Wm. Darlington, Flora Cestrica ; H. W. Ravenel, Fungi Caroliniani Exsiccati ; Lindley's Folia Orchidacea, parts 2-4; Mohl, Cellulose in Vegetable Membranes ; Hoffmann, Circulation of Sap ; Crüger, observations on certain Monocotyledonæ Epigynæ; W. Hofmeister, on Development of Zostera ; Wichura, Winding of Leaves ; Horsfield, Plantæ Javanicæ Rariores; Hooker, Species Filicum, part 6 ; N. B. Ward, Growth of Plants in tight cases. Am. J. Sci., II, xvi, 129-133.
Botanical Notices. Harvey, Nereis Boreali-Americana ; J. Torrey, Plantæ Fremontianæ, on Darlingtonia Californica, on Batis maritima of Linnæus ; A. Gray, Plantæ Wrightianæ Texano-Neo-Mexicanæ, part 2; J. Leidy, Fauna and Flora within living animals; M. J. Berkeley and M. A. Curtis, Exotic Fungi from the Schweinitzian Herbarium. Am. J. Sci., II, xvi, 422-426.

1854.

Botanical Notices. Salad for the Solitary, by an Epicure ; Lindley, The Vegetable Kingdom; De Candolle's Prodromus. Am. J. Sci., II, xvii, 132-133.
Introductory Essay, in Dr. Hooker's Flora of New Zealand, Vol. I. Am. J. Sci., II, xvii, 241-252, 334-350.
Botanical Notices. E. G. Steudel, Synopsis Plantarum Glumacearum, fasc. 1; Lindley's Folia Orchidacea, part 5; A. de Jussieu, Letters of Linnæus to B. de Jussieu. Am. J. Sci., II, xvii, 443-444.
Botanical Notices. J. W. Griffith and A. Henfrey. Micrographic Dictionary; B. Seemann, Botany of the Voyage of the *Herald;* Dr. Hooker's Flora of New Zealand, part 5: A. Gray, Botany of Wilkes's Exped., Phanerogamia. Am. J. Sci., II, xviii, 131-133.
Botanical Notices. Hooker's Icones Plantarum, Vol. X; J. D. Hooker's Flora of New Zealand, part 6; von Esenbeck et al., Genera Plantarum Floræ Germanicæ, etc., Floræ Danicæ Supplementi fasciculus I; Griffith and Henfrey, Micrographic Dictionary, part 2; Linnæa, Vol. xxvi; Bot. Zeitung and Bouplandia; Annales des Sciences Naturelles, etc., Vol. xx, Botanical papers. Am. J. Sci., II, xviii, 284-286.
Botanical Notices. J. F. Allen, Victoria Regia; Miquel, De Vriese et al., Plantæ Junghuhnianæ, fasc. 3; Steudel, Synopsis Plantarum Glumacearum, fasc. 3 ; Seemann's Botany of the Voyage of the Herald, part 5: De Vriese, Pandaneæ. Am. J. Sci., II, xviii, 428-429.

1855.

Botanical Notices. Flora Brasiliensis, fasc. 12; Boussingault on non-assimilatio of Nitrogen by Plants; M. Personne on Lupulin ; Hofmeister, The Fertilization o Ferns; Payer, Traité d'Organogénie Végétale Comparée, livr. 1-4; Griffith and Henfrey, Micrographic Dictionary, parts 3-5. Am. J. Sci., II, xix, 128-130.
Botanical Notices. Hooker's Flora of New Zealand, parts 7 and 8; Seemann' Botany of the Voyage of the *Herald*, part 6; Tulasne, on the Uredineæ and Ustilagineæ

I. A. Lapham, Grasses of Wisconsin; H. G. Reichenbach, De Pollinis Orchidearum Genesi ac Structura, etc.; Micrographic Dictionary on Ergot. Am. J. Sci., II, xix, 439–443.

Botanical Notices. M. J. Schleiden, Poetry of the Vegetable World; De Vriese and Harting, Monographie des Marattiacées; Pritzel, Iconum Bot. Index Locupletissimus; J. Darby, Botany of the Southern States; Dunal et al., Wheat from Ægilops. Am. J. Sci., II, xx, 129–135.

Botanical Notices. Thuret, Sexual Reproduction in the Lower Cryptogamia; Trécul, Formations Secondaires dans les Cellules Végétales; Mohl on Chlorophyll; Miers, Seeds of Magnolia; Bertoloni, Miscellanea Botanica, fasc. 13 and 14; Decaisne on the Wellingtonia of Lindley; Darwin, Does Sea-water kill Seeds? Am. J. Sci., II, xx, 276–284.

1856.

Botanical Notices. A. De Candolle, Géographique Botanique Raisonné; J. D. Hooker and T. Thomson, Flora Indica. Am. J. Sci., II, xxi, 134–137.

Botanical Notices. E. G. Steudel, Synopsis Plantarum Glumacearum, parts 1 and 2; J. D. Hooker, Flora of Tasmania; F. A. W. Miquel, Flora van Nederlandsch Indië; Griffith and Henfrey, Micrographic Dictionary; A. Braun, Algarum Unicellularium Genera Nova et minus Cognita. Am. J. Sci., II, xxi, 282–284.

Botanical Notices. Journ. Proc. Linn. Soc., Vol. I, no. I, 1856, Botanical Papers by C. J. F. Bunbury, C. F. Meisner, R. Kippist, and Zoological Papers; Schacht, Mohl et al., on the Origin of the Embryo in Plants; Pringsheim, Reproduction in Algæ; Flora Brasiliensis, fasc. 15. Am. J. Sci., II, xxii, 134–137.

Botanical Notices. A. De Candolle, Géographique Botanique Raisonnée, etc.; Radlkofer, Origin of the Embryo in Plants; Bentham, Notes on Loganiaceæ; M. Neisler, The Flowers of the Pea-Nut; Flora Brasiliensis, fasc. 16 and 17; L. R. Tulasne, Monographia Monimiacearum. Am. J. Sci., II, xxii, 429–437.

1857.

Botanical Notices. De Candolle's Prodromus, xiv, part 1; W. A. Bromfield, Flora Vectensis, edited by W. J. Hooker and T. B. Salter; Seemann's Botany of the Voyage of the *Herald*, parts 7 and 8; G. Engelmann, Synopsis of the Cactaceæ of the United States Am. J. Sci., II, xxiii, 126–129.

Botanical Notices. A. Henfrey, Origin of the Embryo in Plants. Am. J. Sci., II, xxiii, 278–279.

Botanical Notices. W. S. Sullivant et L. Lesquereux, Musci Boreali-Americani, etc. Am. J. Sci., II, xxiii, 438–439.

Botanical Notices. J. M. Berkeley. Introduction to Cryptogamic Botany; H. Hoffmann, Witterung und Wachsthum; C. Lehmann, Revisio Potentillarum Iconibus Illustrata; R. Caspary, Conspectus Systematicus Hydrillearum; Ad. Chatin, on Vallisneria spiralis, L. Am. J. Sci, II, xxiv, 151–155.

Botanical Notices. Journ. of Proc. Linn. Soc Vol. I, No. 4, Botanical Papers by Berkeley, Currey, Bennett, Seeman, Masters, Lindley, Oliver; Vol. ii, No. 5, containing Higgins on the Cultivation of Mosses; Bentham, Synopsis of the Genus Clitoria; Hooker and Thomson, Præcursores ad Floram Indicam; G. Bentham, on the Principles of Generic Nomenclature; C. Mueller and Walpers, Synopsis Plantarum Phanerogamicarum, etc.; Bertolom, Miscellanea Botanica, fasc. 15 and 16; Harvey, Phycologia Australica; Niesler, Indigofera Caroliniana. Am. J. Sci., II, xxiv, 281–288.

Botanical Notices. A. Henfrey, an Elementary Course of Botany; Naudin's Researches on the Genus Cucurbita. Am. J. Sci., II, xxiv, 434–443.

1858.

Botanical Notices. De Candolle's Prodromus, Vol. xiv, part 2; Hooker's Flora of Tasmania; Journ. Proc. Linn Soc, No 6, papers by Thomson, Hooker and Thomson; De Vriese, Plantæ Indiæ Bataviæ Orientalis. Am. J. Sci., II, xxv, 290–293,

Botanical Notices. F. Boott, Illustrations of the Genus Carex ; Journ. Proc. Linn. Soc., II, No. 7, papers by Henslow, Gray, Wood, Moore, etc.; Lindley, List of Orchids from Cuba ; Andersson Salices Boreali-Americanæ ; Grisebach, Vegetation der Karaiben ; J. Wallman, Essai d'une Exposition Systématique de la Famille des Characées; Parlatore's Eulogy on F. B. Webb; Agricultural Botany in the Western States. Am. J. Sci., II, xxvi, 135-139.

Botanical Notices. H. A. Weddell, Monographie de la Famille des Urticées; Miquel's Flora van Nederlandsch Indië ; Walpers, Ann. Bot. Syst., 2d fasc.; Pringsheim, Jahrbüchei, Vol. I, part 1, papers by Pringsheim and Hofmeister ; Radlkofer, Fecundation in the Vegetable Kingdom : Bowerbank, Natural History of the Spongiadæ; Seeman's Botany of the Voyage of the Herald, parts 9 and 10; J. D. Hooker, Structure and Affinities of Balanophoreæ ; Roussingault, Researches on the part of nitrogenous matters in vegetation, and the nitrates in soils ; J. Decaisne, Structure and Development of Flower and Fruit of Pear. Am. J. Sci., II, xxv, 109-124.

Botanical Notices. Journ. Proc. Linn. Soc., No. 8, Botanical papers by Müller, Hooker and Thomson, Barter, Fée, Bennett; Flora of Australia. Am J. Sci., II, xxvi., 283.

Botanical Notices. Flora Brasiliensis, fasc. 18-20 ; Journ. Proc. Linn. Soc., No. 9, Jameson on Pseudoceutrum ; E. Tuckerman, Lichenes Americæ Septentrionalis Exsiccati, fasc. 5 and 6; Nylander, Synopsis Methodica Lichenum, etc., fasc. 1 ; Miers, Illustrations of S. American Plants, Vol. II ; Bentham, Handbook of the British Flora. Am. J. Sci., II, xxvi, 412-416.

1859.

Botanical Notices. W. H. Harvey, Nereis Boreali-Americana. Am. J. Sci., II, xxvii, 142-146.

Botanical Notices. Wm. Darlington, American Weeds and Useful Plants; Journ. Proc. Linn. Soc., No. 10; papers by Bentham on Leguotideæ; Spruce on Asteranthos; Müeller on Eucalypti of Australia ; Berkeley on Tuberiform Vegetable Productions from China; Grisebach on Abuta ; Dickie on Arctic Plants ; No. 11 of same, papers by Müller, Bentham and Henfiey ; Walpers, Ann. Bot. Syst., Vol. IV; E. Regel, on Parthenogenesis ; L. Vilmorin, Notices sur l'Amelioration des Plantes par le Semis, etc. Am. J. Sci., II, xxvii, 437-442.

Botanical Notices. Non Martius, Eulogy on Robert Brown; F. Mueller, Fragmenta, Phytographiæ Australiæ, Vol. I, fasc. 1-4 ; Journ. Proc. Linn. Soc., Nov. 12, papers by Henfrey, Ralph, Oliver, Spruce, Mitten ; R. B. Van der Bosch, Synopsis Hymenophyllaccarum : Parry, Torrey and Engelmann, Botany of the Mexican Boundary ; Catalogue of Phænogamous and Cryptogamous Plants in Gray's Manual. Am. J. Sci., II, xxviii, 290-293.

Botanical Notices. G. Engelmann, New Genera of Diœcious Grasses of U. S.; W. H. Harvey, Thesaurus Capensis, Vol. I ; Grisebach's Outlines of Systematic Botany ; Henfrey, Structure and Growth of Rootlets ; E. Davy, on the taking of arsenic by plants. Am. J. Sci., II, xxviii, 439-444.

1860.

Botanical Notices. C. Wright, Collections of Cuban Plants; G. Englemann, the Genus Cuscuta; J. G. Cooper, Distribution of the Forests and Trees of N. America. Am. J. Sci., II, xxix, 127-129.

Review of Darwin's Theory on the Origin of Species by means of Natural Selection. Am. J. Sci., II, xxix, 153-184. [The Origin of Species by means of Natural Selection. Darwiniana, pp. 9-16.]

Botanical Notices. C. J. Maximowicz, Primitiæ Floræ Amurensis; Harvey's Thesaurus Capensis, No. 2; Hooker's Species Filicum, Vol. III, part 1; Journ. Proc. Linn. Soc. No. 14, Botanical Papers by Anderson and Spruce ; No. 15 of same, papers by

Cocks, Hooker and Thomson; No. 16 of same, papers by Babington, Caruel, Oliver, Spruce, Moore, and Hogg; Flora Brasiliensis, fasc. 18, 23, and 24; J. D. Hooker's Flora Tasmania; Ogston, Poisoning of Plants by Arsenic. Am. J. Sci., II, xxix, 436-441.

A free examination of Darwin's Treatise on the Origin of Species. Atlantic Monthly, July, Aug., Oct., 1860. Reprinted in 1861 as a separate pamphlet of 55 pages. [Natural Selection not inconsistent with Natural Theology. Darwiniana, pp. 87-177.]

Botanical Notices. A. W. Chapman, Flora of the Southern United States; G. Bentham, Synopsis of Dalbergieæ; G. Suckley and J. G. Cooper, Reports on Natural History, etc., of Minnesota, Nebraska, Washington, and Oregon Territories. Am. J. Sci., II, xxx, 137-139.

Botanical Notices. M. A. Curtis, Geological and Natural History Survey of North Carolina; Thwaites, Enumeratio Plantarum Zeylanicæ, parts 1 and 2; Walpers, Ann. Bot. Syst.; Buek, Index ad De Cand. Prodromum, etc., part 3. Am. J. Sci., II, xxx, 275-276.

<h2 style="text-align:center">1861.</h2>

Botanical Notices. W. H. Harvey, Thesaurus Capensis, No. 4; W. H. Harvey and O. W. Sonder, Flora Capensis, Vol. I; A. H. R. Grisebach, Flora of the British West Indies, parts 1 and 2, and Plantæ Wrightianæ e Cuba Orientali; D. C. Eaton, Filices Wrightianæ et Fendlerianæ; T. J. Hale, Additions to Flora of Wisconsin; J. S. Newberry, Catalogue of Flowering Plants and Ferns of Ohio; E. W. Hervey, Catalogue of Plants of New Bedford, Mass.; E. Tatnall, Catalogue of Phænogamous and Filicoid Plants of Newcastle Co., Delaware; H. W. Ravenel, Fungi Caroliniani Exsiccati, fasc. 1-5; A. Braun, Uber Polyembryonie und Keimung von Cælebogyne; F. Boott, Illustrations of the genus Carex. Am. J. Sci., II, xxxi, 123-132.

Botanical Notices. L. Lesquereux, Botanical and Palæontological Report on the Geol. State Survey of Arkansas. Am. J. Sci., II, xxxi, 431-435.

Botanical Notices. Journ. Proc. Linn. Soc. No. 18, papers by Bentham, Crocker, Hooker, Mitten, etc.; J. Phillips, Life on the Earth, its Origin and Succession; C. R. Bree, Species not Transmutable nor the Result of Secondary Causes. Am. J. Sci., II, xxxi, 443-449.

Botanical Notices. G. Bentham, Flora Hongkongensis; Ann. Bot. Soc. Canada, Vol. I, part 1, papers by Blackie and others; Journ. Proc. Linn. Soc. No. 19, papers by Mitten, Hooker and Thomson; A. Wood, Class-Book of Botany. Am. J. Sci., II, xxxii, 124-130.

Botanical Notices. Flora Brasiliensis, fasc. 25-28; H. Carsten, Floræ Columbiæ, etc., tom. I, fasc. 1; Journ. Proc. Linn. Soc. No. 20, papers by Hooker and Thomson, Welwitsch, Oliver, Bentham. Am. J. Sci., II, xxxii, 289-290.

<h2 style="text-align:center">1862.</h2>

Botanical Notices. H. A. Weddell, Mémoire sur le Cynomorium coccineum, etc.; E. Regel, Monographia Betulacearum hucusque cognitarum; Müller, Ann. Bot. Syst., vols. IV, V, and VI; F. A. W. Miquel, Journal de Botanique Neerlandaise; E. G. Squier, Tropical Fibres; A. Gray, Mexican Boundary Carices; Musci Gubenses Wrightiana, coll. 1856-1858; C. C. Parry, Rocky Mountain Flora; Aroideæ by Dr. Schott; Journ. Proc. Linn. Soc., no. 21, Botanical Papers by Hooker, Masters, Col. Munro and others. Am. J. Sci., II, xxxiii, 139-143.

Botanical Notices. D. Candolle's Prodromus, vol xv, part 1; F. Boott, Illustrations of the Genus Carex; Thwaites' Enumeratio Plantarum Zeylanicæ, part 3; Ann Bot. Soc. Canada, part 3. Am. J. Sci., II, xxxiii, 430-432.

Botanical Notices. C. Darwin, on the Various Contrivances by which Orchids are fertilized; J. D. Hooker, Outlines of the Distribution of Arctic Plants, and on the Cedars of Lebanon, Taurus, Algeria, and India; Weddell's Chloris Andina, vol. II. Am. J. Sci., II, xxxiv, 138-151.

Antherology; Review of Oliver's "Note on the Structure of the Anther." Am. Journ. Sci., II, xxxiv, 282-284.

Botanical Notices. Oliver, on the wood-cells of Hamamelideæ : Journ. Proc. Linn. Soc., nos. 22, 23, papers by Munro, Bentham, C. Darwin, Lindley and Grisebach; Bentham's Presidential Address to the Linnean Society, May, 1862 ; Botany of Northeastern Asia; C. DeCandolle, on the Production of Cork ; Flora Brasiliensis, fasc. 29 and 30; Grisebach, Flora of the British West Indian Islands, parts IV and V. Am. J. Sci., II, xxxiv, 284-288.

Botanical Notices. C. Darwin, Dimorphism in the Genitalia of Flowers. Am. J, Sci., II, xxxiv, 419-420; Seemann's Journ. Bot., I, 147-149 (with corrections).

1863.

Mémoires et Souvenirs de Augustin-Pyramus DeCandolle, Ecrits par luimême et Publiées par Son Fils. Am. J. Sci., II, xxxv, 1-16; Seemann's Journ. Bot., I, 107-120 (abridged, with corrections by the author).

Notice of Boussingault "On the Nature of the Gas produced from the Decomposition of Carbonic Acid by Leaves exposed to the Light." Am. J. Sci , II, xxxv, 121-123.

Botanical Notices. Bentham and Hooker's Genera Plantarum, vol. I, part 1; Hooker's Species Filicum, parts 13, 14. Am. J. Sci., II, xxxv, 134-136.

Botanical Notices. A new character in the Fruit of Oaks, DeCandolle; Review of DeCandolle's "Species, considered as to Variation, Geographical Distribution and Succession "; Harvey and Sonder's Flora Capensis, vol. II ; l'Abbe Provancher's Flore Canadienne; The Tendrils of the Virginia Creeper; Durand's Vites Boreali-Americanæ ; Vegetable Productions of the Feejee Islands; Gray's Manual. Am. J. Sci., II, xxxv 430-449.

Botanical Notices. Notice of Trans. St. Louis Acad., vol. II, part 1 ; Hall and Harbour's Rocky Mountain Plants; Paullinia sorbilis and its products ; Aerial rootlets on the stems of Virginia Creeper (Ampelopsis quinquefolia) ; Flora Brasiliensis, fasc. 31, 32 (note) ; Dr. C. W. Short; Wm. Darlington. Am. J. Sci., II, xxxvi, 128-139.

Botanical Notices. Dimorphism in the Flowers of Linum, Review of a paper by Darwin; Variation and Mimetic Analogy in Lepidoptera ; Bentham and Müller's Flor Australiensis; Oliver's Notes on the Loranthaceæ, with a synopsis of the Gen· era; Parthenogenesis in Plants. Am. J. Sci., II, xxxvi, 279-294.

Botanical Notices. Origin of Varieties in Plants ; Review of Memoirs et Souvenirs de Agustin Pyramus DeCandolle; Hooker on Welwitschia, a new genus of Gnetaceæ; American Tea-Plant. Am. J. Sci., II, xxxvi, 432-439.

1864.

Botanical Notices. Annales Musei Botanici Lugduno-Batavi for 1863; Flora Brasiliensis, fasc. 33-35 ; Agardh's Species Genera et Ordines Algarum ; Harvey's Phycologia Australica and Thesaurus Capensis, vol. II, no. 1; Müller's, The Plants indigenous to the Colony of Victoria ; Brunet's Plantes de Michaux ; Botany of N. W. America along the British Boundary; Ink-Plant (Coriaria thymifolia). Am. J. Sci., II, xxxvii, 281-288.

Botanical Notices. Prior's Popular Names of British Plants ; Saint Pierre's Flore des Environs de Paris; Vilmorin-Andrieux's Des Fleurs de Pleine Terre ; Kindberg's Monographie Generis Lepigonorum ; Andersson's Botany of the Galapagos Islands; Tuckerman's Lichenes Insulæ Cubæ. Am. J. Sci., II, xxxvii, 433-436.

Botanical Notices. Olivier's (Henslow's) Lessons in Elementary Botany ; Göthe's Essay on the Metamorphosis of Plants; Milde's Equisetaceæ ; Brown on Marsilia and Pilularia. Am. J. Sci., II, xxxvii, 124-127.

Botanical Notices. DeCandolle's Prodromus; Mitten's Bryology of British N. W America; Sullivant's Icones Muscorum. Am. J. Sci., II., xxxviii, 290-291.

Botanical Notices. Sullivant's Icones Muscorum. Am. J. Sci., II, xxxviii, 429.

1865.

Botanical Notices. Scott's Functions and Structure of the Reproductive Organs in the Primulaceæ; Mohl's Observations upon Dimorphous Flowers; Naudin and Godron's Essays on Hybrids; Grisebach's Flora of the British West Indian Islands; Bentham's Florula Australiensis. Am. J. Sci., II, XXXIX, 101–110.

Botanical Notices. DeCandolle's Prodromus, vol. XVI, part 1; Hooker's Handbook of the New Zealand Flora, part 1; Flora Brasiliensis, fasc. 36–38; Journ. Linn. Soc., no. 31, articles on Dimorphism and Trimorphism of Plants. Am. J. Sci. II, XXXIX, 359–362.

Botanical Notices. Thwaites' Enumeratio Plantarum Zelaniæ; Harvey and Sonder's Flora Capensis, vol. III; Dr. Torrey, Ammobroma Sonoræ; Harvey's Thesaurus Capensis; Annales Botanices Systematicæ, tom. VI; Child's Production of Organisms in closed vessels. Am. J. Sci., II, XL. 125–127.

Botanical Notices. Welwitschia mirabilis, Hook. fil.; Darwin's Movements and Habits of Climbing Plants. Am. J. Sci., II, XL, 273–282.

1866.

Botanical Notices. Darwin's Movements and Habits of Climbing Plants; Paine's Catalogue of Plants found in Oneida County [New York] and vicinity; Bentham and Hooker's Genera Plantarum, part 2. Am. J. Sci., II, XLI. 125–132.

Botanical Notices. Daubeny's Essay on the Trees and Shrubs of the Ancients. Am. J. Sci., II, XLI, 268.

Botanical Notices. Bentham's Address on Natural History Transactions and Journals; Flora Brasiliensis, fasc. 39, 40; Eichler on the Morphology of the Androecium in Fumariaceæ; Seemann's Flora Vitiensis; Botany of Australia; Müller's Analytical Drawings of Australan Mosses, fasc. 1; Müller's Vegetation of the Chatham Islands; Bunge's Revision of the genus Cousinia; Krok, Monogaph of Valerianæ; Musci Boreali-Americani, Sullivant and Lesquereux. Am. J. Sci., II, XLI, 410–418.

Botanical Notices. Boussingault's Researches on the action of Foliage; Engelmann's Revision of the North American Species of Juncus; Lessingia germanorum; Curtis' Illustrations of the Esculent Fungi of the U. S.; The International Horticultural Exhibition. Am. J. Sci., II, XLII, 126–132.

Botanical Notices. Fournier on Cruciferæ; Salisbury's Genera of Plants; Gray's Hand-book of British Water-Weeds or Algæ. Am. J. Sci., II, XLII, 277–281.

Botanical Notices. De Candolle's Prodromus, vol. XV; E. Boissier, Icones Euphorbiarum. Am. J. Sci., II, XLII, 427.

1867.

Botanical Notices. The Miscellaneous Botanical Works of Robert Brown; J. Mueller on Nature of Anthers; Mémoire sur la Famile des Pepéraciées by DeCandolle. Am. S. Sci., II, XLIII, 125–128.

Botanical Notices. Salices Europeæ Wimmer; Le Specie dei Cotoni descritte da Filippo Parlatore; Tree-labels for arboretum; Ozone produced by Plants, Daubeny's article in Journ. Chem. Soc. Am. J. Sci., II, XLIII, 272–273.

Botanical Notices. Grisebach's Catalogus Plantarum Cubensium; Flora Australiensis, Vol. III. Am. J. Sci., II, XLIII, 409–410.

Botanical Notices. E. Bossier, Flora Orientalis; Catalogue des Végétaux Ligneux du Canada, by l'Abbé Brunet: Rep. of Proceedings of the International Horticultural Exhibition, 1866: Collections of Dried Plants of California. Am. J. Sci., II, XLIV, 122–123.

Botanical Notices. N. J. Andersson, Monographia Salicum; Flora Brasiliensis, fasc. 42 and 43; De Candolle, Lois de la Nomenclature; Miquel, Sur les Affinitiés de la Flora du Japan avec celles de l'Asie et de l'Amerique du Nord; Tall Trees in Australia; Report on destruction of Trees in Wisconsin. by I. A. Lapham and others ; Annales Musci Botanici Lugduni Batavi, Tom. I-III, fasc. 4. Am. J. Sci., II, XLIV, 420-425.

1868.

Review of Darwin's Variation of Animals and Plants under Domestication. Nation, No. 142, pp. 234-236.

Botanical Notices. Miocene Flora of the Polar Regions; Les Fleurs de Pleine Terre, 2ᵉᵐᵉ éd; The Great Dragon Tree of Oiotava, Teneriffe; Geol. and Nat. Hist. Survey of California, Part III, Botany; Bentham and Hooker's Genera Plantarum; Boott's Illustrations of the genus Carex. Am. J. Sci., II, XLV, 269-272.

Botanical Notices. F. A. G. Miquel, Prolusio Floræ Japonicæ; Genera Plantarum, Vol. I; Traité Général de Botanique descriptive et analytique, Le Maout and Decaisne; Gray's Manual, fifth e lition. Am. J. Sci., II, XLV, 403-409.

Botanical Notices. The Book of Evergreens, by Josiah Hoopes; Botanical Works of Robert Brown; Journ. Linn. Soc., Botany, Nos. 42 and 43; Théorie de la Feuille, by C. De Candolle. Am. J. Sci., II, XLVI, 270-272.

Botanical Notices. Flora Brasiliensis, DeCandolle's Prodromus, etc. Am. J. Sci., II, XLVI, 408-409.

1869.

Botanical Notices. J. F. Watson's Index to the Native and Scientific Names of Indian Plants, etc. Am. J. Sci., II, XLVII, 143.

1870.

Botanical Notices. Botanical Notabilia. Bentham's Presidential Address, [Areas of Preservation, Am. Naturalist, IV, 44]; Robert Brown's Works; Master's Vegetable Teratology; Memoir of Harvey; Genera of South African Plants; Flora Australiensis; Oliver's Flora of Tropical Africa, and First Book of Indian Botany; Seemann's Flora Vitiensis; Baker on the Geographical Distribution of Ferns; Hooker's Icones Plantarum; Mitten's Musci Austr-Americani in Vol. XII, Journ. Linn. Soc.; Andersson on Palms; Munro's Monograph of Bambusaceæ; Appendix to French edition of Darwin's Fertilization of Orchids; Baillon's Adansonia and Traité du Development de la Fleur et du Fruit; Bureau's Monographie des Bignoniacées; De Candolle's Prodromus, Vol. XVI; Flora Danica, 47th part; Œisted on Classification of Oaks; Lange on the Pyroleæ and Monotropeæ of Mexico and Central America; Bunge's Monograph of the Astragali of the Old World; Ammobroma Sonoræ; Braun's Monograph of Australian Isoetes; Pritzel's Iconum Botanicarum Index Locupletissimus; Flora Brasiliensis, fasc. 44-46; Rudolph's Atlas des Pflanzengeographie; Pursh's Journal of a Botanical Excursion in N. Y. in 1807. Am. J. Sci., II, XLIX, 120-129

Botanical Notices. Johnson's How Crops Feed; Flora Brasiliensis, fasc. 48; Dickson on Development of Flower of Pinguicula; Geographical Handbook of Ferns, by K. M. Lyell; Bulletin of Torrey Botanical Club, Nos. 1 and 2; Notes relating to Vegetable Physiology, etc. Am. J. Sci., II, XLIX, 403-410.

Botanical Notices. "Miscellaneous Botanical Notices and Observations." De Candolle's Code of Botanical Nomenclature; Baillon's Histoire des Plantes; Hincks on the Arrangement and Nomenclature of Ferns; Bennett on the Genus Hydrolea; Tampico Jalap; Prof. Babington's Revision of the Flora of Iceland; Dr. Ogle on Fertilization of Flowers by Insects; Brunet's Eléments de Botanique; Von Martius' Herbarium; The Michaux Grove Oaks; Bœckler on Scirpeæ; Bunge's Genesis Astragali Species Gerontogeæ pars altera; Flora Caucasia, by Ruprecht; Bentham's Presidential address; Hooker's Student's Flora of the British Islands; The "American Entomologist." Am. J. Sci., II, L, 274-283.

Botanical Notices. Professor Lawson on Oxford Botanists; Hasskar's Monograph of Indian Commelynaceæ; Revision of the Genera and Species of Herbaceous Capsular, Gamophyllous Liliaceæ, by J. G. Baker; Clark on Commelynaceæ of Bengal: Dickie's Notes on Algæ from North Atlantic Ocean; Absorption of Moisture by Leaves; Henfrey's Elementary Course of Botany. Am. J. Sci., II, L, 425-429.

1871.

Botanical Notices. Hohenbühel-Heufler on the Linnæan Hypothesis of the Derivation of Species; Lawson's Monograph of Canadian Ranunculaceæ; Œrsted on characters furnished by the styles in Cupuliferæ and Juglandeæ, etc. Am. J. Sci., III, I, 147-149.

Botanical Notices. Rhododendreæ Asiæ Orientalis, by Maximowicz; Flora Australiensis. Vol. V; Braun's revision of Marsiliæ and Pilulariæ. Am. J. Sci., III, I, 222-223.

Botanical Notices. Von Mohl on Sciadopitys verticillata; Austin's Musci Appalachiani. Am. J. Sci., III, I, 306-307.

Botanical Notices. Flora Brasiliensis, fasc. 50; Prior's Popular Names of British Plants, 2d ed.; Vilmorin-Andrieux, Les Fleurs de Pleine Terre, 3d ed.; Baker's Synopsis of Known Lilies; Hiern on the Distribution of Batrachium Section of Ranunculus; E. S. Rand on the Rhododendron and American Plants. Am. J. Sci., III, I, 475-476.

Botanical Notices. Maximowicz on Diapensiaceæ; Lange on Form and Structure of Seeds. Am. J. Sci., III, II, 62-63.

Botanical Notices. Bretschneider on Chinese Botany; Gœppert on Plants killed by Frost. Am. J. Sci., III, II, 221-222.

Botanical Notices. Flora Brasiliensis, fasc. 51-54; Baillon's Histoire des Plants; Borodin on changes in position of grains of Chlorophyll under Sunlight; Dehérain on Evaporation of Water, etc. Am. J. Sci., III, II, 460-465.

Darwin's Descent of Man. Examiner, Vol. I, 594-600.

1872.

Botanical Notices. Friderici Welwitschii Sertum Angolense; Hooker's Icones Plantarum, III, part 1; Van Tieghem on the Structure of the Pistil in Primulaceæ, on the Anatomy of the Flower of Santalaceæ, on Comparative Anatomy of Cycadaceæ, Coniferæ, and Gnetaceæ, on the Mistletoe; Botany of Clarence King's Survey; Oliver's Flora of Tropical Africa, Vol. II; Heer, Flora Fossilis Arctica. Am. J. Sci., III, III, 58-64.

Botanical Notices. Miers, Contributions to Botany; S. Watson, Botany of Clarence King's Survey; Hall, Plants of Oregon; Saunders' Refugium Botanicum; Warming, Inflorescence or flower in Euphorbia. Am. J. Sci., III, III, 147-152.

Botanical Notices. Scheutz, Prodromus Monographiæ Georum; Baillon, Histoire des Plantes. Am. J. Sci., III, III, 306-308.

Botanical Notices. Bentham, Revision of the genus Cassia; Delpino, on the Fertilization of Coniferæ; J. Müller, on the Cyathium of Euphorbia; Maximowicz, Action of Pollen on Fruit of Fertilized Plant; Grisebach, Die Vegetation der Erde nach ihrer Klimatischen Anordnung; correction to Note on Baptisia. Am. J. Sci., III, III, 376-381.

Botanical Notices. Calletet on Absorption of Water by leaves; change of Habit of a Parasite; Peck's report on Botany before Albany Institute; Cooke, Hand-book of British Fungi; News of Botanists; Journal of Botany: Fossil Flora of Great Britain; "The Garden." Am. J. Sci., III, III, 472-476.

Botanical Notices. Marc Micheli, Recent Researches in Vegetable Physiology; M. T. Masters, Botany for Beginners; C. F. Austin, Musci Appalachiani. Am. J. Sci., III, IV, 72-77.

Professor Babington on Anacharis. Am. Nat., VI, 297.

Botanical Notices. Robert Brown's first Botanical Paper; Prantl's Memoir upon Inuline; Cooke and Peck, Erysiphei of the United States; Kau-Sun, a Chinese Vegetable; Flora Brasiliensis, fasc. 55. Am. J. Sci., III. IV, 149-151.

Botanical Notices. Tuckerman, Genera Lichenum; Hooker, Flora of British India; Grevillea; Linnæa, Vol. III; Flora Brasiliensis, fasc. 57-59,: News of Botanists; Herbarium of the late Dr. Curtis. Am. J. Sci. III, IV, 420-422.

Botanical Notices. Decaisne's Monograph of the Genus Pyrus; Botanical Supplement to Fifth Annual Report of Geol. Survey of Territories for 1871. Am. J. Sci., III, IV, 489-495.

1873.

Botanical Notices. Brongniart on the Theoretical Structure of the Cone in Coniferæ; Zizania aquatica not tuberiferous; Calcareous encrusted Charæ; Origin of the Weeping Willow. Am. J. Sci., III. V, 75.

Botanical Notices. Boissier, Flora Orientalis. Vol. II; Hooker's Icones Plantarum, III, Vol. II, part 1; Journ. Linn. Soc. no. 68; Journal of Botany, Dec., 1872; Discharge of the seeds of Witch hazel; Chlorodictyon, by Agardh; Braun on Marsilia and Pilularia; Baillon, Histoire des Plantes; Triana. Les Mélastomacées. Am. J. Sci. III, V, 142-145.

Seemann's Flora Vitiensis. Trimen's Journ. Bot., XI. 181-182.

Review of Bentham and Hooker's Genera Plantarum, Vol. II, part 1. The Academy, IV, 230-231.

Botanical Notices. Hildebrand, Fertilization in Grasses. Am. J. Sci., III, V, 316.

Botanical Notices. Van Tieghem on the Cotyledon of Gramineæ, etc.; Infelix Lolium; H. C. Wood, Fresh-water Algæ of North America. Am. J. Sci., III, V, 389-391.

Botanical Notices. Van Tieghem, on Nervation of Coats of Ovules and Seeds; Supposed American Origin of Rubus Idæus [repr. in Amer. Nat., VII, 421-422]; a New Textile Plant; Hooker's Icones Plantarum, Vol. II, part 2; Bentham and Hooker, Genera Plantarum, Vol. II, part 1; Wm. S. Sullivant. Am. J. Sci., III. V, 479-481.

Notice of A. De Candolle's Histoire des Sciences et des Savants. Nation, No. 418, p. 12.

Botanical Notices. Flora Brasiliensis, fasc. 60, 61; W. P. Hiern, a Monograph of Ebenaceæ; E. Regel, Animadversiones de Plantis vivis nonullis Hort, Bot. Imp. Petropolitani. Am. J. Sci., III, VI, 75-77.

Botanical Notices. LeMaout and Decaisne's Descriptive and Analytical Botany; Crépin's Primitiæ Monographiæ Rosarum. Am. J. Sci., III, VI, 147-151.

Botanical Notices. Bentham, Notes on Compositæ; Œrsted, System der Pilze, Lichenen und Algen; A. H. Curtiss, Catalogue of Phænogamous and Vascular Cryptogamous Plants of Canada and the Northeastern portion of the United States; A. Pollock, Index to Medicinal Plants. Am. J. Sci., III, VI, 230-231.

Anniversary Address of the President [Bentham] to the Linnean Society, May 24, 1873. Am. J. Sci., III, VI, 241-254.

Botanical Notices. Hanbury on Pareira Brava. Am. J. Sci., III, VI, 315.

Botanical Notices. Bornet on the Composition of Lichenes; Hybridation in Mosses, etc., Philibert. Am. J. Sci., III, VI, 388-390.

The Attitude of Working Naturalists towards Darwinism. [Review of De Candolle's Histoire des Sciences et des Savants, of Bentham's Presidential Address before the Linnean Society, of Bentham's Notes on Compositæ, of Flower's Evidence of Modification of Animal Forms, of Dawson's Story of the Earth and Man.] Nation, No. 433, pp. 258-261. [Darwiniana, pp. 236-251.]

Botanical Notices. Bennett on Movements of the Glands of Drosera; Engelmann, Notes on the Genus Yucca. Am. J. Sci., III, VI, 467-470.

1874.

Notices of the Cessation of De Candolle's Prodromus. Nation, No. 446, p. 42.

Evolution and Theology. [Review of Rev. G. Henslow's Theory of Evolution; of C. Hodge's Systematic Theology, and of J. Le Conte's Religion and Science.] Nation, No. 446, pp. 44-46. [Darwiniana, pp. 252-265.]

Botanical Notices. Contributions to American Botany, Sereno Watson; Characters of New Ferns from Mexico, D. C. Eaton; Botanical Contributions, by Asa Gray, Nov. 18, 1873; Bentham's Flora Australiensis, Vol. vi; Flora Brasiliensis, fasc. 62; Musée Botanique de Leide, Vol. I; DeCandolle's Prodromus, Vol. xvii. Am. J. Sci., III, vii, 63–68.

Botanical Notices. Dr. Regel on Vitis; Hepaticæ Boreali-Americanæ, C. F. Austin; Ilysanthes gratioloides; Synopsis Generis Lespedezæ, C. J. Maximowicz. Am. J. Sci., III, vii, 152–154.

What is Darwinism? [Review of C. Hodges's What is Darwinism?, of A. Winchell's Doctrine of Evolution, of G. St. Clair's Darwinism and Design, and of C. Kingsley's Westminster Sermons.] Nation, No. 465, pp. 348–351. [Darwiniana, pp. 266–282.]

Botanical Notices. Parthenogenesis in Ferns; Hooker's Flora of British India; New views on Lichenes and Gonidia; Decaisne on Eryngium, species with parallel-veined leaves. Am. J. Sci., III, vii, 440–444.

Botanical Notices. Revision of the North American Chenopodiaceæ, Sereno Watson; J. F. Mellichamp on Sarracenia variolaris. Am. J. Sci., III, vii, 599–600.

Owens College Essays and Addresses. [Review of Essays and Addresses by Professors and Lecturers of Owens College, Manchester.] Nation, No. 474, pp. 76–77.

Botanical Notices. Dr. Shawon Changes in the Character of Vegetation Produced by Sheep-grazing; McNab and Dyer on the Perigynium and occasional Seta in Carex; Maximowicz, Diagnoses Plantarum Japoniæ, etc.; Botanical Contributions by Asa Gray, in Proc. Am. Acad., Vol. ix; J. G. Cooper on Influence of Climate and Topography on Trees around San Francisco Bay; O. H. Willis, Catalogue of Plants near New Jersey. Am. J. Sci., III, viii, 69–72.

Manual of Geology, by Jas. D. Dana. Nation, No. 469, pp. 415–416.

Botanical Notices. A. De Candolle on Physiological Groups in the Vegetable Kingdom; W. C. Williamson, Primeval Vegetation in its relation to the Doctrines of Natural Selection and Evolution; J. W. Dawson, Annual Address of the President of the Natural History Society of Montreal, May, 1874; R. Shuttleworth and his collections. Am. J. Sci., III, viii, 147–156.

Notes on the Addresses of the Presidents of the English, French, and American Associations for the Advancement of Science. Nation, No. 481, p. 183.

Note on Prof. Tyndall's estimate of Aristotle. Nation, No. 482, p. 204.

Note on Wurtz's Address on "The Theory of Atoms in the General Conception of the Universe." Nation, No. 482, p. 204.

Notes on Dr. Hooker's Address as President of a section of the British Association on Insectivorous Plants. Nation, No. 483, p. 219.

Notice of the American Naturalist for Oct., 1874. Nation, No. 485, p. 250.

Miscellaneous Notices. Baker's Revision of the Genera and Species of the Tulipeæ; A Sexual Growth from the Prothallus of Pteris cretica, by Farlow; Botany of S. Pacific Exploring Expedition under Admiral Wilkes, etc, Am. Journ. Sci., III, viii, 320–322.

Botanical Notices. J. D. Hooker on the Carnivorous Habits of some Plants; Linnean Society of London; Professorship of Botany at the Jardin des Plantes. Am. J. Sci., III, viii, 395–398.

Botanical Notices. Note on the use of the word Cyclosis. Am. J. Sci., III, viii, 469–470.

Notice of the Address of the President of the Michigan Pomological Society. Nation, No. 493, p. 382.

1875

Botanical Notices. J. Scott, Notes on the Tree-Ferns of British Sikkim; Flora Brasiliensis, fasc. 53, 64: Journ. Linn. Soc., No. 77; Trans. and Proc. Bot. Soc. Edinburgh, Vol. xi; Florida plants for sale; American Naturalist, Vol. viii. Am. J. Sci., III, ix, 65–69.

Notice of De Candolle's Memorial of Agassiz. Nation, No. 504, p. 135.

Notice of Sir John Lubbock's British Wild Flowers considered in relation to Insects. Nation, No. 509, pp. 229-230.

Botanical Notices. Flückiger and Haubury, Pharmacographia; Fries, Hymenomycetes Europæi; Saporta, Miocene Fossil Plants of Greece; Mace. Am. J. Sci., III, IX, 153-154.

Bentham, on the recent Progress and present State of Systematic Botany. Am. J. Sci., III, IX, 346-355.

Botanical Notices. W. S. Sullivant, Icones Muscorum; Attar of Roses; Sir J. Lubbock, British Wild Flowers considered in relation to Insects. Am. J. Sci., III, IX, 323-326.

Notice of Sach's Text-Book of Botany. Nation, No. 519, p. 400.

Botanical Notices. Bentham. Revision of the Suborder Mimoseæ; J. D. Hooker, Flora of British India; Miers, on the Lecythidaceæ; Hooker and Baker, Synopsis Filicum; Grisebach, Plantæ Lorentzianæ; A. Gray, North American Hydrophyllaceæ; S.Watson, Revision of the Genus Ceanothus and Synopsis of the Western Species of Silene; W. G. Farlow, List of the Marine Algæ of the U. S. Am. J. Sci., III, IX, 471-476.

Botanical Notices. M. C. Cooke, Fungi, their Nature and Uses. Am. J. Sci., III, X, 62-63.

Notice of M. C. Cooke's Fungi: their Nature and Uses. Nation, No. 525, p. 62.

A Beginner in Botany. [Review of Ruskins' Proserpina.] Nation, No. 528, pp. 103-104.

Botanical Notices. C. B. Clarke, Commelynaceæ et Cyrtandraceæ Bengalenses. Am. J. Sci., III, X, 154-155.

German Darwinism. Nation, 1875, pp. 168-170.

Notice of Emerson's Trees and Shrubs of Massachusetts. Nation, Oct. 8, 1875.

Botanical Notices. J. L. Stewart and D. Brandis, Forest Flora of N.W. and Central India; Flora Brasiliensis, fasc. 66; De Candolle on Different Effects of same temperature upon same plants under different latitudes; Dr. J. E. Gray's Publications. Am. J. Sci., III, X, 236-239.

Botanical Notices. Rostafinski on Hematococcus lacustris, etc.; E. Tuckerman, Catalogue of Plants growing without cultivation within thirty miles of Amherst College; L. Radlkofer, Serjania Sapindacearum Genus monographice descriptum. Am. J. Sci., III, X, 309-311.

Botanical Notices. The formation of Starch in chlorophyll-grains; G. B. Emerson, Report on the Trees and Shrubs of Mass.; W. T. Dyer, On the Classification and Sexual Reproduction of Thallophytes; F. Buchenau, Monographie der Juncaceen vom Cap. Am. J. Sci., III, X, 392-395.

Botanical Notices. J. Decaisne, Memoire sur la Famille des Pomacées; J. G. Baker. Elementary Lessons in Botanical Geography. Am. J. Sci., III, X, 481-484.

Review of Emerson's Trees and Shrubs of Massachusetts. American Agriculturist, Dec., p. 451.

1876.

Review of Darwin's Insectivorous and Climbing Plants. Nation, No. 549, pp. 12-14; No. 550, pp. 30-32. [Darwiniana, pp. 308-337.]

Botanical Notices. Karl Koch, Vorlesungen über Dendrologie; C. Darwin, Insectivorous Plants and Movements and Habits of Climbing Plants, 2d ed.; Haeckel's Ziele und Wege der heutigen Entwickelungsgeschichte. Am. J. Sci., III, XI, 69-74.

Botanical Notices. Naudin on the Nature of Heredity and Variability in Plants; Rev. H. Macmillan, First forms in Vegetation, 2d ed. Am. J. Sci., III, XI, 153-157.

Botanical Notices. Geo. Engelmann, Notes on Agave; J. Duval-Jouve, Structure of the Leaves of Grasses; B. Renault, Botryopteris Forensis; Brongniart, Silicified fossil Fruits or Seeds; Mayer and Wolkoff, Respiration of Plants; Bornet, Classification of Nostochinæ; Gymnocladus in China; Flora Brasiliensis, fasc. 68. Am. J. Sci., III, XI, 235-239.

Botanical Notices. Botanical Contributions in Vol. XI of the Proc. Amer. Acad., New species and genera from California, by A. Gray, and on the Flora of Guadalupe Island by S. Watson. Am. J. Sci., III, XI, 325.

Botanical Notices. Bulletin of the Bussey Institution, part 5, containing Farlow's Disease of Orange and Olive Trees of California, American Grape-vine Mildew, Fungi near Boston, The Black Knot, and Report of the Director of the Arnold Arboretum. Am. J. Sci., III, XI, 414–415.

Botanical Notices. C. S. Sargent, Tree-planting, Prizes for Arboriculture; A. Blytt, Essay on Immigration of Norwegian Flora during Rainy and Dry Periods; Bentham and Hooker, Genera Plantarum, Vol. II; Botany of California, Vol. I, Polypetalæ, by Brewer and Watson; Gamopetalæ, by A. Gray. Am. J. Sci., III, XII, 73–79.

Notice of A. Koehler's Practical Botany, Structural and Systematic. Nation, No. 579, p. 80.

Botanical Notices. George Engelmann, The Oaks of the United States; M. Gustave-Adolphe Thuret, Equisse Biographique, by M. E. Bornet; F. de Mueller, Fragmenta Phytographiæ Australiæ, Vol. XI; Flora Brasiliensis, fasc. 62 and 69; J. W. Beal, The Forest-products of Michigan at the Centennial Exposition; G. C. Arthur, Contributions to the Flora of Iowa. Am. J. Sci., III, XII, 153–156.

Botanical Notices. C. De Candolle, Structure and Movement of Leaves of Dionæa muscipula; P. B. Wilson, Diatoms in Wheat-straw; Hance, An Intoxicating Grass; Crépin, Primitiæ Monographiæ Rosarum; A. De Candolle, on the Influence of the age of a Tree on the time of Leafing; A. Kœhler, Practical Botany, Structural and Systematic; T. S. Brandegee, Flora of Southwestern Colorado. Am. J. Sci., III, XII, 232–235.

Botanical Notices. J. D. Hooker, Flora of British India, part 4; A. B. Clarke, Compostæ Indicæ; Proc. Am. Assoc., 24th meeting, 1875, Botanical articles by Meehan on Insect fertilization of Flowers; Beal on Carnivorous Plants, Inequilateral Leaves and the Venation of a few odd Leaves; T. B. Comstock on Utricularia vulgaris; J. Hyatt on Periodicity in Vegetation. Am. J. Sci., III, XII, 397–398.

Botanical Notices. Baillon, Dictionnaire de Botanique, fasc. 1; T. Caruel, Nuovo Giornale Botanico Italiano, Vol. VIII; E. Boissier, Flora Orientalis; J. Miers, On the Barringtoniaceæ; G. Vasey, Catalogue of the Forest Trees of the United States. Am. J. Sci., III, XII, 468–469.

1877.

Botanical Notices. T. Comber, Geographical Statistics of the European Flora; J. Sprague and G. L. Goodale, The Wild Flowers of America. Am. J. Sci., III, XIII, 83–85.

Botanical Notices. Baillon, Dictionnaire de Botanique, fasc. 2 and 3; O. Heer, Flora Fossilis Arctica; Proc. and Trans. Nova Scotia, Inst. Nat. Sci. Vol. IV, part 2; containing notes by Lawson on Calluna vulgaris, notes on Rhododendron maximum, and a Catalogue of the Plants of the Province by Sommers. Am. J. Sci., III, XIII, 320–321.

Botanical Notices. C. De Candolle, Observations sur l'enroulement des Vrilles; W. G. Farlow, Onion-Smut; G. Bentham, Classification and Terminology in Monocotyledons; C. Darwin, Various Contrivances by which Orchids are fertilized by Insects. Am. J. Sci., III, XIII, 391–395.

Botanical Notices. O. Beccari, Organogeny of the Female Flower of Gnetum Gnemon L.; C. Martius, Palæontological Origin of trees and shrubs of South of France which are sensitive to Frost in cold winters. Am. J. Sci., III, XIII, 469–471.

Botanical Notices. W. G. Farlow, C. L. Anderson, D. C. Eaton, Algæ Exsiccatæ Americæ Borealis, fasc. 1; Am. J. Sci., III, XIV, 72.

Botanical Notices. A. Cogniaux on Botanical Nomenclature; G. C. W. Bohnensieg, Repertorium Annuum Literaturæ Botanicæ periodicæ. Am. J. Sci., III, XIV, 158–161.

Botanical Notices. W. G. Farlow, Notes on Common plant diseases caused by Fungi; Flora Brasiliensis, fasc. 70; J. Macoun, Botany of British Columbia and Northern Rocky Mountains; S. Kurz, Sketch of the Vegetation of the Nicobar Islands, etc.; A Lavallée, Arboretum Segrezianum; J. G. Baker, Systema Iridacèarum. Am. J. Sci., III. xiv, 426–429.

Botanical Notices. I. Sprague and G. L. Goodale, The Wild Flowers of America, part ii; Cleistogamy in Impatiens; O. R. Willis, Catalogue of Plants of New Jersey; Sir J. D. Hooker's voyage to America. Am. J. Sci., III, xiv, 497–499

1878.

Cook's Lectures on Biology. New Englander, xxxvii, 100–113.

Botanical Notices. C. Darwin, The Different Forms of Flowers on Plants of the same Species; D. C. Eaton, Ferns of North America; G. E. Davenport, Notes on Botrychium simplex. Am. J. Sci., III, xv, 67–73.

Notice of C. S. Sargent's paper on tree-planting in Twenty-fifth Report of the Mass. Board of Agriculture and Hon. B. G. Northrop's Economic Tree-Planting. Nation, No. 665, p. 215.

Phytogamy. Review of Darwin's Different Forms of Flowers on Plants of the same Species, Various Contrivances by which Orchids are fertilized, Effects of Cross and Self-Fertilization in the Vegetable Kingdom. Nation, No. 667, pp. 246–248.

Botanical Notices. F. Parkman, The Hybridization of Lilies; Thuret's Garden; Englemann's Papers in Trans. Acad Sci., St. Louis, vol. iii; Wibbe on new range for two Orchids. Am. J. Sci., III, xv, 151–153.

Botanical Notices. Lesquereux, Contributions to the Fossil Flora of the Western Territories. Am. J. Sci., III, xv, 219.

Botanical Notices. Supplementary Note to the Review of Darwin's Forms of Flowers; J. Smith, Historia Filicum; D. C. Eaton, Ferns of North America, part 2 W. G. Farlow, List of Fungi found near Boston; Journ. Linn. Soc.; Crépin, Guide; du Botaniste in Belgique; I. J. Isaman, Insect-fertilization in Trichostema. Am. J. Sci., III, xv, 221–225.

Botanical Notices. D. C. Eaton, Ferns of North America, parts 4 and 5; Baillon, Dictionnaire de Botanique, fasc. 8; A. E. Carácas, Vargas consideratio como Botanico, etc. Am. J. Sci., III, xv, 483–484.

This Life and the Future. [Review of Dean Church's Human Life and its Conditions.] Independent, June 20th, p. 10.

Botanical Notices. Oliver, Flora of Tropical Africa, vol. iii; D. C. Eaton, Ferns of North America, part 3; L. Lesquereux, Report on Fossil Plants of Gravels of Sierra Nevada; E. M. Holmes, Catalogue of Museum of Pharmaceutical Soc., Great Britain; Thuret's Garden at Antibes. Am. J. Sci., III, xvi, 318–320.

Botanical Notices. A. Gray, Synoptical Flora of N. A.; Sereno Watson, Bibliographical Index to North American Botany; M. T. Masters, On the Morphology of Primulaceæ; G. Henslow, On the Origin of Floral Æstivations; M. M. Hartog, Floral Structures and Affinities of Sapotaceæ; Curtis, North American Plants; Catalogue of Plants within thirty miles of Yale College. Am. J. Sci., III, xv, 400–402, 404.

Botanical Notices. T. Meehan, Native Flowers and Ferns of the U. S.; S. O. Lindberg, Monographia Metzgeriæ and Bryineæ Acrocarpæ; A. Fendler, Ferns of Trinidad; Flora Brasiliensis, fasc. 73. Am J. Sci., xvi, 72–75.

Botanical Notices. J. Williamson, Ferns of Kentucky; J. Robinson, Ferns in their homes and ours; J. Macoun, Catalogue of Plants of Canada; Meehan, Native Flowers and Ferns of the U. S. Am. J. Sci., III, xvi, 155–157.

Botanical Notices. Bentham and von Mueller, Flora Australiensis, vol. vii; J. G. Baker, Flora of Mauritius and the Seychelles; Kurz, Forest Flora of British Burma; J. Miers, The Apocynaceæ of South America; J. D. Hooker, Students' Flora of the British Islands; Botany of Kerguelen Ids.; D. C. Eaton, Ferns of North America, parts 6 and 7. Am. J. Sci., III, xvi, 237–240.

Botanical Notices. A. et C. DeCandolle, Monographiæ Phanerogamarum Prodromi nunc continuatio, nunc revisio; J. D. Hooker, Flora of British India, part 5; A. W. Eichler, Flower-diagrams; G. Bohnensieg et W. Burck, Repertorium Annuum Literaturæ Periodicæ, tome IV; J. G. Baker, Synopsis of Genus Aquilegia. Am. J. Sci., III, XVI, 325-327.

Botanical Notices. Todaro, Relazione sulla Cultura dei Cotoni in Italia, sequita da una Monographia del Genere Gossypium; T. Meehan, Native Flowers and Ferns of U. S. Am. J. Sci., III, XVI, 403-404.

Botanical Notices. A. S. Wilson, Sugar in Nectar of Flowers; D. C. Eaton, Ferns of N. A., parts 8 and 9; Note on a Monstrous Sarracenia purpurea. Am. J. Sci., III, XVI, 485, 487, 488.

Epping Forest and how best to deal with it, by A. R. Wallace in Fortnightly Review. Nation, No. 704, p. 400.

1879.

Botanical Notices. Flora Brasiliensis, fasc. 75-78; Heer, Flora Fossilis Arctica, tome V; A. R. Wallace, Epping Forest. Am. J. Sci., III, XVII, 69-71.

Hooker and Ball's Tour in Marocco. [Review of Hooker and Ball's Journal of a Tour in Marocco and the Great Atlas.] Nation, No. 718, pp. 232-233.

Botanical Notices. W. T. Thistleton-Dyer, On Plant-Distribution as a field for Geographical research; C. F. Nyman, Conspectus Floræ Europææ. Am. J. Sci., III, XVIII, 176-177.

Notices of A. Wood's and J. D. Steele's Fourteen Weeks in Botany, and Arabella B. Buckley's Fairy-Land of Science. Nation, No. 723, p. 324.

Botanical Notices. Strasburger. Ueber Polyembryonie: Bentham, Notes on Euphorbiaceæ; J. D. Hooker, Journal of a Tour in Marocco and the Great Atlas; Eaton's Ferns of North America, parts 12 and 13; Farlow, Anderson and Eaton, Algæ Amer. Bor. Exsiccatæ, fasc, 3; Am. J. Sci., III, XVII, 334-339.

Botanical Notices. Guides for Science-Teaching, Goodale and Hyatt; L. Errera on the Function of the Sterile Filament in Pentstemon; Revue Mycologique, No. 1; Meehan's Native Flowers and Ferns of the United States; F. B. Hine, Observations upon Saprolegnieæ; V. Rattan, Popular California Flora. Am. J. Sci., III., XVII, 410-413.

Botanical Notices. L. Errera on Number of digestive glands in Dionæa; T. F. Allen, Characeæ Americanæ; O. Beccari, Malesia; G. Henslow, On the Self-fertilization of Plants [Bot. Gazette, IV, 182-187]. Am. J. Sci., III. XVII, 488-494.

Concerning a Few Common Plants. [Review of Prof. Goodale's Primer with the above title.] American Agriculturist, July, p. 256.

Botanical Notices. J. T. Rothrock, Botany in vol. VI of Report of U. S. Geogr. Survey west of 100th meridian; Flora of British India, part VI; Reichenbach, Refugium Botanicum, vol II, fasc. 1; Trans. and Proc. of Botanical Soc. of Edinburg, XIII; Botanical Papers in Journ. Linn. Soc. Bot., XVII; F. Darwin, on Nutrition of Drosera; Balfour on the Genus Pandanus; E. Lockwood on the Mahwa Tree, etc.; G. Henslow, Floral dissections illustrating typical Genera of British Natural Orders. Am. J. Sci., III, XVIII, 154-158.

Botanical Notices. J. Ball, on the Origin of the Flora of the European Alps; von Mueller, Native Plants of Victoria, part I. Am. J. Sci, III, XVIII, 236-238.

Notice of S r John Lubbock Scientific Lectures. Nation, No. 746, p. 262.

Instinct and Reason, by F. C. Clark. Am. Nat., XIII, 317-318.

Plant Archæology (Notice of Saporta's "Le Monde des Plants avant l'Apparition de l'Homme"). Nation, 1879, 195-196, 212-213.

Botanical Notices. L. Celakovsky, the Gymnospermy of Coniferæ, by Geo. Engelmann and A Gray [Bot. Gazette, IV, 222-224]; Contributions to American Botany, IX, by S Watson; Musci Fendleriani Venezuelenses; Baillon, Dictionnaire de Botanique, vol. II, part 1; Trans. Linn. Soc. Lond., vol. I; Nouveile Archives du Museum,

II, vol. i; F, Delpino, Revista Botanica dell'Anno, 1878. Am. J. Sci., III., XVIII, 311-317.

Botanical Notices. Kunkel on Electrical Currents in Plants; C. J. Maximowicz, Adnotationes de Spiræaceis; Boissier, Flora Orientalis, vol. IV. Am. J. Sci., III, XVIII, 414-416.

Botanical Notices. Von Mueller, Eucalyptographia; A. et C. DeCandolle, Monographiæ Phanerogamarum Prodromi, etc.; C. DeCandolle, Anatomie Comparée des Feuilles chez quelques Familles de Dicotylédones; Bentham and Hooker's Genera Plantarum, Vol. III, part 1. Am. J. Sci., III, XVIII, 485-488.

Instinct and Reason, by F. C. Clark. Am. Nat., XIII, 317-318.

1880.

Brazil, The Amazons and the Coast. By H. H. Smith. Nation, No. 766, pp. 181-182.

Aroideæ Maximilianæ. Harv. Coll. Library Bulletin, II, 47.

Notice of T. W. O'Neill's Refutation of Darwinism, and the Converse Theory of Development. Nation, No. 766, p. 182.

Review of G. F. Wright's Logic of the Christian Evidences. Nation, No. 771, p. 273.

Botanical Notices. Coulter's Botanical Gazette. Am. J. Sci., III, XIX, 157-158.

Botanical Notices. C. De Candolle and R. Pictet, Seeds endure extreme Cold; Heer, The Genus Giugko; W. H. Gilbrest, Floral Development of Helianthus annuus and Morphology of Vegetable Tissues; J. Peyritsch, Aroideæ Maximilianæ; R. Schomburgk, Naturalized Weeds and other Plants of South America; A. T. Drummond, Canadian Timber-trees; E. L. Sturtevant, Indian Corn. Am. J. Sci., III, XIX, 328-331.

Botanical Notices. Bentham and Hooker, Genera Plantarum, Vol. III; R. C. A. Prior, Popular Names of British Plants. Am. J. Sci., III, XIX, 418-421.

Botanical Notices. G. Englemann, Revision of the Genus Pinus; O. Kuntze, Methodik der Speciesbeschreibung, und Rubus. Am. J. Sci., III, XIX, 491-493.

Notice of D. C. Eaton's Ferns of North America. Literary World, XI, 296.

Botanical Notices. De Candolle's Phytography; D. C. Eaton, Ferns of North America, completion; F. de Mueller, Index perfectus ad Caroli Linnæi Species Plantarum, etc.; A. Rau and A. B. Hervey, Catalogue of North American Musci; Botanical Explorations of the little known West India Islands. Am. J. Sci., III, XX, 150-159.

Botanical Notice. De Candolle's Phytography. Am. J. Sci., III, XX, 241-250.

Botanical Notices. Thomas Meehan, the Native Flowers and Ferns of the United States; C. E. Bessey, Botany for High Schools and Colleges; O. Eventh, Manual of Swedish Pomology; Bidrag till Europas Pomona vid des Nordgräus. Am. J. Sci., III, XX, 336-338.

1881.

The Power of Movement in Plants. By Charles Darwin, assisted by Francis Darwin. Nation, No. 810, pp. 17-18.

The British Moss Flora. By R. Braithwaite. Bot. Gaz., VI, 185.

Botanical Notices. C. Darwin and F. Darwin, Power of Movement in Plants. Am. J. Sci., III, XXI, 245-249.

Botanical Notices. De Candolle, Monographiæ Phænogamarum, Vol. III; A. Lavallée, Arboretum Segrèzianum; R. Braithwaite, The British Moss-Flora. Am. J. Sci., III, XXII, 235-238.

Botanical Notices. John Earle, English Plant Names from the Tenth to the Fifteenth Century; E. Warming, Familien Podostemaceæ. Am. J. Sci., III, XXII, 491-492.

1882.

Botanical Notices. J. Veitch & Sons, A Manual of the Coniferæ; G. C. W. Bohnenzieg, Repertorium Annuum, etc.; A. W. Eichler, Jahrbuch des Königlichen

Botanischen Gartens zu Berlin; Engler's Botanische Jahrbücher; Hooker's Icones Plantarum, Vol. IV, part 1. Am. J. Sci., III, XXIII, 69–71.

The Creed of Science. The Independent, Feb. 2, pp. 9–11. (Notice of Graham's "Creed of Science" and Cellariens's "New Analogy.")

Lyell's Life and Letters. The Literary World, XIII, 53–54.

Botanical Notices. Zool. Soc. of France, Natural History Nomenclature; Maximowicz, de Coriaria, Ilice et Monochasma, etc.; Torsion of Leaf in Compass-plant. Am. J. Sci., III, XXIII, 157–160.

Botanical Notices. Bentham, Notes on Gramineæ; Flora Brasiliensis, fasc. 83, 84; C. J. Maximowicz, Diagnoses Plantarum novarum Asiaticarum, IV; F. Darwin, Relation of leaves to direction of light [Bot. Gaz., VII, 45–47]; W. W. Bailey, Botanical Collector's Handbook; Greenland Flora, edited by J. Lange. Am. J. Sci., III, XXIII, 244–247.

Botanical Notices. W. Turner, The Names of Herbes. Am. J. Sci., III, XXIII, 326.

Botanical Notices. H. Baillon, Monographie des Composées; L. F. Ward, Guide to the Flora of Washington and vicinity; Vilmorin-Andrieux, Les Meilleurs Blés, etc.; H. Devries, The Office of Resinous Matters in Plants; V. Rattan, Popular California Flora, 3d ed. Am. J. Sci., III, XXIII, 492–495.

Botanical Notices. T. F. Allen, Characeæ Americanæ Exsiccatæ distributæ; A. Engler, Versuch einer Entwicklungsgeschichte der Pflanzenwelt insbesondere der Florengebiete seit der Tertiärperiode; G. Englemann, The Genus Isoëtes in North America; A. Clavaud, Flore de la Gironde. Am. J. Sci., III, XXIV, 72–73.

Botanical Notices. S. O. Lindberg, European and North American Peat-mosses. Am. J. Sci., III, XXIV, 156–157.

Botanical Notices. G. Briosi, Sopra un Organo finora non avertito di alcuni Embrioni Vegetali; Van Tieghem and G. Bonnier, Latent Vitality of Seeds; S. Watson, Contributions to American Botany, X; A. Gray, Contributions to North American Botany, Proc. Am. Acad., XVII; Journ. Linn. Soc., Nos. 120, 121. Am. J. Sci., III, XXIV, 296–299.

Botanical Notices. Trees and Tree-Culture, papers by H. W. S. Cleveland and R. Ridgway on Trees, etc.; Am. Journal of Forestry; E. Warming, Familien Podostemaceæ. Am. J. Sci., III, XXIV, 400, 401.

A Dictionary of the Popular Names of Plants which furnish the Wants of Man. By John Smith. Literary World, XIII, 380.

Botanical Notices. J. Smith, Dictionary of Popular Names of Plants. Am. J. Sci., III, XXIV, 476–477.

1883.

Botanical Notices. Brendel, Flora Peoriana. Am. J. Sci., III, XXV, 81, 82.

Botanical Notices. C. F. Nyman, Conspectus Floræ Europæ; Flora Brasiliensis, fasc. 86, 87, 88; J. D. Hooker and C. B. Clarke, Flora of British India, part 9. Am. J. Sci., III, XXV, 162, 163.

Botanical Notices. Marquis de Saporta, Apropos des Algues Fossiles; Vilmorin, Andrieux & Cie, Les Plantes Potagères; Grant Allen, the Colors of Flowers. Am. J. Sci., III, XXV, 235–237.

Review of De Candolle's Origin of Cultivated Plants; with annotations upon certain American species. By Asa Gray and J. Hammond Trumbull. Am. J. Sci., III, XXV, 241–255; 370–379; XXVI, 128–138.

Botanical Notices. A. Lavallée, Arboretum Segrezianum, fasc. 5, 6. Am. J. Sci., III, XXV, 312.

Botanical Notices. A. Engler, Essay on Development of the Vegetable Kingdom; A. G. Nathorst, Bidrag till Japans Fossila Flora. Am. J. Sci., III, XXV, 394–397.

Botanical Notices. Schröter, Morphology of the Androecium of Malvaceæ; Chapman, Flora of the Southern United States; Bentham and Hooker, Genera Plantarum, Vol. III, part 2; A. et C. De Candolle, Monographiæ Phanerogamarum, Vol. IV. Am. J. Sci., III, XXV, 480–481.

Macloskie's Elementary Botany. Science, II, 13–14.

Review of Bentham and Hooker's Genera Plantarum. Nation, No. 942, pp. 62, 63.

A revision of the genus Fraxinus, by Th. Wenzig. Bot. Gazette, VIII, 264–265.

Botanical Notices. E. Häckel, Monographia Festucarum Europæarum; E. Cosson et G. de Saint Pierre, Atlas de la Flora des Environs de Paris; E. Cosson, Compendium Floræ Atlanticæ, and Illustrationes Floræ Atlanticæ, fasc. 1; F. von Müller, Systematic Census of Australian Plants. Am. J. Sci., III, XXVI, 77–79.

Bentham & Hooker, Genera Plantarum. Nation, July 19, 1883. [Am. J. Sci., III, XXVI, 245–247.]

Botanical Notices. Itinera Principum S. Coburgi; Notice Biographique sur M. Joseph Decaisne, par Edouard Bornet. Am. J. Sci., III, XXVI, 247, 248.

Botanical Notices. G. Vasey, The Grasses of the United States; S. Watson, Contributions to American Botany, XI; H. Müller, The Fertilization of Flowers, Transl. by D. W. Thompson. Am. J. Sci., III, XXVI, 322–325.

Some Points in Botanical Nomenclature; a Review of "Nouvelles Remarques sur la Nomenclature Botanique, par M. Alph. de Candolle." Am. J. Sci., XXVI, 417–437.

Botanical Notices. O. Kunze, Phytogeogenesis; J. Jackson, Catalogue of Phænogamous and Vascular Cryptogamous Plants of Worcester Co., Mass. Am. J. Sci., III, XXVI, 486–488.

1884

The Borderland of Science and Faith. [Review of Goodwin's Walks in the regions of science and faith and Drummond's Natural Law in the spiritual world. Science, III, 131–133.

Key to North American Birds, Elliott Coues. Literary World, XV, 216.

Flowers and their Pedigrees. By Grant Allen. Nation, No. 979, p. 304.

Notice of Brook's "The Law of Heredity." Andover Review, I, 208–214.

Review of Dean Church's Francis Bacon. Nation, No. 982, p. 368–370.

Notice of Sophie Herrick's Wonders of Plant-Life under the Microscope. Nation, No. 982, p. 370.

W. A. Kellerman, Elements of Botany and Plant Analysis. Nation, No. 991, p. 558.

Notice of N. D'Anvers' Science Ladders and John Babcock's Vignettes from Invisible Life. Literary World, XV, 167.

Botanical Notices. C. J. F. Bunbury, Botanical Fragments; Bush & Son, Catalogue of American Grape-Vines; W. K. Brooks, The Law of Heredity. Am. J. Sci., III, XXVII, 155-157.

Botanical Notices. O. Beccari, Malesia, part 4; T. Caruel, Thoughts upon Botanical Taxonomy. Am. J. Sci., III, XXVII, 241–242.

Botanical Notices. Carpenter's Tendency in Variation. Am. J. Sci., III, XXVII, 326–328.

Botanical Notices. Bull. California Acad. Sci., No. 1, Botanical Papers by A. Gray on Veatchia Cedrocensis; Behr and Kellogg on Anemone Grayi; Kellogg on Astragalus insularis and Phacelia ixodes., etc., etc.; N. Shepard, Darwinism stated by Darwin himself; I. Sprague and G. L. Goodale, Wild Flowers of America; D. F. Day, of Plants near Buffalo. Catalogue Am. J. Sci., III, XXVII, 413–415.

Botanical Notices. A. Lavallée, Clematides Megalanthes, Les Clématites a Grand Fleurs; Porto Rico plants; V. B. Wittrock, Erythræ Exsiccatæ. Am. J. Sci., III, XXVII, 494–496.

Notice of Sir John Lubbock's Chapters in Popular Natural History and J. Straub's Consolations of Science. Literary World, XV, 217–218.

Biogen, A Speculation on the Origin and Nature of Life. By Prof. Elliott Coues. Nation, No. 992, p. 20.

Botanical Notices. C. B. Clarke, E. Indian Species of Cyperus; C. C. Parry, Revision of the genus Chorizanthe. Am. J. Sci., III, XXVIII, 75–76.

Notices of Lesquereux and James, Manual of the Mosses of North America, and Baldwin's Orchids of New England. Nation, No. 999, pp. 163–164.

Botanical Notices. L. Lesquereux and T. P. James, Manual of the Mosses of North America; H. H. Behr, Synopsis of the Genera of Vascular Plants near San Francisco; Boissier's Flora Orientalis, Vol. v, part 2; J. Ball, Contributions to the Flora of North Patagonia. Am. J. Sci., III, xxviii, 155-158.

Botanical Notices [Gray's Synoptical Flora of North America, part 2]; H. Baldwin, The Orchids of New England; J. D. Hooker, Students' Flora of the British Islands. Am. J. Sci., III, xxviii, 237-238.

Notice of John Fiske's Destiny of Man viewed in the light of his Origin. Nation, No. 1011, p. 426.

Botanical Notices. Flora Brasiliensis, fasc. 93; F. Parlatore, Flora Italiana, Vol. vi, part 1; G. Vasey, Agricultural Grasses of the U. S.; L. M. Underwood, Cata logue of North American Hepaticæ Am. J. Sci., III, xxviii, 402-404.

Botanical Notices. W. Upham, Catalogue of the Flora of Minnesota; G. C. W. Bohnensieg, Repertorium Annuum, etc.; J. U. Lloyd and C. G. Lloyd, Drugs and Medicines of North America. Am. J. Sci., III, xxviii, 472-474.

1885.

Botanical Notices. C. S. Sargent, Report on the Forests of North America; Macoun's Catalogue of Canadian Plants, part 2, Gamopetalæ; A. De Candolle, Histoire des Sciences et des Savants depuis deux Siècles, etc.; A. W. Eichler. Jahrbuch der Koniglichen botanischen Gartens zu Berlin, iii; A. de Candolle, Origin of Cultivated Plants. Am. J. Sci., III, xxix, 264-267.

Botanical Notices. C. S. Sargent, Woods of the United States: F. von Müller, Eucalyptographia; Marquis de Saporta, Organismes Problématiques des Anciennes Mers; E. Koehne, Lythraceæ of the U. S.; O. Kuntze, Monographie der Gattung Clematis; A. Gravis, Recherches Anatomiques sur les Organes Vegetatifs de l'Urtica dioica; J. Fowler, List of Plants of New Brunswick; H. N. Patterson, Check-list of N. American Gamopetalæ; C. E. Cummings, Check-list of N. American Mosses and Hepaticæ; J. H. Oyster, Catalogue of Phænogams and Vascular Cryptogams of N. America. Am. J. Sci., III, xxx, 82-85.

Notices of Bower and Vines' Course of Instruction in Botany, Chapters on Plant Life, Baileys Talk's Afield, and Palmer's Charts of Mushrooms of America. Nation, No. 1050, pp. 138-139.

Botanical Notices. A. Pailleux et D. Bois, Le Potager d'un Curieux; S. Watson, Contributions to American Botany, xii, in Proc. Am. Acad., xx; L. H. Bailey, jr., Talks Afield about Plants. Am. J. Sci., III, xxx, 164-167.

Botanical Notices. Levier, Plantes à Fourmis; Lloyd's Drugs and Medicines of North America; Trans. and Proc. New Zealand Inst., xvii ; N. L. Britton, Revision of N. A. Species of the genus Scleria; P. Zipperer, Beitrag zur Keuntniss der Sarraceniaceen. Am. J. Sci., III, xxx, 245-247.

Insular Floras. [A Review of Vol. i, Botany, of the *Challenger* Reports.] Science, vi, 297-298.

Botanical Notices. J. W. Behrens, The Microscope in Botany, translated by A. B. Hervey and R. H. Ward; Bull. California Acad. Sci., No. 3, Botanical Papers, by Harkness, Mrs. Curran, E. L. Greene, etc.; H. Trimen, Catalogue of Flowering Plants and Ferns. Am. J. Sci., III, xxx, 319-322.

Botanical Notices. Botany of the *Challenger* Expedition, Vol. i. Am. J. Sci., III, xxx, 40?-403.

Botanical Notices. Beccari, Malesia; Cosson, Illustrationes Floræ Atlanticæ; G. L. Goodale, Physiological Botany; K. G Limpricht, Rabenhorst's Kryptogamen-Flora von Deutschland. Am. J. Sci., III, xxx, 487-489.

1886.

Botanical Notices. J. M. Coulter, Manual of the Botany of the Rocky Mountain Region; Sir Joseph Hooker and the Royal Gardens at Kew. Am. J. Sci., III, xxxi, 76-78.

Botanical Notices. Flora Brasiliensis, fasc. 95; T. F. Wood, Sketch of the Botanical Work of the Rev. Moses A. Curtis. Am. J. Sci., III, xxxi, 158-159.

A. De Candolle on the Production by selection of a race of Deaf-Mutes in the United States. Nation, No. 1081, pp. 239-240.

Botanical Notices. J. Ball, Contributions to the Flora of the Peruvian Andes; J. C. Lecoyer, Monographie du Genre Thalictrum; Nathorst, Nomenclature for Fossil Leaves, etc.: Wittrock, Erythææ Exsiccatæ, fasc. 2; F. Buchenau, Synopsis of European Juncaceæ; F. Pax, on genus Acer; R. Spruce, Hepaticæ Amazonicæ et Andineæ. Am. J. Sci., III, xxxi, 231-238.

Sylvan Winter. By Francis George Heath. Nation, No. 1085, p. 326.

Botanical Notices. J. B. Lloyd, Drugs and Medicines of North America, Vol. i; H. de Vries, Leerbœk der Planten-physiologie; Baillon's Dictionnaire de Botanique, fasc. 19; Baillon's Historie des Plantes, Vol. viii; J. Lamie, Plants Naturalized in the Southwest of France. Am. J. Sci., III, xxxi, 313-316.

Botanical Notices. Arthur, Barnes, and Coulter, Handbook of Plant Dissection; Maximowicz, Diagnosis Plantarum Novarum Asiaticarum, fasc. 6; G. Lagerheim, American Desmidieæ. Am. J. Sci., III, xxxi, 477-479.

Botanical Notices. Saint Lager, Histoire des Herbiers; Journ. Linn. Soc., Vol. xxii, containing papers by Ball, Bolus, Henslow, F. Darwin, Ridley, Clark, Masters; xxiii, papers by Forbes and Hemsley; Strasburger on Heterogeneous Grafting. Am. J. Sci., III, xxxii, 79-81.

Botanical Notices. H. Bolus, Sketch of the Flora of South Africa; W. B. Hemsley, Catalogue of North's Paintings of Plants; Guide to the Museums of Economic Botany, Kew; T. Caruel, Filippo Parlatore, Flora Italiana, Vol. vi, part 3; Flora Brasiliensis, fasc. 96; Hooker's Icones Plantarum, Vols. xvi and xvii. Am. J. Sci., III, xxxii, 164-166.

Botanical Notices. Lloyd's Drugs and Medicines of North America; Cypripedium arietinum in China; Index to the Botanical Gazette; W. K. Dudley, the Cayuga Flora, part 1; Catalogue of Plants in Herbarium of College of Science, Tokio. Am. J. Sci., III, xxxii, 244-245.

Florida Fruits, and How to Raise Them. By Helen Harcourt. Nation, No. 1110, p. 297.

Botanical Notices. Hooker's Flora of British India, part 13; Vilmorin, Notice Biographique sur Alphonse Lavalée. Am. J. Sci., III, xxxii, 325-326.

Botanical Notices. Sir John Lubbock, Flowers, Fruits, and Leaves; S. H. Vines, Lectures on the Physiology of Plants; L. H. Bailey, Synopsis of North American Carices. Am. J. Sci., III, xxxii, 411-412.

Botanical Notices. Lamarck's Herbarium; Kamel's Drawings of Manilla Plants; Saint Lager on Botanical Nomenclature; Sir John Lubbock, Phytobiological Observations; Hooker's Icones Plantarum, Vol. XVI, part 2. Am. J. Sci., III, xxxii, 485.

1887.

Botanical Notices. Bulletin of the Congress of Botany and Horticulture at St. Petersburg, containing Notes on the Genus Lilium, by H. T. Elwes; Lynch on Cultivating Aquatic Plants; Baillon on Fertilization of Ovules; Lynch on Tubers of Thladiantha dubia; Wilkins on Peach-stones; Maw's Monograph of the genus Crocus; Jahrbuch des Königl. bot. Gartens zu Berlin, bd. iv; J. C. Arthur, History and Biology of the Pear-blight; Acta Horti Petropolitani, Tom. ix, fasc. 2; Sir Joseph Hooker's Primer of Botany; etc., etc. Am. J. Sci., III, xxxiii, 80-83.

Botanical Notices. N. Loew, Beobachtungen über den Blumenbesuch von Insecten und Frielandpflanzen des Botanischen Gartens zu Berlin; Hooker's Icones Plantarum, Vols. xvi and xvii; Journ. Roy. Hort. Soc., vii, No. 2; Macoun's Catalogue of Canadian Plants, part 3, Apetalæ. Am. J. Sci., III, xxxiii, 162-164.

Botanical Notices. Baillon's Dictionnare de Botanique, fasc. 21; Hooker's Icones Plantarum, Vol. xvii, part 3; H. N. Patterson, Check-list of North American Plants;

Delpino, Prodromo d' una Monografia delle Piante Formicarie; Silphium albiflorum in Bot. Magazine; A. De Candolle on Origin of Cultivated Species of Vicia, Triticum, etc. Am. J. Sci., III, XXXIII, 244–245.

Botanical Notices. Warming, Entomophilus Flowers in Arctic Regions; Flora Brasiliensis, fasc. 98, 99; Hooker's Icones Plantarum, Vol. VI, part 3; Bentham's Handbook of the British Flora, fifth ed.; V. Rattan, Key to West Coast Botany; Wood and McCarthy, Wilmington Flora; Cal. State Board of Forestry, First Report; Dr. Arthur on Pear Blight, etc.; Sympetaleia and Loasella; Index to Plant Names. Am. J. Sci., III, XXXIII, 318–321.

Botanical Notices. Penhallow on Tendril Movements in Cucurbita; A Redwood Reserve; J. Ball, Notes of a Naturalist in South America; E. L. Greene, Pittonia, a Series of Botanical Papers, Vol. I, part 1; A. Gattinger, The Tennessee Flora; Bull. de la Soc. Bot. de France, Vol. XXXIII; Gray, Botanical Contributions, corrections; K. Goebel, Outlines of Classification and Special Morphology of Plants, translated by E. F. Garnsey, revised by I. B. Balfour. Am. J. Sci., III, XXXIII, 425–428.

Notice of Sachs' Lectures on the Physiology of Plants. Nation, No. 1161, p. 259.

Notice of Garnsey's Translation of De Bary's Comparative Morphology and Biology of the Fungi, Mycetozoa, and Bacteria. Nation, No. 1160, p. 239.

Darwin's Life and Letters. [Review of Francis Darwin's Life and Letters of Charles Darwin.] Nation, No. 1168, pp. 399–402; No. 1169, pp. 420–421.

Botanical Notices. J. E. Planchon, Monographiæ Phanerogamarum Prodromi, Vol. V, part 2; Report on Botanical Work in Minnesota for 1886; Bower and Vines, Practical Instruction in Botany; W. J. Beal, Grasses of N. A.; Radlkofer, Serjania Sapindacearum Genus monographice descriptum; Braithwaite's British Moss Flora; E. L. Greene, Pittonia; A. B. Langlois, Catalogue des Plantes de la Basse Louisiana; D. H. Campbell, Development of the Ostrich Fern. Am. J. Sci., III, XXXIV, 490–494.

III.—BIOGRAPHICAL SKETCHES, OBITUARIES, NECROLOGICAL NOTICES, ETC.

1842.

Botanical Necrology, etc. Notices of the deaths of Lambert, Guillemin, Vogel, Amos Eaton, etc. Am. J. Sci., XLIII, 214–216.

1843.

Notice of the Life and Labors of De Candolle, extracted [and translated] from the address delivered before the Royal Botanical Society of Ratisbon at its meeting on the 28th of November, 1841, by the President, Professor von Martius. Am. J. Sci., XLIV, 217–239.

1852.

Botanical Necrology for 1849–'50–'51. Link, Kunth, Hoffmansegge, Hornschuch, Bernhardi, Koch, Sturm, Schauer, Kunze, Ledebour, Wahlenberg, B. Delessert. Am. J. Sci., II, XIII, 44, 45, 48.

1853.

Botanical Necrology for 1852–'53. A. de Jussieu, M. A. Richard, Presl. Am. J. Sci., II, XVI, 426–427.

1854.

Obituary Notices of Dr. Wallich and Professor Reinwardt. Am. J. Sci., II, XVIII, 133.

Botanical Necrology for 1854. Fischer, Moricand, P. B. Webb, King of Saxony. Am. J. Sci., II, XVIII, 429.

1855.

Botanical Necrology. Winterbottom, Stocks, Bischoff. Am. J. Sci., II, xix, 129.
Botanical Necrology for 1854–'55. Dr. Molkenboer and C. A. Meyer. Am. J. Sci., II, xx, 135.

1856.

Obituary Notice of Francois André Michaux. Am. J. Sci., II, xxii, 137–138.

1857.

Botanical Necrology for 1856. Wikström, von Steudel, Don, Bojer, Dozy, Leibmann, Dunal. Am. J. Sci., II, xxiii, 279.

1858.

Botanical Necrology for 1857. C. G. de Buzareingues, A. N. Desvaux, E. Desvaux, F. W. Wallroth, Targioni-Tozetti, W. G. Tilesius, L. W. Dillwyn, H. D. A. Ficinus, M. Graves, Madame de Jessieu, Mrs. Griffiths, J. F. Royle. Am. J. Sci., II, xxv, 293–294.
Obituary of Robert Brown. [In part from the Athenæum of June, 1858.] Am. J. Sci., II, xxvi, 279–283.

1859.

Botanical Necrology for 1858. B. Biasoletto, A. Bonpland, R. Brown, G. A. Eisengrein, H. Galeotti, W. T. Gumbell, Mrs. Loudon, E. H. F. Meyer, C. F. A. Morren, J. B. Mougeot, C. G. Nees von Esenbeck, D. Townsend, D. Turner, C. Zeyher. Am. J. Sci., II, xxvii, 442–443.
Obituary Notice of Nuttall and Dr. Horsfield. Am. J. Sci., II, xxviii, 444.

1860

Botanical Necrology for 1859. C. A. Agardh, A. Henfrey, T. Horsfield, A. L. S. Lejune, T. Nuttall. Am. J. Sci., II, xxix, 441–442.

1862.

Botanical Necrology for 1861. F. Deppe, A. E. Fürnrohr, H. von Donnersmarck, J. S. Henslow, Prince Salm-Dyck, M. Tenore, J. M. C. Marquis de Tristan, G. W. F. Wenderoth, R. B. Van den Bosch, W. H. DeVriese, C. L. Blume, E. James. Am. J. Sci., II, xxxiii, 427–428.

1863.

Botanical Nereology, 1862. Blytt, Borrer, Mackay, von Kieser, Steetz, Tweedie, Benj. D. Greene, Asahel Clapp, M. C. Leavenworth, C. W. Short. Am. J. Sci., II., xxxv, 449–451.

1864.

Botanical Necrology for 1863. Martens, von Steven, Moquin-Tandon, Francis Boott, Jacques Gay. Am. J. Sci., II, xxxvii, 288–292.

1866.

Sir William Jackson Hooker. Am. J. Sci., II., xli, 1–10.
Botanical Necrology for 1864 and 1865. Lessing, Turczaninow, Crüger, Junghuhn, Treviranus, Schacht, Scheele, Sturm, Falconer, Schomburgk, Schott, Paxton, Richardson, Cuming, Bridges, Hooker, Lindley, Riddell, Montague. Am. J. Sci., II, xxvi, 263–268.
Botanical Necrology. William Henry Harvey, Robert Kaye Greville. Am. J. Sci., II, xlii, 273–277.

1868.

Botanical Necrology for 1867. H. P. Sartwell, Chester Dewey, Mettenius, von Schlechtendal, Kotschy, Gasparini, Berg, Mandon, C. H. Schultz, Daubeny. Am. J. Sci., II, XLV, 121–124, 272–273.

¿ Obituary Notice of N. B. Ward and G. A. W. Arnott. Am. J. Sci., II, XLVI, 273.

1869.

Botanical Necrology for 1868. G. A. Walker-Arnott, Nathaniel B. Ward, Edward Poeppig, Dr. Schnitzlein, François Delessert, Horace Mann. Am. J. Sci., II, XLVII, 140–143.

1870.

Botanical Necrology for 1869. Antonio Bertoloni, Guiseppe Moris, J. E. Purkinje. Am. J. Sci., II, XXIX, 129.

Obituary Notice of Prof Francis Unger. Am. J. Sci., II, XLIX, 410.

1872.

Botanical Necrology, 1870–1871. Unger, Lévéillé, Perottet, C. Müller, Ruprecht, von Hugel Anderson, Miquel, Lantzius-Beninga, Schultz-Schultzenstein, Wilson, Hartweg, Rohrbach, Milde, de la Sagra, Lecoq, Reissek, Sowerby, Seemann, Lenormand. Am. J. Sci., III, III, 151–154.

1873.

Botanical Necrology for 1872–'73. M. A. Curtis, A. F. Spring, Hugo von Mohl, de Brebisson, R. Wight, Reuter, Oersted, Gris, Welwitsch. Am. J. Sci., III, V, 391–397.

John Torrey; A Biographical Notice. Proc. Am. Acad., IX, 262–271. [Am. J. Sci., III, V, 411–421.]

Obituary Notice of John Torrey. Nation, No. 403, p. 197.

William S. Sullivant; A Biographical Notice. Proc. Am. Acad., IX, 271–276. [Am. J. Sci., III, VI, 1–6]

Obituary Notice of Elias Durand. Am. J. Sci., III, VI, 316–317.

Louis Agassiz. Nation, 1873, 404–405.

1874.

Botanical Necrology for 1873. John Torrey, W. S. Sullivant, E. Durand, J. L. Russell, H. J. Clark, I. F. Holton. Am. J. Sci., III, VII, 239–240.

Notice of death of Joshua Hoopes. Am. J. Sci., III, VII, 600.

Death of Prof. C. F. Meissner. Am J. Sci., III, VIII, 72.

Obituary. Death of Prof. Jeffries Wyman. Am. J. Sci., III, VIII, 323–324.

Jeffries Wyman. Memorial Meeting of the Boston Society of Natural History, October 7, 1874. Address of Prof. Asa Gray, pp. 9–37. [Am. J. Sci., III, IX, 81–93, 171–177.] Proc. Bost. Soc. Nat. Hist.

Obituary Notice of Jeffries Wyman. Nation, No. 480, p. 170.

Charles Robert Darwin. Amer. Nat, VIII, 475–479.

1875.

Botanical Necrology for 1874. Geo. Aug Pritzel, Rev. R T. Lowe, Mrs. Hooker, J. T. Maggridge. Am. J. Sci., III, IX, 68–69.

Obituary of Daniel Haubury. Am. J. Sci , III, IX, 476

Obituary of Gustav Thuret. Am. J Sci., III, X, 67.

John Edward Gray. An Obituary Notice. Am. J. Sci., III, X, 78–80.

1876.

Botanical Necrology for 1875. I. A. Lapham, F. G. Bartling, A. Bureau, J. E. Gray, J. C. M. Gronier, D. Hanbury, R. F. Hohenhacher, Lieut. Gen. Jacobi, E. F. Nolte, Gustav Thuret, A. Brongniart. Am. J. Sci., III, XI, 326.

1877.

Botanical Necrology for 1876. A. T. Brongniart, J. J. Bennett, C. G. Ehrenberg, L. Fuekel, E. Newman, J. Carson, W. Hofmeister. Am. J. Sci., III, XIII, 237, 238.

Obituary Notices of Lady Smith and Joseph de Notaris. Am. J. Sci., III, XIII, 321-322.

Obituary of Alexander Braun. Am. J. Sci., III, XIII, 471-472.

Obituary Notice of H. A. Weddell and P. Parlatore. Am. J. Sci., III, x.v, 429.

Obituary Notice of George Hadley. Am. J. Sci., III, XIV 499.

1878.

Botanical Necrology for 1877. Mrs. M. E. Gray, Pleasance Smith, G. de Notaris, W. Hofmeister, A. Braun, E. Bourgeau, T. Lestibudois, H. A. Weddell, F. Parlatore, J. Darby. Am. J. Sci., III, XV, 225.

Obituary Notice of Elias Magnus Fries, Am. J. Sci., III, XV, 320.

Obituary Notice of Dr. Thomas Tomson. Am. J. Sci., III, XV, 484.

Biographical Notices. Charles Pickering, Elias Magnus Fries. Proc. Amer. Acad., XIII, 441-454.

1879.

Biographical Memoir of Joseph Henry, prepared in behalf of the Board of Regents. Smithsonian Report for 1878, pp. 143-158; Congressional Record, March 4, 1879, 3-10.

Botanical Necrology for 1878. E. M. Fries, L. Pfeiffer, A. Murray, A. Bloxam, F. V. Raspail, S. Kurz, M. Durieu, Charles Pickering, M. Seubert, T. Thomson, G. Zanardini, R. de Visiani, B. C. DuMortier, E. Borszczow, J. McNab, S. T. Olney, J. W. Robbins, J. Bigelow. Am. J. Sci. III, XVII, 177-180.

Dr. Jacob Bigelow. Am. J. Sci. III, XVII, 263-266.

Obituary Notices of Reichenbach, Itzigsohn, Angström, Buek, Schimper, Grisebach, Koch, Moore, Bigelow, Robbins. Am. J. Sci. III, XVIII, 158.

1880.

Botanical Necrology for 1879. W. T. Feay, J. Bigelow, J. W. Robbins, H. Itzigsohn, J. Angström, H. W. Buek, H. G. L. Reichenbach, H. R. A. Grisebach, T. Irmisch, E. Spach, K. Koch, D. Moore, E. Fenzl, J. Miers. Am. J. Sci. III, XIX, 76-78.

Botanical Necrology for 1879, Additions. F. Lindheimer, C. H. Godet. Am. J. Sci. III, XIX, 158.

Obituary Notice of General Munro. Am. J. Sci., III, XIX, 331-338.

Botanical Necrology for 1880. John Carey, Coe F. Austin. Am J. Sci., III, XIX, 421-423.

1882.

Charles Darwin. Proc. Amer. Acad., XVII, 449-458. [Am. J. Sci., III, XXIV, 453-463; Literary World, 1882, 145-146 (abstract).]

Biographical Notices. Thomas Potts James, John Amory Lowell, Charles Darwin, Joseph Decaisne. Proc. Amer. Acad., XVII, 405-406, 408-411, 449-459.

Botanical Necrology. Thomas Potts James, Joseph Decaisne, Coe F. Austin, Wm. Philip Schimper, Nils J. Andersson, Wm. Munro, Dominique Alexander Godron, S. B. Mead, W. Lauder Lindsay, Ernst Hampe, Alphonso Wood, Gottlieb Ludwig Rabenhorst, Matthias Jacob Schleiden, Theodore Schwann. Am. J. Sci., III, XXIII, 330-333.

1883.

Some North American Botanists. John Eatton LeConte. Bot. Gazette VIII, 197–199.

1884.

Botanical Necrology in part for 1880, 81, 82, 83. C. F. Austin, C. C. Frost, J. Carey, S. B. Mead, A. Wood, T. P. James, E. Hall, J. S. Tommasini, Geo. Wm. Munro, W. P. Schimper, E. Hampe, N. J. Andersson, R. Fortune, L. Rabenhorst, M. J. Schleiden, M. P. Edgeworth, H. C. Watson, P. G. Lorentz, O. W. Sonder, J. Decaisne, G. H. K. Thwaites, C. Darwin, S. Cesati, O. Heer, C. F. Parker, Geo. Engelmann. Am. J. Sci., III, XXVII, 242–244.

George Bentham. Science, IV, 352–353.

Biographical Notices. George Engelmann, Oswald Heer. Proc. Amer. Acad., XIX, 516–522, 556–559; Am. J. Sci. III, XXVIII, 61–69.

Obituary Notice of Alphonse Lavallée. Am. J. Sci., III, XXVIII, 5–76.

Obituary Notice of George Bentham. Nation, No. 1005, p. 2917.

1885.

Memorial of George Bentham. Am. J. Sci., III, XXIX, 103–113.

Botanical Necrology for 1884. Augustus Fendler, George Engelmann, S. B. Buckley, J. Williamson, J. H. Balfour, H. R. Gœppert, George Bentham. Am. J. Sci., III, XXIX, 169–172

Obituary Notice of Charles Wright. Am. J. Sci., III, XXX, 247.

Obituary Notice of Hon. George W. Clinton. Am. J. Sci., III, XXX, 322.

1886.

Botanical Necrology for 1885. Charles Wright, G. W. Clinton, E. Boissier, J. A. C. Roeper. Am. J. Sci., III, XXXI, 12–22.

Botanical Necrology for 1885. Jean-Etienne Duby, L. R. and C. Tulasne. Am. J. Sci., III, XXXI, 312–313.

Louis Agassiz. Andover Review, Jan., 38–44.

1887.

Botanical Necrology for 1886. E. Morren, Rev. W. W. Newbould, W. Hillebrand, H. F. Hance, T. G. Orphanides, J. W. A. Wigand, E. Tuckerman. Am. J. Sci., III, XXXIII, 164–165.

Obituary Notice of W. F. Tolmie. Am. J. Sci., III, XXXIII, 244–245.

Obituary Notice of A. W. Eichler. Am. J. Sci., III, XXXIII, 427.

1888.

Botanical Necrology for the year 1887.—W. E. Tolmie; John Goldie; Albert Kellogg; William Boott; Ezra Michener; Henry William Ravenel. Am. J. Sci., III, XXXV, 260–263.

INDEX.

A.

F.

G.

H.

V.

W.

Y.

Z.

Lightning Source UK Ltd.
Milton Keynes UK
UKHW022229281218
334637UK00013B/1056/P